THE

MARCUS GARVEY

AND

UNIVERSAL NEGRO
IMPROVEMENT ASSOCIATION

PAPERS

SUPPORTED BY
The National Endowment for the Humanities
The National Historical Publications and Records Commission

SPONSORED BY
The University of California, Los Angeles

Marcus Garvey during his trip to the Caribbean

THE MARCUS GARVEY

AND

UNIVERSAL NEGRO IMPROVEMENT ASSOCIATION

PAPERS

Volume III
September 1920–August 1921

Robert A. Hill
Editor

Emory J. Tolbert
Senior Editor

Deborah Forczek
Assistant Editor

University of California Press
Berkeley   Los Angeles   London

University of California Press
Berkeley and Los Angeles, California

University of California Press, Ltd.
London, England

The preparation of this volume was made possible in part by a grant
from the Program for Editions of the National Endowment for the
Humanities, an independent federal agency. In addition, support
was also received from the National Historical Publications and
Records Commission, Washington, D.C., and the University of
California, Los Angeles.

Documents in this volume from the Public Record Office are ©
British Crown copyright 1920 and 1921 and are published by per-
mission of the Controller of Her Britannic Majesty's Stationery
Office.

Designed by Linda M. Robertson and set in Galliard type.

Library of Congress Cataloging in Publication Data
Main entry under title:

The Marcus Garvey and Universal Negro Improvement Association
    papers.

    1. Garvey, Marcus, 1887–1940. 2. Universal Negro Improvement
Association—History—Sources. 3. Black power—United States—
History—Sources. 4. Afro-Americans—Race identity—History—
Sources. 5. Afro-Americans—Civil rights—History—Sources.
6. Afro-Americans—Correspondence. I. Hill, Robert A.,
1943–   . II. Garvey, Marcus, 1887–1940. III. Universal Negro
Improvement Association.

E185.97.G3M36 1984   305.8'96073   82-13379
ISBN 0-520-05257-9

Printed in the United States of America

1 2 3 4 5 6 7 8 9

To
C. L. R. James

CONTENTS

DOCUMENTS

APPENDIXES

ILLUSTRATIONS

Marcus Garvey during his trip to the Caribbean (frontispiece)
Courtesy of the George A. Weston Papers

Capt. Hugh Mulzac
Cleveland Gazette, 6 October 1923

Black Star Line Office
Philosophy and Opinions

S.S. *Phyllis Wheatley*
NW, *19 February 1921*

UNIA Delegation to Liberia, 1921
Philosophy and Opinions

C. D. B. King
Liberia's Past and Present (London: Diplomatic Press, 1959)

Edwin Barclay
Liberia's Past and Present

Momolu Massaquoi
The Republic of Liberia (Hamburg: n.p., 1926)

F. E. R. Johnson
Liberia's Past and Present

Map of the Caribbean area
Courtesy of Army Map Service, Corps of Engineers

Harbour Street in Kingston after the 1907 Earthquake
National Library of Jamaica

Rev. Ernest Price
Courtesy of the Price family

Alexander Bedward
Courtesy of the Institute of Jamaica

J. M. Price
Courtesy of the National Library of Jamaica

Marcus Garvey and UNIA members on a railway car in Costa Rica
Courtesy of the UNIA Hall, Port Limón, Costa Rica

Marcus Garvey addressing a crowd in Port Limón
Courtesy of Amy Jacques Garvey

Isaiah Morter
Philosophy and Opinions

Black Cross Nurses unit
NW, 19 February 1921

Robert Lincoln Poston
UNIA 1922 Almanac

Ulysses S. Poston
NW, 8 July 1922

Sumio Uesugi
Courtesy of Alumni Office, Denison University

George A. Weston
George A. Weston Papers

Marcus Garvey and Adrian F. Johnson in 1921 Convention Parade
Daily News, 2 August 1921

Convention Composite
New York World, 2 August 1921

ACKNOWLEDGMENTS

The editors wish to thank the institutions and individuals whose generous assistance advanced the research and editorial preparation of the present volume. Important documents were provided by the National Archives and Records Service, Washington, D.C.; Washington National Records Center, Suitland, Maryland; Manuscript Division of the Library of Congress; Federal Archives and Records Service, Bayonne, New Jersey; New York County Clerk's Office, New York; Division of Old Records of the Hall of Records, New York; University of Massachusetts Library, Amherst; University of Southern California, Los Angeles; Public Record Office, Kew, Surrey, England; and the Jamaica Archives, Spanish Town. We are deeply indebted to the archivists of these institutions for their responses to our many requests and for their continued interest in the project.

Information used to prepare annotations was provided by the staff of the Library of the Honourable Society of the Middle Temple, London; League of Nations Archives, Geneva; British Foreign and Commonwealth Office Library, London; Baptist Missionary Society Archives, London: Island Record Office, Spanish Town, Jamaica; National Library of Jamaica, Kingston; National Library of Canada, Ottawa; Federal Archives and Records Service, Bayonne, New Jersey; Moorland-Spingarn Research Center of the Howard University Library; Special Collections Division of George Washington University; Louisville Free Public Library, Kentucky; Rhode Island Historical Society, Providence; Detroit Public Library; Museum and Library of Maryland History, Baltimore; University Registrar and Divinity School Library of the University of Chicago; Alumni Office of Denison University, Granville, Ohio; Monmouth County Historical Society, Monmouth, New Jersey; B. F. Jones Memorial Library, Aliquippa, Pennsylvania; Schomburg Center for Research in Black Culture of the New York Public Library; Indianapolis Public Library; Illinois State Archives and Illinois State Historical Library, Springfield; United States Army Military History Institute, Carlisle Barracks, Pennsylvania; National Personnel Records Center (Military Personnel Records), St. Louis; Department of Military Affairs of the Military Records and Research Library, Boone National Guard Center, Frankfort, Kentucky; and the New York City Department of Health. We should also like to thank the reference staff of the University Research Library at the University of California, Los Angeles, for their assistance. The archival staff of the National Historical Publications and Records Commission, Washington, D.C., continues to give indispensable aid to the project, and we gratefully acknowledge their assistance. Even though the staff has greatly decreased in numbers as a result of federal budget cutbacks, they continue undiminished in their dedication.

Helpful data for use in annotations also came to us from Prof. Randall K. Burkett, College of the Holy Cross, Worcester, Massachusetts; Prof. Tom Shick, University of Wisconsin–Madison; and Prof. Franklin W. Knight, Johns Hopkins University, Baltimore. We also wish to thank Prof. Ralph Watkins of the State University of New York College at Oneonta for bringing the *Buffalo American* newspaper to our attention and for providing us with prints of relevant articles; Mother Ella Bell, Newark, New Jersey, for her recollections of her father-in-law, Rev. J. D. Barbour; and Rev. Mark A. Peachey of Triumph, the Church of the New Age, Newark, New Jersey, for kindly arranging the interview with Mother Bell; the late Rev. George A. Weston of Antigua, West Indies, for great generosity with his time over a series of lengthy interviews; Canute Parris, Babylon, New York, and St. Clair Drake, Palo Alto, California, for making available copies of their tapes of interviews with Rev. George Weston; Prof. Gregson Davis, Stanford University, for granting us access to his collection of Rev. George Weston's papers; the Rerrie family, St. Ann's Bay, Jamaica, for information about Garvey's father; the late Rupert Jemmott, Long Island, New York, for his vivid reminiscences about the 1921 UNIA commission to Liberia, of which he was a member; Lionel M. Yard, Brooklyn, for allowing us to use his research materials concerning Amy Ashwood Garvey; Andrew Reed, Point Alfred, South Africa, for material on Bennet Ncwana; and H. P. Jacobs, Kingston, Jamaica, for information regarding various Jamaican personalities and events. We also wish to thank Dr. Peter D. Ashdown, Arundel, Sussex, England, for allowing us to consult his unpublished essay "Marcus Garvey, the UNIA, and the Black Cause in British Honduras." We wish to thank Una Mulzac, New York, for information on her father, the late Hugh N. Mulzac. In addition, we acknowledge with gratitude the research assistance of W. F. Elkins, London. Sharon Burke, New York, also rendered invaluable help in researching UNIA case files in New York City, and we express our appreciation to her.

Permission to publish was gratefully received from the Public Record Office and from the Jamaica Archives. David Graham Du Bois, Cairo, Egypt, kindly granted permission to publish letters by W. E. B. Du Bois. The Federal Bureau of Investigation generously provided the photographic prints of the Black Star Line promotional brochure that is herein reproduced in facsimile. We should also like to thank the family of Rev. Ernest Price, the Alumni Office of Denison University, the Institute of Jamaica and the

National Library of Jamaica for their assistance in our photographic research.

We would like to acknowledge the many debts we have incurred in the promotion and marketing of the first two volumes. We are happy to thank Harlan Kessel, Sales and Promotion Manager, University of California Press, and his exemplary staff: Anne Evers, Marta Gasoi, Patricia Malango, and Amanda Mecke. Special thanks must also be accorded to Kwaku Lynn, KPFK Radio, Hollywood, California, who has been most generous to the project in disseminating information about the volumes. Finally, we would like to acknowledge Bernard Hoyes, Los Angeles, for his oil painting of Marcus Garvey, reproduced on the dust jacket of all of the volumes.

The staff of the Marcus Garvey and Universal Negro Improvement Association Papers project has contributed their usual skill and dedication to the preparation of Volume III. The editors wish to express appreciation for the work of Diane Lisa Hill, Ruth Schofield, Michael Furmanovsky, Margaret Brumfield, and Robin Edelson. We also acknowledge the assistance of Gregory A. Pirio, Assistant Editor of the African series of the edition, for his help with the annotations treating Liberia, South Africa, and the Congo (Zaire).

The National Historical Publications and Records Commission, the National Endowment for the Humanities, and the University of California, Los Angeles, have sustained the project with their support, and we are deeply grateful for their continuing commitment.

INTRODUCTION

The third volume of *The Marcus Garvey and Universal Negro Improvement Association Papers* documents the period between the first and second international conventions of the UNIA. The success of the August 1920 convention justified Garvey's expanded emphasis on African redemption and established his movement's substantial following in scores of black communities around the world. By the time the August 1921 convention came around, the UNIA was the major political force among blacks in the postwar world. Circulation of the *Negro World*, the movement's newspaper, increased from twenty-five thousand at the start of 1921 to seventy-five thousand copies by the middle of the year, so that not only did it become self-supporting, it also contributed over $1,000 every month to the UNIA's general treasury. Counting newspaper employees and distributors, along with officials and staff members of the Black Star Line and the UNIA, William Ferris, the *Negro World*'s literary editor, estimated that by July 1921 Garvey's movement provided employment for nearly two hundred persons in New York and nearly two hundred others in various parts of the world.

Even as the second convention deliberated, however, there arose ominous signs of crisis within the movement. Garvey's lieutenants began to express doubts about the financial health of the Black Star Line and about the wisdom of Garvey's methods in raising money for his Liberian colonization and trade scheme. At the same time, the UNIA's various fund-raising projects had not been able to support the over $70,000 in annual salaries promised to UNIA officials who had been elected by the 1920 convention. By the end of August 1921, the *Yarmouth* (the BSL's flagship) was no longer in service, and the *Kanawha* (a yacht) was disabled and tied up in Cuban waters; the *Shadyside* (the Hudson River excursion boat), meanwhile, was losing money. At this point, the entire BSL enterprise hovered on the brink of bankruptcy. Moreover, a steep general decline in the shipping business made prospects for the Black Star Line even less promising.

The momentum gathered at the August 1920 convention allowed Garvey and his aides to begin a new round of promotional tours devoted to selling Black Star Line stock, shoring up weak UNIA divisions, and chartering new divisions. The current volume documents the activities and growth of UNIA divisions in Buffalo; Chicago and Danville, Illinois; Key West, Jacksonville, and Miami, Florida; Louisville, Kentucky; Los Angeles; Okmulgee, Oklahoma; Philadelphia; Pittsburgh; and Springfield, Massachusetts. Clear evidence of the movement's growth came at the 1921 convention, when the UNIA secretary-general reported that the number of divisions increased from 95 in 1920 to 418 in 1921, with an additional 422 UNIA branches awaiting charters from the parent body in New York.

From September 1920 to August 1921, BSL stock sales totaled $55,147, a difficult achievement in the face of high black unemployment during the postwar economic slump. Garvey introduced new financial schemes during this time. In October 1920 he replaced his Liberian Liberty bonds promotion with the Liberian Construction Loan, a plan to raise $2 million to finance a UNIA loan to Liberia. In order to stimulate sales and contributions, Garvey issued a circular letter on 1 December 1920 calling for $250,000 by mid-January to secure a ship to convey workmen and materials to Liberia. At this point the Black Star Line and the Liberian Construction Loan were, for all practical purposes, one and the same promotion; indeed, the UNIA Liberian loan campaign was as much concerned with staving off the financial crisis of the Black Star Line as with financing construction in Liberia.

J. Edgar Hoover's long-awaited opportunity to remove Garvey from the Afro-American political scene came when Garvey embarked on his promotional tour of the West Indies and Central America in February 1921. Hoover had come to believe that the Garvey movement in America was subsidized to some extent by the British government; another government official voiced the equally farfetched suspicion that Garvey might have been working as part of an international Jewish conspiracy aimed at fomenting revolution. On the basis of these suspicions as well as on evidence of Garvey's radical influence in the black community, Hoover sought the cooperation of the United States State Department to bar Garvey from reentering the United States by denying him a visa. Yet the State Department eventually abandoned the policy of exclusion it had established at Hoover's request and allowed Garvey to reenter the United States. Hoover retaliated by refusing to honor the State Department's request for the Bureau of Investigation's aid in blocking the admission of the UNIA potentate, Gabriel M. Johnson, who arrived from Liberia in July 1921 to attend the August UNIA convention. Johnson's brother, F. E. R. Johnson, was in the United States at that time as a member of the Liberian Plenary Commission negotiating for a United States government loan, and the State Department believed that he was also working on behalf of the UNIA to further its cause in Liberia. Thus, the attempt to keep the UNIA potentate out of the United States supported a larger diplomatic scheme aimed at keeping Garvey and the UNIA from launching their "construction" program in Liberia. In this context, State Department policymakers viewed Garvey's readmission as less significant than Gabriel Johnson's, a conclusion that greatly displeased Hoover.

Garvey faced a curious dilemma in his decision to risk a trip away from the United States despite the sober warnings of his aides, many of his followers, and the black press. Although his advisers anticipated the United States government's attempt to keep him out of the country with the assistance of the British, Garvey knew that without a major fund-raising tour in previously untapped regions, the Black Star Line would soon go under.

Garvey's speeches in the countries that he visited—Cuba, Jamaica, Costa Rica, Panama, and British Honduras (Belize)—challenged local audiences to pursue "a new religion and new politics" and to struggle against "the old-time order of things." Beyond its promotional function, Garvey's tour formed part of a wider UNIA diplomatic offensive: while Garvey was mobilizing support in the Caribbean, UNIA officials in New York were lobbying the visiting Liberian Plenary Commission, which included President C. D. B. King, and the UNIA's delegation in Liberia was asking the Liberian cabinet to set aside land and accommodations for the UNIA construction and colonization program. Garvey's trip also marked a major turning point in the history of the UNIA. Garvey's lieutenants, who were charged with running the UNIA and the Black Star Line during his absence, frequently clashed over unclear lines of authority. At the same time, a quarrel over questions of authority between Cyril Crichlow, Garvey's resident commissioner in Liberia, and Gabriel Johnson and George O. Marke, UNIA potentate and supreme deputy potentate, created severe difficulties for the UNIA, leaving the UNIA's Liberian project at a standstill. Under these circumstances Garvey asked the 1921 convention for control over all UNIA and BSL finances as a means of centralizing authority in his hands. The convention granted him that control and at the same time approved changes in the UNIA Constitution that increased the power of the parent body in New York. According to Garvey's plan, UNIA employees would be recruited from those who passed a UNIA civil service examination, and the executive secretaries of local divisions would be civil servants who would handle all local records and report directly to UNIA headquarters.

When the movement was starting to founder in New York, however, Garvey was preoccupied in the Caribbean with problems of his own. Constant breakdowns of the S.S. *Kanawha* and numerous stops for expensive repairs led Garvey to accuse the ship's captain and engineer of incompetence and sabotage. Garvey also encountered colonial authorities throughout the region who viewed his presence with concern: in the case of Bermuda, where he planned to make the first stop of his tour, officials denied him permission to land. Nonetheless, the tour marked a significant political triumph for Garvey. Large crowds greeted him in Cuba, Jamaica, and British Honduras, and thousands mobbed him in Costa Rica and Panama. In addition, he raised funds by selling substantial amounts of BSL stock and raised even greater sums from the gate receipts at his public speeches.

Prior to Garvey's embarking on his Caribbean tour, his speeches revealed an impressive knowledge of world events and developments on the

African continent, especially those that pointed toward an increasing spread of the movement. Examples of the Garvey movement's impact in Africa appeared in newspaper reports and official correspondence from South Africa and the Belgian Congo (Zaire), as well as in correspondence from UNIA representatives in Liberia. Yet Garvey's speeches on the eve of his departure also revealed his growing concern about the political consequences of leading a "radical movement." American consular officials would later repeatedly deny Garvey's requests for a visa, lengthening his planned five-week tour to over four months. When Garvey finally returned to New York, in mid-July 1921, his Caribbean experience had given him an even greater appreciation of the level of official antagonism that his movement had provoked.

Perhaps as important as the ever-present threat of increased official repression was the financial crisis that faced the Black Star Line on Garvey's return. The decisive blow came when negotiations with the United States Shipping Board failed to produce the long-awaited ship for the African transatlantic route. Garvey went before the 1921 UNIA convention without the long-promised *Phyllis Wheatley*, which many delegates expected to see when they arrived in New York.

Facing these mounting troubles, Garvey announced his intention at the outset of the convention to expose and remove unworthy officials of the movement. A series of important resignations followed, including those of the UNIA assistant president general, Rev. John Dawson Gordon, and the UNIA chaplain general, Rev. George Alexander McGuire. McGuire had played a notable leadership role in the UNIA, and while Garvey was away during the spring of 1921, McGuire wrote two important works for the UNIA, *The Universal Negro Catechism* (New York: UNIA, 1921), which drew heavily from the work of J. A. Rogers, and *The Universal Negro Ritual* (New York: UNIA, 1921).

Garvey also encouraged a freewheeling interrogation of the UNIA's top officials in public sessions of the convention. Garvey himself did not escape criticism, since a number of delegates opposed his methods and ascribed some of the Black Star Line's troubles to his failures. This was particularly the case with the delegates from the UNIA's Los Angeles division.

Garvey's most outspoken challenge at the convention came from the African Blood Brotherhood. The ABB's leader, Cyril Briggs, had joined the Workers' party in the spring of 1921. Shortly thereafter, his offers of unity with Garvey and the UNIA became more tinged with criticism, and his ideological differences with the UNIA's program became more pronounced. Garvey had invited the ABB to send delegates to the 1920 UNIA convention. When he repeated the gesture in 1921, the ABB delegates took the opportunity to raise embarrassing questions about the Black Star Line in convention sessions. Realizing that in 1921 Garvey would not publish official convention news bulletins like those that had appeared during the 1920 convention, Briggs published his own official-looking series of special bulletins, emphasizing controversies on the convention floor. Five days before the convention ended, Garvey expelled the ABB delegates.

With his Liberian plans in disarray and some of his key assistants removed, Garvey launched an aggressive attack at the convention against those black leaders whom he perceived as opponents of the UNIA. He charged them with misrepresenting the UNIA before the United States government and thereby causing his difficulties in reentering the country. Garvey also initiated a controversial campaign to label these political opponents as advocates of "social equality" between the races, while offering as an alternative his philosophy of "racial purity."

Garvey focused his attacks upon W. E. B. Du Bois, whose Second Pan-African Congress opened its first session in London during the final days of the 1921 UNIA convention. Throughout the fall of 1920 Du Bois undertook an extensive investigation of Garvey and of the finances of the Black Star Line, and the results were published in a major two-part article in the December 1920 and January 1921 issues of the *Crisis*. Angered by Du Bois's criticisms and by what he believed was Du Bois's excessive influence on United States officialdom, Garvey hoped to discredit Du Bois and his Pan-African Congress while establishing the UNIA as the sole legitimate vehicle of African redemption, and to neutralize government opposition to his efforts.

The white press began to deepen its coverage of Garveyism during the months immediately after the 1920 convention, and in some cases these publications deviated from the earlier seriocomic approach to the UNIA by examining Garveyism as a major movement contending for support among postwar blacks. A few in-depth reports on the UNIA's history and objectives appeared as a result. During the same months that Du Bois published his report on the Garvey movement in the *Crisis*, a white journal, the *World's Work*, published a two-part article on the UNIA, an article that pleased Garvey so much, he recommended it to *Negro World* readers. Between August 1920 and August 1921, articles on Garvey and the UNIA also appeared in *Life, Current Opinion, Literary Digest, Independent, World Tomorrow*, and *Overseas* (a British journal).

EDITORIAL PRINCIPLES AND PRACTICES

I. Arrangement of Documents

Documents are presented in chronological order according to the date of authorship of the original text. Enclosures and attachments to documents, however, do not appear in strict chronological sequence, but are printed with their original covering documents. Enclosures have been set in italic type in the table of contents for identification.

The publication date of news reports and periodical articles is given on the place and date line within square brackets. In the case of news reports and periodical articles containing the date of original composition, that date chronologically supersedes the date of eventual publication and is printed within double square brackets on the place and date line of the document.

In the case of reported speeches, the date of publication supersedes chronologically the date of original delivery and is printed within single square brackets on the place and date line of the document.

Bureau of Investigation reports that give both the date of composition and the period covered by the report are arranged according to the date of composition.

Documents that lack dates and thus require editorial assignment of dates are placed in normal chronological sequence. When no day within a month appears on a document, it is placed after the documents specifically dated on the latest date within that month. Documents that carry only the date of a year are placed according to the same principle. Documents that cover substantial periods, such as diaries, journals and accounts, will appear according to the date of their earliest entries.

When two or more documents possess the same date, they are arranged with regard to affinity to the subject of the document that immediately precedes them or that which immediately follows them.

II. Form of Presentation

Each document is presented in the following manner:

A. A caption introduces the document and is printed in a type size larger than the text. Letters between individuals are captioned with the names of the individuals and their titles; captions, however, include a person's office only upon that person's first appearance. The original titles of published materials are retained with the documents; however, the head-lines of some news reports are abbreviated or omitted, in which case this is indicated in the descriptive source note to the document.

B. The text of a document follows the caption. The copy text of letters or reports is taken from recipients' copies whenever possible, but in the absence of a recipient's copy, a file copy of the letter or report is used. If the file copy is not available, however, and a retained draft copy of the letter is found, the retained draft copy is used as the basic text.

C. Following the body of the text, an unnumbered descriptive source note describes editorially the physical character of the document by means of appropriate abbreviations. Moreover, a repository symbol gives the provenance of the original manuscript or, if it is rare, printed work. Printed sources are identified in the following manner:

   1. A contemporary pamphlet is identified by its full title, place and date of publication, and the location of the copy used.

   2. A contemporary essay, letter, or other kind of statement that appeared originally in a contemporary publication is preceded by the words "Printed in . . . ," followed by the title, date, and, in the case of essays, inclusive page numbers of the source of publication.

   3. A contemporary printed source reprinted at a later date, the original publication of which has not been found, is identified with the words "Reprinted from . . . ," followed by the identification of the work from which the text has been reproduced. The same applies to any originally unpublished manuscript printed at a later date.

D. Numbered textual annotations that explicate the document follow the descriptive source note. The following principles of textual annotation have been applied:

   1. Individuals are identified upon their first appearance, with additional information about them sometimes furnished upon their later appearance in a document where such data provide maximum clarification. Pseudonyms are identified, wherever possible, by a textual annotation.

   2. Reasons for the assignment of dates to documents or the correction of dates of documents are explained in those instances where important historical information is involved.

3. Obscure allusions in the text are annotated whenever such references can be clarified.

4. Printed works and manuscript materials consulted during the preparation of textual annotations appear in parentheses at the end of each annotation. Frequently used reference works are cited in an abbreviated form, and the complete table may be found in the list of Published Works Cited in the section on Symbols and Abbreviations.

E. Garvey's appeal case (*Marcus Garvey* v. *United States of America,* no. 8317, Ct. App., 2d Cir., 2 February 1925) contains the complete transcript of his original mail fraud trial (*United States of America* v. *Marcus Garvey et al.,* C31-37 and C33-688, U.S. District Court, Southern District of New York, May 1923). Trial documents reprinted in the volume and references to the trial in annotations to documents are taken from the transcript used in the appeal case.

III. Transcription of Text

Manuscripts and printed material have been transcribed from the original text and printed as documents according to the following principles and procedures:

A. Manuscript Material

1. The place and date of composition are placed at the head of the document, regardless of their location in the original, but exceptions are made in the cases of certificates of vital registration and documents in which original letterhead stationery is reproduced. If the place or date of a letter (or both) does not appear in the original text, the information is supplied and printed in italics at the head within square brackets. Likewise, if either the place or date is incomplete, the necessary additional information is supplied in italics within square brackets. Superscript letters are brought down to the line of type, and terminal punctuation is deleted.

   In the case of Bureau of Investigation reports that were submitted on printed forms, the place and date are abstracted and placed at the head of each document, while the name of the reporting agent is placed at the end of the document on the signature line.

   The formal salutation of letters is placed on the line below the place and date line, with the body of the text following the salutation.

   The complimentary close of letters is set continuously with the text in run-in style, regardless of how it was written in the original.

The signature, which is set in capitals and small capitals, is placed at the right-hand margin on the line beneath the text or complimentary close, with titles, where they appear, set in uppercase and lowercase. Terminal punctuation is deleted.

When a file copy of a document bearing no signature is used to establish the text but the signatory is known, the signature is printed in roman type within square brackets.

The inside address, if significant and not repetitive, is printed immediately below the text.

Endorsements, docketings, and other markings appearing on official correspondence, when intelligible, are reproduced in small type following the address, with appropriate identification. In the case of other types of documents, such as private correspondence, endorsements and dockets are reprinted only when they are significant.

Minutes, enclosures, and attachments are printed in roman type following their covering documents and placed after the annotation material of their covering documents. Whenever minutes, enclosures, or attachments are not printed, this fact is always recorded and explained. Whenever a transmission letter originally accompanying an enclosure or attachment is not printed, the omission is noted and the transmission document identified and recorded in the descriptive source note.

2. Printed letterheads and other official stationery are not reproduced, unless they contain significant information, in which case they are reprinted above the date line. In cases where they are not reprinted, they are sometimes abstracted, and the information is placed in the descriptive source note. Printed addresses are reproduced only upon the first appearance.

3. In general, the spelling of all words, including proper names, is preserved as written in the manuscript and printed sources. Thus, personal and place names that are spelled erratically in the original texts are regularized or corrected only in the index. However, serious distortion in the spelling of a word, to such an extent as to obscure its true meaning, is repaired by printing the correct word in italics within square brackets after the incorrect spelling. Mere "slips of the pen" or typographical errors are corrected within the word and printed in roman type within square brackets; however, some typographical errors that contribute to the overall character of the document are retained.

4. Capitalization is retained as in the original. Words underlined once in a manuscript are printed in italics. Words that are underlined twice or spelled out in large letters or full capitals are printed in small capitals.

5. Punctuation, grammar, and syntax are retained as found in the original texts. In the case of punctuation, corrections that are essential to the accurate reading of the text are provided within square brackets. If, however, a punctuation mark appears in a document as a result of typographical error, it is corrected in square brackets or, in some instances, silently deleted.

6. All contractions and abbreviations in the text are retained. Abbreviations of titles or organizations are identified in a list of abbreviations that appears at the front of the volume. Persons represented by initials only will have their full names spelled out in square brackets after each initial on their first appearance.

7. Superscript letters in the text are lowered and aligned on the line of print.

8. Omissions, mutilations, and illegible words or letters have been rendered through the use of the following textual devices:

   a) Blank spaces in a manuscript are shown as [   ]. If the blank space is of significance or of substantial length, this fact is elaborated upon in a textual annotation.

   b) When a word or words in the original text must be omitted from the printed document because of mutilation, illegibility, or omission, the omission is shown by the use of ellipses followed by a word or phrase placed in square brackets in italics, such as: . . . [*torn*], . . . [*illegible*], . . . [*remainder missing*].

   c) Missing or illegible letters of words are represented by suspension points within square brackets, the number of points corresponding to the estimated number of letters omitted. The same holds true for missing or illegible digits of numbers.

   d) All attempts have been made to supply conjecturally missing items in the printed document, according to the following rules:

   (1) if there is no question as to the word, the missing letter is supplied silently;

   (2) if the missing letter(s) can only be conjectured, the omission is supplied within square brackets and printed in roman type. Uncertainty of the conjecture, however, is indicated by a question mark within the square brackets in the document.

   (3) if the conjectured word(s) is highly uncertain, it has been rendered in italics within the square brackets.

9. Additions and corrections made by the author in the original text have been rendered as follows:

   a) Additions between the lines are brought onto the line of type and incorporated into the body of the text within diagonal lines / /.

   b) Marginal additions or corrections by the author are also incorporated into the printed document and identified by the words [*in the margin*] italicized in square brackets. Marginal notes made by someone other than the author are treated as an endorsement and are printed following the text of the document.

c) Words or groups of words deleted in the original, as in a draft, are restored in the printed document. The ~~canceled~~ word or phrase is indicated by ~~canceled~~ type at the place where the deletion occurs in the original text. If a lengthy deletion is illegible, this is indicated by the words [*deletion illegible*].

B. Printed Material

Contemporary printed material has been treated in the same manner as were original texts and has been transcribed according to the same editorial principles as was manuscript material.

1. In the case of originally published letters, the place and date of composition are uniformly printed on the place and date line of the document, regardless of where they appear in the original, and placed within double square brackets. Those elements that have been editorially supplied are italicized.

2. Newspaper headlines and subheads are printed in small capitals. Headlines are punctuated as they are in the original; however, they are reproduced in the printed document in as few lines as possible. Unless the headline would otherwise become distorted, ornamental lines appearing within the headlines are not retained.

3. Words originally printed in full capitals for emphasis or for other reasons are usually printed in small capitals. Boldfaced type that appears within the text is retained.

4. The signature accompanying a published letter is printed in capitals and small capitals.

5. Obvious typographical errors and errors of punctuation, such as the omission of a single parenthesis or quotation mark, are corrected and printed within square brackets in roman type.

6. In the case of a printed form with spaces to be filled in, the printed words are designated in small capitals, while the handwritten or typewritten insertions are designated in italics with spaces left before and after the small capitals to suggest the blank spaces in the original form.

TEXTUAL DEVICES

[ ]	Blank spaces in the text.
[. . .], [. . . .]	Suspension points indicate approximate number of letters or digits missing in words or numerals (not to exceed four) and not conjecturable.
[[ ]]	Double square brackets are used to give the composition date of a published letter or news report if the publication date differs.
/ /	Incorporation into the text of addition or correction made above or below the line by author.
[roman]	Conjectural reading for missing, mutilated, or illegible matter, with a question mark inside the square bracket when the conjectural reading is doubtful. Also used in editorial correction of typographical errors in original manuscript or printed document. Also used to indicate the publication date of a news report or periodical article.
[*italic*]	Assigned date of any undated document; editorial comment inserted in the text, such as [*endorsement*], [*illegible*], [*remainder missing*], [*sentence unfinished*], [*torn*], [*enclosure*], [*attachment*], [*in the margin*]; conjectured reading of any uncertain word(s).
~~canceled~~	Textual matter deleted in the original but restored in the text.

SYMBOLS AND ABBREVIATIONS

Repository Symbols

The original locations of documents that appear in the text and annotations are described by symbols. The guide used for American repositories has been *Symbols of American Libraries*, eleventh edition (Washington, D.C.: Library of Congress, 1976). Foreign repositories and collections have been assigned symbols that conform to the institutions' own usage. In some cases, however, it has been necessary to formulate acronyms. Acronyms have been created for private manuscript collections as well.

Repositories

ADSL	Archives of the Department of State, Ministry of Foreign Affairs, Monrovia, Liberia
AFRC	Federal Records Center, East Point, Georgia
	RG 163 Records of the Selective Service System
CLSU	University of Southern California Library, Los Angeles
DJ-FBI	Federal Bureau of Investigation, United States Department of Justice, Washington, D.C.
DLC	Library of Congress, Washington, D.C.
DNA	National Archives, Washington, D.C.
	RG 26 Records of the United States Coast Guard
	RG 28 Records of the Post Office Department
	RG 32 Records of the United States Shipping Board
	RG 41 Records of the Bureau of Marine Inspection and Navigation
	RG 59 General records of the Department of State
	RG 60 General records of the Department of Justice
	RG 65 Records of the Federal Bureau of Investigation
	RG 84 Records of the Foreign Service posts of the Department of State

	RG 85	Records of the Immigration and Naturalization Service
	RG 165	Records of the War Department, General and Special staffs; Records of the Office of the Chief of Staff
IRO		Island Record Office, Spanish Town, Jamaica
JA		Jamaica Archives, Spanish Town
MU		University of Massachusetts Library, Amherst
N		New York State Library, Albany
NFRC		Federal Records Center, Bayonne, New Jersey
NN		New York Public Library, New York
NNC		Butler Library, Columbia University
NNHR		New York Supreme Court, Hall of Records, New York
NN-Sc		The Schomburg Center for Research in Black Culture, New York Public Library
N-SS		Office of the Secretary of State of New York, Albany
PRO		Public Record Office, London
	CAB	Cabinet Office
	CO	Colonial Office
	FO	Foreign Office
SDNY		Southern District Court of New York
WNRC		Washington National Records Center, Suitland, Maryland
	RG 185	Records of the Panama Canal

Manuscript Collection Symbols

AAG	Amy Ashwood Garvey Papers, Lionel Yard Collection, New York
JEB	John E. Bruce Papers, *NN-Sc*
LC	Lusk Committee Papers, *N*
NAACP	National Association for the Advancement of Colored People Papers, *DLC*
NCF	National Civic Federation Papers, *NN*
TAM	Thaddeus A. McCormack Papers, St. Elizabeth, Jamaica
W	*World* Collection, *NNC*
WEBDB	W. E. B. Du Bois Papers, *MU*

Descriptive Symbols

The following symbols are used to describe the character of the original documents:

ADS	Autograph document signed
ALS	Autograph letter signed
AMS	Autograph manuscript
AMSS	Autograph manuscript signed
AN	Autograph note
ANI	Autograph note initialed
D	Document
DS	Document signed
L	Letter
LS	Letter signed
MS	Manuscript
N	Note
TD	Typed document
TDS	Typed document signed
TG	Telegram
TL	Typed letter
TLI	Typed letter initialed
TLR	Typed letter representation
TLS	Typed letter signed
TMS	Typed manuscript
TN	Typed note
TNI	Typed note initialed
TNS	Typed note signed

Published Works Cited

ATOR	*African Times and Orient Review*
BFQ	*Bartlett's Familiar Quotations*, fifteenth edition
BM	*Black Man*

xlix

CBD	*Chambers's Biographical Dictionary*
CD	*Chicago Defender*
DAB	*Dictionary of American Biography*
DAHB	*Dictionary of African Historical Biography*
DG	*Daily Gleaner*
DNB	*Dictionary of National Biography*
EA	*Encyclopedia Americana*
EB	*Encyclopaedia Britannica*
EWH	*Encyclopedia of World History*
HJ	*Handbook of Jamaica*
JNH	*Journal of Negro History*
NCAB	*National Cyclopedia of American Biography*
NW	*Negro World*
NYB	*Negro Year Book*
NYT	*New York Times*
PP	*Parliamentary Papers*
WBD	*Webster's Biographical Dictionary*
WWCA	*Who's Who of Colored America*
WWCR	*Who's Who of the Colored Race*
WWJ	*Who's Who in Jamaica*
WWW	*Who Was Who*
WWWA	*Who Was Who in America*

Other Symbols and Abbreviations

Included are abbreviations that are used generally throughout annotations of the text. Standard abbreviations, such as those for titles and scholastic degrees, are omitted. Abbreviations that are specific to a single annotation appear in parentheses after the initial citation and are used thereafter in the rest of the annotation.

ABB	African Blood Brotherhood
ACL	African Communities' League
AFL	American Federation of Labor
AME	African Methodist Episcopal church
AMEZ	African Methodist Episcopal Zion church

BSL	Black Star Line, Incorporated
BWI	British West Indies
CSO	Colonial secretary's office
GPO	Government Printing Office
IWW	Industrial Workers of the World
MID	Military Intelligence Division
MP	Minute paper
NAACP	National Association for the Advancement of Colored People
OBE	Order of the British Empire
RG	Record group
UNIA	Universal Negro Improvement Association
USSB	United States Shipping Board

Monetary Symbols

d.	English pence
s. , /-	English shilling
£	English pound

CHRONOLOGY

September 1920–August 1921

1920

2 September	Amy Ashwood Garvey files for alimony increase and legal fees from Garvey.
13 September	Dudley Field Malone speaks at Liberty Hall; proposes alliance with the Irish.
15 September	British ambassador sends circular dispatch to various British consular officers requesting them to submit periodical reports on the UNIA and "Negro activities."
21 September	Garvey begins tour of Pennsylvania, Delaware, New Jersey, Maryland, and Ohio.
30 September	S.S. *Yarmouth*, while at anchor off Bay Ridge in Brooklyn, collides with S.S. *West Pool*; towed away by tugboats.
12 October	Black Star Line forced to defer its August and September installments on the S.S. *Yarmouth*.
ca. 17 October	Garvey launches $2 million Liberian Construction Loan, with promise to repatriate blacks to Liberia.
25–29 November	Garvey speaks in Pittsburgh; returns to New York.
11–24 December	Garvey visits Canada to promote Liberian Construction Loan.

1921

1 January	Original launching date set by Black Star Line for ship to be named S.S. *Phyllis Wheatley*.

2 January	Garvey delivers address at Liberty Hall on "W. E. B. Du Bois and His Escapades."
4 January	Garvey leaves New York on speaking tour of midwestern states.
7 January	UNIA chaplain general, Rev. George Alexander McGuire, leaves on two-month tour of Cuba.
1 February	UNIA six-man delegation leaves for Liberia.
1 February	Amy Ashwood Garvey files renewed motion for increase in alimony from Garvey.
1–5 February	Garvey speaks in Chicago, Cincinnati, and Cleveland.
ca. 14 February	BSL suit for damages against NAACP settled out of court by statement of correction in March issue of *Crisis*.
17 February	Garvey obtains British passport for travel to West Indies.
22 February	Garvey delivers farewell speech at Liberty Hall.
25–28 February	Garvey arrives at Key West, Florida; sails for Havana.
1 March	Charles L. Latham, American consul general in Jamaica, requests instructions from Department of State regarding issuance of visa to Garvey.
7 March	President C. D. B. King of Liberia arrives in New York as head of United States–Liberian Plenary Commission to negotiate loan; five-man welcoming UNIA delegation pays greeting call at Waldorf-Astoria Hotel.
18 March	UNIA mission arrives in Monrovia, Liberia.
ca. 20 March	Hudson Price, associate editor of *Negro World*, meets with F. E. R. Johnson of Liberian Plenary Commission in Washington, D.C., to discuss United States loan.
22 March	Garvey arrives in Kingston, Jamaica, from Santiago, Cuba.
22 March	UNIA delegates to Liberia hold official interview with Liberia's acting president.
23 March	Garvey addresses mass meeting in Kingston, in which he denounces local clergymen as hypocrites, describes Jamaica as most backward country in Western Hemisphere.

25 March	State Department instructs American consul general in Jamaica to refuse Garvey a visa in view of his activities "in political and race agitation."
25–28 March	S.S. *Kanawha* leaves New York for Cuba with forty passengers aboard; returns to New York after valve blowout; resails after two days.
March	UNIA publishes *Universal Negro Catechism*, written by Rev. G. A. McGuire.
1–3 April	S.S. *Kanawha* crashes into government pier at Port Comfort, Norfolk, Virginia, sustaining damage to stern; arrives at Jacksonville, Florida.
7 April	W. E. B. Du Bois submits statement to President C. D. B. King for publication in *Crisis*.
9 April	S.S. *Kanawha* arrives in Cuba.
10 April	UNIA officials in New York announce that ship to be named S.S. *Phyllis Wheatley* will be "floated" on 1 May.
11 April	Garvey applies for visa and is refused by American consul general in Jamaica.
12–15 April	Garvey leaves Jamaica for Costa Rica; holds interview with president of Costa Rica in San José.
18 April	Garvey leaves San José and returns to Port Limón.
21 April	Garvey visits Bocas del Toro, Panama.
ca. 22 April	F. E. R. Johnson, member of Liberian Plenary Commission, addresses meeting of Philadelphia UNIA division.
26 April	Garvey travels to Colón, Panama.
26 April	State Department instructs American legation in Costa Rica to refuse Garvey's request for visa.
28 April	United States Shipping Board grants permit to Black Star Line to inspect former German steamer S.S. *Orion* at Camp Eustis, Virginia; Black Star Line makes offer of $190,000.
30 April	Garvey visits Panama City.
April	UNIA delegates in Liberia stop "construction work" temporarily because of lack of funds.
April	Rev. F. Wilcom Ellegor, UNIA high commissioner,

	meets with President C. D. B. King in Washington, D.C., regarding UNIA Liberian Construction Loan.
4–5 May	Garvey leaves Panama City and returns to Colón; delivers farewell address; sails for Kingston.
7 May	Garvey arrives in Jamaica.
9 May	William C. Matthews, UNIA assistant counselor general, petitions State Department to allow Garvey to return to United States.
10 May	State Department instructs American consul general in Kingston to refuse to visa crew list of S.S. *Kanawha* should Garvey's name appear as crew member.
11 May	J. Edgar Hoover submits brief to Department of State regarding activities of Garvey in the United States.
14 May	Black Star Line's purchase offer for S.S. *Orion* refused by United States Shipping Board.
17 May	S.S. *Kanawha* arrives at Kingston from Cuba.
28 May	Garvey sets sail for Panama as *Kanawha* crew member; after three days at sea, vessel returns to Kingston in distress.
31 May–1 June	Racial violence erupts at Tulsa, Oklahoma, leaving an estimated 270 persons dead and more than one thousand homes owned by blacks destroyed.
1–7 June	Garvey lodges series of complaints against *Kanawha*'s master and crew.
7 June	William C. Matthews confers with State Department's official in charge of visa control.
9 June	Black Star Line transfers deposit on S.S. *Orion* to S.S. *Porto Rico*, with offer to United States Shipping Board to purchase for $175,000.
12 June	Cyril A. Crichlow, resident-secretary of UNIA delegation in Liberia, resigns.
14 June	American consul general in Jamaica carries out investigation of Garvey's charges against *Kanawha*'s master and chief engineer; finds them innocent.
18–22 June	S.S. *Kanawha* leaves Kingston a second time; disabled once more, returns to port.
20 June	Cyril A. Crichlow seeks protection of American consul general in Liberia.

25 June	State Department cables authorization for Garvey to be issued visa in Jamaica.
27 June	UNIA potentate, Gabriel M. Johnson, leaves Liberia for New York to attend second UNIA convention.
28 June	American consul general issues visa to Garvey; he leaves Kingston for Belize, British Honduras, en route to United States.
29 June	State Department seeks to stop voyage of Gabriel M. Johnson.
June	*Crisis* publishes open letter signed by President C. D. B. King renouncing ties with UNIA.
1–5 July	Garvey arrives at Belize; addresses mass meetings and holds interview with governor.
13–14 July	Garvey arrives in New Orleans; detained temporarily by United States immigration authorities; speaks at public meetings.
14–16 July	Gabriel M. Johnson arrives in New York; interviewed by Bureau of Investigation agents; detained for examination by United States Immigration on Ellis Island; finally admitted.
17 July	Garvey returns to New York.
ca. 18 July	UNIA purchases $34,400 worth of BSL stock from funds donated to the Liberian Construction Loan.
20 July	Garvey addresses welcoming meeting in Liberty Hall.
26 July	Second annual meeting of BSL stockholders; meeting adjourned after reading of brief statement.
1 August	Opening of second UNIA convention; keynote speech delivered by UNIA potentate, Gabriel M. Johnson.
2 August	United States Shipping Board accepts BSL offer to purchase S.S. *Orion*.
4 August	Garvey delivers official convention report; writes official letter to President C. D. B. King.
5 August	Charges made against UNIA secretary-general, Rev. J. D. Brooks, for alleged misappropriation of funds.
5 August	Convention reports presented by Elie Garcia, UNIA auditor general, and Rev. G. E. Stewart, UNIA high chancellor; opening of Women's Industrial Exhibit.

8 August	UNIA secretary-general's report presented by J. B. Yearwood, assistant secretary-general.
9 August	Convention reports presented by Rev. G. A. McGuire, UNIA chaplain general, and Rev. F. Wilcom Ellegor, UNIA commissioner general.
10 August	Convention holds Women's Day.
15 August	Delegates of African Blood Brotherhood attend convention.
15 August	ABB head, Cyril V. Briggs, sends letter to Garvey requesting conference with him.
19 August	Rose Pastor Stokes, Communist party leader, addresses UNIA convention.
24 August	S.S. *Kanawha* arrives at Antilla, Cuba; crew forced to abandon ship because of disabled condition.
25 August	Formal charges raised against various UNIA executive officers and debated on floor of convention.
26 August	ABB routed from convention.
27 August	First ceremonial court reception of UNIA held.
28–29 August	Second Pan-African Congress meets in London.
29 August	Election of UNIA officers.
30 August	New York State Supreme Court orders Garvey to be examined before *Pan-Union Company* v. *Black Star Line* begins trial; Garvey fails to comply with the order.
31 August	Bureau of Investigation continues investigation of Garvey for possible Mann Act violation.
31 August	Closing of UNIA convention; Garvey delivers closing address.

THE PAPERS

VOLUME III
September 1920–August 1921

Editorial Letter by Marcus Garvey

[[New York, Sept. 1, 1920]]

To the Negro People of the World, Greeting:

We hereby beg to inform you that acting under instructions from the Universal Negro Improvement Association and African Communities League of the World, an international convention of Negroes, representing every country in the world, was called, and said convention was held in New York, United States of America, in sitting from the 1st to the 31st of August, 1920.

The purpose of the convention was to elect world leaders for the Negro people of the world. After several weeks of discussion and probing into the merits of the most able representatives of the race, the convention elected the following dignitaries as leaders of the Negro people of the world, and now we have it in authority from the convention to present to you these honorable personages that you may know them and govern yourselves accordingly by their ruling. There has been disputed leadership of the Negro people in all countries heretofore, but through the effort of this international convention the problem of leadership has been settled once and for all, and all Negroes in all parts of the world are requested to obey the rulings and advice given by the following dignitaries according to the authority vested in them.

His Highness, Gabriel Johnson, Potentate of the Universal Negro Improvement Association and African Communities League, was elected world leader, and he shall have under his command all the Negro peoples of the world.

His Highness, G. O. Marke, was elected Supreme Deputy Potentate, and ranks second in authority to His Highness, the Potentate.

The Potentate's proclamation on all matters pertaining to the race shall be respected by all Negro[e]s of the world.

His Excellency, J. W. [H]. Eason, was elected leader of the fifteen million Negroes of the United States of America, and his command shall be obeyed in all matters pertaining to the race.

His Excellency, Marcus Garvey, was elected Provisional President of Africa, and his ruling on all things African pertaining to a free and independent republic shall be obeyed by all Negroes.

His Excellency, R. H. Tobitt, was elected Leader of the Negroes of the West Indies, Eastern Province, and his command on all things pertaining to the race shall be obeyed by all in those sections.

His Excellency, John Sydney Debourg, was elected Leader of the Negroes of the West Indies, Western Province, South and Central America, and his ruling in all matters pertaining to the race shall be obeyed by those in the section.

The time has come for the race to establish centralized authority in the control of its own affairs and this convention with the power vested in it through its accredited delegates, did elect and inaugurate into office the

3

dignitaries herein mentioned. The following is a list of the Universal Movement for the Redemption of the Negro Race:

His Highness, the Potentate, Leader of the Negro Peoples of the World—GABRIEL JOHNSON.

His Highness, the Supreme Deputy Potentate—G. O. MARKE.

His Excellency, the President General of the Universal Negro Improvement Association and African Communities League—MARCUS GARVEY.

His Excellency, the Provisional President of Africa—MARCUS GARVEY.

His Excellency, Leader of the American Negroes—JAMES W. H. EASON.

His Excellency, Leader of the West Indies, Eastern Province—R. H. TOBITT.

His Excellency, Leader of the West Indies, Western Province—J[OHN] SYDNEY DEBOURG.

Right Hon. Assistant President General—J. D. GORDON.

Right Hon. Secretary General—J. D. BROOKS.

His Honor, The Assistant Secretary General—J. B. YEARWOOD.

Right Hon. High Chancellor—GABRIEL EMANUEL STEWART.

Right Hon. Counsel General—WILFORD HORACE SMITH.

His Honor, The Assistant Counsel General—WM. C. MATTHEWS.

Right Hon. Auditor General—ELI[E] GARCIA.

Right Hon. Commissioner General—[F]. WILCOM ELLEGOR.

His Grace, The Chaplain General—GEO. ALEXANDER MCGUIRE, D.D.

Right Hon. International Organizer—HENRIETTA VINTON DAVIS.

Right Hon. Surgeon General—D. D. LEWIS, M.D.

Right Hon. Speaker of the House of Convention—FREDERICK AUGUSTUS TOOTE.

Right Hon. Minister of Legions—CAPT. E. L. GAINES.

These are the only accredited leaders of the Negro peoples of the world as elected by the House of Deputies in convention assembled from August 1st to 31st, 1920.

All members of the race will also uphold and give their support to the Declaration of Rights, which is now being published for universal circulation and which is published in another part of this paper. Yours fraternally,

MARCUS GARVEY,
Chairman of Convention.
JAS. D. BROOKS,
Secretary

Printed in *NW*, 11 September 1920. Original headlines omitted.

Reports by Special Agent P-138

New York Sept. 1, '20

NEGRO ACTIVITIES.

Today [30 *August*] marks the end of the actual working session of the Garvey Convention in Liberty Hall. The finishing touches were put on the bylaws which are very numerous. The delegates are now all clamoring for the copies of the so-called "Bill of Rig[hts]" which were to have been printed and a copy or copies handed to each at the end of the convention. However, this was not done, and no one seems to be sure just when they will be ready. At the night session, Garvey gave a lengthy and den[u]nciatory speech against the British Government, and Lloyd George in particular, claiming that the white people were bent on preventing him from entering Africa, but he was going to fool them and beat them to it. He impressed upon his hearers the great necessity of keeping up the fight for the principle of the negro association, even if they were to face death. That the white race were their natural foe, irrespective whether they were American, English, French or Germans.

Great preparation is being made for the grand parade, holiday and reception tomorrow evening which marks the official winding up of the Convention.

P-138

[*Endorsements*] FILE G. F. R.
NOTED W. W. G. NOTED F. D. W.

DNA, RG 65, file OG 329359. TD. Stamped endorsements.

New York 9-2-20

There was a parade on the streets of Harlem by GARVEY to-day [*31 August*], but owing to the rain, it was not as much of a success as they planned. For some reason, the enthusiasm which marked the former parade was lacking in this.

To-night there was a big mass meeting and dance in the Star Casino, Lexington Avenue. Speeches were made by GARVEY, EASTON [*Eason*], MCGUIRE and others.

It would appear, however, that the sole object of this mass meeting was to sell stock of the Black Star Line, as all the speakers dwelt on that subject. The speeches were lacking [in] emotion, as the crowds were attracted there chiefly for the dancing.

The delegates were promised to have a copy of the constitution in a very short while, and many of them are planning to stay over in New York for a week or more.

P-138

[*Endorsements*] NOTED F. D. W.
NOTED W. W. G. FILE G. F. R.

DNA, RG 65, file OG 329359. TD. Stamped endorsements.

New York City 9-4-20

IN RE NEGRO ACTIVITIES. MARCUS GARVEY

On September 1st there was a general meeting at Liberty Hall, but GARVEY was not present. The hall was only about a quarter filled and the speakers confined their speeches to their experiences, etc. . . .

September 2d. I learned that GARVEY's wife filed suit against him for separation, alimony and counsellor fee of a high figure.[1] This is causing a lot of excitement in the Negro section, owing to the fact that his wife was his partner in this "Back to Africa Movement".[2] There are also about eight other cases pending against him in the Seventh District Court, for non payment of debts, etc.

September 3d. . . . The Garvey followers are very bitter against Domingo owing to the attacks of his defunct paper "EMANCIPATOR" on the Black Star Line. These men swore to kill DOMINGO at the very first opportunity.

As a matter of fact they determine to kill anyone who opposes Garvey and his movement in any shape, form or manner.

P-138

[*Endorsements*] NOTED W. W. G.
FILE G. F. R.

DNA, RG 65, file OG 329359. TD. Stamped endorsements.

1. Garvey first brought action against Amy Ashwood Garvey on 11 August 1920. His complaint was presented in two parts: first, that Amy Ashwood had through "fraud, concealment, and misrepresentations" induced him to marry her, and second, that she had been guilty of adultery "with persons unknown to the plaintiff." Garvey requested that the marriage be annulled. His complaint was disallowed, however, because of "improper joinder of causes," a decision that forced Garvey to issue an amended complaint on 23 November 1920. In the meantime Amy Ashwood Garvey went to court on 13 September requesting alimony of $75 per week and counsel fees of $5,000 from Garvey. On 9 October she was granted $12 per week alimony and $250 in counsel fees. She denied Garvey's charges that she drank excessively and continued to correspond with a male friend while engaged to Garvey and after their marriage. (The friend was Allen Cumberbatch, whom she had met in Panama.) On 1 February 1921 she countered with charges that Garvey had been voted a handsome salary at the 1920 convention and could afford to pay a much larger alimony than the court had allowed. She requested that a referee be appointed to investigate Garvey's claim that his income was only $25 per week; this request was granted on 14 February. As the case dragged on without resolution, Garvey became impatient. Claiming that the burden of alimony he had to bear made a preferred status for the case appropriate, Garvey entered a formal request on 7 April. Amy Ashwood's lawyers

answered by claiming that since Garvey had been the aggressor in the case, he should be given no special consideration. Finally, on 18 April Garvey requested that he be allowed to discontinue the suit after paying all court costs as well as paying his estranged wife whatever amount the court considered appropriate. As his justification Garvey stated that in meetings with the board of directors of the Black Star Line and the executive council of the UNIA, he had been advised that the bad publicity the case had generated would affect the credibility of the Black Star Line and hinder the growth of the UNIA (*Marcus Garvey* v. *Amy Garvey*, no. 24028, New York State Supreme Court, September 1920).

2. Bureau of Investigation agent Joseph G. Tucker reported on 4 September 1920 that "the latter's [Garvey's] wife, whom he is suing for divorce, promised within a short time to make some startling revelations that will be of interest to this Bureau" (DNA, RG 65, file OG 208369-A). There is no subsequent report on the matter, however.

New York City 9-7 [*1920*]

Today [*6 September*] while passing GARVEY's office on 135th Street, he beckoned me from his steps, saying he would like to speak to me for a while.

He told me that he was being sued for $20,000 each by R. E. WARREN [*Warner*] and EDGAR GRAY for damages as a result of the outcome of the KILROE case. Both men were complainants in the District Attorney's case, and although GARVEY apologized to them and Mr. Kilroe, thereby getting a withdrawal of the criminal libel, these two men now are entering suits against him for civil action.

Garvey said he was not prepared for this which has taken him by surprise, so he asked me to give him my help and support. He reminded me of an incident long ago, when GRAY collected money from me for advertising in his paper under false pretenses, and asked me whether he could get me to prove that so as to help his side of the case. I told him that I will give him my support as far as I could, but advised him strongly to settle out of court by a compromise, and told him I would see the men and learn their terms of course. Garvey has played into their hands by making a retraction of his newspaper charges against them, which is a trump card in their lawyers' hands, thereby compelling Garvey to pay damages on a compromise. This and the many other cases has got Garvey "up a tree".

Garvey told me that the Bill of Rights and Constitution will be published in his paper this week. He also informed me that he was just about to send out a number of propagandists all over the world to spread his teachings. He said that Domingo's paper "The Emancipator" caused [*cost?*] him and his company thousands of dollars, and Domingo was the most spiteful man he has ever met. He was about to make a big drive for shares in Black Star Line all over the country leaving New York tomorrow, so as to raise money to buy a large ship for the African trade.

P-138

[*Endorsements*] NOTED G. F. R.
NOTED W. W. G. NOTED F. D. W.

DNA, RG 65, file OG 329359. TD. Stamped endorsements.

Editorial Letter by Marcus Garvey

[[New York, September 7, 1920]]

FELLOW MEN OF THE NEGRO RACE, Greeting:

Owing to the pressure of work in the convention I was unable to keep in closer touch with you during the eventful month of August. However, I embrace this opportunity of writing to you to convey the hearty good wishes of the first International Convention of Negroes which assembled in Liberty Hall, New York, United States of America, from the 1st to the 31st of August. This convention will go down in history as an epoch-making event. It is for me to tell you that for the thirty-one days the honorable Deputies who made up the convention and who were sent to us by the scattered electorate of Negroes in the four hundred millions of the race did their work so nobly and well that they have won for themselves the cognomen of "ABLE COUNSEL-LORS." It would have made any race or nation's heart feel glad to listen to these honorable Deputies. They came from the four corners of the world with a message for the convention. It was a message of good-will from their section of the world. Indeed, the assemblage was but a pooling of the heartaches and the fraternal greetings of the Negro people of the world. Retrospectively, methinks I hear the unhappy reports of the delegates from Zululand, from Nigeria, from Nyasaland, and from the Congo in Africa. In the same echo methinks I hear also the sad tales of the sufferings in Trinidad, in Jamaica, in Antigua and the other British West Indian Islands. And what did we do? We had to make laws; we had to formulate and adopt a Constitution, a Declaration of Rights, and, thank God, we have given that Declaration of Rights to the world. We wrote fifty-four articles into the Declaration of Rights, and those articles we have given to the world with the warning, with the understanding, that four hundred million Negroes will sacrifice the last drop of their blood to see that every article comes true. No more fear, no more cringing, no more sycophantic begging and pleading; but the Negro must strike straight from the shoulder for manhood rights and for full liberty. Africa calls now more than ever. She calls because the attempt is now being made by the combined Caucasian forces of Europe to subjugate her, to overrun her and to reduce her to that state of alien control that will mean in another one hundred years the complete extermination of the native African. Can we not remember the extermination of the North American Indian which was practiced in a similar manner to the practices now holding sway on the Continent of Africa[?] This convention of August left us full-fledged men; men charged to do our duty, and by the God Divine, and by the Heavens that shelter all humanity, we have pledged ourselves to bring the manhood of our race to the highest plane of human achievement. We cannot, and we must not, falter. There is absolutely no turning back. There must be a going forward to the point of destiny. Destiny leads us to liberty, to freedom; that freedom that Victoria of England never gave; that liberty that

Lincoln never meant; that freedom, that liberty, that will see us men among men; that will see us a nation among nations; that will make of us a great and powerful people. Do you tell me you cannot make it? And I say, "Shame on you!" Have you not, you British Negro soldiers, made it for British colonization of the west coast of Africa, when, by your prowess, you conquered the innocent and unsuspecting native tribes? Did you not make it, you American Negro soldiers, for the white Americans in the Revolutionary War, in the Civil War, and when you climbed the heights of San Juan? Did you not make it at the battle of Château-Thierry and the Argonne? You French Negro soldiers, did you not make it at the battles of the Marne and Verdun? Then why can you not make it for yourselves, climbing the battle heights of Africa, to plant there the standard of the Red, Black and Green[?] I repeat, you men of the world, there can be no turning back. It means that the Negro must plant the banner of freedom in this twentieth century on the battle plains of Africa or he is lost forever. The world is still in turmoil, the world is still in agony, the world is still in labor. And there will never be a settled world, there will never be a world wherein men will be in peace, one with the other, until the reign of justice is heralded in. But there can be no justice, there will be no ordinary human respect, so long as one race remains at the foot of the great human ladder and the other race sits at the top. It is time that the Negro rise from the foot of the ladder and climb the dizzy heights of fame and meet his brother at the top. What argument, what persuasion, can ever turn us from our course, the course of liberty? Men, be not cowards; men, be not fearful of what the other fellow says. Remember, you are men. God Almighty created us in his image. He gave us all the attributes of men and as men, bearing a semblance to the Divine. Let us rise to the heights that will enable us to say to the race of our brothers, "Indeed, we are of you, and shall remain with you."

The signal honor of being Provisional President of Africa is mine. It is a political job; it is a political calling for me to redeem Africa. It is like asking Napoleon to take the world. He took a certain portion of the world in his time. He failed and died at St. Helena. But may I not say that the lessons of Napoleon are but stepping stones by which we shall guide ourselves to African liberation? We do not desire the conquest of a world; we desire the conquest of Africa; that land that is ours, the land that no one can dispute as being the heritage of the Negro, and for that land I live; for that land I will bleed; for that land I will die, that you have made me its Provisional President. You have also made me President General of the Universal Negro Improvement Association and African Communities League, a social, industrial and commercial organization. This organization seeks no warfare; it seeks not to deprive others of what is theirs; it seeks to build an economic base for the Negro wheresoever he lives. Please give to this organization all the help you possibly can. Help it to become a power of commercial strength so that, as we and our children grow into older manhood, we may be able to find a way by which to live so as to preserve our own existence.

Steamships must be bought and built. In countries like Liberia railroads must be built. Industrial plants must go up if the race is to rise in greatness. Are you prepared to do your part? Men, can you be a commercial power by bowing at the footstools of other races? Can you become an industrial power by giving all energy and wealth to other races? The answer is No. But you can become a great commercial and industrial power by amassing and pooling your own industries and forming your own commercial enterprises. The Declaration of Rights, published in another part of this paper,[1] shall be the Holy Writ of this Negro race of ours. It shall be the very Scriptures by which we shall know ourselves. Alongside the Holy Words of God shall go this Declaration of Rights of this Negro race of ours, and as we pray to Almighty God to save us through his Holy Words so shall we with confidence in ourselves follow the sentiment of the Declaration of Rights and carve our way to liberty. This Declaration of Rights shall take its place alongside of the Declaration of Independence of the United States of America and the Magna Charta of England. Who shall say nay to the Negro in intepreting the sentiment of this Declaration of Rights? He who says nay to the American white man on the principles of his Declaration of Independence; he who says nay to the Englishman on the interpretation of the sentiment of the Magna Charta, then let him say nay to the Negro in his interpretation of this Declaration of Rights, because, as an American white citizen vows that he will give his last drop of blood in defense of his independence and his constitution, and as an Anglo-Saxon will drain the last drop of his blood in defen[s]e of his Constitution and his rights, so I repeat the Negro must drain the last drop of his blood in defense of the sentiments of this Declaration of Rights. Let there be no misunderstanding. The Negro has risen to the fullness of his power. That power he shall preserve down the ages "until the wreck of matter and the crash of worlds."

And now let me say, while we are preparing universally for this new start, let us also remember the Black Star Line Steamship Corporation. The command has gone forth, "Ships and more ships." Africa must be linked to the United States of America. Africa must be linked to South and Central America. Africa must be linked to the West Indies, so that there can be an unbroken intercourse between the four hundred million Negroes of the world. We can only do it by and with more ships, and now is the chance, now is the opportunity for every Negro to do his bit by the Black Star Line Steamship Corporation by buying more shares. Every share you buy is a plate in the great ships of the Negroes' merchant marine. The shares are still going at five dollars each. You may buy two, five, ten, twenty, one hundred or two hundred. The time will come when these shares will bring to you hundreds of dollars. Therefore, while the opportunity presents itself, buy your shares now. Do g[ood] by yourselves in this generation and insure the success of your posterity. You can buy your shares by writing t[o the] Black Star Line Steamship Corporation, 54–56 West 135th Street, New York City, United States of America.

For further information about the Universal Negro Improvement Association, under whose auspices [the first] International Convention of Negroes of the world w[as held] you may write to the Right Honorable Secretary G[eneral,] the Universal Negro Improvement Association, 56 [West] 135th Street, New York. With very best wishes for your success. Yours fraternally,

MARCUS GARVEY

Printed in *NW*, 11 September 1920. Original headlines omitted.

1. See *The Marcus Garvey and the Universal Negro Improvement Association Papers* 2:571–580 (hereafter cited as *Garvey Papers*).

Marcus Garvey to Leo Healy

New York, U.S.A., Sept. 7th 1920

Dear Mr. Healy:

This letter introduces to you Mr. O. M. Thompson, the Vice President of our Corporation.

I am out of town for a week in the interest of my Corporation and he has informed me that he received a letter from Mr. Harris, relative to our note on the "Yarmouth." Please accommodate Mr. Thompson for me in holding over the note as per his arrangement as I am arranging to have same fixed. Your good services in this respect will be highly appreciated.

Relative to the non registration of the Bill of Sale of the "Yarmouth," you and Mr. Nolan[1] will arrange the matter. In any case you can depend that everything will be all right as far as the Black Star Line is concerned. You need not be nervous about the money. Yours faithfully,

BLACK STAR LINE, INC.
MARCUS GARVEY,
President

Marcus Garvey v. *United States*, no. 8317, Ct. App., 2d Cir., 2 February 1925, government exhibit no. 17.

1. Joseph P. Nolan, an attorney whose offices were located at 25 Broad Street, New York, was hired in May or June 1920 by the Black Star Line to handle the bill of sale for the *Kanawha*. The BSL later retained him on salary to handle the negotiations for the *Orion* (*Marcus Garvey* v. *United States*, no. 8317, Ct. App., 2d Cir., 2 February 1925, pp. 1,983–1,989).

Auckland C. Geddes to Earl Curzon of Kedleston[1]

WASHINGTON, September 15, 1920

My Lord:

I have the honour to acknowledge the receipt of Your Lordship's despatch No. 988 (A5761/443/45) of August 25th, and to inform you that I have addressed a Circular despatch to His Majesty's Superintending Consular Officers in those States where the negro question is an active issue, with a view to securing periodical reports on negro activities and the growth of the movement promoted by the various Associations having their headquarters in New York and more particularly by that known as "The Universal Negro Improvement Association". In this connection I have the honour to state that a Negro Conference held in New York in the course of last month appears to have elected Mr. Marcus Garvey, who describes himself as the President General of the Universal Negro Improvement Association, to a position which, according to newspaper reports, is held to constitute him "King of Africa" and which in any case would seem to imply some measure of leadership over negroes both within and without the United States. I have the honour to be with the highest respect, My Lord, Your Lordship's most obedient, humble servant,

A[UCKLAND] C. GEDDES

[*Typewritten reference*] No. 1161

PRO, FO 371/4567. TLS, recipient's copy.

1. George Nathaniel Curzon (1859–1925), British statesman, became Earl of Kedleston in 1911. He served in a variety of diplomatic and government positions, including viceroy and governor general of India (1899–1905), before his appointment by Herbert Henry Asquith to the war cabinet in 1915. In 1919 he became secretary of state for foreign affairs, a position he held until 1924 (*WBD*).

Report by Special Agent P-138

New York City 9-20-20

IN RE NEGRO ACTIVITIES: MARCUS GARVEY

In connection with the meeting held last night [*12 September*] at Liberty Hall I beg to report that this meeting was attended by about 14 Irish sympathizers and Irish men and women who were striking[1] on the d[o]cks against English ships, and for the release of Mayor McSwiney.

DUDLEY FIELD MALONE[2] spoke from Garvey's platform and some Irish leaders as well. They spoke in high terms of Garvey and his movement and pledged their support.

It would appear that on Saturday SELFRIDGE, a Negro local preacher and Garvey's hired field agent and right hand stool pigeon, was sent down to the docks to urge all the Negro longshoremen not to load British ships,[3] which act pleased the Irish strikers, who learned that Garvey had sent him down to aid them. This is the reason for the appearance of Dudley Field Malone and other sympathizers at Liberty Hall Sunday night.

I got in touch with Selfridge today and learned from him that he and another of Garvey's men, named [*Adrian*] JOHNSON, were to have a conference with the Irish leaders at their headquarters this afternoon but Johnson had gone alone.

Selfridge told me confidentially that he was sure Garvey could get money from the Irish, and especially from the Japanese, but Garvey was too slow, as he will be playing his own part and get what he can. He said he is going to keep close to the Irish in the future.

Garvey and all his high officers will leave on a two months stock selling and lecture tour tomorrow, and they bade farewell tonight. Garvey said that New York people were fast asleep regarding giving any more money to the Black Star Line, so he is forced to go out of town. He will be accompanied by a band of music, several singers, etc. and will start in at Maryland, Washington, etc.

Rev. EASTON will go to Canada accompanied by [*Vernal J.*] WILLIAMS, leaving there he will tour the West and Middle Western States, and another lieutenant will invade the New England States, and the New York end of the business will be taken care of by Rev[.] MCGUIRE.

It is admitted all around that finances are very low and things are looking gloomy, hence this big sensational drive for funds.

P-138

[*Endorsements*] FILE G. F. R.
NOTED W. W. G.

DNA, RG 65, file OG 329359. TD. Stamped endorsements.

1. The American Women's Pickets for the Enforcement of America's War Aims, a group connected with the Friends of Irish Freedom, began the strike on 27 August 1920 when five members of the group successfully led a walkout of Irish longshoremen on the New York docks. The International Longshoremen's Association denounced the strike, which had spread to Boston and eventually involved about three thousand men. The British steamship lines countered the strike with black strikebreakers—some of them union members. On 2 September a group of one thousand white workers touched off a race riot when they attacked some five hundred recently hired black longshoremen. Police reserves then forced the black workers off their jobs (*NYT*, 28 August, 29 August, 3 September, 4 September, and 11 September 1920).

2. Dudley Field Malone (1882–1950), an Irish-American lawyer and an early supporter of Woodrow Wilson, became a member of the president's inner circle. Malone married Mary P. O'Gorman, daughter of U.S. Senator James A. O'Gorman. Well-known for his advocacy of liberal causes, Malone supported the NAACP and the women's suffrage movement. In 1913 Wilson appointed Malone third assistant secretary of state, and later the same year Wilson selected him as a collector of the port of New York. In 1917 Malone resigned from this position; he went on to promote a number of political causes for the remainder of his career. He formed the League of Oppressed Peoples in 1919 to "protest against continued imperialist adventures on the part of certain great powers" (Dudley Field Malone to W. E. B. Du Bois, 3 November

1919, MU, WEBDB). The league was primarily interested in promoting self-determination for China, India, Korea, and Ireland (*NYT*, 6 October 1950; *DAB*; *New York Evening Post*, 10 April 1913).

   3. The *Messenger* reported that over 250 black dockworkers joined in the strike by the Irish longshoremen (*Messenger* 2 [October 1920]: 102; Sterling D. Spero and Abram L. Harris, *The Black Worker* [New York: Columbia University Press, 1931], p. 203).

Statement by Edwin P. Kilroe

[*New York*] September 21, 1920

   The defendant [Marcus Garvey] was indicted on the 28th day of August, 1919, on the charge of Criminal Libel. On August 2, 1919 he published in the newspaper "The Negro World" a libelous article concerning Edwin P. Kilroe, Assistant District Attorney, and Edward M. Gray and Richard E. Warner. When the case was called for trial on August 9, 1920, Garvey filed with the Court a retraction of the charges and made a public apology. This retraction was subsequently published on the front page of ["]The Negro World.["] In his retraction Garvey stated that he was satisfied that the statements which he published concerning the conduct of Edwin P. Kilroe in the investigation of the Black Star Line and the Universal Negro Improvement Association were false; and stated that he regretted that the statements had been made. The public apology and retraction is satisfactory to me; and if it meets with the approval of the Court, I respectfully suggest that the indictment against Garvey for Criminal Libel be dismissed. Respectfully submitted,

EDWIN P. KILROE
Assistant District Attorney

The People of the State of New York v. *Marcus Garvey*, cal. no. 27,760, ind. nos. 126535 and 126552, Court of General Sessions for the County of New York, 9 August 1920. TDS.

Report by Special Agent P-138

New York City 9-24-20

IN RE: NEGRO ACTIVITIES. MARCUS GARVEY.

   There are persistent rumors that GARVEY'S BLACK STAR LINE project is bordering on financial ruin; that the two old boats are offered for sale owing to the fact that he is unable to meet his payments due, also to find enough money to make the necessary repairs which will make them seaworthy.

GARVEY is on a tour [*21 September*] in Pennsylvania and New Jersey making desperate appeals for funds to stave off this impending catastrophe.

It must be understood that the foundation and strength of Garvey's anti-white movement rests solely on his retaining ownership of these ships, for just as soon as they are gone, down goes the main prop of his movement, therefore the commercial value of these ships is by far a secondary consideration against their moral and racial value. Hence, if they are lost, Garvey's prestige and power for spreading race hatred will be reduced to a minimum.

P-138

[*Endorsements*] FILE G. F. R.
NOTED F. D. W. FILE W. W. G.

DNA, RG 65, file OG 329359. TD. Stamped endorsements.

Speeches by Marcus Garvey[1]

Washington, D.C., September 24, 19[20]

MEETING OF THE UNIVERSAL NEGRO IMPROVEMENT ASSOCIATION AND THE BLACK STAR LINE STEAMSHIP CO.

PRESIDING OFFICER: H. W. KIRBY (224 ELM STREET, N.W., WASH. D.C.)

. . . HON. MARCUS GARVEY

I have appeared here more than once—many times—and it would appear that every time I speak to you, you hear me and you go away forgetting all I say. I trust you are not going to forget what I say tonight: otherwise I better not come back to Washington. I will leave Washington out and we will redeem the great cause, I suppose, without Washington.

Now what is this Universal /Negro/ Improvement Association? It is a worldwide movement of Negroes having as its purpose the drawing together of every colored man, woman, and child into one great huge body in preparation for a day that is sure to come, a day when the various races of black men will be in one common battleground to settle their differences and to maintain their respective rights. That day threatens as sure as the sun shines every day.

Because this political apportionment of the world means for the people in this age who fail to find a place for themselves, such a people is doomed forever. That is why I waste the time and make the opportunity to come to Washington so often, to speak to you and to make you understand what we are endeavoring to do in other parts of the world. In New York, in Philadelphia, in Boston, in the great eastern states, we have already rolled up an organization of over a million and a half men and women in these United States of America, and the cry is the slogan of Africa for the Africans.

Washington, I say to you, 'awake, awake because the world of Negroes around you is asserting itself to throw off the yoke of the white man of 300 years.['] We, in the convention of August, have elected leaders, and on the first of November we will send into the District of Columbia the first Negro ever elected by the Negroes of the United States of America to lead them. In August we elected the Hon. J. W. H. Eason as the leader of the 15,000,000 Negroes of America. Eason has proved to be one of the ablest men of the race, and we will send him up here in November to occupy the Black House of Washington.[2] And around him we will have men who will be able to rank in the Diplomatic Circle, just as at the French Embassy they have men. As Provisional President of Africa I hope, also, in a few months, to have a Minister Plenipotentiary as an ambassador in Washington. We are going to have representatives of the Negro in Washington, but after November we are going to have a minister plenipotentiary and ambassador in England, Germany, France, and Italy to protect the rights of the Negro.

The Irish were prepared before the war, and what happened after the war? During the war they were promised certain things which, as is customary, England never kept the promises she made, and will never keep her promise.[3] Because Ireland is depending upon England to keep her promise Ireland lost out, and though they lost out they elected a provisional President of Ireland and declared for the freedom of Ireland.[4] Because [*Booker T.*] Washington did not prepare us, because [*Robert Russa*] Moton did not prepare us, there is no Africa for the Negro as there is a Palestine for the Jew,[5] a Poland for the Poles,[6] but what they did not do in the years past we are going to do now. We are contending for the rights of the Negro today, so that when another bloody world war comes it will not be a question of how many Negroes can the United States raise for the Army, or how many Negroes can the British Empire raise for the army, or how many Negroes France can raise for the Army, it will be a question of how many Negroes can the Universal Negro Improvement Association raise for the new Napoleon of the Negro race to march on the battle plains of Africa for the ultimate salvation of this race. I stand and declare to the people of Washington—to repeat what Doctor McGuire said—we are not desirous of asking all the American Negroes or all of the West Indian Negroes to pack up their baggage and go back to Africa. We are asking you to lend your sympathy and your moral and financial and physical support to the building of Africa and the making of Africa a great republic. Make it a first-class nation, a first-rate power, and when Africa becomes a first-rate power, if you live in Georgia, if you live in Mississippi, if you live in Texas, as a black man I will dare them to lynch you, because you are an African citizen and you will have a great army and a great navy to protect your rights.

In concluding I want you to realize this: I am not talking for an untried organization. I am here representing an organization that is a power in the world. The Universal Negro Improvement Association is the only movement among Negroes now that is striking fear in the breast of the nations of the world, and it is no secret. Everybody knows it. They know it in Washington. If you doubt it, go up to the State Department and ask, and they tell you that that movement of Garvey's is hell. They have spent thousands [*and*] thousands of dollars already, following me all over the country, and who can tell that some stool pigeon is not in here tonight. And I have told them all I have to say with the exception of that part I am keeping back for the next war. They will never hear that part until after the victory in Africa. This is the only movement that has caused the great British Empire to be trembling in its shoes, because they can't tell what the outcome will be. When they elected me Provisional President of Africa the other day, the first thing I did was to telegraph David Lloyd George to tell him we were coming, four hundred million strong, and no one better than David Lloyd George—he knows that sixty million of people can not resist four hundred million of people when they come. . . .[7]

DNA, RG 65, file OG 329359. TD.

1. This stenographic transcript of Garvey's speech was prepared by Woolsey W. Hall, a black stenographer who worked in the printing branch of the Treasury Department. He was assigned to cover Garvey's Washington meetings at the request of William J. Neale, the acting chief of the Bureau of Investigation (William J. Neale to P. J. Ahern, 24 September 1920, DNA, RG 65, file OG 329359).

2. This plan was never carried out.

3. An Irish Home Rule Bill was passed by the British Parliament on 26 May 1914, but by an act of 18 September 1914, it was delayed for the duration of World War I. The bill never came into effect and was finally replaced by the Ireland Act of 23 December 1920 (*EWH*).

4. De Valera was unanimously declared president of the Irish Republic at the second session of *Dail Eireann* (Irish parliament), held in secret on 1 April 1919, following his escape from Lincoln Jail. His predecessor, Cathal Brugha, had been elected president in a temporary capacity in January 1919, while de Valera was still in prison (Earl of Longford and Thomas P. O'Neill, *Eamon De Valera* [Dublin: Gill and Macmillan, 1970], p. 91). The first Dail Eireann issued the Irish declaration of independence on 21 January 1919, passing at the same time the provisional constitution of the Dail. Of the seventy-three Republican deputies elected to the constituent assembly, thirty-six were in prison (Dorothy Macardle, *The Irish Republic* [New York: Farrar, Straus and Giroux, 1965], pp. 271–272).

5. Arthur Balfour, British foreign secretary, in a letter dated 2 November 1917 issued the Balfour Declaration, which declared sympathy with Zionist aspirations. The Allies officially approved the declaration in April 1920, and it was incorporated into the British mandate for Palestine in July 1922 (Leonard Stein, *The Balfour Declaration* [London: Vallentine, Mitchell, 1961]).

6. A reconstituted Polish republic was officially proclaimed on 3 November 1918, although its borders were disputed until the end of the Russian-Polish war of 1920.

7. Garvey concluded with a discussion of whether God was white or black and a statement on the necessity of a steamship line to improve communications with Africa.

Washington, D.C., September 25, 1920

Meeting of the Universal Negro Improvement Association and the Black Star Line Steamship Co.

Presiding Officer: Mr. H. W. Kirby (224 Elm Street, N.W., Wash., D.C.)

. . . HON. MARCUS GARVEY, Provisional President of Africa and President of the Universal Negro Improvement Association.

But before the Briton was able to say "Britons never shall be slaves," and to maintain that sentiment, the Britons went to work to build up a power sufficiently strong to protect them in all parts of the world to prevent them from being reduced to slavery. That you must do, and until you do that your sentiment will [be] worth nothing to you. We of the Universal [Negro] Improvement Association have come before you and before the world, therefore, with a program, a program similar to that of the ancient Briton, a program of constructive government. The ancient Briton had a program of constructive government for Brit[ai]n, and we of the Universal Negro Improvement Association have a program of constructive government for Africa, the Africa from which we were robbed 300 years ago—as I said awhile ago—is the Africa, the motherland, the fatherland, that is calling us today, and the country that will save us tomorrow. Without Africa the Negroes in all parts of the world are doomed, and I want you to understand that. You will say "doomed, when we are so successful in Washington?" and I laugh at your sense of security. You will say "doomed, when we are so progressive in New York and Chicago?" and I laugh at your progress. Men[,] let me tell you from my study of the Anglo-American in this country[,] I know this, that the progress, seeming progress of the Negro in the United States at this moment is only superficial progress. It is a progress that will be defeated in a short while, a progress that will be turned over as soon as the white man gets ready. He is not ready yet, but he is getting ready now. I understand that we have about 130,000 Negroes living in Washington. We occupy beautiful homes, and we say we are satisfied. The homes we occupy today, the homes we buy with our own money, is the home that will be occupied by mob violence in the next 50 years, and if you doubt it, wait on, unprepared as you are. Prepared, you will be able to resist them. Unprepared[,] you will have to run for your lives from Washington as some of us have run for our lives from the Southern States to the Northern States. I will prove that to you. Prior to the war, in 1913, there was a disposition on the part of our fellow citizens of the Anglo-American blood in this country to close every industrial and economic door in the face of the Negro in the Northern States. We had the hardest time of our lives up to 1913 in finding economic and industrial openings in the Northern States of the United States of America. It was but the fulfillment of a great plan that the Northern white man had laid for the Negro, a plan whereby he would get rid of the Negro in the Northern States of the United States of America without firing a shot or a shell at him or placing a lynching rope around his neck. I have studied economic conditions prior to 1913, and it revealed itself to me like this: We in New York, Philadelphia, or Boston, o[r] the big Eastern States, or even the big Western States, where hundreds of thousands of Negroes lived—those Negroes there had the hardest time of their lives finding daily employment. In cities like New York, men had to go 10, 15, and 20 times—Negro men—to find jobs that brought them $20, $30, and $40 at the most a month. . . .¹

This cry of America for Americans means that America wants enough bread to fee[d] all white Americans. This cry of Britain means that Britain is endeavoring to grab her share of this stuff to feed her 60,000,000 Anglo-Saxons, irrespective of who dies, and I will say the cry is to grab your portion of the loaf and feed Africa. Except you prepare now as men and as women to play your part, you are doomed. You are doomed, and why I am mixed up with the Negroes of the world, and why I come to Washington to speak to *so people in a church*, is because I am a Negro and can not get away from the destiny that is marked out for you by your Creator. If I could have successfully gotten out of the colored race, I would not be here tonight *speaking to a hard city like Washington*, but I know this, being a Negro like you, whatsoever happens to you as a race is bound to happen to me. If I were a white man I would not give two rows of pins whether you stay at home, or play on the piano, or go to the moving picture. If I were a Jew my interests would be with the Jews; if I were an Irishman my interests would be with the Irish, if I were an Anglo-Saxon, my interests would be with the Anglo-Saxons. Now that I am a Negro, with whom must my interests be but with you[?] After surveying the world, after seeing the trend of events, I realize that except something is done now you and I are doomed. And if I can do anything to prove [*prevent*?] the danger that threatens, it is but right, it is but fair, it is but my duty to do it, and that is why I am here, and that is why I am fighting without any compromise on this question of Africa. If America is to be for the white Americans—as they have plainly told us in more than one way, for Senator Hoke Smith² told us plainly that Negroes are not wanted in the United States of America, they tell us so daily by the lynchings in the South, they tell us so very often in riots like /the/ East St. Louis riot, like the Washington riot, and the Chicago riot. It is told to you in plain words, "This is a white man's country." If you go to Canada they will tell you ["]This is a white man's country.["] If you go to Australia they will tell you ["]This is a white man's country.["] If you go to any of the European States they will tell you ["]This is a white man's country.["] If you go to Asia, if you go to China, the Chinese will tell you ["]this is the Chinaman's country,["] and if you go to Japan they will tell you that ["]this [is] a land of the Japanese.["] My God, you never created four hundred million people to be wanderers all over the world, but you created and gave them a land of their own. That land—Africa, the richest, the most prolific, the most wonderful land, the most mysterious land in the world, that land is ours, and if America is to be for the white Americans, if Canada is to be for white Canadians, if France is to be for white Frenchmen, then Africa shall be for the Africans, those at home and those abroad. And they elected me Provisional President of Africa. I shall but do my duty as de Valera is doing by Ireland, cost him what it may, as Wilson is doing by the United States of America, as David Lloyd George is doing by England, so I have pledged my sacred word and honor to do my duty by Africa and by Africa's citizens, cost me what it may.

The Kaiser lost his dream of a vast German Empire in Africa, and England should also loose her hold upon the weaker races of the world. And now, the world instead of going forward is stationary, and in the stationary situation of the world a call is made for a reorganization, a political reorganization of the world, and in this political reorganization the Jew is running to Palestine, the Pole is running for the Pole, and the Hindoo is saying "a larger share of self-government for us in India." The Irishman is crying out "Ireland for the Irishman." And in this convention four hundred million Negroes cried out "Africa for the Africans." Have you heard the cry? Have you heard the echo? Yes, the cry has gone forth and the echo is resulting [resounding?] all over the world. Methinks I see millions of African citizens on the West Coast with their hands to the[ir] ears catching the cry that goes out from the Liberty Hall (in New York City), "Africa for the Africans." Methinks I see thousands of West Indians putting their hands to their ears catching the cry that goes out, "Africa for the Africans," and around the world the echo spreads. And now I think I see it reach Washington. Have you heard the cry in Washington, "Africa for the Africans"? If you haven't heard the cry you are deaf and you are dead. Men, how long are you going to sleep in idleness? I am here tonight to point you the way to glory or to destruction.

I will come back to what I promised you last night. I told you that I would point you to the future of the Negro of the United States of America. Now this is the future as I see it. Prior to the war there was a disposition on the part of the American white man to invite the white peoples from all parts of the world to come into this country by the hundreds of thousands, by the millions, every year. They came and they scattered themselves in the North for a while, then in the West, and the middle West. The influx had become so great that just a few days before war was declared William Randolph Hearst wrote these words, these pointed paragraphs. "The time has come for the government of the South to replace the Negro laborer with the white laborer from Europe." Those of you who are students of political thought, those of you who are students of current events will recall that he pointed out to the Southern States the time had come for them to get rid of Negro labor and to use white labor that was coming to the country from Italy, Poland, Russia, and from the Eastern States of Europe. The South was about to act when the war came and saved the Negro for another few years. The war came and saved the Southern Negro, the war came and saved the Northern Negro. The war is over and immigration has started again to the United States of America. William Randolph Hearst is still alive. He is more alive now than he ever was. To me William Randolph Hearst is the most experienced, the greatest intellect in this country. To me there is no statesman like William Randolph Hearst. He loves his race. He can see nothing else but his race. It is William Randolph Hearst who has built up the "yellow peril" in this country.[3] William Randolph Hearst is the one sober-minded white man in this country who can see things as they show themselves, and let me tell you that William Randolph Hearst's doctrine is going to be practiced in this country before another five years roll by. They are going to replace the Negro laborer, the Negro worker, with the last arrival of white people from Europe. And it is going to be so. The statistics of New York, the immigration statistics of New York showed last month that the white immigrants of Europe are coming to this country at the rate of two million a year.[4] It means that in the next four years we are going to have at least eight million white men in this country. Today we have ninety million white Americans. They are German-Americans, French-Americans, Russian-Americans, or Anglo-Americans, but they are Americans before you are anything. Although they were Germans a few months ago, they, to the white people of this country, are better Americans than you are—"and ever will be" as somebody (in audience) says. It means in the next three or five years you will have eight or ten million foreigners in America, and it will mean that eight or ten million Negroes will have lost their jobs.

And if America is to be for the white Americans, Africa will surely be for the Negroes, and if the two races can not live in peace in America I can't see how the two races can live in peace in Africa. Therefore, if we have to get out of America somebody must get out of Africa.

(Meeting closed with National Anthem of Africa by singers and Band.)

DNA, RG 65, file OG 329359. TD, prepared by Woolsey W. Hall.

1. The omitted section is a discourse on the international economic situation.

2. Hoke Smith (1855–1931), the North Carolina–born proprietor of the *Atlanta Journal*, served as secretary of the interior in President Grover Cleveland's second administration. He was also the Democratic candidate in a successful campaign for governor of Georgia in 1906, which featured debates on the question of race. The Atlanta riot of 1906 is generally attributed to the increased racial tensions that grew out of that campaign. Smith entered the U.S. Senate in 1911, where he preserved his reputation as a staunch defender of white supremacy (*WBD*; Dewey W. Grantham, Jr., *Hoke Smith and the Politics of the New South* [Baton Rouge: Louisiana State University Press, 1958]).

3. William Randolph Hearst was the most influential American proponent of the idea of an impending race war between "whites" and Asians, specifically the Japanese. In a 9 March 1918 editorial entitled "The Yellow Peril," Hearst warned, "It is more than likely that another great wave of yellow men, bent on submerging the world, will sweep out of Asia. . . . But let the yellow race once succeed in one of these crucial battles between the white and yellow races for world dominion, and the whole fabric of the white man's civilization will be destroyed, the whole structure of moral standards and standards of living, founded on fundamental democracy, will go down in ruin" (E. F. Tompkins, ed., *Selections from the Writings and Speeches of William Randolph Hearst* [San Francisco: San Francisco Examiner Co., 1948], pp. 580–586).

4. The U.S. Immigration and Naturalization Service recorded the arrival of 430,001 immigrants in 1920 and of 805,228 immigrants in 1921. The sharp increase led to legislation to curtail

immigration in 1921 (*Ninth Annual Report of the Secretary of Labor* [Washington, D.C.: GPO, 1921], p. 25).

E. G. Woodford to A. Philip Randolph

PUGET SOUND EXPORTERS & IMPORTERS,
SEATTLE, WASHINGTON, September 25, 1920

My dear Mr. Randolph:

I thank you for your copies of pamphlets on the Negro Question,[1] and later on will write you on the subject.

In the Literary Digest, I read an article upon the "Back to Africa Movement,"[2] which appears to have been organized by a Mr. Marcus Garvey. I am much interested in that question, as for twenty years I have been advocating something of the kind, based upon my thirty years experience in Africa.

Will you kindly inform me of the address of this gentleman, that I may communicate with him on the subject, as I expect to do some speaking before the negro residents o[f] this city in the approaching campaign. Yours faithfully,

E. G. WOODFORD

[*Address*] Mr. R. G. [*A. P.*] Randolph,
70—Fifth Avenue, New York

DLC, NAACP. TLS, recipient's copy.

1. A. Philip Randolph and Chandler Owen had published the following pamphlets: *The Terms of Peace and the Darker Races*, *The Truth About Lynching*, and *The Negro and the New Social Order* (New York: n.p., n.d.).
2. The article, "The Purple-robed Champion of 'Africa for the Africans,'" was published in the *Literary Digest* 66, no. 10 (4 September 1920): 63.

Speech by Marcus Garvey

Washington, D.C., September 26, 1920

MEETING OF UNIVERSAL NEGRO IMPROVEMENT ASSOCIATION

PRESIDING OFFICER: MR. H. W. KIRBY,
224 ELM STREET, N.W., WASH., D.C.

(NOTE—At this meeting, as at the meetings in the Metropolitan A.M.E. Church on September 24 and September 25, the number of people in the house ranged between 50 and 70, all told.)

... THE HONORABLE MARCUS GARVEY—

It is a very long time since I have spoken to such a large audience (about 60 people in The Howard Theatre). It takes my breath away to face such a large crowd. Nevertheless, I am here this afternoon to speak in the interest of the Universal Negro Improvement Association, firstly, and secondly to speak in the interest of the Black Star Steamship Corporation. I have been to Washington several times before and have had the privilege of speaking in this theater and other places, telling the people just of the aims and the objects of this Universal Negro Improvement Association, but there are, I believe, a hundred and thirty-odd thousand Negroes in this city and I don't believe I have met more than a thousand or two up to the present time in all my speeches delivered here. Hence I will embrace this opportunity of explaining, and as briefly as I possibly can, the objects of the Universal Negro Improvement Association. We are endeavoring through this movement to draw into one united whole the four hundred million Negroes of the world. We are endeavoring to do this under the auspices of the Universal Negro Improvement Association, because we realize that the time has come for this race of ours to get together for the same purpose as the other races of the world are getting together. When we survey the world, the world of action, the world of activity, we find all the races of mankind, the white races and the yellow races organizing their forces to protect their individual and collective rights as individuals and as nations. My like experience with the Negro peoples of the world is that they are preparing to remain disunited and disinterested in each other. The American Negro has no interest in the West Indian Negro. The West Indian Negro has no interest in the American Negro, and neither the American nor the West Indian Negro has any interest in the African Negro, and because of that ninety million white people in America have been able to abuse twelve million Negroes in America without the Negroes being able to protect themselves, and the same way in the West Indies, where Englishmen have been able to brutalize and abuse the West Indian Negroes because they have stood apart from the other Negroes of the world. As you in America are not sufficiently strong to fight your own battles in comparison with the white people alongside of you, we of the Universal Negro Improvement Association, therefore—having surveyed the world, having seen the conditions in America, the West Indies, as those conditions affect Negroes—say twelve million Negroes can not successfully combat the forces of ninety million white Americans. If we were to organize, we say, the four hundred million Negroes of the world, we will be not only able to combat the ninety millions of America, but all the white peoples of the world in their attempt to brutalize and take advantage of us. So we come to you with an organization not confined to the twelve million Negroes in America, but we are preaching a doctrine that concerns Negroes everywhere. We are endeavoring to unite Negroes everywhere, and for what? For the purpose of building up a powerful nation on the continent of Africa, a nation in the near future boasting as a first-rate power, and that first-rate power to give us

23

African citizens, who domicile ourselves in America as Afro-Americans, the protection which America does not give us today. That is the larger purpose of this Universal Negro Improvement Association. It is not a religious movement, purely. It is not a social movement, purely. It is not an industrial movement, purely, it is not a political movement, purely, but it is a movement that includes all the wants and needs of the Negro. We are as much political as we are religious, we are as much religious as we are social, we are as much social as we are industrial. We have left nothing out in this Universal Negro Improvement Association because we realize that the other nations have left nothing out where their progress is concerned. We are endeavoring to perform the function of government for our race, just as the Government of America performs the functions of government for ninety million white people. Yet that American Government is already constituted. We have to constitute ours. Before there was a constituted American Government, George Washington had to go out and risk his life and liberty, and that is what some of us are doing now. Some of us are too cowardly even to identify ourselves with the movement, but some of us have absolutely no fear and stand as prepared and ready even as George Washington 140 years ago. I understand that the majority of my people in Washington are composed of that cowardly, sycophantic, cringing lot who refuse to support anything except it[']s led by the white man. Now let me tell you this: The white man has been leading us for 300 years, and he has led us into darkness. If we continue to follow him, follow what he says that we should do, he will not only lead us into darkness but he will lead us into hell. And we are next door to hell now. We are just next door to hell. Just below the Mason and Dixon's line is hell, and we are next door to it now, and he is going to enlarge that hell because he has carried it already to East St. Louis, he brought the hell to Washington a few months ago, he took it to Chicago—not longer than last week he had it there. He is going to start again all over this country until somebody stops him and his gang. And twelve million Negroes in America will not be able to stop the cracker spreading hell all over the world. The cracker took hell to France, that was a heaven up to America's entry a few months ago. France lynched a Negro two-and-a-half months ago through the influence of the cracker. And they are going to spread the doctrine of the white superiority, and the Japanese [are] preparing for any race of people who will tell them that they are superior to them. They are going to show them that there is no man better than the yellow man; that God created yellow and white to play their part in this world. And as much as the white have played their part, the yellow people of Asia will play their part. And after the Japanese-Russian war they started out to respect the yellow man. And not until the Negroes of the world on the battle plains of Africa teach some nation as the Japanese taught the Russians will they stop burning and lynching you in all parts of the world. But the time has come for you to center your opinions, and your thoughts, and your actions about building a government of your own. Let me tell you, if you believe that America will be big enough and large enough in the white man's view to hold himself and the Negro, as the Negro is multiplying now, you will make a big mistake. The white man says that this country is only big enough, only large enough, to hold him; hence, this must be a white man's country. It may not be so today, but he is planning that this shall be a white man's country in the next hundred years at least, and at that time I ask you "What will become of the Negro in the next 100 years?" We have never thought of the tomorrows in our lives, and that is why we are at the foot of the great human ladder. The white man sees hundreds of years ahead and he lays the foundation of his future greatness. What the white man wants to achieve in the next 50 years, he starts out now to lay the foundation for its achievement. The Negro can only see today, and he can only remember yesterday, and he can not see tomorrow. But we of the Universal Negro Improvement Association have caught the vision of the Pilgrim Fathers of America, and whilst we can not be Pilgrim Fathers in America, we shall send out Pilgrim Fathers to the great continent of Africa and there lay the foundation for the future glory of this race of ours. This is a city of intellect. This is a city where all the educated men and women of the race congregate. Yet it is a city that criticizes and condemns everything that seems to them without the leadership of the white man. We of the Universal Negro Improvement Association have absolutely no use for the leadership of the white man where our race is concerned. We have only use for him as a brother to live side by side with him in this creation that God Almighty gave, and we are prepared to let him lead himself, but we say where we are concerned we must lead ourselves. That is the new spirit of the Universal Negro Improvement Association. It is a bold spirit, a courageous spirit, and but very few Negroes can appreciate it, because while the majority of Negroes in this country believe that except the white man leads there is no security—but let me tell you now that wheresoever he leads you as Negroes, you are going to that place that you will find yourself so cornered when you find i[t] out it will be too late.

Wheresoever I have been, and I have been traveling extensively, throughout this nation and throughout Europe, I have traveled throughout the length and breadth of Great Britain, England, Scotland, Wales, and parts of Ireland, I have traveled throughout the continent—France, Italy, Spain, Germany, parts of Austria and Hungary, and Russia. And what have I discovered? What have I discovered? What have I read? What have I seen? I have heard that this is a white man's country. The question was asked in England. What are you doing here? I went to France—What are you doing here? as if I had no right there. I went to Italy, I went to Germany—What are you doing here? And as a journalist and a newspaper man I found out that the attitude of Europe towards alien races was that no alien race had a right of permanent settlement in Europe. No black man, no colored man, had a right to be a permanent citizen or denizen of any of those countries, and when you get your course of education the quicker you get out the better it will please the Englishman or the Frenchman. In Australia the cry is Australia the white man's country, in England the cry is England the white man's country, in France the cry is France the white man's country; in America, where we labored, where we suffered, and where we died for 250 years, the cry is now "A white America," and some of you are playing deaf—that you do not hear the cry. You continue to play deaf. You will get a sudden shock, a sudden shock one of these days. It will be too late to recover from the shock. You will be lost Let me say, too, that the cry all over the world is that this country shall be the country of those who were originally born to it. If America is to be for the whites, if England is to be for the whites, if Canada is to be for the whites, then, in the name of God, Africa shall be for the Africans, and the quicker you get to realize that the better it will be for you. Some of you smart folks say that that man is crazy. I am satisfied to be as crazy as George Washington was 140 years ago. Some say that man was a dreamer. I am satisfied to be a dreamer as Bismarck was over the vision of a vast German Empire. Some of you will say I am a visionary—as the Earl of Chatham was a visionary nearly 200 years ago when he saw the potency of a great British Empire. Let me dream like a Prince von Bismarck of Germany, let me dream like William Pitt of England, let me dream like George Washington of America, and, my God, the spirit that you gave to Bismarck to have his dream come true, the love that you had for Pitt to have his dream come true, the love and help that you gave to Washington to make his dream come true, give that love and help to me. I firmly believe this: That God Almighty never could have made such a terrible mistake—to make four hundred million people black. He never could have made such a mistake. He had a purpose, I understand that. When He made four hundred million people colored folks, that God had a purpose, and I question that God who would create four hundred million folks—I question the love, the majesty, and the omnipotence of that God who would make and create four hundred million folks to be slaves, to be hewers of wood and drawers of water. That would not be a God, that would be a devil. The white man tells us in his lying scriptures—and I want you to understand me clearly on this, I am as much a Christian as any Pope of Rome, I am as much a Christian as the Archbishop of Canterbury, I am as much as Jesus Christ, but I refuse to believe all the lying stuff that the white man put in the Bible. I believe in the fatherhood of God. I believe in the Creed, in the brotherhood of man. I believe in all those things that say that there is a Heaven and that there was a blessed Redeemer, and I say it is a lie that God Almighty ever inspired any man—or wrote himself—that He ever created a race to be hewers of wood and drawers of water. It is a lie. And I would like to see a God, I would like to see a disciple of that God, I would like to see a white man who would come up on this platform and tell me that God Almighty intended me to be a hewer of wood and a drawer of water. That is an impossibility. That is a lie. God Almighty created me to be a man like any other man, and I am going to function just like any other man so long as I live. And that is what our folks must get to realize. Through lying teaching[,] through lying education, we were led to believe that all that was pure, all that was good, all that was noble, came from those who were white, and all that was degrading and debasing came from those who were black. Ah, that lying education got the better of us, so that now in Washington you will not believe anything except it comes from the white race. But we new Negroes who were born out of the great war can see nothing perfect except it comes out of our own race. We have no confidence in anything except it comes out of our own race. If it is [in] industry, in commerce, in religion, it must first come out of our own race before we will bow down and worship.

That will mean that when you start out with ideals of that kind, with lofty beliefs of that kind, the white man's religion, the white man's teaching, the white man's influence over you will lose its potency and you will become a people so noble in your character that no race will ever be able to make an opening into your proceedings and into your progress. Men and women of Washington[,] I want you to understand that the hour is here for the Negro peoples of the world to organize themselves for one mighty and majestic whole. The moment you give in your name and your address and 25 cents as a member of the Washington Division of the Universal Negro Improvement Association, you become a fellow member of an organization of three million five hundred [*thousand*?] people who are now enunciating the principles of the Universal Negro Improvement Association. This Universal Negro Improvement Association is the one movement among Negroes in the world that all governments dread and fear. And in coming to Washington some of the folks said they will arrest you in Washington. Even when George Washington had made up his mind to be shot, so I am prepared to be shot down any time, leaving the host to watch Africa. I want to be understood clearly: I have no revolutionary doctrine to teach in America about America, because I believe America is the greatest country in the world. I believe there is no country in the world with as free institutions as America. I love the Constitution of the United States of America. I love and admire the beautiful democratic institutions of this country, with the exception of the institutions of lynching, and burning, and jimcrowism below the Mason and Dixon's line. But all those things that say "You are equal, you are free and equal," all such institutions based upon such a noble pronouncement, I admire and respect. But I am not endeavoring to make Negroes believe that there is no other country beside[s] America. I want Negroes first to realize that every Negro is an African citizen. Before we were Americans or West Indians we were Africa citizens. Negroes were never born originally to America or the West Indies. Negroes were originally born to Africa, isn't it so? Where did your forefathers come from? Georgia? No, they came from Sierra Leone, West Africa, or they came from the . . . [*word omitted*], West Africa. They were first African citizens before they were emancipated by Abraham Lincoln, who made Afro-Americans, and by Victoria, who made Afro-West-Indians. Now if a Frenchman leaves France—say he has left France 50 years ago and came to America and never asked or applied for naturalization papers. If he lived here for 50 years, what would he be? He would be a Frenchman. He would never be an American citizen until he went through the process of action and applied for naturalization. He has first of all, according to the law of the country, to apply for naturalization papers before he can become a naturalized American citizen. If he lived for a hundred years and never applied for naturalization papers he would always be a Frenchman. Now, sirs, can you remember the time when your forefathers applied for naturalization papers in this country? Your grandfathers never got any naturalization papers. They were gotten from Africa against their will. They were citizens of Africa. Brought them here as slaves and they served as slaves for 250 years and never applied for naturalization papers. Abraham Lincoln set you free, but no law states that emancipation makes you naturalized, and we never went through naturalization, hence we are still and first of all African citizens. And that is why in the convention of August, of last month, we declared that every Negro in every part of the world [is] an African citizen. And they elected me Provisional President of Africa. It was my duty to find protection for every other good citizen, and that is why I am here. Now, as Provisional President I tell you—we must have an African Army second to none. We must have an African Navy second to none. We must have the latest battleships, the latest cruisers, the latest submarines, the latest airships, so that you, an African citizen, whether you be in France, England, or America, if they should lynch and burn you the Ambassador of the African Republic in Africa will send home the news to Africa and we will send our battleships and navy (the rest inaudible by reason of uproar[i]ous applause). You say that is a dream. It wasn't a dream for George Washington 140 years ago when there was no American Navy and no American Army to be appreciated, and today America stands first of all the nations, so that I feel sure that Africa in another half a century will stand shoulder to shoulder among the nations of the world. But you college men, you university men and women in Washington must help to make this thing come true. Instead of your using your college education to be bellboys and spittoon cleaners and butlers, we want you to be ambassadors and to go into the four corners of the world to represent the Republic of Africa. It is no more a dream than George Washington's idea was a dream. Men, wherever the people are determined upon one thing that thing is a possibility so long as the will to act is there, and four hundred million people of the Negro race are determined to be free, and no power in the world, no power in hell, or beneath heaven can prevent the Negroes of the world from being free. I have said enough for this afternoon for the Universal Negro Improvement Association, but I speak here again at 8 o'clock, and I am asking you to return at 8 o'clock to hear me on the subject of the Battle Cry of Africa. Bring your friends, bring everybody you know to this meeting here tonight.

(Meeting closed with National Anthem of Africa—band and singers.)

DNA, RG 65, file OG 329359. TD, prepared by Woolsey W. Hall.

Report by Special Agent P-138

New York City 9-27-20

Conditions among the Negroes in the Harlem and downtown district, 59th, 62d, 63d and 99th Street sections, seem to be alright, especially since GARVEY's removal from the scene, he being on his lecture tour, and the great anti-white agitation is gradually dying out,—at least in a demonstrative way.

It is plain to see that had the Negro race been relieved of all these Fire-Brand, anti-white agitation, who gives them a line of talk, promising to make them Lords, Dukes, Ambassadors and other high officials, at the same time relieving the poor ignorant ones of their hard earned money, conditions in large Negro sections would be O.K. without any fear of race riots, etc., but on the other hand, there is DOMINGO and other Negro radicals preaching and teaching "Class hatred", and GARVEY and his leaders teaching "Race", and above all, "Color hatred". The poor Negro with an undeveloped mind is therefore ready to blame the whites for all his ills, which takes but very little energy to cause him to attack the white at the very least provocation. He goes around with a "chip on his shoulder" and gets more sensitive every time he listens to Garvey and his fire-eating Race hatred speech. Then, after leaving Liberty Hall, the poor creatures are again attracted to another large crowd on street corners, which is being addressed by DOMINGO and other Negro radicals. They tell him that capitalism must be broken down and the Negro must join the "Reds" and take matters in their own hands as the Russian workmen have done. After this comes the "NEGRO WORLD", "MESSENGER", etc. This is the true condition and from my careful observation of affairs I am left to the conclusions that it will take but very little to cause conditions to change over night if methods are not adopted to eliminate these agitators and discourage their propaganda. Of course it must not be forgotten that we have to take into account the intelligent Negroes, conservative Negro newspapers, and sane preachers who are acting as a "balancing power" to counteract all the other detrimental elements.

P-138

[*Endorsements*] NOTED W. W. G. FILE G. F. R.

DNA, RG 65, file OG 329359. TD. Stamped endorsements.

Reports by Bureau Agent H. J. Lenon

Pittsburgh, Pa. 9/27/20

In Re: Marcus Garvey, Universal Negro Improvement
Association, Black Star Steamship Line,
Back to Africa Movement.

Considerable thought was given to the activities of MARCUS GARVEY and his followers and the probabl[e] objects in his campaign when the "Back to Africa" meetings were held in Pittsburgh. A local corporation[1] who employ a number of colored men were interested in the case to the extent that they sent a colored informant to New York to investigate GARVEY and his activities. We have been favored with a copy of his report, which follows:—

New York City, N.Y., Sept. 2–3–4–5, 1920.

The exploits and doings of Marcus Garvey, with his two corporations, the Black Star Steamship Line, and the Universal Negro Improvement Association, have been attracting the attention of the whole of New York City, to such an extent as to excite editorial comment on the part of all of the New York daily papers, as well as an editorial which appeared in the edition of "Life" on September 2nd.

Garvey, and his corporations, have purchased a large plot of ground in this city, on 13[8]th Street, between Lenox and Seventh Avenues, capable of seating five or six thousand people, and during the month in which his convention was held, the writer was informed that every seat was taken and standing room was in demand, at practically every session. On this ground he has erected a one story convention hall, which is to remain there permanently. Though the convention is now over, the hall is still being used for some of the business of the corporations.

In addition to creating sufficient notoriety to c[ause?] editorial comment in the local newspapers, Garvey also had a [talk?] with the District Attorney's office of this city, who investigat[ed] him and all of the business with which he is connected, but could find absolutely nothing which would warrant them in stopping him from the sales of his stock and other things which he is engineering.

The mammoth convention which was held throughout the entire month of August was attended not only by thousands in New York City, but by numbers from all parts of this country, Liberia, East and West Indies, Haiti, British Gui[a]na, all portions of Africa and other parts of the globe. The personnel of this convention was somewhat attracted by curiosity, but on the whole, those who attended were most enthusiastic.

At the session, a colored man was appointed president of "Black America", at a salary of $10,000.00 per year and he is to occupy a building in

Washington, D.C., to be known as the "Black House", though his duties still remain an unknown quantity. Numerous others were elected to fill various positions and in the sessions they are known as "His Grace", or "His Excellency", as the case may be.

On the last day of the convention, a parade was staged in Harlem, and in this parade such banners as "Liberty or Death", "Down with Lynching", etc., were promiscuously in evidence. Instead of this parade being stopped, it seems that special patrolmen were detailed to the sections in which it was being held, to prevent the marchers from being molested. In other words, it seemed that the city officials were co-operating rather than endeavoring to put a stop to these doings. Throughout the entirety of the convention, the writer was informed from numerous sources that all of Harlem, as well as other sections of New York, were very much agitated. Garvey never goes anywhere without a body guard of at least four men and his money getting propensities are positively alarming. It is difficult to conjecture just where he will stop, if he continues at his present rate. He has surrounded himself with colored business and professional men, having had them appointed and elected to official offices in his enterprises, at princely salaries of from $5000[.]oo to $20,000.oo yearly, for doing practically nothing, and whenever a demand is made by him of his followers for additional finance, it is always forthcoming.

Conditions have now reached the stage where Harlem is a veritable hot bed, so far as Garvey is concerned. Garvey himself is a West Indian, and there are now fully five hundred percent more West Indians living in and around Harlem than there were two years ago and all of these people or at least a vast majority, have moved to this country solely because of wonderful promises made by Garvey.

In addition to the Convention Hall on 138th Street, he has executive offices at 54-56 West 135th Street at which place "The Negro World" is edited by him and the Black Star Steamship Line, as well as the Universal Negro Improvements Association are domiciled. There are between seventy-five and one hundred employees in these two buildings, ninety-nine percent of whom are West Indians, all of whom are drawing good salaries.

He is looked upon by these West Indians, as well as numbers of colored Americans, as being a second "Moses", and they swear by him as their salvation. Considering the way that feeling is now, it would be very foolish for anyone to go to New York, and particularly in Harlem, and say [*anything*] against Garvey, he has so many supporters.

The thing which he has promised to do, which is causing so many to line up with him, is to free all black races from the yoke with which they are now oppressed. His "Back to Africa" movement is being met with demonstrated approval and vast enthusiasm by all who have decided to accept him as their leader. It is his plan to start a colony in Africa, to be composed of all of the black races of the world and he is using his steamship company as the means with which to accomplish that end.

This Black Star Steamship Company now has three ocean liners on the waters and another $400,000.00 steamship is to be purchased between now and the last of the current month. All of these steamships are manned exclusively by black people and no other national[i]ties are desired or wanted.

There is absolutely no question about the fact that the things which Garvey is now advocating will eventually be the cause of bloodshed, though technically they cannot be said to be radical. The movement which he has started is so different from anything which was ever promulgated in the past, and he is shrewd en[o]ugh to keep within the law, and as a means of [a]i[d]ing him along those lines he has employed a number of lawyers on yearly retainers, to aid him in keeping within the law.

Both of his corporations, the Black Star Steamship Line, and the Universal Negro Improvements Association, are corporations, having their habitat as Delaware, being registered in New York, and a number of other states, as well as being registered with the British Admiralty.

The writer met Garvey in person and he talked voluminously about his plans, relative to the sale of stock in his corporations and there is not the remotest doubt in the writer's mind that it will be a short while only before he will have a formidable fleet of merchant vessels on the ocean to be used in conjunction with the "Back to Africa" movement, as well as for commercial purposes. There are vague rumors to be heard in and around the colored districts of New York City, to the effect that the Department of Justice is keeping a close watch on Garvey's doings, though no one is able to produce any corroboration for their belief.

The con[s]ensus of opinion of the colored people in New York, whose opinions are really worth while, seems to be that Garvey, if left alone, will be capable of doing much harm. The reason for this belief is because Garvey has so many men of color, colored Americans to be exact, who have heretofore been looked up to as being men of brain.

It seems that Garvey got his start in this city about two years ago, by inaugurating a chain of laundries, grocery stores, etc., in which he let it be known, that cheaper rates would prevail to all patrons[,] further, that the exec[u]tive end of all the business would be handled by black men. The success of these ventures has spurred him to greater ambitions.

In addition to the lengthy convention held in this city, there is another scheduled to be held in Philadelphia, Pa., in the near future. They have already had a parade there, announcing their coming and plans are under way for the purchase of a convention hall there.

It seems, from Garvey's conversation with the writer, that it is his intention to establish convention halls and executive offices in all of the large cities of the country, and unless something unfor[e]seen intervenes and prevents, he is likely to accomplish his desires. He informed the writer that the next large city in which he anticipated launching a large campaign is Pittsburgh. He has the writer's name and address, also the latter's promise of co-operation when he arrives in Pittsburgh, the idea being to get on the inside of his doings, in the event that is po[s]sible.

Part of the editorial comment which appeared in the edition of September 2nd, of "Life" is as follows:—

> Some of the incidents and manifestations of the convention have been funny, but on the whole, it was no joke, and the big Jamaica Negro, Marcus F. Garvey, who is the leader of the movement, talks well and mixes in with his discourse occasional bits of sense. He says the Negroes are being crowded harder all the time—that the radical [*racial?*] prejudice against them is extending from the American South all over the world, and that unless they buck up, they will go under altogether. Force, he says, is the [N]egroes' only hope. ["]If the [N]egro does not show in the next century that he is the equal of the white in capacity, in fighting power, the white man will never give him the chance to show it, but will dominate him, in Africa and out of [it], to an extinction as complete as that of the American Indian. It is the purpose of this movement first to prove the hollowness of the white man's claim to racial superiority by developing within our race capacity for industry, for civilization, for war; then to assert and establish the complete independence of Africa from the white man's rule.["]

Agent is acquainted with the writer of the above and will be in a position to get further information as the case develops. Reports will follow.

H. J. LENON

[*Endorsements*] FILE G. F. R. NOTED F. D. W.

DNA, RG 65, file OG 329359. TD. Stamped endorsements.

1. The Aluminum Company of America, with headquarters in Pittsburgh, sent R. E. Powell, a company employee who was formerly an officer with Military Intelligence, to New York City to prepare a report on black radicals. In a subsequent report, which he also sent to the director of the Military Intelligence Division in Washington, D.C., Powell noted: "They [UNIA] want Africa redeemed from the white man and believe the negro must do it[,] as only then will it be possible to put into force machinery for retaliation. . . . Every time one negro is lynched down in Georgia, the negro's protest would be *seven* white men lynched in Africa. . . . In the United States alon[e], where it [UNIA] is three years old the membership is said to be 1,800,000" (DNA, RG 165, file 10110-2271, 13 January 1921).

Pittsburgh, Pa. 9/27/20

. . . The following report was received from a confidential informant:—

Homestead, Pa., September 16, 1920.

A man, representing himself to be James Young, who is the Pittsburgh head of the Black Star Steamship Line and the Universal Negro Improvements Association, accosted the writer, and requested him to secure a permit for a band belonging to the first named company, to play in the streets of Pittsburgh on October 1st, 2nd and 3rd, and also September 30th. The reason for this request can be explained by a telegram, received by Young, of which the following is a copy:—

James Young,

56 Arthur Street, Pittsburgh, Penna.

Arrange for big mass meeting for Universal Negro Improvement Association and Black Star Line in largest churches and halls in Pittsburgh for nights of 30th of September and 1st[,] 2nd and 3rd of October. Speakers Hon. Marcus Garvey Provisional President to Africa and President of Black Star Line and President General of the U N I A. Band of the Black Star Line and great singers from New York. Admission 50 cents. Have thousands of hand bills distributed and also announce same in all churches. Push advertisement.

(signed) MARCUS GARVEY

The writer now has the original of this telegram in his possession, which of course, will have to be returned to Young, upon his application therefor.

Was informed by the man Young, that he now has plans to secure Labor Temple for one evening, the E[b]enezer Baptist Church for another, and the Watt Street School for the third night. The fourth night they expect to hold a meeting in Braddock, after which Garvey and his crowd will return to New York.

Young intimated that there was a possibility of the writer being employed as the Pittsburgh attorney of the Black Star Steamship Line, and the Universal Negro Improvements Association, in which event, the writer will be able to secure minute details of the inner working of this organization.

There will in all probability be more data relative to this organization a little later on, but at the present, the telegram quoted above furnishes the sum total of practically all information received so far.

H. J. LENON

[*Endorsements*] FILE G. F. R. NOTED F. D. W.

DNA, RG 65, file OG 329359. TD. Stamped endorsements.

Pittsburgh, Pa. 9/28/20

. . . Supplementing my report of September 26th on the above entitled case in connection with the proposed meetings to be held here on September 30th, October 1st, 2nd and 3rd, I called on the Chief of Police of Pittsburgh and inquired as to whether or not he had been requested to grant permits for parade or meetings from the colored gentry of Pittsburgh's black belt. The Chief answered, "Yes, I know all about it. They want permits but they won't get them. We know all we want to know about this gang and if any of them attempt to pull off a meeting or stage a parade here they will all land in the workhouse. We have enough trouble without letting those fellows give us more. You can take it from me, Lenon, there won't be any meetings here for I won't issue any permits unless I am compelled to do so."

I informed the Chief that I had called on him not for the purpose of asking him to stop the meetings, but rather to inform him of the proposed meetings in case he had not already been informed by some of his colored policemen, whom I know are in touch with Negro movements and who are loyal to the city in reporting such matters. Mr. Alderdice assured me that he was ready for the men who might apply for permits and if his orders were disobeyed he would surely throw them into the workhouse. He added, "We will save you the trouble of covering any meetings for they won't be held."

I have been informed that the membership following MARCUS GARVEY in Pittsburgh now amounts to 2000 and they are planning to give him a big reception when he arrives in this city.

H. J. LENON

[*Endorsements*] NOTED W. W. G. FILE G. F. R.

DNA, RG 65, file OG 329359. TD. Stamped endorsements.

A. M. Brookfield, British Consul for Georgia, to Auckland C. Geddes

Savannah, Georgia 30 SEPT. 1920

Sir:—

With reference to Your Excellency's circular despatch of the 15th instant, I have the honour to submit some observations on the "Negro Movement" in the United States, so far as it has come under my notice in the states of Georgia and North & South Carolina.[1]

(1) As regards any specific propaganda by "The Universal Negro Improvement Association" I have at present been unable to hear of any branch or agency of that association which is in actual existence in this part of the United States. I am however still making enquiry and hope to make a further report in due course. The information personally furnished to me by two representative negroes here,—namely the Editor of a (coloured) Newspaper and the Manager of a Negro Bank,—is that "The Universal Negro Improvement Association,"—which is known to exist,—is looked upon as little more

than a money-making scheme for the advantage of the official promoters and is not regarded as a serious movement for the benefit of the race.

(2) An incident that occurred last month at Charleston, South Carolina, throws some light on the subsidiary organization known as "The Black Star Line Steamship Company." In the beginning of August the Vice-Consul at Charleston reported that a vessel belonging to that line called the "YARMOUTH",—(flying the British flag, and vulgarly known as "The Alcoholic Ark,")—had put in at that port in a miserable plight.[2] She was short of coal & provisions; there was small-pox on board; the Master complained of difficulties with his crew, and especially of the conduct of an American stowaway, who, he said, "was eating three meals a day; very costly, and very insolent to him." On August 12th this Master [*Captain Dickenson*]—I believe a Canadian, and the only white man on board the ship,—had become indebted to the amount of nearly twelve thousand dollars, for supplies and other expenses which the owners were at the time unable to pay, and the "YARMOUTH" was thereupon libelled. I have no precise knowledge how she finally got away from Charleston, but it is quite certain that she came there badly found and equipped, badly managed by the owners, badly commanded by the Master, and that if it is not unfair to take this vessel as a specimen of the "Black Star Line Steamship Company's" fleet, it may also be reasonable to conclude that the operations of such a concern are unlikely to accomplish any large commercial or political objects, but are better calculated to weaken the professed cause in view and to confirm prevailing conceptions as to the limitations of the negro race in the conduct of affairs.

(3) With regard to the connection of any Negro movement in this country with social or political developments in the West Indies, I have formed the opinion that the West Indian negroes are in every way so superior to the negroes of the Southern States of which I have any special knowledge, that it is improbable that the former would ever follow the lead of the latter, except, perhaps, as regards some detail of organization which might seem by its success in this country to offer encouragement for its adoption elsewhere. I do not at present know of any such success that has been achieved here; and former Negro movements have been characterized by a feeble policy; bad leadership; want of intelligence, and above all by a conspicuous lack of discipline.

(4) . . . It would be very extraordinary if the almost universal industrial unrest of the world should have failed in any way to affect the Negro race. I am nevertheless of opinion that,—whether from simplicity, laziness, or from a happy state of ignorance,—the Negroes of the states of which I have any special knowledge are in a much less mischievious frame of mind than the majority of the white working classes, and that whether this is the case or not, the only way that they can be incited to take up a dangerous attitude will be by some organization with large funds, controlled by really able, energetic, far-seeing, disinterested men, not necessarily negroes themselves.

From the knowledge that has so far reached me I do not think that these conditions are fulfilled by "The Universal Negro Improvement Association."—I have the honour to be, With the greatest respect, Sir, Your Excellency's most obedient, humble servant,

A. M. BROOKFIELD[3]

[*Endorsement*] COPY TO F. O.

PRO, FO 115/2619. TLS, recipient's copy. Handwritten endorsement.

1. In reply to the same circular dispatch, the acting consul general in Baltimore stated that "no activity in the movement is displayed by the Negroes in the States which compris[e] this Consular district" (acting British consul general, Baltimore, to Auckland C. Geddes, 28 January 1921, PRO, FO 115/2690).

2. The *Yarmouth* made its third and final voyage between May and August 1920, departing from New York with approximately thirty-five passengers. It first stopped in Havana to discharge its cargo. From Havana, the *Yarmouth* sailed to Haiti, remaining there for about four days. The ship next sailed to Jamaica, where its passengers disembarked. The *Yarmouth* remained in Kingston for about two weeks while repairs were made on its engines and boilers. After a stop at Serrana Bank (located approximately two hundred miles off the northeast coast of Nicaragua), the *Yarmouth* returned to New York in mid-August, three days after conditions forced it to recoal in Charleston, S.C.

3. Arthur Montague Brookfield became the British consul for the southern district of Georgia, North Carolina, and South Carolina in 1910 (U.S. Department of State, *Register*, 1918 [Washington, D.C.: GPO, 1918], p. 234).

Report by Special Agent P-138

New York City 10-1-20

IN RE NEGRO ACTIVITIES: MARCUS GARVEY

Conditions are not so good around GARVEY's Liberty Hall, owing to the fact that a large number of the Black Star Line stockholders are getting a bit uneasy over the many and persistent rumors in circulation relative to the doubtful financial condition of Garvey's shipping scheme. I learned from THOMPSON, Garvey's Vice President, Chief Accountant and confidential and right hand man, that the crew of the "YARMOUTH", which is now laid up for repairs, have not received their pay as yet owing to lack of finance, and these men are becoming a little unmanageable, their wives critical, and their friends alarmed. That the ship is libelled with about 6 or 7 law suits pending against Garvey and the Black Star Line.[1]

THOMPSON told me confidentially that he was preparing to quit before the crash came, which in his opinion was a matter of weeks. He claimed Garvey refuses to be advised and is "bull-headed", having been intoxicated with anti-white ideas and the hand clapping of his cheering fanatics for the past year.

REVEREND MCGUIRE, Garvey's spokesman, is trying to keep things together in Liberty Hall, soothing the fears of the skeptics by telling them that the Black Star Line is getting on O.K. despite all rumors.

P-138

[*Endorsements*] NOTED W. W. G.
FILE G. F. R. NOTED F. D. W.

DNA, RG 65, file OG 329359. TD. Stamped endorsements.

1. Only two libels against the *Yarmouth* have been traced, and both were instituted much later than the date given in the documents. They are: *W. J. Hurrell* v. *S.S. Yarmouth*, no. 3272, March 1921, and *National Dry Dock and Repair Co.* v. *S.S. Yarmouth*, no. 3898, December 1921, U.S. District Court for the Eastern District of New York, Brooklyn. There may have been a number of cases brought by former employees for nonpayment of wages.

O. M. Thompson to Louis LaMothe

[*New York*] October 1st 1920

DEAR MR. LAMOTH:

For the last three weeks we have been trying to charter a ship inasmuch as the Yarmouth has not been placed for repairs yet and it does appear as though it will consume all over eight weeks to get her in Sea-worthy condition at the cost of $73,000.00, so we are inclined to believe it would be better for us to keep the Flag on the Seas by chartering a boat as we have 2500 tons of Cargo ready to go out and the sugar which you have engaged to come back, to make it interesting enough for you to continue selling Stock.

Your reference to Captain Richardson[1] is all wrong. Captain Richardson did all in his power to get the Kanawha to Cuba but the ship is a bad purchase, in fact after the fourth attempt to cross to Cuba, the Kanawha is now at Wilmington, Delaware[,] on her way back to New York and we have a salary list of the Crew of 39 for over three months without making a single trip.

"With reference to my mouth being libelled (I guess you meant the Yarmouth)," yes, it is true and in addition to that the accumulation of funds is much too slow to retire the obligations at maturity. This makes the future of the Black Star Line just a little doubtful (of course this is confidential). In order to retain business however, another Corporation is being organized namely the "Black Star Steamship Co."[2] Don't let this get out in Cuba, work as hard as ever, I still believe that we have a wonderful opportunity.

You must tell the people in Cuba when the Mongolia (not sure of this name; the name of the Chartered Ship) gets there that she is on probation for the Black Star Line and if the trip is satisfactory then the Company will buy the Mongolia.

Use your best executive ability and keep the people informed and interested. Personally, I think everything will come out alright only if we work hard. Yours sincerely,

O. M. THOMPSON

Arrange for Cargo of sugar 1st. week in November as we contemplate chartering another boat.

[*Address*] Mr. Louis Lamoth, Aguiar 92
Department 18, Havana, Cuba.

Garvey v. *United States*, no. 8317, Ct. App., 2d Cir., 2 February 1925, government exhibit no. 120.

1. Adrian Richardson (b. 1893) was born in Phillipsburg, St. Martin, Dutch West Indies. Raised aboard ship by a captain and his wife, Richardson became a master mariner in 1919. He first met Garvey during a UNIA rally while the *Yarmouth* was on display in Boston. Shortly thereafter he took a position as port captain for the Black Star Line in New York City. When the *Kanawha*'s first captain, Leon R. Swift, resigned in August 1920, Richardson took his place. His service with the Black Star Line ended when Garvey removed him from duty in July 1921. Richardson was one of twenty-five sailors who brought suit for wages against the Black Star Line; on 16 December 1921 the U.S. District Court for the Southern District of New York awarded a judgment of $12,303.35 (*Garvey* v. *United States*, no. 8317, Ct. App., 2d Cir., 2 February 1925).

2. The Black Star Steamship Co. of New Jersey was formed on 5 October 1920 by Samuel B. Howard, Robert K. Thistle, and A. Roy Myer. These men were probably New Jersey Garveyites whom Garvey enlisted to sign the certificate of incorporation that launched the company. Since it was essentially a means by which the old Black Star Line could continue to do business, the objectives of the new corporation were similar to those of the old. It was capitalized at only $500,000, however, with 100,000 shares at par value of $5 each. Negotiations for a *Phyllis Wheatley* continued under Thompson's direction in the name of the new company (certificate of incorporation of Black Star Steamship Co., *Garvey* v. *United States*, no. 8317, Ct. App., 2d Cir., pp. 2,639–2,647).

Arthur L. Lewis to the Editor, *Buffalo American*

414 Michigan Avenue, [*Buffalo, N.Y.*]
October 2, 1920

Editor Buffalo American:—

Please allow space in your paper for the publication of this article at the request of the Buffalo Branch of the U.N.I.A. and A.C.L.

To the Pastor, Officers, members and friends of the Michigan Avenue Baptist Church:—

It becomes wholly our duty to inform you that the article appearing in last month's issue of the "Negro World" does not meet with the approval of the Buffalo Branch of the U.N.I.A. and A.C.L. We could never endorse any such statement.[1] The article might be the personal opinion of the author. But we know that you and yours are supporters of anything for the advancement of the Race.

Our affiliation with the U.N.I.A. was brought about after a thorough understanding that its principles and ideals sought the universal co-operation of Negroes everywhere, and in every line of endeavor; that it denounces radicalism and has a purpose to destroy the bone of contention.

We, the members of the Buffalo Branch, are positively aware of the fact that such articles as we now try to apologize for, did not or could not have inspired Hon. Marcus Garvey and Dr. Eason to the lofty ideals of this association.

We beg that you and yours do not hold the Buffalo Branch guilty of anything save sad reflection on the publication of this article. We shall see to its correction in the next issue of the "Negro World" and our local ["]American["].

Hoping that this will in some way meet with your approval and gain your sympathy, and here we assure you that we will delightfully attend your leisure at any of our meetings, which are all public.

ARTHUR L. LEWIS
Vice-President and Chairman of Advisory Board
L. T. WILLIS
Sec'y.

Printed in the *Buffalo American*, 14 October 1920.

1. The only extant issue of the *Negro World* for the month of September 1920 is that of 11 September, and the statement mentioned does not appear in it. It is possible that the statement was written and sent to the *Negro World* for publication by a member of the Buffalo UNIA.

Gilbert Grindle to Lord Charles Hardinge,[1] Under Secretary of State, British Foreign Office

[*Colonial Office, London*] Downing Street,
5 October, 1920

Sir,

. . . I am directed by Viscount Milner to state that he would be glad if three or four copies of the Constitution and Book of Laws of the Association could be obtained for the use of this Department and the Director of Intelligence. It is understood to have been published in New York in July 1918. I am, Sir, Your most obedient Servant,

G[ILBERT] GRINDLE

[*Typewritten reference*] 44642/1920.

PRO, FO 371/4567. TLS, recipient's copy.

1. Charles Hardinge (1858–1944), baron of Penshurst, first became permanent under secretary of state for foreign affairs in 1906. He was viceroy of India from 1910 until 1916, when he returned to his previous post. Before the end of 1920 he would be appointed ambassador to Paris (*DNB*).

Report by Bureau Agent H. J. Lenon

Pittsburgh, Pa. 10/6/20

IN RE: MARCUS GARVEY, BACK TO AFRICA MOVEMENT
BLACK STAR STEAMSHIP LINE.

The following reports were received from a confidential source:—

"Thursday, Sept. 30, 1920, Pittsburgh, Pa.

The rain which occurred here tonight had the affect of putting a stop to any attempt on the part of Marcus Garvey and his gang staging a parade, in accord with their original intentions, but it in no measure dampened the enthusiasm of the members who went to hear him at the Labor Temple this evening. The writer would judge, that there were approximately fifteen hundred people present. The band of the Black Star Steamship Line rendered selection[s], as did others who were brought here from New York for the meetings scheduled to take place here.

As was expected, Garvey himself was the center of attraction. His remarks were not in the strictest sense of the term, radical, although he was on the border line on several occasions. At one time during his discourse, he stated that if the League of Nations went through in the manner in which President Wilson desired, that would be the beginning of the end for all the black races of the earth. His "Back to Africa" movement, the Universal Negro Improvements Association, and the steamship line comprised the other matters about which he talked. He claims that on tomorrow night at the Ebenezer Baptist Church, he will have something far more interesting to tell; he is still planning a mammoth parade in Pittsburgh, either with or without permission, if the weather permits."

"Pittsburgh, Pa., Friday, October 1, 1920.

The Garvey meeting, held tonight at the Ebenezer Baptist Church, Corner Wylie Avenue and Devilliere Street, was met with howling enthusiasm on the part of the audience which easily numbered two thousand and more. Every seat in the entire church was filled, and all of the aisles were crowded to capacity. It seems that the pastor of the church above mentioned, Rev. Austin,[1] strenuously objected to Garveyites using his church, but he was overruled by his trustees and deacons, and the meeting proce[e]ded anyway. Austin even went so far as to preach a sermon on last Sunday in which, among other things, he spoke most vehemently against Garvey, and all of his doings, to no avail. Austin was not among those present.

The main speaker of the evening was, of course, Garvey himself, whose remarks were almost the same as those made on the evening previously at Labor Temple. He again touched on the League of Nations, and stated that the object of that instrument was to completely subdue all of the black races of the world. He says that Africa is the birthright of all black races, and that it is his determination to drive out all other races, who are now residing there, and colonize it with black people. The greater portion of his remarks, however, were to the effect that if conditions continue in the manner in which they are now going, the American negro will be completely extermi-nated within the next fifty years. There was loud and prolonged applause throughout the entirety of his remarks. In looking over the audience, it appeared to the writer that fully ninety-nine percent of those present were very illiterate—a type governed very largely by their emotions, which were easily aroused.

Garvey is a West Indian, and a graduate of Oxford College in England. In addition to being a highly educated man, he has a magnetic personality, and the knack of swaying his audiences almost at will. He prefaced his remarks by stating that it was not his intention to make any militant state-ments, and whereas in the strictest sense of the term he could not be called radical, still at the same time the same results are accomplished, so far as his listeners are concerned.

Garvey has adopted an African national flag, which is red, green and black. Numbers of buttons were sold, having bars of each of these colors, and numerous flags of the same colors were in evidence. Garvey and one of his cohorts whom he brought with him from New York were garbed in gowns of red, green and black velvet.

Throughout the entire meeting, people were being importuned to come up to the table and subscribe f[or] stock in the Black Star Steamship Line, which was being sold while the speaking was going on. The musicians who were brought from New York also rendered a number of selections.

Another mam[m]oth meeting is scheduled for tomorrow night, and on Sunday night the crowd will go to Braddock, which temporarily winds up the Western Pennsylvania invasion for the present, although a permanent headquarters has been established here on Arthur Street.

Very little was said about the Universal Negro Improvements Associa-tion tonight, other than casual remarks here and there.

The writer is positive that there is something more back of this man than the public knows about, but it would be well nigh impossible to find that out from this end. There isn't the remotest doubt but that the manner in which he puts his stock before the public will eventually cause trouble, if not bloodshed. The [u]nfortunate feature about Garvey's meetings in general is the fact that he does not cater to the educated classes whatever, for the reason that he finds the illiterate much more easily swayed."

"Pittsburgh, Pa. Saturday, October 2, 1920.

The Garvey meeting held tonight was no different from the others which have been held here for the past two or three days. There was practically the same sort of an audience present, and the remarks of all of the speakers were met with about the same amount of enthusiasm. If matters continue here as they have started, it will not be a great while before memberships in the corporations will number up in the thousands. As has been stated before, Garvey makes his play to the ignorant and illiterate classes who, unfortunately, are many in number. He has little if any difficulty in persuading them that they are being daily persecuted and are rapidly facing extermination in the United States, and that their only hope is to follow him and form colonies in Africa, which he claims is the black man's birthright. The man Young who is in charge of the Pittsburgh headquarters of this concern is himself an illiterate man, but he seems to have quite a deal of influence with his followers.

As is the case in New York, a large percentage of the Garvey followers here are West Indians, who are now fraternizing with American negroes, something which never was done before. It would [*seem*] from all of these things that there is tangible action of some kind being contemplated and unless Garvey is stopped, it is stopped, it is difficult to conjecture what may happen."

"Homestead, Pa., Sunday, October 3, 1920.

Even though the colored Pittsburgh weeklies have run articles about the coming of Garvey, and in addition to that the [*news*] has been scattered broadcast throughout Allegheny County, still there were comparatively few colored mill workers here who k[ne]w anything about the meetings which were being held in Pittsburgh during the latter part of last week, which is all very well and something to be thankful for. The writer has not heard more than a half dozen men in Homestead mention Garvey's name at all, under any pretense whatever, and to date they have absolutely no interest in him or his doings whatever.["]

From statements made by the man Young, plans are now being made by him to start an unlimited campaign throughout the entirety of Allegheny County for memberships, and in the event this is done, the mill towns will not be slighted.

H. J. LENON

[*Endorsements*] H. W. G.
NOTED FILE G. F. R. NOTED W. W. G.
NOTED F. D. W.

DNA, RG 65, file OG 329359. TD. Stamped endorsements.

1. Junius Caesar Austin (1887–1968) soon became an enthusiastic supporter of the Garvey movement. Born in New Canton, Va., Austin was educated at the Virginia Seminary and College at Lynchburg, where he received a D.D. degree in 1910, and at Temple University, Philadelphia, where he earned a B.Th. degree. He became pastor of the Ebenezer Baptist Church in Pittsburgh in 1915, and he quickly developed a reputation as an advocate of foreign missions. During Austin's pastorate at Ebenezer, his national reputation as an orator grew, as did the church membership—from fifteen hundred to over five thousand. In 1919 he was one of the founders of the International League of Darker Peoples. He was also active in the National Race Congress in Washington, D.C., and was a frequent, respected speaker at the National Baptist Convention. In August 1922 Austin would give the opening address at the Third International Convention of the Negro Peoples of the World, delivering a memorable defense of Garveyism. The *Messenger* of May 1923 condemned Austin: "*He is a preacher–business man politician.* He is a fanatic over glory, praise and applause. He jumped into the Garvey movement and rode down Broadway with Garvey at the last convention. When he discovered that there *was to be nothing in it for him*, he jumped out and looked for other worlds to conquer" (p. 694). In 1926 Austin became pastor of the Pilgrim Baptist Church in Chicago, where he remained until his death (Randall K. Burkett, *Black Redemption: Churchmen Speak for the Garvey Movement* [Philadelphia: Temple University Press, 1978], pp. 113–117).

Report by Special Agent P-138

New York City 10-8-20

In Re: Negro Activities: Marcus Garvey

MARCUS GARVEY has returned [*6 October*] from his trip at least I learned that he was forced to return so as to keep his followers in line, who were commencing to ask some very embarrassing questions about the Black Star Line and the investment of their hard earned money.

There was a large crowd awaiting his arrival at Liberty Hall, but owing to the train being late he did not reach there until after 11 P.M. However, he promised them a full explanation tomorrow night.

I find that the anti-white agitation has died away somewhat since the business end of the Black Star Line is rapidly approaching financial ruin.

The prevailing topic is about the probable downfall of the steamship venture.

From my close observations during the past few weeks and from all indications I am strongly of the opinion that the sentiment has changed somewhat against Garvey among a certain group of his followers who are getting a bit nervous about their investment.

From now on I would not be a bit surprised to see a sudden collapse of the steamship proposition, and a decided reversal of sentiment towards Garvey.

If the Black Star Line /ships/ should remain tied up in the docks for the next four weeks, Garvey will be a ruined man and a near riot will start in Liberty Hall. I am very much afraid that the soothing speeches on anti-white topics is not now half as interesting to the members now as the burning question "What is wrong with the Black Star Line", and the true financial condition of the company.

P-138

[*Endorsements*] FILE G. F. R.
NOTED W. W. G. NOTED F. D. W.

DNA, RG 65, file OG 329359. TD. Stamped endorsements.

Report by Bureau Agent S. Busha

PHILADELPHIA, PA OCT. 8, 1920

MARCUS GARVEY, NEGRO AGITATOR & PROMOTER

In compliance with the Bureau's coded telegram dated October 8th 1920, which, decoded, reads as follows:

"MARCUS GARVEY, NEGRO AGITATOR AND PROMOTER OF THE INTERNATIONAL NEGRO IMPROVEMENT ASSOCIATION WILL AR-RIVE PHILADELPHIA TODAY. COVER SPEECHES, ASCERTAIN CONNECTIONS."—

The following has been ascertained in connection with GARVEY's visit in this city. As a result of an invitation by the officers of the INTERNATIONAL NEGRO IMPROVEMENT ASSOCIATION (Philadelphia branch), GARVEY, having arrived in Philadelphia late in the day, attended their business meeting which took place this evening on the second floor of the PEOPLES CHURCH (colored) located at the N.E. Corner of 17th & Christian Streets. There were about 500 colored persons present. From the transpiring events of this meeting, it was disclosed that the Philadelphia branch of the INTERNATIONAL NEGRO IMPROVEMENT ASSOCIATION had requested GARVEY to attend this particular meeting with the object of sett[l]ing various difficulties of the Association, arising out of grievances the members of the association had regarding the handling of the association funds by the officers of said organization.

While the grievances were being presented, the meeting became tumult[u]ous and the members present became profane. GARVEY, after declaring that the audience was composed of "ill mannered persons" left the meeting remarking that the attitude of the members would compel him to revoke the charter of this branch of the association.

This attitude of GARVEY in terminating the meeting and threatening to revoke the charter would have resulted in violence, probably to GARVEY himself as well, except for the presence of a number of uniformed police officers who took a hand in dispersing the gathering.

As it will be seen from the aforesaid events, GARVEY did not make any speeches and immediately after leaving the meeting, he departed from this city. CONCLUDED.

S. BUSHA

[*Endorsements*] FILE W. W. G.
FILE G. F. R.

DNA, RG 65, file OG 329359. TD. Handwritten endorsements.

Report by Special Agent J. G. Tucker

[*New York*] OCT. 9, 1920

NEGRO WORLD

The above paper in its issue of October 9th carries a letter dated Pittsburg[h], October 5th and signed by MARCUS GARVEY which is addressed to "Fellow Men of the Negro Race." The letter is extremely radical and assails the White Race generally.

In discussing the question of White Supremacy over the Negroes, Garvey states in part:

> It is a question of supreme importance, one neither to be evaded or temporized with. Today we find the Egyptians not only clamoring for the right to control their own destiny but actually demanding it and taking steps to enforce that demand.
>
> India with her teeming millions, despite religious differences, is organizing and demanding recognition of her right to independent existence.
>
> The Japanese, with the force of a well organized government and an army and navy which commands respect, move recognition of their right to exist free of the prejudicial conventions now hemming them in.
>
> Africa's teeming millions are awake, wide awake to the power of organized efforts to ameliorate the harsh conditions under which they live. Christians, Pagans and Mohamm[e]dans are all uniting their efforts to this end.
>
> *The millions of Negroes in the West Indies, Central and South America and in the U.S. have ceased to be cringing sycophants. We have ceased to beg and petition to be allowed to exercise our God-given rights.*

We have not only framed our demands for recognition of those rights but have determined to exercise them. . . .

J. G. TUCKER

DNA, RG 65, file OG 208369-a. TD.

Report by Special Agent P-138

New York City 10-9-20

Today [*7 October*] I called Garvey on the phone and congra[t]ulated him on his safe return, etc.

He made an appointment for me to call at his office Monday, 11 A.M. to have a real social talk, as he is desirous of having me help him to bring about an amicable adjustment between him and two men who sued him for $20,000 each, and he is relying on me to put through this matter and keep the men out of court.

My chief reason for making this appointment is to try and question him diplomatically as to whether any Japanese are behind his movement or lending him any support. I am working my way gradually into his confidence on this account.

I learned from one of his henchmen, that two of his campaigners were arrested in Youngstown, Ohio, charged with fraud, and were restrained from speaking or collecting any money out there. The Police tried to arrest Garvey but he slipped away.[1] I learned that so far his tour was a gigantic financial failure.

Tonight I visited Liberty Hall to learn of Garvey's explanation of true conditions of the Black Star Line. He spoke to a very large audience, but to my surprise they were the most nonresponsive I have seen. There was a cloud of gloom of sorrow over the entire audience. Garvey was cheered but feebly and his speech was a failure and his explanation disappointed the audience.

He then read a letter sent to him, threatening him, criticising him, ridiculing him, etc. He pitifully related to his followers what people and his enemies were saying about him, etc. Already there is a fight going on in the ranks between Negroes from different states, county or island, each becoming jealous of the other whenever one is appointed to a high office, and some are calling for their money back out of the Black Star Line.

I joined Garvey on his way home from Liberty Hall tonight and walked with him about 6 blocks, talking to him on general conditions and confirming our Monday appointment. Garvey was accompanied by six of his detectives and two extra guards.

P-138

[*Endorsements*] FILE G. F. R. NOTED W. W. G.

DNA, RG 65, file OG 329359. TD. Stamped endorsements.

1. According to the testimony of Harry R. Watkis, the chief stock salesman for the Black Star Line, Garvey, James D. Brooks, and Watkis were selling stock in Youngstown, Ohio, when Watkis was arrested. Although Garvey and Brooks were also present when the arrest was made, Watkis claimed that they evaded the police by hiding behind a tree and later escaped by train (*Marcus Garvey* v. *United States*, no. 8317, Ct. App., 2d Cir., 2 February 1925, pp. 789–799).

O. M. Thompson to Hugh Mulzac

[*New York*] October 9th, 1920

Dear Mr. Mulzac:[1]

Replying to your letter enclosing Notice from Messrs. Wingate & Brown, Jr., Bankers; my dear Mr. Mulzac[,] we expect you to keep this confidential, but the truth is the Black Star Line is seriously embarrassed financially.

Just at this writing we have the unpleasant news that the YARMOUTH is sinking,[2] however, we were able to get a Tow Boat Company to undertake to pump her. We will write you again very soon perhaps Monday afternoon in detail.

With reference to the balance due you, it[']s a painful fact to record that the Company is practically in a financial suspense, all the more grievous because these Bankers may get the excuse that the reason you could not retire your Note at maturity is because the Black Star Line could not pay you. You know this information spread broad cast is destructive. I have taken up this payment with Mr. Garvey and Mr. Garcia and hope to be able to send you a check on Monday.

If you can make a voyage on somebody's ship and be available in December, this is my advice to you.

It will cost $75,000.00 to make the YARMOUTH sea-worthy and this amount nor any part of it is not yet in sight. Please treat this letter confidentially, if Mrs. Mulzac should read it ask her not to let anybody know about it through her. Yours fraternally,

BLACK STAR LINE INC.
O. M. THOMPSON,
Vice President

[*Address*] Mr. H. Mulzac,
1826 McCulloh St. Baltimore, Md.

Garvey v. *United States*, no. 8317, Ct. App., 2d Cir., 2 February 1925, government exhibit no. 53.

1. Hugh Mulzac (1886–1971) was the chief officer of the *Yarmouth* during its second and third voyages under Black Star Line control, later working as a watchman on the *Yarmouth*. Born on Union Island in the Grenadines, BWI, Mulzac began his career as a sailor at the age of eighteen. He attended Swansea Nautical College, Swansea, England, before serving as a deck

officer on various British and American vessels during World War I. Mulzac became a U.S. citizen in 1918. Although he was passed over in favor of Adrian Richardson to replace Leon R. Swift as captain of the *Kanawha*, he was involved in the attempt to purchase the *Porto Rico*, with the possibility that he would be made its captain. After his service with the *Yarmouth*, Mulzac became a member of a BSL stockholders' committee investigating the affairs of the company. Shortly thereafter Mulzac ended his relationship with the BSL and formed his own steamship company. In 1921 he established Mulzac's Nautical Academy, enrolling fifty-two students, most of whom were seeking to qualify for work aboard Black Star Line ships. When the Black Star Line was declared bankrupt in 1922, enrollment in Mulzac's school quickly declined, and it closed after only one term. Mulzac later served as captain of the Liberty ship *Booker T. Washington* during World War II (Hugh Mulzac, *A Star to Steer By* [New York: International Publishers, 1963]; *Marcus Garvey* v. *United States*, no. 8317, Ct. App., 2d Cir., 2 February 1925, pp. 603–666; *NYT*, 1 February 1971).

2. At 1:37 P.M. on 30 September 1920, a strong breeze blew the *Yarmouth* into the S.S. *West Pool* while both ships were at anchor off Bay Ridge in Brooklyn. No damage was done until 4:00 P.M., when the *Yarmouth* began to sink, rolling into the *West Pool* and denting the *West Pool*'s upper hull plates. At 5:30, tugboats towed the *Yarmouth* away (F. A. Mosher, "Confidential Report of Accident," 14 October 1920, DNA, RG 32, file 553-1410).

Report by Special Agent P-138

NEW YORK CITY 10-10-20

NEGRO ACTIVITIES.

... HINDOO: At Garvey[']s meeting he introduced a Hindo[o] to speak who was silly on the platform. Garvey said that he was looking for help from some one as his organization was out to help any other organization which will help his[,] that the speakers will be a Mr. . . . [*words mutilated*] from Bombay[,] India[,] members of the radical cast[e] Indian movement.[1]

Garvey said that as the Hindoos were fighting for the same thing that he was fighting for hence they welcome them with open arms.

The Hindo[o] spoke no doubt for three quarters of an hour praising Garvey for his courage and determination and also for pr[omising] to give him an[d] his association all the aid possible. He read a pamphlet to denounce all the white race saying that they were the en[em]ies of mankind and that should be fought tooth and nail. He will be given the whole time to speak Tuesday eve., at length on conditions in India and the method of their propaganda. I shall keep a close watch on his movement in the neighborhood.

P-138

[*Endorsements*] FILE G. F. R. FILE W. W. G.
NOTED F. D. W.

DNA, RG 65, file BS 202600-667. TD. Stamped endorsements.

1. In a subsequent report, P-138 indicated that Garvey introduced Mr. W. S. Basuma as a "member of the East Indian radical movement" who resided in Bombay (DNA, RG 65, file BS 202600-667).

Editorial Letter by Marcus Garvey

[[New York City, October 11, 1920]]

Fellow Men of the Negro Race, Greetings:—

We have just returned to New York from a four weeks' tour of Pennsylvania, Delaware, New Jersey, Maryland and Ohio, and we returned with high hopes for the U.N.I.A. Everywhere we saw interest in and enthusiasm for the U.N.I.A. growing. The masses of the race absorb the doctrines of the U.N.I.A. with the same eagerness with which the masses in the days of the supremacy of imperial Rome accepted [C]hristianity. The people seem to regard the movement in the light of a new religion.

The U.N.I.A. has awakened a new race consciousness in the Negro people of the world during the past two years. They realize that they have a destiny which they must work out by and through themselves. They realize that they are created in the divine image, and are not first cousins to the monkey. And they realize that the perverse will of man and not the fiat of the Almighty decreed that color should be the badge of aristocracy and that the natural function of black men was to be chattel slaves and subjects of white men.

The new Negro as he has been inspired by the U.N.I.A. does not believe that God plays any favorites, does not believe that God sets apart any of the garden spots of the world for any particular race. And he believes that just as the Anglo-Saxon in America has redeemed a forest and planted cities by the exercise of his will, so can the Negro by the exercise of his will clear the forests of Africa and plant cities.

But the apostle James has wisely said that faith without works was dead,[1] and our belief that we are sons of God the same as other men, our belief that we are entitled to life, liberty and the pursuit of happiness, that we have a title clear to the good things of this beautiful earth will avail little, unless we have in our possession the material means to realize our ideals and plans. Although the Negro is oppressed in the Southern States of America, underpaid in the West Indies and exploited in Africa, these grievances will not be removed by prayer and supplication.

So selfish is human nature that rights cannot be had for the mere asking. They must be won by toil, struggle and effort. For this reason the Negro Factories Corporation and the Black Star Line have sprung into existence. Through the Black Star Line we will come into trade relations with our brethren on the West Coast of Africa, and transport to Liberia and other African countries, those Negroes who desire to possess and enjoy the fruits of the richest country on God's green earth.

But we cannot fly to Africa at present in airships. We cannot walk across the ocean. The only way that we can get there is through ships, and on January 1, 1921, we plan to launch the Phyllis Wheatley and send the first trading ship manned and owned by Negroes and the pioneers to Africa. For this reason we ask you to send in and buy shares. They are still selling at $5.00 each, and you may buy from one to two hundred. Apply to the Black Star Line, 56 West 135th Street, New York, U.S.A., for your shares now.

With high hopes and expectations for the success of the U.N.I.A. and the Black Star Line. Yours fraternally,

MARCUS GARVEY

Garvey v. *United States*, no. 8317, Ct. App., 2d Cir., 2 February 1925, government exhibit no. 37. Original headlines omitted.

1. James 2:20: "But wilt thou know, O vain man, that faith without works is dead?"

Letter to the Editor, *Negro World*

[[Chunchula, Ala. October 12, 1920]]

Dear Sir:

Although it has been only a short time that we have been receiving your paper, it seems as one of the family. We look forward to its coming with as much joy as we do to one of us, and there is not much done until it is read through and through.

You are doing a good work and I am so glad that you are having much success. Though it has been late, very late for some of us way down here, and especially those of us who are in the "Piney" woods, to hear of it, I think I can say we won't be late in doing our duty towards the uplift of our race.

If all of us could see through your efforts, what it will do for us and ours, and every man and woman should stand up to their manhood and woman-hood, what a great thing it would be.

May God bless and direct you and have mercy on us all.

MRS. SUSIE WILDER

Printed in *NW*, 23 October 1920.

O. M. Thompson to Leo Healy

[*New York*] October 12th, 1920

Dear Sir:

This serves to acknowledge receipt of your letter of October 11th, pursuant to conversation with Mr. Garvey concerning overdue Notes on the "Yarmouth."

We note with much gratitude that Mr. Harris will defer payment of the August and September notes until November 1st, and that you will endeavor to arrange for such instalments as our Financial condition will permit at that time.[1]

We appreciate profoundly your attitude, and beg to remain, Yours very truly,

BLACK STAR LINE, INC.
O. M. THOMPSON,
Vice President

Garvey v. *United States*, no. 8317, Ct. App., 2d Cir., 2 February 1925, government exhibit no. 18.

1. On 3 November 1920 the BSL made a payment of $2,000, leaving an unpaid balance of $34,600 on the contract price of the *Yarmouth*. See *Garvey Papers*, 3: App. II, pp. 775–783, for details of BSL payments on the *Yarmouth*, *Shadyside*, and *Kanawha* for this period.

Reports by Special Agent P-138

NEW YORK, N.Y. Oct. 17, 1920

NEGRO ACTIVITIES

Today [*15 October*] Garvey made an appointment with me over the phone to see me at 2 P.M. next Wednesday for a conference.

I have positive information that the Black Star Line finances are almost gone and things are getting very bad in Garvey's organization.

NEW SCHEME:

Garvey has adopted and put into operation another wild-cat money raising scheme, which is to raise $2,000,000 by notes from his members, the stock-selling plan seems to have been worked to death. From circular enclosed you will see that it is another back-to-Africa plan.

If rumors are true, the financial bottom is sure to be dropped out of his organization very soon. . . .

P-138

[*Handwritten endorsement*] No circular
enclosed F. D. W.
[*Stamped endorsements*] FILE G. F. R.
NOTED F. D. W.

DNA, RG 65, file OG 258421. TD.

Enclosure

ALL NEGROES ARE RELATED BY BLOOD.

All the Negroes in America, Canada, the West Indies, South and Central America, are descendants of the native Africans who were robbed from Africa three hundred years ago. All of us were taken into this Western World to work as slaves, during which period of time we came in contact with the white man's civilization. Out of this contact, we have developed a civilization that has become thought-compelling. The world at large acknowledges the intellectual worth of the present-day Negro. The present generation of Negroes is far removed from the slaves of one hundred years ago. The Negro mixes with a civilization that he understands and is able to cope with, when he does apply himself.

Today the world is undergoing a change. The political boundaries of humanity are being readjusted; and in this readjustment, every Race is endeavoring to find a home sufficiently secured as to protect its own integrity. Hence, the cry of Ireland for the Irish, Poland for the Poles, Palestine for the Jews.

AFRICA FOR THE AFRICANS.

The Universal Negro Improvement Association—the greatest Negro organization in the world—is now making the cry of Africa for the Africans: those at home and those abroad who were torn from her bosom three hundred years ago and worked for two hundred and fifty years as slaves in this Western hemisphere, but who are today to be numbered among the civilized peoples of the world.

CIVILIZED NEGRO MUST FOUND A GOVERNMENT.

With the civilization of the Western Negro, we must found a Government of our own in Africa and build up a new civilization by which the Race may shine out as the leaders in the great ethnic principles of life.

STRONG COMMERCIAL STATE IN LIBERIA.

The Universal Negro Improvement Association has laid its plans for the redemption of Africa by first building up a strong industrial and commercial state in Liberia, West Africa. Liberia was established over one hundred years ago as an independent Negro Republic by run-away and freed Negro slaves from America. This country is dominated by all colored people. The President and entire Government are colored and no white man can be a citizen of the country.

EDUCATE NATIVE TRIBES.

It is now, therefore, for American, West Indian, South and Central American and Canadian Negroes to buy Liberty Loans in the Universal Negro Improvement Association and help to build up Liberia as a strong and powerful African State. Through the Colleges and Universities of Liberia, we hope to educate all the Native Tribes of Africa in the higher principles of self-Government.

Buy a Construction Loan for $20, $30, $40, $50, $100, $200, $400, $500, $600, $700, $800, $900, $1,000, at 5 per cent interest annually. Loan it for 2, 3, 4, 5 or 10 years.

WHY YOU SHOULD SUBSCRIBE FOR BONDS.

Each and every Negro should subscribe to the Loans of the Universal Negro Improvement Association for its constructive work in Liberia, because (1) Railroads are to be built for the purpose of linking up the entire country; (2) Schools and Colleges must be built for the higher training of the populace and for the present and future generations of Negroes who will settle in Liberia; (3) Churches must be built for the spiritual worship of all those who will settle in Liberia; (4) Factories and Mills must be built for the purpose of finding employment for the millions who will repatriate themselves to the grand old country; (5) Docks must be built for the purpose of accommodating the ships of the Black Star Line; (6) Farms must be laid out for the agricultural development of the country; (7) [T]he coal, iron, silver and gold mines of Liberia must be exploited for their hidden wealth; (8) [A] greater Government must be built up in Liberia so as to command the respect of the world.

REASONS WHY YOU SHOULD SUBSCRIBE FOR A LOAN.

All these and many more reasons are sufficient to convince each and every Negro that it is to his or her advantage to subscribe for the Universal Negro Improvement Association's Construction Loan.

If you desire freedom, you will subscribe for a Loan.

If you desire to stop lynching and burning, you will subscribe for a Loan.

If you desire to stop jim-crowism, you will subscribe for a Loan.

If you desire to stop segregation, you will subscribe for a Loan.

If you long to see the Negro respected, you will subscribe for a Loan.

If you would like to see the Negro have a flag of his own, you will subscribe for a Loan.

If you would like to see the Negro having a Nation sufficiently strong to protect him in any part of the world, you will subscribe for a Loan.

If you desire to see the Negro boy or girl with a future, you will subscribe for a Loan.

By subscribing for these Loans, you will raise the standard of the Negro commercially, industrially, politically and socially.

You can subscribe for a Loan in the following amounts: $20, $40, $100, $200, $300, $400, $500, $600, up to $1,000.

All the members of the Race who subscribe for a Loan of from $50 to $100 will receive the Bronze Cross of African Redemption. All of those who subscribe for a Loan of from $100 to $500 will receive the Silver Cross of African Redemption. And all those who subscribe for a Loan of from $500 to $1,000 will receive the Gold Cross of African Redemption.

GOLD CROSS OF AFRICAN REDEMPTION.

The Gold Cross of African Redemption will be to Negroes what the Victoria Cross of England has been to Englishmen, and the Iron Cross of Germany has been to the Germans. There can be no excuse for each and every Negro not supporting the Universal Negro Improvement Association's Construction Loan.

If you are a member of this great Organization, send in immediately to the Universal Negro Improvement Association, 56 West 135th Street, New York, N.Y., U.S.A., and ask for a Liberian Construction Loan in any of the above amounts. With very best wishes, Yours Faithfully,

UNIVERSAL NEGRO IMPROVEMENT ASSOCIATION

THE HOUR FOR UNIVERSAL ACTIVITY.

The hour has struck for universal activity among the Negro peoples of the world. It is for them now to concentrate on the building up of a great industry of their own. It is of no use for the Negro to continue to depend on the good graces of the other Races of the world, because we are now living in a selfish, material age, when each and every Race is looking out for itself.

ALL NEGRO PEOPLE SHOULD UNITE THEIR FORCES.

Because of the scarcity of all that tends to human happiness and human comfort, the Negro should at least make a desperate effort to build up great industrial plants and institutions of his own. The world is large enough for him to operate in; and above all other places, Africa now opens up a golden field of opportunity for each and every progressive Negro who desires his own advancement.

GREAT INDUSTRIAL PLANTS AND INSTITUTIONS.

All the Negro people of the United States of America, the West Indies, South and Central America and Canada should unite their forces and support the Universal Negro Improvement Association's Construction Loan for the building up of Liberia so that the Negro can at least boast of one great State

THE HOUR FOR UNIVERSAL ACTIVITY.

The hour has struck for universal activity among the Negro peoples of the world. It is for them now to concentrate on the building up of a great industry of their own. It is of no use for the Negro to continue to depend on the good graces of the other Races of the world, because we are now living in a selfish, material age, when each and every Race is looking out for itself.

ALL NEGRO PEOPLE SHOULD UNITE THEIR FORCES.

Because of the scarcity of all that tends to human happiness and human comfort, the Negro should at least make a desperate effort to build up great industrial plants and institutions of their own. The world is large enough for him to operate in; and above all other places, Africa now opens up a golden field of opportunity for each and every progressive Negro who desires his own advancement.

GREAT INDUSTRIAL PLANTS AND INSTITUTIONS.

All the Negro people of the United States of America, the West Indies, South and Central America and Canada should unite their forces and support the Universal Negro Improvement Association's Construction Loan for the building up of Liberia so that the Negro can at least boast of one great State able to protect him whether he lives in America, the West Indies or any other part of the world.

Let us have a great Government. Let us help to build it. Now is the time for each and every Negro to pledge his labor, his wealth and his education for the building up of a great country of his own.

The Universal Negro Improvement Association asks you, therefore, to support this Construction Loan. By supporting the Loan of $2,000,000 we will be able in another couple of months to report such progress in Liberia as to make each and every Negro's heart feel glad in every part of the world.

Write to the Universal Negro Improvement Association, 56 West 135th Street, New York, N. Y., U. S. A.

If you desire Liberty you will subscribe for a Loan.

CUT OFF AND MAIL

SUBSCRIPTION BLANK.

Universal Negro Improvement Association.
56 West 135th Street, New York, U. S. A.

Dear Fellow Members:

I hereby subscribe for a $........ Loan for ...... years at 5 per cent interest annually. This money I loan will help to build up a Government of our own.

NAME ....

CITY ....

STATE ....

WHY YOU SHOULD SUBSCRIBE FOR BONDS.

Each and every Negro should subscribe to the Loan of the Universal Negro Improvement Association for its constructive work in Liberia, because (1) Railroads are to be built for the purpose of linking up the entire country; (2) Schools and Colleges must be built for the higher training of the populace and for the present and future generations of Negroes who will settle in Liberia; (3) Churches must be built for the spiritual worship of all those who will settle in Liberia; (4) Factories and Mills must be built for the purpose of finding employment for the millions who will repatriate themselves to the grand old country; (5) Docks must be built for the purpose of accommodating the ships of the Black Star Line; (6) Farms must be laid out for the agricultural development of the country; (7) the coal, iron, silver and gold mines of Liberia must be exploited for their hidden wealth; (8) a greater Government must be built up in Liberia so as to command the respect of the world.

REASONS WHY YOU SHOULD SUBSCRIBE FOR A LOAN.

All these and many more reasons are sufficient to convince each an' every Negro that it is to his or her advantage to subscribe for the Universal Negro Improvement Association's Construction Loan.

If you desire freedom, you will subscribe for a Loan.

If you desire to stop lynching and burning, you will subscribe for a Loan.

If you desire to stop jim-crowism, you will subscribe for a Loan.

If you desire to stop segregation, you will subscribe for a Loan.

If you long to see the Negro respected, you will subscribe for a Loan.

If you would like to see the Negro have a flag of his own, you will subscribe for a Loan.

If you would like to see the Negro having a Nation sufficiently strong to protect him in any part of the world, you will subscribe for a Loan.

If you desire to see the Negro boy or girl with a future, you will subscribe for a Loan.

By subscribing for these Loans, you will raise the standard of the Negro commercially, industrially, politically and socially.

You can subscribe for a Loan in the following amounts: $20, $40, $100, $200, $300, $400, $500, $600, up to $1,000.

All the members of the Race who subscribe for a Loan of from $50 to $100 will receive the Bronze Cross of African Redemption. All of those who subscribe for a Loan of from $100 to $500 will receive the Silver Cross of African Redemption. And all those who subscribe for a Loan of from $500 to $1,000 will receive the Gold Cross of African Redemption.

GOLD CROSS OF AFRICAN REDEMPTION.

The Gold Cross of African Redemption will be to Negroes what the Victoria Cross of England has been to Englishmen, and the Iron Cross of Germany has been to the Germans. There can be no excuse for each and every Negro not supporting the Universal Negro Improvement Association's Construction Loan.

If you are a member of this great Organization, send in immediately to the Universal Negro Improvement Association, 56 West 135th Street, New York, N. Y., U. S. A., and ask for a Liberian Construction Loan in any of the above amounts.

With very best wishes,

Yours Faithfully,

UNIVERSAL NEGRO IMPROVEMENT ASSOCIATION.

able to protect him whether he lives in America, the West Indies or any other part of the world.

Let us have a great Government. Let us help to build it. Now is the time for each and every Negro to pledge his labor, his wealth and his education for the building up of a great country of his own.

The Universal Negro Improvement Association asks you, therefore, to support this Construction Loan. By supporting the Loan of $2,000,000 we will be able in another couple of months to report such progress in Liberia as to make each and every Negro's heart feel glad in every part of the world.

**Write to the Universal Negro Improvement Association,
56 West 135th Street, New York, N.Y., U.S.A.**
If you desire Liberty you will subscribe for a Loan.

CUT OFF AND MAIL

SUBSCRIPTION BLANK.

Universal Negro Improvement Association,
56 West 135th Street, New York, U.S.A.

Dear Fellow Members:

I hereby subscribe for a $...... Loan for ...... years at 5 per cent interest annually. This money I loan will help to build up a Government of our own.

NAME ....

CITY ....

STATE ....

DJ-FBI. Printed circular.

New York City 10-19-20

IN RE: NEGRO ACTIVITIES.

GARVEY, at LIBERTY HALL tonight [*17 October*], opened his drive for the $2,000,000 by voluntary subscription, and by loan. He has revived the "Back to Africa Idea" in a very pointed and persistent manner. He pointed out to the Negroes very forcibly that within a few years the white men will be driving them out of this country, as they, (the Negroes), would be out of employment owing to the full tide of immigration pouring in at Ellis Island,[1] coupled with the inherent hatred of the whites towards the Negroes.

Therefore, urged GARVEY, they should give all the money they had to him, so that he may send it to Liberia for the construction of the foundation of a Negro Empire. He promised to take them back to Africa if they will contribute the money for the buying of more and larger ships.

Of course, from quite reliable information received by me through his Vice President and Chief Accountant, THOMPSON, GARVEY's payments on his ships, lots at Liberty Hall, houses at 56 West 135th St. are now overdue, apart from other pressing financial demands, which must be met hurriedly if disaster is to be avoided, hence Garvey's new and sensational appeal for [a] $2,000,000 loan.

The anti-white feeling which was not so much in evidence since he had left on his tour some weeks ago, has commenced to revive and he has again started to denounce everything that is white so as to appeal to the crude feelings and tastes of his audience. This has always been Garvey's plan whenever he wants to get large sums of money from his people. My candid opinion is, judging from close observations, this fellow GARVEY has very great influence over a wide group of Negroes who are his followers, a hold that cannot very easily be broken except the Black Star Line goes to smash.

I am further of the opinion that this stronghold or influence can either be applied for good or can be turned to a bad purpose overnight.

Whatever Garvey tells those Negroes from the platform of Liberty Hall, they surely will believe it, and if he so orders them, they will act upon it. He is by far the most talked of leader among the Negroes, and caters to the tastes of the less intelligent ones.

P-138

[*Endorsements*] FILE G. F. R.
NOTED W. W. G. NOTED F. D. W.

DNA, RG 65, file OG 329359. TD. Stamped endorsements.
  1. Ellis Island was the major point of entry for immigrants arriving from Europe.

Rev. E. J. Echols[1] to Marcus Garvey

[*Buffalo, N.Y., ca. 20 October 1920*]

To Mr. Garvey or some of his representatives:

. . . As a chosen leader of a part of the Negroes in Buffalo, in order that I may be intelligent before I give further advice to my people who come to me for advice relative to taking membership and purchasin[g] shares, I submit the following questions to be answered for my personal information:

The questions read:

  1. Questions relative to the leader's citizenship:
      (a) Where was the leader of the "Black Star Line" born?
      (b) How long has he been in the United States?
      (c) Is he [a] citizen of the United States?
      (d) If not, then why not?
      (e) Is he a Christian?
      (f) Where was he educated?

2. Questions relative to the "Black Star Line":

(a) Under what laws and what State is the "Black Star Line" chartered?

(b) What is the capital stock?

(c) What kind of stock is the firm selling?

(d) Why does the constitution fail to state the time the dividends are to be declared?

(e) What is the use to have a local branch in Buffalo, if it can not sell all the stock to be sold in Buffalo?

(f) Why did you not use the local secretary when selling shares here?

(g) Who is negotiating for the raw ma[t]erial to which you referred in Africa?

(h) In what part of Africa do you hope to establish trade?

(i) If we say the white man is wrong when he forms a white man's organization, do we not disgrace ourselves when we form a black man's organization?

3. Questions relative to the U.N.I.A.:

(a) Who called the first meeting, where and when was it held?

(b) Why was the world's convention called in New York, rather than the West Indies or Africa?

(c) By whom were the delegates elected? Who were in attendance? Name the governments represented?

(d) Did all of the leading Negro organizations send delegates from the United States?

(e) Is it true that only the local branches of the "Black Star Line," both in and out of the United States sent delegates to the New York meeting?

(f) If the foregoing is true, what effect will the election of a temporary president have upon the people in Africa?

(g) Name ten of the leading Negro educators, born in the United States, who are members of the organization?

(h) Give the name and address of the attorney who has been employed to give legal advice?

(i) Name ten leaders of the governments of Africa who live in Africa?

Please answer as brie[fl]y and early as possible.

REV. E. J. ECHOLS
429 Clinton St., Buffalo, N.Y.

Printed in the *Buffalo American*, 11 November 1920.

1. The following explanatory statement accompanied the publication of Rev. Echols's letter:

Some of the pastors of Buffalo did not approve of the last public meeting held here by the "Black Star Line," because it is a business firm and should not sell its stock on the

Lord's day. Because, Rev. E. J. Echols, the pastor of the First Shiloh Baptist Church, refused to allow them to hold such a meeting in his church, he has been placed among those who are unfriendly toward the institution. Rev. Echols wishes to let the public know his attitude toward this organization, its leader and its system.

Editorial in the *Buffalo American*

[21 October 1920]

THREE GREAT MEETINGS

The three great meetings addressed by Mr. Marcus Garvey, President General of U.N.I.A. and A.C.L., were in many ways the greatest meetings ever held in our city. The attendance was exceptional at every meeting. Interest, after Sunday afternoon [*17 October*], replaced curiosity and many decided not to miss an opportunity to hear Mr. Garvey.

That the fundamental motives of this great organization ... [*words mutilated*] and sound one would readily agree. The organiza[tion of a]ll of the people [of this?] country is a task great enough to undertake, but to organize four millions of people throughout the universe seems to one with less vision than the Great Prophet a task too great to dream of. Yet it is being done. Thus far only success has greeted the efforts of this great organization. The future is not alone in the hands of the leaders, but the disciples as well. For the success of any great enterprise rests not alone on its leaders, as important as this is, but on the followers as well.

As true as it is that no just and far-reaching criticism of any man or movement cannot and should not be made until a thorough study, unbiased and unprejudiced, has been made by the would-be critic[, i]t is equally as important that each disciple, each representative of any man or movement before attempting to represent, have a de[e]p conviction and thorough knowledge of the thing he is selling. For it is too often the case that men with large ideas are misrepresented because they have not been understood.

The idea to build for ourselves everything; to prepare for another day; to stimulate all movements among our Race for progress; and to become an independent, self-sustaining people is the doctrine of the age. Mr. Garvey pointed out that we had helped to develop all of the leading countries of the world and are welcomed in no one of them, thus his back-to-Africa doctrine. Thus an empire controlled by Negroes. Who knows but such may come. Be that as it will or may, today we are clamoring for a place in the country which we have developed, a seat on the throne which we built. Let no doctrine cause us to denounce the Stars and Stripes and this the only home of which we know.

Printed in the *Buffalo American*, 21 October 1920.

Reports by Special Agent P-138

New York City 10-22-20

IN RE: NEGRO ACTIVITIES.

Today [*20 October*] I succeeded in locating [*C. C.*] SIEFERT, the man on whom I reported the other day,[1] at 313 West 137th Street, he being the party who had entertained two Japanese a few months ago. SIEFERT said that these Japs had credentials from the Premier of Japan, and from what they told him they were trying to get in touch with some large organization of Negroes so as to interest them to trade with Japan. They promised to offer their merchandise at prices much lower than what the U.S. could sell, and to convince the Negroes that it would be far more advantageous to throw in their lot with Japan. They were on a special trade mission here but left the country sometime ago, to the best of his knowledge. He said he had their card with their names, somewhere in his desk and promised to give me same.

SIEFERT told me that he introduced these Japs to GARVEY and they had a long talk, but he is of the opinion that they did not come to any definite conclusion, as Garvey seems to have been too slow in grasping the true situation and take advantage of the great commercial opportunity which the Japs were offering. This slow action of Garvey seems to have caused them to be a little displeased. However, they promised to write to him, (Siefert) on their arrival back home.

I had a long talk with Garvey today in my office to cultivate his friendship, so as to approach him as the matter of the Japanese or any foreign aid in his propaganda. He admitted to me that he was passing through troubled financial waters, and he was afraid that he would have to take some radical steps to stave off certain financial disaster. He claims that he /is/ spending every least [last?] chance to defend the many law suits against him and his Black Star Line organization. I have another appointment with him for October 30th.

P-138

[*Endorsements*] FILE G. F. R.
NOTED F. D. W. NOTED W. W. G.

DNA, RG 65, file BS 198940-52. TD. Stamped endorsements.

1. On 21 October P-138 reported that he had attempted to locate Siefert but had been unsuccessful (DNA, RG 65, file OG 258421).

[New Yor]k City 10-23-20

IN RE: NEGRO ACTIVITIES.

. . . GARVEY has opened a big drive for this so-called "African Liberty Loan", which means in simple language a desperate effort to borrow money from his already overworked followers, so as to stave off certain financial disaster which is heading towards him and his Black Star Line. Now that the Negroes failed to answer his call for buying stock, he suddenly phrased this new money getting name "African Liberty Loan", which has a very great psychological ring as touching his "Back to Africa" fanatic. This fellow Garvey is a master mind in knowing how to play on the feeling of his followers and getting the[ir] money. One wouldn't be surprised to see him really succeed in raising large sums over his new pet game.

P-138

[*Endorsements*] FILE G. F. R.
NOTED W. W. G.

DNA, RG 65, file BS 198948-3. TD. Stamped endorsements.

Report by Special Agent J. G. Tucker

[New York] Oct. 23, 1920

UNIVERSAL NEGRO IMPROVEMENT ASSOCIATION

The above organization has issued a one page circular addressed to "Dear Fellow member," which states that "His Highness, the potentate," has sailed and the Executive Council has decided to start construction in Liberia in January, 1921. The Council is, therefore, raising a guarantee fund of $2,000,000 by bond issue of promissory notes from the membership of the organization so as to capitalize the work of construction. The circular then goes on to state the various denominations of the notes to be issued and is signed "MARCUS GARVEY, PRESIDENT." . . .

J. G. TUCKER

DNA, RG 65, file OG 208369a. TD.

John Wesley Cromwell to William H. Ferris

[Washington, D.C., ca. 23 October 1920]

[*Dear Dr. Ferris:*]
. . . The people protesting against persecutions and hardships have at last produced a man, a leader, in the person of Marcus Garvey, towards whom all eyes have been turning the past thirty months. There is no doubt but that the influence of the Universal Negro Improvement Association will be far-reaching. It will also be unmistakably uplifting and of a constructive nature. This is obvious because of the ideals of the leader of the movement as

expressed in his utterances published from time to time in the Negro World. The events during the month of August last compelled the attention of the American statesmen and politicians of this country and the three leading nations of the world.

JOHN WESLEY CROMWELL

Printed in *NW*, 23 October 1920.

Report by Bureau Agent H. S. White

PHILADELPHIA, PA. Oct. 26, 1920

MARCUS GARVEY: UNIVERSAL NEGRO IMPROVEMENT ASSOCIA-
TION & AFRICAN IMPERIAL COMMUNITIES LEAGUE:
NEGRO ACTIVITIES

The following coded telegram was received from the Chief of the Bureau about 7.30 [on] this date (25th): "Marcus Garvey Negro Agitator left New York Four Forty Five today for Philadelphia stop Cover speeches while in City stop Five[.]"

Arrangements were then made to cover the movements and speeches of subject while in this City through an under-cover informant, who reported this morning (26th), that MARCUS GARVEY came to Philadelphia for the purpose of attending a meeting of the Philadelphia Local of the UNIVERSAL NEGRO IMPROVEMENT ASSOCIATION & AFRICAN IMPERIAL COMMUNITIES LEAGUE, at which meeting new officers of this Association were to be elected.

This meeting was held last night, October 25th, at the Bethel A.M.E. Church, 6th & Lombard Sts, Philadelphia. The meeting was presided over by MARCUS GARVEY and there were approximately 250 negroes present.

Reference is hereby made to report of Agent Busha on the above subject, covering the last trip of MARCUS GARVEY to this City on October 8th 1920, which report indicates that the meeting on that date broke up into a general rough house, and that GARVEY told the crowd he was disgusted with them, and after asking for the resignation of the officers in charge he hurriedly went back to New York.

The meeting which took place last night (25th) was for the purpose of ousting the old officers and electing new officers. In the meantime, however, nearly all of the previous officers of the Philadelphia local of this organization ha[ve] resigned. The following were elected at last night's meeting.

E. H. UNDERWOOD, 1st Vice President
E. L. POINTER, 2nd Vice President
PAUL BRANCH, General Secretary

CHARLES STEWART, Treasurer
MRS. O. BROWN, President—Women's Branch

Four women were nominated for Secretary of the Women's Branch but as none of the nominees were present, there was no election to this office.

A man by the name of JEROME was elected chairman of the Trustee Board and FRED PUR[C]ELL[1] was elected chairman of the Advisory Board.

The informant reports that this meeting was a rather stormy session because there seemed to be a great deal of opposition to anyone nominated by GARVEY. There seemed to be some criticism of, and dissatisfaction in Garvey's interference with the matters of the local branch. There was also great dissatisfaction expressed over the sending of a MISS DAVIS from New York by GARVEY after the last meeting, for the purpose of reorganization. This MISS DAVIS has been in Philadelphia as an organizer for this organization since October 9th, and it was finally agreed at last night's meeting that she should remain here until the re-organization is completed and new officers installed.

GARVEY had nothing to say relative to the general plans of his organization, devoting all of his talk to the re-organization of the Philadelphia local, and the election of new officers therefore.

Because of the fact that the last few meetings of this organization have all resulted in "free for all" fights, the trustees of all the negro churches have objected to the further holding of these meetings in the church houses. Arrangements were, therefore, made for the renting of a suitable hall to be used by this organization for its meetings at Philadelphia. GARVEY remained in Philadelphia today for the purpose of arranging for this hall, and will leave for New York this afternoon.

The activities of this organization will be covered as far as possible in the future.

H. S. WHITE

[*Endorsements*] NOTED F. D. W.
FILE G. F. R. NOTED W. W. G.

DNA, RG 65, file OG 329359. TD. Stamped endorsements.
    1. Rev. F. Alexander Purcell, B.A.

Marcus Garvey to Rev. E. J. Echols

[[New York, U.S.A. October 28th, 1920]]

Sir—

I have been handed by Mrs. Lillian Willis of your city, three sheets of paper on which are some typed matter pertaining to be questions you desire answered relative to the Black Star Line, Inc., the Universal Negro Improvement Association and myself. I hereby beg to state for your information that I am a busy man. If I recollect correctly I think I saw you at one of the meetings I addressed in Buffalo. Now if you had not sufficient sense to comprehend what I said at that meeting, then you will readily understand that [w]e have no time to waste with one like you. Some of you preachers seem to think that you know everything pertaining to the Race and the Community, and as far as you are concerned, your questions are so frivolous that even a child in an elementary school would not have asked them.

The Black Star Line, Inc., and the Universal Negro Improvement Association are organizations that have stood the test of intelligent criticisms; therefore, we think it superfluous and foolish to en[t]er[t]ain your questions. If you will spend some time preaching the real Christ and do some constructive work in your community it would pay you better than to try to criticize a constructive and successful organization like the Universal Negro Improvement Association.

I hope I may be saved the worry of having to deal with you in any other matter. Suffice it to say that you are one of those preachers that busy people ought not to waste time over. Yours truly,

MARCUS GARVEY
Per A.[MY] E.[UPHEMIA] J.[ACQUES]

Printed in the *Buffalo American*, 18 November 1920.

Report by Bureau Agents A. A. Hopkins and E. J. Kosterlitzky[1]

Los Angeles Nov. 1, 1920

NEGRO ACTIVITIES
UNIVERSAL IMPROVEMENT ASSOCIATION:

There has been in process of organization in Los Angeles a branch of the UNIVERSAL IMPROVEMENT ASSOCIATION. NOAH D. THOMPSON,[2] an employe[e] of the Los Angeles "Express", is President. REV. J. D. GORDON, who was pastor of the Tabernacle Baptist Church, has resigned his pastorate to become Vice-President and Organizer. E. L. GAINES, of Pasadena, is District Organizer and chief speaker. G. W. SNELL[3] is one of the principal speakers and proponents. Last week GORDON and GAINES went to San Diego to organize among the negro population there. The public meetings are held at the Tabernacle Baptist Church, Los Angeles, after which the Executive Committee of 7 meet at GORDON's home. A confidential informant on negro activities states that this Executive Committee comprises the most radical of the negro residents of Los Angeles. It is estimated that 300 negroes have paid dues to and become members of the organization.

It is noted that practically no negroes are affiliated with or members of the O.B.U.,[4] and kindred organizations, at Los Angeles, nor are they registered as members of, or affiliated with, the Socialist, Socialist Labor, or Farmer-Labor parties. Practically all are registered as Republicans. . . .

A. A. HOPKINS & E. KOSTERLITZKY

DNA, RG 65, file OG 132476. TD.

1. Gen. Ernest J. Kosterlitzky (1853–1928) was the former chief of the Mexican Rurales under President Porfirio Díaz. Born in Moscow, Kosterlitzky came to the United States in 1870. He soon moved to Mexico, where he served as head of the Mexican secret service for thirty years. Returning to the United States in 1913, Kosterlitzky joined the Department of Justice, where he was employed until shortly before his death (*NYT*, 3 March 1928).

2. Noah Davis Thompson was born in Baltimore, Md., and educated at Gregg's Business College, Chicago, and the University of Southern California, Los Angeles. He worked as a clerk at the United States Express Co. in Chicago, from 1888 to 1908, before going to Tuskegee Institute to work for Booker T. Washington. Thompson arrived in Los Angeles in 1911, and in 1912 he published and edited the short-lived *Liberator* (1912–1913). Between 1913 and 1925 Thompson was a member of the editorial staff of the white-owned *Los Angeles Evening Express* and a frequent contributor to the *Los Angeles Times*. At the August 1921 UNIA convention, Thompson represented the Los Angeles division. His frequent speeches on the floor of the convention and his probing questions about UNIA finances caused him to be nominated for the office of assistant president general. Although he was not elected, Thompson became an even more significant figure when he returned to Los Angeles with an unfavorable report on UNIA finances. The uproar that resulted in the local division led Thompson and the majority of members to leave and form the Pacific Coast Negro Improvement Association. Garvey succeeded in partially repairing the rift in the Los Angeles division when he visited the city in 1922. Thompson never rejoined the UNIA, however, and he later established a local chapter of the anti-Garvey Friends of Negro Freedom (Emory J. Tolbert, *The UNIA and Black Los Angeles* [Los Angeles: Center for Afro-American Studies, 1980], pp. 54–56; *WWCA*).

3. G. Walter Snell was later the chairman of the resolutions committee of the Los Angeles UNIA, which drew up a list of complaints against the parent body in October 1921 (*California Eagle*, 29 October 1921).

4. Possibly a reference to the concept "One Big Union," often used as an alternate name for the Industrial Workers of the World. In other bureau reports, Hopkins and Kosterlitzky refer to the O.B.U. as a "radical industrial union" (DNA, RG 65, file BS 202600-5-26x).

Editorial Letter by Marcus Garvey

[[New York, November 1, 1920]]

Fellowmen of the Negro Race, Greetings:

Different ages in the history of mankind have been labeled with a peculiar brand. Some ages have been chara[c]terized as the ages of faith, the ages of unbelief, of discovery, of exploitation, etc. The age in which we are living is also acquiring an individuality of its own. It is the age of unrest, the age of dissatisfaction. Never before in the history of the world has the spirit of unrest swept over as it has during the past two years.

Classes, nations and races which had been quiet for centuries are now asserting themselves and demanding a readjustment of things. The despised Negro who has been kicked about and cuffed for over four centuries, who has been the hewer of wood and the drawer of water for other men, who has meekly borne abuse, insult and humiliation for many generations; whose patience, docility and forbearance can only be compared to the prophet Job, has likewise lifted his bowed head, looked up to God's skies and cried out: "I am a man and demand a man's chance and a man's treatment in the world."

The thoughtful observer will naturally ask: "What is the trouble? Have not men been attending churches, listening to sermons, offering to pray, singing songs and professing to be followers of the lowly Nazarene for centuries?["]

Yes, indeed; what is the trouble then? It looks as if humanity for generations had been attending a masked ball, and that the recent World War rudely tore off the masks and men recognized each other then as they really are. The World War revealed the fact that our much vaunted Christianity was only a dream. It revealed the fact that the Christian church, with its color and class distinctions was not supreme in modern life, and that is why clergymen and philosophers are talking about a reconstruction in theology and religion and ethics.

The Napoleonic wars which disturbed nearly all of Europe did not usher in the universal sway of unrest as did the recent World War. When an American President began to talk about making the world safe for democracy and about the self-determination of peoples and nations, he gave voice and expression to the pent-up thoughts and feelings of men, and oppressed classes, races and nations felt that at last the much-talked-of millennium had come. The failure of the Peace Conference at Versailles and the fact that Ireland, India, Egypt, Africa, the Negroes of the Western Hemisphere and the toiling masses everywhere continued to groan under the yoke of oppression, soon disillusioned men. Then came the recoil and the reaction, and we have as a result the present unrest.

The real trouble is that the justice and humanity which poets sing about and preachers wax eloquent over does not exist as a reality. The classes, races and nations who are down desire a chance to rise, and the classes, races and nations who are on top are endeavoring to keep them down.

That is the whole trouble, and peace on earth will not reign until justice is brought down from the clouds to Mother Earth. Aware of these things, the Universal Negro Improvement Association has adopted a definite program. It has not only preached that the Negro is created in the divine image and is entitled like other men to life, liberty and the pursuit of happiness; but it has also urged the Negro to become industrially fit and commercially strong. As a result of its program the Black Star Line Corporation was organized for the purpose of linking up the Negro on this side of the Atlantic with his brother in Africa. As a further result, the Association is raising a constructive loan of $2,000,000 from its members. The purpose of this loan is to start construction work in Liberia, where colleges, universities, industrial plants and railroad tracks will be erected; where men will be sent to make roads, and where artisans and craftsmen will be sent to develop industries.

In a word, the Universal Negro Improvement Association and Black Star Line are asking the Negro to help himself by mobilizing his financial resources and gaining that commercial strength which is necessary to permanent advancement. . . . Yours fraternally,

MARCUS GARVEY

Garvey v. *United States*, no. 8317, Ct. App., 2d Cir., 2 February 1925, government exhibit no. 39. Original headlines deleted.

O. M. Thompson to Hugh Mulzac

[*New York*] November 2nd, 1920

Dear Mr. Mulzac:

Since writing you last the Corporation has had the awful scare of losing the "YARMOUTH" by auction of Marshall; however, at the last minute we were able to rescue her although there is still a considerable sum to be raised to free her from danger. In the meantime we are negotiating with several Shipbuilding Concerns and might know something with regards to her repairs by the end of this week.

Yes, I did promise to write you and send the balance of money and this promise was made in good faith but the affairs of the Company have not improved, instead they become more threatening day by day. I shall take up the matter of retiring your note with Messrs. Wingate & Brown as soon as Mr. Garvey comes in this morning: it is hard to say with what success inasmuch as there are a hundred similar cases.

It is a pleasure to read that you expect to work on the "KISHOCOQUIL-LAS," please let us know your movements from time to time as it seems at this writing there is no hope of going to sea on the "YARMOUTH" this year, possibly early in the next.

As soon as I have interviewed Mr. Garvey you will hear from me again.

With best wishes for your health and welfare and kind remembrance to Mrs. Mulzac, beg to remain, Yours very truly,

O. M. THOMPSON

Garvey v. *United States*, no. 8317, Ct. App., 2d Cir., 2 February 1925, government exhibit no. 54.

Marcus Garvey to Leo Healy

New York, U.S.A., Nov. 3rd, 1920

Dear Mr. Healy:

Our check which was issued to you in good faith on the 1st inst. to be cashed this morning, has caused me a little disappointment, in that in getting my bank balance from the Chelsea I found that three outstanding checks which we did not expect would have been cashed immediately had just passed through the bank, and reduced the balance to which we hoped to meet the check we issued to you for today. I am sending you by Mr. Thompson $2,000 on account of the check payable on the 1st inst., asking that you hold it over for another two days when the balance will be available at the bank. Please hold the Nov. 4th check until the 11th inst.

Trusting you will be able to help us in this matter. Best wishes, Yours truly,

MARCUS GARVEY

Garvey v. *United States*, no. 8317, Ct. App., 2d Cir., 2 February 1925, government exhibit no. 19.

Reports by Special Agent P-138

New York City 11-5-20

IN RE NEGRO ACTIVITIES.

I met MARCUS GARVEY on the street today [*3 November*] and had a long conversation with him on general affairs. He told me that he was very much upset in view of the fact that his financial obligations were becoming more pressing each day. In trying to overcome them, he appointed several of his men stock selling agents, sent them to various states to sell Black Star Line Stock, but even after selling a large number of shares, they would return to him in New York and present him with a padded expense bill for railroad fare, traveling expenses, etc. which in many cases would be more than the money they took in for stocks. He also said that he had a check of $10,000 to pay a few days ago, but when he sent it in his accounts were short, and this he blamed on his secretary.

He admitted to me that the general Negro public is a little dubious now about all African schemes, so many of them being on the market recently, hence he, Garvey, is not meeting with such great success with his Liberian Liberty Bonds as he thought he would. Of course, he said he might and can easily get all the money he wanted from other big sources, but he hasn't come to that as yet. He admitted that the British Government was a great deal worried over his propaganda as it was affecting them in the Island, and as far as South Africa, where the natives are becoming wise; also, that the British Consul sent up to ask him for a copy of the "Bill of Rights" o[r] Constitution, which was adopted at the convention in August.

The American Government also is getting somewhat weary [wary?] about Liberia, since he, Garvey, is determined to link up with the Liberian Government, help to pay their debt and keep the American and British Governments out. He said that JOHNSON, Mayor of Monrovi[a], Liberia, who was elected High Potentate, sailed for home a few weeks ago and he, Garvey[,] intends to work through him, in keeping [out?] all white men and granting all the concessions to Negroes only. He is determined to make his headquarters in Liberia on January 1, 192[1].

P-138

[*Endorsements*] NOTED F. D. W.
NOTED W. W. G. FILE G. F. R.

DNA, RG 65, file BS 198940-41. TD. Stamped endorsements.

New York City 11-6-20

Today [*4 November*] I had another long conversation with MARCUS GARVEY, and to my utter surprise [he] admitted to me the fact that about a few months ago he was in the act of commiting suicide after he had received news that one of his ships, the "YARMOUTH", had run on a rock off the Coast of Cuba. GARVEY gave me some inside workings of the "BLACK STAR LINE" venture, which was startling, and if his fanatic hero worshippers should ever get these facts he and his officers would either be killed or chased out of town. The following are a few facts as described by Garvey to me:

The ship "YARMOUTH", (the 1st ship) was simply purchased in order to better stir up the Negroes in all parts of the world to invest and a hatred of the white race, this would therefore bring about an upheaval and finally racial equality.

That to chase the white race out of Africa and control the mines and industries was another reason for his newspaper "THE NEGRO WORLD", which was used for propaganda purposes and to spread discontent among the races, not only in America, but in Africa, and the West Indian Island.

That he had had a conference with two Japanese a few months ago in the hope of interesting them in his scheme, especially in the purchasing of ships from them, but for some reason the Japs acted very cautious, refused to commit themselves and so far nothing definite came out of the conference.

The above conference took place months ago while the BLACK STAR LINE was in its financial heights, but since then he has heard nothing more from the Japanese.

GARVEY admitted to me that things have made a desperate plunge for the worst. He is now almost without funds even to pay his bills now due, owing

71

to the fact that he has just discovered that COCKBURN, his first Captain, (Negro), who is now suing him in the Courts for over $6,0000 [$6,000?], had made a lot of graft from the BLACK STAR LINE by acting as the broker in the sale, causing them to pay an exorbitant price for an old 47 year [old] "tramp" like the "YARMOUTH", and now the boat is practically useless and unseaworthy. Cockburn further received graft of thousand[s] of dollars from the whiskey shippers, then afterwards sold some of the whiskey in Cuba, and at sea. This results in the shippers entering suit for thousands of dollars, one $620,000, one $40,000 and another $15,000 for losses.

Cockburn further caused the repair bills to be run up to above 200% of actual work done, he in turn getting graft from the mechanics and they in turn suing the Black Star Line for thousands of dollars.

The result of all this now is that Garvey is very much up against it and pretty nearly lost the YARMOUTH at an auction sale last week. He told me that he feels the last few days like committing suicide on account of his financial worries, and the fear of his followers knowing of the true state of affairs, and turning against him.

P-138

[*Endorsements*] NOTED F. D. W.
NOTED W. W. G. FILE G. F. R.

DNA, RG 65, file BS 198940-40. TD. Stamped endorsements.

W. E. B. Du Bois to *Lloyd's Register*

[*New York*] November 6, 1920

Gentlemen:

I would like to find out the following facts concerning three vessels, some or all of which are of British registry:

Yarmouth
Shadyside
Antonio Maceo

1. When built

2. Present owners

3. Other person[s] who have owned any of these vessels since January 1, 1919.

4. Movements of each of these vessels since January 1, 1919.

Can you undertake to secure this information or any part of it for me? I should be glad to pay any cost. Very sincerely yours,

[W. E. B. Du Bois]

[*Address*] Lloyd's Register,
17 Battery Place, New York City.

MU, WEBDB, reel 8, frame 115. TL, carbon copy.

W. E. B. Du Bois to North American Shipping Corporation

[*New York*] November 6, 1920

Gentlemen:
    May I ask if you own or ever have owned a ship called the "Yarmouth"? If you did own it and do not now[,] to whom have you transferred ownership?
    I shall be obliged for any information. Very sincerely yours,

[W. E. B. Du Bois]

MU, WEBDB, reel 9, frame 165. TL, carbon copy.

Report of UNIA Meeting

[*New York, 7 November 1920*]

Last Sunday night's [*7 November*] meeting was an inspiring one to the many thousands gathered at Liberty Hall to drink in messages of hope and faith and courage that fell from the lips of His Excellency the Hon. Marcus Garvey, Provisional President of Africa, and President General of the U.N.I.A.; Dr. William H. Ferris, literary editor of the Negro World; and Mrs. Lillian Willis, secretary of the Buffalo division. They made clear the duty of every Negro throughout the world to assist by his means the great constructive program that is being launched for the benefit of Liberia and the ultimate redemption of Africa. "Africa Expects Every Man to Do His Duty," was the subject of the Provisional President's remarks tonight, the discussion of which was weighty, timely and effectual. Tonight's address was the last from the President in the present drive to complete New York's quota of $300,000 in the Liberian Construction Loan, as he leaves on a tour of the various branches to give impetus to the efforts being put forth by each to subscribe its quota.

The program, aside from the speeches, was a rare treat, and especial attention must be called to the brilliant playing of the Black Star Line Band under the efficient leadership of Prof. William Isles and the singing of the Liberty Hall Choir and Male Quartet; to the wonderful tenor solo by Prof. Bradley; and the solo by Miss Revella Hughes, who was accompanied by the band. It was a great meeting.

A New Force Launched

["]I am glad to look into your faces tonight,["] began Prof. Ferris. ["]Some of you may have heard counter propaganda, but I desire to inform you that the U.N.I.A. is more talked about and discussed than any other feature of the Negro's life and activities in the world. I was somewhat surprised when I went up to the polls in New Haven to vote, to find the men not only discussing the election, but white and colored men gathered around me and asked me about the Black Star Line and Marcus Garvey and the U.N.I.A. Last week, about a half dozen letters came from Guatemala, Costa Rica, Spanish and British Honduras, telling about new branches of the U.N.I.A. being organized and the impetus which this convention gave to the work there. The world is beginning to realize that in the U.N.I.A. a new force has been launched in the world. Men wonder why it is that some men and some races are talked about. Yesterday's "American" devoted a column to Napoleon Bonaparte who has been dead hundreds of years. Why? It was because he put over big things. Jesus of Nazareth and Napoleon Bonaparte are more talked about than any other mortals, because of what they accomplished. In three hundred years, Jesus of Nazareth launched a tidal wave of religion that swept from Parthia to the British Isles and from the German forests to the Sahara desert, sweeping everything before Him until He had stamped His personality upon the hearts of men. So any race or nation desiring to achieve renown and become a force and factor in the world, must put over big things; and the reason why the entire world was thrilled by the sailing of the "Yarmouth" a year ago last November was not because of the size of the boat, but because a new spirit was manifested in the Negro. Before that, he had been whining, begging, grieving, complaining or threatening, but never had he achieved one definite and concrete result of colossal proportions in the business world.

Construction Work for Liberia

["]Now, in modern life more so than in any other period, you cannot put over big things in a military, commercial and literary, or scientific way unless you have that something which is called the "mazuma," or filthy lucre, to back you up. There comes a time in any movement when the wheels must be greased by that something which is called money—the medium of exchange. Heretofore, I have heard Bishop Walters,[1] Bishop Derrick,[2] Bishop Turner, Bishop Heard,[3] and several bishops wax eloquent upon Africa. I have heard Dr. M. C. B. Mason[4] speak on Africa and the people jumped up and hurrahed and applauded him. But now something else must be done. Once there was a banquet and a man said, "The poor people are outside suffering; let us give three cheers for them." Well, we have been giving Africa and Liberia three cheers heretofore, but the Hon. Marcus Garvey has come with a propaganda which will enable construction work to go on in Liberia, which will accommodate the surplus Negro labor of this country.

THROWING AWAY OPPORTUNITIES

["]Until five years ago, I thought that all of the Negro's misfortunes in this country were due to the malignant spirit of the Caucasian, but when I passed through St. Louis, Chicago, Pittsburgh, Philadelphia, New York and New Haven and saw men who were working for $50 and $90 a week, just throwing it away week after week, buying their girls $20 hats, $10 and $20 pairs of shoes and $75 and $80 dresses, buying champagne and riding in automobiles, I began to think that when the Negro had the economic opportunity which he had been praying for for so long, the majority of them threw it away. It looks to me that the Negro will only have a few months left before he will have to get in the cyclone cellar, and those men who have good jobs now, it will be well for them in this day of reconstruction, in this age of adjustment, when new industries are going out of existence and old industries are undergoing a change, to provide for the inevitable day that is coming. With the influx of foreign immigration, with some of the mills and factories beginning to close, inside of twelve months you will find thousands of men, perhaps hundreds of thousands in this country, walking the streets unemployed. So it well behooves us to husband our resources.

THE COST OF SUCCESS

["]Some of our people get discouraged because they cannot achieve success at a bound. I never belonged to that religious school which believed that.

["]There is hardly any place within twelve miles of New Haven where I have not been on foot, and I have observed the farmers at their work. I saw that if the farmer planted corn, he got corn; I saw that if he plowed under the soil in the fall, put in fertilizers, put in the seed and then cultivated it, he got results. I discovered that farmers get out of the ground just what they put in it, and that is true in all human activities and all human enterprises. None of the great things which you see in the world sprang up in a day. It took years for those magnificent oaks in California to grow and develop. Great animals like the elephant take years to develop. It takes years to build up any great industry. It is unfortunate that our nature is such that if we cannot receive results in a day or a year, we get discouraged. Do you not know that the men who sowed the seeds of this country's prosperity never lived to see the fruit and help harvest it? So it is in all human activities and enterprises, and the thing for the Negro to do is to have faith in his future.

THE NEGRO'S FAITH

["]I believe that the great asset which the U.N.I.A. has given to the Negro is faith in himself. When you touch a man's will power, you touch the springs of his activity. Regardless of a man's brain power, regardless of his physical strength, if he has a weak will, he is just like grass which will sway which ever way the wind blows. But he needs faith and an objective in order to be able to hew out a path and to blaze a way through the wilderness. In the world of physics and mechanics, unless a moving body has power to overcome resistance, it will soon stop. The resistance which has grown up around the U.N.I.A. shows that it has momentum, vitality and a virile force that will plow a way and blaze a path. And in giving the Negro world—the entire world—an exhibition of faith and courage and initiative and will force, the U.N.I.A. has injected in the Negro race that spirit of progress which will enable it to plow on and go on in the face of opposition and ultimately reach the summit of human achievement. . . .["]

"AFRICA EXPECTS EVERY MAN TO DO HIS DUTY"

Hon. Marcus Garvey, taking as his subject, "Africa Expects Every Man to Do His Duty," said:

["]Several decades ago, at the battle of Trafalgar, Horatio Nelson, during that battle, said to his men, "This day England expects every man to do his duty." He said that there and then because he saw that there was about to be the turning point in the life and the destiny of the nation he represented, and each and every man did his duty as England expected it of him. Coming down the ages that sentiment has inspired many a Briton to go forward and do his duty by his nation and by his race. Decades have rolled by; years have rolled by, and a similar situation faces the world. At this time it is not an Anglo-Saxon world; it is a world Negro. Therefore I will not speak to you in the exact words of Horatio Nelson. I will say to you, "Africa expects every man to do his duty." There is a great deal of work to do; the laborers are few, and they are few because those who are most concerned about this great continent of Africa seem to be ignorant of their relationship with the country and with the part that the country must play in their redemption, in their salvation. There are but a few of us who seem to be able to appreciate the fact that Africa holds everything for us. It holds the hope of our future happiness; it holds the hope of our children's happiness. Simple as you may take the question of Africa for the Africans, yet it is the only question that will solve this great problem of our race. Without Africa the Negro is doomed[,] even [as] without America the North American Indian was [l]ost.

["]There is a great international conspiracy at this time to subjugate Africa, to use Africa and to abuse Africa and take away Africa, just as the early settlers of this country—the early colonists of this country came to this country and took it and slew those who owned the country. America affords us a splendid example of the designs that the races and nations of the world now have upon Africa. To draw a picture to you: Several hundred years ago there were no white people living in this country; there were no Negroid people living in this country. This land of which you form a part today was once inhabited by a race of people called Indians. They were the aborigines; the original settlers of the land now called and known as the United States of America. At that time white men lived across the Atlantic in Europe, and after Christopher Columbus discovered this continent and revealed the glories of it to them several of them made up their minds that they would go out to this new world and settle. When they came and found the Indians, they found the Indians stood in their way of peaceful settlement. After they were settled down here, as they did, Indians would congregate around them and make bonfires and probably destroy them; and they made up in their minds that they would take the country away from the Indians by kidnapping and killing them, and ultimately they succeeded. After years and years of fighting, the settlers triumphed and America became the white man's country as you see it now. The people who originally inhabited it, the people who once lived in New York, the native people who were born in this country, are no more. That was the design of the white man to take America centuries ago. It took years, decades and decades, centuries and centuries to take America; nevertheless it is America today. That was his design centuries ago and now he has a similar design, not on America, but where? On Africa. The white man of Europe has a similar design on Africa today, and as the white man had hundreds of years ago when he came and settled in America. He fought the native American Indians, killed them and buried them, and the native American, the aborigines, are no more to be seen; they are dead; they are extinct. Once they were millions, even as Negroes are millions in Africa.

AFRICA'S PLIGHT

["]If you sit quietly, civilized as you are[,] and it would be a great crime because in comparing you with the aborigines of this country, you will find that you today are civilized, cultured people who understand the way of civilization—the way of the world. The aborigines did not understand the way of the world; did not know the white man's civilization, and because of that he . . . [*words mutilated*] and take away his land and his country. You have no such excuse as the Indian had. You in this open day, in this daylight of civilization, are sitting down quietly and allowing the white man to work up a similar design in Africa. He has gone to North Africa, to South Africa, to East Africa, to West Africa, to Central Africa, and is practicing there now just what the early settlers practiced in America years and years ago. It is a question of Africans at home being unable to help themselves because they are not adept in the civilization that confronts them. They will succeed with the native Africans in driving them out and killing them and in taking away their country because the native Africans are innocent of the ways of the civilization that rules the world. But whilst Providence and whilst Nature refused to help the Indian in the white man's onslaught against him, Providence and Nature have not been so unkind to you. Providence and Nature have helped you to understand the man who has his designs upon you. Providence and Nature and the selfishness and wickedness of the world brought you into slavery, and Providence kept you in slavery for 250 years so that coming in contact with the slaveholders you might understand the men with whom you have to deal.

A Sacred Duty

["]Africa, the land that now needs the help of every son and daughter, is the Africa that sent us out 300 years ago—is the Africa that is expecting now each and every one of her sons and daughters to perform the duty that is incumbent upon you. How cold-blooded—how criminal would we not be, knowing as much as we do about the designs of this civilization in which we live—knowing about the designs of the white world against the black world, to sit quietly and do nothing! No Negro in New York or in the United States of America can tell me that he does not know about the designs of the white world against the black world. The Negro child just from the cradle knows that the white man has a design against the entire world that is not white. You know as much as I do, that if we were to sit and follow the propaganda of the other man that he will continue to lead us until we found ourselves in utter darkness. His one purpose is to possess himself of all the land and rule and dominate the world for ever. When Europe was the only part of the world that was known, he settled down there and he exploited Europe for all it was worth. He traveled into other spheres, discovered other continents and worlds, and as he discovered them he went there and settled there for the purpose of ruling and dominating and exploiting. He came to America, he settled and he has exploited. He went to Asia, he has settled, ruled and exploited. And now there is no part of the world that he has not touched. He was not so dangerous 400 or 500 years ago because he had not grown so potent and powerful. Take England, for instance, 400 or 500 years ago; England was not so dangerous to the other nations and races of the world because she was not so powerful. But the strength of England is so almighty today that it is said her dominions extend to every corner of the world. And the design of the Englishman is to own more land at the expense of some one else.

Exploiting Africa

["]The Englishman's designs, the Frenchman's designs, the Italian's designs all are centered about and upon Africa, the land of our fathers, and we will sit down here and say we are not concerned about Africa. But men and women, we are only flirting with our own liberty—our own future.

AMERICA THE WHITE MAN'S COUNTRY

["]You know why I say Africa is the land of our future, because New York is not going to be the land of our future; the United States of America is not going to be the land of our future because it is written in letters bold and it is spoken in words loud and strong, that America is a "white man's country"; and caring not how you try to camouflage the issue—how you desire to pass the issue by, take it now from me, that in the next 50 years you are going to see it really a white man's country except we get busy now.

["]America is the white man's country because he sees and realizes that whatsoever is good within the nation has been brought about by his own initiative. He realizes also that the country is becoming overstocked and over-populated by his own kind and therefore in his racial selfishness he will never think outside of his race, but on the contrary will always think within his race. There is no white man in history, whether he be bishop or priest, who can guarantee that the sentiment of the American white people within the next five or ten or fifteen years will be a sentiment of love towards you or me. By indication it shows that it will be a sentiment of hate; the rising generation cherishes that hate because of race, and it is well that you prepare for it. It will be impossible for you even by your united strength to combat the force of prejudice if these forces are aligned against you. You may make a plea and you may fight to demand the things that are yours, but it is impossible for ten million of people to go up against ninety million and win; and it is only a matter of time when the white man will corner the Negroes in the United States of America and we will have to go and seek salvation or remain here and die. He is going to corner us economically, he is going to corner us industrially. It is the new plan of this country to close out the Negro industrially and economically, and when you close down upon a man's bread and butter you have beaten him. You may talk, you may sing as loud as you care, but whenever your bread and butter is taken away from you, you are beaten; and that is the new campaign that the white man is going to work against the Negro in these United States of America. It was already started, but the war saved the Negro four and one-half years ago. Were it not for the war many of us would not have been in Liberty Hall tonight. The abnormal conditions created by the war saved the Negro for four and a half years and set back the plan of the white man to get even with the Negro in the North and South. It is only a matter of time when he will return to the old-time order of things to work out this industrial plan and campaign against the Negro. You cannot successfully combat him here because he has everything at his command. He has the strength of the nation behind him; he has the wealth of the nation behind him, and it is preposterous for you to think that you can ever combat him single-handed. It cannot be done. The only salvation for the Negro—the American, the West Indian and the South and

Central American Negro—is to unite their intelligence and their resources to use the civilization that they have, to stop the white man in Africa and demand Africa. That is the only program that we should take up now and be serious over, because in the salvation of Africa will rest the salvation of the American Negro, the salvation of the West Indian Negro and the salvation of the Central American Negro.

AN AFRICAN NATION

["]Understand this African program well. I am not saying that all the Negroes of the United States should go to Africa; I am not saying that all the Negroes of the West Indies should go back to Africa, but I say this: That some serious attempt must be made to build up a government and nation sufficiently strong to protect the Negro or your future in the United States will not be worth a snap of the finger. There are many of us here who cannot and will not go back to Africa because of property interests or because of certain conditions, climatic or otherwise. But we are saying that Africa still is your only hope; that without an independent Africa—without a powerful Africa you are lost. You must have an Africa as strong as France; you must have an Africa as strong as Great Britain, so that even as the Frenchman makes up in his mind to live always in America he can get the protection of his government when he needs it, so must you. (Applause.)

["]Africa is the only hope because you cannot claim your rights anywhere else except you can claim it by force of strength and governmental protection. You cannot claim it from the United States of America, because there can be but one government in the United States of America and that shall always be a white man's government. The white man will only respect your rights constitutionally as a citizen of this country or as a resident of this country, when you have some government behind you. When you can compel a nation to respect your rights because of your connection with some government that is sufficiently strong to support you, then and only then will you be respected. What I have seen in my travels throughout the nation is that there is not a Negro in the United States of America that the white man has respect for, whether he be Dr. Du Bois or whether it be Robert Russ[a] Moton, or whether it be Kelly Miller. It is only a matter of time and environment that will make him realize that he [is] no better than the lowest common Negro in the South. Kelly Miller within [the] precincts of Howard University, may be respected by the white man w[ho] visits Howard University. Dr. Du Bois in the section of Fifth avenue where he works may be respected by every white man in that neighborhood, but let Kelly Miller jump on the t[rain] going South, and they see but a black man there and not the dean of Howard University, and see what happens to Kelly Miller if a show do[wn] takes place. They respect you [*less?*] because of your color, because behind your color is no strength, no force, no power of protection; and not until you get behind you that force, that war of protection, will you comp[el] the white, the yellow, and all the r[est] of the world to respect you.

The Ku Klux Klan

["]That is just what [the] Universal Negro Improvement Association is doing. Some Negroes' heads [are] so thick that you cannot put any[thi]ng into them. Their grey matter is [so] dense that no earthquake, no storm, no hurricane can move them; o[nly] the Ku Klux Klan down South. (Laughter.) It takes the Ku Klux Klan to move them and this U.N.I.A. [is] a sort of Ku Klux Klan. I am [*glad*?] the Ku Klux Klan confine their [oper]ations to the South, although [I have] heard they contemplate forming [a] Ku Klux Klan in New York.[5] They [do] not seem to know that there is [a] Ku Klux Klan up here already. They can form a Ku Klux Klan but [the]y had better keep below 116th street or above 166th street or they will [rea]lly have some fun. I think I will [send] the challenge through the columns of the Negro World to the Ku Klux Klan of Virginia and Georgia to come to Harlem, the city of the New York Fifteenth. (Cheers.) If the Ku Klux Klan think they are bad let them go to Chicago, the city of the Eighth Illinois. They can pull off their stuff in the South, but let them come North and touch Philadelphia, New York or Chicago and there will be [lit]tle left of the Ku Klux Klan. (Cheers and laughter.) I feel sure that only [the] "Ku" of the Ku Klux Klan would [be] left.

["]This question of [Afri]ca is dear to each and every man of this race to his thinking; and men and women[,] you must start out to think and you must start some time. What is the use of living without having some purpose and some object. Look at what Edison is doing! Every day Edison is endeavoring to do something for the benefit of his race and humanity. Now he is trying to invent a machine so delicate that he can get messages from the other world. That is characteristic of the white man. He is never satisfied with himself; he is always trying to bring something about for his own betterment. But the Negro is always satisfied with conditions. If you have a good job now you believe you are always going to have that good job; you will make absolutely no effort to secure that job until one day you will find you have no job. Let me say again to you, that the jobs you have now, hold on to; don't give them up, because a Pole is just packing up his baggage in Poland coming over here after that job. An Irish girl is just about packing her grip to come here for that job you have now; and I am advising you to hold out until we can tell you from the platform of Liberty Hall we have better jobs for you in Liberia. We are hoping to do that.["] (Applause.)

Printed in *NW*, 13 November 1920. Original headlines omitted.

1. Bishop Alexander Walters (1858–1917) was born in Bardstown, Ky., and educated at Livingstone College, Salisbury, N.C., where he received a D.D. degree in 1891. He was elected a bishop of the AME Zion church in 1892 and remained bishop of the New York and New England dioceses until his death. He was one of the primary organizers of the Pan-African Conference in London in 1900, and he served as president of the Pan-African Association. The AME Zion General Conference assigned Walters to the church's foreign work in 1908, and he traveled to West Africa in 1910, establishing missions and ordaining several missionaries. He was presiding bishop of the African work until 1917 (*WWCA*; William Walls, *The African Methodist Episcopal Zion Church: Reality of the Black Church* [Charlotte, N.C.: A.M.E. Zion

Publishing House, 1975], p. 238; Alexander Walters, *My Life and Work* [New York: Fleming H. Revell Co., 1917]; *NYT*, 3 February 1917).

2. Bishop William B. Derrick (1843–1913) was bishop of the West Indies, South America, and the Islands of the Sea for the AME Zion church. He was born in Antigua, BWI, but he served in the Union navy during the American Civil War. He received a D.D. degree from Wilberforce University, Wilberforce, Ohio, in 1885. Before he was made a bishop in 1896, Derrick was secretary of the Home and Foreign Missionary Society of the church (*NYT*, 22 April 1913; William J. Simmons, *Men of Mark: Eminent, Progressive, and Rising* [1887; reprint ed., New York: Arno Press, 1968], pp. 88–96; "Rev. W. B. Derrick, D.D.," *A.M.E. Church Review* 10 [October 1893]: 259–264).

3. Bishop William Henry Heard (1850–1937) was born a slave in Georgia. After the Civil War he was educated at schools for freedmen and at the University of South Carolina. He was active in Reconstruction politics, winning a seat in the South Carolina legislature in 1876, and later studied law with an attorney in Athens, Ga. In 1879 Heard chose a career as an AME minister, serving in the South for several years before he was assigned to Allen Chapel in Philadelphia. In 1885 President Grover Cleveland appointed him U.S. minister resident and consul general to Liberia, where he was also superintendent of the AME's Liberian conference. In 1908 he was elected a bishop, serving in West Africa until 1916 (William Henry Heard, *From Slavery to the Bishopric* [Philadelphia: A.M.E. Book Concern, 1924]; *NYT*, 13 September 1937).

4. Rev. Madison Charles Butler Mason (1861–1918) was the first black secretary of the Freedmen's Aid and Southern Educational Society of the Methodist Episcopal church, assuming the position in 1896. Born in Houma, La., he earned a B.A. degree at New Orleans University in 1888, a B.D. degree at Gammon Theological Seminary, D.D. degrees from New Orleans University and Wiley University, and a Ph.D. degree from Alabama State College in 1906. Mason enjoyed a nationwide reputation as an educator and a speaker on the Chautauqua circuit (*WWCR; NYT*, 1 August 1918).

5. The *Negro World* of 13 November 1920 reported that the Ku Klux Klan "is to be organized in New York City." In a letter received by an anonymous New Yorker from Imperial Kleagle Edward Young Clarke, which the *Negro World* quoted, the Klan had announced its intention to choose three hundred men as charter members of the New York City Klan (*NW*, 13 November 1920). Although the suburbs around New York City proved to be receptive to Klan organizing, the city itself was far less hospitable. With a population that was only one-sixth native-born, Protestant, and white, New York confronted the Klan with formidable opposition. The city's press voiced near-unanimous opposition, and in 1927, when fourteen hundred Klansmen attempted to march in Queens, a hostile crowd, unrestrained by the police, attacked them and ended the march (Kenneth T. Jackson, *The Ku Klux Klan in the City* [New York: Oxford University Press, 1967], pp. 174–176).

Report by Special Agent S-A-I-I

[*Philadelphia*] November 7th, 1920

SPECIAL WORK

Gibsons' Standard Theatre, South Street below 12th Street. Benefit for Douglas Hospital. Marcus Garvey, speaker. Subject, "The Call of the Hour." Garvey was introduced by Rev. W. H. Moses. Moses is bedubbed the Garvey of the Baptist Church. In part Garvey said, "I am not a man who interfere[s] with other peoples['] business and I am being criticised by every one. To make it plain to you I want to say, I do not go in to the white man's business or the red, or yellow man's but any concerning the negro I am right in it. Take the case of Africa, today there is /a/ reconstruction period all over the world with the ex[cep]tion of Africa and it is up to the negro to do it. France,

Italy, Russia, Great Brit[ai]n and all the European countries are reconstruct-
ing along serious lines. Is the Negro doing anything? No. American Negr[o]
has been out of Slavery fifty-six years, of the West Indies, eighty some years,
but where have they gotten? Nowhere. (You can go on praying but if you do
not do something but pray and wait on the Lord you will never have
anything.) America is the only country in the world solvent. Great Brit[ai]n,
France, Italy, Germany, Russia and all the countries in the world's war are
bankrupt. It is the world's war that has partly made a New Negro. 1914
before the war, even in the North, were not the doors of all industry closed to
you? During the war the Negro made more money than he had made since
his freedom[,] what did he do with it? I ask you as one[,] not as a whole. The
Italian, Jew, Pole, etc. saved from 60% to 80% of their earnings. Now those
people are going back to help in the reconstruction while those who are over
there are coming here to take [their] place. What have you saved? I am glad
to talk on for anything that is of benefit to my countryman. I am glad of this
Institution that is controlled by our race. (You want to act now, be a man,
stand up for yourself. God did not put you here just by mere chance. He put
you here for a purpose. The time for bowing and scraping and cringing
before any race is over. Stand up be a man.) The white man was a slave once,
look at the slave markets of Rome. It would have been easy for Rome to put
Great Brit[ai]n back in slavery fifty years after her freedom. The white man
has worked from slavery, savagery and infidelity up to something great. (We
are made in the image of God the same as the white man and we can achieve
something great also, don't wait for the opportunity take it.) (Did not the
Anglo Saxon take this country from the Indian, what you want you must
take.) America, England, France and all are afraid that Africa is coming in her
own. I was made Provisional President of Africa a few days ago, I live here
the same as the Provisional President of Ireland lives here, but twenty-five or
fifty years from today the President of Africa, will have his residence in
Africa. You say why do I want a diamond, some gold, a battleship, I say if the
white man has it and wants it[,] I am man same as he is[,] I want it also. All
earthly things white man wants I want also. I am made in the image of God
the same as he is. I do not think God would put four hundred million people
by chance on earth, we are here for a purpose. Do you believe the French
Revolution was a myth, do you believe the American war for Independence
was a joke, then Africa can be won back if some burly Negro the same as
George Washington did, will take a sword and lead the Negro on to victory.
Yes, I say I love the white man as long as he loves me and I hate him as long
as he hates me. Everybody can't be a preacher, or rogue, or politician, there
must be some of all kinds. I did not come here as a preacher as there are
enough here, I will carry on my work and let the preachers get the spiritual
side of it. I challenge any man to say I am not a God fearing man, but God
put us all here for a purpose and since the Irish are going back to Ireland, the
Jews back to Palestine, let the Negro go back to Africa. As David Lloyd
George stands up for England, as Clemenceau stands up for France, so do I

stand up for Africa. (The count[r]y of Liberia wants a loan of $5,000,000[.] The Universal Negro Improvement Association has taken it on themselves to raise that loan. England would not loan the money and America made the conditions so that if Liberia had accepted it would be like Haiti is today. I will talk on Liberia here one day this week.)["]

S-A-I-I

[*Endorsement*] NOTED W. W. G.

DNA, RG 65, file BS 202600-230-7. TD. Stamped endorsement.

Report by Bureau Agents A. A. Hopkins and E. J. Kosterlitzky

[*Los Angeles*] Nov. 8, 1920

UNIVERSAL IMPROVEMENT ASSOCIATION:

Confidential informant on negro activities reports that he attended a meeting at Saints['] Church (Negro) Los Angeles, on the night of November 1st, about 500 people being present. 110 new members were obtained for the UNIVERSAL IMPROVEMENT ASSOCIATION, and paid $2.00 each. The meeting was addressed by REV. J. D. GORDON, Vice-President and Organizer, by E.[*mmett*] L. GAINES, District Organizer, by Rev. E. W. WASHINGTON,[1] and by CAPTAIN E. L. GAINES.

GORDON announced that he was leaving next day for New York to confer with MARCUS GARVEY relative to movement back to Africa and business of the *Black Star Line*. He advised the audience to stop buying silk shirts, high hats and fine clothing and to buy arms. He further advised them to buy black dolls for their babies, and to take down all pictures of white heroes from their homes and put up instead pictures of Black Heroes, "Fred Douglas[s]", Toussa[i]nt O[u]verture, etc.

J. W. COLEMAN[2] spoke and advocated nomination of a negro for President 4 years hence.

A. A. HOPKINS AND E. KOSTERLITZKY

DNA, RG 65, file OG 3057. TD.

1. Possibly Rev. William A. Washington, founder and pastor of Bethel Church of Christ (Holiness) in Los Angeles (*Los Angeles Negro Directory and Who's Who, 1930–31* [Los Angeles: California Eagle Co., 1931], p. 91).

2. John Wesley Coleman was the leading black nationalist in Los Angeles and a cofounder of the local UNIA division. A native of Texas, Coleman graduated from Tillotson Institute in Austin before coming to Los Angeles in 1887. He worked as a policeman, land developer, and realtor before establishing a successful employment agency. He also founded a number of community organizations before organizing the Commercial Council of People of African Descent, which held a convention in Los Angeles in 1920. When the Los Angeles UNIA division split after a dispute with the parent body, Coleman remained with the faction loyal to

Garvey, eventually playing an important part in the division's reorganization (Delilah Beasley, *The Negro Trail Blazers of California* [Los Angeles: Delilah Beasley, 1919], p. 137; Emory J. Tolbert, *The UNIA and Black Los Angeles* [Los Angeles: Center for Afro-American Studies, 1980], p. 51).

Reports by Special Agent S-A-I-I

[*Philadelphia*] November 9th, 1920

SPECIAL WORK

Meeting of U.N.I.A. to raise $2,000,000 as a loan to Liberia and Afro-America for reconstruction.

There were about six hundred present. There were representatives from Liberia on the platform who spoke for the loan. Beside Pres. Gen'l Garvey, there was the Gen'l Organizer, Counselor General. The American leader *Eason* and other high officials whose names I did not catch.

Garvey spoke on what was needed in Liberia. He asked every one to take at least one bond of $20.00 of the loan at 5%. Philadelphia $200[,]ooo, New York $300[,]ooo, Boston $100[,]ooo, Pittsburgh $200[,]ooo and Chicago and Detroit $200[,]ooo each. After this week Garvey goes to another town. He spoke on the question of equality. ["]Let a white man take care of his women and hang any one who bothers them, but he (the white man) must /take/ the consequence if he is caught fooling with negro women.) It is a new negro today. Before the war the negro did not know how to stand up for himself, today though he is not a cringing hat in hand monkey but a man. . . . My subject for tomorrow is 'The New Construction.' (There is going to be a labor crisis here in a few months and the negro will have no place to work. If I can get this loan you all can go to work in Africa.)[1] In a short while you will not have a doubt as some have about Harding, although it happened about one hundred years ago and we have a negro President, elected by the people.[2] You will not have to go back so long to find whether a man is a negro or not if you will get your heads together and claim Africa. I am not here as a Jew or an Irishman but as a negro and what he needs. Not with a hat in hand asking some one to help me build a school but asking you to help yourself.["]

S-A-I-I

DNA, RG 65, file BS 202600-667. TD.

1. In his speech on the following day, Garvey referred to growing black unemployment and stated that "Liberia is the headquarters of the U.N.I.A. and any man who moves to Liberia will get thirty acres of land but he must be a man who works, not a saloon keeper or pool room shark" (DNA, RG 65, file BS 202600-667).

2. Rumors that the Harding family had black ancestry began before Warren G. Harding was born. The stories varied, some claiming that Amos Harding, the future president's grandfather, was a West Indian mulatto. Harding's grandfather claimed that an angry neighbor started the rumor in the small community of Blooming Grove, Ohio, where the family lived for several generations, and that his relatively dark skin made the story plausible to many in the

community. The rumor that Harding had black forebears reappeared during the presidential campaign of 1920 (Francis Russell, *The Shadow of Blooming Grove* [New York: McGraw-Hill, 1968], p. 26; Randolph C. Downes, *The Rise of Warren Gamaliel Harding* [Columbus: Ohio State University Press, 1970], p. 535).

[*Philadelphia*] November 11th, 1920

SPECIAL WORK

Meeting U.N.I.A. and A.C.L. held in Metropolitan Hall, #715 Fairmount Avenue.

Marcus Garvey said, "I am sincerely glad to see so many out this bad evening and it really shows your loyalty to the U.N.I.A. Since this organization started two years ago, we have had hardships of all kinds, but we have done what they say no man could do[—]bring tog[e]ther a few thousand of Negroes who will stick and it won[']t be long before every one of the negroes will come to the cause. Now is the time we need every negro, for it has been said by the whites, that negroes are no good anyway, but since the black star line has been in exist[e]nce a great number have changed their minds. It was once said the negro only wanted [a] menial job so he could be near the white man, but he has proved himself capable of doing anything a white man can do. I want to see him get the education of all white men and I am going to work on this line until I die. Even the crown heads in Europe are worrying about the African Republic, Marcus Garvey is President over /there./ All now concede the negro has power[—]he only wants a little concentration. Look at what the white man has done. Ask him to give an account of himself[,] he will say look at the sky-scraper, locomotive, etc. [W]hat can the negro say? Nothing. We come before you with a constructive plan that[']s why we have this loan. Railroads, water pipes, roads, street cars, etc. are need[ed] in Liberia. Let us get this money by [the] first of January so the boat can sail the last of January. You cannot miss what is due you. The Kaiser wanted everything, did he get it? The whites want everything, so the negro wants everything also. The British think they are smart, but we are smarter. (They tried to put spies with us, we picked them out and blackened both eyes before he could hear or get anything.) Our detective system is better. The slowness of the system is just like they are and it shows that if we work together we can beat the white man at any stage of his game. I go from here to Pittsburgh. I expect to have your $2,000,000 by Sunday. Tonight we want you to get hold of a negro some where, some how and bring him here. Saturday we expect to be at Ca[lva]ry Church but we have not yet heard from the preacher. Sunday afternoon and evening we will be here again. A glorious future awaits you and it is to us to /work to/ our utmost so as to enjoy it. The money comes slowly but surely and as surely as the white man reads his name in gold letters so will you. Those who loan $20 to $100 a bronze cross will be given. $100 to $500 a silver cross. $500 to $1000 a gold cross. This cross will be to you what the Victoria cross is to an Englishman, what the iron cross is to the German. You will be pointed out as you go by as one who help[ed] to reconstruct and built the New Republic. We want recruits of mental ability.["]

S-A-I-I

DNA, RG 65, file BS 202600-667. TD.

[*Philadelphia*] November 12th, 1920

SPECIAL WORK
DRIVE OF U.N.I.A. FOR LIBERIAN BONDS.

Miss Davis presiding. Marcus Garvey the main speaker.

Garvey did not have any particular subject to speak on tonight. He thanked the people for the support they have given the drive for the loan of some $200,000. It is my belief that it will not be secured here and from what Garvey said tonight I am quite certain he does not believe it will be raised either. Garvey said in part. ["]I thank you for the way you have worked in this drive for $200,000[,] your portion of the $2[,0]00,000 loan we are trying to raise to start industries in Liberia. I have not as yet and have not been told just how you stand now. In the bonds of the Black Star Line, Phila. stood fourth. (I am in hopes you will be at least second in the drive for the loan. Of course I know the spies tried to break you up here as they are everywhere. Everywhere I go there are detectives[,] secret service and department of Justice people.) Though they have followed me everywhere[,] even in to Chicago when we were about to launch one of the ships had a frame up on me to try and not let me raise the money which was $59[,]000, there is one place they do not go, Liberty Hall in N.Y.C. There they only have two white men in the Hall, one who stood for Irish Freedom and ran for the Governorship of New York State[1] and the one who has just been elected Governor of N.Y.S.[2] and when this man was there and was making his speech about what good he could do the negro. One man in the front said, ("If you do not do what you say, you had better not come back here.") Yes sir, that is one place where [*they dare*?] not follow me. When that ship was about to be launched we had fourteen days to get $59[,]000. We called a meeting in N.Y.C. and decided that New York City, Phila. and Chicago were to raise this money. New York's first night raised $10,000[.] I was in Phila. one week of those fourteen days and got $6000 and was endeavoring to get Chicago straight when I was locked up. N.Y.C. heard about it, you know what it was and N.Y.C. alone raised the $59[,]000. New York is the town. So you can see that New York City is not worrying about anything and I can raise $10[,]000 from eight o'clock at night by ten o'clock the next day. New York City is the old stand by.

There will be no meeting Saturday as no place could be gotten but Sunday evening and afternoon we expect to have a great time and get all we need.["]

S-A-I-I

DNA, RG 65, file BS 202600-667. TD.

1. Dudley Field Malone ran unsuccessfully for governor in 1920 as the candidate for the Farmer-Labor party, which he helped to organize.

2. Nathan L. Miller (1868–1953), a Republican, had recently defeated Al Smith in the election for governor of New York.

Negro World Advertisement

Report by Special Agent S-A-I-I

[*Philadelphia*] November 14th, 1920

SPECIAL WORK

Meeting of U.N.I.A. and A.C.L. held in Metropolitan Hall, #715 Fairmount Avenue, Phila. in drive for Liberian Loan $2,000,000.

Marcus Garvey the main speaker, Subject "The Loan."

Garvey said we have gone too far now to go back and we will not compromise.

(You want to make the people know this world has as much for you as it has for any other people or race if they are red, white or anything else. None have gotten anything without fighting for it. The Japanese won recognition when they whipped Russia and it does not make any difference to me whether a revolution o[r] any kind of ["]lution["] takes place so we may redeem Bleeding Africa in Africa. We want to make the world so that no matter where a negro is and some thing is done to him he [can] appeal to his Government in Africa for protection. Do not think a white man is going to build a Government in Africa and tell here it is. No, he is not. So you want to work now and fight later.) I see these [*African*] Legion men are very anxious to fight. Hold for the present but you will have your chance later. This thing of saying a white man is better than I am is not so. When he can beat me, logically, physically and politically then he is better than I am[,] not before. I have been to the house of commons and the house of representatives and they have marble and statues but it will not equal to what we are going to have, where they have marble we are going to have gold and diamonds and they will all come to visit and see what we have and at that time we may be able to get even with some of them. Remember this is for your children and your children's children so . . . [*words mutilated*] give till you feel it from $20 to $10[,]ooo for one year to 20 years . . . [*words mutilated*] annually more than you get from any bank. I know you are not near the $200,000 mark but you have a good start and by January 1st, 1921 you ought to be over subscribed to the Freedom Loan.

At the conclusion of his speech a great number responded to his call. Garvey also said that Germany with 60,000,000 held the world at "bay" 4 1/2 years[—]what can we do with 400,000,000 and look what Japan is doing now. We ought to be one of the highest nations in the world in from fifteen to twenty years. This association has done more and has a better constructive plan than [*any?*] association ever formed by either white or negroes. This is the new negro.

Garvey only reviewed the situation as it stood and talked along lines already spoken on. He did not leave the Loan for any side issue. He talked of the good of what the loan would do saying he would not take much time as he had promised that a president of the Phila[.] branch of the Assn. should be elected tonight. Garvey said before the election started that no man concerned in the breaking up of the other or last officers would be considered. It took some time to straighten out the noise after this announcement. Garvey said he wanted a man with sincer[i]ty, honesty and education. A man must have the three qualifications before he be considered. Garvey is in Pittsburgh all next week. Don't you need a good man to go there[?] I will go if you want a good man. A woman was shot at the close of the meeting in the hall.

S-A-I-I

DNA, RG 65, file BS 202600-667. TD.

W. E. B. Du Bois to the Canadian Department of Corporations

[*New York*] November 16, 1920

Gentlemen:

I wish to find out the status of "The Black Star Line" of Canada, 112 St. James Place, Montreal. I should like to know its officials, capitalization, capital paid in and such other information as is open to the public.[1] I will be glad to pay any charges. Very sincerely yours,

[W. E. B. Du Bois]

MU, WEBDB, reel 8, frame 1231. TL, carbon copy.

1. Two weeks earlier Du Bois had requested the same information from the Delaware authorities and had received from Everett C. Johnson, secretary of state for Delaware, a list of the officers and directors of the Black Star Line. Johnson pointed out, however, that corporations incorporated under the laws of the state were not required to file financial statements (Johnson to W. E. B. Du Bois, 4 November 1920, MU, WEBDB).

W. E. B. Du Bois to Messrs. Furners, Withy and Company

[*New York*] November 16, 1920

Gentlemen:

A firm which I am investigating, the "Black Star Line", has advertised that it owns or is buying the steamer "Kanawha" (otherwise called the "Antonio Maceo"). I find, however, that the steamer is registered as belongin[g] to you. Would you be willing to tell me the facts in the case? Very sincerely yours,

[W. E. B. Du Bois]

MU, WEBDB, reel 8, frame 1284. TL, carbon copy.

Report by Bureau Agent William C. Sausele

Jacksonville, Fla. 11/2[2]/20

NEGRO ACTIVITIES

On Sunday, November 14th, Dr. A. P. HOLLEY,[1] a native of Haiti, delivered a fi[er]y speech concerning the revolutionary activities of that country, and Mr. J. H. LE MASHEY, also outlined some of the wrongs to the negroes at /said/ meeting, held in the English Wesleyan Church at Miami. This meeting was attended by Bahama negroes, and resulted in the organization of a Local Chapter of the U.N.I.A. heretofore mentioned in Intelligence Bulletins. This is the Organization in which Marcus Garvey is very active. P. A. Styles, was nominated as Traveling Organizer. He was also chairman of the meeting on November 14th. The names of others active at this meeting are:

Rev. G. E. Carter

G. M. Brown

G. Love

Nathanial Rolls

Leon Davis

L. C. Motherson

Mrs. S. Johnson

Mrs. Maud Farrington

WM. C. SAUSELE

[*Stamped endorsement*] NOTED F. D. W.
[*Handwritten endorsement*] FILE G. F. R.

DNA, RG 65, file BS 202600-10-7. TD.

1. Alonzo Potter Burgess Holly (b. 1865) was born at Port-au-Prince, Haiti, the son of Rev. James Theodore Holly, the Episcopal bishop of Haiti and the first Afro-American to achieve

that rank in the Episcopal church. Alonzo Holly was educated at Harrison College in Barbados, at Cambridge University, and at the New York Homeopathic Medical College, where he received his M.D. degree in 1888. His office and residence were in West Palm Beach, Fla. (*WWCA*).

W. E. B. Du Bois to the New York State Department of Commerce

[*New York*] November 22, 1920

Gentlemen:

I wish to get information concerning a boat called the "Shadyside". It has been used for excursions up the Hudson during the last season. I would like to know its present and former owners, when it was built, its dimensions, etc. Could you tell me where to apply for this information? If you could furnish it to me I should be glad to pay any cost. Very sincerely yours,

[W. E. B. Du Bois]

MU, WEBDB, reel 9, frame 160. TL, carbon copy.

Report by Special Agent P-138

New York City 11-22-20

IN RE NEGRO ACTIVITIES.

The usual crowd was in attendance at Liberty Hall [*21 November*] to enjoy the excitable propaganda of Garvey's lieutenants, MCGUIRE and others.

The anti-white doctrine was touched upon by all the speakers who were pleading for money to put the Liberia Liberty Loan over.

The responses were few, as the people seem to be somewhat tired of being deprived of their hard earned money from time to time, without seeing any tangible result, but promises.

Again, the fact that many of the members are being thrown out of their jobs owing to the general reconstruction period, caused a marked slacking up of liberal collections at Garvey's Liberty Hall, thereby making the future for him not very bright.

P-138

[*Handwritten endorsement*] File G. F. R.
[*Stamped endorsements*] NOTED F. D. W.
NOTED W. W. G.

DNA, RG 65, file BS 198940-36. TD.

W. E. B. Du Bois to the American Bureau of Shipping

[*New York*] November 23, 1920

Gentlemen:

Can you furnish me information concerning the following two boats: The Kanaw[ha], otherwise called the Antonio Maceo, a sea-going vessel, and the Shadyside, a boat used for excursions up the Hudson. I would like to know when these boats were built, what their dimensions are, to whom they belong at present and who the[ir] former owners were.

I should be glad to pay a fee for this information. Very sincerely yours,

[W. E. B. Du Bois]

MU, WEBDB, reel 8, frame 1168. TL, carbon copy.

O. M. Thompson to Leo Healy

[*New York*] November 27th, 1920

Dear Mr. Healy:

Answering your letter of November 26th, in which you seem to center your displeasure on me, please be assured that I am simply a member of the Corporation and am not in any way to be blamed singularly for promises not performed.

I called to see you twice since making the last remittance but unfortunately did not find you in, however, we expect Mr. Garvey in from Pittsburg[h] on Monday, and will then get in touch with you.

We fully realize the situation between Mr. Harris and you but trust that arrangements will be made on Monday which will relieve the tension to our mutual satisfaction.

In the meantime we beg to remain, Yours very truly,

BLACK STAR LINE, INC.
O. M. THOMPSON
Vice President

Garvey v. *United States*, no. 8317, Ct. App., 2d Cir., 2 February 1925, government exhibit no. 20.

Report by Special Agent P-138

New York City 11-27-20

IN RE NEGRO ACTIVITIES.

. . . [T]here are a great many of GARVEY's followers who are very much disappointed at his failure to make the BLACK STAR LINE a success, which has caused a great deal of sadness and in many cases criticism of Garvey and his methods.[1] This is very significant, as up until a few months ago, no one dared to criticize Garvey to those same fanatics who are now doing it themselves.

P-138

[*Endorsements*] NOTED W. W. G.
NOTED F. D. W. FILE G. F. R.

DNA, RG 65, file BS 198940-20. TD. Stamped endorsements.

1. A week earlier, P-138 had reported that despite Garvey's failure "to make good any of his promises," his followers "still continue to follow blindly, even expecting him to perform some miracle by overthrowing the white race" (DNA, RG 65, file BS 202600-667-8).

Editorial Letter by Marcus Garvey

New York City, N.Y., November 29, 1920

Fellow-Men of the Negro Race—Greeting:

It is with pleasure that I inform you of the progress the Universal Negro Improvement Association is making through out the world. Everywhere from America, Guatemala, Spanish Honduras, Costa Rica and Cuba the reports are coming in of new divisions of the U.N.I.A. being formed, charters unveiled and new life and inspiration being infused into old divisions.

The rise and worldwide progress of the Universal Negro Improvement Association during the past two years and a half has been more like a battle than a race. We have continually faced and overcome obstacles. Steadily, step by step, we have advanced, capturing one citadel and then moving forward and capturing another citadel.

The rise of the U.N.I.A. has been like the tidal wave of the sea, moving slowly but surely forward, sweeping everywhere because obeying a powerful gravitational pull. And now the entire world, from the British Isles to the distant ports of Asia and Africa, recognizes the Universal Negro Improvement Association as a reality and not a dream.

Critics who have carefully studied the movement have likened the U.N.I.A. to a religion, because it powerfully appeals to the basic principles of human nature, the desire for freedom, the longing for liberty and the impulse to self-expression and self-development.

But in this world's affairs the spirit, mighty though it may be, is powerless to realize its desires unless it has at its command the tools and weapons to execute its decrees. Those tools and weapons are in the shape of locomotives, steamships, machinery, horse power, steam power and electric power. And these tools and weapons cannot be won by praying, but through the purchasing power of money, the medium of exchange.

We have long grieved over the exploitation of Africa. Our brother across the sea has been robbed of his lands, disfranchised, worked like a beast of burden and frequently flogged unmercifully, sometimes beaten to death. We have long regretted that Africa, with her gold, ivory and diamonds; Africa, with her magnificent forests, her mahogany, ebony, cocoa, kola, rubber, palm oil and coffee, should enrich foreign nations.

And we of the U.N.I.A. have resolved to do our bit in developing the resources of that section of the world known as Liberia. But we cannot walk across the ocean, and when we get there we cannot uproot great trees with our hands and carry them on our shoulders from the plateaus to the coast.

For that reason we have made arrangements with the Black Star Line Steamship Corporation to transport men and materials to Liberia. And the Black Star Line desires to raise $25,000 to equip the ships for the African route.

In order not to be helpless when we reach Liberia, the Universal Negro Improvement Association is raising a construction loan of $2,000,000 from its members. This construction loan is for the purpose of making harbor improvements, making roads, clearing the forests, erecting department stores, saw mills, factories, etc. . . . With best wishes. Yours fraternally,

MARCUS GARVEY

Garvey v. *United States*, no. 8317, Ct. App., 2d Cir., 2 February 1925, government exhibit no. 43. Original headlines omitted.

Report by Special Agent P-138

New York City 11-30-20

MARCUS GARVEY returned to New York today [*29 November*] and is again planning another big mass meeting in Madison Square Garden in his final drive to accomplish the much advertised Liberian Liberty Loan.

This afternoon I spoke to HUDSON PRICE,[1] the Associate Editor of the "NEGRO WORLD", who informed me that GARVEY's financial undertakings, the BLACK STAR LINE, etc. are on the downward sliding scale.

He [*Price*] said that he [*Garvey*] was simply selling stocks and borrowing more money, as so-called Liberia Liberty Loan, so as to meet his bills, as there were no other sources of financial supply.

P-138

[*Handwritten endorsement*] FILE G. F. R.
[*Stamped endorsement*] NOTED W. W. G.

DNA, RG 65, file BS 198940-27. TD.
    1. Price was also the newspaper's business manager.

Circular Letter by Marcus Garvey

The Black Star Line Steamship
Corporation, 56 West 135th Street,
New York City, U.S.A. Dec. 1, 1920

Dear Comrade, and fellow Stock Holder:

The time has come, when every stock holder in the Black Star Line, must become an agent for its greater success. The Black Star Line is the embodiment of the commercial sentiment of the Negro, and we have tried within the last 16 months, to so prop[a]gate the doctrine of commercial preparedness on the part of the Negro, and have succeeded so splendidly that we have cause now to thank our Creator and our loyal Race members for the splendid success we have achieved.

We now have under our control 3 ships, and we are making a desperate effort to acquire the greatest ship of all, the one that is to convey to Africa our workmen and materials for the building up of the great Republic of Liberia for the Race. Africa must be redeemed. Africa must be welded together as a great and mighty nation, controlled by the Negro peoples of the world, and the Black Star Line, as an auxiliary of the Universal Negro Improvement Association, has committed itself to convey workmen and materials and immigrants from the United States of America, the West Indies, South and Central America, to our future seat of Government, Liberia, West Africa.

Our Corporation is endeavoring to raise $250,000 between now and the 15th of January, 1921, and all stock holders are asked to be agents in subscribing for more shares, and in getting their friends and others to buy shares, so we can raise the $250,000 between now and the time mentioned.

For God, and the Race's sake, please let us raise this money in time, so that we can carry out our program for the redemption of Africa, and the Industrial emancipation of our struggling race. The white man takes but a few days to subscribe in the billions to start his own industrial projects. Because of our poverty as a race we have always had to wait to get Capital, but this is one time when we know that every stock holder of the Black Star Line will do his and her duty, to see that we raise the $250,000 by the 15th of January, 1921.

You will find herein enclosed, 6 subscription Blanks. We are asking you to subscribe for more shares yourself, and see that five persons in your community buy shares in the Black Star Line. This is your duty, and this must be your record of service to your race, and to the nation. Africa expects every man to do his duty, therefore there can be absolutely no excuse. You can find time in the mornings, afternoons, and evenings to get five more Negroes to subscribe for shares in the Black Star Line. Tell them that the Black Star Line is destined to be the greatest commercial asset of the Negro race, even as it is now. It is a Corporation that will give the Negro a rating in the Commercial world, a Corporation that has given inspiration to other Negro enterprises, paving the way to racial success.

The Black Star Line is known throughout the world. The Negro in commerce is estimated at the strength of the Black Star Line, so please come forward and put the Black Star among the firmament of stars, never to fall, but ever to shine out with such splendor as to attract in her rays the attention of all men.

We are expecting that 1921 will be a banner year for the Black Star Line. You must do your duty now. We expect to hear from you in another few days, with six subscriptions including yours, for shares in the Black Star Line.

May the Heavenly Master who guides and protects us be with you, and encourage you to continue this grand and noble work for the redemption of Africa.

I also take this opportunity to wish you a Merry Christmas, and a Bright and Prosperous New Year. Yours fraternally,

MARCUS GARVEY,
President of the Black Star Line.

SUBSCRIPTION BLANK

Date ....

BLACK STAR LINE, INC.
56 W. 135th Street, New York City
Gentlemen:

I do hereby subscribe for [   ] shares of Stock at $5.00 per share and forward herewith as part or full payment $[   ] on same, balance to be paid within 60 days.

Name ....
Street ....
City .... State ....

Garvey v. *United States*, no. 8317, Ct. App., 2d Cir., 2 February 1925, government exhibit no. 42, pp. 2,522–2,524.

Report by Bureau Agent H. J. Lenon

[*Pittsburgh*] 12/4/20

NEGRO ACTIVITIES.
IN RE: MARCUS GARVEY.

In last week's report, I stated that a negro had been detailed on the case but failed to locate the meeting place. During the week I was able to obtain the following report from a colored attorney, who attended the meeting:—

There were only about fifty persons at the advertised meeting of Marcus Garvey at the Carnegie Library, November 25th, Homestead, Pa. This includes the speakers and other participants on the program. I am unable to say just how many paid admission.

The meeting was opened by a man dressed in a long black robe, who afterward I learned was the chapl[a]in of the organization. One of Mr. Garvey's company sang a solo entitled, "Mr. Garvey is a God-sent Man". A Reverend Smothers was then introduced. He began his speech by saying that he was glad to be present and that he had lived under two dispensations, i.e. slavery and a limited freedom. He spoke at length of the wrongs inflicted upon the negro race by the white race. He said that he saw the dawn of a new dispensation. Although he claimed that he was not a member of the organization, he was interested in the movement. This man was very radical at times, but before he ended he said that he loved the American government and that he was a veteran of the Civil War. All through his address he appealed to the emotions of the more illiterate of the race by referring to the many injustices and to slavery.

Miss Davis, who was termed the Right Honorable International Organizer, then spoke. She referred to the Negro as an Industrial slave. In part, she said that their organization offered a remedy for this and that the Black Star Line would land the negroes in Mo[nro]via Liberia. She compared this back-to-Africa movement with the present situation in Ireland.

Honorable Marcus Garvey, D.S.O.E., was then introduced as the Provisional President of Africa, President of the Black Star Line Steamship Corporation, and President General of the Universal Negro Improvement Association. Garvey spoke of the many injustices suffered by the soldiers during the recent war. He said that industry merely used the negro during the war because of the shortage of labor, but with the return of normal conditions[,] mills and factories are getting rid of all negro labor. The only solution to this problem, he said, was for the negro to

b[ecome] affiliated with his movement and form a Black Republic. He claimed that the negro would never again fight for any
other country except the proposed Black Republic of Africa. He
openly advocates violence. He said that he was considered radical,
but he did not believe that he was half radical enough. He claims
that his organization has 700 branches with a membership of
4,000,000 covering every country in which negroes live. He, like
the former speakers, appealed to the emotional type of the race.
He is openly antagonistic to the white race in every respect. He
referred to Booker T. Washington, DuBois and Kelly Miller as
hand picked leaders of the white man to do his bidding. He claims
that he is the real leader selected by 400,000,000 negroes from all
over the world. He said that he was encouraged to come to
Homestead by Mr. Wright, president of the branch in Braddock.

While the meeting was very small, it was very enthusiastic. At
every mention of Africa a round of applause was given.

This man is of the very dangerous type, as he used every
opportunity to stir up strife as at last night's meeting when he
continually referred to the race troubles at East St. Louis, Chicago
and Washington, D.C.

H. J. LENON

DNA, RG 65, file OG 329359. TD.

Report by Bureau Agents A. A. Hopkins and E. J. Kosterlitzky

[Los Angeles] Dec. 6, 1920

UNIVERSAL IMPROVEMENT ASSOCIATION:

Confidential Informant reports that the membership in Los Angeles
now is 256 paid up members. Meetings are held regularly. The San Diego
organization has almost 100 paid up members.

A Wom[e]n[']s auxiliary known as the BLACK CROSS NURSES, has been
formed. 56 women are members. They are to nurse negro soldiers in case of a
war and are along the line of the Red Cross.

REV. J. W. GORDON and E. L. GAINES, who went East to confer with
MARCUS GARVEY[,] have not returned yet.

According to informant, NOAH D. THOMPSON, the President, and J. W.
COLEMAN are endeavoring to put over a real estate deal for the Association.
Washington Hall, at the corner of Washington and Center Sts., Los Angeles,
is for sale, price $30,000. 100 members are to put up $300 each to purchase
s[a]me. 10 have already obligated themselves, and informant believes that the

Association will raise the money, as many of the members are very prosperous negroes.

A. A. HOPKINS AND E. J. KOSTERLITZKY

DNA, RG 65, file OG 3057. TD.

Col. Matthew C. Smith, Military Intelligence Division, to Lewis J. Baley, Chief, Bureau of Investigation

[*Washington, D.C.*] December 10, 1920

My dear Mr. Baley:

SUBJECT: NEGRO ACTIVITIES.

The following report received from a reliable source in Chicago is transmitted for your information.

J. W. H. Eason, the new elected leader of the American Negroes, has delivered lectures to more than 60,000 colored people in Chicago according to the Chicago Whip. His lecture tour is under the auspices of the Universal Negro Improvement Association and the African Communities League. Realizing that the darker races are more numerous than the white, Dr. Eason claims that an organization of the majority of the people of the world will surpass and eclipse the present minorities who control, and the darker races shall come into their own again. It is said that over a thousand people joined the local branch of the organization and W. A. Wallace, the president, is planning to build headquarters for the Chicago division at a very early date.

This is given to you for your information. Very truly yours,

For the Director, Military Intelligence Division:

MATTHEW C. SMITH,
Colonel, General Staff,
Chief, Negative Branch

[*Endorsement*] DELIVERED TO DEPARTMENT OF JUSTICE M. A. HARVEY

DNA, RG 165, file 10110-2211/1. TL, carbon copy. Stamped endorsement.

Report by Special Agent P-138

New York City 12-13-20

IN RE: NEGRO ACTIVITIES

Again [*10 December*] GARVEY has sprung another surprise on his followers. He has changed the date of the purchase of another ship from January 1st, 1921, to January 15th, and as a final effort at collecting enough cash, he has sent out another batch of stock selling literature of the Black Star Line.

The large number of men out of work is now reacting on Garvey and his schemes, by reducing the amount of his receipts. His followers stand in groups in front of Liberty Hall until late at night discussing his various schemes.

In case of Garvey failing to live up to his promises, one is at a loss to predict just what course his people will take.

P-138

[*Handwritten endorsement*] FILE G. F. R.
[*Stamped endorsement*] NOTED W. W. G.

DNA, RG 65, file BS 203677-33. TD.

Robert C. Bannerman, Chief Special Agent, Department of State, to Special Agent Robert S. Sharp, New York

[*Washington, D.C.*] December 13, 1920

Dear Sharp:—[1]
Confirming my phone conversation this afternoon, I am told that Garvey (Marcus) is likely to get in touch with the Royal Bank in Montreal as their interests are believed to be favored by agitation at this time against the American occupation of Hayti.

Let Higgins[2] keep this in mind.

Also let him keep his ear open for any whisper of the name of Dr[.] Furnass,[3] who is a negro from Indianapolis and who was our Minister to Hayti in 1910–11. He is now anti-American and will likely hitch up with Garvey to create trouble down there. I will endeavor to get the present address of Furnass and will advise you as soon as received.

R[OBERT] C. B[ANNERMAN][4]
Chief Special Agent

DNA, RG 59, file 000-612. TLI, carbon copy.

1. Robert Sherman Sharp (1869–1932), Tennessee-born politician, reentered government service in 1917 as a special agent for the State Department in charge of investigations of foreign agents in New York (*NYT*, 9 March 1932).

2. Frank C. Higgins was an agent of the Department of State assigned to investigate Garveyism in Canada.

3. Henry Watson Furniss (b. 1868), black physician and diplomat, was educated at Howard University. A practicing surgeon at the Freedman's Hospital in Washington, D.C., and in Indianapolis, he left medicine following his appointment in 1898 to the American consulate in Bahia, Brazil. In 1905 he became U.S. envoy and minister plenipotentiary to Haiti, a position he held until 1913 (*WWCR*).

4. Robert C. Bannerman (1874–1940) was appointed assistant to the under secretary of state in July 1920. A secret service agent, he also had responsibility for protection of distinguished foreign visitors to the United States (*NYT*, 18 February 1940; U.S. Department of State, *Register*, 1924 [Washington, D.C.: GPO, 1924], pp. 8, 24).

J. Edgar Hoover to William L. Hurley

WASHINGTON, D.C. December 14, 1920

Dear Mr. Hurley:

Confirming conversation with Mr. Ruch on the 13th instant, this will advise you that Marcus Garvey left New York, December 11th, 6:45 P.M., for Montreal Canada, and will return to New York about January 1st.

Will you kindly communicate with your representative in Montreal, requesting them to cover the movements of Garvey if possible, and to keep the interest of this Government, in Garvey, from the British authorities.

I will be pleased to receive a report from your office on this subject. Very truly yours,

J. E. HOOVER
Special Assistant to the Attorney General

[*Endorsements*] G. F. R. W. L. H.

DNA, RG 59, file 000-612. TLS, recipient's copy. Handwritten endorsements.

Lewis J. Baley to L. H. Kemp, Jr., Bureau of Investigation

[*Washington, D.C.*] December 14, 1920

Dear Sir:

The Bureau has been advised by a confidential source, that Marcus Garvey has applied for license to sell stock in the State of Virginia. In his application, which is filed in Richmond, he states that one of his ships, namely the "Yarmouth", has made three trips to the West Indies; and another ship, namely the "Kanawha" has made one trip. It is the understanding of the Bureau that this statement is absolutely false, as Garvey's ships have never made a trip to the West Indies.[1]

It is desired that you endeavor to locate this license, and forward copy of same to the Bureau, if possible. Very truly yours,

LEWIS J. BALEY
Chief

[*Address*] L. H. Kemp, Esq.,
Box 721, Richmond, Virginia

DNA, RG 65, file BS 198940-34. TL, carbon copy.

1. At the time of this report, the *Yarmouth* had made two trips to the West Indies. The *Kanawha* had not yet sailed to the West Indies under Black Star Line auspices.

L. H. Kemp, Jr., to Lewis J. Baley

Richmond, Va., December 16th, 1920

Dear sir:—

Replying to yours of the 14th., inst., initial GFR-MMP relative to License of Marcus Garvey for sale of stock in this State, I beg to advise that investigation made at the Office of the State Corporation Commission shows that no license has been issued to Garvey in view of the fact that the required fee of $50.00 for filing his application was not accompanied by a certified check. In his application it states that it is the desire of the Black Star Steamship Line to place on sale $1,000,000.00 worth of stock in this State.

I am informed by Chief Clerk Dunford, State Corporation Commission that it has been said that this negro (Garvey) has already sold stock in the vicinity of Norfolk and Newport News, however this cannot be substan[ti]-ated[;] the following persons are named as Incorporators[:] Marcus Garvey, Edgar M. Gr[e]y, Richard E. W[a]rner, George W. Tobias and Janie Jenkins.

George Tobias being named as Treasurer of the Corporation, with offices at 56 West One Hundred and thirty-fifth Street New York City. Mr. Dunford has in his possession a lengthy report on Garvey made by the Pinkerton Detective Agency of New York City, which shows that Garvey has for some time been interested in Get-Rich-Quick Schemes. Yours very truly.

L. H. KEMP, JR.
Special Agent

[*Endorsement*] NOTED F. D. W.

DNA, RG 65, file BS 198940-112. TLS, recipient's copy.

Special Agent Frank C. Higgins to Special Agent Robert S. Sharp

NEW YORK December 17th, 1920

Sir:—

In obedience to instructions I have passed several days in Montreal, Canada, in an endeavor to unearth the possibility of a connection between the negro agitator, MARCUS GARVEY and the ROYAL BANK OF CANADA.[1]

Operating with great caution and always under cover, I made a careful survey of the negro situation in general in Montreal and found that it consisted of a solidly packed population of some 2,000 blacks, men, women and children inhabiting an area bounded on one side by St. Antoine Street, and on the other by St. James Street, immediately in the rear of Windsor Station of the Canadian Pacific Railway. At least 95 percent of these negroes are West Indians and nearly all of them are employees of the Canadian Pacific and other Canadian railroads, with a strong sprinkling of negro stewards and sailors, also West Indians, from cargo and passenger vessels operating from St. Lawrence ports.

In the almost exact center of the negro settlement on St. Antoine Street is located the Canadian Government Immigration Office and but a few doors away at 144 St. Antoine Street, the Standard Club, a spacious suite of rooms frequented principally by Pullman car conductors of the Canadian Pacific.

On the dates of my visit—the 15th and 16th especially,—I noted a great deal of activity in St. Antoine Street, as for instance the going and coming of groups of important looking and well dressed negroes, who were self-evidently not of the Pullman porter class, but of the type of West Indian merchants and business men. A group of negroes standing by the entrance to the Standard Club at one moment were chuckling audibly as they congratulated each other on the "wonderful meeting" of the night before, the particulars of which did not transpire.

Your Special Agent did his best to ingratiate himself in several negro resorts in St. Antoine Street, being enabled to do so because of the presence of a continuance of prize fighting events in Montreal, which always lead the readily led negroes into conversation. After a number of attempts to settle upon some possible source of information, he succeeded by hanging around a "Black and Tan" tobacco shop frequented by both white men and negroes, in encountering a young and apparently intelligent and well-educated mulatto, who came in to buy a newspaper. Leading this man into conversation and upon his admission that he was a native of Trinidad, it was easy to express a high degree of admiration for Mr. Garvey, as the greatest colored financier of all time.

Your Special Agent told this man that he believed Garvey was going to prove the greatest money maker of the age and he would like to get in touch with him and see if he could get some of his Black Star Line stock, but he was afraid that Garvey's prejudice against the whites would make it pretty hard to do business with him. The mulatto answered that he did not believe that it was as bad as all that and that he would gladly put the speaker in the way of getting in touch with Mr. Garvey, whom he said was not in Montreal at the present time, but that his right hand man could be found over in the Canadian Pacific Railway Station. Asked for particulars, he used a confidential tone in telling your Special Agent to go to one of the "Red Caps" (Baggage Porters), in the station and ask them to point our Mr. Potter. "Who is Mr. Potter?" the mulatto was asked. "Why, Mr. Potter is Mr. Garvey's right hand man; he is the man that receives all his letters and answers all his mail; he does all his advertising and everybody reports to him. There ain't anything connected with Mr. Garvey that he cannot tell you all about. You see him and that is all you need to do."

Your Special Agent later went into the Windsor Station of the C.P.R. and made use of an elderly United States Customs Official of his personal acquaintance, who, an elderly and discreet man, is absolutely trustworthy, giving no intimation of a reason, he asked this man to find out who and what Mr. Potter of the Red Cap Force might be. The informant learned from the transfer man in the station that Potter was one of the so-called captains or leaders of the baggage porters and that his name was Alfred, his common appellation being that of "Fred Potter." Then transferring his inquiry to one of the Red Cap Captains, he asked where Potter was these days, that he had not seen him around lately. "Why, don't you know," said the negro, "He is gone away up. He has been taken away from us on special duty for the officers upstairs and they send him all over the country. He runs down to New York a lot."

The connection between the two foregoing details is obvious and seems to be nothing less than the whole Garvey impetus proceeding from persons closely connected with the Canadian Pacific Railway, of which Sir Herbert Holt,[2] President of the Royal Bank of Canada, is one of the Executive Board.

I have no doubt in the world but that Garvey himself and possibly also Dr. Furnass may be present in Montreal at this moment but close examination of all of the Montreal papers for at least a week back, failed to show any public appearances of such persons, and furthermore, if it be true that they are covered up by the Canadian Pacific officials, in furtherance of a plan involving Garvey propaganda through Pullman car porters running into the United States, it would not be necessary to hold meetings or to attract public attention, as all of the negroes in this section are completely under control of the C.P.R.

In an investigation of this kind a too inquisitive white man would immediately become an object of suspicion and especially if recognized as from the United States, and if investigations along these lines are to be pursued I think that the advantage of employing a trustworthy negro should be taken into consideration.

Upon my return to New York I have ascertained from Mr. [*Hudson*] Price, Garvey's business manager at the office of the Negro World, 56 West 135th St., New York City, that Garvey is away "on a trip," but expects to be back in New York immediately after the Holidays. Respectfully submitted,

FRANK C. HIGGINS
Special Agent

DNA, RG 59, file 000-612. TLS, recipient's copy.

1. The Royal Bank of Canada, which had fifty-seven branches in the West Indies, opened its first Haitian subsidiary at Port-au-Prince in 1919 and its second at Aux Cayes in 1920 (Clifford H. Ince, *The Royal Bank of Canada: A Chronology, 1864–1969* [Montreal: Royal Bank of Canada, 1970], pp. 121–122). Among the major American investors in Haiti were the Wall Street firms of Speyer and Co. and National City Bank of New York. The two firms obtained a controlling interest in the Haitian Banque Nationale in 1911, successfully reducing the influence of Franco-German financial interests. Control of the Banque Nationale, which was made the sole depository for all government receipts, ensured a dominant role for the United States in the internal and external affairs of Haiti. In 1916, a year after the occupation of the island by U.S. Marines, the National City Bank purchased the shares of all other American participants in the Banque Nationale, and in June 1920 it paid $1.4 million to French stockholders to complete the transfer of the Banque Nationale to American financial interests (Hans Schmidt, *The United States Occupation of Haiti, 1915–1934* [New Brunswick, N.J.: Rutgers University Press, 1971], pp. 37–39, 129–132).

2. Sir Herbert Samuel Holt (1856–1941), Irish-born Canadian engineer and businessman, played a major role in the construction of the Canadian Pacific Railway and in 1908 was appointed president of the Royal Bank of Canada (*NYT*, 29 September 1941).

Special Agent Robert S. Sharp to Robert C. Bannerman

NEW YORK December 17th, 1920

Sir:—

. . . You will note from this report that the confidential agent for Marcus Garvey in Montreal, is in the employ of the Canadian Pacific Railway and Agent Higgins' report shows that the officers of this railway have him assigned to special duty all over Canada and that he makes frequent trips to New York.

In addition to the fact set forth by Special Agent Higgins that Sir Herbert Holt, the President of the Royal Bank of Canada, is one of the Executive Board of the Canadian Pacific Railway, the following statements are called to your attention for any bearing which they may have on this report.

Sir Herbert Holt is closely allied with Canadian interests that have been brought into close touch with the activities of James Dunne,[1] Franklin Helm, Pliny Fiske, the British oil man, E. Mackay Edgar,[2] Sperling & Company, Speyer & Company,[3] and Sir William Wiseman.[4] The relationships between Martin Nordegg[5] and the Canadian Pacific Railway are also to be considered in connection with Nordegg's connection with Sir William MacKenzie[6] and the handling of Alien Property Custodian interests in the Canadian Pacific Railroad system.

The connection between Nordegg and Dr. Maloney,[7] and Speyer & Company and the Under Secretary of State of Canada, Mr. Mulvey,[8] as well as the Secretary of State, Mr. Murphy,[9] have been fully set forth in previous reports to your office.

You also are reminded that in the investigation of the interned German ships at Santa Rosalia, California,[10] in which Judah H. Sears was interested, that statements are contained in the files to the effect that the parties who are attempting to procure these ships are railroad officials connected with the Canadian Pacific Railway.

This information should also be considered in connection with the activities of the France and Canada Steamship Company, by which institution Judah H. Sears was employed and for which Franklin Helm also performed numerous services, fully set forth in reports previously sent you.

You are also reminded of a confidential report made by Special Agent Kinsey on November 13th to the effect that one of Mr. Julius P. Mayer's closest personal friends made the statement that Mr. Mayer had refused to accept a salary of $30,000. per annum which had been offered him by the Canadian Pacific Railway. The Julius P. Mayer[11] in question was formerly the General Agent of the Hamburg American Steamship Company in New York City, the same institution which recently made a contract with the Harriman Steamship Interests, which has been the subject of such violent criticism, and in which the majority stockholdings have not yet been developed, but in the control of which the late Jacob H. Schiff[12] seems to have been the leading factor.

Jacob Schiff is reported as having had conferences with Leon Trotsky before he left America for Russia, where he joined with Lenine in creating the Russian debacle, and is a close relative of M. Warburg of the Deutsche Bank interests of Berlin, Germany, and has been in close touch constantly with Felix Warburg, the head of the Jewish Joint Distribution Committee in the United States.[13] Felix Warburg is a brother of Fitz Warburg, connected with the Secret Service of the German Empire during the war, and who is reputed to have had much to do with Lenine's activities in Russia.

From the above brief recital of the files which are in this office, if considered with my letter of December 15th, regarding Sir William Wiseman, and E. Mackay Edgar, and the relationships between this distinguished oil man and Sperling & Company and their Canadian holdings, as well as their direct relations with the English Jewish oil interests, it is not unreasonable to suppose that the close relationship mentioned in Special Agent Higgins' report on MARCUS GARVEY between Garvey's man Potter and the Canadian Pacific Railway officials, is of a sinister character, involving radical agitation in this country among our negro population.[14]

The indications are strong that the same combination of elements that have propagated trouble in Cuba, Mexico, and Canada, and among the Bolshevik elements of the United States, is behind Marcus Garvey and that these elements involve the activities of English Jews, who are closely related to the Rothschilds and Lazard[15] outfit in Europe.

I respectfully suggest that in connection with Agent Higgins' report herewith submitted, that a report of Special Agent Cox dated January 20th, 1920, on the BLACK STAR LINE STEAMSHIP CORPORATION be also considered, as Marcus Garvey appears to be the leading spirit in this enterprise.

During the month of June 1920, the writer was in Liberia, Africa, working under cover and while there he found the name of MARCUS GARVEY was frequently mentioned and he appeared to be, even in that far off little republic, the leading colored man of the world. I have heard statements made by negro citizens of Liberia to the effect that they were opposed to the United States due to information which they had received as a result of statements made by MARCUS GARVEY to the effect that the negroes of Liberia could expect no better treatment from the United States than the negro citizens of the Haytian Republic had received.

This statement should be considered in connection with the fact that Garvey is not a naturalized citizen of the United States, but a native of Jamaica, and a British subject.

It was largely through Garvey's influence that a delegate from Liberia attended the Negro World Congress in New York recently, this delegate being the Mayor of Monrovia, Liberia, and through Garvey's manipulation was elected "President of the Republic of Africa."

If Garvey is working as he appears to be in close connection with British interests, my report submitted to you on the English activities in Liberia and the manner in which they have manipulated that little republic should also be considered in this connection. Respectfully,

R. S. SHARP
Special Agent in Charge

DNA, RG 59, file 000-612. TLS, recipient's copy.

1. James Allan Dunn (1881–1933), Canadian mining promoter, was president of the mining firm of Barry-Hollinger (*Dictionary of Canadian Biography* [Toronto: Trans-Canada Press, 1934] 1: 170).

2. Sir Edward Mackay Edgar (b. 1876), Canadian-born director of the London banking house Sperling & Co., came to the attention of the U.S. government after the publication of an article in September 1919 in which he stated that the bulk of world oil reserves was securely in British hands and that the United States, because of its complacency and high consumption, would soon be forced to import oil from British companies. Sperling & Co. was among the financiers of the Canadian Northern Railway (T. G. Regehr, *The Canadian Northern Railway* [Toronto: Macmillan Co., 1976], pp. 305–307; Anton Mohr, *The Oil War* [New York: Harcourt, Brace & Co., 1926]).

3. Speyer and Co., based in New York and one of three German-Jewish banking houses under the ownership of the Speyer family, was involved in the financing of the prairie west branch of the Canadian Northern Railway. Sir Edgar Speyer (1862–1932), director of the London branch, was accused of disloyalty to Britain during the war, and although initially cleared of the charges by Prime Minister Asquith, he chose to immigrate to the United States.

In 1921 his naturalization was revoked because he maintained financial links with Germany during the war (T. G. Regehr, *The Canadian Northern Railway*, p. 214; Colin Holmes, *Anti-Semitism in British Society, 1876–1939* [London: Edward Arnold, 1979]; *WWW*, 1929–1940).

4. Sir William George Wiseman (1885–1962) served as head of British intelligence operations in the United States from 1916 to 1918. A close friend of Col. Edward M. House, he played a major role in furthering Anglo-American relations after the United States' entry into the war. Wiseman was later appointed chief adviser on American affairs to the British delegation at the Paris Peace Conference (W. B. Fowler, *British-American Relations, 1917–1918: The Role of Sir William Wiseman* [Princeton, N.J.: Princeton University Press, 1969]).

5. Martin Nordegg (d. 1948), German financier and promoter and director of the German Development Co., was associated with the firm Mackenzie, Mann and Co. Ltd. in the development of coal mines in Alberta (T. G. Regehr, *The Canadian Northern Railway*, pp. 250–252; *NYT*, 14 September 1948).

6. Sir William Mackenzie (1849–1923), Ontario-born businessman and financier, became a contractor for the early Canadian railway system in the 1870s, before forming the company Mackenzie, Mann and Co. with his partner Donald Mann. The company obtained its first major contract with the construction of the Canadian Pacific Railway and later played a major role in the creation of the Canadian Northern Railway. Mackenzie and Mann served as president and vice-president of the railway, winning a reputation for their aggressive and effective bargaining (T. G. Regehr, *The Canadian Northern Railway*, pp. 30 ff.).

7. Dr. William J. Maloney, Scottish-born American, testified before the Senate Naval Lobby Investigating Committee in January 1930 that he was the author of the so-called "secret British document" entitled "The Reconquest of America." The "secret document," based entirely on Maloney's unsigned propaganda pamphlet published in 1919, was brought to the attention of the Navy Department in 1928 by a certain "naval expert," William B. Shearer, who published extracts from it in the *Gaelic American*. The pamphlet, issued by Maloney in 1919 and distributed largely through the Friends of Irish Freedom, was designed to offset the pro-British and pro–League of Nations propaganda of Lord Northcliffe. Maloney's authorship of the pamphlet, which he claimed to be merely a "skit" on British propaganda, was known to certain State Department officials, including Robert Bannerman, and to several U.S. senators, including the isolationist Sen. William Borah. However, hearings held by the State Department and the Post Office in their attempt to stop circulation of the pamphlet did not result in any legal action against Maloney. The pamphlet was passed off as a reprint of a report made by a British official and addressed to Lloyd George; the introduction to the pamphlet stated that the essay had been found near 500 Madison Avenue, New York, the residence of William Wiseman, and thus intimated that Wiseman was the author of the program of "Anglicization" of the United States called for in the report. The pamphlet came to the attention of Wiseman in late 1919 and was passed on to Col. Edward House, President Wilson, and the State Department, the department declaring it an obvious forgery. Despite this, certain anti-Semitic elements in the State Department, including W. L. Hurley, continued to monitor the activities of Wiseman, falsely suspecting him of Jewish ancestry. The department also noted Wiseman's alleged connection with American banking interests in Mexico (DNA, RG 59, file 841-139, entry 538; *NYT*, 12 January 1930).

8. Thomas Mulvey (b. 1863) was appointed under secretary of state for Canada in 1909, a position he held until 1933. In 1918 he served as chairman of the Enemy Debts and Reparation Committee, and in 1920 he was named deputy custodian (A. L. Normandin, ed., *The Canadian Parliamentary Guide*, 1933 [Ottawa: Mortimer Co., 1933], p. 626).

9. Charles Murphy (b. 1863), lawyer and Liberal party politician, served as Canadian secretary of state from 1908 to 1911 (Rose Hamilton, ed., *Prominent Men of Canada, 1931–1932* [Montreal: National Publishing Co. of Canada, n.d.]).

10. The disposition of German ships interned by the British and American governments was the subject of considerable controversy in 1919. The British government argued that several interned German oil tankers utilized during 1918 and 1919 by Standard Oil Co. should be distributed to the Allies under the Wilson–Lloyd George agreement. This shipping conflict was closely tied to the Anglo-American commercial rivalry in general and to the conflict over oil reserves and oil trade in particular. In September 1919, officials of the U.S. Shipping Board accused Britain of attempting "to obstruct American-German oil business" (Jeffrey J. Safford, *Wilsonian Maritime Diplomacy, 1913–1921* [New Brunswick, N.J.: Rutgers University Press, 1978], p. 207).

11. The Hamburg-American Line, based in Germany, was directed by the German Jew Albert Ballin and represented in the United States by its vice-director, Julius P. Meyer. In August 1920 W. Averill Harriman, head of the American Ship and Commerce Corp., with the support of Adm. William S. Benson, chairman of the U.S. Shipping Board, arranged a merger with the Hamburg-American Line. Benson, known for his opposition to British commercial expansion, considered the merger as an opportunity to broaden U.S. international commerce at the expense of British and European competitors. The new company, controlled by Harriman and known as the United American Line, received strong criticism from the American Steamship Owners Association and from sectors of the press for helping to rehabilitate the German merchant marine.

12. Jacob H. Schiff (1847–1920), was nationally known for his financing of several railroads. His link with the Harriman interests came to public attention in 1906 and 1907, when he and E. H. Harriman were involved in a battle with James Hill and J. P. Morgan and Co. for control of the Northern Pacific Railroad (*NYT*, 7 September, 13 September, 14 September, and 26 September 1920; Jeffrey J. Safford, *Wilsonian Maritime Diplomacy, 1913–1921*, [New Brunswick, N.J.: Rutgers University Press, 1978], pp. 239–241). Schiff was a founder of the American Jewish Committee in 1906 and played a prominent role during World War I as a contributor to the American Jewish Relief Committee, headed by his brother-in-law, Felix Warburg. In 1920 the *Dearborn Independent*, pointing out that Schiff's company had helped finance the Japanese war against Russia, claimed that this allowed Schiff "to advance his plan to undermine the Russian empire, as it has now been accomplished by Jewish Bolshevism." It claimed that this was done through "the Russian prisoners of war in Japan, who were sent back as apostles of destruction" (Henry Ford, *The International Jew* [Dearborn, Mich.: Dearborn Publishing Co., 1920], 3: 231). The paper also claimed that M. M. Warburg and Co. "is noted in a dispatch published by the United States government as being one whence funds were forwarded to Trotsky for use in destroying Russia" (3: 235). In March 1917 Schiff sent a letter of congratulation to the Russian Menshevik government, but he later opposed the Bolshevik revolution. (*WBD*; Cyrus Adler, *Jacob H. Schiff: His Life and Letters* [London: William Heineman, 1929], vols. 1 and 2).

13. The nature of the allegations here appears to have been determined by the conspiratorial theories voiced by Henry Ford's anti-Semitic newspaper, the *Dearborn Independent*, which began publication in 1920. In a series of articles, later reprinted as *The International Jew* (see n. 12), the paper purported to expose the American banking firm of Kuhn, Loeb and Co., among whose members were the German-born Jews Paul Warburg (1868–1932) and Felix Warburg (1871–1937), who were related to each other and had married into the Loeb family.

14. The influence of Ford's anti-Semitic publications reached its peak in the period of 1920 to 1922, as did the personal popularity of Ford, ranked by a *New York Times* survey as the eighth most admired American in history. It is thus quite possible that his anti-Semitic views, coinciding with a period of strong isolationism, xenophobia, and racism, pervaded the Bureau of Investigation, particularly given the bureau's fear of impending Bolshevism and anarchy and given the currency of numerous Communist conspiracy theories. In the case of the Bureau of Investigation, it also appears that an intermingling of anti-Semitism and anglophobia took place, and this in turn may account for J. Edgar Hoover's belief that the UNIA was being sponsored or aided by the British and Canadian governments (Albert Lee, *Henry Ford and the Jews* [New York: Stein and Day, 1980]; Henry Ford, *The International Jew*, vol. 3; Cyrus Adler, *Jacob H. Schiff: His Life and His Letters* [London: William Heineman, 1929], vols. 1 and 2; *Encyclopedia Judaica* 14: 960–961; *NYT*, 10 April 1917).

15. The Lazard family of German-Jewish international bankers, based in New York, Paris, and London, were among the financiers of the Canadian Northern Railway. During the war Lazard Frères, in combination with the Canadian Bank of Commerce, successfully ousted Martin Nordegg from Mackenzie, Mann and Co. (T. G. Regehr, *The Canadian Northern Railway*, pp. 215–216, 252).

Report by Special Agent J. G. Tucker

[*New York*] Dec. 18, 1920

"Black Star Line"

Marcus Garvey, President of the above corporation, has issued a new lot of circular letters, under date of December 1st, in order to raise Two Hundred and Fifty Thousand Dollars by January 15, 1921. The object of the new loan, the circular states, is to obtain another ship which is to convey to Africa the workmen and materials for "the building up of the great republic of Liberia for the race", and goes on to say: "The Black Star Line as an auxiliary of the Universal Negro Improvement Association has committed itself to convey workmen and materials and immigrants from the United States of America, the West Indies, South and Central America, to our future seat of Government, Liberia, West Africa".

From a confidential source it is understood that Garvey's latest appeal for funds is not meeting with the response for which he had hoped, due partly to the increased number of unemployed Negroes in the Harlem district and partly to the fact that his followers seem to have lost faith in his projects. . . .

J. G. Tucker

DNA, RG 65, file OG 3057. TD.

O. M. Thompson to Leo Healy

[*New York*] December 21, 1920

Dear Mr. Healy:

Herewith enclosed please find cheque for five hundred dollars in favor of Messrs. Harris, Irby & Vose, to be applied to the purchase price of the S/S "Yarmouth."

This remittance is not as prompt as desired but it is the best we could do. Every possible effort is being made to liquidate our account with your client and we believe that during the month of January our business will improve to a state of competency.

In the meantime we beg to remain, with compliments of the season to you, Very truly yours,

Black Star Line, Inc.
O. M. Thom[p]son
Vice President

Garvey v. *United States*, no. 8317, Ct. App., 2d Cir., 2 February 1925, government exhibit no. 21.

Report by Bureau Agent William C. Sausele

Jacksonville, Fla. 12/22/20

NEGRO ACTIVITIES

About 400 members of the recently organized U.N.I.A. at Miami, Fla., met at the Baptist [*Church*], Avenue "H" and Lemon Street, December 5th. Percy Stiles, appear/ed/ to be in charge of the meeting. A general plan for establishing equality with the whites and eventually bringing about supremacy of the Blacks was discussed. Among other things, intermarriage was advocated. A canvass of Jacksonville, to establish to what extent Negroes had armed themselves indicates that about 90% of the Negroes are in possession of fire arms. . . .

WM. C. SAUSELE

[*Endorsements*] NOTED G. F. R.
NOTED F. D. W.

DNA, RG 65, file BS 202600-10-10. Stamped endorsements.

Gabriel M. Johnson to President C. D. B. King of Liberia

Monrovia, Liberia, December 27th, 1920

Your Excellency:

The Universal Negro Improvement Association sends greetings to the Government of Liberia, through me their representative here.

Being deeply interested in the welfare of Liberia; and desirous of assisting her in every possible way to make good, by improving the industries of the country; and augmenting her citizenship by assisting immigrants to migrate to Liberia in appreciable numbers; as well as running a line of steamers from the United States and the West Indies to Liberia; and also being desirous to make its headquarters at Monrovia in the near future, as was intimated to you by the delegate who visited Monrovia in June last;[1] have put on a campaign to raise funds for this purpose and we hope within the next three months to have a ship call at Monrovia and elsewhere along our coast, bringing immigrants and supplies for the beginning of their work.

In view of the facts above mentioned, I should ask your Excellency to kindly give your moral and financial support to the project; and ask that the government would appoint agents to assist in the housing of these immigrants, and locating them in the several settlements, towns and cities as they may desire.

The Association intends bringing such persons as in their estimation are interested in the welfare of our Republic and willing to do their share for its uplif[t] and pro[s]perity, and thereby be a benefit to Liberia.

Thanking you for your favorable consideration of this very important subject, and awaiting your early acknowledgement. I am, your Excellency's Obedient servant,

G. M. JOHNSON
Sup. High Commissioner

DNA, RG 65, file BS 198940-213. TL, transcript.

1. The UNIA sent Elie Garcia as its emissary in June 1920. For his report on the situation, see *Garvey Papers* 2: 660–676.

Report by Special Agent P-138

New York City 12/28/20

IN RE: NEGRO ACTIVITIES

Marcus Garvey is back in town after a trip to Canada and the West lecturing in the interest of his Liberian Liberty Loan.[1] His followers are continuing their bazaar and dance at Liberty Hall where up until now conditions are 'O.K.'

It would appear that this diversion has done a great deal to take their minds off the anti-White propaganda which has been spread by platform speakers every night for over one year.

I spoke to [H]udson Price, associate editor of the "Negro World" today [*24 December*], relative to the policy of the paper. He told me that he had a hard time keeping Garvey from putting more radical anti-racial matter in the paper as he was afraid that it would be debarred from the mails. Respectfully

P-138

[*Endorsments*] FILE G. F. R.
NOTED F. D. W. NOTED W. W. G.

DNA, RG 65, file BS 198940-45. TD. Stamped endorsements.

1. On 4 January 1921 J. Edgar Hoover, in a memorandum to Brig. Gen. D. E. Nolan of the Military Intelligence Division, summarized P-138's report and promised to forward a more detailed report on Garvey's activities in Canada (DNA, RG 165, file 10110-1991).

Editorial Letter by Marcus Garvey

[[New York, December 29, 1920]]

BLACK STAR LINE STEAMSHIP CORPORATION AND UNIVERSAL NEGRO IMPROVEMENT ASSOCIATION PLANNING TO REPATRIATE TO LIBERIA BETWEEN 500,000 AND 1,000,000 NEGROES IN 1921

SURVEYORS, SCIENTISTS AND MEDICAL UNITS TO SAIL IN JANUARY—BULK OF WORKERS AND PASSENGERS TO SAIL IN MARCH.

FELLOW MEN OF THE NEGRO RACE, Greeting:

... The contemplated construction work to be started in our own Republic of Liberia for the commercial and industrial development of that country is to begin shortly. The ships of the Black Star Line which are now being refitted and repaired will be put in service on regular sailings as per announcements that will appear in the columns of THE NEGRO WORLD. Workmen and mechanics who desire to go to Africa are requested to register their names with the presidents of local divisions of the Universal Negro Improvement Association, and also to send a duplicate of the registration addressed to the "Traffic Superintendent, Universal Negro Improvement Association, 56 West 135th Street, New York, U.S.A." The first public sailing of passengers and settlers will take place in March. The first official sailing of surveyors and mechanics will be between the 25th of January and the 20th of February. Let all those who desire to go to Africa register their intentions now, so that a complete list can be made up for early transportation of each and every one. There will be regular sailings of the ships of the Black Star Line from New York and Philadelphia starting from March, 1921. The sailings will be first monthly, then fortnightly and weekly. Liberia offers great opportunities to all men and women who desire to start off independently to build fortunes for themselves and their families. The Universal Negro Improvement Association shall so regulate transportation between the United States, the West Indies, Central America and Liberia as not to cause over-congestion at any one time. Let each and every one start from now to prepare, because between January 1 and December 31, 1921, it is expected that the Universal Negro Improvement Association and the Black Star Line will have transported between five hundred thousand and one million civilized, industrious Negroes from this western hemisphere into the great Republic of Liberia. The great need at the present time is for more ships in the Black Star Line. My advice, therefore, in this new year, is that all those who have not bought shares do so immediately, and those who have bought already that they buy more, if possible, or influence their friends to do so. The more ships the Black Star Line has at its command, the more regular will be the sailings from these points to Liberia. Bigger ships and faster ships must be acquired in this new year. All prospective settlers in Liberia should be shareholders in the Black Star Line. Investment in the Black Star Line will be the safest value in the hands of Negroes in another few years.

Let us all unite to make 1921 a banner year in the [his]tory of the Negro peoples of the world. Let us concentrate on the building up of a great Liberia. Let us all unite and help President King of Liberia to make the Black Republic the greatest of its kind in the world. The Liberian Government needs help and the Universal Negro Improvement Association and the Negro peoples of the world must do it. Let us help to build the railroads of Liberia; let us help to lay out the farm lands of Liberia; let us help to build high schools, colleges and universities in Liberia; let us help to build beautiful homes in Liberia; let us help to build beautiful streets, avenues and boulevards in Liberia; let us help to build subways and elevated railways in Liberia; let us help to build such executive mansions in Liberia as to stand favorable comparison with any such in any other part of the world, and let us build the most beautiful Liberty Hall in Liberia. Let the name of Liberia be written among the nations of the world and let her hold her place as a power to be respected.

We have just spent probably a Merry Christmas on these western shores, but let us hope, a goodly number of us, that we may spend a merrier and a happier Christmas in 1921 on the shores of Mother Africa in the great Republic of Liberia. . . . Yours fraternally,

MARCUS GARVEY

Printed in *NW*, 1 January 1921.

WANTED IMMEDIATELY

Two (2) Architects and three (3) Contracting Builders to Go to

LIBERIA

Must Be Willing to Sail Between January 25 and February 20, 1921

Apply at Once to Office of Commissioner-General

UNIVERSAL NEGRO IMPROVEMENT ASSOCIATION
56 West 135th Street, New York City

[1 January 1921]

WARNING TO THE NEGRO PEOPLE OF AMERICA, WEST INDIES, SOUTH AND CENTRAL AMERICA AND AFRICA

BOGUS STEAMSHIP COMPANIES

It has come to our knowledge that several unscrupulous Negroes have organized Steamship Corporations for the purpose of exploiting the race, and they they are offering their worthless stock under the guise that the people are buying shares in the Black Star Line Steamship Corporation. The public is hereby warned against such unscrupulous persons whose hope of buying steamships is only on paper. They have no steamship, no property, or no guarantee for their stock. This is the time when Negroes should be careful of their investments.

The Black Star Line has no connection with these unscrupulous individuals and corporations, and the people are, therefore, warned that we will not

118

hold ourselves responsible for false representations made by these Corporations or their agents.

The Black Star Line and the Universal Negro Improvement Association has no connection with a certain steamship Corporation that claims that it is running ships to Liberia, as this Corporation has no ships except on paper, and all persons are asked to report these agents to the police when they endeavor to represent themselves as agents of the Black Star Line. Some of these unscrupulous men have been operating in Virginia, South and North Carolina, and other parts south, and in New Jersey.

Report these bogus stocks and their agents to your District Attorney. Pass this notice to your friends.

BLACK STAR LINE, INC.
MARCUS GARVEY
President

FURTHER NOTICE

One, J. M. George, claiming to be a Lawyer and also alleged to be an Agent of one Liberian-American Steamship Corporation,[1] has been selling stock in the South, Virginia and Carolina in the names of the Black Star Line and the Negro World. If you should come across him offering such stock as a representative of the Black Star Line and the Negro World, please hand him over to the police.

Printed in *NW*, 1 January 1921.

1. For a discussion of Pan-African shipping ventures that were contemporaneous with the BSL, see Ian Duffield, "Pan-Africanism, Rational and Irrational," *Journal of African History* 18 (1977): 602–607.

Report by Bureau Agent L. H. Kemp, Jr.

Norfolk, Va. Jan. 3, 1921

MARCUS GARVEY, BLACK STAR S.S. LINE, NEW YORK: ALLEGED
SALE OF STOCK WITHOUT LICENSE; ALSO SAID TO BE
A RADICAL.

At Richmond, Va.

In the 14th ultimo, Chief of Bureau, in a letter initialed GFR-MMP, requested that this office endeavor to [locate] license issued to the above subject to sell stock in the State of Virginia. As stated in Agent's letter to Chief of Bureau under date of December 16, 1920, no license has ever been issued in view of the fact that the $50.00 filing fee was not accompanied by a certified check. This morning Chief Clerk Dunford of the State Corporation

Commission, called over the 'phone and informed Agent that a representative of the Black Star S.S. Line would be in his office, for the purpose of securing the desired license. Agent was present in the State Corporation Commissioner's office when ELIE GARCI[A], representing himself as secretary of the Black Star Steamship Line, was closely questioned by Mr. Dunford. He admitted that his Company had sold between $5,000.00 and $6,000.00 worth of this stock in Norfolk and Newport News, Va., in violation of the State law, and that it was their desire to place $1,000,000.00 worth of stock in Virginia. His financial statement showed $442,625 paid in, while $168,235 were unpaid. Mr. Dunford did not hesitate to tell this negro, in view of the fact that he had been informed by the Pinkerton Detective Agency of New York, that there were nine criminal warrants against GARVEY, and that the cost of promoting this Company was in excess of 20 per cent. Mr. Dunford informed GARCI[A] that his Company would not be granted license and that in the event GARVEY appeared in Virginia, he would be arrested. INVESTIGATION CONCLUDED.

L. H. KEMP, JR.

[*Endorsements*] NOTED W. W. G.
NOTED F. D. W. FILE G. F. R.

DNA, RG 65, file BS 198940-50. TD. Stamped endorsements.

Reports by Special Agent P-138

New York City 1/4/21

IN RE NEGRO ACTIVITIES.

Today [*28 December 1920*] I visited the office of Marcus Garvey where I had [a] lengthy conversation with him along general lines.

He told me he had recently arrived from Canada and had been ill, but is now feeling improved. While in Canada he was lecturing and collecting money for the "Liberia Liberty Loan". He also told me that during the month of De[c]ember his financial condition was very low, but [through?] his Liberia Loan campaign he has succeeded in collecting a few thousand dollars. Garvey is considered (among his followers) a very hard man to reach and his fanatic followers worship him as a god, but for some reason I have worked myself into his confidence. Even when his [high] officers want to reach him and are afraid, they will come to me and ask me to put in a good word for them. They feel that Garvey has great confidence in me and for some unknown reason that I am always able to [reach] him. Garvey is very suspicious and thinks everyone is trying to "frame him up". Of course, the prime reason for his confidence in me is that I once acted as a method by which to settle, out of court, a civil suit pending against him and now he feels obligated to me.

I learned from a lawyer named J. P. Ifill,[1] offices at 139th St. & Seventh Ave., southwest corner, second floor, that Rev. Dr. Easton [*Eason*], recently elected by Garvey convention as 'leader of the Negroes of America', is now accused of attempted rape,[2] on a young married colored woman named Mrs. [*Alice Fraser*] Robinson, whose husband keeps a fruit store at 29 W. . . . [*word mutilated*] St. Mrs. Robinson is a soprano singer employed by Garvey and travels with him on all his out-of-town lecture tours. The lawyer who is conducting the case against Easton told me that while the party (Garvey's party) was at Pittsburgh recently and the three women singers had returned to their room and were asleep, "His Highness, the Right Hon. Rev., Dr. Easton, D.D., leader of the Negroes of America", etc. and Garvey's other right hand man, the "Right Hon. Rev., Dr. Brooks, the Secretary General", attacked these three women and after a fierce three-quarter hour fight, brutally scratched and bruised their victims after an unsuccessful attempt at rape. This is causing a sensation in the Negro ranks and the greatest scandal is pending, which is sure to lower the prestige of Garvey's anti-White organization. The husband is determined to send Easton to jail, while the other high officers are doing all in their power to keep the affair quiet. Respectfully,

P-138

[*Endorsements*] FILE G. F. R.
NOTED F. D. W. NOTED W. W. G.

DNA, RG 65, file BS 202600-667. TD. Stamped endorsements.

1. J. P. Ifill was secretary of the Berry and Ross Toy and Doll Manufacturing Co. and a close associate of its president, H. S. Boulin (P-138).

2. When Eason and Garvey quarreled during the 1922 UNIA convention, Garvey initiated impeachment proceedings against Eason. Garvey claimed at one point that Eason "was charged with breaking into the room of two ladies of the association after midnight, to their great discomfort." When Eason was tried before the convention delegates, Mrs. Barrier Houston testified that the intoxicated Eason had entered a room where she and other women were sleeping and had refused to leave. She accused him of attempting "certain dishonorable acts" before the women managed to eject him (*NW*, 2 September 1922).

New York City 1/4/21

While passing Garvey's offices today [*29 December 1920*], I saw a Hindu entering. I recognized him as the same Hindu whom I heard speak at Liberty Hall on October 10th last, hence I followed him upstairs in an effort to engage him in a conversation. He entered the office of Thompson, Garvey's Vice President and efficiency manager. On going in the room I saw him seated in front of Thompson's desk where they were engaged in an undertone conversation. I was given a chair at the other end of the room where, unfortunately, I could not hear the conversation. After awhile I saw Thompson's stenographer go to a drawer, take out two packages of literature, circulars, etc., and upon instructions from Thompson, gave same to the Hindu. He took the papers and after a brief talk, Thompson said to him, "Well, you must come up more often and don't keep away so long again", to which he assented and left the room. Owing to the fact that I had to wait so as to give Thompson a pretext for my being in the room, the Hindu disappeared before I had a chance to meet him. However, I met Crichlow, one of Garvey's shorthand reporters and asked him what was the name of the Hindu and who he was. Crichlow informed me that he belonged to some great radical association downtown and was a great propagandist. He had reported his speech at Liberty Hall a few months ago, but had forgotten his name.

I shall now keep in close touch with Thompson so as to learn more of this Hindu. Respectfully,

P-138

[*Handwritten endorsement*] Sent State 1/10/21 G. F. R.
[*Stamped endorsement*] NOTED F. D. W.

DNA, RG 65, file BS 202600-667. TD.

New York City 1/4/21

Today [*30 December*] I visited Liberty Hall at the closing night of the fifteen days bazaar. The usual anti-white meetings will be resumed from to-morrow eve.

I had the opportunity of meeting G. O. Marke, a native of Sierra Leone, West Africa, who was recently elected Supreme Deputy and Assistant Potentate of the Negroes. We were engaged in a very lengthy conversation after I discovered that Marke was living in Garvey's house while in New York. He told me, that at times he thinks Garvey is crazy; as, for instance, in this week's "Negro World" he published a lot of untruth about ships which were going to sail to Africa in Jan., Feb. and March, carrying men to Liberia; also, asking people to send in application if they wish to go to Africa. Marke told me that he knows nothing of this false story printed. None of the other officers and directors know anything of it as there is absolutely no ground for such a statement. They have no money to buy a ship and on the whole the thing was a deception engineered by Garvey. However, the Board of Directors called a hurried meeting today and requested him to explain his action. Garvey refused and walked out of the meeting. This misleading newspaper announcement is causing them a lot of embarrassment, as a large number of applicants are already seeking information crowding the office. These applicants are handed an application blank which informed them that they must pay their own passage and go at their own risk. I am trying to get one of these application forms.

JANUARY 1921

CHIEF SAM:

It would now appear as if Garvey's methods are equal to that of Chief Sam and if measures are not adopted to check him I am afraid that from the general outlook he will cause unrest and dissatisfaction. Respectfully,

P-138

[*Endorsements*] FILE G. F. R.
NOTED W. W. G. NOTED F. D. W.

DNA, RG 65, file BS 202600-667-13. TD. Stamped endorsements.

New York City 1/4/21

. . . Garvey, the professional agitator, held a monster crowd spellbound at Liberty Hall to-night [*31 December 1920*]. In spite of the fact that the daily papers announced that De Valera, the Irish leader had left the country,[1] Garvey announced to his followers that De Valera would speak at Liberty Hall where an entrance fee of fifty cents was charged.

Although this speaker failed to put in his appearance, Garvey's followers showed not the slightest sign of disappointment or discontent. This incident only proves the wonderful power Garvey exercises over his followers and just what harm he is capable of doing should he see fit to turn his influence in the wrong direction. Respectfully,

P-138

[*Endorsements*] NOTED W. W. G.
NOTED F. D. W. FILE G. F. R.

DNA, RG 65, file BS 202600-667-14. TD. Stamped endorsements.

1. De Valera's impending departure, after eighteen months in the United States, was rumored on 16 December in the New York press, and shortly thereafter he was reported on board the S.S. *Aquitania* (*NYT*, 16 December and 20 December 1920). De Valera was smuggled into Dublin on the morning of 23 December 1920; ironically, on the very day that his upcoming speech was advertised at Liberty Hall, de Valera sent a cable announcing that he was safely back in Ireland (Patrick McCartan, *With De Valera in America* [New York: Brentano, 1932], p. 220).

Meeting Announcement

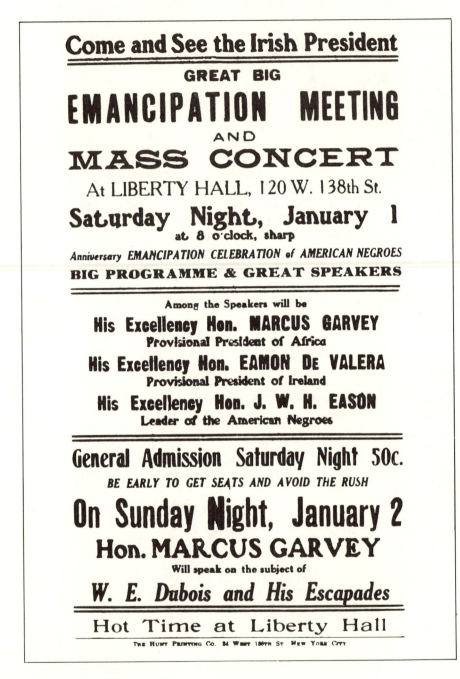

Come and See the Irish President

GREAT BIG

EMANCIPATION MEETING

AND

MASS CONCERT

At LIBERTY HALL, 120 W. 138th St.

Saturday Night, January 1

at 8 o'clock, sharp

Anniversary EMANCIPATION CELEBRATION of AMERICAN NEGROES

BIG PROGRAMME & GREAT SPEAKERS

Among the Speakers will be

His Excellency Hon. MARCUS GARVEY
Provisional President of Africa

His Excellency Hon. EAMON DE VALERA
Provisional President of Ireland

His Excellency Hon. J. W. H. EASON
Leader of the American Negroes

General Admission Saturday Night 50c.

BE EARLY TO GET SEATS AND AVOID THE RUSH

On Sunday Night, January 2
Hon. MARCUS GARVEY
Will speak on the subject of

W. E. Dubois and His Escapades

Hot Time at Liberty Hall

The Hunt Printing Co. 34 West 136th St New York City

(*Source*: NN-Sc, JEB.)

New York City 1/4/21

Garvey gave out at Liberty Hall today [*1 January*] that he had examined the first batch of Negroes whom he says will sail for Liberia, W. Africa on or about January 23rd.

He told the packed hall that he intended to transport between fifty and seventy-five thousand Negroes within the next six months.

To-morrow night he said that he would start a drive in the meeting to collect money so as to build a Liberty Hall in Liberia. He expects to leave the City by Monday and will be away on a secret mission for at least six weeks, something on the order of De Valera.

Of course, he said nothing about the big new ship which he had promised to buy and get ready to sail for Africa on January 1, 1921. To-morrow night Garvey will make a speech in answer to Dr. W. E. Dubois articles in the "Crisis" of December and January.[1] Respectfully,

P-138

[*Endorsements*] FILE G. F. R.
NOTED W. W. G. NOTED F. D. W.

DNA, RG 65, file BS 202600-667-10. TD. Stamped endorsements.
   1. W. E. B. Du Bois, "Marcus Garvey," *Crisis* 21, no. 2 (December 1920): 58–60, and no. 3 (January 1921): 112–115.

New York City 1/4/21

At Liberty Hall to-night [*2 January*], Marcus Garvey denounced Dr. W. E. Dubois before a packed house in which there was not even standing room.

He gave a resume of the entire life of Dubois, cited his many commercial failures with his magazine and newspaper a few years ago. He described Dubois as the "White man Negro", who had never done anything yet to benefit Negroes, claiming, that while Dubois was a [friend?] of the upper 'tens' Negroes[1] he, Marcus Garvey, was along with the working class Negroes. This denunciation was a reply to Dubois' criticism of Garvey in the December and January issue of the "Crisis".

At Liberty Hall every song and poem is made up on the anti-White line. The songs that the choir sing are composed by Garvey's members and the wording of the songs is based on hate for the White race. Then each speaker follows the same line—hate of the White man—every night. In fact, it is almost impossible for those thousands of hero worshippers who attend Liberty Hall every night to be free of this un-American and damnable anti-White doctrine.

I learned that Garvey will be sending about six men to Liberia on or about the 23rd of January as a vanguard of his proposed headquarters over there. Respectfully,

P-138

[*Endorsements*] FILE G. F. R.
NOTED W. W. G. NOTED F. D. W.

DNA, RG 65, file BS 202600-667-11. TD. Stamped endorsements.

1. Du Bois had promoted the concept that a "talented tenth" among America's black population would be best suited for leadership. In his view, black progress would depend on the thorough education and training of this leadership class. (W.E.B. Du Bois, "The Talented Tenth," in Booker T. Washington et al., *The Negro Problem* [New York: James Pott, 1903], pp. 31–75.)

Meeting Announcement

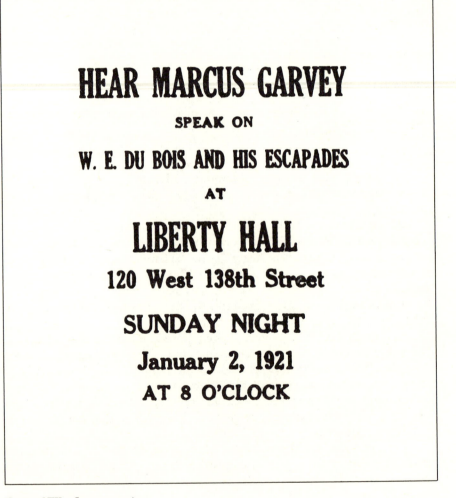

(*Source: NW*, 1 January 1921.)

Editorial Letter by Marcus Garvey

[[New York, Jan. 5, 1921]]

Fellowmen of the Negro Race, Greeting:

I have it in command from the Executive Council of the Universal Negro Improvement Association to convey to you the season's greeting.

That you were good enough to elect us out of the International Convention of August, 1920, as the leaders of the Negro people of the world, commissioning us to carry out your instructions and to initiate plans in your interests, it is for us to say that for the months that we have been in office we have done the best we possibly could. We have absolutely no reason to complain, because you as a people have also done the best you possibly could to propagate the doctrines of the Universal Negro Improvement Association throughout the world.

Nineteen hundred and twenty-one is set down to be a year of universal activity for the Negro peoples of the world, and we are trying through the organization of the Universal Negro Improvement Association to carry through a program that will mean the commercial, economic, industrial, political, social and educational emancipation of the race. We have planned on behalf of all the people to develop the great Republic of Liberia industrially and commercially. In the carrying out of this great plan we have arranged to repatriate Negroes from this Western Hemisphere as skilled mechanics, artisans and laborers. The program calls for a wholehearted support on the part of each and every member of the race, and we are now asking all those who have not yet helped the Universal Negro Improvement Association to carry through its programme to do so immediately. Originally it was planned to raise a loan of $2,000,000 from the members of the organization in two months to carry on the work, but owing to the general financial depression the council has decided to extend the time for the full subscription of the $2,000,000 to March 31, 1921, so as to enable each and every member of the association to pay in his or her subscription. . . .

As stated in my message of last week, the first batch of workm[e]n and mechanics are sailing from New York on or about the 20th inst. Arrangements have been made that the first transatlantic liner of the Black Star Line with passengers will sail on or about March 27, after which time there will be regularly fortnightly and weekly sailings. All those who desire to be settlers in Liberia, the land of our fathers, are requested to start immediately to make arrangements for so doing. Farmers, mechanics, artisans of all kinds and industrial and thrifty members of the race are needed to settle in Liberia. The mineral and agricultural resources of Liberia have never been touched, and it is our desire to develop them. Can we make up our minds for any better purpose than to settle in this great black Republic on the western coast of Africa?

Let Liberia be the boom of 1921! Let Africa be the cry of every Negro in the world, and with such as our object we feel sure that the next twelve months will find the Negro people so prosperous as to demand the respect of all other races and nations. We as a people lost confidence and hope in ourselves for centuries, but through the efforts of the Universal Negro Improvement Association the door of opportunity is opened for every Negro born to the world. There is now absolutely no cause for any Negro to lose hope and confidence in himself.

Let us concentrate on the great plan of building Liberia, helping the people of Liberia and ourselves to become a power in the world. Let us take pattern of the other races of the world who for centuries were in a similar position to us today, but who have made good their own strivings. Let us imitate them, and I feel sure that in a few years the Negro will have absolutely no cause not to feel proud of himself.

I urgently appeal to the members of the Universal Negro Improvement Association to support this great organization. Harken not to what the critics say. Criticism within and criticism without must be expected. Negroes should learn to appreciate criticism. Criticism is a part of human nature. . . .
Yours fraternally,

MARCUS GARVEY

Garvey v. *United States*, no. 8317, Ct. App., 2d Cir., 2 February 1925, government exhibit no. 45. Original headlines omitted.

Report by Special Agent P-138

New York City 1-7-21

IN RE NEGRO ACTIVITIES.

Today [*3 January*] I visited MARCUS GARVEY's office and had about a half hour talk with him. I found him busy signing checks, he explaining to me that he is getting ready to leave for a two weeks trip in the West.

I have reason to believe that MARCUS GARVEY is getting ready to leave for M[o]nrovia, Liberia, West Africa, sometime this month.

During the course of our conversation he said that as soon as he returns from his two weeks western trip, he will be leaving the country on a secret foreign trip. At Liberty Hall last evening he said to the large audience "two weeks from this I shall suddenly disappear from you for six or seven weeks, you won't hear from me during that time, but don't be alarmed because we Negroes will have to adopt the system of underground workings like De Valera and other white leaders." On the street yesterday, CRICHLOW, one of Garvey's official shorthand reporters, told me confidentially that he and a few others were elected by Garvey to sail for Africa about January 23d. G. O.

Marke, Garvey's Deputy Potentate, a native African, who lives in Garvey's apartment, told me that he will sail for Africa about the 23d. I am endeavoring to find out what Garvey's schemes are in connection with this secret trip.

P-138

[*Endorsements*] NOTED F. D. W.
NOTED W. W. G. FILE G. F. R.

DNA, RG 65, file BS 202600-667-16X. TD. Stamped endorsements.

Report by Special Agent J. G. Tucker

[*New York*] JANUARY 8, 1921

"BLACK STAR LINE"

On board the S.S. "Korona" there were recently found several small circulars which bore the caption "The Africans Black Star Spangled Banner", which the circular states is to be sung to the tune of America's battle hymn. The "hymn" mentions the Black Star Line and Marcus Garvey's ideas and is altogether a laudation of Marcus Garvey. The circular states that the "hymn" was composed by Rev. F. ALEXANDER PURCELL, B.A. . . .

J. G. TUCKER

DNA, RG 65, file BS 202600-33-140. TD.

Report by Special Agent P-138

New York City 1/10/21

(1) Garvey has left the City today [*4 January*] on a western trip. (2) This Chaplain General Rev. McGuire, a rabid agitator, is preparing to sail for Havana, Cuba on Friday. (3) Garvey is preparing to send about twelve (12) anti-White propagandists to Africa, Liberia and other points between now and the 23rd of January. These men, so as to avoid the suspicion of the American and British Consuls, will be travelling under assumed names and different nationality. Some will be going as Haitian, Brazilian, Cuban and under other nationality than that which they actually are. They are preparing to outwit the scrutiny of the authorities here, as they feel strong opposition is d[irect]ed aga[in]st Garvey and his movement. I learned the above from Rev. Helliger,[1] one of Garvey's officials and the master planner of the s[ch]eme for the secret departure of these propagandists. We had lunch together at a restaurant today and he outlined the entire scheme to me. He is the man who is arranging for their passages by way of Spain and on Spanish ships. This

fellow has travelled nearly all over the world and is well up and conversant with world conditions. Rev. Helliger is a Negro preacher and was once employed as head of the Liberian state schools in Monrovia, Liberia, West Africa. He is a graduate of a London university. Respectfully,

P-138

[*Endorsements*] FILE G. F. R.
NOTED W. W. G. NOTED F. D. W.

DNA, RG 65, file BS 198940-52X. TD. Stamped endorsements.

1. Probably a reference to Francis Wilcom Ellegor.

O. M. Thompson to Leo Healy

[*New York*] January 11th, 1921

Dear Sir:

Answering your letter of January 10th, we regret very much to learn of Mr. Harriss' attitude and have asked Mr. Nolan to get his address from you and cable him.

If only Mr. Harriss would permit us to resurrect ourselves by sending out one of the boats, we would be able to create interest for the purchasing of stock and to repair the "Yarmouth."

We trust the reply through Mr. Nolan will be favorable to our plans.

In the meantime, beg to remain, Yours very truly,

BLACK STAR LINE, INC.
O. M. Thompson
Vice President

Garvey v. *United States*, no. 8317, Ct. App., 2d Cir., 2 February 1925, government exhibit no. 22.

William L. Hurley to J. Edgar Hoover

WASHINGTON January 11, 1921

Dear Mr. Hoover:

With reference to your letters to me of December 14, 1920, and January 4, 1921, requesting information covering the movements of Marcus Garvey, I would advise you that I have recently received a report from an agent of this Department at Montreal in which it is stated that one Fred Potter, a socalled captain or leader of the Baggage Porters in the Canadian Pacific Railway Station at Montreal, is Garvey's righthand man; that he receives all of Garvey's mail, does all of his advertising, and is cognizant of all of Mr. Garvey's connections. In answer to an inquiry made by the agent as to where Potter could be found, he was advised that this important personage was on special duty "for the officers upstairs, and they send him all over the country. He runs down to New York a lot."

There is not a doubt in the world but that Garvey and possibly Doctor Furnass may have been present in Montreal at the time of this investigation which was instituted about the middle of December, /but/ a close examination of all of the Montreal papers for a week preceeding that time failed to show any public appearances of such persons, and furthermore, if it be true that they are covered up by the Canadian Pacific officials in furtherance of a plan involving Garvey propaganda through Pullman car porters running into the United States, it would not be necessary to hold meetings or to attract public attention, as all of the negroes in and around this section are completely under the control of the Canadian Pacific Railway.

In an investigation of this kind a too inquisitive white man would immediately become an object of suspicion and especially if recognized as from the United States.

It would therefore, seem necessary, if investigations are to be pursued, to employ a trustworthy negro in the furtherance of all investigations along these lines. /Can you arrange for this?/

Any information which may come to my attention will be promptly communicated to you. Very truly yours,

W. L. HURLEY

[*Handwritten endorsement*] Sent Hurley
1/17/21 G. F. R.
[*Stamped endorsement*] NOTED F. D. W.

DNA, RG 65, file BS 198940-59. TLS, recipient's copy. Handwritten corrections.

Rev. C. S. Smith to the Editor, *World's Work*

[[Detroit, Michigan January 14, 192[1]]]

To the Editor of the World's Work:

In your issue of December, 1920, there appeared an illustrated article by Truman Hughes Talley under the caption of "Marcus Garvey—The Negro Moses?" It is not my purpose to deal with the article *per se*, which at the best is but a spectacular write-up of an ephemeral show, for the material of which the writer evidently drew largely on his imagination. I wish to rivet your attention on the editorial note leading to the article in which, among other things, you said, "he (Marcus Garvey) is the best point at which to study what is going on inside the heads of the ten million colored people in the

United States." In that statement you have unwittingly discredited the intelligence and common-sense of the American colored people. Marcus Garvey does not interpret the thoughts of 1 per cent. of colored Americans. To my knowledge, there is only one of that group, of whom it can be said that he is in any sense a national character, who is numbered among the followers of Marcus Garvey, namely, John E. Bruce, of Yonkers, N.Y., whose *no[m] de plume* is "Bruce Grit."[1]

Marcus Garvey is the Moses (?) of a group of West Indians, resident in and around Harlem, a section of New York City, of whom there are thousands; and, in this instance, it is a West Indian leading West Indians. In more than an hour's interview which I had with Marcus Garvey in my home less than three years ago, I sought to impress on him that he had started out to follow a will-o'-the-wisp, particularly as it related to an African Empire on the basis of the plan which he unfolded to me.

Mr. Garvey prates about Liberia as if it were "No Man's Land," to be seized and exploited by any and everybody. My knowledge gained during two visits to that Republic does not justify any such conclusion. However, on this point, I beg to refer all who may desire information to Dr. Ernest Lyon,[2] Baltimore, Md., the American Consul-General for Liberia.

C. S. SMITH

Printed in *World's Work* 41, no. 5 (March 1921). Original headline omitted.

1. John E. Bruce answered Bishop Smith's charges in his *Negro World* columns of 26 March and 2 April 1921. For other responses to Bishop Smith's letter by supporters of Garvey, see James N. Lowe, "Bishop Smith and Garvey—Bishop Smith's Attack on Garvey Analyzed and Answered," *NW*, 19 March 1921; James D. Brooks, "Negro Leadership of America and Elsewhere," *NW*, 9 April 1921; and James G. Horsford, "Bishop Smith Ably Answered by Puerto Rican," *NW*, 30 April 1921.

2. Ernest A. Lyon (1860–1938), Liberian consul general to the United States, was born in Belize, British Honduras. Educated and naturalized in the United States, he became pastor of the John Wesley Church in Baltimore, in 1901; in this capacity he founded the Maryland Industrial and Agricultural Institution of Colored Youths. In 1903 he was appointed minister to Liberia by President Roosevelt, a position he held until 1911. While serving in Liberia, Lyon helped to establish the New York–Liberia steamship line, and following his return to the United States, he served as Liberian consul general in Washington, D.C., until his retirement in 1926 (*WWCA*; *Negroes in Public Affairs and Government* [Yonkers, N.Y.: Educational Heritage, 1966]).

Report of Marcus Garvey's Speeches in Cleveland

[15 January 1921]

. . . GARVEY VISITS US AND WINS CROWDS

Marcus Garvey, the New York "whirlwind" visited the local division of the Universal Negro Improvement Association last week, making several addresses in behalf of his ventures.

Meetings were held at Lane Metropolitan C.M.E. Church Friday and Saturday nights and on Sunday [*9 January*] at Spira Hall, East 38 and Scovill avenues.

"The Back to Africa" movement was given a boost in all the Garvey speeches, and from evidences of approbation given by the hand-clapping at the meetings, it can be hazarded that "the seed fell on good ground."

Whatever may be said of Garvey by his detractors, one must admit that the man [h]as a wonderful personality and "bubbles over" with the elements of leadership. This assertion will be better digested when it is understood that hundreds of people paid an admission of fifty cents to be given an opportunity to enter the hall where Garvey was endeavoring to sell stock in the Black Star Line. And what's more, the pilgrims to the Garvey shrine bought freely of the investment, when they were loosed from under the influence of his spell-binding oratory. The masses are with Garvey. It is a fact that cannot be denied.

Whatever becomes of his schemes for conquering Africa and the like, it is a certainty that at the present time his worshippers believe him capable of doing all that he says.

Garvey and his aides left for Detroit Monday morning.

Printed in the *Cleveland Advocate*, 15 January 1921; reprinted in *NW*, 26 February 1921.

Report by Bureau Agent H. J. Lenon

Pittsburgh, Pa. 1/18/21

MARCUS GARVEY, PRESIDENT, UNIVERSAL NEGRO
IMPROVEMENT ASSOCIATION

The following report received here from a confidential source, although belated and in addition may have reached you through other channels, is passed on to assure having it on record and further because of the assertion by GARVEY contained in the seventh line[1] of the third paragraph:—

"Philadelphia, Pa.

"This evening I attended a farewell mass meeting given to Marcus Garvey at Musical Fund Hall, 6th and Locust Sts., Philadelphia[.]

["]The early part of the evening was taken up by juvenile speakers of the Universal Negro Improvement Association. Many older persons also spoke on the doctrines of the U.N.I.A.

["]At nine o'clock Garvey arrived accompanied by what they call his secret service legion. He began his address by saying: "I am here tonight to say good-bye to Philadelphia. I am going away for months. I start for the West Indies and Central America, then for Africa. I am about to put into operation the plans laid at the August Convention in New York, namely, the construction and probably the conquest of Africa. *We are sending men there from New York, January 20th, 1921.* The time has come to cease talking and do something. This nation must be built between 1921 and 192[2]. We are planning to accommodate 1,000,000. The U.N.I.A. is here to stay until all negroes have liberty or all have passed away. Do not question my being away as I am about to bring you success. Be ever ready as the call may come at any time.

"I have at my command statistics that prove the British Empire is about to go bankrupt. This is something we have been waiting for for a long time. If they are in that condition and 2,000,000 former soldiers who are out of work and who will positively never fight for England again—do you understand what I mean? Get together from now on and be ready to get into Africa, build battleships and raise armies, after we get a good foothold in Africa, which must positively be in the next twelve months. I am very well posted on foreign internal conditions and I know that the time is near for concerted action.

"They said that they are going to keep me out of Africa. They said they were going to keep De Valera out of Ireland, but he is there, I will be in Africa also, but I will not tell my mother how I am going to get there, so do not ask me.

"In two years I predict we will have ten to fifteen million negroes ready for action in Africa. They will tell you while I am away that Garvey is a bad man. Reply [']that for once I am satisfied to follow a bad man.['] I am positive that the interpretation in the Bible—"Eth[i]opia shall stretch forth her hand"—the time is nigh. I have gone so far in this movement I cannot turn back. When the bugle sounds for the final conflict I expect to be there and not to be ninety years old either. No human agency can stop the U.N.I.A. now. Liberia offers thirty acres to every negro who lands in Africa. When I get in the West Indies I expect the negro there to be ready to a single call. That will be my final visit there. So buy Black Star Line bonds and help float the Liberian Loan so we will have millions of dollars to help this movement. I will not lead you into unnecessary danger. Remember my command should be your pleasure. Good-bye".

H. J. LENON

[*Endorsements*] NOTED W. W. G.
NOTED F. D. W. FILE G. F. R.

DNA, RG 65, file BS 198940. TD. Stamped endorsements.

　　1. The "assertion by Garvey," originally from the third paragraph, is rendered in italics.

Marcus Garvey to Gabriel M. Johnson

New York, U.S.A. January 18, 1921

May it please your Highness:—

By this letter you will be informed that the Executive Council has decided to take a practical step in carrying out their construction plan for Liberia, and for that reason they have decided that His Highness the Supreme Deputy should take up his residence along with you in the Capital City of Monrovia. His Highness sailed on the 22nd inst., from New York for Monrovia via Cadiz, Spain, in company with Mr. Cyril A. Crichlow, who is appointed resident Commissaire and Secretary to our Headquarters in Liberia, Mr. Israel Mc[L]eod, Surveyor General, Mr. A. N. Henry, Minister of Agriculture, Mr. R. Jemott,[1] Builder and Director of Public Works, Mr. F. P. Lawrence, Pharmacist, Mr. Crichlow will be in charge of the Commissariat. That is[,] he will be responsible to the Executive Council for the business correspondence and the proper accounting for the receipts and disbursements of moneys under your supervision. Mr. Crichlow shall pay to the men employed their salaries and receive such vouchers, and take the proper records for business purposes. All moneys of the Universal Negro Improvement Association shall, under your instructions be lodged in the most responsible bank in Monrovia in the name of the Universal Negro Improvement Association and said Crichlow, and in your absence that of Mr. G. O. Marke. You will therefore have a letter written to the Bank conveying that much information. Mr. Crichlow, the Secretary, shall not be at liberty to draw any moneys from the Bank, without your signature, and in your absence that of Mr. Marke's. That Mr. Crichlow shall not employ any help or incur any expenses without your approval, and in your absence that of Mr. Marke. That the men who are sent out to work will be continuously employed and shall put in nine or ten hours work every day. Their salaries are as follows: Mr. Crichlow, $2500, and residence, at the Commissariat. Mr. Israel McLeod $1000. Mr. A. J. Henry $1000. Mr. R. Jemott $1500. Mr. F. P. Lawrence $1000. [W]ith the exception of Mr. Crichlow all the other men will have to find their own lodgings. His Highness Hon. G. O. Marke will also live at the Commissariat. We are asking that you interview the Government immediately for the purpose of securing from them a concession in land in Monrovia or near by Monrovia for the purpose of starting agricultural work. We would like Mr. Henry, Minister of Agriculture [to] start immediately planting for the earliest crop, so as to be able to take care of the other workmen, who will be sent out in March and April, and also to enable Mr. Jemmott to start putting up buildings to accommodate the other workmen who will be sent to you. Try to get as large a concession as possible. If we can succeed in getting 1000 acres of land in any part of Liberia we could start a township of our own. Try to use your good offices with President King, in getting this concession.

We will cable the necessary amount of money on a requisition to meet the progress of the work initiated by the men.

Please send us a report of conditions up to date.

With very best wishes, I have the honor to be Your highness obedient servant,

UNIVERSAL NEGRO IMP. ASSN
MARCUS GARVEY
Pres. Gen.

DNA, RG 65, file BS-198940-213. TL, transcript.

1. Rupert Jemmott (1893–1981) was born in Barbados, BWI; in 1914 he left Barbados for Panama, where he was a construction worker for the Panama Canal project. He served with the British army in Canada during World War I; in 1918 he traveled to Boston, later arriving in Harlem. Job opportunities in Detroit soon led him to leave New York temporarily, but in early 1920 he returned to Harlem and joined the Garvey movement. Jemmott received diplomas from the Extension Division of the Chicago Technical College and from the American Technical Society of Chicago in April and May 1920. He was trained in building construction and estimating, skills that the UNIA needed for its Liberian work. In 1921 the UNIA chose Jemmott out of twenty-three applicants for the position of building engineer on its six-man Liberian team. Although he ended his service for the UNIA after six months, Jemmott remained in Liberia for an additional sixteen months, returning to the United States in 1923 (Robert A. Hill, interview with Rupert Jemmott, Patchoque, Long Island, 9 November 1978).

Report by Bureau Agent Adrian L. Potter

Springfield, Mass. Jan. 18, 1921

UNIVERSAL NEGRO IMPROVEMENT ASSOCIATION
(SPRINGFIELD, MASS.)[1] MASS MEETING: SPEAKERS: W. W.
SIMONDS; MR. THOMAS MARION; COL. ADRI[A]N JOHNSON;
DR. H. W. DU BISSETTE.

Jan. 14th, evening at Liberty Hall a mass meeting for negroes was held. The meeting had not been publicly advertised. [Agent] attended in company with Agent V. J. Raffney[.] W. W. Simonds of 72 Congress st., presided, and announced that at a secret meeting of the Springfield Division he had been elected president; that he was proud of the honor conferred and intended to devote his time to furtherance of interests of the organization, and predicted that: "We are going to win. The colored race of people are going to be on top. We are going to fight".

Thomas Harten (introduced by Simonds as "Rev. Dr. Harten[,] president of the Division of Cambridge, Mass.") delivered a speech and among his statements said: "I asked thousands of Negroes to buy Liberty bonds during the world war, but I will answer the general roll before I do such a thing again in [the] coming war with Japan. I feel like banding my race together, join the Japanese and advance on the Mason and Dixon line and mop up the devilish 'crackers' down there. We are used but little better here in the North". He urged that colored men and women join the association and stated that the Cambridge and Boston Division were greatly prosperous in numbers and finances. Dr. Du Bissette[,] a Dentist of North st., spoke briefly urging that Negroes discuss their affairs in regular and secret meeting. He urged that Negroes [pr]esent spread the "glad tidings" among acquaintances to the end that a large attendance might be had on Sunday afternoon Jan. 18 mass-meeting.

Johnson introduced by Simonds as Colonel in the African Legion speaking with a French accent and interjecting into his remarks several French phrases stated that it was a joke to allow one fifth of the world's population to control the colored four fifths. "This would not be so if we had racial or class consciousness," he shouted. "This country, what does it give you?" he asked, and continued, "We colored men can [n]ever become president of the United States! Why are you so blind? We must unite financially, socially, economically and then physically and make the whites respect our race. We must become a unit and if we fail to force recognition in America we shall remove to Africa. We must fight to make the world safe for Negroes['] democracy." The speaker eulogized Marcus Garvey[,] "that man of mystery from the island of the sea," and declared that Garvey had organized seven million Negroes throughout the world who would be loyal to the end. "We have today three steamships on the seas. Our flag is the red[,] black and green—red for the blood we have and may shed; black—for our color[']s distinction, and green representing the foliage of our native land in tropic climes." He pleaded for a large attendance at Sunday's meeting. About forty persons joined the association.

Sunday afternoon Jan. 15th, a mass meeting of negroes was held in Liberty hal[l] and about 450 Negroes attended. Simonds presided and rehashed remarks [o]f previous [date], concluding by saying "when we get together by ourselves in secret meeting we enjoy full Liberty; then we can talk and explain things that you don't get here.["] He announced that new officers could be chosen anytime and said "I am not anxious to be a martyr but so help me God I will do my best until the new despised colored race reigns supreme throughout the world." "Colonel" Johnson then introduced himself saying "I represent Marcus Garvey and the great African Legion known in some localities as the Negroes Universal Improvement Association and in some localities by other names.["] He denounced the white race, praised Japan and predicted war between this country and Japan and declared that Negroes should know but one flag, red, black and green, now flying on the West and East coasts of Africa where he predicted there is soon to be "one hell of a time[.]" He declared that Africans once dominated in world affairs and would, assisted by peoples of color, dominate, again. He stated divisions of the U.N.I.A. have been established throughout the United States and Canada; in South America, Mexico, London, Paris, Tokio, Calcutta, east, west, north, and south Africa and islands of the sea. He gave a lurid and horrible word picture of the slave-trade in various countries of the world and especially as relating to the United States. He declared every diamond worn by white millionaires and the[ir] mistresses belonged to the black men of Africa[.] "Where are three million of organized workers of the white race who will aid us when the time comes[?]" he cried and then applause was noisy. He stated that all colored races were of one mind save possibly some of the "high yellows" or "seal gray" Chinese who consider themselves white. "[We] have powerful people of influence working in our behalf[,] Madam Henrietta Davis is in Washington, D.C. and she is with us and for us. She knows all that transpires," he asserted and urging his hearers to join the movement at once concluded by saying[,] "On a bloody field of battle somewhere someday, sometime we will win our Liberty!"

About 75 signed cards before the meeting adjourned.

Agents of this office noted that few of the respectable Negroes of the city were in attendance.

Jan. 19th, Agent's investigation shows that Simonds is a person of low-character[,] unemployed and an associate of Russians and Jews known to be identified with radical organizations. Simond[s] has stated that he is to go to New York city for instructions and is to then travel in the South as an organizer for the U.N.I.A.

[Du] Bissette is a recent arrival in this city, resides with Edward LeCount[,] an alien negro tailor of 178 Sharon, a close associate of persons known to be radicals. Survey of mail received by Simonds[,] also known as Manuel Simons, Du Bissette and LeCount requested at P.O. this date.

Case continued.

ADRIAN L. POTTER

[*Endorsements*] J. E. H.
FILE NOTED F. D. W. NOTED W. W. G.

DNA, RG 65, file BS 202600-824-1. TD. Stamped endorsements.

1. The Springfield, Mass., division of the UNIA, with a reported membership of 1,204 in May 1921, appears to have had some connection with the Socialist movement in that city. Dr. Hyacinthe Du Bissette, the leading figure in the division, attended a meeting of the Russian Progressive Club in April 1921, and a few weeks later a UNIA meeting was held at the club's headquarters, at which members were urged to attend a forthcoming Socialist rally. On 16 June the division also participated in an unemployed workers' parade. Du Bissette aroused the suspicion of the Bureau of Investigation by meeting regularly with a Japanese-Hawaiian student suspected of radical activities at the local YMCA college. (DNA, RG 65, files BS 202600-22-65; BS 202600-1804-2X).

Raymond Sheldon to the Director, Military Intelligence Division

GOVERNOR'S ISLAND, NEW YORK CITY
January 21, 1921

From: Assistant Chief of Staff for Military Intelligence.
To: Director, Military Intelligence Division.
Subject: Negro Activities. . . .

2.   The editor of the "Crusader", Cyril V. Briggs, volunteered the information that the racial question, from a radical point of view, was progressing very favorably. The Universal Negro Improvement Association, according to his statements, has a membership at the present time of approximately 600,000, and, while not as radical as he would wish, still they are doing good work. He stated that Marcus Garvey, who is the president-general of this association, while trying hard to make a perfect ass of himself, nevertheless had done a lot of work indirectly inasmuch as he had aroused the colored population out of their state of dormancy to the fact that they control considerable amount of power if solidarity could be accomplished among the various factions.

3.   When asked if he knew anything about a salary supposed to have been paid Garvey as provisional president of the Republic of Africa, he stated that it had been contemplated to pay him a certain salary which would have been raised by popular subscription, but as far as he knew the project had not been carried out. However, he stated that Marcus Garvey received a very good income from the publication called "The Negro World" which had a circulation at the present time of about 45,000, and also as president of the Black Star Steamship Line. . . .

RAYMOND SHELDON

[*Endorsement*] A. C. DUNNE M.I.4

DNA, RG 165, file 10218-412-50. TLS, recipient's copy. Stamped endorsement.

Sir James Willcocks, Governor General of Bermuda, to the British Secretary of State for the Colonies

[*Hamilton, Bermuda*] 26th January 1921

With reference to your Secret despatch of August 23rd[1] a party of the leaders of the negroes association is advertised to leave New York 30th instant in a Black Star Line vessel visiting American ports in West Indies and Cuba Central America as well as Bermuda and Jamaica.

If the party should include official representatives of the Association I propose to prohibit their landing under the Government [C]ontrol Act 1919 since the Association is openly revolutionary as is shown by their charter signed in New York last August, Addressed to Secretary of State for the Colonies[2] copy sent to Governor of Jamaica[3] for information.

WILLCOCKS[4]

[*Endorsement*] GOV/26426/20

PRO, CO 318/363. TG (paraphrased).

1. On 23 August 1920 the secretary of state for the colonies transmitted to the governors of the various West Indian colonies copies of a dispatch received from the governor of British Honduras, who, on 10 May 1920, reported about the circulation of the *NW* and the activities of the UNIA in that territory. In his dispatch, the governor of British Honduras stated: "It is possible that the whole movement underlying the Universal Negro Association and African Communities League was originated by German propaganda and money, and probably is still supported by German Americans. On this point it seems to me that His Majesty's Ambassador at Washington should be able to make enquiry and give advice" (PRO, CO 318/354). In turn, the British ambassador at Washington, D.C., was sent the copies of the correspondence on 25 August 1920, with the instruction that he was to "continue to report from time to time on the negro movement in the U.S., especially in so far as it affects the West Indies" (PRO, FO 371/4567).

2. Winston Churchill acknowledged receipt of the telegram on 16 February 1921; the following day copies of both the telegram and Churchill's reply were sent to the Foreign Office, in keeping with a Foreign Office request of October 1920 that the Colonial Office keep it informed of Garvey's activities (PRO, FO 115/2690). In turn, copies were also forwarded to the British ambassador in Washington, D.C. While one Foreign Office official viewed the UNIA as "an I.W.W. organization," another noted that "the 'Nation' or 'New Republic' may talk if such exclusion takes place." At the same time, it was noted that "the C. O. are very cautious. They do not say whether they approve the Governor's action or not" (PRO, FO 371/5684).

3. On 18 January 1921 the governor of Jamaica's private secretary notified the Jamaican colonial secretary of the following: "A Cable Message has been received from the District Intelligence Officer, Bermuda, through the Government of Bermuda, to the effect that an announcement has appeared in the 'Negro World' that the Black Star Liner 'Antonio Maceo' leaves New York on or about the 23rd January and will visit the following places: Bermuda; Havana, Cuba; Port au Prince, Hayti; Kingston, Jamaica; Colon, Republic of Panama" (JA, CSO 1B, file 1169).

4. Gen. Sir James Willcocks (1857–1926) was governor of Bermuda from 1917 to 1922; he was also the author of *From Kabul to Kumasi* (London: John Murray, 1904); *With the Indians in France* (London: Constable, 1920); and *The Romance of Soldiering and Sport* (London: Cassell, 1925) (*WWW*).

Wilford H. Smith to Arthur B. Spingarn

New York, January 27th, 1921

Dear Mr. Spingarn:—[1]

Replying to your favor of the 21st inst., in the case of Black Star Line, Inc. vs. Dubois and N.A.A.C.P., I am glad to find that there is a disposition on the part of the publishers of the "Crisis" to make a retraction and thereby to dispose of the case now pending.[2]

I submitted your letter to the President of the Black Star Line Co. and he is not satisfied with the precise form of the retraction proposed in your letter. He requests me to submit instead the following working of the retraction:—

> Under the caption of "Marcus Garvey" we published in our December and January Numbers, two articles which pertained to a criticism of the Black Star Line Steamship Corporation. We are sorry that certain statements were made which might be construed as a reflection upon the business management of the said Black Star Line. Our reference to the Steamship "Yarmouth" being a wooden ship, is incorrect, as the Yarmouth is in truth a steel vessel, and it was not our intention in any way to embarrass this corporation in its successful business and operations.

If your clients can see their way clear to publish the retraction in the language above stated, it would be very pleasing to the Black Star Line management, and we would be very glad to discontinue the action without costs. Kindly advise me if the retraction will be made as proposed in this letter. Very respectfully

WILFORD H. SMITH
Counsel-General

MU, WEBDB, reel 10, frame 748. TLS, transcript.

1. Arthur Barnett Spingarn (1878–1971), a lawyer, was born in New York City and educated at Columbia University. Arthur Spingarn and his brother, Joel Spingarn, were among the most important whites in the leadership of the NAACP. They joined in 1910, and Arthur Spingarn headed the NAACP's Legal Committee until 1939. Both were active in early antilynching cases and suits challenging discrimination in public accommodations. In 1939 when Joel Spingarn died, Arthur Spingarn succeeded him as president of the NAACP (Charles Flint Kellogg, *NAACP: A History of the National Association for the Advancement of Colored People* [Baltimore: Johns Hopkins University Press, 1967], pp. 61–62, 123; B. Joyce Ross, *J. E. Spingarn and the Rise of the NAACP, 1911–1939* [New York: Atheneum, 1972], pp. 57–58).

2. *Black Star Line* v. *W. E. B. Du Bois and NAACP*, no. 1944, New York State Supreme Court, 1 January 1921. The damages asked for were $100,000; on 25 January, however, the action was discontinued. The BSL Corp. brought suit because of the two articles entitled "Marcus Garvey," published in the December 1920 and January 1921 issues of *Crisis*. Garvey particularly objected to the following statement: "The *Yarmouth* is a wooden steamer of 1,452 gross tons, built in 1887. It is old and unseaworthy; it came near sinking a year ago and it has cost a great deal for repairs" (W. E. B. Du Bois, "Marcus Garvey," *Crisis* 21, no. 3 [January 1921]: 112–113).

O. M. Thompson to Leo Healy

[*New York*] January 28th, 1921

Dear Sir:

This serves to acknowledge receipt of your esteemed letter of January 25th, showing a balance of $32,546.00 due on the purchase price of the "Yarmouth."

Under the present ratio of income, the promise of $500 a week will be a strain but please be assured that you will receive this amount even though the "Yarmouth" is a hopeless proposition without the expenditure of $150,000.00 worth of repairs.

We hesitated replying to your letter sooner because our Mr. Garvey was away, he has read and appreciates your arbitration and success in getting your clients' sanction to the rate of $500.00 per week. In order to meet the payments promptly he has arranged for a stock selling tour of the Islands and possibly South America which supplies the confidence expressed to you in making these payments weekly.

We shall send you a check on Monday for $500.00.

In the meantime, with much gratitude for your several courtesies, [I] beg to remain, Yours very truly,

BLACK STAR LINE, INC.
O. M. THOMPSON
Vice President

Garvey v. *United States*, no. 8317, Ct. App., 2d Cir., 2 February 1925, government exhibit no. 23.

Report by Special Agent P-138

New York City 1/28/21

IN RE: NEGRO ACTIVITIES

G. O. MARKE, Garvey's Deputy Potentate, a [nat]ive African, called on me today [*27 January*] and during our conversation I learned from him that he (Marke) and about six or seven other Garvey propagandists will sail for Liberia on a Spanish ship via Spain on Feb. 1st.

This route was chosen so as to outwit the British authorities. Marke is one of Garvey's highest officers.

He also informed me authoritatively that Garvey has planned to go on a propaganda trip to the West Indies. He will sail on his own ship the S.S. "Kanaw[h]a".

Marke said that there were a lot responding to Garvey's invitation for men to go to Liberia. The poor dupes think that there will be a ship to take them free. Some are selling their belongings in anticipation of this fake trip. Respectfully

P-138

[*Endorsements*] NOTED W. W. G.
FILE G. F. R. NOTED F. D. W.

DNA, RG 65, file BS 198940-7XX. TD. Stamped endorsements.

Madarikan Deniyi to the *Richmond Planet*

New York, January 29 [1921]

LIBERIAN LIBERTY LOAN

The greatest money making scheme ever attempted by any black man in the United States is the latest "Liberian Liberty Bond," which was signed by Marcus Garvey and the Universal Negro Improvement Association in New York City a few months ago, without any seal of Liberian Government on it. President King and the Legislatures in Liberia, West Africa[,] did not authorize Marcus Garvey to sell such a bond to poor and needy people in the United States and Canada. Many ignorant Negroes are selling their farms and houses in Canada to buy this 'Liberian Bond' and redeem Africa when the president of the Universal Negro Improvement Association himself couldn't redeem the Negroes in British West Indies, who are getting eighteen cents a day for hard labor. Some of the American and West Indies Negroes had bought lots of bonds [in?] the United State[s] but only God knows when Marcus Garvey and the Universal Negro Improvement will be able to pay those poor and needy people back their money because the Liberian Government is not responsible for this money making scheme of Marcus Garvey according to my investigation through secret messages from West Africa.

President King and the Legislatures in Liberia are not ignorant Negroes because they were educated in the best colleges and universities in Europe and America. They studied the African, European and American laws and know how to use them to improve the black Republic of Liberia better than Marcus Garvey who has never traveled in any part of Africa to study the condition in that continent. I do not believe that they will depend on the poor and needy Negroes in America to loan their money to the Liberian Government. It is true that Gabriel Johnson, the Mayor of Monrovia, Liberia, West Africa[,] was elected as Potentate of the U.N.I.A. in New York city last August 1920 but it would be impossible for him to authorize Marcus Garvey to sell such a Liberian Liberty bond to the Negroes in the United States and Canada without the consent of President King and the Legislatures. I discovered through my investigation in New York city that the U.N.I.A. is to

loan the Liberian Government two million dollars. ($2,000,000.) This money
is to be used for the purpose of building beautiful houses, streets[,] railroads[,]
telegraph lines, subways, trolley cars[,] automobile factories, schools[,] machine shops, colleges[,] electric plants, cablegram lines, universities and ammunition factories to kill all the white people in Liberia.

To my great surprise, I read in some of the American newspapers that
Marcus Garvey was born at St. Ann, Jamaica, British West Indies[,] about 1885.
How can he from the sugar cane plantation of these islands be able to redeem
Africa and establish [a] new black republic for the U.N.I.A. in Liberia, West
Africa? Will the President and Legislatures stand for such conspiracy in
Liberia? I should say no because they won't stand for the unbridled audacity of
this Marcus Garvey. The greatest trouble for him and his followers is that they
talk too much. That's why lots of Negroes lost their good positions in New
York [o]n account of Garvey's conspiracy but it seems to me that Marcus
Garvey is sugering for [*suffering from*?] cerebral spinal [men]inigitis, and needs
a specialist to examine his cranium cavity.

It has been published and advertised in the Negro World that the Black
Star Line Steamship corporation would send a ship to Liberia this January
1921 but January is almost gone and the steamship Yarmouth is still broke
down at the dry dock in New York. When will this corporation quit using
the mails to defraud poor and needy people in Africa by selling them their
shares? I am not opposing the American and West Indies Negroes for having
their own ships to carry people to Africa but will oppose any steamship
corporation in America that will use the mails to deceive the natives in
Africa. Therefore I will advise the natives in Africa not [to] buy any more
shares in the Black Star Line unless Marcus Garvey[,] president of the
corporation[,] can prove to them that he bought and paid for the steamship
Yarmouth. This ship [is] an old wooden ship and too old to [m]ake any safe
voyage from New York city to Liberia, West Africa on [the] high seas. The
Black Star Line [S]teamship corporation had sold enough shares and
Liberian Liberty bonds to lots of Negroes in Africa, America and Canada to
buy a large steel ship instead of using the peoples' money to pay for a wooden
ship about 40 years old on installment plan from the white people. [It is] a
shame for Marcus Garvey and the U.N.I.A. to be using the name of the
Liberian government.

The "Free African Movement" is another problem to be solved but I did
solve it at Liberty Hall on West 135th street, New York city in August 1[2?],
1920[,] having stopped Marcus Garvey from electing himself as President of
Africa and rule 400,000,000 black people of the world.[1] Therefore the
members of the U.N.I.A. elected him without any vote from the black kings,
chiefs and presidents in Africa as Provisional President of the U.N.I.A. in
Africa and America. He also made the correct statements to his followers
after reading my article in the New York Times of August 15, 192[0] that he
was not elected to rule the natives in Africa or dictate to any of the African
leaders in that great continent. If he had not obeyed me, I could have put him

in Federal prison through the help of the American post office inspectors and detectives for his conspiracy and ambitious scheme of getting rich quick. But it is not too late yet for the Federal authorities to investigate the 'voodoo' power of Marcus Garvey. Many stockholders in the Black Star Line Steamship corporation are too scared to demand their money from the corporation, thinking that Marcus Garvey would '[v]oodoo' them with his 'rabbit foot' in the office. One of the Negro Captains went to the Black Star Line office [a] few months ago to demand his money after bringing the steamship Kanaw[h]a back to New York city from Norfolk, Va., but somebody had to draw a gun on him in Garvey's office instead of a rabbit foot. That's the kind of man who is planning to redeem Africa in this New Year 1921. If I were the Captain I could have reported the matter to Mayor Hylan[2] and the policemen in New York because it is against the Sullivan law in New York State for any white or colored person to draw a loaded gun on another person in his office. I hope the Negroes will take notice of this principal fact because there will be a race riot and revolutional war in Africa if any of Garvey's followers is to draw a loaded gun on the natives in Liberia, West Africa.

How can Marcus Garvey and the U.N.I.A. redeem Africa without the consent and cooperation of the black kings, chiefs and presidents who were born and elected to rule the natives in Africa? As it is impossible for a camel to pass through the eye of the needle in Jerusalem, so it will be impossible for Marcus Garvey to rule in any part of Africa. He will have to return to St. Ann, Jamaica, British West Indies, and rule the Negroes there, because no slave is allowed to rule in Africa. I read in the Negro World that he and members of the U.N.I.A. had sent five Negroes to Liberia to act as spies for the organization but I am quite sure that President King and the natives in Liberia will treat them as the African leaders always do to the spies in Africa. They used to cut the spy's head off and hang it on the tree in public market where every native could see the traitor but the King don't do that anymore since the American and European Missionaries brought Christianity to Nigeria, West Africa; but still they won't let any spy escape without punishment. Let us hope that these Negroes will not [seem] to be traitors on their arrival in Liberia. They left New York in January 1921 but there is no available chance for Marcus Garvey to disappear with the people's money.

The President and officers of the Liberian Exodus Association disappeared with the people's money in North Carolina in 177[8?][3] and did not leave any record behind for the members where to find their money. The Chief Sam movement also disappeared in the United States in 1914 and we haven't seen Chief Sam and his steamship Liberia but we are going to make the United States detectives and policemen use their power and help poor and needy Negroes to demand their money from the Black Star Line before Marcus Garvey disappears to No Man's Land with his red, black and green flag.

The writer of this article lives at 33 West 132nd street, New York City and would like to hear from all the readers, who are interested in Africa.

Printed in the *Richmond Planet*, 19 February 1921. Original headlines abbreviated.

1. Responding to Deniyi's article in a letter to the editor of the *Richmond Planet*, John E. Bruce described Deniyi at the 1920 UNIA convention: "He has appeared in a gorgeous robe and turban at times, and when the UNIA Convention met here in August last he was resplendent in his African royal pompery and marched with the marchers with heaving breast and the pride born of fiction" (*Richmond Planet*, 5 March 1921).

2. John F. Hylan (1868–1936) was a two-term mayor of New York, holding office from 1918 to 1925.

3. Deniyi's historical information was incorrect. The Liberian Exodus Joint-Stock Steamship Co. was organized in 1877 and based in Charleston, S.C. Under the leadership of Rev. B. F. Porter, the company purchased the *Azor* and transported a group of Afro-Americans to Liberia in 1878. The "Liberia fever" among many blacks at the end of Reconstruction led hundreds to seek passage on the *Azor*. The *Azor*'s Atlantic crossing was plagued with unexpected expenses and a number of deaths. Its funds exhausted, the company was unable to organize a second trip. Nevertheless, the enthusiasm for emigration continued for years among many black Americans (Nell Irvin Painter, *Exodusters* [New York: W. W. Norton Co., 1976], pp. 139–141; Edwin S. Redkey, *Black Exodus* [New Haven, Conn.: Yale University Press, 1969], p. 22).

Reports by Special Agent P-138

New York City 1-31-21

The only thing of interest in the Negro section at the present time [*28 January*] is the GARVEY "Back to Africa" scheme. I learned that volumes of requests are pouring in from all over the country concerning Garvey's invitation to take Negroes to Liberia, and believe that these people are laboring under the impression of securing a free passage, but Garvey's high officers informed me that it is just propaganda in order to excite the fanatics who in turn will contribute more of their hard earned money.

Of course this "Back to Africa" scheme will cause quite an unrest among the Negroes, causing them to sell their belongings and quit their work.

P-138

[*Endorsements*] FILE G. F. R.
NOTED F. D. W. NOTED W. W. G.

DNA, RG 65, file BS 198940-58. TD. Stamped endorsements.

New York City 1-31-21

Today [*29 January*] I had a long talk with MARCUS GARVEY in his office. He told me that he will be leaving for the West Indies on a propaganda trip within three weeks, on his ship "KANAW[H]A". I asked him if he was not afraid of the British Government taking him off when he lands there and the American Consul refusing to vise his passport, and he told me he was all covered and safe, as he would leave here as a seaman or an officer on his own ship, thereby outwitting the two Governments. He expects to sail for Africa in March on his return from the West Indian trip. I learned that his other officials endeavored to persuade him not to take the trip on account of his chances of not returning, but they have not been able to convince him.

P-138

[*Endorsements*] FILE G. F. R.
NOTED W. W. G.

DNA, RG 65, file BS 202600-667-26. TD. Stamped endorsements.

Marcus Garvey to Gabriel M. Johnson

NEW YORK, N.Y. January 31, 1921

Hon. Sir:

This is to inform you that your communication of November 27th, owing to an oversight, has just reached my hands, for which please accept my thanks.

I am more than sorry that this letter reached me after all arrangements had been made for men, as well as materials, leaving for Liberia. I had expected this letter from you so as to know your requirements at that end, but as I said already, it is rather late to ship your requirements, and just at this moment, I am leaving town for about 2 weeks, but I promise that on my return to town I will fill the order and ship same to you at the earliest possible date.

You will please do you best to foster the work of the Association as much as you can.

Relative to the $2,000, when Mr. Crichlow reaches there, you can give a full account to him of the disbursements of this amount, so that he can enter same through the books of the Association, and we, at this end, be kept posted with current expenditures.

Thanking you very much for your letter, and hoping to hear from you within a short time, I beg to remain, Yours fraternally,

UNIVERSAL NEGRO IMPROVEMENT ASSOCIATION
MARCUS GARVEY
President-General

DNA, RG 65, file BS 198940-213. TL, transcript.

J. D. Gordon to John Milton Scott

NEW YORK, U.S.A. January 31, 1921

Dear Brother Scott:

Your letter to hand. I note with interest your words on despo[li]ation and my necessary limitation. To state in clear terms, our position,—here it is.

No Negro can lead the Race while seeking favors at the hands of the race from whose bondage he is seeking to lead them. Now, everything in accordance with that basis, you can work it out yourself and see my limitation. We do not object to receiving help from the white people. Any white man who feels like helping the Cause of the Race can do so but the Negro who *seeks* this help can only be pronounced a Splendid Brilliant Beggar, but our leaders—our Race leaders—must come in an entirely different class. Leading now is a work of God Divine—men whose hearts are pledged for Racial up-lift. Here we will not allow ourselves to be tampered with by those who seek gifts. As Assistant President General I would not be at liberty to seek favors of anyone but still if anybody could give a business loan that would be all right. If the matter could be properly presented to our Executive Counsel I think we could come to some helpful conclusions about the matter but at the time being we have on a $2,000,000 Drive for the Liberian Construction loan and in this we must not fall down. We are dealing with African Governments creating proper impressions with them. Therefore, we cannot fail. When that is in the way, I am certain we can turn our attention to things of that type.

Gorgeous robing or anything that attracts the eye—anything to lift the people from the stupor of the ages—and expense means nothing with us now. If we had to hire a man and pay him a hundred dollars a week just to beat a drum and the beating of that drum created the proper impression, we would be glad to hire him. We have money to spend for gorgeous ro[b]es. Our people have been so completely destroyed by propaganda that we are taking every possible method to relieve the situation. The Catholic Church, even though white is mightily affected by ro[b]es. Anything that is pompous, grand and gorgeous, while it may not be economical, yet is very effective among any simple people, and as one who knows, I say to you, the ro/b/e is not out of place.

Some of the papers write about us to belittle us. We don't mind that. Let them keep thinking that there is nothing to it. When they wake up to what it is, it will be too late to stop it.

The New York Independent was around the other day getting some fundamental information and I had the privilege to fill the writer full. If he writes under the inspiration I gave him, he certainly will give the world a great article.[1] He told me that the way I put it so enchanted him that he regarded it the most romantic thing of the ages. So you may expect to hear something else from the New York Independent soon, but if you want to see something well written and very justly handled, get the December and January issues of the World's Work.[2] I don't know whether you can find any on sale there or not, for the man wrote up here that if he had a thousand copies he could dispose of them all in Los Angeles.

So, yes, the ro/b/es are rather gorgeous just like the gorgeous tail of a rooster but, there, God let loose his gorgeousness to attract the hens. Seems unnecessary but in the mind of the hen, it plays a very important part—and his loud voice and the glittering red around his head, all serve the purpose in the great mind of God.

We are only sending the mechanics into Africa this time who are going to do the building that we have planned. . . .

J. D. GORDON

[*Address*] Mr. John Milton Scott,
518 Wesley Roberts Bldg.,
Los Angeles, Calif.

CLSU, Poet's Garden Collection. TLS, recipient's copy, on UNIA stationery. Hand-written corrections.

1. See Rollin Lynde Hartt, "The Negro Moses and His Campaign to Lead the Black Millions into Their Promised Land," *Independent* 105 (26 February 1921): 205–219.
2. A reference to Truman Hughes Talley's series of articles.

Speech by Marcus Garvey

[[CHICAGO, ILL. Feb. 1 [*1921*]]]

. . .Hon. Marcus Garvey visited here and spoke as follows:

Mr. President and fellow citizens: It is indeed a pleasure for me to find myself here this evening. I have come to this your beautiful city to speak in the interest of the Universal Negro Improvement Association. I can remember coming to your city some fifteen or sixteen months ago, for the purpose then of giving you an insight into this great world-wide movement and to tell you of its activities. Tonight, I am here to tell you of the dimensions of the movement. But before I speak on the movement, I want to clarify the minds of some of the curious persons in this hall. I want it plainly and clearly understood that there is absolutely nothing in the wide world—in the great universe—to intimidate Marcus Garvey. It takes more than human power, more than human effort, to drive fear into my soul. (Applause). I fear God, and know no other fear. Therefore, if anyone comes here this evening expecting to listen to a coward or to one who is going to apologize for something, they have mistaken their man. There is nothing of fear in the make-up of the Universal Negro Improvement Association. We feel that the time has come for the Negro to strike the blow for his freedom; and, by all the Gods that be, we are going to strike that blow when the time comes.

I have not come [to] Chicago to stir up strife among the races, nor to preach revolution, because I am not an anarchist nor a socialist, even though they try to picture me as one of these. I know nothing about them. I am a Universal Negro Improvement Association man from the bottom of my foot to the top of my head. We of the Universal Negro Improvement Association stand for the freedom of the Negro, and we have no apology to make for that, neither to men nor nations. Negroes have been bowing and cringing, dying here and dying there for three hundred years; now they are preparing to die when the time comes for their liberty. I came to the city of Chicago some fifteen months ago—I believe some of you who are here tonight heard me—and some reporters concocted lies about what I said. If there is any man who knows at all [times] w[hat] he says that man stands here tonight. What I said then I will say now. I am not against this government; I have nothing to say against any government; I have no time to talk about other peoples' governments whether it be that of England, France, Germany or any other nation. The government that I am talking about now is the new government that is to be, the government of Africa from whence my father and grand-fathers, against their will, were brought years and years ago. I am talking now about the new government which will be the government of Africa, which we shall give to, and carry throughout, the world and compel them to respect. That is the government I am interested in, and I want everybody to understand, therefore, what I have to say. Perhaps hundreds of you will have to go into court to substantiate what I say here tonight. Garvey can fight to a finish. I am not afraid of any jail; no jail in the world is big enough to make me afraid of it. I am afraid of nothing where the liberty of the Negro is concerned. I do not fear death. How can a man die more gloriously than fighting for the cause and for the liberty of the race? (Applause). Tell them that Garvey has no fear of jail, in Chicago, New York, nor anywhere. So please take that much from your ideas about my being fearful and intimi-dated. You can have a million policemen here, and I shall talk the better. I have been talking over the country for five years, and I know I have said nothing against the government of the United States. In fact, I think Uncle Sam is very pleased with the fact that the Negro is getting ready to protect himself and not bother Uncle Sam so much. We have held numerous mass meetings, and president after president has told us "We can do nothing; the white populace will be dissatisfied." We are not going to worry Uncle Sam nor any other nation for that matter; we are going to build up in Africa a government of our own, big enough and strong enough to protect Africa and Negroes anywhere. Men do not respect mass meetings and petitions; men respect that thing that everybody is afraid of. The white folks have it here and everywhere, the yellow men have it in Asia, and Negroes must get it. God Almighty created us all—white, yellow and black—and when he did so he did not give us any guns and swords to take along with us. All mankind came into this world naked; yet some of these folks have written that they had something then. I have been looking at them daily, and becoming more suspicious. Here you have three men, one white, one black, one yellow, all came into the world at one and the same time. The white man has guns and swords, daggers and other implements and keeps them with him; the yellow man does the same, and this foolish black man stands up in the middle— between these two men—with two bare hands. You must realize that you are flirting with your own future, your destiny, and your [race]. If the white fellow and the yellow fellow found cause to have those things, you should find cause to have them also. And we should have those things for a purpose. What is the idea of Japan having a big navy? The idea is to protect the rights of the yellow man in Asia. The nations of Europe have navies to protect the rights of the white man in Europe. Negroes, the time has come for you to make and create a nation of Africa and have the greatest army and navy in the world. I do not care what white men or yellow men say; I want to see freedom for the Negro everywhere; I want to say that I am a citizen of Africa.

I have no apology to make to any other man, whether he comes from Europe or from Asia. If you are interested in Europe or Asia that is your business. I am interested in Africa. I am not going to try to stop you talking about Europe; I am not going to try to stop you talking about Asia; so please don't interfere with my talking about Africa. (Applause). I have travelled all over the world and white folks have told me "This is a white man's country!" The Asiatic has told me "This is the yellow man's country." I am prepared to meet somebody somewhere and tell him "This is a black man's country." (Applause). Africa must be redeemed. There is no doubt about it, it is no camouflage. The Universal Negro Improvement Association is organizing now, and there is going to be some dying later on. We are not organizing to fight against or disrespect the government of America. I say this plainly and for everybody to hear—we are organizing to drive every pale-face out of Africa. (Applause). Do you know why? Because Africa is mine; Africa is the land of my fathers; and what my fathers never gave to anybody else, since they did not will it to anybody, must have been for me. The right of possession comes to four hundred million Negroes to claim Africa. Some of you turn up your noses against an Africa of Africans. Africa was the land from whence our foreparents were brought three hundred years ago into this Western Hemisphere. They did not probably know what the consequences would be. But that God who rules, that God who sees and knows, he had his plan when he inspired the Psalmist to write: "Princes shall come out of Egypt, and Ethiopia shall stretch forth her hand unto God." He knew centuries ago what he meant. Tonight in Chicago I can see Ethiopia stretching forth her hand unto God. You young men of Chicago, I can see in your eyes that princes shall come out of Egypt; and coming from all parts of the country, coming from all parts of the world, I can see Ethiopia stretching forth her hands unto God. The time has come, the hour has struck, for Negroes all over the world to organize for their liberty.

Some white people and some Negroes think that this movement is radical[.] They say "Garvey's movement is too radical: he should be more conservative." What has the Negro to conserve? He has nothing but Jim Crowism to conserve. If anybody should be a radical it should be the Negro. We are not radicals, even though some men think that we are. The I. W. W. are radicals, and so are some Socialists; but they are white people, so let them "raise Cain" and do what they please. We have no time with them; we have all the time with four hundred million Negroes, and have absolutely no time to waste with anybody else. So, please understand that Marcus Garvey is no I. W. W.; he doesn't even know what it means; he is no Socialist, he doesn't know what it means; he is no anarchist, as far as Western civilization is concerned; but if anarchism means that you have to drive out somebody and sometimes kill seriously, to get that which belongs to you, then when I get to Afric[a] I am going to be an anarchist. Africa has been calling for three hundred years, and who should tell me now that I shall not talk for my right. Look at me, a man knowing myself, and knowing my relationship to my creator. Tell me that I must close my mouth when I see the other fellow taking away that which is mine? You are crazy. (Applause). As I said in my opening remarks, there is but one fear in my soul; no man[,] be he Pope of Rome, Archbishop of Canterbury, Emperor of Germany, President of France, King of England, there is no man who is broad and big enough to drive fear into my soul. Therefore, I say to you all: Know thyself, know that God Almighty created you as men, know that he created you for a purpose, and [find] that purpose. Ethiopia never found that purpose, but the new Negro has found his purpose, and it is interpreted in these few words of Patrick Henry: "I care not what others may say; as for me, give me liberty or give me death." (Applause.)

Look at Africa, the land from whence my father came three hundred years ago. We despise her today because we do not know her history. Three hundred years ago no Negroes were to be found in these United States of America on this North American continent, in the West Indies and South and Central America. Just about that time a large number of white men, calling themselves colonists, settled in this country. In their desire to develop the country they searched the world for laborers that they could use to build up the country, the nation of their dreams. They went to Europe and were unsuccessful in recruiting from that part of the world the laborers they needed to help them in the building up of America, so they turned to Asia where they also failed to secure the required help. John Hawkins, with a committee, then asked permission of Elizabeth, Queen of England, to take the blacks of Africa into her colonies in the West Indies and this Western Hemisphere for the purpose of developing the colonies. Queen Elizabeth inquired of John Hawkins and his committee: "What consideration will you give these blacks, should I sign the charter giving consent to take them from Africa into my colonies of the Western Hemisphere?" Their answer was:

"We will civilize and christianize them. In their own country they are savages and cannibals." The Queen signed the charter, and John Hawkins and his committee transported across the Atlantic forty million black men, women and children, whom they scattered all over these Americas and the West Indian islands. Shiploads after shiploads were sold in the slave markets of the West Indies and to the slave masters of Georgia, Alabama, Mississippi and throughout the Southern states. The slave holders of the West Indies, Jamaica, Barbados, Trinidad and Cuba all bought according to their likes and dislikes of the slaves who were brought to them; and in that way brothers were separated from sisters, and parents were separated from children. Those sold in the West Indies were kept in bondage for 230 years, and those in America for 250 years. Eighty-three years ago Victoria of England, known as "Victoria the Good," signed the Emancipation proclamation that set free hundreds and thousands of Negroes in the West Indies, and the Declaration of Independence set free over 4,000,000 in America. Negroes were brought into this Western Hemisphere three hundred years ago for the purpose of being civilized and Christianized. The price was paid. My father and your fathers paid the price for 250 years in these Americ[as] and 230 years in the West Indies, to make us what we are tonight; and, by God, the price they have paid I will appreciate and fight out; and if any white man or yellow man [should] turn me back from taking that which my foreparents paid, they are making a big mistake. (Applause.) I was brought over here for a purpose; I did not bring myself here; I did not ask them to bring me here; if I make trouble for somebody they will have themselves to blame, and not me. Three hundred years ago my foreparents were brought here; and they never asked anybody to bring them here; these white people themselves went there and brought us over here. If we have sense now it is not our fault, it is theirs. The sense we have we are going to use, that's all. I am going to use the sense of political science, because they sent me to school. I went to school and I paid dearly for going. Two hundred and fifty years ago, I will remember, I paid for it, so as to be able to get to school. I met in the classroom David Lloyd George, N[itti,][1] Clemenceau, von Bethmann Hollwegg,[2] and Woodrow Wilson. All of us studied out of the same textbook; they studied political science. Bethmann Hollwegg said: "I will apply my political science for the good of my race and the good of my country." Lloyd George said: "I will use my political science for the good of my people and the good of my nation." Clemenceau said: "I will use my political science for the good of [my] race and for the good of my country." Nitti said: "I will apply my political science for the good of my race and the good of my country." Woodrow Wilson said: "I will use my political science for the good of my race and good of my country." Marcus Garvey said: "I will apply my political science for the good of my race and good of my country." (Applause.) Let David Lloyd George go his w[ay] and let ther[e] be a greater Britain; let Clemenceau go his way and let there be a greater France; let Nitti go his way and let there be a greater Italy; let Marcus Garvey go his way and let there be a free and redeemed Africa. In saying that I have no apology to make to anybody in Chicago, New York, London, Boulogne[,] Paris nor anywhere in the world. I have absolutely [*no*] apology to make, and in saying this I am fully conscious of it. Those who are slaves must strike the blow for their freedom. In all the history of the human race I have never heard of a race begging for their freedom and getting it; they have had to fight for their freedom and then winning it. Abraham Lincoln made us free here fifty-six years ago; Victoria in the West Indies eighty-three years ago. But the new Negro is not satisfied with the kind of freedom he has now; he wants a larger freedom so that if he desires to [be] a great general in the army, or the president of a country he can do so. If it is right for the white man and the yellow man to rule in their respective domains, it is right for the black man to rule in his own domain. Remaining here you will never have a black man as president of the United States; you will never have a black Premier of Great Britain; you need not waste time over it. I am going to use all my time to establish a great republic in Africa for four hundred million Negroes so that one day if I desire to be president, I can throw my hat in the ring and run as a candidate for the presidency. So, understand me [you] gentlemen from the Department of Justice, understand me well, I have not come to Chicago to preach revolution as some of you desire. Marcus Garvey and those who support the doctrine of the Universal Negro Improvement Association are prepared to go to the last court. (Applause.) I know I have come to Chicago where I have some very good (?) friends who have been "laying up" for me all the time, and who have been trying to do ever so much for me and would be happy to see me on the other side of Jordan. But folks[,] you are waiting for long.

Now I am going to give an illustration of the Negro. The Negro is like the Jew. There was a man called Jesus, who came to earth as the saviour of mankind, the saviour of his race, the Jews, and those Jews, when he came just got together and said: "We are not satisfied with this man, we want him put away." The Jews had no power, they were just living in the great Roman empire, but had no power, just as Negroes have no power today; they could not do anything with Jesus, because they were nobody in the Roman state. But those Jews played politics, and they went to those Roman prefects, the Roman chief of police, and lied against their brother Jew Jesus. They said: "He has preached against Caesar and against the state[.] Put him to jail." The Roman judges said they found no fault in him, but the Jews replied: "He is a bad man; if you put him in jail you will please us so much." They took him before the governor of the state and before Pontius Pilate who both said: "We have found no fault in this man." But the Jews still cried: "Crucify him! crucify him! crucify him!" And then those Jews, because they could not accept the doctrine of Jesus Christ, were not satisfied until they had crucified their blessed Lord and Saviour on the Cross of Calvary. There are many such Negroes in Chicago now; they are no[t] judges, nor mayors, nor governors, nor police captains; they are the heads of nothing in the state, yet they say: "Here comes the man Garvey; put him in jail; put him in jail." But let me tell you this: In all ages men who have come before the people to help them have always been regarded as agitators, but they always prepared themselves for the extreme of everything.

I want to say, good friends in Chicago, whether any of you desire to see Garvey in or out of jail, it is immaterial to Garvey. If you are afraid of jail Marcus Garvey is not, when he knows he goes there for a righteous cause. Some of you Negroes go to jail for robbing another Negro; but when Garvey goes he goes fighting the battles of four hundred million Negroes all over the world. I do not care what lies you tell the police captain, judge, mayor, governor, or nation. I know there is a God who means that Ethiopia shall stretch her hands; and no police captain, judge, mayor nor anyone else can stop Ethiopia from stretching forth her hands at this time. We have already organized the world. Let Marcus Garvey die, and you have two thousand Negroes willing to take his place. (Applause.) The work must go on. As I speak to you in Chicago tonight, four million Negroes are listening. Put me in jail in Chicago and somebody may be going in jail somewhere else. The Negro has reached the point where he is going to take care of himself. What is life to me, if I must live a life of beggary, bowing and cringing? Life is dear to me when it is the life and spirit of a free man. (Applause) I look on the world around me and I see a great civilization that I admire. I am not angry with the white man nor the yellow man. But I want this much understood: If the white man loves me, I love him; if he hates me, I hate him. I have no more to give him than he has to give me. I have been playing [the] fool for three hundred years, somebody has got to play the fool now. You have to show me how much of a brother you are before I accept your brotherhood.

Now, I admire your cities. I admire the civilization of this great America, the greatest republican country in the world. I see it as a great accomplished fact, a reality coming to us by the sufferings of hundreds and thousands of the Pilgrim fathers, the early settlers, who came to suffer and to die. I have nothing but praise for the man who lays down his life for his country. The fault that I have to find with Negroes is that we are too lazy.

I have not come to Chicago to compliment you, because you have not done anything. We have learned, we have labored for the other fellow to build a country entirely his own. The Universal Negro Improvement Association would build up and is working for a country to give you as your own[.] When you are to build up a nation in Africa, a great industrial nation, and have an army in Africa second to none in the world, then I will come out in the world and compliment Negroes. Until then I have no praise for you, I have no compliment for you. I believe that what white men have done Negroes can do. So I am here to inspire you to greater actions. The Universal Negro Improvement Association is now taking the work under its own leadership. That is my message tonight. This is no apology nor compromise to any man. We are going forward and shall continue to go forward until Africa is redeemed. (Applause.)

Printed in *NW*, 12 February 1921. Original headlines omitted.

1. Francesco Saverio Nitti (1868–1953), Italian economist, author, and statesman, succeeded Vittorio Orlando as prime minister on 19 June 1919. He resigned on 9 June 1920 (*EWH*).

2. Theobald von Bethmann-Hollweg (1856–1921) became chancellor of the German Empire in July 1909. Hindenberg and Ludendorff forced him out of office in 1917, when he failed in his attempt to prevent unrestricted warfare (*WBD*).

Marcus Garvey to Cyril A. Crichlow, UNIA Resident Secretary to Liberia

New York, U.S.A., February 1, 1921

INSTRUCTIONS TO MR. CRICHLOW

On arriving at Cadiz, rebook passage immediately for Monrovia, Liberia. On arriving at Liberia, interview the Honorable Gabriel Johnson, present your credentials and have him find for you and men a place to stop. Get busy immediately and have Commissariat put in order for your accom[m]odation and for the starting of work. See that all monies are lodged immediately in the bank on your arrival and drawn from the bank according to the instructions sent to the Honorable Gabriel Johnson; that is, all monies shall be lodged in the name of the Universal Negro Improvement Association and drawn only under the signature of the Honorable Gabriel Johnson and yourself. You shall make arrangement to pay the men fortnightly or monthly. All requisitions for help must be made through your office and confirmed by the Honorable Gabriel Johnson. None of the heads of departments shall employ any labor without first acquainting you and the Honorable Gabriel Johnson of same and getting your approval. You shall see that the men perform their work regularly day by day; and any negligence of duty shall be reported immediately to the Honorable Gabriel Johnson and to the Executive Council through me. Should the men not put in enough work commensurate with the salary received, you shall make such deductions from their salary to cover the time that they do not put in; and should they express any dissatisfaction, you shall report immediately to the Honorable Gabriel Johnson, and if it is not then satisfactorily settled, you shall report same immediately to the Executive Council through me. You and the Honorable Gabriel Johnson have the right to suspend such men from active work if they refuse to carry out their part of the contract entered into with them. You shall not contract any debt on account of the Universal Negro Improvement Association without first consulting the Honorable Gabriel Johnson.

MARCUS GARVEY,
President General

DNA, RG 84. TL, carbon copy.

Marcus Garvey to Gabriel M. Johnson

New York, U.S.A., February 1, 1921

May it please Your Highness:

This letter introduces to you Mr. Cyril A. Crichlow who is appointed by the High Executive Council of the Universal Negro Improvement Association as the Resident Secretary of our Commissariat in Liberia. He will carry out all your instructions in the matter of the Construction work and upbuilding of Liberia through the program of the Universal Negro Improvement Association. He is charged to be responsible for all our records and all data and reports pertaining to the interests of the Universal Negro Improvement Association in Liberia. He shall keep all such records and reports under his custody according to your direction. He is authorized to sign checks along with you for the withdrawal of the funds of the Universal Negro Improvement Association from the bank to meet the regular demands according to approved expenditures. He shall submit to you for your consideration and approval all matters pertaining to the business of the Universal Negro Improvement Association. He is instructed to acknowledge the authority of His Highness the Supreme Deputy in your absence or according to your special designation. Mr. Crichlow is to live at the Commissariat and you will please accom[m]odate him the best you can until the same is fixed sufficiently for his accom[m]odation and for him to start his work. Mr. Crichlo[w] held the position of Official Reporter to the Convention and to the Universal Negro Improvement Association. With very best wishes, I have the honor to be, Your obedient servant,

MARCUS GARVEY,
President General

DNA, RG 165, file 10218-261-71-78. TL, carbon copy.

Credential for Cyril A. Crichlow
from Marcus Garvey

New York, U.S.A., February 1, 1921

TO WHOM IT MAY CONCERN:

This is to certify that the bearer of this letter—Mr. Cyril A. Crichlow—is appointed by us as RESIDENT SECRETARY of the Commissariat of the Universal Negro Improvement Association in Monrovia, Liberia. He is engaged at a salary of Twenty Five Hundred ($2500) Dollars a year. He shall live at the Commissariat and shall take charge of all the records and reports and attend to all business transactions initiated through His Highness the Potentate and carry out all instructions of the High Executive Council of the

Universal Negro Improvement Association. His appointment shall continue as long as he continues to give satisfactory services to the Universal Negro Improvement Association and such services shall be judged according to his honesty and attention to duties. He shall receive instructions from His Highness the Potentate the Honorable Gabriel Johnson and through the Executive Council. He shall be held responsible for all cash in his hands and shall keep such records and vouchers as to show the faithful discharge of his duties.

> FOR THE HIGH EXECUTIVE COUNCIL OF THE
> UNIVERSAL NEGRO IMPROVEMENT ASSOCIATION:
> MARCUS GARVEY, Pres. Gen.

DNA, RG 165, file 10218-261-71-78. TL, carbon copy.

Marcus Garvey to Gabriel M. Johnson

New York, U.S.A., February 1, 1921

May it Please Your Highness:

This is to inform you that we have this date despatched from New York a number of men for the purpose of starting our Construction Work in Liberia. These men sail under the guidance of His Supreme Highness the Honorable G. O. Mark and Mr. Cyril A. Crichlow. On the arrival of these men in Liberia, you will do your best to temporarily accom[m]odate them and start them off to work immediately. Mr. Crichlow is the commercial and responsible head of the office, and all these men shall work under your direction and be controlled by the office of Mr. Crichlow. Their salaries shall be paid fortnightly or monthly according to local arrangements and they shall be paid their salaries through the office of Mr. Crichlow for which they shall give proper vouchers. Mr. Crichlo[w]'s salary shall be paid through you—Eighty Dollars ($80) of said salary per month shall be deducted by you, as he has made arrangement to draw that much monthly in New York; that is to say, Mr. Crichlow has a standing arrangement with the Chancellor in New York to pay out on his account the sum of Eighty ($80) Dollars per month. If there should be any change, Mr. Crichlow will notify you and same will be confirmed by the Chancellor. And, further, for the first two and a half months of Mr. Crichlow's salary, an additional Forty ($40) Dollars per month shall be deducted until the sum of One Hundred and Five ($105) Dollars is paid. You will make requisition to us through cable and letter for the necessary amount of money to continue the work in Liberia.

You will see that Mr. Crichlow make[s] monthly statements of his transactions for the Executive Council and have them posted to my office, so that we will be able to keep a correct account at Headquarters here of the transactions at that end. You will please do your best to help all the men start work immediately—putting up new buildings and starting farms, etc. The pharmacist is to start a drug store immediately on his arrival so as to sell and furnish medicine to the local public. The agriculturist is to start farming immediately.

You will please interview the Government and try to get the best concessions of land you can so as to start off these men doing some practical work. What you cannot get in the city for nothing you will please purchase on the cheapest terms possible for the organization and set Mr. Jemmott the builder at work immediately. He should employ native laborers and help so as to make the construction as cheap as possible. Please instruct Mr. Crichlow to make out a list for all the materials that are necessary that cannot be obtained locally for carrying on our construction work, and see that such reports are sent weekly to New York so that we can compile same and make a shipment.

We are hoping to have our first ship leave here sometime in March or April with a complete shipment of goods to continue the construction work which they will start until then. Please do your best to encourage this work and foster the good interests of the Universal Negro Improvement Association. With best wishes, I have the honor to be, Your obedient servant,

MARCUS GARVEY,
President General

DNA, RG 165, file 10218-261-71-78. TL, carbon copy.

Editorial Letter by Marcus Garvey

[[Chicago, Ill., February 2, 1921]]

FELLOW MEN OF THE NEGRO RACE, *Greeting*:

One month out of the New Year is gone, and still there are millions of Negroes who have not yet started to do their duty by themselves. As I have said in my previous articles, this is a year of universal activity on the part of all races and nations, and no people can well afford to ignore the "signs of the times," which portend to a greater consummation of human energy in every field of life. The Negro, like all other races, must play his part in this universal movement of the betterment of humanity and the stabilizing of the economic conditions of the world.

The reorganization of industries everywhere means that those who have no plans will be left out in the cold avenues of speculation. The Universal Negro Improvement Association has planned a great spiritual and physical revival among the Negro peoples of the world for 1921, and already there are hundreds and thousands who have joined in this revival, the desire of which is to awaken the sleeping consciousness of scattered Ethiopia to the fact that a new and worthy race must be established out of the 400,000,000 of our people who have for centuries dragged out an existence as serfs and peons under the domination of alien forces and alien races.

When we come to consider the question of man it is as plain as we can argue it that the Negro, like the rest of mankind, has a place in the world. His place, however, will not be given to him by others, but he must take and occupy it.

For centuries he has lived at the mercy of those who are willing to dole out to him sympathy and charity. With that much he has been unable to reach the pinnacle of human quality and greatness. That is to say, he has been unable to establish his claim to those higher human developments known to us in the civilization of the age.

But with the new hope that has taken hold of the world through which all races of mankind are looking forward to a brighter and a more glorious day, we of the Universal Negro Improvement Association think that the time is also opportune to inspire in the heart and soul and mind of every Negro the vision of a brighter Ethiopia—an Ethiopia whose glories will be so resplendent as to shine throughout the age.

But this can only be done when each and every member of the race realizes the consciousness of self—that each and every one has a part to play. And 1921 is the time which we of the Universal Negro Improvement Association have set for all the members of the race to get hold of that spirit of activity that will place them in the vanguard of human progress.

One month of the New Year is already gone, and millions have not yet rallied to the colors of the red, the black and the green—the standard of this organization. It is for us, therefore, to sound a warning through my message of this week and let the world of Negroes know that it is not the time for us to argue and dispute the questions that may confront us within our own ranks that will cause division, but it is just the time for us to unite—one and all—and make one desperate effort towards our own salvation.

Th[a]t question of a free Africa looms up as the biggest issue in the Negro universe. Why should there be a division on this question of Africa? All Negroes, whether in America, the West Indies, South and Central America or Africa, have but one common parentage—a parentage that has bequeathed to us within recent centuries a heritage of hardship and sufferings of all kinds. But in the days of our foreparents the world was so organized as to make it impossible for them to free themselves. Today the world is reorganizing itself. New political boundaries are being laid out—new laws are being instituted, and in this change of political confines and of the systems of government under which man lives it is but time that the Negro also think of a readjustment.

Wake up, Ethiopia! Wake up, Africa! and let us work towards the one glorious end of a free, redeemed and mighty nation. . . .

Lincoln and Victoria, in their large-heartedness, assisted us in throwing off the yoke of chattel slavery in this Western world, but chattel slavery still continues in Africa; and whilst we suffer not from chattel slavery in this western hemisphere, we are suffering from industrial slavery. The fight should be more determined now in that we have to strike the blow for our own freedom, that not only there should be an industrial emancipation of Negroes in this western hemisphere, but there should also be a universal emancipation of Negroes.

Let Africa be our guiding star. Yes! Let her be the star of destiny! Each and every race—each and every nation—has a guiding purpose. The purpose of England is to be a mighty and powerful empire on which the sun will never set. The purpose of France is to build up a mighty state that will rank the first among the nations and empires of the world. The purpose of the Universal Negro Improvement Association is to make Africa the greatest star in the constellation of nations. . . .

Remember, also, that Liberia—the Lone Star[1] in the constellation of nations—is beckoning to us to come to her rescue commercially, industrially and educationally. The plans of the Universal Negro Improvement Association are well laid for the development of this, our dear country; but it rests on each and every one of us to give the support, moral and financial, that is necessary. . . .

MARCUS GARVEY

Garvey v. *United States*, no. 8317, Ct. App., 2d Cir., 2 February 1925, government exhibit no. 49.

1. This phrase probably originated with the title of a book by Frederick Alexander Durham, *The Lone-Star of Liberia, Being the Outcome of Reflections on Our Own People: [A Reply to "Black America" by W. L. Clowes]*, with an introduction by Mme la Comtesse C. Hugo (London: Elliot Stock, 1892).

Speech by Marcus Garvey

[Cincinnati, 4 February 1921]

. . . The white man has been fooling us for 300 years, and I am on strike of being fooled any longer. He has done all kinds of things to make us feel that we are an inferior kind of people; he has tried to make us believe that we were created to be "hewers of wood and drawers of water." How could God create 400,000,000 people to be "hewers of wood and drawers of water?" These white people got this thing in their brains and tried for 300 years to make us believe that God said so, and some of us are crazy enough to believe it. God has no printing office up in heaven. He has no linotypes or typesetting machines; the angels are not compositors. God inspired the apostles to write and say certain things in those days; but the white folks got hold of all those things that the apostles said and put them in a book and changed them to suit themselves. They have put in that book things that God said and thing[s] that God never said to carry out their propaganda of white superiority. Hence they have made God a white man and Jesus Christ a white man, and the angels beautiful white peaches from Georgia. Everything up in heaven is white according to the white man's teaching.

Every Negro believes that God is white and that the angels are white. God is not white or black; angels have no color, and they are not white peaches from Georgia. But if they say that God is white, this organization says that God is black; if they are going to make the angels beautiful white peaches from Georgia, we are going to make them beautiful black peaches from Africa. How long are we going to stand for this propaganda of white superiority and black inferiority? The Universal Negro Improvement Association says not one day longer. God created me to be a man, and I know and feel that I am a man and shall die as a man. When Negroes get that kind of spirit they will be free. We have encouraged that old-time spirit of being born to be slaves too long; now we want to be free. I want to be as free as any other man in the world; no white man has a right to be freer than I am, because this world does not belong to any one man; it belongs to all of us. (Applause.) What right has another man to find things for me? You have never had the manhood to go out and do things for yourself, that is why white folks have got the idea that they are superior to us. You should not expect a chance; you should go out and take a chance. White folks did not expect chances; they went out and took chances. That is why there is a great America today. White men did not wait for God to come down to help them build the city of Cincinnati nor any of the other big cities. If they did they would have been waiting till now. Negroes are always waiting for God to stretch out His hand first before they stretch out theirs, but you will wait until eternity. To you colored men of Cincinnati and of the world[,] the Universal Negro Improvement Association says get ready to build for yourselves in Africa great cities and set up a great nation. When you do[,] no man can tell you you cannot have a job in another nation. Otherwise you are going to ask him the reason why. Give a little reflective thought to what I have said. Look all over the United States of America—Boston, Washington, Philadelphia, Cincinnati and other cities—and you see no statues of black men. You see that the black man has done nothing. All that we have done was to carry mortar for the other fellow when he was building up his property. The time has come for us to build up in Africa. I am very serious about it, because it is my only hope. If Negroes sit quietly down and pay no attention for the next fifty years until Africa is taken by England, France, Spain, Italy and Belgium, here and in the West Indies we are doomed. I am longing for the day, the mighty day, when we shall plant the standard of the red, black and green on the hilltop of Africa. . . .

Printed in *NW*, 26 February 1921. Original headlines omitted.

Bureau of Investigation Report

[*Los Angeles*] Feb. 5 [*1921*]

NEGRO ACTIVITIES

UNIVERSAL NEGRO IMPROVEMENT ASSN.:

Confidential informants report that this organization now has branches at Riverside, Bakersfield, and San Diego, and that the approximate membership in Southern California is now 2500. Effort is being made to bring the membership up to 6000 by May 1st.

MISS VINTON DAVIS came from headquarters at New York arriving in Los Angeles December 26, 1920. She has been actively engaged organizing women's auxiliaries, such as Black Cross nurses, etc. A MRS. BOSS [*Bass*][1] has been appointed as local organizer of women's auxiliaries. The organization meets in Los Angeles every second Tuesday night. The "African flag", consisting of alternate stripes of black, Red and White, with the letters U.N.I.A. superimposed on the white stripe, are being widely sold, not only to members of the UNIA but to other negroes at $1.00 each.

MONROE TROTTER, so-called negro envoy to the Paris Peace Conference, is on a speaking trip in Southern California. It is reported that the U.N.I.A. are endeavoring to secure his [adhesion] and services for their organization.

Confidential informant states that evidently all is not running smoothly at New York Headquarters. The *Rev. Gordon*, who resigned his pastorate in Los Angeles to accept an appointment at Headquarters, has written back asking for reinstatement as pastor of his old church.

CAPT. E. L. GAINES, "Minister of Legions", in a letter to confidential informant, stated that his organizing trip in Virginia was not altogether successful; that he was frequently ordered out of towns, and escorted to trains with the warning not to return. He states that he is starting on another organizing trip through Pennsylvania.

FERGUSON, HOPKINS &
KOSTERLITZKY

DNA, RG 165, file 10218-261-60. TD, carbon copy.

1. Charlotta Spears Bass (1880–1969) published the oldest and largest black newspaper on the West Coast, the *California Eagle*. She and her husband, Joseph Bass, were charter members of UNIA Division 156 in Los Angeles, and Mrs. Bass served as lady president of the division and state organizer. Born in Sumter, S.C., Charlotta Bass took courses at Brown University, Providence, R.I., Columbia University, and the University of California before and during her stint as editor and publisher of the *Eagle*. She moved to Los Angeles in 1910, and when the *Eagle's* founder, John Niemore, died two years later, she acquired the paper. When the Los Angeles UNIA division was organized in 1920, the *Eagle* became its unofficial organ. When Noah Thompson led a dissident group into forming the Pacific Coast Negro Improvement Association in 1921, however, the Basses became active in that group, eventually condemning Garvey and the New York parent body of the UNIA. Always active in politics, Mrs. Bass was also an organizer for the Republican party, later serving as the western regional director of Wendell Wilkie's 1940 presidential campaign. After World War II, Mrs. Bass became a found-

ing member of the Progressive party, and in 1952 she was the party's vice-presidential candidate (Barbara Sicherman and Carol Hurd Green, eds., *Notable American Women: The Modern Period* [Cambridge, Mass.: The Belknap Press, 1980], pp. 61–63; Emory J. Tolbert, *The UNIA and Black Los Angeles* [Los Angeles: Center for Afro-American Studies, 1980], pp. 63, 67; Theodore Vincent, *Black Power and the Garvey Movement*, pp. 170–171; Charlotta Spears Bass, *Forty Years: Memoirs from the Pages of a Newspaper* [Los Angeles: Charlotta Bass, 1961]).

Speech by Marcus Garvey

[[New York, February 6, 1921]]

Hon. Marcus Garvey spoke as follows:

I am pleased to welcome the members and friends to Liberty Hall tonight.[1] I have just returned from a trip to Chicago and Cincinnati, visiting two of the branches of the Universal Negro Improvement Association in the midwest, and I bring a message to you from the great Windy City of Chicago. Chicago in the West has become another stronghold of the Universal Negro Improvement Association. (Applause.) Those of you who have been following the Universal Negro Improvement Association in New York for the last eighteen months will remember the fight we had to enter Chicago. Well, we entered Chicago, and we have captured Chicago. (Loud cheers.) In Chicago you will find domiciled corrupt Negro politicians. You will find men there who control the entire city through the politics they play, and they can keep anybody and anything out of Chicago; but for the first time they made an attempt to keep something out of Chicago, and despite all they did that something went into Chicago and took Chicago, and that something is the Universal Negro Improvement Association. (Cheers.) The politicians in the West have tried their best to keep me out of Chicago for eighteen months—I mean the Negro politicians—and they went to the extreme of having me indicted up there for sedition, and I had to face that much indictment in the State of Illinois. They calculated that by that indictment they would have been able to keep me out of Illinois and prevent us carrying the great city of the West as we carried New York. Well, I remained out of Chicago because of the convention and other work I had here for nearly seven months and then I made up my mind before I leave I would go to Chicago, and I went to Chicago last Tuesday and found an indictment against me along with other indictments against twenty or thirty other men, some Socialists, I.W.W.'s and Anarchists. All of us were linked up together. I believe one man got ten years and I got away with the bunch who got away. (Laughter and cheers.)

When the records which were given out showed that the indictment against me was withdrawn, the Negro politicians got annoyed and they went up to the political captains and asked that the indictment be reinstated against me so as to prevent me speaking in Chicago, and half an hour before the meeting at which I was scheduled to speak I was besieged with alarmists from all quarters asking me "What am I going to do"; because it was said that a whole army of detectives and policemen were to be at the armory to greet me. I told them to go back to the armory, because I would be there on schedule at 8 o'clock, and when I went into the armory I saw another Liberty Hall. It was the Seventh Regiment Armory of Illinois, which I believe is nearly twice as large as Liberty Hall, and as far as I could look I saw men wearing the colors of the Red, the Black and the Green. (Cheers.) I believed that the Chicago African Legions include half of the famous Eighth Illinois boys (Cheers) and besides that big battalion of African Legions, we have the finest display of Black Cross Nurses I ever saw. (Cheers.) The Legions and the Black Cross Nurses were ready for action, and therefore those who came changed their minds, and I spoke to the people in Chicago in that armory on Tuesday night just as I spoke to them before, I believe—eight or nine months ago—and as I speak in Liberty Hall night after night; and I can tell you that the enthusiasm of that city is something that each and every one of you should see and realize for yourselves, because it is something wonderful. The U.N.I.A. that night brought out men of all walks of life in Chicago—I mean Negro men and women and white men and women, too. The police came under the command of what is known as the Big Six, and when the Big Six put in their appearance we took care of them, and when the meeting was over the Big Six had a conference at one of the street corners and they were overheard to say, "You better not trouble those 'niggers'; those 'niggers' will kill anybody up there." (Laughter.) And so I remained in Chicago for two nights and spoke to as large a gathering as I am speaking to tonight, and I have to say that the Hon. W. [A]. Wallace, who came to the convention representing the Chicago Division, has done wonderful work in the West for the Universal Negro Improvement Association. He and Mr. Orain and others have worked up the membership to 4,800 since they left the convention, and there is no place in Chicago large enough now to hold the membership of that division of the Universal Negro Improvement Association.

CINCINNATI STRONG FOR THE U.N.I.A.

I went from Chicago to Cincinnati, and there again I saw quite a splendid manifestation of the determination and interest of another delegate who came to the convention of the U.N.I.A. in the person of Mr. William Ware, who came to the convention representing about twenty people who had then formed themselves into the Universal Negro Improvement Association, and now it has a membership of 1,000 persons. He had a terrible fight in Cincinnati also to ward off the politicians who are endeavoring to get the U.N.I.A. out of the State; but before I left last Friday night we converted half of them and they have all pledged to support Mr. Ware and carry the colors of the Red, the Black and the Green in that section of Ohio. (Cheers.) I left Cincinnati for New York and missed my train by one hour and stopped off in Cleveland, and there again I saw the splendid work of the delegate to the convention, Mr. Shedrick Williams. He came to the convention representing an organization of about 400 members in Cleveland; at the present time he has over 3,000 members. Since he went back he bought a Liberty Hall, two houses and an office for the Cleveland Division of the U.N.I.A., and my party had the pleasure of remaining over at the official residence of the Universal Negro Improvement Association in the city of Cleveland.

That gives you an idea of the work that is being done in the Mid-Western States by the other divisions of the Universal Negro Improvement Association. And let me reaffirm to you men and women in Liberty Hall that the Universal Negro Improvement Association has taken hold of the country like wildfire. It is sweeping everything before it, and white men and black men, critics and supporters, everybody now are falling in and supporting the red, the black and the green, because they believe that we are on the right track. The criticisms of Dr. Du Bois reached Chicago before I got there and it did wonderful work for us in Chicago, because I believe it made about 500 new members (cheers) for the Chicago Division of the U.N.I.A. Outside of the Chicago Defender, all the papers in Chicago are allied to the Universal Negro Improvement Association in that they publish the news and they support the U.N.I.A. and the editors themselves spoke at the meetings which I addressed while I was in the city. (Cheers.) And we have had this much satisfaction out of the Chicago Defender—that one of the members approached the editor relative to the Universal Negro Improvement Association and he said, "That man Garvey and the Universal Negro Improvement Association—I have nothing to do with them any more." (Laughter and cheers.) Through the Chicago Defender we were somewhat hampered in our first entry into the city of Chicago.

I want you to realize, men and women of Liberty Hall, that your movement has reached the stage when we must stand solidly behind it and put it over, because we are just now at the cross roads—the cross roads . . . [*words mutilated*] will pass from one sta[ge to the] other, and those of you who [have stuck] by the U.N.I.A. and stood by the organization in the years past, you have the satisfaction now of seeing a small thing grow into a mighty Colossus. There are some of you present tonight who are old members, joining two or two and a half years ago, when we used to hold our meetings in four by six rooms around here; and tonight you have the satisfaction of knowing that you have not only one Liberty Hall in New York but you have Liberty Halls all over the world; not only in the Western States and other parts are they buying and building their Liberty Halls, but the news that comes to us from Cuba reveals the fact that nearly every week a new Liberty Hall is bought by some of the divisions there. In Panama and in other parts and in Africa they are also buying and dedicating their Liberty Halls, and I feel sure that the time is not far distant when we will have not one, two or one hundred, but we will have thousands of Liberty Halls scattered throughout the world, from whose platforms the same doctrine will .

be propagated as we are propagating from the platform of Liberty Hall in New York City. We have the satisfaction of knowing that we have done a practical thing; we have done the practical thing in that we said a couple of years ago that our program was for the redemption of Africa. We talked it and now we have actively gone out and in a practical way to redeem Africa. At this hour, whilst we are in Liberty Hall, we have our pioneers at sea on their way to Africa. In another couple of days they will land on the bright and sunny shores of our own motherland, there to start that construction work that we have planned. (Cheers.) . . .

Printed in *NW*, 12 February 1921. Original headlines omitted.

1. The meeting was called "for the purpose of honoring those who have subscribed to the Construction Loan in New York" (*NW*, 12 February 1921).

Report by Special Agent P-138

New York City 2-8-21

IN RE NEGRO ACTIVITIES:

MARCUS GARVEY is back in New York once more. He spoke at Liberty Hall tonight [*6 February*] before a crowded house and informed them that he was getting ready for his trip abroad. He told them that he will be in New York until at least next Monday and during his stay in the city will straighten up his affairs; speak in Liberty Hall, Friday, Sunday and Monday night, then he will sail afterwards.

I mixed in among the members after the meeting just to get an idea of how they felt about his trip. Many of them seem to think that there is some danger as to his meeting with opposition in the West Indies—others think that the British Government is liable to detain him as a dangerous propagandist, and others think that he is smart enough to beat both the U.S. and the British Governments.

Undoubtedly, his presence here after his trip, has again awakened that anti white feeling and talk among his followers[.]

P-138

[*Handwritten endorsement*] FILE G. F. R.
[*Stamped endorsement*] NOTED F. D. W.

DNA, RG 65, file BS 198940-72X. TD.

Editorial Letter by Marcus Garvey

[[New York City, February 8th, 1921]]

Fellow Men of the Negro Race, Greeting:

It is my duty once more to write to you asking your cooperation in the great work we have started in the interest of the Universal Negro Improvement Association and African Communities' League. Reports from all parts of the Western World reveal the fact that thousands of our men are out of employment. My personal experience through my travels [reve]als to me that thousands are in desperate need. Thou[sa]nds have been thrown out of employment through the great [in]dustrial setback that is now sweeping the entire world.

If you will remember, for over four years I preached the doctrine of preparedness among the Negro peoples of the [w]orld. I pointed out to them that the time of reaction indus[tr]ially, and economically, would come. That it was neces[sa]ry for them then to save and conserve every bit of surplus cash worked for and invest a part of same in responsible and well-meaning Negro corporations like the Black Star Line, and the Universal Negro Improvement Association, as out [of] these organizations would come the salvation of the Negro during the time of the present industrial setback. Very few [N]egroes heeded the plea, whilst men in America and other [pa]rts of this Western Hemisphere earned $100 every week as [sk]illed and unskilled workers and laborers. The majority [cav]orted at the highest, indulged in pastimes that were unnecessary, and the full one hundred per cent of the money earned was spent in riotous living. No preparation was made for the rainy day, everybody believing that every day would be a day of harvest. I preached, and preached the doctrine of preparedness all over the United States of America. My utterances were published in the columns of the Negro World, so that those who did not hear, at least read what I had to say, and now we are confronted with the terrible reaction. What are we going to do? Should we fold our arms and sit down in this condition? Are we waiting on some imaginary saviour to come and relieve the situation? Are we waiting for some spiritual being to help us? We will wait until doomsday, and the miracle will not be performed. You must now be up and doing, having a heart for any fate. By your own actions, if initiated now, shall we be saved the fate of threatened disaster. Whilst conditions a[re ba]d among a large number of our race, yet through unity in America, the West Indies, Central America and Canada, we who are employed can do something worthy of the name of the race, through which we can ward off universal want within our ranks.

Whilst you did not heed my pleadings of years ago to help organizations like the Black Star Line, and the Universal Negro Improvement Association, I am now repeating my plea. Whatsoever you can do, do it now. You men of the Negro race who have $1,000, invest at least $500 in the Black Star Line now, and right now, and help us to buy more ships, so that we can transport the unemployed from this Western Hemisphere to Africa. Keep the $1,000 for another twelve months, then at the end of that time you will find yourself as penniless as the man who was unemployed; and then neither of you will be able to help the other. You men who have $500, invest $250 in the Black Star Line, and if you have $100, invest $50 now.

If every man and woman of the Negro race does this in the next thirty days, the $10,000,000 capital of the Black Star Line will be subscribed. The corporation will be able to buy bigger ships, and more ships, and then we will be able to transport from this Western Hemisphere at least 3,000 men every week for work in Africa, and thus relieve the stagnation of unemployment among Negroes in this hemisphere. Men if you do not see and hear, it is not the fault of Marcus Garvey. He has been telling you for over four years to prepare. It is not an alarmist cry. It is the handwriting on the wall. Remember, men and women of the Negro race, this is no sentimental age; this is a practical, material, soulless age when man knows no kindness, when man knows no love, when man's one desire is to grab and take away from his brother that which Nature and God gave him. . . .

MARCUS GARVEY

Printed in *NW*, 12 February 1921. Original headlines omitted.

Marcus Garvey v. *Amy Garvey*

COUNTY OF NEW YORK
9th Day of February, 1921

MARCUS GARVEY, being duly sworn deposes and says: I am the Plaintiff in the above entitled Action and have read the Affidavit of the Defendant filed herein as the basis of a new Motion for an increase of alimony and counsel fee.[1] Nearly all of the statements contained in the Affidavit of the Defendant were also contained in the original application and are mere repetitions of the statements in the original application.

The Defendant dwells upon the meeting of the Universal Negro Improvement Association held in August of last year and the fact that a per capita tax of $1.00 (One dollar) was levied upon the members of the Organization throughout the world. While that is true, returns from this assessment have been so slow in coming in that the Organization has been compelled to borrow money from its members with which to carry on its construction work in Liberia and other portions of the country.

The levied $1.00 (One dollar) assessment, however, was never intended by the Convention to be applied especially to the payment of salaries. The salaries voted to the officers of the Executive Council, alleged in the Defendant's Affidavit were fixed at the figures mentioned by her merely to give tone and dignity to the offices of the Association and with the hope that the

Organization might be built up to such a high standard and to such large numbers that all such salaries might be in fact realized in the near future. It was perfectly understood by all the parties participating in the said Convention that the Universal Negro Improvement Association had no funds or means with which to pay any such salaries. If such salaries are to be realized and actually paid the officers understand that it must come after the Organization has been built sufficiently strong and the business of the Organization carried to such an extent as would justify the payment of such salaries.

The Organization itself is only about three years old and has had to spend a great deal of money for travel, expenses and propaganda work, besides providing places of meetings for the members and it has not been able to accumulate any considerable money for salaries. Besides, as President General of said Organization I would have no right to use the funds of the organization for my personal ends, and whatever is paid me, must be voted out by the Executive Council and cannot be appropriated by me.

The Defendant is misinformed because it is not true as alleged by her that the assessment of $1.00 (One dollar) on the members of the Organization has been steadily flowing into the coffers of the Parent Body, from the Branches all over the world. On the contrary, we will not be able to know what Branches have paid their assessment until the next meeting of the Convention in August of 1921.

I deny giving my personal check for $500.00 (Five hundred dollars) in payment of any subscription to the Liberian Liberty Loan as stated by the Defendant. The fact is, I subscribed for $1,000.00 (One thousand dollars) of the Liberian Liberty Loan, but the payment was to be made in instalments from time to time out of my salary.

I am not receiving any salary yet from the Black Star Line, because that Corporation is still undergoing readjustment of its affairs. My salary from the Universal Negro Improvement Association depends wholly upon the amount of work I do and in order to earn a living wage out of it, I have constantly to travel from place to place and speak in the interest of the Organization: That out of my salary I have to pay back the money that I borrowed from my friends while the Organization was unable to pay me any salary and also I was indebted for loans received and rents that I was unable to pay, and I am paying up now from month to month.

Besides, I had to pay off a Judgment obtained against me at my home in the West Indies. Besides, I am paying to my Sister, who is my house-keeper, $35.00 (thirty-five dollars) per week for taking care of my home and for the necessary help in the up-keep of the home. My rent of my apartment is $96.00 (ninety-six dollars) per month, exclusive of gas bills and electricity bills. Besides I have to pay an instalment of $125.00 (One hundred twenty five dollars) a month to the Harlem Furniture Company on a bill of furniture which I purchased when the Defendant and I were living together and at present I owe a balance of $2,500.00 (Two thousand five hundred dollars) on such furniture. I have not purchased any furniture since this action was commenced.

I am further indebted to the Insurance Company, about $500.00 (Five hundred dollars) past due premiums on my insurance and I am likely to lose my Policy because of my indebtedness to the Company for premiums.

With all my expenses to meet and the debts which I have incurred, the salary I am receiving from the Universal Negro Improvement Association is not sufficient and I am hoping that the condition of the Black Star Line and other kindred Organizations will soon be in shape so that I may receive enough money to make my financial condition easy. At present I have to work sixteen hours per day and am on the Road practically all the time trying to bring in sufficient money to the Organization to enable it to pay me a living wage for my services.

I forg[o]t to mention, also that I am indebted to the Bloomingdale Company to the amount of $600.00 (Six hundred dollars) for [a] piano which I purchased having paid about $100.00 (One hundred dollars). I have purchased no piano since this Action was begun and the piano referred to by the Defendant in her Affidavit is the same piano that was purchased as mentioned.

I deny that the Defendant is in frail health and is unable to earn anything towards her support. The truth is that she is in perfectly good health but that she is lazy and will not work. That she lives in expensive style buying new dresses every month. She also travels a great deal, going long distances from New York to other states and Canada. She is also frequently seen in the company of George S. Johnson, alias Solomon, who was mentioned in my previous Affidavit which was before the Court in which we charged her with being guilty of criminal relations. We have evidence in abundance to establish the fact that her criminal relations are still continuous with this man Johnson.

The Defendant's father and two brothers live in the city and her father is employed and presides over a home where she could live and be protected, but instead of living with her father and her b[ro]thers, she prefers to live in a furnished room, entirely among strangers and lives exclusively to herself where she can receive whom she will.

The Defendant also is a regular attendant upon the theaters of the city and goes to the shows two and three times per week, sometimes three and four times per week and goes in expensive style, as though she had the income of a milliona[i]re.

I am firmly of the belief that the Defendant is in league with my enemies not only to extort money out of me, but to destroy my good name and reputation and standing and to break down the reputation and standing of the Organization, which I am trying to build up.

That the Defendant is under the influence of her Attorneys, one of whom is an enemy of myself and my Organization[2] and has made public declarations of his hostility to me and my Organization so that the efforts of the Defendant and her Counsel, of continually harassing me with Motions is largely the result of a scheme to blackmail and to extort money from me on account of newspaper reports of matters appearing in their papers filed in Court.

Besides, the Defendant is unnecessarily and too frequently in consultation with her Attorneys which she is doing in order to make the charges for legal services larger, and in order to extort money from me.

Besides, I am receiving anonymous letters which the Defendant, I am sure, caused to be sent me and which I have traced to the Defendant, threatening my life and threatening to destroy my reputation and to break up and destroy the Organization which I am devoting my life to; So that this Motion is a part of the scheme to keep up the plan of harassing and annoying me in order to force me to pay large sums of money to the Defendant and her lawyer.

MARCUS GARVEY

Marcus Garvey v. *Amy Garvey*, no. 24028 New York Supreme Court, 9 February 1921. NNHR. TDS. Notarized.

1. On 1 February 1921 Amy Ashwood Garvey renewed her original application for $75 per week alimony and $5,000 in counsel fees (*Marcus Garvey* v. *Amy Garvey*, no. 24028, New York Supreme Court, 9 February 1921).
2. A reference to attorney Pope Billups, who was second vice-president of the rival UNIA formed in New York in January 1918 and who was the rival UNIA's attorney as well.

Arthur B. Spingarn to Wilford H. Smith

[*New York*] February 10, 1921

Re Black Star Line, Inc. vs. *Du Bois and N.A.A.C.P.*

My dear Mr. Smith:—

Referring to your letter of January 27th, immediately upon Dr. Du Bois's return, I took up with him the retraction proposed in your letter. For reasons which must be obvious to you, it is not feas[i]ble to print it in the exact form suggested by you. The CRISIS, however, is quite willing to correct any misstatements it may have made and would be pleased to insert in its next issue either of the following:

Under the caption "Marcus Garvey" we published in our December and January numbers, two articles which incidentally discussed the affairs of the Black Star Line Steamship Corporation. We regret that certain statements therein might be misconstrued. Our statement that the YARMOUTH is a wooden vessel was incorrect as it is in fact steel. We have, naturally no intention to embarrass this corporation in its business or operations.[1] OR

We regret that in our articles on "Marcus Garvey" an error occurred in regard to THE BLACK STAR LINE, INC., which we are glad to correct: the YARMOUTH is a steel vessel and not wooden and is at present seaworthy. The CRISIS, as stated in the articles, wishes every success to this corporation and has no desire to embarrass it in any way.

I am authorized to say that the retraction will be printed in the same type and in as conspicuo[u]s a position as the original articles and that it will appear in the table of contents at the beginning of the number as "A Correction." The March number is already in page proof, but the forms can be held open until Monday, the 14th for the insertion of this correction. May I ask that you send me an immediate reply so that its [in]sertion in the March number may be assured. Very truly yours,

ARTHUR B. SPINGARN

MU, WEBDB, reel 10, frame 749. TLS, recipient's copy.

1. This first statement was the one eventually published in the March 1921 issue of the *Crisis* (21, no. 5: 200). The minutes of the NAACP Board of Directors' meeting on 14 February 1921 read: "Mr. Arthur B. Spingarn, Chairman of the Legal Committee, reported that the $100,000 suit of the Black Star Line against the National Association and Dr. Du Bois has been settled out of court by the Legal Committee of the Association agreeing to have inserted in the next issue of the Crisis the fact that the Yarmouth is a steel vessel and not a wooden one as stated in the January issue" (DLC, NAACP).

Report by Bureau Agent James O. Peyronnin

Chicago, Ill. February 10, 21

UNIVERSAL NEGRO IMPROVEMENT ASS'N MEETINGS:

MARCUS GARVEY OF NEW YORK CITY (NEGRO) PRINCIPAL SPEAKER. ALLEGED RADICAL ACTIVITIES

In company of Special Agent Wolff of this Bureau Office, Employe proceeded to the 7th Regiment Armory, 3400 Wentworth Ave., Chicago, to cover a meeting at 8:00 P.M., February 1, 1921, under the auspices of the above named association, Chicago Division, and at which meeting MARCUS GARVEY, President of said association, and well known New York agitator, was to make an address. The Armory was extensively decorated with American Flags, and on the speakers['] platform the American Flag was hung along side of the so-called African or Liberian Flag, "Red, Black and Green". Approximately 3,500 negroes were present. Six police officers (negroes) covered the meeting for the Police Department. Employe attended the meeting for the express purpose of taking short-hand notes of any remarks which "GARVEY" might have made of interest to the Department. Garvey was introduced by the Chairman of the meeting as "His Excellency" MARCUS GARVEY, Provisional President of the Republic of Africa. During his discourse, GARVEY stated that he was fully aware that the U.S. Department of Justice had agents present, as well as police reporters, to take notes of his speech, but that the Government, as well as the Police Department, should have no fear of his advocating violations of the laws of the country, as he was not a "Red" or Bolshevik, nor was he a Socialist, and that he could not explain Socialism if he was called upon to do so, that he was not an I.W.W. or connected in any way with such kindred organizations, and further that the Universal Negro Improvement Ass'n was in no way connected with the Abyssinian movement, members of which movement in June 1920 burned an American Flag and which resulted in a riot, bringing about the death of a sailor and a citizen; that he loved the Stars and Stripes, and that in time to come there would be only two Republics in the world, the grand and glorious republic of the United States of America and the Republic of Africa. Of course, as usual, GARVEY harang[u]ed his audience about the old kind of negro disappearing and that the "new" negro was born with the same ideas and ambitions of the white man, and that the time has come for the negro to strike the blow for his freedom, and by all "Gods" we the new negroes are ready to strike that blow when the time comes. However, GARVEY told his audience that he did not come to Chicago to stir up trouble among the races, that he believed in the laws and obeyed them. Following are some of his remarks:

> I am nothing but a UNIA, (Universal Negro Im[p]. Ass'n) from the bottom of my feet to the top of my head, and you also as members of the organization stand for the freedom of the negroes, for the negroes who have been bowing and slaving for 300 years, but now have made up their minds to die for Liberty. They accuse me of saying things about the Government; I have nothing to say about any Government, all I have to say is for the Government of Africa. All I say is that the negro is getting ready to protect himself; we are going to build up a Government in Africa to protect the negroes everywhere. God Almighty created Yellow, Black and White men alike. He never gave us swords, guns and deadly weapons; all men came to the world with naked hands. This white fellow takes up guns and weapons to protect his interest, the Yellow fellow imitates him, and this fellow the Black Man stands up in the middle with two bare hands. If the white and yellow men can have cause to have these things you should have cause, the same power to use these things. They have these things for a purpose; they have these things to protect the rights of their nations. Negroes[,] the time has come to make the greatest Navy and Army of the world in Africa. I want to say that

as a citizen of Africa, if you are interested in Europe, that is your business, if you are interested in Asia that is your business, I am interested in Africa. I am not going to stop you talking about Europe or Asia, so please don't stop me from talking about Africa. I am not organizing the negroes to fight America, but I say this plain for everybody to hear, we are organizing the negroes to drive every white race out of Africa, you know why because Africa is mine, the land of my father, and by God what my father had I never gave to anybody, and since I never gave it away it must therefore be for me. The Universal Negro Imp. Ass'n is not a radical movement. Understand me now[,] I do not hate the white man, but I do say if the white man loves me I love him, but if he hates me I hate him. I have no more to give to him than he has to give to me. I admire the white man for his civilization when [I] look at this great America, the greatest Republic and country in the world. The white man has laid down his life for his country; the fault that I find with the negro is that he is too lazy. The negro has done nothing. With the Universal Negro Improvement Association you have got a start now to work for a country of your own. I have no praises for you, what the white man has done you can do.

It appeared that the main object of GARVEY's visit to Chicago was to strengthen membership in the association and to subscribe loans for the construction of Liberia. Garvey stated that the first group of men, such as engineers, surveyors and railroad builders have already left New York for Liberia to do construction work, and that in order to continue the great work already started it was necessary to have funds, and that this was the object of the loan. He also urged those present to purchase shares in the Black Star Line.

On February 2nd a second meeting of the association was held at the 7th Regiment Armory at 2:00 P.M., and a third meeting of the association was held at 8:00 P.M. at Quinn Chapel, 2400 S. Wabash Avenue. About 3,000 negroes attended these two meetings. The price of admission at each meeting was 60 cents. It was stated by members of the association that the Chicago membership is 4,500. GARVEY in his speeches stated that there were four million members in the association throughout the world, and that New York City alone had a membership of 30,000 (Thirty thousand). GARVEY's remarks in his second and third speeches on February 2nd were in substance the same as his first speech on February 1st.

Concluded.

JAMES O. PEYRONNIN

DNA, RG 59, file 000-612. TD, carbon copy.

Report by Bureau Agents A. A. Hopkins and E. J. Kosterlitzky

[*Los Angeles, ca. 10 February 1921*]

... The Universal Negro Improvement Association.

Strong branches of this radical negro organization exist in California, particularly in Los Angeles, Riverside, Bakersfield, and San Diego, with auxiliaries such as "Black Cross Nurses", etc., and a membership of approximately 2,500. They hold frequent meetings. Considerable radical and racial talk [and] utterances have been reported by our confidential informant. One of the local negro papers is the official mouthpiece of the organization.[1] A real estate transaction is in process, to purchase a tract valued at $30,000 in Los Angeles, California, as a permanent home for the organization. Considerable money has been contributed to Marcus Garvey at the New York headquarters. The negro population of Los Angeles has a large number of exceedingly prosperous individuals, and the above organization has been well supported financially. The membership of this radical organization are a much larger and more enthusiatic group than those of the conservative negro societies that are working alon[g] lines of cooperation with the whites for the uplift of the race.

The two principal organizations working along conservative lines, and opposed to the U.N.I.A., are the National Association for the Advancement of Colored People and the Commercial Council of People of African Descent.[2] The latter is a local organization.

Negro organization activities in the Eighth Division are confined to California, there being no record of such activities in either Utah or Nevada.

[A. A. Hopkins and
E. J. Kosterlitzky]

DNA, RG 65, file BS 202600-5-26X. TD. This report originally appeared as an enclosure to a letter from R. B. Pierce, eighth division bureau superintendent, to the Bureau of Investigation (10 February 1921).

1. The *California Eagle* regularly published reports from local UNIA division meetings.

2. The Commercial Council of People of African Descent was organized in 1920 by Los Angeles blacks to encourage business interests among blacks. The council's principal founder, John Wesley Coleman, was a cofounder of the Los Angeles UNIA division in January 1921. Under the sponsorship of the council, Los Angeles blacks held a convention and an industrial parade in September 1920. The parade featured two thousand participants and over one hundred floats. Coleman decreased his activities with the council after he helped to organize the Los Angeles UNIA division, and he brought many members of the council with him into the Garvey movement (DNA, RG 65, file OG 132476; Emory J. Tolbert, *The UNIA and Black Los Angeles* [Los Angeles: Center for Afro-American Studies, 1980], p. 51).

J. Edgar Hoover to Lewis J. Baley

WASHINGTON, D.C. February 11, 1921

MEMORANDUM FOR MR. BALEY.

It is my desire to call your attention to the departure from this country, of MARCUS GARVEY, the well known negro agitator, publisher of the "Negro World" and president of the Universal Negro Improvement Association.

The activities of Garvey have been covered for some time in the past, in a confidential manner, and it has now come to our attention that he is contemplating leaving this country February [7th?] aboard the Black Line steamer "Ka[n]a[w]ha." Garvey who is a British subject, also contemplates securing a seaman's passport, in order that same will warrant his return to this country. I understand that his trip will take him to the West Indies.

For your further information on this subject, I desire to advise you that I have been under the impression for some time, although with a limited amount of proof, that Garvey's movement in this country, is subsidized to some extent by the British Government, further, that he through his emissaries, has been responsible to a considerable extent, for the negro disturbances.

In view of the above it is my desire, should Garvey leave this country, that he be denied entry in the future, and it is suggested that some such arrangement be made with the State Department in this matter.

Will you kindly advise this office as to the final disposition of this matter. Respectfully,

J. E. HOOVER

[*Handwritten endorsements*]
RETURNED FROM CHIEF FILE G. F. R.
[*Stamped endorsement*] NOTED F. D. W.

DNA, RG 65, file BS 198940-72X. TLS, recipient's copy.

Report by Special Agent P-138

New York City 2-11-21

Today [*9 February*] I learned from one of GARVEY's close associates, that the chances are he might not be leaving on the "KANAW[H]A" as was planned. He told me that he thinks Garvey is trying to go by way of Florida, then by boat to Cuba. He expects to ascertain the facts within a few days.

I was also informed that nearly two thirds of GARVEY's members are prevailing upon him not to take the trip as they are afraid of his being captured by the British, thereby putting his whole propaganda to an end.

Of course, it is evident that should Garvey be taken away from the scene, within two months the bottom would be dropped out of his anti-white propaganda, as none of his officers would be able to hold the followers together, as they are hero worshippers.

I also learned that the REV. DR. MCGUIRE, Garvey's Chaplain General and Chief Advi[s]er, is now in Cuba[1] where he is organizing and spreading Garvey's propaganda.

P-138

[*Endorsements*] FILE G.F.R.
NOTED F.D.W.

DNA, RG 65, file BS 202600-667-29. TD. Stamped endorsements.

1. McGuire left for Cuba on 7 January 1921 and was the first member of the UNIA's executive council to make an official trip to the Caribbean after the 1920 convention. McGuire conducted a series of meetings in various parts of the island, visited fourteen divisions, sold shares in the Black Star Line, and collected contributions to the Liberian Construction Loan. McGuire returned to New York in early March 1921 (*NW*, 18 March 1921).

Speech by Marcus Garvey

[[Liberty Hall, New York, Feb. 11, 1921]]

HON. MARCUS GARVEY ON "UNEMPLOYMENT"

I desire to speak to you this evening in a heart-to-heart manner, because just at the time we are facing critical conditions, and it is but right that we should talk to each other, counsel each other, and get to understand each other, so that all of us may be able to work from one common understanding for the good of all.

I desire to appeal to the memory of the members of this association. You will remember that in the years immediately preceding the great war in Europe there was a great industrial stagnation among Negroes in the United States of America, and that we then faced a hard and difficult task industrially, economically, and we saw no hope, and we had none. Then immediately, whilst undergoing our hard and difficult experience, the war broke out in Europe. Germany declared war, and nearly all of the European powers were dragged into the bloody conflict. Immediately the war started in Europe the participants rushed a large number of orders for war supplies and munitions to the United States of America, that was then neutral in the war. By the abnormal demands for the industrials of these United States of America, a great industrial wave swept the country, and untold opportunities were opened up to Negroes everywhere in these United States of America; not only to Negroes, but these untold opportunities were opened up to all races, to peoples within the confines of this country. Factories and mills and industrial plants sprang up everywhere in the great industrial centers, and men who never had employment, men who never had any occupations prior to that time, found opportunities then. Men for years who never had the chance of earning a decent wage, found jobs ranging in weekly salaries or wages from $25 to $100, and some $200 a week. Men everywhere were employed, and even the peons and the serfs of the South broke loose from the South and ran North, where these great industrial opportunities had opened up themselves for each and every one.[1] Men came from the West Indies; men came from all parts of the world to America to enjoy the benefits of the new industrial opportunities offered in America. These opportunities opened up larger and larger, and out of the wealth that was poured out of the great war some of the people who enjoyed the distribution of that wealth conserved the portion they got or received, such as the Jews, the Italians, the Irish and the Poles. Their leaders in the pulpits, through periodicals, through magazines, and from platforms and classrooms, taught their respective groups the value of conserving the wealth that was then poured out into their pockets in the form of salaries and wages, to prepare for the rainy day that would come. Negroes, however, in the most loose, the most slack, the most indifferent manner, received their portion of the wealth that was poured out, and they made absolutely no effort to conserve it. They distributed it as quickly as they received it; they paid it out back to the employer, or to his friend, or to his brother, or some of his relatives, as quickly as they received it from him. And just at that time a large number of the leaders of the country said nothing. They had no advice to give. The preachers said nothing, and they gave no advice to the people.

Just about that time the Universal Negro Improvement Association came upon the scene, with an active propaganda. It taught preparedness—industrial preparedness among the Negroes then. It warned them, and told them that they should prepare to start industries of their own, to save their money, and to make every effort to protect themselves; because after the war there would be a great industrial dearth; there would be a great industrial stagnation. We taught that doctrine; we preached it; we wrote it in the newspapers; we scattered it near and far; we sent the doctrine everywhere and everywhere we got the retort that we were crazy; that we were a bunch of lunatics. The man who inspired the movement was a crazy man and a fit subject for the lunatic asylum. They said all manner of things against him, because we dared then, when no others would do so, to teach the doctrine of industrial, economic preparedness. The people, however, could not see, and they believed we were crazy. But we stuck to our doctrine, we adhered to our belief, and we were able to convert four million people scattered all over the world to our doctrine and to our belief. But we did not convert the four million people at one time; it took us four years to convert them. Some became converted immediately, and assumed the burden and responsibility of carrying and conveying the doctrine to others. Hence tonight I am able to look into the faces of some of the people who started with me when we organized the Universal Negro Improvement Association; people who have made the sacrifices I made—sacrifices in money and in time. They bore the brunt of the situation, because on them laid the responsibility to finance and support the propaganda so as to carry the propaganda to others. And they have borne the price of the propaganda for four years reaching the four millions. But it reached the four millions only too late, because the war and the opportunities were over, and when it reached them they could ill afford to support the doctrine to convey it unto others. Hence the present situation that confronts us now.

There are hundreds and thousands, and later on millions of men in this country of Negro blood who will be thrown out—thrown into the cold. We anticipated it; we saw it, and we warned the people against it. We did it with the feelings of our sympathies for our own; we did it with the feelings of conviction that the men with whom we mingled during the war paid us large wages, paid us large salaries with a vengeance, but they were forced, they were compelled to do so, and they did it with a spite and with a vengeance. Some did not see it, and did not appreciate the fact of those who saw it and warned the people against it. The attitude of the employers in this country was to pay the Negro as small a wage as possible on which he could hardly subsist or hardly live, because he desired to keep the Negro as an industrial peon, as an industrial serf, and make it impossible for him to rise in the great industrial, economic ladder of life. He kept him down, not because the Negro before the war was not worth more than he was paid for his labor, for at all times the Negro is worth more than twenty, thirty or forty dollars a month. Yet that was all that was paid to us prior to the war, and all of you know it. It was paid to the elevator men, to the porter men, and everybody nearly got the maximum of forty dollars or fifty dollars, or sixty dollars a month from his employer prior to the war, not because we were not worth more than that for our labor, but because the other man was prejudiced against paying us more than that. He desired not to give us a chance to rise in the industrial and economic world. But the war came, and we compelled him by conditions, we forced him by conditions to pay us $100 a week, to pay us $50 a week, to pay us $60 a week, and some of us mechanics forced him to pay us $200 a week, and he paid it, but with a bitter anguish; he paid it with great reluctance; he paid it with a vengeance and he said: "I am going to get even with the Negro." He knew the Negro better than the Negro knew himself. He knew the Negro would spend every dollar, every nickel, every penny he earned which he was compelled to pay him. He laid the plan by which the Negro would spend every nickel but the Negro hadn't sense sufficient to see it and know it. Now, what was the object and purpose of it? To take back every nickel that he paid him. When he raised the cost of living, when he raised the cost of bread, when he raised the cost of butter and of eggs, and of meat, and of other necessities of life, what did he mean? He meant that we should return to him every penny of that which we got from him, and the Negro had not sense enough to see it. He raised the price of everything; he raised the price of luxuries, for he knew well that, above all other peoples, Negroes love luxuries, and he taxed us in the districts where Negroes live, for you paid more for the luxuries you received in your district than the white folks paid for the same luxuries in their district. The white people planned to get every nickle that they paid to you; and we fell for it. We bought silk shirts at $10 apiece, and $15 apiece. We bought shoes at $30 and $25 a pair. We bought ladies' dresses at $100 a suit; we bought the most expensive hats, silk socks at $3 a pair, at $2 a pair, and $1.50 a pair (laughter), and we took automobile rides and paid $24 for a Sunday afternoon ride, and we did all kinds of things of that sort. Some of us had six girls and gave presents to each of them. (Laughter.) Thus we spent every nickel of what we received.

How Much Did We Save?

Did anyone else live at the same rate at which the Negro then lived? Did the Italian live at that rate? Did the Jew live at that rate? They did not. The Jews saved at least fifty per cent of what they earned. The Italian saved at least sixty per cent of what he earned. The Irish saved at least fifty per cent of what he earned. And at the end of the war every one of them had a bank account to show. Every one of them had some investment in Irish interests to show. How much did we save? What interest have we to show? Absolutely none. Whose fault is it? It is the fault of the people; it is the fault, more, of the leaders. You cannot so much blame the people, because the bulk of the people do not think, the bulk of the people follow the advice of their leaders, and the people of that Race that has no leaders is a Race that is doomed. Negroes never had any leaders at any time. That is why we have always been doomed. When we preached the doctrine of preparedness, men like Du Bois criticized the U.N.I.A. and its leader. All of you can remember that when we started the propaganda of the U.N.I.A. and the Black Star[,] every newspaper and magazine in New York tried to down us. "The Amsterdam News" wrote against us; the "New York News" wrote against us; the "Crusader" wrote against us; the "Challenge" wrote against us; the "Emancipator" wrote against us; everyone of them wrote against us, and discouraged the people. Whose fault is it now?

That is the question, and you yourselves must give the answer. They all said, and pointed to us, saying that we were a crazy bunch of people. What did we tell you during the war period? And immediately following the war, when you were still employed? Didn't we tell you that there was a Black Star Line? Did we not tell you that its capital was $10,000,000? Did we not throw away, during the war, $50 and $100 and more at different times for mere pleasure and expensive, fashionable clothing? And had we invested that money which we then spent so lavishly and foolishly, to subscribing to the capital stock of the Black Star Line, what would have happened? With $10,000,000 of its stock subscribed and paid for, we would tonight have twenty ships that would belong to us as ours, each worth half a million dollars. And what kind of ships would they be? They would be ships of a tonnage of five thousand to eight or ten thousand tons. They would be ships each able to accommodate at least 500 to 1,000 passengers. If we had twenty ships, each able to accommodate a thousand passengers across the Atlantic Ocean, what would happen today? Every day in the week, or every other day of the week, a ship of the Black Star Line would sail out of New York port with at least a thousand unemployed men from New York to Liberia, West Africa. (Applause.) That is what we saw. That is what we tried to tell the people and teach the people. How many of us would be unemployed tonight if the capital stock of the Black Star Line had been subscribed for two years ago? I hardly believe that there would be an unemployed Negro here. Because if we have ten thousand unemployed Negroes in Harlem tonight, we could call up ten ships of the Black Star Line, and say to the captains of those ships that we have ten thousand Negro men unemployed to send to Liberia. Take them! But you did not subscribe the capital; you paid it out in silk shirts; you paid it out in expensive socks. And who made those factory silk shirts and those fancy silk socks that you purchased and paid for? White men. Who sold them to you? White men. Where is the money you paid for them? Gone back to white men, and you are still the paupers that you were prior to the war in 1914. Whose fault is it? That is the answer you must give yourselves.

It pains me, it grieves me, it brings tears to my eyes when I see a race, not of children, but of matured minds, of full grown men and women, playing with and threatening their lives and the destiny of themselves and of posterity. What more can we do as leaders of the Universal Negro Improvement Association than to open the eyes of the people by talking to them, preaching to them, pleading with them, and writing to them concerning that which we know, that which we see? That is all we can do. Some of you are crazy now, as crazy as you were, some of you, four years ago. (Laughter.) And those of you who are old members of the U.N.I.A. can remember Marcus Garvey in the streets of Harlem. When you had your fat jobs downtown, earning $100 a week, and in other parts of the country, I could have done the same. But I saw the threatening disaster. And what did I do? I had as much ability as the average man; I had as much skill as the average man. The average man was going his way, making his pile, and enjoyed himself when he was at leisure. People would walk up and down Lenox avenue and see Marcus Garvey on a stepladder, and would say: "Look at that crazy black fool!" (Laughter.) (They called me all kinds and all manner of names standing up there talking about Africa!) Look at his coat! Look at his shoes, and everything he has on! They said all those things about me. But I saw the future collapse. I saw the results that would follow the then period of prosperity that was only transitory. I saw the day when the very big Negro who then got his pay envelope on a Saturday night of $100 and believed he was the biggest thing in Harlem—I foresaw when he would be the smallest thing in Harlem; that he would be the man without a nick[el] because I knew the war would soon be over, and I knew the white man would then throw him aside as soon as hostilities were over and there was a slackening in the demand for the commodities or munitions he was then making and give the preference to white men; and that has been the white man's policy ever since his contact with the Negro. That has been his program, and that will be his program always, so long as Negroes are foolish enough to allow him to use them for what he wants.

A Needed Warning.

I am sounding this second warning, and I want you to take it from a man who feels the consciousness of what he says. I am not pretending to be a prophet; I am not pretending to be a sage or a philosopher. I am but an ordinary man with ordinary common sense who can see where the wind blows, and the man who is so foolish as not to be able to see and understand where the wind blows, I am sorry for him; his senses are gone. I can feel; and the man who cannot feel now I am sorry for his dead sense. I can see where the wind is blowing, and it is because of what I see that I am talking to you like this. There are some Negroes in Harlem who are working and some who save money. They believe they are always going to have jobs; they believe they are always going to have money. You will always have money if you know how to use it. There are some men who have money and then lose all they have because they never know how to use it. There are some men who never had and they get and always have it. Now, I want you to realize this one truth that I am endeavoring to point out to you. There are a large number of unemployed Negroes in New York and there are hundreds of thousands of unemployed Negroes in different parts of the country. I have been traveling for the last couple of months and in all of the Western states I have been I have seen Negroes out of work by the hundreds in centers like Pittsburg[h], Detroit, Cleveland, Columbus, Youngstown and Chicago—all around the Western and mid-Western states. So that whether we live in New York or somewhere else, conditions are just as bad. So you might as well stay where you are and face the situation. What we want Negroes who are still working and who have money to do, is to decide upon some wise plan to save the situation. Negroes do not like to help Negroes anyhow; but perforce we will have to help each other or otherwise something will happen to surprise us. I told you but recently that when a man is hungry he is the respect[e]r of no person. A hungry man forgets the look of his father. Understand that. There are some Negroes who believe they should not take interest in other Negroes. Now let me tell you that we are going to face a situation, the most critical ever experienced by this race of ours in these United States of America. I told you some time ago that it is a question of dog eating dog. You know how bad a situation that must be. What I mean by it is just that: that there are some Negroes who are too big, who are too aristocratic and too dicty to take interest in other Negroes. I am going to tell you what I believe will happen to such Negroes later on, if they do not get busy now and do something for all Negroes irrespective of what class these Negroes belong to. No community is safe if in its midst there are thousands of hungry men. I do not care where that community is, it is an unsafe community and especially at midnight. Let the big dicty Negroes say, "What do I care for that good-for-nothing Negro; he is nothing." That poor Negro who has never had a square meal for four days goes to that big dicty Negro—I am trying to picture the conditions later on—he goes to that big dicty Negro and asks for a quarter or 50 cents and he drives him away. That Negro after not having a square meal for two, three or four days, turns away and loses heart and nothing in the world is too desperate for him not to do. To find bread a man is driven to the farthest extreme and at midnight or even in the daylight he resorts to violence and cares not what the result be so long as he finds bread to satisfy his hungry heart and soul. I have just come from Chicago and there I heard of a hungry Negro who never had a square meal for two or three days. He had begged everybody around town and everybody drove him away. He said, "Why should I die for hunger when somebody can give me bread? Since they have refused me, I will take it," and he goes to the house of a preacher somewhere in the outskirts of Chicago and he gets into the house where sleeps the lonely preacher and at midnight what did that hungry Negro do? He took a razor or some sharp instrument and severed the head of that sleeping preacher from the body to get two dollars.[2] He got $2, and killed a man for $2 so as to find bread. When he had spent that two dollars and could not get any more bread he called the police and said, "I will confess to you what I did if you give me a square meal." He was given a meal of chicken and something else and confessed that he killed the man. Those are the conditions that hungry men are not responsible for. I do not care how religious a man is or how many Sunday schools he goes to; I do not care how long he can pray, when that man is hungry he is a dangerous character. And that is the practical common-sense issue that you have to face in a practical common-sense way. White folks have stopped looking out for Negroes; they stopped before there was a war.

The war robbed them of all that there was in the world. Now they have nothing because they have used up all that is in the world. It is a question now of every man looking out for himself. That is all. The white man is deaf to your sympathy and to your cries. You may cry and beg for jobs he will not give you except you are the only fellow who can fill that job that he wants done. But the first man of his own race he finds able to fill that same job with the same ability as you have, you are gone. And he does not wait to ask where the white man comes from. He only wants to know he is a white man, and out you go. He does not wait to know where you are from. He says you are a Negro, and out you go.

Now what [must we] do? We are saying to the men of the Universal Negro Improvement Association and to the Negro race. I am speaking only to those who have confidence. If you do not have any confidence in yourselves, if you do not have any confidence in your own race movements, I am sorry for you, and I would ask you to go your way. Men must have confidence in something and in some one. Without confidence the world is lost. Mankind has retrograded and the world has gone back. The world is built upon confidence—confidence in some one, confidence in some institution, confidence in something. We live as rational human beings, social human beings, because we have confidence in people and in God the creator. Let a man lose his confidence in his people and in a God, and chaos is ushered in and anarchy sweeps the world and human society is destroyed. It is only the belief and the confidence that we have in a God why man is able to understand his own social institutions and move and live like rational human beings. Take away the highest ideal—the highest faith and confidence in God, and mankind at large is destroyed. As with your confidence in God, as with your confidence in religion, whether it be Christianity or any other religion, so must you have confidence in your institutions that mean anything to you as individuals and as a community.

Now I am saying to you who have confidence in the Universal Negro Improvement Association—and if you have no confidence you should not be here. I am here because I have confidence that the men and the women who make up the movement will continue and continue until victory be written on the banner of the red, the black and the green. (Cheers.) I am here because I have confidence in humanity; I am here because I have confidence in God, and I expect that all those who wear the red, the black and the green are here because they have confidence in the ultimate triumph of this great cause of ours. (Cheers.) If you have confidence; if you have faith in it as you have confidence and faith in your religion, therefore it is time for you to support the movement and make it the success that you want to be, make your support not a half-hearted one, but make it a whole-hearted one. You have seen the first practical demonstration of the utility of the Universal Negro Improvement Association. You have seen the first mistake made by this race of ours, as I have tried to preach to you in these few years—the mistake during the war period. I am asking you now not to repeat or not to make the same mistake. I know as I look into the face of many of you that there are hundreds of you members of the Universal Negro Improvement Association who have not done anything yet for the practical carrying out of the program of this organization. I have asked many of you if you have your Liberty bonds, and you say no. I ask why? You say, well, because you are not able just now to buy. You rate your ability to buy on the surplus money you have. When you bought a share or two in the Black Star Line for $5 or $10 two years ago you did it when you were getting a salary of probably $100 or $50 a week, and you said, "I will invest $10 in the Black Star Line because you had your work and so much surplus cash." Now it is not a question of surplus cash; it is a question of duty. It is a question of your own interest. I am saying to the men and women of the Negro race, there is but one salvation for the Negro as I see it now, and that is the building of Liberia, West Africa. The only salvation for Negroes now is opening up industrial and economic opportunities somewhere, and I don't see it around here. You will have to create another war for it, or you will have to get another kaiser before I will see it around here. I have no objection to seeing another kaiser, and I feel sure you would have no objection either, whether he comes from Japan or anywhere, but on the second coming I believe you will be better prepared than the first coming. "Once bitten, twice shy." But you have to bite Negroes a hundred times before they get shy. We have been bitten for 300 years and up to now we are not shy yet. What do I mean? I want you members to act as living missionaries to convince others. There are still Negroes here who can help and buy shares in the Black Star Line. Those of you who have done your duty, I am not speaking to you; but there are thousands who can subscribe to the Liberian Construction Loan. There is a hungry man, he has not a nickel in his pocket and he is begging bread. There is another man with a thousand dollars. The one man without money to buy bread can neither help himself nor his fellow men. The man with a thousand dollars cannot only help himself, but he can help dozens of others; but he is too selfish. He, like the other man, has no money, has no job, and he says: "I have a thousand dollars, but I have no job. I am just going to hold on to this thousand dollars." And every day he spends $3, $4, $5 out of it and still has no job. Every day $5 has gone and he is too selfish to think about the other man.

He is too selfish to think about anybody else he meets, and every day $5 goes out of his thousand dollars, and at the end of the year he still has no job. His thousand dollars is gone, and he is [just] like the other fellow, without a nickel. Both of them face each other—two hungry men; one cannot help the other; but that man who had the thousand dollars, if he were a wise man, a man of common, ordinary sense, what would he have done when [he] finds himself without a job and with a thousand dollars only left out of his years of earnings? He would say: Is there an organization around that is endeavoring to do some good? Are there any other men around who want to do some good? If so, I will go and link up with them and do some good. Yes, he would say, there is an organization over there. What are they trying to do? They are trying among other things to raise two million dollars or ten million dollars to put a line of steamships on the ocean to carry hundreds of men from these ports of the world to Africa, where they are going to build factories, mills, railroads, etc., and find employment for hundreds of men. They are crying for money to put over the scheme. I will find out how far they have gone, and if it is possible that they can carry it through I will put in $500, and if the other fellow who has his thousand will also put in $500 and others will do likewise $10,000,000 will be subscribed to buy ships and $2,000,000 will be subscribed to buy railroad and building materials, and we will be ready to ship men to Africa to work from January to December and open up opportunities immediately. That is what I am trying to get you to understand. A thousand dollars in your pocket without a job may find you worse off at the end of six months. A thousand dollars or $200 or $100 invested in an organization in which you have confidence may save yourself, your children and posterity. If you have no confidence I cannot advise you because I will do nothing myself except I have confidence in it. A man's confidence is his guide; a man's faith is his guide. I am only speaking to those who have faith in the Universal Negro Improvement Association. If you have faith, if you respect the success that we have made in three years when we started without anything and have reached where we are now; if you have faith that we can continue where we are to the greater success to be, I am asking you to support the program of the Universal Negro Improvement Association. I want to find out how many of you have confidence and faith in the Universal Negro Improvement Association. Hold your hands up. (Simultaneously hands went up from all parts of the hall.) I thank you for your faith. I thank you for your confidence; but men and women, remember it is not a question of Marcus Garvey or any other man. It is a question of yourselves. What will you do to save yourselves[?] Marcus Garvey cannot save anybody because Marcus Garvey is but human like every other man. Jesus Christ is the only man who has the power to save. I am but a man. I cannot save you; you must save yourselves. I am only trying to advise you the way how all of us can save ourselves. If you do not heed it will not be my fault. I have stood by; I have listened and I have heard all kinds of people blaming me for what I never . . . [*words mutilated*] somebody is crazy. How can Marcus Garvey prevent Negroes . . . [*words mutilated*]? What can I do? I have advised you all the time how to get jobs. That i[s] all I did. If you do not have jobs now it is not my fault. I advised you to put the money you saved into a great corporation—into a great corporation of which you are members; not in some strange thing that you did not know anything about—but in your own organization. Every member of the organization has a right to know everything about the organization, so that when you put your money into it you are putting your money in your own hands. I am but one individual who helped to carry on the work of the organization, and if you do not trust yourselves who is to blame? You did not have confidence in yourselves.

I am giving you a message that you may impart it to others and tell them there is still a chance; because we have not reached the worst yet; but that chance you must grasp in the next sixty days. I have met men coming to the office who have been out of work for three months and two months and one month. It brings tears to my eyes to see them. I saw a fellow whom I believe four years ago was raising "Cain" up in Harlem. He used to look at me on the street and laugh and walk on; but now he has been reduced to dire straits, and he came to the office and would not leave until I gave him 50 cents. That is the way with the majority of Negroes. That fellow earned as much money as any other men around here, and every evening you saw him on the avenue with a new [. . .] and a new girl. (Laughter.) The girls are belonging to somebody else [now] and he is down and out. (Laughter.) And that is the situation, not with one man but with hundreds of our men.

WE PRESERVED AMERICAN FREEDOM.

I am going to give this one advice. I have been waiting for the last 60 days to see what the politicians would do in making an effort to present the case of the Negro to the proper authorities. I have searched all the papers, and I have not seen anything done—no attempt made; and because they have done nothing I have to start to do something. You will all understand that I am an African citizen, and I am not supposed to interfere in domestic politics; but if the other fellow will not start out, before I see the people perish, I will take my chance. I know that this nation owes a solemn obligation to the Negro, and I could not stand and see the Negro perish without a hearing; and since the politicians have not spoken we shall send a delegation of the Universal Negro Improvement Association to the Governor of New York to find out what he means by allowing Negroes to be closed out of jobs,[3] when Negroes and especially the boys of the New York 15th fought so nobly in France and Flanders for the preservation of American freedom. What does the State mean by allowing the politicians and citizens of the State to close out Negroes and give alien enemies jobs now? (Cheers.) We will send a deputation to Albany to ask Albany, will you want us again? And we will expect an answer from Albany. We will ask Albany, "Will you want us in the American-Japanese war? Will you want us in the Anglo-American war?["] Because David Lloyd George is scheming now to write off the war debt,[4] and no American citizen is going to stand for it. Therefore it may end somewhere else. "Will you want us then?" And we will listen for the answer from Albany; and from Albany we will send the same deputation to Washington a couple of days after to ask the same question. (Cheers.)

This is no time for bowing and scraping and pussyfooting. It is time to let the other fellow know that you are alive (great applause). Negroes do not want to beg jobs; Negroes must demand jobs; that is all there is about it. (Applause.) But you must demand jobs in the proper way. Let the leaders of the race, if they are leaders, as Du Bois, and men like Mot[o]n, go out and let President-elect Harding know that ten or fifteen million Negroes stood behind the country in time of war, and they must now stand behind those ten or fifteen million Negroes. (Applause.) If you have any men posing as leaders who are going about among white people bowing and scraping they will brush you aside. You must have as your leaders and representatives men who will let our high officials and other influential white people know that you are alive, and that you are going to stay alive. I cannot see the philosophy of taking any other stand but this. I cannot see the reason for it—that Negroes should be drafted and sent three thousand miles away to fight and die at the command of their country, to help make conditions and life safe for other people; that Negroes, those whom their Government did not send to war, remained at home and engaged in making munitions and other necessities for carrying on the war, so as to win the victory—I repeat, I cannot see wherein Negroes who have made sacrifices such as these for their country, now that the war is over and a condition of business depression exists through the country, should be discriminated against, and in favor of other men who were their country's foes, and who have no other claim to preferential consideration than that the color of their skin happens to be white. I cannot see the consistency, the right of it. You men must not [y]ield up your jobs so easily. You have [a] right to them, and it is a question what you must make up you minds to [d]o; and that is, to demand what is yours; that is all. If you are too cowardly you will never get anything. It is better to die demanding what is yours than starve getting nothing. That's how I feel, and since they have done nothing, in another ten or fifteen days we will have a delegation up in Albany, and from Albany the delegation will go to Washington and ask what do they mean. We preserved the nation and the nation must preserve us.

Men, you have the balance of power in America, and we are the balance of power over the world. Do not let the world blu[ff] you. The American writers themselves acknowledge that the only people they could depend on in America for loyalty to the flag are the [fi]fteen million Negroes in America (applause); because they cannot tell the enemy in that he is white; the German is white; and they have had a hard time finding Germans. But they could tell who were Negroes, and the Kaiser was not from the Negro, either. So they knew the Negro was their friend. When the white man came, they had to ask: "Who comes there?"—and he had to answer: "Friend." But they did not have to ask that when they saw the black man coming, they knew before he came that he was a friend. However, we are going to ask them a question, as I told you a while ago, for since the politicians have not done anything we have got to play a little politics now. But, above all, men, I want you to remember that now is the time for you to support the Universal Liberian Construction Loan—you men who have fifty dollars; you men who have a hundred dollars; you men who have three hundred dollars or two hundred dollars. Now is the time for you to invest part of your money so as to enable us in another couple of weeks to secure the ship which we want to go to Africa. The ship is right down at the foot of Eighty-second street now. We can have it under contract this very hour; but the ship has to go for another twenty-six days, because we haven't the money to sign up the contract.[5] The ship costs $500,000. Oh, some of you think a ship can be bought for $500. (Laughter.) Ships in these days cost a million, two million dollars, five hundred thousand dollars, two hundred and fifty thousand dollars, and so on; and when you get a ship for $250,000 you have got a cheap ship. We have been [negoti]ating for the ship, the kind of beautiful ship that we want—a ship with everything on it that we want; but we just had to look and wait awhile, because Negroes wouldn't subscribe enough to buy it.

If we had the money with which to buy the ship we could send three hundred men tomorrow morning to Africa. The ship can carry three hundred passengers at one time; and the money for it is right here in Harlem! Some of you say we are crazy. I can not do better than tell you what we are planning, what we are hoping, what we are doing, what lies before us all in the future, and what we should do to attain the destiny that God has mapped out for us. We are hoping that we will realize the money between now and the 19th of March to complete the contract. But God Almighty knows it depends upon the people. If they will not support the Universal Liberian Construction Loan I cannot work miracles; I cannot take blood out of a stone. Therefore, for this reason I have spoken to you tonight, and I am asking you to advise your friends, those of you who have already subscribed, or who have already invested in the Universal Liberian Construction Loan, to appeal to them and urge them to join in the support of this very necessary and much needed and most worthy object, by subscribing to the Loan and investing whatever money they can at this time in the enterprise so that we can put this great program over.

I thank you very much for your attention. Good-night, all! (Great applause.)

Printed in *NW*, 26 February 1921. Original headlines abbreviated.

1. Industrial production in most areas of the economy increased during the period 1914 to 1918, with the largest growth in mining, manufacturing, and transportation. The gross national product rose by 15 percent during the same period, although output in nonwar production actually decreased. Average weekly earnings rose from $14 in 1916 to $27 in 1920, but a rapid increase in prices kept the real increase at about 6 percent. During the years 1918 and 1919, weekly wages for black industrial workers ranged from $14.22 for unskilled female cannery workers to $57.24 for highly skilled cattle slaughterers. A majority of black industrial workers earned between $15 and $30, although considerably lower wages were prevalent in nonindustrial labor and in the South. Black agricultural workers earned between $3 and $6 a week in 1917, and thus, wage increases of from 500 to 1,000 percent for migrants to the North were not uncommon (George Soule, *Prosperity Decade: From War to Depression, 1917–1929* [New York: Rinehart and Co., 1947], pp. 54, 221; George E. Haynes, *The Negro at Work During the World War and During Reconstruction* [1921; reprinted, New York: Negro Universities Press, 1969], pp. 10, 46–49).

2. The *Chicago Defender* of 5 February 1921 reported that Roscoe Thompson, an unemployed black man, confessed to killing Rev. L. W. Burbridge, pastor of the Macedonia Baptist Church, a black church in Chicago.

3. No record of this proposed delegation has been found.

4. On 5 August 1920 Lloyd George wrote to President Wilson suggesting the cancellation of all inter-Allied war debts. The proposal was rejected by the Wilson administration (James Thayer Gerould and Laura Shearer Turnbull, *Selected Articles on Interallied Debts and Revision of the Debt Settlements* [New York: H. W. Wilson Co., 1928]; Marc Trachtenberg, *Reparation in World Politics: France and European Economic Diplomacy, 1916–1923* [New York: Columbia University Press, 1980]).

5. At Garvey's mail fraud trial, Orlando Thompson testified that the Black Star Line began negotiating for a British vessel, the S.S. *Tennyson*, in January 1921, before Garvey left for the Caribbean. The Lamport and Holt Line owned the ship, and the Oceanic Freighting Co. served as brokers. The BSL's overtures ended shortly after Garvey's departure, when Thompson received a letter from the owners breaking off negotiations (*Marcus Garvey v. United States*, no. 8317, Ct. App., 2d Cir., 2 February 1925, p. 1,201).

UNIA Division News

[*Negro World*, 12 February 1921]

Since the August convention of the U.N.I.A., nearly one hundred new divisions have received and unveiled their charters and scores of divisions formed which have not yet been chartered. We have endeavored as far as possible to publish the division notes[1] in the Negro World for the purpose of encouraging the various divisions and letting the world know that the U.N.I.A. is sweeping over the world like a tidal wave. Last week we devoted nearly half of our reading space to the work of the divisions in different sections of the world. We will be glad to publish interesting news items of the various divisions, such as the formation of new divisions, the unveiling of charters, the presence of speakers from the parent body and special mass meetings. But we cannot publish, for lack of space, the weekly reports of the various divisions. It would require a newspaper twenty times as large as the Negro World to publish the weekly reports of all the divisions. So please remember that we have space for special reports from a few divisions, but not weekly reports from all.

Printed in *NW*, 12 February 1921. Original headlines omitted.

1. In 1921 the *Negro World* regularly printed two full pages of reports from selected UNIA divisions. Edited by William Ferris, the reports often described special meetings of local divisions featuring speeches by visiting UNIA officials. These pages were later given the title "News and Views from UNIA Divisions."

UNIA Announcements

SEND IN FOR CHARTERS AND INFORMATION NOW

ALL NEGRO COMMUNITIES OF THE WORLD

(of America, Africa, the West Indies, Central and South America)

ARE REQUESTED TO FORM THEMSELVES INTO BRANCHES OF THE

UNIVERSAL NEGRO IMPROVEMENT ASSOCIA- TION and AFRICAN COMMUNITIES LEAGUE OF THE WORLD

FOR THE CONSOLIDATION OF THE SENTIMENT AND ASPIRATIONS OF THE 400,000,000 OF THE NEGRO RACE

ORGANIZE FOR RACIAL PROGRESS, INDUSTRIALLY, COMMERCIALLY EDUCATIONALLY, POLITICALLY AND SOCIALLY

ORGANIZE FOR THE PURPOSE OF BUILDING A GREAT NATION

Any Seven Persons of Liberal Education of the Negro Race Can Organize Among Them- selves and Apply to the International Headquarters for Necessary Instructions and Charter

All Colored Churches and Lodges Are Requested to Organize Chapters.

2nd INTERNATIONAL CONVENTION OF DEPUTIES

From the Branches and Chapters of the Association of Every Country in the World, Will Assemble on the 1st of August, 1921, at Liberty Hall, New York

THE GREATEST MOVEMENT IN THE HISTORY OF THE NEGROES OF THE WORLD

The Universal Negro Improvement Association and African Communities League

wants every black man and woman to become an active member of the organization. If you have pride, if you feel that by co-operation we can make conditions better, if you believe that the black boy or black girl is the equal of other boys and girls of other races, then prove it now by co-operating to demonstrate our manhood and womanhood, not by talking, but by doing things.

The general objects of the Universal Negro Improvement Association and African Communities League, are:—

To establish a universal confraternity among the race; to promote the spirit of pride and love; to administer to and assist the needy; to assist in civilizing the backward tribes of Africa; to strengthen the nationalism of independent Negro States in Africa; to establish commissionaries or agencies in the prin- cipal countries of the world for the protection of all Negroes, irrespective of nationality; to establish uni- versities, colleges and schools for the racial education and culture of our young men and women; to con- duct a worldwide commercial and industrial intercourse for the benefit of the race; to work for better con- ditions among our people; to promote industries and commerce for the betterment of Negroes. If these objects do not appeal to you, then you are dead to all sense of race pride and race manhood.

Address All Communications to

UNIVERSAL NEGRO IMPROVEMENT ASSOCIATION AND AFRICAN COMMUNI- TIES' LEAGUE, Inc.

56 WEST 135th STREET   NEW YORK, UNITED STATES OF AMERICA

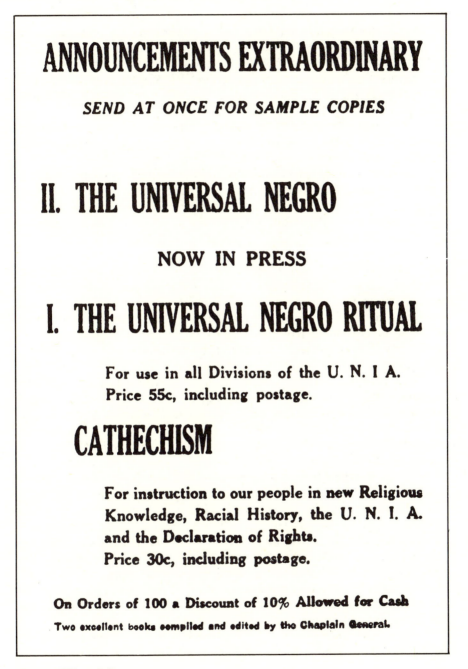

ANNOUNCEMENTS EXTRAORDINARY

SEND AT ONCE FOR SAMPLE COPIES

II. THE UNIVERSAL NEGRO

NOW IN PRESS

I. THE UNIVERSAL NEGRO RITUAL

For use in all Divisions of the U. N. I A.
Price 55c, including postage.

CATHECHISM

For instruction to our people in new Religious
Knowledge, Racial History, the U. N. I. A.
and the Declaration of Rights.
Price 30c, including postage.

On Orders of 100 a Discount of 10% Allowed for Cash

Two excellent books compiled and edited by the Chaplain General.

(*Source: NW*, 12 February 1921.)

Marcus Garvey v. *Amy Garvey*

[*New York*] 12 February 1921

MARCUS GARVEY, being duly sworn, deposes and says: I am the Plaintiff in the above entitled Action and have read the Affidavit of the Defendant herein. I have promptly complied with the Order of this Court, signed by Mr. Justice Finch, and am now paying the Defendant $12.00 (Twelve Dollars) per week alimony and have paid her Attorneys their fee of $250.00 (Two Hundred and Fifty Dollars) required by said Order.

I have made these payments, although I have never yet been served with a certified copy of the Order of this Court; neither has there been any written or other demand made upon me by the Defendant.

The fact is I have been compelled to be out of the City most of the time, traveling in the interests of my Organization and it has not been convenient for me to make the payments in any different manner, and in view of the fact that I received my salary fortnightly. However, I am not in arrears with my payments and expect to make the payments promptly in the future.

The first I knew of any dissatisfaction on the part of the Defendant was a few days ago when I was informed by my Attorney that the Defendant's Attorney had made a demand upon me for the payment of her alimony in advance in the event I went away on a trip to the West Indies. I, at that time, suggested to my Attorney to inform the Defendant's Attorneys that I had made arrangements to pay the Defendant's alimony promptly each week during my absence but that I would not consent to any payment in advance, as I cannot afford it.

I am planning to go on business to the Republic of Panama to be gone not more than three weeks. I am leaving on one of the Company's boats which will take me to Panama and bring me back. I will only stop at the port in Panama long enough to transact my business and perhaps stop at one or two other ports in the West Indies or Central America, and will immediately return on the same ship to New York.

It would appear from the Defendant's Affidavit that I was leaving New York for good, with no intention of returning. On the contrary the fact is that all my interests are in New York and I have no intention of leaving New York permanently. The Defendant is fully aware that I am only going on a business trip and that I will shortly return to this City. Since the Order was granted giving the Defendant alimony, I have been on trips to Canada and other places in the West where I have remained away quite three weeks and she has suffered no loss by my absence and there is absolutely no reason for her making this Motion to secure her alimony during my absence on a trip to the Republic of Panama.

I have made arrangements with my Attorney to pay the alimony that will be due the Defendant each week during my absence which will be not more than three weeks and the Defendant will receive her alimony promptly each week as the same becomes due.

MARCUS GARVEY

Marcus Garvey v. *Amy Garvey*, no. 20408, New York Supreme Court, 12 February 1921. TDS. Notarized.

Speech by Marcus Garvey

[[LIBERTY HALL,
NEW YORK, Feb. 13, 1921]]

Before I enter into the burden of my speech tonight I desire to read a newspaper clipping that comes to me from Canada, revealing the activities of the British and Canadian government in the designs on the exploitation of Africa.[1] In reading the clipping I will do so with a heart full of sorrow because of the inactivity and the careless indifference the Negro has shown towards his own interests while others alien to him have been busying themselves organizing for the purpose of taking away from and depriving the Negro of all that is belonging to him. Again I must say, as I have often said, that Negroes are the most lazy, the most careless and indifferent people in the world, and it simply sickens one sometimes to feel that he is identified with a people who cannot see while the whole world is seeing and realizing in its own interests. I will read the clipping and I will comment afterwards. (He then read the news article, as follows):

MUCH CANADIAN MATERIAL TO BE USED.

BY LUKIN JOHNSTON.

Fifty million dollars will be entrusted by the British Government to the Canadian firm of Stewart & MacDonnell, headed by Major-General J. W. Stewart, C.B., to be spent on vast engineering works in the Gold Coast Colony, West Africa. General Stewart returned from England on Monday evening after making final arrangements for the carrying out of the first unit of the great harbor works at Takoradi.[2] This unit will cost $17,000,000, and will take from five to six years to complete.

The fact that this huge undertaking has been committed to the hands of a Canadian firm of engineers is a matter for congratulation to the Dominion, but it has much deeper significance than appears on the surface. It is the first concrete evidence that the British Government is ready and anxious to recognize and develop the true economic and imperial unity of the British Empire.

"I am weary of the cry of 'Australia for the Australians!' 'Canada for the Canadians!' and so on," Viscount Milner, until recently Secretary of State for the Colonies, is reported to have said on one occasion. "Why should Canadians stay at home? Let Canadians, Australians, New Zealanders and South Africans realize now and always that the crown colonies of the British Empire are part and parcel of their heritage just as much as they are of the people of Great Britain."

This is the deeper significance of the undertaking which has been committed to General Stewart and his colleagues. It is a part of a great plan, conceived by a man of broad vision, to further unify the empire and to strengthen the intangible cord which binds all parts of it together.

TELLS OF VAST PROJECT.

General Stewart sat in this office in the Winch Building and discussed this great project in West Africa, nearly 9,000 miles distant from his own home.

It is a platitude to say that General Stewart is a remarkable man. Any one who has followed his career, particularly during the war, when he was in command of the Canadian railway construction troops, must realize that here is a man of most unusual capacity. With the quiet voice and retiring manner of the student rather than the man of action, General Stewart talked calmly in millions while he told of the vast project which he and his associates will direct.

The Gold Coast colony is a huge territory lying between the British colony of Togoland and Nigeria on the east, and Ivory Land on the west. Roughly speaking it has a coast line of 350 miles and extends toward the hinterland of Central Africa for a distance of 300 miles. Its population consists of 6,000 whites and 6,000,000 Negroes. The value of its natural resources is beyond estimate. Even today 400,000 tons of manganese ore are shipped annually from the colony. There are great forests of mahogany; there are gold and silver and mines and immense stretches of tropical country which in years to come will produce crops of rubber, rice, sugar and cocoanuts of much value. Today all these things which may be turned to good use for man's welfare are either inaccessible or undeveloped.

To a Canadian firm it has fallen to make the first big move in developing the Eldorado of equatorial Africa.

The first unit which will be constructed under the supervision of General Stewart's firm comprises a breakwater one and a half miles long. It will protect the area decided upon for the harbor of Takoradi from the prevalent western winds and currents. Within this harbor will be dredged a deep-water harbor of a minimum depth of 22 1/2 feet.

To an outsider such a vast project must be of great interest. To those directly concerned, as are Canadians, it is a matter not only of interest but of great commercial potentialities. General Stewart states that, as far as possible, Canadian material and equipment will be used in the work. Canadian cars, steam shovels, locomotives, cement and iron will be shipped in immense quantities, while British Columbia Douglas fir will have an important place in the array of material needed. The first cargo of B.C. timber will be shipped from Vancouver as soon as a vessel is available.

B.C. FOR AFRICAN PRODUCTS.

Ships which carry to the Gold Coast these vast stores of rolling stock and equipment will return laden with the produce of Africa. Mahogany, cotton, rubber and other produce will come back to Canada in exchange, and there will be openings for the building up of a valuable export and import trade.

While for the most part Negro labor will be employed, the heads of departments will be Canadians, most of them at present engaged with Messrs. Foley, Welch & Stewart, in this province. The first party of thirty officials will leave British Columbia in time to reach the Gold Coast by April. In charge of the work for the first year or so will be Hon. Angus MacDonnell, a well-known resident of British Columbia. Probably in the autumn General Stewart will go out and take charge when the plant is assembled and ready to start operations.

It will be of interest to many British Columbians to learn that Admiral Sir John Parry, K.C.B., known in British Columbia waters as Commander Parry, in charge of the hydrographic survey vessel Egeria until 1914, has been working with Mr. MacDonnell in the Gold Coast on the preliminary survey work for the undertaking. He has been of the greatest assistance, says General Stewart. General Guggisberg,[3] the governor of the colony, is also a Canadian, his wife being the sister of Miss Eva Moore, who was here recently. It is to General Guggisberg probably as much as to any other man that Canada owes the honor which has fallen to her, for he has shown himself keen from the first to see the methods employed by Canadians in France adopted in the country over which he rules.

MR. GARVEY COMMENTS.

Commenting on the article, Mr. Garvey said: Not longer ago than last Sunday night, I believe, I told you that we had but very little time to work in for the next six months would be eventful in the life of the Negro; and probably some of you went away and you forgot about it. Just at this time the entire bankrupt states and nations of Europe are making a mighty and desperate effort to get hold of new fields for exploitation. I told you on several occasions that Europe no longer offers a chance or opportunity to any of the great powers for exploitation. Europe is over exploited and Asia is keenly protected by Japan, hence no encouragement is offered for those who desire new fields for exploitation in Asia. The only part of the world left then is Africa. Africa during the war and Africa immediately after the war—I am speaking of native Africa—did absolutely nothing to protect its own interests. No effort was made to establish political rights and ownership hence the white bankrupt world saw the chance, saw the opportunity to concentrate on the exploitation of Africa. No longer than a couple of weeks ago Italy published through the newspapers a similar news item which revealed the fact that Italian capitalists backed by the Italian government were about to open up new spheres and fields of exploitation in Africa similar to this Canadian and British project. What does it mean? It means that the last hope—the [last] stronghold of the Negro is being torn from him, and when it is gone, it is as well he says his prayers and go home to his God. The words of Lord Milner that the slogan of Australia for the Australians and Canada for the Canadians and New Zealand for the New Zealanders is all bosh and that these Colonials—those people of the great dominions—should realize that the Crown Colonies of the Empire belongs to them as much as it is belonging to other Britishers—is very significant.[4] It is an encouragement to those colonials to leave their barren spheres and go into the more productive spheres of the Crown Colonies where Great Britain holds sway and dominion. Simultaneously with this project of sending out these Canadians with a capital of $[5]0,000,000 to lay the foundation for the exploitation of the Gold Coast, they have made the greatest Negro hater in the British Empire, Winston Spencer Churchill, Secretary of the Colonies.[5] Winston Spencer Churchill just a couple of days ago was made Secretary for the Colonies. Those of you who have been following the utterances of British and other statesmen will remember that not very long ago Winston Churchill said somewhere in England when the question of the return of the German colonies to the natives was being discussed, he asked the question: "What reasonable Englishman would turn over the colonies we have wrested from Germany in Africa back to the savages of Africa?"[6] Winston Churchill, a close pupil of Christian Smuts of South Africa,[7] is known to be one of the greatest Negro haters of the world, and the Crown Colonies are now placed under his control; and they have capitalized a Canadian expedition with $50,000,000 to go and exploit all the Gold Coast. They then admit that the wealth and the riches of the Gold Coast passes all estimates and that is all to be theirs, because Negroes have been lazy and indifferent for 300 years. The wealth that you desire to bring you food and clothing—the wealth that belongs to you, you sit down and allow another man to take it away from you. Talk about calling on God Almighty; talk about praying to the Lord Jesus Christ—what has God Almighty and Jesus Christ to do with the gold dust on the Gold Coast? What has God Almighty to do with a corporation capitalized at $50,000,000[?] God Almighty is the Creator of the Universe. He did his job thousands of years ago. He created the Universe and gave a portion of it to you. If you allow someone else to take it from you[,] you ought to die. And that is just the situation now.

For four years we have been preaching this doctrine to Negroes. A meagre $50,000,000 for that the Gold Coast must be exploited because the Gold Coast for years and years has been looking to the Negroes of the Western Civilization to come to her rescue. The men in their innocence in the Gold Coast and other parts knew not of the wiles of Western commerce; they heard of it, they saw part of it, but they knew not the conduct of it, and they were ever waiting and longing for men of their race to teach them the value of the minerals—the value of everything in their own land, and Negroes kept away all the time. God Almighty gave us five years of chance not to get $50,000,000 but to get hundreds of millions of dollars; because did you not send $250,000,000 during the war for Liberty Bonds?[8] You spent $250,000,000 for Liberty Bonds. In the same way you did that you could have saved and started some organization to the extent of $100,000,000, and tonight it would be a fight between British exploiters and the Universal Negro Improvement Association to get into the Gold Coast. But we preached the doctrine to you and you said we were crazy. We preached the doctrine to you and you would not hear and now you are lost from your home; it is about to be taken away from you, which makes your fight the harder. . . . [*remainder of paragraph mutilated*]

LIBERTY HALL MESSAGE.

Now I want to send this message from Liberty Hall. It is a question of the survival of the fittest, and if the Negro peoples of America, the West Indies and this civilized Western world sit down for another five years as they have sat down for the years past they are doomed, because the world organized as it is now has no mercy for weak and unprepared men. America as she reveals herself becomes more prejudiced towards Negroes every day. Canadians for the first time are going [9],000 miles away. What does it mean? It means a new grasp on Africa, and whatsoever we have to do we must do it now—now or never. They say it will take six years for them to build up to usefulness the project that they have. I pray it will keep them that long. I pray God will give 400,000,000 men strength enough to go out and conquer and take Africa. I want you to note how the white man works. This man who is to direct operations on the Gold Coast is a valuable man; he is the master mind. What is he doing? He is doing just what the American Government did a few years ago when it started to build the Panama Canal. They kept the engineering geniuses until all was prepared for them. The plan of the white man is to work Africa with the labor of the Negro. They say they are going to use Negro labor. These thirty white men are going out to use those Negro laborers in making the Gold Coast sanitary and habitable for the white man, and when those white men send a message back that everything is well, others will follow with their mighty force. West Indian Negroes were sent for to work in the swamps and bushes of Panama and when they had made the place sanitary it was then that the white American engineers under the leadership of General Goethals went out and built the Panama Canal.[9] And so they have a design again to use Negro laborers in the Gold Coast to make the place sanitary and habitable and then these other Canadians will go in large numbers and occupy the land.

I tell you men, there will be a toss up some day. Some people think I am anti-British; some people think that I am anti-white. I am neither anti-British nor anti-white. I am pro-Negro, and I want to say this from Liberty Hall tonight—come the world in arms, South Africa shall be won for the white man only when Marcus Garvey with 400,000,000 lay down their lives. (Cheers.) It is my last hope and I shall give the last drop of my blood for that last hope. Men, it is your last hope. When Winston Churchill, as secretary for the colonies, with men goes out with a desire only to exploit what does it mean? It means that in another 50 years Negroes will be as rare in Africa as North American Indians are rare in this United States of America today.

This advice of Lord Milner to Canadians and Australians to go out and take advantage of the Crown Colonies means that Africa is the hope of the white man. But before Africa was the hope of the white man Africa was created the home of the black man. And it is a question of a man proving himself fit to live. I say to you in here tonight that if you are fit you will live; if you are not fit you will die.

PROVE YOUR FITNESS.

We of the Universal Negro Improvement Association are calling upon you to prove your fitness[.] God Almighty created you men: he never created you weaklings or puppets. God Almighty bequeathed to you the same rights as he bequeathed to other men. It is for you 400,000,000 Negroes of the world to go out, look at the world and demand your place in the world. (Cheers.) But how can you do it[?] Englishmen and Canadians and Frenchmen and Italians do not go about things they want in a half-hearted manner; they do not only talk about it, but they go about it; and whilst we have been talking here in this whole-hearted manner for four years, what have we done? We have not subscribed the $10,000,000 capital of the Black Star Line; we have not even subscribed $2,000,000 to the Liberian Construction Loan. How do we expect ever to win? Overnight the Canadians got $50,000,000. It is not a case of your not having it. If you had not got it[,] it would be quite a different thing; but you have it, as much as they have it, and if you have not got it[,] it is your fault. You are to get it from the same source they got it. You had it and what did you do with yours? You gave it back to them. How long will this slackness continue among Negroes? I wish I could convert the world of Negroes overnight to the tremendous possibilities of the Universal Negro Improvement Association. The things I have dreamed of; the things I foresaw four years ago are now coming true and the people I preached to, I talked to, I wrote to have not helped to realize the dream. It pains me every moment of the day when I see Negroes losing the grasp they should have on their own. You of Liberty Hall[,] I must ask you to go out as missionaries and preach this doctrine again of the Universal Negro Improvement Association. Let all the world know that this is the hour; this is the time for our salvation. Prayer alone will not save us; sentiment alone will not save us. We have to work and work and work if we are to be saved. I would not spend one minute with you if I were to preach a sermon to you because Jesus Christ preached his sermon nearly two thousand years ago which converted me. What I want you to understand is not so much preaching about beatitudes, but it is the preaching about your bread and butter that will cause you to live whilst you are down here. Jesus Christ preached and taught the beatitudes and every man born in the Christian dispensation ought to know and realize it. The time now is to preach the beatitude of bread and butter. I have contributed my bit in preaching this doctrine. What is the idea of men going 9,000 mile[s] away? For fun? Just to see some new god? No! For what? To see gold, to see all the minerals, the copper, iron, gold, rubber and everything that is of material value. That is why they are going 9,000 miles away and as they are prepared to go 9,000 miles away to rob what is not theirs, I am prepared to go 15,000 miles to stop some one taking away from me what belongs to me. (Cheers.)

Some of us are made up too cowardly. There is no place in the world for cowards. What right has Winston Spencer Churchill to stand up in the Guild Hall, or in the Caxton Hall, or in the Royal Albert Hall, or anywhere in London, and tell me and tell my brothers that they should not have the country that God Almighty gave them? What right has he to say that he believes such a thing? But if he believes it, it is for me to disprove that right; and that is just what we are organizing for[.] Negroes, understand, there are 400,000,000 of you in the world, and if you are too cowardly to stand up for what belongs to you, if you are going to let 60,000,000 Anglo-Saxons take away that which God Almighty gave you, you ought to die! But here is one man (the speaker here refers to himself) who will measure arms with and meet any Anglo-Saxon anywhere, at any time. Every day and night I feel sure I will meet him and bring away what belongs to me and let him go on his way. That is the determination I want each and every one of you to make up in your minds, for it's your last chance. You despise Africa, some of you, but let me tell you that Africa is going to be the greatest spot in the world in another fifty years. When you hear of progress, when you hear of h[um]an success, when you hear of wealth, you will hear of Africa, even if it is fifty years from now, for these Canadians are going there to make it, and these Italians are going there to make it, but before they get there the Universal Negro Improvement Association will be there! (Applause.)

THE SOUTH AFRICAN ELECTION.

To change my thought for a while, news has also come from South Africa that Smutts has been victorious in carrying the election.[10] Smutts, you know, is the successor of the late General Botha. Smutts stands for a white South Africa.[11] Smutts stands for South Africa as a part of the British Empire. The elections indulged in the other day brought out a rivalry between himself and Gen. Hertzog, the leader of the Nationalist party of South Africa.[12] Gen. Hertzog's desire is to have an independent South Africa—a free and independent South Africa, and at the time of election he had a majority in the South Africa Parliament, as against the party represented by Smutts.[13] The election came off, and a rigid campaign was waged, Hertzog and his men campaigned on the question of an independent South Africa, and Smutts waged a campaign on a united South Africa as part of the British Empire. Smutts succeeded in the election with a majority because he preached to the people there—the white people—that it would be dangerous to have an independent South Africa at this time, since there are but one million white settlers in South Africa, while there are about six million natives, and that owing to the new trend of thought among the natives it was unsafe to have an independent South Africa at this time. He was therefore counting upon the support of the Empire of Great Britain to back him and his government should the natives attempt to take advantage of the establishment there of a free and independent South Africa. Because of his campaigning tactics in that direction, many of the Nationalists who would have otherwise voted for an independent South Africa voted for Smutts' party, and he is again returned to power in South Africa.

I am not sorry that he has been returned to power with his party. Do you know why I am not sorry? It is because we are not prepared. I have always been looking at that South African question with a close eye. I am always anticipating the day when the South Africans themselves, as a National Party, will cut loose from Great Britain, and then will come a great chance for the Negro peoples, if they are organized. What could you do if South Africa were declared independent tomorrow? What would you do? The Boers would take us and beat us and do everything else that is cruel and brutal, the same as they have done ever since they first settled in South Africa, because we are not prepared and not ready.

The world is still in the balance. Wilson talks about peace while the world is just next door to war. Why? The machinations of the various Allied Governments, especially Great Britain, led by David Lloyd George, who are seeking to have America wipe out their war debt to us, is but a sounding of the sentiment of war. Ten billions of dollars were loaned by the United States of America to England, France, Italy and Russia, and the premiers of all these countries are coming to us and saying: "Please cut out that war debt of ten billion dollars we owe you (laughter). You know what that means. It is a threat of war. That is all. England has not paid one cent of her interest on her war debt to the United States for the first year. What does it mean? It is only provoking the United States to anger; and if you had another man for president than Wilson, probably a short, curt note would have gone to Westminster ere now. Such a note would by now be in the hands of the British Premier, but because of Wilson's disposition nothing has been said about it. But we anticipate that something about it will be said when Harding gets into power[14] (applause). The ten billion dollars of war debt to us these nations want us to cancel. Just think of it! But it will not be canceled by the American working man, because he had to slave and starve himself for over five years to subscribe that ten billion dollars, and he wants it; because when he gets it back, it means that his burden of taxation will be lifted. If the ten billion dollars is not paid back by these Allied Governments who borrowed it he will be taxed another ten billion dollars to make up for it and to keep the nation agoing. The American nation will not do that. England is simply trying to hide-and-seek about it: they are preparing to dodge their portion of this great war debt. I believe they got four billion out of the ten billion, and they are trying to dodge the issue of paying it back.

If they don't pay it back, something is going to happen. If they don't pay it back, if the bankrupt powers of Europe do not pay back their indebtedness to the United States something is going to happen and you know what that will be. France will say: "I cannot pay back the money I borrowed from the United States of America." England will say to France: "I cannot pay back that money I borrowed from the United States of America." And Italy will say: "We cannot pay back that money we borrowed from the United States of America." And then they will all say: "Let us get together and start something!" That's how war comes about—get together and start something: and, brothers, I am laying up for that day when they do start that something. (Laughter and applause) When they start that something, we will be ready to start something too. (Renewed applause and laughter).

Printed in *NW*, 19 February 1921. Original headlines omitted.

1. Lukin Johnson, "Much Canadian Material to Be Used—General Stewart Tells of Great Contract Secured on Gold Coast—British Government Entrusts Vast Project to Soldier-Railway Builder," *Daily Province* (Vancouver), 2 February 1921; see also "Great Task on Gold Coast," *Daily Province*, 8 February 1921.

2. Consulting engineers employed by the British government first suggested the construction of a deep-water harbor in Takoradi Bay in 1895. Following his appointment as governor of the Gold Coast, Frederick Guggisberg worked to secure a loan for the construction of the harbor. After obtaining African and colonial legislative support, he appointed Messrs. Stewart & McDonnell, a company headed by Maj. Gen. J. W. Stewart (b. 1882) of Canada, to make a survey of the area. The British government's first estimate of expenditure for the harbor at Takoradi was £500,000, but by February 1921 that figure was brought down to £100,000; then in September 1921, the official agreement with Stewart & McDonnell was further modified to £20,000 per year for three and a half years, starting July 1921, for work in connection with the harbors at Takoradi, Sekondi, and Accra (PRO, CO 96/628). On 20 July 1921 Winston Churchill, the British colonial secretary, gave final approval. Three years later, however, Messrs. Stewart & McDonnell, whose initial estimate of £1.6 million had now risen to £2.5 million, resigned from the contract, apparently because of restrictions limiting the purchase of certain materials to the United Kingdom (R. E. Wraith, *Guggisberg* [London: Oxford University Press, 1967], pp. 101–107; David Meredith, "The Construction of Takoradi Harbour in the Gold Coast, 1919 to 1930: A Case Study in Colonial Development and Administration," *Transafrica Journal of History* 5 [1976]: 134–149).

3. Sir Frederick Gordon Guggisberg (1869–1930), Canadian-born engineer and statesman, was appointed governor and commander in chief of the Gold Coast in 1919, where he served until 1927. He began his career with the British Colonial Office in 1897 as chief surveyor of the Gold Coast and Ashanti, and he remained in West Africa until the First World War. The publisher of several works on West Africa, Guggisberg in 1927 visited the United States at the invitation of the Phelps-Stokes Fund, and in 1929 he coauthored, with Rev. A. G. Fraser, *The Future of the Negro* (New York: Phelps-Stokes Fund, 1929), a discourse on his visit to the Tuskegee and Hampton institutes. In the book, he called for similar educational opportunities for black Africans and expressed his belief that "the Negro races are capable of the highest development." The *Negro World*, however, took issue with Guggisberg's statement that the Africans were "suspicious of the American Negro" and also pointed out that the paper was banned from British West Africa (*WWW*; R. E. Wraith, *Guggisberg*, p. 288; *NW*, 4 February 1928).

4. Alfred Milner (1854–1925) was the British governor of South Africa who played an important part in bringing about the Boer War (1899–1902). At the conclusion of the war he continued to serve as British high commissioner. Milner was the leading proponent of "imperial unity," and perhaps the first British statesman to conceive of an empire transcending the countries or races of which it was composed. In 1906 he stated that "every white man of British birth . . . can be at home in every state of the Empire" (Viscount Milner, *Imperial Unity* [London: Compatriot's Club, 1907], p. 21). In 1918 he became secretary of state for the colonies and was succeeded by Winston Churchill in 1921 (*DAHB*; Vladimir Halperin, *Lord Milner and the Empire: The Evolution of British Imperialism* [London: Odhams Press, 1952], p. 182).

5. Winston Leonard Spencer Churchill (1874–1965) was appointed secretary for the colonies and air on 12 February 1921, a position he held until his defeat in the general elections of November 1922 (*WBD*). In 1920 Churchill asked to be relieved of his position as secretary of state for war and air because of disagreements with Lloyd George, the prime minister, over the running of the army and the Royal Air Force. He preferred the Office of the Exchequer, but was also interested in the Foreign Office and the Colonial Office. Unwilling to lose the most talented member of his cabinet, Lloyd George appointed Churchill colonial secretary (William Manchester, *The Last Lion* [Boston: Little, Brown and Co., 1983], p. 695).

6. Churchill strongly opposed the return of the captured German colonies to Germany, but he did not participate in the debate in Parliament over their disposition. He did, however, oppose efforts to give nonwhite colonists increased self-government and generally attributed unrest in the British Empire to Bolshevik subversion. During the period of 1919 to 1920, Churchill was the architect of the policy of counterrevolution against the Bolshevik government in Russia, and he frequently ridiculed the Soviet call for self-determination for smaller European nations and for Asian and African colonies. In a March 1921 Liberty Hall speech, Garvey said of Churchill, "His illegal, unconstitutional intrigues in Russia cost the British many millions of dollars in taxation and no less of reputation" (*NW*, 12 March 1921). He was a staunch upholder of the British empire; as one recent commentator notes, "Churchill's 'finest hour' oration in 1940 wound up with a call to defend not Britain but the British empire, and keep it intact for the next thousand years" (V. G. Kiernan, *From Conquest to Collapse: European Empires from 1815–1960* [New York: Pantheon Books, 1982]; Robert Rhodes James, ed., *Winston S. Churchill: The Complete Speeches* Vol. 3 [New York: Chelsea House Publishers, 1974], p. 2,920; Prosser Gifford and William Roger Louis, eds., *Britain and Germany in Africa: Imperial Rivalry and Colonial Rule* [New Haven, Conn.: Yale University Press, 1967]; Peter Kenez, *Civil War in South Russia, 1919–1920: The Defeat of the Whites* [Berkeley, Los Angeles, London: University of California Press, 1978]).

7. Churchill was an admirer of and occasional correspondent with Jan Christian Smuts (1870–1950). In March 1917, on Smuts's arrival in London to take up his appointment to the Imperial War Cabinet, Churchill praised him for his leadership of the East African campaign; on 18 November 1918 Smuts wrote in turn to Lloyd George, recommending Churchill for promotion to a cabinet post (J. C. Smuts, *Jan Christian Smuts* [London: Cassell and Co., 1952]; Jean Van Der Poel, ed., *Selections from the Smuts Papers* [Cambridge: Cambridge University Press, 1973] 3: 687). In the Asian context Churchill has also been viewed as "a notable but idiosyncratic racist." (Christopher Thorne, *Allies of a Kind: The United States, Britain, and the War Against Japan, 1941–1945* [London: Hamish Hamilton, 1978], p. 6).

8. Blacks contributed an estimated $225 million to the U.S. war effort by purchasing Liberty bonds and war savings stamps (*NYB*, pp. 45–50).

9. Shortly after the American government took over the Panama Canal project in 1903, the growing colony of newly arrived American engineers and their families was swept up in a

devastating yellow fever epidemic. Three-quarters of them left soon after arriving, and the American physician in charge of controlling malaria and yellow fever in the Canal Zone, William C. Gorgas, was finally given sufficient funds and personnel to launch a campaign of fumigation and sanitation. The fumigation teams, who went door to door in Panama City and also worked in swamps and wooded areas, were made up largely of black West Indians and Panamanians. Even after significant numbers of Americans returned, blacks continued to suffer an appalling mortality rate, with deaths of blacks in 1906 reaching a rate three times that of whites. Blacks were continually employed in the work of digging drainage ditches, cutting grass, hauling garbage, and pouring oil on streams and swamps, labors that partially accounted for the higher mortality rate (David McCullough, *The Path Between the Seas* [New York: Simon and Schuster, 1977], pp. 500–501).

10. Smuts had become prime minister by appointment when his predecessor, Louis Botha, died. In February 1921 Smuts was the victor in a national election, remaining prime minister and increasing his parliamentary majority (Monica Wilson and Leonard Thompson, eds., *The Oxford History of South Africa* [New York: Oxford University Press, 1971], pp. 378–380).

11. Smuts made his most comprehensive statement on South African "native affairs" in a speech delivered in London on 22 May 1917. Calling for cooperation between the English and Afrikaners and for strict racial separation between black and white, he stated that: "It has been our ideal to make it a white man's country, but it is not a white man's country yet. It is still a black man's country. . . . There are people in South Africa . . . who are not certain that the white experiment will be a success, or that we shall ever succeed in making it a white man's land. We are going to make the attempt" (*Times* [London], 23 May 1917).

12. James Barry Munnik Hertzog (1866–1942) was an Afrikaner general in the Boer War and founder of the Nationalist party in 1914. Hertzog's party opposed conciliation with the British, and it gradually gained strength until 1924, when he was able to form a coalition government. He assumed the post of prime minister and served until 1939 (*DAHB*).

13. The forty-four seats won by the Nationalist party in 1920 formed a plurality. The South African party won forty-one seats, the second largest number. (Monica Wilson and Leonard Thompson, eds., *The Oxford History of South Africa*, pp. 378–379).

14. Harding had been elected president, but he was not inaugurated until 4 March 1921.

Report by Special Agent P-138

New York City 2-14-21

IN RE: NEGRO ACTIVITIES.

Owing to the fact that there were several rumors relative to the exact date of MARCUS GARVEY's departure to the West Indies, I today [*11 February*] had a conversation with Marcus Garvey at his private office, 56 West 135th Street, and he told me that he should have been well on his way now, but the "KANAW[H]A" is undergoing repairs and the mechanics told him that the new boiler tubes were late in arriving at the shipyard, thus causing a delay. He expects, however, to leave about the end of next week as soon as the ship repairs are completed. This delay has upset his itiner[ar]y, inasmuch as he had made speaking dates with many of his local organizations in the West Indies, who were expecting him.

P-138

[*Handwritten endorsement*] FILE G. F. R.
[*Stamped endorsement*] NOTED F. D. W.

DNA, RG 65, file BS 202600-33-167X. TD.

Speech by Marcus Garvey

[[Liberty Hall, *ca. 16 February 1921*]]

... We are not the only ones who feel that the Prime Minister of England and the British Government have made a bad selection or choice in naming Winston Spencer Churchill as the Secretary of State for the Colonies. I spoke about Winston Spencer Churchill last Sunday night, and Brisbane, of the Hearst newspaper, speaks about him today. And this is what Brisbane had to say under the caption of "Selection of Churchill a Bad Sign." "The appointment of Winston Churchill to the control of British colonial administration has a very ominous porten[t] for the return of decency and justice and economy so much needed in the British Empire for the restoration of its financial and moral credit. This temperamental, unscrupulous and audacious and irresponsible person has done more than any ten men in the British Empire to bring disrepute and bad credit morally and financially upon the British Government. His illegal, unconstitutional intrigues in Russia caused the British many millions of dollars in taxation and no less of reputation.[1] He will succeed to the control of the British policy in Egypt, Mesopotamia, Persia and those Near-Eastern countries where British imperialism is so flagrantly giving the lie to British pretense[2] during the war that Britain was fighting Germany to make the world safe for democracy. This unscrupulous and irresponsible man can, by virtue of the powers and opportunities of his office, continue his ceaseless intrigues against Russia in the Near East as Liberal newspapers in England point out in their dismay at the appointment of Churchill to this delicate and responsible office. It portends the end of the announced British plan to carry out Britain's solemn oath in Egypt given thirty years ago, and again solemnly during the war, and renewed as solemnly since the close of the war.[3] It portends some intrigue throughout the Near East and constant embroilment, confusion and ferment in other parts of the world. It has succeeded in the Balkans as the powder magazine of the white race. For the sake of the British people and for the sake of the people of the Near East, we hope that this man will not have freedom to follow his natural bent, and that his appointment has not the direct significance of its present appearance."

While the white world is lamenting the appointment of Winston Spencer Churchill as Secretary of State for the Colonies, the English people have their reason and their purpose for appointing this man to that high office. Winston Spencer Churchill in England is like Tillman and Vardaman in the United States of America, a rank Negro hater and hater of all peoples who are not white, and David Lloyd George, in his wisdom, I believe, appointed him to this office because he is the man that will carry out that savagery and brutality among the darker and weaker races of the world through a system of exploitation that will bring to bankrupt Britain the solvency that she so much desires.[4] Because this is a period of exploitation for Britain, and she has searched her entire empire to find a man to do the job of exploitation, and they have singled out the Negro hater Churchill to do the job.

As I have often said from the platform of Liberty Hall, the war has left the world in bankruptcy. I said that long before the American papers realized it, and wrote about it. I said that even before the war came to a close that the end of the war would see universal bankruptcy among the nations of Europe. And it has come true. Europe and the world is bankrupt today, and every nation is endeavoring to find new openings, new outlets for exploitation—that exploitation that will bring to them the resources, the revenue and the power necessary for their well being. Among the bankrupt nations today are Great Britain, France, Italy and Belgium. I speak of these because they are great colonizing powers in Africa. Germany is also a bankrupt nation, but we are not very much concerned about Germany now; Germany cannot do any harm. (Laughter.) Germany is too hemmed in by British greed, by British selfishness, that she can hardly attempt to do anything even if she desired to. But Great Britain, France, Italy and Belgium are great colonial powers; they have great territories in Africa, and recently the utterances of their statesmen and the persuasions of their journals and magazines and periodicals inform the world that they are now making a desperate attempt—a desperate effort to exploit the fields of Africa. Africa from north to south, from east to west, Africa centrally, Africa's 12,000,000 square miles open up untold opportunities and advantages for these bankrupt nations of Europe, and they are mobilizing all their powers, all their strength, all their energy to carry out systematically this exploitation of Africa which will, as I said last Sunday night and several weeks ago, settle a plan to monopolize Africa. Italy is sending out under the patronage of great Italian corporations hundreds and thousands of men into Italian Africa to exploit and take away from Africa the wealth that Africa contains. And while Italy is now sending out her greatest colonial exploiters and explorers, so England has placed in authority this great Negro hater, this great imperial genius of theirs, who will map out a program for the next five years, for the life of the present David Lloyd George's cabinet that will mean the subserviency of every inch of land and every ounce of wealth that Africa contains.

REDEEMING AFRICA.

In having Winston Spencer Churchill as Secretary of State for the Colonies we have a dangerous and desperate foe. But even as the English people have concentered upon him the right and power to carry out their imperial program, so we—400,000,000 of us—have concentered upon the Universal Negro Improvement Association the right to redeem Africa (Cheers). Not many of us take interest in international affairs; but those who are leading this movement have perforce to take cognizance of international happenings. Some of us cannot see things further than in Harlem; but that will not take us very far. Some of us cannot see things further than [*what is?*] happening within the bounds of the United States of America. We have to mingle with international problems so as to be able to cope with international situations; because humanity is an international, and universal being, and when a man becomes dissatisfied in any one part of the world he reaches out to other parts. In Europe these Caucasians after having exploited others, robbed and killed others[,] are now dissatisfied with their own native habitat and are endeavoring to reach beyond Europe. As I said last Sunday night, they are endeavoring to reach beyond Europe into Asia; but there stands Japan saying "Hands off!" hence they are reaching somewhere else. They cannot reach into this Western Hemisphere because the United States Government through the Monroe Doctrine says "Hands off!" So the only part of the world that they can reach out to is the great continent of Africa. They are reaching their hand out and they seemingly have heard no voice saying "Hands off!" but if they keep their hand stretched out one of these days they will have but the stump left—the whole hand will be gone and the stalk alone will be left. We of the Universal Negro Improvement Association say—"insignificant as we are; insignificant as they count Negroes to be; mark it, that 400,000,000 Negroes are warning the world." We are not warning the world that we are going to do anything to outrage the world; we are not warning the world that we are going to do anything to outrage humanity; we are not warning the world that we are going to do anything that will cause human suffering; but we are warning the world that we are coming 400,000,000 strong to take from the world what the world has for us (cheers). And in surveying the world and determining what the world has for us, we know that the world has 12,000,000 square miles of land belonging to us, and whatsoever bankrupt race or nation has a portion of that twelve million square miles of land, if they persist, if the insist, if they continue, if they desire to interfere with what is not belonging to them, what happened to them they will have no one else to blame, but themselves (cheers). I think it utter foolishness on the part of any man after being forewarned about danger to go into danger and into trouble. Such a man is a fool. I cannot for the life of me see where white people get their reasoning and their logic from that they must keep Europe, that they must take Asia and this Western Hemisphere and then take Africa and say to Negroes to get out of everywhere. I cannot understand where they get their logic from. I cannot understand where they get their prejudice and foolhardiness from—looking into the faces of men and taking so long to realize that they are men. Up to now the white man is not convinced that the Negro is a man; because if he were convinced that the Negro was a man he never would play the "pranks" he is playing with the Negroes today. The idea of Canadians leaving far off Canada going 9,000 miles into the black man's count[r]y and talking about it as his empire. In that very place they want to go there are about 6,000 white people and 6,000,000 Negroes; and they look into the faces of these 6,000,000 Negroes and say "this place belongs to us 6,000 white people and more must come in." I cannot understand where they get the nerve from. Where did they get their nerve? They must have got it from our original and ancient spirit of bowing and scraping and cringing. They have not yet realized the New Negro.

I feel sure that if Winston Spencer Churchill had met the [N]ew Negro he would never be mapping out the program he has before him now for the conquest of Africa, because he would know it was an impossibility. I do not care how powerful you believe England is; I do not care how powerful you believe Italy and France are; it is only a question of time. Why we had Carthage; we had Rome; we had Greece; we had Egypt; we had these great empires and nations of ancient history as our guide and inspiration. England today is no more powerful than Rome was when Rome was in her glory. Rome lived in an age when civilization had not developed to the extent it is today. But in the same proportion of human development Rome occupied a power that was regarded to be unconquerable; and so of England today. But Rome fell; Greece fell; Carthage fell; Syria fell; and I know Great Britain will fall like Lucifer, never to rise again, unless she changes her policies towards the darker races. (Cheers.) And with a man like Winston Spencer Churchill at the helm of the Colonial dominions, it is only a question of time when India, when Egypt will rise in revolt because they are not going to stand for his domination and for his iron rule. We are awaiting the time when the war clouds will again rise on the horizon and then there will come the glorious opportunity for the 400,000,000 of African blood to strike a blow for their freedom and for their independence.

Let no preacher persuade you; let no philosopher or prophet tell you otherwise. There are going to be wars and rumors of wars, and the best thing you can do during the time of peace is to prepare for war. I do not care what preacher or priest say to me, I am preparing for war, and when that war comes somebody will have to run, and I hope it won't be me. (Laughter.) I will only pray to the Lord, "if you don't help me, don't help the other fellow."

It is only a question of time. Let those fellows from Canada go out. Sometimes I take it amusingly, and sometimes I take it in a serious vein and say that those men are going out before us to prepare things and then we can go and take that which we should receive. Sometimes I think that God is just working out the plans of our destiny—sending them to prepare the way. You know before Christ came there was a John the Baptist as his forerunner who preached and prepared the way. And I believe these Canadians are going out as John the Baptist to prepare the way for 400,000,000 people to go and clean them out and take everything. We have no $50,000,000 now, so they are advancing it for us; that is all about it. Some of you are fearful that the time will never come for you to whip the white man. You will never whip the white man except you have a man's spirit and a man's courage. The white man, and not only the white man, but any man will whip you if you have the spirit of cowardice in you. But when you have the spirit of a man not even the devil can whip you. And this is the kind of spirit we want to have; we want to get rid of that spirit of cowardice and fear no man. There are some

British Negroes who think George V and David Lloyd George and Winston Churchill are little gods and that certain other men are little gods because they are white and kings and presidents. My God, if he has color, looks like me, and anybody who does not look like me will have to wait until I pay any respects to mine. This fear and this trembling that England is a power is amply demonstrated to you[,] is what someone said from the platform a few minutes ago about David and Goliath. There was a giant Goliath who killed and destroyed everything that came in his path and he thought that nothing in the world could intimidate or overpower and conquer him, but a little boy (David) went up with a slingshot and slew him and took the life of the great giant Goliath. And so tonight I think that we Negroes are the little Davids playing around the Goliaths of the nations of the world, and whilst they think they are unconquerable, it won't be slingshots that will conquer them, but it will be something more deadly than slingshots. David did not know anything else but slingshots, but Negroes know how to use every implement of war in the world.

I want to leave you in Liberty Hall with this one determination: That as men you have a part to play in the drama of life. You have a place to take and occupy in the avenue of life, and it is no use putting it off and saying that you will do tomorrow what you ought to do today. It is for us to make up our minds now. The world is undergoing a change; nations and races everywhere are reorganizing themselves, hence these changes in government. There was someone else before Winston Spencer Churchill as Secretary of State for the Colonies, but they wanted a better man, a man who could better interpret the spirit of the nation, and they appointed Winston Spencer Churchill. So the whole world is undergoing a change everywhere and we have to change, too. We must read down those old-time Negroes who have been preaching all religion and put up Negroes who will teach us the way to freedom—industrial freedom. We want Negroes who can [sn]atch men like Winston Spencer Churchill of England here in America and all the men that the different governments of Italy and Canada and Germany and France are putting up to lead. We want men of brain power; we want men of vision; we want men of nerve force; we want men who will not tremble; we want men who will not go down on their knees like weak sycophants; we want men who will strike out straight from the shoulder and demand for the Negro what is belonging to the Negro. (Loud cheers.)

Give us a chance! Give us a chance! Let the Canadians go to Africa; let Smutts and his party carry on in South Africa, whilst General Stewart and his battalion of workers carry on in the West Coast of Africa. Let the Italians, and the Portugese and the Belgians carry on in East Africa until we get there; because until we get there I have made up my mind to one determination, and that is, I am going to fight somewhere for my life, and when I get down to fighting for my life I'm going to carry everything I see before me until I go down! (Applause.) If they are wise, they will keep that $50,000,000 and spend it in Canada; but if they want to be philanthropic—some white folks, you know, are very philanthropic. I have heard of some very kind white folks, such as the men whom Dr. Du Bois goes to and associates with, who give away large sums of money for charity and for sympathy. They give away millions every year for charity. So, as I have said, I have heard of these folks. Remember, those are the kind of folks going out from Canada with this $50,000,000, and who want to do some philanthropic work to help the Negro over there. (Ironically.) That is what I believe when they go over, and we are getting ready to go over there when they are through with their work, so that we can enjoy whatever they will have done. And when we meet them there we are simply going to ask them to leave, as the place may not be large enough for two sets of people to occupy. (Laughter.)

AFRICA THE CONTINENT OF LIGHT.

They seem to think that Africa is still the "Dark Continent." Africa is today the most brilliant continent on the globe—the continent of light. There is no darkness about Africa. Africa is so much lit that it is attracting the world. Like the moon and the sun, it attracts the world, because of its brilliancy. Africa, I say, is full of light, because diamonds are there. Africa is full of light, because gold is there. Africa is full of light, because copper and tin and iron and coal and everything you can think of is there; and the white man wants light wherever he sees it shine. That's why he is going to Africa. Yet they are still trying to camouflage you about the "Dark Continent!" Let it be dark until it lights itself up. Sometimes you play the fool in the dark, and somebody tries to surprise you and flashes a light on you, when in reality it is your trick. He tries to hide behind the white light, but you fool him. I believe that one of these fine mornings the flash of light of African powder will shine out, and somebody will run from his dirty darkness. I have nothing to hide from, I have no camouflage. I have but one truth to tell where Africa is concerned. It is the land of my fathers. They never gave it to anybody, and by my rights, legal and moral, it belongs to me; that's all. I cannot argue with the white man about Canada. I won't argue a second with the white man and tell him Canada is mine. I won't argue with him a second trying to convince him that America is mine. I wouldn't argue with the Englishman two minutes, telling him that the great British Empire is mine. But I will spend eternity fighting with any man who wants to talk about Africa; because it is mine. Let the Canadians have Canada. Let the Americans have America. When we are through, then we will go to Africa. We are not there yet. (Laughter). You, when you take someone from somewhere, you are responsible for that person until that person gets back. (Laughter). That is just what we want our American fellow-citizens and brothers in the Lord, brethren in Christ, to do. I can remember what the Bishop told the Rev. Dr. McGuire, who belongs to the same communion and the same Church and the same Diocese.[5] This white Bishop came to Dr. McGuire, preaching about "We are all brothers," and so forth. And Dr. McGuire said, wanting, as a

Negro, to find out the reality of this brother's religion—he went up to him, in a secluded moment, and said: "Bishop, are you my brother?"

The Bishop scratched his head. Dr. McGuire repeated the question: "Bishop, are you my brother?" "I—I—," and he scratched his head again, as he was asked, "Now, Bishop, I want to find out; Are you my brother?" Finally, the Bishop answered: "Yes—my brother in Christ." Now, I am willing to admit of the brotherhood in Christ; but Christ has gone a long time ago and He is coming back some time; we cannot tell when. When he comes back we will be willing to report then, and only then, that we are all brothers in Christ. But for the time being, when we do not see him, and while we are living down here, and the other fellow has part of what belongs to us we are going to suspend the idea of brotherhood and talk something else. (Laughter and applause.) I believe in the brotherhood of Christ when all of us get into heaven. That's time enough for all of us to be brothers in Christ. What do you say about that, Dr. Paul (turning to and speaking directly to Rev. Dr. Paul)? (Renewed great laughter.) When we get into the pearly gates and all of us have on those same white long robes and shiny slippers, with golden crowns on our heads, and all our robes look alike, and all the crowns look alike, then all of us will be "brothers in Christ." But while Morgan[6] and Hearst have a hundred million dollars down here and I have nothing[,] I can't see wherein the brotherhood comes in—not until I get fifty per cent of what he has. Then we are brothers well met. And as long as some one is depriving us of our fifty per cent, or whatever it is, whether it be fifty per cent, or whatever it is, as long as some one, I say, is depriving us of our portion and our job, there cannot be any talk about brotherhood. Tell the yellow man about brotherhood when some one is encroaching upon his rights in Asia? There is no brotherhood when one man is robbing the other fellow, and that is just what is happening to Negroes now; the other fellow has his hand in their pockets, taking the last nickel, the last copper away from them; and if you will stand up and let him take it from you, and then talk about his being a brother to you, when he has gone away and left you without a nickel with which to buy bread, then you are crazy, indeed; for if you are deprived of the wherewithall to buy bread and you are left alone, you will simply stay there and die unless you will go after the other fellow and fight for what is ours. And that's the kind of man the white man is. He has made a bankrupt of himself in Europe; he is penniless. Take it from me[,] Great Britain is penniless; France is penniless; Italy is penniless and they have no mercy and no sympathy, and anywhere they can get wealth they are going there and will take it. That's why they are trying to gain a release from the obligation of that loan of $10,000,000,000 which Wilson lent them. But I believe that so long as Hearst is alive they will have a fine job on their hands in trying to accomplish anything like that with the United States. Hearst is the greatest power in the United States of America. Hearst can make war and Hearst can make peace.[7] That's why I like Hearst so well. I have been just waiting, and I know the time is coming when Hearst is going to start up something. Hearst is going to get some President, or somebody here, whether i[t] be Democrat or Republican; but later on he is going to start something, because Hearst loves England.[8] (Laughter.) I love England. Don't you know that? I love the British because they love me. I have often told you that if the other fellow loves me I will love him. If he hates me I hate him. Now, I know England loves me; therefore I love England.

THE QUALITY OF MERCY.

When our civilization is given to the world we will startle mankind. Give us a chance! Give us fifty years, and we will show them a civilization that will startle the universe. We did it once, and we gave it to them on trial. They have abused it, however; they have wrecked it. They have made it a bankrupt civilization, and we are going to start out anew and show them something fresh. That's what we are going to do. We are going to show them the quality of mercy—after we get even with the "crackers." I don't believe there can be any dispensation of mercy until you "get even" with the "other fellow." I believe in the "eye for an eye" principle, and the "tooth for a tooth" business; I believe in that religion, and I believe in showing the other fellow mercy—after I "get even" with him; only then. I want to feel satisfied that he feels what I felt, and then, after that, we can call it quits, for we then can appreciate each other's feelings. So that when we get to Africa—and we must get there—those of you who say you are not going to Africa, you will have to follow us. You are going to follow the crowd. Once we had but thirteen people in the room, and 4,000,000 have followed the thirteen people! And as 4,000,000 have followed the thirteen people, so 400,000,000 will follow the 4,000,000. It is like the rats following the Pied Piper of Hamlin. You know the man who went through the town with the flute and who blew all around with it. The scientists and the physicians, nobody could get rid of the plague of rats, and the Pied Piper of Hamlin took his flute, and he started blowing through the streets, and gave forth such beautiful and sweet tones that all the rats from everywhere followed him. He kept right on, with the rats following on behind, and marched into the sea, and all the rats were drowned. Now, the Universal Negro Improvement Association, when the question comes to lead, like the Pied Piper, will follow the tune of the national anthem of "Africa!" and every Negro will rise, everywhere, and where the Black Star Line Band leads (because, you know, we are going to put Prof. Isles in front), and wheresoever the Black Star Line band leads, with the national anthem, the other 400,000,000 Negroes will follow, and if we come across Churchill in the march, good-bye!

So, this is my message to you tonight: Be courageous. Don't talk about "Africa can't be won." Africa can be won, and if you will make up your minds to win it, Africa is already won. Do you know why? It is because the spirit of the Universal Negro Improvement Association is all over Africa today. Those Canadians going out there, and General Smutts talking about a "white

South Africa!" They don't know anything. Why, Africa already has caught the spirit of the Universal Negro Improvement Association, and it is only a question of time when Africa herself will free herself from the bondage of the white man. All that Africa wants now are soldiers; not so much soldiers in the rank and file, as military geniuses to lay out the plans. We want the Napoleons, and I think we see them here tonight. We want the strategists; and looking into your faces, men, I see a Napoleon at the bridge of Lodi.[9] I see a Brutus reading in his tent at Philip[p]i. I see a Richard Coeur de Lion bearing down upon the white armies of Saladin. I see a Drake crowding his sails off the galleons of Spain.[10] Yes, I see a crown prince storming the forts at Verdun; then I see a Marshal Joffre marshalling the artillery in counter attack. I see in you the new princes that shall come out of Egypt. (Applause.) You took your stand in the last war in France, in Flanders, and in Mesopotamia. You fought like Trojans; you died like men. Well, the hour is fast approaching when we will call you again to fight, but not as auxiliaries or mercenaries of war, but to fight, as freemen, for your liberty. (Great applause.) Why should you lose courage, when a world stands before you to be conquered—a world of 12,000,000 square miles, that God Almighty originally gave your forefathers—a world that still beckons to you, "Come"—a continent from which you were torn 300 years ago, for the purpose of getting the enlightenment that you now have? What are you going to do with your psychology and your university education? Why sit at the foot-stool of the white man, and be trampled upon? The answer is, "No!" for we shall rise like men, from the class rooms of the universities, trusting in God, and go forth and lead 400,000,000 Negroes on to victory! (Applause.)

THE PATHWAY OF GLORY.

Tell me now to turn back while humanity is at the cross roads of time? Why should I turn back while the other fellow journeys on? On and on is a pathway that leads to glory. That pathway the white man has followed for thousands of years—that pathway he is still treading today—that pathway that leads to glory and fame shall be followed by 400,000,000, and when the end of the journey is reached and the white man answers "Here," and the yellow man answers "Here!" simultaneously the black man shall answer "Here!" (Uproarious applause.)

I send a challenge to the world—weak as this race is and divided as it is, we send a challenge to the world, "Despise us not, because we are black! Despise us not because we are comely, but fear us because we are coming!"[11] (Cheers.) Men, prepare in the way that all men have prepared before. The Romans before they ascended into their glory prepared for conquest; the Greeks before they ascended to their glory prepared for conquest; Great Britain before she reached the heights of her imperial glory was prepared for conquest; she is still making conquest. You[,] before you reach the end of your grand and glorious journey[,] must prepare for conquest but not the conquest of Rome; not the conquest of Greece; not the conquest of Great

Britain, because their conquest was an unjust one and that is why Rome fell and Greece fell and that is why Great Britain will fall unless she changes her policy towards the darker races. (Loud cheers.) The conquest I want you to make is not the conquest of Europe; not the conquest of alien races; not the conquest of Asia. I want you to make the conquest of Africa—that which is yours.

They tried to lie to us about Africa. Every new discovery brought to light about Africa that reveals the glory of ancient Africa and attests to the power of the black man centuries ago, the white man turns around and attributes it to some other race. If they discover the Pyramids they were not the black man's handiwork; if they discover some new hidden tables or records that attest to the civilization or the ancient glories of Egypt or Alexandria, they attribute it to some other race but the Negro. All historians have tried to bring down the Negro. That is why I read the white man's history with disgust. When I take the white man's history in the class room and read it, I read it with disgust, because of lies from start to finish as far as the Negro is concerned.

You men of Liberty Hall[,] you must rise to fill your place in the world. We want historians of our own to write in burning letters of gold the achievements of our fathers and our achievements today and the achievements of tomorrow.

THE RISE OF THE JEW.

To change my thoughts for a few minutes. The Jews are another people who have been despised for several centuries. Some of us thought the Jews had no program. The Jews had the biggest program in civilization in the last 200 years. The Jew several decades ago found himself a despised individual— a despised person—a despised race in Europe. A couple of decades ago wheresoever a Jew showed himself or displayed himself, he was kicked about; he was buffeted worse than the Southern Negro today. There was a time when it was a disgrace to be a Jew in England; it was a disgrace to be a Jew universally; it was a disgrace to be a Jew all over Europe and in all parts of the world. Even in this country it was a disgrace to be a Jew. What did the Jews do? The Jews were but 12,000,000 people. They knew they could not carry out any physical conquest; they were too few to carry out any physical conquest; and the Jews thought they would carry out a financial conquest of the world; and these Jews planned for several years—probably a couple of centuries to carry out a conquest, and the conquest of the Jews was realized in the last war. Let me tell you: it was not the Kaiser who made the war; it was not the English statesmen who made the war; it was the Jew who made the war and it was the Jew who stopped the war. Jewish financiers, Jewish capital in London, in Paris, in Berlin and in Petrograd financed and started the war[12]; and it was Jewish capital when Russia tumbled down, that came forward and said "Let the war be stopped; I won't finance it any more," because the Jew had his promise of Palestine.[13] Jews in Poland were restored to power[14]; the Jews in Russia were recognized[15] because Trotsky—I believe the master mind of Russia—is a Jew; the Russia that carried out her pogroms day after day and slaughtered millions of Jews.[16] The Jew by his finance destroyed the Czar and placed a Jew in power and he is running the government of Russia now. The Jew has gone back to Palestine and the Jew it is that has the world in the palm of his hand. Where is the Jew who was despised? In England 20 years ago you found a Jew in the White Chapel district in the East End of London a despised individual. He had to go to the garbage pail to find bread because no one would employ him and no one would consider him. The Jew had no other district to live in England than the east [end] of London—the slums of London.[17] What has he done? He has made such a complete conquest of Great Britain that Sir Rufus Isaacs who was but "Rufus Isaacs" 20 years ago, rose from the legal profession to the Attorney Generalship of Great Britain. As a Jew he rose from the Attorney Generalship of Great Britain to be Lord Chief Justice of Great Britain. From Lord Chief Justice of Great Britain he rose to be Minister Plenipotentiary and Ambassador of Great Britain to the United States of America. And where is that Jew now? He is on his way on the high seas to India as Viceroy of India, the representative of the King of England in the great dominion of India.[18] That is what the Jew has achieved in the space of a couple of decades. The Jew has made a financial conquest of the world[.] They did it though plans. You need not desire to make financial conquest because you have the physical strength[.] I am not talking about financial conquest; I am talking about physical conquest because we are 400,000,000 people; and if any whipping ever is to be done, I believe a few of us will be left after all are gone. What I mean by this is this: That we are the second largest number of people in the world, and when the famine is through with China[19] you will be the largest group of people, because I understand the famine in China is killing out one or two millions a week, and if it continued for another month you will be the largest group of people in the world. So that if the world is wiped out by a war of the races, a few Negroes will be left while everybody else is gone. So I am not talking about financial conquest; I am talking about physical conquest—not of America, not of Europe, but physical conquest of Africa. (Loud and prolonged applause.)

Printed in *NW*, 12 March 1921. Original headlines omitted.

1. A small British contingent and arms for 250,000 men were supplied to forces led by the White Russian leader, General Denikin. In November 1919, however, Lloyd George announced that Britain could no longer "afford to continue so costly an intervention in an interminable Civil War," and in the following months he withdrew most military assistance. Lloyd George in 1919 estimated the cost of the war at £100 million (Henry Pelling, *Winston Churchill* [London: Macmillan London Ltd., 1974], pp. 261–265; Peter Rowland, *Lloyd George* [London: Barrie and Jenkins Ltd., 1975], p. 502).

2. During his tenure at the Colonial Office, Churchill was often occupied with problems in the Near and Middle Eastern mandates allocated to Britain after the war. In 1921 he succeeded in placing the Emir Feisal of Arabia on the throne of the newly created kingdom of Iraq. British imperialism in this area met with considerable but largely unsuccessful resistance from Egyptian, Iraqi, and Persian nationalists (Henry Pelling, *Winston Churchill*, pp. 261–265).

3. British troops occupied Egypt in 1882, following the nationalist revolt led by Arabi Pasha. The British offered a severely limited measure of Egyptian self-government, but the nationalists rejected this circumstance, and agitation for independence mounted in the following decades. In December 1914 Egypt, nominally under the suzerainty of Turkey, was declared a British protectorate, and a harsh repression of nationalist dissent followed. The British refusal to allow Egypt a voice at the Paris Peace Conference and the exile of the nationalist leader Saad Zaghlul led to the uprising of 1919. In 1920, following a lengthy investigation by Lord Milner, negotiations between British and Egyptian officials began. These negotiations collapsed early in 1921, and on 28 February 1922 the British government unilaterally declared independence for Egypt on British terms and allowed the sultan to proclaim a monarchy and assume the title of King Fuad I (Peter Mansfield, *The British in Egypt* [London: Weidenfeld and Nicolson, 1971]; M. Travers Symons, *Britain and Egypt: The Rise of Egyptian Nationalism* [London: C. Palmer, 1925]; Letitia Wheeler Ufford, "Milner Mission to Egypt, 1919–1921" [Ph.D. diss., Columbia University, 1977]; Afaf Lutfi al-Sayyid-Marsot, *Egypt's Liberal Experiment, 1922–1936* [Berkeley, Los Angeles, London: University of California Press, 1977]; John Darwin, *Britain, Egypt, and the Middle East: Imperial Policy in the Aftermath of War, 1918–1922* [London: Macmillan, 1981]).

4. In fact, Lloyd George appointed Churchill as colonial secretary after Churchill recommended that the Royal Air Force be used to police Britain's newly acquired territories in the eastern Mediterranean. At the same time, Churchill recommended that a rejuvenated Colonial Office should take control of the new territories. Lloyd George was quick to accept both recommendations. Churchill was widely known for his interest in colonial questions, and his new position as colonial secretary gave him complete responsibility for all Near and Middle Eastern policy. However, Lloyd George and Churchill frequently disagreed later in Churchill's tenure in office (*DAB*, 1961–1970, p. 202; Lord Beaverbrook, *The Decline and Fall of Lloyd George* [London: Collins, 1963], pp. 30–33).

5. McGuire left the United States in May 1919 and returned to his native Antigua, BWI, at the invitation of Bishop Edward Hutson, Anglican bishop of Antigua. On a tour of Barbados and Antigua the year before, McGuire had "delivered lectures to immense audiences on Industrial Education in the United States of America and the part which the American [Episcopal] Church is taking in this movement through its Institute for Negroes" (Church Historical Society Archives, Austin, Texas, report of field agent, 1 May 1912–30 April 1913). Bishop Hutson chaired McGuire's lecture in Antigua and invited him to return to Antigua in order to foster industrial education locally. In addition to setting up the Antigua School of Domestic Science and Nursing, McGuire became parish rector of the Anglican churches in Falmouth, Liberta, and his own native Sweets. Sometime in 1919 McGuire "handed in his resignation but gave no reasons" (Gavin White, "Patriarch McGuire and the Episcopal Church," *Historical Magazine of the Protestant Episcopal Church* 38 [June 1969]: 117). For eighteen months prior to his return to the United States, McGuire worked as a physician and "in the pursuance of other duties . . . was brought in daily contact with the masses"; he also served "on various committees having as their object the economic improvement of the laborer" ("Antigua: Corroborating Dr. McGuire," *NW*, 23 October 1920).

6. John Pierpont Morgan (1837–1913), the most famous American financier of his day.

7. Hearst competed vigorously with Joseph Pulitzer (1847–1911) for preeminence among American newspaper publishers before the outbreak of the Spanish-American War. To attract readers, Hearst's *New York Journal* and Pulitzer's *New York World* printed anti-Spanish propaganda that included lurid stories of Spanish atrocities against Cubans. They are considered to have directed American public opinion toward support for a war against Spain (W. A. Swanberg, *Citizen Hearst* [New York: Charles Scribner's Sons, 1961], pp. 79–169).

8. Hearst was noted for his anti-British stance in the years before America's entry into the First World War. A strong opponent of American involvement in the war, Hearst was widely criticized in the American and British press for the pro-German slant in the editorials printed in his newspapers. The British government responded by attempting to censor news reports sent by Hearst's news service in England. When Hearst resisted, his newspapers were banned from using the transatlantic cable, which the British government controlled. Hearst also sympathized with the Irish struggle against England. In addition, he was anti-Japanese, and his opposition to Britain increased when the two nations signed a treaty of alliance (W. A. Swanberg, *Citizen Hearst*, pp. 294–295; Edmond D. Coblentz, *William Randolph Hearst* [New York: Simon and Schuster, 1952], p. 83).

9. On 10 May 1796 Napoleon gained control of Lombardy by defeating the Austrians at the Battle of Lodi in northern Italy (*EWH*).

10. Sir Francis Drake was the most celebrated British seaman during the period of conflict between England and Spain for maritime supremacy. Drake was famous for his plunder of Spanish ships and ports in South America and the West Indies. In addition, he was credited with inspiring the English victory against the Spanish Armada in 1588.

11. A loose paraphrase of Song of Sol. 1:5–6. In these verses a Shulamite girl, who is the object of Solomon's love, says, "I am black, but comely, O ye daughters of Jerusalem. . . . Look not upon me, because I am black, because the sun hath looked upon me."

12. The belief that a worldwide conspiracy of Jewish bankers was responsible for the outbreak and financing of the First World War derived in part from the impact of the forged "Protocols of the Elders of Zion" and from the general increase in anti-German and anti-foreign sentiment in the United States during the war. This in turn was fueled by the anti-Semitic statements of such prominent figures as isolationist Sen. Henry Lodge and by proponents of American racial homogeneity and exclusivity, most notably the Ku Klux Klan. The conspiracy theory gained additional impetus as a result of the publication of Henry Ford's violently anti-Semitic paper, the *Dearborn Independent*, in May 1920 (Nathan C. Belth, *A Promise to Keep: A Narrative of the American Encounter with Anti-Semitism* [New York: Times Books, 1979], pp. 73–76).

13. When the British issued the Balfour Declaration of 2 November 1917, they hoped that an appeal to Russian Zionist sentiment might win Russia's support for the allied cause and help to dampen the growth of pacifism in revolutionary Russia. Russian Zionists welcomed the declaration, but the majority of Jews were preoccupied with consolidating their liberties under the Bolshevik government and largely ignored it (*Encyclopedia Judaica*; Isaiah Friedman, *The Question of Palestine, 1914–1918* [New York: Schocken Books, 1973], p. 295; Frank Hardie and Irwin Hermann, *Britain and Zion: The Fateful Entanglement* [Belfast: Blackstaff Press, 1980]).

14. The peace settlement, which included provisions protecting the national rights of minorities in multiethnic nations, required the newly reconstituted Polish state to protect the rights of Jews and all other non-Poles. Although the revised Polish constitution abolished all discrimination based on religious, racial, or national differences, Jewish hopes for the development of their own national institutions and for an end to anti-Semitism were soon discarded. During 1919 and 1920, thousands of Jews were killed or injured in battles between the Poles and their Ukrainian and Bolshevik enemies, a fact that prompted the creation of investigating commissions by the British, French, and American governments. In November 1920 Henry Ford's *Dearborn Independent* published an article, "Jews Use Peace Conference to Bind Poland," which claimed that the peace treaty, calling for Poland to respect the Jewish sabbath, had humiliated Poland and given the Jews unwarranted power. In addition, Ford's newspaper accused the Jews of having collaborated with both the Bolsheviks and the Ukrainians (*Encyclopedia Judaica* 13: 738; *The International Jew* [Dearborn, Mich., n.p., 1921] 2: 232–243).

15. All discriminatory laws based on national, religious, or ethnic origin were removed following the formation of the Russian provisional government in March 1917. On 15 November 1917 the Russian Bolshevik government issued the "Declaration of the Rights of Peoples," proclaiming the right of self-determination for ethnic minorities and repudiating anti-Semitism. Jews received a measure of cultural and political autonomy in 1918, but by August 1919 the government had closed most of the Jewish schools and cultural institutions and had adopted a policy of cultural assimilation. In the Ukraine, the newly created *Rada*, or central council, enacted laws in March 1917 guaranteeing non-Ukrainian minorities, including Jews, 30 percent representation. In January 1918 the Rada proclaimed the Ukraine an independent "People's Republic" and formally recognized the rights of Jewish, Polish, and Russian minorities to national autonomy and self-government. Despite these promises, however, tens of thousands of Jews were massacred by Ukrainian military forces and peasants in the course of the civil war during 1918 to 1920 (Oscar I. Janowsky, *The Jews and Minority Rights* [New York: Columbia University Press, 1933], pp. 211–240; *Encyclopedia Judaica* 15: 1,518; 14: 459–463).

16. Pogroms were a regular feature of Jewish life in prerevolutionary Russia. Not until the period from 1915 to 1921, however, did the number of deaths reach into the tens and hundreds of thousands. During these years, approximately 250,000 Russian Jews died as a result of pogroms, starvation, or exposure. The majority of these were murdered in pogroms conducted by Ukrainian guerrilla forces during the Russian Revolution and civil war (Paul E. Grosser and Edwin Halperin, *The Causes and Effects of Anti-Semitism: The Dimensions of a Prejudice* [New York: Philosophical Library, 1978], pp. 247–250).

17. Although the majority of Jewish immigrants to Britain from Eastern Europe settled in the slum-ridden East End of London, large numbers were also attracted to the northern industrial cities of Manchester, Leeds, Liverpool, and Glasgow (*Encyclopedia Judaica*).

18. Rufus Daniel Isaacs, first earl of Reading, was appointed viceroy and governor-general of India in January 1921. He held this position until 1926 (*DNB*, 1931–1940, p. 466).

19. The *New York Times* reported in February that famine in northeastern China, caused by several consecutive years of drought, threatened the lives of fifteen million peasants by the spring of 1921. In the ensuing months, however, international relief organizations, led by the American Relief Committee, succeeded in obtaining adequate food and other aid for China. Nevertheless, by the end of the famine in 1922 several hundred thousand Chinese peasants had died from starvation and disease (Herbert H. Gowen and Josef Washington Hall, *An Outline History of China* [New York: D. Appleton and Co., 1929], p. 82; *NYT*, 13 February 1921; "Appeal to Aid Starving China," *Gleaner*, 24 March 1921).

Gloster Armstrong to Auckland C. Geddes, British Ambassador, Washington, D.C.

NEW YORK, February 17th, 1921

Sir,

With reference to my telegram No. 3 of the 27th ultimo,[1] reporting that Marcus Garvey, the well-known leader of negro opinion in this city, had applied for a passport, I have the honour to report that a passport has now been issued to this individual and that a circular, copy of which is enclosed, has been addressed to certain British authorities who may be interested.

I took the opportunity [to] interview Garvey, who is an alert negro of the aggressive type. I questioned him as to his loyalty to British rule and pointed out the benefits which have accrued to the Negro Race under British administration in Africa and elsewhere.

I think that he was surprised at the conciliatory attitude which I adopted towards him, and I am not without hopes that my policy will eventually have the effect of causing him to be less radical in his attacks on constituted authority. I have asked him to come and see me again after his return from Panama, and hope then to be in a position to influence him further in the right direction. I have the honour to be, Sir, Your obedient servant,

GLOSTER ARMSTRONG
H. M.'s Consul General

PRO, FO 115/2690. TLS, carbon copy.

1. Gloster Armstrong's cable to Sir Auckland Geddes of 27 January 1921 informed him: "Marcus Garvey has applied for a passport to travel to Costa Rica and Panama and return. I propose to issue passport on morning of January 31st subject to above limitations unless I receive instructions otherwise from you." On 31 January the British ambassador decided to "take no further action in the matter but to leave it to the discretion of the passport authorities at New York." This went against the advice given a couple days earlier, however, when it was recommended on 29 January that "we should refuse visa and inform [the] F.O." (PRO, FO 115/2690).

Enclosure

[*New York*] February 17th 1921

CIRCULAR

H.B.M. Consul General at New York presents his compliments and begs to report that Mr. Marcus Garvey, the well-known negro agitator, has been provided with a passport to enable him to travel from New York to Panama and Costa Rica and return, touching at intermediate ports. The passport has been further endorsed to the effect that it is not valid for other destinations unless a fresh endorsement is obtained.

It is not definitely known whether Marcus Garvey will travel in one of the Black Star steamers or by ordinary passenger boat.

Sent to: Havana
Port Limón
Panama
Bermuda
Barbados
Jamaica

[*Address*] British Embassy, Washington, D.C.

PRO, FO 115/2690. TD, carbon copy.

J. Edgar Hoover to Lewis J. Baley

WASHINGTON, D.C. February 18, 1921

MEMORANDUM FOR MR. BALEY.

Supplementing my memorandum of 1st instant concerning MARCUS GARVEY, I desire to advise you that we are in receipt of information that this individual will leave this country February 27th.

The above is referred to you for your information and such attention as you may deem advisable, and it is desired that this office be advised of the final disposition made by the Bureau of this case. Respectfully,

J. E. HOOVER

[*Endorsement*] NOTED F. D. W.

DNA, RG 65, file BS 198940-72X. TLS, recipient's copy. Stamped endorsements.

Negro World Editorial Cartoon

(*Source*: *NW*, 19 February 1921.)

Negro World Advertisements

THE FIRST UNIVERSAL NEGRO ALMANAC FOR 1921

Issued by the Association Is Now Ready

The Almanac contains some Excellent News Features and Portraitures, and is really a work of Art

It contains statistics of the Negro population in the United States, the West Indies and Liberia. A brief historic sketch of some of the most prominent men in Negro history and the photo of every member of the executive staff and the editors of The Negro World. etc., etc., etc.

It is a fine New Year gift.

Price in New York 25 Cents :: Outside New York 30 Cents

Orders will be received at the office for mailing copies any part of the world at 35 cents

ONLY CASH ORDERS WILL BE EXECUTED

Apply Commissioner-General's Office

UNIVERSAL NEGRO IMPROVEMENT ASSOCIATION

54-56 WEST 135th STREET

Mark Letters Outside: ALMANAC ORDER

WE HAVE IN RESERVE JUST A FEW THOUSAND COPIES FOR OUR FOREIGN MEMBERS AND FRIENDS

(*Source: NW*, 19 February 1921.)

Report by Bureau Agents A. A. Hopkins and E. J. Kosterlitzky

[*Los Angeles*] Feb. 19, 1921

NEGRO ACTIVITIES

UNIVERSAL NEGRO IMPROVEMENT ASS'N.:

HENRIETTA VINTON DAVIS. National Organizer for the U.N.I.A. and African Community League is now organizing in Missouri, and was at Carthage and Jop[l]in, Mo. this week. . . . A poster with a picture of the "African Flag" in colors, and the words "Long live the U.N.I.A.", has been printed and is being distributed in Los Angeles (Copy attached to Washington report.)

NOAH D. THOMPSON is President, W. L. KIMBROUGH,[1] Secretary, and T. A. HARRIS, Treasurer, of the Local Branch of the U.N.I.A. According to confidential informant, these men are not extreme Radicals and as long as they maintain their leadership ultra radicalism or race clashes are not anticipated. In a recent speech NOAH D. THOMPSON said, "This movement means that every person not white is behind every other person not white, regardless of his standing intellectually, socially, or financially. When we said we intended to stand as one, we never mentioned fighting to do it, consequently we are not talking about fighting. We are simply going to learn to stand when the other fellows fight, and when he comes facing us, he will change his mind and go the other way."

[A. A. HOPKINS AND E. J. KOSTERLITZKY]

DNA, RG 65, file BS 202600-5-32X. TD.

1. Wiley L. Kimbrough became one of the leaders of a dissident Garveyite faction in Los Angeles which formed the Pacific Coast Negro Improvement Association. Kimbrough joined Noah Thompson as a Los Angeles delegate to the 1921 UNIA convention. When Noah Thompson returned to Los Angeles with accusations of financial mismanagement by the UNIA parent body, Kimbrough endorsed his report (*California Eagle*, 10 September 1921).

Marcus Garvey's Farewell Speech

[[New York, Feb. 22, 1921]]

. . . Mr. Garvey's opening and closing formal addresses were as follows:

. . . Now, you have two gigantic propositions that call for your support. Each of them is equally important, but you may take your choice in supporting either of them, if you cannot support both at one and the same time. The Black Star Line is a commercial investment. Outside of buying shares in the Black Star Line for the purpose of helping the organization to build up a merchant marine to convey cargoes of the commerce of Negroes from one part of the world to the other to the open markets of the world; outside of the purpose of having us build up a name in the commercial and maritime world of which we can be proud and of which our children and posterity may be proud; outside of all that, there is another reason why we should support the Black Star Line, just as other men in other walks of life belonging to other races support institutions, corporations and industrials of their own. The reason is the financial benefit that will accrue to you from investing your money in buying shares to float the ships.

The Black Star Line is a business organization—a corporation. At the close of each financial year of its successful operation, it is supposed to declare a dividend out of whatever profit it has made during that year. The directors of the corporation are elected annually by the shareholders, and annually these directors report to the shareholders the condition of the corporation, whether the corporation has made money or has lost money [or] whether it is just where it started in the beginning.

The Black Star Line is not an old established institution or corporation, it is only about twenty months old as a business venture. Yet it is the biggest, the most gigantic business venture ever undertaken by Negroes in the last five centuries. (Applause.) Nothing engineered by Negroes within the last 500 years has been as big or as stupendous as the Black Star Line. The Black Star Line being only twenty months old and having been able up to the present to hold its own, reveals a wonderful change in Negro advancement. That Negroes have been able to hold together a corporation of the[ir] own of such magnitude and proportions reveals the new business acumen of the Negro. (Applause.) The steamship business is one fraught with many rivalries, and only those who ar[e] strongly capitalized can survive in the steamship business; because when properly capitalized it is the most profitable business in the world. It yields a profit of 50 per cent at least in comparison with other business which yield a much smaller percentage of profit. When the steamship business starts to pay it pays more than any other business venture or investment. (Applause.) And that is why all steamship corporations are so heavily capitalized. If you turn to the United Fruit Company you will find them capitalized at more than $100,000,000, all fully subscribed. If you turn to the White Star Line you will find it capitalized for over $100,000,000. The Cunard Line or any of the other big lines [are] capitalized in the hundreds of millions of dollars, so as to be able to hold their own; and the Black Star Line, capitalized at $10,000,000, and not having more than three-quarters of a million dollars of its capital stock subscribed for, that it should be able to hold its own in the midst of all these big corporations shows that we have the business acumen to put the thing through. (Applause.) We started out in competition and rivalry with old established lines with millions and millions of dollars at their command. They have crushed hundreds and probably thousands of their own who made the effort we have made. Since the Black Star Line started many other steamship corporations were forced out of business by the bigger white companies.[1] But the Black Star Line has a place all its own in the world; a place whose market is peculiarly its own (applause), that no combination of corporations or steamship companies can destroy. And do you know why? It is because we have a world exclusively our own. (Applause.) Whereas white ships have to compete with white ships, black ships can compete with white ships successfully and win out. (Applause.) There are white sections of the world and there are black sections of the world; and whereas they can easily squeeze out another white company, it will be impossible for them to squeeze out a black company appealing to black men. (Applause.)

That's why I am leaving the United States of America just now—to lay the foundation on the other side of the Atlantic, across the Caribbean, for a solid, commercial link and connection between the black peoples of America [and] the black peoples of South and Central America and the West Indies. (Applause.) The fruit industry and the many other industries exploited in South and Central America and the West Indies by the white steamship lines are now to be exploited by the Black Star Line (applause), and for that I go to lay the foundation, because 1921 and 1922 will be a bloody year of rivalry between black and white men and yellow men the world over. (Applause.) The Negro, therefore must prepare himself now; must prove himself fit to survive. That's why I'm asking you to support the Black Star Line tonight.

I tell you, men, from my vision, from my deep conviction and from the spirit of my communion with my God, speaking to you in the presence of the Almighty, I have the greatest faith. I have the greatest confidence in the ultimate success of the Black Star Line. As a commercial venture I am staking my all, almost, in the Black Star Line, because I know we are bound to succeed if we stick to the colors of the Black Star. (Applause.)

THE AFRICAN TRADE.

Now, I appeal to you for the last time for probably four or five or six weeks to support the Black Star Line. Caring not what may have been said against or about the Black Star Line, the fact remains that the Black Star Line started twenty months ago without a hundred dollars, and today we control three-quarters of a million dollars (applause); not three-quarters of a million on mere paper, but in property value—money that can be realized in twenty-four hours if the stockholders desire that their money be refunded to them. By a majority vote at any meeting we can sell out the property of the Black Star Line and realize every nickel we have placed in it. (Applause.) So that with the full confidence we have in the future I am asking you tonight to support the Black Star Line by buying more shares. We need a ship for the African trade worthy of the name of the Black Star Line, and worthy of the race. Africa, with her teeming millions, is extending her hands toward us. Africa is beckoning to us to come forward, to go forth and rescue her from the conquest now being made by the alien races of the world to exploit and rob her of her wealth.

In sending the first ship to Africa in another few weeks I feel sure that we will take from Africa the precious minerals and materials that have been allowed to rot and waste there for decades and decades, because black men have withheld the [s]ite and value of the natural wealth of Africa and have refused to give or sell it to white men, knowing them as they do now. They are waiting for black men to come and to enjoy the fruit of the land that they themselves have prepared. And in sending forth the ships of the Black Star Line we have full assurance that they will come back to us laden with precious wealth—precious goods. So tonight I am asking each and every one of you to buy more shares in the Black Star Line and bonds for the Liberian Construction Loan.

The Black Star Line, as I have said, pays a dividend at the close of every successful financial year. It may be 6 per cent; it may be 10 per cent; it may be 100 per cent; there is no limit to the dividend to be declared at the close of any year, because this depends upon the success the corporation meets with in the year that is past. One year you may get 10 per cent, or 15 per cent, interest on your money or profit on your money, next year you may get 20 per cent, and the next year more, or much less. So, when you invest your money in the Black Star Line you will realize that you are investing to reap as much benefit and profits from the corporation as the corporation makes in that one year.

THE LIBERIAN CONSTRUCTION LOAN.

As for the Liberian Construction Loan of the Universal Negro Improvement Association, the association offers to pay you an annual interest of 5 per cent. That is to say, if you lend the association $100 for one year, at the close of that one year you get $5 for the year on the $100 loaned. If you lend it for ten years you will get $5 interest for every year, and so on. If you lend it $1,000 dollars you get that much more interest. I am asking each and every one of you in the hall to loan to the association whatever money you can invest for the Liberian Construction Loan or buy shares in the Black Star Line. If you feel you will be satisfied with getting 5 per cent interest on your money, then subscribe to the bonds for the Liberian Construction Loan. If you put your money in the bank you will get only 3 per cent or 4 1/2 percent, and the white man will use your money for his own purposes all during that year; but when you invest your money in the Universal Negro Improvement Association or in the Black Star Line, of which you are a member, the $100 or the $1,000 that you invest you are lending to yourselves to be used by yourselves for the building up of a nation and a government of your own, and at the same time getting anywhere from 15 to 25 or 30 per cent or more interest on your investment. (Applause.) When you put your money in the white man's bank it remains there for the year and he lends it out to other white men or to other governments. When Britain comes over to America and goes down to Wall Street and says to the bankers there, "We want to borrow a million dollars from you," the American banker lends it to England for ten years, or maybe twenty years or longer, to enable England to devote it to certain national and colonial schemes. It is your money that you have put into the various banks of the country that the American bankers lends to England or to France or to Italy to build up those countries; yet when you get there they tell you that it is a white man's country, when your own money helped build it up, simply because you haven't the sense to use your own money for your own purposes and benefit. I am trying to explain it to you as plainly as I can, so that you can clearly grasp the point, which is that when you lend your money to the other man, who is prejudiced against you, he does not use it to help you; on the contrary, it weakens you, makes you weaker, rather than helps make you stronger. So that is my argument tonight, and those of you who love your race, those of you who feel like the Negro has a right to a political place in the sun, I am asking you to support the Liberian Construction Loan as also to share in the Black Star Line.

Men and women of Liberty Hall, remember this: It is your work, the work we have planned out to do as the program of the Universal Negro Improvement Association, and if you want the work done you must support it. There is nobody here too poor not to subscribe for at least one share in the Black Star Line; there is no man or woman in Liberty Hall tonight who is not able to subscribe for at least one bond for the Liberian Construction Loan of the Universal Negro Improvement Association. If you cannot pay all the money in cash now, pay what you can, and make part payments on the balance. Do this rather than keep your money tied up in the white man's bank, where he uses it not for your benefit, but for his own; not for your protection and benefit, but to help keep you down and in a state of industrial and economic servitude.

THE EXPLOITATION OF SOUTH AFRICA.

Mr. Garvey in his closing address began by reading an extract taken from a publication, entitled "The Black Man,"[2] of South Africa, which, he said, is edited by the president of the Cape Town division of the Universal Negro Improvement Association.[3] Said Mr. Garvey:

It is the Negro World of South Africa. (Applause.) I am sorry Mr. Platje is not here tonight. Since he left Africa the Africans have thrown away their prayerbooks and have taken up something else. I will not tell you what just now (laughter), but as an indication of the new spirit of the South African, as inspired from the propaganda of the Universal Negro Improvement Association, I will read to you a news item from "The Black Man." South Africa (as you know) was regarded, and probably is still regarded as the worst spot in the world for Negroes; worse than the Southern States, where the Negro has been regarded as an animal, a beast of burden. The white people there, the Boers and the British and the Dutch, have absolutely no respect for the natives of South Africa. They brutalize them; they murder them; they do everything to them, and nothing has been said about it until the Universal Negro Improvement Association got into South Africa. (Applause.) These men, who probably had lost hope and courage for years and years, have within recent months found new hope and new courage and gathered new faith; and as the editor of the paper I have mentioned, he is now waging an active campaign throughout South Africa to prepare the people at that end, just as we are preparing them here. (Applause.)

General Smuts, as you know, is the successor of General Botha. General Botha stood for a white South Africa, and he bequeathed the heritage of that doctrine to General Smuts, and he stands now not only for a white South Africa, but for a white world. He has been conducting his politics and his political campaigns on the policy of a white South Africa, and recently he published and said many things about South Africa, as to that country being a white man's country; and what I shall now read from "The Black Man," edited by the president of the Cape Town Division of the U.N.I.A., is in reply to General Smuts' propaganda:

"General Smuts' policy of white South Africa. We are prepared to respond to General Smuts' appeal. But we will not permit him to catch votes [at] our expense. White South Africa can never be! (Applause.) It is ridiculous for the leaders of the white population of one million to talk of white South Africa, irrespective of the seven million blacks who own the country. (Applause.) We must put it plain to General Smuts (laughter) that this country is not a white man's country; it belongs to the black man. (Renewed applause.) We agree that the white race should live side by side with us until (listen!) we can be in position to hold our own (laughter and applause), but we are afraid that if it is the policy of the Constitutionalists to make our country white, we shall not wait for that time to mature. (Applause). It shall be compulsory for us to dispute the white man's claim to Africa by every possible means." (Applause.)

Now, the Negro World of the Universal Negro Improvement Association [is] speaking right in the heart of South Africa; and if we have achieved nothing else during the three years of our campaign we have at least waked up South Africa to the consciousness of itself. You people in Liberty Hall are the ones who have done it (applause), and if you could awaken South Africa you can wake up hell itself! (Renewed deafening applause.) You have not only wake[ne]d up South Africa, but you have wakened up the white man himself to the consciousness of his own danger. I will now read you what a white man says on this subject. It is an article published under the editorial column of the Negro World of South Africa.[4] The caption to the article is "Warns against wars of the races. Speaker says economic imperialism must go."

"The policy of economic imperialism of the past, if continued during the rebuilding of the world, will bring on a world war between the white and colored races within the next generation, and destroy the chance of the white races to rule the world. Dr. Blank, correspondent of the New York Times in

Switzerland during the war and student of international countries, declared in an address before the Industrial Association of College Men at Hotel . . . . on February 15: 'The way is open to you. You can have anything you want, everything in the business world, but do not do business anywhere in China, Mexico, South America, Africa or Asia, unless you take your heart there, else that will mean death to the next generation. Dr. Buckle[5] says that the "big stick" won't work any more in the world.' "

You know what the doctor means by the "big stick." He means that bluff won't work any more. That is what I told you before, the white man's rule of the world has been bluff. He bluffed our fathers and our forefathers, but he will have a hard time bluffing the new Negro. (Great applause.) He will have to "come across with the goods" now. He will have to lay down his superiority on the table. He will have to prove it. That white man is wise; he is sensible, because we have been telling them in South Africa and in West Africa and those Canadians who are going down there, that "you are only going to carry out a course of philanthropy; you are only giving away what you can hardly afford now." These white people went down to South Africa, built up the country, and those South Africans had the sense to allow them to stay there until the place is looking so beautiful now that they say, "It is ours." Who said the African had no sense? (Laughter.) The African is the most sensible being in the world; a man who was satisfied to wait for five hundred years to get what he wants is "some man!" And the Negro is the only man who has the patience to wait and get what he wants. We have had patience on this side of the Atlantic for three hundred years, suffering the white man's slavery, withstanding his abuse, and suffering the torture of his lynching and burning us, without even uttering a cry. But they never knew why (speaking ironically). Another ten years will tell them why; we were just looking on, and waiting for the opportunity, the chance, and the chance is coming now; the whole world has gone Red, Black and Green! (Great applause.) Now, if Africa can be "going" so strong, and I haven't got there yet, when I get there how will it be? (Applause and laughter.)

THE WEST INDIES AND PANAMA.

Now, men, I am going to leave you for a while. I am going to the West Indies, to Central America, and will be there for about five or six weeks, speaking in the interests of our movement. We have hundreds of branches there, and in Cuba, Jamaica, Costa Rica and Panama, of the Universal Negro Improvement Association. Panama did splendidly for us when we launched the idea of the Black Star Line. Panama is preparing to do a hundred times more now. (Cheers.) To put over the Black Star [Line] and the Liberian Loan[,] Cuba has already gone over the top, but Cuba sends a message to me. In Havana alone they say they have $20,000 waiting for the first night I arrive there for the Construction Loan. I believe I can spend only one night in Havana, but they have cabled me asking for three, and they want to do for me what I do not want done. They want to take me to the President.[6] I do not want to get there just now. I do not like too many public functions; but I know that the President of Cuba is one of the many friends we have. It was the President who received the captain and the crew of the Black Star Line in right royal manner, honoring the Universal Negro Improvement Association and its achievements. (Cheers.) And it was the President who sent a message of encouragement to us not very long ago. Therefore, on my arrival in Cuba I will have to fall in with the arrangements made by the Havana Division of the Universal Negro Improvement Association. Suffice it to say, however, that all Cuba is organized into the U.N.I.A., and His Grace the Chaplain General has sent message[s] to me saying that Cuba is even more warm than Liberty Hall for the colors of the Red, the Black and the Green. He has had a successful time in Cuba, and he will arrive back in this country and will speak in Liberty Hall on the 9th of next month. I am asking you to arrange for a big meeting for his Grace the Chaplain General on the 9th of next month, when he will report to you his successes in Cuba for the six weeks he has been there.[7]

I will go from Cuba to Jamaica and spend five days there speaking to the different divisions of the association in that island. I will leave Jamaica and then go to Colón or Panama, where I will spend four days. From there I will go to Costa Rica where I will spend two days. From Costa Rica I go to Bocas del Toro and spend two days there. From Bocas del Toro I will sail for New York via Jamaica, hoping to be back in New York around the 4th of April, when I will speak in Liberty Hall, God willing.

Now I want to leave with you my heartiest wishes. I want to wish you the very best prosperity during my absence. I know of the hard industrial times through which we are passing in this country; nevertheless we of ourselves must make an effort to relieve the situation. It is for the relieving of the hard economic pressure among Negroes that I am going abroad to make arrangements at those ends—in Central America and the West Indies—so that the Black Star Line can be more actively engaged for the balance of this year and all next year and for all times. Immediately after my return from the West Indies and Central America I am planning to leave for Africa, where I will also make connections there in the interest of the Black Star Line and the Universal Negro Improvement Association. In Africa we have hundreds and hundreds of branches of the U.N.I.A. (Cheers.) We have branches not only among the English speaking people, the French speaking people and the Belgian speaking people, but we have branches among the native tribes (Cheers) in the hinterland of Africa—East Africa, West Africa, Central Africa and all Africa is organized into the Universal Negro Improvement Association, and all we have to do now is to mobilize the financial and the moral and physical strength of the people for the deliverance of Africa. And that is one of the reasons why I am going to the West Indies and Central America to encourage the people there; to let them understand our plans so that all of us between America, the West Indies, South and Central America and Africa can work for the same purpose during this year and in the future.

You need not entertain any fear of anything happening to me. I am going because our plans are well laid and the Universal Negro Improvement Association is such a power today that not only men but Governments fear the result in dealing with the Universal Negro Improvement Association. As I said, I will be going to my native land for the last time. I want you to understand that I, before I became an African citizen, was a citizen of the world. The world was my province. I was born there only by accident. The choice of my nativity is Africa. It is said somewhere in Scripture that you must be born again before you can be saved.[8] Well, I believe I am born again because I want to be free, and the second birth has made me a citizen of Africa. So I will be going to Jamaica not to speak as a Jamaican, but I will be going there to speak as an African citizen, and I will speak to my fellow countrymen not as Jamaicans but as citizens of Africa. And I want it clearly understood in leaving Liberty Hall that I go to the Negro peoples of the world not with any national limitation but with the broadest spirit of African freedom. I go from you as a citizen of Africa and I shall return to die as a citizen of Africa. (Loud cheers.)

When I went for my passport—in that I cannot give passports yet—probably in another couple of years we will give our own passports—it was granted on condition that I could only go from here to there and come back. They made it clear that I could not go to Europe. They know I do not want to go to Europe; but they know this; that to go to Africa you have to sail out of New York and under present conditions you have to pass that way. They did not want to tell me "you must not go to Africa"; they say "you must not go to Europe," and that is because to their knowledge the only ships that leave New York are white ships and if you have to go to Africa you have to sail via Liverpool or some other European port. But later on we can sail from anywhere and reach Africa; and that is just why I am appealing to you tonight to give us sufficient money to buy ships that we can sail from anywhere and everywhere.

I must say good-bye because the hour is late and I hope to meet you all again in another four or five weeks. I want you to pray for me as I will pray for you and for your success. I will ever remember Liberty Hall and wherever I go I shall make it my duty to send you a cable to reach you every Sunday night. Those of you who want to know about the success of my trip you can go to Liberty Hall every Sunday night and I will ask the presiding officer to read to you my cable message. (Loud and prolonged applause.)

Printed in *NW*, 5 March 1921. Original headlines omitted.

1. The Armistice of 11 November 1918 was followed by an eighteen-month period of considerable prosperity in the shipping industry, with higher prices for tonnage and freight. This was largely because of the U.S. government's continued spending on foreign trade and the paralysis of former European rivals. An enormous glut of ships, however, many of which were built immediately after the war, soon led to a rapid decline in prices, which was exacerbated by competition from British shipping and the general trade depression of 1920 to 1922. After the U.S. Shipping Board returned the wartime merchant fleet to private industry, the shipping industry collapsed, with 35 percent of the USSB's ships lying idle by March 1921.

Tonnage prices also declined rapidly, with ships that had cost over $200 per ton to manu-
facture selling for $150 per ton in 1921—and as little as $30 per ton in 1922. The ships most
severely affected were coal- and oil-powered vessels (the Black Star Line ships were coal
powered), which were being made obsolete by the new diesel engine (Jeffrey J. Safford,
Wilsonian Maritime Diplomacy, 1913–1921 [New Brunswick, N.J.: Rutgers University Press,
1978]).

2. The *Black Man* was originally the official organ of the Cape Town–based Industrial
Workers and Commercial Union (ICU). The editor was Samuel M. Bennet Ncwana, president
of the Cape Town division of the UNIA; its business manager was the leader of the ICU,
Clements Kadalie. The prospectus distributed in 1920 concerning the Black Man Co., capitalized at £1,000, was signed jointly by Ncwana and Kadalie. Articles published in the *Black Man*
were also reprinted in the *Negro World*. Ncwana split from the ICU in 1922 and helped to
organize a rival union, the Industrial and Commercial Colored and Native Workers' Union
(ICWU), for which the *Black Man* became the official organ. The only known copies of the
newspaper are from the period of July to December 1920 (South-West Africa Government
Archives, file A. 68/1; P. L. Wickins, *The Industrial and Commercial Workers' Union of Africa*
[Cape Town: Oxford University Press, 1978], pp. 66–67; Les and Donna Switzer, *The Black
Press in South Africa and Lesotho* [Boston: G. K. Hall, 1979], pp. 28, 31).

3. Samuel M. Bennet Ncwana (b. 1892?), was born a Pondo in Natal, South Africa. He
served in the South African Native Labour Contingent in France during World War I, and
after his return to South Africa in 1918, he became a militant leader of the Cape Town
association of former contingent members. He was a founder in 1920 and president of the
Mendi Memorial Club, formed to honor those members of the contingent who had perished in
the sinking of the S.S. *Mendi* on its voyage to Europe during World War I.

In addition to his role as a leader of the ICU and UNIA, Ncwana was also a Cape provincial
leader of the South African Native National Congress (changed to the South African National
Congress [ANC] in 1925). In the early 1920s Cape Town had five UNIA divisions: Cape Town,
Claremont, Goodwood-Parow, Woodstock, and West London.

In June 1921 Ncwana traveled to Luderitz, Namibia (South-West Africa), where he helped to
establish both the ICU and UNIA. After his split with the ICU in 1922, he collaborated with
two leading Cape Town Garveyites, James S. Thaele and Ben Impey Nyombolo, in organizing
the African Land Settlement Association, the objective of which was to resettle landless urban
Africans on land of their own. Ncwana also coedited *Izwi Lama Africa (African Voice)*, an
English and Xhosa newspaper that was founded in Queenstown in May 1922. Ncwana was also
general organizer for the Griqualand West Native Voters' Association during his period of
residence in Kimberley in 1923. He was then associated with the Cape Native Voters' Convention. He was a frequent contributor in 1925 and 1926 to *Imvo Zabantsundu*, the King William's
Town newspaper controlled by the politically influential Jabavu family.

In December 1928 Ncwana was cofounder (with A. M. Jabavu) of the Advisory Board's
Congress of South Africa. In 1931 in east London he edited a new version of *Izwi Lama Africa*,
and in July 1931 *Izwi* became the unofficial organ of the Independent ICU movement led by
Clements Kadalie (Brian P. Willan, "The South African Native Labour Contingent, 1916–1918,"
Journal of African History 19 [1978]: 83; P. L. Wickins, *The Industrial and Commercial Workers'
Union of Africa*, pp. 66–67; South-West Africa Government Archives, file A.68/1; *APO*, 8 April
1922; *Imvo Zabantsundu*, 5 June 1923).

4. A reference to the *Black Man*.

5. George Earle Buckle (1854–1935) was editor of the *Times* (London) from 1884 to 1912
(*CBD*).

6. Dr. Alfredo Zayas y Alfonso (1861–1934) was first elected president of Cuba in November
1920. Accusations of fraud led to a new election in March 1921, which Zayas also won. He
served until 1925 (*WBD*).

7. McGuire was welcomed with full ceremonies and a packed audience at Liberty Hall on 8
March 1921 (*NW*, 19 March 1921).

8. John 3:3.

Report by Special Agent P-138

New York City 2/23/21

IN RE: NEGRO ACTIVITIES:

From careful observation of the Garvey movement for the last few months, coupled with the various conversations I have had with Garvey, his Deputy Potentate G. O. MARKE, Rev. HEYLEGAR [*Ellegor*], Vice Chancellor, and other leading lights of the Black Star Line and Negro Improvement (U.N.I.A.) Association, I am in a position to give the following positive information which I think is of importance:

(1) The Government of Liberia is secretly behind this Garvey movement.

(2) President King of Liberia has been trying to get a loan of $25,000,000. from the U.S.A. and knowing the attitude of the U.S.A. towards Garvey's anti-white propaganda, he is afraid to come out boldly and indorse Garvey's scheme.

(3) GABRIEL JOHNSON (Mayor of Monrovia)[,] who is now Garvey's High Potentate, is the spokesman and actually acting for (secretly) Liberia officially.

(4) Mayor Johnson (Garvey's Potentate) is related to President King by marriage. I learned that the King married Johnson's sister.

(5) G. O. MARKE, Deputy Potentate, is a school mate of Johnson and a very close friend. Marke is also the contributing editor of a number of the leading Negro newspapers in Sierra Leone.

(6) Johnson's daughter is married to a very prominent ex-chief who was ousted by the British as a trouble-maker in Sierra Leone, but now lives in Liberia.

(7) Rev. Heylegar [*Ellegor*] was employed for many years by the Liberian Government as a teacher. He has travelled extensively in Africa and Europe. Today he is the master schemer in getting Garvey's propagandists out and in this country. He takes care of passports, passages, steamship routes, etc.

During my last conversation with Garvey I asked him why he didn't first go to Africa before going to the West Indies; also, whether President King is behind his movement. Garvey told me that *Mayor Johnson is acting for President King in all matters, as Liberia was trying to get a $25,000,000 loan from the United States and if the U.S.A. finds out that President King was in sympathy with his anti-white movement, Liberia would have no chance of getting a cent; so, the King has secretly arranged with him (Garvey) to put Johnson in the limelight to act for him in all matters and as Johnson was not a Liberian Government official* *the U.S.A. could not object to his activities or suspect the King in the least.* But he has sent his advance guard of propagandists and President King has arranged to give them and all members of the Black Star Line the welcome band. Garvey also told me that the King was expected back in the U.S.A. shortly on a mission relative to the loan, but he will have to arrange to see him privately so as not to ruin his chances of getting it.[1] He finally assured me that the King has endorsed and given his movement entire support, secretly, through Johnson, so as to get the loan.

Cuba. Rev. McGuire, Garvey's Chapl[a]in General and chief propagandist, is now in Cuba lecturing and is expected back shortly and will take charge while Garvey is on his trip.

G. O. Marke. G. O. Marke also assured me of the President King's support of Garvey's movement and cited the loan as his reason for acting secretly for the time being. Marke is a native African and a school mate of the President King. He has returned to Africa a few weeks ago. Respectfully,

P-138

[*Endorsements*] FILE G. F. R. NOTED F. D. W.

DNA, RG 65, file BS 198940-72X. TD. Stamped endorsements.

1. President King arrived in the United States on 7 March 1921. Thus far, no evidence has been found of a meeting between the Liberian president and Garvey.

J. Edgar Hoover to Anthony Caminetti, Commissioner General of Immigration

[*Washington, D.C.*] February 24, 1921

Dear Mr. Caminetti:

I am today in receipt of information that Marcus Garvey, the notorious negro agitator who has for many months been a cause of disturbance in this country, is departing for Key West and the presumption is that he will make an effort to leave the country. My purpose in communicating with you is to ask your cooperation and assistance in having the immigration authorities, at the various ports of entry on the Atlantic and Gulf coasts, on the lookout for the return of Garvey, who is a British subject and who should be closely questioned and examined before being allowed to again enter the United States.

I have communicated the same information to the Department of State for its guidance. Very truly yours,

J. E. HOOVER
Special Assistant to the Attorney General

DNA, RG 65, file BS 198940-76. TL, carbon copy.

J. Edgar Hoover to William L. Hurley

WASHINGTON, D.C. February 24, 1921

Dear Mr. Hurley:

Referring to our phone conversation of the 23rd I have to advise you that I have today communicated, by telegraph, with our Key West office informing the agent in charge of the contemplated visit of Marcus Garvey, the notorious negro agitator. I assume that he is making an effort to reach Cuba or some gulf point. He is a British subject and would not therefore require an American passport, but I assume would have to be fortified with other documentary evidence required by the British authorities. I am communicating with the immigration authorities in order that should this individual actually depart from our midst the Labor Department may have their ports of entry scrutinized for his return. Very truly yours,

J. E. HOOVER
Special Assistant to the Attorney General

[*Endorsement*] List under prev[*ious*] file number 000-612

DNA, RG 59, file 000-612. TLS, recipient's copy. Handwritten endorsement.

Lewis J. Baley to the Bureau of Investigation, Jacksonville, Florida

[*Washington, D.C.*] February 24 1921

Marcus Garvey notorious negro agitator left New York today for Key West stop[.] Cover movements thoroughly stop[.] [F]ive[.]

BALEY
Chief

[*Address*] Sauselle[,] 607 Sisbee Bldg., Jacksonville Fla[.]

DNA, RG 65, file BS 198940-74. TL, carbon copy.

BSL Announcement

(*Source*: Archives of Senegal, Dakar.)

Report by Special Agent P-138

New York City 3/1/21

IN RE: NEGRO ACTIVITIES

There are still a lot of doubts as to whether Marcus Garvey intended to sail on the "Kanaw[h]a", or it was a camouflage to make his 'getaway'.

To-night [*26 February*] I had a talk with James Watson, a negro attorney with offices at 240 Broadway, who was once Garvey's right hand legal adviser. Watson told me that Garvey came to his offices some weeks ago and asked him advice relative to the fixing up of his passport. He was then accompanied by a girl named AMY JAKES [*Jacques*], his secretary whom he thinks will accompany Garvey on his trip. This girl, Amy Jakes [*Jacques*], is the woman who caused all Garvey's marital troubles, being the cause of separation from his wife and an impending divorce. This girl is commonly known as the woman whom Garvey lives with. They occupy the same apartments on West 129th St. and caused a lot of criticism and scandal as they can always be seen walking arm in arm to and from his office. He takes her on all his trips over the country and his followers always entertain fears that some day he may be arrested [*for?*] white slavery. The leading officials have always tried in vain to discourage this state of affairs, but for some unknown reason she exercises a wonderful influence over Garvey. Of course she travels with Garvey under the guise of private secretary to cover him, but it is common knowledge that they live together as man and wife. Respectfully,

P-138

[*Endorsements*] NOTED F. D. W. FILE G. F. R.

DNA, RG 65, file BS 198940-78X. TD. Stamped endorsements.

Charles L. Latham, American Consul, Kingston, Jamaica, to Charles Evans Hughes,[1] United States Secretary of State

Kingston, Jamaica, March 1, 1921

SUBJECT: PROPOSED VISIT TO JAMAICA OF MARCUS GARVEY.

SIR:

. . . An item appearing in to-day's issue of the "Daily Gleaner" announces that Marcus Garvey is due to arrive in Kingston on or about March 9, 1921, on board the s.s. MACEO, a ship of the Black Star Line, of which Company he is reported to be president.

His visit is said to be purely of a commercial nature in connection with the above named steamship line and the Negro Factories Corporation, both incorporated in the United States, but plans are underway for the holding of several functions in his honor by local negro associations.

As his activities for the past several years have been conducted in the United States and are understood to have been the subject of police or governmental investigation,[2] instructions are requested as to the visa of his passport in event that he intends returning to the United States. I have the honor to be, Sir, Your obedient servant,

C. L. LATHAM[3]
American Consul

DNA, RG 59, file 000-612. TLS, recipient's copy.

1. Charles Evans Hughes (1862–1948) was secretary of state in the Harding administration. A former governor of New York, Hughes was the Republican candidate for president who lost to Woodrow Wilson in 1916 in one of the closest elections in American history (*NYT*, 28 August 1948).

2. On 22 March 1921 William L. Hurley forwarded a copy of this dispatch to J. Edgar Hoover (DNA, RG 65, file BS 198940-85X) and to Brig. Gen. Dennis E. Nolan, Military Intelligence Division (DNA, RG 165, file 10218-418/2).

3. Charles L. Latham (1881–1960) had served in the U.S. Consular Service in Colombia, Chile, Brazil, and Scotland before his appointment to Jamaica (*NYT*, 11 March 1960).

Editorial Letters by Marcus Garvey

[[Cuba, March 5, 1921]]

Fellow Men of the Negro Race, Greeting:

The mainspring of success for Negroes will be found in unity. A community of interests binds us together in an indissoluble tie, and it matters little whether we are in Africa, North, Central or South America or the West Indies, we are, none the less, bound by these interests. We of the Universal Negro Improvement Association have fully realized the efficacy of organization and each member of this association shall bend every effort to interest every other member of the Negro race with whom he comes in contact in the cause of the Universal Negro Improvement Association. In the final analysis it will be found that the powers opposed to Negro progress will not be influenced in the slightest by mere verbal protests on our part. They realize only too well that protests of this kind contain nothing but the breath expended in making them. They realize, too, that their success in enslaving and dominating the darker portion of humanity was due solely to the element of force employed. In the large majority of cases this was accomplished by force of arms. Pressure, of course, may assert itself in other forms, but in the last analysis whatever influence is brought to bear against the powers opposed to us must contain the element of force in order to accomplish its purpose, since it is very apparent that this is the only element they recognize. Four hundred million Negroes organized with a firm determination to occupy as good a place as any man in the world with no other limitation than his abilities, will have the weight of numbers that the world must reckon with. Four hundred million Negroes organized for one common purpose would constitute a force in itself that would command respectful attention. Organization among Negroes under the banner of the Universal Negro Improvement Association is, therefore, immeasurably influential and absolutely indispensable in combating the elements opposed to Negro progress.

Whatever influence lies back of current propaganda against the Universal Negro Improvement Association and its allied interests it has greatly miscalculated the temper of the Negro people. I am proud to state that everywhere Negroes are flocking to our banner by the thousands, and in the not distant future we hope to see every Negro in every part of the world alive to his personal interest and to the interest of his race and joining [with his]

239

brother in black under the colors of the Red, Black and Green. Today I am proud to convey to the fifteen million Negroes of America greetings from the Negroes of Cuba who express the hope that through unity we will, in a short time, reach the summit of our hopes, A FREE AND REDEEMED AFRICA. Let me impress upon you the importance of your giving unstinted support to the Black Star Line and the "Liberian Construction Loan" by purchasing shares in the former and bonds in the latter. It is absolutely essential to the success of our program that the Black Star Line have more and bigger ships. These ships can only be purchased through our loyalty in subscribing for shares.

Send in and purchase yours now from the Black Star Line, Inc., 56 West 135th Street, New York City, U.S.A. With kind personal regards, I have the honor to be, Your humble servant,

MARCUS GARVEY

Printed in *NW*, 12 March 1921. Original headlines omitted.

[[Cuba, March 5, 1921]]

. . . FELLOW MEN OF THE NEGRO RACE, *Greeting*:

Three years ago last month thirteen Negroes gathered in a small hall in Harlem and formed the New York Division of the Universal Negro Improvement Association. The movement in New York City grew by leaps and bounds, and then began to spread over the United States of America, Canada, the West Indies, Cuba, Hayti, Santo Domingo, Central America, South America, England, West Africa and South Africa, until the chain of U.N.I.A. divisions encircled the globe.

The underlying idea of the Association was the bringing together of the Negro peoples of the world in one confraternity for the purpose of establishing a community of interests.

We soon found that the condition of the Negro was everywhere the same; his color was a bar to the advancement. In some sections of the world it was a bar to his economic progress; in other sections a bar to his enjoying the rights and privileges of citizenship. And we desired the world to bestow upon the Negro that liberty and freedom for which he fought and died in Flanders, France, and Mesopotamia. But the oppressed peoples of the world gained little from the Peace Conference at Versailles.

We soon realized that the Negro, like other men, must work out his own destiny. For that reason we established the Black Star Line Steamship Corporation and the Negro Factories Corporation. We felt that industrial and commercial strength would be a powerful asset to the Negro race in its upward striving.

Then we looked across the sea and saw the wonderful commercial possibilities of West Africa, especially Liberia, with its virgin soil, valuable forests and undeveloped resources. We felt that money, wisely invested in opening up the interior of West Africa, in time would yield a splendid income.

Then, again, we felt that the pride and self-respect, the prestige and standing of the Negro peoples of the world would be increased by developing a strong, progressive and self-governing republic in Africa.

The Black Star Line and the "Universal Construction Loan" are the means by which we plan to transport men and material to Africa, to develop her wonderful resources. By purchasing shares in the former and bonds in the latter you will help provide a future for your children and your children's children. We need more ships and bigger ships. Cuba is loyally responding, and we ask the Negro peoples of the world to follow suit.

The world is looking to see what the New Negro will achieve in the field of commerce. We firmly believe that a brighter day is dawning for men and women of African descent.

Send in and purchase shares from the Black Star Line, Inc., and bonds from the Universal Negro Improvement Association, 56 West 135th Street, New York City, U.S.A. With kind personal regards, I have the honor to remain, Your humble servant,

MARCUS GARVEY

Printed in *NW*, 19 March 1921.

BLACK STAR LINE

SAILINGS FOR

LIBERIA, WEST AFRICA

Sailings with cargo and passengers from New York on or about the 27th March, 1921, at 3 P. M.

Other ships of the Line will sail with cargo and passengers on or about the 2nd of April, 1921, at 3 P. M.; May 8th at 3 P. M.; May 29th at 3 P. M.; June 12th, 3 P. M.; June 26th, 3 P. M. Sailings thereafter will be announced later.

For rates and further information apply
Traffic and Passenger Dept.,

BLACK STAR LINE STEAMSHIP CORP.

56 West 135th Street, New York, U. S. A.

(*Source*: *NW*, 5 March 1921.)

Report by Special Agent P-138

New York City 3-7-21

IN RE: NEGRO ACTIVITIES.

As far as I have been able to gather [*4 March*], President KING will be in New York on or about the 5th or 6th and the GARVEY Association will be sending a delegation to meet him.[1]

The question is being asked by Garvey's followers why he made it a point to be away from the U.S. just when President King of Liberia is expected, in view of the fact that he is selling Liberian Liberty Bonds.

It is expected the Rev. HEYLEYEN [*Ellegor*], Garvey's High Commissioner, who was formerly in charge of the Liberian Public Schools, will represent Garvey here in negotiating with President King.

Of course, Garvey had already informed me that it was imperative that he should not see King or be seen or known to be in his company while he is a guest of the U.S. as this would spoil the chances of his $25,000,000 loan.

P-138

[*Endorsements*] FILE G. F. R. NOTED F. D. W.

DNA, RG 65, file BS 198940-78X. TD.

1. King arrived in New York on 7 March 1921 as the head of a four-man Liberian commission to negotiate with the U.S. government for a $5 million loan. A five-man delegation of UNIA officials paid a welcoming visit to President King at the Waldorf-Astoria Hotel on the day of his arrival (7 March 1921); the delegation consisted of Wilford H. Smith, Elie Garcia, J. B. Yearwood, H. V. Plummer, and Rev. G. E. Stewart (*NW*, 12 March 1921). The American minister in Liberia reported to the Department of State prior to the Liberian president's visit: "At heart President King is probably pro-British. He has actually said, by reliable report, that he personally does not desire the American loan. His acceptance of it would therefore be based on the fact that the Liberian people desire it and not because he favors it. He will not take advice unless it coincides with his views" (DNA, RG 59, file 882.51/1259).

Report by Bureau Agent Adrian L. Potter

Springfield, Mass. Mar. 8–14, 1921

WEEKLY CONFIDENTIAL REPORT

NEGRO AFFAIRS:

Saturday evening Mar. 12, meeting of Universal Negroes Improvement Association held in hall at 685 North St.

"Capt" Leslie Truiaz and Madame L. Elois Trauchette, the latter of Chalmette, La., were the principal speakers. Trui[az] rehashed his talk of Mar. 3rd and 5th relative to Brazilian colonization s[c]heme.[1] The woman, a comely and intelligent young person, exhorted her hearers to perfect an organization in every large and small center of colored population and advised against publicity. She declared: ["]The whites hate us; and we hate the whites. Let us go forward to victory hand in hand with our friends but let us be sure that we be not made fools of at the end." She recited many instances of lynching, burning and alleged brutal treatment of negroes of the South and exclaimed "The Southern states belong to the negro and Iceland belongs to the whites!"

Truiaz stated that the members of the colored race outnumbered the whites in Cuba in the ratio of 12 to 1[2] and that "the island whose soil is soaked with the blood of the black man will soon be governed by one of us, under the black, red and green flag of the U.N.I.A.["] He likened Marcus Garvey to Jesus Christ and declared that Garvey did not need divine assistance something no colored race had ever received. 350 were in attendance.

ADRIAN L. POTTER

DNA, RG 65, file BS 202600-22-59X. TD.

1. The Springfield UNIA division was also involved in a Brazilian-American colonization scheme, originating in Chicago, to settle black Americans in Brazil. The State Department, investigating reports of the scheme in February 1921, was informed by the Brazilian embassy in Washington, D.C., of the existence of a syndicate that sought to colonize American blacks in the Brazilian states of Matto Grosso and Goyaz. To prevent this the Brazilian government had instructed its consuls in the United States to discourage such emigration. In May 1921, however, the Bureau of Investigation reported that seven black families had recently left for British Guiana en route to homes in northern Brazil and that Du Bissette was in correspondence with a Walter B. Anderson, secretary and treasurer of the syndicate (DNA, RG 59, file 000-2259; DNA, RG 65, files 202600-22-65, 70, 77, and 99, and 202600-1804-4).

2. According to the 1919 census, the black and mulatto population of Cuba was 27.2 percent. This figure has been the subject of considerable dispute, and estimates of the black population of the island have been as high as 70 percent for the 1953 census. This wide divergence can be attributed to the "often subjective nature of Cuban racial classification" (Rosalie Schwartz, "Afro-Cuban Mobility in the Republican Era, 1910–1940" [Paper presented at the annual meeting of the American Historical Association, New York, December 1979]; Wyatt Mac-Gaffey and Clifford R. Barnett, *Cuba, Its People, Its Society, Its Culture* [New Haven, Conn.: HRAF Press, 1962]).

Howard P. Wright, Bureau Agent in Charge, to Lewis J. Baley

Miami, Fla. March 11, 1921

ATTENTION MR HOOVER

Dear Sir:

I beg to call to your attention the second paragraph on page three of attached report.

If it is the wish of the Bureau that an effort be made to keep Marcus Garvey from re-entering the United States, any evidence which might be used before the Immigration Inspector handling the matter, should be forwarded before April 1, when Garvey is expected to return to the Port of Key West, Fla.

I have taken this matter up personally with the Immigration Inspectors at Key West, and have been assured of their hearty co-operation. Very respectfully,

HOWARD P. WRIGHT
Agent in Charge.

[*Handwritten endorsement*] Report attached
[*Stamped endorsements*] FILE G. F. R.
NOTED F. D. W.

DNA, RG 65, file BS 198940-81. TLS, recipient's copy.

Enclosure

Miami, Fla. 3/11/21

MARCUS GARVEY: JAMAICA NEGRO AGITATION

February 24 agent received the following telegram from the Agent In Charge at Jacksonville: (in code)

["]Following wire received from chief today quote Marcus Garvey negro radical left New York today for Key West stop Cover movements thoroughly unquote Will cover hard and keep you advised."

Upon receipt of above agent immediately got into communication with negro informants Newbold at Miami and Hardy at Key West, and gave them instructions. I found that Newbold had already heard that GARVEY was to come to Miami to speak, and that his route included a trip to Key West, Cuba, some of the British isles including his former home in Jamaica, and probably Nassau, N[ew] P[rovidence] Bahama Islands.

I then got into communication with N.J. CONQUEST, colored, pastor of WA[L]KER'S MEMORIAL A.M.E. ZION CHURCH, Corner 18th St. and First Place, where the U.N.I.A. have been holding meetings every Sunday. Without arousing his suspicions, I learned that GARVEY would probably speak in his church. CONQUEST recently came to Miami from Los Angeles, and is an ardent supporter of GARVEY. I attempted to find PERCY A. STYLES, who has recently been appointed to the position of district organizer for the U.N.I.A., but was unable to find him.

Late March 9, agent learned GARVEY was not coming back to Miami, my informant stating that he had been warned not to come here by some one in Key West.

Agent proceeded to Key West March 10.

The movements of GARVEY in Key West were as follows:

He arrived the morning of the 25th, and was driven to the home of P.S. GLASHAN,[1] a Jamaica negro, living at 318 VIRGINIA STREET. GLASHAN is president of the U.N.I.A. organization at Key West. Accompanying subject was CLEVELAND A. JAGNES [*Jacques*] and AMY E. JAGNES [*Jacques*], who were supposed to be secretaries. GARVEY spoke the night of the 25th.-26th.-and 27th.-at SAMARITAN HALL, 7th. and WHITEHEAD STREETS.[2]

At the meetings GARVEY spoke principally of the necessity for the economic freedom of the black race, and devoted most of his time to soliciting subscriptions for stock in the BLACK STAR LINE. He stated that the boat line now had three ships in commission, and would [*soon*] float a fourth: that soon the line would put a ship in commission every three months until it covered the world. He spoke of his aims in the Liberia project, and the necessity of trained mechanics and experts in all lines of industry, emigrating to Liberia.

DR. A. J. KERSHAW, an American negro, spoke at all three meetings giving his endorsement to GARVEY's plans. Agent interviewed KERSHAW, who stated that GARVEY had expressed surprise that several government agents had not bothered him in Key West. He then gave me the information that GARVEY expected to return to Key West the first week in April, going from there to Miami; thence to Nassau. KERSHAW is the financial secretary of the U.N.I.A. at Key West. He [*seems*] to be suspicious of GARVEY's financial ability, and mentioned criticisms of GARVEY made by DU BOIS in the CRISIS. KERSHAW stated he believed GARVEY expected to meet other officials of the U.N.I.A. in Havana.

Agent then talked to S. A. MOUNTS, corresponding secretary of the U.N.I.A. at Key West. He is a naturalized Bahama negro. He gave me the information that GARVEY left no record with the local organization of how many shares of stock he had sold. MOUNTS stated that about thirty persons subscribed for stock at each meeting, each subscription from five to thirty dollars each. He seemed suspicious of GARVEY's business methods, but stated that each subscriber was given a receipt for his money by one of the secretaries accompanying subject.

GARVEY sailed from Key West for Havana Feb. 28 on the GO[v] COBB, P. & O. Steamship Company. He had a British passport, as he is a citizen of Jamaica. Agent's information of GARVEY has largely come through intercepted copies of the [NEGRO] WORLD, and I did not until this time know he was not an American citizen. I immediately went to the office of the Immigration Inspector in charge at Key West, with the intention of asking the office to co-operate in trying to keep GARVEY out of the United States. I found that Mr. Hoover, of the Bureau, had already asked such action. The inspectors, however, have no knowledge of GARVEY, and requested agent to obtain whatever evidence of disloyalty, or membership in a radical organization, that was in the possession of the Bureau.

Agent requests that any evidence which should be placed before the Immigration Inspectors be forwarded to agent at once in order that I can appear against GARVEY. This should reach us before April 1. I am this date requesting this by telegraph.

Agent has made an effort to learn who warned GARVEY not to come to Miami, and I believe this warning came from DR. A. P. HOLLY, a former Ha[i]tian revolutionist, and consul from Haiti to the Colonial Government of the Bahamas. HOLLY has been covered in reports of agent on the OVER-SEAS CLUB.[3] . . .

For the information of the Bureau, the U.N.I.A. has about 600 members in Miami, 300 in Key West, and more than a thousand in the city of Nassau, N.P. Bahamas. Nassau members have bought heavily in the steamship line, the principal occupation of Bahama negroes being that of operating sail boats. CASE OPEN.

[LEON E. HOWE]

DNA, RG 65, file BS 198940-81. TD.

1. The *Negro World* refers to Rev. T. C. Glashen (*NW*, 30 April 1921).
2. The *Negro World* of 30 April 1921 reported on Garvey's Key West visit: "He was met at the station by one of the crack bands of the city and escorted uptown. Long before the hour arrived the Samaritan Hall, where his Excellency spoke, was filled to overflowing with hundreds of eager and enthusiastic Negroes."
3. The Overseas Club and Patriotic League was an international society of British subjects with headquarters in London. About thirty-three hundred of the organization's twenty-one thousand members resided in the United States, with slightly over six hundred living in the southeastern states. All of the members of the Miami branch of the club were black Bahamians, with the exception of the president, Archdeacon P. S. Irwin of the Wesleyan church. Bureau of Investigation agents viewed the club with suspicion, one claiming that the club taught "its negro members particularly contempt for American institutions." The same agent reported that the club's leaders told members that "they are the social equals of the whites," concluding that racial conflict in Miami would be the result (DNA, RG 65, file OG 360202).

Gabriel M. Johnson to Marcus Garvey

Monrovia, March 11th, 1921

Your Excellency,

I conform my letter of February 10th. and now beg to acknowledge yours of the 18th. and 31st. of January. The steamer with His Highness The Supreme Deputy has not yet arrived but may be here within the next week. The decision of the Council re expenditure of funds and work here, has my approval; and I shall insist on them being carried out. I will write more fully on this matter after arrival of the officers.

The office building with Co[m]missariat in lower story, is not yet completed, but hope to be in a few weeks. It is ready to receive the Secretary and His Highness, as the . . . [*word mutilated*] apartments are quit[e] ready[.] I note the decision, that the officers are to furnish their own lodgings. I may mention here that this is a very difficult problem but I shall do all I can to assist them in this respect.

I am sorry to say there is no possibility of getting any lands from the Government in Monrovia, there [is] no public land in or [ne]ar Monrovia and as to the township of our own that is alright; but as I mentioned to Mr. Garcia, while he was h[e]re, also to the Council at our meeting; this township will have to be in the rear of the other towns already laid out. I wrote concerning two settlements in Maryland County, near Cape Palmas, that have been already surveyed by Government and the road leading there is in fair condition only need[ing] improving a bit and the local Government and Citizens there have promised all assistance possible for them to render. I have put forth effort to organize a division there and hope to visit that point soon as possible. The township near Monrovia which may be about 30 or 40 miles away, has some roads partly built and we can get laborers to complete it here, much cheaper; therefore, the Council ought not send out a large number of workmen in the begin[n]ing as the feeding and housing problem have to be solved; a few m[e]n to instruct these we can hire here; until we get a good start, will be more advisable.

I am afraid it is late for any extensive planting; except in places already cleared; the clearing time is almost past; and farms are now being plant[ed], but we will be the best we can. The building I mentioned in my last letter for a hotel ha[s] been thoroughly examined and I have now the proposal of the owners which I enclose. As I before stated this will be a paying ventur[e] and advise that the council accept it. Monrovia has only one hotel at present and it cannot meet the demands of the present traf[f]ic here; if accepted please remit one year rent by cable thru [Bank] that is $280.00 and sufficient funds to purchase materials and begin the work immediately. After arrival of the Builder, we shall make calculation for materials and workmen, and send /on 1/ but in the meantime if the remittance by Cable can be sent say about $1500.00 this would start the work while we are making out the statement.

Mr. J. Milton Marshall who was instructed by Mr. Garcia whil[e] in Liberia to proceed to organize divisions, up on the St. Paul river and elsewhere has done very good work. I have given the best part of the past three weeks in visiting these d[i]visions and find they are coming on very well: it only remains some one who can visit them regularly to get them properly enthused and instructed as to the real meanings and intentions of the Organization, there are a good many knockers here, as in other parts /among them is Mr. Cyril Henry/ and it takes a good bit of my time trying to prevent them from doing harm to the association, but I can safety say we are moving on finely now, and with the coming of these officers we will be able to do a good work, and I am sure I will be able to give an encouraging report at the Convention.

Refer[r]ing to Mr. Marshall I think some thing [o]ught to be done for him; as he has given so much of his time to th[e] w[or]k, and is a real good worker and deeply interest[ed] in the cause.

The association in Liberia was charted by the national legislature during its last session. I will send a copy of the Act as soon as possible; after consulting with some of the best law[y]ers here they suggested it as a better course than simply registering the articles of Incorporation you sent out: that it would be more effectual.

We had to mention the Monrovia division as the parent body of Liberia, and all charters to other divisions must be approved by it; therefore, we will send over for the charter in the near future and some other charte[r]s for the other divisions.

Conditions here are becoming encouraging; I have been able to get each division to agree to assist in housing persons coming over to settle in the various settlements; and also to render any other assistance they find necessary to promote the interest of the movement. With sentiment of esteem, I am, dear Sir, Yours fraternally,

G. M. JOHNSON

Payne & Jones
Building offered for $500. per annum for first five years and $600 for next five years, one-half each year to go to repairs. After ten years, rent for further term to be agreed on.

DNA, RG 65, file BS 198940-213. TL, transcript.

Alfred Hampton, Assistant Commissioner General, Bureau of Immigration, to J. Edgar Hoover

WASHINGTON March 11, 1921

Dear Mr. Hoover:

Referring to your letter of the 24th ultimo regarding Marcus Garvey, a notorious negro agitator, I desire to advise you that information has been received from our Key West office to the effect that this man departed for Havana, Cuba, ex SS "Governor Cobb" on February 28, 1921. Garvey at that time gave his future permanent residence as the United States.

The Inspector in Charge at the above named port is very anxious to secure all available information from an immigration standpoint concerning this man for use in case of his return. Will you, therefore, kindly furnish whatever facts you may have which might be used as a basis for excluding

Garvey should he attempt to again enter the United States. Please expedite. Very truly yours,

[ALFRED HAMPTON]
Assistant Commissioner General

[*Handwritten endorsements*] Ack 3/17/21
G. F. R. FILE G. F. R.
[*Stamped endorsement*] NOTED F. D. W.

DNA, RG 65, file BS 198940-80. TLS, recipient's copy.

Edgar Collier to James Weldon Johnson, Secretary, NAACP

2381 E. 43rd, St.,
Cleveland, Ohio 3/12/21

Sir:,

Is This, Marcus Garvy, Really In earnest, about His work? is it Safe to Deposit Money with him, for Stock? Should the Colored People Follow his Doctoring? Could the Colored People Stand the African Climate? is he taking the right Steps, by which People of african Decent will be able to demand Recognition From Other Races?. The Reason why i'm Asking these Questions, is because i hear a lot of Mr. Garvy's, Plans and work. and i have had the occasion to hear Quite a Few people, of the race speak against His idea. and i thought You Would Give me a little information Concerning Same. as i am very interested in the facts of the Matter. Of course i dont mean to agitate, i want to know only the facts. i hear a lot of people say, Oh' i wouldn't Go to africa, Oh' I wish i had my money Back. i would like to know wheather they are right, or not by making Those wishes?, I'm Only a race /man,/ & citizen. But Very interrestd.[1]

Mr. Johnson, your Honor, This is a private Letter. i beg to remain, Very Truly, Yours,

EDGAR COLLIER

DLC, NAACP. TLS, recipient's copy.

1. Johnson had received other correspondence concerning Garvey and the UNIA. On 9 January 1921 John A. Melby of Gary, Indiana, stated his view that the UNIA "should be suppressed. There is only one way to reclaim Africa and that is to buy her back piece by piece. A big movement to take Africa en masse would kill all the good work of the past year" (John A. Melby to James Weldon Johnson, 9 January 1921, DLC, NAACP).

MARCH 1921

Archibald Johnson to the *Richmond Planet*[1]

Montreux, Switzerland.[2]
[*ca. 12 March 1921*]

Editor of the Planet:

I heartily endorse and support the fair, just and common sense view you take of the "Black Star Line" venture and its founder. He is entitled to this liberal, broad-minded, sensible reception of his plans and not narrow-minded, jealous criticism, predicting failure and defeat. His venture is the thin entering wedge, so I take off my hat to Mr. Garvey, wherever born or however black, and shout to him across the seas: Go on! And God speed your efforts! For in all the book of time there is no record of any man of African blood having put ships of merchandise on the broad oceans, navigated and manned by men of African brain and blood.

Therefore, honor to whom honor is due! For why should the brainy men of the race stand by and see this man set upon by some man with a swelled head,[3] simply because Garvey has never had higher university education? He has made a very practical application of what education he has attained and has gotten ahead of some of us who have sweat[ed] long and eagerly by the midnight lamp.

Two Good Reasons.

Two good reasons, therefore, present themselves for accepting Mr. Garvey's plans at their face value: (1) We owe respect to the man himself for his courage and daring in attempting to transport African goods in his own ships. (2) We should patronize and help the [line] to encourage Africans to unite along economic and commercial lines.[4] . . .

The press laughed over Garvey's words in Madison Square [*Garden*], but the English laughed over Arabi Pasha's war and said he "was only a barber," but the kick Arabi put into Egyptian affairs is still there, just as England is giving them a constitution.

But colored men fight each other too much. Let us have peace. We are healing the breach the noble white man has made in our ranks, then shoulder to shoulder. Much to be thankful for! Sixty years ago we were property; cattle in the market. But now—Gerald Mass[e]y,[5] an English poet, has written:

He gave us only over fish, flesh, fowl,
Dominion absolute,
But man over man He made not Lord,
Such title to Himself reserving,
Human left from human free.

ARCHIBALD JOHNSON

251

Printed in the *Richmond Planet*, 12 March 1921; reprinted in *NW*, 23 April 1921. Original headlines omitted.

1. Archibald Johnson reported that he was a regular contributor to "papers and Magazines of my colored *confrères* in America and the West Indies," among them the *Richmond Planet*, the *New York Age*, and the *African Methodist*. Johnson was a native of Bermuda. He was admitted to study law at the Middle Temple in London in November 1901, but he was not called to the bar. He was the only son of Andrew Johnson, a colonel of the Highland Regiment in Bermuda, who later became a sugar merchant (Archibald Johnson to René Claparede, 12 and 17 November 1924, League of Nations Archives, Geneva; Archibald Johnson, "The Ubiquity of the Negro," *A.M.E. Church Review* 9 [1893]: 258–277).

2. Johnson claimed to have studied in Paris and Berlin prior to residing at Montreux, Switzerland (Archibald Johnson to René Claparede, 12 November 1924, League of Nations Archives, Geneva).

3. Possibly a reference to W. E. B. Du Bois.

4. In the *New York Age* of 21 May 1921, Johnson would write, "So long as he [Garvey] confined himself to barter and trade I was in sympathy with him." His changed view of Garvey formed part of a wide-ranging attack against Du Bois and Du Bois's upcoming Pan-African Congress. Referring to Garvey, Johnson declared: "Garvey must remember [George William] Gordon of Jamaica, and how promptly the English Governor Eyre hung Gordon for trying his hand at reforms. Well, England is only waiting for Garvey to come where she can clap a hand on him. . . . It is a great shame to let this fellow [Garvey] humiliate and disgrace all the colored men on the planet."

5. Gerald Massey (1828–1907), English poet, was a proponent of spiritualism (*WBD*).

Report by Bureau Agents A. A. Hopkins and E. J. Kosterlitzky

[*Los Angeles*] Mch. 12, 1921

NEGRO ACTIVITIES

UNIVERSAL NEGRO IMPROVEMENT ASS'N:

Confidential informant reports the membership in Southern California as of March 1st, 1921, as follows:

Los Angeles—964
San Diego—360
Riverside—188

Total—1512

He further reports that the Radical Element is almost without exception West-Indian Negroes. . . .

[A. A.] HOPKINS & [E. J.] KOSTERLITZKY

DNA, RG 65, file BS 202600-5-32X. TD.

Robert Adger Bowen to J. Edgar Hoover

New York, New York March 17, 1921

My dear Mr. Hoover:

In response to Miss Trovillion's request for three bad articles by Marcus Garvey in The Negro World, or for editorials therein, I send you now copies of those utterances from this paper which I embodied in my report on the Negro's radicalism in his press.[1] I also send an article which I reported at the time in full quotation to Mr. Keohan, as well as certain other articles I have today dug out from subsequent issues of The Negro World.

Perhaps, as interesting as any is that from the issue of March 12, 1921[,] which was lying on my desk at the moment that I received your request. It implies the necessity for the use of force in the Negro's aims, and is approximately of current date.

I left The Negro World on list III, prepared the other day, but purposely excluded it from List II of present day out-right radical racial papers. In view of this article of March 12, 1921[,] I am not so sure that we should be amiss in including The Negro World as an ultra-radical paper of the moment as it certainly has been in the past. Very truly yours,

ROBERT A. BOWEN

[Endorsement] NOTED F. D. W.

DNA, RG 65, file BS 198940-81X. TLS, recipient's copy. Stamped endorsement.

1. See DNA, RG 28, file B-240, 2 July 1919, printed in Garvey Papers 1: 487–489; see also DNA, RG 28, file B-500, 22 August 1919, printed in Garvey Papers 1: 497.

Reports by Special Agent P-138

New York City 3-18-21

IN RE: NEGRO ACTIVITIES.

Tonight [13 March] it was given out from the platform at Liberty Hall that sometime next month GARVEY intends to send a Negro Ambassador to take up his headquarters in Washington, D.C.[1]

This representative is to be REV. EASTON [Eason], who was elected Leader of the American Negroes at the last Garvey convention. This idea is, according to the report, that Garvey will try to compel the U.S. to recognize a Negro Ambassador who will speak for the American Negro, thereby giving the Black Star Line movement more prestige.

They are planning a big parade and demonstration in Washington next month, which they term an "inauguration of the first Negro President". Rev. Easton was also elected by Bridges['] Liberty Party[2] as Negro President.

P-138

[*Endorsement*] NOTED F. D. W.

DNA, RG 65, file BS 198940-123. TD. Stamped endorsement.

1. This was never carried out.
2. The Liberty party, formed in August 1920 by Hubert Harrison, William Bridges, and Edgar Grey, was a continuation of Harrison's earlier Liberty League of Negro Americans. It was formed partly in response to the Tulsa, Okla., race riot of May 1920; in street meetings of the party in Harlem, Harrison urged blacks to arm themselves for future confrontations and to vote only for black candidates in the forthcoming elections. Although never formally constituted as a political organization, the Liberty party in October 1920 held a meeting of about 150, at which the names of prominent black figures, such as W. E. B. Du Bois, James Weldon Johnson, Kelly Miller, William Pickens, Monroe Trotter, and Rev. J. W. H. Eason, were placed in nomination for president. Eason secured the most votes and was announced as the party's candidate. The original call for a black president had been made by Bridges in an editorial in his *Challenge* magazine and had been officially endorsed by the *Negro World* in June 1920. In September 1920, however, Bridges made a visit to Wisconsin to gain the support of the Socialist party and the IWW, and following an apparently successful meeting with Victor Berger, in which Berger assured the party of moral and financial aid, he returned to New York and began to call for black support for the IWW and the Socialists. Partly as a result, Bridges was expelled from the party, and he subsequently became associated with Tammany Hall. The Liberty party continued to hold occasional street meetings but appears to have attracted few members, and no record of it has been found after August 1921 (DNA, RG 65, files OG 329359, 272451, and 202600-667; *NW*, 19 June 1920; *Messenger* 2 [October 1920]: 105–106).

New York City 3/18/21

There is a strong feeling existing among a number of the leading business men (Negro) to find out from President King whether he approves of the Garvey Liberian Loan or whether it is an independent scheme of Garvey's to fleece the public. They seem to feel that Garvey should be openly denounced by King.

However, there is a great effort on the part of Garvey's officials to keep King quiet.[1] From the latest report Garvey is still in Cuba. Respectfully,

P-138

[*Endorsements*] FILE G. F. R. NOTED F. D. W.

DNA, RG 65, file BS 198940-112. TD. Stamped endorsements.

1. On 23 March, P-138 reported that "there is a strong effort to induce President King to come out openly for Garvey and his movement, thereby improving the U.S.A. loan" (DNA, RG 65, file BS 198940-95X).

J. Edgar Hoover to George F. Ruch

WASHINGTON, D.C. March 18, 1921

MEMORANDUM FOR MR. RUCH

I am attaching hereto some material which has come to hand upon Marcus Garvey.[1] You will note that it is reported that Garvey is scheduled to arrive at Key West on April 1st of this year. Whether or not he will actually endeavor to enter at this point remains to be seen, but I desire that there be prepared at once a summary memorandum upon the activities of this individual, giving particular attention to utterances either by word, or mouth, or in writing, advocating the overthrow of the Government of the United States by force or violence, or urging the unlawful destruction of property. The files of the M.I.D. and State Department should be thoroughly gone into and the memorandum prepared in final form not later than Monday, March 21st at noon. Mr. Bowen of New York,[2] and Miss Trovillion should be called for assistance in this matter. Very truly yours,

J. E. H[OOVER]

[*Endorsement*] FILE G. F. R.

DNA, RG 65, file BS 198940-80. TLI, recipient's copy. Stamped endorsement.

1. This material has not been found.
2. Robert Adger Bowen, director of the Post Office's Bureau of Translation.

George Cross Van Dusen, Military Intelligence Division, to J. Edgar Hoover

[*Washington, D.C., 19 March 1921*]

MARCUS GARVEY

INFORMATION EXCLUSIVELY FROM THE FILES OF THE MILITARY INTELLIGENCE DIVISION AND STATE DEPARTMENT

PERSONAL HISTORY.

Marcus Garvey was born in St. Ann's Bay, Jamaica, 1887 and lived on the island for twenty years attending the Church of England school although a Roman Catholic. He learned the printing trade and followed it for years until he went abroad, although he had the reputation of never sticking to one job long. He attended Berdeck [*Birkbeck*] College in England graduating in 1913. He travelled in England, France and the Central European countries, returning to Jamaica shortly after graduating from Berdeck [*Birkbeck*]. While abroad he conceived his idea of organizing the Negro Improvement Society. On his return to Jamaica he organized, together with his sweetheart Amy Ashwood, the Jamaica Improvement Association which appears to have been a sort of Forum for the agitation of Negro questions. Garvey acquired debts he could not pay and moved from place to place finally leaving for Port Limón, Costa Rica, coming to New York in 1916. He arrived penniless and devoted himself at once to matters affecting his race. He announced himself to be Marcus Gar[ve]y Jr. of the Jamaica Improvement Association, Kingston, Jamaica, W.I. and collected some money for schools to be established on the Island for colored girls. He posed as a Roman Catholic, securing the use of their churches to lecture in, acquiring the confidence of colored people and even their financial support and that of the Catholic Church. The schools were never built. At the same time he started his soap box campaign for the "back to Africa" idea and for the Negro control of the continent. He next raised "a large sum of money" to build a school for colored children in New York to teach them anti-white ideas. The school was never built. He obtained loans to start a negro daily paper and then bought out "The Negro World", a weekly. Until June 1919 he was about bankrupt and had seven "convictions" for non-payment of wages.

He then launched his "Black Star Navigation Co" project and began raising money to build ships to be controlled by a negro company, manned by negroes, run to Africa and to carry negro made goods.

FORM OF EARLY PROPAGANDA, AND HIS CHANGE OF ATTITUDE.

Before leaving Jamaica he agitated the establishment of a negro industrial school which did not materialize but after his arrival in the United States he changed his form of agitation and took the attitude that industrial education would merely mean the eternal submission of the black to the white race and that complete independence of the black race from the white was the only object to be sought for.

He even went so far as to denounce the Pope to the Catholic colored people as it meant the submission to the white race in religious matters.

His popularity was greatly heightened after the formation of the Universal Negro Improvement Association by the organization of the Black Star Navigation Company and the Negro Factories Company.

BLACK STAR NAVIGATION COMPANY.

This is a Delaware corporation with an authorized capital of [$]10,000,000 divided into 2,000,000 five dollar shares. He and a corps of promoters have been active selling the stock among negroes and have been extravagant in their statements as to [what] the company has accomplished and what it is to do. They [have] three ships; two small [steamers] and one small Hudson River excursion boat. They have been in continuous trouble and litigation, the Yarmouth which is the largest, having been libeled and all the boats requiring extensive repairs.

Trade with the West Indies is to be established and then a line of passenger and freight steamers operated to Africa.

Garvey claims two trips have been made by his ships to the West Indies but the only clear record of a trip is the start made by the Yarmouth for Cuba with a cargo of liquor in 1920(?)[.] The ship sprung a leak and was towed into Norfolk and libeled for extensive repairs and towage charges. The Hudson [R]iver boat was used as an excursion steamer during the convention of negroes in New York in 1920.

Garvey and his Black Star Navigation Company have been in trouble twice for stock selling in violation of state laws, once in Illinois where Garvey was arrested and fined $100.00 and [. .] costs for selling stock without a license and once in Virginia where he had applied for a license to sell stock and it was denied because his representative had already sold stock (about $5,000) around Norfolk. The Post Office Department states that there had been no violation of the postal laws.

NEGRO FACTORIES COMPANY.

This is a corporation with an authorized capital of a million dollars. Its purpose is to stimulate the manufacture of any article of trade by negroes by the production of which the economic status of the negro race can be improved.

UNIVERSAL NEGRO IMPROVEMENT ASSOCIATION.

Little information is contained in the M.I.D. files as to the actual organization of this association. It is essentially a propaganda agency through which Garvey carries on his agitation. Its official publication is the Negro World. I will not go into detail in regard to the Negro Factories Company, the Universal Negro Improvement Association or the Negro World as they are fully covered by Department of Justice files.

CRIMINAL RECORD OF GARVEY.

I find no record of Garvey's ever having been convicted of a felony in or out of the United States. Mention has been made above of his having been in trouble because of stock selling on behalf of the Black Star Navigation Company in violation of the laws of Illinois and Virginia. He has been the defendant in numerous civil actions arising out of debts he contracted and it is reported he was found guilty of criminal libel on August 28, 1919 in New York in an action brought by District Attorney Kilroe based on an article published in the Negro World. I have also heard this action was compromised out of court and never went to trial.

RECENT REFERENCES.

The following two recent references to the activities of Garvey are of interest:—

1. Under date of January 21, 1921 the Intelligence Officer at Governor's Island writes as follows:—

> Cyril V. Briggs, Editor of the "Crusader", when interviewed by an operative of the M.I.D. states in regard to Garvey that the racial question from a radical point of view was progressing very favorably. The Universal Negro Improvement Association has a membership of 600,000 and while not as radical as he (Briggs) would wish still is doing good work. Says Garvey has done good by arousing negroes out of their lethargy and making them realize their power. Says Negro World has a circulation of 40,000 and that Garvey gets a good income from it.
>
> [*File*] 10218-412

2. An article in the New York Call of March [1]9, 1921:—

> Garvey is reported in Havana, March 8th as agitating among Cuban negroes despite the disapproval of the Cuban Government to "fight and die for liberty". Government objections merely passive and based on fear of race friction. Garvey said to intend touring the West Indies.

EXTRACTS FROM HIS SPEECHES.

He has advocated that for every negro lynched in the south, the negro ought to lynch a white in the north. This statement is reported as made at a mass meeting held by the Universal Negro Improvement Association in Harlem, New York, December 1918. At this meeting, he also preached that the next war would be between the negro and the whites, and with Japan's assistance, the negro will win. He has frequently stated that the balance of power in the wars to come will be the negro.

[*File*] 10218-261-53

Extracts from Garvey's address at Bethel A.M.E. Church, Baltimore, Maryland, December 18, 1918:

> "We, like Josephus Daniels, believe that the next world war will be a war of the races, and I believe that that war will start between the white and the yellow peoples. Negroes should make no compromise with either the white men or the yellow men. We have become the balance of power between the white men of Europe and the yellow men of Asia.

"Can die on the battlefields of France and Flanders to give liberty to an alien race and cannot die somewhere to give liberty to himself.

"Out of this war we have produced the American, or the West Indian, or the African Napoleon who will ultimately lead the 400,000,000 black people of the world to Victory.

"Must organize to know what we are to get out of the next war and see that we get it before one sacrifice is made."

[*File*] 10218-261-38

"A big reunion of negroes of America, Africa, the West Indies, South and Central America and Canada, the biggest ever staged in the United States of America" was widely advertised to be held in Carnegie Hall Monday night, August 25th, 1919, attracting the attention of Assistant District Attorney Archibald Stephenson, of counsel for the Lusk Committee, who attended with detectives of the Bomb Squad and stenographers who took notes of the speeches. It is expected that action will be taken against Garvey for he had previously promised the District Attorney to sell no more shares in the Black Star Line, and to "tone down" his public utterances. Garvey's speech in part was as follows:

"Within the next few months our organization will be in such condition that if there is a lynching in the South and a white man cannot be held to account down there, the button will be pushed here and a white man in New York will be lynched. . . .¹ shall continue the war until we get democracy. Woe betide the man or nation which stands in the way of the negro. The negro shed his blood in the great war and that same blood will continue to be sacrificed until we get the rights we demand. We are striving to make Africa a republic, and the white man here harries us in this plan. In America and England the negroes are asked by the white man 'What are you doing here?' The negro in Africa will soon ask the white man, 'What are you doing here?' We are out to get what belongs to us politically, economically, socially and in every other way. . . . The white man is the barrier to a black republic in Africa, and it is for his interest to clear out of there. . . . [We] are not Bolshevik, I.W.W., Democratic, Republican, or Socialists, we are pro-negro and our fight is for the new negro race, that is to be."

[*File*] 10218-344-3

Address Peop[le']s Church, 16th and Chris[tian] Sts., Phila. September 22, 191[9].

"The masses are going to rule. The few little despots and robbers who used to run the world are now being sent to their graves, and before another ten years roll by all of them will be buried by the hands of the masses."

[*File*] 10218-364-7

The following letter from Marcus Garvey, dated Chicago, Oct. 1st, and addressed to Fellowmen of the Negro Race, was published in the "Negro World" issue of Oct. 11, 1919 under the caption "Black Men All Over the World Should Prepare to Protect Themselves"—"Negroes Should Match Fire with Hell Fire."[2] . . .

[*File*] 10218-364-13

At a meeting at Liberty Hall, New York on February 1, 1920, Garvey said:

"We are engaged in a great warfare. It is a fight that must be fought to the finish; it is a fight that will take the last drop of blood of some of us, but we are prepared to give it. . . . So, in conclusion, I adjure you to be courageous, I ask that you continue the fight. Cease not until victory comes."

[*File*] 10218-364-22

SUGGESTIONS.

John E. Bruce of Bruce and Franklin, publishers of negro literature 2109 Madison Avenue, New York should be interviewed as to Garvey's statements as he has followed Garvey's activities for some time and is opposed to his plans for the future of his race.

Bruce should be especially interrogated in regard to Garvey's having left Jamaica with "several hundred pounds" he had collected for a school there and which he appropriated for his own use.

This could perhaps be connected up with his other fake school projects for which he raised money in the United States.

It would seem as though an investigation of the affairs of the Black Star Navigation Company would develop a violation of the postal laws.

There is, in addition, the possibility of violation of the Mann Act on the part of Garvey which seems to be more than merely suggested by the Justice files.

STATE DEPARTMENT FILE.

J. E. H. please refer to my confidential memorandum to you on this subject dated March 19, 1921.

GEO. C. VAN DUSEN

DNA, RG 65, file BS 198940-107. TDS.

1. Ellipses throughout this document appear in the original.
2. Printed in *Garvey Papers* 2: 41–42.

First *Negro World* "Spanish Section"

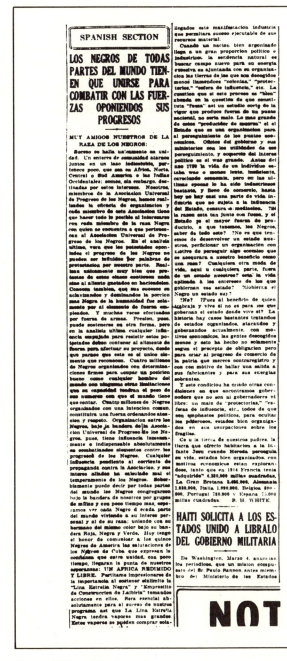

(*Source: NW*, 19 March 1921.)

J. Edgar Hoover to William L. Hurley

WASHINGTON, D.C. March 21, 1921

Dear Mr. Hurley:

I have been advised by a strictly confidential source, that MARCUS GARVEY, who is now in Cuba, if prevented from returning to the United States, will attempt an illegal entry.

The Black Star Steamer, Kanawha, has been ordered to proceed to Cuba at the earliest possible moment, and if Garvey is prevented from returning to the United States, he will board this steamer and be placed ashore somewhere along the south-east Atlantic Coast, at night.

Our various Bureau offices have been instructed to give this matter close attention. Very truly yours,

J. E. HOOVER/G. F. R.
Special Assistant to the Attorney General

[*Endorsement*] (Confidential) Mr. Welles[1] file

DNA, RG 59, file 000-612. TLS, recipient's copy. Handwritten endorsement.

1. Sumner Welles (1892–1961) became assistant chief of the Latin American Affairs Division of the Department of State in 1920. He was promoted to chief in March 1922, and in later years he won a reputation as an architect of the American "good neighbor" policy toward Latin America (*WBD*, p. 1,557; Hugh Thomas, *Cuba: The Pursuit of Freedom* [New York: Harper & Row, 1971], pp. 605–614).

Walter C. Foster to Lewis J. Baley

PHILADELPHIA March 23, 1921

RE: MARCUS GARVEY

Dear Sir:

Referring to Bureau letter dated March 17, 1921, and initialed GFR:MMP, which directs our special attention to the probable illegal entry into the United States of Marcus Garvey, upon very reliable information it looks as though GARVEY will be here on Monday night, April 11th, at the Bethel A.M.E. Church, 8th Street below Pine, where he will debate with a Dr. W. [E.] B. Du Bois on "Race Leadership."[1] This debate was scheduled to take place on Monday night, April 4th, but it looks as though it may not take place on that night.

From inside information we have learned that if GARVEY does come it will be under-cover, and we are almost sure to know of it. We have made arrangements to keep him covered but it may be late at night when we will be notified that he is in town. Have you any further information to give us as to what we should do in case he comes here? He will, no doubt, get into communication with Dr. Francis, President of the Philadelphia Division of the Negro Improvement Association. Respectfully,

WALTER C. FOSTER
Special Agent in Charge

[*Typewritten reference*] JFMCD/AG.
[*Endorsements*] NOTED F. D. W. FILE G. F. R.

DNA, RG 65, file BS 198940-86. TLS, recipient's copy. Stamped endorsements.

1. Dr. R. R. Wright, Jr., editor of the *Christian Recorder*, arranged a debate at the Mother Bethel AME Church. Du Bois spoke there on 4 April. Garvey was scheduled to speak on 11 April. One of Garvey's representatives was to speak for him in the event he could not return by that date (*NW*, 9 April 1921).

Report by Bureau Agent Erle O. Parrish

Baltimore, Md. March 23, 1921

IN RE: MARCUS GARVEY (NEGRO) RADICAL AGITATOR NOW IN CUBA WHO WILL ATTEMPT ENTRY INTO THE U.S.

Upon instructions from this office, I received two pictures of SUBJECT, over the caption of Hon. Marcus Garvey, D.S.O.E.; one of which I delivered to the Commissioner of Immigration and the other was delivered to Mr. Hayward of the Customs Service, with the request that a careful watch be had on all Immigrants, in order that SUBJECT may be apprehended and detained. Investigation Continued.

ERLE O. PARRISH

[*Endorsement*] FILE G. F. R.

DNA, RG 65, file BS 198940-95. TD. Stamped endorsement.

News Report of Garvey's Arrival in Jamaica

[*Gleaner*, 23 March 1921]

Dressed in a dark brown palm beach suit, with a Panama hat, and wearing on his vest the insignia of his office, Mr. Marcus Garvey, President of the Universal Negro Improvement Association, and the acclaimed leader in the United States of America of the coloured race, arrived here yesterday afternoon from Santiago on the s.s. La Belle Sauvage of Messrs. Lindsay Swan Hunter Ltd., Cuba-Jamaica service.

It was thought that Mr. Garvey was coming on the Black Star Line steamer, Antonio Maceo, and so when the good ship La Belle Sauvage swung alongside Mr. Frank Lyon's Mark Lane Pier, there were no representatives of the U.N.I.A. present. There was however on the pier the usual wharf staff and a few Water-policemen, as also Depot Inspector O'Sullivan, whose alertness on the waterfront must have drawn him hither. There was a slight breeze on and the vessel was a little time in docking. Mr. Garvey stood on the upper deck and soon recognized one or two old acquaintances to whom he extended a hearty salutation. Then there arrived Mr. Adrian Daley, the Secretary of the local branch of the Association with one or two other office bearers.

Before the vessel had been made fast, a representative of the Gleaner was on board as also Depot Inspector O'Sullivan who had a short interview with Mr. Garvey, whom apparently he had known many years ago in St. Ann, as they quickly recognized one another and exchanged greetings. Mr. Daley then introduced to Mr. Garvey other members and office bearers of the local branch, with whom he shook hands.

INTERVIEW WITH MR. GARVEY.

The pressman who was also acquainted with Mr. Garvey had at this stage a short interview. Mr. Garvey's features had not changed a bit except that he had grown much stouter. He was not looking his best, however, as the night before the vessel met rough weather, and Mr. Garvey as he said himself was not feeling quite himself.

"How is Kingston[?]" asked Mr. Garvey somewhat anxiously of the pressman.

"Much the same as when you left it," the pressman replied. "And how long will you be staying here?" he added.

"Well," said Mr. Garvey "I will be staying here for about seven days. I would have come over on the Black Star Line steamer, but it was late in reaching Santiago and as I had to keep my appointment here I came over by this vessel, accompanied by one of my Secretaries, Mr. Jacques. Miss Vinton Davis will be here on the vessel in the course of a few days."

"Do you propose to tour the country during your stay?" asked the pressman.

"Yes," said Mr. Garvey "I have arranged so far to visit Morant Bay, Port Antonio and St. Ann's Bay. I have some engagements too in Kingston."

"Yes," said the scribe, ["]I understand you are down for a welcome meeting at the Collegiate Hall to-night."

"Well, I thought I would have a quiet time until to-morrow night, especially as I had a rather rough passage. However I am ready for it."

"How did you get along in Cuba, Mr. Garvey?" asked the pressman.

"Well, I had a very grand reception in Cuba. I was received on my arrival at Havana by President Menocal, members of the Government and members of the Municipality. I went from Havana into the interior—on the estates where there were thousands of Jamaican labourers on the cane farms. I spent about ten days there and I spoke with them. I need hardly say I had a very warm reception from them and the cause which I am advocating received their heartiest support. As I have said I had a rather rough voyage and I should like to have a little rest to recuperate."

"I can well understand that," said the scribe, "and I suppose you will have to devote a little time to the office bearers of the society who are rather anxiously awaiting you," added the pressman.

"Yes" said Mr. Garvey, "I must go and see them and we shall meet again."

The pressman thanked Mr. Garvey and withdrew.

After Mr. Garvey had talked with Mr. Da[le]y and others he left the ship and proceeded along with the office bearers to York House in East Street where he will be staying during his visit.

At the entrance to the wharf in Port Royal Street, where it had got known that Mr. Garvey had arrived, a few people gathered to have a glimpse at him as he passed out for his lodgings from the wharf premises. The motor cars, however, slid by very quickly and there was not much time for anything more than a bow or a wave of the hand.

Thus did Mr. Garvey, President of the Black Star Line and Universal Negro Improvement Association set foot once again on his native soil. . . .

Printed in the *Gleaner*, 23 March 1921; reprinted in the *Panama Star and Herald*, 1 April 1921. Original headlines omitted.

Marcus Garvey to the *Gleaner*

York House, 80 East Street, Kingston,
Jamaica, March 23rd 1921

THE EDITOR,

Sir,—In your to-day's paper, you published a letter above the signature of Henry [F.] Godden[1] to which was attached a copy of a letter written against me by Rev. C. S. Smith of Detroit, Mich., U.S.A., which was published in the World's Work of New York.[2]

For your information, let me say that the Rev. Bishop Smith has absolutely no influence over the American Negro people. He is merely an old preacher, who may be known among his "shouting church folks," but in the life politic, he is as offensive as a red herring. No one pays any attention in America to what fellows like Bishop Smith says.

When I return to the United States and to Detroit, I will deal with Bishop Smith, although he has been already nicely handled by Dr. William Ferris M.A., (Harvard and Yale) Literary Editor of the Negro World. There are two million members of the Universal Negro Improvement Association in America, and in a Negro population of ten million, surely that's not one per cent.

As for Henry F. Godden, the envy and malice of this Jamaican is quite characteristic. Very few Jamaicans can appreciate the success of one of their own. Jamaicans are like crabs; no one must climb out of the basket, or out of the barrel. All will unite to pull him back as he climbs. Jamaicans of the type of Godden tried to pull me down in America, and have been defeated. I would not waste time with Godden. He knows nothing about me. I have never met the man. He must have known my father.[3] What has that to do with me? My father, I believe, lived in St. Ann's and spent his own life there. I lived abroad and away from where I was born, for over seventeen years. But, I shall be in St. Ann's Bay at noon on the 31st March, and if Henry F. Godden wants to know me, he can meet me there, and I shall surely let him have what he may be looking for.

I may take this opportunity of saying to all Jamaicans, Brown, Yellow, and Black men like Henry F. Godden, (although this man may be trying to pass off as white) "You will have a very hard and difficult task trying to pull me down because negroes the world over, have ceased to think in the narrow channel of the Jamaica colour question."

Any negro of ability and education, can lead in the outer world, be he black, brown, or yellow. In Jamaica it is a question of colour worship so Godden can now take notice, that I have not come to Jamaica to lead brown and yellow men, who have no better self-respect than to call themselves coloured. I am a negro, and proud to be one. I have come here to speak to self-respecting negroes, be they black, brown or yellow. I am etc.,

MARCUS GARVEY

Printed in the *Gleaner*, 26 March 1921.

1. Harry Godden was the half brother of Anthony Bayley Dougall Rerrie (1864–1937), the owner of the Winders Hill property adjacent to Garvey's childhood home in St. Ann's Bay. The previous year Rerrie had also acquired the small piece of land owned by Garvey's late father and added it to Winders Hill. Godden had lived in the United States, where he worked for a time as an actor; after his return to Jamaica, he was employed as the manager of the St. Andrew Golf Club in Kingston, a bastion of upper-class Jamaican whites (Robert A. Hill, interview with the Rerrie family, St. Ann's Bay, 1977).

2. The first part of the Truman Hughes Talley article, which Bishop Smith responded to in his letter, was reprinted by the *Gleaner* for local readers on 5–6 January 1921.

3. Godden had written in his letter, "I, personally, knew his [Garvey's] old father pretty well, but 'that's another story' " (*Gleaner*, 23 March 1921).

Gabriel M. Johnson to Marcus Garvey

[*Monrovia, Liberia*, 24 March 1921]

Have received favorable news concessions. Are progressing fairly with the work. We cannot give you any information by cable or letter. Will have to make special report in person. Remit by telegraph immediately $5000 and

$5000 more April. Complete sawmill equipment needed immediately. Hurry on provisions immediately, also wire-screening and mosquito netting. Ship by an early steamer, the first if possible. Coal cannot be obtained here. What is present quotation for palmoil and kernels. Further information by first mail. Please wire reply to our telegram.

[GABRIEL M.] JOHNSON

DNA, RG 165, file 10218-261-78. TG (coded).

Schedule of Garvey's Speeches

BIG MEETINGS & CONCERTS

ARRANGED ALL OVER THE ISLAND TO HEAR HON. MARCUS GARVEY

Elected Provisional President of Africa, President General of the Universal Negro Improvement Association and President of the Black Star Line Steamship Corporation.

The Hon. Marcus Garvey

He will be in Jamaica nine days and will speak as follows :---

TO-NIGHT, March 24th at 8 o'clock **Ward Theatre,** Kingston.

SUBJECT :---" Jamaica, her needs and the Negro Problem." Admission Dress Circle and Parquette 1s 6d, Gallery 1s.

SUNDAY NIGHT, March 27th, at 8 o'clock **Ward Theatre,** Kingston.

SUBJECT :---" The Man Jesus Christ as understood by the New Negro." A Sunday Night as celebrated in Liberty Hall, New York. Mr. Garvey as President General of his Organization will appear on these nights in his robes of office. Admission to all parts of building 1s.

MORANT BAY, Saturday Night, March 26th at 8 o'clock and Sunday afternoon, March 27th at 2.30 o'clock.

MONTEGO BAY, Tuesday night, March 29th at 8 o'clock and Wednesday night, March 30th at 8 o'clock.

ST. ANN'S BAY, Thursday noon at 12 o'clock, March 31st

PORT ANTONIO, Thursday night, March 31st at 8 o'clock and Friday night, April 1st at 8 o'clock.

All are invited to hear the greatest Orator of the Negro Race.

Marcus Garvey was elected by twenty-five thousand delegates to the World Convention of Negroes in New York last Summer, as the First Provisional President of Africa.

He is the foremost Leader among Negroes in the United States, the West Indies and Africa.

(*Source*: NW, 24 March 1921.)

Report of UNIA Meeting, Kingston, Jamaica

[*Gleaner*, 24 March 1921]

Mr. Marcus Garvey, President General of the Universal Negro Improvement Association and African Communities League, and President of the Black Star Line and Negro Factories Corporation, was given a hearty reception by the Jamaica Division of the Association at the welcome ceremony held in his honour in the Collegiate Hall on Tuesday night [*22 March*].

The hall was crowded to its utmost seating and standing capacity, and around the entrances and approaches the people that gathered would have filled the room again. All were eager to catch a glimpse of the man they had assembled to honour and welcome. Eight o'clock was the time fixed for the start of the proceedings, but Mr. Garvey did not arrive in the hall until about half an hour later, when the low murmur of conversation spontaneously swelled in an outburst of applause. Previously Mr. Garvey was met at the northern gate of the premises by the office bearers and some of the members of the Association and a procession formed, headed by their banner, marched into Church Street and entered the hall by the Western door.

As the procession entered the building, the opening hymn of the Association, "From Greenland's Icy Mountain," begun, led by the U.N.I.A. choir and a special orchestra. Mr. Garvey took the seat of honour on the platform, which by this time was besieged by the crowd and packed uncomfortably.

After the singing of the hymn, Mr. Edwin E. Reid, President of the local branch of the Association addressed the gathering. He said:—

Ladies and Gentlemen:—We have assembled here this evening to witness the presentation of an address to the Hon. Marcus Garvey, President General of the Universal Negro Improvement Association and President of the Black Star Line and Negro Factories Corporations. Honour may be conferred on any man or woman who has manifested enough laudable things to attract esteem, respect of another individual or individuals. Brutus was an honourable man, according to Mark Antony. Marcus is an honourable man according to his people. (Cheers.) This human encyclopedia and invincible democrat is a native of our beautiful island, Jamaica. (Cheers.) He had in his possession the wide open privilege of education, a free choice of religion, etc. Ac[c]ording to his natural good demeanour and being of a fair mood of optimism, he has now become one of our real cosmopolitan[s]. (Applause.) You will remember some time ago, some time in 1914, he founded the above mentioned society, and had received hearty assurances and aid from many well-known personages, including the then Governor[,] also the General Commanding the Forces.

After finding greater opportunities could be pursued in other places, he travelled; then lastly found himself in the United States of America, where, with his indomitable and indefatigable efforts, he succeeded in developing the Association which has given birth to the Black Star Line and its allied corporations. (Cheers.) The Association has auspicated to endeavour us to support it unequivocally, which must certainly put us in a full state of hom[o]genial development, under the exemplification of the principles of the better Caucasians. To whom this may concern, kind friends, may eliminate anything adverse in their minds against this Association and welcome him that is in our midst. Then render to Caesar that which is Caesar's and unto Garvey that which is Garvey's. (Loud cheers.)

ADDRESS BY REV. W. GRAHAM.

The orchestra gave a selection, after which the Rev. W. Graham, pastor of the Scotch Kirk, addressed the congregation. He said he hardly expected to have had the honour of saying a few words to this large meeting, but as he had the opportunity he would like to speak, preferably with regard to the gentleman they were welcoming back to Jamaica. (Cheers.) A prophet was not without honour, save as they knew, in his own country, and he was pleased to see that they had broken through for once that rule or that prophecy, and that they were here in large numbers to give Mr. Marcus Garvey welcome. And he thought Mr. Garvey deserved it. As he (the speaker) knew well, Mr. Garvey had ever from the beginning the advancement of his own race at heart and he (the speaker) admired a man who stuck to and laboured and spent for the advancement of his own people. (Cheers.)

When Mr. Garvey was much younger than he was to-day, he used to come to him for advice; and on those occasions he gave Mr. Garvey the very best possible advice in sympathy with the Negro Race of Jamaica. It was being whispered and said that this Negro Improvement Association was somewhat disloyal. As a Minister of the Gospel, who had laboured here for 25 years and had been in touch with Mr. Garvey from the very beginning of his career, he would be very much surprised that anything that Mr. Garvey should do or wanted to do, would in any respect whatever be disloyal to the British Empire. Mr. Garvey knew as well as he did (because he was going back to a conversation he had with him), what the Negro race owed to his race; and there was nothing that offended him more than to hear speakers speak against the principle of a general advancement, spiritually and mentally of the Negro race in this island of Jamaica. He wanted to emphasise that he did not for a moment believe that the man they were honouring that night would ever utter a word of disrespect or disloyalty to the Throne of Great Britain. He knew Mr. Garvey had difficulties and that he had overcome many difficulties and he would have difficulties, but so long as he trusted in the Great Master Who ruled all nations, he (Mr. Garvey) was bound to succeed and overcome all the difficulties. (Applause.) They would excuse him for what he was going to say, for he had some experience in dealing with the people; and the greatest difficulty Mr. Garvey would have would be the disloyalty of themselves to themselves. (hear, hear.) What he meant exactly was this; in his own work he had found Jamaica people, not all of them, but such a large number of them, ashamed to be known as natives of Jamaica. He had found it so, and was persuaded that probably the great difficulty Mr. Garvey would find he had to contend with would be the disloyalty of his own people to his own people. They have not got into the co-operative spirit, the spirit of unity, and every man and woman (especially the women) have got to work and labour for the great cause of bringing up their people, bringing them up into the higher stage of civilisation and giving them the best education, especially the best religious training. And if they went along the lines laid down by the Great Master, they would get, as had been in the past, a people that would do good in the world and spread the gospel of their Master. (Turning to Mr. Garvey): "I give you welcome, Sir, and hope you will succeed among your own people, that you will succeed in bringing them up to a higher stage of life, an honour to themselves, an honour to man, and an honour to God."—(Cheers.)

A beautiful solo, entitled, "Rose in the Bud", was rendered by Mr. R. B. Evans, in so effective a manner that it brought forth thunderous applause from the audience and repeated calls for a repetition. In response, Mr. Evans gave with equal effect, another song, entitled, "As you pass by."

ADDRESS OF WELCOME.

Mr. Adrian Daley, the General Secretary, next read the address of welcome, as follows:—

"Kingston, Jamaica, B.W.I., March, 1921.

"Hon. Marcus Moziah Garvey, President General of the Universal Negro Improvement Association and African Communities League, President of the Black Star Line and Negro Factories Corporations.

["]Hon. and Dear Sir,—We, the officers and members of the Jamaica Division of the Universal Negro Improvement Association and African Communities League extend to you our warmest greetings and a right hearty welcome to this the land of your birth—our beautiful 'Isle of Springs.'

"As your fellow-countrymen, we are unfeignedly proud of your wonderful achievements, which feeling is intensified by the fact that this colossal organization, from which has emanated steamships and factories, was founded in Jamaica by you only seven years ago. And besides paving a way for the negro, our Association now stands out boldly in the noonday light of world-wide recognition.

"Those of us who were associated with you in those bygone days, conscious of your untiring zeal, expected of you great things when you set sail for that Land of Opportunities—the United States of America—five years ago; but never in our wildest dreams did we foresee such mighty deeds—unprecedented in Negro history—as those you have wrought within such a comparative brief space of time.

"Guided by the Almighty Arms of our Common Father 'Who created of one blood all nations of men to dwell upon His fair earth,' you have courageously and successfully piloted your barque o'er billowing seas, and to-day the scattered sons and daughters of our luxuriant Fatherland have awakened to a consciousness of race pride and love—the salient characteristics of the New Negro, and the eternal heritage of all the civilised peoples.

"The territory of commerce which seemed at one time an impossibility to the Negro Explorer, becomes now an actual living reality; and just here we pause in humble thanksgiving to our Heavenly Guide Who weakened the hands of your would-be assassins ere you had perceived these the first fruits of your toil—the floating of the S.S. 'Yarmouth,' first ship of the Black Star Line. Surely, no language of ours can adequately prove our congratulations towards you; we can only trust that your short stay amongst us will be enjoyed right heartily.

"By his blood, which has watered the battlefields of France and Flanders, Egypt and Mesopotamia, the Negro has now emerged into the light of a new-born day. He fought, and bled, and died. He took a man's chance then; he claims a man's chance now. And so the Negro is only striving towards that haven which will place him on the same social, economic, industrial and intellectual plane as those who were his comrades-in-arms in that titanic struggle against the selfish Hun.

"This, and this alone, do we accept as the tenet of the Universal Negro Improvement Association, which demands the support of every ambitious Negro and the commendation of other civilised races. And in this struggle we will press on. Imbued with this spirit of determination, with you as our leader, we hope to soar into further regions of success, and pray God that He will lavish you a furtherance of His Guiding Care until life's latest evening bell shall summon you to your eternal rest.

"On behalf of the Jamaica Division of the U.N.I.A. and A.C.L., We are, Yours for racial uplift,

> EDWIN E. REID, Acting President; ADRIAN A. DALEY, General Secretary; T. A. McCORMACK, Assistant Secretary; U. LEO GRANT, Treasurer; W. E. WILSON, P. H. NICHOLAS, J. M. REID, LINCOLN WILSON, M. GRAHAM, NATHAN CAMPBELL, C. [A.] CAMPBELL, GEORGE S. McCORMACK. Members of the Hon. Advisory Board.["]

... MR. GARVEY'S REPLY.

Mr. Garvey on rising to reply, was greeted with clamorous applause. "Mr. President," he said, his voice reverberating through the hall, ["]Members and friends of the Universal Negro Improvement Association: It is indeed a pleasure for me to find myself once more in the beautiful island of Jamaica." Continuing, he said he left this country between 4 1/2 and 5 years ago for the United States. He went there primarily for the purpose of seeking aid for the Jamaica Division of the U.N.I.A. to build an industrial school after the pattern of Tuskegee in the southern part of the U.S.A. but on arriving in America he received an unwelcome response from the Jamaicans and West Indians who lived in the city of New York. He left the city of New York and travelled through 5 or 6 of the States for the same object. He met other West Indians who discouraged him in the idea of receiving help in the U.S.A. to build an industrial institution for Negroes in Jamaica. He was forced, therefore to change his object. Nevertheless, he was deeply interested in the development of the Negro. He saw before him in America then a grave problem, and immediately went into a sociological study of conditions of the Negro in the United States, which caused him to travel through thirty-eight of the States. He lectured in some of the churches, passed on from place to place, returning to New York in the latter part of 1917 with the intention of coming back to Jamaica. But just at that time something happened that caused him to render certain assistance and he gladly gave it. Immediately after that assistance was rendered, he found out that the people there desired of him a longer stay in New York. He was, therefore, encouraged to start the U.N.I.A. and he assembled 13 men and women in 1917 and founded the New York Division of this Association. (Cheers.) Thirteen members under his leadership grew into 600 in the space of one month. In the space of six months it improved into a membership of 10,000, in the space of three years they had grown into a membership of 35,000 in the city of New York. The Association he started in New York four years ago had now a membership of four millions. (Cheers.) Seven hundred branches were scattered all over South and Central America, the West Indies, in every State of North America and the continent of Africa. He found it impossible, therefore, to return immediately to Jamaica, for his work was laid out for him in the city of New York. He was elected permanently President of the New York organisation as well as the International Organiser of the movement. He travelled through the 48 States of America and organised branches, and now they had 2,000,000 members in the United States. The Organisation had grown by leaps and bounds and that night he was there, not representing the American Organisation, or the West Indies or the South or Central American Organisations, but an International Movement of Negroes. (Applause.) He was here not speaking to them as a British born subject, but as a citizen of Africa. He had to thank them for their address of welcome. He was commissioned by the High Executive Council of his Organisation to go to Africa—to go to Liberia to lay out there certain plans for the redemption of their Motherland. But prior to taking that journey, he thought that he would pay his island home a visit for the last time; hence in mapping out the Central America and West Indian tour, he included the island of Jamaica. Before he left New

York, 35,000 members of that division asked him not to visit Jamaica because of certain rumours they heard—rumours to the understanding that the British Government regarded him as a disloyal subject—as a seditionist and that should he arrive in Jamaica certain things would happen. He could not really understand why such a rumour should be abroad because he had never been disloyal to any government in his life. (Cheers). He had no time to be disloyal to Governments. (Uproarious applause). All this time, every minute of his life, every second of his life was given to the glorious and grand cause for the redemption of Africa. (Cheers). On the 13th of August last year, 25,000 delegates, representing the negro peoples of the world (four hundred millions of them) elected him as the FIRST PROVISIONAL PRESIDENT OF AFRICA. That job and that responsibility was given him and he would not shirk it. Africa, the land that God Almighty gave them, was robbed and bespoiled by the nations of the world and shall be redeemed by the four hundred million negroes in the world. In saying so, he meant no disrespect or any discourtesy to any nation, to any race, but any nation or any race that desired to take it as such, they were welcome to it. There were four hundred million negroes in the world—they robbed four million of them from Africa 300 years ago, they brought them in slavery to the Western Hemisphere; when the matter was brought before Queen Elizabeth it was represented that the negroes were taken for civilising and Christianising them. After 300 years if they were civilised and Christianised, they would use that same civilization and Christianisation—(Here the applause was so great that the last words of the sentence w[ere] not distinctly heard.)

After the applause had subsided, Mr. Garvey said, in thanking them for the address of welcome, they would understand that he had come to Jamaica not for the purpose of stirring up discord among the races in the Island. He came here to [speak] to the negro and to unify the hundreds of negroes who lived in this country. He realised there were many races living in Jamaica— they had the white race, the yellow race, and the black race—who had lived in peace for so long. He did not come here to create any disturbance, but for the purpose of speaking to his people. No power of hell or on earth could stop him from so speaking to them. By accident, he was born in this country, not through any choice of his or of his father or mother, who by some slave master, years and years ago, brought his foreparents into this country, causing him to have been born here and not in Africa. If he had the choice of birth, his choice would have been in Africa, but since he was born here by accident (laughter), he believed he had the right of speaking in this country as any man born in this country or came to this country. The President and officers of the Kingston U.N.I.A. would understand that the Association had nothing to apologise for or compromise. This was a movement made up of men and women who gained a new birth out of the last world war. All races and nations fought for freedom and democracy and liberty in the last world war and two million negroes from America, the West Indies and Africa were drawn into the war; they fought most nobly and splendidly in France,

Flanders and Mesopotamia and after the war they were pushed back. But the U.N.I.A. said they shall not stay back but go forward. (Cheers). He came to them, not as a Jamaican, he came to them as a Negro interested in negro humanity everywhere. (Cheers). "I cannot understand why they should say I am disloyal," he said. "I have never been disloyal to any Government in the world. I am more than loyal, first of all to this race of mine because, by God! if there is a race which needs loyalty, it is the Negro Race." In coming to Jamaica he was not scared, he was a negro that could not be scared, he refused to be scared. He believed in the grand and noble utterance of Theodore Roosevelt, "Fear God, and you have no need for fear." (Cheers). He was out in the world to meet all men of human equality, whether you were white, or yellow, or black, if you were a man he respected you, because you also were created with the image of God Almighty. And he believed that the white man was entitled to certain rights and privileges, the yellow man was entitled to certain rights and privileges, and he believed the black man was also entitled to certain rights and privileges. So they would understand him well; he did not come to Jamaica to stir up strife, the State of Jamaica was too small a place for him. (Cheers). He was just wasting time here. They would understand why they said he was disloyal. He was not only President General of the U.N.I.A. but they had given him the biggest political job in the world—Provisional President of Africa, and he had to speak at times in the interest of his republic, and if in speaking in the interest of his republic he displeased other statesmen, it was not his fault, it was their fault. Warren Harding, the President of the United States[,] had to speak for his Government. Clemenceau of France had to speak for his, and why should not he speak for his? (Cheers). All he was concerned with were politics and economy. He was interested in the economic development of the Negro, that was why they had the Black Star Line, their social and moral growth, and that [was] why he was interested in the U.N.I.A. He had three jobs— President of an industrial corporation, President General of a social and moral movement, Provisional President of a big republic, and sometimes he had to speak differently. When he was making a political speech he made no apologies, when he was speaking on industry it was a different talk. He was not there that night to speak [on sedition?], the next night he would speak to the citizens of Kingston, and he welcomed white citizens, coloured citizens and black citizens. He welcomed His Excellency the Governor, he welcomed everybody, and if they were coming to hear him speak sedition they would be mistaken. (Cheers). He was goi[n]g to speak on his work and responsibility, and he hoped to meet them the next night. (Prolonged applause.)

"Auld Lang Syne" was pathetically sung, after which a collection was taken, during which the orchestra gave a selection. Mr. George S. McCormack rendered a baritone solo, "Asleep in the Deep," in his usual style, and was encored, to which he responded.

Mr. T. A. McCormack gave the closing address. He said from the evidences of that evening he was sure they had the true spirit and appreciation towards the Association. Now that they had honoured the man they had to welcome back to the land of his birth—the land where Mr. Garvey had first dream[t] of his mighty task, he hoped that this visit might infuse fresh zeal and courage in the hearts of members and friends. He believed he voiced the sentiments of all present when he expressed the wish that this would not be the last time they would have the pleasure of having the President General in their midst and that his visit might be an annual event. (Cheers). He thanked them for their presence and for the enthusiasm shown. "Long live Marcus Garvey" he concluded.

Mr. A. Bain Alves called for three cheers for Mr. Garvey, whom he styled the "greatest reformer of the world." The cheers were vociferously given. The hymn "Now thank we all our God," was sung, and the enthusiastic meeting was brought to a close with the singing of "God save the King."

Printed in the *Gleaner*, 24 March 1921. Original headlines omitted.

J. Edgar Hoover to William L. Hurley

WASHINGTON, D.C. March 25, 1921

Dear Mr. Hurley:

I desire to refer to my communications of December 14, 1920, January 4th, and January 17, 1921 concerning Marcus Garvey. This individual is now stated to be either in Cuba or the West Indies, with a prospect of his return some time during the early part of April. I am preparing the material in this office upon Marcus Garvey at this time with a view to excluding him from the country upon his application to enter. In my communications above referred to I requested certain information concerning his trip to Canada in December 1920. I am particularly anxious to ascertain Garvey's connection with financial interests in Canada and write to inquire whether or not there was any information obtained as to his connections in Canada, and the persons interested in him. Very truly yours,

J. E. HOOVER
Special Assistant to the Attorney General

DNA, RG 59, file 000-612. TLS, recipient's copy.

Wilbur J. Carr to Charles L. Latham

[*Washington, D.C.*] March 25, 1921

Sir:

The Department has received your despatch No. 901, of March 1, in which you request instructions as to whether or not a visa should be granted to Marcus Garvey who was due to arrive in Kingston on or about March 9th, and who may desire to return to the United States.

In view of the activities of Garvey in political and race agitation, you are instructed to refuse him a visa and to inform at the same time the Consul at Port Antonio of your action. I am, Sir, Your obedient servant, For the Secretary of State:

WILBUR J. CARR[1]

Vi/JPD/es

[*Address*] Charles L. Latham, Esquire,
American Consul, Kingston, Jamaica.
[*Handwritten endorsements*] JPD. #MCB
U-H LAW
[*Stamped endorsements*] A true copy of the
signed original
ALVEY A. ADEE.

DNA, RG 59, file 811.108 G 191/2. TLR, carbon copy.

1. Wilbur J. Carr (1870–1942), an attorney, was a career employee of the Department of State. He was director of the Consular Service as well as a ranking budget officer in the department (U.S. Department of State, *Register*, 1924 [Washington, D.C.: GPO, 1924], p. 105).

Report by Special Agent P-138

New York City 3/26/21

IN RE: NEGRO ACTIVITIES.

I had a conference [*25 March*] with Hudson Price, Associate Editor of the "Negro World". He told me that the "Kanaw[ha]" had sailed for Cuba at 2:30 this afternoon from Staten Island, having on board about forty passengers including MRS. VINTON DAVIS and TOBITT, the two propagandist[s].

According to Garvey's announcement in the Negro World for months, a large ship was to sail for Africa on March 23rd or 27th and all these who wanted to go back to Africa were to be ready with their baggage. Hudson Price told me that for the past three weeks a large number of persons (members of the U.N.I.A.) arrived from Detroit, Georgia, and other cities and towns with their baggage ready to sail to Africa. Some wrote the office informing them that they were selling their properties and belongings so as to leave. Now that these people are here in New York and after visiting the office and told that the ship was not yet ready, but would be ready next month, Garvey's officials here are a bit puzzled as to just what to do for them. To prevent others from coming into New York on the same wild-cat mission, they have decided to alter the Negro World advertisement to read that they will have the ship ready to sail for Africa next month. Of course, Price told me that there is not even any sign of a new ship in sight and the whole thing is preposterous. He said it[']s a shame to be fooling the poor people like that.

Price went to Washington last week to visit the King mission in the interest of the Negro World. He had a chat with Johnson, one of the members.[1] Johnson told him that Liberia was greatly in need of the loan and must get it from some place. He asked Price to use the Negro World in appealing for aid. The result was a front page article in this week's issue of the Negro World, boosting the loan.[2] He did not see President King but will return to Washington again to see him.

Price also told me that he has worked out a plan for the floating of the Liberia loan which he wanted to present to King. . . .

P-138

[*Endorsements*] NOTED F. D. W. FILE G. F. R.

DNA, RG 65, file BS 202600-667-21X. TD. Stamped endorsements.

1. Frederick Eugene Richelieu Johnson (b. 1862) was associate justice of the supreme court of Liberia and a brother of Gabriel M. Johnson, UNIA potentate. Johnson was listed among the dignitaries who were seated on the platform of a UNIA meeting in Monrovia, Liberia, on 30 December 1920 (*NW*, 26 March 1921). Johnson's grandfather, Elijah Johnson, was one of the founders of Monrovia, while his father, Hilary R. W. Johnson, was a four-term president of Liberia (1884–1892). The following assessment of him was made by the American minister in Liberia prior to the visit of the Liberian commission:

> Justice Johnson is inclined to be egotistical and has rather an exaggerated opinion of Liberia's importance. While he doubtless feels that the best interest of Liberia calls for a close friendship with the United States yet he believes that Liberians are self-sufficient and need very few American agents and these should have as little power in Liberian affairs as possible. He might be called lukewarm toward the United States but it is not thought that he is pro-British (DNA, RG 59, file 882.51/1259).

2. "United States Government Loan to the Liberian Government," *NW*, 26 March 1921; see also *NW*, 9 April and 7 May 1921, for reports on the Liberian Plenary Commission.

Report by Bureau Agents A. A. Hopkins and E. J. Kosterlitzky

[*Los Angeles*] March 26, 1921

NEGRO ACTIVITIES

U.N.I.A.:

Confidential informant states that the projected real estate deal for the purchase of the property at Washington and Central Ave., Los Angeles, to be used as a home for the local unit of the U.N.I.A., and for a cooperative store to be run by the U.N.I.A., has failed. Not more than 10 would put up the money, so the scheme fell through. (See Weekly Intelligence Report, Los Angeles, for December 6, 1920, page 45). He further states that efforts to sell stock in the BLACK STAR LINE and other MARCUS GARVEY ventures, have been unsuccessful;[1] that in spite of the large membership of the Local U.N.I.A. and the prosperous condition of many of its members, very little enthusiasm is shown in backing the financial schem[e]s of GARVEY. However, the sale of stock in the LOWER CALIFORNIA MEXICAN LAND AND DEVELOPMENT COMPANY[2] (See Weekly Intelligence Report, Los Angeles, for November 1, 1920, February 18, 1921, and March 18, 1921, re NEGRO ACTIVITIES) is meeting with considerable success. A party of about [30] North Carolina Negro[e]s are expected to reach Los Angeles about April 15th enroute to the colony. The promoters claim that there are over 400 negro[e]s already settled on their lands in Lower California.

Informant further states that the present conservative leadership of NOAH WEBSTER [*Thompson*] seems to be firmly established and he is holding down all efforts at Radicalism, racial or otherwise. Meetings are held regularly, but there has been no appreciable growth in membership during the last few weeks. . . .

HOPKINS & KOSTERLITZKY

DNA, RG 65, file BS 202600-5-33X. TD.

1. A few months later, UNIA solicitations and sales in Los Angeles improved. On 5 July 1921 Bureau of Investigation agent A. A. Hopkins reported that Noah Thompson said the Los Angeles UNIA contributed "approximately $100.00 per month to the parent organization in New York." Another confidential source added that "about $30,000 in UNIA bonds have been sold in this district in the past three months" (DNA, RG 65, file BS 202600-2126-30).

2. The Lower California Land and Development Co. was founded in December 1919 by Theodore W. Troy, a black Los Angeles promoter and businessman. Troy moved his family to the Santa Clara Valley in Baja California, Mexico, where he planned to develop a black farming community that would engage in the type of truck farming that the Japanese successfully undertook in California. By 1923 Troy's company claimed to control eight thousand acres of land and had petitioned the Mexican government for aid in establishing a farm demonstration bureau (*California Eagle*, 6 December 1919; NW, 24 March 1923).

Speech by Marcus Garvey

[*Gleaner*, 26 March 1921]

A monster mass meeting was held in the Ward Theatre on Wednesday night under the auspices of the Jamaica Division of the Universal Negro Improvement Association and African Communities League, at which Mr. Marcus Garvey, President General of the Association, was the speaker. The building was packed from pit to dome with an enthusiastic audience. Mr. Garvey was cheered to an echo as he stepped on the platform. He delivered an oration, lasting over one hour, dealing with the aims and objects of the association. His striking eloquence riveted the attention of his hearers. The vast multitude caught his enthusiasm, and as he spoke the ceiling echoed and re-echoed with the thunder of their applause. . . .

Mr. Garvey then spoke. He said it was indeed a great pleasure to find himself there that night. He had come from the United States of America on a tour of the West Indies and Central America for the purpose of speaking to them in the interest of the great movement he represented (Cheers.) The Universal Negro Improvement Association was a world movement of Negroes. They were endeavouring through this association to draw into one united whole the four hundred million negroes of the world for the purpose of establishing in the continent of Africa a dominion of Negroes (cheers). They believed the time had come in the history of the Negro people of the world like in the history of the White race and the Yellow race, for the Negro to pave a way and to blast a way to Negro independence (Applause). The U.N.I.A. believed if it was right for the white man to dominate in Europe, and the yellow man to dominate in Asia, it was right for the black man to dominate in Africa. Nations had sprung up out of Europe and Asia and the time had come for nations to spring up out of Africa. The U.N.I.A. had no apology to make to nations or races, the one desire was to blast a way for the motherland. Three hundred years ago forty million negroes were taken from Africa as slaves to the Western Hemisphere and the time had come for the Negro to use his civilization and Christianization to redeem the motherland (cheers). The world in which they lived was re-organization itself. The world had just passed through a bloody war, fought on the sacred principle of democracy. Two million black men with white men fought for the cause, held the Germans at bay and threw them across the Rhine. But for the assistance of the negro in the war a different tale would have been told (cheers), and when the war was over all the people who fought in it demanded their share and received consideration, but the negro alone got nothing. What did they think? Did they think that the men who suffered and died, their brothers and his, in France and Flanders and Mesopotamia were going to shed their blood for nothing? "You will understand, negroes of Jamaica!" he shouted, "The world is re-organizing itself politically, and men and races and nations everywhere are clamouring for and demanding their rights. Hence the Universal Negro Improvement Association has organized itself and call[s] upon the four hundred million negroes in the world to demand their rights. What was the matter with Jamaica? The whole world was organizing [itself]. Negroes everywhere were [answering] the call of the motherland. She was now bleeding and crying [out to] her children for aid and her Negroes everywhere had answered. Are you going to answer in Jamaica?" (Cries of "yes!"). He continued: "I have come here to have your answer. Yes or no. I have been made to understand that Jamaica is made up of cowards. Fellows are afraid to talk because they are afraid to die! Were you afraid to die in France and Flanders? Talk wherever you are! Talk for your constitutional rights! I understand there is a trembling fear in Jamaica. Trembling for what? God Almighty created you as men, as men you live, as men you must die! (Applause). Are you afraid of men? I would like to see a man who dared make me afraid. You men of Jamaica, you want backbone! Take out the weak bones you have and put in backbones! Don't let anybody cow you! You have your constitutional rights! Demand them! Englishmen in England demand their constitutional rights; Irishmen in Ireland demand their constitutional rights, throughout the whole Empire men speak for their rights! You lazy, good-for-nothing Jamaicans, wake up!" (Cheers).

In stirring language and warmly gesticulating, he almost yelled, "If for your constitutional rights, they will not hear you in Jamaica, then carry it to the foot of the Throne in England! It looks like this is a country of blind one-man rule, because in my survey of world politics and international matters,

JAMAICA IS THE MOST BACKWARD COUNTRY

in this Western Hemisphere. Men dare not talk in Jamaica! What is the matter with you, men? I am glad to let you know that a change is taking place and you must join in the change now, otherwise you will lose forever. I have no respect for men who are too cowardly to demand their rights."

In an easier tone he went on, "Some have been scattering rumours that I am coming to Jamaica to stir up some sort of strife. Why so nervous about my coming here if they have done no wrong? A man with a clean conscience is ready to welcome a man and a friend at any time. I have not come to Jamaica to stir up any revolution or race strife but come to speak to the men and women and children who look like me, and I would like to see the man who would stop me do it! I never brought myself here, they brought me here, and I am here until I am ready to go (cheers). Little did they calculate 300 years ago when they robbed black men and women from Africa that black men would strike terror into their hearts to-day (cheers)." Continuing, he asked to whom did this world belong? It belonged, he said, to the Great God, the Great Architect of the Universe Who created Man His Masterpiece and gave him to the world, the "Lord of creation." He said, "Man, thou are perfect!" God never said white men as against the privileges and rights of black men or yellow men. God said, men! "Are you men?" he thundered, as he paused to wipe the perspiration from his face. "Do you still believe in the Darwin theory that [*the black*] man is a monkey or the missing link between the ape and man? If you think it is, that theory has been exploded in the world war. It was you, the supermen, that brought back victory at the Marne![1] (Cheers). If you believed yourself monkeys prior to 1914, then your achievements in the world war [were] such that [*they*] will restore your confidence. If you are men, if you are the 'lords of creation,' what right have you 'lords of creation' to allow other 'lords of creation' to take away what belongs to you and make slaves of you? You have as much right in the world as any other man whatever his colour. White men know their right and claim it! Here is one negro who represents four million negroes who feel and think like me, who feel and think that we are 'lords of creation' and as the white man is exercising the jurisdiction of his over-lordship, so we are organizing negroes to exercise the jurisdiction of our over-lordship. Hence as we are willing to see Europe for the white man and Asia for the yellow man, so we demand Africa for the black man" (Applause).

He went on: "Negroes, you want men, you want leaders to point you the way to destiny. The way is long, the road is rocky, it calls for not so much prayers as sacrifice. You negroes in Jamaica pray too much! (Laughter and cheers[.]) With all your prayers you have hurricanes, earthquakes, droughts and everything! You know why! Because God is not satisfied with prayers alone[.] God says you must work and pray! And you people seem to give up the world to the white man and take Jesus! The white man has the world and gives up Jesus! Don't you know the white man has a right to Jesus, too? Jesus belongs to everybody so you are foolish to give up the world and take Jesus only. You must take part of the world and part of Jesus, too! You negroes have not got into your head the scientific idea of worshipping God!

EMOTION AND SENTIMENT DOES NOT COUNT

in a world like this. They cannot move the world. This world can only be moved by practical achievements. Unless you work with your prayers, you will be too late here or anywhere else. Can't you see you have a part of the world, too? Along with your prayers do some work and that is what the U.N.I.A. is here to advise you to do. What kind of work? We want you to do ennobling work. White men have statesmen, able leaders in science and literature, men who control and dominate Governments, we want negroes to do the same (cheers). The hour has struck!" He said he was not endeavouring to divide loyalty in any way. He was not here to preach disloyalty to any Government but to preach loyalty to the negro race. To-day his race was down-trodden and oppressed the world over and he was calling upon his race for a new emancipation that would make them men among men, an emanci-

pation which in the near future (and not far) they would find white statesmen, yellow statesmen and black statesmen (cheers). The time had come for
negroes to point themselves to a more glorious destiny. Was their race to be
always slaves and serfs? If there was no better for him but to be a lackey, let
him die. No one could tell him that he must bow and cringe and scrape to a
man because that man was white! It was insulting to his Creator that he
should do so. Why? But he could not blame the people of Jamaica, he said, or
the negroes of the West Indies for the lethargy in which they found themselves now because they had had the wrong kind of education. For 83 years
they taught them to believe in a white God and a white Jesus Christ and
white Angels and a black devil. They taught them to believe that the angels of
hell were black and hideous. "Who told those liars that God is white?" he
cried, "that Jesus Christ is white, that the angels are white women? God has
no colour. He is a Spirit. Jesus Christ was not white, black or yellow. He was
the embodiment of all humanity. If He was Jesus the Christ, the Redeemer, if
He came to save fallen mankind and He came as a white man then He did not
come to redeem me. Jesus Christ is the Son of God Who took our physical
form, that physical form bore in it a link of every race. The line from which
He came had connection with every race existing, hence Jesus Christ is the
embodiment of all humanity, otherwise He could not have been the Christ.
Who told them the angels were white women? Angels are spiritual beings,
they have no physical form or flesh. If they reject God as a Spirit and Jesus
Christ as the embodiment of all races then the U.N.I.A. shall make God and
Jesus Christ black. (Cheers). Men and women of Jamaica! I want you to
understand that you are living in a thinking age; you are not living in a
sentimental age but an age of thought and facts!" Continuing, he said the
negroes of Jamaica wanted to work some more and make some of those
preachers do some hard bustling. They had too much religion in Jamaica. He
defied any man to be a better Christian than he was. They wanted men in
Jamaica with more sympathy. Nobody seemed to have sympathy for black
people in Jamaica. He was sorry for this island and for the black people here
and he was sorry he could not remain here to help them for a wider world
called him. He had come for the last time and he hoped what he had said
would inspire some one to carry the torchlight of Christianity. "Your Gordon Somers and your Wilsons and the great bunch of negro preachers ARE A
BUNCH OF HYPOCRITES," he said, "I say so without any hesitation, because
if they were not hypocrites they would have led. They are men with superior
education, but they have no backbone.[2] If they were not cowards they would
lead you, but they bow and cringe before a man because he is white. You
want men!" The difficulty in Jamaica was [the] colour question. Why, they
only had two races in the country (he did not mean the Chinese and Syrians
with whom he would deal the next night)[,] the white race and the negro
race. Where did they get this coloured race from? There was no coloured
race. Colour meant nothing. Some people did not like to be called negroes.

"Why," he said, "some people in Jamaica would just shoot you dead if you call them a negro." (laughter). What was beating Jamaica was that they had too much "white-black" men in Jamaica. (cheers). How ignorant they were? How foolish? A race that was ashamed of itself was a race that displeased the God who created it. Were they going to continue in the same ignorance? That was what the UNIA [set] itself out to do, to change the current of thought and to make them realise that they belonged to one race and to one common destiny. If they rise they must rise as a race and not as individuals. Individual effort had never yet done anything for humanity or saved any great situation; it took co-operative effort to save any situation. In Jamaica they had been individualistic too long. They wanted co-operation and they wanted their Gordon Somers and their Wilsons to pitch in as men.[3] He refused to believe that any man was his superior because of colour. He believed in superiority not of colour but of intellect and achievement. He was willing to admit any white man was better than he, if the white man could whip him in intellect and given the same chances and opportunities the white man was able to forge ahead of him. They had to use an American colloquialism, "to come across with the goods and deliver it." Continuing, he asked, "You think now that I have sense I believe everything in the Bible? You people don't know how to diagnose things and analyse things. What is the Bible? It is the Holy word of God but God never wrote every word in the Bible[.] Inspiration came to the prophets and good men of the world and they wrote certain things and gave it to the Christian world. Men got hold of these manuscripts and they have been revising them for over 1,000 years and are you so foolish as to trust white men with this property for 1,900 years? I want you to think this over and hear my speech on the Man Jesus Christ on Sunday night." He said he refused to believe the white men who revised the Bible that God said to him, "Servants obey your Masters," or that God created his race to be "hewers of wood and drawers of water." The old world was gone and things were making a new start. He said he was surprised to find on his return to Jamaica that Jamaica had not been improved. All he found here was dust. But he would speak on conditions in Jamaica the following night, his subject being "Jamaica and her problems." He then described the aims and objects of his association, how it was started, the difficulties he met, how he overcame them and his successes at present, to all of which he attributed the grace of God. He made a point of it, that when he was trying in Jamaica, his own race "turned him down" and all the assistance and encouragement he received were from men of the white race, mentioning specially the Rev. William Graham, Sir William Henry Manning, Brigadier General Blackden and Mr. Bourne, late Colonial Secretary. He referred to what Bishop Smith wrote with respect to him in the "World's Work," and reproduced in the Gleaner. He said he knew Bishop Smith well and when he returned to America, he intended calling on Bishop Smith in Detroit and make him tell the people about what he had written in the "World's Work."

He thanked his hearers for their attention and hoped to meet them again. (Applause.)

The meeting was then brought to a close.

Printed in the *Gleaner*, 26 March 1921. Original headlines omitted.

1. In July 1918 the 369th Infantry Regiment played a key role in the battle to repel the German forces at the Marne bulge. Sixteen men from the 369th were among the volunteers who remained on the front lines while French and American forces retreated. Afterward, the volunteers fired flares to inform the French artillery units of German troop locations. When the German army launched its attack, the white commander of the 369th remarked that the black regiment was "all there was between the German Army and Paris." The black unit repelled the German forces until they were relieved by fresh troops (Florette Henri and Arthur E. Barbeau, *The Unknown Soldiers* [Philadelphia: Temple University Press, 1974], p. 118).

2. Garvey makes an ironic reference here to the title of a book by Charles T. Wilson, one of the clerics he is criticizing: *Men with Backbone and Other Pleas for Progress* (Kingston, Jamaica: The Gleaner Co., 1913). Wilson's later book, *Men of Vision* (Kingston, Jamaica: The Gleaner Co., 1928), included a highly complimentary chapter on Garvey.

3. Somers and Wilson had been social activists in Jamaica for a number of years. At the time of Garvey's speech, both were affiliated with the Jamaica League, Somers as president and Wilson as general secretary. Wilson founded the Jamaica League in August 1914, establishing benevolent and fraternal goals similar to those of the UNIA; their slogan was "Jamaica's Welfare First." By 1921 the league had established cooperative stores and a bank. Among the league's goals were the industrial development of Jamaica, legislation against monopolies, and a minimum wage to stabilize the island's labor force (*Jamaica Times*, 1 August 1914; *Gleaner*, 14 April 1921; PRO, CO 137/748).

John A. Soulette to the *Gleaner*

23 Church Street, Kingston,
March 26, 1921

THE EDITOR,

Sir,—As a leader of thought amongst the labouring and common people of this island, I cannot allow the barbarous and uncalled-for onslaught of this prodigal son of Jamaica, Marcus Garvey, to be abusing all and sundry, and especially his betters as I observe in the Gleaner of to-day. It is very evident he has not improved either in culture or refinement; the vulgar tirade he has made on such worthy citizens as the Rev. Gordon Somers, and Rev. Wilson, makes me come to the conclusion that it was the flotsam and jetsam of the United States he must have been associated with during the four years of his sojourn, and perhaps he does not know that refinement and ability and not colour are the qualities that count in Jamaica. Vulgarity and disloyalty are things we discount, and it might not be out of place to tell him that he is not capable of accomplishing anything for his countrymen by the methods which he is propagating.

We in Jamaica would like very much to see a balance sheet published in the Gleaner of the Black Star Line, so that a nod of approval or congratulation could be given, but until then our disgust and disapproval are the only things he will get out of us.

As far as Africa and the triumphal return of the race is concerned, I question whether the owners of Africa would permit this Black Moses to enter it whether by land, sea, or volplaning from the air. I am, etc.,

JOHN A. SOULETTE[1]

Printed in the *Gleaner*, 29 March 1921.

1. John A. Soulette (d. 1946) was born in Haiti and came to Jamaica sometime in the early 1890s. He was a watchmaker who was also active in numerous social and political movements. He was one of the founders, along with Dr. J. Robert Love, of the Phillippo, Knibb, and Burchell Memorial Fund Association, of which he was also secretary (*Gleaner*, 2 August and 25 August 1894). The association had as its aim "the erection in the island of Jamaica of a suitable Public Memorial, commemorative of the personal labours, sacrifices, and successes" of the well-known English missionaries for their part "in the Work of Evangelization, Education and Emancipation" (*Gleaner*, 25 August 1894). Soulette also served as secretary of the Jamaica Representative Government Association for many years. He was an alderman of the Kingston and St. Andrew Corp. and a friend of the popular Legislative Council member, J. A. G. Smith (*WWJ*).

Negro World Front Page

Inspector McGerrity to the Inspector General of Jamaica

Constabulary Office
St. Ann's Bay [*Jamaica*] 27/3/21

Inspector General,

REF. YOUR CONF. OF 25/3/21

Marcus Garvey's father was an inmate of the St. Ann's Bay Alms House from 28th May to 8th Dec 1917. He was removed from there by a man named Bellamy[,] an ex-soldier of the B W I R and also a friend and supporter of Garvey's and died in St. Ann's Bay some time last year (1920.)[1] I understand Marcus Garvey defrayed the funeral expenses. The Inspector of Poor took out a maintenance summons against Marcus Garvey who altogether for the support of his father owes the Parochial Board £46-4/-. He saw Marcus Garvey when Garvey was /last/ in Jamaica, but he said he wouldn't pay a farthing as his father had done nothing for him. This £46-4/- is still unpaid and if the Parochial Board desired they can proceed against him for the amount. In my opinion it would be an excellent way of exposing Garvey publicly if the Parochial Board did so. If you desire any further information, I can obtain it without any knowledge of it becoming public.

McGERRITY
Inspector

JA, CSO. ALS, recipient's copy.

1. Garvey's father died on 9 April 1920, at the age of eighty-three; the cause of death was listed as senile debility. At the time of death, he resided with his granddaughter, Adassa Harvey, at Musgrave Street in St. Ann's Bay.

Report of UNIA Meetings at Kingston and Morant Bay, Jamaica

[*Gleaner*, 29 March 1921]

As briefly announced in Saturday's Gleaner, Mr. Marcus Garvey, President-General of the Universal Negro Improvement Association and African Communities League, who is now on a visit to Jamaica, delivered another powerful address at the Ward Theatre on Thursday night on "Jamaica, her needs and the Negro Problem." There was a large turnout, and an excellent musical programme was rendered. Those who contributed to the programme were Mr. and Mrs. G. McCormack, Mr. Evans and Professor Barnes (Pianist).

At the outset of the meeting Mr. Adrian Daily explained the objects of the Negro Improvement Association.

Mr. Garvey, who was received with cheers, said Jamaica was an island that was somewhat isolated from world activities. In all his travels he had never [c]ome across a country that was more backward than Jamaica. Whilst in Jamaica the negroes made no progress, they had the Chinese and Syrians coming here and making wonderful progress (cheers). Why was it that Jamaicans had to leave their country?[1] Why was it that men had to leave and go abroad to make a living[?] It was because of the backward condition in which the country was. If they had good statesmen in the island, Jamaica would be more prosperous. In England they had statesmen like David Lloyd George, Winston Spencer Churchill. In France they had a Briand; in America they had a Warren Harding[;] then in Cuba they had statesmen. In Jamaica they had no statesmen (cheers). They had a bunch of ignoramuses. They wanted men

WITH EXPERIENCE, MEN WITH VISION.

He then pointed out how dependent Jamaica was in respect to foreign trade, and said he was there to warn them how cautiously they should move. The United States of America had developed such islands as Porto Rico, San Domingo and Haiti. It was not [un]likely that prohibitive tariffs would be raised against this island, and what Jamaica needed was men of backbone— men of vision who would lead them through any impending crisis. He was interested in the 800,000 negroes who lived in Jamaica. His future lay in the Continent of Africa. When he looked at the undeveloped resources of the island, he could not help thinking that what they wanted was more men of vision but unfortunately there was too much selfishness—a selfishness that was not known abroad. The spirit which pervaded the average Jamaican was that he did not like to see the other Jamaican rise (cheers). What they wanted was real leadership. They had too many hypocrites and a bunch of religion, which was doing no real good for the people (cheers). If the negroes in this country would unite, they would achieve greater things. The[y] did not want a man who occupied an honorary position. They wanted to have a paid leader—a man who would devote himself to the cause and interests of the people—whether he was a J. A. G. Smith[2] (cheers) or a Gordon Somers. They wanted a leader who would be able to maintain a lasting co-operation, a leader who would be able to carry out their aims and desires. It was a shame that men in this civilized age should go about naked and not be able to earn enough to feed themselves whilst the other fellow lived in luxury and affluence (cheers). They had in this country all the elements which, if developed, would mean material progress to the country. What had the men who had made money out of the people done for the country? (A voice: None). They had no factories, no industries here. Nearly everything they needed came from abroad. This was probably his last visit to Jamaica as he would be proceeding to Africa where he had a big and important job and he wanted them to co-operate and improve themselves. From what he could understand, there was no desire of their Governor to see that people were living in a state of starvation[,] were badly housed and poorly clad. "Negroes of Jamaica" he proclaimed "don't allow yourselves to remain in a process of stagnation. Arouse yourselves. Do not make fools of yourselves (cheers)."

Proceeding, Mr. Garvey said they could not get anything by merely praying for it. The negroes had been kept under and it was all

Due To Their Own Inertness.

People who came here from abroad were able to make substantial progress. They had a Chinese J.P., a Coolie J.P., and soon they would have an Assyrian J.P. Could a negro go to China and be appointed a J.P.? (Voices: No). He wanted them to think. They should arouse themselves and cease begging for what justly belonged to them. There was no reason why the negro should not advance economically, socially and politically. He wanted to see negro statesmen, negro magnates, negro admirals and negro Field-marshalls (cheers). And that hope would eventually be achieved when they set up the great republic in Africa (cheers). The Englishmen, he pointed out, had years ago been held in bondage by the Romans. To-day what was the position of Britons—"Britons, Britons never shall be slaves." This was their song; and when the negroes returned to Africa, their motherland, they would sing: ["]Ethiopians, Ethiopians never shall be slaves." (prolonged cheers). He had brought the message from the [12],000,000 negroes of America of be of good cheer, and to look forward to the day when the four hundred millions of negroes in the world would unite under the one standard and would be under one vine and fig tree (cheers). In Liberia they had been laying the foundation for the great cause. He then proceeded to refer to the Black Star Line and the value of owning stock in the company. They had a White Star Line and a Red Star Line and the negroes were now having a Black Star Line. What the negroes wanted was to co-operate and to advance themselves, socially, economically and politically; and he threw out the hint that he had a scheme under consideration which he would submit to his associates in New York for the establishment of a big Departmental Store in Kingston where black girls would be employed just as white girls were employed in other stores. (cheers).

At the conclusion of his address, Mr. Garvey was lustily cheered; and the proceedings terminated with the singing of the National Anthem.

At Morant Bay.

Mr. Marcus Garvey spoke to an audience numbering about 100 at the Court House, Morant Bay, on Saturday night. Mr. Louis Duff presided, and in a ten minute speech introduced Mr. Garvey as a leader who had come forward to help the Negro Race on the path of progress.

Mr. Joshua N. Gordon of the local branch of the Universal Negro Improvement Association then presented Mr. Garvey with an address, in which his organizing abilities, as shown by the success and great speed of the Association Mr. Garvey had founded, [were] praised and the final success of the meeting hoped for.

Mr. Garvey spoke for about 90 minutes, traversing in the main the points he had dealt with in his Kingston meetings. He commenced by briefly outlini[n]g the aim and objects of the Universal Negro Improvement Association which was to "draw into one united whole the 400,000,000 negroes of the world. To link up the negroes of the West Indies with the negroes of North America, with the negroes of South and Central America, with the negroes of Africa for the purpose of founding on the continent of Africa a Government of our own." They were organizing for the industrial, commercial, educational and social development of the negro race, and they believed that the negro like other races should play an important part in world affairs, and now when the other races of the world were engaged in reform and reconstruction and new nations were being born, the negro should become a great nation himself.

The speaker then went on to point out what the white and yellow races had done in the development of civilization, and asked what had the negro contributed in this direction? The race had done nothing. It had been content to be the servant all the time, had shown no ambition. The race had done nothing because it had never united in effort, and had no race pride. The Englishman, Frenchman, American, the German, the Japanese and Chinese and the others were all proud of their nationality and their race. The negro was not, hence he could do nothing for its uplift nor for the progress of the world. They were now seeking to change the order of things, to teach the negro race-pride, and to mould the 400,000,000 members of the race into a mighty nation. The negro should build cities and railroads, and operate steamships and run great businesses, just as the other races had done, and this was what the Universal Negro Improvement Association had set itself out to accomplish—and his mission to Jamaica was to bring the negroes of this island into line in the movement. In vigorous and fluent language he urged his hearers to get out of the lethargy in which they had lived so long, and take on themselves the ambition to be men in their own land and to help in the formation of a negro nation in Africa.

In conclusion he recommended the taking of shares in the Black Star Line, and participation in a $2,000,000 loan being raised by the Association to start building a nation for the negro people of the world.

SUNDAY NIGHT'S MEETING.

On few other occasions has the Ward Theatre been so crowded with people as on Sunday night at the meeting of the Jamaica Division of the Universal Negro Improvement Association, when Mr. Marcus Garvey, President General of the Association, spoke on his subject "The Man Jesus Christ as understood by the New Negro." Every seat was occupied and standing room in the building was hard to be obtained.

Mr. Garvey appeared in his robes of office made up of the emblem[atic] colours of the association—red, green and black. He entered on the stage in a procession formed of office bearers of the association with banners aloft and of members of the Jamaica Labour Union[3] also carrying their banner, while the choir sang the hymn, "Now thank we all our God."

Mr. Adrian Daily, Hon. Secretary of the Association made a few remarks thanking the people for attending the meetings in such large numbers and inviting new members to join.

Mr. and Mrs. George McCormack rendered a short programme of song and their performance was heartily appreciated.

Rev. E. Seiler Salmon,[4] who was in his robes, beg[a]n giving a discourse on Easter, but the audience refused to hear him. Mr. A. Bain Alves also started to address the audience and was well received, but when he attempted to picture the old days of slavery and to give an account of the origin of the people of mixed colour the crowd showed their disapproval and silenced him with clapping.

MR. GARVEY SPEAKS.

Mr. Garvey who was suffering from a cold and the exertions of the past week rose to speak amidst generous applause. He said: ["]Over nineteen hundred years ago, the Man, Jesus Christ was born in the world. His mission was to redeem fallen mankind. After nineteen hundred years they were taught the doctrine that Jesus taught during His time. Men everywhere bowed at the footstool of the Christ Who was crucified for the [redemption] of fallen men. Whereso[e]ver they turned their eyes within [christen]dom they found man professing Christ. Jamaica like everywhere else in christendom believed in the Christian idea, in the Christian dogma as taught by the Man Jesus. For over 300 years in this part of the world they taught them the way of Christ and Him crucified, and got them to believe that Jesus, His Father God and all belonging to the Heavenly hosts were spiritual Beings, whom they should revere in trembling and in every other way; that this God they worshipped, that this Jesus they adored had no special mission for them but that of making 'Men hewers of wood and drawers of water,['] that this Jesus and this God they were taught about and believed in, had no other mission for them but that of servants, and as servants they should obey their masters.["] He was there that night to give them an insight into the new meaning by which Negroes everywhere were worshipping Jesus Christ and were worshipping God whom all men revered and honoured. In Jamaica it would appear that they had a very slavish and peculiar notion of Jesus and of God. They had been taught to believe in Jesus and God as Beings who had no sympathy with them for a better economic condition in this world in which they lived, but as Beings who were preparing a throne for them, and all that they expected to get out of life would be given to them when they got to heaven. He was there that night to give an idea of how Jesus and God were being worshipped by all intelligent human beings. Negroes because they had been forced to accept teaching by an alien race seem[e]d to think there was no hope for them on this side of Jordan, the hope they aspired to was all in the world beyond. This doctrine had been taught by an alien race for purposes of their own. Jesus Christ who came into the world over 1900 years ago was human even as He was divine; He came for the purpose of redeeming fallen humanity and fallen humanity was of such a nature, of such a character then as to cause disgust; it was through the disgust of God why it became necessary for Him to send His Blessed Son to redeem the world. When He came here, one class—the privileged class—did not receive Him, such class as governed the world, such class as they had in Jamaica who had no sympathy with the lowly, the humble, the meek and despised ones. Those people who preached the gospel to-day were like the very class Jesus found when He came to the world over 1900 years ago. Those people were privileged to oppress the weak and unfortunate and among those they would find those who subsidised others of their own to preach Jesus and Him crucified. Religion had been prostituted ever since Jesus left this world (Hear, hear). When Jesus came they mocked Him, they cried out: Crucify Him. And who mocked Jesus? Were they black men? (Cries of: No!) Were they Negroes? They were

THE VERY CLASS

of people who preached Jesus Christ to-day; the very class of people who ruled and dominated the world (cheers), the very class of people who were distorting the name of Jesus, who were commercializing the name of God— those were the people who crucified Jesus. And they were the people who crucified and would crucify and would condemn everything that aimed for human uplift. To-day they did not crucify anybody but they destroyed every principle Jesus Himself would teach if he was here. And they carried their propaganda through the pulpit! Jesus Christ Himself would deny! If Jesus Christ were to come to the world to-day, he felt sure there were many pulpits He would not occupy. If Jesus were to come to Jamaica His sympathy would be with the lowly, the humble and the despised. They as a people had suffered and were still suffering but there was still great hope for them. Men might despise them, but the God whom they worshipped and adored, and the Jesus who was crucified would never forsake them, for God was grateful. Why should God be grateful to the Negro and why should Jesus Himself be grateful to the Negro? Because when God sent His Son into the world to redeem man, when humanity despised and rejected Jesus and sought His life, who was [it] that rendered assistance? Was it the white man? When the white man in the person of the Jews cried: Crucify Him, when the white man in the person of the Roman soldiers pierced Jesus in His side,

IT WAS THE NEGRO IN THE PERSON OF SIMON THE CYRENE

who went to His assistance, who took up the cross and relieved Him! (Cheers). Just at this Easter time it was the Negro that rendered the greatest assistance to His Master when the world rejected Him and the U.N.I.A., knowing the gratitude of Jesus Christ had chosen Him as their Standard Bearer, and whereso[e]ver He led they followed (cheers). No human power, no human agency could have made the association what it was to-day; no human power could have brought into the association four million Negroes, the hardest of all people to organize in the world. In his experience and that of others they could not get Negroes to organize, they could not get 12 Negroes anywhere to agree on any matter whatever, but here was an association of four million Negroes all agreed on destiny. That night he came to them—the scattered sons and daughters of Ethiopia, asking them to stretch forth their hands simultaneously with other Ethiopians. That night he

SAW IN THEIR FACES

the image of their Great Creator, if God has created them in His own image why should any one despise them? Why should they give them a back place in the world? Why not preach the good doctrine? Why all this hypocrisy and lies? He could not understand it, but more lies were told in the pulpit of Jamaica than anywhere else (hear, hear). They wanted more God, more Christ in their pulpits. The Chaplain-General of the U.N.I.A. told him that wanting to find out the right attitude of the Bishop of the West Indies he asked him the question, "Bishop, are you my brother?" The question was put to the Bishop four times before he replied "Yes, brother in Christ." He [want]ed them to understand that the white man had a different notion about God and about Christ and that they (the hearers) had the sentimental, emotional idea about Jesus and about God. The white man had the scientific idea. He wanted them to change their emotionalism and sentimentalism and give some of the scientific application. There was science in religion. It took a good suit of clothes, a clean and tidy home and good food to be a christian, otherwise they were going to be villains. The kind of christianity the U.N.I.A. wanted them to follow was the christianity Jesus taught in the sermon on the Mount, the true and undefiled religion that made all men equal (cheers). They wanted the kind of religion that would help them to rise and find happiness on earth. He could not understand how this beautiful and resourceful country could allow its people to live in rags, half starved and diseased. Who was to bring about the change? Not the doctors and lawyers, it was the preachers, but they seemed worse than anybody else, because though the people were poor, these preachers sought to take away their last penny. The people of Jamaica wanted to demand of their preachers to preach Jesus Christ, to preach the real religion and if the preachers did not do so they should shut up the churches and select a leader to preach Jesus to them. They could not get the right kind of understanding because they had too much theology, they wanted more of Christ and less of theology (cheers). He was no preacher, he was a publicist, but he saw "some of the fellows not doing their work and he had to help them do it." He then exhorted the people to unite and co-operate to rise. He bespoke a hearty welcome for Miss Vinton Davis, the Right Honourable International Organizer of the Association, who would soon be in the island to carry on the work he had begun. Liberty was not gained without fighting, liberty was not got by petitions, deputations and mass meetings. They must be prepared to die for their liberty; he was one Negro prepared to die, even now on the spot, for the cause he thought just and righteous. This might be his last public appearance in Kingston and he bade them farewell (cheers).

The National Anthem was sung and the gathering dispersed.

Printed in the *Gleaner*, 29 March 1921. Original headlines omitted.

1. A total of 146,000 Jamaicans emigrated from the island between 1881 and 1921. Of this number, 46,000 settled in the United States, 45,000 in Panama, 22,000 in Cuba, and 33,000 in other areas (George W. Roberts, *The Population of Jamaica* [Millwood, N.Y.: Kraus Reprint Co., 1979], p. 466).

2. James Alexander George Smith (1877–1942), a barrister, was elected in 1917 as representative in the legislative council for the parish of Clarendon. He was one of the few black members of the council and a harsh critic of the practice of placing "imported" officials from England in power. In August 1921 Smith formed the Jamaica Representative Government Association. Smith was among the most popular of Jamaican politicians of the period, and he, along with Garvey, is often credited with founding the nationalist movement in Jamaica (*HJ*, 1918; James Carnegie, *Some Aspects of Jamaica's Politics, 1918–1938* [Kingston, Jamaica: Institute of Jamaica, 1973]).

3. The Jamaica Trades and Labor Union was affiliated with the American Federation of Labor. Founded in 1907, the union was the first to offer sick benefits to Jamaican workers. When the union first appeared, it was designated Affiliate No. 12575 of the AFL. Its organizers encountered government resistance, however, which forced many of them to emigrate. By 1921 the Jamaica Trades and Labor Union had been reorganized as AFL Affiliate No. 16203 and had registered its rules with the government under the Friendly Societies Law. The Jamaica Trades Union, along with the Longshoremen's Union and others, was active in the labor strikes of 1918 through 1920 in Jamaica, which were caused by the declining living standards workers suffered after World War I (George Eaton, "Trade Union Development in Jamaica," *Caribbean Quarterly* 1, no. 8: 48–52).

4. Edward Seiler Salmon (b. 1864) was born in Westmoreland, Jamaica, and educated at Fairfield College. After teaching for the Church of England in Jamaica, Costa Rica, Trinidad, and several other West Indian islands, Salmon attended General Theological Seminary in New York. He was ordained a deacon in the Protestant Episcopal church in June 1911 and became a priest the following year. Salmon served as rector in a church in Port Limón, Costa Rica, for five years, but he was forced to resign because of his agitation against the British. In 1923 to 1924, Salmon joined the African Orthodox church and supervised several of the church's missions in New Orleans before being discharged by Archbishop George Alexander McGuire in 1925 (*The Negro Churchman* 2, no. 5 [May 1924]: 3–4).

Report of Meetings at Montego Bay and Port Antonio, Jamaica

[[Montego Bay, March 30, 1921]]

As was announced, Mr. Garvey arrived here yesterday and beg[a]n his series of meetings in the town hall last night. Outside the building was a large crowd gathered to see the Provisional President of Africa and in the hall there was an appreciable gathering swelled by visitors from neighboring towns and districts. At the approaches of the hall, Mr. Garvey was met by the representative of the local branch of the Universal Negro Improvement Association, together with Dr. Henry J. Evans who conducted Mr. Garvey to the platform.

Mr. J. A. Brown was voted to the chair and with other preliminaries carried through was a short musical programme.

The Chairman introducing Mr. Garvey referred to his indomitable courage and said he was bold enough to tell Mr. Garvey that he was not a disciple of his, but whatever might be his methods they were bound to admit that Mr. Garvey was a great man, a unique man, a man inspired to work among his race, a man with strong determination, with the spirit of [perse]-verance and the ability to . . . [*word mutilated*] men.

Mr. Garvey's Address.

Mr. Garvey rose amidst prolonged cheering to address the audience. He said: ["]It is indeed a great pleasure to find myself in your midst to-night. I have come to this town to speak to you in the interests of the world-wide movement I represent. The Negro Improvement Association is a world-wide movement of negroes who are endeavouring to draw into one united whole the four hundred million negroes of the world thus linking the negroes of the West Indies with the negroes of the North and South America for one common purpose and dominated by the negro peoples of the world (cheers). You will understand, therefore, that I am not here to preach a sermon because I am no preacher. I am not here to talk domestic politics for I am not a politician. I have come to you in Jamaica to give new thoughts to the eight hundred thousand black people in this island. Your chairman said a while ago that he did not agree with all the things said by me or printed in the public press. When I contemplated coming to Jamaica I knew that Jamaica had no thought, it was for me to give Jamaica thought. Montego Bay being only a part of Jamaica I knew you had no thought save that given to you 83 years ago, as sycophants looking up to the white man as superior and master. I am not here with any sympathy for the old spirit of Jamaica, I am here to give you if I can a new spirit of manhood. Not the spirit to bow and cringe, to apologize, but the spirit to strike forward for the rights of the negro people of the world, and the rights belonging to them. Jamaica negroes are too apologetic. I don't understand what is the matter with the negro people of this country. In comparison, they cannot favourably compare with the negro peoples in other parts of the world, especially of the other West Indian Islands. Compare the Jamaican with the Barbadian, with the Trinidadian and he is a coward. He is always apologizing for something—it is no wonder when conditions of the people are as they are. A man who wants things does not apologize—he demands things! (Hear, hear). As a people you have been buffeted and tossed about for too long! The time has come when your voice must be heard throughout the length and breadth of this land—and throughout the world. You must not expect [a] speech of compromise, of apologies; that is not in me; I am not made that way. I represent a manhood movement—a movement with backbone and only men of backbone we appreciate. We are living in a new age and in a new world—the old world is gone. This has been brought about by the war with the Central Powers and subsequent victory of the Allies and with this change all races and people are clamouring for freedom of speech and the rights of demo[cracy.] I am here to represent the [move]ment of four hundred million negroes, one of the strongest groups of people in the world. I, like the majority of you, was born in this country 33 years ago, circumvented by the conditions of the country— the environment of this country, an environment that sits on black men that he must be merely a hewer of wood and carrier of water—a servant looking up to the white man as superior and master—who was born to [be]lieve himself inferior to other races—born not to have hope for himself. Under this environment I was born myself—you all know of this. But I did not confine myself to this environment. I refuse to be enslaved by an environment which keeps a black man at the foot of the ladder. I was entitled to climb as any other man, be they white, yellow or black. I was determined to climb the ladder of success, equal with every other man because God created all mankind and gave mankind the overlordship of the world—not to colour, but to the special man—not designating that white men should be lord and black men slaves or serfs. I have to disabuse the mind of some of you who came here as black-white and brown-white, men who are everything else except what they are. I know Montego Bay is not different from any other township in Jamaica, that St. James is not different to any other parish in Jamaica.

WE HAVE IN JAMAICA A PECULIAR RACE COMBINATION

which calls for some explanation. I want to give that explanation and those who may be satisfied can remain and those not desirous of being what they are can take the privilege of doing whatsoever they care, I came here to speak to negroes. I am not here to speak to white people. I want this clearly understood that this peculiar race question is going to destroy Jamaica— destroy the economic and industrial well-being of this country because this peculiar race question of yours is driving abroad more Jamaicans than you have in Jamaica. And when any country drives its native population abroad that country is doomed. I am here to give you my wide experience and to settle this ignorant race issue of yours. In this country the white man can raise no issue; he is at a discount. Whatever harm is done you are to blame; it is engineered by yourself. Fourteen thousand people could not in the wildest dreams stand in the way of eight hundred thousand people if those people had common sense, if they had even horse sense. Conditions racially depend on yourselves because some of you negroes refuse to admit what you are, you want to be everything else except what God created you to be. I want you to understand that you are not living in a world exclusively your own, you are living in a world made up of great groups of humanity, and these divide themselves into races and each race has a name. In Jamaica every man represents a race to himself—the most peculiar country for the race question I have ever met. The Universal Negro Improvement Association is a world-wide movement of negroes, black men and coloured men, who have enough self respect to call themselves by a race name. What is the movement for? For the industrial, commercial, social, educational and political betterment of the race—not only in one country but everywhere. Why do we call it the Universal Negro Improvement Association? Because after careful study and analysis we have discovered that negroes nowhere, [wherever] they be, represent anything of power and negroes everywhere are ignored and badly treated simply because they represent no power of their own. Hence if all are universally backward let us organise and go forward. Hence I come before you representing the Universal movement of negroes. We are going home to destiny. And what is destiny? Destiny is the point to be reached by every individual race and nation. And the destination of the black people shall lead them on to a great African Empire.["] (loud and prolonged cheers).

The speaker, continuing, appealed to the manhood of his hearers. He showed that they had not the excuse of their fathers. The white people were using their knowledge of political science to improve themselves. What were negroes doing? Some were using their knowledge for blacking some white man's shoes or cutting sugar canes.

Mr. Garvey then went fully into the origin and settlement of the republic of Liberia, outlining the objects aimed at by the U.N.I.A. He showed the progress now under way, and the intention of raising two million dollars in loans for developing the country. Mr. Garvey continued at length to show some of the possibilities of the race, and criticised the negro's knowledge of business in that he banked his money disadvantageously, and was lacking in co-operation. He dealt with the progress of the Black Star Line, and the intention of establishing a large fleet of steamers. After urging the audience to take shares in the Black Star Line and loans for the improvement of Liberia, Mr. Garvey concluded his address amidst loud cheers.

Dr. H. J. Evans moved a vote of thanks, and with the singing of the National Anthem, the proceedings terminated.

Meeting At Port Antonio.

[[Port Antonio, April 1.]]

Over two hundred persons attended at the Church Hall last night to listen to the speech given by Mr. Marcus Garvey, President General of the U.N.I.A., and who is at present on an 8 weeks' tour addressing large audiences in Kingston and elsewhere. The meeting was called to order at 8 P.M. by Mr. L. Thomas, druggist of the town. After the singing of the opening ode, "From Greenland's Icy Mountain", Mr. Garvey was presented with an address from the Port Antonio division of the U.N.I.A. A few musical items were rendered, which helped to make the proceedings lively.

Mr. Garvey rose amidst a lot of applause and spoke for fully two hours. During the course of his remarks he explained the aims and objects of the U.N.I.A., and also the workings of the Black Star Line. The Universal Negro Improvement Association, said Mr. Garvey, is a gigantic world-wide movement of negroes endeavouring to draw into one mighty whole the four hundred million negroes scattered all over the world, to link up the negroes of the West Indies, South and Central America, and negroes everywhere for the purpose of establishing a Government to be owned, controlled and dominated by negroes. (Hear, hear). Continuing, the speaker said we are endeavouring to organise for the economic, industrial, commercial, social and political emancipation of the Negro race. The U.N.I.A. is 3 1/2 years old in America and about six years old in this island of Jamaica. Mr. Garvey continued, "Many of you will remember that six years ago, when I was in Jamaica I started the U.N.I.A. immediately after my return from a continental tour. After I had propagated the doctrine of the organization for about two years, I found that I had little scope in this island. I therefore left for the United States of America, the land of opportunity, to study the condition of the Negroes. I started a division of the U.N.I.A. 3 1/2 years ago with 13 members, and tonight we have an active membership of four millions, scattered the world over. We started in New York with one branch, and to-day we have 700 branches. (Cheers).

The meeting was brought to a close with the singing of the hymn "Onward, Christian Soldiers." Mr. Garvey will deliver another address in the Town Hall to-night at 8 o'clock.

Printed in the *Gleaner*, 4 April 1921. Original headlines omitted.

UNIA to Cyril A. Crichlow

[*New York, 30 March 1921*]

Wired $2000 balance. Money required will be supplied by short time. Now making every arrangement for sawmill. We write you full particulars.

UNIVERSAL

DNA, RG 165, file 10218-261-78. TG (coded).

Elie Garcia to Cyril A. Crichlow

[*New York, 30 March 1921*]

Wired $730 salaries up 15th day of March. It is as follows: Johnson $250, Mark[e] $250, Jemmott $62.50, yourself $44.50, others $41.50 each.

GARCIA

DNA, RG 165, file 10218-261-78. TG (coded).

J. Edgar Hoover to William L. Hurley

WASHINGTON, D.C. March 30, 1921

Dear Mr. Hurley:

Replying to your communication of the 22nd instant concerning Marcus Garvey, in which you enclose a despatch from the American Consulate at Kingston, Jamaica, will you kindly advise me at the earliest possible moment as to the reply the State Department intends to make to the Consulate's request for instructions as to the visa of Garvey's passport. Very truly yours,

J. E. HOOVER

Special Assistant to the Attorney General

DNA, RG 59, file 000-612. TLS, recipient's copy.

Article in the *Chicago Whip*

[[New York City, Mar. 30. *1921*]]

... It is strongly rumoured in immigration circles here that Marcus Garvey will not be allowed to re-enter the United States at the end of his present tour of the West Indies.[1]

Garvey expects to return to New York in April, but it is believed that on account of his agitation for black rule in Africa, Mr. Garvey will be excluded as an undesirable alien.

The District Court has ruled in the divorce case of Mrs. Garvey against Mr. Garvey, that he must show that his present income is not more than $25 per week, or increase the alimony he is now paying to her.[2] Mrs. Garvey claims that her former husband has an income of 25,000 dollars per year.

Printed in the *Chicago Whip*, 2 April 1921; reprinted in the *Gleaner*, 17 April 1921; reprinted in the *Daily Argosy*, 21 May 1921.

1. The Associated Negro Press had released a statement entitled "Will Garvey Get Back?" which was reproduced in several black newspapers. It was reprinted, accompanied by extensive editorial commentary, under the caption "Garvey's Rights Under the Constitution" in *NW*, 9 April 1921.

2. On 22 March 1921 Maurice Wormser, an attorney, was appointed by the court as a referee to determine whether Marcus Garvey had sufficient income to pay the increased alimony and counsel fees Amy Ashwood Garvey had requested. Marcus Garvey ended his suit before a final ruling was made (*Marcus Garvey* v. *Amy Garvey*, no. 24028, New York Supreme Court, 22 March 1921).

Universal Negro Catechism

[*New York, March 1921*]

UNIVERSAL NEGRO CATECHISM[1]

A COURSE OF INSTRUCTION IN RELIGIOUS AND HISTORICAL KNOWLEDGE PERTAINING TO THE RACE

COMPILED BY
REV. GEORGE ALEXANDER McGUIRE, M.D.

ISSUED BY
AUTHORITY OF THE HIGH EXECUTIVE COUNCIL,
UNIVERSAL NEGRO IMPROVEMENT ASSOCIATION

1921

CONTENTS

1. Religious Knowledge
2. Historical Knowledge
3. Constitution and Laws of the U.N.I.A.
4. Declaration of Independence

RELIGIOUS KNOWLEDGE

Q. What is God?

A. God is a spirit, that is to say, He is without body, or visible form.

Q. Are there more Gods than one?

A. No; there is but One living and true God.

Q. Mention some of the attributes of God.

A. He is everlasting, omnipotent, omniscient, omnipresent, and of infinite wisdom, goodness, truth, love, holiness, justice and mercy.

Q. By what title do we address God?

A. "Our Father in Heaven."

Q. Why is God called "Father"?

A. Because He is the Creator of all beings, visible and invisible, and the Maker of all things in the natural world.

Q. Are all human beings then the children of God?

A. Certainly; He is the great All-Father, and all members of the human race are His children.

Q. How did God create man?

A. Male and female created He them after His own image, in knowledge, righteousness, and holiness, with dominion over all the earth and the lower animals.

Q. Did God make any group or race of men superior to another?

A.   No; He created all races equal and of one blood, to dwell on all the face of the earth.

Q.   Is it true that the Ethiopian or Black group of the human family is the lowest group of all?

A.   It is a base falsehood which is taught [in] books written by white men. All races were created equal.

Q.   What, then, is the chief reason for the differences observed among the various groups of men?

A.   Environment; that is, conditions connected with climate, opportunity, necessity, and association with others.

Q.   What is the color of God?

A.   A spirit has neither color, nor other natural parts, nor qualities.

Q.   But do we not speak of His hands, His eyes, His arms, and other parts?

A.   Yes; it is because we are able to think and speak of Him only in human and figurative terms.

Q.   If, then, you had to think or speak of the color of God, how would you describe it?

A.   As black; since we are created in His image and likeness.

Q.   On what would you base your assumption that God is black?

A.   On the same basis as that taken by white people when they assume that God is of their color.

Q.   Who is Jesus Christ?

A.   The Redeemer of all mankind.

Q.   What does the name "Jesus" mean?

A.   It means "a Saviour."

Q.   What does the name "Christ" mean?

A.   It means "Anointed."

Q.   Why is Jesus Christ spoken of as "God's only Son," when we are all sons of God?

A.   Because He is the only-begotten Son, begotten of His Father before all worlds, while we were created since the world began.

Q.   Who was His mother?

A.   Mary, the Virgin, blessed among women.

Q.   Who was His foster-father?

A.   Joseph, the carpenter of Nazareth.

Q.   Where was Jesus born?

A.   In Bethlehem, a town six miles from Jerusalem.

Q.   Who came from far to worship the infant?

A.   Wise men, called "Magi."

Q.   How many Magi came?

A.   It is generally believed that there were three: Caspar, Melchior, and Balthazar, and that Balthazar was of the Negro race.

Q.   Who sought to slay the infant child?

A.   Herod, King of Jerusalem.

Q.   Where did His parents take Him for refuge?

A. Into the land of Egypt, on the Continent of Africa.
Q. How long did He live in Africa?
A. Until He was two years of age.
Q. Where did He spend the rest of His life?
A. In Palestine, the Holy Land.
Q. How old was He when He was crucified?
A. Thirty-three (33) years.
Q. Upon whom did they lay His cross as He ascended Mount Calvary?
A. Simon, the Cyrenian, a man of Africa.
Q. How many times then in His life do we find mention of Africa?
A. Three times: when the wise men visited Him at His birth; when He was taken to Egypt for safety, and when He was about to be crucified.
Q. Of what race was Jesus Christ?
A. The Hebrew race, through Abraham, Judah, David and others.
Q. Of what larger group is the Hebrew race a part?
A. The Sem[i]tic.
Q. Was there any admixture of other blood than Sem[i]tic in the veins of Jesus?
A. Yes.
Q. Give an instance.
A. Pharez, the son of Judah, and an ancestor of Jesus, was born of Tamar, a woman of Canaan and a descendant of Ham.
Q. Mention another instance.
A. Rahab, the mother of Boaz, who was the great-grandfather of David, was also a Canaanite woman.
Q. For what purpose did Jesus die?
A. For the salvation of all men without distinction.
Q. What contains the sum of His teachings?
A. The Sermon on the Mount.
Q. Where is that to be found?
A. In the 5th, 6th and 7th Chapters of the Holy Gospel according to St. Matthew.
Q. In which verse do you find the essence of that sermon?
A. In the 12th verse of the 7th chapter.
Q. Repeat it.
A. "All things therefore whatsoever ye would that men should do unto you, even so do ye unto them; for this is the law and the prophets."
Q. What name is usually applied to this verse?
A. The "Golden Rule."
Q. How did Jesus Christ summarize the Ten Commandments, which were given to the world by Moses?
A. "Thou shalt love the Lord thy God with all thy heart, and with all thy soul, and with all thy mind. This is the first and greatest commandment. And the second is like unto it; thou shalt love thy neighbor as thyself. On these two commandments hang the Law and the Prophets."

Q.   What did Jesus Christ teach as the essential principle of true religion?
A.   The universal brotherhood of man grow[s] out of the universal Father-hood of God.
Q.   Did His Apostles preach the same truth?
A.   Yes; especially St. Paul, who is known as the great Apostle to the Gentiles.
Q.   Mention a verse in this connection from the writings of St. Paul[.]
A.   Colossians 3rd chapter, 11th verse (R.V.) "There cannot be Greek and Jew, circumcision and uncircumcision, barbarian, Scythian, bondman, free-man: but Christ is all, and in all."
Q.   Did St. Peter also proclaim the same doctrine?
A.   Yes; for in the Book of the Acts of the Apostles, 10th chapter, 35th verse (R.V.), he says: "Of a truth I perceive that God is no respecter of persons: b[ut] in every nation he that feareth Him, and worketh righteousness, is acceptable to Him."
Q.   Will there be any separation of men in Heaven?
A.   No; for the Book of the Revelation of St. John the Divine, it is written in the 7th chapter, 9th verse (R.V.), "After these things I saw and beheld a great multitude, which no man could number, out of every nation, and of all tribes and peoples and tongues, standing before the throne and before the Lamb."
Q.   Is it true that Noah cursed his son Ham?
A.   No; he cursed Canaan, the youngest son of Ham, saying, "Cursed be Canaan; a servant of servants shall he be unto his brethren."
[Q.]   Who are the descendants of Canaan?
A.   The Canaanites who dwelt in Palestine before the Jews took possession of it.
Q.   Are Negroes concerned in this curse of Noah?
A.   Certainly not.
Q.   How are the people of our race described in the Holy Scriptures?
A.   As Cushites or Ethiopians.
Q.   From whom did they descend?
A.   From Cush; who was the first son of Ham and the grandson of Noah.
Q.   Who was the most famous son of Cush?
A.   Nimrod, the first mighty man of the earth.
Q.   What saying concerning him became a proverb?
A.   "Like Nimrod, a mighty hunter before the Lord."
Q.   What is really the fact about Nimrod?
A.   He was the pioneer explorer and nation builder.
Q.   Of what Kingdoms was he the founder?
A.   Babylon and Assyria.
Q.   What great city in Assyria did he build?
A.   Nineveh, its capital.
Q.   Who was Ishmael?
A.   The son of Abraham and Hagar.

Q. Who was Hagar?

A. An African from the land of Egypt.

Q. How were Hagar and Ishmael subsequently treated?

A. They were driven out of Abraham's house into a wilderness to provide for themselves.

Q. Who was the wife of Moses, the great leader of the Jews?

A. Zipporah, an Ethiopian woman.

Q. Who was her father?

A. Jethro, a prince and priest in Ethiopia.

Q. When did Moses go to Ethiopia?

A. When his life was threatened by Pharaoh, king of Egypt, for having slain an Egyptian.

Q. Was Moses' marriage pleasing to his relatives?

A. No; Miriam, his sister, who was a prophetess, and Aaron, his brother, who was a priest, both upbraided him for having married an Ethiopian woman. Read Numbers 12:1.

Q. What does this show?

A. That race prejudice is as old as the human family, and that even religious teachers are not free from it.

Q. What punishment came to Miriam for speaking against the Ethiopian woman?

A. She became afflicted with leprosy, and was placed in quarantine for seven days until Moses prayed for her restoration.

Q. What appears, then, to be the most effective cure for race prejudice?

A. Leprosy.

Q. From whom did Moses first receive instruction in the principles of civil government?

A. From Jethro, his father-in-law. Read Exodus, 18th chapter.

Q. Who was the guide to Moses when he led Israel through the wilderness?

A. Jobab, his brother-in-law, the son of Jethro. Read Numbers 10:29–32.

Q. Who is responsible for the color of the Ethiopians?

A. The Creator, and what He has done cannot be changed. Read Jeremiah 13:23.

Q. Mention a verse in the Bible in which a person of black color was proud of the fact.

A. "I am black, but comely, O ye daughters of Jerusalem." Solomon's Song 1:5.

Q. Explain the connection.

A. Shulamith, daughter of Pharoah, king of Egypt, betrothed to King Solomon, thus describes herself to her Jewish rivals.

Q. How do the best Negro scholars translate the words mentioned above?

A. "I am dark, and comely." It seems that white translators use "but" in preference to "and" to create the impression that one who is *dark* is not expected to be *comely*.

Q. Who first informed David of the death of Absalom, his son?

A. A fleet runner of the Cushite or Ethiopian race. Read 2 Samuel 18:21, 23.

Q. What person went from Africa to visit King Solomon?

A. Balkis, the wise and wealthy Queen of Sheba.

Q. What African people claim that their emperors are descended from Solomon and the Queen of Sheba?

A. The Abyssinians.

Q. By what name are the Abyssinian Emperors usually known?

A. Menelik.

Q. When the prophet Jeremiah was in prison, who was it that brought about his release?

A. A God-fearing Ethiopian official by the name of Ebed-Melech. Read Jer. 38:7, 10, 12.

Q. What distinguished African personage was baptized by St. Philip?

A. An Ethiopian eunuch, a high official in the Court of Candace, Queen of the Ethiopians. Read Acts 8:27.

Q. Who was the first great military genius whose deeds are recorded in the Bible?

A. Zerah, an Ethiopian general, who commanded an army of a million men and 300 chariots.

Q. Mention a verse of Scripture which refers to the precious stones of Ethiopia.

A. "The price of wisdom is above rubies, the topaz of Ethiopia shall not equal it." Job 28:18, 19.

Q. What is the first Book of Enoch?

A. It is a sacred book as old as others which were included in the present Bible, but which was left out of the collection intentionally by white men.

Q. Why did they not include it in the Bible?

A. Because it was taken from the literature of the Ethiopians, and was known as Ethiopic Enoch.

Q. Mention one thing stated in this Book of Enoch about our race.

A. "We are true sons of God."

Q. Was not this Book read by the early Christians?

A. Yes; it was read by them for 300 years.

Q. What prediction made in the 68th Psalm and the 31st verse is now being fulfilled?

A. "Princes shall come out of Egypt, Ethiopia shall soon stretch out her hands unto God."

Q. What does this verse prove?

A. That Negroes will set up their own government in Africa, with rulers of their own race.

HISTORICAL KNOWLEDGE

Q. Whom did the ancients call Ethiopians?

A. All men of dark-brown or black color.

Q. Why did they select this name?

A. Because "Ethiopian" is derived from a Greek word which means "sun-burnt."

Q. To whom was the name more particularly given at a later period?

A. To the inhabitants of the countries south of Egypt and west of the Red Sea, in Africa, along the upper Nile Valley.

Q. What place was the first important capital of Ethiopia?

A. The island of Meroe, formed by the junction of two tributaries of the River Nile.

Q. What celebrated oracle was located there?

A. The oracle of Jupiter Ammon.[2]

Q. Tell what you can of Meroe.

A. The extraordinary fertility of the soil, the abundance of animals and metals, made it the chief resort of all inhabitants of adjacent parts, as well as the emporium of Egypt, Carthage, Arabia, and India. Even as early as 1000 B.C. it was counted as one of the most powerful states of the world.

Q. What connection had the Ethiopians with the Egyptians?

A. They were kindred nations, but were constantly at war, sometimes the Egyptians being subject to the Ethiopians, and sometimes the Ethiopians to the Egyptians. Later, both nations emigrated freely into each other's country, and the greatest kings of Egypt, especially Rameses I, II, and III were Ethiopians. We cannot separate the early civilization and accomplishments of the Egyptians and Ethiopians. Their religion, art and form of government were identical, and both of these African nations contributed to build a high civilization when Europe was still a continent of barbarians.

Q. Name some of the ancient university cities of Egypt.

A. Memphis, Thebes, Heliopolis.

Q. Where was Memphis located?

A. About nine miles south of where Cairo now stands.

Q. Describe Memphis as it was 4000 years ago.

A. It was the seat of the highest culture of the world. Its avenue of sph[i]nxes compelled the admiration of the world; its magnificent temple was thronged with pilgrims from over the world. In its university, Moses, the leader and lawgiver of Israel, received theological and scientific instruction. Greece sent her Homer, Thales and Solon to Memphis to receive the finishing touch, and Plato himself spent thirteen years there getting inspiration.

Q. What shepherd race lived in Egypt as slaves during this time?

A. The Hebrews.

Q. Were the Hebrews regarded as social equals when they first came into Africa from Asia?

A. No; the cultured Egyptians looked upon them as an inferior people and considered it an abomination to eat at the same table with the shepherds.

Q. What unrivalled monuments of African architecture are still the wonder of the world?

A. The pyramids and sph[i]nxes.

Q. What are hieroglyphics?
A. The ancient African characters or system of writing on stone by which our early achievements have been preserved.
Q. Who destroyed the ancient Ethiopian capital on the island of Meroe?
A. The Romans under Augustus and Nero, during the first Christian century.
Q. What is the most powerful Ethiopian state in existence?
A. Abyssinia, whose emperors are known as Menelik, the first being a son of Solomon and the Queen of Sheba.
Q. What was the fate of the African people other than the Egyptians and Abyssinians?
A. Dwelling in the Hinterland, and their civilization destroyed by the Romans, they lapsed into a wild and nomadic life. Multiplying rapidly, they formed numerous tribes and soon peopled the whole African continent. For over a thousand years they lived unknown to white men.
Q. Did they lose all their knowledge of the civilization, arts and sciences of their ancestors?
A. No; they retained the tribal form of government with Kings and Chiefs; they pursued such arts as agriculture, smelting of iron, and the weaving of cotton. They also practiced medicine, and knew certain medical facts and treatment which white men have since learned in Africa and claimed as their discoveries.
Q. Mention one of these medical facts.
A. They knew that sleeping sickness was caused by the bite of the tse-tse fly, and Koch, a German physician learned this from them and published it to the world as his discovery.
Q. To whom do foreigners resort for the most effective treatment of African fevers?
A. The native herb-doctors.
Q. Who were the first Europeans to get in touch again with the Africans who had then covered all of West, Central, South and East Africa?
A. The Portuguese, who were great navigators.
Q. Were the Africans heathen when these white men visited them?
A. No; most of the tribes had very clear ideas about God, or gods, and worshipped after their own rites.
Q. Were they immoral?
A. No; the native Africans are the most moral people in the world. Their vices have come from contact with immoral white people. Wherever white men go they sow the seeds of immorality.
Q. What terrible institution began with the visits of the Portuguese to Africa?
A. Slavery.
Q. What European nations conducted the traffic in African bodies and souls?
A. Portugal, Spain, England, Holland, and others.

Q. Where were these slaves chiefly taken?
A. To the West Indies and North and South America.
Q. How long did slavery last in the Western Hemisphere?
A. For over 250 years.
Q. When and how were the West Indian Negroes emancipated?
A. In some islands on August 1, 1834, and in others on August 1, 1838; by an Act of the British Parliament.
Q. How and when were American Negroes emancipated?
A. By Proclamation of President Abraham Lincoln, January 1, 1861 [*1863*]; although this proclamation did not become generally effective until after the close of the Civil War in 1865.
Q. Have Western Negroes benefited from their forcible exile from Africa?
A. Yes; they have progressed wonderfully in the arts and sciences, in industrial skill, and in the possession of property.
Q. Do they enjoy all their civil rights in the alien countries in which they live?
A. No; while in theory they possess all the rights and privileges of other citizens, they are denied the full enjoyment thereof in practice.
Q. Will Negroes ever be given equal opportunity and treatment in countries ruled by white men?
A. No; they will enjoy the full rights of manhood and liberty only when they establish their own nation and government in Africa.
Q. What great event occurred in 1492?
A. Christopher Columbus made his first visit to the West Indies.
Q. Was Columbus the real discoverer of the West Indies and America?
A. No; it has been recently proven by a professor of Harvard University[3] that Negro navigators crossed the Atlantic from Africa to the Western Hemisphere, visiting several of the islands of the Caribbean Sea and the mainland of America.
Q. What proof of this fact exists?
A. Tobacco and peanuts were brought by these Negroes from Africa and given to the Indians, who soon learned to cultivate and use the same.
Q. What event of importance occurred in 1619?
A. The landing of the first cargo of African slaves in Jamestown, Va.
Q. Mention some important Negro national holidays.
A. In Liberia, July 26th is observed as Independence Day and December 1st as New Port Day; in the West Indies, August 1st is Emancipation Day; in the United States, January 1st is Emancipation Day; August 31st was set apart by the great International Convention which met in New York City, in 1920, as the International Holiday for Negroes.
Q. Who was Edward Wilmot Blyden?
A. The most learned Negro of modern times; born in the Danish West Indies in 1831, but was identified with Africa for fifty years; he was a distinguished statesman, philosopher, linguis[t] and Arabic scholar; the author of

several works on Negro history and sociology; he died on February 7, 1912, in Sierra Leone, West Africa.

Q.   Who was James Africanus Beal Horton?

A.   A native of Sierra Leone, West Africa, who became a surgeon-major, the highest rank ever granted a Negro in the British Army; he published a work on Tropical Diseases which was considered the highest authority on the subject; he died in 1880.

Q.   Who was Sir Samuel Lewis?

A.   A native of Sierra Leone, and for nearly a half century the greatest jurist of British West Africa; he was the second Negro to be made a Knight in the British Empire; he died in 1903.

Q.   Who was the Right Reverend Samuel D. Ferguson?

A.   The first Negro Bishop of Liberia; he died August, 1916.

Q.   Who was Sir Conrad Reeves?

A.   The first Negro to be made a Knight in the British Empire; a native of Barbados, B.W.I., and later Chief Just[i]ce; he died January, 1901.

Q.   Who was Toussaint L'O[u]verture?

A.   A distinguished soldier, statesman and martyr, born in Haiti, May 20, 1743; became emancipator of Haiti and the conqueror of the European forces.

Q.   Who was Crispus Attucks?

A.   A Negro who led a mob in Boston against the British troops in the struggle for American liberty and freedom; he was the first to shed his blood for the cause of Independence, being killed in the streets of Boston, 1775.

Q.   Who was Frederick Douglas[s]?

A.   A great Negro orator and statesman of international fame; born in Maryland in 1817; escaped from slavery in early manhood; lectured in America and England against slavery; died in Anacostia, D.C., February, 1895.

Q.   Who was Booker T. Washington?

A.   A famous Negro leader and industrial educator; founder of Tuskegee Institute; born in slavery in Virginia, 1858; trained at Hampton Institute; died in 1915.

Q.   Who was Prince Hall?

A.   The founder and organizer of Negro Masonry in America; he was born in the West Indies.

Q.   Who was Reverend Alexander [C]rummell?

A.   A distinguished clergyman of the Protestant Episcopal Church; born in New York City in 1819; his father was a prince of an African tribe; he received his early education in America, and later graduated from Cambridge University, England; was missionary in Liberia for several years; wrote several books on Africa; was a ripe scholar and the founder of the American Negro Academy.

Q.   What are the independent Negro governments?

A.   The Abyssinian Empire, the Liberian Republic, the Haitian Republic.
Q.   In what other countries do Negroes have a large share in the government?
A.   In Santo Domingo, Cuba and in several of the South and Central American Republics.
Q.   What is the present Negro population of the United States?
A.   About 15,000,000.
Q.   What is the Negro population of the West Indies and adjoining provinces?
A.   About 10,000,000.
Q.   What is the total Negro population of the Western Hemisphere?
A.   About 50,000,000.
Q.   What is the total Negro population of the world?
A.   About 400,000,000.

THE UNIVERSAL NEGRO IMPROVEMENT ASSOCIATION

Q.   What is the Universal Negro Improvement Association and African Communities League?
A.   It is a social, friendly, humanitarian, charitable, educational, institutional, constructive and expansive society, organized for the general uplift of the Negro peoples of the world.
Q.   What pledge do the members make?
A.   To do all in their power to conserve the rights of their noble race and to respect the rights of all mankind, believing always in the brotherhood of man and the Fatherhood of God.
Q.   Who founded the Universal Negro Improvement Association and African Communities League?
A.   The Honorable Marcus Garvey in Jamaica, B.W.I. in 1914, and in New York, U.S.A. in 1918.
Q.   What is the motto of the organization?
A.   "One God! One Aim! One Destiny!"
Q.   What other motto has been selected?
A.   "Pro Deo, Africa et Justitia"; which means, "For God, Africa and Justice."
Q.   What is the slogan?
A.   "Africa for the' Africans."
Q.   What is the jurisdiction of the Universal Negro Improvement Association?
A.   Its jurisdiction includes all communities where people of Negro blood and African descent are to be found.
Q.   Who are the ordinary members of the Association?
A.   All people of Negro blood and African descent are regarded as ordinary members, and are entitled to the consideration of the organization.

Q.   Who are the active members?

A.   Those who pay monthly dues for the upkeep of the organization, and who in consequence have first claim for all benefits to be dispensed.

Q.   What are the objects of the Universal Negro Improvement Association and the African Communities League?

A.   To establish a united brotherhood among the race; to promote race pride and loyalty; to assist the needy; to aid in the civilization of the native tribes of Africa; to develop independent Negro nations and communities; to establish diplomatic agencies in the principal countries and cities of the world for the representation and protection of all Negroes; to build educational institutions in Africa; to promote a conscientious spiritual worship among the native tribes; to conduct world-wide commercial and industrial intercourse for the good of the race; to improve conditions in all Negro communities.

Q.   How may a charter be secured to establish a Division of this Organization in any community?

A.   Seven or more citizens of intelligence, having the respect of the educated and cultured people of their community, on application, may be given a charter; provided there is no chartered Division already existing in such community. Chapters and branches of divisions may receive charters for work under the auspices of the chartered Division in any community where circumstances justify the existence of such chapters and branches.

Q.   What is the governing body of the Universal Negro Improvement Association and African Communities League?

A.   The International Convention which meets annually unless otherwise provided for.

Q.   How is the Convention composed?

A.   Of Deputies and Delegates from the various Divisions, and kindred Organizations, Societies and Orders subordinate to the Universal Negro Improvement Association and the African Communities League, such Deputies holding office for four years after election.

Q.   Who are the High Officials and Rulers of this Association?

A.   A Potentate, a Supreme Deputy, a President General, an Assistant President General, a Secretary General, an Assistant Secretary General, a High Chancellor, a Chaplain General, a Counsel General, an Assistant Counsel General, a High Commissioner General, a Speaker in Convention, an International Organizer, an Auditor General, a Surgeon General, and a Minister of Legions.

Q.   What body do these High Officials form?

A.   The High Executive Council, which is the ruling Body of the Organization in the interim between sessions of Convention.

Q.   What is their term of office?

A.   The Potentate and Supreme Deputy hold office permanently; all other

High Officials hold office for four years, provided their conduct conforms at all times with the laws and principles of the Association.

Q. What are the qualifications for office in the Universal Negro Improvement Association and the African Communities League?

A. Candidates must be registered active members with all dues paid up; shall be Negroes; shall not be married to anyone of alien race; shall be conscientious in the cause of race uplift; shall be free from criminal conviction, and shall be of reputable moral standing and good education.

Q. From what source is the revenue of the Universal Negro Improvement Association and African Communities League derived?

A. From monthly subscriptions of not more than 25 cents per month, being the authorized dues of each active member, [don]ations, collections, gifts, profits derived from business, entertainments, functions or general amusements of an innocent nature.

Q. How is this revenue employed?

A. To defray the general expenses of the Organization, and to carry out its objects.

Q. How is money transmitted from the Local Division to the Parent Body?

A. The Secretary of each Division and subordinate Organization remits at the end of each month, through the Secretary General, to the High Chancellor, one-fifth of all monthly dues, and the net profits from local business under control of said Division, as also from all donations, grants, gifts, and proceeds of amusements, entertainments, and other functions, to be applied to the general fund of the Organization.

Q. Is there any tax levied on members of the Universal Negro Improvement Association?

A. Yes; a tax of one dollar is levied on every member, payable on January first, for the purpose of defraying expenses of the High Officials of the Organization and the leaders of the Negro peoples of the world.

Q. What is the entrance fee?

A. Each person pays an entrance fee of 25 cents when joining the Association.

Q. Who is the working-head of the Universal Negro Improvement Association and the African Communities League?

A. The President General, to whom all Divisions and subordinate Organizations are responsible, and on whom rests the general administration of all Local Divisions.

Q. May the Divisions admit any member of an alien race to active membership?

A. They shall admit none to active membership who is not of Negro blood.

Q. What descriptive emblem is worn by the members of the Universal Negro Improvement Association and African Communities League by which they may be known to other members?

A. They were on their coats or blouses a button, with the colors red, black and green, which are the authorized colors of the Association.

Q. Is a charitable fund maintained by the Association?

A. All Local Divisions or Societies maintain a charitable fund for the purpose of assisting distressed members or needy individuals of the race.

Q. Are any loans made to members?

A. Each Local Division is required to maintain a fund for rendering assistance by way of loans of honor to active members.

Q. Does the Organization help its members to find employment?

A. Each Local Division is required to manage an employment bureau for the purpose of finding employment for the members of the Universal Negro Improvement Association and African Communities League.

Q. Where are the meetings of the Association held?

A. Each Local Division is required to maintain as far as possible a building of its own (rented, leased or purchased), in which the general meetings shall be held every Sunday afternoon or evening, presided over by the President; meetings shall also be held on weekday evenings.

Q. Has the Organization a Weekly Journal?

A. Yes; the "Negro World," controlled and directed by the President General, and circulated among Negroes everywhere, giving regular accounts of the progress of the Association, and spreading propaganda of the Movement.

Q. Who are the subscribers to this Journal?

A. Each member of the Universal Negro Improvement Association and the African Communities League is required to be a regular subscriber to this Journal, in addition to paying the monthly dues and taxes.

Q. What provision is made for children and juveniles in the membership of this Association?

A. Infants are required to be brought by their parents to be dedicated by the Chaplain of the Division not later than three months after birth, at which time they enter the general membership of the Organization. In every Division a Juvenile Branch shall be formed, in which moral, spiritual, and racial instruction shall be given to the members.

Q. What is the African Legions Society?

A. An allied organization under the direction of the Executive Council and Potentate, for the purpose of giving military training to the men of our race between the ages of 18 and 55.

Q. What is the Black Cross Nurses Society?

A. It is another allied organization having for its purpose the training of women of the Negro race in First Aid to the Injured, and in promoting the charitable objects of the Organization as may be required of them by the High Executive Council.

Q. What commercial and industrial organizations are allied with the Universal Negro Improvement Association and A[frican] Communities League?

A. The Black Star Line Steamship Company Inc., which trades between the

United States, the West Indies, Central America and West Africa; the Negro Factories Corporation, which conducts a laundry, a millinery store, and other establishments.

THE DECLARATION OF INDEPENDENCE

Q.   When was the Declaration of Independence of the Negro people of the world drafted and adopted?
A.   At the first International Negro Convention, held in Liberty Hall, New York City, U.S.A., from August 1 to August 31, 1920.
Q.   Who presided over this Convention?
A.   The Honorable Marcus Garvey, President General of the Universal Negro Improvement Association, the Organization under whose auspices the Convention was held.
Q.   Who composed this Convention?
A.   Negro Deputies from every country of the World inhabited by people of our race.
Q.   By what name is this Declaration known?
A.   The Declaration of Rights.
Q.   What were the causes for the Declaration?
A.   The reports brought by representatives from all over the world concerning the wrongs and injustices which our people suffer at the hands of white men; their determination in the future to secure their just rights, and to demand equal opportunity and treatment with other men.
Q.   When was the Declaration signed?
A.   At 5:00 P.M. on August 13, 1920, beneath a display of flags of many countries, including those of the United States, the Provisional African Republic, Liberia, Haiti and Abyssinia.
Q.   What were some of the grievances reported by the various delegates?
A.   Discrimination in public hotels because of race and color; denial of the right of public trial when accused of crime; lynching and burning by mobs; discrimination in public conveyances in the southern part of the United States; inferior education for our children in separate schools; denial of an equal chance to earn wages for the support of our families; exploiting of the Continent of Africa, and inhuman treatment of the natives by European nations; denial of the privilege to vote in some southern states, and of a voice in the administration of the laws; discrimination in the Civil Service, and other departments of the Government; secret and cunning devices in the British and other West Indian Islands and colonies to deprive our people of those fuller rights of government which white citizens enjoy; peonage and serfdom both in the West Indies and the southern states of America.
Q.   What decision was arrived at after the Convention had listened to these grievances for a space of one week?
A.   That the Deputies should emphatically protest against all such inhuman, unchristian and uncivilized treatment, and invoke the condemnation of all mankind in order to encourage our race all over the world to overcome the

handicaps and difficulties surrounding us, and to push forward to a higher destiny.

Q. What does the first clause of the Declaration of Rights state concerning the citizenship of Negroes?

A. It declares all men, women and children of our blood throughout the world free denizens of the countries in which they live, but claims them as free citizens of Africa, the Motherland of all Negroes.

Q. On what principle do we claim Africa for the Negro people of the world?

A. On the principle of Europe for the Europeans, and Asia for the Asiatics, we also demand Africa for Africans at home and abroad.

Q. Should the Negro endeavor to possess himself of Africa?

A. We believe it his inherent right so to do, and that such possession shall not be regarded as an infringement on any claim made by any race or nation.

Q. What is our attitude towards those nations who have seized the territories and natural wealth of Africa?

A. We strongly condemn their cupidity, and place on record our solemn determination to reclaim the treasures and possession of this vast continent of our forefathers.

Q. What protest do we make against the treatment accorded the natives of Africa?

A. We protest against depriving them of their lands, and exercise of free citizenship within their own country; against the atrocious crimes of whipping, flogging, and overworking of such natives, and demand that all such barbarous practices be abolished.

Q. Mention one such atrocious and disgraceful practice.

A. The shaving of the heads of Africans, including females, when placed in prison as a punishment for crime.

Q. Should Negroes demand the right to elect their own representatives in the Legislature?

A. Wheresoever they form a community among themselves they should be given the right to elect their own representatives in all law-making bodies, councils, or other institutions which exercise control over that particular community.

Q. Should Negroes be represented on juries?

A. We declare it unfair and prejudicial to the rights of Negroes in communities where they exist in considerable numbers to be tried by a judge and jury composed entirely of an alien race, and demand that in all such cases members of our race be given representation on the jury.

Q. What do we declare concerning "taxation without representation"?

A. We declare it unjust and tyrannical and that there should be no obligation on the part of Negroes to obey the levy of tax by any lawmaking body in which they are denied representation.

Q. What do we believe about any law discriminating against the Negro?

A. That it is not only unfair and immoral, but an insult to the race as a whole, and therefore should be resented by the entire body of the Negro people.

Q. How should the word "Negro" be written?

A. Always with a capital "N"; we should demand that all newspapers, periodicals, and books published should observe this rule.

Q. Should the Negro endeavor to live in peace with all other men?

A. Undoubtedly so; but when other races and nations provoke our ire by infringing upon our sacred rights, war becomes inevitable, and any attempt on our part to free ourselves and protect our rights and heritage becomes justifiable.

Q. What does the Declaration of Rights say concerning lynching?

A. That the lynching of human beings by burning, hanging, or any other means is a most barbarous practice, and a shame and a disgrace to civilization, and that any people guilty of such atrocities should be considered outside the pale of civilization.

Q. What does it state concerning the "Freedom of the Press"?

A. That we believe in the doctrine of the "Freedom of the Press," and protest against the suppression of Negro newspapers and periodicals in various parts of the world, and call upon our people everywhere to employ all available means to prevent such suppression.

Q. Ment[i]on some further conditions against which protests are made.

A. Boycotting of Negroes from industry and labor in any part of the world; the system of education which denies Negroes the same privileges and advantages as other races; segregated districts; separate public conveyances and accommodations by land or sea; curtailing of free speech; the publication of scandalous and inflammatory articles by the white press tending to create racial strife; the exhibition of picture films representing the Negro as a cannibal, and the caricat[u]res on the stage which hold up our race to ridicule.

Q. Mention some important rights which we demand in the Declaration.

A. Self-determination of all peoples; freedom of religious worship; the right of an unlimited and unprejudiced education for ourselves and our children; the right of free emigration of Negroes to any country or state without molestation or discrimination, especially when they pay equal fare with travellers of other races.

Q. Did the International Convention choose any Leaders for our race?

A. Yes; it elected a Provisional President of Africa, a Leader for the American Negroes, and two Leaders for the Negroes of the West Indies, Central and South America.

Q. Why were these Leaders elected?

A. To look after the welfare of our people everywhere, and to demand from the various governments under which they live equal opportunity and equal treatment with other races of people.

Q. What are the National Colors of the Negro Race as selected by the Convention?

A. Red, black and green.

Q. What do these Colors represent?

A. Red is the color of the blood which men must shed for their redemption and liberty; black is the color of the noble and distinguished race to which we belong; green is the color of the luxuriant vegetation of our Motherland.

Q. What National Anthem did the Convention authorize for our race?

A. That which begins "Ethiopia, thou land of our Father," composed by Burrell and Ford. . . .[4]

Q. What will this Declaration of Rights accomplish for Negroes?

A. It will secure for them their complete rights and privileges and the unlimited enjoyment of liberty.

Q. Did not an Act of the British Parliament and the Emancipation Proclamation of President Lincoln give freedom to Negroes in the West Indies and in the United States?

A. Only in the sense of freedom from compulsory labor and servitude.

Q. What is our attitude to the League of Nations?

A. We declare it null and void in that it deprives millions of Negroes of the right of liberty, self-determination and self-government.

Q. Do we believe in the "Golden Rule"?

A. Yes; we cheerfully accord to all men their rights and privileges and in turn make the just demand that they do unto us as we would unto them.

Q. What declaration do we make concerning our women and children?

A. That, with the help of Almighty God, we swear to protect their honor and virtue even with our lives.

Q. Should Negroes engage in any war which alien races are waging against each other?

A. Only in case of the defence of the country in which they live from external aggression, and only when given consent by the chosen Leader of the Negro people of the world.

Q. What do we declare concerning the seas?

A. We believe in the absolute freedom of the seas for all peoples and demand a free and unfettered ocean intercourse with Negroes everywhere.

Q. What International Holiday for the Negroes of the world was ordered by the Convention?

A. August 31st of every year.

Q. Do Negroes intend to support this Declaration of their Rights and Independence?

A. They pledge to maintain it as the Magna Charta of their race and solemnly swear to defend it with their lives, their fortunes, and their sacred honor. . . .[5]

Printed in the *Universal Negro Catechism*, March 1921.

1. In a speech at Guabito, Cuba, on 21 April 1921, Garvey referred to the catechism: "Now we are going to cut out all in the Bible that does not suit us. We are just completing a new Bible which is the first Bible of the Universal Negro Improvement Association and African Communities League" (*NW*, 18 June 1921).

2. Jupiter Ammon (or Amon or Amen) was the name given by the Romans to the Egyptian god Ammon. In 332 B.C. Alexander the Great visited the temple of Jupiter Ammon in the Siwa Oasis, where the famous oracle called Alexander "son of Ammon." Shortly thereafter he was crowned king of Egypt (Anthony S. Mercante, *Who's Who in Egyptian Mythology* [New York: Clarkson N. Potter, 1978], p. 79).

3. Leo Wiener (1862–1939) claimed that Arabs, along with their Mandingo slaves, had traded with Mexico many years before Columbus. A philologist at Harvard University, Wiener claimed that his studies in history and philology had also proven that "the Negroes of Guinea and the Congo discovered America" and that "yams, sweet potatoes and peanuts" were introduced to the New World by early African explorers (*NW*, 23 October 1920). In December 1921 Wiener addressed the American Negro Academy on the topic "The Problems of African Civilization." The next year he published three volumes expanding his theory of African discovery of the New World (Leo Wiener, *Africa and the Discovery of America*, 3 vols. [Philadelphia: Innes and Sons, 1922]; Ivan Van Sertima, *They Came Before Columbus* [New York: Random House, 1976]; *NW*, 24 December 1921).

4. The text of the "Universal Ethiopian Anthem," which has been printed in *Garvey Papers* 2: 575–576, has been omitted here.

5. The document concluded with the names of the signers of the declaration, which can be found in *Garvey Papers* 2: 571–580.

Elbert W. Moore to W. E. B. Du Bois

Pittsburgh, Pa., April 1, 1921

My dear Dr. Du Bois:

. . . I need not assure you that many of the best friends of the Negro are somewhat apprehensive concerning the Garvey movement in its affect on the situation here at home as well as abroad. I know however, that they are all in accord with your views and with your attitude in regard to the same. I remain Very Truly yours,

E. W. MOORE[1]

MU, WEBDB, reel 9, frame 432. TLS on "American Baptist Home Mission Society" letterhead, recipient's copy.

1. Elbert W. Moore was the director of the American Baptist Home Mission Society, a group devoted to religious and community service. The American Baptist Home Mission's main headquarters were located in New York City.

Report by Bureau Agents A. A. Hopkins and E. J. Kosterlitzky

Los Angeles Apr. 2, 1921

UNIVERSAL NEGRO IMPROVEMENT ASSN: NEGRO ACTIVITIES

Confidential informant on negro activities states that REV. EDWARD DRIVER[1] has been appointed Pacific Coast Organizer for the U.N.I.A., under direct commission from MARCUS GARVEY. He states that the REV. DRIVER is inclined to be radical, and is not in sympathy with the present conservative leadership of the U.N.I.A. in Los Angeles.

MRS. BASS, the State Organizer of the U.N.I.A., works in harmony with NOAH WEBSTER [*Thompson*] and other conservatives. For this reason informant states the appointment of REVEREND DRIVER has not been publicly announced, and not known outside of a limited circle and will probably cause considerable dissention when it becomes known.

Reference is made to Weekly Intelligence Report, Los Angeles for March 26, 1921, page 77, and other previous reports re LOWER CALIFORNIA MEXICAN LAND AND DEVELOPMENT CO., the Negro Colonization project in Lower California.

Under date of March 4th, H. E. MACBETH,[2] one of the principal organizers of this colony, wrote to J. D. GORDON, "Assistant President General" of the U.N.I.A. at New York, asking for the co-operation and authorization of the U.N.I.A. in the scheme. Following is the reply received:

New York, U.S.A. March 14, 1921.
Universal Building, 56 W. 135th St. . . .

Mr. H. E. Macbeth,
My Honorable and Esteemed Sir:

Your letter of March 4th reached me a few moments ago. I had to be out of the City, and my mail was held until my arrival.

I am more than pleased to know that you have given this movement a thought from that fertile brain. I am aware of your ability to think and do, for certainly you have demonstrated your ability to bring things to pass. The same spirit, however, that moved Mr. Garvey to start his wonderful organization, is the same spirit that moved you to form this liberation settlement in Lower California. Both of your purposes were identical, even though your methods differ somewhat.

I am well enough acquainted with you to mark you as an hundred percent Negro. You are in every way an ideal member of the U.N.I.A. We hold all Negroes as members, some operative and some unoperative. You were just simply so engaged in your own great undertaking that this is the only reason why you have not been in the foremost ranks, of this movement and I am certain, that had you taken hold of this movement, you would now be occupying a position of honor and trust, and that even now your Land Company by no means incapacitates you for the furtherance of this cause, that I know to be dear to your heart. For among all the Negroes of America, there are none that I know should rejoice more at this movement than yourself. There is evidently a similarity and ought to be a harmony between this Movement and Your Movement, for every independent stroke of the Negro for the assertion and establishment of individual and racial manhood, as one. Were the matter left to me, it would be my purpose forthwith to formulate some plan of general cooperation, but as it is, all affairs like that go before our Council of Sixteen, and would have to secure the President's indorsement, and the indorsement of this Body before such a thing would be impossible, but profitable to all parties concerned.

For certainly these Negroes going to Lower California will thereby keep themselves in touch with the great body of Negroes of the world, having freedom there, more than they could enjoy in America, and they would play a most telling part.

I know, also the President of your organization, MR. TROY, whom I have known for many years, and have loved equally as long. I know what is the burden of his heart. Racial uplift is the one supreme thought of his spirit. Also A. J. Roberts, you know I have always regarded him too as one of the Prince of Negroes.

It might be well for you to consider one thing, that it is not our purpose to have every Negro go to Africa, but just such ones as can build Africa up. We have an empire dream. We hope to found an Empire as the ultimate aim of the U.N.I.A.; and from this Empire we can make Negroes safe everywhere, and they can live where they please under more favorable conditions than they can live now.

I am just delighted to have this letter from you, and shall take it home to read it to my wife, that she, too, may enjoy the fact that the great minds of the West co-operate with the great minds of the East and the world.

Again thanking you for this kind missive. Love to the Madam. I am glad to remain.

Your Brother in the Great Cause of Human Uplift.

J. D. GORDON
Ass't. President General

[A. A. HOPKINS AND E. KOSTERLITZKY]

[*Handwritten endorsements*] FILE G. F. R.   H. G.
[*Stamped endorsement*] NOTED F. D. W.

DNA, RG 65, file BS 198940-113. TD. Copies of this report were furnished to the bureau's Washington, D. C., and San Francisco offices.

1. Edward R. Driver was a former teacher and lawyer who came to Los Angeles in 1914; a year later he founded the Saints Home Church of God in Christ. He was pastor of Saints Home during his service as an organizer for the UNIA (*Los Angeles Negro Directory and Who's Who, 1930–31* [Los Angeles: California Eagle Co., ca. 1931]).

2. Hugh E. MacBeth was a black lawyer and activist in Los Angeles and a promoter of the Lower California Mexican Land and Development Co. MacBeth became a major supporter of the dissident Garveyite faction that formed the Pacific Coast Negro Improvement Association in 1921 (*California Eagle*, 20 October 1919, 24 June 1921).

Open Letter by Rev. Ernest Price

[*Gleaner*, 2 April 1921]

An Englishman Comments on the Speeches and Methods of Mr. Marcus Garvey

To all the people of Jamaica who hear or read the speeches of Marcus Garvey.

Brothers,—At the present time, when you are being assembled in great numbers to hear the words of one who is hailed by many as a national deliverer, I venture to address you in a few simple words to explain why many of the best friends of Jamaica and its people are unwilling to follow Garvey as a leader, and believe rather that if he is a leader at all, he is a blind leader, who will lead any who are mistaken enough to follow him into a very dirty ditch.

You will all agree, I am sure, that before anyone's leadership is accepted by a people he and his message should be closely scrutinised. It is only a few weeks since Bedward, giving himself out to be somebody, by his promise of a heavenly paradise to his disciples, brought many into poverty and ridicule.[1] The fact that Bedward is perhaps a sincere man made no difference to his failure. In the same way Mr. Garvey may be sincere, in his promise of an earthly paradise, but if the foundations he lays are in the sand, great will be the fall of the house he tries to build thereon.[2]

A hundred years ago my predecessors found the people of Jamaica in slavery. With magnificent courage, unquenchable hope, and unmatchable patience they with many equally heroic missionaries of other churches, worked for Jamaica, suffered for it, and in many, many instances died for it. They made no boast of this, but to-day we all glory in their works. Their successors, in the century afterward, have bravely tried to help you realise and enjoy the freedom that was then given to your fathers. They do not claim to have been perfect or to have made no mistakes, but they have done their best, and I do not think you have any reason to be ashamed of them. Perhaps in their name and for their sake, you will let one of their further successors, who tries daily to do his little task for Jamaica, say why he knows the promise[s] of Garvey are false, and his exhortations delusive.

I. His claims to be a representative of 400 million negroes are absolutely baseless. No one knows that there are so many for there are no means of counting them, and there may be many more, but more or less the great majority of them have never heard of Marcus Garvey, and therefore cannot [have] elected him their leader. They speak many, many different languages, some of which have never been put in writing, and of them all

I CHALLENGE MR. GARVEY TO NAME ONE

that he has mastered, except the one non-negro language in which he del[i]vers his addresses. The African people do not know English, and the only people who have mastered their languages are the very white missionaries whom Mr. Garvey scorns. Those men at great risk to . . . [*word mutilated*] and life have lived among negroes and have begun to uplift them socially, morally, spiritually, but Mr. Garvey has never so much as trodden their coasts, much less explored their territory or learned their tongue.

The people of Africa do not acknowledge Garvey as their leader, and further if he dared to land in Africa and claim to be so, his life would be very short, for African tribes have chiefs, fierce and strong, who would make very short work of anyone who claimed to be above them.

I do not stop to discuss at length his talk about the European Governments in Africa, but I would just ask you to consider this one simple fact. During the great war, the Allies tried to turn out of German East Africa the comparatively few German forces that were there. They were successful, but the task was long and difficult[3] though they had with them all the resources of Europe. How then do you think that Garvey could turn out of Africa not one nation only but many, English, French, Belgian and Dutch and afterwards get all the differing tribes, who even now are always quarrelling among themselves, to forget all their quarrels, put down their own kings and leaders, and elect as President a man who does not know their customs, their laws, their religions, or their languages.

Indeed an apology is needed for even explaining all this to many of you, because your own intelligence has made you laugh it all to scorn long ago, but I appeal to those of you who understand to explain what you know to those of your fellow-citizens who do not understand, and to those who cannot read, or have not read enough to know that all Garvey's boasting[s] are just idle, empty words.

II. His record is, so far, empty. What has Mr. Garvey really done? Done, not "said." He has said plenty but as the saying goes, "words are cheap." A few years ago, Mr. Garvey had the idea, he tells us, of a Jamaica Tuskegee. I know that this is so for I was one of those whom he consulted on the subject and to whom he confided his hopes. The scheme was a good one, and if it had succeeded Jamaica would have been all the better for it. But as Mr. Garvey himself tells us, he failed. I do not blame him for that. All of us who attempt difficult things fail in at least some of them, and few succeed in even the majority of their attempts, but the leaders of men are those who succeed in some. Now what has Mr. Garvey achieved? The Jamaica Tuskegee he never even began, because his own people would not supply him the money.

THE BLACK STAR LINE IS SUCH AN UNRELIABLE THING

that he does not even come to Jamaica himself on a Black Star ship, but on one owned by white men. The U.N.I.A. has not united the Negro people, for in America the majority of negroes have nothing to do with it, and in Jamaica there has already been a split from it.[4] So I press this question upon you, "What has Mr. Garvey done to warrant him in appealing to you to follow him?" You have read, have you not, that he who is faithful in that which is least is faithful also in that which is much? The leaders of the negro people will come—and are coming—from the doers, not the talkers, and I would rather cheer the men who like Booker T. Washington, have built the Tuskegees than men who have to admit that they tried to build them, but failed.

III.   No really great man vilifies other men or sneers at their endeavours. Jamaica has already proved that there are great potentialities in the negro race. In the realm of physical valour one of her sons won the Victoria Cross[5] and thousands of her sons have proved themselves men in France, and Italy and Palestine. In the realm of scholarship her sons and daughters have done her credit in [halls?] of arts, science and medicine. In the sphere of pastoral service and in teaching both in pulpit and at desk many have done valiantly, and a few have exceeded them all. Among these few are Wilson and Gordon Somers. Of the latter I know most,[6] and can say most, though the abilities of both are admirable. These two men (and they are not alone) command the respect of all Jamaicans, black and white, for their character and work. They have risen from the ranks of sheer ability and industry. Mr. Somers could have had far better remuneration by going abroad, but he chose rather to suffer loss with his own people and share their hardships than to enjoy pleasures which he might have had by lowering his ideal of unselfish service. But what does Mr. Garvey say of these men[?] They are "hypocrites." That is the dirtiest word with which to assail anyone. Mr. Garvey has an undoubted right to differ with them. He may think their ideals mistaken, or their methods harmful. That however is not his criticism; he claims to read their heart's motives and expose them to the populace, and he does so in the word "hypocrite."

Men and women of Jamaica, are you proud of Gordon Somers or are you ashamed of him? I do not [pick] out his name because he is my friend. Garvey picks out his name, and calls him "hypocrite." Do you think, as the chairman of the welcome meeting said, that "Marcus is an honourable man" when he calls one of the most respected Jamaicans amongst us a hypocrite? For my part, I think it a most dishonourable cry, and I want you to face the question whether you consider a man who can talk like that about his own brethren, worthy to be a leader of yours.

IV. No man is worthy to be your leader who teaches you to despise your Bible. Mr. Garvey's remarks about the [B]ible would be very amusing to people who know anything about the various translations of that book, if it were not for the fact that many of his hearers are uneducated people, not through their own fault may be, but still uneducated. They may know nothing about translations of the Bible, or the manuscript of the original languages, and when they read Mr. Garvey's insinuation that these translations have been made by white men, and therefore have been altered to encourage black people to subservience, they may not understand that all his words on that point are utter rubbish.

Even if it were true (which of course it is not) that white men would insert such commands as "servants, obey your masters," it does not alter the fact that in the countries where the white men's translations are made, there are no black servants kept. In the earliest days of the church there were, it is sadly true, many slaves, but they were white, not black.[7] If you once grasp this, you will realise how vain Mr. Garvey's words about the Bible are.

But they are worse than vain, for when he quotes it, he misleads you, or rather tries to, about the context of the passages he quotes. I know that you Jamaicans

READ THE BIBLE MORE THAN ANY OTHER ONE BOOK

so I hope you have already remember[ed] the passage about "hewers of wood and drawers of water." This passage is indeed in the Bible, and white men translated it, but they did not apply it to Mr. Garvey's race, as he suggests, but to the race called Gibeonites, the people who deceived Joshua, and who were not black at all.[8]

It would be possible to go through Mr. Garvey's speeches line by line and show similar absurdities in most of them, but the game would not be worth the candle. What do you think of the colossal conceit of the man who can name himself in the same sentence with Clemenceau and Warren Harding, as consulting his Government as they consult theirs. They have got a Government acknowledged and obeyed by millions, and able to enforce its decisions. This so-called Provisional President can't even call upon the solitary little steamer of his Black Star Line to carry him to Jamaica in time. He is a President without a republic, and a commander without an army.

People of Jamaica! Do not be misled. Do not trust this political Bedward. He is not going to ascend.

You have doubtless heard the lines:—

> The heights by great men reached and kept,
> Were not attained by sudden flight,
> But they while their companions slept,
> Were toiling upwards through the night.[9]

The same thing exactly is true of nations. Jamaica is backward. Mr. Garvey says it is the most backward on earth, but there he is wrong again. It is not so backward as all that. But it is backward[.] You can help it advance. Not by calling your most honoured ministers "hypocrites," not by believing that a man who has so far failed even to build a single school is going to found a world wide republic. All that sort of thing is too cheap and easy to be effective. But by honest toil, by the saving of money and its wise investment, by honourable marriage and the founding of lawful families, by sexual purity, by truthfulness of words, and by faithfulness of promise, by fair labour when you are employed and by just wages when you employ others,— thus, and thus only, will you build up a great people, and be worthy of rule and leadership.

It is untrue, as you know, but as he tells you, that your ministers, whether black or white distract your thoughts from earthly improvements by thoughts of heaven! Is it not the ministers to-day who manage your schools without a penny of salary, and preside over your Agricultural Societies without reward[?]

It is true, unfortunately, and as he tells you, that you are not as free as you might be. How can you be, when seventy percent of the children of the land [are illegitimate] and the country reeks with venereal disease bearing testimony to a slavery to lust on the part of so many? How can you be when praedial larceny is the crying evil of the land, proving that many are slaves of laziness? How can you be when thousands of people can be got to pay a shilling and two shillings each to listen to the empty boasting of a man who has never done a thing for his country but who denounces those of his own country men who do most?

Men and women, it is not that way that true freedom lies. When it can be said that a Jamaican's word is his bond; when it can be seen that a Jamaica man honours his own . . . [*several words mutilated*] Jamaican's work is as thorough behind his master's back as in his presence, then you will be free men indeed. Thank God, there are some of whom it can be said[.] I believe it is true of the two men whom Garvey calls hypocrites. It is true of others whom all of us, white and black, are proud to know. They are your true friends, they are the harbingers of the country coming dawn . . . [*words mutilated*] me, as one also of the Englishmen who are trying to serve you and your children beg you to follow such and let the boasters and the self-advertisers go their way. Yours for Jamaica's sake

ERNEST PRICE[10]

Printed in the *Gleaner*, 2 April 1921.

1. Alexander Bedward (1859–1930) led over seven hundred of his followers on a march to Kingston on 27 April 1921. Bedward was a black Jamaican prophet and faith healer and the founder of the Jamaica Native Baptist Free church. He was born in St. Andrew Parish, Jamaica, and reportedly worked as a cooper on the Mona estate. While living in Colón, Panama, Bedward was instructed in a dream that he was to return to Jamaica for a special work. In 1891 Bedward declared the waters of the Hope River, near August Town in St. Andrew, to have healing power, and after numerous reports of miraculous healings, thousands began to attend

Bedward's services and baptisms. Bedward's predictions of black self-government drew the interest of colonial authorities, who arrested and briefly detained him in the insane asylum in 1895. When Bedward led his famous "manifestation" in 1921, over two hundred of his followers were arrested before they reached Kingston and were jailed for vagrancy. Bedward was held for medical examination, declared insane, and incarcerated in the Bellevue Hospital until his death in 1930 (*Gleaner*, 27 April, 28 April, and 30 April 1921 and 11 November 1930; Roscoe M. Pierson, "Alexander Bedward and the Jamaica Native Baptist Free Church," *Lexington Theological Quarterly* 4, no. 3 [July 1969]: 65–76; Martha Beckwith, *Black Roadways: A Study of Jamaican Folk Life* [Chapel Hill: University of North Carolina Press, 1929]; Claude McKay, "Garvey as a Negro Moses," *Liberator* 5 [April 1922]: 8–9).

2. Because of the coincidence of Bedward's march to Kingston and Garvey's return to Jamaica, there were other comparisons of the two men. In a letter from A. A. Keating of Swift River published in the *Jamaica Times*, the following appeared:

> Then his [Garvey's] scheme to gather together the Negroes from all parts of the world into Africa is preposterous. The black race has such a firm footing in every nook and corner of the civilized world that they scorn the idea of going to a dark, unknown uncivilized land. I would advise all unthinking persons to remember Bedward of August Town and the consequences brought down on them by their folly. (*Jamaica Times*, 16 April 1921)

3. A relatively small force of native troops commanded by the German strategist Col. Paul von Lettow-Vorbeck was able to hold back for over four years a 250,000-man British army in German East Africa. During the so-called Battle for the Bundu, German soldiers used sophisticated guerrilla tactics to create an extremely high casualty rate among the poorly led British troops (Charles Miller, *Battle for the Bundu: The First World War in East Africa* [New York: Macmillan Publishing Co., 1974]).

4. A reference to the Ethiopian Progressive and Co-operative Association Ltd., founded in July 1920 by J. Manasseh Price and Alfred A. Mends after they left the UNIA. Price had been appointed president of the Kingston UNIA division when Henrietta Vinton Davis reorganized it in December 1919. Four months later when Davis returned, the Kingston division was in turmoil because of complaints from other division officers about Price's handling of the organization's money. At a 19 April 1920 meeting of the Kingston membership, Cyril Henry, who had accompanied Henrietta Vinton Davis to Jamaica, claimed that the local division had not made any of the monthly contributions to the parent body required by the UNIA constitution. Adrian Daily, the local UNIA secretary, claimed that only a portion of the money raised by the division had been deposited in the bank, whereupon Price admitted that he had deposited funds in a separate account in his own name but insisted that he had done so to protect the local members. The members voted to remove Price from office and to bring legal proceedings against him. On 23 April 1920 Price filed suit against Henrietta Vinton Davis for illegally entering his office and removing account books. Davis left Jamaica shortly after the meeting in which Price was deposed, and Price was unable to proceed with his suit until Davis returned a year later (JA, file 12185, 24 April 1920; *Gleaner*, 10 February, 21 April, and 23 April 1920; *Jamaica Times*, 24 July 1920).

5. The Jamaican contingent of the British West Indies Regiment was awarded a total of sixty-three military decorations during World War I, including one Victoria Cross and one croix de guerre (*HJ*, 1921, p. 588).

6. Rev. Gordon Somers was educated at Calabar High School, a school founded by Rev. Ernest Price. Somers also was secretary of Calabar for ten years (*HJ*, 1921).

7. Recent estimates suggest that several hundred Africans, most of them slaves, were resident in Britain in the half century before the publication of the King James Bible in 1611. In 1596 Elizabeth I ordered the expulsion of all "suche blackamoores . . . within this realme with the consent of their masters" (Folarin Shyllon, *Black Slaves in Britain* [London: Oxford University Press, for the Institute of Race Relations, 1974], and "Blacks in Britain: A Historical and Analytical Overview," [Paper presented at the African Diaspora Studies Institute, Howard University, Washington, D.C., 26–31 August 1979], pp. 6–8).

8. In the biblical story, Joshua was instructed to destroy all the people of Canaan when the Israelites took the land, but the Gibeonites tricked Joshua into making a treaty with them by pretending not to be natives of Canaan. As a condition of the treaty, the Gibeonites were made bondmen to the Israelites and were required to be "hewers of wood and drawers of water" (Josh. 9:21).

9. From the tenth stanza of Henry Wadsworth Longfellow's poem, "The Ladder of St. Augustine."

10. Known as "Mr. President" of the Baptist church in Jamaica, Price was for many years the senior local representative of the Baptist Missionary Society in England. He was also the founder of Calabar High School, one of Jamaica's leading secondary schools, and its head-master for twenty-five years. He was appointed chairman of the Jamaica Baptist Union in 1924 ("Rev. Ernest Price: Friend of Man," *Star*, 9 November 1965; C. G. Webb-Harris, "Tribute to Rev. Ernest Price," *Sunday Gleaner*, 7 November 1965).

John E. Bruce on Bishop C. S. Smith

[*Negro World*, 2 April 1921]

Some one has called my attention to Bishop C. S. Smith's article in the "World's Work" for March in which he has paid me the doubtful compliment of being the "only nationally known character in the Garvey Movement." This is, of course, news to me, and I have a right to doubt its accuracy, and to suspect the motive which impelled the Bishop to make the statement. I haven't seen Bishop Smith in more than thirty years. At that time he was a Democrat and a receptive candidate for the position of Minister to Liberia. Cleveland was then President.

I met Dr. Smith by appointment and at his request in the parlors of Perry Carson's Hotel in Washington, D.C. He wanted some publicity in my newspaper, the "Washington-Grit," which he didn't get. I have never claimed, and I have never aspired, to be a national character. I have always preferred to be a Gad fly and free lance, journalistically. . . .

Marcus Garvey is not disturbed over Bishop Smith's opinion concerning the organization of which he is the head—the moving spirit—and I don't mind telling the Bishop, sotto voce, that his flattering allusion to myself does a great injustice to other gentlemen who are more intimately associated with Mr. Garvey than myself. I am only a contributing editor of The Negro World. There are two ways of interpreting the Bishop's reference to myself, and I prefer to believe that he is honest and sincere in what he has said of me, because I do not desire to indulge the thought or suspicion that a Christian Bishop is capable of juggling with the truth, by saying the thing that is not. But if he is indulging in sarcasm at my expense I promise to hand him a Roland for his Oliver.[1] The question, therefore, is was Bishop Smith joking or just funning, when he singled po' me out as the biggest item in the Black Star Line outfit, when, as a matter of fact, I am only a small stockholder, standing loyally by my leader[2] and fighting the insidious enemies of the organization who like to go to white newspapers and magazines to deposit the bile they have in their systems and on their chests.

[JOHN E. BRUCE]

Printed in *NW*, 2 April 1921.

1. A figure of speech from the eleventh-century *Song of Roland*, meaning a blow for a blow (*BFQ*).

2. A short time earlier, Bruce remarked: "Marcus Garvey will live in the ages to come, despite the opposition[,] the sneers and jeers, and suspicions of the worldly wise of the race who have lost the vision, and are content with their present condition, because this new Apostle to the blacks did not come with a fanfare of trumpets, nor out of their circle. They see nothing good in the man, though he has wrought a work, the consequences of which are almost beyond human calculation" ("Bruce-Grit," *NW*, 26 March 1921).

Colonial Secretary, Kingston, to Clerk, Parochial Board, St. Ann's Bay, Jamaica

[*Kingston, Jamaica*] 2nd. April, 1921

Urgent. Understand that Garvey is liable for £46. 4. 0 in respect of maintenance of father now deceased at Alms House. If so immediate steps should be taken to recover amount due. Suggest you instruct legal agent at Kingston. Acknowledge receipt.

JA, CSO 1B/1/5. TG.

Hon MARCUS GARVEY

—AT—

WARD THEATRE AGAIN

On Sunday Night 3rd inst.

By special request, so as to facilitate those who were unable to gain admission on Sunday Night last through big rush.

If S.S. "ANTONIO MACEO" second ship of the Black Star Line arrives on Sat., 2nd inst. as expected this will be

MR. GARVEY'S FAREWELL MEETING

In Kingston, and Miss Henrietta Vinton Davis. International Organizer and High Commissioner of the U.N.I.A. along with the leader of the West Indian Divisions of the Association, Mr. J. DeBourg will also address the Meeting subjected to "Maceo's" arrival.

High-Class Musical Programme.

ADMISSION:

DRESS CIRCLE & PARQUETTE 2s.   GALLERY 1s.

Doors open from 6:30 o'clock.   Meeting begins at 8:15.

Printed at Gray's Book Room, 98 Oxford St, Kingston.—1656.

(*Source*: Jamaica Archives.)

Capt. Adrian Richardson to O. M. Thompson

Jacksonville, Fl[a.] April 4 1921

O [M] THOMPSON

Wrote full details. Expect to sail tonight[.] Repairs[1] will be finished at 6.
Have them rushing repairs[.] As soon as finish am leaving if it is midnight[.]

RICHARDSON

Garvey v. *United States*, no. 8317, Ct. App., 2d Cir., 2 February 1925, defendant's
exhibit GG. TG.

1. The *Kanawha* crashed into the government pier at Old Point Comfort in Norfolk, Va., on
the night of 1 April 1921. The stern of the ship was damaged, and the damage to the pier was
estimated at about $2,000 (DNA, RG 65, file OG 215356).

Marcus Garvey to the *Gleaner*

[[York House, Kingston, April 5, 1921]]

THE EDITOR

Sir,—In your issue of Saturday's date, you published a letter from Rev.
Ernest Price attacking the Universal Negro Improvement Association, the
Black Star Line, and myself, which attack grew out of the lectures I delivered
in the Ward Theatre since my advent in Jamaica.

In starting his tirade against me, he addresses the Negro people in
Jamaica as "Brothers." This man well knows that he uses this salutation as a
camouflage. I hate hypocrisy and in this case, I cannot but characterize the
writer of such a salutation, being himself a white Englishman, as anything
else but an arch hypocrite. When certain white men desire to deceive
Negroes, they call them "brothers," and "brethren"; when they meet them in
certain parts of the world where they are independent of their support, they
call them "Niggers." I am well accustomed to the methods of such men as
Ernest Price. He claims to be a friend of the people of Jamaica, thus advising
them against me as a Leader, saying that "If he is a leader at all he [is] a blind
one, who will lead any who are mistaken enough to follow, into a dirty
ditch[.]"

Your reporter, and those who heard me speak at the Ward Theatre, can
well remember my saying that I did not come to Jamaica to lead white
people, or even to advise those who do not claim to be Negroes, but that my
visit here, was specifically in the interest of the people who are proud to
know themselves, and call themselves Negroes. I cannot understand why
Ernest Price a white Englishman, should interfere with a proposition that
does not concern him. Why won't these dabblers leave Negroes alone? Do
they not know that Negroes are competent to handle their own affairs?

The gentleman endeavours to classify me with Bedward, speaking of Bedward's movement, as a spiritual one, and of mine, as a political one. He, by that reference seeks to prejudice the minds of the people in Jamaica against the intelligence that rules the Universal Negro Improvement Association, likening it to the Bedward movement. He ought to know—if he is the student he says he is—that the Universal Negro Improvement Association, reflects the highest intelligence in the Negro Race, a[n] intelligence that can be compared with that of any other race anywhere. That the men who head the Universal Negro Improvement Association, and form its Executive Council, are men who are all capable of teaching Ernest Price how to use the English language, as not to make himself ridiculous, in criticising anyone on things said conveying meanings that are quite different from the criticisms.

To go back to the Bedward reference—if there is any movement in Jamaica that is practically similar to that of the Bedwardites, I believe it is the religious cult represented by the Rev. Ernest Price. His dete[r]mination [*denomination?*] I think, is the nearest to Bedwardism that I think there is in Jamaica; the only difference is that he and his predecessors have been preaching the doctrine of Bedward, long before Bedward appeared, and that they give a longer period for their ascension than Bedward gives for his.[1]

He among other things said "One hundred years ago my predecessors found the people of Jamaica in slavery. With magnificent courage, unquenchable hope, and unmatchable patience, they worked for Jamaica, suffered for it, and in many instances died for it. They made no boast of this, but to-day we all glory in their works." I take it for granted that the Reverend Gentleman means that his predecessors worked for the abolition of slavery in Jamaica, speaking of fellows like Wilberforce and Buxton. If he knew anything of history[,] claiming to be a B.A. as he is, he would have known that Negroes did not bring themselves into slavery, that slavery was imposed upon them by his own predecessors, therefore if the said predecessors liberated the said Negroes from slavery

They Were But Performing a Duty

that would have to be done at some time or the other, to save their own skins. With what happened in Hayti, and the threatening attitude of the Jamaica Negro slaves at that time, Wilberforce and Buxton and the rest, saw the handwriting on the wall, and knew well if they had not done something to bring about the emancipation, the people whom their brothers kept in slavery, would have ultimately emancipated themselves, to the loss of certain people not only in cash, but in something more dear to them.

He challenges my claim to be a representative of the four hundred million Negroes of the world, stating that the statement is baseless. What does Price know about Negro movements, and present day Negro attitude? To my knowledge, he is only interested in the Baptist movement of which he is President of one of their colleges, an institution that seeks to get the pennies and pounds from Negroes on Sundays, at special Missionary meetings, and other such festivities, but as for their political and social uplift, I cannot remember coming across anything ever done by Ernest Price, for me to recognise him as a student of Negro movements. If he were well informed, he would have know that on the 1st August last, 25,000 delegates of the Negro Race from all parts of the world assembled in New York City at the greatest Convention ever held by any race group and that they continued in Convention for 31 days and 31 nights, during which time they elected certain leaders of their own, among them the writer who was elected as the First Provisional President of Africa, and the President General of the Universal Negro Improvement Association. He would have also known that a constitution of Negro rights, and liberty was framed at this Convention, and that this constitution now stands as the guiding principle of the Negro peoples of the world.

He further states "The people of Africa do not acknowledge Garvey as their leader, and further if he dared to land in Africa, and claim to be so, his life would be very short, for African tribes have chiefs, fierce and strong, who would make very short work of anyone claiming to be above them." Again I have to attack the scholarship of Ernest Price. If he is really a B.A., he passed his examination more by chance, than by merit, because all sensible people know that the African chiefs, although fierce and strong, have not made short the life of even the robbers who have despoiled their land, because these very chiefs are the most friendly, charitable, and merciful men, that one could hope to come in contact with. If it were not for such many of the predecessors of Price would have lost their heads in Africa centuries ago. For the world of me, I cannot see how a cousin or a brother of mine would make short my life, for attempting to help him, whilst he protects and prolongs those of the villains who seek to rob him. The Rev. Price knows nothing of the present attitude of the people of Africa. If he did, he would have known, that all Africa from South to North, East to West, and Central, is made up of branches of the Universal Negro Improvement Association.

Mr. Price may be playing "smart" to find out the method the Universal Negro Improvement Association is to use in reclaiming Africa for Negroes but smarter men than he have tried for the same thing, and have failed in gathering the information. I, in no way as an individual, intend to turn anybody out of Africa. When the time comes, Africans themselves will be able to protect their own country, and I, being a humble citizen of Africa, shall but contribute my bit along with four hundred million Africans, to preserve the rights of their motherland.

Mr. Price claims that my record is empty. Pray, will he tell us about the record? All that I can gather from the record of this gentleman, is that for the last few years he has found it to his advantage to be moralizing the Negroes—the philosophy he would like to impart to them in a word means "hand me as much cash as you can get, I will sit in the college, and you will go and work." If he has any other achievement, I will be pleased to be informed. It is not for me to speak of what I have done, but the achievements of the Universal Negro Improvement Association and of the Black Star Line, stand out as a monument to the sacrifice, energy, and ability of some one. Everybody knows that the Universal Negro Improvement Association, has a membership of four million active members. Everybody of sense ought to know that it takes some ability to organise four million people in the space of three and a half years. Everybody knows that the Black Star Line owns three ships and in another couple weeks will own [the fourth] ship, and ships are not bought by mere cheap words but by hard American dollars and English pounds. The tonnage of ships range from $90 to $160 a ton, hence ships of large tonnage ought to represent tall figures in present day currency, and any individual or individuals who can make a line of ships possible ought to possess some ability, and would not be regarded therefore as empty brawlers.

Rev. Price referred to my failure in starting a Tuskegee Institute in Jamaica. He suggests that it would have been a good thing to have. I can really understand why Mr. Price draws the line at the present time—he would much prefer to see an industrial school where Negroes are taught to plough, hoe, wash plates, and clean pots, rather than to have Negroes thinking about building up empires and running big steamships across the ocean. Ah! a Tuskegee in Jamaica, would be but the

CARRYING OUT OF THE PHILOSOPHY OF MR. PRICE.

"Servants obey your masters." But in reference to my failure in building a Tuskegee in Jamaica, which Mr. Price labours so hard, may I not ask Mr. Price what has he really done as a constructive builder. Can he give us his record from England? [W]here he has living monuments to his energy and ability? Can he tell us how many Tuskegees he built in England? Can he tell us how many steamship companies he successfully floated? Can he tell us how many Englishmen he converted to the Baptist Denomination? When he can give us a record better than the one he criticises in me, I shall be pleased to take advice and counsel from the Rev. Ernest Price.

Price says the U.N.I.A. is not uniting the Negro people, for in America, the majority of Negroes have nothing to do with it and in Jamaica there has already been a split from it. Can Price tell me of any one thing in the worl[d], including Christianity, that all the people of a race are in? Can he tell me being a B.A. of any instance in human history where all the people have ever agreed on any one opinion or point of view? If this man is really a B.A. should he not exhibit a better appreciation for movements that have been successful in bringing about an organised sentiment among large numbers of people, without exposing such a movement to ridicule, scorn and contempt?

Mr. Price asks "What has Mr. Garvey done to warrant him appealing to you to follow him?" If Mr. Price had any modesty he never would have asked this question. It is not in the province of an Englishman to ask Negroes such a question. To my way of thinking, I think Mr. Price a rude and unwelcome intruder in interfering in matters that do not concern him. As an English-man, and as a white man, it is quite in his province to dabble in all things pertaining to white people, but when it comes to things that affect Negroes, he ought to have the common decency to allow Negroes to attend to their own affairs. Mr. Price ought to know that there are Negroes in Jamaica far more intellectual than himself, far more able to analyse and handle public sentiment that affect the Negro race, than he Mr. Price can. Why not leave therefore, the things that pertain to Negroes to members of the race to handle, without interfering? Mr. Price ought to know that intelligent, edu-cated Negroes resent the idea of men of other races interfering in matters pertaining to our race.

Mr. Price charges me of vilifying Messrs. Wilson and Gordon Somers. How he arrives at that, I cannot tell. Surely, this B.A. is in sore need of being taught how to analyse an English sentence, because the sentence in which I referred to Wilson and Gordon Somers, could not be misconstrued in any way as being a vilification of the two gentlemen.

Mr. Price tries to camouflage us about our physical valour and about one of our sons winning the Victoria Cross, and thousands of others proving themselves men in France, Italy, and Palestine. Will he as a straightforward honest Christian (?) gentleman tell us what have those poor fellows received materially for all the services they have rendered for the last 300 years? For Mr. Price's information, and a guide to a better study of the English lan-guage, may I not say to him that in my reference to Messrs. Wilson and Gordon Somers I meant no harm. On the contrary, I desired to bring home to the men a conviction of their responsibility to the poor struggling people of Jamaica whom they represent. I referred to them as a class of leaders, not as individuals.

Mr. Price makes out that he is so much interested in Rev. Somers, and that he believes that the Rev. Somers has made a sacrifice to be at home, and that he could do much better abroad. Oh! for the hypocrisy of this world!! Does Mr. Price really mean this? From his Christian (?) soul, can he tell me that he means well by the Rev[.] Somers? If so, why did he not recommend him for the Pastorate of the East Queen Street Baptist Church, being the ablest Baptist Preacher in the country? Why did he encourage his denomina-tion to send all the way to England for the Rev[.] Tucker,[2] a man who could not loose the shoes of the Rev. Somers, in the pulpit of any church? Do you, Rev. Price, really mean to tell me and the people of Jamaica that the people of England would hand out a cure or charge in any Diocese in England to Rev. Somers, and that he would be better appreciated speaking from an English pulpit in England, than from the pulpit from which he preaches in Spanish Town? Oh! for the sins of this world, how many of us shall see salvation!

Rev. Price says "no man is worthy to be your leader who teaches you to despise your Bible." Why does the Rev. Price so misrepresent me? Did I advise anybody to despise the Bible? I, like the majority of Jamaican Chris-tians, have a great deal of respect for the Holy Bible, that is, that part that was inspired by our Heavenly Master, but Mr. Price well knows if he is a scholar and a B.A. that the Bible has been handled by man for hundreds of years, and that man makes so many mistakes especially when he sees he can gain certain advantage by saying certain things, and saying them in certain ways. He, as a scholar and a B.A. must know that the Bible has been handled by the classes ever since the first edition was printed, and that the classes even though religious, have always had a prejudice against the masses, whether those masses be white or black, that it has always been the desire even of our modern day preachers to get the masses to be as subservient as possible, and anything that would lead them to subserviency would naturally find a place in the Scriptures that they themselves control and interpret. Mr. Price does not mean to tell me that the Bible was not printed on earth!! Everybody knows that it was printed on earth with human hands, and it is but human to err. Who can well interpret the ways of God? What man is there who is audacious enough to be able to convey to [us] the Spirit of God as God himself intends it?

Mr. Price says that it would be possible to go through Mr. Garvey's speeches line by line, and show absurdities. It is also possible for me to go through Mr. Price's letter, word by word, and pick him to pieces, as a scholar, and more than all as a B.A.

Mr. Price seems to be very sore about people paying money to h[elp] me. Why, I did not invite white people to come and hear me!! I invited Negroes who are interested in themselves to hear what I had to say about the development of the race. But why should Mr. Price be envious of the people paying 1/- or 2/- to hear one of their own? Mr. Price and his class have been getting thousands and thousands of pounds from the said people for over eighty three years, just as Bedward has been doing, and nobody ever raised a voice of protest!! Why should Mr. Price be so selfish? Does he not know that the shilling or two that the Negroes pay to hear me speak go into the funds of the Universal Negro Improvement Association

FOR THE PROMULGATION OF THE WORK,

and not to me as an individual? If Mr. Price wants to see the accounts of all the meetings held since I have been here, he can consult my private Secretary and he will know what has become of the money; but to exchange courtesies, would Mr. Price let me know what becomes of the collection received in the various Baptist Churches from morning services to evening services? I would just like to know who gets it on Monday morning, whether it is laid at the Altar of the Lord or in the pockets of men like Mr. Price? It is a pity Mr. Price writes as an Englishman, because he only brings to light the arrogance of certain Englishmen, who are doing much harm to the Empire. Arrogant, bombastic, and intruding Englishmen like Mr. Price, are doing great harm to the British Empire in India and Egypt and in the foreign outposts. They do this harm by their assumption of being Englishmen, and

Englishmen with rights and privileges to ignore, tr[am]ple under foot, and despise all other races of people, treating them as inferiors as they come in contact with them. I cannot understand the audacity of Mr. Price, in saying that I should not refer to Clemenceau and myself in the same breath. Who is Clemenceau—but an elected and constituted leader of the French people? [A]nd who is Marcus Garvey—but an elected and constituted leader of the Negro people? Is it because Mr. Price despises Negroes so badly, why he thinks a Negro should not be mentioned in the same breath as the white man? I can well see behind all of Mr. Price's intentions, I can well see behind his mind, I think I know him for what he is. As much as he despises Negroes, so do all intelligent and self-respecting Negroes, despise him. I feel sure also that Mr. Price's advocacy of the cause of Messrs. Wilson and Gordon Somers is nothing else but a camouflage, in that I believe his intention is more to attack me, and destroy public confidence in the Universal Negro Improvement Association, so as to cause its downfall, rather than to espouse the cause of the other two gentlemen.

I will mention this so as to intimate to Mr. Price that I know more about his intention than he seems to think. Mr. Price, I know of the Rev. Stone, a fellow Englishman of yours. He is in Banes, Cuba. He comes in contact with the Universal Negro Improvement Association in Cuba, and he had a tale to tell you when he came here the other day. Didn't he? Behind the defence of Messrs. Gordon Somers and Wilson, methinks I see the Stone matter.

Mr. Editor, in this same letter, I may as well say a few words about Mr. John Soulette, in that I have no time to write many letters. This gentleman attacked me a couple days ago,[3] and in his communication he tried to make out that he is a loyal son of Jamaica, he loves Jamaica, a leader of Jamaica people, and that I have never done anything for Jamaica.

If my memory serves me right, Mr. Editor, may I not ask: Is not this the Mr. Soulette who collected and gave evidence for the Insurance Companies against the Policy holders of Jamaica during the last earthquake? Is not he the same Soulette who stood out against Jamaica when Jamaica was in sore need? Can you not remember sir, that the policy holder's backs were to the wall during the last earthquake, when they fought, and fought to collect on their policies, so as to be able to restart business? Wasn't it this "patriot" of Jamaica who stood up for these foreign countries and gave evidence which tended to deprive the policy holders of their collections? Mr. Editor, I also passed through the earthquake. At that time, I occupied the position as manager of the Benjamin Printing Dept., which business was situated in King St., just opposite the Photographic Studios of Messrs. Cleary and Duperly. I saw the fire started.[4] I knew of its origin. If I had volunteered to give evidence on behalf of the Insurance Companies the policy holders would have lost; but for the love of my country and my interest, I closed my mouth. I never got a penny. Mr. Soulette may be able to say how much he got—if he is the same Mr. Soulette—for giving evidence in that case against his country and against his countrymen. When this gentleman can clarify this matter, then I will be able to take him seriously. I am, etc.,

MARCUS GARVEY

Printed in the *Gleaner*, 6 April 1921. Original headlines omitted.

1. Between five and six thousand of Bedward's followers came to August Town, Jamaica, from throughout Jamaica, Cuba, and Central America on Friday, 31 December 1920. Bedward had promised to ascend into the sky to prepare a place for them and to return the following Monday to take them back with him (*Gleaner*, 15 December 1920, 3 January 1921).

2. Rev. Leonard Tucker was educated at London University College, where he received an M.A. degree. He first went to Jamaica in 1889, serving initially at Montego Bay, and later on the staff of Calabar College. In 1902 he became secretary of the Young People's Missionary Association; five years later he became secretary of the Young People's Department of the Baptist Missionary Society. He was invited to become pastor of the East Queen Street Baptist Church in Kingston in 1918 and remained there until 1923 (Alan E. Easter, Baptist Missionary Society, London to Robert A. Hill, 2 February 1983).

3. John A. Soulette, "The Propaganda of Mr. Marcus Garvey," *Gleaner*, 1 April 1921, and "The Financial Aspect of Mr. M. Garvey's Schemes," *Gleaner*, 12 April 1921.

4. A reference to the fires that followed the Kingston earthquake of 1907, which reduced the city to ruins. The fire, which started in the city's commercial center, spread quickly. According to H. P. Jacobs of the *Gleaner*:

> The great difficulty was the absence of earthquake insurance. Property had been insured against fire, but not against earthquake; and while much of the damage had been done by fire, the companies denied liability on the ground that the earthquake had preceded and caused the fire. Litigation followed, and it was not until 1909 that the companies agreed to pay eighty-five percent of the face value of policies. (*From the Earthquake to 1944* [Kingston, Jamaica: Pioneer Press, n.d.], p. 103)

In a more recent account, H. P. Jacobs revealed: "Witness after witness declared that he had seen fire before the earthquake took place. Indeed there was only one man in Kingston who continually and loudly maintained that this was not true: Mr. John Soulette, a business man who was one of the leading city politicians in the next generation" (H. P. Jacobs, [untitled, unpublished MS]; see also *HJ*, 1908, pp. 588–589).

John A. Soulette's reply to Garvey was immediate; his letter describing the fire and his subsequent role in the litigation was published in the *Gleaner*, 7 April 1921.

Robert P. Skinner,[1] American Consul General, to J. Butler Wright,[2] American Chargé d'Affaires

[*London*] April 5, 1921

Sir:—

With reference to your letter of the 31st ult. in regard to Mr. Dusé Mohamed Ali,[3] it will probably interest you to know that the person named called upon me yesterday afternoon and again discussed his commercial projects which appear to have no relation to political matters of any character. . . .

The mention of Marcus Garvey to Mr. Ali aroused his manifest irritation. He explained that Marcus Garvey was a West Indian, a native of

Jamaica, who was his messenger in London in 1913, having applied at his office for employment as a destitute person. After being so employed for a short time Marcus Garvey proved to be so lazy and generally worthless that he was discharged. This Mr[.] Garvey is now in New York and seems to have written an article in the "World's Work," which I have not seen and which brings Mr. Ali's name into the Garvey enterprise. My informant says that when he reaches New York he intends to bring suit for libel against the "World's Work," if he can find the slightest ground for taking steps of this character. He ridicules a recent organisation formed among the negroes as a result of which the members have given themselves bombastic titles, and I rather gather that the persons engaged in this movement are not American negroes at all.

The suggestion that Marcus Garvey is an alien may perhaps be of some utility to the Department of Labor, since if he is an objectionable person, he might very properly be deported.[4] I find by experience that the West Indian negroes differ very greatly from the negroes of the American states, and usually conceal the fact of their West Indian origin as much as possible. I am, Sir, Your obedient servant,

ROBERT P. SKINNER.
American Consul General

[*Address*] J. Butler Wright, Esquire,
American Chargé d'Affaires, 4, Grosvenor
Gardens, S.W.1 [*London*].

DNA, RG 59, file 811.1 TL, carbon copy.

1. Robert P. Skinner (b. 1866), a career diplomat, became consul general of the American Embassy in London in October 1914 (U.S. Department of State, *Register*, 1924 [Washington, D.C.: GPO, 1924], p. 188).

2. Joshua Butler Wright (b. 1877) was assigned as the counselor to the American Embassy in London in September 1918. He served there until October 1921 (U.S. Department of State, *Register*, 1924, p. 208).

3. Dusé Mohamed Ali applied to the American consul in London for a U.S. visa in January 1921. His purpose was to raise funds from American businessmen for a proposed new banking house in West Africa, to be operated by West Africans in competition with the established Bank of British West Africa. He was also interested in meeting with President King of Liberia to discuss his Inter-Colonial Corp. Ltd., which he intended to compete with Lever Brothers Ltd. On 28 February 1921 Ali wrote President King to "MARK TIME until I can get over to the United States," when he would seek "some satisfactory solution" to the unfavorable terms proposed in the $5 million American loan, which, according to Ali, "would only mean a throttling of the Republic, and those Africans who are patriotic cannot possibly be satisfied with such a condition of affairs." As his principal contacts in the United States, Ali listed John Mitchell, president of the Mechanics Savings Bank of Richmond, Va., and owner of the militant *Richmond Planet*, and his longtime colleague and correspondent John E. Bruce. Both Mitchell and Bruce became subjects of an investigation by the State Department. Ali received a visa in March 1921, but because the State Department suspected him of having ties with Garvey, his visa was canceled on instructions from the secretary of state (DNA, RG 59, file 880-L-3). Ali was finally granted another visa, but after he arrived in the United States in October 1921, his West African trading plans failed to materialize. Bruce subsequently introduced Ali to R. R. Moton of Tuskegee and also paved the way for Garvey to appoint him head of the African Affairs Department of the UNIA and to make him foreign affairs columnist for the *Negro World* in 1922, a position he held until July of that year (DNA, RG 59, files 880-L-2 and 880-L-3; Ian

Duffield, "Some American Influences on Dusé Mohamed Ali," Paper delivered at the Colloquium on Pan-African Biography, African Studies Center, University of California, Los Angeles, 12 April 1982).

4. Lawrence Lanier Winslow, secretary of the American Embassy in London, sent a copy of this letter to William Hurley of the State Department on 6 April 1921, adding that: "In view of the undesirable activities of Marcus Garvey in connection with Negro Agitation, it might be worthwhile for you to consider Mr. Skinner's suggestion in regard to his deportation provided he is, as Ali suggests, a native of Jamaica" (DNA, RG 59, file 880-L-2).

Rev. Ernest Price to the *Gleaner*

Calabar College, Kingston,
April 5th, 1921

THE EDITOR,

Sir,—I see that Garvey adds to his charge of hypocrisy against one of our most honoured ministers, the charge of being actuated by the desire for money. He also suggests a debate with me. I would like instead to ask him the following questions—

I   When he was last in Jamaica did he hire a motor car for which he was unable to pay?

II   Did he, in his distress, when he was unable to pay and was pressed for the money, go to Mr. Gordon Somers and beg for help[?]

III   Did Mr. Somers help him?

IV   Has he been asked to repay the money?

V   When he called Mr. Somers a hypocrite in the theatre, was he at that very moment indebted to Mr. Somers' generosity?

VI   If the answers to the above questions are in the affirmative, does he consider himself a low-down scamp?

VII   If he is, why does he invite the poor black people of this island to entrust him with their money to invest in the Black Star Line? I am, etc.,

ERNEST PRICE

Printed in the *Gleaner*, 6 April 1921.

W. E. B. Du Bois to C. D. B. King

[*New York*] April 7, 1921

Dear President King:

I regret that I was unable to find you at home while in Washington and that I could not get to Baltimore to confer with you and Dr. Lyon. . . .[1]

I am enclosing a statement[2] which I also laid before Dr. Lyon. Would you be willing to [publish] this statement or a similar statement in The CRISIS with your signature.[3] I[f] [not] could we publish some such statement as this and [s]ay that it was "official"[?] I should be glad to hear from you at your convenience. With best regards, Very sincerely yours,

[W. E. B. Du Bois]

[*Address*] Hon. C. D. B. King, Liberian
Legation, Z Street, N. W.,
Washington, D.C.

MU, WEBDB, reel 9, frame 957. TL, carbon copy.

1. Here Du Bois expressed the hope that President King would attend the forthcoming Second Pan-African Congress, where he planned to "give the public a correct opinion concerning such movements as that of Mr. Garvey."

2. Neither the original nor the copy of this statement has been found.

3. A statement signed by President King was published in the June 1921 *Crisis* ("An Open Letter from the President of Liberia," *Crisis* 22, no. 2:53).

THE CRISIS

Vol. 22. No. 2　　　**JUNE, 1921**　　　**Whole No. 128**

Opinion *of* W.E.B. Du Bois

AN OPEN LETTER FROM THE PRESIDENT OF LIBERIA

SOME wrong impressions seem to exist about the present conditions in Liberia. I take this opportunity of making the situation clear to our many American friends. Liberia has been an independent country since 1847 and naturally it has never considered the surrender of its sovereignty to any nation or organization. On the other hand Liberia has always regarded itself as the natural refuge and center for persons of Negro descent the world over. As a country whose greatest development is just beginning we are not, of course, in condition to receive large, miscellaneous numers of immigrants. Our present need is especially for strong young men trained as artisans, engineers and merchants who can bring with them some capital for investment. To such immigrants and their families we offer a vast and rich country waiting for the application of hard work and brains and money. It goes without saying that in this development Liberia respects the integrity of the territory of her neighbors in the same way that they must respect hers. Under no circumstances will she allow her territory to be made a center of aggression or conspiracy against other sovereign states. She proposes to develop Liberia for Liberians and to live at peace with the rest of the world.

★　*[signature]*

PRESIDENT OF LIBERIA.

THE RISING TRUTH

SINCE the founding of THE CRISIS one of the criticisms against it which has been hardest to bear has been that of deliberately exaggerating the mistreatment of Negroes, suppressing the favorable truth and seeking to foment race trouble. While the Nashville *Banner*, the Macon *Telegraph*, the Columbia *State*, and men like Weatherford, Bolton Smith a n d Brough have deliberately spread this false impression, we who sit and see and hear the truth know that far from exaggerating we were more often consciously suppressing and concealing the horrors of southern oppression. Month after month we go through the sordid and horrifying details—the letters, the newspapers. the personal visits and appeals—and say in despair: if we publish all this—if we unveil the whole truth, we will defeat our own cause because the public will not believe it, and our own dark readers will shrink from our pages. And

53

(*Source*: *Crisis*, June 1921.)

Charles L. Latham to Julius D. Dreher,[1]
American Consul General, Colón, Panama

[*American Consulate*] Kingston, Jamaica,
April 7, 1921

CONFIDENTIAL.

Sir:

I have to inform you that this consulate has received an instruction from the Department of State not to visa the passport of Marcus Garvey, a British subject, native of Jamaica, and at present in this Island.

Marcus Garvey is the President of the Black Star Line of New York. He is also President of the Universal Negro Improvement Association, and has lately become well known as a speaker of a radical type, alleging himself the leader of a new movement to gather negroes all over the world into a nation to be established in Liberia.

He is likely to proceed from this Island to some nearby South or Central American country before seeking to return to the United States. The Department's instruction states the refusal of visa is in view of the activities of Garvey in political and racial agitation. Very respectfully yours,

CHARLES L. LATHAM
American Consul

DNA, RG 84, file 811.1. TLS, carbon copy.

1. Julius D. Dreher (b. 1846) was appointed the American consul general to Panama in 1915 (U.S. Department of State, *Register*, 1924, p. 119).

Alfred E. Burrowes to the *Gleaner*

[[St. Ann's Bay, 8th April, 1921]]

THE EDITOR,

Sir,—In your issue of the 7th instant, I notice that Mr. John Soulette has again published some unfounded statements regarding the alleged ill-treatment Garvey's father received at the hands of his son; as also an imaginary account of what took place on the occasion of Mr. Garvey's visit to his native town and parish.

In justice to Mr. Garvey, and from my personal knowledge, I may say that he might not have been in the position at some time of his life to support his father; seeing that he was then engaged in a struggle to educate and fit himself for something better than what the old man aspired to. During this said period the old man was then in a position to look after himself as he parted gradually with what property he had and lived off the proceeds therefrom. Eventually this source of revenue was exhausted, then it was that the old man became an inmate of the Poor House. During this period Mr. Garvey was not in a position to do anything for his father. As soon, however, as I realized that Mr. Garvey could assist I wrote to him, and in justice to him, and for the information of Mr. Soulette, I may say Mr. Garvey not only sent me instructions for the disposal and care of his father, but sent me monies to do so, and to have him properly buried when he died. The old man was thereupon removed from the alms house and was properly cared and tended till the time of his death, which, through the instrumentality of his son—Marcus Garvey—was not permitted to be that of a pauper.

I publish this fact for the information of those persons who may have accepted the statements of Mr. Soulette.

As regards police protection (?) and the kind of welcome given Mr. Garvey on his recent visit here, as depicted by Mr. Soulette, I may say this is also not correct.

Mr. Garvey had quite a warm and most enthusiastic welcome extended him on his recent visit to St. Ann's Bay. I had some job trying to regulate the dense crowd that gathered at my office for the express purpose of seeing and greeting Mr. Garvey. Despite the fact that the time fixed for his meeting was very unsuitable from my experience of St. Ann, I venture to say that no man other than Mr. Marcus Garvey could have had the number of persons in attendance at the court house at that hour to hear his lecture.

Mr. Marcus Garvey is a wonderful Jamaican, who, as the "African and Orient Review" puts it, "has presented to the world the Black Star Line, which though it should meet with loss, would still be a source of inspiration to the Black millions for generations to come." I am,

ALFRED E. BURROWES

Printed in the *Gleaner*, 13 April 1921. Original headlines omitted.

Marcus Garvey to the *Gleaner*

York House, Kingston, April 8, 1921

THE EDITOR,

Sir,—By your issue of the 7th, I observe that John Soulette has tried to make out a defence for himself in the matter of his connection with the insurance companies during the earthquake. I am not disposed to waste much time with Soulette because he is not worth it. You can never convince ignorant people against their will. If Soulette will go back to school and learn to write the English language, it would pay him much better than trying to criticise his intellectual "betters." His construction is so poor, that it would reflect disgrace on a school boy in the 4th standard! Soulette ought to know that when he speaks of "betters" he could not even be my office boy, because any of my office boys is supposed to reflect a higher grade of intelligence than he. Whatsoever can be understood out of his jumble of one column of your paper, it goes without saying that the man is guilty of standing up against his country, and his countrymen during the time of need. He tries to hide himself under the so-called scholarship of Rev. Ernest Price, claiming that ["]Mr. Price has placed the laurel wreath on my grave." I wonder if Soulette knows what this means? I thank you for the compliment[,] Mr. Soulette[,] of winning laurels, so that after all, you admit defeat. Suppose you use your dictionary some more[,] Soulette! I think you would be better off in another five years. If there are no night schools in Jamaica, I suggest that you take a correspondence course. That would help you somewhat.

Mr. Editor, I may also say a few words in reply to the questions of the Rev. Ernest Price as asked of me in your publication of the 6th. First of all, let me say that Mr. Price's attitude is not in keeping with the Christian religion. To imagine Christ speaking or writing as Ernest Price!! If this man knows really what he is trying to be, he would never more append Reverend to his name, thereby meaning that he is an Apostle of the Spirit of our Lord and Saviour Jesus Christ. To imagine Christ speaking in terms as abusive and vulgar as this Baptist divine! I may now state for Mr. Price's information that I have never been obligated to Rev. Gordon Somers for any loan in money, or otherwise that he may claim to have given me. I know one can hardly trust the honesty of some preachers now a days, but I do not believe the Rev. Gordon Somers could be so bold as to say he ever loaned me any money. What

REALLY HAPPENED WAS

this. Before I left Jamaica last, I was engaged in the work of the Universal Negro Improvement Association, and had occasion to travel between Kingston and St. Ann's Bay in a motor car. Through some prejudice on the part of those who owned the motor car that I travelled in from Kingston, it was plotted to damage or destroy the car, so as to have me pay the cost of it, because these people were against my work! Whilst I was a few miles out of Spanish Town the chauffeur damaged the car. He returned to Spanish Town under the guise that he was going to seek help for repairing the damage. I gave him money to buy certain things he claimed that he required. He took the money, paid his fare on a train that was leaving the Spanish Town station back to Kingston, and left me on the road waiting for him. I was scheduled to speak that night in St. Ann's Bay at 8, and it was then 6 o'clock. Since the man did not appear, I made enquiries, and found out that he had deserted me. I was then forced to engage another car, from a Mr. Ellis in Spanish Town. The car took me to St. Ann's Bay and back. When we arrived in Spanish Town, Mr. Ellis demanded immediate payment for the use of his car. I told him I had not the money there, but in a few days I would settle the matter with him. He said that I should give him a reference as a security for the money. I gave him the name of the Rev. Gordon Somers, and the Rev. Somers did act as reference for me. On the day that I set for paying the bill of Mr. Ellis, I was unable to meet it, because of the lowness of funds in the Universal Negro Improvement Association. I wrote Mr. Ellis and asked him for time, during which time, Mr. Somers started a campaign of vilification against me stating to my many friends in Kingston and elsewhere, that he had had to pay a bill of £7 for me for motor car hire. I suffered so much from the misrepresentations of Rev. Somers, that I felt that he ought to be punished for the money that he had to pay.

I subsequently left Jamaica under the impression that Rev. Somers had paid the bill, and when I arrived in the U.S.A. I also suffered from the Rev. Somers making representations to other people in the U.S.A. in the same way he did whilst I was in Jamaica. I still laboured under the impression that Rev. Somers had paid the bill, and therefore I decided I would take my own time in paying him back the money, since he did me so much harm.

It was surprising to me on my arrival in Jamaica, at which time I really meant to pay the Rev. Somers, to find that he had never paid the money to Mr. Ellis, and that at no time did Mr. Ellis ever collect one penny from him out of the £7. I therefore immediately gave Mr. Ellis my personal check for £7 and liquidated the debt.

Those are the facts in the case of the Rev. Somers and myself which the Rev. Price wrote on by way of queries in your paper of the 6th. I am, etc.,

MARCUS GARVEY

P.S. Mr. Editor, relative to the reference of Soulette to my father,[1] it is for me to say, that I, as a poor man, did all that was possible for me to do to assist a father who had money to provide for himself and made no good use of it. My father gave me at the age of fifteen the care of my mother and an elder sister when he himself was in a position to care for his family. He squandered his money and made ill use of his properties, without even providing for his lawful children, educationally and otherwise; yet when he was in need, I did the best for him, and more than Soulette would have done for such a father. When he appealed to me for money, I gave it to him out of my meagre means. Before he was dead, over forty pounds was cabled by me, and was actually spent for his care and burial. I did more for him that he did for me, and if he were alive I would have done my best for him.—M. G.

Printed in the *Gleaner*, 11 April 1921. Original headlines omitted.

1. Soulette claimed that the elder Garvey had "languished in [St. Ann's] alms house whilst you [Garvey] were masquerading as 'Honourable' in a foreign land" (*Gleaner*, 7 April 1921).

Memorandum by the Division of Western European Affairs, Department of State

[*Washington, D.C.*] April 8th, 1921

Mr. Wiley[1] called upon President King this morning at the latter's request.

President King discussed the so-called Marcus Garvey movement and the U.N.I.A., expressing grave concern with regard to the nature of this movement, its political aspirations, its financial integrity and the danger that existed, perhaps unwittingly, /that/ Foreign countries, particularly France and England, might become anxious with regard to the position of Liberia in connection with this movement.[2] Both President King and Mr. Morris,[3] especially the latter, declared that the time had come to announce publicly and definitely that the Liberian Government disapproved of the aforesaid association, and asked Mr. Wiley for his advice. Mr. Wiley replied that as he had no official knowledge of the U.N.I.A., he was not in a position to give any official advice.

Incidentally, President King said that he had discussed the matter at some length with a negro named Major Murray who, he said, had impressed him the most of any negro he had met in the United States, and that Murray had advised him against the U.N.I.A. As Murray, judging from what King said, may play a big role in advising the Liberian Delegation, it might be well to look him up. He is said to be the head of the State School for Negroes at Savannah, Georgia, and to have a son who is cashier of some negro bank in Philadelphia.[4] I think he impressed President King with his ability to raise large sums of money for Liberia among negroes in the United States.

DNA, RG 59, file 811.4106/55. TD.

1. John Cooper Wiley (1893–1967) entered the diplomatic service in 1915, serving in a number of American embassies in South America and western Europe. He was briefly assigned to the State Department from February to October 1921 (U.S. State Department, *Register*, 1927–1928, [Washington, D.C.: GPO]).

2. The American minister in Liberia prepared a lengthy assessment of President King for the Department of State as part of his larger memorandum on the personnel of the Liberian Plenary Commission. He stated, *inter alia*: "Indirection is his [King's] favorite device to conceal his true motives. It is very difficult to get a positive decision from him. By taking refuge in the indefinite and uncertain he often attempts to twist from one side of a proposition to the other according to his convenience. Politics has occupied the whole of his attention during the last twenty-five years. He knows and uses all the tricks of the game" (DNA, RG 59, file 882.51/1259).

3. John L. Morris, Liberian secretary of the interior. He was born in 1882 and educated in mission schools and at Liberia College. He had twice previously visited the United States. After entering public service, Morris was appointed successively to the positions of chief clerk of the General Post Office, auditor and secretary of the treasury, and secretary of war and the interior. He was married to the daughter of the Liberian consul general, Dr. Ernest Lyon. The American resident minister in Liberia noted: "Mr. Morris probably understands the American point of view with reference to Liberian affairs better than any other member of the [Liberian Plenary] Commission. It may be expected that he will be considerably influenced by his

father-in-law. But he will hardly be dominated by the President [C. D. B. King]" (DNA, RG 59, file 882.51/1259).

4. From the description given in the document, the person referred to as Major Murray was undoubtedly Maj. Richard Robert Wright (1855–1947). A graduate of Atlanta University in 1876, Wright was to become one of the best known black American educators of the period as the founder in 1891 of Savannah State College in Savannah, Georgia, and its head until his retirement in 1921. He served in the army during the Spanish-American War and was one of the two black Americans whom President McKinley appointed as special paymasters with the rank of major. He returned to Savannah State College after the war and was instrumental in organizing the National Association of Teachers in Negro Schools. Following his retirement in 1921 as head of Savannah State College, he moved to Philadelphia and there established the Citizens and Southern Bank and Trust Co., on the corner of South and Nineteenth streets. When the Philadelphia UNIA division held a special mass meeting at the Standard Theatre on 25 April 1921, Major Wright was among those who delivered addresses (*NW*, 30 April 1921). Rev. R. R. Wright, Jr., who had earlier been secretary of the People's Savings Bank of Philadelphia, also served as treasurer of his father's bank. The Citizens and Southern Bank and Trust Co. expanded until it eventually became the largest black-owned and operated bank in the north. From his position as president, Major Wright helped organize the National Association of Negro Banks, and for sixteen years he was president of that organization. During the Depression, Wright organized a drive that succeeded in having Booker T. Washington honored on a special postage stamp issued in 1939 (W. S. Robinson, *Historical Negro Biographies* [New York: International Library of Negro Life and History, 1967], pp. 147–148; William Newton Hartshorn, *An Era of Progress and Promise* [Boston: Priscilla Publishing Co., 1910], p. 423; R. R. Wright, Jr., *Eighty-seven Years Behind the Black Curtain: An Autobiography* [Philadelphia: Rare Book Co., 1965], chap. 14; William H. Ferris, "Travel Notes," *NW*, 16 July 1921; *NYT*, 3 July 1947).

Marcus Garvey to the Black Star Line, New York Office

Kingston JA April 8th 1921

Why won[']t you answer my cable[?] Send Maceo Kingston[.]

GARVEY

Garvey v. *United States*, no. 8317, Ct. App., 2d Cir., 2 February 1925, defendant's exhibit GG. TG.

T. M. Reddy to Lewis J. Baley

New York, N.Y. April 9, 1921

ATTENTION MR. HOOVER.

Dear Sir:

Your attention is invited to the report of confidential employee P-138, covering April 4, 1921, in which he states that Marcus Garvey, who is said to be at this time in Jamaica, B.W.I., is accompanied on his present speaking tour by a girl known as Amy Jacques, with whom he is said to have been living in New York since his separation from his wife and with whom he is said to have left this country. The woman is generally supposed by Garvey's followers to be his private secretary.

The above is transmitted for such action as the Department may deem advisable to take in the circumstances. Yours very truly,

T. M. REDDY,
Acting Division Superintendent

JGT:FJK

[*Handwritten endorsement*] FILE G. F. R.
[*Stamped endorsement*] NOTED F. D. W.

DNA, RG 65, file BS 198940-113. TLS, recipient's copy.

Report of UNIA Meeting

[[LIBERTY HALL, New York, April 10, 1921]]

BLACK STAR LINE STEAMSHIP "PHYLLIS WHEATLEY" TO BE FLOATED MAY 1—RALLY TO RAISE $40,000 NEEDED TO MAKE LAUNCHING OF BIG SHIP POSSIBLE BY THAT DATE

. . . On the speakers['] stand sat the Presidents of the various branches throughout this country and in the West Indian Islands; in all, about forty, among them being: From Massachusetts, Mr. Chas. A. Stewart, Mr. B. J. Brown, of Springfield, from Connecticut—Mr. G. W. Wilson, of Hartford; from Maine—Mr. Holman, of Portland; from New York State—Mr. A. Lewis, of Buffalo, Rev. Dr. G. E. Stewart, Rev. Dr. Geo. Alexander McGuire, and Mr. Samuels, of New York City; Mr. R. G. Austin of Brooklyn; from New Jersey—Mr. J. B. Sutton, of Jersey City; Mr. N. Cavaza of Roselle; Mr. A. W. Jolley, of Elizabeth; Mr. John McLaughlin, of Newark; from Pennsylvania—Mr. Lloyd [*Lionel*] F. Francis, of Philadelphia; Mr. J. Sla[pp]ey, of Pittsburgh; Mr. Wilson, of Harrisburg; Mr. J. H. Harvey, of Germantown; Mr. Harry Lewis, of McKeesport; Mr. A. Wright (by proxy) of Braddock; for Ohio—Mr. W. D. Harper, of Youngstown; Mr. Wm. Ware, of Cincinnati; Rev. J. C. West, of Columbus; from Illinois—Mr. W. A. Wallace[1]; from Maryland—Rev. J. J. Scranton [*Cranston*], of Baltimore; from Haiti—Mr. Napoleon J. Francis; Mr. Philip Van Putten, of San Domingo. They were introduced to the audience, one by one, and as each one stood upon his name being called by the Chancellor, the audience applauded. They were here, the Chancellor stated, by reason of a call issued by the High Executive Council of the U.N.I.A. to engage in a conference of great importance concerning the Association in connection with the purchase of the steamship "Phyllis Wheatley" and the plan for her launching by May 1. They seemed greatly impressed—in fact, so expressed themselves at the close of the meeting—with the great audience that filled the hall, the presence of the members of the Black Cross Nurses, the members of the Motor Corps, the African Legions, all dressed in their respective uniforms; while as for the presence of the Black Star Line Band under Prof. Isles' direction, and the wonderful choir of the U.N.I.A., they were carried away with ecstasy by the extraordinary programme rendered by these two branches that have contributed so much and are still contributing largely to the success of the Sunday night meetings in Liberty Hall. The programme rendered was choice and of the best, and consisted of the following numbers: Selection by the Black Star Band; Anthem ("The Heavens Are Telling") by the choir; soprano solo by Mme. Bertha Jackson; recitation by Mr. Andrew Josephs; selection by the Liberty Hall Quartette; soprano solo ("I Will Extol Thee") by Mme. Alice Fraser-Robinson; selection by the band. It is hard to say which number was the best; they were all good. . . .

Rev. Dr. Stewart was the master of ceremonies, and conducted the meeting in his typically able and delightful manner, keeping the audience in good humor, and saying pleasant things to them and about them, that prepared the way for the stirring appeal he made in the opening speech of the evening for the purchase of more shares to help put over the top the launching of the ["]Phyllis Wheatley["] on May 1. The Doctor was very adroit in making his appeal. He asked the audience, "Do we need the ship for the African trade?" The loud response was "yes." Then he asked: "Can we buy the ship only by saying yes?" to which again the answer was "no." "How then," he went on[,] "can we get the ship?" The cries to this last question were "By getting the money." "All right now," said he, evidently having gotten his hearers to the point he wanted to lead them to, "I want to see you come forward tonight with the money in generous and liberal fashion. I expect each man and each woman in this hall tonight to come forward and buy one share of stock in the Black Star Line." Seeing his adroitness in the appeal he made, the audience roared with laughter and good humoredly came forward instantly in a rally, the like of which has never before been witnessed in this Negro cradle of liberty.

The Rev. Dr. J. D. Brooks, secretary general, who had just returned from an extended trip to the Southwestern States, where he had had a remarkable experience in the interests of the Universal Negro Improvement Association, having, as the high chancellor said, gone down into the lion's mouth and come out alive, was next introduced. Dr. Brooks looked none the worse, however, for his experience with the so-called lion (the "crackers" of the South, the chancellor doubtless meant), and spoke with his wonted fire and earnestness. He spoke on: "What Does the Future Hold in Store for the Negroes of the World?" He first al[luded] to the Hon. Marcus Garvey as the leader of the Negroes of the world, and referred to the fact that it had been rumored by some that the president general would not be permitted to return to this country, because he was regarded as an undesirable alien. "Mr. Matthews, the assistant counselor general of the association, however," he said, "had assured him that no stone would be left unturned to see to it that His Excellency does come back in due time into the United States." This statement caused the house to shake and resound with applause. Continuing with his subject, that if the Negroes will combine and organize, they will become a living force in the world. Only in this way can they hope to accomplish their deserved place in the affairs of the nations of the earth. His argument was a logical and forceful one, and a rich exposition of how the Negro can attain an independent status, freed from the things by which he is today kept down because of his lack of organization and lack of a government of his own, discrimination, injustice and oppression.

Counsellor Wilford H. Smith and Capt. [E.] L. Gaines, Minister of Legions, were also on the platform, and when called upon by the High Chancellor, made brief, effective addresses of appeal to their hearers to come to the assistance of the Executive Council at this crucial and important time to help make possible the achievement of launching of the fourth steamship to the new rapidly augmenting line of vessels owned by the Black Star Line.

Announcement was made by the Chancellor that on tomorrow evening, Monday, April 11, all the presidents from the various branches of the U.N.I.A. that were present tonight would again attend Liberty Hall and that an opportunity would be given them to address the friends of Liberty Hall. It is expected that it will be a rousing meeting and one of exceptional interest, as such a meeting has not been held since the days of the big convention in August a year ago. Additional meetings will also be held throughout the balance of the week in the interest of aiding in the rally for the needed funds in connection with the launching of the great "Phyllis Wheatley."

REV. DR. STEWART SPEAKS.

Hon. Dr. G. E. Stewart, in welcoming the gathering and introducing the speakers, said in part:

We are indeed glad to greet you in Liberty Hall tonight. Day by day we are undertaking great things. Prior to the month of August last the whole weight of the Universal Negro Improvement Association was on the head of one individual, the Hon. Marcus Garvey. During that great convention you in your wisdom selected and elected men to fill different offices. These men comprise the great Executive Council of the Universal Negro Improvement Association. Now that the president general is away in the West Indian Islands doing great work, I feel sure wherever he is tonight his heart is at ease, because he knows that he has men left behind who can shoulder the burden. And in the wisdom of these men whom you have elected, while meeting some time during the past week they came to a great problem—the greatest problem in the history of the Executive Council of the U.N.I.A.— and, finding it impossible to tackle it by ourselves, we invited the presidents from different parts of the country to meet us in conference this afternoon. And here they are—great, wise, tactful men—sitting before you tonight. This is the first time in the history of the Universal Negro Improvement Association that the presidents have had the opportunity to meet in conference with the Executive Council. But this is just the beginning of the great things we have planned to do.

The speaker then introduced one by one the presidents of the various divisions who were summoned and had responded. "These are the men," he said, "on whom the work of the Universal Negro Improvement Association is depending for success. We can do nothing if these presidents stand in the way. But if they co-operate with us we must take this country by storm, and let it be known through the world that we are working in full co-operation.["]

Continuing Dr. Stewart said:

Dear Friends: We have reached the point tonight where we are determined by the help of Almighty God and your assistance and the assistance of these presidents before us, to put on the waters before the president general comes back to the city of New York the ship that we have been so longing to see, the "Phyllis Wheatley." We found the task was an arduous one; therefore we have sent for them. They have come here tonight to see what New York will do, and we want to show them what kind of people we have in Liberty Hall, because we want them to go back to their different divisions and tell them "We have never seen things after this fashion before." (Applause.)

DR. BROOKS SPEAKS

Hon. Dr. J. D. Brooks, Secretary General of the U.N.I.A., was the first speaker introduced. Having just returned from the sunny South, where he had been working in the interest of the U.N.I.A., organizing new branches and making converts to the cause, Dr. Brooks expressed his great pleasure to be again back in Liberty Hall. He paid a tribute to his co-workers in the field and urged for more appreciation of the telegrams and other communications that they send in to Liberty Hall from time to time. . . .[2]

Printed in *NW*, 16 April 1921. Original headlines abbreviated.

1. William Alexander Wallace (1867–1946) was born in Port Deposit, Md., and educated at Lincoln University in Pennsylvania, where he received a B.A. degree. He operated a wholesale and retail bakery in Chicago from 1904 until 1924. In March 1926 he became UNIA secretary-general. In 1931 Wallace worked for the Cook County Recorder's Office, and after a series of positions with the county, he was elected state senator for the Third District of Illinois in 1938 (*Who's Who in Chicago and Illinois* [Chicago: A. N. Marquis Co., 1945], p. 867; Illinois Department of Public Health, certificate of death no. 11,399).

2. Dr. Brooks's address on "The Future of the Negro," has been omitted.

Report by Bureau Agent A. A. Hopkins

Los Angeles, California 4/11/21

. . . Confidential informant reports that there has been a split in the Los Angeles local of the Universal Negro Improvement Association, and about 125 members have formed a group which is meeting separately, and have appealed to MARCUS GARVEY, and the headquarters of the U.N.I.A. at New York for support. This group is composed of the Radical element and is under the nominal leadership of J. W. DUPREE, who is president of the Colored Car Cleaners Union, but informant states the real leader is R. L. RICHARDS, a [W]est Indian Negro, heretofore reported. Another leader is "Professor" MCKINNEY,[1] a brother of "CAPTAIN" MCKINNEY, heretofore reported in connection with pro-Japanese activities among negroes.

Informant states that this seceding group includes almost all the radicals, including practically all the West Indian Negroes in Los Angeles. This group is also receiving the quiet support of REV. EDIE DRIVER, lately appointed Pacific Coast organizer of the U.N.I.A. by MARCUS GARVEY. However, DRIVER has not yet openly affiliated with the radical group. INVESTIGATION CONCLUDED, pending further information.

A. A. HOPKINS

[*Endorsements*] FILE G. F. R. NOTED F. D. W.

DNA, RG 65, file BS 202600-824-3. TD. Stamped endorsements. Copies of this report were furnished to the bureau's Washington, D.C., and New York offices.

1. J. A. McKinney was a music teacher who offered private lessons on stringed instruments (*California Eagle*, 4 October 1919).

Rev. T. Gordon Somers to the *Gleaner*

Spanish Town, April 11, 1921

THE EDITOR,

Sir—There appeared in your issue of this date a reference from Mr. Garvey to the questions asked by Mr. Price touching a money transaction between him (Mr. Garvey) and myself over five years ago. It is necessary for me to make some observations on Mr. Garvey's statements.

Mr. Ellis, at Mr. Garvey's request, drove the latter to my house on the occasion referred to. He was accompanied by his then Secretary, Miss Ashwood. He made out a promis[s]ory note for £7 to be paid in seven days, and begged me to endorse it. I was unwilling to do as he desired, until assured by him and his lady secretary in the following words: "Do not be afraid, Mr. Somers, the money is in the bank, but we cannot get it until our committee meets." I then endorsed his paper, whereupon Mr. Ellis released the Kingston car which he had locked up in his garage. Everybody knows that this act of mine made me morally and legally responsible for the payment of that money in case Mr. Garvey failed. A week after the paper was due, I wrote to Mr. Garvey, then called several times at his office, only to be put off with ready excuses. And to my surprise, he confessed to me that at the time the paper was signed, his Association had at its credit only £2. This statement compared with the one made in my study [by] his secretary and endorsed by himself, was to me very significant. Soon after he left for America, Mr. Ellis kindly offered to compromise with me by my paying so much on the account, but reserved the right to await a favourable opportunity to collect the full amount from Mr. Garvey himself, when any payment of mine would be refunded, and this arrangement had actually been carried out before Mr. Garvey settled the bill with him; so that had he not paid up I would have been out of pocket for so much.

It is absolutely untrue that I ever told any one that I paid £7 for Mr. Garvey. I mentioned the transaction exactly as it went to agents of his, and officers of the Universal Negro Improvement Association, who on several occasions invited me to take part in their meetings, and gave it as a reason why I could not associate myself with any movement at the head of which Mr. Garvey stood. In every case I pointed out that I was left to face the legal responsibility, but never said I actually paid £7. When Mr. Garvey was in, I think, Philadelphia, I wrote to him asking him to settle the matter. He replied with an insult on a picture post card. Was that act an evidence of his intention to pay the bill? The only person to whom I wrote in the United States on this subject was a Mr. C. Gentle or Gentles, who sent me a lot of Mr. Garvey's paper[s] and hand bills on the unused spaces of which the sender wrote extolling Mr. Garvey's virtues and lecturing me for not taking an active part in his propaganda. My reply, which I asked him to show Mr. Garvey, contained a statement of that transaction, giving it as one of the reasons which prevented me from taking part in the work of the U.N.I.A. If these are acts of vilification, then, in the circumstances, Mr. Garvey must blame himself, not me. I am satisfied that the money is paid, though I am still wondering if it is the result of my own request to him contained in a letter sent him after his arrival, [or] if it was because Mr. Ellis actually took steps to collect it. I am, etc.

[REV.] T. GORDON SOMERS

Printed in the *Gleaner*, 13 April 1921.

Charles L. Latham to Charles Evans Hughes, Secretary of State

Kingston April 12, 1921

Referring to the Department's instruction of March 25th concerning Marcus Garvey, visa for the Canal Zone refused. Sailing to-day on the steamer CORONADO touching at Cristobal [*Panama*]. Passage paid to Port Limón.

As he may attempt to land at the Canal Zone I have telegraphed Consul General at Panama. Garvey's activities here indicate that he would arouse considerable racial antagonism among the negroes at the Canal Zone and in the Republic of Panama.

[CHARLES L. LATHAM]

DNA, RG 59, file 811.108 G 191/5. TL, recipient's copy.

E. Blackwell, British Home Office, to the British Colonial Under Secretary of State

WHITEHALL, [*London*] 12th April, 1921

CONFIDENTIAL

Sir,

In reply to your letter of the 31st ultimo,[1] I am directed by Mr. Secretary Shortt[2] to acquaint you, for the information of Mr. Secretary Churchill, that it is understood that a meeting was held at Liberty Hall on the 12th September, 1920, under the auspices of the Universal Negro Improvement Association and the African Community League in order to obtain for Sinn Fein the support of the Negro Movement in the United States and that the Meeting appeared to have been successful. Negro supporters claimed that within a few years there would be a vast Negro Republic in Africa, but there was nothing in the speeches to show what action was to be taken in support of this African Negro policy. I am, Sir, Your obedient Servant

E. BLACKWELL

PRO, CO 583/106/18121. TLS, recipient's copy.

1. The background to this letter is complicated. It began when Gilbert Grindle of the Colonial Office received a confidential letter dated 4 December 1919 from David Boyle, the assistant director of the British Mission in New York, who was also formerly a member of the Gold Coast civil service. Boyle disclosed that his intelligence-gathering work had produced evidence of a concerted movement among American blacks "to join with the more lawless American element in fomenting a Race War in Africa." Additionally, he observed that "one of the chief points at which their attack is to be directed is (through Liberia, of course) the

conquered Colonies" of Togoland and the Cameroons (PRO, CO 583/86/282). In a secret dispatch on 15 April 1921 the Colonial Office directed Sir Hugh Clifford, the governor of Nigeria, to communicate directly with the director of the British Mission in America, Lt. Col. N. G. Thwaites, regarding the nature of the evidence upon which the statements in Boyle's letter rested. On the same day that he wrote to Thwaites for this information, 17 May 1921, Sir Hugh Clifford wrote to the colonial secretary, Lord Milner, that he did not "regard Mr. Boyle and his communication very seriously," since, as he said, "self-advertisement has, too often in my experience of him, furnished to this gentleman a principal incentive to action," leading the governor to "the suspicion that this may have been a contributory factor to the genesis" of Boyle's supposed findings of a movement among American blacks to foment a race war in Africa (PRO, CO 583/86/282). After failing to receive any response for several months, on 20 January 1921 the Colonial Office wrote to the Foreign Office to request that it inquire "as to whether Lieutenant-Colonel Thwaites received Sir Hugh Clifford's letter and, if so, whether a reply may be expected" (National Archives of Nigeria, Ibadan, CSO 1/36/9). The reply that came from the Foreign Office on 28 February 1921 stated that Thwaites, indeed, had not received the letter; it pointed out, however, that "further information on the subject is in possession of the H[ome] O[ffice]" and suggested that the Colonial Office should communicate directly with the Home Office's director of intelligence, Sir Basil Thomson. On the basis of this recommendation, during the following month the Colonial Office wrote to the Home Office (31 March 1921) forwarding copies of Sir Hugh Clifford's original correspondence on the subject (PRO, CO 763/9).

2. Edward Shortt (1862–1935) became the British chief secretary for Ireland in April 1918. While in office, Shortt faced a Sinn Fein uprising, which he countered by arresting 150 members of the group. In January 1919 he was transferred to the Home Office, where he remained until 1922 (*DNB*).

Charles L. Latham to Charles Evans Hughes

Kingston, Jamaica, April 12, 1921

Subject: Passport Visa of Marcus Garvey

SIR:

I have the honor to refer to the Department's instruction of March 25, 1921, and to report that Marcus Garvey, President of the Universal Negro Imp[ro]vement Association, Negro Factories Corporation and Black Star Line, called at this office yesterday morning and applied for visa for travel to the United States via the Canal Zone.

He was accompanied by Cleveland Augustus Jacques and his sister Amy Euphemia Jacques, who stated that they were chauffeur to Marcus Garvey and Secretary to the Negro Factories Corporation, respectively.

These three persons desired their passports to be visaed for travel to the United States via the Canal Zone in time to enable them to sail for Cristobal that afternoon on the American Steamship ["]Sixaola["].

Garvey's application was taken and the fee of One Dollar collected therefor and receipt in the prescribed form given him. He was informed that we would be unable to grant him visa without due consideration and that he should return to this office at noon on the following day, April 12, 1921.

The passports of his two companions were visaed as they had already been in the United States and there were no instructions against their being granted visas. The passages booked on the "Sixaola" by Garvey and his companions were cancelled and they did not sail.

This morning we learned that they sailed on the British Steamship "Coronado" for Port Limón, Costa Rica, which vessel touches at Cristobal, C.Z.

The Consular Officers in the Caribbean ports were notified by mail of the Department's instruction to this office and the action of this Consulate. Letters were sent to the Chief Immigration Offiicer at Cristobal, C.Z. through the Masters of the "Sixaola" and "Coronado", respectively, advising him fully in the matter.

The American Consulate General at Panama was this day cabled to in the matter with request that the Immigration authorities of the Canal Zone be advised of Garvey's sailing on the "Coronado" and possible attempt to land at Cristobal. I have the honor to be, Sir, Your obedient servant,

C. L. LATHAM
American Consul

[*Endorsements*] File LAW H/s London MID
DJ 5/16/21

DNA, RG 59, file 811.108 G 191/8. TLS on printed form. Handwritten endorsements. A copy of the dispatch was transmitted by the State Department to Brig. Gen. Dennis E. Nolan of MID on 16 May 1921 (DNA, RG 165, file 10218-418/14).

William L. Hurley to J. Edgar Hoover

[Washington, D.C.] April 13, 1921

Dear Mr. Hoover:

Please refer to your letter of March 30, 1921, and previous correspondence concerning MARCUS GARVEY.

I have recently been advised by the Consulate at Kingston that a visa was refused Garvey for the Canal Zone. He was to have sailed from Kingston on April 12 on the s.s. CORONADO touching at Cristobal. His passage was paid to Port Limón. The Consul General at Panama has been advised in case Garvey may attempt to land at the Canal Zone. His activities while in Kingston indicate that he would arouse considerable racial antagonism among the negroes at the Canal Zone and in the Republic of Panama.

Similar information is being furnished M.I.D. Very truly yours,

W[ILLIAM]. L. H[URLEY].

DNA, RG 165, file 10218-418-3. TMI, carbon copy.

Gabriel M. Johnson to the UNIA

[*Monrovia, Liberia, 14 April 1921*]

In accordance with our telegram 24th day of March, we must have $5000 at once and $5000 about middle of May. Please expedite. Please pay [*Emily Christmas*] Kinch in future according to arrangement. Please inform Ellegor the goods cannot be traced as being shipped Nassy; please make inquiry about it.

JOHNSON

DNA, RG 165, file 10218-261-78. TG (coded).

Walter C. Thurston to Charles Evans Hughes

San José, CR. April 15, 1921

Marcus Garvey, negro leader, has arrived at San José.

[WALTER C.] THURSTON[1]

[*Endorsements*] file LAW noted H/S MID DJ
London 4/20/21 MEF

DNA, RG 59, file 811.108 G 191/7. TL, recipient's copy. Handwritten endorsements.

1. Walter C. Thurston (b. 1894) was the first secretary of the American Embassy at Costa Rica (U.S. Department of State, *Register*, 1924 [Washington, D.C.: GPO, 1924], p. 197). The information in the cable was furnished by the State Department's William L. Hurley to Brig. Gen. Dennis E. Nolan of MID (DNA, RG 165, file 10218-418/5).

Stewart E. McMillin, American Consul, to H. Boschen, Manager Agent, United Fruit Company, Port Limón, Costa Rica

Port Limón, Costa Rica, April 16, 1921

In pursuance of instructions received[,] Consul Guyant[1] at San José has just informed me by telephone, through Vice Consul [Thurston?], that he must refuse to visé the passport of Marcus Garvey, [negro?] race agitator now in Costa Rica, for entry into the United [States] and the Canal Zone. At his request I have also promised [not to] visé his passport.

You are being informed of this matter at the request of the San José office. Very truly yours,

STEWART E. MCMILLIN,[2]
American Consul

DNA, RG 84. TL, carbon copy.

1. Claude E. Guyant (b. 1886) was assigned to the American Consulate at San José, Costa Rica, in October 1920 (U.S. Department of State, *Register*, 1924 [Washington, D.C.: GPO, 1924], p. 134).

2. Stewart E. McMillin (b. 1889) became U.S. consul at Port Limón, Costa Rica, in September 1919 (U.S. Department of State, *Register*, 1924, p. 159).

Elie Garcia to Gabriel M. Johnson

[*New York, 17 April 1921*]

Cash in six days.

GARCIA

DNA, RG 165, file 10218-261-78. TG (coded).

Walter C. Thurston to Charles Evans Hughes

San José [*Costa Rica*] April 19th, 1921

Please instruct me at once whether or not Marcus Garvey may be aided in entering Panama. He desired Panaman[ian] visa from Consul McMillin at Port Limón who holds Panama consular representation.

THURSTON

[*Endorsements*] Tel. Ans. 4/20/21
J. P[reston]. D[oughten].[1]-ES File

DNA, RG 59, file 811.108 G 191/9. TL, recipient's copy. Handwritten endorsements.

1. J. Preston Doughten (b. 1886) was a career employee of the Department of State, serving in various consular posts before he became attached to the Visa Office. He subsequently became the chief of the Visa Office, on 20 December 1921 (U.S. Department of State, *Register*, 1924 [Washington, D.C.: GPO, 1924], p. 119).

Memorandum from the Military Intelligence Division

[*Port Limón*] Costa Rica April 21, 1921

SUBJECT: COSTA RICA. ECONOMIC.

No. 87.

Marcus Garvey, negro leader, desires to go from Limón to Panama. The Panaman[ian] archives are now in the hands of the American Consul at that port. Garvey must wait in Limón, pending instructions from the State Department, Washington, as to whether he is to be aided in entering Panama.

DNA, RG 165, file 10218-418-10. TM, carbon copy.

Article by William Pickens

[*New York Dispatch*, 22 April 1921]

GARVEY AND THE REST OF US

Marcus Garvey, Provisional President of Africa, is now in the West Indies somewhere, and there is talk of excluding him permanently from the United States, as "an undesirable alien." Some colored folk who do not agree with Garveyism may make the pitiable mistake of sympathizing with an effort to exclude Garvey. They may forget that when it comes down to the question of human rights, of the rights of a black man to go and come in the world so long as he obeys the laws of the land; they may forget that when it comes down to the question of common rights, we are all inseparably linked with Garvey and he with us.

Garvey has lived here for many years, and unless he has committed crimes against society here, no colored man of ordinary self-respect and of brains will abet any efforts of anybody to "exclude him" as an undesirable alien. That generality has worked a lot of injustice to white people already. There is no reason why colored people should countenance it. We are always likely, however, to make the mistake of rejoicing when an injustice is done to our enemy opponent—forgetting that whatever wrong is done another man can be done to any of us. It would be just as sensible for us to rejoice when a mob burns a Negro that we do not personally like or who happens to be our rival in some way. A few people have no more brains than that.

We may disagree with some of Garvey's ideas, but we are not a coward, and do not seek a coward's advantage. Some white people, however, are very cunning; they write long magazine articles about Mr. Garvey, and tell many lies and make many exaggerations about his work and the holdings and doings of colored people—not altogether calculated to help either Garvey or the colored people—and when they really turn in the dark and show what they really intend by an effort to take advantage of both Garvey and the rest of us. Some of us have had sense enough to know that much of what has been appearing in certain magazines and papers was not really meant to HELP but to HURT. They have hoped that by exaggerating certain oddities and pecularities of "Garveyism," they would really do great harm to certain other movements of the American Negro, of which they are far more afraid than they will ever be of an attack upon Africa. It is like military trickery: they hoped by directing attention to what they think is a futile attack upon AFRICA, that they will thereby divert energy from what they fear one hundredfold more—the attack upon the Barbarians of Texas, the slave system of Georgia and the Cannibalisms of Arkansas.

And now they show their real hand by making suggestions to "keep Garvey out," and they expect the rest of us Negroes to be such poor fools as to join in and help at this stage of the scheme. We won't do it. We will rather fight for Garvey's right as a citizen of the world and as a property holder and accredited resident of the United States, to go and come at his will. We are tired of being inveigled into fighting each other in the interest of our REAL COMMON ENEMY. We won't be fooled both ways.

Printed in the *New York Dispatch*, 22 April 1921.

Capt. Adrian Richardson to the Black Star Line, New York Office

Havana April 23, 1921

Burkley[1] and the engineer[2] has balled up everything[.] Coal bill and repair have to be paid before I can sail[.] For God sake send it[.] Need three thousand more[.] Answer[.]

RICHARDSON

Garvey v. *United States*, no. 8317, Ct. App., 2d Cir., 2 February 1925, defendant's exhibit GG. TG.

1. A. G. Buckley, traffic manager of the BSL in Cuba ("A Rousing Sunday Night at Havana," *NW*, 19 February 1921); see also " 'Antonio Maceo' Arrives in Cuba in Blaze of Glory; High Cuban Officials Go on Board Ship and Heartily Welcome Officials of U.N.I.A. Aboard," *NW*, 30 April 1921. The *Kanawha* arrived at Havana on 9 April 1921.

2. Charles C. Harris received his license (serial no. 93432) as chief engineer from the U.S. local inspectors at Providence, R.I., on 25 June 1921, subsequent to his employment on the S.S. *Kanawha*. His address at that time was given as 3 Masterson Street, Pawtucket, R.I.

Report by Bureau Agent Claude P. Light

Louisville, Ky. Apr. 23 [*1921*]

The Black Star Line—Marcus Garvey & U.N.I.Assn.

Information was received from a confidential informant that a conference was held by I. Willis Cole,[1] editor of the Louisville Leader (Colored man's paper), during the first part of March with a negro named Rev. J. A. WILSON (D.D.) of New York City, personal representative of MARCUS GARVEY. Cole reports that Garvey was said to intend to visit Louisville in interest of his ten million dollar steamship line which was to represent the capital and executive genius of colored men. Rev. Wilson was selling shares of stock in the Black Belt [*Star*] Line at $5.00 per share and reported some success. A local negro preacher named Rev. Andrew W. Thompson, pastor of the Church of the Living God, 1821 W. Walnut St., took an active interest in the matter and it was announced that meetings would be held at his church every Sunday afternoon at 5:30 P.M. They reported stea[m]ers running between Jamaica, Garvey's home, and the West Indies, Liberia and Monrovia. They expect soon to have money enough to get a steamer to ply between New York and Jamaica.

Rev. Wilson left about the 8th of March saying he would return in a few weeks but no information of such return has been received. Meetings are reported at this church but no radical activity is complained of. The Nat. Assn. for the Imp. of the Colored Race is rather strong here and is discouraging the movement.

CLAUDE P. LIGHT

[*Endorsements*] NOTED F. D. W.
FILE G. F. R.

DNA, RG 65, file BS 198940-131. TD. Copies of this report were furnished to the bureau's Washington, D.C., office. Stamped endorsements.

1. I. Willis Cole (b. 1887), born in Memphis, Tenn., established the I. Willis Cole Publishing Co. and the *Louisville Leader*, a small black weekly, in 1917. By 1926 the paper had a circulation of twenty thousand. Cole also served as regional director of the National Negro Business League and honorary delegate to the Republican national conventions of 1920, 1924, 1928, and 1932. In 1921 he ran unsuccessfully for the state senate on the black Lincoln party ticket (*WWCA*).

Report by Bureau Agent H. B. Pierce

[*Los Angeles*] April 25, 1921

NEGRO ACTIVITIES

UNIVERSAL NEGRO IMPROVEMENT ASSOCIATION:

DR. J. D. GORDON, Vice President-General of the U.N.I.A., is in Los Angeles in an endeavor to heal the split in the U.N.I.A. between the Radical and Conservative wings, and, incidentally, raise $20,000 for the Black Star Line.

He spoke at a meeting of negroes April 17th in Los Angeles. About 1800 were present. 125 new members were enrolled in the Local U.N.I.A. and he has raised between 3 and 5 thousand dollars. He advised the U.N.I.A. to continue under the leadership of NOAH WEBSTER [*Thompson*], but advised WEBSTER and his following to be a little more radical.

(COMMENT:—Perhaps the raising of the $20,000 had something to do with the upholding of WEBSTER, as most of the well-to-do negroes are of his faction[.])

According to confidential informant who attended the meeting, in his speech he advised his hearers not to countenance or assist the Anti-Alien Land Law[1] and Anti-Japanese Movement. He said the Japanese are our best friends because they injected into the peace conference the equality of races, without regard to color, and now this country is trying to prevent them having what they won and the allies gave them. (The Island of Yap).[2]

H. B. PIERCE

DNA, RG 65, file BS 202600-5. TD.

1. The Alien Land Act of 1920 was designed to plug the loopholes in the previous act of 1913 by prohibiting any further transfer of land by any corporation in which Japanese held a majority of the stock. The act proved largely ineffective, and parts of it were eventually declared unconstitutional (Roger Daniels, *The Politics of Prejudice* [Berkeley and Los Angeles: University of California Press, 1962]).

2. The Micronesian island of Yap in the western Pacific Ocean was sold to Germany by Spain in 1899 and transferred to Japan in 1919 as a League of Nations mandate. It became the subject of a dispute between Japan and the United States in 1919 and 1920, but this was settled by an agreement concerning cable rights at the Conference on the Limitation of Armaments held in Washington in 1921 (*EA*).

Capt. Adrian Richardson to the Black Star Line, New York Office

Havana April 25 1921

Burkley in Santiago[.] I can do nothing[.] Have no money to wire Garvey[.]

RICHARDSON

Garvey v. *United States*, no. 8317, Ct. App., 2d Cir., 2 February 1925, defendant's exhibit GG. TG.

O. M. Thompson to Marcus Garvey

[*New York, ca. 25 April 1921*]

Wire Havana three thousand[.] Situation desperate[.] First instalment Phyllis Wheatley paid[.][1] Delivery May twenty fifth[.][2]

THOMPSON

[*Address*] Garvey, care of C H Bryant, Port Limón, Costa Rica.

Garvey v. *United States*, no. 8317, Ct. App., 2d Cir., 2 February 1925, defendant's exhibit GG. TG.

1. The Black Star Line announced the imminent purchase of a ship for the transatlantic African route, which was to be renamed the *Phyllis Wheatley*. The ship to be purchased, the *Hong Kheng*, was in dry dock in Greece at the time. The Black Star Steamship Co. of New Jersey, formed in October 1920, would represent the BSL as the purchaser, and A. Rudolph Silverston, a white man who headed his own brokerage company, the New York Ship Exchange, would be the company's agent. Silverston agreed to purchase a ship from the United States Shipping Board for $200,000 and to sell it on credit to the Black Star Line for $325,000. Silverston required the Black Star Line to produce $25,000 as the down payment on the ship by 16 April 1921. According to BSL records, payments to Silverston began on 11 March and were as follows:

$500	11 March 1921
$1,200	21 March 1921
$2,000	8 April 1921
$15,000	19 April 1921
$1,300	19 April 1921
$5,000	18 June 1921
$25,000	

On 23 April the BSL signed a contract with the U.S. Shipping Board to purchase the *Hong Kheng*, but shortly thereafter Elie Garcia, BSL secretary, learned that the ship would not be delivered within the expected sixty days. The BSL Board of Directors quickly decided to drop negotiations for the *Hong Kheng* and to begin negotiations for the *Orion*, a ship that Silverston had found in the meantime (*Marcus Garvey* v. *United States*, no. 8317, Ct. App., 2nd Cir., 2 February 1925, pp. 1,766–1,783 and 2,042–2,052; DJ-FBI, Thomas P. Merrilees, "Summary Report of Investigation of the Books of the Black Star Line, Inc.," pp. 36–37).
2. The negotiations for the *Orion* were never successfully completed.

Marcus Garvey to the Black Star Line, New York Office

[*Colón, Panama*] Apl 25 1921

To which individual must I cable money Havana[?] [R]eply Colón[.]

GARVEY

Garvey v. *United States*, no. 8317, Ct. App., 2d Cir., 2 February 1925, defendant's exhibit GG. TG (sent via New Orleans).

O. M. Thompson to Marcus Garvey

[*New York*] April 26, 1921

Cable money Captain Richardson Slib [*Black Star Line*] Havana[.]

THOMPSON

Garvey v. *United States*, no. 8317, Ct. App., 2d Cir., 2 February 1925, defendant's exhibit GG. TG.

O. M. Thompson to the Black Star Line, Havana

[*New York, 26 April 1921*]

Get money Garvey Jamaica[.]

THOMPSON

Garvey v. *United States*, no. 8317, Ct. App., 2d Cir., 2 February 1925, defendant's exhibit GG. TG.

O. M. Thompson to Capt. Adrian Richardson

[*New York*] April 26th, 1921

Garvey sending money from Colón[.] Prepare to clear[.][1] Inform when money received[.]

THOMPSON

Garvey v. *United States*, no. 8317, Ct. App., 2d Cir., 2 February 1925, defendant's exhibit GG. TG.

1. The *Kanawha* was further delayed and did not arrive at Kingston, Jamaica, until 17 May 1921.

Charles Evans Hughes to the American Legation, San José, Costa Rica

Washington, April 26, 1921

Refuse aid in securing visa for Marcus Garvey. Inform Port Limón.

[CHARLES EVANS] HUGHES

[*Handwritten endorsements*] Green U. H.
W[*illiam*]. L. H[*urley*].
J. P[*reston*]. D[*oughten*].
[*Stamped endorsement*] *Signed by*
A. A. Adee

DNA, RG 59, file 811.108 G 191/9. TL, carbon copy.

Report by Special Agent P-138

New York City 4/26/21

IN RE: NEGRO ACTIVITIES

Garvey's adherents and chief officials continue to meet every night at Liberty Hall and discuss the racial question.

Of course, the crowds are not large, except on Sunday nights when they come out to hear whether there is any letters or cables from Garvey. Apart from this fact, the great amount of enthusiasm has dwindled down considerably since Garvey's departure. His propagandists are still scattered over the country. Among the most prominent is Vernon [*Vernal*] Williams, a negro law student who is stationed permanently in Washington, D.C., with headquarters in the Whitelaw Hotel. Respectfully,

P-138

[*Endorsements*] FILE G. F. R. NOTED F. D. W.

DNA, RG 65, file BS 198940-122. TD. Stamped endorsements.

Marcus Garvey to the Black Star Line, New York Office

Colón April 27th [*1921*]

Have sent three thousand to Richardson to clear to Jamaica[.]

GARVEY

Garvey v. *United States*, no. 8317, Ct. App., 2d Cir., 2 February 1925, defendant's exhibit GG. TG.

Speeches by Marcus Garvey at Colón, Panama

Labor Union Hall, Colón, April 27, 1921

FIRST MEETING HELD IN COLÓN

President, Officers, members and friends of this Association—I am pleased to meet you here in this, our hall, for the first time, and I am glad of this opportunity, as I intend to tell you the reason and object of my being here from the United States of America. My aim and object is to improve the Negro Association and to bring four hundred million negroes together to build a nation and an Empire of our own. I will further state that I am appointed as Provisional President of Africa, and I am doing my best to improve the nation so that we will join hands and redeem our mother-land, Africa. You may remember that four years ago we started with only a few, and now we are four million strong, so you see, brothers and sisters, we are well organized. If you think I am not telling the truth, let any man touch a member of the U.N.I.A. Let me tell you, dear people, that the governments are all my friends. I have nothing against them, and no personal ill-feeling for anyone, but I want to have what is mine, and I am claiming my rights.

I will further tell you that all Europe is trembling today over our movements, in fact all the Governments of the entire world. You can see that they are so scared of me that they do not want me to land in certain parts—but the more they look the less they see. We will let them know that the Negro Association stands this time for good, and that this race of negroes is not going to give up, for we now have our backbone. Gentlemen, Europe for the White, China for the Chinese—then I can say, brothers, that Africa is for the Africans and we must get what is ours. We are not offering any fight but we say we must get our belongings. Remember we did not sell Africa—we were taken away from there three hundred years ago. At least 30 million negroes were robbed of their fatherland, were fooled by the white people when they said they were bringing about civilization. We thank them if they

368

.

have done any good for us but now we are civilized we want what was taken from us for we can take care of ourselves. We know the world will criti[c]ize us and they will say a lot of things about us, but we don't care, we are going strong because we are united. You won[']t be surprised to know that today all the Governments all over the world are taking their hats off to us. God placed and made you with the object of making yourselves men and women, and besides that you were made a race and also a nation, so you see now we have nothing to do with anyone but to look out for ourselves, and the only way we can make ourselves right is by going back to our fatherland. I am not going to allow people who don't like me to rule me—I must rule myself or be ruled by someone of my own race. I am tired of that sort of business. My father and grandfather stood for ruling. White men ruled us for three hundred years. Now we are not going to beg them but we are going to rule ourselves. I will tell you this—white is for white, red for red, yellow for yellow, and now I say negroes for negroes.

A few years ago in the European conflict, had it not been for the negroes the German[s] would be laughing at them today, so you see that since we can fight, we won't fight for anybody anymore but we will fight for ourselves when we get to Africa. I met all I had been looking for in all parts of the world. They did all kinds of things to me—they laughed at me—but now I am laughing at someone. Remember we are not going to cut the cane nor plant the bananas anymore—we are going to our fatherland. Don't worry about me—if they try to keep me out of the United States, or any part of the world, there are about two thousand Marcus Garveys left, so you see we are playing their own game. In days gone by anyone could leave gold or diamonds in the streets or waysides of Africa and it would remain there for months, but since the white man took the negroes as slaves to do as they liked with them they learned to do everything that is wrong.

Now brothers and sisters, as I am about to close let me say to you that we are going strong, and about the end of this month or the first of next month our next ship will be launched—her name is the "Felix Witney" [*Phyllis Wheatley*] and she will leave direct for Liberia, Africa, taking our own machines and our own engineers to do the work, and within a few months from then she will be here also to take passengers for our native land. Now we want two million dollars to build ourselves and to make a nation, and the only way we can do that is to subscribe to the cause. It is no use going back—we must go ahead. If we stop they are going to laugh at us.

Now I am going to close and before I do so I want to see about ten of you people come right up here to this table where my Secretary is sitting and buy yourselves all the shares you can. Each share costs five dollars, and the more you buy the better it will assist and help the cause. My next meeting will be called at 8 P.M. during which time I will be able to say more about Africa and our Black Star Line Co., so good-bye until later, but you must remain and buy your shares at the table.

DNA, RG 165, file 10218-418-21. TD.

Colón, April 27, 1921

Second Meeting Held at the Universal Negro Improvement Association Hall

Officers, Members and Friends—I am pleased to be in your midst, as a representative of the negro race. Please allow me to inform you that I am here from the United States of America for a cause, aim and object—and that is to organize 40 million Africans to blast and fight for their rights in Africa. I am not a preacher—neither am I a politician. I am not here to criticize Panama nor any Government whatsoever but I am only here to show to you dear people that I want a square deal and I must have it, or I am going to fight for it. All over the world they call me a Radical, and I like that for when people can't do as they like with you they call you all kinds of names. I am a radical, but do you know what for? Because I fight for my rights. Brothers, I am one of those men who believes much in the new doctrine—that is, if a man hits me on the right jaw I am going to hit him on the left, irrespective of who he is, and I am sure that I am going to hit him above the belt. I am not here to speak to Christians, but to New Negroes, and let me tell you that I have no objection to traveling with you on the roads going to Africa, but you do the praying and I will do the work and the fighting. My job is to build a nation and an Empire. I am not going to stand for that sort of thing—seeing you people going to plant bananas, cut cane, and all kinds and sorts of things. You go to Africa and do what you can down there. I say you won't have to dig any more Canals if you now get together and help the Universal Negro Improvement Association. We want you now to build your own Empire and let me tell you again that we are not going to beg for what we want, but we are going to have what is ours. Now brothers, just think, our Organization is only four years old and we have 700 branches all over the world, that is, in the West Indies, South and Central America and other parts of the world. There are right now, today, forty million negroes gathering in Africa so why not do for yourselves wh[a]t you should do. Do you remember the great War in Europe a few years ago—do you remember how the white men tried all they could to stop the Germans and could not succeed until they decided to send the negroes, who, without doubt, did win the World War[?] The white men have been tal[k]ing for several years now and we don't want them to talk for us any more—we are going to talk for ourselves—we are going to make ourselves Officers. You people had a bad principle and that is, to be loyal to someone and not to yourselves. First start your loyalty at home. I am not going to give the pick and shovel to my boy and girl. Now you can see that all the white man does is to build great empires; they are lords, and we, the negroes, do nothing but cut bananas and plant cane—anyhow, better late than never. We are not going to apologize to anyone. Some of you may be timid of Great Britain—now let me tell you, my belief is that the white man has no right to rule me. The Englishman sings "Rule Britan[n]ia," now we are going to sing, "Rule Eth[i]opia." Ethiopia never shall be slaves. Now brothers, let me tell you something—I have no objection to becoming a citizen provided you will let me go fifty-fifty. That is, if I go to England I must be elected or nominated Pr[emier] of England. No man can place a limit over my ambition. Let me work out my destiny according to my ambition. If any man tries such things with me he will say he is my master after five rounds. Don't let the Whites bluff you; let him deliver the goods. There are two kinds of negroes, the Old and the New Negroes. The Old were buried in 1914, and I am here now in Colón to dig up those who are practically dead, and make them new. Dear people, I am not doing this to stir up strife, but because we love ourselves. All nations in the world have theirs and we, the negroes, must get our empire. We won't nor do we intend to trouble the President of any Empire or country, neither do we want them to trouble us. We are only trying to go to Africa and help those who want help there. The other day, say a few months ago, I nearly lost my life in the U.S.A., but I can say, Thank God it was not my time to die. I hope when the next war comes I shall be in Africa and not in Europe. Your forefathers and mine danced the tread-mill in all parts of the world where they were taken as slaves. Don't forget that you too were slaves, but we won't always be slaves, we won't be slaves anymore, we will be back in Africa. Again I say, don't think me radical. My radicalness is only because I want a change. For 31 days and 31 nights in the month of August last year we were engaged in making the constitution, the same that governs you today. Once more let me tell you that all other nations respect this[,] the negro, a nation to themselves. Just think of it, Japan, America, England and all other nations have battleships— we too must have our own battleships, and let me say to you that before ten years pass we shall have the largest and best battleship afloat. I will not stop until I invent all the implements that our nation should have. The boys born, including myself, never came into this world with any box of war implements. Now if I were to find myself between two white boys and we grow up to be men and I see them with guns and ammunition and I have none, brother I am gone, I am not going to take a chance. You negro women, you don't appreciate yourselves; if so you would not be scrubbing the white women's floors.

I thank you for your splendid support and your aid in behalf of the Black Star Line Co. We are improving wonderfully because we believe in God. Now brothers, remember I told you that next month our ships will be going to Liberia. Now at the end of this meeting I want you to come and buy your shares; remember I told you they cost each five dollars, and you can buy as many as you want. Now I can tell you that you will get an interest of 5% and I am sure that no bank pays you that amount. Now I say, start with me right now. I want two million dollars to support our cause and build our nation. As I said, our first set of men have gone down and we want to support them and pay them while they are making good there, so it is your duty to come across and do your best. Those of you who can't buy tonight can come tomorrow to Dr. Hamlet's residence where you can buy the shares you want.

DNA, RG 165, file 10218-418-20. TD.

COLÓN, April 28, 1921

THIRD MEETING HELD IN
OPEN LOT IN COLÓN

Ladies, gentlemen and children, I am indeed glad to be in your midst once more and to tell you that I am here from the United States of America to swell the cause and rights of the negro race. As I see the flying banners of our race and the sons and daughters of mothers and fathers it gives me more impetus to go ahead with my noble work. Let me say to you that I am going to fight to the last. I don't intend to give up and I know that you will stand by me and soon, very soon, I shall see these spangling banners with the colors Red, Black and Green flying on the highest mountain in Africa. I must say that in all my travels among the West Indies, South and Central American ports[,] Colón has flagged the field for the kind assistance and attendance of the school children and I only hope that you all will continue your noble work so that in later years you may not only be in Liberia but you may be the wives of some of the great lords and husbands of some of the princesses of this great nation. I give you my hearty thanks and hope to see you tonight at the Hall, as usual at 7:30 where I will tell you something more about our cause and nation. So after the Anthem is sung you can retire to your respective homes until 7:30, God bless you.

DNA, RG 165, file 10218-418-19. TD.

COLÓN, April 28, 1921

FOURTH MEETING HELD IN
UNIVERSAL NEGRO IMPROVEMENT ASSOCIATION HALL

Mr. President, Officers, members and visiting friends, Again I am glad to see you, and I must give you thanks for your kind attendance and attention. This may be my last public meeting as tomorrow night I shall hold a meeting for the members alone, which will be private. There will be quite a lot to discuss as regards our aims and objects in the improvement of our nation. We want to build a nation of our own and a language of our own. A few years ago the world took everything I said and did as a joke, but now that they see everything is on foot, brothers, don't you think they are trembling now? So you can see, we are playing their own game, and at the same time we are holding our own. About 145 years ago the leaders of revolution in the U.S.A. succeeded. We may not have one government to fight[,] for they are all looking at us, but remember we are four millions strong. We do not care what others may say—"Give me Liberty or Give me Death." We are going forward and not backward. We must find liberty, and we can find it nowhere else but in Liberia and under the flag of the negroes. Now brothers, let me tell you that in all parts of the world where I go I find the negroes pulling against each other, Jamaicans against Barbadians, Trinidadians against St. Lucians, and all the negroes against each other—even in the United States the negro Americans against the West Indian negroes. You know why— because we were not organized. Do now or die—I started four years ago and I am not dead yet, and allow me to tell you, brothers, that I mean to go ahead until I die. If they put me in prison, if they put me on the gallows, if they cut my head off, it is all the same to me, but I mean it from the bottom of my heart and soul and everything in me, I am not going to stop until I get what I want, and that is what is mine; that is, my rights that have been taken from me. Now in the U.S.A. we have thousands of people of our race organized, and I have come to Colón to get you to organize and that you should stop clamoring at each other on account of where you are from. I must say that the place where I was born was not the place I should have chosen, it was an accident there, I should have been born in Africa but as it has happened so I will bring it about myself. The Scriptures say so and now I am born again. We are speaking of a new birth. Some of you still love England—my mother never came from there. Those fellows make a joke at me when they ask me if I am not going to my mother's country, England. We have to fight a hard battle—I don't mean with the white men but with the fellows of our own ranks and color. I mean the black-whites, brown-whites. The whitest man I met in Jamaica was as black as my coat. I will tell you something that is true, there are some of our own race who call themselves aristocrats because they wear fine pairs of shoes and fine cut pants; others because they buy an automobile. They pull themselves away from us and call themselves aristo- crats, but don't mind them, they will come here soon. In ages gone by the Great Duke of Cumberland and several others who had great honors were called lords. I will tell you how they got such great names—they gave their services to swindling the rights of others. They did succeed and that is where their nobility came from. You men of service in scientific affairs, we will give you a Cross of Africa—not a St. George's Cross. They, the whites, stole what they got. The poor black man who did not steal and won't steal[,] he is the aristocrat. For the last 83 years the preachers have been getting rich out of us—now they are not going to get any more out of us for we are not going to pay any more homage to them. I am not against a man for his color, but for his injustice. I admire the white man's spirit for he boosts for race and nation. The white man dies for his color and his race but the negro he will die for any flag rather than his own, and sings, "Rule Britan[n]ia". Churchill said no negro is competent to rule himself. Now we have been waiting for 83 years—brother[,] I can't wait any longer. I am going to do for myself.

Now I will tell you about three boys who went to school—one was white, one brown and the other one black. The black one was Marcus Garvey. All were trained the same way and we all came out at the top in the examinations. The white boy went to Europe, the brown one to Japan and I went back to Africa. We are four hundred million strong—better late than never. The race is not for the swift nor the strong but for him who endures to the end. The first shall be the last and the last shall be first. I love myself first. If I give help to someone when I need it for myself then something must be wrong in my upper story. You know what the preacher says—he says, wait, treasures are up there. I have no objection to going with him if he will let me go half and half. God made you, he gave you the seas, and the lands—they are yours. Now I will ask you, if I have twenty shillings or twenty dollars and you were all broke and I should give each of you a share and one of you let another take away your share and then you come back to me for more money—Brother, I would drive you away and tell you to go and hold the fellow and take away what is yours.

Now things are getting serious. We are in the last stages of human development. England, Germany and all the other great powers took Africa away from you while you were sleeping. God is good to you. Now help yourselves. Now suppose there is one spot of land where one man can stand and it is his and several others want to stand there—there is going to be war. Brothers[,] that is what is going to happen. Now you get ready for the other fellow. Don't mind the ring that is dancing around you but get ready and hit him always over the belt. You negroes have dug the Panama Canal—you have joined two oceans—now you are not going to dig anymore Canals. Rise in your manhood, you men and women, with hopes for achievement. I have a job now until I die and that is to work for the redemption of Africa, all my life for the freedom of my race and country.

I know that through sacrifice some of us must die, but remember all won't die. Where I die let me die. If I live, then let me live free. Leaders, prepare to pay the price of leaders. Remember Patrick Henry's words, he says, "Liberty or death." I only hope that after awhile I shall see someone of you who sit[s] here as President of Africa. Now remember that your mind makes you what you are. It is your chance, so catch it right now. I hope to teach some of those white guys a lesson and I am going to do it too. Now, tomorrow night at 8 o'clock we will have a meeting here for the charter members; also for C. Moore Branch at 3:00 P.M., where if anyone has any troubles or worries I shall settle same.

Our S.S. Messio [*Antonio Maceo*] will arrive here within seven or eight days time and she will take passengers between Colón, Jamaica, Costa Rica and Cuba. The S.S. Yamo [*Yarmouth*] is now on dock but as soon as she is off she will also take passengers between Colón, Jamaica and Cuba. Our boats will also go direct from here to Liberia, so that those of you who want to go will have the direct line.

Now I want you to do your best and buy all the shares you can to swell our cause. In regard to buying of shares and bonds, I will now take the honor of pinning this silver emblem, a medal of honor, on Mr. and Brother John Wilcher who has bought the first hundred dollar bond for and in aid of the liberation of his suffering race. And Sir, may you wear it not only for its beauty but as an honor confer[r]ed on you for your noble works on behalf of humanity.

All who would like to make your loan and buy your bonds come right to the table here and spend half an hour after we dismiss and you will be attended by my Secretary. Now we will close, wishing you God Speed until Wednesday night when I will give you my farewell meeting. I intend to go to Panama on Saturday so you won[']t see me before Wednesday. Good night, brothers, sisters and friends.

DNA, RG 165, file 10218-418-18. TD.

Gabriel M. Johnson to the UNIA

[*Monrovia, Liberia, 28 April 1921*]

We are entirely without money. Operations compelled to stop. Telegraph immediately the total amount. Please pay Mrs. Crichlow $40 monthly additional from 15th day of May.

JOHNSON

DNA, RG 165, file 10218-261-78. TG (coded).

George Washington to Harry Daugherty, Attorney General[1]

615 Thomas St., Key West, Fla[.]
Apr[.] 28th [19]21

Sir:

I am writing you to inform you of an alien organization which is disseminating bolshevick prop[a]ganda throughout this country amongst Negroes and especially so in this city of Key West, this organization is known as the U.N.I.A. and has for its leader an alien by the name of Marcus Garvey[.] After careful investigation I have found out that this organization is in Lea[gu]e with some Japanese who are behind of this propaganda against our Government in this city, I am asking that you send to this city at once some Government investigators in order that they may run down these West Indie[s] Aliens that are connected with this organization as they are fomenting a lot of unrest amongst i[gn]orant negroes in this city against our government, and most of these negroes that are members of this organization in this city are employed by our government at the U.S. Naval Station in this city without Even being citizens of this country, while the[re] are a number of loyal Americans[,] many Ex service men walking the streets without any work to do[.] The head of this organization in this city is a Mr[.] Glashen who recently came here from the West Indies and organized this organization in this city, other prominent members are Edward Roberts[,] A. J. Kershaw[,] Charles Dixon[,] a Rev. Edmonds[,] Samuel Mounts[,] Edwin Heil[,] Dewey Finder[,] Anthony Sawyer[,] James Andrews, these are just a few of the names of 500 members that compose this organization in this city, these people are displaying a red[,] black and green flag[;] this they hoist on a mast at their meetings, and each of them are wearing in the lapels of their coats an emblem of their flag and going around Preaching to other Negroes that it is the only flag that they honor. [N]ow sir I think that it is time that the U.S. gov[er]nment take some steps to make these aliens bolshiveicks no [*know*] that this is America and that they will have to stop this kind of prop[a]ganda in this country and respect American Institutes. [H]ere I want to give you the name of two men identified with this organization, one a watchman at the Naval Station and the other a mail carrier at the local office[:] Joseph Wake watchman[,] S. D. Leggett mail carrier[.] As a good loyal American I have did my duty and hope that you will do yours by sending investigators to the city at once and put down this Alien Prop[a]ganda in our city[.] Yours Resp[,]

GEO. WASHINGTON

[*Endorsements*] Mr. Baley Ack & Jacksonville 5/19/21 GFR FILE G. F. R.
NOTED F. D. W.

DNA, RG 60, file 198940-123. TLS, recipient's copy. Handwritten endorsements.

1. Harry Micajah Daugherty (1860–1941) was attorney general in the Harding administration; he held that position until President Calvin Coolidge forced him to resign in 1924 as a result of the Teapot Dome scandal (*NYT*, 13 October 1941; Burl Noggle, *Teapot Dome: Oil and Politics in the 1920s* [Baton Rouge: Louisiana State University Press, 1962]).

Report by Special Agent P-138

New York City 4/29/21

IN RE: NEGRO ACTIVITIES

I learned from Hudson Price, associate editor of the Negro World, that Johnson, a member of President King's Liberian Mission, has commenced to take an active part in Garvey's Association. He spoke at a meeting of the Philadelphia division of Garvey's Association last week.[1] Price is expecting Johnson to speak before the Association at Liberty Hall within the next few weeks.

Conditions are "O.K." with no sign of foreign interference. Respectfully,

P-138

[*Endorsements*] FILE G. F. R.
NOTED F. D. W.

DNA, RG 65, file BS 202600-667-41. TD. Stamped endorsements.

1. Johnson addressed a special mass meeting of the Philadelphia UNIA division in the Standard Theatre on 25 April 1921 (*NW*, 30 April 1921), the same meeting at which Maj. R. R. Wright, Sr., also spoke.

Walter C. Thurston to Stewart E. McMillin

[*San José*] Costa Rica [*29 April 1921*]

Have received instructions from Department not to facilitate travel Marcus Garvey. If he has not left do not visé his passport.

THURSTON

DNA, RG 84, file 840.1. TG, recipient's copy.

Stewart E. McMillin to Walter C. Thurston

Port Limón, Costa Rica, April 29, 1921

Sir:

Acknowledging receipt of your communication today I have to inform you that the subject of it left Costa Rica days ago without my assistance and under visé given him by the Panamanian Consul General in New York last February. I understand that a B.S. [*Black Star?*] boat will pick him up at Bocas and take him to the Canal Zone. I refused him a visa to Panama. I am, Sir, Your obedient servant,

STEWART E. McMILLIN
American Consul

DNA, RG 84, file 840.1. TLS, carbon copy.

Lt. Comdr. C. M. Hall to Rear Adm. M. Johnston[1]

15th Naval District, Colón, Canal Zone
29–30 Apr. 1921

Intelligence Report

Marcus Garvey, President of the Black Star Steamship Company and so called President of Africa and The Negro Republic arrived in Colón, Panama, on April 26 from Jamaica via Port Limón, Costa Rica. Six meetings under the auspices of The Universal Negro Improvement Association, all of which were well attended by the negroes of the Canal Zone and Panama, were addressed by Garvey between April 27 and April 30 on which date he left Colón for Panama City. . . .

All meetings were conducted with the great pomp and dignity necessary to impress the negro mind, but each speech was ended by Garvey's practically ordering those present to buy shares in his Steamship Company and there is no doubt but that he raised a great deal of money. At four of the meetings an admission fee of one dollar was charged.

There has been no evidence of unrest among the negroes since Garvey's appearance as many of them still remember how they were induced to strike on the Canal Zone a year ago when they not only lost the strike but lost all the money they had contributed toward the Union.

Several letters written by negroes have appeared in the local paper the past week in which the writers urge the blacks to continue as they are and not to spend their money foolishly on Garvey's schemes.[2]

[Lt. Commdr. C. M. Hall]

DNA, RG 165, file 10218-418-16. TD, carbon copy.

1. Marbury Johnston (1868–1934), a graduate of the United States Naval Academy, was appointed rear admiral in November 1918 (*WWWA*).
2. See the letter published in the *Panama Star & Herald*, 30 April 1921.

Elie Garcia to Gabriel M. Johnson

[*New York, 30 April 1921*]

Cabled $730 salaries 31st day of March.

Garcia

DNA, RG 165, file 10218-261-78. TG (coded).

Walter C. Thurston to Charles Evans Hughes

[*American Legation*]
San José, Costa Rica, May 2, 1921

Sir:

I have the honor to inform the Department that prior to the receipt of its instruction number 28 of April 26, 4 P.M., Marcus Garvey, the negro leader, had departed from Puerto Limón for Bocas del Toro, Panama. He entered Panama under a visa granted by the Panaman[ian] Consul at Boston.

So far as I have been able to ascertain Garvey did not conduct any radical propaganda while in Costa Rica, although he several times addressed the many negro laborers of the United Fruit Company. He was received by President Acosta,[1] who states he spoke to him only of the African Commonwealth he hopes to establish.

The General Manager of the United Fruit Company states that the voluntary and continued subscriptions in favor of Marcus Garvey, of the negro employees of that Company in Costa Rica are approximately $2,000 monthly, and it is reported from other sources that as a result of this personal visit he received over $30,000. I have the honor to be, Sir, Your obedient servant,

WALTER C. THURSTON

[*Endorsement*] MID DJ 5/23/21

DNA, RG 59, file 811.108 G 191/11. TLS, recipient's copy. Handwritten endorsement.

1. Julio Acosta (1872–1954) was president of Costa Rica from 1920 to 1924.

Speeches by Marcus Garvey in Panama

[Variedades Theatre, Panama City,
2 May 1921]

. . . Mr. Chairman, ladies and gentlemen:

Once more I have the good fortune to be in your midst and probably for the last time in Panama in speaking to you tonight. I desire to elaborate some more on the work of the association, which I have the honor to represent at this time. It has become a power and force. Its object is to unite 400,000,000 negroes scattered throughout the world. To establish a government second to none in the world; to protect negroes everywhere; to demand the respect of all races; to make them men among men. The U.N.I.A. and A.C.L., has an ambitious program and every member of the association is ambitious. We are fighting men and women. We have no use for cowards, but brave men and women, who will be prepared to die now for their freedom (cheers). The time has come when we must pray and work. We want men with broad minds and back bones. My father has been begging for 250 years and I am not prepared to beg not even one minute. If a man has that which is justly mine I will ask him for it, if he refuses to give it to me, I will take it that he is hard of hearing and ask him again in louder tones, then if he still retains it, I am going to pitch into him, for I am not responsible if he has lost one of his senses. I understand that there are some professional men here who say that we cannot achieve anything, but let me tell them, that this is a fighting association. They say we are a crazy lot of people. We are no more crazy than Britain a few centuries ago when she succeeded in defeating the Romans; than Washington when he gained the Independence of North America; than France when she established her own autonomy. We of the U.N.I.A. believe in the temporal law of man divided in race groups—white, yellow and black. If they say a government for Europe, a government for Asia, then we say a government for Africa. We believe in a new age—a "stand up and demanding age." Ask and demand and if you do not get it then fight for it and take it. Some are scared. We are not concerned about those who are scared. Cowardice ha[s] never done anything for any man or people. We have to fight until we get what is ours. Every coward is an enemy to the U.N.I.A. Sometimes he is the ordinary man, sometimes the middleman and sometimes the professional man. Some of them criticize me and they have never seen me. I do not want to see them. I have no use for them. I will pause right here and give 10 mins. to any man, whether he be a lawyer, doctor or a dentist, who has anything to say against this association. If he does not do so now, then he will hereafter keep his peace.

No one came forward and the speaker continued:

You professional men try to impede the progress of this movement, you are the lowest in the Negro family. We want men with back bone. Not men who are afraid of a white face. I have no apology to make for the aims of this association. The white man has nothing to apologize for. He is a national entity and power and I admire him for it. Why should you apologize to a God so powerful and good. You good for nothing negroes, are you afraid to stand up for your right and die if it becomes necessary? The Irish men are fighting for their independence. The Jews fought for a restored Palestine and they have succeeded in getting it. Negroes! shouted the speaker, have you not got sufficient proof to see that no other race will protect you. In Guatemala, Ecuador, Port Limón, you are ill treated. If they will not protect you, have you not got the common sense to protect yourselves? We want such a nature as to make any other man afraid of us. I repeat our program is an ambitious one. A man without ambition is not fit to live. We are ambitious men. What is good for the other fellow is good for us too. The other fellow has held on to things temporal. We want some of it too. If I refuse to live up to the requirements of civilization the police will take me to the calaboose. If organization is good enough for one man it is good enough for the other. If the other fellow need[s] food for the body and a home I need it too. I believe in civilization and whatsoever is belonging to it. I want some of it. There should be a consciousness of self. Why should you think you are inferior to some other man. You are insulting God. Why do you think you cannot go further. God never made you inferior. He alone demands that you bow down and worship Him. It is outside of your province to bow down and look up to any other man as supreme except the God of Heaven. I prefer to die, and every negro to die rather than to live and think that God created me as inferior to the white man.

Right here, Mr. Garvey with arms outstretched and looking heavenwards most earnestly and fervently said: "O God!—if thou created me inferior I do not want the life thou gavest me. I prefer to die now."

Continuing, he said:

Knowing myself as a man, I meet every man as a man and expect every man to meet me as a man. That silly, stupid talk of color must be destroyed. Why should you worship others because they are white. Before the white man became a national entity he was a savage, a pagan, a barbarous cannibal. When you were in palaces on the Nile in Egypt, Ancient Brit[o]ns were barbarous and filled with paganism, but through evolution of matter they came out of their barbarism. Fifty-five years before the birth of Christ when Rome swayed the world with her might and power the early Brit[o]ns were subjected to many attacks. Several Britishers were taken to Rome as slaves. As a result of the fall of Rome Britain got her full civilization. Now, they have a national anthem and they sing: "Britons, never, never shall be slaves."

The idea of the anthem brings to them that they were once slaves. The Negro failure is due to the fact that he forsakes his history. He has no guide for the future. No guide to posterity. The reason why I fight so tenaciously is because I know the history of the world and I have no compromise to make. I will only compromise with God. He speaks to me. He says: "Go on because I lead." (Some one shouted Allelulia.) The professional men say a Negro cannot lead. Do they expect some white man to lead[?] The white man took my father 4,000 miles and kept him as a slave 400 years. He was beaten and killed. You weak-kneed Negroes! shouted the speaker, there is a David Lloyd George, a Bonar Law and a Winston Churchill in England; a Clemenceau in France; a Ebert[1] and Hollwegg in Germany; a Harding and Hughes in America; a Ishi in Japan. All these are statesmen. Where are the Negro statesmen? (Voices: None). Where is our national freedom? Lloyd George, Clemenceau, Ebert, Ishi, are speaking for their national integrity and dignity. If no other Negro will speak (dramatically striking his chest) I shall do it by the help of God for the Imperial freedom of Africa. (Cheers.) I have an everlasting love, an everlasting devotion and an everlasting faith and belief in the Majesty of my God and the scriptures: "Princes shall come out of Ethiopia["] (Vociferous applause). Shall I wait any longer for that which my father had waited long enough? My father had been begging and praying and I do not believe in wasting all that energy. God gave us this life to make good use of it, and I am going to use every minute to further this movement. The impulse of the moment says: "There is a world political re-organization. It is not a question of begging and worrying God for what we can get ourselves." I do not believe in worrying my God for things temporal. God has millions of worlds, Saturn, Jupiter, Mars, to attend to, so that they may not come in contact with each other. After God created you He was through with you, with the exception, that He says you must worship Him in spirit and in truth. God says I will help those who will help themselves. I love the God of justice. It is not a question of size but justice. I have an abiding faith in the U.N.I.A. Africa is going to play the David. The sensible white man is not afraid of us, for he can protect himself. But it is the good for nothing "cracker" white man who has nothing to rely on but his color. Some people can only see physical power. But I can remember history. Some of the greatest wars that have been fought and won w[ere] not a result of great battalions, but strategy. We are going to use strategy to redeem Africa. (Cheers.) Some are asking: "How is Garvey going to free Africa?" What nonsense!! No general gives away his strategic plans. I would advise those lawyers and doctors to take a 6 months' course in logic[,] then they will see through this movement. This association consists of cultured, cultivated and educated men, who are well versed in political economy and political science and although I am alone here tonight, I challenge any man who can come on this platform and give a better discourse than I can, on either of these subjects. Lloyd George and other statesmen went to the best universities to study political science. I have been to a university and used the same text-books that they have used. They have made plans for the development of their country and empire. I shall expect no apology from them and they shall expect none from me. Black man as I am, I shall cho[o]se my way for the building of my empire. (Cheers.) There must be freedom and autonomy for all races. Some people say that this is a radical movement against the white people. I believe in conserving time and it takes time to hate a white man. Britain has her salvation and protection and the others have got to look on and walk around. Why? Because she has her dreadnoughts, cruisers, etc., I am determined to establish a government which will make the nations of the world walk around Africa. (Thunderous applause). The Anglo-Saxons will not beat me in the race of life. Whenever you hear Garvey is licked he is well licked.

After wiping the perspiration from his face and refreshing himself with some water, the speaker, in declamatory tones, said:

I can see my counterpa[rt] in Britain, France, America, Germany, Russia and Japan and I am going to give them the race of my life.

The race is not for the swift, but for those that endure to the end. The greatest diplomats in the world are Negroes. (Here he narrated the history of the defeat of the North American Indians and the tricky embrace of the African Negro. How the latter instead of shooting at a distance with his bow and arrow at his enemy surrendered, and as a result succeeded in acquiring a first class knowledge of the mechanism of the gun which he can now use better than his enemy.)

Three hundred years ago the Negro studied at the feet of his so-called master and his apprenticeship was declared up in 1914. It was Negro strategy that brought the war to a close. Men of Panama[,] prepare for the call in Africa. Women of Panama[,] you will be needed not as Red Cross nurses but as Black Cross nurses.

I understand that some of you professional men say that I am here to stir up revolution. I am not here for disturbance, but to speak to African citizens.

Before I bid you farewell, I want to give you a closing thought. I shall take the most pleasant recollections of my stay here. I thank the Panamanian government for the protection I received here, as also Colón and Bocas del Toro. I appreciate the hospitality extended to the Negroes living here. In the future the Negro will not forget her in time of need (perhaps the next 25 years), when we shall send the African fleet to support her. I hold the best appreciation for the Panamanian Government. I am not here to disrupt the autonomy of her government. If there is no government to protect weaker nations the Government of Africa will. A glorious day await[s] us when we shall throw away color prejudice. We shall have liberty and democracy by your moral and financial support. I appeal to you in the name of God and in the name of reason. Liberia will soon be free. If you do not heed the call it will not be Garvey's fault.

The meeting was brought to a close by the singing of "Onward Christian Soldiers" and the pronouncing of the Benediction by Mr. H. E. Wynter.

Printed in the *Panama Star & Herald*, 4 May 1921. Original headlines omitted.

1. Friedrich Ebert (1871–1925) was a leader of the German Social Democratic party and the first president of the German Reich (1919–1925). He was elected president by the national assembly at Weimar in February 1919, and the following year he suppressed the Kapp putsch; later he was responsible for suppressing the attempt by Hitler and Ludendorff in 1923 to establish a dictatorship in Bavaria (*WBD*).

[*Calidonia, Panama, 3 May 1921*]

. . . Mr. Chairman, Ladies and Gentlemen: Before I address you, I desire to correct a mistake of the statement from your chairman. He said I said last night, that the professional men are the least in my estimation. I never said that last night. I said words to this effect. That there are some of the professional men who criticise—your doctors, your lawyers and so forth, [*who*] in my estimation are more ignorant than the people who make up the Universal Negro Improvement Association, in spite of their college and university training. I do not refer to all the professionals. As far as education is concerned with the people of the U.N.I.A., they were far more educated than such men. This is what I said last night, so I trust my learned friend (Mr. A. B. Thompson) will take back that correction to his colleagues for the members of the U.N.I.A. (Applause).

I am indeed pleased to be among the prospective chapter of the U.N.[I.]A. I have to thank you for your address of welcome. I have to thank you for the hospitable and friendly manner in which you have received me. I desire to say that the U.N.I.A. embraces Negroes everywhere; that the U.N.I.A. has no national bar, no color bar, where [N]egroes are concerned. The U.N.I.A. is not insular; is not parochial, is not national, is not Barbadian, is not Jamaican, is not Trinidadian, is not American: it is purely a Negro institution. When you join the U.N.I.A. you will not join it as a Barbadian, Jamaican, Trinidadian, American, you join it as a Negro. (Applause). And we recognize any one as a Negro who has one-sixteenth drop of Negro blood in his veins. If he does not claim to be a Negro he may stay to himself and we welcome him to stay there; hence you realize I am here representing not an insular institution, not a parochial institution, not a national institution, but a universal movement for the Negro, that is, Universal Africa for Negroes, by Negroes[,] a government of our own. Barbadians can work for it; Jamaicans can work for it; Americans can work for it; just as you worked for the Panama Canal.

Nobody can tell what part of the Panama Canal the Barbadian dug; what the Trinidadian dug, but everybody can tell that it was the Negro who dug the Panama Canal. (Applause). Now there is similar work for you in Africa to do as you did at Panama, whether you be Barbadian, Jamaican, or Trinidadian you will be the man selected to do that job. That is the spirit of the association.

Those of you who can lay railroads, those of you who can build buildings, will have that work to do. Those who are educated to be clerks and school teachers will find that work to do; and those who are lawyers will practice their law. So you realize that the U.N.I.A. is not against the laboring man; is not [against] the work of the artisan and [is not] against the professional man; but, if he is against the U.N.I.A., naturally we may have something to say to him as I did say to the professionals last night; but I feel sure that in the ultimate achievement of our work you will find all of us Negroes pulling together, whether professionals, workingmen, artisans, or ordinary laborers. Because this call has stood out without any dispute. You cannot get away from race. I do not care how far you go, how far your travels be, you cannot get away from your race. You will have to come back some day or the other; it is only a question of time and we will be driven back to the race.

I do not know of any of our people who thought best to be with other races who did not express afterwards a feeling of disgust and dissatisfaction from the treatment received from them, whether they marry white men or keep white men's company. Some time or other the white man states something that makes him feel that it was better to be among his own folks.

The latest report is that the Cuban government has passed a law that only native labor must be employed on the plantations in Cuba.[1] During my last trip to Cuba, I saw nearly sixty to seventy thousand West Indians who ran from the Panama Canal, from Bocas del Toro, from Costa Rica, from Nicaragua. Where next are you going? You cannot go back home except you are prepared for something—you cannot go back to Jamaica, or back to Trinidad, because your economic conditions at home are where you left them—the white man at the top. And the only way you can go back to your home, to your land, to your country, is to encourage that courage and spirit of true manhood. The next is to educate those who have never left home, who are still asleep deep down in ignorance, who are as blind as a bat because they can see nothing more than the hypocritical teachings which they get. You have to give them a new religion and new politics. Are you prepared for that? Very few of us are prepared for it, because I left my country four and a half years ago. When I was ready to go back, my own countrymen said I could not get back because I would interfere with the old time order of things. Just imagine that people speak such things to anybody who sees anything and reported the conditions or description; but I went back home and told them a part of my mind. But the trouble was that I had no time to remain. If I had time to remain at home, probably the[re] would be a change of conditi[ons] there.

Therefore, we have come to [the] conclusion that we must concentrate our forces and our energy the same way we did in Panama in the construction of the Canal, and on the plantations in Costa Rica and on the plantations in Guatemala so as to build for ourselves a permanent government of our own in Africa, and thereby not let any government or race be able to prescribe how much each of you should work for, but show and let them know that we are masters of our own destiny and we will decide our own economical affairs. That is what the U.N.I.A. seeks to do.

In my few remarks to you this afternoon, I hope you have understood what we are endeavoring to accomplish. I have said enough for the most illiterate man to understand. I did not speak in high classical terms; I did not speak that only students of colleges and universities could understand. I have made it my duty to speak in plain English that every man can understand me. If any man fails to understand me, then it is no fault of mine. I feel sure that you understand what I am endeavoring to explain to you. We are not endeavoring to encourage hatred between races, we are not endeavoring to create hatred among our people and other people, neither are we trying to disrupt good feelings in any way. This association wants to link up every man, woman and child of the race. The only way we can accomplish anything for ourselves is to work while we live for the construction of an autonomy on the continent of Africa so that our children can enjoy those things which [we] ourselves do not enjoy. That is the policy of the U.N.I.A.

There is one disadvantage—we never look for the tomorrows in our lives; we always look for the todays. [You] will have to change that [phil]osophy; you will have to change [your?] views of living for today; you . . . [*word mutilated*] also see that you look for tomorrow and the existence of your . . . [*words mutilated*] to live up to this standard will not be able to ride in his own automobile and to live in a beautiful home and to have good concerns and to make himself a happy man.

If you have no country you can never be free. As soon as I landed here I was made to understand that whenever a West Indian go[es] before the courts of justice because he is a West Indian, he is fined heavier than the other fellow after he has committed the same crime. Can you not see it is necessary to have a government of your own? The U.N.I.A. seeks to establish that government that will give us rules of our own, courts of our own, for the good and welfare of Africans.

God has given me five senses: has He not given you the same? Then what is the matter with you[?] Whether you be doctor, lawyer, or otherwise, you should link hearts and hands together, and thus show service rendered because of humanity. The clergy or the lawyer is no better than the ditch digger. I give you encouragement; you cannot tell what your position in life will be. But you follow and never had a hope for the future. Who's to tell that some of you ladies now sitting before me will be the wives of some of the greatest statesmen of Africa[?] Who's to tell whether any of the little girls now before me will become the first empress of Africa?

In conclusion I hope that the officers and members of this prospective chapter will continue to support the red, the black and the green; because through this organization, U.N.I.A., we hope to have aims of our leadership accomplished (Applause.)

Printed in the *Panama Star & Herald*, 5 May 1921. Original headlines omitted.

1. An earlier ban on nonwhite immigration into Cuba, known as Military Order No. 155, was passed in 1910. It was lifted, however, in response to the sugar boom of World War I, and it is estimated that as many as 170,000 Haitians and Jamaicans entered Cuba between 1910 and 1927 (Robert B. Hoernal, "Sugar and Social Change in Oriente, Cuba, 1898–1946," *Journal of Latin American Studies* 8, no. 2 [November 1976]: 215–249). However, many West Indians were forced to leave Cuba following the collapse of the sugar market in 1920. The *Negro World* of 19 March 1921 carried a report that the sugar planters of Cuba were complaining about the poor quality of the work done by Jamaican and Haitian laborers. According to the report, Cuban planters paid Cuban workers in currency, while foreign workers received "bits of paper to procure them food at the commissariats." The 7 May 1921 issue of the *Workman*, a newspaper for the West Indian community in Panama, lamented:

> Thousands of West Indians, principally Jamaicans, are walking daily from province to province looking for jobs. Some have not even got as much money as would enable them to leave the country. This is a fact, and the situation is still worse because the President has sent out circulars to all the centrals and working places to lay off West Indians to employ natives of Cuba, who are out of work.

Gabriel M. Johnson to the UNIA

[*Monrovia, Liberia, 3 May 1921*]

Will leave in about a fortnight. Remit by telegraph $600 traveling expenses. In great need of $5000. We are entirely without money; therefore, work is entirely stopped in consequence of.

JOHNSON

DNA, RG 165, file 10218-261-77. TG (coded).

Report by Bureau Agent Adrian L. Potter

Springfield, Mass. May 3–9, 1921

BRAZILIAN AFFAIRS.

Several negro families, the heads of which have been more or less identified with Universal Negro Improvement Association of this locality have secured American Passports for Brazil.[1] At New York City, the Brazilian Consul has refused to visé said Passports. These negroes now intend to enter Brazil via Georgetown, British Guiana.

ADRIAN L. POTTER

DNA, RG 65, file BS 202600-22-59. TD.

1. See George D. Creese, "The Black Man's Progress in Brazil," *NW*, 12 March 1921.

Memorandum from the Military Intelligence Division

[*Colón*] Panama, May 5th 1921

SUBJECT MARCUS GARVEY IN PANAMA. (POLITICAL FACTOR NO. 75) MONOGRAPH REPORT.

Marcus Garv[e]y arrived in Panama about a week ago. Since then he has spoken in Bocas del Toro, Guabito, Colón and Panama. He is boosting the Black Star Line and urging "Africa for the Negroes." The only thing objectionable in his speeches is his repeated statement that "the whites must bedriven from Africa, even if armed force is required."

It is clearly evident that the primary object of Garvey's presence here is to get some easy money. He charges a dollar admission to each lecture and all are more than crowded. He sells stock in the Black Star Line on every occasion, and in fact "grabs" money in the most brazen way. The working negroes here are all enthusiastic about him, but the more influential seem to see through his game and are publishing criticisms and warnings against him. From his actions here I should class him as a pure grafter, agitating only for the money in it, and with no real convictions at all on what he preaches.

To date Garvey has taken in the following sums:

	Admissions.	Stock sold.
Bocas del Toro.	$ 300.00	None.
Guabito.	700.00	$ 5000.00
Colón.	4000.00	10000.00
Panama.	5000.00	10000.00
TOTAL	$10,000.00	$25,000.00

Source of information: Newspapers and personal observation.

DNA, RG 165, file 10218-418-13. TM, carbon copy.

Newspaper Report

[*Workman* (Panama), 7 May 1921]

THE ACTIVITIES OF MARCUS GARVEY IN CITY OF PANAMA MEET WITH BIG SUCCESS

Last Saturday [*30 April*] on the 12.45 P.M. train there arrived in Panama City from Colón the Honourable Marcus Garvey, Provisional President of Africa, President General of the Universal Negro Improvement Association and President of the Black Star Line Corporation.

Long before the time of arrival of the train, the crowds commenced to assemble in the vicinity of the passenger station, eager to catch a glimpse of this great leader. When at last the whistle blew announcing the approach of the train and the gates were thrown open the people flocked to the platform in such numbers, that it was with great difficulty the members of the reception committee could get to him. In a second the first class coach in which he traveled, was packed, some even climbing through the windows lest they should lose the first opportunity of seeing this great man.

When at last he was able to get out and into the waiting automobile, the crowds started after him up J Street to the headquarters of the Association where the reception was to be held. But here again, it was impossible to manage them, seeing which, it was arranged to call off the reception and the car drove away bearing its precious burden accompanied by his stenographer, Miss Jacques, and President Graham, of the local branch.

However, the crowd not knowing of the arrangements still hung around, despite a pretty heavy shower which fell at that time, and so fly sheets were distributed from the balcony of the building, giving particulars as to the place and time of meetings and prices of admission.

The first meeting at which he appeared was held in the tent of a Circus company now showing here on the grounds of the old cockpit and a monster crowd it was that was there to hear him. He spoke for one hour and 20 minutes, explaining the aims of the U.N.I.A., and the reasons which actuated him to start the Back to Africa movement. His opening remarks were directed to his critical friends who, he had been informed, had made representations to the Governments of Panama and the Canal Zone that he was coming here to stir up revolution. This, he said, was not the case. He had come to speak only of the one government in which he was deeply interested, the government of Africa, so that they would be disappointed if they thought that he was going to interfere with the political autonomy of this place.

The U.N.I.A. to-day had a membership of four million and operates 700 branches scattered all over the United States, Central and South America, the West Indies, and the great continent of Africa. The movement seeks to unite the four hundred million Negroes of the world for the purpose of forming on the continent of Africa the greatest republic ever known or seen in this world.

He was considered by some a hater of the white race but he had no time even to consider the white man far less to hate him. What he believed was that there was no such tommy rot as the superiority of any race. God had created all men equal and just as the white man had a right to rule in Europe, and the yellow to rule in Asia, so he believed that the Negro had a right to rule in Africa and he was here to appeal to their national pride.

He referred to a book written some 60 years ago by an Irish-American, entitled "The Negro a Beast in the Image of God," in which the writer inferred that the negro was like a horse, or a cow or a mule, ordained to carry out the bidding of the white man and with no constructive genius of his own, but the new negro of today is proving to the world that he is intellectually equal to any Race and can do what has been done by any other Race, and as a proof of this they were today able to boast of 4 ships flying the Black Star and sailing the seven seas, the result of negro initiative and negro support.

But it was not their purpose only to buy and sail 4 ships, it was their purpose to build up a great republic in Africa, to build up the greatest government in the world, to train discipline and maintain the greatest army in the world in Africa and to build up Africa to the greatest industrial state in the world.

He failed to see the reason why people should leave Europe, thousands of miles away, to go to govern down in Africa. They once said it was charity and love of humanity that caused them to come to our help. But all the Africans today are christianized and civilized and he thinks that it was time for them to leave. But the liars and the vagabonds never meant any christianity, they never meant to civilize. They wanted to rob the diamonds and gold and silver and agricultural wealth of Africa. They went there with the Bible, the medium of the white man's deception. Whenever a white man wanted to deceive the negro, he comes with a [B]ible and a bottle of rum, first gets you drunk and then robs you. But I am [from] the United States where prohibition laws are in force, so all I take is cold water and they won't be able to get me that way.

The speaker then referred to the achievements of the Negro in the Great World War, how Germany had France and England and Belgium beaten so badly that the Kaiser was preparing to take his Christmas dinner in Paris and to drink champagne in Buckingham Palace at Easter. Then came the cry from Asquith,[1] help, help, help, and 2,000,000, Negroes from Africa and the West Indies rushed to their assistance and in a short time had the Germans going across the Rhine. And in a similar manner will they fight for the redemption of Africa.

He was homeward bound, back to the home from which he was stolen 300 years ago. He had already sent word that he was coming and if those who are now occupying the place have any sense they would get out before he got there. He had come to encourage them to buy more shares in the Black Star Line and to assist the great Construction Loan. With good backing they could have several more ships by the end of this year which will be necessary to handle the rush to the great republic. Just a few days yet and the *Ph[y]ll[i]s Wheatl[e]y* will be on her way to Liberia with a force of 300 mechanics who are going forward to construct homes to be ready for you when you get there.

He closed his address by thanking the people for their presence and inviting them to the meetings which were to be held on the following day.

On Sunday, May 1, the meetings were held in the Bull Ring, one at 3.30 and another at 7.30 P.M. On both occasions the attendance broke the record. The speeches were nearly on the same order of the previous day, the status of the Negro to-day, the reason why he should seek a government of his own, and requesting the purchase of more shares.

On Monday, two meetings were again held, this time in the Variedades Theatre. At the 7.30 meeting, the sale of tickets had to be suspended long before the commencing hour, as many as 500 people failing to obtain admission.

On Tuesday afternoon at 3.30 he was the guest of the Guachapali Branch, now known as the Prospective Chapter, and addressed them and their friends in their hall at the grade crossing at Calidonia. The same privilege was given the Chartered Branch in their hall in J Street at 7.30 P.M. Admission to both these meetings was free of charge.

On Wednesday morning he left for Colón on the early train and sailed for the States via Cuba on Thursday by the U.F. Co. [*United Fruit Company*] steamer *Abangarez*.

Printed in the *Workman* (Panama), 7 May 1921.

1. Herbert Henry Asquith (1852–1928), first earl of Oxford, prime minister of England, 1908–1916.

Maj. Norman Randolph to the Director, Military Intelligence Division

Quarry Heights, C[*anal*]. Z[*one*].,
May 7, 1921

SUBJECT: MARCUS GARVEY.

1. The subject arrived in Colón aboard the launch "Linda S" from Bocas del Toro, R. de P., on April 26th and remained on the Isthmus until May 5th when he sailed for Kingston, Jamaica aboard the S.S. "Carrillo."[1]

2. Garvey's first activities in the Republic of Panama were at Bocas del Toro, Almirante and Guabito where he was received very cooly and left after wordy altercations with the negroes there. The negroes became incensed over the fact that Garvey raised the price of admission to his lectures from fifty cents, the advertised price, to one dollar, (see enclosure #2).[2] The negroes in that locality put Garvey down as another "faker" in the class with Severs[3] and other agitators who have "bled" the negroes here.

3. Garvey's arrival was unannounced here and at first it appeared that his work would be a total failure but, as is characteristic of the West Indian, the curiosity of the lower class of negroes was aroused and many paid their dollars to hear him and having heard him, they were aroused and influenced by him so that they paid to hear him again, joined the Universal Negro Improvement Association and bought shares in the Black Star Line. The better class of negroes, including doctors, lawyers, clerks, etc., would have nothing to do with Garvey and did all in their power through speech and press to warn the lower classes not to let Garvey influence them and take their money, so that Garvey's efforts did not meet with the degree of success which he expected.

4. During his stay in Colón and Panama, Garvey and his secretaries collected the following amounts:

Stock sold in Colón	$600.00
Stock sold in Panama [*City*]	905.00
Admission fees in Colón	950.00
Admission fees in Panama [*City*]	1738.00
Total	$4193.00

These figures do not show the amounts collected in Colón during Garvey's last twenty-four hours there and they do not show stock sold privately so that it is estimated that he left the Isthmus with about $5,000.00 collected from the poorest class of negroes. In Panama City, Garvey had to lower his admission charge to fifty cents as he could not draw the crowd with the dollar charge.

5. No difficulties arising from Garvey's preachings are anticipated as what enthusiasm he aroused is already waning. He was not received by influential and representative negroes who, on the contrary, are combating his efforts.[4] Negroes here have been fooled too often by men of his type to make this a very fertile field for such activities.

6. Copies of speeches made by Garvey are enclosed herewith.[5]

NORMAN RANDOLPH
Major, 14th Infantry

DNA, RG 165, file 10218-418-32. TLS, recipient's copy.

1. The Panama Canal Zone military intelligence had also notified Matthew C. Smith, director of the Military Intelligence Division in Washington, D.C., that Garvey had left for Jamaica (Smith to William L. Hurley, 7 May 1921, DNA, RG 59, file 000-612).

2. "Marcus Garvey in Bocas del Toro," *Panama Star & Herald*, 30 April 1921; see also "Pilgrim Wilkins' Impressions of Marcus Garvey's Visit to Isthmus," ibid., 3 May 1921.

3. Severs was a white American organizer for the AFL and a representative for the AFL affiliate in the Panama Canal Zone, the United Brotherhood of Maintenance of Way Employees and Shop Laborers. Severs, along with another white American recruiter named Allen, held a number of meetings in the Panama Canal Zone shortly before the United Brotherhood strike of 1919. Their goal was to promote equality in the terms of employment for blacks and whites. American and British authorities believed that Severs's organizing efforts were a factor contributing to the strike (PRO, CO 318/350/02504).

4. Additional letters critical of Garvey were published in the *Panama Star & Herald*, 3 May, 4 May, and 5 May 1921.

5. The speeches were the five that Garvey made in Colón, four of which are printed in *Garvey Papers* 3: 368-375, and newspaper reports that appeared in the *Panama Star & Herald*, 30 April, 4 May, and 5 May 1921.

Charles L. Latham to Charles Evans Hughes

Kingston, Jamaica, May 7, 1921

SUBJECT: MOVEMENTS OF MARCUS GARVEY

SIR:

I have the honor to refer to the Department's instruction of March 25, 1921 (File No. 811.108 G191/2), and my telegram of April 12, 1921, concerning the movements of Marcus Garvey.

He arrived in Kingston this morning from Cristobal, Canal Zone, on the American Steamship CARRILLO and disembarked at this port.

I have been informed that the Black Star Line Steamer KAN[AW]HA is in Havana, Cuba, and expects to arrive shortly in Kingston and it is possible that he may attempt to return to the United States on this vessel as a member of the crew, I have therefore to request telegraphic instruction as to what I should do in case this attempt is made. I have the honor to be, Sir, Your obedient servant,

C. L. LATHAM
American Consul

DNA, RG 59, file 811.108 G 191/13. TLS, recipient's copy.

William C. Matthews, UNIA Assistant Counsel General, to the Department of State

[*New York*] 9 May 1921

On behalf of Marcus Garvey, we submit; that he should be allowed to return to the United States of America for the following reasons:

FIRST: Having been a resident of the United States of America for about five years and during that time he has succeeded in organizing the Universal Negro Improvement Association and African Communities League which is a fraternal and charitable organization composed exclusively of Negroes whose membership in three years has increased to about four millions and which organization has branches throughout the world. In addition to that he has incorporated and organized the Black Star Line and Negro Factories Corporation which corporations have been transacting business in New York for about three years and have accumulated considerable property. He is not only the organizer and promoter of these enterprises among Negroes but he is also the president and general manager and they are dependent upon his personality for their very existence and growth. Thousands of dollars have been invested in these enterprises and their success is largely dependent upon his personal attention.

SECOND: His trip to Cuba and the West Indies was purely in the interest of these enterprises under the direction of the Board of Directors of the Black Star Line with no intention of remaining out of the country but with the full intention of returning to the country when he completed the business arrangement which required him to leave the country.

He will be returning in one of the ships of the Black Star Line and he is not a laborer but a business man with ample means but returning to his own business which he was promoting by his trip to the West Indies.

THIRD: Having resided in the United States about five years, Mr. Garvey's character is well known and established. Not only his business associates testify to his good character but the millions of his followers throughout the United States all citizens of the country are living witnesses to his character and leadership.

We also submit the evidence of the Vice President[,] the Treasurer and the Attorney of the Black Star Line[1] in addition to the foregoing and urge that upon these reasons and this proof that there should be no objection raised by the Government to the return of Mr. Garvey to his business and to the United States, Respectfully submitted,

WILLIAM C. MATTHEWS
Ass. Counsel-Gen.
Universal Negro Improvement Assn.

DNA, RG 59, file 811.108 G 191/33. TD, recipient's copy.

1. The three affidavits were identical.

Enclosure

COUNTY OF NEW YORK
Ninth day of May, 1921

IN THE MATTER OF MARCUS GARVEY RETURNING TO THE UNITED STATES OF AMERICA.

STATE OF NEW YORK) SS.:
COUNTY OF NEW YORK)

O. M. Thompson, being duly sworn, deposes and says:

I am the Vice President of the Black Star Line, a corporation duly organized and incorporated under the laws of the State of Delaware, and that Marcus Garvey is its president and general manager. That among the stockholders of said Corporation are thousands of citizens of the United States, scattered over many states of the Union who have invested thousands of dollars in said corporation.

That said corporation is engaged in the business of purchasing and operating a line of steamships between the Port of New York and the West Indies and Monrovia, Liberia and ports along the west coast of Africa.

That on or about the 25th day of February, 1921 the business of said Corporation required the said Marcus Garvey, its president, to make a trip to Cuba and to the West Indies and Central America, where he went at that time under the express orders and direction of the Board of Directors of said corporation for the purpose of raising funds with which to purchase a new vessel and to make arrangements for cargo and for the coaling of said vessel.

That it is now essential that the said Marcus Garvey be allowed to return to the United States in order to protect the large sums of money invested in said corporation and to carry forward the business plans and operations of said corporation and that without his presence in this country and his personal management of said corporation it will not be able to carry out successfully its business plans and operations and will be likely to fail and the vast sums invested by the citizens of this country would be lost.

Affiant further says that there are a great many cases pending in the Courts of the State of New York and in the Courts of the United States in which said corporation is a party, plaintiff or defendant,[1] involving large sums of money which cases could not be tried successfully without the presence, advice and testimony of the said Marcus Garvey, president and manager of said corporation; and if said cases were tried without the presence and testimony of the said Marcus Garvey they would in all probability be lost which would entail consequent loss of thousands of dollars upon the stockholders, a large portion of whom are citizens of the United States.

That I have known Marcus Garvey intimately for five years and have been associated with him on the Board of Directors of said Corporation for the past three years and can testify cheerfully to his good moral character and general qualifications and fitness and say that he is a worthy person and entitled to return to the United States of America.

O. M. THOMPSON
Vice Pres't

DNA, RG 59, file 811.108 G 191/33. TD, recipient's copy. Notarized by Hudson C. Pryce.

1. The cases pending involving the BSL were:
   Black Star Line v. *Irvine Engineering Co.*, no. 21-190, U.S. District Court for the Southern District of New York, January 1921; *Black Star Line* v. *W. E. B. Du Bois and NAACP*, no. 1944, New York County Supreme Court, 1921; *Black Star Line* v. *New Negro Publishing Co.*, no. 8242, New York County Supreme Court, May 1920; *Black Star Line* v. *New York News Publishing Co.*, no. 8814, New York County Supreme Court, 1920; *Black Star Line* v. *Fred D. Powell*, no. 8340, New York County Supreme Court, June 1920; *Gerald B. Rosenheim* v. *Black Star Line*, Seventh District Municipal Court of New York, August 1920.

Cyril A. Crichlow to Marcus Garvey

[*Monrovia, Liberia, 10 May 1921*]

This in confidence. Have private information for Council which cannot be forwarded at present, cable or mail. Traveling expenses needed by June 1st. Potentate's presence New York unnecessary.

[CYRIL A. CRICHLOW]

DNA, RG 165, file 10218-261-77. TG (coded).

William L. Hurley to J. Edgar Hoover

WASHINGTON May 10, 1921

Dear Mr. Hoover:

I have recently received information under date of May 7, 1921, to the effect that MARCUS GARVEY arrived in Kingston, Jamaica, from the Canal Zone on that day. It is thought that he will probably attempt to enter the United States shortly by shipping as a member of the crew of the s.s. KA[N]A[W]HA of the Black Star Line.

The Consul at Kingston has been instructed to refuse to visa the crew list of the s.s. KA[N]A[W]HA if Garvey's name appears thereon unless it is removed.

I shall not fail to keep you advised of any further information which may come to my attention.

Similar information is being furnished M.I.D. Very truly yours,

W. L. HURLEY

[*Handwritten endorsement*] FILE G. F. R.
[*Stamped endorsement*] NOTED F. D. W.

DNA, RG 65, file BS 198940-129. TLS, recipient's copy.

Charles Evans Hughes to Charles L. Latham

Washington, May 10, 1921

Urgent, Secret.

Your May 7, 3 P.M. Refuse visa crew list S.S. KA[N]A[W]HA, if Garvey's name appears thereon, unless his name is removed therefrom. Keep Department informed.

HUGHES

[*Endorsements*] V.I./McB[*ride*][1] WLH.

DNA, RG 59, file 811.108 G 191/10/10. TG. Handwritten endorsements.

1. Harry Alexander McBride (1887–1961) was chief of the Visa Office in the Department of State for the period from 1 January to 13 September 1921. In 1913 he was deputy consul general at Boma in the Belgian Congo, after which he was sent to Angola to investigate commercial conditions. In August 1918 he was appointed to Liberia as acting receiver of customs and financial adviser, remaining there until May 1919. He resigned from the State Department in 1939, but in 1942 President Roosevelt appointed him as his special representative to the conference that negotiated the United States–Liberian defense agreement of that year (U.S. Department of State, *Register*, 1938 [Washington, D.C.: GPO, 1938], p. 136; *NYT*, 13 April 1961).

J. H. Irving to the Detective Inspector, Jamaica

Detective Office, Kingston, 10 May 1921

Detective Inspector,

I have the honour to report that last night 9th instant, I attended a Public Meeting at the Ward Theatre held by Mr. Marcus Garvey. As on previous occasions his chief point was the building up of an African Republic in Liberia. He exhorted all who were present to join in the movement by supporting the Black Star Line, and the Construction Loan for Liberia, whether they were employed to the Government or not. If they were turned out of their jobs, they should be prepared to make sacrifices, as he had sacrificed the whole of his time for 4 1/2 years, which sacrifice has now put him in a position to draw from the Universal Negro Improvement Association $10,000.00 per annum. He also told the audience that at last convention $12,000.00 was voted as his salary per annum, as first Provisional President of Africa and also $5,000.00 per annum as President of the Black Star Line, making altogether $[2]7,000.00 per annum, but he has only accepted the $10,000.00 as President General of the U.N.I.A. and $1,000.00 from the salary of President of Africa, making $11,000.00. The salary of $5,000.00 for President of the Black Star Line he has given over to the Co-operation [*Corporation*] to foster its aims, and he said these words: "So you will see that I am getting more pay than the Colonial Secretary of Jamaica, and that's a job for life".

He will hold a members' meeting at St. Mark's Hall tonight to re-organise the Kingston Branch of the Universal Negro Improvement Association.

J. H. IRVING
Detective Sergeant

[*Endorsement*] Gov. Secret 28.5.21.

JA, CSO, file 10063. TL, carbon copy. Handwritten endorsement.

J. Edgar Hoover to William L. Hurley

WASHINGTON, D.C. May 11, 1921

Dear Mr. Hurley:

Inclosed herewith you will find, copy of resume and exhibits, of in-formation in our files concerning the activities of MARCUS GARVEY.

You will note from the inclosure, that exhibits No. 1, 2, 3 and 5 are missing. We were unable to secure affidavits from these individuals because Davidson and Jeffreys could not be located and Louis Cantor would not agree to make an affidavit, in view of the lapse of time in these speeches. Very truly yours,

J. E. HOOVER
Special Assistant to the Attorney General

DNA, RG 59, file 000-612. TLS, recipient's copy.

Enclosure

[*Washington, D.C., ca. 11 May 1921*]

MARCUS GARVEY

Birth:
    Jamaica, West Indies, August 17th, 1888 [*1887*].
Religion:
    Catholic.
Citizenship:
    British (by virtue of his birth in a British possession).

Education:

Graded and High Schools, Jamaica. Course in Journalism, Jamaica. College, (Burbeck college), England.

Entry into the United States:

Not Known.

Present business address:

45–46 West 135th Street, New York City.

Brief of Business Ventures Prior and Subsequent to Garvey's Arrival in the United States.

1. Edited a negro publication in the West Indies and Central America before coming to the United States.

2. School in Monrovia, Liberia.—Soon after Marcus Garvey's arrival in the United States he endeavored to raise funds to establish this school, but this proposition failed in a short time.

3. Chain restaurants.—Garvey organized a corporation and sold stock for this business venture at 54 West 135th Street, New York City. The entire proposition failed in one year.

4. Universal Negro Improvement Association—Headquarters, 56 West 135th Street, New York City. Purpose—to bring the four million (Garvey's figures) together throughout the world. Present membership—one hundred thousand.

5. Liberty Hall. 138th Street, between Lenox and 7th Avenue, Purchased by Garvey to be used as a public meeting place for the negroes of New York.

6. Black Star Line. Purpose—to purchase ships and establish a regular line of negro steamships between the West Indies and the United States. Company—incorporated under the laws of Delaware, with capital stock of $2,000,000. Ships—"in and out" of operation.
    a. Yarmouth (still in British registry)
    b. Shady Side.
    c. Kanawha.

7. Negro Factories Corporation. Purpose—to build factories to employ thousands of negroes.

8. Construction Loan Bond. Purpose—to raise $2,000,000 for construction in Liberia.

9. "Negro World." Garvey's propaganda sheet. Circulation, United States, Central and South America, Africa and the West Indies.

From the above business schemes, Garvey has extracted thousands of dollars from the working negroes of this country, and has given them in return, stocks, and to date not one cent of dividend has been paid by any of the corporations.

Marcus Garvey is at the present time in Cuba, where he is selling Construction Loan Bonds, with the expectation of returning to the United States with approximately $100,000 for his movement.

Private Life:

In December of 1920, Marcus Garvey married a West Indian girl, Amy Ashwood, but he has since left her and pays a small alimony.

Violations of State Laws:

Marcus Garvey was arrested in Chicago in September of 1919, for violation of the state statute which prohibits the sale of fraudulent stocks. There is also a warrant for his arrest in Newport News, Virginia, for the same offense.

Garvey was indicted in Chicago, in January 1920 for violation of the State Criminal Syndicalist Law.[1]

Evidence showing Garvey to be amenable to Section of the Criminal Laws:

A. Extracts from a speech of Marcus Garvey in the Palace Casino, 135th Street and Madison Avenue, on November 10, 1918, in the interest of the Universal Negro Improvement Association.

> Brethren: We are assembled here tonight for the purpose of furthering our fight for that negro democracy. We have been slaves for four hundred years and we now come not to compromise but to demand that we be recognized as a nation and a people. We are backed by four hundred million, who we will mobilize if necessary and fight for what is our just rights. Not one of the big men which include Premier Asquith, Lloyd George, Premier Clemenceau, Robert Lansing or President Wilson and many others have mentioned the future of the negro race. The time has come for the blackmen to mobilize his forces against these whites. We are now as civilized as our former white masters who called upon us to aid them in this present war. Have we not attended the same schools and colleges as the whiteman not only equaling his mental strength but in many instances excelling it[?] Concerning our physical strength of that they are well aware. No nation is safe in war when part of its internal population is dissatisfied. *I do not say there will be but there may be a revolution if we are not recognized.* Do not follow the dictates of men like William Randolph Hearst. We are determined to get liberty even at the cost of our lives. No nation is safe in having twelve million dissatisfied people within their borders.[2]

Affidavit of Mr. Davidson, reporting on this subject, is attached hereto and marked "Exhibit No. 1.["]

Attached hereto and marked "Exhibit No. 2["] is affidavit by Lewis Cantor, reporter for the New York Tribune.[3]

B. On December 1, 1918, Garvey spoke at the Palace Casino, 135th Street, between Fifth and Madison Avenue. Ralph A. Jeffreys, who was employed at the Palace Casino, gave the following extracts from Garvey's speech:

> That if the American Negro did not get their rights the next war would be between the Negro and the White man and that with Japan to help the Negro they would win the war. (When he said this a lot of white people got up and left the hall, followed by the jeers of the Negroes[.]) The cessation of lynching is one of the principles which our delegates at the Peace Conference will demand. For every Negro lynched by the Whites in the South the Negroes ought to lynch a white man in the North.
>
> Parents should learn the children to save their pennies up and learn to use fire-arms so that when the time came they would be able to go to war against the Whites.

G[eorge] Washington Mills, 322 Mott Avenue, Bronx, New York, who attended the same meeting at the Palace Casino, gave the following extracts from Garvey's speech:

> That Japan was combining with the Negro race to overthrow the white race because the blackman was not getting justice in this country (United States). That it was time for the blackman to mob[i]lize his forces against these former white masters who were not giving the blackman a square deal. That it is a crime to lynch blackmen in the south and the Negroes ought to lynch a White man in the North for every Black man they lynch in the South.

Lewis Cantor, reporter for the New York Tribune covered his meeting and corrob[o]rates the statements of the aforementioned Ralph Jeffreys and G. Washington Mills, in his article appearing in the New York Tribune, December 2, 1918.

The affidavit of Ralph Jeffr[ey]s is attached hereto and marked Exhibit No. 3. [*marginal handwritten note: Unable to secure affidavit*]

The affidavit of G. Washington Mills is attached hereto and marked "Exhibit No. 4."[4]

The affidavit of Lewis Cantor, is attached hereto and marked "Exhibit No. 5."[5]

C. The July 26, 1919, issue of "The Negro World" bore an editorial which closed with these words—

> It is true that all races look forward to the time when spears shall be beaten into agricultural implements, but until that time arrives it devolves upon all oppressed peoples to avail themselves of every weapon that may be effective in defeating the fell motives of their oppressors.
>
> In a world of wolves one should go armed, and one of the most powerful defensive weapons within the reach of Negroes is the practice of Race First in all parts of the world.

[D.] In the September 20th, 1919, issue of the Negro World, there occurred an exchange of letters between Claude McKay, the author of a much quoted poem about the negro with his back against the wall and fighting to the death and W. H. Ferris, literary editor of the Negro World. McKay advocates Bolshevism as a means of freedom for the negro in these words:

> Every Negro who lays claim to leadership should make a study of Bolshevism and explain its meaning to the colored masses. It is the greatest and most scientific idea afloat in the world today that can be easily put into practice by the proletariat to better its material and spiritual life. Bolshevism (as Mr. Domingo ably points out in the current Messenger)[6] has made Russia safe for the Jew. It has liberated the Slav peasant from priest and bureaucrat who can no longer egg him on to murder Jews to bolster up their rotten institutions. It might make these United States safe for the Negro. When the cracker slave frees his mind of the nightmare of race equality, when he finds out that his parasite politicians have been fooling him for years, when he takes back the soil from his Bourbon exploit[ers] and is willing to till it alongside of the Negro and tries to forget that he is a "nigger", while the latter ceases to think of him in terms of poor trash, when the Vardamans[7] and Cole Bleases[8] find themselves jobless, then the artificial hate that breeds lynchings and race riots might suddenly die.
>
> If the Russian Idea should take hold of the white masses of the Western world, and they should rise in united strength and overthrow their imperial capitalist government, then the black toilers would automatically be free! Will their leaders educate them no[w?] to make good use of their advantages eventually?

E. Statement by Marcus Garvey given at Newport News, under date of October 29, 1919, entitled "Marcus Garvey sends Message to Negro People of the World from the South"—appeared in the Negro World for November 1, 1919:

VIRGINIA SUPPORTING THE BLACK STAR LINE

Fellowmen of the Negro Race, Greeting:

Away down in Virginia I have been for a few days testing out the sentiment of our people as touching their outlook on things temporal, and I have discovered that the Negro of the South is a new and different man to what he was prior to the war.

The bloody war has left a new spirit in the world—it has created for all mankind a new idea of liberty and democracy, and the Southern Negro now feels that he too has a part to play in the affairs of the world. A new light is burning for our brothers at this end. They are determined that they too shall enjoy a portion of that democracy for which many of their sons and brothers fought for and died for in France.

The New Negro manhood movement is not confined to the North alone, it has found its way far do[w]n South and there are millions of black folks here who mean to have all that is coming to them or they are going to die in the attempt of getting same.

I cannot but encourage the spirit of my brothers all over the world who are struggling for manhood and freedom rights.

This is the age of helpful action, and it falls to the province of every Negro to help his brother to a fuller realization of the opportunities of life. Now is the time for all of us, fellowmen, to join in and help in the spreading of the doctrines of the Universal Negro Improvement Association. We have to utilize every energy we possess to redeem the scattered millions of our race. There is no time to waste about East, West[,] North or South. The question of the Negro should be the only question for us. We have remained divided long enough to realize that our weakness as a race is caused through disunity. We can no longer allow the enemy to penetrate our ranks. We must "close ranks" and make up our minds all over the world either to have full liberty and democracy or to die in the attempt to get it.

The salvation of our race depends upon the action of the present generation of our young men. We fellows who could have died by the millions in battle fighting for the white men, must now realize that we have but one life to give and since that life could have been given in France and Flanders for the salvation of an alien race, we ought to be sensible enough to see and realize that if there is to be another sacrifice of life, we shall first give that life to our own cause.

Africa, bleeding Africa, is calling for the service of every black man and woman to redeem her from the enslavement of the white man. All the sacrifice that must be made, therefore, shall be of the Negro, for the Negro and no one else.

Whether we are of America, Canada, the West Indies, South or Central America, or Africa, the call for action is ours. The scattered children of Africa know no country but their own dear Father and Motherland. We may make progress in America, the West Indies and other foreign countries, but there will never be any real lasting progress until the Negro makes of Africa a strong and powerful Republic to lend protection to the success we make in foreign lands.

Let us therefore unite our forces and make one desperate rush for the goal of success.

And now that we have started to make good by uniting ourselves, let us spare no effort to go forward. The Black Star Line that we are giving to the world calls for the support of every Negro, and it is pleasing for me to say that our people in Virginia are doing most splendidly their part to help this Corporation fly the colors of the Negro on the high seas.

Buy all the shares you can now in the Black Star Line and make money while the opportunity presents itself. You may buy your shares today at $5.00 each; in the very near future you will have to pay more. Write or call on the Black Star Line, 56 West 135th Street, New Yor[k], and purchase all the shares you want. With very best wishes for your Success, Yours fraternally,

MARCUS GARVEY.

Newport News, October 29, 1919.[9]

F.   Excerpts from an address given by Marcus Garvey at Madison Square Garden, October 30, 1919, as published in the Negro World, November 8, 1919:

"NEGRO MUST RECEIVE LIBERTY."

The message I have to tell to the world for the New Negro is that there is no longer any cowardice from ourselves, and if the white or yellow man expects to find cowardice in the Negro he is only making a terrible mistake with himself. The boys of the New York Fifteenth Regiment were not cowards in France: the boys of the Illinois Eighth[10] were not cowards in France: the boys of the West Indies Regiment from the West Indies were not cowards in France: the boys they took from Africa were not cowards in France. We the men who have returned as Americans, as Canadians, as West Indians, as South and Central Americans and as

African Negroes from the battlefields of France and Mesopotamia have one declaration to make to the world; we went out to live our lives for the sacred cause of democracy, and in view of the fact that we have not received that democracy upon our return from the battlefield we intend to carry on the war until the Negro has received liberty and democracy.

The war that I speak of that we intend to carry on will not be a war in Europe or America, but it will be a bloody war between black and white on the African battlefields. The New Negro has made up his mind to find a place in the sun, and it is that place in the sun 12,000,000 square miles called AFRICA. (Cheers).

THE TEACHING OF THE WHITE MAN.

The white man taught us for three hundred years to despise Africa, and he has kept us in the bonds of slavery for 250 years, and for fifty years we were satisfied with the white man's leadership. We were misinformed about Africa for 300 years, but the New Negro is well informed about Africa now, and he knows that Africa is the richest continent in the world. (Cheers). He knows that Africa is the bone of contention between the white man and the yellow man. He knows that, caring not what England says, caring not what France says, the fight between Great Britain and Germany was a fight for African aggrandizement. The Allies whipped the Kaiser to his knees with our assistance, and had it not been for the Negro the Kaiser would have been giving them trouble up to now. It took the boys of the New York Fifteenth, the Illinois Eighth and the soldiers of the West Indies and of Africa to bring the Kaiser to his knees. (Cheers) We brought the Kaiser to his knees because we believed we were fighting for a just and sacred cause. But after we 'licked' the Kaiser, after we had brought him to his knees, we found out that crackerdom was universal, that crackers were in England as well as America, in France as well as Germany, in Italy as well as Russia. Therefore, we fought under a farcical idea of democracy, in that we defeated the Kaiser for England and her allies and have received nothing for ourselves, not Africa, because they have divided it up among themselves. So we intend to take back Africa for the 400,000,000 black folks of the world. From Madison Square Garden tonight I give a challenge to the white man, to the world. If you think you are having the greatest fight now you have another thought coming as far as that is concerned, because you have used the black man, 2,000,000 strong, to help you win out in the greatest war you have ever seen. But the greatest fighter up to now the world over is a black man, and he has not started out yet to fight himself.

It will be a terrible day when black men start to fight for their liberty. And that day is coming. We are not hiding it from the white or yellow races of the world; that day is coming, and we can see Japan preparing for that day. We can see Europe preparing for that day—The day of the war of the races. Japan has been sharpening the sword of the East for over fifty years in preparation for that day. The sword of Europe is already sharpened. But 400,000,000 black men have just started to sharpen their swords (cheers) and I believe in that Bible saying 'The last shall be first and the first shall be last.' (Cheers).

ADVANTAGE OF THE NEGRO.

I speak in this way not because I hate white men; I speak in this way not because I hate any of God's children. No; I hate no man, because it is not the nature of the Negro to hate anybody. It is because the Negro has been so charitable; it is because the Negro has been so merciful why the white man has been able to take advantage of the Negro for over 500 years.[11]

G. The following article appeared in Garvey's Negro World, for October 11, 1919, entitled:

BLACKMEN ALL OVER THE WORLD SHOULD PREPARE TO PROTECT THEMSELVES.

NEGROES SHOULD MATCH FIRE WITH HELL FIRE.

SO SAYS LEADER OF GREAT MOVEMENT.

Fellowmen of the Negro Race,

Greeting: Once more the white man has outraged American civilization and dragged the fair name of the Republic before the Court of Civilized Justice.

Another riot has visited the country and Omaha, Nebraska, has placed her name upon the map of mob violence, so it can be seen that the mob spirit is spreading all over, going from South to East, to mid-West and then to the West.

Mobs of white men all over the world will continue to lynch and burn Negroes so long as we remain divided among ourselves. The very moment all the Negroes of this and other countries start to stand together, that very time will see the white man standing in fear of the Negro race even as he stands in fear of the yellow race of Japan today.

The Negro must now organize all over the world the 400,000,000 negroes to administer to our oppressors their Waterloo.

No mercy, no respect, no justice will be shown the Negro until he forces all other men to respect him. There have been many riots in the United States and England recently, and immediately following the war of Democracy, there will be many more as coming from the white man. Therefore, the best thing the Negro of all countries can do is to prepare to match fire with hell fire. No African is going to allow the Caucasian to trample eternally upon his rights. We have allowed it for 500 years and we have now struck.

Fellowmen of the World, I here beg of you to prepare, for a great day is coming—the day of the war of the races, when Asia will lead out to defeat Europe and Europe and the white man will again call upon the Negro to save them as we have often done. The New Negro has fought the last battle for the white man, and he is now getting ready to fight for the redemption of Africa. With mob laws and lynching bees fresh in our memories, we shall turn a deaf ear to the white man when Asia administers to him his final "licking," and place and keep him where he belongs.

If the White man were wise, they would have treated the Negroes differently, but to our astonishment they are playing the part of the dog by biting the hand that feeds. If it were not for the Negro, the White man would have been lost long ago. The black man has saved him and the only thanks we get today is mob law.

Let every Negro all over the world prepare for the new emancipation. The Fatherland, Africa, has been kept by God Almighty for the Negro to redeem, and we, young men and women of the race, have pledged ourselves to plant the flag of freedom and of Empire.

Our forces of industry, commerce, science, art, literature and war must be marshalled when Asia or Europe strikes the blow of a second world war. Black men shall die then and black women shall succor our men, but in the end there shall be a crowning victory for the soldiers of Eth[i]opia on the African battlefield.

And now let me remind all of you, fellowmen, to do your duty to the Black Star Line Steamship Corporation, of 56 West 135th Street, New York City, United States of America. This corporation is endeavoring to float a line of steamships to handle the Negro trade of the world, to run a line of steamships, between America, Canada, South and Central America, the West Indies and Africa, to link up the Negro peoples of the world in trade and commerce. The shares are now going at $5.00 each, and I now ask you to buy as many shares as you can and make money while the opportunity presents itself. You can buy from one to two hundred shares right now.

Send in today and buy 5, 10, 20, 40, 100, or 200 shares. Write to The Black Star Line Steamship Corporation, 56 West 135th Street, New York, N.Y. U.S.A., With very best wishes, Yours fraternally,

MARCUS GARVEY
Chicago, Ill., October 1st, 1919.[12]

H.   Attention is directed to an article appearing in the "Negro World" for December 6, 1919, entitled: "NEGROES OF THE WORLD, THE ETERNAL HAS HAPPENED[.]"

Extracts from the aforementioned article written by Garvey, are as follows:

> I beseech you, men and women of the race, to steel your hearts, your minds and your souls for the coming conflict of ideals. The whole world is in turmoil and a revolution threatens. Asia and Europe are preparing for this revolution. It will mean the survival of the fittest, and I now declare that Africa must also prepare, for in the triumph of the forces of white, yellow or black men in this coming revolution will hang the destiny of the world.
>
> Sons and daughters of Africa, scattered though you may be, I implore of you to prepare. Prepare in all ways to strengthen the hands of Mother Africa. Our mother has been bleeding for centuries from the injuries inflicted upon her by a merciless foe. The call is for a physician to heal the wounds, and there can be no other ph[y]sician than the dark hued son of the mother, and there can be no other nurse as tender and kind as the daughter of this afflicted mother.

Photostat copy of the entire article is attached hereto and marked "Exhibit No. 6".[13]

I.   The following are extracts from Marcus Garvey's speech given on October 20th, 1919 the People's Church, corner of Fifteenth and Christian Street, Philadelphia, Penn[a].

WHITE MAN'S IMPERIAL MAJESTY . . . . . .

The White man comes before you in his imperial and majestic pomp and tries to impress upon you the idea that he is your superior. Who made him your superior? You stick his face with a pin and blood runs out. You stick the black man's face with a pin and blood runs out. Starve the white man and he dies. Starve the black man and he dies. What difference is there, therefore, in black and white[?] If you stick the white man, blood comes out. If you starve the white man he dies. The same applies to the black man. They said the white man was the superior being and the black man was the inferior being. That is the old time notion, but today the world knows that all men were created equal. We were created equal and were put into this world to possess equal rights and equal privileges, and the time has come for the black man to get his share. The white man has got his share and more than his share for thousands of years, and we are calling upon him now to give up that which is not his, so that we can have ours. Some of them will be wise enough and sensible enough to give up what is not theirs to save confusion. You know when a man takes what is not his, the one from whom he took that thing is going to take him to court so as to recover his loss. Now, the Negro is going to take somebody to a court of law one day. This court is not going to be presided over by the white man. It is the court to be presided over and decided by the sword. Yes; the sword will decide to whom belongs the right.

Garvey's entire speech appeared in the Negro World for November, 1919.[14] This issue is attached hereto and marked exhibit No. 7.

J. The following are extracts from a speech given by Garvey on October 24th, 1919, at the First Baptist Church, Newport News, Virginia.

U.N.I.A. SERIOUS MOVEMENT.

As I have told you in many addresses before[,] the Universal Negro Improvement Association is a very serious movement. We are out for serious business. We are out for the capturing of liberty and democracy. (Cheers) Liberty is not yet captured, therefore we are still fighting. We are in a very great war, a great conflict, and we will never get liberty, we will never capture democracy, until we, like all the other peoples who have won liberty and democracy, shed our sacred blood. This liberty, this democracy, for which we Negroes of the world are hoping, is a thing that has caused blood as a sacrifice by every people who possess it today.

THE NEGRO AND THE GUN AND POWDER.

If we had not a complete training in knowledge before 1914, in that we only knew the book and were only able to read and write, they of themselves gave us training and placed two million of us in the army and gave us gun and powder and taught us how to use them. That completed the education of the Negro. Therefore, tonight the Negro stands complete in education. He knows how to read his book, he knows how to figure out, and he knows how to use the sword and the gun. And because he can do these things so splendidly, he is determined that he shall carve the way for himself to true liberty and democracy which the white man denied him after he was called out to shed his blood on the battlefields of France and Flanders.

THE NEGRO MUST PROTECT HIMSELF.

Every ship, every house, every store the white man builds, he has his gun and his powder to protect them. The white man has surrounded himself with all the protection necessary to protect his property. The Japanese Government protects the yellow man, and the English, German, French, and American Governments protect the white man, and the Negro has absolutely no protection. And that is why they lynch and burn us with impunity all over the world, and they will continue to do so until the Negro starts out to protect himself. The Negro cannot protect himself by living alone—he must organize. When you offend one white man in America, you offend ninety millions of white men. When you offend one Negro, the other Negroes are unconcerned because we are not organized. Not until you can offer protection to your race as the white man offers protection to his race, will you be a free and independent people in the world.

The entire report of Garvey's speech appeared in the November 1st, issue of the "Negro World".[15] Photostat of this issue is attached hereto and marked Exhibit No. 7.

K. Extracts from editorial appearing in the Negro World for April 10, 1920.

It may be argued that race first is racial selfishness, and as such will not remove the reasons that called it into being; [b]ut this argument loses its validity when recognition is taken of the fact that certain problems seem to suggest their own remedies. Fire is regarded or reputed to be an effective agent in fighting, while steel is principally relied upon to cut steel. To say that because Negroes are the victims of organized race first sentiment on the part of white people they should not organize along lines o[f] race first to defend themselves is to inferentially condone their present oppression and counsel meek submission to its perpetuation. Failure on the part of the oppressed to organize in terms of self as opposed to similar kinds of organizations on the part of their oppressors must naturally make their oppression more thorough.

"Race First[,]" "Negro First," or whatever the shibboleth adopted by Negroes may be, finds its highest justification in the practices and methods of their oppressors.

It is true that all races look forward to the time when spears shall be beaten into agricultural implements, but until that time arrives it devolves upon all oppressed peoples to avail themselves of every weapon that may be effective in defeating the fell motives of their oppressors.

In a world of wolves one should go armed, and one of the most powerful defensive weapons within the reach of Negroes is the practice of RACE FIRST in all parts of the world.

The entire editorial is attached hereto and marked "Exhibit No. 8."

L. Extract from statement by Garvey, dated August 17, 1920, which appeared in the August 21st issue of the "Negro World", entitled: "NEGROES SHOULD ENFORCE THE PRINCIPLE OF AFRICA FOR AFRICANS AT HOME AND ABROAD."

Today the nations of the world are aware that the Negro of yesterday has disappeared from the scene of human activities and his place taken by a New Negro who stands erect, conscious of his manhood rights and fully determined to preserve them at all costs. They may not be prone to admit this, but they are aware of the fact none the less.

This entire article is attached hereto and marked "Exhibit No. 9."[16]

M. Statement by Marcus Garvey issued under date of August 9, 1920, appeared in the Negro World for August 14, 1920, entitled "THE NEW SPIRIT OF THE NEGRO ASSERTS ITSELF IN GREAT WORLD CONVENTION."

Fellowmen of the Negro Race, greeting:

Today the spectacle of millions of Negroes from Africa, America, the West Indies and other parts of the world, stretching forth their hands to each other in token of blood-brotherhood, with grim determination to break down the bars that impede their progress, haunts the dreams of their oppressors and strikes terror to their hearts. It is a fact of common knowledge that where there is unity there is strength, and if I mistake not the tone and temper of the white nations of the world, they undoubtedly recognize the power of organization. Let no man deceive you; 400,000,000 Negroes when united constitute a power that must be reckoned with. That this fact has been recognized is evidenced in the strenuous efforts put forth to prevent the consummation of unity among the Negroes of the world. That these efforts have failed and are forever doomed to failure is evidenced in the Greatest Convention of Negroes now holding its sessions in Liberty Hall and numbering among its delegates men and women from all parts of the world who are discussing the various problems confronting us, with a view to taking remedial action for their soluti[on]. That Negroes have learned the value of organization and the necessity for racial unity and integrity is further evidenced in the splendid response now most strikingly manifested in the unparalleled achievements of the Universal Negro Improvement Association and its associate bodies.

As I write, your delegates are laying before this convention the conditions under which you live—the injustices perpetrated against you for these hundred years.

The conditions they describe—the sufferings they depict—cry aloud to high heaven to witness these damnable outrages against a suffering people. Since we are convinced that "God helps those who help themselves," we are determined that we shall not labor under these conditions any longer, but shall rise in the majesty of our manhood and break asunder the shackles that bind us.

Have no fear, "men like nations, fail in nothing they boldly attempt when sustained by virtuous purpose and firm resolution."

The sleeping giant, now fully awakened, conscious of his strength and the rectitude of his actions serves notice on the world that henceforth and forevermore he demands his rightful heritage. [F]or the first time in history Negroes from all parts of the world have met under one roof for the most serious purpose it has ever been the lot of man to pursue; and when this convention shall have entered its closing stages, when the Magna Charta of Negro liberty shall have been written, a new day will dawn for the Negro. A new future opens before him, a future in which, rising to the full stature of manhood, and in the glory, the majesty of that manhood, history shall record a free and redeemed Africa. And now let me again invite your attention to the Black Star Line. Delegates coming from overseas have complained of the difficulties encountered in obtaining steamship accommodations. Today there are thousands of Negroes in different parts of the world who are unable to secure passage on steamships leaving those places. You and I know why. The only answer is "Black Star Liners[.]" The need for more and bigger ships for the Black Star Line is evident. A trade route between America, the West Indies and Africa must be established. Give the world your answer.

BUY SHARES IN THE BLACK STAR LINE and enable it to launch more and bigger ships. I am asking those who have already bought shares to buy as many more shares as possible, and those who have not bought shares to buy t[h]em now. The shares are five dollars each, and you may buy from one to two hundred. Write to the office of the Black Star Line, 54–56 West 135th Street, New York City. U.S.A. With kind personal regards, Yours fraternally,

MARCUS GARVEY
New York, August 9, 1920.

N. Excerpts from statement made by Marcus Garvey under date of August 31, 1920, entitled "GREAT CONVENTION OF NEGROES CLOSES AFTER MAKING HISTORY FOR THE RACE," which appeared in the September 4, 1920, issue of the Negro World:

> The war wrought many changes in the lives of men and things, and so has the Universal Negro Improvement Association with its branches reaching into the uttermost parts of the world. The greatest change of all was the transformation of Negroes from cringing persons, pleading for rights and privileges cruelly denied them into upstanding men and women demanding those rights and privileges and determined to exercise them regardless of consequences. In the light of this transformation it is not only reassuring but refreshing to be a member of the Negro race in this day and time.

The entire statement of Garvey is attached hereto and marked "Exhibit No. 10[.]"

O. Extracts from statement by Marcus Garvey dated September 21, 1920, entitled "NEGROES MUST LAY AN ECONOMIC FOUNDATION FOR THEMSELVES," which appeared in the September 25th issue of the Negro World:

> Now comes the Negro through the medium of the Universal Negro Improvement Association demanding the right and taking unto himself the power to control his own destiny. Immediately the hue and cry go up from the ranks of our oppressors that this organization must be suppressed. All sorts of devices have been employed in an effort to accomplish this. A few Negroes have even been cajoled into giving expression to the lie that we are satisfied with existing conditions. It must be difficult for even these few Negroes to keep up the illusion of being thoroughly satisfied with conditions. To them submission is a custom and servitude a pleasure. Men who begin by losing their independence will end by losing their very souls.

Attached hereto and marked "Exhibit No. 11,["] is the entire statement by Garvey.

P.   Extract from statement by Marcus Garvey at Chester, Penna., September 29th, 1920, entitled:

THOUSANDS ARE FLOCKING TO THE STANDARD OF THE UNIVERSAL NEGRO IMPROVEMENT ASSOCIATION.

These discussions, however, left our problems without solution. A remarkable change in attitude toward petitioning and begging for rights has developed among us during the last two years. We are no longer content to plead for those rights. We are now organized to demand and exercise them. It seems incredible that the Governments which prate so much about democracy are unwilling, nay, positively opposed to granting us full measure of democracy but it i[s] the record of the British and American governments—the governments of the Southern United States particularly—and is indeed the record of all white governments.

The entire statement by Garvey is attached hereto and marked "Exhibit No. 12.["]

Q.   Extracts from statement by Marcus Garvey, made at Buffalo, New York, October 18, 1920, entitled "THE MARCH OF EVENTS," which appeared in the October 22nd issue of the Negro World.

There is something in the composition of this demand which makes it imperative that particular attention be given it. Today the white man is confronted with a racial force which it can neither frighten b[y] its show of superior armament nor trample under foot as has been its wont.

After long years of furious struggle and rough insolence towards us, the white world beholds the spectacle of millions of determined men united for the purpose of arresting and permanently checking its domination. The spectacle looms large[r] in his vision than most of us suspect.

Taking into account the forces which events are quickening throughout the world, nothing in the book of fate is more clearly written than that the days of white world domination [are] already numbered. Nothing is surer than that this domination is fast approaching its end.

The entire statement by Marcus Garvey is attached hereto and marked "Exhibit No. 13."

R. Extracts from a statement made by Marcus Garvey in Cuba, March 5, 1921, which appeared in the Negro World for March 12, 1921, entitled:

NEGROES THROUGHOUT THE WORLD MUST UNITE TO COMBAT THE FORCES OPPOSED TO THEIR PROGRESS.

In the final analysis it will be found that the powers opposed to Negro progress will not be influenced in the slightest by mere verbal protests on our part. They realize only too well that protests of this kind contain nothing but the breath expended in making them. They realize, too, that their success in enslaving and dominating the darker portion of humanity was due solely to the element of force employed. In the large majority of cases this was accomplished by force of arms. Pressure of course may assert itself in other forms, but in the last analysis whatever influence is brought to bear against the powers opposed to us must contain the element of force in order to accomplish its purpose, since it is very apparent that this is the only element they recognize. Four hundred million Negroes organized with a firm determination to occupy as good a place as any man in the world with no other limitations than his abilities, will have the weight of numbers that the world must reckon with. Four hundred million Negroes organized for one common purpose would constitute a force in itself that would command respectful attention. Organization among Negroes under the banner of the Universal Negro Improvement Association is, therefore, immeasurably influential and absolutely indispensable in combating the elements opposed to Negro progress.

The entire statement by Garvey is attached hereto and marked "Exhibit No. 14."

DNA, RG 59, file 000-612. TD.

1. A person using Garvey's name was arrested. The indictment, however, was later dropped. See *Garvey Papers* 2:215–216.

2. Printed in *Garvey Papers* 1:286–290.

3. These exhibits have not been printed.

4. Exhibit not printed.

5. Exhibit not printed.

6. W. A. Domingo, "Did Bolshevism Stop Race Riots in Russia?" *Messenger* 2 (September 1919): 26–27. A year later Domingo also published in the *Messenger*, "Will Bolshevism Free America?" 3 (September 1920): 85–86.

7. James Kimble Vardaman (1861–1930), populist demagogue, was governor of Mississippi from 1904 to 1908 and U.S. senator from 1913 to 1919 (*DAB*).

8. Coleman Livingston Blease (1868–1942) was governor of South Carolina from 1911 to 1915 and U.S. senator from 1925 to 1931. Known for his outspoken racism and defense of lynching, Blease was also a strong opponent of the League of Nations (*DAB*).

9. Printed in *Garvey Papers* 2: 121–122.

10. The Eighth Illinois National Guard, which was made up of black soldiers from the Chicago area, was known as the 370th Infantry Regiment during World War I and was the only black regiment in the U.S. Army whose officers were all black, including the commanding officer, Col. Franklin A. Denison. Although it was the object of considerable criticism by the white American press and of numerous complaints by white American military officers, the 370th received more citations for bravery in battle than any other American regiment (W. E. B. Du Bois, "An Essay Toward a History of the Black Man in the Great War," *Crisis* 18 [June 1919]: 63–87). Criticism of the 370th centered around white doubts regarding the competence of black officers to lead an all-black unit. At the conclusion of the war, despite their commendable record, American military intelligence investigated the officers of the 370th as a result of reports that they were "interested in the formation of a secret organization or society among all colored troops in the A.E.F. [American Expeditionary Force] whose object is the promotion of social equality between colored and white after demobilization." The report was never substantiated (DNA, RG 120, entry 177, general correspondence, box 5987, folder 110 (181–190), file 110-188; Emmett J. Scott, *Scott's Official History of the American Negro in the World War* [Washington, D.C.: Emmett J. Scott, 1919], pp. 214–230).

11. The Bureau of Investigation transcript of the speech is printed in *Garvey Papers* 2: 123–133.

12. Printed in *Garvey Papers* 2: 41–43.

13. Printed in *Garvey Papers* 2: 159–161.

14. Printed in *Garvey Papers* 2: 89–98.

15. Printed in *Garvey Papers* 2: 112–121.

16. Printed in *Garvey Papers* 2: 599–601.

Memorandum by John Cooper Wiley, Division of Western European Affairs, Department of State

[*Washington, D.C.*] May 12, 1921

Memorandum for Mr. Bliss,[1] Mr. Harrison,[2] Mr. Hurley.

In an envelope marked "Coopers' Limited", a person signing himself as "Charley"[3] has written President King stating "The U.N.I.A. is making a big demand on the Government for 5,000 square miles of land in Leve Cess[4] and Grand Cape Mountain.[5] Many leading people are against this and strongly protest. Only two members of the Cabinet are for it, namely, Massaquoi and Walker.[6] The rest are absolutely against this move. So am I. We must be careful about this U.N.I.A."

The U.N.I.A. (Universal Negro Improvement Association) is the subversive negro movement headed by Marcus Garvey. The Walker mentioned is presumed to be the brother-in-law of Morris, a member of the Liberian Plenary Mission and a son-in-law of Dr. Lyon, former American Minister to Liberia—now Liberian Consul-General at Baltimore. Massaquoi is the son of a native chief, now acting as Minister of the Interior. ([H]e is specifically prohibited from holding public office by the Reform Program of 1917[.])[7]

J[OHN]. C[OOPER]. W[ILEY].

DNA, RG 59, file 000-612. TNI, recipient's copy. Handwritten insertions.

1. Robert Woods Bliss (1875–1962) became chief of western European affairs in the U.S. Department of State in 1920.

2. Leland Harrison (b. 1883) was a diplomatic secretary assigned to the Department of State in March 1921. A year later he was made assistant secretary of state (U.S. Department of State, *Register*, 1924 [Washington, D.C.: GPO, 1924], p. 136).

3. A possible reference to Gen. Charles Garrette Cooper of the Monrovia militia. There was also a Charles Cooper who was appointed Liberian consul general to Great Britain in 1921 (Fatima Massaquoi-Fahnbulleh, "Bush to the Boulevards: The Autobiography of a Vai Noblewoman," in the Writings and Papers of Fatima Massaquoi-Fahnbulleh [Center for Research Libraries—Cooperative Africana Microfilming Project], MF-3699, p. 410).

4. No information on an area in Liberia with the geographical name Leve Cess has been identified. It may be noted, however, that the Cess (or Cestos) River traverses Liberia, emptying into the Atlantic near a town named River Cess. One of Liberia's five counties during this period was also called Grand Bassa with River Cess Territory (Stefan von Gnielinski, *Liberia in Maps: Graphic Perspectives of a Developing Country* [New York: Africana Publishing Corp., 1972], pp. 32–33).

5. Grand Cape Mount, which was contiguous with Sierra Leone on Liberia's northern boundary, was one of Liberia's five counties. Its eastern boundary was only forty miles inland during this period, and it was inhabited principally by Vai-speaking people (ibid.).

6. On 22 March 1921 three UNIA commissioners, Gabriel M. Johnson, George O. Marke, and Cyril A. Crichlow, met with the Liberian cabinet in Monrovia to discuss plans for the immigration of UNIA members from the Americas. Among the cabinet members who met with the UNIA commissioners were Momolu Massaquoi, the acting secretary of war and of the interior, and Walter F. Walker, secretary of education (DNA, RG 165, file 10218-261-78).

7. In April 1917 the U.S. State Department sent a note to the Liberian government urging it to enact a program of reforms that would streamline their governmental system as a step in reestablishing Liberia's financial solvency. "The American Reform Program," as it was called in Liberia, was enacted by the Liberian legislature in July 1917. American officials, however, held that many of its provisions were never enforced. The reform program gave to the general receiver of customs, who was an American official, considerable control over the exportation of Liberian laborers, over Liberian fiscal policy and procedure, and over the Liberian Frontier Force. It also mandated that "a simple, modern and effective plan of administration of the Hinterland," including the consolidation of the Interior and War departments under one head, be accomplished. The reform program specifically stipulated that Momolu Massaquoi was not to be employed in connection with "native" affairs, which included any involvement with the administration of the Department of the Interior. The American disapproval of Massaquoi stemmed from the 1915 accusation, which had been made by U.S. military attaché Maj. Charles Young, that Massaquoi, who was then serving as a commissioner general of the Liberian Frontier Force, was guilty of maladministration. Massaquoi was subsequently vindicated of the charge (Nancy Kaye Kirkham Forderhase, "The Plans That Failed: The United States and Liberia, 1920–1935" [Ph.D. diss., University of Missouri, 1971]; DNA, RG 59, 882.00/562A and 882.00/753).

Précis of Correspondence[1]

[*Kingston, Jamaica, ca. 14 May 1921*]

It was reported to the Governor [*of Jamaica*][2] that Marcus Garvey's father was an inmate of the Alms House at St. Ann's Bay. The Inspector General was asked for a report and was instructed that if this was the case it should be arranged that Garvey should be questioned on the point at one of his public meetings.[3]

The Inspector General reported that it had been ascertained that Garvey's father had been an inmate of the Alms House at St. Ann's Bay from

28th. May to 8th. December, 1919; that he had been removed from the Institution by a friend of Garvey's and had died in St. Ann's Bay in 1920; that a summons had been taken out by the Inspector of Poor against Garvey who owed the Parochial Board £46. 4. 0. for the support of his father; that the Inspector of Poor had seen Garvey when he was last in Jamaica but Garvey would not pay anything; and that the amount of £46. 4. 0. was still owed by Garvey. The Inspector General also reported that it had not been found possible to question Garvey on the point at his meeting in St. Ann's Bay, but that he would endeavour to arrange for questions to be put at some other meeting.[4]

The Parochial Board was then informed that steps should be taken to recover the amount owed by Garvey. The Board's legal Agent in Kingston consulted the Attorney General and the latter reported to the Government that in the present state of the Law the procedure contemplated by the Board could not be followed. (It subsequently transpired that this procedure was that Garvey should be arrested on the ground that he was about to leave the Colony.)

Later on, as a result of further enquiry by the Police, it was learnt that the amount of £46. 4. 0. owed by Garvey to the Parochial Board was for maintenance of his father in the Alms House for 924 days *from 1916 to 1919* and that the summons that had been taken out against Garvey was one for £1. 8. 6. taken out *in 1915* for disobedience of an Order of the Court for maintenance of his father. It was also reported that a Warrant of distress had subsequently been issued against Garvey in respect of this amount in 1916 but had not been served owing to Garvey's absence from the Island. This Warrant was accordingly obtained from St. Ann by the Police and served on Garvey in Kingston, and the amount in question was forthwith paid.[5]

The Inspector General in reporting as above stated that it had not been found possible to have questions on the subject put to Garvey at any of his meetings.

PRO, CO 137/747. TD.

1. The "precis of correspondence relating to certain facts connected with the recent visit to this Colony of Marcus Garvey, the Negro Agitator" was sent by Governor Probyn of Jamaica to Winston Churchill, colonial secretary, on 14 May 1921, together with an extract from the *Gleaner* of 18 April (PRO, CO 137/747).

2. Born in England, Leslie Probyn (1862–1938) had been attorney general of British Honduras, governor of Sierra Leone, and governor of Barbados before assuming his post in Jamaica (*Times* [London], 19 December 1938).

3. On 21 March 1921 the colonial secretary of Jamaica inquired about the rumor that Garvey's father was in the poorhouse at St. Ann's Bay, adding that "it should be arranged that he [Garvey] shall be questioned as to the fact . . . at some public meeting." At the colonial secretary's request, the Jamaican inspector general made an investigation of the rumor and reported that the parochial board of St. Ann's Bay had interviewed Garvey earlier and that Garvey had refused to pay the amount owed for the care of his late father. The board was not, however, prepared to pursue the matter and seemed content to let the case be closed until the inspector general intervened (JA, CSO 1B/5/52, 1916–1924).

4. "Efforts were made both in St. Ann's Bay and in Kingston to have the question suggested in His Excellency's minute of the 24/3/21 put to Marcus Garvey at a public meeting, but

without success" (inspector general to colonial secretary, 12 April 1921, JA, CSO 1B/5, conf. 92/21).

5. The detective inspector served a warrant on Garvey in Kingston on 11 April 1921. According to the inspector general, "The amount of £1.8.6. for which the warrant called, was paid instantly by Marcus Garvey" (ibid.).

Report by Bureau Agent C. E. Breniman

Los Angeles May 16, 1921

NEGRO ACTIVITIES

UNIVERSAL NEGRO IMPROVEMENT ASSOCIATION:

Reverend J. D. GORDON, whose activities have been heretofore reported, now signs himself as PRESIDENT GENERAL of the UNIVERSAL NEGRO IMPROVEMENT ASSOCIATION a title heretofore held by MARCUS GARVEY. He left Los Angeles enroute to New York, May 10, 1921. He was very successful in raising money. According to confidential informant, he obtained $30,000 in cash and pledges for $20,000 additional, which was secured through the sale of "First Series Parent Body of Universal Negro Improvement Association Construction Loans". The purpose of these bonds, as given, is "for use in the further[a]nce of the Industrial, commercial, and agricultural purposes of the Association in the construction plans in America and Africa." GORDON left as his representative in charge of finance and collections, JAMES A. WEBB.[1] . . .

A considerable increase in the Local membership of the U.N.I.A. is reported, and the Los Angeles membership is now 1400, and a big membership drive is scheduled to start June 1st, 1921.

NOAH WEBSTER [*Thompson*] and the conservatives, are still in the saddle, but the fight against the conservative leadership, started by the West Indian Negroes and other radicals, which was suspended during the visit of GORDON, has again broken out.

C. E. BRENIMAN

DNA, RG 65, file BS 202600-5-51. TD.

1. James Morris Webb was an evangelist and lecturer on biblical history who became a strong supporter of the UNIA. He lived in Seattle, where he joined the Garvey movement in 1921, but he soon became active in San Francisco and Los Angeles as an organizer for the UNIA. Webb made motion pictures of Marcus Garvey and also filmed biblical pageants, showing them to Liberty Hall audiences in New York in October 1921. He preached at Liberty Hall in November 1921 on the theme "God is Waiting for the Gathering of Ethiopia" (*NW*, 5 November 1921). The ultimate black religious nationalist, Webb asserted that Garvey was the Moses of the modern age and that "the Black Man Will Be the Coming Universal King" (*NW*, 29 July 1922). His lectures on the part blacks played in the Bible were especially popular among UNIA members (*NYT*, 15 September 1924; James Morris Webb, *The Black Man: The Father of Civilization Proven by Biblical History*, 2d ed. [Chicago: Fraternal Press, 1924]; James M. Webb, "The Garvey Movement Is Biblical," *NW*, 17 December 1921).

Gabriel M. Johnson to the UNIA Executive Council

[*Monrovia, Liberia, 17 May 1921*]

Work is entirely stopped in consequence of waiting your reply to our telegram of [*3 May*]. We are entirely without money; please send immediately.

JOHNSON

DNA, RG 165, file 10218-261-77. TG (coded).

M. B. O'Sullivan, Acting Deputy Inspector General, to the Inspector General, Jamaica

Detective Office, Kingston,
18th, May 1921

Inspector General,

I have the honour to report that the S.S. Kanaw[h]a of the Black Star Line arrived at this Port from Cuba at 8.30 P.M. on the 17th, May 1921, with 41 passengers exclusive of Mr. /Marcus/ Garvey and his party as under:—
Henrietta Vinton Davis, Cleveland Jacques and Amy Jacques, (Private and Assistant Secretaries) Wilfred James, John De-Bourg and Thorton Frederick.[1]

I understand that Mr. Garvey will hold a public meeting at the Ward Theatre this evening and also tomorrow evening at the same place.

Mr. Garvey's movements and also that of his party will be unostentatiously watched.

M. B. O'SULLIVAN
Ag. Deputy Inspector General

JA, CSO, file 10063. TLS, carbon copy.
  1. This was Augustus Fredericks.

Charles L. Latham to Charles Evans Hughes

Kingston, Ja May 18, 1921

Your telegram of May 10, 3 P.M. Garvey shipped on the KANAWHA as purser at Santiago de Cuba by master, not before American Consul at Santiago; ship's papers now deposited this consulate, very extraordinary, proposes to leave for Costa Rica about May 20th. Master states that vessel

Capt. Hugh Mulzac

Black Star Line office

The proposed S.S. *Phyllis Wheatley*

UNIA Delegation to Liberia, 1921 (Bottom row, left to right): G. O. Marke, Cyril A. Crichlow; (Top row, left to right): Israel McLeod, A. N. Henry, F. P. Lawrence, and Rupert Jemmott

Sumio Uesugi, a speaker at the 1921 UNIA convention

George A. Weston

Marcus Garvey (right) and Adrian F. Johnson (left) in the 1921 convention parade

Convention composite

returns to Kingston, doubted by me[.] Bill of Health probably will not be called for. Request instructions as to action to prevent Garvey travelling on the steamer to Port Limón as of the crew or a passenger.

LATHAM

[*Endorsements*] Tel. to Port Limón Tel. to
Kingston 5/20/21 J.P.D.-E.S. File Letter
Com. MP/JBM(?).

DNA, RG 59, file 811.108 G 191/12. TG, recipient's copy. Handwritten endorsements.

Report by Special Agent P-138

New York City 5-18-21

IN RE: NEGRO ACTIVITIES. MARCUS GARVEY

This day had lunch with REV. HEYLEGAN [*Ellegor*], (Garvey's right hand man) in an endeavor to secure information concerning the exact plans of Marcus Garvey, who is now on his West Indian tour.

He told me that he keeps Marcus Garvey well posted as to conditions here, and that as far as he knows Garvey is keeping the place of his landing a secret. He did say, however, that he was of the opinion that Garvey would sail from some West Indian port to a point somewhere in Florida, so as to evade the authorities at Ellis Island, as there were plans on foot by the Government and others to prevent his landing. Heylegan [*Ellegor*] also stated that the Black Star Line organi[z]ation has sent Counsellor Matthews (Negro), who is Garvey's Assistant Counsellor General, to Washington, with an affidavit to swear that Garvey was not an agitator. Matthews will be stationed there for the purpose of trying to use political influence, in an effort to assure Garvey's safe landing. Heylegan [*Ellegor*] also said the people are not sending in much money since Garvey's departure.

The high officials of the Black Star Line were afraid that the first report that the Government was stopping Garvey from coming back to the United States, would cause a sure collapse and a run on the Black Star Line Office by members for their money, so on that account they are doing all in their power to keep the rumors down and the members in an optimistic state of mind. Heylegan [*Ellegor*] told me also that he went to see President King of Liberia, now in Washington, a few weeks ago and had a three hours conference with him on the Garvey movement, and King told him he objected to Garvey's method of telling the white people just what he is going to do, and that while he, as a Liberian would like to see the Negroes own Africa, he would be a fool to tell them so openly.

Heylegan's [*Ellegor*] visit was primarily to urge President King not to say anything for or against Garvey's Liberian Loan, as it would cause a panic and a run on Garvey's office, and probably his life, if the poor people who subscribed found out that the Liberian Government was not behind it, as was the general impression among all of Garvey's followers. President King promised not to say anything although since his arrival in Washington the representatives of British, French and American Governments persistently asked King whether he endorsed it or not.

Today I saw about 15 men, women and children, poorly clad, apparently from the country, entering the office of the Black Star Line[.] I inquired from Heylegan [*Ellegor*] as to the trouble and he said that these poor people were from somewhere in California, had read an advertisement in the "Negro World" about securing passage to Africa and had sold their belongings and come to New York to book passage on Garvey's imaginar[y] Black Star Line "Back to Africa Ship". There were a large number of other people from the South who had also sold their homes and are now in New York, but who are disappointed at not seeing any Black Star Line ship. They have all paid their passage money to the Garvey office, and the question of finding lodging for them is now becoming a problem for that office. Today the high officials of Garvey were compelled to send telegrams to West and South warning those who booked passage, not to come to New York until further orders.

P-138

[*Handwritten endorsements*]
State 5/26/21/ GFR FILE GFR
[*Stamped endorsement*] NOTED F. D. W.

DNA, RG 65, file BS 198940-137. TD.

Charles Evans Hughes to Stewart E. McMillin

Washington, May 20, 1921

Marcus Garvey supposed to be member of crew or passenger steamer "KANAWHA". May apply to you for visa which should be refused. Inform Department of his movements.

HUGHES

[*Handwritten endorsement*] Gray Gergy 5pm
[*Stamped endorsement*] Signed by A. A. Adee

DNA, RG 59, file 811.108 G 191/12. TG, recipient's copy.

Reports by Special Agent P-138

New York City 5/21/21

In Re: Negro Activities.

I was informed by Plummer, Garvey's Chief of Field Force, or Secret Service Staff, that he was having quite [*a*] difficult time explaining the situation to men and women who had arrived from all over the country after having bought their tickets in readiness to sail for Africa on the proposed ship. Another of his troubles was to find lodgings for them. Plummer blamed this condition on the foolish way in which the officials place[d] their advertisement in the "Negro World[,]" thereby misleading the people.

He is firmly of the opinion that Garvey must get a ship of some kind for Africa, so as to avoid trouble with these people. Respectfully,

P-138

[*Endorsement*] NOTED F. D. W.

DNA, RG 65, file BS 202600-667-45X. TD. Stamped endorsement.

New York City 5/21/21

I learned from Rev. Heylegan [*Ellegor*] (A Garvey Official) that they have already contracted for the sale of a ship to run from here to Africa; that the Black Star Line has paid down $20,000. as first deposit and expect to pay another installment shortly.

The name of the ship and owners and where located I will endeavor to ascertain later.

They are all worrying about the probable debarring of Garvey from the U.S.A., which would cause a panic and a run on the office, resulting in a collapse of the entire movement. Respectfully,

P-138

DNA, RG 65, file BS 198940-140X. TD.

Marcus Garvey to William H. Ferris, Literary Editor, *Negro World*

[*Kingston, Jamaica*] May 21st, 1921

My dear Dr. Ferris:—

This is to inform you that I have seen several copies of the Negro World since I left New York, and I am indeed pleased with the get-up of the paper. You are doing it splendidly—keep it up. Some of the editorials I have read I hardly believe were yours. They were [so?] peppery, especially the one on Dr. Du Bois.[1] It seems that your trip to Canada[2] has given your work more pep. I hope you will add to it, so that at the next Convention you may be able to blaze out as one of the [chief?] exponents of the [new?] radicalism of the U.N.I.A.[3]

Relative to reports from Cuba, I want you to take special notice of this, that there are two men operating there by the name[s] of Radway[4] and Davidson.[5] Suppress any news that comes through their[6] . . . [*words illegible*]. These men are not in very good standing with the [Negroes?] there, and they are only using the medium of the Negro World, to foist themselves upon the public in Cuba.

You will please govern yourself accordingly. Yours truly,

MARCUS GARVEY

DNA, RG 65, file BS 198940. TLS, recipient's copy.

1. W. H. Ferris, "Dr. Du Bois and His Ebony World," *NW*, 7 May 1921, written in response to Du Bois's editorial in the May issue of the *Crisis*, entitled "The Drive" (p. 8). Du Bois included in his editorial a denunciation: "Into the field have jumped a hoard of scoundrels and bubble blowers, ready to conquer Africa, join the Russian revolution, and vote in the kingdom of God tomorrow." Ferris's editorial retort to Du Bois appeared with an accompanying editorial entitled "Is the Negro a Man?" (*NW*, 7 May 1921).

2. Ferris spoke in Montreal on 15 and 16 April and in Toronto on 17 and 18 April 1921. These meetings were sponsored respectively by the Montreal and Toronto divisions of the UNIA (*NW*, 9 April 1921; 30 April 1921; and 7 May 1921). The topic of his lectures was "Negro History and [the] UNIA."

3. On 2 March 1921 Bureau of Investigation Special Agent P-138 reported the following: Mr. Ferris, Garvey's editor of the Negro World, spoke before the [Negro Radical] forum today on the subject of Negro Radicalism and Garveyism, after which he was asked questions. Of course, he praised Garveyism and said it was the only method the Negro can use to get recognition from the White. He objected to White supremacy and told them it was all a fake, saying that Garvey was the only Negro who can fight the White man. . . . He also praised the Negro radicals and offered to help them, although he did not know enough about Bolshevism. (DNA, RG 65, file BS 202600-667)

P-138 described the forum, held in room 4 of Lafayette Hall, located at 121st Street and 7th Avenue, as "the uptown Negro branch of the Bolshevic free lecture room conducted by Domingo, Moore, Campbell, Potter, Randal [*sic*], Owen[,] Reid and other members." He noted that "Domingo and Moore are the executive officers and invite all the speakers from other sections."

4. Samuel Percival Radway (b. 1872), a herbalist, was an early activist in anticolonial movements in the West Indies and Central America. Born in St. Ann, Jamaica, Radway traveled to England and the United States as a young man and reportedly received diplomas from several schools, including the Jacksonian Optical College in Chicago and the American College of Naturopathy in New York. He lived in Central America in 1918 and 1919, first in Port Limón, Costa Rica, and then in Colón, Panama. When the dockworkers of the Panama Canal struck in 1919, Radway was chairman of the UNIA in Colón; although officials blamed Radway and a colleague, J. Henry Seymour, for the strike, they failed to deport him from Panama. Radway soon left voluntarily for Cuba, however, where he became an active UNIA organizer. In March 1921 he organized UNIA branches in Port Pastelillo (*NW*, 19 March 1921) and Jobabo (*NW*, 26 March 1921). When Henrietta Vinton Davis and J. S. de Bourg arrived in Cuba in May 1921, Radway acted as their official UNIA reporter and escort (*NW*, 7 May 1921). A month later he delivered a speech at the unveiling of the charter for the UNIA division in Santiago de Cuba. Later the same year, Radway returned to Jamaica, where he formed political alliances with Alfred A. Mends, A. Bain Alves, and J. Mannaseh Price, all of whom were formerly associated with the Garvey movement. In August 1923 he was elected secretary of the Jamaica Reform Club, which he and Mends organized. The club supported a new constitution for

Jamaica, a minimum wage for laborers, and religious and medical freedom, an important issue for often-harrassed herbalists such as Mends and Radway. Meanwhile, Radway skirmished with colonial authorities, who accused him of practicing medicine without a license and agitating against local conditions. In 1924 Radway left Jamaica for Haiti and the Dominican Republic, where he promoted the Afro–West Indian Settlers Association and Publishing Co., which he had founded a few years earlier. He later formed the West India Soil Producing Association, with headquarters in British Guiana, but encountered considerable opposition from governments in British Guiana and the Dominican Republic. By 1934 Radway was in Liberia, distributing literature on his Afro–West India Round Trip Association. He also set up a sanitarium there. He visited London in 1935 and finally returned to Jamaica in 1938. In 1949 Radway was president of the local chapter of the Universal African Nationalist Movement, Inc., in Jones Town, St. Andrew, Jamaica. Based in New York, this movement promoted Afro-American immigration to Liberia (William F. Elkins, *Street Preachers, Faith Healers, and Herb Doctors in Jamaica, 1890–1925* [New York: Revisionist Press, 1977], pp. 68–91; JA, CSO 172/1935; Dr. S. P. Radway, *To All Whom This May Come, Greetings in His Name* [Kingston, Jamaica: Star Printery, 1946]; I. K. Sundiata, *Black Scandal*, p. 119).

5. Prof. Dave Davidson traveled with Radway to UNIA organizing meetings in Cuba from March through May 1921. He delivered speeches in English and Spanish, often introducing Radway to audiences (*NW*, 19 March and 26 March 1921). In 1919 Davidson was vice-president of the UNIA in St. Thomas, Virgin Islands (*NW*, 11 October 1919).

6. Garvey wrote this letter in reaction to a long report, written by Radway and published in the *Negro World* of 7 May 1921, describing meetings organized by Henrietta Vinton Davis and J. S. de Bourg at various locations in Cuba. Because this letter was found in the files of the Bureau of Investigation, it is not possible to determine whether Ferris ever actually read it. It may have been intercepted in the mails before reaching UNIA headquarters, or Bureau of Investigation Confidential Informant 800 (James Wormley Jones) may have removed it from the incoming mail at UNIA headquarters. The *Negro World* continued to print reports from Radway as late as August 1921, indicating that Garvey's advice was either not received or not heeded.

Robert Woods Bliss to Joseph L. Johnson,[1] United States Minister Resident and Consul General, Liberia

WASHINGTON May 25, 1921

CONFIDENTIAL.

Sir:

You are instructed to watch closely and report fully all activities of the United Negro Improvement Association in Liberia.

The Department desires to know the names of persons in Liberia connected with this apparently subversive movement and wishes to be informed especially with regard to Gabriel Johnson, Mayor of Monrovia, who is reported to have taken an active part in furthering the aims of this movement. I am, Sir, Your obedient servant, For the Secretary of State:

ROBERT WOODS BLISS

[*Address*] The Honorable Joseph L. Johnson, Minister Resident and Consul General, Liberia.

DNA, RG 84, file 113. TLS, recipient's copy.

1. Joseph L. Johnson (1874–1945) was United States minister resident and consul general to Liberia from 1918 to 1921. He later served as the president of the board of trustees of Wilberforce University, Wilberforce, Ohio. He was educated at Ohio Northern University, Ada, and at Howard University, where he received his M.D. degree in 1902 (U.S. Department of State, *Register*, 1918, p. 129; *NYT*, 20 July 1945).

Marcus Garvey to the *Gleaner*

[[York House, Kingston, May 26, 1921]]

The Editors

Sir.—Having been in Jamaica for several weeks, after an absence abroad of nearly five years, and having had cause to observe the native life of the country industrially, commercially, socially, religiously and politically, it is for me, now that I am about to leave the island, to make a few comments.

To me, Jamaica is like a country of blind men where the one eye man rules. To me, Jamaica is misinformed and grossly ignorant in the things that tend to be [for] the general development of modern governments.

Jamaica, as I can see, is controlled by a few inexperienced "imported strangers," whose positions in Jamaica as officials and heads of departments have come to them as "godsends". These fellows know well that they could find no place in the body politic of their own native lands because of their inferiority and inability to perform technical work, yet through the system of any white man being better than a native, these "imported gentlemen" are continuously being sent out to the Colonies ("dumping ground") to administer the affairs of our governments. It is time that a halt be called. If Jamaica is to be saved, if Jamaica is to take her place among the progressive and successful nations of the world, then we must have a change of policy. Jamaica is void of that national spirit that should characterise every country, such as the nationalist spirit of Canada, Australia, South Africa, India etc. Everybody in Jamaica seems to be looking to the "Mother Country" for everything[,] even the black people speak of England as the Motherland. I never knew black mothers were born in England. I say black mothers, because this is the sense in which a large number of the people who refer to motherland and fatherland mean it. The poor black people of this country are taught a multitude of meaningless terms, politically and religiously, hence the gross ignorance of Jamaica.

I feel that Jamaica wants a political awakening, and it should come from within, and not from without. You want a better and more competent Legislative Council. You want able legislators and not mere prattlers. With the exception of a few of the elected members you have no real statesmen in the Council.

Your President of the Council[1] talks too much, he talks back at everything that is said by a member and instead of hearing what the member has to say, he tries to put words in his mouth and thereby change the line of discussion. I have never seen or heard of any legislative or debating body where the chairman has so much talk as in Jamaica. It doesn't appear that you follow rules of debate in your Council. Your Chairman here is everything, and it is apparent that the majority of the members of the Council go there to be told what to do and what to say by the President. Imagine the Speaker of the House of Commons in England, or the Speaker in the United States Senate having so much talk. Why won't Jamaica do things properly? How long are my countrymen going to allow Tom, Dick and Harry to come here and tell them what they ought to do politically and religiously? Must we admit that we are still children politically and religiously[?] Those of us who have been trained refuse to admit that we are children. We feel that we are quite competent to handle the affairs of our country, and now all that we ask is a chance, but if we don't get a chance, we should take a chance and I am here advising the people of this country to adopt a more aggressive attitude in handling the affairs of the island.

NATIVE LEADERS

The native leaders of Jamaica are too much afraid of giving offense to Mr. So and So. Mr. So and So be hanged[,] [i]f Mr. So and So is doing things to the detriment of the country. Real leaders don't care whom they offend, if in offending they are serving the cause of humanity and working for the good of their country. Jesus Christ was the greatest offender when He was on earth, and we ought to take a leaf out of His book in this respect.

Jamaicans, as I can see, worship too much that which comes from abroad and from anywhere. If a thing, a man, or an animal is imported, it is supposed to be better than the native product. How silly[!] As for individuals, I have seen some of the greatest idiots abroad[;] as for things, I have seen so many inferior articles abroad, when compared to native ones. Jamaicans want to have more confidence in self.

I would recommend that the poorer classes of Jamaica, the working classes get together and form themselves into unions and organizations and elect their members for the Legislative Council. With few exceptions the men in the Council are representing themselves and their class. The workers of Jamaica should elect their own representatives and if the Government here will not pay the legislator, as is done in England and America, then the unions and organizations should pay these men so they can talk out without caring whom they offend. The legislators in Jamaica should be paid at least £500 (five hundred pounds) per annum. If this was done you would have had a better class of legislators, and more independent ones. Poor, honest men like Messrs. Wint,[2] Lightbody,[3] Young[4] and Smith can't afford to waste four or five months annually away from their work and paying high living expenses without feeling it. That suits the wealthy legislators of today.

427

Religiously, I believe the poor Negro people of Jamaica are being deceived by a large number of the men who are attempting to preach Christ. Christ is being sold to the poor of Jamaica at a higher price than paid anywhere else. One who receives 1/6 per day has to pay 12/- annually for each member of his family to be in good standing with the "imported preacher" who preaches Christ, and this tax doesn't include collections at all meetings, harvest festivals, anniversaries, missionary meetings, special envelopes, pew rents, communion tax etc. Would Christ so tax the poor black people of Jamaica as they are so being taxed in His name today? If Christ saw the condition of the people he would have preached against it as he did in the days of old, but the "imported Jamaica preachers" tell the people to lay up their treasures in Heaven whilst they (the preachers) enjoy theirs down here. Jamaica needs a spiritual revival, not the Gypsy Pat Smith's sort.[5]

The people of Jamaica want advanced religion today. The religion that will prepare them for heaven, by having them live clean[,] healthy[,] happy and prosperous lives down here. No hungry man can be a good christian. No dirty[,] naked[,] civilized [man] can be a good christian. No shelterless civilized man can be a good christian for he is bound to have bad, wicked thoughts[,] therefore it should be the duty of religion to find physical as well as spiritual food for the body of man and when your preachers ignore the economical condition and the moral depravity of the people, they are but serving themselves through their preachings and not representing the spirit of God.

In my way of thinking I believe that there will be more Jamaican preachers in hell after judgement than any other kind of people, because I believe they deceive more and speculate more of the Holy Name of God than any other class of preachers. I am not blaming the native preachers for they culled their religion, their methods and their systems from the established Churches as introduced and presided over by the "imported preachers". What I would like to see, is that the negro preachers of Jamaica get together and preach to their own people the real religion of Jesus Christ.

Industrial and commercial Jamaica is so bankrupt that I will have to treat it in another letter as also social Jamaica.[6]

I hope this letter will be taken in the spirit in which it is written, and that critics won't try to import foreign matter and personalities into the discussion that will follow the publication. I am, etc.

MARCUS GARVEY

Printed in the *Gleaner*, 2 June 1921. Original headlines omitted.

1. Under the Jamaican crown colony constitution, Sir Leslie Probyn, as governor of Jamaica (1918–1924), was president of the council.
2. Dunbar Theophilus Wint (1879–1938) was one of the leading planters in St. Ann. He was born in Snowden, Manchester, and was elected to the Legislative Council as representative for St. Ann in 1920. He was formerly a teacher and editor of the *Jamaica Tribune*. In 1926 Wint became editor of the *Jamaica Critic*, and in 1930 he published an editorial strongly criticizing Garvey for his attacks against the Jamaican government in the *Black Man* newspaper (*HJ*, 1938; D. T. Wint, "Garveyism," *West Indian Critic* 5 [January 1930]: 7–8).

3. Philip F. Lightbody, editor of a small newspaper, was the member of the Legislative Council for St. James.

4. George Lewis Young (d. 1924) was a minister in the United Methodist Free church and for a time chairman of the Jamaica Union of Teachers. He served for several years on the parochial board of St. Catherine, and he represented the parish in the Legislative Council from 1920 until his death (*HJ*, 1924).

5. Gypsy Pat Smith was a white American evangelist preaching at the time in Jamaica. On 26 May 1921 the following letter by Marcus Garvey appeared in the *Gleaner*:

> Sir,—It has come to my notice that Mr. Gipsy Pat Smith is advising the poor black people of the island to throw away their jewelry, namely, bangles, earrings, broaches, etc.[,] for with such things they will not enter heaven, and that they should store up their treasures in heaven.
>
> Mr. Editor, this is nothing short of a crime, and if Pat Smith says these things he ought to be jailed or confined in the insane asylum even as [Alexander] Bedward is because he would be a dangerous enemy to the progress of the black people of this country.
>
> Why won't Pat Smith call a revival meeting for the wealthy men of the country and advise them to throw away their wealth to the poor, as no rich man can enter heaven.
>
> Black Jamaica is tired of the Gipsy Pat Smith's brand of religion.

6. It does not appear that this letter was ever published.

Report by Special Agent P-138

New York City 5/27/21

IN RE: NEGRO ACTIVITIES.

Today [*24 May*] visited the office of the Black Star Line and interviewed THOMPSON, Garvey's Vice President and General Manager, of said line, using the pretext that I was interested in African produce and had quantities of cocoa beans and mahogany ready to be transported from West Africa to New York. Thompson exhibited the photo of the new ship which they are purchasing,[1] to be put in service in July, and wanted 4,000 tons of cargo, and said he would be glad of the offer of freight.

He was getting ready to go to Newport News or Norfolk on the evening train to make an inspection of the ship, and return by Saturday, when he would go more fully into the matter.

P-138

[*Endorsement*] FILE G. F. R.

DNA, RG 65, file BS 198940-142. TD. Stamped endorsement.

1. Two weeks earlier the U.S. Shipping Board had rejected the Black Star Line's offer to purchase the former German steamship *Orion* for $190,000 "as is, where is." Some days later, however, the Black Star Line submitted a revised offer of $225,000 (J. Harry Philbin to chairman, U.S. Shipping Board, 25 May 1921, DNA, RG 32, file 1091-1250, pt. 1).

Constantine Graham, British Chargé d'Affaires, Panama, to Earl Curzon of Kedleston

BRITISH LEGATION, Panama, May 27, 1921

My Lord,

I have the honour to report that Marcus Garvey, President of the Universal Negro Improvement Association and African Communities League, arrived at Colón from Port Limón, Costa Rica, on April 26th, and, in the course of his stay on the Isthmus, delivered a series of lectures on the aims of the Universal Negro Improvement Association and the reconstitution of Liberia as a nucleus for negro power in Africa. Garvey claims to be President-Elect of Liberia, and the practical object of his tour was the collection of funds for a $2,000,000. loan for his purpose.

In the course of his lectures Mr Garvey made constant appeals to sentiments of race solidarity and equality based on the achievements of negroes in the past on [in?] analogy with the struggles of other races and peoples. He made particular reference to the negro effort in the recent war which, he alleged, was won by their collaboration, and to the Panama Canal which, he claims, was dug by their work.

Mr Garvey advocated enthusiastically the support of an African State whose future he portrayed in very highly coloured terms. While much that he said was crude and even ludicrous, his speeches were interesting as showing a determined movement to escape from race subjection, and eventually to place negroes on a footing of at least equality with other races as an independent force.

No official reception appears to have been given to Mr Garvey's mission, but he drew large audiences and is understood to have collected considerable funds, mainly from West Indian sources, in subscriptions to the loan[,] one of the objects of which is also the support of the Black Star Line, a negro shipping concern which has so far not shown any very great practical activity.

He proceeded from the Isthmus of Panama on May 5th for Jamaica and Cuba, but I understand that difficulties may arise as to his readmission to the United States of America.

A copy of this despatch has been sent to His Majesty's Ambassador at Washington. I have the honour to be, with the highest respect, My Lord, Your Lordship's most obedient, humble Servant,

CONSTANTINE GRAHAM[1]

PRO, FO 371/5684. TLS, carbon copy.

1. Constantine Graham (1882–1934) assumed charge of the British consulate at Colón, Panama, in 1920. The same year he was British chargé d'affaires at Panama (*WWW*).

Lewis J. Baley to William B. Matthews, Bureau of Investigation

[*Washington, D.C.*] MAY 28, 1921

Dear Sir:

The bureau desires that you make an immediate confidential investigation of the activities of W. A. Matthews, of the Whitlaw Apartment House, of this city.

Matthews is personal representative of Marcus Garvey, in this city, and is making every possible effort to effect the return to this Country of Marcus Garvey.

Kindly give this matter immediate attention, forwarding your report under confidential cover, to the attention of Mr. Hoover. Very truly yours,

LEWIS J. BALEY
Chief

DNA, RG 65, file BS 198940-149. TLS, carbon copy.

Lewis J. Baley to William B. Matthews

[*Washington, D.C.*] May 28, 1921

Dear Sir:—

The Bureau is advised by strictly confidential source that one Van Cronburgge, of 1780 Massachusetts Avenue N.W., is a subscriber to the "Negro World." The nature of the recent activities of this individual would be of interest to the Bureau. Very truly yours,

LEWIS J. BALEY
Chief

[*Address*] William B. Matthews, Esq.,
[1330 F?] Street, Washington, D.C.

DNA, RG 65, file BS 202600-1993-1. TL, carbon copy.

Henry P. Fletcher, Under Secretary of State, to Herbert Hoover, Secretary of Commerce[1]

[*Washington, D.C.*] May 28, 1921

Sir:

The Department has been advised by the American Consul at Kingston, Jamaica, that a seaman named Marcus Garvey was shipped on the American steamship KANAWHA at Santiago de Cuba by the master of the vessel[2] without the sanction of the American Consul at that place.

This matter is referred to you for such action as you may desire to take when the vessel returns to the United States. I have the honor to be, Sir, Your obedient servant, For the Secretary of State:

HENRY P. FLETCHER[3]
Under Secretary

DNA, RG 59, file 811.108 G 191/12. TLR, carbon copy.

1. Herbert Clark Hoover (1874–1964), engineer, administrator, businessman, and thirty-first president of the United States, won an international reputation for his direction of the Commission for Relief in Belgium after World War I. In 1919 he served as an adviser to President Wilson at the Paris Peace Conference and played a major role in planning the economic reorganization of Europe. Following his acceptance in 1921 of the position of secretary of commerce in the Harding administration, Hoover was responsible for the controversial decision to alleviate famine in the Soviet Union through food and other relief (*DAB*, supp. 7, pp. 358–360).

2. Adrian Richardson, captain of the *Kanawha*, testified at Garvey's mail fraud trial in 1923 that "he [Garvey] said that he had trouble to get back in the United States at that time; that it would be good if I could sign him up as a member of the crew then he would have no trouble" (*Marcus Garvey* v. *United States*, no. 8317, Ct. App., 2nd Cir., 2 February 1925, pp. 452–453).

3. Henry P. Fletcher (1873–1959) directed the State Department's Division of Latin American Affairs in 1920. The following year President Harding made him under secretary of state (*NYT*, 11 July 1959).

Report by Special Agent J. T. Flournoy

[*Washington, D.C.*]
May 28 to June 4, 1921

NEGRO ACTIVITIES:

. . . At the request of Robert Silvereruys, "Secretaire d'Ambassade de S. M. le Roi des Belges", Washington, D.C., I called at the Belgian Embassy and was furnished information as to negro agitators from this country stirring up strife among the negro natives of Belgium especially in Belgian Congo and Liberia. The files of the Embassy contain considerable information on the subject and are courteously offered to the Department for any information of value which they might contain. The Ambassador stated that he would hesitate hereafter to visé the passports of negroes leaving this country to enter any of these possessions. . . .

J. T. FLOURNOY

DNA, RG 65, file BS 202600-9-18. TD.

Report of Liberty Hall Meeting

[[Liberty Hall, N.Y. May 29, 1921]]

GARVEY SENDS MESSAGE OF APPRECIATION TO MEMBERS AND FRIENDS OF LIBERTY HALL—EARLY RETURN NOW EXPECTED

. . . DR. STEWART SPEAKS.

Rev. Dr. G. E. Stewart, High Chancellor, spoke as follows:

Right Honorable Speaker in Convention, Officers and Members of the New York local of the Universal Negro Improvement Association, and Friends. We are happy to greet you again tonight. I do not intend to make a speech tonight, as I am compelled to hold a little. I have been going too much, night and day, and I am beginning to feel the effects of it; therefore, I must hold up a little.

But I have a little message for you that I shall read:

"I have read of your work in Liberty Hall. Let me thank you for what you have done in representing me during my absence. Keep up the good work the best you can, and let the people of Liberty Hall know that everything is O.K.; that I hope to be with them within a couple of weeks.["]

This is a message from the Hon. Marcus Garvey (Applause). It was a letter written on the 20th of this month, and I feel sure—I know that you are longing to see him and hear his voice again.

I must take the privilege of thanking you for the manner in which you supported these meetings. I have such good news to tell him that it will take me a whole day to tell him about you; everything went on nicely and smoothly all the time and I want you to continue on that way until he returns. You have all done well. The choir from the manager down, has indeed been faithful in carrying on the work assigned to them: the band continues onward and onward without failure. I must commend the Legions, the Black Cross Nurses, and the Motor Corps for their punctuality. We asked them to be here at ten minutes to 8 o'clock and they are always here promptly. If we have done nothing else, we are learning punctuality (Applause). We promised to begin our meetings at 8:00 during the week, and you are always here waiting when I come. You were indeed liberal in your offerings during the absence of the president, and now I know more about you than I knew before. You have been tested, and I venture to say, weighed in the balance, and not found wanting. (Applause) No longer are you simply depending upon the presence of the president; you have learned your duty—that whether he is here or not, you must be here.

Sometimes on Sunday nights I wonder where we will put the people during the coming convention. If at ordinary meetings this place is so packed, where will you be placed when the president returns? Some are going to charter their seats from 5 o'clock in the afternoon. I think I see some who are sitting in their seats more firmly than ever, determined to hold them, I suppose for that occasion.

Before I sit down, having made these scattered remarks I want to read just this to you: In the British Parliament, not very long ago, David Lloyd George arose and with enthusiasm said "Gentlemen this world-wide trouble is fast growing beyond human control. But I see before me a government which is founded upon Justice; a government to which all religious prejudices and racial distinctions shall cease. (Applause) I see growing up before me a government that is founded upon justice, whose workings are based upon love. This government comes not from the hands of feeble men but from the power of Almighty God." (Renewed applause.) If David Lloyd George confesses that this government that he sees in the future is built by the hand of Almighty God, then the Negro is safe, for the Negroes' hope is built on nothing less than Jesus' blood and righteousness; and if he believes that it is built on that, and through God, then we know we are safe, because we are in God's hands. God's promises are sure, and I am glad that David Lloyd George sees a greater movement than that of which he and the people of England have boasted so long and still boast of.

The world is looking up. You may think me selfish in saying that the Universal Negro Improvement Association has caused Negroes to speak what they never would have thought of speaking many years ago. But one thing, Negroes, be careful; be careful how you may be bribed. A Negro met me this week, and told me the Negroes don't want a republican form of government; that Negroes want a monarchical government. Just think of it—a Negro saying such a thing! And that man is living right in America now; yet he has the presumption to talk about monarchical government! But he is a type of some of the cringing Negroes that there are amongst us. I would to God he was here now. He did not know I was going to talk on the subject and about him in public.

THE STARS AND STRIPES

But I will take them all to task who I hear make such utterances, and expose their ignorance in the midst of all their boasted education. (Applause) Here is a man living now under the American government, yet talking about monarchial government! He should be driven out of the country. Under this American flag, how can any man take a stand for a monarchial form of government? It is the only flag under which the Universal Negro Improvement Association can stand (applause), and while I am here I will respect the Stars and Stripes. (Applause.) The Universal Negro Improvement Association believes in loyalty to that flag, under which and by which it is receiving protection, and if I felt that I could not be loyal to the flag of the United States, I would get out of America at once. So long, however, as I am here, I must be and will be loyal to it. When you are in my house you must obey me (applause), and what I put before you, you must eat (laughter); if you cannot do as I say in my house, and cannot eat what I offer you, you can walk out of it, and I will close the door after you. (Continued laughter) Simple though that is, yet it is logical.

Another thing I must tell you is this: I had been thinking very seriously about this paper called the Negro World, and I began to wonder about it, that wherever I would go in New York I looked and saw bundles of newspapers thrown away, but I never saw even a single sheet of the Negro World torn up or thrown into the street. It would appear that the Negro World is regarded by the people as being too precious to be thrown away. And do you not know that in communities where men and women are brought up under the Christian religion, a man or a woman on seeing in the street or on the ground a leaf of the Bible will stop and pick it up, such is his reverence and regard for the Holy Book? It is the same, it seems, with the Negro World: if a person happens to see a sheet of the Negro World anywhere, he will stop and pick it up and read it and preserve it, or pass it on to someone else to read. All newspapers are wasted except the Negro World. (Applause.) Can't you see that God Almighty is in this whole movement? He is in it, and since God has a hand in it, I am not afraid. Whatever may be hard to bear, He will make right, and He is [s]o wise and so great that every mountainous difficulty that stands in the way of the people He removes miraculously. I have known some seemingly insurmountable obstacles to be removed in such a way that I have wondered over it, although I love and serve God, and do you know that sometimes God does things and answers prayer so quickly that we can hardly believe that is a fact; we can scarcely believe that He has really answered our prayer? Peter once did not believe that God had answered his prayer, and those who were praying for Peter could hardly believe that God would have answered their prayer so quickly, that when they heard it was Peter they said: "Impossible; it must be Peter's angel." But it was so, and my brethren, God is going to answer our prayers. His ears are not deaf; His hands are not shut tight; His blessings are ready to be poured upon us, because giving does not impoverish Him, neither does withholding enrich Him. God's blessings are upon the Negro race, and if His blessings were not on us, we would not have survived until now and coming together as we do. (Applause.) Let us, therefore, give God the praise and the glory and let us, with one voice send up the supplication: "God save Marcus Garvey. God enable him to carry on the great work that he has begun. God put more wisdom in him, that he may be able to plan and carry on the work." Where God leads, we will follow, and if the Hon. Marcus Garvey follows God, a nation will be following him, 400,000,000 strong. (Great applause.) . . .[1]

Printed in *NW*, 4 June 1921. Original headlines abbreviated.

1. Other speakers at the meeting were William H. Ferris and Fred A. Toote.

Charles L. Latham to Charles Evans Hughes

Kingston, Jamaica May 30, 1921

SIR:

I have to refer to my despatch No. 1057 of May 7, 1921, and to my telegram of May 18, 1921, in regard to Marcus Garvey and to report that Garvey sailed for Cristobal and Port Limón, Saturday, May 28th., as a member of the crew of the Black Star Line steamer KANAWHA.

I have cabled the Department to this effect on this day, and have also notified the Consulate General at Panama.

As stated in my cablegram of May 18th., Garvey was signed on as a purser on the Articles of the s.s. KANAWHA while the vessel was at Santiago, not before the American Consul, but by the Master, after the ship had cleared. Three other men were signed on in the same way at the same time.

The Master stated that the KANAWHA will return to Jamaica before it returns to the United States, but this course may not be adhered to, the vessel possibly going directly to the United States from Cristobal or Port Limón. In case the KANAWHA does return to Jamaica and seeks to sail direct to the United States this office will, unless instructed to the contrary, refuse to visa the crew list unless Garvey is removed therefrom. Instructions are requested as to whether this office may refuse to give a bill of health, or return the Ship's papers until the requirement of the law that the crew list be visaed has been complied with. I have the honor to be, Sir, Your obedient servant,

C. L. LATHAM
American Consul

DNA, RG 59, file 811.108 G 191/17. TLS, recipient's copy.

J. Edgar Hoover to William L. Hurley

WASHINGTON, D.C. May 31, 1921

Dear Mr. Hurley:

I am inclosing herewith a photostat copy of an article in the "New York Amsterdam News" for May 25th, being a statement by PRINCE DENIYI upon MARCUS GARVEY, the notorious negro agitator.[1] Very truly yours,

J. E. HOOVER

Special Assistant to the Attorney General

[*Endorsements*] hold prev pls any rec of
Deniyi? *No*

DNA, RG 59, file 000-612. TLS, recipient's copy. Handwritten endorsements.

1. See also "Native Brands Back to Africa Move a Farce," *Chicago Defender*, 14 May 1921.

Enclosure

[*Amsterdam News*, 25 May 1921]

AFRICAN PRINCE FLAYS GARVEY

MADARIKAN DENIYI IN SWORN STATEMENT, CALLS BLACK STAR LINE CROOKED STEAMSHIP CORPORATION

To the Editor of New York Amsterdam News.

Sir: Prince Madarikan Deniyi, noted writer and lecturer, who has opened the eyes of the Negroes in Africa, Europe and America by writing interesting articles against [the] Garvey movement to the Associated Press and Negro Press for publication, is the grandson of the late Balogun Ijemo, a powerful Yoruba chief at Abeokuta, Nigeria, West Africa. He was born in Lagos, Nigeria, West Africa, March 2, 1892, and came to the United States of America, May 5, 1914. He is a registered druggist, a licensed embalmer, and a learned scholar. But as a writer and lecturer Deniyi grew so that his fame rises above the mountains and forests of America. The current of his personal magnetism and occult power is so great that Marcus Garvey and Bruce [G]rit failed to turn him into a frog in New York City with their fake Black Star Line "hoodo" and West Indies "Obio" [*Obeah*]. Prince Deniyi lives at 33 West 132d street, New York City, and would like to hear from all people who are interested in Africa. He is not a member of the Universal Negro Improvement Association, and doesn't believe in investing his money on any crooked Black Star Line steamship corporation in America. Some of his articles about the conspiracy and fraudulent stock schemes of Marcus Garvey were published in the New York Times, August 15, 1920, and Richmond Planet, February 19, 1921. The leading newspapers in Europe, Africa and America

437

helped this Nigerian hero to open the eyes of the Negroes all over the world about the fake "Free Africa movement."

"Let not your heart be troubled[,]" [wrote?] Prince Deniyi. "I am the African writer, who is able to straighten Marcus Garvey as the Colored women are using the hot iron to cultivate their kinky hair in America. Garvey [*is*] detrimental to the Black Race and very stubborn like the Balaam ass. He talks too much, but I will stop his unbridled audacity this year 1921, before allowing his conspiracy and fraud[u]lent stock schemes to put the Negroes back in slavery bondage. Buying an old second-handed steamer on installment plan from white people in the United States is not easy as chasing wild monkeys on the cocoanut trees in West Indies. Why did Garvey fail to send a ship to Liberia, West Africa, in January, February, March, April and May, 1921, as it was advertised in the Negro World by the Black Star Line Steamship Corporation? The Negro World is the greatest Negro lie newspaper in the United States of America.

"The Black Star Line Steamship Corporation and Universal Negro Improvement Association have been trying to buy the old steamship Yarmouth on installment plan from the white people for the purpose of carrying the Negroes from America to kill all the white people in Africa, but old Yarmouth is now almost completely wrecked at Staten Island, in New York, and too old to carry the Negroes from America to hell. Marcus Garvey himself had to ride on the white folks' ship from the United States to Cuba and British West Indies last March, 1921. If the Black Star Line couldn't give the Negroes' dividend since 1919, how many more ignorant Negroes in Africa, Europe and America are going to be stockholders in this fake Negro steamship corporation? I am not a monkey chaser, but it is ridiculous for a monkey chaser like Garvey to be using his fraudulent stock schemes to fool the Negroes. If Bruce Grit[1] and Marcus Garvey don't [*like*] my protest articles, I will advise them to sue me for damages. But I will prove to the American judges and lawyers that it is a great conspiracy and forgery for the Universal Negro Improvement Association to issue and sell fake Liberian Liberty Bonds to the Negroes in America for the purpose of redeeming Africa on false doctrine without the proper seal of the Liberian Government on the bonds. Garvey is an undesirable subject, and ought to be exterminated from the United States."—Advt.

MADARIKAN DENIYI

State of New York.
    City of New York. SS.:
County of New York.

On this 23rd day of May, 1921, before me, a Notary Public in and for the County and State of New York, personally appeared Madarikan Deniyi, to me known and known to me to be the person mentioned and described in the foregoing article, and he did upon his oath acknowledge to me that he is the author of the foregoing article and signed the same fully knowing the contents thereof.

SADIE E. PARHAM

Notary Public, New York Co. Clerk's No. 273, N. Y. Register No. 3245. My commission expires March 30, 1923.

DNA, RG 59, file 000-612. Newspaper clipping.

1. John E. Bruce wrote in the 26 February 1921 issue of the *Negro World*, "I have in my possession two letters from Lagos from a gentleman who ought to know, which brand this 'Prince' as a fraud and adventurer and says that he is unknown in Lagos. This man, like a good many other Africans who have come to this country and posed as sons of native kings, princes or the relatives of prominent merchants and traders, has many imitators all over the country." Deniyi became the target of numerous editorials, news reports, and irate letters that appeared over many months in various issues of *NW*: " 'Prince'? Madarikan," 16 April 1921; " 'Prince' Madarikan Deniyi Takes to His Heels in New Jersey City," 4 June 1921; H. Hodge, "A Word Regarding 'Prince' (?) Deniyi," 4 June 1921; J. N. Bridgeman, "Answer to 'Prince' Deniyi's Attack on Black Star Line," 25 June 1921; "Adeoye Deniyi, a Real Prince Exposes Madarikan Deniyi, a Fake Prince," 10 September 1921; "Fake Prince Flogged in Philadelphia," 29 October 1921; "Philadelphia Negro Put 'Prince' to Flight," 26 November 1921.

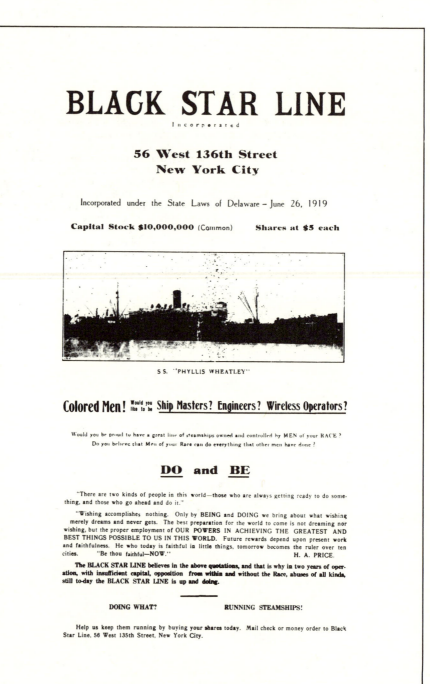

BLACK STAR LINE

Incorporated

56 West 136th Street
New York City

Incorporated under the State Laws of Delaware – June 26, 1919

Capital Stock $10,000,000 (Common)   **Shares at $5 each**

S S. "PHYLLIS WHEATLEY"

Colored Men! Would you like to be Ship Masters? Engineers? Wireless Operators?

Would you be proud to have a great line of steamships owned and controlled by MEN of your RACE?

Do you believe that Men of your Race can do everything that other men have done?

DO and BE

"There are two kinds of people in this world—those who are always getting ready to do something, and those who go ahead and do it."

"Wishing accomplishes nothing. Only by BEING and DOING we bring about what wishing merely dreams and never gets. The best preparation for the world to come is not dreaming nor wishing, but the proper employment of OUR POWERS IN ACHIEVING THE GREATEST AND BEST THINGS POSSIBLE TO US IN THIS WORLD. Future rewards depend upon present work and faithfulness. He who today is faithful in little things, tomorrow becomes the ruler over ten cities. "Be thou faithful—NOW."   H. A. PRICE.

The BLACK STAR LINE believes in the above quotations, and that is why in two years of operation, with insufficient capital, opposition from within and without the Race, abuses of all kinds, still to-day the BLACK STAR LINE is up and doing.

DOING WHAT?   RUNNING STEAMSHIPS!

Help us keep them running by buying your shares today. Mail check or money order to Black Star Line, 56 West 135th Street, New York City.

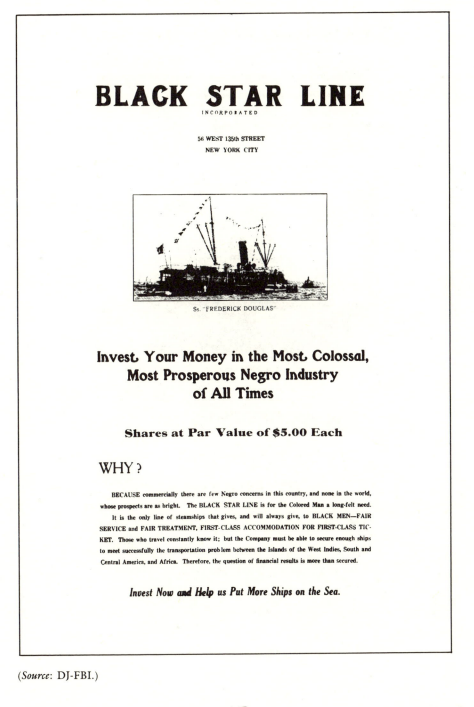

BLACK STAR LINE

INCORPORATED

56 WEST 135th STREET
NEW YORK CITY

Ss. "FREDERICK DOUGLAS"

Invest Your Money in the Most Colossal, Most Prosperous Negro Industry of All Times

Shares at Par Value of $5.00 Each

WHY ?

BECAUSE commercially there are few Negro concerns in this country, and none in the world, whose prospects are as bright. The BLACK STAR LINE is for the Colored Man a long-felt need.

It is the only line of steamships that gives, and will always give, to BLACK MEN—FAIR SERVICE and FAIR TREATMENT, FIRST-CLASS ACCOMMODATION FOR FIRST-CLASS TIC-KET. Those who travel constantly know it; but the Company must be able to secure enough ships to meet successfully the transportation problem between the Islands of the West Indies, South and Central America, and Africa. Therefore, the question of financial results is more than secured.

Invest Now and Help us Put More Ships on the Sea.

(*Source*: DJ-FBI.)

Management

Whatever might have been the errors of the past, the present administration of the Black Star Line is composed of trained business men and specialty service help, unquestionably equal to their responsible tasks; and improvement will always be gladly considered.

Remember: Criticism is Cheap and Can not Feed Hungry Men.

Ss. "SHADYSIDE"
(River Excursion Steamer)

Has the Black Star Line been Successful?
Read This:

"When I speak of success I do not mean it in the sordid sense. A successful man is one who has tried, not cried; who has worked, not dodged; who has shouldered responsibility, not evaded it; who has got under the burden, not merely stood off looking on, giving advice and philosophizing on the situation.

The result of a man's work is not the measure of success. To go down with the ship in the storm and tempest is better than to paddle away to Paradise in an orthodox canoe.

To have worked is to have succeeded, we leave the results to time. Life is too short to gather the Harvest, we can only sow.   E. Hubbard.

Now we have worked day and night, it is for you to do something now by investing RIGHT NOW in the BLACK STAR LINE.

SHARES .... $5.00 EACH

Buy 5, 10, 20, 50, 200. Cash or instalments. Ten (10) per cent with subscriptions, balance equal monthly payments.

N. B.—We are entirely open to investigation and will be glad to furnish information upon request

Black Star Line, Inc.

56 West 135th Street, New York.   MARCUS GARVEY, President

Marcus Garvey to Charles L. Latham

37 Orange Street, Kingston [*1 June 1921*]

COPY

Dear Sir:—

As President of the Black Star Line an American Corporation, incorporated under the laws of the State of Delaware, United States, owning the Steamship Kanawha of New York, I hereby beg to lodge the following complaints against the Master and Crew for the d[e]structive mismanagement of the said Steamship Kanawha, and especially to lodge complaint against Charles C. Harris of Washington D.C. Chief Engineer of the said Kanawha and his Assistants Cyrus M. Yarter[1] of New York and Charles S. Sauncy[2] of Oklahoma.

That our boat the Kanawha sailed out of New York harbor on the 25th March 1921 in perfect seaworthy condition with her engines and boilers in perfect order, and having a certificate of American inspection, and making a speed of over 14 knots per hour, in a trip that should have consumed but 30 days, but which has now taken over 10 weeks and not half completed, and that since the 25th March the said Charles C. Harris and his Assistants have criminally damaged and destroyed parts of the engines and boilers and have in the most criminal manner handicapped and embarrassed the Black Star Line in causing the Corporation to spend unnecessarily thousands of dollars in having the boat call at nearly every port on /the/ route from New York, including American and Cuban ports, which ports were not on the entry of Call. Reasons given that the said engines and boilers needed repairs, and even after such repairs were done, whilst not more than, in some cases 6, 10, or 12 hours at sea, that a repetition of the previous destruction and other damage would take place, causing the boat to put in at other ports as above outlined, and in many cases to imperil the lives of those on board. I hereby charge these men as conspiring to do the said damage.

That the said Charles C. Harris outside of the destruction done to property reveals himself as being drunk, as also his Assistants, having in his possession, and being under the influence of spirituous liquor, on board the boat. And that he from what can be gathered is grossly incompetent, which incompetency has inflicted terrible loss to the extent of over thirty-five thousand dollars on the Corporation.

The said Charles C. Harris is further accused of using indecent and obscene language, as also other members of the crew to the hearing of passengers and all aboard the boat.

That the engineers would all be seen on deck at one and the same time even though the boat is on high sea, and whilst it has already been reported that the boat needed then more than ever, careful attention of the Engineers in consequence of previous breakdown to parts of the engine.

Before the said Charles C. Harris leaves a port, he would be asked what are the requirements for the safe conduct of a voyage. After making requests for such requirements, and after they have been supplied, he would in 6, 10, or 12 hours after leaving port, place the boat in an alarming condition. Through this conduct untold hardships have been inflicted upon the Black Star Line in an endless waste of supplies and wages to a crew, that proves itself absolutely incompetent and undi[s]ciplined.

This complaint is lodged as a protest against /paying/ the crew and the said Charles C. Harris and his Assistants any wages that they may further claim until the matter has been thoroughly investigated by the marine authorities in the United States of America.[3] And that the Black Star Line Corporation now asks your protection and help so as to safe guard the Corporation from the conspiracy and destruction which has been brought about by the action of the men as herein outlined.[4]

The Black Star Line is in a position to support these statements by proofs that can be submitted in evidence.

Trusting that you will take cognizance of this complaint and protest, and that you will give the protection necessary. I have the honor to be,

Black Star Line Inc.
MARCUS GARVEY
President

DNA, RG 59, file 811.108 G 191/18. TL, carbon copy. This letter was an enclosure to a letter from Charles L. Latham to Charles Evans Hughes (secretary of state), 4 June 1921, DNA, RG 59, file 811.108 G 191/18.

1. Cyrus M. Yarter, of 35 Poplar Street, Brooklyn, was granted his license as second assistant engineer of ocean steamers when his original license (no. 88640, 22 July 1919) as chief engineer of steam vessels of 150 gross tons was endorsed by the U.S. local inspectors of New York on 13 April 1920.

2. No record of a license being granted to Charles S. Sauncy (or Sauncey) has been found.

3. In a later action on 21 September 1921, twenty-five former crewmen from the *Kanawha*, claiming that they had not been paid, filed a libel against the Black Star Line for $11,267.78 plus additional costs in the U.S. District Court for the Southern District of New York. By 15 December 1921 four additional plaintiffs had joined the original group. On that date the court awarded them their wages to the time they finally arrived in New York City on 7 September 1921, compensation for the money they had spent for provisions while in Jamaica, and $75.00 each for the time they spent waiting for their wages. The total award was $12,303.35, and the Black Star Line was given sixty days to pay. On 7 January 1922 attorney Wilford Smith, representing the Black Star Line, told the court that receipts for the wages previously paid to the seamen had been misplaced, but that during the time since the court's ruling they had been found, enabling him to prove that the men had actually already received their compensation. The court was unimpressed, however, and awarded two more seamen from the *Kanawha* their unpaid wages plus money for waiting time. On 20 February 1922 the court ordered the marshal of the Southern District of New York to recover the required amount from the Black Star Line. On 5 November 1923, however, the marshal reported to the court that there were no "goods, chattels, lands or tenements" owned by the BSL that could be seized to satisfy the debt. The seamen later sued for a portion of the $22,500.00 that the BSL left on deposit with the U.S. Shipping Board during the unsuccessful negotiations for the *Orion* (*Albert A. Zink* v. *Black Star Line, Inc.*, no. 80/279, U.S. District Court, Southern District of New York, 18 October 1921).

Garvey's charges against the crew members of the *Kanawha* were eventually investigated by the Department of Commerce's Steamboat-Inspection Service. On 31 October 1921 the board of the inspectors ruled in favor of the crewmen, refusing to revoke the licenses of the officers who served on the ship (DNA, RG 41, U.S. Department of Commerce, Steamboat-Inspection Service, file 14677).

4: Charles Latham, the American consul in Kingston, Jamaica, informed Garvey that he would have to present proper credentials to the consulate, establishing his power to act on behalf of the Black Star Line in dismissing the *Kanawha*'s captain and chief engineer. Normally, when a shipowner discharged a captain and crew, he paid them their full wages to the date of discharge plus one month's salary and transportation back to the United States. No extra wages or transportation costs would be paid if Garvey could prove his charges of incompetence, however. Garvey could also deduct the cost of the damages from the wages of the captain and engineer if he could substantiate his charges to the satisfaction of the consul (Charles Latham to Marcus Garvey, 1 June 1921, DNA, RG 59, file 811.108 G 191/18). After receiving Garvey's complaint, Latham wrote to Charles Evans Hughes, the secretary of state, requesting instructions on how to handle the case (Latham to Charles Evans Hughes, 1 June 1921, DNA, RG 41, file 122539-N). Hughes instructed Latham to cooperate with Garvey if Garvey presented evidence of his authority to act on behalf of the Black Star Line; if Latham decided to sustain Garvey's charges, he was to remove the captain and the ship's officers. Hughes ordered Latham to make an investigation even if Garvey did not present proper evidence of his authority, however, and added that Latham should send a report to the State Department (Hughes to Latham, 4 June 1921, DNA, RG 41, file 122539-N).

Affidavit by UNIA Members

City of New York 2nd day of June 1921

STELLA HARRIS, CLAUDE HARRIS, LIZZIE JOHNSON and JOSIE GATLIN, being duly sworn, depose and say:

That they are members of the Universal Negro Improvement Association with offices at Number 56 West One Hundred and Thirty-fifth Street, Borough of Manhattan, City, County and State of New York, of which Marcus Garvey is represented to be the head;

That they were assured before becoming members of the said Universal Negro Improvement Association that if they could get as far as the water (meaning New York City) from Oklahoma, they would be given free transportation to Africa, in consideration of their having paid membership fees in the said Universal Negro Improvement Association;

That upon presenting themselves at the offices of the said Universal Negro Improvement Association, they were informed that passage to Africa would cost, for children the sum of One Hundred and Ten Dollars ($110.00), and for adults the sum of Two Hundred Dollars ($200.00), despite the fact that they presented badges and other evidences of membership in the Universal Negro Improvement Association;

That Mrs. Josie Gatlin, one of the deponents above named owns five (5) shares of stock bearing the name of the Black Star Line Steamship Company, the steamship line of the Universal Negro Improvement Association.

X CLAUDE HARRIS
JOSIE GATLIN
STELLA HARRIS
X LIZZIE [JOHNSON]

DLC, NAACP. TD. Notarized.

W. E. Wilson to Marcus Garvey

Kingston, Jamaica, June 4th, 1921

Dear Mr. Garvey,

Herein I enclose a letter received from the Master of the "Kanawha".[1] From fact within my knowledge it is advis[a]ble that we act very cautiously inasmuch that it must be patent to you that there are enemies in our camp and the letter speaks for itself. The signer must have got the joint concurrence of the men under him to have written such a letter.

Before asking your opinion or knowing what would be your mode of action I desire to let you know in my opinion the best way out of the difficulty in the interest of the Corporation.

I would entirely disregard the $2,000[.00] asked for as advance and instead try to get the amount owing to the crew so that if possible we could meet their demand of immediate payment and sign off the entire crew in Jamaica.

I beg to assure you that you will receive my heartiest support financially and otherwise, in this decision.

I am not unmindful of the fact that you feel /it/ incumbent on you to fulfil[l] certain promises you made to shareholders in South America and other quarters, nevertheless I feel that when matters are brought to their knowledge that there are traitors in our camp and on board the vessel judging from the time she has left New York and the expenses incurred through what appears to be a contra-propaganda, they will readily understand and appreciate the fact that our actions are in the best interest of the stockholders and Corporation.

I should be obliged if you will be good enough to arrange a meeting before noon to-morrow with Miss Davis, Mr. deBourg, myself and any other independent persons whom you feel are interested and qualified enough to advise in the cause. I am taking the liberty of inviting Mr. T. Aiken,[2] an engineer employed by the Government and a trustee of the U.N.I.A.

As it may not be convenient for me to see you to-night I will send my son to wait on you about 7.30 to-morrow morning when you will send me your views on this matter as I have tried but failed to find any other alternative. Believe me to be, Yours sincerely and fraternally,

W. E. WILSON

[*Address*] Hon. Marcus Garvey,
York House, Kingston.

TAM. TLS, recipient's copy, on Black Star Line letterhead.

1. Not retained.

2. Percival Augustus Aiken (1885–1967) was born in Kingston, Jamaica, and educated at Mico Primary School and Wolmer's Boys School. After working as an electrician for the United Fruit Co. at Port Antonio from 1905 to 1916, Aiken returned to Kingston, where he was a mechanic and electrician for the Jamaica Government Railway Service. Aiken became presi-

dent of the Kingston UNIA division in the late 1920s, after he had developed a successful business as an electrical contractor. He later married Mme M. L. T. De Mena, his second wife and the international organizer of the UNIA. Garvey named Mme De Mena officer-in-charge of the American Field in 1930 (*NW*, 23 January 1932).

C. H. Calhoun, Chief of Division of Civil Affairs, to the Chief Customs Inspector, Cristobal, Panama Canal Zone

Balboa Heights, C.Z. June 4, 1921

Sir:

Information has been received from the American Consul at Kingston, Jamaica, to the effect that the American steamship KANAWHA, of the Black Star Line, cleared from that port for Cristobal Saturday afternoon last, and that Marcus Garvey, negro agitator, is a member of the crew, having been signed on as Purser at $50.00 a month on May 16, 1921, at Santiago de Cuba.

Consuls have been instructed to refuse visa for the return of this man to the United States, and also to refuse visa to the crew list on which he may appear as a seaman.

The Governor has directed that the KANAWHA shall not be cleared for a United States port with Garvey aboard. Will you please be governed accordingly, and if Garvey is on board the vessel either as a member of the crew or passenger, when clearance is requested you may inform the Master that clearance will not be granted in the circumstances. There is no objection to clearing this vessel for a United States port if Garvey is not aboard. Respectfully,

C. H. CALHOUN,
Chief, Division of Civil Affairs

WNRC, RG 185, file C-61-H-3/B. TL, carbon copy.

Report by Special Agent P-138

New York City 6-6-21

IN RE: NEGRO ACTIVITIES.

Today [*3 June*] again had conversation with some of the officials of the Black Star Line, but none of them were able to give me any definite information regarding Garvey's whereabouts, and as a matter of fact they all seem to be at a loss and are afraid of the members getting suspicious and panicky, thereby causing a run on their office and treasury.

Discouraging rumors are still in the air of his not being allowed to re-enter the U.S.

P-138

[*Endorsements*] NOTED F. D. W. FILE G. F. R.

DNA, RG 65, file BS 198940-152. TD. Stamped endorsements.

Marcus Garvey to Charles L. Latham

Kingston, June 7th 1921

Dear Sir:—

In keeping with previous communications sent you, I hereby beg to make a formal and specific charge against the Master of the s.s. KANAWHA, and Mr. Chas. Harris, the Chief Engineer and those under their control. As outlined in my previous communications, the Captain has in a most wil[l]ful, and destructive manner, mismanaged our boat through his incompetency, neglect, and conspiracy, as to inflict heavy financial loss to the owners of the Black Star Line. For this, we are asking his dismissal from the boat, /as/ Master, and that he be tried before the Marine Authorities of New York, the Port from which he signed, for his misconduct after you have investigated same.

In asking the dismissal of the Captain, I am asking that in view of the fact that he has done excessive damage to the boat, in the smashing of the stern of the boat, the repairs of which will cost more than his salary, that if a demand is made by him for his pay, up to date, should you find it necessary to have him dismissed, that you grant us the privilege to pay him this salary under protest, so that the Company can be protected in the recovery of the damages done to the boat, through the neglect and incompetency of the said Captain.

As for /Mr./ Chas. Harris, the Chief Engineer, I am hereby on behalf of the Black Star Line, laying a charge of incompetency[,] neglect, and criminal destruction of property, in that he, on more than one occasion since the boat sailed out of New York Harbour on the 25th. of March, did, through his neglect, and incompetency, cause damage to be done to the Engines and Boilers of our boat, which have caused a loss of thousands of dollars to the Corporation for repairs. Through the incompetency, neglect and criminal destruction, as caused through the Chief Engineer and through the incompetency of the Captain to control the boat and crew, our boat has been unnecessarily delayed in its voyage, a voyage that was undertaken to consume 30 days has now extended to three months and not yet half completed.

You will understand, Sir, that this boat left New York on the 25th. March 1921 fully equipped in a seaworthy condition, being just from dry dock, and having aboard a certificate of seaworthiness granted by the Marine Authorities of the port of New York. That all damage to the boat has been done since the boat has been at sea, and under the control of the Master herein charged, and the Chief Engineer. These men have shown an utter disregard for discipline, for good behaviour aboard the boat, which are necessary adjuncts to the high integrity of the American Merchant Marine. These men have done everything that can be imagined to disgrace the Marine service of the United States whilst they have been in control of this boat.

The following statements are facts which will guide you in the charge we are now making, and in the enquiry we are asking you to make:—

1—The S.S. KANAWHA of the Black Star Line sailed out of New York on the 25th. March 1921, at 6.45 P.M. in perfect seaworthy condition, making a speed of 15 or 16 knots an hour. Between 11 O'clock, and 12 O'clock in the night of the 25th. a valve in the engine room blew out, which brought the ship to a stand still, and the Chief Engineer whose watch it was, [was] nowhere to be found in the engine room, and never appeared in the engine room, until he was called by the water tender.

2—The boat returned to New York to have check valve renewed, and re-sailed out of New York at 2.45 on Monday the 28th.

3—Between Norfolk and Jacksonville, the dates March 31st, to April 3rd, the Fan engine broke down. Prior to the breakdown of the fan engine, indications were given that something was wrong with the engine. The water tender on one occasion reported that the cross head was knocking, and the Chief Engineer said "it is alright let it remain." No attention was paid to the fan engine until it broke down.

4—The boat arrived in Jacksonville on Sunday the 3rd. April, and on Monday the 4th, repairs were done to the fan engine and again rendered the boat seaworthy. She sailed on Tuesday the 5th, at about 2 P.M. and at about 4 the next morning, the fan engine broke again.

5—Although the KANAWHA carries an evaporator which gives an indefinite supply of water after fresh water has been taken in, the Chief Engineer took in salt water in the boilers within 24 hours after the boat left Jacksonville, even though he took in water at New York, Norfolk, and Jacksonville.

6—Through the use of salt water in the boilers, excessive damage was done to the boiler tubes, two dynamos, and other parts of the machinery. There was absolutely no cause for the use of salt water, in that the ship carries an evaporator.

7—On the arrival of the boat in Havana on the 9th, repairs were given out to the parts of the engines and boilers damaged which work was completed to render the boat seaworthy. Immediately after the repairs were done, and before the boat sailed, the 1st Assistant Engineer, tampered with the fan engine, and immediately after leaving port, the fan engine broke down again. The tampering with the fan engine by the 1st. Assistant, produced the same signs of defect on the fan engine, as has always been indicated before a breakdown.

8—Although the fan engine broke down in sailing out the Port of Havana, the ship continued its voyage, its destination being Santiago. After the vessel was about five hours out of Havana Harbour, the Starboard L. P. Cylinder Dome was blown off, and the Piston Rod broken. This damage was caused particularly through the previous use of salt water and through neglect.

9—On the night of the 28th, the dynamo went out of commission, through negligence.

10—The ship arrived in Sagu[a] La Grande on the 29th, and underwent temporary repairs, taking in fresh water.

11—The ship sailed out of Sagu[a] at 1.30 P.M. on the 30th. April for Santiago. Whilst she was about three and a half hours out of Sagu[a], the port Low Pressure Cylinder cover blew off, and the Piston Rod broke. No engineer was in the engine room.

12—On the night of the 1st. May, at about 8 P.M. the water tender going on his watch, discovered that the temperature of the boiler room was higher than it should be. There was no engineer in the boiler room at the time. On observation he discovered that the boiler was out of water, and red hot. The relieving water tender, asked the water tender on watch, why the boiler was so neglected, and he said that he called the Engineer on watch, and he refused to come. The cause of the neglect has resulted in serious damage to the boiler, and, but, for the action of the relieving water tender, there would have been a serious collapse of the boiler which [would] have resulted probably in the setting of the ship afire. This boiler was out of commission because of the destruction caused through neglect.

13—Although water was taken in Sagu[a], on the 30th. April, the Engineer caused ship to put into port of Gibar[a] for water on the 2nd. May, and remained there until the 4th. May, sailing out of Gibara at 4 P.M. on the 4th.

14—On entering the port of Santiago, at 10.40 P.M. on the 6th. May, the engineer used salt water in the boilers.

15—On the arrival of the boat in Santiago, further repairs were effected, to enable the boat to continue her journey.

16—On the arrival of the ship in Kingston, it was found that the fan engine was out of order, as also four boilers, were damaged, joint air pump was out of order. Reverse gear port engine was out order. Dynamo engine was out of order. Port starboard engine was out of order, also jacking gear and rachet; drain pipe in starboard engine; forward feed pump; L. P. Piston rod for starboard engine, as also cover; port engine, destruction to piston ring in port engine. Bilge pump out of order. All this caused through the improper handling of the boat, neglect, and incompetency on the part of the

Engineer. All the last named damages were repaired in the port of Kingston, to render the boat seaworthy for the continuance of her voyage.

17—Sailed out of Kingston for Colón on Saturday the 28th. May at 4 P.M., the Chief Engineer making a statement that he had water aboard the boat to serve him indefinitely. After thirty hours at sea, the Engineer demanded that the boat return to Kingston, and not continue her voyage to Colón, because he had no water. About five hours after he turned back to Kingston, he started to use salt water in the boilers, and continued the trip to Kingston using salt water.

18—After the boat sailed out of Kingston at 4 P.M. and was about three hours at sea, Assistants in the engine room, drew the attention to the fact that there was a banging on the port engine and that the engineer should endeavor to locate the cause. He replied that he could not locate it. The engine was subsequently closed down by the chief, without an effort made to locate or discover the cause. At the time this port engine was closed down, the ship was making a speed of about five knots an hour, starting out from Kingston, with only the port engine in operation. The speed of the boat with the two engines, is about 16 knots. No effort was made to keep the two engines going, so as to maintain the speed of the boat to reach her destination, but that the port engine was positively closed down without an investigation made into the cause of the banging, and on the closing down of the port engine, the starboard engine was brought into action, thus confining the speed of the boat to not more than 5 knots, by not having the two engines in active operation.

19—On Sunday the 29th, whilst the boat was at sea, an Assistant hears the fan engine giving out unusual sounds and drew the matter to the attention of the engineer, and the engineer instead of fixing the fan himself, ordered the assistants to do so. The fan was fixed and was in running order. The 1st. assistant engineer allowed the fan to race at an abnormal speed which increased the draught, and raised the steam on the boiler to 200 lbs, and at the same time made no effort to release the pressu[r]e which resulted in the blowing of a tube in the boiler, and thus putting the boiler out of commission.

20—After the boat turned back on Sunday night the 28th, making a quicker speed back to Kingston, than she was making to her destination, the Starboard engine piston gland blew out, which caused the immediate stoppage of the starboard engine. After the packing of the glands, the engines started and immediately after the start, the drain pipe to the throttle valve was broken off, which necessitated the stopping of the engines again. After this there started a banging in the starboard engine low pressure cylinder, and the engine stopped of itself. At which time the engine[er] opened the starboard engine L. P. Cylinder and discovered the piston rod broken. He attempted to start up again on compound, the starboard engine, but because of the piston rod being bent, the engine would not turn. At this time, the port engine which was thoroughly neglected because the boat was at a stand still, was now resorted to, and fixed to run on compound, and that the boat returned to Kingston on the port engine compound, which port engine was thoroughly neglected when the starboard engine was in working order and to which engines, if repairs had been done, would have kept the two engines running.

21—On the various watches of the engineers, the boat would make different speed; under the control of certain engineers she would go at 15 knots; other engineers at 8, 9, and 10 knots, and still under others she would go at 4, and 2 knots, and sometimes come to a perfect standstill.

22—That the Chief Engineer continually on the trip from New York used the most obscene and filthy language, on the main and other decks of the ship to the hearing of the passengers and the crew, passengers including ladies of refinement and culture.

23—That on Sunday the 29th. ult, whilst the boat was at sea, and whilst it was reported that the engines were in a dangerous condition and needed the careful and proper attention of the engineers on watch, that the three engineers absented themselves from the engine room; the Chief Engineer sleeping in his bunk, the 1st assistant holding a conversation at one end of the deck, and 2nd assistant standing on deck looking over into the sea, and the engines throbbing in a most alarming condition. The same occurrence was repeated on Monday the 30th. ult, and on several occasions since the boat left Kingston on its voyage to Colón, the engineers have been absent from the engine room during the course of the voyage.

24—That the Chief Engineer on Saturday the 28th. was drunk aboard the boat and that he had rum in his cabin, and did offer a drink of such liquor to Mr. W. E. Wilson, agent of the line in Kingston. That he carried this rum as also whisky on the voyage from the port of Kingston, and that he was under the influence of liquor during the voyage.

25—At 12 O'clock noon of the 6th. Inst. the Chief Engineer attacked aboard the boat on the open deck the 2nd. mate, after using the most obscene language to him, he slapped him in the face, because the 2nd. mate did not join the chief mate, the Captain and other officers in making an unreasonable protest to the Consul in Kingston.

26—That although the Chief Engineer was employed aboard the s.s. KANAWHA nearly three months before she sailed on the 25th March, and had at his command men working in the engine room, and although he has had command of the engine room for nearly three months at sea, the said engine room is kept in a filthy and dirty condition, that absolutely no care has been given the engines and boilers although he has under his command more men than the Marine regulations call for.

27—That in Port or out of Port, the engineer makes no effort to regulate or fix any defects in his engine room, and that the boat has, and is being [u]nnecessarily delayed by such neglect of the engineer.

28—That whatsoever is being done by the engineer, is more to destroy and obstruct, than to help in the successful running of the boat.

29—That although the boat has been laid up in ports since she left New York, for periods of three weeks, two weeks, one week, and on occasions several days respectively, and at different ports, that the engineer gives no time so in port, to fix and regulate his engine room in preparation for his voyage.

30—At the present time, the boat has been in Kingston for seven days, returning as claimed by the engineer for repairs, and he has done nothing of himself and by his assistants to get under control and prepare for sea, the boat in such work that could be undertaken and done by him and his assistants, as apart from that work that should be done by contract.

31—That the engineers are constantly idle in port, often under the influence of liquor, and that the Company loses by such conduct in having on boa[r]d, and paying these men, for duties they do not perform.

In view of the foregoing charges that can be supported by the evidence of witnesses, I charge the Chief Engineer with incompetency[,] with criminal neglect, and Conspiracy as herein set forth.

The following persons will testify to the truthfulness of what has been herein stated:—

Percy Griffiths,
Joshua Parris,
Harold Warren,
Richard Tomlinson,—all members of the crew.
Clarence Pearce, who was temporarily signed on.
Mr. Sydney De Bourg,
Miss Henrietta Vinton Davis[,]
Mr. W. E. Wilson,
Miss Amy Ja[c]ques,
Mr. Augustus Fredericks—all passengers, as also other members
of the crew whose names will be submitted.

I am asking on behalf of the Black Star Line, that, if you are satisfied with the evidence given, and the statements herein laid, that you permit us to dismiss from our service, Chas. Harris, and pay his wages up to date under protest, so that we may be able to recover from such wages, at least a part of the damage sustained through his incompetency and neglect, as shall be determined by your investigation, and the investigation of the Authorities in

New York, and I am further asking on behalf of the Black Star Line that all others who may be guilty be likewise treated according to your determination, and the determination of the authorities when the matter is finally investigated in New York.

The following are the charges against the Master of the s.s. KANAWHA:

1. That Captain Adrian Richardson as Master of the s.s. KANAWHA against the wishes of the Black Star Line did sign on on his trip between New York and Kingston more men than necessary for the crew, and far in excess of what the American regulations calls for. The inspection calls for the services of twenty-five men and the Captain carries on his articles and otherwise over forty men, including men who were discovered on the ship as stowaways, and who should have been handed over to the police authorities at the nearest port. These men are now being paid at the highest wages without the consent and approval of the Company. The wages of these men is hereby protested and asked to be charged against the Master.

2. That the Captain's neglect did cause unnecessary delay to the boat the s.s. KANAWHA at several ports, even though the boat was ready to proceed to sea. As on the occasions when the boat returned to New York Sunday 27th. March for repairs, which repairs were completed immediately the said Sunday, whilst the Captain absented himself from the boat, never returned until 2 P.M. Monday the 28th. March. During which time boat was unnecessarily delayed.

That the boat was unnecessarily kept at a standstill in the ocean under steam the entire day and night of the 26th. March thereby causing unnecessary delay and expense.

That from Wednesday morning the 30th. March to Thursday morning 31st. the Master did cause the vessel to remain at anchor off Hampton Roads again causing unnecessary delay, and that subsequently he went into Norfolk under the guise of needing supplies etc. even though the boat was nearest to the port of Charleston. The Captain going ashore and remaining all night not returning to the boat until the following day. It is hereby charged that the Captain put into Norfolk and not into Charleston because of his desire to see his wife at this port, even though it caused the Black Star Line such ill-convenience and loss.

That between the ports of New York, Santiago and Kingston the destination of the s.s. KANAWHA that the Chief Engineer did cause extreme delay to the sailing of the boat in that she did put into three ports in the United States of America for repairs and unnecessary supply of water and coal, and did put into at least four ports in Cuba for the same purpose, causing loss of time and money to the Company, as well as delay to the boat. And with all this knowledge the Captain took no steps to hold a thorough investigation and to probe into the competency of the engineer, and his ability to handle the Steamship KANAWHA, in spite of the fact that the said ship sailed out of New York her engines being in perfect order. And that up to the present the Captain has caused no investigation to be held into the conduct of the Chief Engineer and his department to safe guard the safe conduct of the vessel under his control.

3.   That on Thursday 31st. March immediately before the boat sailed out of Norfolk, after they had taken on supplies, that a gentleman, a friend or acquaintance of the Captain, not a passenger on the boat, did board the boat and was conveyed by the Captain to a destination entirely out of the course of the boat, and which place was not a port of call as ordered by the Black Star Line, and that in landing this gentleman he did go out of his way, and in the act of landing him almost came into collision with a double decked ferry boat, and did in the act of landing him did back the stern of the boat into the pier damaging the stern of the boat to the extent of over $1000. for repairs, and also damaging the pier, the owners of which are expecting to file a bill of claim against the Black Star Line as owners of the s.s. KANAWHA. That the said damage to the boat has not been officially reported to the proper authorities.

4.   That the Master took the boat into Jacksonville, a port not on the ship[']s destination on the 3rd. April. He went ashore immediately and never came back until 3 P.M. the following day. At this port he ordered supplies, including coal for the boat. The coal was sent to the boat, and was refused by the Chief Engineer, because it was discovered to be worthless, and not the kind of coal that could be used for a seagoing vessel. In spite of the fact that the engineer protested against the purchase and taking of the coal, the Captain ordered the coal received, even though the coal was not good. The use of which coal caused further delay to the boat between Jacksonville and Havana, in that the boat could make no speed under the consumption of the coal which was not good.

5.   That on the voyage between New York and Jamaica the Captain was seen by passengers and others to be gambling on the deck of the ship with bone dice with sailors and other members of the crew.

6.   That the Captain of the ship between New York and Jamaica was often heard to use obscene language to the hearing of passengers and crew. And did allow other members of the crew to use such obscene language without establishing order on board the boat.

7.   That between the ports of Kingston and the sailing of the boat on the high seas on Saturday 28th. and 29th. May[,] the Captain did have in his possession a bottle of rum or whisky and that he did indulge in drinking of such liquor between himself and two passengers who were aboard the boat. This was done to the open view of the passengers and other members of the crew.

8. That the Captain has no discipline and as Master of the boat has been unable to establish discipline, in that members of the crew from time to time whilst they should be at work, assemble and congregate on the deck using foul language etc. and absolutely no effort made by the Captain to establish discipline or order.

9. That the Captain most improperly did sign on as Chief Steward his brother, who is unable to read and calculate sufficiently to order, supervise, receive and control the stores and the rationing of the men of the KANAWHA.

10. That on Saturday the 4th. June at 8 o'clock two members of the crew did engage themselves in a fight on the open deck of the KANAWHA in the port of Kingston in the presence of the Captain, and that the men did fight for over fifteen minutes one of the men hitting the other slightly thereby inflicting a wound, from which blood was seen to gush, and when the President and Representative of the Black Star Line called upon the Captain and asked him if he permitted such scenes to happen on the ship, without establishing law, order and discipline, he retorted "Let the men fight it out on the open deck, if they have anything among themselves."

11. That because of the improper handling of the ship and the lack of discipline the majority of the member[s] of the crew have absolutely no respect for the Master, and that he cannot properly control them.

12. That the s.s. KANAWHA under the command of the Master sailed out of New York on the 25th March to make an immediate trip to Santiago, Kingston, Port Limón, and Colón, and return to New York in thirty days, and that up to now nearly three months have been consumed on the journey and the voyage is not half completed. The boat not going further than Kingston, and that the Captain has taken absolutely no steps to have the unnecessary delay, which has been caused through the incompetence of himself and the Chief Engineers and his department, investigated. And which delay of time has seriously embarrassed the Black Star Line in doing unnecessary repairs to the boat for damages which ha[ve] been done, and paying the men above time, also supplying the boat with food, fuel and taking on engine and deck stores.

13. That the Captain did improperly turn back the ship on the voyage started between Kingston and Colón on Sunday 29th. May, which voyage should have been continued, and that the excuse given for the return of the voyage by the Chief Engineer was that he had not sufficient water, and that was not sufficient cause for [t]he return of the boat. In view of [t]he fact that the Chief Engineer gave assurance that the boat could make the voyage, and that there was sufficient water taken on at Kingston, and that on previous occasions he used salt water to continue the voyage, and when there was an evaporator on board the boat. And that the Chief Engineer did use salt water on the return of the boat to Kingston, and that no investigation was made by the Captain to find out if the excuse of the Chief Engineer was justifiable.

And as a proof of the incompet[e]ncy of the Captain he did remark on nearing the port of Kingston, if he [h]ad known he would have gone straight on.

These charges can be supported on the evidence of John Hunt, John Laviscount, William King, T. Richards, William Rummeyer, R. Lema, Henry Bailey and other members of the crew. As also Miss Henrietta Vinton Davis, Messrs. Sidney D[e] Bourg[,] Augustus Fredericks and Amy Ja[c]ques. Passengers on the boat.

In view of the foregoing charges against the Master of the KANAWHA, the Chief Engineer and his assistants, I hereby ask on behalf of the Black Star Line the owners of the s.s. KANAWHA that the men herein charged be relieved of their duties, and that they pay back to the Black Star Line Corporation damages done through their negligence, incompetency and mismanagement. And that their wages be attached as a safe guard for the financial loss to the Corporation. And that the men be brought before the Marine Authorities of New York, the port from which they signed on, and that their license or tickets be investigated.

I hereby beg to state that from observations made and from my best belief, I believe that there is a conspiracy of fraternal relationship which prevents the true and honest conduct of affairs in the matter of these officers complained against, and that although this may be irrelevant to this communication, it is my belief that it is a direct abuse of the privileges of such orders by the individuals.

Trusting that after the enquiry you will find our charges and complaints to be just, and that you will give us the protection necessary. I have the honor to be, Yours truly,

> BLACK STAR LINE INC.
> MARCUS GARVEY
> President

DNA, RG 41, file 122539-N. TL, carbon copy.

Report by Special Agent J. T. Flournoy

Washington, D.C. 6-7-21

TITLE AND CHARACTER OF CASE: RENE A. M. VAN CROMBRUGGE, CHANCELLOR OF THE BELGIUM EMBASSY

Facts Developed:

I called at No. 1780 Massachusetts Ave. N.W. and found this to be the home of the Belgian Ambassador to the United States. There is no such person at this address as "VAN CRONBURGE[.]" There is, however, at this address a Mr. RENE A. M. VAN CROMBRUGGE, who is, no doubt, the person referred to in the memorandum. I found that he is the Chancellor of the Belgian Embassy. He stated that he is the party who subscribed for the "NEGRO WORLD," and it was on behalf of the Belgium Ambassador for the purpose of ascertain[ing] what the contents of the paper is from time to time, as he found that this paper was being circulated in the Belgium possessions and was stirring up the negro inhabitants by the circulation of propaganda against this country and Belgium.[1] He stated that they are having considerable trouble at the present time with negroes in Belgium[2] and attributes it to the "NEGRO WORLD" being circulated among them.

Investigation closed.

J. [T.] FLOURNOY

DNA, RG 65, file BS 202600-1993-2. TD.

1. Belgian colonial authorities reported that catechists of the American Methodist missions had been discovered distributing copies of the *Negro World* in the region of the lower Congo. Many of the same catechists were also known to have joined in the anticolonial millenarian movement known as Kimbanguism, which emerged during this period. (Simon Kimbangu [1890?–1951] was the leader of the most important independent Christian religious movement in central Africa. He was a member of the Kikongo group, born at Nkamba. After receiving a vision in March 1921, Kimbangu immediately began to preach and, according to many witnesses, performed miraculous healings. In September 1921 Belgian colonial authorities arrested Kimbangu and imprisoned him until his death.) Clandestine groups of Garveyites were also established in Leopoldville (Kinshasa), Stanleyville (Kisangani), Coquilhatville (Mbandaka), and Lisala. They were drawn from the ranks of the skilled work force in the Belgian Congo, which consisted largely of migrant workers from Senegal and British West Africa. An ordinance of the governor-general of the Belgian Congo, issued in April 1922, prohibited the circulation of the *Negro World* ("Le garveyisme en action dans notre colonie," *Congo*, 2d year, 2, no. 4 [November 1921]: 575–576; Archives nationales, Paris, Section d'outre-mer, slotfom 88, série 3, C84(2) [letter of 5 October 1920]; Damaso Feci, "Vie cachée et vie publique de Simon Kimbangu selon la littérature coloniale et missionnaire belge," *Cahiers du CEDAF* [Centre d'étude et de documentation africaines] 9–10 (1972): 2–84; Octave Louwers and Iwan Grenade, *Code et lois du Congo Belge* [Brussels: M. Weissenbruch, Imprimeur du roi, 1927]; Cecilia Irvine, "The Birth of the Kimbanguist Movement in the Bas-Zaire," *Journal of Religion in Africa* 6: 23–76; Marie-Louise Martin, *Kimbangu, An African Prophet and His Church* [Oxford: Basil Blackwell, 1975]). The *Negro World* gave a prominent place to wire service reports of the suppression of the African rising at Kinshasa in the Congo ("Congo Natives Revolt," 26 March 1921, and "Great Revolt in the Congo—Equatorial Blacks Rise in Mass," 9 April 1921).

2. Belgian officials believed that the founder of the *Union Congolaise* in Brussels, M'Fuma Paul Panda Farnana, was collaborating with Garvey and the UNIA. While no direct evidence of contact between Garvey and Panda has been discovered, it may be noted that Panda played an active role in the Brussels meeting of the Second Pan-African Congress in 1921 ("Le panafricanisme," *Congo*, 2d year, 1, no. 2 [February 1921]: 274–275; *Correio de Africa*, 22 May 1922; W. E. B. Du Bois, "Worlds of Color," *Foreign Affairs* 3 [April 1925]: 426–428).

Sen. William B. McKinley to the Department of Justice

[*Washington, D.C.*] June 8, 1921

Dear Sir:

From time to time I have seen more or less in the newspapers in regard to the scheme for colored people owning a ship line to Liberia, and a propaganda to sell stock to the colored people in this Ship line. For twenty years I have been well acquainted with a very responsible colored man at Danville, Illinois. He advises me that representatives of, as he pronounces it, Marcus Garvis, are working in and around Danville, talking to the colored people he thinks in a very disloyal manner and stirring up race prejudice. At the same time capitalizing this talk by selling stock in the so-called Ship line.

I am wondering if you can do anything to check this? Sincerely,

W. B. McKINLEY[1]

DNA, RG 65, file BS 198940-159. TLS on U.S. Senate letterhead. recipient's copy.

1. William Brown McKinley (1856–1926) was a Republican senator from Illinois from 1921 until his death.

A. J. Tyrer, Acting Commissioner of Navigation, Department of Commerce, to Collector of Customs, New York

[*Washington, D.C.*] June 8, 1921

Sir:—

The Department of State reports that a seaman named Marcus Garvey was shipped on the American steamship KANAWHA at Santiago de Cuba by the master of the vessel without the sanction of the American Consul at that place.[1]

It is believed that the steamship KANAWHA to which reference is made is the steam screw KANAWHA (161123) owned by the Black Star Line of your port. Should this vessel arrive at your port you may report the master for violation of R.S. 4517 and 4518.[2] Respectfully,

A. J. TYRER
Acting Commissioner

DNA, RG 41, file 122539-N. TLR, carbon copy.

1. At Garvey's mail fraud trial, Captain Richardson testified that he had asked the American consul at Santiago, Cuba, for permission to sign on a new crew member but that he had not mentioned Garvey's name (*Garvey* v. *United States*, no. 8317, Ct. App., 2d Cir., 2 February 1925, p. 453).

2. Revised Statute 4517 required every shipmaster who engaged seamen outside of the United States to obtain the sanction of the American consul before the ship returned to sea (*United States Compiled Statutes,* 1918 [St. Paul, Minn.: West Publishing Co., 1918], p. 1,309). R.S. 4518 set a penalty of $100 for violating R.S. 4517, for which the ship was to be held liable.

Charles Evans Hughes to Charles L. Latham

WASHINGTON June 10, 1921

American Consul, Kingston, Jamaica.

If any seaman is discharged from the steamship KANAWHA without his consent and without cause, the owner must pay him extra wages of one month. You should hold ship[']s papers until the law is complied with. In order to enforce the master's claim for wages the ship[']s papers should not be withheld. If the demand is made by Garvey for discharge of master you may render proper assistance, submitting facts in the case to the Department. A foreigner should not be permitted to take command of vessel but if master is removed a duly qualified American citizen must be appointed as master.

[CHARLES EVANS] HUGHES

DNA, RG 41, file 122539-N. TG.

Charles L. Latham to Charles Evans Hughes

Kingston, Jamaica June 11, 1921

Secretary of State, Washington.

Reference Department's telegram of June 10th. I have been asked by Garvey whether the license of first assistant engineer, who is an American citizen, and license Chief Mate, also an American citizen, may take steamship KANAWHA to Cristobal, these officers acting as chief engineer and master respectively. I believe neither of these men are very competent. Garvey also asks whether under the circumstances [*the*] alien chief engineer and mates may be signed on the vessel.

[CHARLES L. LATHAM]

DNA, RG 41, file 122539-N. TG.

Charles L. Latham to Charles Evans Hughes

Kingston, Jamaica, June 11, 1921

SUBJECT: COMPLAINT OF MARCUS GARVEY AGAINST THE
CAPTAIN AND CHIEF ENGINEER OF THE S.S. KANAWHA.

Sir:

I have the honor to refer to the Department's telegram of June 10, 1921, in regard to complaints made by Marcus Garvey as President of the Black Star Line, Incorporated, against the captain and chief engineer of the s.s. KANAWHA.

I have to report that on June 1, 1921, after the s.s. KANAWHA returned to this port in distress (three days after clearing Kingston for Port Limón and Colón) Mr. Garvey appeared at this office and made general complaints in writing against the master and chief engineer of the s.s. KANAWHA and later submitted a long list of specifications, much of which was irrelevant and high flown.

He has furnished evidence of authority to act which seems to be authentic. At his request an investigation was begun, which is still in course, to determine whether the master and chief engineer are incompetent to continue in their positions.

The investigation of the charges by this office is nearly completed. The witnesses have all been produced by Mr. Garvey, as the officers themselves have not as yet desire to present any. The witnesses are all negroes, the principal ones being passengers on the s.s. KANAWHA on its journey from New York to Jamaica, and who are officers or members of the Universal Negro Improvement Association and Black Star Line, Incorporated, and who are traveling in the interest of these negro enterprises. The rest of the witnesses are members of the crew.

The evidence as given by these witnesses has been contradictory in material points, and frequently has been evidently biased by personal interests and animosities. Most of the facts submitted by Mr. Garvey are not in themselves serious enough to weigh as proof of the charges, and the evidence as to their truth is so conflicting as to indicate that they are either exaggerated or false. In my opinion, so far, the charges are not proven.

Since Mr. Garvey has been on board, and especially since his laying of charges against the two officers, there has been such division of authority between Mr. Garvey and the Master and so much animosity has been aroused between the persons on board that the conditions are seriously disturbed on board the vessel.

The master will doubtless be discharged by Garvey, probably without payment of wages, in which case, unless cabled instructions to the contrary are received, he will be given assistance and transportation to New York as a destitute seaman.

The chief engineer and probably other officers will not be willing to continue on the ship in view of the extraordinary conditions and circumstances.

A further report is being promptly compiled. I have the honor to be, Sir, Your obedient servant,

C. L. LATHAM
American Consul

DNA, RG 41, file 122539-N. TLS, carbon copy.

William C. Matthews to Harry A. McBride, Visa Control Office, Department of State

303 OLD SOUTH BUILDING BOSTON
June 11, 1921

ATTENTION OF MR. McBRIDE

My dear Sir:—

Referring to a conference I had with you on Tuesday the 7th of June relative to the return of Marcus Garvey, permit me to advise you that the Board of Directors of the Black Star Line, Inc. has requested Mr. Garvey to return to the United States in order that arrangements might be completed for the taking over of the ship to be named "Phillis Wheatley" by the above named Corporation.

Arrangements for cargo and passengers have already been completed by our agents. Officers and crew have been tentatively engaged. This ship will sail by way of West Indies, the Cape Verde Islands and Liberia. Among its cargo will be a complete saw-mill equipment for construction work our society is planning in Liberia. Many of the passengers are workmen who will be employed in this construction service. This work we are attempting is of course through permission of the Liberian officials.

I would thank you to do what is in your power to facilitate Mr. Garvey's immediate return to the United States. I am advised that he will apply for the VISA of his passport at the port of Kingston, Jamaica during the coming week.

Thanking you very much for the interest and assistance you have shown and assuring you my highest personal regards, I am, Respectfully yours,

WILLIAM C. MATTHEWS
Assistant Counsellor General

[*Address*] Department of State, Visa Control, Washington, D.C.
[*Endorsement*] Garvey, Marcus File

DNA, RG 59, file 811.108 G 191/29. TLS, recipient's copy. Handwritten endorsement.

Gabriel M. Johnson to Cyril A. Crichlow

Monrovia, June 11th, 1921

Dear Mr. Secretary:

Enclosed is a copy of a cable received from the Executive Council, New York, at 2:10 P.M. I have instructed the Counselor of the Association to write you. Yours respectfully,

G. M. JOHNSON

DNA, RG 165, file 10218-261-77. TL, carbon copy.

Enclosure

[*New York, ca. 10 June 1921*]

$480 cabled. Salaries five men 30th April. Must be paid. Instruct Crichlow do not come here on any account.

UNIA
[EXECUTIVE COUNCIL]

DNA, RG 165, file 10218-261-77. TG (coded).

Arthur Barclay, UNIA Legal Adviser in Liberia, to Cyril A. Crichlow

[*Monrovia, Liberia, 11 June 1921*]

Sir:

I am instructed by the Potentate as Counsel here for the U.N.I.A. to call your attention to the fact that it has now been ascertained by cable just received that the remittance of $480 which the Potentate learned from you was sent last week to pay your expenses to New York, was not sent as you intimated. It was remitted to pay salary of Staff. It is therefore requested that you pay over the money to the officials for whom it was intended. Kindly reply to this at once. Yours faithfully,

ARTHUR BARCLAY
Counsellor at Law

[*Address*] C. Crichlow, Esq., Secretary,
Commissariat, U.N.I.A., Monrovia.

DNA, RG 165, file 10218-261-77. TL, carbon copy.

Cyril A. Crichlow to Gabriel M. Johnson

[*Monrovia, Liberia*] June 11/21

My dear Mr. Potentate:

Yours to hand and noted. I am glad my action has smoked them out of their indifference and neglect (apparent) and made them say something—only they haven't said enough. By prolonging the situation, we might hear further.

However, that's business; they should never send money without forwarding instructions as to its uses. It's not my fault that I have refused to spend it until I first learned specifically what it was for.

By the way, the Offices of the Association are over here in this Building—not elsewhere. Do you intend to keep official messages away from the offices of the Association; or am I to be just a figurehead and not really responsible for the records according to my instructions? Please advise. The copy of the cable you send me is not official, and I refuse to take cognizance of it in an official way.

I have already seen Counsellor Barclay. Was your approaching me through him intended as a threat? It's just a step from where you are to where I am to see me. I shall now await his seeing you in turn before acting. Thanking you for the information, &c., &c., Yours,

C. A. CRICHLOW

DNA, RG 165, file 10218-261-77. TL, carbon copy.

Cyril A. Crichlow to the UNIA Executive Council

[*Monrovia, Liberia, 12 June 1921*]

Please accept resignation, President General approving.

CRICHLOW

DNA, RG 165, file 10218-261-77. TG (coded).

Charles L. Latham to Charles Evans Hughes

Kingston, Jamaica June 14, 1921

Secretary of State, Washington, D.C.

The charges made by Garvey against the captain and chief engineer have been investigated and I have found that these men have not shown themselves to be incompetent and they have not committed any neglect of duty. Garvey and officers concerned are being informed to this effect. The American chief mate, holding a master's license is superceding captain. At his own request the Chief Engineer has been discharged.

[CHARLES L. LATHAM]

DNA, RG 41, file 122539-N. TG.

Report by Bureau Agent L. J. Barkhausen

Oklahoma City 6-14-1921

DR. A. O. WILLIAMS, (COLORED) OKMULGEE, OKLAHOMA.[1]
VIOLATION OF POSTAL REGULATIONS

Reference is made to the above initialed letter [*letter of chief GFR:JWM, 31 May 1921*] relative to the activities of subject, who is President of the Okmulgee Division of the Universal Negro Improvement Association of Okmulgee, Oklahoma, who was alleged to have made misrepresentations to colored people of his vicinity with respect to their travel to Liberia. Investigation was requested to ascertain if violation of the Postal Laws were found, and if so, instructing that the Postal Inspector be communicated with and furnished with the result of our investigation.

DICK FARR, Chief of Police, Okmulgee, stated that he had known subject for nearly fifteen years, that he had been law-abiding, and that he considered him one of the foremost negroes in that vicinity. That he was a property owner, owned considerable residence property and business property, in which there were white tenants.

The Postmaster at Okmulgee stated that he did not believe that there was any postal violation by DR. WILLIAMS, and that he was an old fellow who had never been known to violate any laws, and was considered to be highly honest and respectable.

A number of colored people in this vicinity were interviewed who remembered this Improvement Association.[2] They stated that there was absolutely no business carried on by WILLIAMS as President through the mails; that they had a meeting every Sunday at three P.M., at the Knights of Pythias Hall, at which time WILLIAMS was the principal speaker, and while he made many references to their travel to Liberia, it was strictly in accordance with instructions and literature sent out by the Black Star Line, Incorporated, Universal Building, 56 West 135th St., New York City, of which MARCUS GARVEY is President. They further stated that WILLIAMS had never solicited subscriptions or stock for the purpose of traveling to Liberia, that that was done by MRS. JESSIE KENNEDY, who was Secretary of the Okmulgee Division of the Universal Negro Improvement Association. They claimed to have a membership of three hundred in this Division, and that none of their business, even by the Secretary, was transacted by mail.

DR. WILLIAMS, when interviewed, stated that he was interested in the movement of negroes in this country to Liberia, though he felt that not very many negroes now living would ever succeed in getting to Africa. He gave a list of trustees, or Board of Directors of the Okmulgee Division of the Universal Negro Improvement Association No. 133: SAM LOVETT, HENRY MCMILLION, S. T. KENNEDY, JOHN EZELL, and B. J. JONES. He said that they charge monthly dues of twenty-five cents, in addition to ten cents a month, which is called a death tax. He explained this death tax by saying that it insured the membership of $75.00 burial. This burial, however, was only given to members who had been in the Association for six months prior to their death. He showed a button of red, black and green, which he stated was the colors of the national flag of Liberia, the red standing for loyalty, black for the black race, and green for the continent of Africa. He stated that he had been practicing medicine in Okmulgee for sixteen years, and prior to that time had lived at 1413 Hawkins Avenue, Raleigh, North Carolina. He stated that in 1920 he made a trip to his old home, North Carolina, from there going to New York City, where he conferred with MARCUS GARVEY and other officers of the National Association, for the period of seven days. He denied absolutely that he had ever used the mails to make any representations to his membership relative to travel to Liberia, or for any other reason.

He stated that about two weeks prior to Agent's visit, that a member of his association by the name of GADLIN, present whereabouts unknown, brought a negro to his office, who claimed to have come from Africa, about seven years ago, who stated that he wanted a recommendation from WILLIAMS to MARCUS GARVEY, which was refused him. He stated that some few days afterwards he, WILLIAMS, received information that this negro had gone among his membership and had stated that they should be prepared to leave for Liberia at an early date; that he would send a train for all the colored people in that vicinity, and for them to have $15.00 at the station to pay their passage to New York City. WILLIAMS states that he is positive that this man did not collect any money from any of his fellow members, simply telling them that they should have the $15.00 at the station.

WILLIAMS described this negro as unusually large, black, with pop-eyes, with a double fold to his lip, about five feet ten inches, 45 or 50 years of age, and spoke with a brogue. He gave an African name, which WILLIAMS does not remember. (Agent made inquiry relative to the visit of this African amon[g] the other negroes, and did not find anyone who had seen him.)

WILLIAMS stated that the following Sunday afternoon he issued a warning to his membership at their regular weekly meeting.

In addition to the directors or trustees before mentioned, WILLIAMS stated that W. F. COTTREL, farmer, was Vice President, P. H. OWENS, also a farmer, was Secretary, J. C. KENNEDY, farmer, and his wife, JESSIE KENNEDY, act as Treasurers.

Agent searched the records of this Division in DR. WILLIAMS' possession, with his permission, and secured circular letter issued by the Black Star Line Steamship Corporation, under date of December 1, 1920, by MARCUS GARVEY, also letter from the Black Star Line, Incorporated, signed by GEORGE TOBIAS, Treasurer, New York City, addressed to MISS JESSIE KENNEDY, 604 East Main Street, Okmulgee, Oklahoma, under date of January 21, 1921, the following of which is a copy:

DEAR MISS KENNEDY:—

Your letter of the 10th inst., enclosing $45 for stock for various persons, has been received, for which please accept our best thanks.

Enclosed herewith you will find the following certificates:

CERTIFICATE NUMBER	NAME	NO. OF SHARES
30648	H. M. MEEKS	1
30649	H. HAGLER	2
30650	MATTIE MEEKS	1
30651	ANNIE KENNEDY	1
30652	JIM MALONEY	2
30653	JESSIE KENNEDY	1
30654	J. B. AMBRES	1
	TOTAL	9

Attached to certificates are receipts, which please have signed and return to us, as it is to show that the certificates reached your hands.

We appreciate very much the interest you manifest in the corporation, and hope you will continue to do your best for us.

Hoping to hear from you soon again, and with best wishes, we are Yours very truly,

BLACK STAR LINE, INC.
GEO. TOBIAS.

Also another letter, also from the Black Star Line, Incorporated, signed by P. PREMDAS, Chief, Correspondence Department, addressed to MR. JESSIE KENNEDY, under date of February 15, 1921, following of which is a copy:

MR. JESSIE KENNEDY
604 Main Street
Okmulgee, Oklahoma

DEAR MR. KENNEDY:—
    Your letter of the 12th of February enclosing $10.00 for shares for various persons has been received.
    Enclosed herewith we are forwarding you Stock Certificates:—

CERT. #	NAME	NO. OF SHARES
32665	L. Baker	1
32666	S.W. Williams	1

    Attached to the Certificates are receipts which please get signed and return to us as it is to show that the Stock Certificates reached their hands.
    The fare to Monrovia, Liberia, is $225.00—$5.00 war tax making a total of $230.00. Port of sailing will be from New York.
    We appreciate the investment and hope to hear from you again. Yours very truly,

                                BLACK STAR LINE, INC.
                                P. PREMDAS,
                                Chief, Corr. Department.

Also, subscription blank for shares of stock at $5.00 per share, in the Black Star Line, Incorporated, and a constitution and book of laws for the Government of the Universal Negro Improvement Association, and the African Communities' League, Incorporated, of the World. All attached and made a part of this report.

Agent could find no indication that there was the slightest violation of the Postal Regulations on the part of DR. WILLIAMS. Many of the other negroes, after talking with Agent, expressed a doubt as to the trustworthiness and honesty of the Black Star Line, Incorporated, but showed the utmost confidence in DR. WILLIAMS. They stated that they felt that if they were sending their money to New York City to this organization, and that nothing would come of it, in other words, that they would not be able to travel to Liberia, that they were being duped. They wanted Agent to assure them of the character of this organization.

DR. WILLIAMS' confidence in this Association could never be shaken, but he did wish to be advised relative to the Government's attitude concerning this organization of which he is President.

Concluded.

[L. J. BARKHAUSEN]

[*Endorsement*] NOTED F. D. W.

DNA, RG 65, file BS 36-723-1. TD.

1. Okmulgee remained a center for black emigration movements long after Chief Sam's movement of 1912 to 1914. In the *Negro World* of 24 March 1923, a report revealed that fifteen black families had left Okmulgee for Mexico, where a black-owned real estate concern, the International Community Welfare League, had claimed settlement rights to over 450,000 acres of land in three states. This real estate company had headquarters in Los Angeles, Mexico City, and Okmulgee.

2. See "Okmulgee U.N.I.A. Holds Monster Meeting," *NW*, 19 March 1921.

UNIA Executive Council to Gabriel M. Johnson

[*New York, ca. 15 June 1921*]

We have not accepted Crichlow resignation. Please cancel our previous telegram and substitute the following: You may come America. Cabled yesterday $800.

UNIVERSAL

DNA, RG 165, file 10218-261-77. TG (coded).

H. M. Daugherty, Attorney General, to Sen. William B. McKinley

[*Washington, D.C.*] June 15, 1921

My dear Senator:

I have the honor to acknowledge the receipt of your communication of the 8th instant advising me of agitation among the negroes in the vicinity of Danville, Illinois. The activities of MARCUS GARVEY and his associates have been receiving the attention of the department for some time. They have generally been confined to the vicinity of New York City and the extension of their propaganda to the middle western states is indeed interesting, and I want to assure you that I appreciate your action in calling it to my attention.

I have caused the Bureau of Investigation to conduct an inquiry into the situation reported.[1] Faithfully yours,

H. M. DAUGHERTY
Attorney General.

DNA, RG 65, file BS 198940-159. TLR, carbon copy.

1. Lewis J. Baley, in a memorandum to J. P. Rooney, instructed Rooney to send an agent to Danville on 1 July to "make a thorough investigation of the activities of Garvey's representatives, keeping in mind possible postal fraud being perpetrated upon various negroes in this vicinity" (DNA, RG 65, file BS 198940-178).

Report by Special Agent J. G. Tucker

NEW YORK, N.Y. 6-16-21

MONTHLY REPORT OF RADICAL PRESS

... "THE CRISIS" (RADICAL NEGRO MONTHLY)

The above magazine, in its June issue, carries an article which notwithstanding reports from confidential sources that President King of Liberia is in s[ym]pathy with the movement of Marcus Garvey, seems to be in strict opposition to Garvey's "Back to Africa" scheme. The article, which is signed by "C. D. B. King, President of Liberia", follows: ...

The above statement is in striking contrast to the promises made by Garvey to his followers, the general sense of which has been to the effect that those who returned to Africa would be assured of plenty of work and a good living. As has previously been reported, a number of Garvey's followers have sold their belongings in order to pay for passage to Liberia where Garvey, through his publication "The Negro World," had stated that a ship was to sail some time ago. Many of these unfortunates have come to New York after having first paid their passage to the Black Star Steamship Co. and are at present in destitute circumstances.

J. G. TUCKER

DNA, RG 65, file BS 202600-1628-88. TD.

Charles L. Latham to Charles Evans Hughes

Kingston, Jamaica June 17, 1921

Secretary of State, Washington.

Sufficient funds have been advanced by Garvey /to master/ at the master's request to return to the United States and Garvey has given him a letter to the Black Star Line at New York City, with reference to balance of wages. Return satisfactory to the captain. In consequence of animosities and insults while on board and a nervous breakdown in collection of extra wages the Chief Engineer has been discharged. Protests have been made by Garvey in the matter of payment of both wages and extra wages. It is considered advisable to discharge all persons desiring by mutual consent to return if agreeable to captain. Otherwise in view of the disorganization on board the vessel discharge with extra wages payable.

[CHARLES L. LATHAM]

DNA, RG 41, file 122539-N. TG.

Report by Bureau Agent Madison Ballantyne

Washington, D.C. 6-17-21

W. C. MATTHEWS, WHITLAW APARTMENT HOUSE (NEGRO): IN CONNECTION WITH MARCUS GARVEY.

Acting under instructions of Agent in Charge Mr. Matthews, I learned from reliable confidential source that [*William C.*] MATTHEWS was considered a very fine man; that informant knew MATTHEWS did not approve of the radical activities among the negroes, although he was acting as attorney and adviser of MARCUS GARVEY in relation to the Black [S]tar Steamship Line, and had stated to informant that for such service he was receiving a salary of $6000 per annum. He further stated that MATTHEWS was a graduate of Tuskegee Institute, later of Andover and finally of Harvard University. Informant stated that MATTHEWS was held in very high regard by President Eliot of Harvard,[1] and that he had made a wonderful record while attending the University; that MATTHEWS was formerly Assistant United States Attorney at Boston, and he (informant) was under the impression that MATTHEWS was now endeavoring to receive a political appointment.

Informant further stated that he would endeavor to obtain additional information from MATTHEWS as to the relationship between GARVEY and MATTHEWS, and would let me know as soon as he found anything further. Investigation concluded.

MADISON BALLANTYNE

[*Endorsement*] NOTED F. D. W.

DNA, RG 65, file BS 198940-106. TD. Stamped endorsement.

1. Charles William Eliot (1834–1926) served as president of Harvard University from 1869 until 1909 (*WBD*).

Report by Special Agent J. G. Tucker

New York, June 18, 1921

NEGRO ACTIVITIES

BLACK STAR LINE

From a confidential source it has been learned that there is considerable trouble brewing in the ranks of the above corporation and it is not improbable that if Marcus Garvey does not return to the United States soon, there will be an expose of Garvey and his assistants and their methods and that some of them will meet with bodily [h]arm.

The Black Star Line occupies No. 56 and 58 West 13[5]th St. which were formerly three story dwelling houses and which have been broken into one large building.

Including the officers of the Company there are about thirty employees, all of whom, it is understood, are receiving fair sized weekly salaries to say nothing of the considerable field for[ce] which is also under salary.

From the same source it has been learned that financially the Company is in a very bad way for the reason that the weekly collections taken up at the meetings of the Universal Negro Improvement Association which have been previously used to help defray the expenses of the Black Star Line, have fallen off very materially during the absence of Garvey and nothing that his assistants have been able to do seems to have helped the financial situation to any appreciable extent. One of Garvey's assistants recently made a confidential statement to the aforementioned informant to the effect that he (Garvey's man Helliger) [*Ellegor*] had recently been to Norfolk where he made a small deposit on a boat which is to be called the "Phyllis Wheatley" and which, through the advertising of the Black Star Line, its supporters and stock subscribers have been led to believe the Company owns. Within the past week a large number of people have at times congregated around the offices of the Company seeking booking on one of its ships to sail to Africa.

The general fe[e]ling amongst Garvey's assistants at this time is, that if he does not return within a short time the stockholders of the Black Star Line and members of the Universal Negro Improvement Association will take matters into their own hands and all those officially connected with the Line are very likely to meet with physical violence.

No one connected with either of Garvey's ventures seems to have any idea when he will return and all seem to share the opinion that he has been unable to obtain a passport to return to the United States.

J. G. TUCKER

DNA, RG 65, file BS 202600-1628-91. TD.

Report by Special Agent P-138

New York City 6-18-21

IN RE: NEGRO ACTIVITIES.

Today [*16 June*] again saw another group of men gathered in front of the Black Star Line Office, and inquiries developed the fact that they were also trying to get signed on as a crew on a ship, the negotiations for the purchase of which are now pending. They have been waiting over a week and many of them are commencing to become doubtful. There is every reason to believe that if Garvey does not return in a comparatively short time, a reaction is bound to set in, thereby causing a run on the office for their money. There are hundreds of his followers out of work.

P-138

[*Endorsements*] FILE G. F. R. NOTED F. D. W.

DNA, RG 65, file BS 202600-667-54. TD. Stamped endorsements.

Negro World Editorial

[18 June 1921]

BISHOP SMITH'S BIG BLUFF.

Bishop C. S. Smith of the A.M.E. Church, who resides in Detroit, Mich., has sent an advertisement to several newspapers, claiming that he will give $1,000 to the party who will give him information about the Black Star Line owning absolutely and in fee simple any boats which trade between the United States and the West Indies. A couple of months ago the celebrated divine published another advertisement stating that he would give $500 to anyone who would inform him from what port the pioneers of the U.N.I.A. sailed for Africa, when they sailed and where they arrived. We gave the information in an editorial about a month ago, and have not yet received the $500. It would come [in] very handy and expedite the publishing of a book which is in the hands of a publisher, or enable us to attend Dr. Du Bois' Pan-African conference or to take a trip to Monrovia.

First as to the $500 proposition. The Industrial Pioneers of the U.N.I.A. sailed from New York on the Buenos Aires for Cadiz, Spain, on February 3. They arrived in Cadiz, Spain, on February 17. They sailed from Cadiz, Spain, for Monrovia, Liberia, the last week in February and arrived in Monrovia the first week in March. The Negro World three or four weeks ago published the account of the reception tendered them by citizens of Monrovia. The party consisted of two officials of the U.N.I.A. and architects and mechanics. An agriculturist had preceded them to Monrovia. If Bishop Smith doubts our word, let him send a cable to Monrovia, for he evidently has money to burn, and verify our statement. Now that we have given him the desired information, he can send the check or money order of $500 to the Literary Editor of The Negro World, 56 West 135th St., New York City, N.Y., U.S.A. . . .

Printed in *NW*, 18 June 1921.

Charles L. Latham to Charles Evans Hughes

Kingston, Jamaica, June 18, 1921

Secretary of State, Washington

GARVEY exhibits cablegram from Wilford Smith, New York City, reported to be consul for U.N.I.A. and affiliated organizations stating that he cannot work longer with Thompson, Vice President Black Star Line, and requests Garvey to return New York at once.

[CHARLES L.] LATHAM

[*Typewritten reference*] Recd. 5:03 P.M.

DNA, RG 59, file 000-612. TG, carbon copy.

Charles L. Latham to Charles Evans Hughes

AMERICAN CONSULATE. Kingston, Jamaica,
June 18, 1921

SUBJECT: COMPLAINT OF MARCUS GARVEY AGAINST THE
CAPTAIN & CHIEF ENGINEER OF THE S.S. KANAWHA.

SIR:

I have the honor to supplement my despatch No. 1086 of June 11, 1921, relative to the complaint of Marcus Garvey against the Captain and Chief Engineer of the s.s. KANAWHA.

The following is a more detailed report on the subject:

On June 1, 1921, Mr. Garvey filed in this Consulate a letter in which he lodged a general complaint against the Master and crew of the said steamship KANAWHA for the destruction and mismanagement of the vessel, and especially against Charles C. Harris, Chief Engineer, Cyrus M. Yarter and Charles S. Sauncey, second assistant Engineer.

As this complaint was only general in character, I requested Mr. Garvey to specify in detail the grounds for the complaint. On June 7, 1921, Mr.

Garvey filed a letter (copy enclosed) in compliance with my request. The charges as outlined in this letter were placed in the hands of the Master and Chief Engineer and they were requested to answer each and every charge in detail. Their answers are enclosed.

Mr. Garvey later on submitted a list of witnesses which he was ready to produce to prove /the/ charges brought. These witnesses were as follows:

> Sidney De Bourg, Henrietta Vinton Davis and Augustus Fredericks, all of whom are officials of the Universal Negro Improvement Association and who were passengers on the vessel from New York to Kingston. Summaries of their evidence in the form of statements are also enclosed.

Mr. Garvey then produced as witnesses the following members of the crew:

> Percy Griffith, water tender; William Rommeyer A.B.; Norman Neuville, fireman; Joshua Parris, fireman; John Hunt A.B.; Richard Tomlinson, coal passer.

A sworn statement of each of these witnesses is also enclosed.

Several other witnesses who were in the same position as those mentioned in the first group were also examined but their stories were not considered sufficiently important for record in full.

After carefully investigating the whole matter I concluded that Mr. Garvey's charges of destructive mismanagement, incompetency, neglect of duty and conspiracy to inflict heavy financial loss to the owners of the vessel were not sustained and he was so informed.

During the investigation various disturbances occurred on board the vessel so that a great deal of animosity was aroused between the officers of the ship and Mr. Garvey.

The entire crew also complained of a shortage of food and upon investigation it was found that, while Mr. Garvey had substantially complied with the requirements of the law in this respect[,] the quantities of certain foods supplied were not sufficient for the wants of the men and he was informed that proper steps should be taken to see that the men were sufficiently supplied with food.

The outcome of the whole matter has been the super[s]ession of the master and the discharge of the Chief Engineer and the first Assistant Engineer. These three men are leaving Kingston for New York to-day on the SIXAOLA. The Master will take up the settlement of his accounts at the office of the Black Star Line in New York: the Chief Engineer was discharged at the request of this Consulate because of the animosities aroused by Garvey's charge and interference resulting in a nervous breakdown, and one month's extra wages were collected. Mr. Garvey, however, on behalf of the owners, protested at paying any money at all to the Chief Engineer as he still maintained that the officer, because of his neglect, was responsible for the various mishaps to the machinery of the vessel, which resulted in loss, and he stated that his Company would place the matter before the proper court in the United States for adjudication. I have therefore sent to the Department with separate despatch the sum of $748.40, which represents the wages due from March 1, to June 15, 1921 amounting to $443.40, and one month's extra wages amounting to $305. In the case of the first assistant engineer he was discharged by mutual consent. I have the honor to be, Sir, Your obedient servant,

C. L. LATHAM
American Consul

ENCLOSURE (4)[1]

Copy of Letter & Answers.
Statements.
Sworn Statements.

DNA, RG 41, file 122539-N. TLS, carbon copy. Sent in quadruplicate.

1. The enclosures have not been printed.

J. Preston Doughten, Visa Office, to Richard W. Flournoy, Jr., Office of the Solicitor, Department of State, and William L. Hurley

[*Washington, D.C.*] June 18, 1921

Mr. Flournoy:[1]
Mr. Hurley:

Please express your views on the advisability and legality of our instructing the American Consul at Kingston, Jamaica to refuse Bill of Health and ships['] papers as mentioned in the last paragraph of the Consul's despatch of May 30, 1921 of the steamer "KANAWHA", should the master refuse to discharge Marcus Garvey from the crew.

J. P[RESTON]. D[OUGHTEN].

DNA, RG 59, file 811.108 G 191. TMI, recipient's copy.

1. Richard Wilson Flournoy, Jr. (1878–1961), became acting chief of the State Department's Bureau of Citizenship (later the Passport Division) in 1915. He was a drafting officer with the Office of the Solicitor in 1921 (U.S. Department of State, *Register*, 1924 [Washington, D.C.: GPO, 1924], p. 126).

Cyril A. Crichlow to the UNIA Executive Council

[*Monrovia, Liberia, 19 June 1921*]

On account of serious personal differences with and imposition by Potentate and Supreme Deputy, position untenable. I am very ill, Doctor orders home. Will expenses be allowed? Hold important information. Vigorously I protest against ex-parte hearing. I am anxiously waiting an answer personal.

CRICHLOW

DNA, RG 165, file 10218-261-77. TG (coded).

Reuben Vassall, Detective and Acting Corporal, to the Deputy Inspector General, Kingston, Jamaica

Water Police Station, Kingston.
19/6/21

CONFIDENTIAL.

Deputy Inspector General,
I beg to report that the S.S. Kanawha of the Black Star Line left here yesterday 18.6.21 for Colón, Bocas Del Tor[o] and Port Limón. She had on board 23 passengers for Colón including Mr. Marcus Garvey, President General, Miss Henrietta Vinton Davis, Second Vice President, and Mr. De Bourge. The ship is captained by Mr. O'Neil who was former mate on the ship. The former Captain, Mr. Richardson, the chief Engineer, Mr. George [*Charles*] Harris, and the Second Engineer Mr. A. S. Durrant left by the S.S. Sixaola of the United Fruit Company yesterday afternoon for New York. Having been sent away by the American Consul to face their trial at New York before the American Shipping Board on charges preferred against them by Mr. Marcus Garvey, for breach of discipline. There were allegations that the Captain and Chief Engineer were tampering with the boiler and engine of the ship which resulted in the delay. The Kanawha is expected to return here in about three weeks time, and then back to New York.

REUBEN VASSALL,
Detective & Actg. Corporal

[*Stamped reference*] Colonial Secretary's
Office 12779

JA, CSO, secret and confidential file, 1B/5, 12207/n. TL, carbon copy.

Cyril A. Crichlow to Joseph L. Johnson

Monrovia, Liberia, June 20, 1921

Sir:

Owing to my inability to adjust matters pertaining to our organization here in Liberia, I find it quite impossible to proceed further without complaint. I have endeavored to do the best I could to adjust matters in such a way that it would not be necessary to approach my Government; but as so many things have developed from day to day that I now find my position intolerable and unbearable—so much so that there is nothing left for me to do but fall back on my Government to see that I get a square deal: and this, too, in face of the fact that you have told me on several occasions to try and manage the affairs of the Association in such a way that the Government you represent will not have to be called upon to participate in any of its affairs.

My reasons for complaint are as follows:

(1) My instructions issued and signed by the President General in New York have been violated to such an extent that I am no longer functioning in the way and to the extent that it was intended that I should function.

(2) My authority as commercial head of our organization in Liberia has been supplanted by persons here who have no authority to supplant me.

(3) The affairs of the Association are being conducted outside of the Commissariat contrary to the orders of the President General and in such a way as to make it impossible for me as Resident Secretary to keep the records properly.

(4) Efforts have been made to prevent my drawing money from the Bank on my own signature along with that of Mr. G. O. Marke, or to receive cables from the organization at New York by specific instructions being given at the Bank and at the Cable Station by some one who had no authority to give such instructions or to interfere in any way with my duties as Commercial head of the organization in Liberia.

(5) The outcome of all this has been to "ditch" me here with scarcely enough money to pay my passage home and no possibility of getting messages to New York except by paying for them out of my own pocket, thus reducing the amount of money I now have on hand—a fact which will, if continued, make it quite impossible for me to return home at all.

In view of the foregoing, I have the honor as an American citizen to request that you use your good offices to see to it that I am fairly dealt with in the premises. I have the honor to be, Sir, Your obedient servant,

C. CRICHLOW

[*Address*] Dr. Joseph L. Johnson, Minister
Resident and Consul General of the
United States, Monrovia.

DNA, RG 59, file 882.00/705. TLS, recipient's copy.

W. E. B. Du Bois to the Editor, *New York Age*

[[New York City. June 20, 1921]]

Editor of THE NEW YORK AGE:

I am glad that THE AGE is giving its columns to a frank discussion of the Pan-African movement. A great question like this needs discussion and clarification and for this reason I venture again to trespass on your kindness in answer to Bishop [*Charles Spencer*] Smith. Bishop Smith mingles the Pan-African Congress and the Garvey movement as practically one idea.[1] This is a grave mistake. The Pan-African Congress has nothing to do with any "Africa for the Africa[ns]" movement.[2] The object of the Pan-African Congress is simply to bring representatives of the various people of African descent into knowledge and common acquaintanceship, so that out of such conferences general policies and actions can be evolved. . . .

Many colored persons know this, but have been restrained by the Garvey movement. Mr. Garvey's African program has been dangerous, ill-considered[,] impracticable, and for that reason the Pan-African Congress has not invited him to participate.[3] On the other hand we must be generous enough and give Mr. Garvey the credit of having foreseen the necessity of a union in business and social uplift between all the African people. He is not the man to carry this out because he lacks poise and business ability; all the more reason therefore for Bishop Smith and others to push a wise program. . . .

. . . It does not matter a picayune whether the initiative in this movement comes from a man born in New York or Capetown or Kingstown [*Kingston?*]. . . .

W. E. B. DU BOIS

Printed in the *New York Age*, 25 June 1921. Original headline omitted.

1. In his letter regarding the "Pan-African Congress" published in the *New York Age*, 18 June 1921, Bishop Smith declared: "Du Bois' plan for a Pan-African Congress squares with that of Marcus Garvey's scheme for an African Empire. Both are delusionists and dreamers as it relates to Africa." At the conclusion of his letter, Bishop Smith stated that his views were "largely" those that had been set forth by Archibald Johnson in the *New York Age* of 21 May 1921 regarding Du Bois's Pan-African Congress.

2. In a letter to Charles Evans Hughes, Du Bois reemphasized the purposes of the Pan-African Congress, stating that "it has nothing to do with the so-called Garvey movement and contemplates neither force nor revolution in its program" (W. E. B. Du Bois to Charles Evans Hughes, 23 July 1921, MU, WEBDB, reel 10, frame 554).

3. William H. Ferris responded to this statement with the following comment:
    We do not believe that Mr. Garvey will lose any sleep because Dr. Du Bois did not invite
    him to participate. Had he been invited he might have sent a representative, but he
    would not have gone in person. He is a man of action, not a theorizer; a doer of deeds,
    not a dreamer. And we believe that he would be like a fish out of water in one of Dr. Du
    Bois' congresses, where there would be considerable criticism, speculation, poetic
    vaporings and plaintive wailings, with no practical program outlined and no practical
    results achieved. ("The Pan-African Congress and the U.N.I.A.," *NW*, 2 July 1921)
Ferris's lengthy editorial sought to answer the statements made in the letter by Du Bois in the
Age. For other *NW* comments about Du Bois during this period, see *NW*, 7 May, 9 July, 16
July, and 1 October 1921.

Richard W. Flournoy, Jr., to
J. Preston Doughten

[*Washington, D.C.*] June 21, 1921

Mr. Doughten.

It appears from the reports in the attached file that Marcus Garvey is an
undesirable, and indeed a very dangerous, alien. It appears that he is not only
attempting to organize all of the negroes in the world against the white
people, but that he has been doing everything that he could to stir up
animosity among the negroes in the United States against the white people.
His advice to American negroes, if followed, would make them all disloyal to
this country. Moreover, he is constantly speaking of resorting to forcible
means to accomplish the aims of his organization. It is evident that he should
be kept out of the United States if possible and the instructions to the consul
at Kingston to refuse him a visa were well warranted. However, it is at least
doubtful whether the Department would be warranted in instructing the
Consul to refuse, unless Garvey is discharged, to grant a bill of health to the
steamer on which he is employed as a member of the crew. The law governing the action of American consuls in granting bills of health to vessels
clearing for the United States is found in the Act of Congress of February 15,
1895, Section 2. . . .

The bill of health, as its names indicates, relates solely to the health
conditions of the vessel and persons on board. There seems to be no authority of law for refusing to grant a bill of health except for failure to comply
with the health requirements. If a member of the crew of a vessel has a
dangerous or loathsome contagious disease, it is evidently the duty of the
consul to refuse to grant a bill of health until he is removed, but such refusal
would hardly be warranted by the objectionable character of a member of the
crew or his political views.

For the reasons mentioned, it would seem sufficient in the present case
for the consul to refuse to visa the crew list [*In the margin*: This is modified
by Mr. Nielsen's[1] memo of June 23, herewith] and to inform the Master of

the vessel that all of the alien members of the crew will be kept on the vessel if it arrives at a port of the United States without a visaed crew list. However, before instructing the consul to this effect it would seem desirable to take the case up with the Bureau of Immigration and make certain that they will see that the members of the crew are kept on the vessel if it arrives without a visaed crew list.

R[ICHARD]. W. F[LOURNOY].

[*Endorsement*] FILE J. P. D.

DNA, RG 59, file 811.108 G 191/31. TLI, recipient's copy. Marginal insertion and endorsement are handwritten.

1. Fred Kenelm Nielsen was appointed solicitor for the Department of State in June 1920 (U.S. Department of State, *Register,* 1924 [Washington, D.C.: GPO, 1924], pp. 170–171).

Charles L. Latham to Charles Evans Hughes

Kingston, Jamaica June 22, 1921

Secretary of State, Washington.
On account of boiler trouble and lack of coal and water, the KANAWHA arrived today at noon at Kingston, being unable to reach Port Limón.[1]

[CHARLES L. LATHAM]

DNA, RG 41, file 122539-N. TG.

1. Gov. Leslie Probyn of Jamaica, in a dispatch to Winston Churchill, gave a fuller account of the *Kanawha's* difficulties, stating that "an attempt to sink the ship was reported to have been made by the Chief Engineer . . . whereupon the crew became mutinous, and demanded that the engineers and Mr. Marcus Garvey should leave the vessel." Garvey subsequently announced that he would not make a return visit to Colón but would proceed to New York (Leslie Probyn to Winston S. Churchill, 11 July 1921, PRO, CO 137/749).

Marcus Garvey to Charles Evans Hughes

Kingston Jca June 22 1921.

Hon. Charles Evans Hughes, Washington, D.C.
Could you instruct Consul here to visa my passport[?]

MARCUS GARVEY

DNA, RG 59, file 811.108 G 191/30. TG, recipient's copy.

Wilford H. Smith to Marcus Garvey

[*New York*] June 23rd 1921

Marcus Garvey
    Money sent by cable Royal Bank[.] [R]eturn at once very much needed[.]

[Wilford H.] Smith

Garvey v. *United States*, no. 8317, Ct. App., 2d Cir., 2 February 1925, defendant's exhibit GG. TG.

Fred K. Nielsen, Solicitor, Department of State, to Richard W. Flournoy, Jr.

[*Washington, D.C.*] June 23, 1921

Dear Mr. Flournoy:
    I agree with what you say regarding bills of health. So far as concerns the objectionable character of a member of the crew, I think that we should merely refuse to let his name be on the visaed list. A Consular Officer can always be directed to telegraph the Department if, according to his information, any member of a crew is sailing who is not on the visaed list. Then, if necessary, we can warn the port authorities. I think it would be rather high-handed and not within the law to refuse to visa all of the crew when only one member is regarded as ineligible for the list.

F[red]. K. N[ielsen].

DNA, RG 59, file 811.108 G 191/14. TMI, recipient's copy.

William W. Heard, American Vice-consul, Kingston, Jamaica, to Charles Evans Hughes

Kingston, Ja. June 23, 1921

Secretary of State, Washington, D.C.
    Garvey exhibits cablegram from Smith New York City instructing him to request us request the Department again at his expense permission visa his

passport[.] KANAWHA may now return to the United States via Cuban ports.

[WILLIAM W.] HEARD[1]

[*Endorsements*] Tel. to Kingston 6/24/21
J[ohn] P[reston] D[oughton] ES File.

DNA, RG 59, file 811.108 G 191/19. TG, recipient's copy. Handwritten endorsements.

1. William W. Heard (b. 1887) was U.S. vice-consul at Kingston from May 1920 to September 1922 (U.S. Department of State, *Register*, 1924 [Washington, D.C.: GPO, 1924], p. 138).

William L. Hurley to Harry A. McBride

[*Washington, D.C.*] June 24, 1921

Visa

Dear Mr. McBride:

Things are so shaping themselves with reference to Marcus Garvey that I really think by insisting upon exclusion, we would martyrize him.

I have learned that prior to his departure he evolved some sort of an insurance scheme[1] which he put before his followers with the result that considerable money passed through hi[s] fingers. It appears, however, that the scheme does not exactly fit in with the insurance laws of the state of New York. It is just possible that in connection with this, he may have violated our Postal laws. I have good reason to believe that he has, so I suggest that he be allowed to return and his case will receive the undivided attention of the Department of Justice with a view to taking up this matter and if possible secure a conviction thereby, utterly discrediting him once and for all.

What do you think?

[WILLIAM L. HURLEY]

DNA, RG 59, file 000-612. TN, carbon copy.

1. Art. 3, sec. 28 of the UNIA's "General Laws" (1920) stated that a "death tax of 10 cents per month shall be levied on each member." This fund was to be separate from the dues normally paid by members. When a member died, if his or her dues were paid up, the death fund granted a burial benefit of $75. This arrangement was to become controversial in later months, when several divisions complained that the families of deceased members had not received the burial funds.

Cyril A. Crichlow to Marcus Garvey

Commissariat, Monrovia June 24, 1921

Your Excellency:

I have the honor to submit the following report covering that portion of my services as Resident Secretary for the Association at Monrovia that has brought me into serious personal differences with His Highness the Potentate and His Highness the Supreme Deputy. . . .

Reverting to the question of personal differences, I have to say that I foresaw an inevitable cleavage between myself on the one hand and the Potentate [*Johnson*] and Supreme Deputy [*Marke*] on the other hand. From the outset of our journey from New York, I was quite aware that the Supreme Deputy did not favor the position in which I was placed, whereby the $2000 for the traveling expenses of the party were placed in my possession. I undertook to humor and flatter him and undertook no expenditure unless with his approval and sanction. This soothed him a bit, but from time to time during the trip he expressed dissatisfaction with Your Excellency, after promising to give him written instructions, did not give him any; that Your Excellency maneuvered him into riding second-class from New York to Cadiz and Garcia helped to fool him into it by some sort of tale that he would be made uncomfortable by the prejudice he would meet in the first-class; that all his life he had always been accustomed to traveling first-class, and he could not see, being the Supreme Deputy and of a higher rank than Your Excellency, why he should have to do it now, whereas Your Excellency always travels the best, Pullmans and the like; that Your Excellency did not recognize him in providing for his signature along with those of the Potentate and myself, or otherwise along with that of the Potentate only; that when he got to Monrovia he would try to have all that changed.

From our arrival in Monrovia, I gradually sensed that the Potentate and the Supreme Deputy were putting their heads together and that, thru the machinations and intriguing of the latter, would do all in their power to embar[r]ass me so that in the end I would be forced out or my wings clipped so the two of them together could control the expenditures. There was already a sentiment in Monrovia hostile to Americans on my arrival; Americans believed they knew too much and were more aggressive and progressive in their methods than the Liberians: and the Liberians were in league to tame them down. That is why Col. Young's[,] the American Military Attache's, wings had to be cut; that is why Mr. Bundy, the Secretary to the American Legation was *persona non grata*; that is why Dr. Ross, President of the College of West Africa, was forced out; that is why several others have been gotten rid of; that is why I was a marked man from the start.

The Supreme Deputy grumbled considerably against His Excellency the President General because, as he stated, the Council was little and sometimes never consulted on vital and important affairs; and he moreover declared on more than one occasion that "we were a part of the Council over here and would alter and modify things to suit ourselves, Garvey notwithstanding." He said: "The American and West Indian Negroes could control things on their side of the water; we Africans will run things over here. We hold the trump cards; we can make or break them; they have got to come by us."

From all these circumstances, I knew and perceived from the first that gradually my authority and instructions would be over-ridden and the men encouraged in all possible ways to go over my head and come to them direct. They artfully sought to range them against me, showing them that I was not their friend.

The first serious difference arose over the question of the employment of the Potentate's son (Mr. Hilary R. W. Johnson) as clerk in the office to assist in the handling of the paper work. It was due to my suggestion that the son was employed as a clerk, because of his higher intelligence and ability than the average Liberian young men. In doing so, I relished the danger that might ensue as the result of nepotism, which events did not take long to confirm. But still, there was no other qualified person available, so that my suggesting him was unavoidable to a certain extent.

On the water side the Johnson family and interests own a large river launch called the "Rachel Agnes." The Potentate came to me privately, called me aside, and told me that his son would have to be off about a couple hours every day to go to the water side to attend to the despatching and incoming of the boat. I was quite aware that Your Excellency had expressly warned me orally that none of the men, not even the Potentate himself, were expected to engage in any other work or line of business outside the Association's; and to report to Your Excellency confidentially what each man was doing if engaged otherwise than upon the Association's work. But I agreed to his suggestion so as to see what the ultimate outcome would be. The office hours were from 8 to 12 and 1 to 4.

The son started at once by coming to work late, and sometimes never showing up until late in the afternoon, and sometimes not showing up at all. There was a picnic one day and the son stayed away to attend same, and never said a word to me as the business head of the office to let me know that he wanted to be off or intended to be off. I did not understand from the potentate that his son's hours would be so irregular and impossible; and after calling his attention several times to the situation, finally reported him to his father. In taking that step, I committed the unpardonable sin and I have been *persona non grata* ever since with both father and son. Instead of just sitting down and drawing my salary and taking things easy, I was like the rest of Americans trying to be too strict.

I had a time sheet made out in which he was to fill in beside his signature his "hours in and hours out." This he treated with contempt, signing it when he pleased and sometimes not signing it at all at the proper time, thus putting in the hours to suit his convenience when he did sign. Then at the end of April when I looked for the time sheet for that month, it had disappeared. I managed to secure a partially filled out report for May which I submit herewith. I saw there was no use in complaining further to the Potentate, so I simply allowed matters to take their course. And that course was soon to take the form of a conspiracy on the part of the Potentate, his son, and the Supreme Deputy, to show me up.

The son's constant grumble was that he was educated in the United States, graduated from some college or other, and had more ability than any of the other men, and he did not think it was fair to only offer him $50 a month. He thought he was superior to Jemmott as a Builder and Architect, and to Mr. Donaldson as my assistant, whom he said could ne[i]ther type-write nor compose a letter, and so expressed himself often. In this connection, he undertook to tell the unsuspecting Liberian public that he was the Resident Secretary at a salary of $5000 a year, with attendant complications and confusion. In writing letters, he often undertook to sign for me, without my knowledge or consent, in such a way that people got the impression he was the real secretary; also, in addition to that, he often wrote letters and filed away the duplicates without letting me know just what was passing along through the correspondence. I called his hand with respect to this on several occasions. His father, moreover, encouraged his attitude by bringing over correspondence and mail and giving it direct to his son to be answered, and I was thus kept ignorant of the affairs of the Association. The position thus became intolerable and in the interests of my own self-respect and not deciding to accept the situation and become a figurehead, there was nothing left for me to do but to offer my resignation and return to the States.

I have been told confidentially that the son expects that his father will succeed in having me removed from my position as Resident Secretary and get it for him, as he is expecting to get married soon and must have a good job by which he can support a wife. Besides being a clerk in the Commissariat, he is engaged as a Despatcher for his father's boat, he is an Architect and Builder, he is a Y.M.C.A. Secretary, Secretary of the Monrovia Division of the U.N.I.A., etc. He is depending on his father to find him a soft berth.

His Highness has been very inactive in the Association's affairs since his return to the States, so much so that it is the wonder among many elements of the Liberian public what he was elected Potentate for and voted so large a salary as $12,000 a year. For the whole time since our arrival at Monrovia on March 18th, he has made only one trip on behalf of the Association, and that was the trip we made on Sunday April 3d, to Louisiana, where we did not address over 50 persons. His time is largely devoted to his private interests—his boat and other personal affairs.

I understand that he has a number of little pet schemes that he intends to combine with the Association's program in order to make some money for himself. He has an old, leaky bui[l]ding on Broad St., that had funds come as requested, he would have repaired and sold or leased to the Association for the Drug Store. I did not approve this. He also had some arrangements whereby settlers would be turned over to certain persons who would board and lodge them, paying His Highness a consideration. I also did not approve this. It is felt that the property leased from Mrs. Moort for the farm was not the best land for the purpose; Mr. A. J. Henry, our Agriculturist, complains that the land is poor and worn-out, and no good, and will not be able to give satisfactory results, and there is a feeling that the property was palmed off on the Association as a personal favor by His Highness to Mrs. Moort.

The plans for the distribution of the settlers, it is felt, will not be for the best interests of the Association; but will be in line with the purposes of the one-party political system to maintain its existence and power unimpaired. That is to say, instead of being concentrated in settlements together, the settlers will be parcelled out among the older settlements in such a way as to allow the Liberians to be in the ascendancy politically and dominate in the political elections. It is important that Your Excellency know these facts, in order that you may understand to what extent it is proposed to waive aside the political program of the Association.

As attention has hitherto been called, the arrival of settlers in . . . [*word mutilated*] is not greatly desired by Liberians; Americans especially are not particularly wanted, unless they have money. Their money is loved but they themselves are not loved. Americans arriving here with money are usually planted in the "sands;" they are parted from their money by such smooth practices that there is nothing left for them to do but lay down and die, because the economic situation is so deplorable that in order to eke out an existence they would be forced to live on less than a shilling a day, in the event they did not have any other independent means of making a living.

My relationship with the Potentate was further aggravated by a trip I undertook up the river to Careysburg in the effort to locate coal. The President General had suggested that I make such a trip in order to size up conditions generally and as the Commercial head to gain some acquaintance with the people and the practical possibilities of profitable enterprise and trade with them. The Potentate endorsed the trip, sanctioned the preliminary expenditure of £20 for expenses in Monrovia covering certain food supplies, etc., and was notified by me in a letter which he asked for that additional expense money would be needed to carry out the necessary plans.

There were eight men to go in the party, including Mr. Cyril Henry whose valuable experience and knowledge in chemistry, mineralogy and agriculture added to the success of the trip. Also, a Mr. Maxwell, a recent arrival from Brazil and a prospector, was included in the party at the instance of the Potentate after all the expenses had already been calculated. From what I understood the Potentate wanted Mr. Maxwell to do, being informed by Mr. Maxwell himself, I sent him a blank check hurriedly one morning as he was hurrying to get up the river to Brewerville or Louisiana (I forget which), which he signed. I drew the check for £30 which I had spoken to His Highness the Supreme Deputy as being the sum of money necessary to meet the expenses of the trip, and asked him to notify the Potentate concerning the same, which he promised to do. Later, he denied knowing anything about the matter on my return when the question came up. Words fail me to characterize this denial, but to me the motive was plain, and I began to perceive the dangerous ground on which I was treading in the determination of His Highness to queer me in every possible way.

The Potentate accepted the Supreme Deputy's denial, which was perfectly natural for him to do, of course, and at once began to speak of his particular honesty in business, because Liberians were always criticized by foreigners as being particularly tricky and dishonest, especially in their dealings with foreigners, and at once launched an attack against Americans in general. Colonel Young, the Military Attache of the American Legation here, and other Americans were personated, and in a private conversation later on both His Highnesses launched an attack against the Assistant President General (Dr. Gordon), whom they declared as unfit for the position, especially should something happen to Your Excellency and it became necessary for him to succeed you. Reference was made to him that he had been to Liberia once upon a time and had perpetrated some dishonest practices here at the expense of Liberians and that his record here was so unsavory he could never come to Liberia, and in the President General's place could have but little influence in Liberia. His Highness the Supreme Deputy took occasion to express himself with reference to The American Leader (Dr. Eason) and the Secretary General (Dr. Brooks) whom he stated were whiskey-heads and small-change thieves.

I fully believe that trip has netted the Association some very valuable mineral samples, which I have brought with me, and which if followed up could lead to profitable enterprise. Money was spent for digging here and there, and dash money had to be given to the native carriers and diggers to get them to work fast, so our stay would not be too long; and in the circumstances, being out in the bushes among untutored people, it was impracticable to secure vouchers for expenditures. The expenses of the trip were £50.15.6, the difference (15/6) being advanced by Mr. Cyril Henry so the rest of the party could get down the river to Monrovia from White Plains, which I repaid him out of my own private funds, credit for same not being asked from the Potentate in view of the position he had taken in the matter.

I call your Excellency's attention to the Petty Cash Account Statement for May, 1921, attached herewith. The Potentate's son was responsible for the Petty Cash, and he [k]ept it so irregularly that it became necessary for him to credit himself with salary to the amount of £5.10.11, in order to make his statement balance.

I call Your Excellency's attention to the enclosed letter from the Bank of British West Africa, concerning the deposit of £5.4.2 which Mr. Milton Marshall paid in on account of the Brewerville Division and which was entered upon our books and given to the Potentate's son to be deposited in the Bank to the credit of the Association. Instead, it was deposited to the personal account of G. M. Johnson's. The Potentate's attention has been frequently called to this mistake, and he has refused to listen to me, telling me it was none of the Association's business.

Between the Potentate and myself, there is a clear case of incompatibility of temperament; he being extremely conservative, and I with a disposition to do things in the go-ahead American way. When asked about doing things, his frequent reply would be: "Let's cable to New York and find out what they think about it."

If the Association should send a man out here to fill my position, he should be a man capable of adjusting himself to the haughty, aristocratic, dogmatic, domineering, conservative manner of the Potentate; but by no means should the Potentate and the Supreme Deputy be authorized to control the expenditures and the signing of checks. It is not saying anything that Your Excellency has not observed already when I say that the Supreme Deputy as a business man is totally impractical and unfit. As backwards as Liberians are in their own business and governmental affairs, I do not hesitate to state that no self-respecting American or West Indian would tolerate being placed under any Liberian for the execution of business; you will be certain to have things accom/plished in the/ good-old-fashioned Liberian way, which is beautifully less than nothing.

The Universal Negro Improvement Association is the only foreign concern that attempts to place its major affairs under a Liberian head; all European and American concerns have a European or American national at the head; even the missionary organizations are operated on that basis. Liberians are not accustomed to business on the same huge scale and business methods of the European or American business man; so that to place any American or West Indian, who is a first class, business man, under the Potentate and Supreme Deputy, is to handicap him before he starts.

The practical side of the Association's program should be separated from the propaganda side. The Potentate properly should be the head of the propaganda side, but an American or West Indian should be place[d] unfettered at the head of the practical side of the Construction work, in order that things may be done from the concept of the New World and not that of the Old World.

In view of the foregoing, it is at once obvious that my position as Resident Secretary is no longer tenable and that the best interests of the Association, whose ideals I shall ever cherish, can best be served by my immediate withdrawal. Without in any way attempting to do me any injustice, the Association's best course is to support the Potentate in all things calling for diplomacy; otherwise the clannishness and sensitiveness of Liberians will be their trump cards to make or break, which will but lead to irrecoverable disaster and failure. This would be unfortunate from any angle. Liberia must be developed and the world of Negroes must accomplish it. It would be regrettable if the Association could not be the means to accomplish this glorious result. I can afford to overlook any personal differences for the larger welfare of the race and the Universal Negro Improvement Association. I have the honor to be, Sir, Your Excellency's obedient servant,

C. A. Crichlow
Resident Secretary

DNA, RG 165, file 10218-261-78. TL, carbon copy.

Henry P. Fletcher, to Charles L. Latham

Washington, June 25, 1921

American Consul, Kingston, (Jamaica)
Your twenty-third. Visa authorized Marcus Garvey. *Cable name of steamer and date of sailing.*[1]

[Henry P.] Fletcher
Acting [Secretary of State]

DNA, RG 59, file 811.108 G 191/19a. TLS, outgoing copy. Handwritten insertion.
1. The italicized portion of the cable was handwritten.

Report by Special Agent J. G. Tucker

[*New York*] June 25, 1921

. . . Negro Activities

. . . Nothing new has been heard of regarding the looked for arrival of Marcus Garvey. Subscribers of the Black Star Line and members of the Universal Negro Improvement Association continue, however, to show marked anxiety as to the time of his return and the general feeling amongst his followers seems to be that the vise of his passport has been held up by the British Government. As has been previously remarked, the temper of those who have subscribed for shares of the Black Star Line seems to have been sorely tried and according to confidential advices there is a daily congregation of disgruntled shareholders awaiting the departure of one of the ships which the Black Star Line claims to have under operation and for passage on which these persons have already paid.

J. G. Tucker

DNA, RG 65, file BS 202600-1628-96. TD.

Report by Special Agent J. T. Flournoy

[*Washington, D.C., ca. 28 June 1921*]

... PASSPORTS

I am advised by Mr. Hurley, of the State Department, that a letter has been received under date of June 11 from W. A. Mathews [*William C. Matthews*], attorney for Marcus Garvey, stating that Garvey is now in Jamaica and will apply at the Port of Kingston for visa of passport to enter this country. Mathews states that Garvey is needed in this country to assist in straightening out the affairs of the stockholders of the "Black Steamship Line", of which he is president. Mr. Hurley states that no doubt the State Department would grant permission for Garvey to enter this country again, on account of Garvey's financial entanglements which seemingly are about to end up in a general collapse of his various enterprises. He believes to refuse him admission at this time would be used by his sympathizers here to make a martyr of him.

J. T. FLOURNOY
Special Agent

DNA, RG 65, file BS 202600-9-24. TD.

William W. Heard to Charles Evans Hughes

Kingston. June 28, 1921

Department's telegram of June 25, noon. Garvey's passport visaed to-day.[1] He sails for Belize to-day steamship CANADIAN, Fisher to secure passage there for New York.

[WILLIAM W.] HEARD

[*Endorsements*] No list(?) JPD File
DJ DL 6/30/21 MEF

DNA, RG 59, file 811.108 G 191/20. TL, recipient's copy.

1. Amy Jacques, her brother, Cleveland Jacques, and Garvey's secretary, Enid Lamos, were also granted visas. The American consul arranged for them to be "specially examined" upon entry into the United States, however, and in the case of Amy Jacques, he informed her that her passport did not guarantee readmittance (Charles L. Latham to Charles Evans Hughes, 30 June 1921, DNA, RG 65, file 198940-200). In September 1923 Cleveland Jacques, who was returning to the United States from Jamaica, was described by Latham as "highly undesirable" and a "racial agitator." The American vice-consul in Jamaica had mistakenly visaed Cleveland Jacques's passport, and Latham warned the State Department that he was due to arrive in Philadelphia on 19 September 1923 (Latham to Hughes, 17 September 1923, DNA, RG 59, file 000-612). Latham's letter was passed on to William Burns of the Bureau of Investigation and to W. W. Husband, the commissioner of immigration. Neither acted to exclude Jacques, since

they "had nothing of a sufficiently definitive nature concerning him . . . to recommend his exclusion" (DNA, RG 59, file 000-612).

John C. Wiley to William L. Hurley

[*Washington, D.C.*] June 29, 1921

URGENT
Mr. Hurley:

RE PROPOSED VISIT OF GABRIEL JOHNSON, "HIGH POTENTATE OF GARVEY MOVEMENT" AND MAYOR OF MONROVIA.

Gabriel Johnson is a brother of F. E. R. Johnson, Associate Justice of the Supreme Court of Liberia who is now in the United States as one of the four members of the Liberian Plenary Mission to negotiate for the $5,000,000. loan. The latter is believed to be very anti-American and opposed to the loan. The former is a member of the Garvey Association and, of course, opposed to the loan, and is probably being brought over by the Garvey people in an endeavor to negative [negate?] the Department's plans.

This Division considers it important that immediate steps be taken to stop Gabriel Johnson's voyage.

The SAN CARLOS belongs to the Compaña Transatlantica. She is to-day at Fernando Po, presumably enroute for either the Canary Islands, Cadiz or Barcelona. It is hoped that cable instructions can be sent immediately to those three places in an endeavor to have Johnson intercepted, either by refusal of visa, or if visa has already been granted, by cancellation thereof.

J[OHN]. C[OOPER]. W[ILEY].

DNA, RG 59, file 880-L-2. TMI, recipient's copy.

William L. Hurley to J. Edgar Hoover

WASHINGTON, D.C. June 29, 1921

Dear Mr. Hoover:

Please refer to my letter of June 25, 1921, relative to information received from Monrovia, Liberia, regarding GABRIEL (DONNEY?) (JOHNSON?).

I have recently received information from the same source under date of June 27, 1921, to the effect that GABRIEL JOHNSON* sailed on the S.S. SAN CARLOS for New York. It has been reported that he will tranship in Spain or the Canary Islands.

Any further information which may come to my attention will be promptly forwarded to you. This is for your information and as being of possible interest. It might be well, however, to have your agents notified of Johnson's contemplated arrival in this country.

Similar information is being transmitted to M.I.D. and D[*epartment of*]. L[*abor*].[1] Very truly yours,

W. L. HURLEY

Name Confirmed

DNA, RG 65, file BS 198940-113. TLS, recipient's copy.

1. On 25 June Hurley sent letters to Gen. Dennis Nolan of MID and to Walter W. Husband (1872–1942), who was appointed commissioner of immigration in 1921 by President Coolidge. Husband served throughout the Coolidge and Hoover administrations (*NYT*, 1 August 1942; DNA, RG 59, file 800-2-2, 29 June 1921).

Report by Bureau Agent Leon E. Howe

Miami, Fla. 6/29/21

REV. T. C. GLASHAN [*Glashen*] (HONDURAN NEGRO) ALLEGED RADICAL U.N.I.A. AT KEY WEST FLORIDA

Reference is made to report of agent dated March 11, 1921, under Caption MARCUS GARVEY, JAMAICA NEGRO AGITATOR, and to letter from the Chief of the Bureau dated May 11 initialled GFR with reference to negro radicals at KEY WEST FLORIDA.

June 11 agent learned that prominent citizens of KEY WEST FLA were interesting themselves in the activities of the U.N.I.A. and its local president REV T. C. GLASHAN. Following the visit of GARVEY to KEY WEST the movement grew considerably, and the organization held many meetings. GLASHAN always s[po]ke, and informant gives the following as a sample of his ranting: "We have been under the White people's control long enough. The time has come for us to strike, and all of us negroes must let the world know that we are a power, strong and ready to defend our rights. If we can't suc[c]eed with words, we will [*use?*] other methods, and never mind what happens. If blood is need[ed, let it be] shared. We fought to help this and other countr[ie]s to be free, so let[']s fight to free ourselves."

In speaking of GARVEY, whom he called "our Moses," he said they should demand that he be allowed to go to the halls of Congress and speak for negro recognition. He bitterly [*criticized*] the American negroes because they would not join the U.N.I.A.

About June 16 a warrant was sworn out charging GLASHAN with "inciting a riot" under the state laws. Shortly afterwards DR. A. J. KERSHAW, financial secretary of the U.N.I.A. at KEY WEST, was arrested, charged with stealing the funds of the organization. KERSHAW turned over the books and papers of the organization to agent's informant, and is at present at liberty under bond. KERSHAW is an AMERICAN negro.

KERSHAW has resigned from the U.N.I.A. GLASHAN has been given the option of leaving KEY WEST by way of CUBA, or of standing trial on the charge of inciting a riot. It is my understanding that he has already left for CUBA. The case against KERSHAW, which was instituted by the U.N.I.A., is still standing, and agent will be advised of all matters in this connection by KERSHAW himself.

The books and minutes of the U.N.I.A. at KEY WEST have been examined by agent, and only two things of interest appear therein. One is the fact that the membership numbers 690, and agent has a list of all these members, which is being forwarded with copy of report to Jacksonville.[1] The other is an entry with reference to some action which was proposed at a meeting, and action was not taken "because it would be in violation of the Federal Law." What this entry refers to agent has not yet been able to learn. One informant states there was a debate one night with reference to the serving of some liquor at a meeting, and this may be the truth.

The new president of the U.N.I.A. at KEY WEST is GILBERT ALBREY and the financial secretary is [D.] HEALD. The organization is operating a bakery on a cooperative plan, and the delivery wagon is painted in the U.N.I.A. colors.

Agent has carefully refrained from having anything to do with the activities of the citizens of KEY WEST in the foregoing matters, and have obtained my information largely from KERSHAW. There is likely some question of the legality of ordering GLASHAN to leave Key West via Cuba, but it was done by a judge of the Circuit Court, Judge Hunt Harris. Practically all members of the U.N.I.A. at KEY WEST are aliens, as is the case of MIAMI and WEST PALM BEACH.

LEON E. HOWE

[*Endorsement*] NOTED F. D. W.

DNA, RG 65, file BS 198940-175. TD. Stamped endorsement.

1. The list was not retained with the report.

A. Rudolph Silverston to Albert D. Lasker, Chairman, United States Shipping Board

NEW YORK SHIP EXCHANGE, 115 BROADWAY,
NEW YORK, June 30, 1921

Dear Sir:—

Imperative reasons compelled my return on the Congressional Limited to New York yesterday, and, I take this opportunity to immediately confirm my telegram to you, which reads as follows:

Washington, June 29, 1921.

Al[bert] D. Lasker, Chairman,[1]
U.S. Shipping Board,
Washington, D.C.

That you are a man of action is creating a new and favorable impression among shipping interests which leads me to respectfully solicit your decision on following matter that has been dragging along for about four months   Stop   I hold power of attorney to act for Black Star Line controlled by over four million colored citizens   Stop   We bid two hundred and twenty five thousand dollars for Steamer Orion to be employed in New York African trade where we control freight and passenger business but Board decided to charter her   Stop   Your sales department and others suggested we purchase Porto Rico which while not as adaptable to our service needs we acquiesced placing deposit on price said to have been fixed by then Chairman   Stop   All formalities except Board[']s approval have apparently been gone through   Stop   We have foreign tonnage offered at lower prices but as Americans prefer to own and operate American ship Stop   We are ready to conclude the transaction and would appreciate advice of Board[']s definite decision today.

A. RUDOLPH SILVERSTON
Room 505, Shoreham Hotel.
Washington, D.C.

In elucidation and explanation of the above telegram, we briefly beg to state, that, after a number of trips to Washington, or as a preliminary step to open negotiations with the U.S. Shipping Board for the purchase of a suitable steamer, we finally obtained a permit to inspect the Ex-German Steamer "Orion", dated April 28th, located at Camp Eustis, Va. After due inspection, a firm offer of $190,000. "As is and where is", was made to the Board, accompanied by a certified check of $15,000. as earnest money. This offer was declined under date of May 14th, on the ground that the bid was considered too low.

It subsequently was indicated to us that $225,000. would be acceptable to the Chairman of the Board. We consented to the price and deposited as earnest money 2 1/2%, as suggested, or $5,625. by certified check. In the meantime, it developed that the Chartering Division of the Board had committed itself to one "K. E. HURLBURT", and, it developed afterward that he used to be Secretary to a former member of the U.S. Shipping Board by the name of "MR. SCOTT."

On or about May 26th, the writer was urgently requested to look at and take under consideration the Steamer "PORTO RICO", Ex-Prinz Joachim, and a permit for inspection was issued under that date. This steamer, on inspection, was found to be most suitable for our purpose, but, action was held in abeyance, pending a decision on the Steamer "ORION". Positive assurance was given that the s/s "PORTO RICO" was ordered sold by the Board; that the Board had sustained a great loss by reason of having been under charter to the NEW YORK & PORTO RICO LINE, and had for that reason been withdrawn by the Board from their service. She was, according to rules, duly advertised; on opening of bids, one bidder appeared, "MOORE & MCCORMACK", of New York, with a bid of $20.00 a deadweight ton. Her official deadweight capacity is supposed to be 4700 tons; but investigation will prove that the "PORTO RICO'S" cargo capacity is less than 3500 tons, with only 163 passengers. In other words, the best price offered, assuming she is of 4700 tons capacity, was $94,000. and that on easy terms.

Finally, on or about June 9th, we were definitely informed that the s/s "ORION" had been chartered to Mr. Hurlburt, formerly Secretary to Commissioner Scott, and, we were earnestly requested to transfer our deposit on the "ORION" to the "PORTO RICO". We did so, offering $175,000. on terms 10% on delivery and 10% monthly thereafter, secured by mortgage and performance bond to be approved by the Board. Shortly thereafter, we were informed that the then Chairman considered the price too low and $225,000 with 10% on delivery and 10% monthly thereafter, secured by mortgage and approved performance bond, was named as satisfactory. We accepted immediately and increased our deposit to $12,500. or more than 5%.

On or about June 22d, the Sales Department informed us definitely in the presence of C. M. Barnett, President, Clinchfield Navigation Company, and another gentleman, that the sale was duly approved[2] and recommended in writing by the Sales Division, by the Operating Department and by the Construction and Repair Department, and that the balance was merely formal in character, and that the Legal Department, of course, would duly attend to the legal end, approving the forms, etc., all of which would be but a question of a day or two.

We are acting under and by virtue of a general Power of Attorney, for and on behalf of the "BLACK STAR LINE, INC." organized under the laws of the State of Delaware, with a capital of $10,000,000.00 and is composed entirely of colored citizens and its stock is owned by the Universal Negro Improvement Association which has a membership exceeding four million colored citizens who are making monthly contributions for the development of their own steamship service.

These people have their *own* cargo and passengers, both ways, opening a new trade route between West African Ports and New York, about the only people who can, under existing laws, make a fair profit, as they control freight nobody else can obtain.

There are four and a half million of loyal, peaceful Americans, who, I, the writer, personally represent as their attorney in fact and deed. It has cost me several months of my time and large sums of money to procure an *American* steamer for American citizens and I feel I cannot afford to do any more "Pusseyfooting". We have complied with all the requirements but it seems as if I am "bucking-up" against the "color line" or some "underground" wires, pardon the slang.

I appeal to you as a fair-minded man; this is a business proposition and "pussey-footing" and "parlor-politics" should be cut out. After all this time spent and money wasted, we are still put off and have had no action.

However, the writer has interesting data and facts on hand, in writing, that may clear the situation, which, if you so desire, is at your disposal. I can get first-class English tonnage for $20.00 a ton, but it would be a dog-gone shame to have to resort to foreign bottoms.

Awaiting your prompt action in the matter; in other words, it[']s just a case of "fish or cut bait", Very Respectfully yours,

NEW YORK SHIP EXCHANGE, REG.,
A. RUDOLPH SILVERSTON

DNA, RG 32, USSB, file 605-1-653. TLS, recipient's copy.

1. Albert D. Lasker (1880–1952) was chairman of the United States Shipping Board from 1921 to 1923. During that time he directed the liquidation of more than $3 billion worth of investments held by the USSB after World War I. A pioneer in the field of advertising, Lasker later became a well-known philanthropist (*NYT*, 31 May 1952).

2. On 22 June 1921 the manager of the USSB's Ship Sales Division recommended acceptance of the Black Star Line's offer to purchase the *Porto Rico*, and this decision was forwarded for consideration to the office of the general counsel of the U.S. Shipping Board (DNA, RG 32, USSB, file 605-1-653).

William L. Hurley to J. Edgar Hoover

WASHINGTON June 30, 1921

Dear Mr. Hoover:

URGENT.

Under date of June 18, 1921, the American Consul at Kingston, Jamaica, reported the exhibition by GARVEY of a cablegram from Wilford Smith of New York City, U.N.I.A. and affiliated organizations. The cablegram requested that Garvey return to New York City immediately, and further stated that he (Wilford Smith) could not work longer with Thompson, Vice President of the Black Star Line.

Under date of June 28, information was received from the same source to the effect that MARCUS GARVEY's passport was vis[a]ed on that date. He was to have sailed the same day for Belize on the S.S. CANADIAN. Passage was to have been secured there for New York by Fisher.[1]

The foregoing information is transmitted to you in case you may wish to give Garvey a thorough overhauling upon arrival.

Similar information is being transmitted to D[epartment of]. L[abor]. Very truly yours,

W. L. HURLEY

[Endorsement] FILE G. F. R.

DNA, RG 65, file BS 198940-172. TLS, recipient's copy. Stamped endorsement.

1. Because of a punctuation error in the American Consulate's cable to the Department of State regarding its grant of a visa to Garvey, the relevant portion read, "He (Garvey) sails for Belize to-day steamship CANADIAN, Fisher to secure passage there from New York." The insertion of the comma in the name of the steamship *Canadian Fisher* obviously created the misreading of the cable (DNA, RG 59, file 811.108 G 191/19a).

William Smith to Charles Evans Hughes

New York, July 1, 1921

In the matter of Marcus Garvey the negro agitator, British /subject/ seeking readmission from Jamaica into the United States. He is married to Amy Garvey, formerly Amy Ashwood residing in New York. He left here in company of Amy Jacques an unmarried woman negress residing at 133 West 129 New York where her people still live. She is traveling as his wife by rail and his steamer KANAWHA over protest of all negroes he represents. He is guilty under Mann Act and publicly declares would never consider becoming American citizen. A committee of decent negro delegates during negro convention here last year at Madison Gardens tried to compel him quit that woman but after fight he left convention in disgrace. Garvey is dangerous agitator preaching force of arms against whites everywhere. Entirely unfit represent American loyal negroes. Is also actively fomenting troubles in British possessions on a wide scale.

WILLIAM SMITH[1]

[*Endorsement*] DJ/7/5/21/MEF

DNA, RG 59, file 811.108 G 191/21. TG, recipient's copy. Handwritten endorsement.

1. Possibly William H. Smith, secretary of the American Commission of the U.S.-Canada International Commission.

William L. Hurley to Harry A. McBride

[*Washington, D.C.*] July 1, 1921

Dear Mr. [Mc]Bride:

I have just talked this matter over with Mr. Bliss and seem to think that the best plan to follow would be for your office to get in touch with each Consul abroad at the various points at which the steamer might touch, instructing them to be on the lookout for [*Gabriel*] Johnson and if he is in possession of a visa to cancel it and if not, upon application to refuse him one notifying the Department immediately of the action taken.

W[ILLIAM]. L. H[URLEY].

DNA, RG 59, file 800-L-2. TNI, recipient's copy.

Cyril Henry to O. M. Thompson

c/o M. E. Mission, Monrovia, Liberia,
West Coast Africa, July 1st 1921

Dear Friend Thompson:—

Knowing your intense interest and connection with U.N.I.A. affairs and its vital connection with the Republic of Liberia, I am taking advantage of this opportunity and confidence in our friend Crichlow whom I have entrusted with this, to write you at length confidentially touching upon the conditions obtaining here.

Strange as it might seem one dares not send through the regular mail letters of comment or criticism which in the mind of the Liberian born would be other than complimentary. I have not really conclusively verified this charge, but it is currently and persistently stated by old residents that letters of foreigners—Negroes from elsewhere are classed in manner as whites just the same—especially of newcomers are subjected to a sort of censorship. That is, letters mailed and awaiting the mail steamer are opened and perused by some postal clerk at leisure, any adverse criticism would be revealed, and the author of the same would be spotted as a "marked man". One such instance has been cited to me. So, taking it for what it is worth one is bound to be careful nevertheless, and not risk exposure by criticising. Hence the true condition of affairs existing here is usually obscured, for none but the good side is played up to those abroad. You see my reasons for making above observations don't you?

It has long been my desire to write you as I am now doing but until now I had no opportunity to send the same. So at the outset I must say that by substantiating in greater part what may be Crichlow's final report it is rather a coincidence. However, it is a happy one for I am glad that by so doing I am able to render him some service in the defence of his conduct and the conscientious discharge of his trust.

I have already told you that by reason of my previous experiences, aversion to exaggerations, propaganda, and superficial bias, I would not say anything re conditions here until I had allowed impressions to soak in.

Before going further I want to say that I am well aware of the principles and objects of the U.N.I.A. to which I have given and you are still giving conscientious service. I must frankly say that the difficulties met already and still to be reckoned with are largely due to three principal causes[,] viz:—

(1)   Open and glaring propaganda—too blatant a disclosure of our ultimate aims.

(2)   Launching of too many large schemes and plans in rapid succession. The U.N.I.A., A.C.L., Black Star, Convention Plans, Negro Factories Corp., Liberia Loan, and other minor appeals for money.

(3)   The burden of a ponderous official salary list. Whether these salaries be paid in full or not I have noticed that the moral effect has been adverse to the continued support of old members, and the proper bearing of some officials.

Criticism #1 is commonly expressed here. It is the chief cause of official opposition.

Re #3 they also argue that it cannot be seen why the Potentate should draw such a large salary—larger than that of the President.

It is quite apparent in the face of these things that there must be some vital change in policy and plans in order that we may achieve the success wished for, and so I hope that these criticisms will be taken in confidence and referred to fit parties only.

Touching the work of the U.N.I.A., I regret to observe the state of painful inactivity into which the pioneers are apparently forced. Their growing reserve and quiet discontent—not spoken, but can be seen nevertheless—the apathy, and waning interest of the Liberians, are plainly evidenced. Indeed, there has been set up a current of opposition which is gaining rather than diminishing.

It is a glaring error to neglect the needs and just dues of those whom you have appointed and sent out to carry on your plans.

Don't imagine that any information has been furnished me beyond what my present status warrants; but one with past and even present connections such as I have, must surely know. I vividly recall my own experiences upon the voyages of the "Yarmouth" and sojourn in Panama. But for my ready sales of stock to liquidate debts, we would have met disaster on more than one occasion.

Here there is neither enthusiasm nor the money to raise by the sale of stocks; hence you see how badly is the position of your workers here when urgent requests they would send go unheeded. Lack of support breeds indifference, discontent and final disruption.

Notwithstanding all you might hear to the contrary, /such as/ the abundance of fish, fruits, and vegetables, the existence of large tracts of fertile land, mineral deposits, and the little need of and ease in procuring shelter, living conditions are indeed irksome and for a very long while must be so to the Negroes of the Western Hemisphere into whose system for at least four generations has been bred an attachment more or less to Western ideas and ideals.

One sad discovery I find—sad I mean as far as the ability to adjust oneself to present conditions is concerned—and that is, *Africa is more Oriental than Occidental*. Immediately on one's coming here, there is set up in the mind a conflict of ideas: what we should or should not adopt is always a source of great concern. Inasmuch as the newcomer to Europe is gripped by the influence of Europe, in America by the influence of America, in Asia by the Asiatic influence, so too in Africa he slowly and surely is gripped by the influence of Africa.

The food of the African aborigines is invariably rice, /cassava,/ palm-oil and fish when obtainable. Meats are obtained only as the result of a hunt or discovery in the bush. Owing to its precarious supply, every form of meat is then readily relished; so besides what we would consider fit—that is beef, mutton, pork, venison and poultry,—such things as snakes, monkeys, leopards, dogs, rats, snails, worms and insects are eaten.

The clothes of the African vary from the graceful flowing robes of the Mohammedan to a mere rag around the loins /and/ absolute nothing.

Their shelter is either beautifully plastered round mud-huts or mere palm thatches.

The special customs of the African are in the main based on strict observance of the laws of the chiefs who see to the carrying out of all rites, ceremonies, plays, agreements, etc., etc.; and the inescapable "palaver" or councils where cases are heard and penalties imposed. Peonage is both an inflicted penalty and a self-imposed method of buying wives or paying debts. Polygamy is an institution and cannibalism really obtains in remote places. These are not given for publication. I merely enumerate them in order to point out where the conflict of ideas must and do obtain. Hence our inability to fall in *in toto* with such tastes as above must be contrary to what is distinctly African; and what we should introduce must be Western or European.

The Liberian as an off-shoot of the Westerni[z]ed American in this conflict of ideas strives to maintain himself in a class separate and distinct; but he either draws entirely from his brother native in sympathy or, given time, reverts to his ways. By this you will readily see why so much is reported to obtain in Liberia. All is true. Everything African and everything European and Western is to be found; and according to our estimate of fitness is the feeling as to how irksome conditions are.

You will not be surprised when you imagine a mere handful of partly Westernized Negroes as compared with the millions of aboriginal inhabitants seeking to establish a government with all the virtues and defects of European and African ideals to contend with. Power is largely vested in political bodies; hence this minority in accordance with first principles is very jealous of its control of affairs, yet wishing for and inviting aid from abroad. Therein lies a snag to the plans of the U.N.I.A. "You are welcome," they say, "but your numbers, your influence and combined power should not be sufficient to supplant our political preferments; i.e., the presidency, the secretary-ship, consulships abroad, customs service, etc. You must adopt our ways, be scattered amongst us, not combined, be not over-zealous about the welfare of the aborigines—us first! And do not place us at odds with the white governments from whom we expect favors."

The traps and pit-falls laid for the foreigner are numerous. The slightest error in contravention of the law on the part of the foreigner meets with /the/ infliction of a heavy fine. Bishop [*Matthew*] Clair of the M.E. Church has been the latest victim; he was fined for landing without the examination of his effects although coming from another part of the country and not from abroad. Revenue is needed, you know, and rich foreigners are considered a prey. (smiles)

The whole future of this Republic and operations therein hinges upon the result of the present loan negotiations. But as I see now, the chances of the U.N.I.A. succeeding in its program are becoming more and more remote—let us hope that something will /int/ervene to off-set this adverse tide.

I daresay you have received my cable, in which I stated "Please advise Council act with great caution. Await arrival of Crichlow." This brings me to observe the regrettable break which has occurred between the Potentate and Supreme Deputy on the one hand and Crichlow on the other. The Potentate as you already know is an ultra-conservative. He has allied himself with the U.N.I.A., it is true, and so honored; but, remember, he is /a/ Liberian official first, and in very close touch with his associates in office[,] many of whom are his near relatives, and—I hate to be so critical—would foster the work of the U.N.I.A., only so far as it will lend itself to the will of this coterie of Liberians.

I have heard both Crichlow's side and that of the Honorable Marke, and would say that to me the root of the matter is really an attempt to transfer as full powers as possible to themselves on this side. *Crichlow was in the way.* You can put things together for yourself.

That I have not done much in active co-operation with the fellows was really due to the attitude of the Potentate towards me at the outset. I placed myself at his disposal upon my arrival, but he seemed somewhat cold or chary as to my intentions; and so, in a spirit of independence and above-board principles, I would not further intrude myself upon his notice. My only participation was my trip which I mentioned to you in my previous letter. In company with Crichlow, we undertook that trip in order to trace down information as to coal, diamond and gold deposits. We had three in the party, in addition to two boys and three carriers—eight (8) in all. The trip lasted eight days, hard traveling /afoot/, and kept fairly within estimated expenses, Fifty (£50) Pounds, the extra costs (15/6) I gladly loaned, which has since been refunded. Though fruitless as far as obtaining what was desired, from another standpoint it was highly satisfactory, for it gave splendid material for publication and established definitely the reported coal, gold and diamond deposits, which in reality proved to be dolomite, iron sulphate and quartzites respectively.

Dear Friend, I frankly could not advise our people coming out here under present conditions. One can live in Liberia all right, but only in effective and profitable work can a true man find real happiness. These opportunities must first be created. Africa's problems are large, very large, and to tackle it largely is the only sure road to success—in short, is the only solution of the problems. We must bide our time. Au revoir! Yours truly,

CYRIL HENRY

DNA, RG 165, file 10218-261-78. TLS, recipient's copy.

Elie Garcia to J. Harry Philbin,[1] Manager of Shipping Sales, United States Shipping Board

[*New York, 2 July 1921*]

Dear Sir:

In the course of our investigation at the United States Shipping Board office, of 45 Broadway, New York City, Mr. Foster, head of the Contract Department has referred us to you for information in the following matter.

About two months ago, the above named company [*Black Star Line*] entered into a contract with Mr. Rudolph Silverston, doing business under the name of the New York Ship Exchange, to purchase for it a ship from the said Exchange. After some negotiations with Mr. Silverston, he stated to us that he could purchase for us from the United States Government the steamship Porto Ric[o], then in Dry Dock at Brooklyn and after several trips to Washington he came back and stated that the said steamship Porto Ric[o] has been awarded to the Black Star Line, Inc., through his efforts. He further stated that he had deposited with the United States Shipping Board $5,625. on an option, which was 2 1/2% on the sum of $225,000., the purchase price of said ship. He stated that the United States Shipping Board required a cash payment of $25,000., which amount was turned over to him to secure title to said steamer and a certified check of $5,000. of said amount was made payable to the order of the said United States Shipping Board.

After receiving the said $25,000, the said Silverston reported that the papers for the full transfer of said steamship would be signed and approved within ten days and on June 17, 1921, the said Silverston signed a contract that the full transfer and delivery of said ship would be made not later than June 23, 1921. On June 23, when questioned about the progress of the negotiations for said ship, Mr. Silverston stated that as the new Heads of the Shipping Board were in New York, the papers could not be approved before Monday, June 27th, when they would return to Washington. On June 27, the Black Star Line was informed by him that owing to developments we would have to continue to wait longer, before the ship could be transferred and from time to time we have been put off.

In view of the fact that the acquisition of this ship is urgent and that more than five weeks have elapsed since we began negotiations for the purchase of the same, we would be very grateful to your Department if you would furnish us with information concerning the nature of Mr. Silverston's transactions with the Shipping Board and what results we may expect from the same.

We would like further to know if the said steamship Porto Ric[o] is still for sale,[2] and if there is any possibility of the same being purchased by the Black Star Line if it should turn out that the negotiations claimed by Mr. Silverston did not take place.

Hoping that you will oblige us with a prompt reply, we beg to remain, Yours respectfully,

BLACK STAR LINE, INC.
ELIE GARCIA
Secretary

DJ-FBI. TL, transcript. Included in the report by Thomas P. Merrilees of 26 October 1922, "Summary Report of Investigation of the Books and Records of the Black Star Line, Inc.," DJ-FBI, file 61.

1. Joseph Harry Philbin was the manager of shipping sales for the U.S. Shipping Board and the person with whom A. Rudolph Silverston, Orlando Thompson, Elie Garcia, William

Matthews, and other Black Star Line agents and officials met in 1921 while negotiating for a ship for the transatlantic route to Africa (*Marcus Garvey* v. *United States*, no. 8317, Ct. App., 2d Cir., 2 February 1925, pp. 1,875–1,894).

2. Garcia went to Washington, D.C., to deliver this letter to Philbin in person. Philbin informed Garcia a few days later that the U.S. Shipping Board had leased the *Porto Rico* to the Porto Rico Line, Inc., and that Silverston's offer on behalf of the Black Star Line had been rejected. Silverston had refused to take back the $12,500 he had placed as an option on the *Porto Rico* but had instead shown an interest in the S.S. *Freedom*. The BSL Board of Directors then voted to end their relationship with Silverston and demanded the return of the $25,000 they had advanced him for the purchase of a ship. At the 2 July 1921 meeting of the board, however, O. M. Thompson, the BSL vice-president who had represented the company in negotiations with Silverston, expressed his confidence in Silverston and signed a statement declaring his belief that Silverston has "as much opportunity to secure either the Prinz Joachim or the Prinz Oskar [*Orion*] for the Black Star Line as ever." In his statement Thompson also requested that the BSL delay its decision to withdraw from any association with Silverston. His request was not granted (Thomas P. Merrilees, "Summary Report," DJ-FBI, file 61, pp. 39–40).

Report by Special Agent P-138

NEW YORK CITY 7-2-21

NEGRO ACTIVITIES.

I had a talk [*29 June*] with Hudson Price[,] associate Editor of the Negro World on the subject of the Black Star Line and Group companies in general.

Price told me that 6 months ago the [N]egro [W]orld[']s circulation was only 25,000 copies but now it had increased to over 75,000[,] that the [N]egro [W]orld was the only payable of the Gar[ve]y[']s undertakings but the other departments were eating up all the profits.

P-138

[*Endorsement*] NOTED F. D. W.

DNA, RG 65, file BS 202600-667-63. TD. Stamped endorsement.

Albert D. Lasker to A. Rudolph Silverston

[*Washington, D.C.*] July 5, 1921

ATTN: MR. A. RUDOLPH SILVERSTON.

My dear Mr. Silverston:

I have your letter of June 30, wherein you set forth at length your aspect of the situation concerning your proposal on behalf of the Black Star Line, Inc., to purchase a combination cargo and passenger ship.

I have to advise you that negotiations were under way for the chartering of the ORION quite some time before any offer for her purchase was received from you. The Board had given the prospective charterers definite assurance that under certain conditions the ORION would be chartered to them. For a while it appeared that these conditions might not be met, and under these circumstances tentative negotiations for the purchase of the ORION by the Black Star Line, Inc., were entertained. The corporation which had been negotiating for the chartering of the ORION fulfilled the terms which had been outlined to them almost simultaneously with the receipt of your definite offer of $225,000. Every circumstance was considered at this time, and the Board after mature deliberation determined that the prospective charterers having satisfactorily fulfilled the terms which had been demanded by the Board, were entitled to have the vessel; and accordingly your offer for the ORION was rejected.

Likewise in the case of the PORTO RICO, which vessel your clients also offered to purchase, tentative arrangements had previously been made to effect a charter for this vessel. The consummation of this charter had been held in abeyance pending the settlement of several questions which had presented themselves. The Board has at all times been favorably inclined towards the disposition of any of its ex-German tonnage where a fair offer for each has been received. It was upon this basis that you were requested to submit a proposal for the PORTO RICO. Your clients being unable to make such a bid, it was suggested that a proposal be made on a performance bond basis. Thereafter the PORTO RICO was duly advertised for public sale. As you were advised in my letter of June 29, all of the factors surrounding the status of the PORTO RICO were considered by the Board on June 29, after which it was determined that none of the offers received, including yours, was sufficiently attractive to warrant the sale, instead of the charter, of the PORTO RICO.

The substance of this information was communicated to the Black Star Line, Inc., on July 1, in answer to their inquiry of June 30.[1] This Company was advised that details concerning the remaining ex-German passenger and cargo vessels had been given to you and that you were then in the process of determining whether any of them would be suitable for the contemplated trade.

I note with interest your statements concerning the extent of the organization supporting the Black Star Line, Inc.

I should suggest that in submitting any further proposals to the Board, you include therewith a complete financial statement of this organization and of the Black Star Line, Inc. Very truly yours,

A. D. LASKER
Chairman

ADL;JHP;M;H
Approved by J. Harry Philbin.

DNA, RG 32, USSB, file 605-1-653. TLR, carbon copy.

1. This exchange of correspondence has not been found.

Report of Interview

Belize 5th July 1921

Memorandum of Interview with Mr. Marcus Garvey at Government House, Belize, at 2 p.m. on Tuesday 5th July, 1921.

His Excellency the Governor [*Eyre Hutson*] received Mr. Marcus Garvey, the President of the Universal Negro Improvement Association, who was accompanied by Mr. W. A. Campbell, Mr. H. H. Cain and Mr. C. N. Staine.

The Colonial Secretary and the Private Secretary were present. His Excellency the Governor:—

Mr. Marcus Garvey, you have asked for an interview with me to-day. I claim the privilege before you address me on the subject of your visit, to make a statement and to ask you to favour me with some information.

I desire first to call your attention to the fact that, as the interview is of some importance, I have a shorthand writer present. I shall be glad to supply you with a record of the interview, and to supply a copy to the leader of the local branch of the Universal Negro Improvement Association and African Communities' League.

You are, I understand, a native of Jamaica?

Marcus Garvey.   Yes Sir.

H. E.   Are you still a British subject?

M. G.   Yes Sir.

H. E.   Your official position in the Association and League is, I understand, "President of the Provisional Republic of Africa and President General of the Association and League".

M. G.   Yes Sir.

H. E.   I have had the privilege of reading the Laws of the Association and League, and I have noted the great authority conferred on yourself and on "The High Potentate of the League and Association."

M. G.   Yes Sir.

H. E.   I noted that the newspaper "The Negro World" is stated in the Laws as the official organ and publication of the Association and League. Am I correct?

M. G.   Yes Sir.

H. E.   Who is the Editor?

M. G.   William Lietch Ferris[,] but I have the controlling supervision.

H. E.   Now I am, or I claim to be, the first to recognise and support, if it be in my power to do so, the praiseworthy aims of the Association, to promote the material, social and educational advancement of the people of the Negro Race so long as such movement proceeds by proper and loyal methods, I have so stated publicly in this Colony, and I have recently endeavoured to assist Dr. Simon in the medical education of nurses. I have, however, of course noted other aims of the Association and League so forcibly placed before the people of this town and elsewhere by yourself.

I have noted the religious character of your meetings and the singing of the British National Anthem at the conclusion of the meetings.

Having in view your replies and assurances to my questions asked, I shall esteem it a favour if you can explain and justify the following account of your speech at a meeting held in Philadelphia, U.S.A. on the 3rd December last, which appeared in the issue of the "Negro World" of the 18th December 1920, it being admitted that the paper is the official organ of the Association and League.

EXTRACT FROM "THE NEGRO WORLD", SATURDAY
18TH DECEMBER, 1920. ADDRESS DELIVERED BY
HON. MARCUS GARVEY ON 3RD DECEMBER 1920, IN
PHILADELPHIA, U.S.A.

I am looking for the time to come when there will be another world's war. The time will come when the nations who are controlling Africa will look down in disgrace. Working men in Europe drove the city council out of the city the other day and took charge of the city. It is mentioned that England's doom is at hand. And those men who drove the council out are only paving the way. And as the Czar lost his throne some years ago, so I fear George of England may have to run for his life, and that will be the chance for the Negro. I have prayed for it, and all the Negroes have done for the last few years, was to pray. The white man starts to work and pray. Because we are such great prayers; let us pray for the "downfall of England". Why do I want the downfall of England? Because I want the freedom of Africa. (Cheers).

I want it clearly understood that the ideas of the Universal Negro Improvement Association are one. If these big Negroes and dickty Negroes knew what I do, they would come into this movement now. Africa will crown you for what you do for Africa.

In the years to come your picture will be hanging in the gallery of Africa. And your children will be able to see what you did in the great construction work of Africa.

The paper from which this extract was taken is now in the hands of the Secretary of State in London; but if it becomes necessary it is possible to have it returned. I have read from a certified true copy.

I consider it only fair to you to give you an opportunity of removing from my mind a very strong impression and feeling caused by a perusal of that article, which is as offensive to me as it is to every other loyal subject of His Majesty the King.

M. G.   I may say, for Your Excellency's information, that the first time the article was brought to my notice was shortly after my arrival in Jamaica about two months ago, when Detective Inspector King, who was on the eve of departure to Nigeria, asked me to call and see him, and in the course of conversation he presented the article and I read it. This is the first time I saw the article.

It happened that I did speak in Philadelphia on that day, but I am fully persuaded and I am fully conscious of the fact that I never said the things that are reported there. I did say certain things concerning the political situations of several countries in Europe, but I am afraid the reporter's article is an incorrect statement of what I did say. Your Excellency will realise that we are seldom reported correctly in the press. It is usually just a summary of a speech, and when you see your speech the next morning it is as strange to you as it is to a stranger who had never heard you.

As proof that the speech was not properly and correctly reported as you read there, you will find that I am reported to have said that the working men took over the city council in Europe. A very broad statement "the city council in Europe". I must have said something to at least bear upon that, whether in England or somewhere.

At no time have I ever made such statements as made there. There are times when I do not see "The Negro World" for months, and /at/ that time I believe I was engaged in a tour in America, and I never saw that article until I went to Jamaica two months ago. Had I known that such statements were reported in "The Negro World" I would certainly have corrected them.

I admit I did say things, but not in the crude and disloyal manner reported. If these things were said under my signature I am responsible.

H. E.   Have you taken any steps to have those incorrect statements corrected in "The Negro World", and to deny having made the[m]?

M. G.   No Your Excellency: but I intend to do so on my return to the United States.

H. E.   I am glad to receive that assurance from you.

M. G.   As Managing Editor of "The Negro World" and President of the Universal Negro Improvement Association I have often written on the policy of the organisation from my point of view, but at no time can anyone accuse me of anything disloyal, as a British subject, over my signature: but as you realise it is very hard and difficult to get oneself correctly reported in the newspapers, especially when the report is not made by a competent man.

H. E.   If the article had appeared in any other paper than the "Negro World" which is the acknowledged official organ of your association I should have taken no notice of it. I should have given you the credit of having been incorrectly reported.

M. G.   Why I desired an interview with Your Excellency is because I understood on my arrival here that there was a misunderstanding and a misapprehension attached to the aims and objects of the association, and I would like it clearly understood that the Universal Negro Improvement

Association stands solely for the uplifting in every way, morally, socially, educationally and industrially, of the negro people of the world.

In certain parts it stands for the liberty of the people, but where they are already free, such as in this Colony, we are doing our best to strengthen the moral life of the people.

We have absolutely no political interference, we are only interested in the moral, social and educational development of the people. Each country has to work out its own problems. Throughout colonies such as British Guinea [*Guiana*] we can educate and we are interested in the better moral, and social grounds. I feel sure that Your Excellency will not deny the right to any race to educate itself on the best possible lines.

H. E.   The Governor of a British Colony must be very careful not to say /or do/ anything to identify himself with the entire objects and aims of your association, because they are to a certain extent political as referring to the United States of America.

M. G.   I have to thank you in the name of the organisation for the help you have given and I thank you also for the interest you have taken in getting a complete explanation of a statement reported to have been made by one whom you expected to be a loyal subject. It is no desire of mine to be disloyal to any man. I am a British subject, and a large number of us are British subjects, and it is foreign to our aims to be disloyal and to disrupt the Government, but to help the Government to bring about a better state throughout. There have been charters and religious institutions that have been trying to christianise for nearly three to five hundred years. We are endeavouring to help all such agencies to bring about the speedy realisation of these aims, and we claim that we have some of us reached the standard of civilised life to help in some way to bring about what we have so long desired.

I know the movement is misrepresented because of the demands of its programme but whenever we are given a chance to explain we have always done so to the satisfaction of all those concerned in the interests of the negro people.

H. E.   I note it is your desire to assist other[s] and to relieve others of the great responsibility which they have had to assume for many years. I am glad that I have had this opportunity of meeting you and to have heard your explanation and I appeal to you to correct that statement in your paper.

I wish to say this. I do not know whether any account of this interview will appear in the local press. I have no wish to publish it unless you desire it but I will have a copy of the record sent to Mr. Campbell who can forward it to you. I reserve to myself the right to publish the record if there appears in the public press any garbled or incomplete account of your interview with me.[1]

PRO, FO 371/5684. TD.

1. On 14 July 1921 Governor Hutson sent to Winston Churchill reports of Garvey's four mass meetings in Belize as well as the report of his interview with Garvey (PRO, FO 371/5684).

W. J. H. Taylor, British Vice-consul, to Tom Ffennell Carlisle,[1] British Consul, New Orleans

Key West, Fla. July 5th 1921

Sir:

I have the honour to refer to your CIRCULAR no 161/21 "NEGRO ACTIVITIES IN THIS DISTRICT" and beg to further report to you on this subject as follows:

A negro Marcus Garvey said to be editor of the "Negro World" published in New York U.S.A. came to Key West from New York and started the organization of a secret society to be called the United Negro Improvement Association. Garvey was successful in obtaining n[u]merous applicants and after the organization it is said information started to leak out disclosing its purpose to be to incite the negroes to use violence to obtain its assumed rights. It was said that threats were made to the negro population here to join this organization otherwise the organization would use its efforts and prevent them from obtaining or h[o]lding positions in the community.

It seems that the better class of the negro element resented the efforts of this organization or organizer and the Society and readily supplied information to the authorities upon which his Secretary one T. C. Gla[s]hen was arrested together with others and after the arrest of Gla[s]hen he concluded to leave Key West and departed for Havana Cuba.[2]

During the time of the arrest conditions looked bad but calmness on the part of the authorities together with riot drills held by the Marines prevented any trouble in this Community.

One [R.] H. Higgs[,] pastor of one of the coloured churches in this city for years, came under the influence of Garvey and went to Miami and there created some trouble as will appear by a clipping taken from the Miami Herald of July 3rd 1921. Copy of same is enclosed herewith.

It is said that Higgs expects to leave M[ia]mi for Nassau and it is anticipated that no further difficulty will be had and it is reported that the organization [ha]s broken up.

I may also say that the United States has sent an additional of eight[y] (80) soldiers to the post here.

I have the honor to be sir, your most obedient servant

W. J. H. TAYLOR[3]
British Vice Consul

No. 70/21

PRO, FO 115/2690. TLS, recipient's copy.

1. Tom Ffennell Carlisle was the British consul general for Alabama, Louisiana, Florida, and Mississippi from January 1917 (U.S. Department of State, *Register,* 1918 [Washington, D.C.: GPO, 1918], p. 234).

2. Bureau of Investigation agent Leon Howe reported that "Rev. T. C. Glashen, former president of the U.N.I.A. at Key West . . . expects to sail from Cuba for New York soon. Efforts are being made by the U.N.I.A. members at Key West, which has a membership of 490 to raise money for Glashen." Howe also stated that Garvey "stayed at Glashen's home in Key West for three days in February, just before he sailed for Cuba" (DNA, RG 65, file BS 198940-181). Glashen, who was born in British Honduras, was still under Bureau of Investigation surveillance in August 1923, when an agent reported: "Letters were intercepted from the Rev. R. H. Higgs, Coconut Grove, Fla., which is a suburb of Miami. These letters from Higgs to Glashen contained advice to Glashen to organize the negroes in Key West and on the given date poison everybody and take possession of the island" (DJ-FBI, file 61-746). Glashen was appointed UNIA commissioner to Tennessee in 1922 (*NW*, 26 August 1922).

3. William John Hamilton Taylor served as British vice-consul of Key West and Miami, Fla. (U.S. Department of State, *Register*, 1924 [Washington, D.C.: GPO, 1924], pp. 268, 283).

Reports by Bureau Agent Leon E. Howe

Miami, Fla. 7/6/21

REV. R. H. HIGGS (BAHAMA NEGRO) FORMER VICE-PRES. U.N.I.A. AT COCONUT GROVE, FLA. DEPORTED BY K[U] KLUX KLAN.

Subject left MIAMI July 5 on the British gas boat MAISIE, for NASSAU, BAHAMA ISLANDS, N.P., following a whipping given him by four masked men, and orders to leave the United States within 48 hours.

OSCAR JOHNSON, Financial Secretary of the Miami branch of the U.N.I.A., was a passenger on the same boat. He is also an alien. Agent is informed that he became frightened on account of the treatment given to HIGGS at COCONUT GROVE and to GLASHEN at KEY WEST. In the opinion of agent, JOHNSON was not warned to leave as was HIGGS. Further Report.

LEON E. HOWE

DNA, RG 65, file BS 217184-2. TD.

Miami, Fla. 7/8/21

U.N.I.A.—MIAMI BRANCH

Reference is made to previous reports of agent on the U.N.I.A. activities in this section under captions "MARCUS GARVEY[,]" "T. C. GLASHEN" and "R. H. HIGGS". Owing to the threatening attitude of white toward colored persons in this section, agent devoted the past few days to ascertaining the extent of the activities of the U.N.I.A. in Miami, COCONUT GROVE, HOMESTEAD and vicinity. In general, my investigation has shown that over 95 per cent of the members and officers of the U.N.I.A. in these places are aliens, mainly Bahama negroes, and hence, BRITISH CITIZENS. A few are from the BARBADOS, HAITI, and JAMAICA. Of the membership in MIAMI, which numbers about 1,000, I have found only seven American negroes. Of the 690 members at KEY WEST, the proportion of American negroes is slightly larger. This condition is what has aroused the action of citizens in ordering GLASHEN and HIGGS to leave the United States, as negroes from the British islands are not accustomed to being restricted to certain districts, and bitterly resent the color line as drawn in Florida. Of the approximately 10,000 negroes in Miami, more than 7,000 are aliens.

In continuing the investigation of the Miami Branch of the U.N.I.A.[,] agent obtained all the books and papers of the organization for examination. These books contain detailed information of every meeting, financial status of each member, and extracts from speeches of various men including three speeches of JOTHAR W. NISHIDA,[1] an alleged HAWAI[I]AN, who is well known to the LOS ANGELES office of the Bureau as the owner of a revolutionary book shop in that city, and whose activities in MIAMI were covered in previous report of agent.

The official roll gives the following as officers: (All are aliens except those marked otherwise)

President REV. J. A. DAVIS (Am.), G. M. BROWN, J. R. TAYLOR and S. C. MCPHERSON, 1st., 2nd. and 3rd. vice-presidents, FINANCIAL SECRETARY OSCAR E. JOHNSON, ASSISTANT SEC. PERCY A. STYLES, TREASURER J. H. HOWARD, TRUSTEES—G. E. CARTER (Am), R. A. ROBERTS, PERCY A. STYLES, W. D. ROBINSON, F. BATES. ADVISORY BOARD—REV. S. H. CLARKE (Am.), E. C. GIBSON, HANNAH TAYLOR, J. H. HOWARD, G. M. BROWN, NATHANIEL ROLLE, S. C. MCPHERSON.

Ladies Division

PRESIDENT LILY FARRINGTON, VICE-PRES. NETTIE TROUBLEFIELD, SECRETARY EMMA ROLLE, ASST. SEC. OLGA MINUS, TREASURER ALICIA JOHNSON, (advisory board composed of men, all Bahama negroes).

Agent is forwarding copy of list of all members to the Jacksonville office of the Bureau as soon as it can be completed.

From a partial reading of the minutes of the organization, which go into minute detail, J. A. DAVIS and REV. DR. BROOKINGS,[2] Presiding Elder of the Florida District A.M.E. Church, attended the first meeting and were influential in forming the organization. J. A. DAVIS, apparently had been soliciting members, and mention is made of both having attended the national convention held in WASHINGTON in August, 1920. The first meeting held was September 16, 1920, so evidently DAVIS was appointed a district organizer, and immediately returned to Miami and went to work. From the speech of BROOKINGS, DAVIS evidently attended the convention on his own responsibility, and was not an elected delegate.

With the exception of DAVIS and CARTER, American negroes, all the active work of the organization was in the hands of the BAHAMA negroes, especially the financial matters. In this connection, OSCAR E. JOHNSON who left for NASSAU on the same boat with R. H. HIGGS of COCONUT GROVE, is suspected of being short in his accounts. CARTER told agent that he had been

elected delegate to the National Convention to be held in NEW YORK in
AUGUST 1921, and that $300 had been raised to defray his expenses, but that
he believed that the money had been stolen by JOHNSON. As chairman of the
trustees, he said it was his duty to audit the books and find out the shortage.
CARTER is secretary of the colored Y.M.C.A. and says he entered the organization in order to strengthen his own work, but the minutes of the meetings
indicate that he took an active part in everything, and made a speech every
meeting.

The financial records indicate the organization took a year's lease on
what is known as the old Airdrome Building in colored town, bought
benches for the place, placed a huge sign on it reading "U.N.I.A. Miami
Branch", purchased a motion picture machine, and otherwise seemed to be
in a flourishing condition. The minutes indicate the average collections
amounted to about $25, this including subscriptions for stock in the BLACK
STAR LINE, dues, and buttons, pamphlets, and copies of the [Negro] WORLD.
At one time the organization seems to have had $1,848.00 in the treasury.
The meeting place was known as LIBERTY HALL.

The situation is very strained between white and colored citizens of the
Miami district, and agent is expecting a recurrence of the race troubles which
occurred during July and August last year. Reports from informants in
colored town indicate the negroes are well supplied with arms and ammunition, which is no doubt the result of the action of city and state authorities in
obtaining machine guns, riot guns, and ammunition in large quantities.
When any race trouble threatens as in COCONUT GROVE recently, the American Legion, two companies of the National Guard, and hundreds of private
citizens seize their guns, and any event might precipitate a riot. All white
citizens seem to be convinced that a race war is sure to occur.

Since the affair at COCONUT GROVE the U.N.I.A. has not been meeting,
and it is agent's opinion that they have been warned by citizens not to meet.

Agent will keep in touch with negro activities, and make further report
from time to time.

LEON E. HOWE

[*Endorsement*] NOTED F. D. W.

DNA, RG 65, file BS 198940-183. TD. Stamped endorsement.

1. Nishida was the Los Angeles agent for the *Messenger*, and reportedly the publication's
most successful salesman. The War Department's intelligence reports also claimed that he was
a member of IWW as well as a translator of IWW publications into Asian languages (DNA, RG
165, file 10110-1241; DNA, RG 165, file 10218-364).

2. Probably Rev. Robert Burns Brookins (1859–1943). Born in Camac, Ga., he was pastor of
several AME churches in Florida in the 1880s and 1890s (Richard Robert Wright, *Encyclopedia
of African Methodism* [Philadelphia: Book Concern of the African Methodist Episcopal Church,
1947], p. 49).

A. Rudolph Silverston to J. Harry Philbin

At Washington, D.C., July 8, 1921

ATTENTION: MR. J. HARRY PHILBIN MANAGER,
SHIP SALES DIVISION.

Gentlemen:

On behalf of the Black Star Line, Inc., we hereby offer to purchase the steamship ORION,[1] ex-Prinz Oskar, "as is, where is", for the sum of $225,000, on terms of 10% cash on delivery of vessel, 10% each month thereafter until entire purchase price is paid, with interest on deferred payments at 5% per annum. We further propose to furnish a performance bond, satisfactory to the Shipping Board, guaranteeing the fulfil[l]ment of our contract.

It is understood that this steamer will operate under the American flag. She will be engaged in the New York/Liberian and other African trades, carrying passenger and freight business which the company exclusively controls.

Certified checks (3) in the amount of $12,500,[2] or more than 5% of the amoun[t] of bid, are deposited with this offer as evidence of good faith.

The Black Star Line, Inc. was organized under the laws of the State of Delaware, with a capital of $10,000,000 and is composed entirely of colored citizens, and its stock is owned by the Universal Negro Improvement Association which has a membership exceeding four million colored citizens who are making monthly contributions for the development of their own steamship service.

We understand that the ORION is a combination cargo and passenger vessel, having 3 decks, bridge and poop; 403'4 long; 49'2 breadth; 29'6 depth; d.w.t. 5610; gross 6026; passenger accommodations, 134 first class, 1500 steerage; 2 quad. expansion engines IHP 3000; 2 D.R. Scotch boilers; built in 1902 at Bagesack, Germany.

Trusting that our offer will receive favorable consideration by the Shipping Board, we remain, Very truly yours,

NEW YORK SHIP EXCHANGE, REG.
By A. Rudolph Silverston

DNA, RG 32, USSB, file 605-1-653. TLS, recipient's copy, on New York Ship Exchange letterhead.

1. Albert D. Lasker, chairman of the USSB, later acknowledged receiving a letter from Silverston dated 6 July 1921. This letter apparently discussed the possibility of a new Black Star Line offer for purchase of the *Orion*. This letter, which probably would explain why the *Orion* was once again available, has not been located (Lasker to A. Rudolph Silverston, 15 July 1921, DNA, RG 32, file 605-1-653).

2. BSL records indicated that checks totaling $25,000 had been sent to Silverston between 11 March and 18 June 1921, but he submitted only $12,500 to the Shipping Board (Thomas P. Merrilees, "Summary Report," DJ-FBI, file 61, pp. 36–37). The U.S. Shipping Board, however, required $22,500 as a deposit for the *Orion*. The additional $10,000 was finally paid on 22 December 1921 by Joseph Nolan, a lawyer who occasionally represented the BSL. In his

testimony at Garvey's mail fraud trial, Nolan said that he and Orlando Thompson, BSL vice-president, had arranged to borrow the $10,000 using the BSL's equity in the *Kanawha* and projected income from the *Orion*'s cargo as collateral (*Marcus Garvey* v. *United States*, no. 8317, Ct. App., 2d Cir., 2 February 1925, pp. 1,983–1,989). Although the transaction for the *Orion* was never completed, the ownership of the $22,500 deposit held by the USSB was a matter of controversy for years to come (DNA, RG 32, file 605-1-653). Silverston claimed that a portion of the $12,500 he had received but not submitted to the USSB was used to cover the expenses incurred during the transaction (*Marcus Garvey* v. *United States*, pp. 1,983–1,989).

Report by Bureau Agent Louis Loebl

Chicago, Ill. July 8, 1921

IN RE: MARCUS GARVEY—BLACK STAR LINE; UNIVERSAL NEGRO IMPROVEMENT ASSOCIATION; AFRICAN COMMUNITIES LEAGUE; LIBERIAN CONSTRUCTION COMPANY.

Pursuant to instructions Agent proceeded to Danville, Illinois and there made a thorough investigation of the activities of Garvey's representatives keeping in mind possible postal fraud being perpetrated upon various negroes in that vicinity.

Besides the various interviews had with the persons mentioned below, Agent made undercover inquiries among a number of negroes living within the colored belt[,] many of them being members of Garvey's organization. A summary of the information thus secured is as follows:

GARVEY's movement was first introduced in Danville and vicinity [in] the latter part of March, 1921, when one BURTON, claiming to be a [West] Indian and one CASCHAY, a Liberian, came to Danville and opened a series of meetings under the auspices of the Universal Negro Improvement Association of which MARCUS GARVEY of New York was termed Superior President. Burton and Caschay conducted meetings every night for about [six] weeks and succeeded in getting a great number of negroes interested in the so called "Back to Africa" movement. These men were in Danville about five weeks when they were joined by A. D. WILLIAMS and H. B. WILLIAMS, the first claiming to be the superior traveling representative of Marcus Garvey while the latter called himself the secretary to A. D. Williams. Shortly after the arrival of Williams, Burton and Caschay departed from Danville; it is alleged that they had returned to Africa since then. It seems that the doctrines preached by these men were different in character from the propaganda spread by Williams. Burton and Caschay did not seem to have been interested in the selling of shares of the Black Star Line[,] their main object being to propagate in behalf of the Back to Africa movement. It is alleged that they were decidedly radical in their talks and advocated preparedness against the white race. They predicted a great war to break out in the near future between the white and the colored races, the conflict to take place either in

Africa or in this country; they made disparaging remarks about the United States Government and its people accusing them with dealing unjustly with the negroes. They stated that the negroes in this country ought not [to] have anything to do with the white race, that they should either organize and provide themselves with arms and ammunition to protect themselves against the atrocities perp[e]trated upon them by the white people, or concentrate in Africa, expel the white folks from there and establish an independent negro government. The departure of Burton and Caschay was brought about by the intervention of some of the prominent negroes in Danville who anticipated race trouble if the propaganda of Burton and Caschay was permitted to continue. A. D. WILLIAMS conducted meetings since the latter part of April until about three weeks ago when he left Danville to return east. He came back to Danville on two or three occasions since then and is expected again in Danville within the next few days. It is said that the sole object of his propaganda was to solicit membership for the Universal Negro Improvement Association and to sell shares of the Black Star Line Corporation. Up to the time of his departure from Danville, Williams initiated 425 members and sold about 200 shares at $5.00 each share. After his departure which came rather sudden and unexpected, some of the investors became suspicious and restless and they with the assistance of some prominent negroes called the attention of JOHN LEWMAN, Prosecuting Attorney of Vermillion County to Williams' manipulations with the result that a warrant was issued for the arrest of Williams for violating the Illinois State Securities Law. Since the issuance of the warrant the movement is at a standstill at Danville. The sentiment against Williams is rather bitter and the members and investors are anxiously awaiting the outcome of this case fearing that they had been fleeced and loaded up with worthless stocks.

The following are the present officers of the Danville Division of the Universal Negro Improvement Association and the African Communities League: W. B. BESS, President; CLARENCE F. WHITE, General Sec'y.; JULIA DOWNING, President, Ladies' Section and THELMA MORTIS, General Sec'y. Ladies' Section. It is generally stated that the movement had lost a great number of the followers in Danville and that the present activities of the Danville Division is absolutely dormant.

Agent interviewed the following persons in particular:

JOHN KELLY, Chief of Police, states that he had caused two of his colored policemen [to] join the U.N.I.A. and that they had attended their meetings regularly. They report that Williams' talks were not anti-American or otherwise objectionable and that the entire movement has proven to be a money making scheme in which large amounts of money is being extorted from the ignorant negroes in collections and for membership fees and shares. Chief Kelly claims that an exclusive negro assemblage of this kind has the tendency to create antagonism between the whites and negroes and that he keeps a close watch over their activities.

FRANK BARNES, colored, 504 East Williams Street. States that he was a member of the U.N.I.A. and that he is not a member anymore as he came to the conclusion that the whole movement was a graft. He was thinking of buying some shares of the Black Star Line and of the Liberian Construction Company, and inquired from the State Department whether or not the sales of such stocks were permissible. The State Department advised him that the securities of those companies have never been qualified for sale and that their sale was in violation of the Illinois State Securities Law. (Letter dated Springfield, June 9, 1921, signed L. Emerson, Secretary of State.) Barnes subsequently became instrumental in securing a warrant for Williams. Barnes claims that while he was very close to the inside manipulations of Williams, he didn't know of an instance where the mails were used for the offering or selling of shares. However, he heard Williams advising his audience at the meetings that anybody who didn't care to give him money could send it to the parent body at New York whence the shares would be fort[h]coming directly.

GEORGE R. TILTON, Postmaster. States that he had never heard of Garvey's corporations or of similar negro activities in Danville; that his attention was never called to the mail being used for any fraudulent purpose by the negroes.

DAVE LYONS, Post Office Inspector, was out of the city and could not therefore be interviewed. Mr. Tilton stated to Agent that if a case of such character would have been brought to the attention of Mr. Lyons, that he, (Mr. Tilton) would necessarily know about it.

ABE OUTLAW, colored Police Officer. States that the main object of the movement outside of being a very shrewd money scheme, seems to be to colonize negroes in Africa and to build up there a government of their own. He never heard Williams criticize the United States or talk disrespectfully against the white people. He heard Williams state on many occasions that the U.S. was their only protection and that harmony between the whites and blacks must be the main factor for which the negro ought to strive while he is living in the United States.

W. M. THOMPSON, colored, 323 E. Van Buren St., quite prominent among the negroes in Danville. States that Garvey's men have a fertile field in Danville to prey upon the ignorant negro and that no matter how little mentioning is made at those gatherings about the white people, it nevertheless has the tendency to create ill feeling. Most of the race riots in the past were preceded by propaganda of similar character, Mr. Thompson states. He claims that he is in touch with some of the members of the U.N.I.A. and that they say that the movement in Danville is going backwards rapidly due to the fact that the negroes begin to realize that they had been swindled.

W. H. BEELER, colored, 205 S. Main Street, one of the most influential negroes in the community. States that the propaganda of Burton and Cas[c]hay had such a strong effect upon some of the negroes that they quit

their own church and joined the nonsectarian church under which camouflage Burton and Caschay carried on their propaganda work. Of late, Mr.
Beeler says, he didn't hear of any agitation of unamerican character, and it
seems that the main object of Williams was to get as much money out of the
negroes as possible, and then take "French Leave". Mr. Beeler was one of the
committee that called upon State Attorney Lewman.

Dr. LEWIS A. FRAZIER, colored dentist, 5 1/2 North Jackson Street.
States that he had joined the U.N.I.A. after he was told by some of his
patients that he would be boycotted unless he became a member. He attended two or three meetings at which Williams spoke but didn't he[a]r any
remarks that were of inciting nature. However, Dr. Frazier states, the movement ought to be stopped for it is bound to cause ill feeling among the races.
Garvey's scheme is an attempt, and apparently a successful one to play upon
the ignorance of the negro; a great number of them were fleeced of their last
Dollar and given shares and bonds that seem to be worthless.

Dr. JAS. H. RACHELS, colored physician, 606 Perysville St. States that he
was threatened with boycott unless he would become a member of the
U.N.I.A. He was a member two months but recently withdrew as he clearly
saw that the entire movement was a fraud. A movement of this kind, Dr.
Rachels claims, goes a long way to poison the minds of the negro and make
him antagonistic towards the white people.

G. W. FOSTER, colored, 716 E. Seminary St. States that he was treasurer
of the Danville Division of the U.N.I.A. from its inception until May, 1921;
he resigned after he realized that Williams was acting fraudulently and that
the entire movement was a fake. Of the total membership of 425, only about
45 are still with the movement, apparently on account of the money they have
invested in shares of the Black Star Line. Mr. Foster states that all the
transactions were had between Williams and the purchasers of stocks and
that to his knowledge no solicitations were made through the mails. The
Danville Division owns 20 shares of the Capital Stock of the Black Star Line.
Mr. Foster showed Agent this certificate as he was on his way to turn the
same with the books over to the State Attorney. The certificate bears serial
number 29754, dated April 19, 1921, and is signed by "[O]. M. Thompson",
president and by the secretary whose signature is illegible.

J. C. SMITH, colored police officer. States that he attended several meetings where Burton and Caschay spoke and that they were decidedly radical
advocating the gathering of arms by the negroes for protection against the
white folks. Williams was not radical and his remarks were restricted to
advising his audience to invest money in the Black Star Line and Liberian
Construction enterprises. Smith claims that W. B. Bess, who is the president
of the Danville Division, is still holding meetings but that his activities do
not amount to anything and the meetings are attended by very few men,
mainly by those who are more interested in getting back their invested
money than in the progress of the movement.

JOHN CHAVIS, prominent negro business man, 521 E. Harrison St. States that the movement has fallen off considerably since Williams left the city. His propaganda, Mr. Chavis says, had a tendency to keep the white and colored people apart and to create dissension among the negroes.

R. MAYBERY, colored grocer [13?], E. Madison Street. States that his patronage consists mostly of members of the U.N.I.A. and that he was urged on several occasions to join but did not do so. It seems that the members are getting wise and begin to see the fraudulent purpose of the whole scheme. They do not seem to be enthused anymore to emigrate to Africa and they appear to be anxious to break away from the movement save for the money they had invested in shares and bonds.

JOHN BUFFORD, colored, 407 Union Street, a strong supporter of the movement, being interviewed by Agent undercover, stated that the Danville Division is not as strong as it started out to be due to the fact that Williams had misrepresented certain things relative to the financial side of the movement. The aims of the Universal Negro Improvement Association and the African Communities League is to hold the colored race together, to get them interested in co-operative enterprises and to help toward the freedom and nationalization of the negroes. He claims that the movement tends to draw the white and the colored race closer together and to wipe out certain differences that had caused frictions in the past between the two races. Investigation Concluded.

LOUIS LOEBL

[*Stamped endorsement*] FILE G. F. R.
NOTED F. D. W.
[*Handwritten endorsement*] Senator McKinley
8/[1]/21

DNA, RG 65, file BS 198940-182. TD.

Cable by Marcus Garvey

[[At Sea, July 10, 1921]]

FELLOW MEN OF THE NEGRO RACE GREETINGS

In order to make this convention as great a success as the first, held on last August, the Universal Negro Improvement Association is requesting all Negro communities, societies, lodges, churches, fraternities and newspapers to send delegates to this convention.[1]

The task of organizing the four hundred million Negroes of the world is gigantic and requires the combined wisdom of all our forces.

We are, therefore, appealing to all the loyal men and women of the race to rally to this cause and to send delegates to represent them in this convention, which is to be a CONFERENCE OF THE NEGROES OF THE WORLD.

Great problems confronting the race will be discussed. Legislation will be enacted for the future guidance and protection of the race.

His Excellency, the Provisional President of Africa, the Honorable Marcus Garvey, will address the convention regarding his official visit to the West Indies, the Republic of Panama and South Central America.

New departments will be created and new heads of bureaus selected. Fraternally yours,

MARCUS GARVEY

Printed in *NW*, 16 July 1921. Original headlines omitted.

1. A message from Garvey, read at the conclusion of a Liberty Hall meeting on 13 June 1921, reportedly declared, "This convention (the U.N.I.A.) is destined to be the greatest recorded in the history of the Negro, and will accomplish inestimable benefit to the race" (*NW*, 25 June 1921).

Report by Special Agent P-138

New York City 7-11-21

IN RE: NEGRO ACTIVITIES.

Learned [5 *July*] from Rev. HEYLEGEN [*Ellegor*], an officer of the Black Star Line, that the Garvey organization was bordering on financial ruin in view of the fact that very little money is being received. He also stated that he had not received his salary for over two months, and they have again lost a few thousand dollars on a prospective ship. He stated he was thinking very seriously of resigning.

P-138

[*Endorsement*] NOTED F. D. W.

DNA, RG 65, file BS 198940-184. TD. Stamped endorsement.

Charles J. Scully to Frederick A. Wallis, Commissioner of Immigration, Ellis Island

[*New York*] July 12, 1921

Dear Sir:

This office is in receipt of information to the effect that Gabriel Johnson, of the Universal Negro Improvement Association, is a passenger aboard the S.S. "Leon the XIII", scheduled to arrive at this port on the 13th instant.

Johnson is enroute from Liberia and is associated with Marcus Garvey, head of the Black Star Steamship Line and a widely known Negro radical, and it is therefore requested that a thorough examination be made of this man's effects and this office be notified upon his arrival, so that a representative may be present at that time. Thanking you in advance, I am, Yours very truly,

CHARLES J. SCULLY
Acting Division Superintendent

[*Stamped endorsement*] NOTED F. D. W.
[*Handwritten endorsement*] FILE G. F. R.

DNA, RG 65, file BS 198940-186. TL, carbon copy.

Charles J. Scully to Lewis J. Baley

NEW YORK, N.Y. July 12, 1921

ATTENTION: MR. HOOVER.

Dear Sir:

From inquiries made in this city as a result of the telegram received to the effect that Marcus Garvey is due to arrive in this city aboard the Steamship "Suriname," it has been learned that this ship is owned by the United Fruit Company and operates between Porto Barrios, Guatemala and New Orleans.

The "Suriname" left Porto Barrios for New Orleans on the ninth instant and is expected to arrive there on the thirteenth.

The New Orleans office has been notified by telegram to have a thorough examination of Garvey made in the presence of a representative of this Department and that this office be advised of his destination when he leaves that city.

Confidential Employee P 138 states that the Reverend G. E. Stewart, High Chancellor of the Universal Negro Improvement Association, recently received a cable from Garvey at Belize, British Honduras, in which Garvey stated that he expected to be in New York in plenty of time to address meetings in this city on the 17th, 18th and 19th instants.

Stewart also stated that Garvey had received a passport at Jamaica, West Indies, and it had been vis[a]ed by the American Consul at that place through the efforts of friends of Garvey's who had recently been in Washington and visited the State Department. Yours very truly,

CHARLES J. SCULLY

Acting Division Superintendent

[*Stamped endorsement*] NOTED F. D. W.
[*Handwritten endorsement*] FILE G. F. R.

DNA, RG 65, file 198940-185. TLS, recipient's copy.

Marcus Garvey to Charles Evans Hughes

New Orleans, La., July 13, 1921

May it please your honor that my two secretaries Amy Jacques [*and*] Cleveland Jacques and I who have all been residents of the United States for several years Amy Jacques being secretary of Negro [F]actories Corporation of Delaware of which I am president doing business at 56 W 135 New York as also private secretary and Cleveland Jacques an employee and special secretary of the Black Star [L]ine corporation of Delaware doing business at 56 W 135 New York of which I am president left New York four months ago on a business trip to West Indies and Central America in the interests of the corporations[.] [W]e have personal and other properties in the state of New York where we lived respectively for several years[.] Our passports were vis[a]ed at the American consulate Kingston Jamaica for return to the United States and arriving at New Orleans this morning we have been detained not permitted to land to continue our journey to New York by the immigration authorities here without our committing any offense against the laws or constitution of the United States[.] My business in the United States is of a responsible nature to four million negro people who have invested their hard earned pennies in the corporations I am head of[.] [B]ecause of the success of my efforts in the United States in helping the people of my race in America and other parts of the world many enemies members of my race and others have made false representations against me and there has been an organized effort to prevent me returning to the United States through their jealousy which they calculate to cause the ruin of my efforts for struggling humanity[.] I have an abiding faith in the justice of American institutions and in view of the fact that I have business interests in the United States unsettled involving millions of dollars to American citizens and others and that I have also several cases before the courts of the United States not yet called or settled and in view of the fact that we are all loyal to the laws and constitution of the United States and in consideration of the fact that we have just passed through the following countries where /we/ have done business on our way to the United States without hindrance—Cuba[,] Jamaica[,] Panama[,] Costa Rica[,] British Honduras and Guatamala—we ask that your honor be good enough to admit us back into the United States even for the period of enabling us to give a true and honest report of our transactions to our corporations and to settle our property interests[.] Awaiting your honor[']s reply.

MARCUS GARVEY
Care Immigration Authorities
New Orleans

[*Endorsement*] Granted entry at noon
July 14th [*13th*] 1921

DNA, RG 59, file 811.108 G 191/32. TG, recipient's copy. Handwritten endorsement.

Report by Special Agent P-138

NEW YORK, N.Y. 7/13/21

RE: NEGRO ACTIVITIES.

I learned positively from PLUMMBER, the propaganda agent of the Black Star Line, that they had received a cable from Jamaica yesterday [*8 July*] from MARCUS GARVEY which said that he would probably arrive in the U.S.A. within ten days.

PLUMMBER told me that very little cash was being received by the BLACK STAR LINE on account of GARVEY's absence. That owing to the big salaries of so many officials, preachers, etc., it was impossible to keep up with expenses, hence many of them had received no pay for weeks, while others got theirs. That there is great danger of not being able to purchase the proposed ship, thereby disappointing the members and stockholders.

P-138

[*Endorsement*] NOTED F. D. W.

DNA, RG 65, file BS 198940-191. TD. Stamped endorsement.

Charles J. Scully to Lewis J. Baley

New York, N.Y. July 13, 1921

Attention five. New Orleans office reports Marcus Garvey arrived there today from Jamaica via Belize was released from Immigration station at noon and is now under surveillance.[1]

[CHARLES J.] SCULLY, Acting

[*Handwritten endorsement*] NOTED G. F. R.
[*Stamped endorsement*] NOTED F. D. W.

DNA, RG 65, file BS 198940-198. TG, recipient's copy.

1. Bureau agent J. A. Condon, on instructions from bureau agent Toliver, questioned Garvey on his arrival in New Orleans; he also attended Garvey's meeting on 14 July. Condon reported that "there were about fifteen hundred negroes present of the ignorant class" (DNA, RG 65, file BS 198940-202).

Speech Announcement

RALLY   RALLY

TO HEAR

HON. MARCUS GARVEY

THE MOSES OF OUR RACE

AND FOUNDER OF

U. N. I. A. ASSOCIATION
& BLACK STAR LINE

AT THE

NATIONAL - PARK

Corner Third & Willow Sts.

Wednesday and Thursday Nights,
July 13 and 14, 1921, 8 P. M.

——

Carney Print, 1912 Dryades St.

(*Source*: DNA, RG 65.)

Speeches by Marcus Garvey

[*New Orleans*] July 13, 1921

MARCUS GARVEY held meeting at 8:30 P.M., Wednesday, July 13, 1921, NATIONAL PARK, Corner 3rd and WILLOW STS.

"THE UNIVERSAL NEGRO IMPROVEMENT ASSOCIATION."

"The time has come for the strongest race of people on earth, bar[r]ing the Chinese, to break the bonds of oppression. Oppression everywhere clamoring for freedom. I mean no disloyalty to the Government in preaching antagonism of race. Two Masters cannot rule in one country. Let the whites rule ENGLAND, FRANCE AND AMERICA, and let the negro rule in AFRICA. Our ancestors were taken from Africa against their will in chains and sold into slavery. They have never relinquished their rights to the country, and it is still ours. The negro race is too strong to be whipped. I am not preaching radicalism. I advise you to obey the laws of your country, or you wish you had. Will respect ownership of whites in ENGLAND, FRANCE and AMERICA, but if all are not our color in AFRICA, we will recognize no one. We have favored and aided by the hundred, but favor has not been returned. Time now to pay attention to our own interest. Look out for yourselves. We are the most charitable people on earth, but charity begins at home.

["]Propaganda has been circulated by the explorers of Africa for three hundred years. Propaganda is very valuable. So valuable that with the aid of the negro it whipped the Kaiser, who, would now have whipped ENGLAND, FRANCE and AMERICA if it had not been for them. Propagandists, explorers of Africa calling negroes thieves now. The thieves in Africa fell out in 1914—Four hundred million negroes now reach to back Africa up. We have talked enough. FIGHT FOR YOUR RIGHTS—FOR EQUALITY.

["]There is some great reason for creating some black and some whites. The bible says that princes will come out of EGYPT. You are the princes that shall come out of EGYPT. Everything under the sun is possible for you. What the whites have done you can do. Let no other permit the master to exploit us. Boss with whites 50–50[.] Establish the greatest republic in the world in AFRICA. Call its Leader—PRESIDENT. You must do or the negro must die. Dispute every inch of your right until death. The world owes you a living. It is your fault if it gets away. Negroes look out for yourselves. The fittest race is the question of the ages. Negroes are waking up. The world is without sympathy. You must form your own future. Do for yourse[lv]es what others have done for themselves. You get equal rights with birth. It is your own fault if you let others take your rights. We are not organizing to fight the whites, but to protect what is ours if it takes our lives. The next one hundred years means elimination of the weaker race. It is now to call the surviving of the fittest."

His closing words were—

"Touch one negro and you touch four hundred million. We live to die together."

DNA, RG 59, file 000-612. TD.

[*New Orleans*] July 14, 1921

IN RE: MARCUS GARVEY: MEETING NATIONAL PARK—3RD AND WILLOW STS.

In introducing MARCUS GARVEY, MRS. HENRIETTA VINT[O]N DAVIS, INTERNATIONAL ORGANIZER FOR THE UNIVERSAL NEGRO IMPROVEMENT ASSOCIATION, made a very radical talk, in which she denounced the whites in every way. She stated that after the REPUBLIC IN AFRICA was established, the whites would be given whipping for whipping, lynching for lynching. This woman is an educated and able speaker, and a very dangerous agitator. She has personality, and a very forceful way of expressing her views.

TALK OF MARCUS GARVEY.

The first set of purposes is to establish an exclusive government of their own in AFRICA. We have four million members since starting this movement four years ago. We have seven hundred branches extending all over the world. We have made up our minds not to die separately but together. If any one kills a member you will have to kill us all. Grievance to one is a grievance to all. We will fight to the last of our four hundred million. When the whites lived in caves, negroes were leaders of the world. What whites tell us to do, negroes told them thousands of years ago. We have been asleep, but we have awakened. We are so much awake that we refused to sleep longer. We have buried the scraping negro. We have given to the world a new negro very much awake.

When I /arrived in/ New York four years ago, no one paid any attention to MARCUS GARVEY. Now I cannot move an inch without every one knowing that I am in town. Crown heads of all countries have their eyes on me. Nothing was read in the past except of lynching negroes. Now they will read that negroes are working for redemption of the race. The chance is here. When we start to redeem AFRICA what will they say[?] We have no hatred for the Southern White Man[.] I believe that the Southern White Man is the best friend the negro ever had[.] But for the Southern White man the negro would still be asleep. He "JIM CROWED" you, and he KICKED you. That aroused class consciousness. If it were not for the attitude of the white man I would be addressing negro congregations with white wives. Lynching did more to arouse consciousness in the negro than anything else. HOKE SMITH, TILLMAN and SMUT [*Smuts*] are the negroes['] best friends. Their attitude towards the negro caused the negro to wake up to class prejudice. I am a SMITH, SMUT [*Smuts*] and TILLMAN all in one word. If we had not been

529

lynched and jim-crowed, we would never have awakened and started a Republic in Africa.

In the WEST INDIES negroes outnumber whites one hundred to one. They do not lynch negroes because the odds are too great. White man goes up to the negro with a bible in his hands instead of a rope. He tells you that you are as good as he, but he sees to it that you never get above the station in life that he intends. He makes economic conditions such that he keeps you too poor to mix up in his society and join his clubs. The higher class negro in the WEST INDIES holds the poor class down. The white man rules the Negro there, but exploits him. It causes me great pain to be jim-crowed and lynched, but it is a boo[n] to the negro, for it wakes him up to the situation. Blacks of AFRICA and WEST INDIES were not /class conscious/ till the negro world told him of the lynching of negro women, children and men in America, and that the whites were not the negroes' friends, but his enemy. No matter how much property you have in America you cannot prosper until you have forced a protection. You never see any race driven out on account of prosperity, but in Africa the negro prospers and i[s] driven out. Behind the other races are large armies and navies to protect their people. The negro has no such protection. We are going to put up in AFRICA a negro Government—the Greatest government on earth—to protect the negroes from the world. I would like to see peace, and all races get together, but the time for that is ten thousand years away. Time of race equality will come with the return of JESUS. It is too long to wait. If you say that whites and blacks are brothers you are crazy; if I call MORGAN my brother, he would call a policeman, but if I was a millionaire in Africa, he would welcome me as his brother. Whites hate blacks because they are ignorant. Physical force demands respect. The negro is too ignorant to demand it. If we get power, the whites will respect us. There will be no more race prejudice because you will be too powerful. We will sometime stand on a plain of equality. I am not preaching revolt, but trying to organize and strengthen ourselves, and unite the negro. All honor to the flags of the UNITED STATES, ENGLAND, and FRANCE, but all supreme honor to the RED, BLACK and GREEN FLAG. We want the numerical strength of the race with the Government to support us. Before the Japanese-Russian War, the Russians called the Japs "LITTLE YELLOW MONKEYS." The "Monkey" made up his mind to show the Russian what he could do, and gave him a whipping. The Russian now calls the "Little Yellow Monkey" his brother. You see it takes force to demand respect. The white man is jealous. He is afraid of the man who has nothing, fearing he will take from him his worth. If you have not riches you have nothing commendable. You are ashamed that you are a negro, but in five years from now you will be glad of it. When we get our Government in Africa, I will advocate "Jim-crow" laws for the whites. They will get a dose of their own medicine. I am called an alien. We are not aliens. We were taken away from Africa in chains against our will, and scattered around the world in slavery. We are now searching for one [an]other.

DNA, RG 59, file 000-612. TD.

Report by Special Agent P-138[1]

NEW YORK CITY 7/19/21

IN RE: MARCUS GARVEY

MARCUS GARVEY arrived in New York, at the Pennsylvania Station, 9:35 A.M. [*17 July*]. I met him there. Among others present who met him were REV. STEWART and GARCIA, the Secretary of the Black Star Line.

GARVEY was accompanied by MRS. HARRIET V. DAVIS, Miss AMY JAKES [*Jacques*], her brother and three other men, members of the U.N.I.A.

GARVEY, MISS DAVIS, MISS JAKES and myself rode in a Taxi from the Station to his home at 135 West 129th Street. I learned from th[em] that he had had quite a lot of trouble getting his passport vis[aed]; that to evade the authorities who refused to vis[a] his passport direct to the U.S.A. he had taken a roundabout tour, going to British Honduras, then to Guatemala, then to the U.S. He was met everywhere, he said, with questions as to his objects in launching the BLACK STAR LINE and organizing the negroes. He feels that DR. DU BOIS, MOTON, EMMIT SCOTT and others of his enemies tried to embarrass him by writing letters to the authorities. He seemed to know but very little relative to the proposed new ship as he inquired of me: "What about the 'Phylis Wheatley' and when and where will she sail? Is she in New York? Has she been taken over?

He is prepared to proceed with his campaign, get rid of some of his officials and push the BLACK STAR LINE.

He also inquired as to whether PRESIDENT KING was still in the U.S. and about the progress of his loan.

We parted at his door with the hope of having another interview early next week.

P-138

[*Endorsement*] NOTED F. D. W.

DNA, RG 65, file BS 198940-205. TD. Stamped endorsement.

1. P-138 was instructed by bureau agent Charles J. Scully to meet Garvey at the station and to "ascertain his future plans" (Scully to Lewis J. Baley, 15 April 1921, DNA, RG 65, file BS 198940-195).

Memorandum from Clifford Smith, Secretary, United States Shipping Board

WASHINGTON July 19, 1921

MEMORANDUM FOR SHIP SALES DIVISION.

The Shipping Board today considered your recommendation that the Board accept the offer of the Black Star Line, Inc., to purchase the SS ORION on the terms set forth therein, and deferred action thereon, pending the receipt of a detailed report of the financial responsibility of the proposed purchasers and their financial ability to carry out the conditions of the proposed contract of purchase.

Please arrange to secure such report immediately and transmit same, with appropriate recommendations, through the usual channels, to this office, in order that the matter may be again presented to the Board at the earliest date possible.

CLIFFORD W. SMITH
Secretary

CC General Comptroller
Treasurer
Acting Director of Operations
Contract Bureau
Mr. Farley.

DNA, RG 32, USSB, file 605-1-653. TMS, recipient's copy.

Speech by Marcus Garvey

[[Liberty Hall, New York, 20 July 1921]]

. . . May it please your Highness, the Potentate, Right Hon. Members of the Executive Council, Members and Friends of the New York Division of the Universal Negro Improvement Association:—Again it [is] my good fortune to address you. Tonight I am supposed to explain to you my experience as gathered from my trip to the West Indies and Central America in your behalf. As I said last night, I took my departure from this country, leaving New York on the 23d of February for Key West, arriving there on the 28th, where I spoke in the Key West division of the association on two occasions. From Key West I journeyed on to Havana, Cuba, where I met the Havana Division of the Universal Negro Improvement Association. I was entertained by the division in a manner that was characteristic of the spirit of the membership of the U.N.I.A. in all parts. I spoke for them three nights at one [of] the Savan[n]ahs of Havana. The people turned out by the thousands to hear me on these occasions, not only the West Indians and American Negroes who were domiciled in Cuba, but the native Cubans came by the hundreds and by the thousands to hear me at these meetings. They were attended by not only the ordinary citizens, but they were attended by some of the biggest officials in the Cuban Government, as also members of the Cuban Senate. After remaining in Havana for two days, it became widely known throughout the Island that I was then speaking in Havana. A special message was sent throughout the length and breadth of Cuba to the various municipalities to extend to me the freedom of these municipalities wherever I should visit. Hence my trip through Cuba was a most enjoyable one, in that wheresoever I appeared, wheresoever I went, throughout Cuba, the officials of the communities, as well as the populace, received me with open arms. I was presented to His Excellency, the then President of Cuba, President Menocal, and also to the President-elect at that time, who is now the governing president of Cuba.[1] I met both of them in the National Palace at Havana. They gave me a hearty welcome to the Republic and for a few minutes we discussed the question of the Universal Improvement Association; and I gathered from both presidents that they were in hearty sympathy with the work of the organization for the liberation of Africa for the Negro peoples of the world. (Cheers).

From Havana, after receiving a hearty reception and watching the people respond most nobly in a financial way to the Black Star Line, and for the Liberian Construction Loan, I went to Moron, little town in the province of Oriente—I had two meetings in Moron where I was also splendidly entertained by that division. They also supported the Black Star Line and the Construction Loan. From Moron I went to the little city of Nuevitas, and there also I received another hearty response, and there the people "Went Over the Top" 100 per cent. for the Black Star Line and the Liberian Construction Loan, even though his Grace, the Chaplain-General, Dr. McGuire had been there, and as an Archbishop, naturally he had cleaned up all Cuba and left not even a brass nickel there. But when I arrived in Nuevitas, the ladies went down into their "National Banks" and they brought out all the reserves they had, and they went over the top 100 per cent. for the Black Star Line shares and for the Construction Loan for the industrial development of Liberia.

From Nuevitas, I went to the great stronghold of the Universal Improvement Association—Preston. In Preston I also received a warm reception. Dr. McGuire had proceeded me there, and I believe in two nights took away all the savings of the people in Preston. So when I arrived there to get some more they did the best they could, and I think that best can be measured with the best of any other center of the Universal Improvement Association, because they open-heartedly did every thing they possibly could to make my trip there a success. From Preston, I went to another great stronghold, the stronghold of Barnes, where Dr. McGuire, I believe, in two nights got $4,000 for the Black Star Line.

I must say that I was sick all during my stay in Cuba, because I contracted a very bad cold, having gone immediately from the cold in the North to the warmth of the tropics down in Key West. I took a very bad cold and having to speak every night it developed seriously and I was very much embarrassed in my speeches in Cuba because I suffered nightly from the effects of the bad cold. Nevertheless, I was sent out to represent the Universal Improvement Association, and the first night hundreds and thousands of people assembled in the biggest theatre [in] the city of Barnes, and I was suffering terribly while I spoke. I sold thousands of dollars worth of stock at the meeting, and we received a large amount of money for the door admittance, because all the meetings that I addressed during my stay from New York the people paid a dollar to attend. That amount was paid in Cuba, in Jamaica and in all the places that I spoke. Miss Jacques collected $14,000 for door receipts alone, outside of dozens of meetings I addressed for nothing so as to accommodate all the people of the various communities I visited. As I said last night, in Panama, when I was about to leave there the people were so anxious (those who were closed out because of the overtaxed capacity of the building), they were willing to pay $50 just to hear me for the last time in Panama. That will give you an idea of the enthusiasm of the people in Cuba, Jamaica and the Panama Republic in hearing me as the representative of the Universal Improvement Association. The second night I was unable to continue my meetings in Barnes; even though I was determined to go out, yet the Black Cross Nurses there under the direction of Mrs. Collins, refused to let me get out of bed. When I was preparing to get out they barred the door so that I could not get out. That was the only meeting I was unable to address during the time I was away even though I suffered all the time. I was thankful, however, that they kept me away from that meeting, because I suffered that night, and at one time I thought I was going across on a long journey, not on the ship of the Black Star Line, but on the spiritual ship. Nevertheless, Mrs. Collins worked on me all night and I recovered enough to continue the journey next morning to Antilla and I spoke in Antilla the following night.

From there I journeyed to Santiago where I met a large band of men and women working in the interest of the U.N.I.A. The people are doing splendid work at that end of Cuba for the carrying through of this great cause of ours.

In leaving Cuba for Jamaica, I left a country 100 per cent. working in the interest of the U.N.I.A. When I arrived in Jamaica some time late in April I was received most heartily and enthusiastically by the citizens of Kingston. My advent into the city was not well known; that is, the hour and the date of my arrival was not known beforehand. Nevertheless, they were looking out for me at any time, and in the space of a couple of minutes the news flashed around the city that I had arrived; so they came from all parts so as to greet me and bid me welcome to my own native land. The first night when I landed there I calculated I would take a rest because I was suffering, but they refused to let me rest, and arranged a welcome meeting for me, and that night hundreds and thousands were turned away from the Collegiate Hall where the welcome was tendered to me. The next night I spoke to them in the largest public building in Jamaica, the Ward Theatre, and it was said it was the first time in the history of that theatre that so many people were crowded into it, and although the capacity of the theatre was overtaxed we turned away thousands, and each person inside had paid 2 shillings and 6 pence to enter that building. Notwithstanding the poverty of the country the people overtaxed the building to demonstrate their enthusiasm for the Universal Improvement Association. I addressed large meetings at the Ward Theatre and stirred the entire Island of Jamaica in the name of the Universal Improvement Association, insomuch so that for several days—Jamaica being the most critical country in the West Indies—no critics dared to attack me; they were afraid. Then after several days passed by[,] some of the bolder critics of the country came forward and attacked me, and those of you in the United States who have received communications from Jamaica will realize how we handled ourselves in the name of the U.N.I.A. (Cheers.) We handled ourselves in Jamaica so splendidly that I hardly believe there is one man in Jamaica bold enough to attack the Universal Improvement Association. We silenced the critics of Jamaica forever.

From Jamaica I journeyed to Costa Rica, and in Costa Rica I received a warm reception on my arrival by 15,000 residents of that republic—West Indian residents and American Negro residents, men and women who were domiciled there for 40, 30, 20, 15 or 10 years,[2] and they gave me a welcome that I will never forget. Costa Rica is the country that really gave us to believe that the Universal Negro Improvement Association cannot die, because people there are willing to sacrifice their last so that this association will accomplish the task of giving us a free and redeemed Africa. The people of Costa Rica were so enthusiastic—the large majority of them are employees of the United Fruit Co., scattered in all sections of Costa Rica working on the farms; they have been working there, as I said, for 40, 30, 20 or 15 years—and when they heard that Marcus Garvey, representing the Universal Association, had arrived in Costa Rica, every man threw down his cutlass, every man threw down his hoe and other instruments of labor and said that there was going to be no more work until Marcus Garvey got out of Costa Rica. (Cheers.) Well, the United Fruit Co. had about three ships which were to be loaded with bananas and they were up against it, so I believe they came to a compromise with me and they said, "Look here, we don't want to embarras[s] you; we want you to have all the money you want to get so as to carry on the work, so we are going to have a special pay-day that these folks can get money to do what you want them to; but you must help us in this way: you must go out to the capital for three days and stay out there, during which time they will load all the bananas on the ships, and by the time the ships are loaded we will send a special train for you and bring you down and have a pay-day so that they will have money to support your cause.["] (Cheers and

535

laughter.) I did not go there to embarrass anybody; I went there for the purpose of doing business; so I accepted the arrangement and took the special train. Outside of the satisfaction it gave to me in that they paid a compliment to me not as Marcus Garvey but as representative of the Negro peoples of the world, I am pleased at the satisfaction it gave to the people of Costa Rica; because never in the history of Costa Rica was a black man or a dark man allowed to ride on certain cars of the railroad that runs from Port Limón to San José; in that a certain class of people are allowed to ride in a certain class of coach going from Port Limón to the capital, San José. And when I arrived there I was the first black man who ever had a special train. (Cheers.) And that gave satisfaction to the people of Costa Rica for having put it over for once, and I was glad to help them anyhow. We had a special train all during the time I was there. The United Fruit Co. was very kind; they not only gave us a special train but they also arranged for a special launch to take me from Costa Rica to the province of Bocas del Toro and I accepted it because the people demanded it. And let me tell you a joke. The morning I was to leave for San José, the capital, before I arrived they brought out a certain coach, and I believe there were a few dirty spots on the outside of the coach, and the people refused to have that coach. They said: "This coach is not going to move from here until you bring the best coach you have down in Limón," and so the railroad had to shunt it off and put on one of the brand newest coaches they had so as to accommodate the Provisional President of Africa. (Cheers.) In Limón they had a holiday lasting for several days; they ran special trains for the people from all sections of Costa Rica to bring them down to Port Limón, [3] and the day that I was going to San José so as to address a meeting in the afternoon in Port Limón I saw miles of cars stretched on the railroad track all the way down through certain sections of Costa Rica to Port Limón. The people came down from all sections by the thousands; they were inside the coaches, they hung outside of the coaches at the doors and windows, and they sat on top of the coaches; the coaches could not hold them; they did not have enough coaches to bring them down from the different parts of the line to Port Limón. They came by the thousands and there was no place large enough in Port Limón to accommodate them; therefore they rented a stand on the plaza—I believe they call it the Open Plaza—of several acres of land, and I spoke to the thousands of people there. They had a time of it all day and all night. The house they arranged to accommodate me was immediately opposite the Plaza and they had the house decorated with the flags of the African Republic, the Red, the Black and the Green; and they enjoyed themselves at the Plaza all night and all day. They had electric lights; they had music and they played and danced all day and all night for four days; there was no work in Costa Rica; all the Negro people were on strike celebrating the forthcoming emancipation of Africa. We did a splendid business in Costa Rica. The young man I took with me (Mr. Jacques) was occupied all day and all night writing out shares in the Black Star Line and selling bonds of the Liberian Construction Loan, and Miss

Jacques, my secretary, was working all the time counting money received as entrance fees to the meetings and contributions they gave to the cause of the U.N.I.A.

From Costa Rica I went to Bocas del Toro and there again I had another beautiful time in the province of Almirante, up in the woodlands of Bocas del Toro; there you will find hundreds and thousands of West Indian Negroes, chiefly Barbadians and Jamaicans—the majority Jamaicans. They had saved their money there and had kept it on tap until I got there to buy shares in the Black Star Line and bonds in the Liberian Construction Loan. There again we did great business, and the enthusiasm was warm. There again the United Fruit Co. could not get the people to work until I was out of the country, and they gave us special trains and ran them at midnight and did everything to accommodate us so we could have a successful time in order that I should get out and allow some work to be done.

I left Bocas del Toro for Colón. I arrived in Colón some time in April, and there again I went unannounced because I did not want any trouble with the Canal Zone Government. They were looking for me somewhere and I was determined to get there from under the sea; so I took a submarine, and I just got out of the water one afternoon and dropped on shore in Colón and checked my baggage and stood up beside a man. I said to him, "Sam, go and call Mr. Morales." He said, "Who are you?" I said go and tell Mr. Morales Marcus Garvey wants him and in two minutes after there were about ten thousand people around me. By that time the Canal Zone heard I was there, but there was ten thousand around me so they could not get to me through the crowd. Mr. Morales came in an automobile and took me to the place they had prepared for me—the residence of Dr. Mammlet, a kind-hearted man, and a loyal member of the U.N.I.A., from Barbados; he is now a citizen of Panama. He entertained me and my party royal[l]y and we enjoyed our stay in his home. The first afternoon when I arrived the people forced me to come out on the veranda to make a speech and I had to make a speech and inform them that I would speak that night. Night came and it was arranged for me to speak in Liberty Hall. Liberty Hall of Colón is a beautiful structure and can accommodate 800 or 900 persons, and when I went there at 7 o'clock the place was overcrowded. I believe they had a thousand people in the hall, all having paid a dollar apiece, and there were about 5,000 outside trying to get into the hall; there were about 2,000 on the veranda of another building outside, and the crowd was so immense they tore the veranda down, and the verandas all around that building [were] overcrowded with people trying to hear something of my voice as giving an explanation of the aims and objects of the Universal Improvement Association. I delivered six addresses in Colón, each night and every afternoon, and we did a splendid business there.

From Colón we journeyed up to Panama City, and as I said last night, when I arrived in Panama City I met the largest crowd of people I have ever seen at any one time—at least Negro people. They came from all directions. They overcrowded the city. From the time I arrived I met crowds of people and they made such a rush on me that they lifted me from the [*railroad*] car, smashed the windows of the car, took me out, lifted me and carried me to the automobile, placed me in the automobile and they all got in the automobile. (Cheers and Laughter.) You can just imagine the work of that poor automobile. They got into the automobile, punctured the tires and put the automobile on the rims, and they were not satisfied until they had to get out and push it all the way. (Laughter.) They had a gala day in Panama. On my arrival in the city it was said by the Panama newspapers that it was the largest assembly of people ever yet seen in the Republic of Panama. I addressed the people that night in the circus tent. A circus company was performing there and they gave over the tent to us for that night where I addressed a large crowd. The following Saturday afternoon and Sunday night I addressed a large concourse of people in the "Bull Ring." Thousands of people assembled, because it was the largest place they could get. The meetings were so successful that the news went all the way down the [*Canal*] Zone and everybody wanted to hear me. On Monday night everybody came out to hear me for the last. They got a theatre with a seating capacity, I think, of 1,800. The meeting was scheduled for 8 o'clock, and by 6 o'clock the theatre was overcrowded and over two thousand people were outside clamoring to get in. At 8 o'clock when I got there I had to go through a dense crowd of people, and at that time they were offering $50, $25, $20, $10, and $5 just to get a peep in to hear me for the last time in Panama. I was very sorry that all the people could not be accommodated and they went away at 11 o'clock when I dismissed the meeting, back to the Canal Zone. They came in automobiles from all parts of the Zone. In returning from Panama to Colón I boarded a ship of the United Fruit Co. for Jamaica.

On my return to Jamaica I addressed another series of meetings, and then made up my mind to return to the United States of America. The day prior to arranging for my passage to the United States of America, I received a cable from Miss Davis in Santiago asking me to come immediately to Santiago because there was trouble there with the members determined to discipline the captain and crew of the Kanaw[ha] who had displeased them by their actions and the stockholders there had called a meeting, and if I did not go down[,] there would have been serious trouble, because somebody would have been lynched in Santiago. I went there in time to save the situation and took the ship from Santiago to Jamaica. The explanation about the ship I will give to you tomorrow night in my discussions of the Black Star Line. I want all of you to turn out tomorrow night to hear me on the subject of the Black Star Line. Tomorrow night you will get all the information you desire about our ship, the Kanaw[ha], and about the business relationship of the Black Star Line and what has been done since my absence.

But suffice it to say that from Jamaica I traveled with Miss Davis, Miss Jacques and her brother to Belize, British Honduras, with the intention of going by that way to the United States of America. We were heartily received in Belize, British Honduras, by the people of that country. In Belize they

have a beautiful Liberty Hall. They bought that Liberty Hall proper for
$2,100, and they had paid off all but a couple of hundred dollars. It is a
splendid hall and is living testimony of the loyalty and devotion and the
splendid spirit of the people living in that city of Belize in British Honduras.
I spoke there for several nights and won the confidence of the people. There I
was the guest of a black man who is known as the "Coconut King" of Central
America. He is known to be a millionaire—a man who is coming up to the
convention to be presented to you—a loyal member of the Universal Negro
Improvement Association. His name is Mr. Isaac Morter.[4] He is known as
the "Coconut King" of Central America; so we have already started to make
"coconut kings," and soon we will have diamond kings in Africa. We were
his guests for the time we remained in Belize.

From Belize we went to Puerto Barrios, Guatemala, and there we saw a
beautiful division of the organization. There are people there from all parts
of Jamaica, Barbados and other West Indian Islands and from America. They
are domiciled there and work for the United Fruit Co. They have banded
themselves into a division of the U.N.I.A. and are doing splendid work.
They sent out with me on the ship [on] which I came their deputy, Mr.
Clifford Bourne, who was here at the last convention as their representative—a splendid man, a man who has done great work for the U.N.I.A. in
Guatemala as well as in other parts of Central America. Later on during this
week I will take the pleasure and honor of introducing Mr. Bourne to you,
because he has come to you representing one of the strongest divisions of the
Universal Negro Improvement Association that stands 100 per cent. for the
cause that you represent. Again, in Barrios, I had the privilege and good
fortune to be entertained by another "prince" of the race. I was entertained
by Mr. Ren[e]au,[5] who is known as the uncrowned king of Guatemala—a
black man; when you think of money you think of that man in Barrios. He is
a 100 per cent. U.N.I.A. and has bought to the limit in shares of the Black
Star Line. I was entertained by him most hospitably.

From Puerto Barrios I sailed for New Orleans and arrived there last
Wednesday morning [13 July]. Before I departed for the West Indies and
Central America I gave an itinerary to all the men of the council and to the
men of the field corps, and sent them out into different sections of this
country; and among the men I sent out was Colonel Adrian Johnson. All of
you are acquainted with Mr. Adrian Johnson during the convention here and
during the time preparatory to the convention when he was around Liberty
Hall and did splendid work for the cause. I sent him to the far South—New
Orleans, La. There were just about 100 or 200 members down there who
were not properly organized. I sent him to organize New Orleans, La.,
Mississippi and Alabama. He spent a couple of months in New Orleans, in
the heart of the South, and he took the 200 members to 2,500 when I arrived
there. (Cheers.) Johnson did splendid work in the South, and I do hope that
all the members of the Executive Council who were sent out will have a
record as good as Johnson's to present to the convention, because we have to

recognize men for their work and for their merit. Johnson was not satisfied only to be in New York; he went into the heart of the South; he went into jail, came out of jail and organized the U.N.I.A. for the better (Cheers), and I understand now that he has the heart to go into Texas, and from there I hope he is coming back to the convention. So you will see the stuff he is made up of.

When I arrived in New Orleans I found hundreds of loyal men—good men and true men—who were waiting to receive me through the great work that Johnson had done preparatory to my getting there. We had a time in New Orleans. I spoke for two nights in the National Park in New Orleans, where we had thousands of people, and there they celebrated the occasion just as they did in Costa Rica. They had a large plaza and they had midnight dances and other amusements. They had music, and they danced all night.

From New Orleans I journeyed to New York and arrived here at 9.15 last Sunday morning. I rested up on Sunday, because I was too tired to come out on Sunday night, and last night I appeared before you for the first time after being away for five months.

Now let me say in summing up my trip to the West Indies, that the Universal Negro Improvement Association stands now as a mighty rock. There is no speculating about it; there is no doubt about it. It stands as the "Rock of Ages," as far as anything human can stand for such a time. (Cheers.) Nobody dares think that they can permanently boycott or interfere with the success of the Universal Negro Improvement Association. (Cheers.) As I have often said from the platform of Liberty Hall, the Universal Negro Improvement Association is like a mighty avalanche which sweeps on and on. We have already swept the world; all that is left for us to do is to conquer Africa (cheers), that is all. We have already swept the world. There is no doubt about it, the U.N.I.A. is the strongest living force among Negroes. (Cheers.) It causes men, it causes races, it causes governments to tremble and to live in fear. But they need not tremble; they need not live in fear, because we do not want to do anybody harm. All that we want is a square deal. (Cheers.) I repeat what I said last night, we have no animus against any race; we are not organizing to fight any race, but we are organized to demand the things that are ours, and we are not going to give them up, we do not care how much you preach to us. We do not care how much you beg us to be quiet, we are not going to be quiet until you give us 100 per cent. of what we ask for. (Cheers.) And now let me tell you that you are the strongest point, and that is why you have so many enemies now—because you have become so significant, you have become so powerful they cannot afford to ignore you. Can you not remember four years ago Marcus Garvey standing on a step-ladder on Lenox avenue? Can you not remember that not even the ordinary policeman on the beat paid any attention to Marcus Garvey? What a change! To think that at that time the ordinary policeman would not notice Marcus Garvey, and today the governments of the world are noticing and are afraid of the Universal Negro Improvement Association. (Cheers.) This

Marcus Garvey that the ordinary policeman would not notice four years ago is causing governments to spend hundreds of dollars every day in cables asking where is Garvey. (Cheers.) Again I say, Garvey is still here, and "the more you look, the less you will see," and I feel that with the grace of God and with the blessing of our Divine Master I will still be here until we see the Promised Land. (Cheers.) And let me tell you, men, the vision of the Promised Land is not so far off after all. We have brought pressure to bear; and let me tell you, there are certain things that I cannot say and you may better understand them not said, but let me tell you, you are at your strongest point, and that is why the fellows are so worried; keep up the work, keep it up! You cannot af[f]ord to lose time and the money and the sacrifice you have made, because you are coming near the turning point. They are feeling your pressure. Remember it is not only Liberty Hall, but it is the world of organized Negroes; that is where the pressure comes from. There was once Garvey talking on Lenox avenue; now it is a matter of Garvey and the Universal Negro Improvement Association talking to the world over. Some tourists went to Jamaica the other day and paid me a compliment by coming back to New York and writing in the New York World, I believe, that when they arrived in Jamaica all they could hear was discussions of President Wilson and Marcus Garvey. Before I got there some other tourists said all they could hear about was Marcus Garvey and the Black Star Line. Wheresoever they have gone and they have come back, they have said that. It shows that you have made an impression the world over. That is what we wanted; that is what we were organized for, and the question is now not only Liberty Hall, New York, it is Liberty Hall everywhere. (Cheers.) They have been worried about Africa. My good friends, the British have said: "But why, this provisional president of Africa?" That is the thing that is troubling them. They do not know what part of Africa, and I won't tell them. (Laughter.)

That is all they are worried over. You have every cause to be satisfied with the work you have done. I have not given enough in money and in sacrifice to the Universal Negro Improvement Association because what has been done here already is enough satisfaction for me for all that I have done for the cause. Because wheresoever I go I see the change that has come about among Negroes. Negroes who used to submit to a kick and insult with a smile are standing up now and saying: "Man, what do you mean by it?" Not only in America, but through the West Indies and all through Central America; and if you once wear the colors of the Universal Negro Improvement Association—the red, the black and the green—nobody will molest you in Central America and in the West Indies. Do you know that during the war between Panama and Costa Rica the Costa Ricans invaded the Panamanian territory in Guabito, in the province of Almirante, in one particular section, and when they came they were looking for every Panamanian under the Panamanian flag, and the Panamanians ran out of the town and there was but one flag seen in that town in Guabito. It was the flag of the African republic—the red, the black and the green—and in the house over which that flag floated Panamanians and West Indians sheltered themselves for protection. When the Costa Ricans approached and asked what flag is that, the president of the division said "That is the flag of the republic of Africa." The Costa Ricans turned away and said "All right." (Cheers.) And for over forty-eight hours that was the only flag that gave protection to the Negro people who lived in that section called Guabito.[6] It was the only recognized flag, and any man who sheltered himself under that flag was not disturbed. It proves to you the force and the potency of this great movement. And as the Costa Rican soldiers had to turn away from the flag, in another few years we are going to have any government who dares to think of insulting the Negro turn away from it.

The movement is strong and that is why we have so many enemies at work. And the other people—I am not blaming them for it because they are great diplomats and because they might be misinformed—they may be adopting methods to protect themselves, but they have nothing to protect themselves against, because we are not trying to interfere with them. We are endeavoring to do them no harm; we are only trying to organize ourselves in a peaceful manner for our own protection. So white folks need not fear of Negroes, because if Negroes did not trouble them in the past they will not trouble them now. If when they were beating Negroes and killing Negroes we did not get even with them, I do not see why Negroes should interfere with them so long as they go about their business and allow Negroes to go about their business. (Cheers.) What we are suffering from now is not the enmity of the white man; we are suffering from the treachery of Negroes. We are our own enemies; that is all. The trouble we have had came not from the white man. Even in a few isolated cases where the white man shows up as the prosecutor he never originated the prosecution; it was the treacherous Negro who went there and begged him and worried him and induced him into doing what he did not care to do. Therefore I am not blaming the white people, because they are looking out for themselves, and Negroes will be fools if they do not look out for themselves. What I am engaged in doing is looking out for Negroes, because other folks are looking out for themselves. My embarrassment in not arriving in America before was because not through the white government of this country—not through the white men of this country—but because of the Negro traitors. The moment I left this country a certain class of men who had been fighting us all the time organized themselves into a band to influence this government by making misrepresentations to them to keep me out of the country because they feared the growing strength of the Universal Negro Improvement Association and the destruction of their hypocritical leadership. They found out that the people were getting away from them and that their positions were becoming unsafe, and they attributed it to the propagation of the Universal Negro Improvement Association, and for that reason they tried to destroy me, believing that if they smote the shepherd they would scatter the sheep.

But, thank God, there are many shepherds of the Universal Negro Improvement Association, and though they may not be shepherds of long occupation they are shepherds anyhow who can hold the fort until somebody comes. And I think when I delegated the Right Hon. the High Chancel[l]or the position of presiding over the meetings in Liberty Hall I struck a shepherd who had backbone. (Turning to the High Chancellor) Sir, I am to thank you and all those who helped you for so successfully conducting the meetings of Liberty Hall. I waited longingly for every copy of The Negro World to see what was going on in Liberty Hall, and as I said last night, I decided to remain out for so long simply because of the splendid reports I saw from Liberty Hall. I saw you had control over the people here and I was satisfied that Liberty Hall was safe. About three weeks ago when I saw that you were admonishing the enemies and encouraging the members who were somewhat restless, it was only then that I decided that it was time to come home, and I came home in time to help and rescue the situation. I am here now and I am ready for the enemies.

Let me say, as heretofore, to the "big" Negroes of this country who have been fighting the Universal Negro Improvement Association; let me say to Dr. Du Bois; let me say to Bishop Smith of Detroit, that I am here, and you will have to reckon with me here for another four years. It may not be permanently four [y]ears, because I have to go and come between here, Africa and other parts; but you will have to reckon with me because when Marcus Garvey starts a fight he will not stop until he has finished completely. I never interfered with Dr. Du Bois; I never interfered with Bishop Smith, but I am willing to fight them to the bitter end, and I am saying to Dr. Du Bois, "I accept your challenge between here and Paris." I accept Dr. Du Bois as the leader of the opposition to the Universal Negro Improvement Association's policy and program. There is much more in Dr. Du Bois' writing than you may see on the surface. Dr. Du Bois is the exponent of the reactionary class of men who have kept Negroes in serfdom and peonage. (Cheers.) My life is staked on the liberty and the freedom of the Negro everywhere. Dr. Du Bois will have the bitterest foeman in Marcus Garvey in putting over his program to the detriment of the Negro peoples of the world. I realize that he represents a party of compromise; I realize that in this African proposition many projects are advanced for the purpose of destroying the ultimate aim and object of the U.N.I.A. and many methods are adopted to forestall us in this work in which we are engaged. I can see that beneath the surface of Dr. Du Bois' writings. He may be scholarly; he may be from Harvard; he may be from Yale, but Marcus Garvey has been through some of the best schools of the world, and above all the schools, he is a graduate of the "academy of the world." (Loud and prolonged cheers.) I feel sure that the final analysis—the official reckoning—that the Universal Negro Improvement Association will have nothing to be ashamed of, because millions of us have pledged that the Red, the Black and the Green shall never trail in the dust.

We have carried the association for four years, until today it is a recognized emblem everywhere. It is not only recognized by Negroes, but it is recognized by all other races, and it is more than all recognized by governments. We have nothing to be ashamed of. They talk about intelligence; they talk about education; if they want to see intelligence; if they want to see education, they will have to come into the ranks of the Universal Negro Improvement Association. (Cheers.) Their talk about education is all a farce—is all bosh. It is only one of the ways and one of the methods for the purpose of prejudicing the minds of the people against the leadership of the Universal Negro Improvement Association, though they know well they cannot stand against the intellectuality of the U.N.I.A. I did it several months ago, and again I give out a challenge to Dr. Du Bois, graduate of Harvard and Yale as you are, to meet me on the platform of Liberty Hall at midnight, at noon time, or any time, and I will make you look like a bit of cotton. (Cheers.) If you think your education so superior this is your chance to defeat Marcus Garvey and close his mouth forever. That is my challenge to Dr. Du Bois and the class of men who call themselves intellectuals. Let them meet me if not on the platform of Liberty Hall, anywhere. I am willing to meet them anywhere, at any time, under any circumstances. I will be satisfied even to give them their own judge and jury. That is as far as I can go.

Let it be known, men, that before this convention of 1921 adjourns we feel sure that we will so legislate and so act that it will be impossible for traitors to be able to damage the Universal Negro Improvement Association after the 31st of August. I have to thank you for your presence here tonight, and let me reassure you that the Universal Negro Improvement Association is a moving power that has already encircled the world. I have again to thank you for the splendid support, morally and financially, that you have given this great cause. I pray God's blessing on you. I trust He will guide and help you so that you will continue the work you have started. Good night! I hope to see you tomorrow night, when I will speak on the subject of the Black Star Line. (Cheers.)

Printed in *NW*, 30 July 1921. Original headlines omitted.

1. Dr. Alfredo Zayas y Alfonso.

2. The 1927 census listed 17,245 Jamaicans living in Costa Rica, most of whom were employees of the United Fruit Co. in Limón Province. Jamaican immigration to Costa Rica and Panama was cyclical, beginning in the 1870s and reaching a peak in the decades from 1881 to 1891 and from 1911 to 1921 (Michael D. Olien, "The Adaptation of West Indian Blacks to North American and Hispanic Culture in Costa Rica," in Annon Pescatello, ed., *Old Roots in New Lands* [Westport, Conn.: Greenwood Press, 1977]; Roy S. Bryce-Laporte, "West Indian Labor in Central America: Limón, Costa Rica, 1870–1948," Paper presented at the symposium "The Political Economy of the Black World," Center for Afro-American Studies, University of California, Los Angeles, May 1979).

3. The *Workman*, a black-owned West Indian newspaper published in Colón, Panama, reported on the meetings in Costa Rica: "It is understood that free trains were given and there was a rush of both white and colored people to hear him [Garvey], paying without scruple $2.00 for front seats" (23 April 1921).

4. A reference to Isaiah Morter, the wealthy black planter from Belize who bequeathed property valued at about $100,000 to the UNIA. Morter was knighted by Garvey, who made

him a knight commander of the Distinguished Service Order of Ethiopia. When Morter died in 1924, the UNIA became involved in a lengthy legal battle to secure the property he had left. The UNIA eventually divided into two factions after Garvey was deported to Jamaica, with one group having its headquarters in New York City and the other group under the leadership of Garvey in Jamaica. The New York City–based group, called the UNIA, Inc., eventually won control over Morter's property (Amy Jacques Garvey, ed., *The Philosophy and Opinions of Marcus Garvey* [New York: Universal Publishing House, 1923 and 1925; rpt., Atheneum, 1969] 2: 90–92).

5. George C. Reneau was a black merchant in Puerto Barrios who purchased two hundred shares of BSL stock in 1920 (*NWCB*, 7 August 1920).

6. The long-standing border dispute between Costa Rica and Panama erupted on 21 February 1921, when a small contingent of Costa Rican troops invaded the town of Coto in the province of Chiriqui. Panama recaptured Coto, prompting a Costa Rican retaliation on Guabito and Almirante on 4 March 1921. The United Fruit Co., whose headquarters at Port Limón had been attacked, provided food and transportation to the Costa Rican forces (William D. McCain, *The United States and the Republic of Panama* [New York: Russell & Russell, 1965]).

J. Edgar Hoover to William L. Hurley

WASHINGTON, D.C. July 20, 1921

Dear Mr. Hurley:

Reference is made to previous correspondence concerning GABRIEL M. JOHNSON.[1] For your information I have to advise you that this individual was admitted at the port of New York by the immigration authorities on the 16th instant.

There is inclosed herewith copy of a report of AGENT STARR under date of the 14th instant, which shows the result of this investigation from the time this individual arrived at Ellis Island. Very truly yours,

J. E. HOOVER
Special Assistant to
the Attorney General

DNA, RG 59, file 880-L-2. TLS, recipient's copy.

1. Hurley had advised J. Edgar Hoover to instruct the customs authorities to give Johnson "a thorough medical examination" with the possibility that he might be excluded on medical grounds (Hoover to George F. Ruch, 14 July 1921, DNA, RG 65, file BS 198940).

Enclosure

NEW YORK, N.Y. 7/14/21

RE: HON. G. M. JOHNSON, K. C., POTENTATE OF THE
U.N.I.A. (AFRICA) NEGRO ACTIVITIES.

Pursuant to instructions of Special Agent J. G. Tucker, and accompanied by Agent Drennan, Agent proceeded to Pier 8, East River, and after conferring with Customs authorities, boarded the Spanish Royal Mail Steamship "LEON XIII", locating Immigration Inspector FEDER, who informed us that he had interviewed subject, GABRIEL M. JOHNSON, who arrived on this vessel from Liberia, via Spain.

Mr. FEDER informed us that subject had denied knowing MARCUS GARVEY and also denied having any connection with GARVEY's organization.

Agents interviewed subject, who in answer to questions stated that he was and is acquainted with Garvey and with REVEREND ELLEGOR and also with CHANCELLOR STEWART, all of whom are connected with the GARVEY organization,—the UNIVERSAL NEGRO IMPROVEMENT ASSOCIATION.

Mr. Johnson further stated that he is himself an officer in the organization but did not know whether he could continue to belong to it, as he did not agree with the modus [ope]randi of the organization; stating that while in the U.S. he will visit Baltimore, where he can be reached through MISS LOUISE PARN, a cousin, of 1915 Druid Hill Avenue.

He further stated that he will visit Philadelphia and can be reached there thru Mrs. E. C. KINCH, 2416 MOLE STREET; that he will also visit Boston; that during his stay in New York City he can be reached at #2106 MADISON AVENUE, c/o MRS. TOMPKINS.

Subject stated that he is a citizen of Liberia, born in Monrovia; fifty-one years of age; occupation—contractor and builder (this is also the occupation given on the passport); stated that he had been employed at times as an accountant and bookkeeper.

Subject has made two visits to the United States, according to his answers, one in 1911 when he spent six weeks in the States, arriving on the s/s ARABIC some time during July or August; again in 1920 he spent two or three months here, arriving about the middle of July on the Steamship ISLE DE PANAI of the Spanish Royal Mail Line. On this latter trip part of his expenses were paid by a group of persons in Liberia who were interested in ascertaining the nature and purpose of the GARVEY organization. Mr. Johnson stated that this trip was made with the approval of PRESIDENT KING of Liberia.

The present trip is made at his own expense and was not discussed with PRESIDENT KING, owing to the latter's absence from Liberia. In this connection it is deemed important to call attention to an admission made by Mr. Johnson in reply to a question as to whether or not he had sent a wireless message from the "LEON XIII." He replied that he had sent a wireless message to REV. ELLEGOR of Yonkers, New York, and under further questioning admitted that the wireless message had been addressed to the UNIVERSAL NEGRO IMPROVEMENT ASSOCIATION thru their cable address: UNIMPRO, New York.

Subject informed us that PRESIDENT KING of Liberia is married to subject's niece and that "JUSTICE" JOHNSON, who is on the Liberian Commission now in the U.S. with PRESIDENT KING, is subject's brother.

Subject has a wife and six children in Liberia and has some distant relatives in various parts of the United States.

He stated that the purpose of his present visit is as given on his visa application—"to visit relatives and friends for a period of about four months." It will be noted that in answer to the question on the application— "Address of last residence in U.S.?" subject answered, "None". When this was called to his attention he stated that that was the way it was filled out at the consulate and that the U.S. Consul in Liberia knew that he (Johnson) had made a previous trip to the U.S. as they had crossed on the same boat.

Subject admitted that he is a small stockholder in the BLACK STAR LINE but is not an officer of the organization.

While subject answered all other questions willingly and frankly, he would not answer a question as to the amount of salary which he received from GARVEY's organization, altho he did admit that he is—and was—on the payroll.

In answer to the question concerning his salary, he stated that the MRS. E. C. KINCH (of Philadelphia) above referred to is his agent in the U.S. and has documents authorizing her to draw whatever funds may become due him from the organization as required. He stated to agent that this question was one he could not and did not feel inclined to answer.

He informed us that his purpose in visiting the country was purely commercial; that he expected to sell some African products and purchase general merchandise and that he would probably sever his connection with the GARVEY organization.

While awaiting the arrival of the Steamship, Agent observed several colored individuals who constituted what appeared to be a reception committee for subject. One of these telephoned to "HARLEM 2877" (the telephone number of the headquarters of the UNIVERSAL NEGRO IMPROVEMENT ASSOCIATION) and endeavored to get in touch with COUNC[I]LLOR SMITH. He was referred to a COUNC[I]LLOR MATTHEWS. During the conversation—such of it as your agent was able to overhear—the speaker referred to himself over the phone as CHANCELLOR STEWART. Al[th]o agent was unable to overhear all the conversation, it was evident that they were discussing the detention of MARCUS GARVEY upon his arrival at New Orleans and they were seeking to get in touch with COUNC[I]LLOR SMITH to prevent a rep[e]tition of such a delay in the arrival of subject JOHNSON.

Also waiting—and obviously noticeable by the resplendency of their full military regalia—were some other five or six colored dignitaries who devoted the waiting time to practise of proper and formal reception. This military detail was still waiting for subject's arrival when Agents left the pier.

Subject was detained by the Immigration authorities for further examination. Agent conferred with Landing Officer, Mr. Moulton, and learned from him that subject will be landed at ten o'clock tomorrow morning, the 15th inst. and sent to Ellis Island,[1] at which time his baggage will be examined.

Agent, with Agent Drennan, left the dock about 1 P.M. and returned to Bureau office, the reception committee and "military escort" still waiting for subject's arrival. . . .

GEO. J. STARR

DNA, RG 59, file 880-L-2. TD.

1. At the request of the Bureau of Investigation, Gabriel Johnson was taken before a special board of inquiry at Ellis Island. The bureau informed the immigration authorities that the State Department had filed a complaint against Johnson. The special board of inquiry indicated that it would detain Johnson if data regarding the radicalism of the UNIA could be furnished. Charges against Johnson were soon dropped, however, since Garvey himself had been readmitted three days earlier (Charles J. Scully to Lewis Baley, 16 July 1921, DNA, RG 65, file 198940-197; Mortimer J. Davis to J. Edgar Hoover, 27 July 1921, DNA, RG 65, file BS 198940-214).

William C. Matthews to William H. Ferris

[[303 Old South Bldg., Boston, July 20, 1921]]

My dear Professor:

I would like to have the members of the Universal Negro Improvement Association throughout the world to be advised of the excellent services rendered them by Colonel Henry Lincoln Johnson, the only member of our race who is a member of the Republican National Committee (and lately named by President Harding as Recorder of the Deeds for the District of Columbia) in the matter of valuably assisting me in securing the admission into this country of His Highness, the Potentate, Gabriel Johnson, Mayor of Monrovia. Colonel Johnson gladly and willingly assisted me in bringing to a successful termination this splendid piece of work, and it was made possible by the high regard in which he is held by the Secretary of Labor, Hon. James J. Davis.[1] Very truly yours,

WILLIAM C. MATTHEWS
Assistant Counselor General

Printed in *NW*, 30 July 1921. Original headlines omitted.

1. James John Davis (1873–1947) was appointed secretary of labor by President Harding in March 1921. He continued in the same position under presidents Coolidge and Hoover, leaving office in 1930 (*WWW*).

Speech by Marcus Garvey

[[NEW YORK, July 2[4], 1921]]

... Right Hon. Members of the Executive Council, Members and Friends of the Universal Negro Improvement Association: I am pleased to be with you tonight. I desire to speak for a short while from the subject of "Leadership"; that is, as far as that leadership relates to the great movement known as the Universal Negro Improvement Association, and as that leadership affects the Negro race at large. ...

The world has reached the turning point of humanity. The world has reached the crossroads of humanity, when each race will travel in its own direction, when each national group will travel in its own avenue. Let the Anglo-Saxon go the way he desires to go. Let the Frenchman go the way he desires; let the Teuton go the way he desires to go; we are now organizing the 400,000,000 Negroes so that they can go the way they desire to go. (Cheers.) Now, we cannot travel that way without leadership. Where is the leadership? I call upon Du Bois, who for years represented himself as a leader, and I ask him, "In what direction are you traveling?" and his answer is, "Wheresoever the white man bids me go there shall I travel." (Laughter.) I call upon Moton and ask him, "Whither leadest thou?" and he says, "Wheresoever my master leads I will follow." I call upon Kelly Miller and ask him, "Whither leadest thou?" and he says, "By the bidding of my master shall I follow." And I come back to the 400,000,000 Negroes of the world and I ask, "Are you prepared to be led that way?" and a universal answer comes to me, "No! We shall not be led in that direction." And by that answer I realize that you demand a new leadership—a leadership that will not compromise, a leadership that will not falter, a leadership that will not give up when the hour seems dark; a leader that will start and continue the journey until victory perches upon the banner of the Red, the Black and the Green. (Cheers.) A leadership that counts not for a dark hour is a leadership misplaced, because in all leadership that leads to liberty, freedom and human emancipation there has always been a dark hour. All victories have been won just at the turning point of the dark hour. There is always a silver lining, and the leader who thinks that the dark hour will not come in the struggle of the Negro is a leader who is indeed misplaced. We have seen experiences and trials in the Universal Negro Improvement Association, but our dark hour has not yet come. The dark hour is the hour when you apparently seem to be losing out, yet you have courage enough to fight on until victory comes your way. That is the dark hour which each and every one of you must prepare for. That dark hour may be tomorrow; that dark hour may be five or ten years or twenty years from now; but I want you to realize that you must prepare for the dark hour. It may meet you in America; it may meet you in the West Indies; it may meet you on the battle plains of Africa; but wheresoever it meets you you must be ready. (Cheers.) And you would not be true and loyal members of the U.N.I.A. if you did not count for a dark hour. The dark hour may never come, but it is best to prepare for that hour as you march on from one success to the other, because the history of the Universal Negro Improvement Association reveals one continuous line of successes—one triumph after another. How many fights and battles have we won? Innumerable battles and fights we have won and there are other battles still to be encountered—other fights still to be won. Let us prepare for them.

If I can interpret correctly the spirit of Negroes, it is for me to say that Negroes everywhere are determined to be free, determined to be liberated; liberated from lynch law, liberated from mob rule, liberated from segregation, liberated from Jim Crowism, liberated from injustice. That is the spirit of Negroes everywhere. It is not found in any one country because Negroes have been taken advantage of everywhere. It is a universal desire and it is a universal program that seeks to liberate Negroes everywhere.

It is well the world knows and understands that as men we are determined to live as men and determined to die as men. (Cheers.) We recognize no superman in creation; we recognize the [e]quality of men and because man is equal we feel that man has no right to take advantage of man. Thus it would be a conflict between men where advantage is hurled at man by man. Let the world understand that 400,000,000 Negroes are determined to die for liberty. If we must die we shall die nobly. We shall die gallantly fightin[g] on the battle heights of Africa to plant the standard that represents liberty. (Cheers.)

Some people seem to misunderstand us in this African question. They desire us to locate the part of Africa we intend to fight. (Laughter.) Now, you know that no general is going to give away his plans, and we never told anybody we are going to fight, anyhow. We only say that if you remain there until we get there, what happens to you is not our fault. That is all we say. If you want to interpret that as fighting, that is your business. Now listen, some people try to misrepresent us by saying that we are going to locate ourselves at a certain place in Africa and start fighting from there. I want to disavow any knowledge of any particular place where we are going to start from, because anywhere I land I am going to start to fight right there. (Cheers and Laughter.)

We feel that the time has come for universal action. I really would like to have the world understand the Negro so that there can be no blame given to the Negro for hiding his attitude, for suppressing his intention, for stultifying his desires. The old leadership represented us as a race of beggars. The old leadership represented us as wanting only an industrial school and a few churches; the old leadership said we were satisfied to shout, "Give me Jesus and take the world." (Laughter.) The old leadership represented us as wanting to have no hand in politics, but that we were satisfied to cast our vote for Tom, Dick and Harry of any other race without trying to exercise it in our own behalf. That is a misrepresentation of the new Negro, and if any of the old leaders make any such representations they are misinterpreting the spirit of the new Negro. That is a warning to civilization; that is a notice to the world. We no longer are satisfied with industrial schools and churches only; we are no longer satisfied to have the vote and not to exercise it in our own behalf. The vote represents political liberty and the new Negro desires to give his ballot for an alderman of his race, for a congressman of his race, for a senator of his race, and for a president of his race. (Loud Cheers.) He says if you will not give me an opportunity because you outnumber me by mob violence—if you will not give me an opportunity to cast my vote for my own alderman, congressman, senator or president in one part of the world, I will make it possible to cast it in another part of the world. (Cheers.) The new Negro says, not only churches, not only industrial schools, but we want parliament houses, houses of Congress, national museums, national art galleries, great institutions of learning of our own. The old Negro representing the Negro as being satisfied to be a subject without rights, is a misrepresentation. The new Negro demands a leadership which will establish his right to rule. If it is right for the yellow man to rule, it is also right for the black man to rule. (Cheers.) We say rule on, great white man; rule on, great yellow man, and we are now saying rule on, great 400,000,000 black men. Creation opened with many distinct races; I cannot enumerate them, but creation will also close with those many distinct races, and when the end comes and other races answer here, I am quite sure the Negro will be among those who will answer "here." They may exterminate the North American Indian; they may exterminate the aborigines of Australia; they may exterminate the aborigines of the various countries they have conquered, but there is one race that they shall never—will never exterminate, and that is the Negro race. (Cheers.) I would like to see the race that would be so audacious as to make the attempt to exterminate the black race of today—a race of warriors who have never fought—warriors whose deeds in war have never been reckoned because they have never been performed. They talk about the New York 15th; that was only an experiment in warfare. (Cheers.) They talk about the Illinois 8th; that was only a pastime for the boys. They talk about the prowess of the West Indian regiments; those fellows were only having a picnic; it was a gala day. No man has ever yet seen the Negro fighting at his best, because the Negro has never yet fought for himself. (Loud and prolonged cheers.)

Civilization and statesmanship have flattered themselves that there shall be peace, but intelligent students of political economy and political science know that there will be war and rumors of war. And all political students know that the world is more preparing for war today than ever before. And all students of political history and political science know that at any moment humanity will face its common battleground. The world of political scientists know that the conflict may originate in Asia as well as it may originate in Europe; but to be originated we know it will; and all races and all peoples are preparing for it. The old leadership of the Negro prepared for nothing. We foresee the conflict of races, and we know that no conflict in the future or at the present can be successfully decided except the Negro casts his vote. I do not only mean politically this time by going to the ballot box, but cast his vote on the battlefield. No conflict can be successfully decided until the Negro has put his hand in it. And I am warning the races and nations of the world not to forget and not to ignore the Negro.

The old leadership of Negroes recorded nothing. They have no record of lynch law; they have no record of mob violence; they have no record of injustice; they have no record of segregation; they have no record of brutalizing the Negro; but the New Negro has a record of everything that is done to him (Cheers) and when anything goes on later on, the first thing the Negro is going to do is to present his record, and he is going to ask you what you are going to do about it, and you have to decide clearly and positively before he will lend his hand. We appreciate and we love the civilization that we gave to the world. Thousands of years ago when the white man was a savage the Negro was the custodian of civilization. The Negro held civilization and in turn handed it to the white man to keep. You will always love your property anywhere you see it. If I have a suit of old clothes and I give it to somebody, anytime I see that suit I smile, because I loved it before I bought it. And this civilization that the white man has was not originally his. The Negro gave it to him; therefore the Negro loves the civilization as held today by the white man, and the Negro when fighting will always fight to preserve the civilization that he gave to the white man, that is, to maintain it and keep it; but since the white man has it and claims it, we want him to understand that we are going to fight for it on condition. It is an easy thing to take away something you gave to somebody else. We do not want to take away civilization; we want to share it up. We say to the white man, take a part of civilization and give us our part. We will help you to live with your civilization and whenever your civilization is in trouble you can call on us and we will help you out of it; but the condition is, give us what is belonging to us. That is all we ask. I feel sure that there is no statesman in the world foolish enough to ignore the fighting force or power of the Negro. I cannot see where narrowminded men get their argument from; brutalizing the Negro and legalizing it; Jimcrowing the Negro and legalizing it, when they know that the Negro is a man and nothing can be decided in the world except the Negro is in it. (Cheers.) In the time of peace you kick down a man, you slap him in the face, and when you are in trouble you want that man to help you; are you not a fool? I trust the world will understand the new attitude of the Negro. We are not giving to you more than you give to us. Give us a kick and we return the kick; give us a smile and we return the smile—and you know nobody can smile like the Negro. (Laughter.) He smiles broadest and he fights longest.

I feel that we are nearing the point where all the races will get together and compromise the issue of life; but not until the Negro is lifted to the highest standard of humanity; not until the Negro is given the privileges and opportunities of other races; not until then will we sit around the table of peace—the table at which humanity will end its troubles. This is my message to you tonight, and I trust you will keep it with you and transmit it to your friends or colleagues or coworkers in the cause of African freedom. Realize, men, that the call of this hour is for new leadership, not the leadership Du Bois gives, not the leadership Moton gives—the leadership that is satisfied with industrial schools and the leadership that is satisfied with an annual donation from the white philanthropists, and so long as that donation comes regularly we are satisfied and come to a compromise and want us to "close ranks" at a time when we ought to open ranks. Remember that the Negro cannot be bought by charity alone; in fact, we want no charity; we are not beggars, we are not paupers, we are not lepers; we only want a chance.

At this time some of the white people say "you Negroes are getting too impertinent and, because of that, we are going to turn you out of your jobs and give them to white folks." They don't know that they are doing a dangerous thing. Do you know what government means? Government means the protection of human rights. Government means the protection of the property of the people who make up the nation. Do you know why they keep soldiers and battleships? Not for ornaments, but to protect the nation's property. Just a few years ago the property of the world was in danger, and they would have lost every penny they ever had were it not for the fact that 2,000,000 black men went to France and Flanders and drove the Teutons out of France and Belgium when white men failed to do it. (Cheers.) Do you know that were it not for the 2,000,000 Negroes who fought in the war the white men who fought on the side of the Allies would have lost everything they had; they would have had to pay over to Germany a huge war indemnity? Do you know that 2,000,000 black men left their business in Africa, in the West Indies and America and went over to France and Flanders and Mesopotamia and fought and saved the Allied nations? Let me tell you this: If you are employed by white men and they choose to dismiss you because of color tell him, "Brother, you remember the last war; all right, another one may come." That is your trump card. You are not begging for jobs; you demand jobs because you made it possible for them to live in peace (Cheers), otherwise the Germans would have been at their door. You have a fair exchange for the money that is given to you. Let them know this: that your future service depends upon their present good treatment.

Now I must close for tonight. On Monday, the 1st of August, the biggest convention of races will assemble in New York with 50,000 delegates representing the Negro peoples of the world, who will assemble here to sit for 31 days and 31 nights to discuss the problems that confront this race of ours. We are coming to create new legislation for the government of 400,000,000 Negroes, and already some of the delegates are here, and they are coming from all quarters. By next Saturday we will have between 30,000 and 50,000 delegates here in New York. Monday week at 9:30 we will assemble in this hall for a religious service to open the convention. At one o'clock we will—50,000 of us—join in a great parade and march through the district of Harlem. At 8 o'clock the same night we will assemble at the 12th Regiment Armory at 62d street and Columbus avenue, where we will officially celebrate the opening of the second International Convention of Negroes. It will be declared open by His Highness, the Potentate, Hon. Gabriel Johnson, Mayor of Monrovia, Liberia. I trust all of you will do your best to scatter the information to advertise the convention so as to make a success of it. . . .

Printed in *NW*, 30 July 1921. Original headlines omitted.

Report by Special Agent P-138

NEW YORK, N.Y. 7/25/21

IN RE: MARCUS GARVEY

I had a short talk with GARVEY today [*22 July*] in his private office. He told me that he was about to make a radical change in his organization by discharging some of his high officers. Just as soon as the convention convenes he will start reorganization. He stated that some of his men were working against him and to the detriment of his organization. He left to speak in Philadelphia tonight.

P-138

[*Endorsement*] NOTED F. D. W.

DNA, RG 65, file BS 198940-210. TD. Stamped endorsement.

Second Annual Report of the Black Star Line

[*New York*] July 26, 1921

BLACK STAR LINE, INC. OF DELAWARE

MINUTES OF REGULAR MEETING OF STOCKHOLDERS

The Stockholders of the Black Star Line, Inc., met in annual meeting at 120 West 138th Street at 8.30 P.M., July 26, 1921.

The meeting was called to order and presided over by the Right Hon. Marcus Garvey, President of the Company. The Secretary of the Company Mr. Elie Garcia, acted as Secretary of the meeting.

The minutes of the preceding annual meeting were then read and approved.

The President of the Company gave to the stockholders a lengthy report of his trip to the West Indies and Central America for the purpose of developing new business for the Company and bringing new investment. He related some of his unfortunate experience on board the S/S "Kanawha" due to the incompetency and disloyalty of the crew. Before closing his address, the following letters were read by him to the stockholders.

Hon. Marcus Garvey
President, B. S. L., N.Y. City,
Honorable Sir:
    Owing to the numerous transactions pending for settlement, it is almost impossible for me to furnish you with a balance sheet which will reflect the true conditions of the Company, therefore I am asking that you use your influence to bring about an adjournment of the stockholders' meeting. Respectfully yours,

ELIE GARCIA
Secretary

Same letter signed by Tobias, Treasurer.

On the strength of the above letters the President placed the request with the stockholders for an adjournment.

It was moved by Mr. R. Hicks and seconded by Mr. Nicholas Carter that the meeting be adjourned until October 26th, 1921.

The motion was carried by a large majority of votes and the meeting adjourned.

[MARCUS GARVEY]
President
ELIE GARCIA
Secretary

Garvey v. *United States*, no. 8317, Ct. App., 2d Cir., 2 February 1925, government exhibit no. 144.

E. R. Conners, Master, S.S. *Kanawha*, to Charles L. Latham

[*Kingston, Jamaica, 27 July 1921*]

Sir:
    Confirming my statements to you of July 26th. and of this morning, I have to state that the steamer KANAWHA has been ordered to sail for New York, and that I am unwilling to sail on the vessel under the present conditions.

    I wish to make formal protest to you that I do not consider the KANAWHA seaworthy and safe for the proposed voyage. The matter is not only one of personal risk for I consider that I have the responsibility for the thirty or forty persons on board who would be in jeopardy of their lives.

I have reached the conclusion that the vessel is unseaworthy from careful observations extending over a period of four months, and especially upon observation and reports made to me during the past month that I have been acting as Master. The vessel is continually blowing out boiler tubes even while at dock and without full normal pressure of steam. In addition to this, it appears the KANAWHA has been unable recently to make even short trial runs without shortage of fresh water for the boilers occurring. She has a record of having often to make port in distress on account of water shortage and has twice left Kingston and had to return back. If the vessel sails as she is, I believe it will in a very short time lie helpless at sea on account of boiler and engine trouble and exhaustion of fresh water.

A local pilot has refused to take the KANAWHA even to and from the dock on account of his knowledge that the engines are not working properly and that the vessel was unable to make (on July the 25th) even a short run to Port Royal, in this harbor, without a break-down on the way back.

I hereby make a formal complaint and protest that the vessel is in an unsuitable condition to go to sea and I request you to appoint surveyors to make an examination of the vessel.

In view of the risk to lives of crew and passengers, please appoint the strongest surveyors available. I understand that Mr. McInnes who has made certain surveys in connection with previous repairs to the vessel is not available at the present time on account of his confinement to bed due to illness. I think it is well that some, at least, of the surveyors be new men to the case so that their judgment will be additional to those previously given. I am, Sir, Very respectfully yours,

E. R. CONNERS[1]
Master Steamship KANAWHA

DNA, RG 41, file 122539-N. TL, carbon copy.

1. E. R. Conners's letter and a similar written statement by A. A. Zinc, chief mate of the *Kanawha*, were forwarded by Charles Latham to the U.S. secretary of state on 28 July 1921 (DNA, RG 41, file 122539-N).

Marcus Garvey to E. T. Chamberlain, Commissioner of Navigation

New [Y]ork NY. July 29, 1921

American consul Latham at Kingston Jamaica has constantly acted within the last two months to detain in Kingston Jamaica the American ship Kanawha by unfair rulings and by prejudice against the Black Star Line Corporation. His action has detained this boat with a crew of forty two men for over two months preventing the boat to sail for her destination to New York much to the loss of the corporation[.] Charges against his action are being prepared but immediate release of boat is requested so as to save the terrible expense of keeping the crew and detaining passengers in a foreign port after everything has been done to live up to the marine regulations of this country. Please be good enough to order consul Latham to release boat to continue trip to New York destination and port of registry.

BOARD OF DIRECTORS OF BLACK STAR LINE
MARCUS GARVEY, Prest.

DNA, RG 41, file 123858-N. TG, recipient's copy.

O. M. Thompson to Marcus Garvey

[*New York*] July 29th, 1921

Dear Sir:

For your information, a Contract has been drawn up by Mr. Nolan between Black Star Line and the D. F. Leary Company[1] of 45 Pearl Street, to take care of loading the "Phyllis Wheatley" on her outward trip to Africa.

Cargo will be received from any of the ports along the route covering Havana, St. Thomas, Barbados, Demerara, Trinidad and West Africa, providing the cargo offered is of sufficient quantity to warrant stopping at the West Indian ports mentioned.

The final requirement of the Shipping Board in order for us to take the title to the "Phyllis Wheatley," is a Performance Bond, this Bond has been applied for and the matter is now before the Board and will be dealt with at their next meeting which we expect will take place today. Very truly yours,

O. M. THOMPSON

Marcus Garvey v. *United States*, no. 8317, Ct. App., 2d Cir., 2 February 1925, defendant's exhibit VV, p. 2,717.

1. The Black Star Line signed a contract with the D. F. Leary Co. on 3 May 1921. Under the agreement, the Leary Co. would become the loading agent for the *Phyllis Wheatley*, receiving a commission of 5 percent on the gross amount of the steamer's manifest. While the Black Star Line retained the right to book cargo on the ship, hire stevedores, and arbitrate union disputes, the Leary Co. would handle the details of engaging the freight, loading the ship, collecting payments for shipping the freight, and paying all expenses from the money collected. After all of these financial matters were completed, the Leary Co. would take its 5 percent, and the Black Star Line would receive the balance of the freight money (*Garvey* v. *United States*, no. 8317, Ct. App., 2d Cir., 2 February 1925, pp. 2,728–2,730).

Reports by Special Agent P-138

New York, N.Y. 7/30/21

NEGRO ACTIVITIES.

. . . For some unknown reason all the officials of the BLACK STAR LINE and Garvey's other organizations seem to have undergone a change of mind. They are very patriotic in their speeches and have eliminated all the anti-white talks and in its place preaching loyalty to the U.S.A.

P-138

DNA, RG 65, file BS 198940-217. TD.

New York, N.Y. 7/30/21

There must be something which has caused MARCUS GARVEY to change his views so suddenly. I called on him today [*24 July*] and while waiting to see him I could hear him dictating a speech loudly to his stenographer. He spoke of the kind treatment which the government had accorded him and praised Secretary Hughes for allowing him to reenter the U.S.A. pledging his organization's support to the U.S.A. always. He said he is not against any white government but was against DR. DU BOIS and EMMETT SCOTT who were instrumental in trying to keep him out. GARVEY is now more patriotic and is preaching nothing but loyalty to the flag. His recent experience must have taught him to take another sane[*r*] course. However, I shall see how long he will keep it up.

P-138

[*Endorsements*] FILE G. F. R.
NOTED F. D. W.

DNA, RG 65, file BS 198940-218. TD. Stamped endorsements.

NEW YORK, N.Y. July 30. 1921

I visited a stockholders meeting at the BLACK STAR LINE tonight [*26 July*] where over 2,000 were present.

GARVEY asked them to postpone the meetings for 90 days owing to the fact that there were a lot of stealing and robbery by his employees, especially those who were entrusted in getting the new ship.[1] He intimated that O. M. THOMPSON, his vice-president and general manager was double-crossing him[,] also his ex-captain named RICHARDSON.

The stockholders were so enraged they threatened to mob them. The meeting broke up into a free-for-all fight and the police had to be called in.

P-138

[*Endorsement*] NOTED F. D. W.

DNA, RG 65, file BS 198940-220. TD. Stamped endorsement.

1. The *New York News*, an anti-Garvey newspaper, reported that Garvey asked for a postponement of the meeting "until better investigation could be made as to [why] they had not got the 'Philis Wheetly' " (*New York News*, 30 July 1921).

NEW YORK, N.Y. 7/30/21

There is quite a lot of discontentment growing in the ranks of Garvey followers [*27 July*], especially those who invested in the Black Star Line. They are disgusted after last night stockholders meeting. They feel it is a losing game and their money is gone. Just what will be the reaction is hard to say but from the general outlook something is bound to happen.

P-138

DNA, RG 65, file BS 198940-221. TD.

Article by John E. Bruce

[*Negro World*, 30 July 1921]

The "middle class" having struck out for itself under the splendid leadership of the intrepid Marcus Garvey, without the aid or consent of white wet nurses, or the O.K. of the self-styled "better class," calling itself "colored," which takes itself very seriously, quite naturally must excite the fears and apprehensions of the former as to its ability to function without its superior guidance and the wise and sapient counsel of the latter—whose much learning hath made it mad. The middle class will continue to go on in the even tenor of its way, regardless of either of these superfluous elements now that it has gotten its stride and only requests that they will attend to their own business and permit it to do the same. We are a little bit surprised at the learned and self-sufficient John Crosby Gordon's deliberate and gratuitous slander that a color line exists in the U.N.I.A.

There never was an organization of black and colored people in America in which the color line is so conspicuous by its absence and so unpopular as in the U.N.I.A. There is absolutely no friction or fooling, and no intention to encourage this crass nonsense. Mr. Gordon is badly advised, and as a gentlemen of light and leading, he ought to apologize, unless he can give specific proofs of his mischievous (I will not say malicious) statement. Produce your facts, Mr. John [C]rosby, and be specific. "No, 'tis slander whose edge is sharper than the sword, whose tongue out-venoms all the worms of Nile." The people who comprise the membership of the U.N.I.A. are at least intelligent enough to understand that the destiny of all the peoples of the Negroid races, whether their hair is straightened or crisp, is identical. They have neither the time nor the patience to quibble about color or class. This is left to the "intellectual" snobs among us who are constantly in word and act quarreling with the Almighty because he made them black or colored, and who are trying by artificial means to improve on his handiwork. Mr. John Crosby Gordon will act the part of a very wise man by preserving a discreet silence as to what the U.N.I.A. is and stands for. We deny emphatically that the condition precedent to admission to its ranks is color. Mr. Gordon affirms that it is. Let him give a specific case, supported by facts, since he knows so much about the workings of the organization, or keep silent.

Printed in *NW*, 30 July 1921.

A Membership Appeal from Marcus Garvey to the Negro Citizens of New York[1]

[*New York, July 1921*]

Fellow men and women:

I greet you in the name of the Universal Negro Improvement Association, and African Communities League of the World.

You may ask what Organization is that? It is for me to inform you that the Universal Negro Improvement Association, is an Organization that seeks to unite into one solid body, the 400 million Negroes of the world, to link up the 15 million Negroes of the United States of America, with the 20 million Negroes of the West Indies, the 40 million Negroes of South and Central America, with the 280 million Negroes of Africa for the purpose of bettering our industrial, commercial, educational, social and political condition.

As you are aware, the world in which we live to-day, is divided into separate race groups, and distinct nationalities. Each race, and each nationality endeavoring to work out its own destiny, to the exclusion of other races, and other nationalities. We hear the cry of England for the English, of France for the French, of Germany for the Germans, of Ireland for the Irish, of Palestine for the Jew, of Japan for the Japanese, of China for the Chinese. We of the Universal Negro Improvement Association are raising the cry of Africa for the Africans, those at home and those abroad.

There are 400 million Africans in the world who have Negro blood coursing through their veins, and we believe that the time has come to unite these 400 million people for the one common purpose of bettering their condition.

The greatest problem of the Negro for the last five hundred years, has been that of disunity.

No individual or no Organization ever succeeded in uniting the Negro race, but within the last four years, the Universal Negro Improvement Association has worked wonders in bringing together in one fold, four million organized Negroes, who are scattered in all parts of the world, being in the 48 States of the American Union, all the West Indian Islands, and the countries of South and Central America, and in Africa. These four million people are working to convert the rest of the 400 millions scattered all over the world, and it is for this purpose that we are asking you to join our ranks, and do the best you can to help us to bring about an emancipated race in the strictest sense of the word.

You will realise that this an age of Organization. The individual cannot live by himself, he can accomplish very little by himself. If anything praiseworthy is to be done, it must be done by united effort; and it is for that reason that the Universal Negro Improvement Association calls upon every Negro in the State of New York to rally to its standard. We want to unite the Negro race in this State. We want every Negro to work for one common object, that of building a nation of his own on the great continent of Africa. That all Negroes all over the world are working for the establishment of a Government in Africa, means that it will be realised in another few years.

We want the moral and financial support of every Negro to make the dream a possibility. Already this Organization has established itself in Liberia, West Africa, and is endeavouring to do all that is possible to develop that Negro country into a great industrial and commercial commonwealth.

Pioneers have been sent by this Organization to Liberia and they are now laying the foundations upon which the 400 million Negroes of the world will build. If you believe that the Negro has a soul, if you believe that the Negro is a man, if you believe the Negro was endowed with the senses commonly given to other men by the Creator, then you must acknowledge that what other men have done, Negroes can do. We want to build up Cities, Nations, Governments, Industries of our own in Africa, so that we will be able to have a chance to rise from the lowest to the highest positions in the African commonwealth.[2]

The Universal Negro Improvement Association does not seek to set race against race, but seeks to elevate the Negro. We have no time to preach race hatred, because all of our time is given to the spreading of the doctrine of unity among Negroes everywhere. In our desire to build a nation for Negroes, we are doing so without prejudice to any other nation, Government, or race in the world. If the Englishman has [the] right to rule himself, if the German has the right to rule himself, if the Frenchman has the right to rule [hims]elf, if the Chinese has the right to rule himself, if the Japanese has the right to rule himself, on the [same pr]inciple, we believe that the Negro has the right to rule himself. When God created the world He gave . . . [*words mutilated*] common rights and intended that all of us should be the lords of creation. Under our common [*right?*] therefore as a race, we demand a place in the political sun of the world. We demand our portion, which is Africa. The Almighty Architect, when He created the world, designed that black men should inherit the land of Africa. Our country is being robbed and despoiled by the avaricious races and nations of the world, but by their injustice, and by their unrighteous methods, they will fall, and by their fall will come the rise of the African Empire upon which the sun will never set. Let us work toward the end of the glorious cause of African freedom caring not how long we have been out of Africa. Although we have been slaves in these parts for nearly three hundred years, it goes without argument that we are still citizens of Africa. From Africa our parents were robbed three hundred years ago. Nevertheless, when they were robbed from Africa, they never gave over their rights of ownership in the land to any other race or any individual. By right of heritage therefore, each and every Negro in the Western world has a moral and a legal claim to Africa. As Africans abroad, we should lend out assistance morally and financially for the redemption of our Motherland.

This is what the Universal Negro Improvement Association seeks to do by inculcating race pride, and race consciousness in the mind and heart of every Negro. There are some Negroes who think themselves too educated, too successful to lend an ear to the common plea, and the common cry of Mother Africa. How unfortunate that this should be. These people are indeed narrow minded, and have no vision, because every careful student of political science can foresee a future world of tears for those who are not prepared to defend themselves by strong political organization. When we say political organization we do not mean as confined to one's domestic district, where you live, as a subject or as a citizen of the Government that is controlled by an alien race. We mean political organization that is indeed independent to race, that political organization that will make you an independent political unit among the nations and races of the world. We mean the political organization called independent Government. No Negro with all his success, is secure in any community where the Government is vested in an opposite race, when that opposite race is prejudiced to the Negro. There is no guarantee of the safety of any such Negro, because by mob violence and by lynch law, the outcome of race prejudice, one's success can be overthrown overnight, and one transformed from a prosperous subject or citizen, to a refugee. That has been demonstrated in many communities and it should act as a warning to the educated and prosperous Negro, and let him realise that the best thing for every one to do, is to unite, and so fortify ourselves by building up a strong Government in Africa, that as citizens of that Government we can claim protection in any part of the world we happen to find ourselves. Why should not Africa have a Navy? Why should not Africa have a standing Army? Why should not Africa have a Government second to none in the world, controlled and dominated by Negroes? Do you mean to say that 400 million Negroes cannot govern themselves? Do you mean to say that 400 million Negroes cannot work to build up themselves, and to protect Civilization? Men and women of the race in New York, the Universal Negro Improvement Association appeals to you at this hour, for unity. "United we stand, divided we fall."

This, we believe, is your last chance to come together as a race, because if, in the reorganization of the world, you do not demonstrate your fitness to exist, you shall be completely wiped out in the question of the survival of the fittest. We of the Universal Negro Improvement Association are longing for the day, when the other races of the world will respect Negroes for what Negroes have done on their own initiative to demonstrate their ability as a race. We are longing for the day when Presidents and Princes shall come out of Africa. We are longing for the day when the children of Africa will have respect and homage paid to them, even as are paid to the other races of the world to-day. We can do it, but we cannot do it living sep[a]rately and individually. We can only do it when we work collectively and unitedly, so let all the Negroes of the State of New York come together and join the Universal Negro Improvement Association and African Communities League, and support the program morally and financially. It is only by the pooling of our own resources your dollar with mine, and our dollars with the other fellow[']s, that we can accumulate sufficient money to put over big programs, industrially, commercially and politically, in the name of our race.

The Universal Negro Improvement Association is the strongest Negro Organization in the world. It has no selfishness about it. It is not for one class of Negroes as against another class, it is for all Negroes. If you are poor, you can come into the Universal Negro Improvement Association, if you are rich you can come into the Universal Negro Improvement Association, if you are educated, you can come into the Universal Negro Improvement Association. It is for everybody, so long as you have one drop of Negro blood in your veins. We want to build factories. We want to build and run steamships, and that is why we have the Corporation known as the Black Star Line with its shares selling at $5.00 each. Already those who have joined our Organization have bought their shares, some one, some two, some ten, 20, 50, 200, and by what they have done by purchasing shares in this Corporation, we have been able to place ships on the ocean, thus demonstrating to the world, that Negroes are able to enter into maritime commerce, but we want more money now, to build and buy more ships. We want more money now to build factories. We want more money now to finance our industries in Africa. Why not make up your mind to come over and help the Universal Negro Improvement Association carry through this program, so that you and your children can be insured forever.

We are asking you to communicate at once with, or call at the office of the Universal Negro Improvement Association, 5[6] W. 135th street, New York City, N.Y., U.S.A., for all information about the Universal Negro Improvement Association, and for membership. You can send $1.00, which will, if you are a Negro, make you a member of the Organization, with all the necessary supplies furnished for membership. If you desire shares in the Black Star Line, so as to enable us to float a bigger merchant marine, you can write to the Black Star Line Steamship Corporation, 56 W. 135th street, New

York City. You can send from $5.00 to $1,000.00 for shares, in that the shares are sold at $5.00 each, and you can buy as many as you want. In buying shares in the Black Star Line, you will be investing to make profit which will be declared by way of dividends, once a year, according to the success of the Corporation for that year. Outside of the profits they will give to you as individuals, there is the satisfaction that you have helped to build up a great merchant marine, to be owned and controlled by the Negro race.

Men and women of New York, let us be up and doing, turn not a deaf ear to this place, but right away let us make up our minds to be whatsoever we can for the glorification of this race of ours.

Write, or call, Department of Information, Universal Negro Improvement Association, 56 West 135th street, New York City, or Department of Information, Black Star Line, 56 W. 135th street, New York City. If you want to help this movement, you may also send us a donation for the continuance of our work.

This Organization meets in Liberty Hall, 120-148 W. 138th street, New York City, every night at 8:30. Yours for racial uplift,

UNIVERSAL NEGRO IMPROVEMENT ASSOCIATION
MARCUS GARVEY, President General

APPLICATION BLANK FOR MEMBERSHIP IN UNIVERSAL
NEGRO IMPROVEMENT ASSOCIATION

Secretary, Universal Negro Improvement Association.

56 W. 135th street, New York.

Dear Sir:—Enclosed and attached hereto please find one dollar. For this amount register me as an active member of the U.N.I.A. and send me all supplied by an officer of the organization.

NAME ....

ADDRESS ....

DNA, RG 165, file 10218-261. TD.

1. With certain omissions, this appeal also appeared in a phonograph recording that Garvey made in July 1921 with the title "Explanation of the Objects of the Universal Negro Improvement Association." On the other side of the record, Garvey recorded another speech, entitled "Hon. Marcus Garvey on his return to the U.S.A." (DNA, RG 59, file 811.108 G 191/25). The C. N. Bourne Recording Co. produced the record.

2. The original recording ended at this point.

ORDER OF DIVINE SERVICE

FOR THE OPENING OF

Second International Negro Convention

LIBERTY HALL

Monday, August 1st
At 9.30 A. M.

AND

PROGRAM FOR PARADE
At 1 P. M.

AND

PUBLIC MEETING
At 8 P. M.

❋

Universal Negro Improvement Association

❋

1 9 2 1

(Source: DNA, RG 165.)

Convention Parade of the U.N.I.A.

[[*Negro World*, 1 August 1921]]

The great parade of the Universal Negro Improvement Association as a feature of the program in connection with the opening of the International Convention of Negroes of the World, having been heralded in advance far and wide, all Harlem prepared itself to welcome and view the marchers. Long before the hour of starting huge crowds lined the [s]idewalks from below 128th street to 145th street, both on Lenox and on Seventh avenues, while the windows of all the houses along these two great thoroughfares were filled with spectators, eagerly and patiently waiting the pageant as a long-expected feast to their eyes. Buntings and streamers in black, red and green (the colors of the association) and of the American flag could be seen in almost every window, and all along the route everywhere, the entire community [was] wearing the aspect of a public holiday in honor of the greatest movement inaugurated among Negroes for their racial uplift and advancement. . . .

First came a guard or escort of seven mounted policemen, followed by Captain E. [L.] Gaines, Minister of Legions, on horseback, and Adrian Johnson and several members from the African Legion, also on horseback, as his aides. Then followed the full complement of the Black Star Line Band and the Liberty Hall choir (50 in number) on foot, dressed in their white surplices. Then came the officials of the High Executive Council, all in automobiles in the following order: Hon. Gabriel M. Johnson, High Potentate and Mayor of Monrovia, Liberia; the Rev. Dr. G. A. McGuire, Chaplain General; Hon. Marcus Garvey, President General of the U.N.I.A. and Provisional President of Africa, accompanied by a member of the African Legion in uniform; Hon. Dr. J. W. H. Eason, Leader of American Negroes; Eli[e] Garcia, Auditor General; Rev. Dr. J. D. Gordon, Assistant President General; Miss Henrietta Vinton Davis, International Organizer; Hon. Fred. A. Toote, Speaker in Convention; Prof. Wm. H. Ferris, Editor of the Negro World; Rev. P. E. Paul and Bruce Grit. In addition to these high officials there followed automobiles bearing the wives of many of them, including Mrs. Gaines, Mrs. Garcia, Mrs. Gordon, Mrs. Alexander Walters and Mrs. Maria Johnson (who has charge of the Negro Women's Industrial Exhibit).

Then followed an automobile containing some of the crew of the S.S. "Yarmouth," dressed in uniforms of immaculate white; then an automobile the occupants of which carried a beautiful life-size oil painting of the Hon. Marcus Garvey. On foot were the uniformed members of the New York Division of the African Legion (75 in number), 30 women of the Motor Corps in their blue uniforms, followed by 100 Black Cross Nurses dressed in white, with black crosses on their white caps. These units presented a unique spectacle, their military bearing eliciting great applause from the crowds as they passed by.

Then followed the Juvenile Corps of boys and girls ranging in age from 6 to 15, the boys in blue uniforms and caps, the girls in green dresses.

The marchers on foot included representatives from the various Divisions of the organization both in America and from abroad. The Philadelphia Division was strongly represented with a large complement of Legion men, Black Cross Nurses and Motor Corps women. The banners of several contingents of the U.N.I.A. were displayed and included Canada, Jamaica, Grenada, Bahama Islands, Antigua, St. Kitts, Newark, N.J., and Boston.

The parade was divided into two groups, the second group being led by the High Chancellor, Rev. Dr. G. E. Stewart, in an automobile, followed by the famous 15th Infantry Band,[1] which gave added life to the marchers and delighted the crowd with that jazz music peculiar to the 15th.

The inscriptions on the banners distributed at various points throughout the march were as follows:

"The Negro woman is the greatest mother."
"Down with jim-crowism!"
"Long live the republic of Liberia!"
"Africa a nation, one and indivisible."
"The time has come for all Negroes to unite."
"Negroes shall never be slaves."
"Honor to the Stars and Stripes!"
"Freedom for all."
"Why a Pan-African Congress in Paris?"
"Scattered Africa united."
"The Negro will form an alliance with civilization."
"Negroes everywhere must be free!"
"Centuries of hidden mysteries have been revealed to the Negro."
"The Negro will build battleships and cruisers."
"Toussaint L'Ouverture was an abler soldier than Napoleon."
"We have mastered the hidden arts of Africa."
"The Negro gave civilization to the world."
"What will France do in Africa?"
"The Negro as a soldier has no peer."
"By the science of perpetual motion the Negro will conquer."
"We demand a true democracy."
"The mysteries of Africa will be revealed in the coming racial conflict."
"The Negro won the war."
"Negroes, hitch your wagon to the Black Star!"
"The Negro's fighting strength is not known."
"African scientists will play an important part in the next world war."
"Africa is calling her 400,000,000 sons and daughters."
"Duty requires every Negro to fall in line."

"Princes shall come out of Egypt."

"All hail to the New York 15th Regiment and the 367th Regiment!"

"Africa must be redeemed!"

"Africa's star is rising."

"Africa resurrected."

"Africa, the mother of civilization."

"African scientists are prepared to use the arts of their forefathers in the coming conflict."

"Can aliens fight Negroes in Africa?"

"Remember the New York 15th."

"Let the Negro have the vote!"

"Africa, the land of hope."

"In the righteousness of our cause we triumph."

"The Negro will build aeroplanes."

"Free Africa; free Ireland!"

"The Negro leader who begs for a donation does not represent the race."

"God and nature saved Africa for this day."

"The South will change, for the new Negro is here."

"400,000,000 black men shall be free!"

"Africa shall be redeemed."

"The Negro will build dreadnoughts and submarines."

"Stop lynching in Georgia and we will not lynch in Africa."

"United we stand for African liberty!"

Among the flags carried in the parade were the American flag and the new, beautiful, large size flags of the New York local of the U.N.I.A. and the New York Division of the African Legion. These were carried by two men of the legion, and attracted much attention.

Each automobile in the parade carrying the distinguished high officials were beautifully decorated with streamers in the American and the U.N.I.A. colors. In addition to these automobiles there were several, as many as ten[,] large sight-seeing auto buses used in the parade carrying friends and members of the association.

The parade having created a new landmark not merely in colored Harlem, but in the work of the Universal Negro Improvement Association and in the progress of the Negro as a race, the event will long live in the memory of all who witnessed it, reflecting, as it did, credit to all our people and to those who took part in it and contributed to its success.

Printed in *NW*, 6 August 1921. Original headlines omitted.

1. The Fifteenth Infantry Band, founded by James Reese Europe, played an important part in the early popularization of jazz in the United States and France (Florette Henri, *Black Migration* [Garden City, N.Y.: Doubleday, 1975], p. 298; David Levering Lewis, *When Harlem Was in Vogue* [New York: Alfred A. Knopf, 1981], pp. 30–34).

Article in the *Negro World*

[*New York, 1 August 1921*]

CONVENTION REFLECTIONS

. . . We should judge that it [*the parade*] was nearly two miles in length.[1] When the auto containing Mr. Noah Thomson, of Associated Press fame; Bruce Grit, H. V. Plummer, Dr. Duvall, Rev. Dr. Paul and the writer reached 120th street and Lenox avenue, the head of the procession had gone down Lenox avenue, rounded 116th street, Fifth avenue and 120th street and was turning up Lenox avenue, thus indicating that nearly a mile of paraders were in front of us. And as far back as the eye could see there were nothing but streaming banners and marchers, thus indicating that nearly a mile of paraders were back of us. In the down town section of Harlem we noticed children of the Caucasian races leaning out of windows, standing in doorways and by the curb stone eagerly watching the magnificent pageant. They had read in school geographies, histories that the Negro in his native state in Africa was a naked savage, and that he had been the slave for centuries. And they saw the Potentate riding in his auto looking like an emperor, the Chaplain General looking like a Pope, the President General like a king, the American leader like a cardinal and the International Organizer like a queen. With the exception of the Potentate, who rode with the Chaplain General, each member of the Executive Council was the sole occupant of the auto, save for his body guard. The dignified manner in which the dignitaries, clad in their gorgeous and resplendent robes sat back in their autos, added to the impressiveness of the parade. Then the choir and Black Cross Nurses, who were gowned[,] the children, motor corps, legions and bands who were in uniform, the thousands of enthusiastic marchers and hundreds of automobiles added to the brilliance and splendor of the paraders.

The Minister of Legions rode his horse like a trained and veteran rider. New York city has never seen a greater parade.

Tuesday morning the New York World published the photos of Potentate Johnson, Dr. McGuire and the Hon. Marcus Garvey in their autos. And the Daily News published the photos of Marcus Garvey and Jack Johnson. Why? Because Jack Johnson and Marcus Garvey had put across more spectacular performances than any living Negroes. . . .

W[ILLIAM]. H. F[ERRIS].

Printed in *NW*, 13 August 1921.

1. According to a Bureau of Investigation report, the parade numbered "some ten thousand negroes" (DNA, RG 65, file BS 202600-33-292).

Keynote Speech by Gabriel M. Johnson, UNIA Potentate

[[Liberty Hall, New York, 1 August 1921]]

His Excellency, Hon. Gabriel M. Johnson, Mayor of Monrovia City, Liberia, High Potentate of the Universal Negro Improvement Association, delivered the opening address of the convention as follows: Members of the High Executive Council, Delegates to the Second International Convention of Negroes of the World: I now declare this convention officially opened to the transaction of business for the year 1921. Fellow men of the race, in accordance with the constitution governing this association, I am here to make the first potentate speech. I must first thank you for the confidence imposed in me by electing me to the high office I now hold in the Universal Negro Improvement Association. I am aware that there have been many comments with reference to this position and its importance and status of the movement, and knowing, as I do, what it really means, I am convinced that it was due solely to my connections in Africa which induced the convention to make the selection, as I am sure there were many persons better fitted intellectually for the post. I am not unmindful of the great responsibility the office carries with it, nor had I the slightest idea that I was equal to the task, but it was the desire of the convention and I could but yield my wishes to the will of such a great body. I am not one of those who think that nature has bestowed all wisdom upon any one individual. My motto is: "There is wisdom in counsel," and I am impressed that this was the intention of the founder and original organizers of this great organization, consequently they suggested the creation of the High Executive Council.

One year has elapsed since we last met in a similar capacity—a year that is fraught with happenings in connection with the Universal Negro Improvement Association. A year very remarkable in the history of the Negro race; therefore let us unite in giving praise to the great arbiter of all human events for what we have been able to achieve, praying that He will continue to give us His blessing and such a measure of His grace and wisdom that we may be enabled to deal soberly and discreetly with the many problems that confront us as a race, and as an association.

It is with great praise and gratitude to the Almighty God that we have not had the need to mourn the loss of a single official of the parent body during the past year, although so widely dispersed as we have been. We have lost several very important members and officers of some local divisions; these, no doubt, will be given in the report of the secretary-general. I would like just to specially mention one in the Liberian field, the Rev. G. W. Parker, president of the Liberia division. He was a zealous member and an ardent supporter of the movement in Liberia, and one whom we looked forward to with much pride. He was untiring in his efforts to assist in pushing forward the movement in that field. His death was very sudden and much regretted by all of his friends and relatives. In his death the organization has lost a very enterprising and energetic member. He was mentioned in the report sent to The Negro World some time in April last, and I sincerely hope that the services of such men will have a lasting effect upon the cause. May they all rest in peace!

Coming, as I do, from Liberia, I have to mention that the headquarters of the movement just established in Monrovia under my direction is doing all that is possible to impress the government and peoples of the country of its sincerity of purpose and deep interest in the welfare of the republic. I can also say that the most friendly relations exist between the government and our association, and already all of the men who have gone out during the past year have ingratiated themselves into the good feelings of the old settlers and bid fair to succeed. Our industrial work, although just begun, has a very bright future before it, and with your hearty support financially [*it*] will soon become a potent factor in the life of [the] country.

Ours is a great trust and should not be lightly regarded by any one of us. We should remember that great trusts carry with them great responsibilities, but I am afraid that many of us too lightly regard the interests that have been entrusted to our care, and therefore fail to measure up to the requirements that such a position demands of us. I am sure you will agree with me when I say that the Universal Negro Improvement Association is the greatest movement in the history of our race; in fact, it is the greatest movement in the world today. Unlike many of the other movements in other parts of the world today, we stand for good government and loyalty to the flags under which we all live. We are only contending for a "square deal" and equal opportunity with other races under similar conditions. If this is given to us, we shall surely demonstrate by our actions that we are not an inferior race, intellectually or industrially, as the enemies of this race of ours have endeavored to establish. But in our zeal to push forward the movement we must be very careful not to disseminate false ideas in the minds of the uninformed and raise their hopes upon a frail foundation, so that they will not be disappointed in not realizing their hopes. This mode of procedure if adopted will have a tendency to do more harm in the end than good. We cannot be too careful in our utterances and the ideas established, therefore it requires great minds to handle the big problems that it must encounter. We cannot maintain this organization nor can we expect to successfully propagate its teaching unless we become fully conscious of the needs of such a movement. Get into the spirit of the organization and endeavor to carry out its aims and purposes in full accord with the present age.

We are living in a very strenuous and exacting age—an age that demands of those of us holding high, responsible positions to be true to our trust and responsibilities, giving of the best that is in us in order that we may lift up a standard unto the people that shall see and follow in its train, and that we use no deception in order to gain the favors of those whom we are called to lead.

It is necessary therefore for us to be true to God who created us, true to our fellowmen whom we are to lead, and, lastly, true to ourselves as men.

Conditions everywhere in the world during the past year have been of a very trying nature. The readjustment of the world's affairs in its various aspects of human activities has brought about some of the most trying circumstances and conditions unequaled even by the conditions that existed in some parts during the terrible world war. Therefore it is necessary that we should seriously consider the problems and issues that confront us at this session in a sane, sober and dispassionate manner, in order that we may not create a condition for our people that is worse than that with which we are confronted at the present moment.

The principles as set out in the preamble of our Constitution are: Social, industrial and commercial improvement. The idea of social equality between the whites and Negroes in America and other parts of the world has been discussed over and over again by many writers, many of whom I consider more able to deal with the subject than I am. That there is need for social improvement among the members of our race in many parts of the world goes without saying and cannot be denied, but I am afraid in many instances more stress is laid on the desire to be considered the social equal of such a set or individual rather than on the idea of equipping or improving ourselves in that respect. If an individual or a set of individuals in any community make it a plan to conduct themselves in strict conformity to the rules of social order and set to work to become efficient in these rules and demean themselves in a fitting manner at all times, they will have no need to ask for social recognition. No matter where they go their actions and demeanor will be their pass, and they will be the means of inducing others to imitate or copy their example.

The Negro is without a doubt an industrious race, despite what has been said and is still being said to the contrary, that the native African is lazy and indolent. If this statement was true where would the English, German, French, Spanish, Italian and American steamers get their loads of thousands and thousands of tons of African produce, timber, etc., that is shipped to Europe and America, to load their numerous ships that go to Africa[?] Does the white man go out into the forest and make the oil, gather the nuts and prepare the fiber, or does he bring saw-mills and machinery to get the timber from the woods to load his ships? No, this is all done by the native African, and this impression is given out for a special purpose, and the Negro is the first to accept it. Most Negroes who go to Africa from America or the West Indies go with that impression, but they are soon convinced otherwise. This is no more true of them than the idea that all white Americans hate the Negro. That the African or the Negro in Africa, as a rule, has not made very great advancement in recent years in the arts and sciences as compared to other races is no doubt true, but this does not prove that he is not capable of doing so; his past history proves the contrary. His position in the world for the past century or more, also his present condition, have very much to do with this. The Negroes in the United States and the West Indies have done wonderfully well in this sphere of activity, when we consider what they have had to encounter, and if the idea of a combined effort in the various industries as has been exhibited by the other races, and which this movement is endeavoring to teach, is taken hold of in the right spirit and put to practical use, there is bound to be greater achievements in the next few years.

I have never visited any other country outside of Africa but the United States of America that has a large colored population, but my conclusions from reading and from the reports given out at the convention last August are that practically the same conditions exist in each of these countries where the white man is the controlling element. When we consider the position of China today, how a small nation like Japan has control of so much of its territory and how the Chinese are treated in these districts by the Japanese, we are led to conclude that human nature is the same the world over, and the policy of the strong dominating and oppressing the weak runs throughout the universe. Not only among alien races, but it applies to sects, clans and tribes of a same race. Therefore, the only remedy against this is to get strong; but this cannot be done in a day nor a year. And not only by preaching and talking about it, but by active work and proper management. And if we would be a great people we must seriously consider our present condition and acquit ourselves like men; be willing to suffer privations, as other races and peoples have done in the past, and not expect to accomplish great things simply by agitation without putting forth efforts to improve ourselves and our conditions.

Commerce is the greatest factor in modern civilization for bringing together the scattered nations of the globe. The Negro, scattered as he is to the four corners of the earth by the ruthless hand of a domineering Anglo-Saxon, will take years to get together again. Certainly the most optimistic leader of this movement of ours must have his own peculiar views as to how this is to be accomplished. I consider the commercial venture of this association carried on by one of its auxiliaries, the "Black Star Line" Corporation, is the most important factor for carrying out the purposes and principles of the organization. With the scattered millions of our race in all parts of the world, this should be made the rallying point of every member and division of this grand movement, for it must be remembered that a successful "Black Star Line" will mean everything to the Negro race; although every effort has been made by enemies in our race and also of the other races to prevent it from "going"; but when once it succeeds, you will have very little to fear from any source.

It is not necessary that we should antagonize the members of other races and peoples because we desire to conduct a purely Negro venture; certainly not. We can show that we have race pride and ambition and still not be antagonistic in our methods. This is a new field for us, and there are a great many ideas as well as much material we will need to secure from the controlling element of the white race, and we will have need of many things they possess for many years to come to carry out our own plans. If we will demean ourselves properly and not be found guilty of the very things we are denouncing in others—stirring up race antipathy—we will get all we want without begging or cringing and thereby be none the worse for it. I do not, for one, profess to have any special love for the white race any more than for the other races of the world, but it is an undeniable fact that they have what it takes to make a people great materially, and while we have thousands of capable men in our race today, as well as the means necessary to do great things, still these forces have not yet been properly welded together in one great whole, as with the dominating races, and therefore if they're not willing to share it with us it makes the task all the more burdensome. But there is one thing certain, we cannot build up a successful organization that has for its aim the complete emancipation of our race upon the fragments of envy, hate, greed, retaliation and such other foul interests. It will not succeed. We must be completely emancipated from the fetters of ignorance, superstition, prejudice, avarice and greed before we can expect to build up a healthy organization on high ideas that will give that dignity and prestige to the race, an organization that is essential to the successful accomplishment of all that is grand and great in this noble race of ours. The history of the Central Powers in the past decade is quite proof enough. In speaking of this state of affairs, hear what a prominent writer has to say concerning it and the German people. He says: "They must feel in their own body and purse that decency, fairness, kindness and humanness in everyday life, bring also palpable monetary advantage, and that far behind them lie[s] the time when lasting power was given to the man who glared at his neighbor with the eyes of a wolf craving for robbery and human flesh."

This proves that the world today is being run on different lines, and we must adopt methods in keeping with the trend of thought of the world. The clearing house of the world has a power verging on omnipotence, and we are sure to meet with disaster and ruin and failure if we attempt to antagonize all other races in our propaganda. Therefore what we decry in others we should not agitate or induce them to follow. I am not of the Booker T. Washington type, nor do I follow altogether in the line of thought of some of the other leaders. I realize that the Negro should regard himself as an equal of any other race and that every race has a claim to some section of the globe, but great things and great movements cannot be attained in a day, nor can talking and prating about the other man accomplish our work.

We must be trained in all phases of public life before we can attempt to govern and control ourselves, and this is one of the main features of the Universal Negro Improvement Association and must be emphasized. Therefore social improvement, industrial training and commercial development must first be emphasized and a keen conception of the national idea with a combination of these views thoroughly impressed upon the members. Not the industrial training of the Washington type, only just enough to be useful to the other race, but carried to its fullest extent in order to maintain and control our own concerns; to build factories and navigate our own ships on the seven seas. This is what the Universal Negro Improvement Association stands for, and must teach and emphasize. Arousing the feelings of a people and bringing them together is not always combination. To bring a race of people or community or nation together on one subject is one thing, and being able to combine them in their ideas, their thoughts and their actions and keep them together is absolutely another question altogether. The Negro having been trained under different environments—some in America under a democratic government, some under British rule in England and the islands and British West Africa under a constitutional monarchy, some in France and French Africa under a monarchical democracy, and others under their own rule in Abyssinia, Haiti and Liberia—certainly they cannot all be expected to see, think or act alike in a short space of time.

A movement of this nature must certainly appeal to each in a different way, and what suits one may be found objectionable to the other. While on the whole the general idea may be acceptable by all, there would certainly be points of objection by many of those even who view the association with favor; certainly, then, it will require much time and effort on our part as leaders to give a clear and proper explanation and information to the several classes as above mentioned in order that they may be better able to give that support necessary to the cause.

The editor of "The World[']s Work" for March, in his comment on the letter from Bishop Smith, among other things, said that "any man who seeks to set up a new allegiance for this part of our population, and especially one so intangible as an African Empire, is no true friend to his race, and may become a danger to our domestic peace and security."

The idea of a "new allegiance" is really amusing, but the reference to a "domestic peace" is really more so. Since the abolition of slavery—by proclamation—there has been no domestic peace between the two races in America and will never be, as long as the immigrants from the slums of Europe are given preference to the Negro, who has done so much to make the United States what she is, by his brawn and muscle, and who continues to carry a large portion of the responsibility of feeding, not only America, but starving Europe. That there is a strong allegiance between the Negroes of America and Africa goes without saying. In the same manner that the white race in America is strongly allied to Europe and Asia in many ways. The same refers to the colored population of America with Africa. Many of them have their kith and kin there, and only circumstances prevent a union in many cases. I must admit though, that there are a great many also who know very little about Africa—"In fact have lost nothing in Africa"—is the popular expression, and make no effort to learn the truth about it, but there are millions, I may say, who are ready and willing to do all they can to assist their brethren in realizing their fullest ambitions and raising them to the highest plane of civilization and enlightment.

One can discern from the trend of this article what is intended to be conveyed, but this great movement of ours has no intention to disturb the domestic peace of this great Republic, nor any other country where the

Negro is sojourning; but such articles are worthy of note, and it is with us as leaders to read, mark, learn and inwardly digest what is written therein, and also what can be read between the lines, in order to be able to deal with the situation more effectively and sagaciously.

In conclusion, ladies and gentlemen, let me urge upon you the necessity of considering all matters that will come before you in a calm and dispassionate manner, in order that we do nothing to place a damper on this great and grand movement, or hamper its progress. The President General and Administrator, who is charged with the administration and management of the affairs of the organization shall put before you, from time to time, during your sitting, suggestions for the better working of our grand movement, and I ask for him your hearty support in all matters that have for their aim the emancipation of our race and the redemption of our Motherland, Africa.

Printed in *NW*, 6 August 1921. Original headlines omitted.

Opening Speech of the Convention by Marcus Garvey

NEW YORK, Aug. 1, 1921

. . . May it please your Highness, may it please your Grace, Right Hon. Members of the Executive Council of the Universal Negro Improvement Association, Deputies and Delegates to the International Convention of Negroes of the World. It is my good fortune to find myself before you this evening representing the Universal Negro Improvement Association. I am supposed to deliver the address of the evening. On behalf of this organization I desire to thank you for the loyal and hearty support you have given the cause since the convention of last year. You are assembled tonight as the representatives—not the nominated, not the appointed, but the elected representatives of the 400,000,000 Negroes of the world. As one of the representatives you will not expect me to "close ranks"[1]; as one of the representatives of the new Negroes you will expect me to "open ranks." I am not Dr. Du Bois.[2] You will understand that I am Marcus Garvey. I therefore have nothing to apologize for as far as the aims and objects of the Universal Negro Improvement Association goes. We are assembled in this second annual convention for the purpose of legislating in the interests of 400,000,000 Negroes. We are to legislate for the freedom of Africa. We desire as a race that opportunity, that freedom, that democracy that is common to humanity—that for which we fought in France and Flanders and Mesopotamia, but that which is denied us by the people for whom we fought and with whom we fought.

We realize that the world discounts us because we have always been compromising. We have always been begging for the things that are ours, not only morally but by right divine. Because we have begged for these things the world ignored us. But tonight we are assembled to beg no more. (Cheers.) We are assembled to demand—demand from all races and from all nations; demand from all governments the things that belong to Negroes by right morally and right divine. We as the representatives of the 400,000,000 Negroes of the world desire to make it known to Asia, to Europe and to the Americas that we are coming, we are coming, we are coming 400,000,000 strong. We are coming, we are coming, and our destination is Africa— 12,000,000 square miles. We are coming with a great determination to conquer, not to beg for, not to apologize for, but if needs be to die for the freedom of Africa. (Cheers.)

Before I go farther on this African question I should like every one to understand me clearly as a representative of the Universal Negro Improvement Association. Several people have charged us with an intention of entering Africa at a certain place that is known for the purpose of creating disturbance in Africa. They charge us with desiring to convert Liberia into a battleground. I deny any such intention on the part of the Universal Negro Improvement Association. I desire to let the world know that we recognize not only Liberia as belonging to the Negro, but all Africa. (Applause.) And since Liberia is already occupied by Africans we have no need to make an entry through Liberia, but we shall make our entry wheresoever we place our feet in Africa. Whether we land in the South or the West or the North or in Central Africa there shall be the battleground for African freedom. And it does not mean that American Negroes are going to do it. It will be done in Africa even without our going there. Smuts is somewhat scared; he is scared of his own shadow. Smuts seems to be the spokesman of the white race. I would advise the white race to get another statesman than Smuts, because Smuts is one African that the 400,000,000 Negroes intend to get square with in Africa. Smuts represents the idea that Negroes have no rights anywhere.[3] Smuts represents the idea that Negroes should not walk on the same sidewalk like other races, even in their own country. Smuts has the wrong idea, because Negroes are going to walk anywhere they desire in Africa. (Cheers.) Smuts, a Boer; Smuts, a Dutchman, may well understand that we are not depending on the statesmanship of fellows like Du Bois to lead this race of ours, but we are depending on the statesmanship of fellows like the New York Fifteenth, the West Indian regiments and the Eighth Illinois, who fought their way in France. (Cheers.) I desire the permanent existence of the British empire, as I desire the permanent existence of all governments, but I would advise the statesmanship of Great Britain to get rid of Smuts. Smuts is a dangerous representative of the Anglo-Saxon race. He is dangerous because he hates Negroes; and if Negroes start to hate, mind yourself. Negroes have never hated, and that is why they seem to miscalculate and misunderstand the Negro. The Negro in all history has never hated; he has always returned a smile for a kick; he has always returned a smile for abuse. Let me say to the world that was the characteristic of the old Negro. We are dealing with the new Negro today, the Negro who intends to return a blow for a blow. (Cheers.) Mark well! There are 400,000,000 Negroes in the world, and it is a question raised not with 15,000,000 American Negroes, not with 20,000,000 West Indian Negroes. The question rests not with 40,000,000 South and Central American Negroes. The question is one that concerns 400,000,000 black men. (Cheers.)

We are tired of being kicked about; we are tired of being tossed around. The hour has come for a definite decision and we are about to take the step of decision. In this convention assembled we would like the world to understand that the Negro is prepared to be as peaceful now as he has always been, but nobody knows that the Negro is preparing to demand the things that are his. Yield up the things that are belonging to the Negro and we will have everlasting peace and abiding peace. It may seem strange to hear the Negro talk in the terms of war, but that is the only medium through which men can get salvation. I do not care what the philosophers say and theologians say—war to me is the only medium through which man can seek redemption. Now understand me well. We are gathered as an international body not to start war in any country where government is already constituted, but we are organized the world over first of all to demand the things that are belonging to Negroes in Africa, and if you refuse them[,] what you get, please take. (Cheers.) Now there are some Negroes who are very nervous, while other Negroes get up and talk boldly for their rights. Let me say to you nervous Negroes that you are barnacles hanging around the neck of this race of ours. We are determined to bury you even as we buried our enemies. A compromising coward has never won anything yet, since the dawn of creation. The civilization that you enjoyed, the democracy that we enjoyed in this country was brought about not by cowardice, but by the valor of fellows like George Washington and Patrick Henry. I like America because it reveals to me the way in which all men should go who desire liberty. Patrick Henry—I can see him now; I can see him now in the Virginia Legislature of 140 odd years ago when he stood up among his fellow legislators and said: "I care not what others may say, but as for me, give me liberty or give me death." Tonight, as representatives of 400,000,000 Negroes of the world we re-echo the words of Patrick Henry, "We care not what others may say, but as for us, give us liberty or give us death." (Cheers.)

The world tries to ignore and minimize the power and potency of the force of the Universal Negro Improvement Association. Let them continue to live in a fool's Paradise. Yes; we are as serious in this intention of ours as George Washington was, Garibaldi[4] was, as Mirabeau[5] was, as Madame Roland[6] and Voltaire[7] were, as Tolstoi[8] was, as Lenine and Trotsky were; we are serious because we desire liberty and we want it now. Some people—some foolish white men and ignorant Negroes, some of them—believe that

Negroes should not talk big. Brother, I want to ask you where do you get that idea from? Where do you get that notion from that Negroes should not talk big? This is the time, this is the age for big talk. Talk on Lloyd George, I can hear you. I can hear you talk for the rights of Englishmen. Talk on Clemenceau, I can hear you talking for the rights of Frenchmen. Talk on Charles Evans Hughes, talk on Warren G. Harding, I can hear you talking in the interest of 90,000,000 white Americans. You would be untrue to your race if you did not speak for them. Talk on Sonnini, talk on Orlando, I can hear you talking in the interests of millions of Italians. Talk on Ishii, I can hear you talking in the interest of 60,000,000 Japanese. I say talk on New Negro, talk without stopping; talk on, talk on, and let there be a free Africa; and if any one dares stop you, use the power that God Almighty gave you to battle your way through the world. Black men, white men, yellow men— God made me a man. God made each and every one of us in His own image. God Almighty when He created us gave us a common right, a common heritage. My right, my heritage I shall demand and if any one attempts or dares to intrude upon my rights I shall fight and die in defense of those rights. (Cheers.)

Let me go back to another phase of this question. Some people seem to think that the Universal Negro Improvement Association encourages animus against white people and against other races. It is for me to declare emphatically against that. We love all humanity, whether humanity be black, yellow or white; we love humanity because all of us are creatures together; but we say to you what you would like for yourself we also would like for ourselves. What you have won by your activities, what you have won by your labor, what you have won by your skill, what you have won by your genius we are now making an effort to win for ourselves. That is all we are about today; and we therefore give to you your Europe, we give you your Asia, we give to you when you want it your American continent, but we demand our Africa. (Cheers.) We are not going to quarrel with you over Europe; we are not going to quarrel with you over Asia; we are not going to quarrel with you over America, but we are going to die alongside with you on the African continent. Somebody is crazy if you think the new Negro is going to allow himself to be a slave perpetually. No sir; the new Negro is a man; if he cannot live a man he prefers to die a man. (Loud cheers.) Understand, we recognize humanity; we love humanity, and we are about to bring about an alliance with all humanity, that is as far as that section and portion of humanity will ally itself with us. There are 400,000,000 Negroes in the world. Now I want you puny-hearted Negroes to listen to what I am saying, and I trust there is no prejudiced white man in this building. I trust all the white people in this building will enter into the spirit of this meeting as if it were a white meeting, and was a white man speaking to white people in the interests of white people. Now there are 400,000,000 Negroes in the world. The world is in terrible confusion and turmoil now, and all the political scientists predict a war of the races. Our Josephus Daniels several years ago said that the next world war will be the war of the races. White men, think that over; yellow men, think that over, because black folks are thinking it over. (Cheers and laughter.) There are more colored people in the world than white people. We love white people because they have been our children, you know. They have been our proteges. You know, when a father has an old suit and he does not care to wear it any longer, he gives it to his son. We once had civilization and we got tired of it, and we called in the white man and gave it to him, and he has been keeping and using it for us for several hundred years, but we have just changed our minds now. We ask and demand a part of that civilization for ourselves. We are not going to be unfair about it; we are not going to collect any interest. What do I mean by we love the white man? We love him because he was once a cannibal; he was once a savage, and we took hold of him and taught him and gave him our civilization. The fellow got so audacious that he wants to keep it all for himself. Yet we love you all the same, and we have to love you twice because we love our civilization first, and since he is now the custodian of that civilization that we gave to him we have to see that he is properly protected within reason. And that is why we do not want to get away from the white man; but day after day he is forcing us away from him. I want the white man to get a little sense. Don't you believe your political scientists that the next world war will be a race war? White man, do you think you can stand up against the combined forces of Japan, China, India and Africa? White men, why are you so crazy? Why are you driving away from you your best friend, your well tried and true friend? Why are you driving him away from you with lynching, and burning, and Jim Crowism, and segregation, and of late throwing him out of jobs that you should give him because of your obligation to him? White men, don't you know that when the war of the races comes, if the Negro is not on your side you are "burnt up." (Cheers and laughter.) Do you know that throwing Negroes out of jobs is encouraging hatred and animus for you, and when you get in trouble they will not help you? We don't want to be revengeful; we like you because you have been our child for centuries; we have nursed you when your own mothers turned you down. We have done everything for you because we loved you so much, because you have been unable to do things for yourselves. Now why are you driving us away from you? I trust the white people of this country and the white people of Europe will get sense to know that the Negro is civilization's best friend.

We must call an alliance because we have been too careless with ourselves in the past. The New Negro is going to form an alliance somewhere. We have no objection to forming an alliance with white people; we are willing to form it now; but in forming that alliance we say: what is good for you is good for us too. (Cheers.) That is the principle of our alliance, and listen, you cannot ignore us, because we are 400,000,000 strong, and the manhood of this race is made up of fellows like the New York Fifteenth— good for anything at any time, anywhere.

I trust that the white people of this country and the white race at large will understand that they have to calculate with a new leadership among Negroes today. I am not blaming the white people for misunderstanding the Negro, because all properly organized governments, races and nations and institutions treat with representatives or organizations or governments; they do not treat with organizations as a whole; they treat with the representatives of this government or this organization or this race; and we have been having some bootleggers who for years and years have been going in our name claiming to be our representatives; and because we did not say anything to the contrary—in that silence gives consent—the white people accepted the bootleggers as our representatives. The illiterate preacher with a long coat, hat in hand, who went up and said: "Boss, I represent my people and I am asking for a few dimes to help me to buy a church"; the white man really believes that we were represented in these individuals and they treated us as a mass according to the representation we presented to them. They are not yet acquainted with the change. Let me tell you now there is a change. Du Bois and Moton are no more; we buried them in 1914. The New Negro demands a leadership that refuses to beg but demands a chance. The New Negro presents a leadership that will not go down in supplication but will stand up and demand the things that are belonging to the race. Hence we are acting with our own leadership on our own initiative. And that is why we open ranks and do not close ranks. We have been closing ranks for five hundred years; we are going to open them now. Open ranks in the leadership of the Negroes of the world means that we shall present our own leaders, thanking the race for all the leaders they have given us in the past. We get our leaders not by appointment from any other race but by popular election from our own race. We deal no longer with individuals; we deal with measures; we deal not with men but with measures. So when I speak of individuals you will understand that I speak of them simply because they are interfering with certain measures that tend to the detriment of Negroes, and I am a Negro.

I refuse to be misrepresented to the world; I love honesty; I love righteousness; I refuse to allow any bootlegger or Jacklegger to go and say Garvey is satisfied when Garvey is not satisfied. Garvey is not satisfied because Garvey is not given a fair chance. What is true of Garvey is true of 400,000,000 Negroes the world over. The New Negro therefore demands a chance; we are not praying for a chance; we are going to demand a chance or we are going to take a chance, and if needs be we are going to die taking a chance. We are the friends of humanity; we are the friends of civilization; but we desire just this; we desire equality from humanity and from civilization. That is what divides the Old and the New Negro. So tonight when we are assembled in this second Annual Convention of Negroes of the World we would like it clearly understood by races, by nations, by governments everywhere that our desire is not to foment trouble in any country where we live as subjects and citizens, but our desire is to free and liberate ourselves on the great continent of Africa. We have naturally as a race desiring government to present to the world from our ranks the ablest and the best within us in intelligence, in foresight, in statesmanship. In every branch of human activity we have to present the best within us, and I am going to present before you a resolution.

You may not see anything on the surface of any one holding a Pan-African Congress in Europe, but I want you to understand that if the Negro is to be properly led he must go beneath the surface. In analyzing questions and issues that confront a race I want to point out to you a treacherous bit of conspiracy to defeat the aspirations, the aims and the hopes of this struggling race of ours. A world conspiracy is launched to again enslave this race probably for another century or for eternity. We are living in an age when humanity in itself sees no love, sees no charity, gives no sympathy. Humanity everywhere divided up into separate and distinct race groups is looking out for itself; hence the cry of Germany for the Germans, England for the English, Italy for the Italians. I want to warn you of the kind of leadership that we have had; it is being used today so as to return us to serfdom and peonage and slavery from which we were emancipated by great philanthropists like Abraham Lincoln and Victoria of England. Certain Negroes are being used today to defeat the aspirations and the hopes of the New Negro. I feel sure that those of you who will pay keen attention and study to political events will realize that a dangerous scheme is now being engineered in Europe to defeat the plans of Negroes in redeeming Africa. Africa is to become a common battleground of the exploiters—the exploiters who are now looking toward Africa as the only redeemer, as the only savior, and they realize that a change is coming about among those who claim ownership in Africa. The change is that those who claim ownership of Africa are crying out "Africa for the Africans," and those people who desire Africa have entered into a conspiracy to further darken or becloud the eyes of Negroes and turn their attention from independence in Africa. They talk about mandatories in Africa; it means nothing else but another hundred years of merciless exploitation of the natives and of the wealth of Africa; and they are now about to use certain colored men—certain Negroes to defeat the intention of the far-seeing members of this race of ours. In view of that, therefore, I am going to move a resolution which I ask you to support as delegates representing the 400,000,000 Negroes of the world. You have been honored here to represent the true interests of Negroes everywhere; they expect you to exercise statesmanship; they expect you to match your intelligence, your intellect with that of David Lloyd George and Clemenceau. Clemenceau sees down the ages; Lloyd George sees down the ages and you will have also to see down the ages, otherwise you are lost to the ages. And penetrating this scheme we see nothing else but an attempt to enslave the Negro for another 500 years by compromising the issue of Negroes' intentions and desires at this time. This is the resolution which I will read, and I trust that you will follow me word by word, line by line, and get the intention of this resolution:

Be It Resolved: That we, the duly elected representatives of the Negro peoples of the world, from North America, South America, Central America, West Indies, Asia, Europe, Australia and Africa, assembled in open conclave on this 1st day of August, 1921, at the 12th Regiment Armory, New York City, United States of America, in Second Annual International Convention of the Negro peoples of the world do hereby place on record our repudiation of a Pan-African Congress to be held in London, England, Sunday and Monday, August 28 and 29; Brussels, Belgium, Wednesday, Thursday and Friday, August [3]1, September 1 and 2; Paris, France, Sunday and Monday, September 4 and 5. As also the Special Committee of the said Congress to visit the Assembly of the League of Nations, Geneva, Switzerland, after September 6.[9]

Our repudiation of this Congress, as representatives of the Negro peoples of the world, is based upon the fact that W. E. B. Du Bois, Secretary of the so-called Pan-African Congress, and those associated with him, are not representatives of the struggling peoples of the world, and that the men who have called the said Congress have not consulted the Negro peoples of the world of their intention, and have received no mandate from the said people to call a Congress in their name.

That the said W. E. B. Du Bois and his associates who call the Congress are making an issue of social equality with the white race for their own selfish purposes, and not for the advancement of the Negro race, and that the idea of their holding a Congress in European cities is more for the purpose of aggravating the question of social equality to their own personal satisfaction, than for the benefit of the Negro race.

That we believe the motives of the Congress are to undermine the true feeling and sentiment of the Negro race for complete freedom in their own spheres, and for a higher social order among themselves, as against a desire among a certain class of Negroes for social contact, comradeship and companionship with the white race.

We further repudiate the congress because we sincerely feel that the white race, like the black and yellow races, should maintain the purity of self and that the congress is nothing more than an effort to encourage race suicide by the admixture of two opposite races.

That we appeal to the sense of race pride among the white people of Europe not to encourage this congress in misrepresenting the attitude of the Negro. The Negro feels socially satisfied with himself, and means to maintain the dignity and purity of his race, and therefore denounces any attempt on the part of dissatisfied individuals who by accident are members of the said Negro race in their attempts to foster a campaign of miscegenation to the destruction of the race's purity.

This convention desires also to place on record for the information of the white race that the Negro is a friend and protector of civilization and that all the ills that attend civilization affect him. That the Negro is not racially a beggar, as represented by a worthless class of race leaders who have in the past made capital out of the Negro's poor economic condition to beg the philanthropists of other races for donations in the name of the Negro, but which donations have been used more for the personal aggrandizement of such leaders than for the cause in whose name they begged.

All that the Negro desires is a fair chance to work for his livelihood, and if he is given that chance the entire race problem will be solved. The Negro objects to and denounces its old leadership, that has fattened at the race's expense and that now seeks to foster propaganda that aims at the destruction of the purity of the white and black races.

And be it further resolved that a copy of this resolution be sent to and filed with all those concerned, including the press of Europe, Asia, America and Africa.

Printed in *NW*, 6 August 1921. Original headlines and portions of the report are omitted.

1. A reference to an editorial written by W. E. B. Du Bois for *Crisis* magazine and published in the July 1918 issue under the title "Close Ranks" (*Crisis* 16, no. 3 [July 1918]: 1).

2. In an appeal issued shortly before the August 1921 convention, Garvey invited Du Bois and other members of the older Afro-American leadership to the convention: "This is not a time for personal differences; this is not a time to ask where a man was born, what country he came from, what organization he is attached to, and the college he graduated from; but this is the time for every man—let him be Du Bois, Moton, Garvey, Kelly Miller—to pitch in now to save the Negro race from the doom that threatens" (*New York Call*, 1 August 1921).

3. Smuts's political career was marked by his advocacy of racial segregation and white supremacy. He was responsible in 1902 for drafting article 8 of the peace treaty concluding the Boer War, which left the question of the native franchise to be settled by the white minority "after the introduction of self-government" (*Parliamentary Papers*, 1902, cd. 1,284, p. 12). Smuts was also the architect of the color bar regulations issued under the Mines and Works Act of 1911: "These reserved thirty-two categories of work for whites and prohibited the issue of certificates of competence in the Transvaal and Orange Free State to any person of colour" (H. J. Simons and R. E. Simons, *Class and Colour in South Africa, 1850–1950* [Harmondsworth, England: Penguin Books, 1969], p. 174). In a May 1917 speech in London, Smuts warned against arming Africans as soldiers in European conflicts, which he believed threatened the maintenance of civilization. He also defended the South African policy that kept the native population "apart as much as possible in our institutions, in land ownership, in forms of government, and in many ways" (*Times* [London], 23 May 1917). Later, in 1920, Smuts inaugurated a "don't hesitate to shoot" policy and enforced it against striking African workers in Port Elizabeth. When police opened fire following the dispersal of demonstrators, 20 demonstrators and 3 white bystanders were killed, and 126 others were wounded. Earlier in 1920 Smuts piloted through parliament the Native Affairs Act, "to side-track the African demand for the right to sit in parliament" (Simons, *Class and Colour*, p. 251) by creating a native affairs commission and local councils in the African reserves. Smuts would also be responsible for enacting the Natives (Urban Areas) Act of 1923, which legalized compulsory segregation and instituted the registration of all labor contracts in urban areas (Simons, *Class and Colour*, p. 315).

4. Giuseppe Garibaldi (1807–1882), Italian patriot, was instrumental in establishing the kingdom of Italy (*WBD*).

5. Honoré Gabriel Victor Riqueti, comte de Mirabeau (1749–1791), was an influential figure during the early years of the French Revolution (*WBD*).

6. Jeanne Manon Roland (1754–1793), whose salon was a gathering place for French Republicans and Girondists, was later guillotined after the Girondists fell from power (*WBD*).

7. Voltaire was the assumed name of François Marie Arouet (1694–1778), French writer, philosopher, and political thinker (*WBD*).

8. Leo Tolstoy (1828–1910), the leading Russian novelist and social philosopher of his time (*WBD*).

9. According to Du Bois, "The [Pan-African] Congress directed its executive officers to approach the League of Nations with three earnest requests, believing that the greatest international body in the world must sooner or later turn its attention to the great racial problem as it to-day affects persons of Negro descent." They made four requests: the appointment of a black member of the Mandates Commission; the creation of a section of the International Bureau of Labor "to deal particularly and in detail with the conditions and needs of native Negro labour, especially in Africa and in the Islands of the Seas"; the direction of the league's attention to "the condition of civilised persons of Negro descent throughout the world"; and the initiation by members of the league who were colonial powers of "an International Institute for the study of the Negro Problem, and for the Evolution and Protection of the Negro Race" (W. E. B. Du Bois to the president of the Council of the League of Nations, Geneva, 15 September 1921, League of Nations Archives, Geneva, I/15863/13940).

Marcus Garvey to Warren G. Harding

New York City [*1 August 1921*]

WE, THE REPRESENTATIVES OF THE 400,000,000 NEGROES OF THE WORLD ASSEMBLED IN THIS OUR 2nd ANNUAL INTERNATIONAL CONVENTION, BEG TO CONVEY TO YOU THE BEST WISHES OF OUR RACE, AND TO PLEDGE TO YOU AND YOUR GOVERNMENT THE HEARTY SUPPORT OF OUR PEOPLE EVERYWHERE, IN THE CAUSE OF JUSTICE, EQUALITY AND HUMAN RIGHTS.

2ND INTERNATIONAL CONVENTION OF NEGROES
MARCUS GARVEY
President

[*Endorsement*] Received Neg[*ative*] Br[*anch*]
8-8-21 3:45 PM

DNA, RG 165, file 10218-261/70. TG. Handwritten endorsement.

Marcus Garvey to Charles Evans Hughes

New York City [*1 August 1921*]

We the Representatives of the 400,000,000 Negro peoples of the World assembled in this our 2nd Annual International Convention, GREET YOU as one of the greatest STATESMEN of the Age, and wish for you a successful career as Secretary /of State/ of the greatest Republic in the World.

2ND INTERNATIONAL CONVENTION OF NEGROES
MARCUS GARVEY
President

DNA, RG 165, file 10218-261/69. TG. Handwritten correction.

Marcus Garvey to Eamon de Valera

New York City [*1 August 1921*]

We the Represent[a]tives of the 400,000,000 Negroes of the World assembled in the 2nd Annual International Convention, send GREETING, and pray that you and your fellow COUNTRYMEN will receive from the hands of the British your merited freedom.

2ND INTERNATIONAL CONVENTION OF NEGROES,
MARCUS GARVEY
President

[*Address*] Eamon de Valera, Dublin, Ireland

DNA, RG 165, file 10218-261/68. TG.

Marcus Garvey to George V of England

New York City [*1 August 1921*]

SIRE:

On principle, nothing would please the 400,000,000 Negro peoples of the World more, except the freedom of Africa, than the granting of freedom to the four and a half million people of Ireland, as also the emancipation of the poor people of India, and Egypt. Our Representatives fought in the last World War for Democracy, and the Self Determination of the weaker peoples, and we, assembled in the 2nd International Convention of Negroes, ask your Majesty to use your influence to prevent /future/ race wars by being just to all races.

> 2ND INTERNATIONAL CONVENTION OF NEGROES
> MARCUS GARVEY
> President

[*Address*] HIS MAJESTY GEORGE V, BUCKINGHAM PALACE,
LONDON, ENGLAND

DNA, RG 165, file 10218-261/67. TG. Handwritten correction.

Marcus Garvey to Mahatma Gandhi[1]

New York City [*1 August 1921*]

Please accept best wishes of 400,000,000 Negroes through us their representatives, for the speedy emancipation of India from the thraldom of foreign oppression. You may depend on us for whatsoever help we can give.

> 2ND INTERNATIONAL CONVENTION OF NEGROES,
> MARCUS GARVEY,
> President

[*Address*] MAHATMA GANDHI, AHMEBARAD,
BOMBAY, INDIA

DNA, RG 165, file 10218-261/66. TG.

1. Mohandas Karamchand Gandhi (1869–1948) was the leading figure in the Indian struggle for independence (*WBD*).

Report by Special Agent P-138

NEW YORK, N.Y. 8/1/21

MARCUS GARVEY—BLACK STAR LINE

NEGRO ACTIVITIES.

I called at the office of the Black Star Line today [*29 July*] and spoke to O. M. THOMPSON the Vice-President and he told me that he is expected to be killed any day by stockholders who were enraged by not getting the new ship the Phillis Wheatley which was promised them several times only to be disap[p]ointed. That on account of the temper of the people he was compelled to walk with two guards wherever he goes on the street. He said that

Garvey has turned the sentiment of the people against him accusing him of stealing and double-crossing on the matter of the purchasing of the ship.

P-138

[*Endorsements*] NOTED F. D. W.
FILE G. F. R.

DNA, RG 65, file 198940-222. TD. Stamped endorsements.

Article in the *New York Globe*

[2 August 1921]

"The Negro race is not a violent race. It is not addicted to fighting," said Marcus Garvey, "provisional president" of Africa and leader of the Universal Negro Improvement Association, a world wide Negro movement that is holding a thirty-day convention at Liberty Hall, in 138th street, Harlem, with delegates from America, Europe, Asia, and Africa, when seen to-day by a Globe reporter.

"Violence will only be an extreme resort," declared the Negro leader. "But history has shown that races that have enslaved other races will never willingly give up their slaves. In the past they have listened to nothing but force."

Mr. Garvey speaks with an English of which many a university professor might be proud.

DON'T LOOK TO TUSKEGEE.

"We have been misrepresented by our leadership," he complained. "We have been taught to beg rather than to make demands. Booker Washington was not a leader of the Negro race. We do not look to Tuskegee. The world has recognized him as a leader, but we do not. We are going to make demands."

Asked as to definite steps in the immediate future looking toward the enforcement of these demands, Mr. Garvey said that just as Europe is a conglomeration of races, so Africa must be one, but that the black race there is to be absolutely dominant. ["]The English, Portuguese, and French do not need to be expelled; they can remain in Africa as aliens now remain in Europe and America," he added.

"Do you mean the whole of Africa, Mr. Garvey?" he was asked.

"Yes, all of it, except the Mediterranean coast, which has been occupied by varied races so long."

The Negro is no longer to fight in some one else's wars, he declared. The Negro flag—red, black, and green—the flag of the provisional African republic, is to be his flag all over the world. This is not an American movement; it is a world movement, and the Negro everywhere is to respond to the call of that flag.

WHEN THEIR CHANCE WILL COME.

"Our chance will come," said Mr. Garvey, "when some war breaks out and the races of the world are disorganized. That will give the Negro his freedom. When there is a war between Asia and Europe, then we will make our demands."

The Negro is no longer going to fight, except in his own interest, is the idea permeating this convention. In the case of war between England and the United States, two nations containing millions of the Negro race, the Negroes will not fight each other. They will fight for any nation only if granted political status and in case the nation is threatened by a power that would destroy that status.

"The Negro is not contemplating the initiating of a fight," said the African president, "but we must protect our interests. We are going in for mass organization. In the past we have worked separately and individually, now we are going to organize, in three and a half years our organization has obtained 5,000,000 active members in Africa, Australia, Asia, and the Americas.["]

TO WIN BY EVOLUTION.

Asked about the movement's intentions with regard to the exercise of force, Mr. Garvey said:

"We are not distributing arms; we are not supplying implements of war. We are preparing the Negro race mentally and physically, and the Negro will win out by evolution. This convention feels that it must have friends. Humanity has found that it cannot exist of itself. It must have allies, and we are trying to get allies, white, and yellow, by diplomatic means."

"How long will it be before the Negro is free, Mr. Garvey?"

"How long? To-morrow, or it may be a hundred years. It depends on the evolution of the world. Our opportunity may come any time, or it may be long delayed, but we are going to fight for our rights in America by constitutional means and in Africa openly."

The time is not to be hastened by the sending of all American Negroes to Africa, he added, but pioneers among American Negroes and East-Indies Negroes are to go to Africa to forward the cause of emancipation.

BASED ON AMERICAN DEMOCRACY.

"Is the African republic to be socialistic?" asked the reporter.

"No," said Mr. Garvey, "It is to be based on American democracy. I think the state should own those things that are necessary to human exis-

tence." Asked as to the public ownership of such commodities as coal, [ ]
and railroads, Mr. Garvey expressed himself as in favor of it to some extent,
but said the republic was to be essentially a democracy and not a soviet.

Many of the delegates from other continents have not yet arrived here.
Those already here are happy and hopeful.

Printed in the *New York Globe*, 2 August 1921. Original headlines omitted.

Convention Report

[[*New York, 2 August 1921*]]

. . . The great congress began its business at 10 o'clock, the Right Hon.
Speaker-in-Convention Fred A. Toote presiding. Seated with him on the
rostrum were the members of the High Executive Council of the U.N.I.A.—
His Highness the Potentate, Mayor G. M. Johnson of Monrovia, Liberia;
His Excellency the Provisional President of Africa and President General of
the U.N.I.A., the Hon. Marcus Garvey; His Excellency the American
Leader, Dr. J. W. H. Eason; the Rt. Hon. the Asst. President General, Dr.
J. D. Gordon; His Excellency the West Indian Leader, R. H. Tobitt; His
Grace the Chaplain General, Dr. G. A. McGuire; the Rt. Hon. the Interna-
tional Organizer, Mrs. Henrietta V. Davis; the Rt. Hon. the High Chancel-
lor, Dr. G. E. Stewart; the Rt. Hon. the Counsel General, Wilford H. Smith;
the Rt. Hon. the High Commissioner General, F. Wilcom Ellegor; the Rt.
Hon. the Auditor General, Eli[e] Garcia; the Rt. Hon. the Minister of
Legions, Captain E. L. Gaines; His Hon. the Asst. Counsel General, William
Matthews, with His Hon. the Asst. Secretary General, J. B. Yearwood.
Hundreds of delegates were in attendance seated within the inclosure, while
beyond the barrier there was a large and enthusiastic crowd of spectators.

The Speaker welcomed the delegates and then introduced the Provisional President, Hon. Marcus Garvey, who struck the keynote in an inspiring address. After announcing that his official speech would be delivered at
the Tuesday morning, and expressing his pleasure at seeing so many delegates present, he continued:

A UNITED BODY

"We are assembled in this second annual international convention to
discuss business relating to this downtrodden, oppressed race of ours. We are
assembled here not as sectional groups, but as a united body. We are
assembled as coming from no particular section, but as coming from a race.
(Hear, hear.) I trust, therefore, that we will enter into the spirit of this
convention without prejudice to any location or locality, but that we will

discuss our questions, our problems solely in the interests of the entire Negro race.

"No one section of the Negro race can progress or develop without the assistance of the other sections of the Negro race. We have tried it in the past and we have failed. It is time that a change be brought about, and the Universal Negro Improvement Association comes into existence to bring about that change, and I feel sure from what has happened, from our experience of the past, that the Universal Negro Improvement Association has nothing to complain of, nothing to regret, as far as the change is concerned, because the change has really redounded to our interests and the interests of Negroes everywhere. (Applause.)

"Once upon a time [we] were wont to meet in convention as Elks, as Pythians, as little clubs and little [leagues?], and nobody ever paid any attention to what we said and what we did. But today when the Universal Negro Improvement Association [me]ets the whole world stands on tip t[o]e listening for the news. (Applause.) Already we have set the cables working and the news has gone to the four corners of the world that the four hundred million Negroes are together agai[n] in convention.

"You saw some white folks in here this morning. Did we go and look for them? No! They came and looked for us. (Applause and laughter.) I tell you th[e] Negro is now coming; he is right h[er]e. (Applause.) It was a pleasure [for] me to read just a li[ttle] different to the things we used to read. Last Sunday we read a bit of news about Jack Johnson preaching in a church.[1] They tried to make fun at the expense of the Negro, and we had a long bit Sunday morning also about two Negro thieves downtown holding up some people there—the old time order of things. But, thank God, this morning we gave them new news. We gave them news to think over, so that they can realize that Negroes are not only frivolous, not only thieves, but Negroes are statesmen (and frivolous men and thieves are to be found in all races, as well as statesmen). But they gave us credit in the past for being only frivolous, thieves and bootleggers; now they have to admit we have statesmen.

GOING FORWARD

"I spoke to a reporter this morning. He said: 'You are going to form an alliance. With whom are you going to form an alliance?' Is that not a change from a bootlegger? We have brought them to it. Let us go it the whole length. As for me, there will be no turning back. (Applause.) As an African citizen there shall be no turning back for me until the Red, the Black and the Green perches on the hilltops of Africa.

"The interviewer asked me another question this morning. He said: 'Do you mean to take all Africa? Are you not going to give some portion of Africa to the settlers there, for instance, those in South Africa?' I said, 'No, not even that, because they got it by slave labor, by force, by conspiracy, by fraud, by cheat, and, therefore, we do not recognize their ownership.' We mean that, too, and are going to stand behind that. (Applause and laughter.)

"We have come from all parts. We have come from the oppressed Southlands, as far as the Negro is concerned. We have come from the prejudiced sections of the North, we have come from the prejudiced sections of the West Indies, of South and Central America. We have come from the oppressed sections of Africa. We know our grievances. We know all our complaints, all our sufferings, and we are here to legislate against them. Remember, men, cowardice and weakness have never won anything in the world. (Cries of "no.") If you come from the South as cowards, you will go back to the South as cowards. If you come from the West Indies as cowards, you will go back to the West Indies as cowards. If you come from your respective spheres as cowards, you will go back as cowards. But if you come as bold men, you will go back as liberators of the race.

THE WORK MUST GO ON

"This work must be done, must be carried on, even at the sacrifice of the life-blood of some of us. And if you are going to be afraid of the South, the South will always be oppressed. If you are going to be afraid of conditions in the West Indies, the West Indies will always be oppressed. If you are going to be afraid of the oppressors in Africa, Africa will always be oppressed. But when you become bold enough to see the right, know the right, and demand the right, the world will consider you.

"We want the South to understand that the Southern Negroes must be emancipated. It is all well these Southern crackers talking about Negroes getting fresh up North, but I want them to understand that the safety of America depends upon the loyalty of Negroes in America, whether in the South or the North. And since the safety of this country depends on the Negro, whether of the South or the North, the Negro is entitled to a voice anywhere. And he is going to be heard now. He was not heard through N.A.A.C.P. because they compromised, but they shall be heard through the Universal Negro Improvement Association without any compromise. We must be heard, not as beggars, hat in hand, but as men demanding our rights because we are entitled to them. The question of humanity is a complex one and one that must be settled in this very age, and we are prepared to settle our part of it now. (Applause.) The South with its prejudice, its lynching and burning, is nothing else but a huge [b]luff. The world is run on bluff. That is all. The whole world is run on bluff. No race, no nation, no man has any divine right to take advantage of others, and if the other fellow takes advantage of you it is because he has bluffed you into deeming him a better man than you. The Negro realizes now that it is a question of bluff, and we are going to bluff for bluff. (Loud applause.)

"The interviewer, who saw me a while ago, asked me: 'What do you mean by fighting?' I replied: 'We mean just what it literally means: we are going to fight, constitutionally in certain places and politically and militarily in other places.' (Laughter and applause.) He said: 'What do you mean?' I said: 'You see in p[l]aces like America we recognize the Constitution and we want those things which belong to us under the Constitution; we will fight constitutionally, but in Africa we do not recognize.' (Cheers.) So he said to me: 'At what time are you going to fight?' I said: 'It may be tomorrow, it may be one hundred years.' He said: 'Do you mean to fight with the implements of war?' I said: 'I am not going to tell you that; we are getting ready, that is all.' So at the close he shook my hand and said: 'I sympathize with you, I feel your cause is just, and I am gone.' But do you think I am crazy to believe any white man telling me a thing like that?

THE GREATEST CONGRESS

"So we are assembled here as legislators. We cannot go into the congress hall, nor the House of Representatives, nor Parliament, but we are in the greatest congress, the greatest parliament in the world. It is right here now, and in thirty-one days the world will hear from us and will never forget us after that.

"As I said, I am not delivering my official speech yet, so I cannot touch on the business of the organization for the past year, and I cannot make recommendations for the ensuing year until Thursday morning, when I speak in answer to the High Potentate, but I am trying to get you in shape for the great work you have before you. Men, let us come to this convention with clean hearts. (Applause.) The world of Negroes oppressed is looking toward us for freedom and liberty. They have sacrificed to make this convention possible. They have sacrificed all their meager means, their meager earnings, to send us to this convention. For God's sake, let us be fair and just to them. You come from your churches, from your lodges, you come from your fraternities, from your different organizations, from the divisions of the U.N.I.A.; let us come as brothers and sisters ready to pool our intelligence, to pool our ability, and to see what we can do by so pooling to emancipate this troubling, oppressed race of ours. As representatives of the churches you are welcome to the convention, as representatives of the various fraternities, you are welcome to this convention. We want the best in you in intelligence, in interest and in purpose.

"This convention, I hope, will bring out the best in the Negro. We want men, we want leaders; not fellows who will malign leaders, but real leaders; and I hope that the branches will send out this year their most intelligent men, their most intelligent representatives; because we need intelligence to lead this movement to the success it deserves. Why, we need more intelligence to lead the U.N.I.A. than any government needs in the world. That is right. Because this organization represents a larger group of people than any government. We represent the interests of four hundred million people and our dear government here represents one hundred million. Therefore we have four times more business at stake. And if this government needs such intellectuals to lead, we want super-intelligence. No mediocre character can lead. We want fellows of ability. Fellows of light and learning.

PROMISED TO SERVE ONE MASTER

"And I will tell you something. Somebody is going to get hurt in this convention, if, when he comes to give his report as an executive officer, if he took the confidence of the people at the last convention, if that report is not clean and he cannot give a good account of himself. The Negro who deceives the Negro, when the Negro is in earnest, is a vagabond. For him you should have no respect. (Cheers.) We stood up before you here at the close of the convention last year and swore by the God Divine, by the Almighty God, that we would serve you to the end without faltering, that we would serve as one master, knowing no two masters, and, I trust each and everyone will be able to give a good account of our stewardship, that we served but one master during the twelve months. You, the delegates, you, the deputies from the different parts of the world have seen us, because we have been sent to you, and 'by their works, ye shall know them.' (Applause). You are the masters of the situation, you elected the men, the men we sent back to you; whatsoever you know of the men, let us know. (Applause.) We are not expecting you to hide anything, or to cover anything, otherwise, you are as guilty. If at any time you have met a representative of this council who was dishonest, immoral, who was untrue to this cause, it is for you, let him be High Potentate, President-General, let him be Secretary-General, Minister of Legions, or any member of the Executive Council, bring your charge against him at the bar of this convention. (Loud and prolonged applause.) Let him justify his actions; let him justify himself before this convention; and when you acquit him, it means that you are satisfied with his defense. So I expect you to come here with clean hearts, because you are not representing yourselves. Remember that. Hundreds of people in your divisions, in your churches, in your organizations, subscribed their dollar, their half dollar, their quarter, their five dollars to send you here, not for fun or sport, but with the prayer of God that you may do something to alleviate their condition. Therefore, I trust you will not recognize personal friendships in this convention, because, if you are looking to me for friendship to protect you, you are looking to the last man.

WARNS TRAITORS

["]Before this convention opens for business proper, let me say, as far as the U.N.I.A. is concerned, I have no friends. I have no brother, I have no mother, I have no father, I have no wife where the U.N.I.A. is concerned. When it comes to life outside, I have my friends. If you want a dollar and I have two, I will slip you one. But if it comes to the U.N.I.A., and you have taken a dollar and I know it, you are going to jail, as far as Marcus Garvey is concerned. And when you are gone to jail, as your personal friend I will be sorry for you and try to get a bond man to take you out of jail, but first of all I will have done my duty to the Universal Negro Improvement Association, to the post I hold, to the people and my God. If you are dishonest and you know it now, clear out of this convention, because you are going to be exposed. You are going to be exposed. There is nothing to be covered here. We are going to expose everybody who has something to expose.

"So that I trust you will enter into the spirit of this convention as I have advised you. I expect great things out [of] this convention. My life, the life of my race is bound up in this convention. This convention is going to live through the thirty-one days during which the U.N.I.A. is going to get a fillip, a new impetus to go out after the thirty-first of August and do greater work in the future than in the past.["]

Delegation Sent to Connectional Council

A vote of thanks was accorded the President-General and the Speaker-in-Convention for the excellent keynote they had struck in their opening speeches.

Dr. Eason moved the following motion which was carried: That the convention send a delegation to the Connectional Council of the A.M.E. Zion Church,[2] which was then in session a few blocks away, to bear greetings from the second Convention of Negro Deputies of the World.

The order of the day was then proceeded with.

Delegates and deputies were called upon to address the Assembly from the rostrum, stating the complaints, grievances and conditions existing in their several localities. The remainder of the day was occupied with this business.

A feature of the delegates' accounts was the generality of the statement that the greatest opposition the organization had to encounter was from Negro preachers who, as one honorable member said, no longer wanted the people to go to heaven, but to keep away from the U.N.I.A. There were a few, however, who stated that in their communities the preachers had greatly co-operated with them. . . .

Printed in *NW*, 13 August 1921.

1. Jack Johnson spoke at the New York Baptist Tabernacle, protesting his innocence concerning charges of violating the Mann Act (*NYT*, 1 August 1921; Al-Tony Gilmore, *Bad Nigger!: The National Impact of Jack Johnson* [Port Washington, N.Y.: Kennikat Press, 1975]; Randy Roberts, *Papa Jack: Jack Johnson and the Era of White Hopes* [New York: The Free Press, 1982]).

2. The Connectional Council was established in 1900 to make annual appropriations to departments within the church (Bishop William J. Walls, *The African Methodist Episcopal Zion Church: Reality of the Black Church* [Charlotte, N.C.: AME Zion Publishing House, 1974], pp. 107–108).

Speeches by Marcus Garvey and Charles H. Duvall

[[*Liberty Hall*, Aug. 2, 1921]]

The meeting tonight, the first of the series to be had in the evenings during the 31 days sitting of the Second International Convention of Negroes of the World, was a successful one. A large crowd, consisting of delegates, members and friends, was in attendance, and the enthusiasm and interest displayed in the proceedings were an echo of the brilliant meeting of the preceding night at the Twelfth Regiment Armory.

But two addresses were made: One by the Provisional President of Africa, who presided; the other by the Rev. Dr. Duvall,[1] of Malden, Mass., a delegate to the convention, and ardent sympathizer and supporter of the U.N.I.A. They were of a character, however, as aroused the highest emotions and feelings of the audience, an indication bidding fair for the success throughout the month of the convention's evening meetings.

Mr. Garvey announced that dozens of cablegrams had been received from various foreign divisions of the U.N.I.A. to the effect that they are celebrating simultaneously the opening of the convention, thus showing that the hearts of Negroes the world over at this time are beating in unison.

A COMMON COMPLAINT

Continuing, he said we have a common complaint to make at the bar of civilization, and we are not only going to make that complaint now, but we are going to demand redress. This remark was a signal that brought forth great cheering. The world ought to know, he further said, that it could not keep down forever 400,000,000 Negroes. In the past we were accustomed to address white people as our master, to come before them with hat off, and in a bowing, cringing manner, but today we recognize no master, for we are now masters of ourselves. We refuse, he went on, to bow and cringe as a race any longer. They promised concessions in the matter of Africa, but we are not satisfied; we want no concessions; we want everything in Africa, and will be satisfied with nothing less.

These and other epigram[ma]tic utterances delighted the audience immensely. It seems that Mr. Garvey has an inexhaustible mind of saying upon the great question of the redemption of Africa and the progress of the race; expressions that are original and forceful, and which the people never tire of hearing—in fact they always expect it from him whenever he rises to address them. Tonight he was in a humorous vein, and poked much fun here and there at the Anglo-Saxon race, saying that we had, for three hundred years, been in the academy of experience and hardships, and now that we are full graduates, we are going to teach the world; that it would be well to let it be known publicly that the Negro has changed his attitude toward the world.

Negroes heretofore, he remarked, have been accustomed to use the Bible only in solving their problems, and, in consequence, had failed; but from now on he will use, in conjunction with the Bible, the material forces and weapons used by the white men in gaining and maintaining his supremacy, in fighting his way to the top.

World Disarmament

He touched upon the subject of world disarmament, and said that President Harding has a big job on his hands in trying to induce the nations of the world to adopt this plan of bringing about world peace.[2] Each nation is waiting for the other to take the step first, of reducing its armament, while none is willing to take the initiative. He was glad, he said, that we are not engaged in the disarmament plan; for we have nothing to disarm now, excepting the Bible, and this we would not disarm ourselves of because of the many beautiful passages it contains of hope held forth to the Negro race.

In conclusion, he said that, whereas other people and other races had used their physical power to oppress others, he hoped that as a race we would never at any time use our physical prowess to oppress the human race, but that from now on we shall use our strength physical, moral and otherwise, for the preservation of humanity and for the preservation of civilization.

The second speaker, the Rev. Dr. Duvall, a new speaker in Liberty Hall, showed that he, too, possessed in marked degree the powers of an orator. He is not a West Indian, and deprecated the fact that the American Negro is inclined to hold aloof from the movement. It was the West Indian who, as a teacher, came to this country, he said, in the early years after the emancipation of the Negro and helped educate the Negroes in the South. This the West Indian did at a sacrifice of his life and through many deprivations and the suffering of much humiliation. But he did it to help his brother here. This the American Negro should not forget. He went on to show that the instrument known as the Declaration of Rights adopted at the convention last year was a document that ranked, in his opinion, even above the Declaration of Independence. He analyzed it, paragraph by paragraph, and proved its broad humanitarian spirit and that it expressed principles founded upon according justice and equality of opportunity to all mankind the world over. He had made a contribution of $100 to the cause, he stated, not as an investment in shares of the Black Star Line, from which to realize dividends or profits, but as a gift to help the cause in its forward march, and that he purposes to propose to the convention before its close that he be permitted to endeavor to raise, as a patriotic fund, $100,000 to the association by the people of New York. He is not interested so much, he said, in the Black Star Line as a business enterprise connected with the Association as he is in the cause which the Association represents of securing justice and freedom for the race and its emancipation from race hatred, lynching, segregation and the like throughout the world. He spoke in tones of great earnestness, impressed his hearers and sat down amid a salvo of cheering and applause that was indeed a very flattering comment to him as a speaker and loyal worker in the U.N.I.A.

MR. GARVEY'S ADDRESS

Members of the High Executive Council, Members and Friends of the Universal Negro Improvement Association, Ladies and Gentlemen:—We are pleased to welcome you to Liberty Hall tonight, the second night of the second international convention of Negroes of the world. As delegates to this great convention, you have come here to do the best you can to bring about a solution of the great problems that confront the Negro. The Negro, suffering not in any one land nor in any one country, but throughout the universe, has grasped the opportunity, now that the world is reorganizing itself, to play an important part in the reorganization. Hence we are assembled here from the four corners of the globe to give expression to our feelings, to give out to the world our intentions and to formulate plans by which we shall ultimately save ourselves.

Yesterday His Highness the Potentate opened this convention. It is for us, the delegates, to continue the convention and bring about the result that we so much desire as the representatives of the 400,000,000 of our race. Just at this hour the whole world has become acquainted with the fact that we are meeting in convention. The world will look each and every day, expecting much from us, and we are preparing to give much to the world.

DIVISIONS CELEBRATING

We have received dozens of cablegrams from foreign divisions which are celebrating simultaneously with us the opening of the convention. They are not only satisfied that we shall celebrate the convention in Liberty Hall, New York, but they themselves also desire to celebrate at home the opening of the convention. It shows that the hearts of Negroes the world over are beating in unison. (Applause.) We have had to travel a long way to get where we are; nevertheless, we are here. (Applause.)

You know, as much as I do, that it was a difficult proposition to get Negroes to see through one common spectacle, as far as their own interest was concerned; but today, thank God, all of us have one common outlook, because we have been suffering from one common oppression. That the Negro is oppressed goes without saying, and he is oppressed not in any one country, but throughout the world. That is why this organization is organizing, not only as a national movement, but as a universal movement, because we have a universal and not a national problem to solve. We are so positioned, we are so hemmed in, we are so environed, that if the Negro goes from America to the West Indies, he sees injustice, he finds oppression. If he goes from the West Indies to America, he sees injustice, he finds oppression. If he goes from this western Hemisphere to Africa, he sees oppression, he finds injustice. Our suffering, and the oppression against us, is universal; that, I say, is why we are organizing a universal, rather than a national movement. (Applause.) We have a common grievance, and we are making a common complaint. And we are not only going to complain, but we are going to demand redress. (Applause.) How long must we continue to be insulted, to be abused, to be tossed about, and to be kicked about by all other races in the world?

RACES ON STRIKE

All other races are on strike now. The Japanese struck over sixty years ago. The Chinese are striking now. The Hindus are striking now. The Egyptians are striking now. Four hundred million Negroes are striking (applause) and we are striking now with a vengeance, never to be abused, never to be tossed about, never to be kicked about again, because we have found the way to liberty. We have found the way to liberty, and we know it is only through climbing the battle heights that we can get to the destination of liberty. (Applause.) We are preparing ourselves to climb the battle heights, and rugged though the path may be, we are going to climb on until we reach the top; and you know that we can climb the battle heights. We climbed it in France and in Flanders; we climbed it in the Civil War; we climbed it in the Revolutionary War; we climbed it in the tribal wars of Africa, fighting for Great Britain. We shall climb it again, but this time with the goal in view of reaching the destination that is dear to our hearts as a suffering, struggling race.

The world ought to know that it could not keep down 400,000,000 Negroes forever. There is always a turning point in the destiny of every race, in the destiny of every nation, in the destiny of all peoples, and we have come now to the turning point of the Negro, where we have changed from the old, cringing weakling, and transformed into full grown men. We are talking in a strange tongue now, apparently to some. Why, we surprise some folk now, the way we speak. (Laughter.) White people hitherto have been accustomed to hear the Negro address them in that old-time, subservient manner, with hat in hand, a bending of the body, a shrinking look, and bowing, as he says: "Yes, boss; yes, master," to every remark that comes from the "master." But today we know no masters; we are masters of ourselves. (Applause.)

REFUSES TO CRINGE

And we refuse to cringe as a race any longer. We realize, we feel, that we are men, and we are demanding respect and our portion as men. (Applause.) How glorious a day it will be when humanity will settle down to deal out justice to all! How glorious a day it will be when Asia will have a right to rule itself, when Europe will have a right to exercise the right to rule itself, and when Africa will have the right to rule itself! (Applause.) We ask no more; we desire no more, and when that day comes I feel sure we will see the brotherhood of man, and realize the fatherhood of God; but until then we see no brotherhood. We are fighting for that objective, the objective of a free and redeemed Africa. (Applause.) In traveling toward that destination we will be deaf to all people whether they be of our own race or of any other race for postponing our travel toward that destination. There can be no postponing of this great issue.

Other men and other races everywhere whose eyes have been turned toward Africa are endeavoring to postpone for us the question of African freedom. They are using many subterfuges to bring about that result; but, fortunately, we have men among us whose vision is clear; we can see beneath the surface of every proposition. They may propose to a Du Bois to postpone the ultimate redemption of Africa by promising him certain considerations and he may be blind enough not to see beneath the surface, but the Universal Negro Improvement Association can analyze any proposition laid before the Negro race. (Applause.)

WANTS ALL OF AFRICA

They may promise concessions in Africa. We are not satisfied; we want no concessions; we want everything in Africa. They may promise a place in the mandatories of Africa; we want no such place; we want all. (Applause.) Like the Irish, we say we desire complete independence. That is what we want, and no Smuts and no David Lloyd George and no Winston Spencer Churchill and no Italian statesman and no French statesman need come to the Universal Negro Improvement Association with any compromising program. There can be no compromise, because we have suffered for too long. If Africa seems good to you, it should seem good to us, too. Why all this concession about Africa when they tell us Africa is a dark continent—a continent of savages and cannibals? What do you want there? Why don't you leave those cannibals? Why don't you leave those savages to themselves? Now, we are satisfied to transform the dark continent into the continent of light. There we see the star—the star of Ethiopia shining most brilliantly; the star beckons to us and we are traveling in the direction of that star. (Applause.) Europe ought to know that she cannot rule the world forever. Africa once ruled the world; Europe wants to rule the world and I believe Europe's time is up now. Africa shall, if not rule the world again, rule herself, and the scattered children of Ethiopia are preparing to exercise such a rule. Why, we have paid dearly for our college experience. We have paid dearly for our education. You know the average child when he goes to school gets the tamarind rod or he gets the strap, and in the process of five or six years he passes from that stage into another stage. We have had the tamarind rod and the strap to us for 300 years; we have been studying in the schools of adversity for 300 years; we have been studying in the academies of hardship and now we are full graduates tod[a]y, and we can teach now. (Laughter and applause.) And it is well that the world now knows that Negroes have changed their attitude toward the world. Once it was: "Give me Jesus and take the world," but the new Negro's attitude is "Give me part of the world and part of Jesus." (Applause.)

PRAISES NEW YORK FIFTEENTH

They caught us once in Africa with the red flag. 300 years ago they used the red flag to catch our foreparents in Africa; then afterwards for 300 years they used the Bible to temper down the Negro, and he had been well tempered down. Then afterwards they started to use the sword to keep us down; but they were not artful enough in the use of the sword in that they allowed us to use the sword also. We [learned?] everything of the Bible from Genesis to Revelations; in[as]much [as] nobody can preach more than a Negro Baptist preacher (laughter), and no one can fight more tenaciously than a Negro soldier. (Cheers.) As an example, we have the New York 15th. We can just "eat up" the Bible. Any Negro in here can tell you and explain to you some of the most beautiful passages in the Scripture. We have more graduates in theology than any other race. If you doubt it, just turn this meeting into a prayer meeting now (laughter) and you will hear more old religion this very night than you have ever heard before.

Yes, we have mastered everything in theology. We have studied the Bible from cover to cover, and, thank God, we have mastered the art of warfare. They tell us the Bible and the sword must rule the world, and we are going to follow them in their own example.

Now, understand, I believe in the sword. I am not one of those Christians who believe that the Bible can solve all the problems of humanity. It cannot be done; the Bible is good in its place, but we are men; we are the creatures of God and we have sinned against God, and therefore it takes more than the Bible to keep up with the age in which we live. Man is becoming so vile; man is becoming so criminal that you have to write other codes besides the Bible. You have to build jails so as to confine man because man is so bad. You have to build asylums of correction so as to confine man because man is so bad. Man is such a vagabond that you have to watch him all the time.

MAN MUST BE WATCHED

Once we could afford to watch man just with our physical bodies and selves, but today you have to watch man with implements of destruction because man is so vile. Therefore you will realize that it takes more than a Bible to handle man. Negroes have been using the Bible alone to handle this human problem, and that is why Negroes have failed. You have to get something other than the Bible. You have to get the material carnal weapon, because man is too vile to be dealt with otherwise, and, late though it be, I am appealing to Negroes everywhere to imitate the other races in their methods of protection. I am willing to preach the Bible and the Bible only if President Harding is successful in bringing about disarmament among the races and nations of the world. But I know he has a hard job on his hands, and I am telling him this: That there are no crazy people nowadays in large groups. You may find an individual in the nation crazy, but outside of Germany I do not believe you have many crazy nations. You understand what I mean. No nation is crazy enough to throw away the implements of protection, because each nation knows the villainy of the other nation. To think that Japan is going to throw away her implements first! You are crazy. Nobody is going to start, you understand; none of them is going to start discarding implements of war. England is waiting on Japan; Japan is waiting on America; America is waiting on France, because all of them know the other's tricks[.] (Laughter.) If you are waiting for disarmament you will wait until Gabriel blows his horn. (Laughter.) I am glad that we are not engaged in this disarmament plan. We have no time to waste; we have nothing to disarm now except the Bible, and we are not going to disarm the Bible because it has in it some beautiful passages of hope.

ETHIOPIA SHALL STRETCH FORTH HER HAND

It tells us that "Princes shall come out of Egypt and Ethiopia shall stretch out her hands unto God," and if for no other passage but that we will not disarm the Bible. So that while we are not engaged in this disarmament plan we will be glad if other races and nations will disarm, because it will prevent a lot of folks dying later on. (Laughter.) Let them throw away their guns; let them throw away their deadly gas; let them throw away all the implements of destruction, and there will be very little dying in Africa when we get there. All that they will have to do is—we will be generous enough to give them some of the ships of the Black Star Line on which we go to Africa to take them back to Europe or back to America to take some more Negroes back to Africa. So we are not against the disarmament plan because it will prevent certain folks dying later on.

MYSTERIES OF AFRICA

I was very pleased to see some of the banners in the parade yesterday. One of the banners read this way: "Negroes have mastered the hidden mysteries of Africa." (Applause.) I am glad that our scientists have discovered the hidden mysteries of Africa, and you know what that means— men can shoot at you and you do not die. (Laughter.)

The hidden mysteries of Africa have been the wonder of the world. For centuries explorers have been to Africa year after year, decade after decade, century after century, trying to unfathom the mysteries of Africa; but, thank God! the banners said yesterday that we ourselves have discovered the hidden mysteries. Others in the future will fight with their aeroplanes and we will fight with our hidden mysteries. Let them find out what that is. They hid it away for 300 years, and we will hide it away until we meet on the battleplain. Suffice it to say that the Negro has found out the art of his protection and we are journeying towards this destination of a free Africa with a full consciousness that the Red, the Black and the Green will one day perch on the hilltops of our motherland. (Applause.) All honor to the Stars and Stripes; all honor to the Union Jack as far as it will confine itself to Europe among the Anglo-Saxon folks; all honor to the Tricolor of France, yet, above all, all honor to the Red, the Black and the Green (Applause), our flag of hope, our flag of destiny. Wheresoever that flag be we will follow 400,000,000 strong. (Applause.) Our best wishes to the nations and races of the world; our best wishes to the Jew; our best wishes to the Italian; our best wishes to the Poles; our best wishes to the English; our best wishes to the Chinese; our best wishes to the Japanese; we admire you for what you have done. Late though it be, 400,000,000 of us are attempting to do for ourselves what you in the past have done for yourselves. (Cheers.)

Press Is More Intelligent

I am glad that the press of this country and the press of Europe has become more intelligent towards the objects of the Universal Negro Improvement Association. Once they said that we were anarchists, I.W.W.'s and revolutionists, and up to last year they printed some monstrous, hideous things about us; but I am glad now that they have a sober intelligence of our intention. Our intention is not to create race hatred; our intention is not to create race warfare; our intention is to work among ourselves for our own interests, in our own development. In doing that we do not mean to ignore the rights of other races. We yield the right to every race to develop on its own lines. Let the white man develop as he desires. Let the yellow man develop as he desires. If his God be of his race let him worship his God as he desires; if the white man has the idea of a white God, let him worship his God as he desires. We have found a new ideal. Whilst our God has no color, yet it is human to see everything through its own spectacles; and since the white people have seen their God through white spectacles, we have only now started out and, late though it be, to see our God through our own spectacles. The God of Isaac and the God of Jacob, let him exist for the race that believes in the God of Isaac and the God of Jacob; we believe in the God of Ethiopia (Cheers), the everlasting God; God the father, God the Son and God the Holy Ghost; the one God in all ages. That is the God we believe in, but we shall worship Him through the spectacles of Ethiopia.

A Radical Change

That has been a change—a radical change—you may say in our theology, but nevertheless a new man in every walk of life is here in the Negro race. We have a new Negro theology as well as we have a new Negro teacher and the new Negro statesmen; everything is new in this race today. We have changed the jackleg preacher for the new theologian, and in every sphere we have changed. We have to thank the white people for what they have done for us, that is, after they have found out their mistake. You know it was a mistake when they took Negroes into slavery. It took them 300 years to find it out. They never found it ou[t] until we told them a year ago that we were coming, sharpening our swords, 400,000,000 strong.

It was only then they found out that slavery was a big mistake. They did not see the diplomacy of the Negro. As I have often told you, the Negro is the greatest diplomat in the world. Several hundred years ago the white man came to this American continent from Europe, saw the land and coveted it. But at the time when he arrived here the land was occupied by a race called the North American Indian. The white man in quest of this land examined the land and formulated plans through which he would ultimately conquer the land and possess the land. He started warfare; he started war against the Indians—the aborigines. The poor innocent aborigines had no sense, had no diplomacy. These foreign invaders came with guns and powder and sword and shot and shell—implements that the Indians themselves did not have. All they had was the bow and arrow. They had not enough sense not to resist the men who came with all these dangerous weapons. They started with bow and arrow to fight the men with gunpowder and shot and shell. Naturally the men destroyed him because he was able to kill from a distance. The Indian did not have diplomatic sense enough to find out what the strange man had and how he used it. Because he did not have sense enough to find out that[,] the intruder successfully destroyed him, took away his country and today everybody knows that America is the land of the white man. He tells it to you everywhere it is a white man's country. Is it not so? (Cries of Yes! Yes!) Because the Indian did not have sense enough to resist him when he came here, [t]hey ultimately conquered America. They went with the same trick to Africa.

ADEPT IN DIPLOMACY

They went with gun and powder and shot and shell. The native African had the same bow and arrow as the North American Indian, but the Negro had so much sense; the Negro was such an adept in diplomacy that when he saw the stranger with this strange thing, he said: "Use that thing and let me see!" and the white man fires his gun and kills a deer half a mile away. The black man scratches his head and says: ["]That thing kills far." The black man levels his bow and arrow at the deer and finds that the arrow could not go as far as the gun went; it was non-effective in killing at long range. The white man demonstrated his intention to use that gun, not only against the deer and the animals of Africa, but against human beings in Africa, and the Negro scratched his head again and says: "I have nothing to fight that man with; I am not going to resist him." "I am going to let him believe that I am so foolish and ignorant as to follow him anywhere he wants to lead me"; and he allows the white man to go with his gun and powder and refused to fight him and allowed the white man to have his way. The white man thought he was doing a great thing by taking Negroes from Africa to work on the cotton plantations of America and the West Indies for 250 years. They did not know that the Negro was laying up to make himself a liability. The Negro followed them all the way to America and all the way up to the West Indies. Do you know what for? Just to find out how to use that thing. (Laughter.) And the Negro was so artful that when he started to use the thing for the first time in the Revolutionary War of America, he said: "Boss, let me go with you." They could not tell why the Negro wanted to follow the boss to the Revolutionary War. The Negro wanted to find out how to use that thing, (Laughter and Applause). They took him into the Revolutionary War and he learned how to use the thing. Then afterwards he started a Civil War and the Negro says: "Boss, I must go with you." They could not understand why this Negro—a slave—[was?] offering and so willing to fight and die alongside his boss. The Negro has had the world beat all the time for diplomacy. And we followed him all the journey for 300 years seeing how to make the thing and use the thing. And thank God, you cannot find men anywhere better able to use a rifle than the men of the New York Fifteenth. (Loud applause).

NEGROES HAVE GAINED EXPERIENCE

We have traveled a long journey; we have come a long way to get our experience, but nevertheless we have it and we are not going to give it up for all the Bibles in the world.

So that I thank you for your presence here this evening, the second night of our second international convention. You have learned not only the Bible, you have l[e]arned the strategy of warfare, but I am appealing to you to use power, your physical power 400,000,000 strong, not for aggression, but for human justice. Other people have used their physical power to take advantage of the Negro. I pray God that we will never at any time use our physical prowess to oppress the human race, but we shall use our strength, physically, morally and otherwise, for the preservation of humanity and for the preservation of civilization. The white race need have no fear of us; the yellow race need have no fear of us; we are not going to hurt anybody. Why, we have been the kindest people in the world—the most charitable people in the world, and we are going to be as charitable in the future as we have been in the past—but after we have won the freedom of Africa; not until then. When we build up a free Africa we will invite future Presidents of the United States to come and stay with us for a while in the Black House of Africa. (Applause and laughter.) When we build up our African republic we will some time send an invitation to the future Prince of Wales to come and stay with us a while in Africa, because we will send out also some of our counts and dukes and earls and peers to the foreign courts of the world. They will be stationed at the Court of St. James, of Washington, at Berlin and at all the diplomatic courts of the world. What is good for others is good for us. If the name of king sounds good to white folks, if the name of president sounds good to white folks, they also sound good to Negroes of the twentieth century. That is my message to you tonight at this second international convention, and I trust you will take it home. (Applause.)

THE PAN-AFRICAN CONGRESS

The president-general announced that the resolution that was moved and carried on the previous night at the Twelfth Regiment Armory relative to the pan-African congress, was dispatched by cable last evening to the different governments of Europe, and we had full assurance that today and tomorrow the press of Europe will publish the resolution for the information of the people domiciled in that part of the world. "We are determined," he said, "to take the 'pan' out of the African congress, because we feel there is no need for a pan-African congress in Europe. We can appreciate a pan-African congress in Africa, or a pan-African congress in America, where 15,000,000 Negroes live, or a pan-African congress in the West Indies, where 20,000,000 Negroes live, but we cannot see the reasonableness of a pan-African congress in Europe; and for that reason and for others, we consider that it is only a subterfuge. The idea of Negroes having a congress for their freedom and inviting white folks to be the spokesmen. Du Bois tells us that the delegates will come from the colonial offices of Europe; that England, Italy, France, Portugal and Belgium are to send delegates to this congress. Just imagine that! It reminds me of the conference of rats endeavoring to legislate against the cats and the secretary of the rats convention invites the cat to preside over the convention. That is a fair analogy for Du Bois' pan-African congress.[3] Just imagine these little lions—400,000,000— desiring to free themselves from the wolves and lions that have been eating them up for 300 years, and now we come to this convention we are calling a lion to preside. I am surprised at the philosophy of Dr. Du Bois. Why, he is a disgrace to Harvard. (Applause.) But men, let me tell you, people sometimes play fool to be wise, especially when their pocketbooks are at stake; and I can see a big pocketbook in somebody's hands. You must learn to see beneath the surface of things. This African proposition of the U.N.I.A. is causing many pocketbooks to become fat. Men are being paid handsomely to turn the tide of the Universal Negro Improvement Association's intention to redeem Africa completely; but we have enough statesmen in the U.N.I.A. to see beyond a ten-inch wall, and these fellows will have to come with some more new tricks, because we have studied in their own school for 300 years and know all their tricks now. The Negro has evolved a new statesmanship of his own, and they have to come with better than a pan-African congress to defeat the objects of the U.N.I.A. I am glad you did so splendidly in carrying the resolution unanimously last night. You have carried out the intention of the U.N.I.A. in defeating the designs of our enemies. . . .[4]

Printed in *NW*, 13 August 1921. Original headlines omitted.

1. Charles Harris Duvall (b. 1858) was the author of two books: *A Lecture: The Building of a Race* (Boston: Everett Printers, 1919) and *Twenty Years in the Pulpit; or, the Author's Greatest Secret* (Pittsburgh: City Mission Publishing Co., 1917). By November 1921 Duvall was UNIA commissioner for the state of New York. In July 1922, however, Duvall resigned (*NW*, 3 December 1921, 15 July 1922). On 13 February 1923 Andrew M. Battle, a Bureau of Investigation agent, interviewed Duvall. In his report Battle said: "Dr. Duvalle [*sic*] stated that Garvey should be convicted for using the mails to defraud, that if he (Duvalle) were called on to tell what he knew of Garvey and the U.N.I.A. in general, he would be glad to appear and bring with him letters that Garvey had written to him, which would assist in proving the conversion of monies pledged by the negro race for the purpose of purchasing stock in the Black Star Line, and that he, Duvalle, had resigned from office immediately on finding out that Garvey was traitor and hindrance to the progress of the black race." Battle also reported having interviews with Duvall on 18 February and 19 February 1923, in which Duvall reemphasized his willingness to testify against Garvey. Duvall did not testify during Garvey's mail fraud trial (DJ-FBI, file 61).

2. President Harding did not view the Washington conference as a vehicle for world peace but simply as a means to "relieve the crushing burdens of military and naval establishments" faced by the Western powers (Thomas H. Buckley, *The United States and the Washington Conference, 1921–1922* [Knoxville: University of Tennessee Press, 1970]).

3. On the eve of the congress, Du Bois published a statement asserting that "the Pan-African Congress is expecting representatives from the Colonial Offices of Great Britain, France, Belgium and Portugal" ("The Second Pan-African Congress," *Crisis* 22, no. 3 [July 1921]: 119). On 16 June 1921 Du Bois had written to the British ambassador, Sir Auckland Geddes, informing him that the Pan-African Congress had no connection with Garvey and the UNIA. He requested, as a measure of official British cooperation, that the London meeting of the congress have "some representatives of the colonial office who will explain frankly the present government attitude toward Africa and its future" (PRO, FO 371/5708). The Foreign Office in London endorsed this request and recommended to the Colonial Office that "an expert should attend their meeting in London and say what is thought fit" (ibid.). The Colonial Office decided, however, to turn down Du Bois's request, a decision that the Foreign Office viewed as "rather unfortunate in that they [the delegates] represent the more moderate U.S. Negroes"; in a message to Du Bois, the Foreign Office justified the negative decision "on the score of time," while at the same time giving him "a non-committal assurance of our friendliness" (ibid.). The records of the Brussels and Paris meetings of the congress do not indicate that official representatives of either the Belgian or the French colonial ministries attended. The *Negro World* later published a report that the congress had adopted a resolution "to summon him [Garvey] to be present at the next Congress to explain his program and enable this Congress to adopt a just attitude towards him" (*NW*, 17 December 1921).

4. Dr. Charles Harris Duvall's closing remarks have been omitted.

Convention Report

[[*New York, 3–5 August 1921*]]

SECOND DAY

[*3 August 1921*]

Wednesday was occupied in the same way as the previous day, the various delegates giving very interesting accounts of the progress of the work in their localities, their trials and difficulties. The unemployment prevailing everywhere was given as the cause of the failure of many divisions to do even greater work. Considerable enthusiasm was evoked by the narrative of a delegate from South Nigeria, West Africa, who assured the assembly that the Negro in Africa was now fully awake, thanks to Garvey, and urged that more support be given to the Black Star Line, Inc.

A delegate told a harrowing tale of conditions in Spanish Honduras where educational and medical facilities were very bad. He suggested that the convention take steps to have a Negro physician and surgeon and a minister of religion sent there.

Delegates from the Southern States complained of the lynching and of the antagonism of some of the white people to the organization, chiefly through ignorance of the real aim of the organization.

Exceedingly interesting was the address of an African chieftain who declared that there were hundreds of Africans who desired to come to headquarters this month, fired as they had been with enthusiasm by the U.N.I.A., but who could not do so, as difficulties were put in their way when it became known that they were coming to fall actively in line with the U.N.I.A.

He appealed to the assembly to stimulate the buying of shares in the Black Star Line, stating that the people in Africa had produce earmarked for the Black Star Line ships, which they had begun to withhold from other ships. Members of the U.N.I.A. would be surprised to know to what depths and how extensively the people of Africa had been stirred by the Garvey movement.

THIRD DAY

[*4 August 1921*]

Thursday was a highly interesting day. Immediately after prayer, His Excellency the President-General and Provisional President of Africa delivered his official speech.

A vote of thanks was unanimously accorded the Provisional President for his "statesmanlike, comprehensive and fearless report," the assembly rising in doing so. Discussion of the report was deferred.

Considerable discussion was provoked by a motion to the effect that delegates from the Southern States should be allowed to withhold their names and the names of the States from which they had come if they so desired.

Several Southern delegates as well as the President-General expressed strong disapproval of the motion, giving as their reason that the motion savored of cowardice. His Excellency said he felt that the Negro had entered upon a new era—an era of fearlessness. Four hundred million Negroes should not be afraid of any Southern State. As a matter of principle and policy he was against the motion.

The assembly then resumed hearing delegates on the conditions existing in their communities.

HARROWING TALES OF HARDSHIP

A recital of hardships through the bad economic condition and the prejudice of white fellow citizens followed, punctuated with some heated exchanges between members, as some protested against delegates addressing the house on any subject other than that laid down in the order of the day.

When the convention resumed business after the luncheon interval the Hon. Speaker in Convention announced that at a meeting of the Executive Council, just held, he had been appointed to act as Secretary General and his Excellency the President-General had been appointed to act as speaker. He thereupon relinquished the chair in favor of the new appointee.

His Excellency the President-General, on taking up his new office, explained, in answer to a question by a delegate, that since his return to the United States he had been informed that the Rt. Hon. Secretary General, J. D. Brooks, had absented himself from New York for six weeks[1] without the authority of the Executive Council and had visited several branches of the organization, holding meetings. He had given the Secretary General time enough to report, and as he had not appeared the Executive Council had suspended him from office pending an impeachment by the convention.

The delegates then resumed their statement of conditions.

In the course of his remarks a delegate, digressing, stated he had noticed there was an inclination on the part of the Negroes living in New York to be factious, some saying that the movement was a West Indian one. It mattered not to the people of his locality who were at the head of affairs. The movement was one for Negroes—it did not matter in which country they had been domiciled—and should be supported by all Negroes.

Shortly before adjournment was taken the delegation which had been sent to take the greetings of the convention to the Connectional Council of Bishops of the A.M.E. Zion Church reported that they had had a most cordial reception and that the bishops were willing, after they had given due consideration to the aims and objects of the U.N.I.A., to fall in line with the movement.

FOURTH DAY

[*5 August 1921*]

Two more official reports were presented on Friday—the High Chancellor's and the Auditor General's.

Consideration of the report was deferred.

The Hon. Auditor General then read his report.

On a delegate asking for further information re the item "$46,556.20— goodwill, 'Negro World'," the Auditor General explained that before the existence of the parent body of the U.N.I.A.[,] The Negro World was owned by the New York local, a branch of the organization. Under the constitution it was necessary that ownership should pass from the New York local to the parent body, and so The Negro World was bought by the parent body for the sum of $60,000, its estimated cost.

Consideration of the report was deferred.

It was announced that the report of the Secretary General's Department[2] would be delivered on Monday, August 8.

The order of the day was then proceeded with.

A few more delegates having told of the condition of things in their divisions the luncheon adjournment was taken.

On the resumption on the suggestion of the acting spea[k]er, His Excellency the President-General, it was moved and carried that the convention adjourn until 10 o'clock Monday, August 8, so as to permit the delegates to attend the opening of the Women's Industrial Art Exhibition held in conjunction with the convention.

He then introduced Miss Mary Johnson, the secretary of the Exhibition Committee.

Miss Johnson delivered a stirring address, in which she expressed the determination of the women to do their share in the redemption of Africa.

The meeting then adjourned.

Printed in *NW*, 13 August 1921. Original headlines omitted.

1. See "Dr. J. D. Brooks Makes Okmulgee His Headquarters," *NW*, 9 April 1921. On 25 June 1921 the *Negro World* reported that Brooks had "addressed a mammoth meeting in Cleveland, Ohio," and that he had then traveled to Cincinnati. There were no further published reports of his activities before the August 1921 convention.

2. According to a Bureau of Investigation report, on the same day the convention was informed of the change, "It was announced that Rev. Brooks, the Secretary General, cannot be found, hence the financial report of the U.N.I.A. was not given. They charged him with misappropriation of funds and efforts are being made to issue a warrant for his arrest" (DNA, RG 65, file BS 198940-230).

Editorial Letter by Marcus Garvey

New York, August 3, 1921

FELLOW MEN OF THE NEGRO RACE, *Greeting*:

We are now celebrating the opening of the second annual convention of the Negro peoples of the world. This convention is to continue its sessions in Liberty Hall for 31 days and 31 nights. It is expected that 50,000 delegates will take their seats during the entire month of the convention. These delegates are sent as the representatives of the 400,000,000 Negroes of the world, and they are charged with the sacred duty of discussing the problems that confront the race and legislating in the race's interests.

As a people we have never had the privilege of a voice in government. We have lived under separate and distinct flags, claiming separate and distinct nationalities, but we have never been called by those flags or governments to give expression to our feelings in any legislative chambers of such governments. But today we are glad to be able to assemble among ourselves as a congress of men and women, determined to pass legislation in our own interest.

The Negro has reached the cross roads of Time, when he must strike out on his own account. Humanity everywhere has studied to exhibit that selfishness which characterizes the individual as well as the collective whole. Groups everywhere are endeavoring to take advantage of conditions and circumstances to suit their own group ideas. And when we come to contemplate the fact that there are 400,000,000 Negroes in the world, we cannot but admit that it is right, that it is fair, that it is just that we should in our own protection, seek to gather around us those ideas, those principles, that will lead us on to that goal that is sought by the many independent groups that are striking out in their own interest.

The Universal Negro Improvement Association, under whose auspices this convention is being held, desires to see the Negro taking a place in the world that will enable him to demand the respect of other races, and, at the same time, to continue his existence as an independent human entity. In the program of self-protection we seek the building up of a nation; hence, the cry of "Africa for Africans," those at home and those abroad. We desire a free Africa, a greater Africa. With the argument that Asia belongs to the Asiatics, that Europe belongs to the Europeans, the 400,000,000 Negroes feel that Africa belongs to the Africans, and everything that has been done by the other peoples to enhance their own interest should also be done by the Negro in his own behalf, if he is to continue his existence as a man.

It is no use complaining against the other races that they will not give us a chance. It is no use sending up petitions to other races asking them to give us a hearing. It is the right of every race, it is the right of every nationality to strike out in its own behalf, and we of the Universal Negro Improvement Association, through this convention, are calling upon Negroes everywhere to exercise their moral, financial, physical strength to demonstrate to the world that the time has come for us to establish ourselves as an independent national force.

The holding of this convention is an opportunity that the Negro should seek to support in every way. So I appeal to every Negro to send to the Secretary-General of the Universal Negro Improvement Association at 56 West 135th Street, New York, United States, during the month of August whatsoever financial help is possible, so that the delegates attending the convention may be able to legislate the necessary requirements out of the finances of this organization.

Trusting that each and every one will do his or her best during the month of August to support the Universal Negro Improvement Association and the Black Star Line, I have the honor to be, Your humble servant,

MARCUS GARVEY

Printed in *NW*, 6 August 1921. Original headlines omitted.

Capt. Adrian Richardson to Marcus Garvey

Kingston Ja Aug 3 1921

Surveyors pronounced Kanawha seaworthy[.] Stores exhausted. Require not less fifteen hundred immediately[.] Replenish same[.] Satisfy crew wages[,] captain Crew better mood[.] All anxious re sailing[.]

[ADRIAN RICHARDSON]

Garvey v. *United States*, no. 8317, Ct. App., 2d Cir., 2 February 1925, defendant's exhibit GG. TG.

J. Harry Philbin, United States Shipping Board, to A. Rudolph Silverston

[*Washington, D.C.*] August 3, 1921

My dear Mr. Silverston:

I have to refer you to your communication of July 8, 1921, offering to purchase on behalf of the Black Star Line, Inc., the ex-German steamship ORION.

I have to advise you that on August 2, 1921, the Board by formal resolution accepted the offer of the New York Ship Exchange on behalf of the Black Star Line, Inc., to purchase said steamship ORION, ex-Prinz Oskar, "as is, where is", for the sum of $225,000, payable 10% cash on delivery, and 10% each month thereafter until the entire purchase price is paid, with interest on deferred payments at 5% per annum, the purchasers to furnish a performance bond satisfactory to the Shipping Board to guarantee fulfillment of contract.

Prior to the delivery of this vessel to you it will be necessary for you to deposit with the Board a certified check for $10,000 covering the balance of the initial 10% payment. Furthermore, the requisite performance bond guaranteeing the fulfillment of the contract must be furnished, together with cover notes indicating that appropriate insurance has been arranged in favor of the Board.

Upon receipt of the performance bond, the same will be submitted to the Legal Division for examination following which appropriate documents will be prepared for execution covering the transfer of this ship to you. I am requesting the Director of Insurance to advise you of the requirements of the Board concerning the form of policy to be obtained.

After the foregoing details have been attended to, arrangements will be made by this Division to effect immediate delivery of the ORION to the buyers. Very truly yours,

J. HARRY PHILBIN
Manager Ship Sales Division

DNA, RG 32, USSB, file 605-1-653. TLS, carbon copy. Copies were sent to general counsel and Insurance Division.

J. Harry Philbin to the Treasurer, United States Shipping Board

[*Washington, D.C.*] August 3, 1921

SALE OF S.S. ORION

There are transmitted herewith certified checks, as listed below:

$5,625.00, drawn on the American National Bank of Washington
1,875.00,   ''   ''   ''   ''   ''   '' ''   ''
5,000.00,   ''   ''   '' Chelsea Exchange Bank of New York

The total amount of these checks, $12,500, is to apply against the purchase price of the ex-German steamer ORION, sold to the Black Star Line, Inc., for the sum of $225,000.

Before delivery of the vessel, however, it is necessary for the purchasers to furnish a performance bond, satisfactory to the Board, guaranteeing fulfil[l]ment of their contract. Will you therefore kindly hold the checks transmitted herewith in escrow until you receive further advice from this division.

Details of this sale are given in a separate memorandum.

Kindly acknowledge receipt.

J. HARRY PHILBIN
Manager Ship Sales Division

DNA, RG 32, USSB, file 605-1-653. TLS, carbon copy.

Official Convention Report by Marcus Garvey

[*New York*] August 4, 1921

May It Please Your Highness and
Delegates of the Convention:

As President General of the Universal Negro Improvement Association, elected by your popular vote, a year ago, it is for me to present to you this, my first report, of the work carried out under my administration for the past year.

Before our convention met a year ago our organization existed only as a scattered number of branches organized through my instrumentality. The convention brought all the branches together, and in open conclave we elected an Executive Council of which I became a member. We also adopted our constitution in which authority was given me as President General to supervise the work of the minor officers and to be general administrator of the affairs of the organization as elected for four years.

I must say that the past twelve months have been brimful of great results for the Universal Negro Improvement Association and the cause Afric. Whilst last year we had a scattered membership of four million, not thoroughly organized, I am now able to say that pains were taken to reach them through their various divisions and to have them live up to the principles of our constitution. In the prosecution of this purpose I visited several of the branches in the United States of America, especially in the Eastern, Midwest and Western centers. I found the branches ready to receive me and the people enthusiastic everywhere to fall in line with the principles of the Universal Negro Improvement Association. I was successful in building up strong followings in centers like Philadelphia, Pittsburgh, Boston, Chicago, Detroit, Cleveland, Cincinnati, Buffalo and Toronto. Whilst these branches mentioned, and others not mentioned, multiplied themselves in membership, after each and every one of my visits, I have discovered that other officers of the council had been through these divisions after my visits, and in many cases have destroyed the morale and solidarity of the members; in some instances they have practically ruined the work of the U.N.I.A. In many cases where they were called upon to investigate the conditions of branches and to honestly bring about reorganization, that they purposely and wilfully showed partiality to friends and acquaintances as against the true interest of the organization and those concerned.

This is borne out by the many complaints I have received from the branches everywhere where some of these officers have visited. This tends in a great way to handicap the work in the U.S.A. I have discovered also that great confusion exists among the branches everywhere, caused principally through the dishonesty of some of the local officers, involving, in some instances, presidents, secretaries and treasurers. Many cases have been reported to me where presidents acted as their own secretaries and treasurers, and kept all the funds of the divisions, and where secretaries would receive funds without turning same over to the division, and where the treasurer would abscond from divisions with the funds of the division. Through the actions of such men the millions of members whom we had and those who would have joined, became suspicious and satisfied themselves to be inactive rather than to be active members of the organization. I may say, however, that up to the 23d of February we had the American field, to my knowledge, under control. We had succeeded in establishing hundreds of new branches, and we were getting new members by the thousands. Because of the satisfaction afforded me through the enthusiasm of the people in America I made plans to pay an official visit to the branches in Central America and the West Indies, leaving New York on the 23d of February with the intention of remaining for five weeks in the various parts mentioned. In my trips to the tropics I visited several of the branches in Cuba, in Jamaica, in Panama, in Costa Rica, in British Honduras and in Guatemala. I found that the branches, several of them in Cuba, Jamaica and the other countries, suffered in like manner as the American branches from dishonest leadership. In many instances where presidents and secretaries and treasurers at times would misappropriate the funds of the divisions, making it difficult for the members to establish confidence in their administration. I was forced to remain in the West Indies and Central America over the five weeks contemplated; in fact, I had to remain away from America for nearly five months, caused principally through several enemies, both personal and enemies of the organization, using their influence with the government after I had left the country to prevent my return.

I have learned that not only enemies from without did make representations to the government against my returning to the United States, but that members and officers of the Universal Negro Improvement Association did encourage and engage themselves in such representations to the government. Through the misrepresentations made to the State Department, all the American Consular Agents in Central and South America and the West Indies were instructed by the State Department not to vise my passport for a return to this country. Through the various Consuls refusing to vise my passport I was prevented all during that time from returning to America to take up the ends of my work. During this absence a great state of demoralization set in as by information supplied us, and complaints made. No respect was shown for the authority of some of the members of the Executive Council, who acted just to suit themselves rather than to foster the work of the organization.

According to complaints that I have received, some of these officers conducted themselves in such a manner as to have caused the branches where they visited to have lost respect for them. All this tended to hamper the work of the U.N.I.A. for the last five months, through which we have suffered immensely.

I desire to inform you, most honorable delegates, that the time has come for us to be more critical in the selection of the men who are to lead this race of ours and to carry on the work of this organization.

We need men who have the conviction of service to the race, men who will not feel themselves above the people when elected to high positions. I have had to deal with men since the convention who felt that because they were elected to positions that it was not necessary for them to do any work to enhance the cause of the U.N.I.A., but that they should collect salaries by just sitting down without making any effort to reach the people on whom we have to depend for the upkeep of this movement.

I must say that among the executive officers I have found some honorable and worthy colleagues. I have received great assistance during the past year from His Highness the Potentate, His Highness the Supreme Deputy, the Right Hon. International Organizer, His Excellency the American Leader, High Chancellor, the Right Hon. Commissioner General, the Right Hon. Auditor General, the Right Hon. Counsel General, the Right Hon. Asst. Counsel General, the Right Hon. Assistant Secretary General, His Grace the Chaplain General, the Minister of Legions, Hon. Speaker in Convention and several members of the Field Corps, yet in one or two instances a few of the above mentioned officers have given me more than ordinary trouble to get them in proper working shape, whilst the rest of the above officials did everything possible to carry out the commands of this convention. They gave me no trouble in carrying out the commands given them and it is for us to consider them in the best way possible. Other officers have been a source of disappointment to me, and I feel sure that this convention will take steps to create better conditions under which we can continue the great work we have before us.

From my varied experience with the branches and with individuals, officers and officials of this organization, I think it is wise to suggest to this convention that we take immediate steps to establish a civil service for the Universal Negro Improvement Association, out of which we will train, discipline and place our men for the work that we have to accomplish. I am suggesting that this civil service prepare the men and women who are ambitious and desirous to serve, and send them out as executive secretaries to the various branches; that is to say, many complaints have come from divisions of the dishonesty of presidents and secretaries and treasurers and the disloyalty of the officers generally causing at times resignation among the officers or a general reorganization of the division, that it is wise that to prevent such an occurrence in each and every branch, that an executive secretary from the civil service of the U.N.I.A. be sent from headquarters to each and every branch and that the executive secretary be responsible to the parent body in protecting the interest of the members of that locality as against graft, dishonesty or disloyalty of any local officer elected by the people through confidence. This executive secretary would keep in his custody the records of the local division so that should the people of that local division call upon their officers to resign or should they desire a reorganization of the division, that the elected officers would not remove the records and documents pertaining to that division to the loss of that division, but that said records and documents would always be in the custody of the civil service of the U.N.I.A., and would be available to be handed over to any new set of officers as elected by the people.

I have also marked the embarrassment of our members in identifying themselves at different parts of the world where they have been refused help and protection not by other branches only, but by institutions and governments. In that our organization is recognized as a world power, and appreciated not only by ourselves but by established governments of the world[,] I am recommending that this convention pass legislation to establish a passport identification service for the benefit of our members. That is to say, we will issue passports of identification to each member of the U.N.I.A. in good standing, and that passport will be used by that member traveling to any country, or any part of the world. That passport identification will also recommend him to the consideration of all divisions, as a bona fide financial member of our organization. I am also suggesting that steps be taken immediately to raise a large sum for the purpose of financing and carrying out the bigger plans of our organization.

Relative to our work in Liberia, it is for me to inform you that in February we sent a contingent of men under the leadership of His Highness the Supreme Deputy to start operations. According to the report of His Highness the Potentate, the men arrived and were directed by him to start immediately in putting through the plans of the organization. From the report we have gathered everything is working splendidly in Liberia.[1]

During the past year the Executive Council, so as to be able to finance the great work we have before us, decided to raise a loan of $200,000 from our membership, under the heading of the Liberian Construction Loan. From reports received from the Auditor General I believe $137,458.22 were subscribed by the membership through this loan.[2]

Owing to my absence in Central America and the West Indies, there seems to have been a falling off in the loan drive because of the demoralized condition of the branches as visited by some of the officers referred to in the earlier part of this, my address.

At the present time there is a great financial depression among the Negro peoples everywhere. Millions of our men are without employment in America, the West Indies, and Central America, and it is therefore necessary for this organization to make desperate efforts to put through this African programme so as to alleviate the sufferings of the race in these parts.

I would also like to bring before this honorable convention the fact that legislation should be enacted for the purpose of creating a veto power on the part of the administrator of this organization, against any unreasonable demand that may happen to pass through the Executive Council, which would in a way embarrass the finances of the organization. This suggestion originates from my experience of the council and individual executive officers at times creating bills and ordering the paying of bills or the increase of wages, etc., or salaries, without taking into consideration the financial resources available for the proper liquidation of such liabilities.

It is for me to assure you, very honorable delegates, that the U.N.I.A. in sentiment and in fact has grown since last convention by leaps and bounds. We have taken complete possession of the minds of the people, and millions are ready everywhere in these United States of America, South and Central America, the West Indies, and Africa, to do everything possible for the realization of the objects of our organization.

But the great difficulty is to find honest, upright, sincere leadership to take care of these millions of willing souls. As far as financing the movement goes, the people are willing to do everything, but because of past experiences in other organizations, and even in some of our divisions, where the leaders have been dishonest, people are somewhat reluctant to immediately respond to the financial demands of the Universal Negro Improvement Association. They desire first to be convinced that our leaders are strictly honest and when they prove them, it will not be a question of money, because they will give millions for the successful carrying out of the plans that we have all laid. The fault, therefore, is not with the people, because, as I know, they are conscientious, willing, true, and they will sacrifice their all for the principles of the Universal Negro Improvement Association. The fault is with the leaders. It is for this convention, therefore, to see to it that honest leaders are elected to lead those poor suffering people out of their woes and tribulations.

From the experience I have received through my contact with the people everywhere in Central America, North America, the West Indies and South America, I feel sure that we have a bright year before us. We can treble our membership in the ensuing year because the people are willing to join everywhere, but that this convention is the most representative body of the entire organization, I am asking you to take steps right here to enact legislation as will enable us to guarantee the honesty and sincerity of those who are to serve us as leaders. You have nothing to be discouraged over. The U.N.I.A. is climbing, and I feel sure that this is only a question of a few more years when we will perch our banner on the hilltop of success.

It is for me to also report to you fellow deputies that oral charges have been made against many members of the Executive Council who swore at the last convention to be loyal and true to the trust of this organization, that they have been using the time that they should have devoted to the work of the organization for their own personal business and that in some cases that they have been unfair enough as to use the funds of our organization in paying their way to their own personal business. That the complaints have come from the delegates, I trust you will bring the matter up in convention and have it rectified immediately.

As an incentive to better service on the part of certain of the high officers of the organization, I would suggest that legislation be passed to better regulate the salaries of such officers. I would suggest that instead of each officer getting an absolute maximum salary, provisions be made that his salary be started at a minimum and a maximum, the minimum to rise by increments to the maximum, according to the ability of each officer.

I feel sure that we have been encouraged by the ringing message of His Supreme Highness the Potentate. It is for us in the ensuing year to be as loyal to him and his government of this organization as we have been in the past. As the President General and administrator I renew my pledge to do all within my power to carry out the commands of this convention, representing the interest of four hundred million Negroes of the world, and to be loyal to the commands of His Highness the Potentate, whom we have sworn to obey, in the execution of his duty as the head of the four hundred million Negroes of the world. Yours very truly,

MARCUS GARVEY
President General

Printed in *NW*, 13 August 1921.

1. At the time of Garvey's report, work in Liberia had apparently been halted. Crichlow returned to New York at his own expense, and in September he asked Garvey for back pay due him for service in Liberia. When Garvey refused, Crichlow sued. In February 1922 Crichlow won a judgment of $700 (*NW*, 4 February 1922).

2. According to a confidential report by the Bureau of Investigation, President Harding's proposed $5 million loan for Liberia interfered with Garvey's effort to collect money for the UNIA's Liberian Construction Loan (DNA, RG 65, file BS 202600-33-292). On 3 August President Harding urged the U.S. Congress to approve the loan, stressing the commercial and military potential of the port of Monrovia for the United States. In the end, Congress rejected the loan (Nancy Kaye K. Forderhase, "The Plans That Failed: The United States and Liberia" [Ph.D. diss., University of Missouri, 1971]).

Marcus Garvey to President C. D. B. King

[*New York, 4 August 1921*]

To His Excellency, the President of
the Republic of Liberia and His
Honorable Associates on the Plenary
Commission.

Greetings: Respectfully represents that we, the Executive Officers, Deputies and Delegates of the Second International Convention of the Universal Negro Improvement Association in Convention assembled, do hereby desire to express to you and to the people of your noble Republic, our earnest desire to be of service in whatever way, industrially and commercially, you may wish.

That, in consequence of certain misrepresentations as to the political aims of this association toward Liberia, this convention wishes to emphasize and reiterate the views and ideas as expressed by the Potentate and President

General, that the purpose of the Universal Negro Improvement Association with respect to the Republic of Liberia, is solely and purely industrial and commercial, with a view of assisting the peoples of Liberia in strengthening and improving their country, generally.

That, with respect to the loan sought by the Liberian Republic from the Government of the United States, we, the delegates, here assembled, congratulate your Honorable Plenary Commission on the success so far attained, and pray that the ultimate result may be as your Honorable Commission may desire.

MARCUS GARVEY
President General

Printed in *NW*, 20 August 1921. Original headline omitted.

UNIA Auditor General's Report

[*New York, 5 August 1921*]

TO THE HONORABLE DELEGATES AND DEPUTIES TO THIS CONVENTION

Honorable Gentlemen:

It is not customary for the auditor of a company or an organization to submit any detailed report of his own, when statements and balance sheet submitted by the treasurer of said concern, are satisfactory to those who represent the financial interest of the business.

However, I may say that I have audited the reports as read by the High Chancellor, and that I have found all the items mentioned in the statement of receipts and disbursements to be true and correct and supported by proper vouchers and that all payments were made by the order of the President-General of the Association according to our constitution.

Nevertheless, it is always the duty of the auditor when such statement and reports have passed through his hands, to convey to the interested parties the impression that said report and balance sheet has made upon him, and also the true significance of the figures as lined up in the reports. It is also his duty to reveal to those in authority the various reasons why the report is good or bad, also the causes of loss of profit as found out by him, throughout his investigation and auditing of the transactions of the concern.

For the benefit of those who may not have fully understood the true significances of the report read by the chancellor, I will make the following comments:—

REPORT OF PARENT BODY

You have noticed that two separate and distinct reports have been made for the funds received by the parent body. The general funds, and the construction funds. The general funds include the natural resources of the parent body coming from the branches, such as membership fees, dues, assessment tax, and so forth, while the construction funds represent only the amount of monies received through sales of bonds for construction in Liberia.

The disbursements made from the funds of the parent body need no comment, as they are entirely in keeping with the maintenance and operation of the association.

In the expenses made out of the construction funds, the items of $4,000. represent the amount invested in materials for the building of our headquarters in Liberia.

The item of $4,463.42 represents the cost of a saw mill equipment, which was purchased by the Executive Council on the request of his Highness, the Potentate, and which is at the present time, in Hoboken, N.J., ready to be shipped to Monrovia, Liberia, at the first opportunity.

The items of $17,206.42, as also the one of $9,740.61 represent the salaries of the staff, both members of the Council and ordinary employees, who have labored for the sales of the bonds.

The items of $10,872.19 is the cost of railway tickets, car fares, and other conveyances of the staff throughout this country, and abroad, also for the disposition of the bonds.

The item of $6,400.00 for the advertising is self explanatory.

The item of $34,440.00 represents the investment of the parent body in the Black Star Line, Inc.

The item of $46,555.20 represents the cost of purchase of the good will of the Negro World, the official organ of the Universal Negro Improvement Association, from the New York Local for $60,000.00[.]

BALANCE SHEET—ASSETS.

The general funds of the parent body and the construction funds amounts to $10,913.67, which was the bank balance as per July 31st.

There is also a bank balance of $1,436.00 to the credit of the Negro World which is also to be credited to the parent body by virtue of the purchase of the good will of said Negro World.

The item of $2,154.00 for furniture and fixtures, represents the value of the furnitures of the various offices of the parent body, less a reasonable amount for depreciation.

The item of $3,494.30 mentioned as uncollected checks represent the aggregate amount of numerous checks returned by the bank and not yet collected from the makers.

The item of $4,463.42 is, as stated, the value of the saw mill equipment, which, being new, has no depreciation.

The item of $4,500 mentioned as inventory represents the cost value of the supplies on hand in the Chaplain General's office, the Commissioner General's office and the Secretary General's office, to be sold to the various branches of the U.N.I.A.

AMOUNTS RECEIVABLE.

The item of $37,690.52 represents the balance due by the various branches of the U.N.I.A. to the parent body of the 20 per cent dues.

The item of $68,664.80 represents the correct amount of death tax due by the various branches to the parent body. The amount which should have been received from death tax is $88,227.60, and only $19,562.80 have been received, which gives the uncollected balance of $68,664.80 above stated. Therefore the total assets of the parent body as per balance sheet is $233,340.71.

LIABILITIES.

The parent body has no other liabilities except the amount of $144,450.58, which is the amount of bonds sold during the year. This liability is extended over a period of ten years and the books show that there will be no more than $20,000 to be paid out in one year. The computed interest on said notes is $6,500. The total liabilities being, therefore $150,950.58, showing a net worth of $82,390.13, on July 31, 1921.

Before closing my comments I should like to say that the net worth of $82,390.13 is only the net worth of the central office of the association, but is not the net worth of the Universal Negro Improvement Association, which is to include the net worth of all the branches of the Universal Negro Improvement Association throughout the world.

I want also to call the attention of the honorable delegates to the important fact that the parent body has no other income but what is paid by the branches to its treasurer, and when the branches fail to maintain their obligations or fail to keep up their payments the parent body receives nothing.

I want also to bring to the attention of the honorable delegates that it is important for the presidents of the various branches to devise means and ways by which they can collect dues and death tax from the largest number of members in their branches.

The Secretary General's report shows a large membership throughout the world, but I have found that only a portion of the membership is financially connected with the parent body.

In conclusion I want to state that owing to the economic condition of the world at this time, and especially of our people, it is my opinion that the year just ended has been a successful one and that the operations carried out as well as the investments made are all going to bring great profit in the future. It must be understood that to maintain an organization as broad in its scope as the Universal Negro Improvement Association, large sums of money are required to meet the expenses.

If I should base my estimation on the experiences of the previous year I would say that a budget of no less than $300,000 a year is to be met by the Universal Negro Improvement Association if our construction work in

Liberia is to go on and if we are to have a large enough staff to attend to the work and if we are to maintain the propaganda that we have launched throughout the world.

I therefore recommend to the honorable delegates that before the rising of this convention you take into consideration the discussion of the budget for the following year, so that each branch or each district of the country where the Universal Negro Improvement Association is represented can be allotted a certain portion of the total amount, and that on your return to your respective homes you may see to it that they carry their part as decided by you at this convention. Respectfully yours,

ELIE F. GARCIA
Auditor General

Printed in *NW*, 13 August 1921.

Annual Report of the UNIA High Chancellor

[New York, 5 August 1921]

His Highness the Potentate, His Excellency the Righ[t] Honorable President General, Honorable Members of the High Executive Council, and Honorable Deputies: . . .

Since I took up my position I have visited Philadelphia twice, Pittsburgh and Boston. I was confined to my office work, which required me daily.

For five months out of nine I was in charge of Liberty Hall during the absence of the President General, which kept me busy day and night. It was indeed strenuous work in order to keep up the morale until the President returned. He found everything in full action. He took up from where I stopped and continued to the present. We have no complaints whatever. The members of Liberty Hall are indeed loyal.

RECOMMENDATIONS

1. I recommend that the officers of the various divisions, on whom we depend for the success of this organization, show the members the necessity of paying the $1 per year assessment tax which was voted for at the convention of 1920.

2. That the death tax be sent to the parent body regularly.

The work of the U.N.I.A. is not to be carried on by so many fits, but by constant course of progress; still gaining ground upon our opponents, still approaching nearer to the goal. Let not your exertions end in tears; mere weeping will do nothing without action. Get on your feet, you who have voices and power; go forth and publish the doctrine of the U.N.I.A. in every street and alley. You that have wealth, go forth and spend it for the poor, the sick, the needy, the uneducated, the unenlightened. Help us in establishing a free and redeemed Africa. You that have time, go forth and spend it in deeds of goodness. Everyone to his post, everyone to his gun in this day of battle for God and my race. Men who have not depth of integrity are like comets—they blaze for a time—but fixed stars are always in the firmament; they never vary—so true men are like fixed stars in their integrity.

There are some if they cannot leap into the highest position they will leave it alone, as if it is to be ascended by leaping and not by climbing. Others are unwise that, having got up many steps of Jacob's ladder and finding difficulties in some of the uppermost steps, whether wrestling with assaults and troubles or looking back upon their old environment, descended with Demas.[1]

Even the most sparkling and shining grace cannot take you to heaven of itself without perseverance; nor faith, which is the champion of grace, if it be faint and fail; nor love, which is [the] nurse of grace, if it decline and wax cold; nor humility, which is the adorner and beautifier of grace; nor obedience, nor patience, except they have their perfect work of perse[v]erance.

Perseverance crowns every grace and commands every duty. It is not only faith and hope, but the holding f[a]st our confidence and the rejoicing of our hope firm to the end that God looks at. Not the seeming zeal and swiftness of our emotion at the first start, but the constancy of a well breathed soul in holding on in our cours[e] till the race is finished. Let us not be weary in working for this organization, for in due season we shall reap if we faint not. Respectfully submitted,

G. E. STEWART, D.D.K., C.A.R.,
High Chancellor

PARENT BODY UNIVERSAL NEGRO IMPROVEMENT ASSOCIATION

CHANCELLOR'S REPORT[2]

September 1, 1920 to July 30, 1921.

General Funds:

Balance in bank September 1, 1920	$ 3,324.31
Membership fees	3,891.84
Sales supplies to branches	9,043.49
Death tax	19,562.80
Twenty per cent due from branches	7,471.26
Convention funds	3,993.37
Sales from almanacs and pictures	2,102.10
Dollar assessment tax	8,996.66

Fees of charters	5,901.40	
Contributions voluntary	19,802.56	
Collections for Black Star	5,959.11	
		$90,048.90

Expenditures:

Petty cash expenses for coal, gas, light, telephone bills, postage, expressage, minor repairs and general	5,735.67	
Furniture and fixtures	1,154.00	
Returned checks	3,494.30	
Salaries of officers	35,519.74	
Salaries of employees	10,105.00	
Travelling expenses	5,346.39	
Printing, stationery & adv.	9,930.56	
Cost of supplies	4,956.37	
Loans to N.Y. Local	643.89	
Purchase of stock Negro F [C]	3,019.71	
Loans, sundries	227.00	
Death benefits paid	1,275.00	
Telegrams and cables	1,258.00	
Refund Black Star Acct., Dollar Drive	5,000.00	
		87,665.57
Balance in Bank July 30		$ 2,383.33

G. E. Stewart
High Chancellor U.N.I.A. and A.C.L.

[Construction Loan]

Construction Loan

Notes sold	$137,458.22
	6,992.36
	$144,450.58

Expenses:

Building Liberia	4,000.00
Sawmill equipment	4,463.42
General expenses	2,238.40
Cost of various sales campaigns—	
Salaried officers	17,206.42
Salaried employees	9,740.61
Travelling expenses	10,872.19
Advertising	6,400.00
Invested in B.S.L. stock	34,440.00
Purchase acct. Negro World good will	46,555.20

	135,920.24
Balance in Bank	8,530.34

Condensed Statement of Receipts and Expenses:

General receipts	90,048.90	
Sales of bonds	144,450.58	
		234,499.48

Disbursements:

General expenses	87,665.57	
Construction funds	139,920.24	
		223,585.81
Balance in Bank		10,913.67
Balance Parent Body		2,383.33
Balance Acct. Loans		8,530.34
		$ 10,913.67

G. E. STEWART
High Chancellor U.N.I.A. and A.C.L.

UNIVERSAL NEGRO IMPROVEMENT ASSOCIATION

Balance Sheet as of July 31, 1921
Assets:

Balance in bank July 30	10,913.67
Furniture and fixtures	2,154.00

Uncollected checks	3,494.30	
		16,561.97
Machinery:		
Sawmill equipment	4,463.42	
		4,463.42
Investment in building material, Liberia	4,000.00	
		4,000.00
Inventory:		
Supplies on hand	4,500.00	
		4,500.00
Stocks:		
6,888 shares common stock B.S.L.	34,440.00	
604 shares common stock N.F.C.	3,020.00	
		37,460.00
Good Will:		
Negro World estimated worth		60,000.00
Accounts Receivable:		
Arrearages from branches on dues	37,690.52	
Death tax unpaid by branches to be collected	68,664.80	
[Total assets]		233,340.71

Liabilities:

Notes payable	144,450.58	
Computed interest	6,500.00	
		150,950.58
NET WORTH		$ 82,390.13

G. E. STEWART
High Chancellor U.N.I.A. and A.C.L.

Printed in *NW*, 20 August 1921; financial portion of the report printed in *NW*, 13 August 1921. Original headlines omitted.

1. The Apostle Paul said of Demas, "For Demas hath forsaken me, having loved this present world, and is departed unto Thessalonica" (2 Tim. 4:10).

2. A copy of this report was kept in the NAACP administrative file, with the following note attached:

> We had often heard expressions of doubt as to the financial responsibility and business integrity of the Garvey Movement. It is charged that many people have been led on by false promises of early financial returns and that there is no adequate accounting for money received and expended. We have heard the same thing about every other large movement of colored people. We applied to the High Chancellor and the Secretary, who keep the money and the records and they gave us copy of a printed statement of accounts of all the various departments, which they claim to have circulated at the August Convention. They produced also a copy of one issue of the Negro World, a weekly which circulated among all their members, in which this same statement of the finances of the year was printed. While we still believe that it will be wise for the institution to take any honorable steps to convince the general public of its business integrity, we wish to confess as an individual that the frankness with which our questions were met and the statements which we were shown removed some of the misgiving which rumor and unsigned report had given us. ("Marcus Garvey," 25 September 1920–27 December 1921, DLC, NAACP, administrative file, box C-304)

Speech by Marcus Garvey at the Opening of the Women's Industrial Exhibit

[*New York, 5 August 1921*]

... Ladies and Gentlemen: I have been requested by the executive secretary of the Women's Industrial Exhibition[1] to open this exhibition. This second international convention of the Universal Negro Improvement Association desires to demonstrate the usefulness and the ability, industrially, of the women of our race. For that purpose they have made a feature at this second annual international convention of showing to the world the handicraft that the women of this race of ours [*are*] capable of producing. The women in the various divisions of the Universal Negro Improvement Association in different parts of the world have sent articles for exhibition here such as will prove to you and to others also that Negro women are capable of the finer arts.

I took it as a pleasure to accede to the request of the executive secretary to say a word, not only of encouragement to the women who sent articles, but also to encourage our women everywhere to emulate the example of these women who have demonstrated their ability and their determination to do things for the honor and glory of this race of ours[.]

The Universal Negro Improvement Association, as you may know, is a world-wide movement that seeks to encourage the Negro in the pursuit of the higher arts, and we have to be grateful to the women for helping us to demonstrate that we are capable in all lines. Those of you who visit this exhibition will be more than satisfied that the women of the Negro race are able to acquit themselves as creditably in the finer arts as the women of other races. The women, however, seek the encouragement of the men of the race. They are asking you to give them your whole-hearted support, because they are unable to put over their great program—the program which the Universal Negro Improvement Association has entrusted to them—without your assistance. Those of you, therefore, who will visit this exhibition will be given ample proof of the ability, of the genius of the women of the race, in doing things in a manner that compares very favorably with the work of the women of other races.

The international convention meets for the entire month of August in New York. The exhibition to be opened here today forms a feature of the convention, and I feel that the delegates and the members of the organization and our friends and visitors will attend this exhibition and will purchase some of the articles made and manufactured by your own women. It is for you to encourage them. We have adorned ourselves with articles manufactured by the women of other races—by the women of Japan, by the women of China, by the women of the countries of Europe, and I think you will find in here articles manufactured by Negro women that will reflect great credit on the race. (Applause.) The exhibition will reveal to you the great possibilities. Through the Universal Negro Improvement Association we are hoping to establish industries, not only in one centre, but in all centres where Negroes live. We want to establish hives of Negro industry throughout the United States of America, in Africa, in the West Indies, in South and Central America. The articles you will see will give you an idea of the work we intend to do. If the articles please you, we will manufacture them in the future by the millions, and by manufacturing on a large scale we will find employment for the hundreds and thousands of our race who are unemployed. (Applause.) We are asking your help in every way so that these women can continue the work under the leadership of the Universal Negro Improvement Association until we have accomplished the liberation of this struggling, oppressed race of ours.

THE WOMEN'S PART

The women have a part to play in the ultimate success of the Negro race, and they have started to play their part; and I want the men to realize that we men also have a part to play. We want you who have never heard of the Universal Negro Improvement Association to realize that it is an uplift movement among Negroes. We desire the social, industrial, commercial, educational and political development of this race of ours. For over three hundred years we have been sojourners in foreign parts. We have lived only in the environment in which we have been placed by others. Now we are endeavoring as a race to emancipate ourselves from this environment. We desire to build up a culture and civilization of our own, and in prosecution of that ideal is the Universal Negro Improvement Association engaged. But the Universal Negro Improvement Association will be unable to carry out its program successfully unless it gets the co-operation of Negroes everywhere. We desire to link up four hundred million Negroes of the world. We desire to secure the industrial, social, commercial and political liberation of the race. Already we are doing it. We have succeeded in impressing the world with the commendable character of this movement. The Universal Negro Improvement Association is the only Negro organization that claims the respect of all the peoples of the world. Whether it be in the United States, whether it be in Great Britain, in France or Italy, or whether it be in Japan, India or China, the whole world has already started politically to recognize the Negro as a moving force through the Universal Negro Improvement Association. (Applause.)

In fact in certain parts of the world we are already recognized as a government. And we who are leading this organization are determined not to stop, not to abate our efforts until we have established for ourselves on the continent of Africa a government controlled and dominated by Negroes.

WANTED: TRUE CITIZENSHIP

We do not desire to subvert the government of any other nation, but we are dissatisfied with our political condition. We are not accorded the privileges of true citizenship and desire a government of our own, and we are working toward that end. We want politically the power that will enable us to use our influence and exercise it on the other nations of the world. We believe the British should have a government of their own, we believe the Americans should have a government of their own, we believe the Italians should have a government of their own, we believe that the Japanese should have a government of their own, and we believe that the Negro people should have a government of their own. We believe that the government of the Negroes should be second to none. It should be as great and powerful as the government of the white race or the yellow race. Since there is a great Great Britain, since there is a great Japan, we want a great Africa. (Applause.) We want greater opportunities, political and economic; we have been limited in the past both politically and economically. For instance, though regarded as citizens, we cannot be President of this country, and the new Negro is dissatisfied to be a citizen without the rights and privileges of the citizen. If it is right for the Negro to be a citizen, then he must have a chance to be a President also. This is the feeling of the new Negro. And since we are outnumbered by whites, and they will not give us a chance, we are going to establish a government of our own. That is the object of the Universal Negro Improvement Association.

And these women who have fostered this industrial exhibition are in their own way helping this organization to bring about the great ideals I have explained to you. I thank you for your presence and declare this exhibition open. (Loud applause.)

Printed in *NW*, 13 August 1921. Original headlines omitted.

1. A description of the exhibit published in a Unitarian journal read: "In a building across the street [from Liberty Hall] there is yet more proof of this new unity [among blacks] in the

Women's Industrial Exhibit. There samples of dress-making, millinery, and cookery of American Negro women are displayed next to the intricate basketry, weaving, and leatherwork of native African women, and the fancy work and grass-plaiting of the West Indians" (Worth Tuttle, "A New Nation in Harlem," *The World Tomorrow*, September 1921, p. 279).

Joseph A. Yard to Warren G. Harding

Freehold, N.J. August 5, 1921

My dear President—

Undoubtedly you are acquainted with the Marcus Garvey movement inciting colored American[s] to return to Africa. You are undoubtedly further acquainted with the fact that Garvey is a West Indian and a British subject. His agitation is not only commercially selfish, but savours of international political subterfuge which has a far distant political objective, namely, to alienate the Colored Americans' patriotism and Americanism to the degree that in case of a crisis they will be negligible in their patriotism. I believe the Marcus Garvey propaganda to be a diplomatic blind alley on the part of foreign interests. It is germanic in effect and purpose.

It is of the utmost national importance that every racial unit in this country remain absolutely unified and loyal.

For the durability of America, the Colored people must be cooperated with in the solution of the most delicate and pivotal American problem, namely the so called Negro problem. . . .

[JOSEPH A. YARD][1]

DNA, RG 59, file 000-612. ALS, on *Monmouth Democrat* letterhead.

1. Joseph A. Yard (1866–1939) and his father, James Sterling Yard, were the owners and editors of the *Monmouth Democrat*, one of the oldest weeklies in New Jersey, which was published in Freehold, approximately twenty-five miles east of Trenton, from 1834 until 1942 (*NYT*, 28 November 1939). President Harding also received a nearly identical letter from an employee of the *Monmouth Democrat* (F. G. Fenderson to Warren G. Harding, 5 August 1921, DNA, RG 65, file 198940). William J. Burns, director of the Bureau of Investigation, answered Fenderson's letter, promising that Garvey's activities "will be given thorough consideration" (Burns to Fenderson, 12 October 1921, DNA, RG 65, file BS 198940-271).

Reports by Special Agent P-138

New York City 8/5/21

IN RE: NEGRO ACTIVITIES.

Marcus Garvey was not at the day session of his convention today [*3 August*]. He was present at the evening general mass meeting when the hall was crowded.

Marcus Garvey introduced a Japanese to the audience who spoke for some time. This Japanese was very much enthused at the welcome accorded him. He quoted several passages of scripture and gave the impression that he is a missionary or local preacher. He claimed to have attended Columbia University and had visited Chicago and other cities. He told of his experiences with white people when he called at their homes and they found out that he was a Japanese they refused to hear him irrespective of the fact that he was a Christian local preacher. He said that the white man's Christianity was not sincere and that he was disgusted with them and all Japanese were 'fed up' and ready to pack up and leave the country.[1] However, now that he found a place that was congenial and gave him a hearty welcome, he would go home and tell his friends so that they may come back to Liberty Hall with him. It was impossible for me to learn his name, but I shall endeavor to do so. I learned that he also spoke at another Convention of Negro Methodists at 136th St. and Seventh Avenue, a few days ago. Respectfully,

P-138

[*Endorsement*] FILE G. F. R.

DNA, RG 65, file BS 198940-227. TD. Stamped endorsement.

1. The adult population of the Japanese-American community in California had reached 47,566 in 1920, the year of the Alien Land Act prohibiting Japanese land ownership in the state. The act, which was passed as a result of a successful ballot initiative, reflected a widespread belief that the Japanese were an inferior race, loyal only to Japan. Anti-Japanese sentiment continued to grow in the postwar years culminating in the exclusionary Immigration Act of 1924 (Roger Daniels, *The Politics of Prejudice: The Anti-Japanese Movement in California and the Struggle for Japanese Exclusion* [Berkeley and Los Angeles: University of California Press, 1962]).

New York City 8/6/21

In Re: Negro Activities

. . . *Japanese*: Today [*4 August*] I met the Japanese who spoke at Garvey's meeting last night. I saw him coming out of the office of the Black Star Line. We fell into a conversation and I complimented him on his splendid speech last night. His name is Sumio Uesugi,[1] M.A.B.D., a graduate of the University of Chicago, Theological Dept. He now lives at 510 West 124th St., telephone Morningside 0880. (Card attached to N.Y. office copy.) He told me that the white people were hypocrites who called themselves Christians, but always turn him down on account of his color. He told me of the hard time he had while in Chicago in finding and retaining a suitable lodging owing to his color; that the white people were afraid of the Japanese Government on account of their growing power and strength hence President Harding was calling a conference[2]; that everywhere he goes he will tell the negroes of the hypocrisy of the white race; that he will be back to Japan after a few years to spread Christianity among his people; that he had been speaking at many negro churches recently; that he never knew of Garvey's organization and he is sure that his Government is not aware of the great strength which lies in Garvey's movement; that he had gone to the office and secured some papers and other literature dealing with the Black Star Line and the U.N.I.A. and had forwarded them on to the Japanese newspapers and his government. That, Marcus Garvey was a wonderful man whom he admires; that he was going to open a stand near Liberty Hall so as to introduce and sell Japanese articles; that he has been in this country fifteen years and was now glad to mix with the negroes especially after the welcome he received at Liberty Hall.

1.   Garvey's followers are all enthused and feel (after his talk at Liberty Hall last night) that this fellow is really a representative of the Japanese Government whom they feel also will help them to carry out their aims. . . . Respectfully,

P-138

[*Stamped endorsements*] FILE G. F. R. NOTED F. D. W.
[*Handwritten endorsements*] 800 and Bulletin 8/16/21

DNA, RG 65, file BS 202600-667-76. TD.

1. Sumio Uesugi (1882–1943) was born in Japan; he received his A.B. degree from Denison University, Granville, Ohio, in 1912. Four years later he earned an A.M. degree in practical theology from the University of Chicago Divinity School. In 1918 he completed a B.D. degree but apparently continued to take courses at the university until 1920. He resided in New York City from 1922 to 1938, working as a lecturer on Japan and a Japanese interpreter.
2. President Harding first considered the idea of a conference on general disarmament (as an alternative to United States participation in the League of Nations) in 1921. Congress debated on the conference after passing in May 1921 the legislation designed to build up the United States Navy, a move in response to the increasing strength of British and Japanese naval forces and the possible renewal of the Anglo-Japanese alliance. The Washington conference on naval disarmament, held 12 November 1921 to 6 February 1922, brought together representatives from the United States, Great Britain, France, Italy, and Japan; Belgium, China, Portugal, and the Netherlands were present for the debate on Far Eastern questions. The final agreement called for recognition of colonial possessions in the Pacific, an end to the Anglo-Japanese alliance, and an agreed ratio of naval tonnage for the major sea powers. In an editorial in the *Negro World*, John Haughton gave the UNIA view of the conference: "A diplomatic shroud to veil certain ignorant people so as to give Europe a chance to repair its naval forces and to prepare the minds of Europe for certain propaganda—'White Supremacy and the Rising Tide of Color,' while they exploit those weaker nations of Europe to support the new machinery" (*NW*, 4 January 1922; Thomas H. Buckley, *The United States and the Washington Conference, 1921–1922* [Knoxville: University of Tennessee Press, 1970]).

Negro World Front Page

PROVISIONAL PRESIDENT OF AFRICA AT
OPENING OF 2nd INTERNATIONAL RACE
CONVENTION ASKS FOR SUPPORT OF NEGROES
EVERYWHERE FOR A FREE NATIONALITY

Send Support to Movement Now and Save Yourselves

BIG EVENTS FOR NEGROES DURING THE MONTH OF AUGUST

We are now celebrating the opening of the second international session of the Negro peoples of the world. This convention is to continue its sessions in Liberty Hall for 31 days and 31 nights. It is expected that 50,000 delegates will occupy these seats during the entire month of the convention. These delegates are sent as the representatives of the oppressed Negroes of the world, and they are charged with the sacred duty of discussing the problems that confront the race and legislating in the race's interests.

As a people we have never had the privilege of a voice in government. We have lived under separate and distinct flags, claiming separate and distinct nationalities, but we have never been called by those flags or governments to give expression to our feelings in any legislative chambers of such governments. But today we are glad to be able to assemble among ourselves as a congress of men and women, determined to pass legislation in our own interest.

The Negro has reached the cross roads of Time, when he must strike out on his own account. Humanity everywhere has studied to exhibit that selfishness which characterizes the individual as well as the collective whole. Groups everywhere are endeavoring to take advantage of conditions and circumstances to suit their own group ideas.

And when we come to contemplate the fact that there are 400,000,000 Negroes in the world, we cannot but admit that it is right, that it is fair, that it is just that we should in our own protection, seek to gather around us those ideas, those principles, that will lead us on to that goal that is sought by the many independent groups that are striking out in their own interest.

The Universal Negro Improvement Association, under whose auspices this convention is being held, desires to see the Negro taking a place in the world that will enable him to demand the respect of other races, and, at the same time, to continue his existence as an independent human entity. In the program of self-protection we seek the building up of a nation; hence, the cry of "Africa for Africans," those at home and those abroad. We desire a free Africa, a greater Africa. With the argument that Asia belongs to the Asiatics, that Europe belongs to the Europeans, the 400,000,000 Negroes feel that Africa belongs to the Africans, and even as duty has been done by the other peoples, therefore the same special should also be done by the Negro in his own behalf, if he is to continue his existence as a man.

It is not complaining against the other races that they will not give us a chance. It is no use sending up petitions to other races asking them to give us a hearing. It is the right of every race, it is the right of every nationality to strike out in its own behalf, and we of the Universal Negro Improvement Association, through this convention, are calling upon Negroes everywhere to exercise their moral, financial, physical strength to demonstrate to the world that the time has come for us to establish ourselves as an independent national force.

The holding of this convention is an opportunity that the Negro should seek to support in every way. So I appeal to every Negro to send to the Secretary-General of the Universal Negro Improvement Association at 56 West 135th Street, New York, United States, during the month of August whatsoever financial help is possible, so that the delegates attending the convention may be able to legislate the necessary requirements out of the finances of this organization.

Trusting that each and every one will do his or her best during the month of August to support the Universal Negro Improvement Association and the Black Star Line, I have the honor to be.

Your humble servant,

MARCUS GARVEY.

New York, August 1, 1921.

"Warning to the Negro Public of America"

[*Negro World*, 6 August 1921]

A man claiming to be PRINCE MADARIKAN DENIYI, alleged to be a native prince of Lagos, Nigeria, West Africa, is travelling through the United States lecturing to colored people and asking for financial help. This man appeared in Liberty Hall, New York, some months ago and received a public collection from the Negroes of this city, stating that he was a native prince of Africa and that he was about to return to Africa to work in the cause of his people.

Information to hand proves that this man is not a prince from Africa, he is an imposter. It is now alleged that he is a propagandist receiving money to preach disunity among American and West Indian Negroes so that the educated Negroes of this Western Hemisphere may not concentrate upon the redemption of Africa, but allow the White Nations of Europe to control and exploit the continent.

All Negro organizations and churches are asked to look out for this man.

All colored newspapers please copy.

NEGRO WORLD

Printed in *NW*, 6 August 1921. Original headlines abbreviated.

Negro World Advertisement

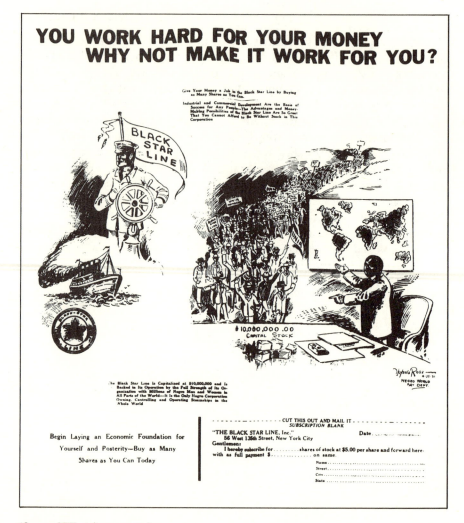

Article by the African Blood Brotherhood

[*Negro Congress Bulletin and News Service*,[1]
New York, 6 August 1921]

Plan of Having All Negro Organizations in a Mighty Federation To Make Race a World Power is Supported by Many Leading Delegates

The program offered by the African Blood Brotherhood, especially the plan pertaining to the formation and the necessity of one all powerful Negro World Federation,[2] composed of all Negro organizations, is arousing considerable enthusiasm among the delegates to the Second International Negro Convention now in session at Liberty Hall, New York.

While Mr. Garvey and other officials of the Congress have not yet publicly declared their attitude on the matter, Mr. Garvey and several others when privately approached, expressed themselves as heartily in favor of the plan. Most of the delegates approached received the idea with enthusiasm, some expressing themselves as already having it among the measures they propose to press for adoption by the Congress.

Many of the delegates were also interested in other portions of the Manifesto,[3] such as those planks calling for the devising of means to organize and prepare our people; to raise and protect the standard of living of the Negro people, to stop the mob-murder of Negroes, whether members of our organizations or not, and to protect them against sinister secret societies of cracker whites. A number of delegates were interested enough to call at our headquarters at 2299 Seventh Avenue for further information on certain of the planks contained in the Manifesto. . . .

The Results So Far

While nothing substantial or positive has been accomplished thus far by Congress, the signs are encouraging. The delegates are all of them intelligent and unselfish persons and are in a receptive mood to all suggestions and motions bearing on the important subject of the liberation of Africa and the redemption of the Negro race. Then too, this Congress right at the opening took a step far in advance of anything done by the first Congress when it adopted Parliamentary rules as every convention of self respecting men and women must. The working machinery of a convention are its committees. Without them any convention is just so much buncomb[e] and lost time. The most important of these committees is a Program Committee whose duty it is to reform program and tactics in accordance with the experiences gained since the last convention. Issues change as well as tactics, conditions and ideas and a program shall always embody the best of them. Such a committee must not be composed of too many men. At a large congress twenty are quite enough. Needless to say, such a committee must really represent all the organizations present at the congress.

Another important committee is a Constitution Committee to draw up rules and laws for the efficient and honest administration of all funds, etc. Such a committee is indispensable for a sound organization. The powers of the various officials and committees must be defined to prevent usurpation, arbitrariness and dishonesty.

There must also be a Resolution Committee to express in proper language the attitude of the Congress towards various problems and organizations.

And, of course, there must be an Auditing Committee to audit the accounts of the last year and during the coming year and to render an impartial report to all concerned. This committee is absolutely necessary to ensure honest administration. No paid officials should be elected to this committee, but only disinterested members and known opponents to the present administration. This committee must be elected, not appointed.

A wholesome sign at the Congress is the determination of many delegates to root out dishonesty in the movement. Several delegates threatened not only to throw out dishonest [memb]ers, but to put them in jail for usurpation and mismanagement of funds whether this accusation is correct or not it is absolutely necessary, in the interests of a healthy organism which all people can respect and to which the Negroes of the world can rally, that all such charges be investigated and the findings made public.

Printed in the *Negro Congress Bulletin and News Service*, 6 August 1921.

1. The ABB convention bulletins were the topic of testimony by Joseph Kornfeder (1893–1963) in his appearance in 1957 before a state of Louisiana joint legislative committee investigating Communist activities. A Hungarian-born immigrant who helped in 1919 to organize the American Communist party, Kornfeder stated:

> He [Garvey] was holding one of those show conventions that he held every two years [*sic*] to which he invited also the African Blood Brotherhood. That was his big mistake. So we sent a large delegation, of course, demanding an accounting of his income, funds and other things. Meanwhile we had created a bulletin which was dressed up as a news bulletin in such a way as if it was coming from Garvey's organization. And the bulletin was sending news about the doings at that convention. The Negro papers, of which there were several hundred weeklies, thought it was news from the convention. But it was gradual criticism of Marcus Garvey—subtle, but positive. So he got excited and decided to expel the delegates of the African Blood Brotherhood. (*Subversion in Racial Unrest: An Outline of a Strategic Weapon to Destroy the Governments of Louisiana and the United States*, part 1, Public hearings of the state of Louisiana Joint Legislative Committee, Baton Rouge, 6–9 March 1957, pp. 38–39; Brauko Lazitch, *Biographical Dictionary of the Comintern* [Stanford, Calif.: Hoover Institution Press, 1973])

A Bureau of Investigation report on Briggs's activities at the 1921 convention stated that at one point he had local newsboys sell the delegates copies of his bulletin; it was also said that "these circulars are printed by the Communist Press downtown." Briggs also gave his newsboys copies of the anti-Garvey *Chicago Defender* to sell to the delegates (DNA, RG 65, files 202600-2031-11 and BS 202600-667-78). On 5 August it was reported that "the African Blood Brotherhood continues to distribute their circular, and seeking new members for their organization" (DNA, RG 65, file BS 198940-230).

2. The African Blood Brotherhood intended to "organise the Negroes in the coast districts (of Africa), and bring all Negro organisations in each of the African countries into a worldwide Negro Federation." For blacks in the United States, the ABB proposed that "all Negro organisations should get together on a Federation basis, thus creating a united centralised movement" ("Programme of the African Blood Brotherhood," *Communist Review*, April 1922, pp. 449–454). The goal of a black federation led Cyril Briggs to cultivate Garvey in 1921. For a brief time in 1923 Briggs succeeded in forming a coalition of black organizations which he

called the United Negro Front. It included the African Blood Brotherhood, the Friends of Negro Freedom, the NAACP, the National Equal Rights League, the National Race Congress, and the International Uplift League (DLC, NAACP, the Crusader News Service, 8 January 1924).

3. In a pamphlet published on 6 August 1921 with the title "To New Negroes Who Really Seek Liberation," the African Blood Brotherhood issued a manifesto stating its aims for the UNIA convention:

> This Congress shall devise means to organize and prepare our people so that they shall be ready when needed to defend themselves, that they may be ready after the downfall of Capitalism to establish their own governments.
>
> This Congress must devise means to raise and protect the standard of living of the Negro People.
>
> This Congress must take a stand and devise means to stop the mob-murder of our People and to protect them against sinister secret societies of cracker whites, and to fight the ever expanding peonage system.
>
> Out of this Congress there must emerge a federation of all existent Negro organizations, molding all Negro factions into one mighty and irresistible factor, governed and directed by a Central Body made up of representatives from all the major Negro organizations. (DNA, RG 38, misc. records, military government of San Domingo, 1914–1920, box 5, M201–202)

ABB Bulletin

NEGRO
CONGRESS BULLETIN
AND NEWS SERVICE

Published Every Week During the Second International Negro Congress By the African Blood Brotherhood, from its offices at 2299 Seventh Avenue, New York City, Phone 2056 Morningside.

VOL. I NO. I   AUGUST 6, 1921   Whole NO. I

Plan of Having All Negro Organizations in a Mighty Federation To Make Race a World Power is Supported By Many Leading Delegates

(*Source:* DJ-FBI.)

Official Report by the UNIA Secretary-General's Department

[[*New York*, AUGUST 8, 1921]]

OFFICIAL REPORT OF SECRETARY-GENERAL'S DEPARTMENT FROM SEPTEMBER 1, 1920 TO AUGUST 1, 1921

May it please Your Excellency, Rt. Hon. Members of the High Executive Council and Delegates to the Second International Negro Convention:

As Assistant Secretary-General, elected by you at the Convention of 1920, I have the honor to submit this report on behalf of the Secretary-General's Department for your information and consideration.

The year under review has been a checkered one, and we have had some experiences that cannot be described as altogether pleasant, but I think we have a lot to be thankful for in the great increase of divisions and membership we have had, and also for the deep interest and enthusiasm that have been aroused and maintained among our members.

MEMBERSHIP

Prior to the last convention there was but a scattered membership here and there; now we have an organized membership extending over four of the continents of the world: Europe, Africa, America (North and South), and Australia, to say nothing of the islands of the sea; and although there is a great financial depression among all races everywhere, there has been, amidst all the difficulty, marked improvement and interest shown on the part of the officers of local divisions in sending in their monthly reports within the past six months.

The Secretary-General's office has always endeavored to point out to the delinquent ones the absolute necessity of reporting regularly and keeping their members on a good financial standing, so as to avoid any inconvenience and embarrassment in [cas]e of death. It is a pleasure to note the progress in this direction. We have only about six divisions that have fallen out of the ranks through loss of membership. We have to contribute their failure to the great economic crisis through which they have been passing during the past year.

DIFFICULTY

Up to the month of March, the various divisions were under direct control and were satisfactorily operating, but not many weeks after the President-General went abroad visiting the various divisions in Cuba, Jamaica, Panama, Costa Rica, British Honduras and Guatemala, a spurious atmosphere was engendered, some claiming it was not his intention to return and others that he could not return. This, coupled with a demoralization of some of the divisions, caused through one or two field workers and, in some instances, even officials, split several divisions in various factions. These two factors were responsible for the swelling of the department's correspondence to unusually large proportions and demanded all the tact, energy and skill that could be possibly mustered to readjust same through correspondence.

DIVISIONS

The organization has grown by leaps and bounds, hundreds of divisions having been organized during the year.

Number of chartered divisions up to August 1, 1920 95

Number of chartered divisions up to August 1, 1921 418

Showing an increase of 323

Besides the number of chartered branches, there are in existence 422 branches not yet chartered.

There were no chapters in existence up to August 1, 1920; up to August 1, 1921, there were 19 chapters.

DEATHS

We regret that we have to report the loss of some of our very active and very influential members by death during the year under review. The Secretary-General's office has been notified officially of the death of 45 members. Of these 12 have been financial and their claims have been paid. A few are still pending investigation. The others have not been sustained because of failure to comply with the law as laid down in the constitution.

Special mention must be made of some of our ardent workers who have passed to the great beyond:

Hon. F. F. Smith of Philadelphia, Pa.
Mr. Wm. Passley, secretary Hartford, Conn., Division.
Mr. James Spear, secretary Camden, N.J. Division.
Mr. L. C. Shiver, organizer and ex-president of Newport News,
Va. Division.
Rev. G. W. Parker, president Louisiana Division, Liberia, W.A.

In every instance the parent body tendered to the bereaved relatives and friends of late members its sincere condolence in their irreparable loss.

Finance

I may here make a few comparative statements relative death tax and dues for 1920 and 1921.

The highest receipts over the period of a single month were as follows:

June, 1921, death tax $2,347.70

June, 1921, dues 1,068.35

June, 1920, death tax 1,482.04

June, 1920, dues 861.56

Total receipts for death tax for
the year 1921 .... $19,562.30

Total receipts for death tax for
the year 1920 .... 3,833.86

Showing an increase of $15,591.18

This office has received during the months September 1920, to July, 1921, inclusive, the amount of $90,048.90 for general funds, death tax, etc. and $144,450.58 for bonds. These amounts had from time to time been turned over to the Chancellor, and the office holds receipts to cover same.

There is [yet?] an outstanding amount to be collected. I regret to state that the greater portion of this is for assessment tax and you, the honorable delegates, are requested to urge the prompt remittance of same immediately on return to your various divisions.

Staff

When the Executive Council took up office on November 1, 1920, the parent body had then to take care of 130 divisions with a membership less than one-third of its present strength, and there was then a staff of nine, composed of a chief clerk, a bookkeeper, 3 stenographers, 2 filing clerks and 2 shipping clerks. We have endeavored to be as economical as possible in the employment for the running of the office and at present we have a staff of the same nine, including 1 chief clerk, 1 bookkeeper, 3 stenographers, 3 filing clerks and 1 shipping clerk, to take care of 418 divisions instead of 130, and 19 chapters in addition; also 422 unchartered divisions in the majority of cases at a smaller salary.

I have the control of the department, the Secretary-General being frequently in the field, and must commend the members of my staff for their help and willingness in assisting me to achieve the almost impossible task that I had to handle. Speaking of myself as a unit in the Secretary-General's office, although our work for the past 12 months has been a success, I am compelled to say I would have done yet more effective work were it not for the fact that I was so often embarrassed and my hands actually tied under the guise of superior authority. I have to make special mention of the Rt. Hon. Counsel General, the Rt. Hon. Commissioner General and the Rt. Hon. Auditor General, who being regularly in their office during the absence of His Excellency the President General on his tour abroad, and other members of the council spared no pains to give me all the aid they could. Respectfully submitted,

[J.] B. YEARWOOD,
Asst. Secretary-General

Printed in *NW*, 20 August 1921.

Lewis J. Baley to Frank X. O'Donnell

[*Washington, D.C.*] August 8, 1921

Dear Sir:

Reference is made to your past investigation of Marcus Garvey.

The Bureau has been advised from time to time from a confidential source that evidence could be secured warranting prosecution of Garvey for violation of the Mann Act. We are advised that Captain Richardson, who lives at 19 West 136th Street (second floor), and who was formerly captain of the s.s. KANAWHA, has important information along this line. Richardson was recently dismissed by Garvey from the Black Star Line.

We are also informed that Garvey recently discharged Cleveland Jacques, an individual who accompanied Garvey on his recent trip to the West Indies. Jacques is now stating that Garvey paid someone $2,000.00 to return to the United States and that he, Jacques, knows who that "someone" is; also that he knows that Garvey violated the Mann Act with his sister, Amy Jacques, who has accompanied Garvey on nearly all of his trips. Jacques' address is 156 West 136th Street, New York City, c/o Gordon.

Kindly make an immediate investigation, giving especial attention to ascertaining the name of the individual to whom Garvey paid $2,000.00, also to secure evidence which will warrant prosecution of Garvey for violation of the Mann Act.

The Bureau desires to caution you that the above information was secured from a strictly confidential source, and discretion should be used in handling same, in order not to disclose this source. Kindly render reports promptly on this matter. Very truly yours,

LEWIS J. BALEY
Chief

[*Address*] Frank X. O'Donnell, Esq.,
Box Number 241, New York, N.Y.
[*Typewritten reference*] GFR:KEM

DNA, RG 65, file BS 198940-229. TLS, recipient's copy.

Convention Reports

[[*New York, 8–13 August 1921*]]

. . . FIFTH DAY

REPORTS OF OFFICIALS

On the resumption on Monday, the 8th inst., the delegates continued their reports on conditions existing in their various communities, the Hon. Marcus Garvey, acting speaker, presiding.

The day's proceedings were interesting and eventful.

The assistant secretary general, Hon. J. B. Yearwood, read his report on the working of the secretary general's department during the past year. (The full text of this report appears elsewhere in this issue.)

The report was printed and circulated among the members.

The assistant president-general also read his report. He gave a detailed account of his activities in the field during the year, and asserted that in the absence of the president-general he did not function, that power having been delegated to others.

He ended by stating that since making his report he had read the annual address of the president-general, in which the charge had been made that some officers had taken charge of other work for which they had received remuneration. He pleaded guilty to that charge. He had found it impossible, being a minister for thirty-five years, to exist without a troubled heart, if he did not preach. He had, therefore, accepted the pastorate of a small church at a salary of $75 per month. Besides, he wanted to keep himself in touch with the 4,000,000 Baptists of America.

Dr. Gordon then asked permission to read his resignation.

The resignation paper proved to be very lengthy, containing no less than fifteen reasons for resignation. There was much that was contentious and, perhaps, curious in the document.

A heated discussion followed, in the course of which the president-general stated his reasons for coming to the conclusion that his assistant was, in his absence, incapable of functioning as administrative head of the organization.

It was finally agreed that the resignation paper be thoroughly considered by a committee of five, which would carefully examine the various charges and statements made therein, and report its findings to the convention.

The Hon. R. H. Tobitt, leader of the Eastern Province of the West Indies, then made an exhaustive report on his work for the past year. He spoke of the conditions existing in the places he had been called upon to function, namely, Philadelphia and Brooklyn, in the United States, and the islands of Bermuda, Dominica, Ba[r]bados, Trinidad, Demerara, Antigua and St. Lucia, in the West Indies. In most of the West Indian islands, he stated, he had encountered considerable opposition from the government as well as from individuals.

Several delegates made very entertaining reports.

A favorable report was made of conditions in Haiti, where, the delegate said, the antagonism of a white newspaper had been overcome and permission obtained from the Minister of the Interior for the holding of meetings throughout the country.

The delegate from Jamaica gave a report of satisfactory progress of the work in that island, the movement having received a great fillip through the recent visit of the president-general.

Delegates from Canada spoke very encouragingly of that country as a good field for the association, declaring there was little or no opposition to the movement, the chief difficulty being the serious economic conditions existing.

Several delegates from various States of the Union of America also spoke and, as did others during the first week's session, ascribed what difficulties were being experienced to the prevailing unemployment, dissension among the members themselves, and the attitude of some of the preachers. They emphasized the need for earnest work on the part of field workers in helping to push the progress of the various divisions.

[*9 August 1921*]

SIXTH DAY

DEPARTMENTAL REPORTS

Tuesday was also devoted to hearing reports.

Before business was begun, the Hon. Marcus Garvey, Acting Speaker, said he desired to correct the statement that was being made by some enemies of the movement that the U.N.I.A. and A.C.L. was against religion and the Church. The association realized the good influence and power of the Church and the debt society owed it; but the Association was up in arms against certain unworthy persons who professed to represent the Church.

Chaplain General's Report

His Grace the Chaplain-General, Dr. G. A. McGuire, read his report.

The first duty imposed upon him, he said, was the preparation of a Universal Negro Ritual for use in meetings of the Divisions of the Association throughout the world and a Universal Negro Catechism, for instruction of the general membership. He was happy to report that not only had the Ritual received almost unanimous commendation from all sections of the U.N.I.A., but from those without the fold. Moreover, it had become a steady source of Revenue to the Association. The demand for a Musical Edition of the Ritual had been made in several quarters. If, in the judgment of the convention, the Ritual was a necessity, he would ask Negro Hymn Writers among the membership to send in immediately their sacred compositions adjusted to the accepted and established meters, or with music to the hymns, if the music was peculiar. The Catechism also had received universal endorsement. Many Chaplains were using it weekly in the instruction of their Juvenile Departments and making it the basis of their addresses to the adult members.

He then referred to the secular work he had done in several States of the U.S.A. by the instruction of the President-General, and to his special duties in Cuba.

He then made a forceful denial of the statement, which he said was being made by mischief-makers, that they desired to make any one denomination the protege of the U.N.I.A. He believed that in time there would be a united Negro Race with a United Negro Government and a United Negro Church. Some day there would be a Universal African Church. It would not be any of the existing denominations, and yet it would include them all. It would have its Methodist, Baptist, Presbyterian, Episcopal, Catholic and other connections or rites, each one prescribing its own form of Government, its own form of worship, and its own symbols of Divine Truth. There would even be a Mohammedan branch or connection, if it was to be really a Universal African Church.

He ended with an appeal to the organization that it use whatever talents it might possess to spiritualize the movement, to direct its ethical affairs and to win for it the co-operation of Negro ministers and denominations; to preach anniversary and other special sermons in the divisions, to visit and stir the hearts and souls of Negroes everywhere, to receive the free-will offerings and collections of the people, and to convert and evangelize with the Gospel of a Free and Redeemed Africa the millions still untouched.

Commissioner General's Report

The Hon. High Commissioner General [*Ellegor*] also read his report.

He pointed out that on his department had fallen very many important duties which had not been envisaged when his duties were defined in the Constitution last year. They had been responsible for the compilation of the

Universal Negro Almanac and had circulated throughout the world 10,000 copies. Arrangements had been made, by establishing agencies abroad, to increase the circulation to 20,000. They had edited the Blue Book for the convention of 1920, which was now ready for publication. The department was also in charge of the correspondence with reference to the immigration to the Republic of Liberia, and thousands of letters had been received from various parts of the world. Those communications helped the office to find out the status of hundreds of people who really wished to go to Africa to domicile.

The office also kept all correspondence with the pioneers now in Liberia; was responsible for the beautiful map of Monrovia by the young surveyor, who is now in Monrovia. The map was to be corrected and struck off in print for the benefit of members, and, it was hoped, would bring Liberia before the world as it had never been brought before. The office was also respo[n]sible for the correspondence with the Liberian Plenary Commission during the whole period of their sojourn in this country. Among other duties the department assumed the work of designing in connection with flags, buttons, etc., and conducting the sale of same. The department was also responsible for the arrangement of the Women's Industrial Exhibition. It was his idea that records had been obtained of the Ethiopian National Anthem and of Mr. Garvey's address on his return to the United States.[1]

Several delegates gave accounts of the work in their divisions.

Of great interest was the account of a delegate who had been doing missionary work in various parts of Africa.[2] He had succeeded, he said, in dispensing propaganda in Egypt, in Somaliland, in Abyssinia and other parts, besides at various ports in France on his way to Africa. He found the Egyptians crying out for liberty. The 3,000,000 Negroes in French Somaliland were badly treated. Many of them were starving. They became very interested in the movement and bade him convey to th[e] convention their complete sympathy with its aspirations. The Abyssinians, too, were greatly impressed. They were hoping that some day there would be one great Universal Church in Africa. The U.N.I.A. could count upon the support of 25,000,000 black people there.

Other delegates e[m]phasized the need for more intelligent leaders and members in the various divisions, and stated that in many cases the work of the organization suffered, chiefly because those at the head were unable to expound, to the satisfaction of intelligent inquirers, the principles of the movement.

SEVENTH DAY

WOMEN'S DAY

Wednesday, Women's Day, in connection with the Women's Art and Industrial Exhibition, was, with the exception of the first hour of the session, given over to the lady delegates to make their reports.

The Hon. the International Organizer, Miss Henrietta Vinton Davis, made her departmental report.

She gave a detailed account of her work in the field, in the U.S.A. and overseas, and recommended that more care be exercised in the appointing of organizers, that proper arrangements should be made whereby only duly authorized persons could interfere with the work of branches, and stressed the necessity for strict obedience to the President-General's orders.

A number of very inspiring reports from the various lady delegates followed.

Many told of excellent work done in their communities by the Black Cross Nurses, and particularly striking was the report of a delegate from C[l]eveland, O[hio], that a committee of women was looking after the feeding of about 138 to 148 out-of-work men and women per day. In a little over two months about 6,000 persons had been fed.

Shortly after the day's session was begun the Hon. Marcus Garvey, as the president of the New York local, gave a glowing account of the financial standing and general spirit which prevailed in the New York local, the model branch of the association. He pointed out the great assistance it had given to the Black Star Line with investment[s] and also substantial support rendered to the Liberian Construction Loan, and emphasized that the prosperous condition of the New York local was due to the fact that its officers inspired and held the confidence of its members.

GOOD WISHES FROM CHINA

Immediately after he announced that the following cablegram had been received from Manchuria, China:

Darien, Aug. 19, 1921

Chairman[,] Second International Negro Convention, New York:

In gratitude for mankind for your great enterprise to bathe God's love and humanity in radiance of freedom and independence on absolutely equal footing I fervently pray for your lasting success.

HEIKICHI KANEKO,
President Tatiung Jihpao
("Oriental Daily"),
Darien, Manchuri[a].

A motion was then moved and carried unanimously that a cabled reply be sent immediately.

[*11 August 1921*]

EIGHTH DAY

THE CIVIL SERVICE PROPOSITION

A considerable portion of Thursday morning was spent in discussing a motion to the effect that the convention go into secret session to discuss the official reports which were then before the house for consideration.

Among others the Hon. Marcus Garvey expressed his disapproval, stating that he saw no reason why the gallery should be cleared. The reports concerned the people and should be discussed before the people. He did not see why delegates should anticipate that there was something wrong and which required concealment.

The motion was lost.

The Hon. Marcus Garvey then vacated the chair, giving place to the Hon. F. A. Toote, the speaker in convention, as his report was about to be discussed.

Several questions were asked the President-General concerning the statement made in his report that some of the officers had been unfaithful, had destroyed much of the good work he had done in several divisions and had encouraged others to make representations against his return to the United States.

The President-General would not mention the name of the individual who, he said, he had learned had been engaged in trying to keep him from returning to the United States, stating that the matter was still under investigation. As soon as it was completed he would give the information to the convention.

He further stated the names of [t]he members of the Executive Council who, in his opinion, had undone his work in some of the divisions. He also mentioned the names of the officers who had given trouble.

The afternoon session was a stormy one.

MANDATES TO DELEGATES

Immediately on resumption the Hon. Marcus Garvey said it had been brought to his notice that an attempt had been made by a delegate to bring about the recall of another delegate from the same division. He wanted the convention to rule whether it was in the power of a division to recall a candidate because, as it had been stated, that delegate had disobeyed the mandate of the division.

The Assistant Counsel-General, Mr. William Matthews, gave it as his opinion that under the Constitution a division could not recall a candidate, even though he may have disobeyed the mandate given.

A motion was then moved and carried unanimously that no division had any right to recall an accredited delegate.

Discussion of the President-General's report was continued.

He answered several questions relating to his estimation of several of his colleagues.

THE CIVIL SERVICE

In reply to questions concerning the civil service proposition mentioned in his speech he said he deemed it advisable to create a civil service where men could be trained and sent out to every branch of the organization as executive secretaries, with authority to keep in their possession at all times the records of the organization, so that if at any time the officers left the organization the records might be secure in the hands of the executive secretary. They should be paid according to the financial ability of the local division. In case a division was unable to pay the parent body should contribute to the salaries. Officers of local divisions would be allowed to sit for the civil service examinations,[3] and if they met the requirements would be returned to their branches as civil servants.

In reference to identification passports mentioned, he stated that considerable difficulty was sometimes experienced by some in traveling from one country to another. To relieve the embarrassment he recommended that passports be issued to every financial member of the U.N.I.A., by which they would not only be able to prove their identity when traveling, but also to recommend them to the consideration and respect of the various branches.

LIBERIAN DELEGATION

Relative to the work of the delegation sent to Liberia, he said he was informed by His Highness the Potentate that splendid work was being done. The Surveyor's Department was busily engaged, the Agricultural Department had purchased a farm of about 200 acres and was now working on it in the interests of the organization. The Medical Department had reported that they had established medical service in Liberia. The secretariat was functioning as the official headquarters of the U.N.I.A. in Liberia.

In regard to the African program, if they were to be able to put it through, the unemployment in this country among Negroes could be relieved by sending some of the unemployed to work where the U.N.I.A. had chosen.

Shortly before the meeting was adjourned His Grace the Chaplain-General tendered his resignation on the ground that he could not give his entire time and service to the organization during the ensuing year, the resignation to take effect from the rising of convention.

The motion was tabled by the unanimous vote of the house, several delegates apparently not regarding the matter seriously.

[*12 August 1921*]

NINTH DAY

A LIVELY SESSION

There were lively exchanges on Friday morning when the delegates continued to elicit information from the President-General on his report.

The question of the dishonesty of certain past officers of divisions and rumored improprieties on the part of high officials occupied chief attention, and was productive of acrimonious discussion.

After the luncheon adjournment the High Chancellor [*Stewart*] and the Auditor-General [*Garcia*], were interrogated about certain items of their reports and answered to the entire satisfaction of the house.

The remainder of the afternoon was occupied with investigating certain charges made by the President-General against the leader of the Eastern Province of the West Indies [*Tobitt*], so far as his competence to fill the post and the results of his year's work (which the President-General held were poor and placed the West Indian leader in the position of a liability rather than an asset to the organization[)], were concerned.

When the session was adjourned, the investigation was not concluded, and it was decided that the convention should assemble on Saturday morning to conclude it.

[*13 August 1921*]

The convention assembled at 10 o'clock on Saturday morning, when the West Indian leader was subjected to a rigid questioning by the house.

It was finally decided that the charges of the President-General be upheld.

Printed in *NW*, 20 August 1921. Original headlines omitted.

1. The 27 August 1921 issue of the *Negro World* advertised a variety of convention souvenirs. Besides medallions featuring pictures of Garvey, Eason, and other UNIA officials, there were banners for the various UNIA divisions. Three phonograph records were also on sale. One featured "Marcus Garvey in his two famous speeches 'The Aims and Objects of the Universal Negro Improvement Association' and 'his reply to his enemies. . . .'" On a second record a soloist sang two songs written by Arnold Ford, the "Universal Ethiopian Anthem" and "Shine on Eternal Light." The Black Star Line Band performed on the third album, which offered an instrumental version of the "Universal Ethiopian Anthem" and a rendition of "Hostrauser's March" (*NW*, 27 August 1921).

2. J. D. Barber (1878–1933) was a delegate to the 1921 convention and a former adviser to the late Bishop E. D. Smith, founder of Triumph, the Church of the New Age, popularly known as

the Triumph Church. Barber, who was secretary of the church, had accompanied Smith on a mission to Ethiopia in late 1919 "to effect a closer relation between the dark races of the Earth" (*Youngstown* (Ohio) *Triumph*, 25 September 1919). R. D. Jonas, an informer for British intelligence, stated that Barber had "adopted the policy of Mr. Garvey" before going to Ethiopia (DNA, RG 65, file OG 44062). While in Ethiopia, Smith and Barber held meetings where, according to a British intelligence report, "attention was drawn to the position of the black races throughout the world." The report continued: "The American and South African colour bar [was] emphasized. Discrimination against educated and responsible members of the coloured races, solely on account of colour, was pointed out: the failure even of Japan to secure at the Peace Conference racial equality 'which union and *strength* can alone obtain' " (J. E. Philipps, "Ethiopian Religious Movement," 27 September 1920, PRO, FO 371/4399). The Ethiopian prince regent decorated Barber with the Order of the Star of Ethiopia during his visit. After Bishop Smith died in Ethiopia in April 1920, Barber returned to the United States to assume the position as head of the church. Barber was also a delegate to the UNIA convention of 1924, held in New York, and to the 1929 convention in Kingston, Jamaica.

3. A civil service examination for the UNIA was held on 15 September 1921 at Liberty Hall. At that time, Garvey argued that a civil service staff would not constitute an added expense for the UNIA, since the new civil servants would see to it that more funds were sent to the parent body from local divisions (*NW*, 1 October 1921). In January 1922 the UNIA announced that an additional one thousand civil servants were needed and that examinations would be held in New York, Buffalo, Detroit, Chicago, St. Louis, and Pittsburgh. The announcement added: "The Civil Service of the (UNIA) carries with it great advantages, in that it opens up the opportunity for higher industrial and commercial occupations within the organization. It also carries the advantage of a pension list, confined to those who have given consistently faithful service to the race through the organization for periods of ten to fifty years" (*NW*, 7 January 1922).

J. Edgar Hoover to William L. Hurley

WASHINGTON, D.C. August 9, 1921

Dear Mr. Hurley:

I am transmitting to you herewith a copy of a memorandum prepared in this office upon the result of the investigation and examination of GABRIEL JOHNSON, known in the Universal Negro Improvement Association as "His Highness, the Potentate". Very truly yours,

J. EDGAR HOOVER
Special Assistant to the Attorney General

DNA, RG 59, file 880-L-2. TLS, recipient's copy.

Enclosure

[*Washington, D.C.*] August 4, 1921

GABRIEL JOHNSON.

Johnson, known in the Universal Negro Improvement Association as "His Highness, the Potentate", is from Monrovia, Liberia. He is the father-in-law of a very prominent ex-chief, who was ousted by the British as a trouble maker in Sierra Leone, but who now lives in Liberia. President King of Liberia married Johnson's niece, which, of course, makes our subject rather prominent in that country.

Little is known in regard to Johnson's activities, as he has only been in this country on two previous occasions, the first time in 1909 and the second time in July of 1920.

He arrived in this country again on the s.s. LEON XIII, July of this year. He went first in review before the Immigration authorities. He denied having any connection with Garvey's movements when questioned by the Immigration authorities. However, he informed agents of this Bureau that he was connected with Garvey's movements.

Johnson was held for a board of special inquiry at Ellis Island, where he was given a close examination by United States Immigration Inspectors.

A copy of report of his examination before the board of special inquiry is attached hereto.[1] Briefly, he submitted the following information:

> That he is mayor of Monrovia, Liberia, where he resides with his wife and six children; that his main purpose in coming to the United States was to inquire into the Universal Negro Improvement Association; that the Universal Negro Improvement Association has established offices in Liberia and that he is at the head of same; that the purpose of the Universal Negro Improvement Association is for the social and industrial improvement of its members; that President King of Liberia does not disapprove of the Universal Negro Improvement Association, but does not look with favor upon the political side of same; that there is an African Legion in connection with the Universal Negro Improvement Association; that he, Johnson, has only received four or five hundred dollars salary from the Universal Negro Improvement Association since last April.

Copies of letters taken from Johnson, showing his connection with the Universal Negro Improvement Association are attached hereto,[2] and also have been forwarded to the Department of State, as well as other reports on this subject. Respectfully,

Inc. No. 105675.

DNA, RG 59, file 880-L-2. TD, carbon copy.

1. Not printed.
2. Printed above.

Gabriel L. Dennis, Secretary, Liberian Plenary Commission, to William C. Matthews

[[WASHINGTON, D.C. August 12, 1921]]

Dear Sir:

I have the honor by direction of the President of Liberia to acknowledge the receipt of your note addressed to the Liberian Plenary Commission dated August 4, 1921, covering a letter expressing the sentiments of the Second International Convention of the Universal Negro Improvement Association now assembled at 120 West 138th street, New York City, with regard to the Republic of Liberia and its people.

In reply, I am further directed to say that the President and the Commission while appreciating the kind sentiments of your association with regard to the Republic of Liberia and its peoples are also pleased to note the declaration made over the signatures of the official heads of the association to the following effect: "That the purpose of the Universal Negro Improvement Association with respect to the Republic of Liberia is solely and purely industrial and commercial, with a view of assisting the peoples of Liberia in strengthening and improving their country generally."

The President is of the opinion that this declaration of the association is most opportune, in view of the representations that have become current as to its political aims in Liberia and Africa generally.

That the Republic of Liberia, as a sovereign state with corresponding international responsibilities, could not permit its territories to be used as a center of hostile attacks upon other sovereign states, by any organization now operating or which may desire to operate within its political and territorial jurisdictions, is a fact which the President of Liberia hopes that your association will fully appreciate. With sentiments of respect, I have the honor to be your obedient servant,

GABRIEL L. DENNIS[1]
Secretary, Liberian Plenary Commission

[*Address*] William C. Matthews, Esq.,
Assistant Counsel-General,
Universal Negro Improvement Association,
New York City, N.Y.

Printed in *NW*, 20 August 1921.

1. Gabriel L. Dennis was a graduate of Syracuse University, Syracuse, New York, and a prominent Liberian businessman (*NYT*, 7 March 1921). He was described by the American resident minister in Liberia as "a young Liberian without any political or public experience" whose appointment as a member of the Liberian Plenary Commission was simply "to do the clerical work and attend to the business arrangements." The American minister said he was "pro-American in his sentiment" (DNA, RG 59, file 882.51/1259).

Report by Bureau Agent Leon E. Howe

Miami, Fla. 8/12/21

NATIONAL CONVENTION—NEW YORK CITY—REPORT
OF DELEGATE. U.N.I.A. & A.C.L.

Agent is this date in receipt of the following letter from G. E. CARTER,[1] an American negro, who is now in NEW YORK attending the national convention of the U.N.I.A. as a delegate from the MIAMI[,] FLA[.] DIVISION. The letter gives indications that there is a coming split between the American and the alien, especially British element, of the order. This is in line with agent's previous reports on the alien character of this order.

> For one week it has been my good fortune to sit in the deliberations of the U.N.I.A. and A.C.L. Conventions as a delegate from the Miami Division. There are 200 accredited delegates and about the same number of deputies from all parts of the world in attendance. The negroes from the British possessions are in the majority. The American negro, who is in attendance, is not the average, but the intellectual, who appears to be here to study the movement and to investigate every phase of its operation. The reports of the Chancellor and Auditor will be printed and put in the hands of the delegates. This was obtained through the motion of American negroes.
>
> The temperament of the speakers is seasoned at all times with impassionate language, as it is thoroughly understood and recognized that the eyes of organized government are upon the movement, its adherents, and its operations. Naught was said of Miami[,] saving that brought by me. My report will appear in the Negro World of next week. Our following is astounding. Over 6,000 persons attending sessions three times a day. The routine of the day consists in reports from all local divisions, and short addresses at night. Every southern delegate has been a man of real training or a woman of wide experience, and each seems to realize what is necessary to put over a program in the southland, and they have asked that only some persons come to represent the parent body in the south, and that whenever it is practical, that it be an American Negro.
>
> We will place the affairs of the organization on a solid financial basis, or else withdraw our (American) influence from the Body. Any such a movement as this on the part of Americans now identified with the body, would mean its collapse. Mr. Garvey is an unusual character, a born organizer, possessing the cunning of a fox and the doggedness of a bull. Gifted with [gab?] and some

depth of thought, witty and very responsive to praise. My honest impression is he is sincere in his dreams, but equally as mindful of providing for his welfare, should his dreams fail to come true. Handsome salaries are provided for all Executive officers, and employees are paid from $20 weekly upward, and this in itself commends the organization to the common people.

Judging from reports, a state of depression exists broadcast throughout America and abroad, and in some instances, the dismission of servants has been charged to their identity with the Garvey movement. I find many foolish persons here as followers, who do not understand Mr. Garvey no[r] his movement, and they are constantly issuing wild silly statements, believing firmly that the movement is a provisional government already and that the Executive Council are in a position to carry out the prerogatives of a government within this government. My conclusion of the whole matter to date is that the whole movement is calculated to accomplish a real good in organizing the colored folks of the world to do something in a commercial way, because when ships are purchased and put on the high seas, the[y] will find much trade in Africa and the colonies abroad. There is nothing revolutionary in the movement nor any secret affiliation with any foreign powers. An Irishman spoke last evening bringing greetings from the organization that sympathizes with their fellow men in England. Should anything develop that tinges of sedition or arguments thereto, I will feel free to write you. Will also endeavor to get hold of any literature that may be of future service to you.

The writer of the foregoing is a rather intelligent American negro, who was secretary of the colored Y.M.C.A. at Miami, and one of the five American negroes who were members of the U.N.I.A. at MIAMI. He is a northern negro, and has been in MIAMI about a year. He is not as bitter towards the British negroes in Florida as are the native American negroes. For his letter it appears that if a little anti-British talk was injected into the convention, a split would occur which would bring the U.N.I.A. out into the light for what it really is—an alien order, with alien members.

Closed.

LEON E. HOWE

[*Endorsement*] NOTED F. D. W.

DNA, RG 65, file BS 202600-667-77. TD. Stamped endorsement.

1. G. Emonei Carter was to become assistant to the UNIA president general at the following year's convention (*NW*, 19 August 1922). Carter worked as a check writer at the Royal Poinciana Hotel in Palm Beach, Fla., before moving to New York. In 1923 he was first vice-president of the New York local UNIA division (Carter to Calvin Coolidge, 21 August 1923, DLC, CC). He was appointed UNIA secretary-general in 1924, after the death of Robert L. Poston, and held the position until he was ousted from it at the emergency

convention of the UNIA held in Detroit in March 1926. Carter was secretary of the Black Cross Navigation and Trading Co. in 1925. He was also the author of "Weekly Sermon," one of the longest-running features in *NW*, which began in 1921 and continued until his ouster in 1926. In 1927 he was director of religious education at Williams Institutional Colored Methodist Episcopal Church.

Report by Bureau Agent F. M. Ames

Pittsburgh, Pa. Aug. 13, 1921

WALTER GRAVES, (GREAVES), #241 Todd Street, Woodlawn, Pa. President, Woodlawn Division, Universal Negro Improvement Association, (Black Star Line).

Information was received at this office from the Chief of Police, Michael Kane, at Woodlawn, Pa., that an organization was being organized by the negroes at Woodlawn, Pa. This organization is known as the UNIVERSAL NEGRO IMPROVEMENT ASSOCIATION. A request was made by the Chief of Police of Woodlawn to investigate the nature of this organization.

Based upon the above information and pursuant to instructions of Agent in Charge McKean, I proceeded to Woodlawn, Pa., and interviewed Chief of Police Michael Kane, also Harry G. Mauk, Chief of Police of the Jones & Laughlin Steel Company, concerning the organization referred to and ascertained the following information:—

The Chief of Police informed me that on January 28th, 1921 the organization named in the caption of this case was organized at Woodlawn, Pa., and the officers are as follows:—

WALTER GRAVES, President, Woodlawn Pa.
IRVIN FRANKLIN, Vice-President, Woodlawn, Pa.
R. B. SEARCIE, Secretary & Treasurer, Woodlawn, Pa.

The meetings are held in a hall located at Wykes and Davis Streets, Plan No. 11, Woodlawn, Pa., every Sunday at 3:00 P.M.

After obtaining this information I interviewed WALTER GRAVES, the President of the organization in question, under a suitable pretext without disclosing my identity, and ascertained the following information:—

1st—The strength and membership of the organization at Woodlawn, Pa., is two hundred members, who were organized by WALTER GRAVES, the President of the organization at the present time.

2nd—Thirty-five (35¢) cents a month dues are paid by each member.

3rd—A charter granted by the state of New York on January 28th, 1921, authorizing the Woodlawn Division of this organization to organize. The application for the charter in question was made by WALTER GRAVES,

IRVIN FRANKLIN, JAMES HILL, M. W. OWENS, LAWRENCE BRADLEY and M. REDRICK.

A communication was received by one WALTER GRAVES, written by MARCUS GARVEY, President General, #56 West 135th Street, New York City, New York, which is as follows:—

"Office of the
UNIVERSAL NEGRO IMPROVEMENT ASSOCIATION
56 West 135th Street
New York, N.Y.,
U.S.A.

["]DEAR FELLOW-MEMBER AND COMRADE:
The time has come for each and every member of the UNIVERSAL NEGRO IMPROVEMENT ASSOCIATION and of the race to do his and her duty for the redemption of Africa. Africa means everything to the Negro at this time. The entire world is re-organizing itself, and all races and nations are endeavoring to secure themselves against threatening disaster. We of the UNIVERSAL NEGRO IMPROVEMENT ASSOCIATION are making a desperate effort to do everything possible to protect the entire Negro race. Nothing has ever been done to protect the Negro; hence, he is lynched and burned and abused and reduced to industrial peonage and serfdom in all parts of the world. But the UNIVERSAL NEGRO IMPROVEMENT ASSOCIATION is now making an effort to make of Liberia, West Africa, a great commercial and industrial commonwealth as well as to start industries in different parts of the world for employing the millions of Negroes who will be thrown out into the cold in another short time when the other races have organized themselves thoroughly in their own self-protection.

"The Universal Negro Improvement Association is, therefore, raising a Loan of $2,000,000 from its members, in amounts of $20, $30, $40, $50, $60, $70, $80, $90, $100, $200, $300, $400, $500, $600, $700, $800, $900 up to $1000, bearing an annual interest of 5%, for the periods of 1 year, 2 years, 3 years, 4 years up to 10 years, for the purpose of financing its great industrial program.

"You are, therefore, requested through this letter to do your very best in subscribing for a Loan. Send in immediately for your Loan to whatsoever extent you can afford. This is a time when every Negro must do something for his own salvation and for the protection of his children and future generations. All of us cannot indulge in "watchful waiting", as it will never take us anywhere; but we must make efforts to bring about conditions satisfactory to ourselves.

"God Almighty in his own plans preserved the Negro up to this time. We ought, therefore, to unite in one great body for the purpose of founding a nation sufficiently strong to protect us. The cry, therefore, is "Africa a Nation One and Indivisible."

"But before Africa can be sufficiently strong to protect all the peoples of the world with her navies, her armies, her great parliaments and her great industries and commercial prestige, we of the present generation must work for its realization. Hence, no member of the UNIVERSAL NEGRO IMPROVE-MENT ASSOCIATION or member of the race will have any excuse for not doing his or her duty at this time.

"As you receive this circular, send in immediately for your Construction Loan to the UNIVERSAL NEGRO IMPROVEMENT ASSOCIATION. Write to the office, 56 West 135th Street, and secure your Loan immediately.

"With very best wishes for your success, I have the honor to be, Your humble servant,

MARCUS GARVEY,
President General.

"P.S.—Your money in the bank used by another man in his own business will not help you; but your money in the hands of your own organization and your own race, using it in your own interest, will help you to become economically independent and nationally to become a better and a stronger man. If all the Negroes of the world were to have their money in the banks of other races, then those banks would loan their own race that money to build up themselves, and the Negro whose money is used would be just as poorly off as he was before he lodged his money in the bank. Hence, let the UNIVERSAL NEGRO IMPROVEMENT ASSOCIATION use what surplus cash you have for the betterment of yourself and for the building up of a nation of your own. In remitting for the Loan send cheques or money orders if possible.

M.G."

The National Officers of the UNIVERSAL NEGRO IMPROVEMENT ASSOCI-ATION and AFRICAN COMMUNITIES LEAGUE, Post Office address, Universal Building, 56 West 135th Street, New York City, New York, are as follows:—

MARCUS GARVEY, President General.
J. D. GORDON, Asst. Pres. General.
J. D. BROOKS, Secretary General.
J. B. YEARWOOD, Asst. Secy. General.
G. E. STEWART, Chancellor.

A communication addressed to WALTER GRAVES from the BLACK STAR LINE, INC., Post Office address, Universal Building, 56 West 135th Street, New York City, written by MARCUS GARVEY, the President, was received, copy of which I was unable to obtain. Information obtained from the letter-head of this communication is as follows:—

MARCUS GARVEY, President, BLACK STAR LINE, and GEORGE TOBIAS, Treasurer. Cable address "Slib", New York. Telephone: Harlem 2877.

On further questioning WALTER GRAVES I ascertained that REV. JACOB SLAPPY (colored), was the principal speaker at different times at Woodlawn, Pa. The address of REV. JACOB SLAPPY is Liberty Hall, Caldwell and Miller Streets, Pittsburgh, Pa. At the present time REV. SLAPPY is visiting MARCUS GARVEY in New York City, on a special mission.

I also learned that a paper entitled "THE NEGRO WORLD" is being subscribed for by the different negroes at Woodlawn. A copy of the paper in question is attached to copies of this report furnished Washington, for their information.

I wish to call attention to the fact that during the month of September, 1920 a race riot occurred at Woodlawn, Pa., during which time there were twelve members of the Pennsylvania State Police force called to Woodlawn for the purpose of preserving law and order.[1] During this time there was an organization in progress by the colored people known as the "COLORED PROTECTIVE AND PROGRESSIVE LEAGUE OF WOODLAWN". The President of this organization, at the time of the race riot referred to, was IRVIN FRANKLIN, who is Vice-President of the UNIVERSAL NEGRO IMPROVEMENT ASSOCIATION at the present time.

Arrangements have been made by me to keep this organization under surveillance and in the event anything of interest to this Department develops this office will be notified immediately.

An investigation will be made concerning one REV. JACOB SLAPPY, of Pittsburgh, concerning his activities[,] etc., and a further report made.

Continued.

F. M. AMES

[*Endorsements*] NOTED F. D. W.
FILE G. F. R.

DNA, RG 65, file BS 198940-235. TD. Stamped endorsements.

1. No race riot actually occurred, but on 27 September 1920 the fear of a riot brought a posse of thirty Woodlawn, Pa., police into "Plan Eleven," an area of the town where twelve hundred blacks resided. Rumors that local blacks had purchased a cache of weapons in Pittsburgh and were planning an uprising brought the police patrols (*Beaver* (Pa.) *Daily Times*, 28 September 1920).

Speech by Marcus Garvey

LIBERTY HALL, Aug. 14 [1921]

. . . Delegates to the Second International Convention, Members and Friends: Tonight we are assembled as followers and supporters of a great cause. Four years ago, realizing the oppression from which we suffered, realizing the hardship from which we suffered, we organized ourselves into an organization for the purpose of bettering our condition, for the purpose of founding a government of our own. The four years of organization have brought great results, in that from an obscure, despised race we have grown into a mighty power, a mighty force whose influence is being felt throughout the length and breadth of the world. The Universal Negro Improvement Association existed but in name four years ago. Today it is known as the greatest moving force among Negroes. We have accomplished this through unity of effort and unity of purpose. It is a fair demonstration of what we will be able to accomplish in the very near future, when the millions who are outside the pale of the Universal Negro Improvement Association will have linked themselves up with us.

By our success of the last four years we will be able to estimate the grander success of a free and redeemed Africa. In climbing the heights to where we are today we have had to surmount difficulties, we have had to climb over obstacles, but the obstacles were stepping stones to the future greatness of this great cause we represent. Day by day we are writing a new history; day by day we are recording new deeds of valor performed by this race of ours. It is true the world has not yet valued us at our true worth, but we are climbing up so fast and with such force that every day the world is changing its attitude toward us. (Applause.) Wheresoever you turn your eyes today you will find the moving influence of the Universal Negro Improvement Association among Negroes from all corners of the globe. We hear among Negroes the cry of Africa for the Africans. This cry has been a positive, determined one; it is a cry that is raised simultaneously the world over because of the universal oppression that afflicts the Negro. You who are congregated here tonight as delegates representing the hundreds of branches of the Universal Negro Improvement Association in different parts of the world will realize that we in New York are positive in this great desire of a free and redeemed Africa. We have established this Liberty Hall as the centre from which we send out the sparks of liberty to the far corners of the world, and if you have caught the spark in your section we want you to keep this spark burning for the great cause we are supposed to represent.

FREEDOM THE CRY OF ALL RACES

There is a mad rush among races everywhere toward national independence; everywhere we hear the cry of liberty; everywhere we hear the cry of freedom; everywhere we hear the cry and demand for democracy. In our corner of the world we are raising the cry for liberty, for freedom and for democracy. Men who have raised the cry for freedom and liberty in ages past have always made up their minds to die for the realization of that dream of democracy and that dream of freedom. We who are assembled in this convention as delegates representing the different peoples of the world give out the same spirit that the fathers of liberty in this country gave out over a hundred years ago. We give out a spirit that knows no compromise; we give out the spirit that refuses to turn back; we give out the spirit that says liberty or death. And in prosecution of this great idea—the idea of a free and redeemed Africa—men may scorn, men may spurn us, men may say that we are on the wrong side of life, but men, let me tell you the way in which you are traveling is just the way all peoples who are free have traveled in the past. If you want liberty you yourselves must strike the blow for liberty. If you must be free you must become so through your own effort, through your own initiative. Those who have discouraged you in the past are those who have enslaved you for centuries, and it is not expected that they will admit that you have a right to strike out at this late hour for freedom, liberty and democracy. But I have to thank you, the delegates, and thank you, the members, for being able to see liberty through your own spectacles. I have to thank you for your being able to realize that your destiny lies in your own hands.

At no time in the history of the world for the last 500 years was there ever a serious attempt to free Negroes. We have been camouflaged into believing that we were made free by Abraham Lincoln, that we were made free by Victoria of England; but up to now we are still slaves. We are industrial slaves; we are social slaves; we are political slaves, and the New Negro desires a freedom that has no boundary, that has no limit. (Applause.) We desire freedom that will make us as men and nothing less than men; we desire a freedom that will lift us to the common standard of all men, whether they be the white men of Europe or yellow men of Asia. That is the standard we desire to lift ourselves to. Therefore in our desire to lift ourselves to that standard we shall stop at nothing until there is a free and redeemed Africa—a great African empire upon which the sun shall never set. (Applause.) Men are endeavoring to turn you from the idea of a free Africa, but let me tell you your destiny for freedom and for liberty lies in the emancipation of Africa. Without Africa free Negroes everywhere are doomed—doomed now and forever.

GREAT LEADERS

Great influence is being brought to bear against the objects of the Universal Negro Improvement Association and the plan of a free and redeemed Africa, and the objects and plans of an emancipated race, but let me tell you that we who make up this organization know no turning back. We have pledged ourselves even to the last drop of our sacred blood that Africa must be free. (Applause.)

I understand that just at this time, while we are endeavoring to create public opinion and public sentiment in favor of a free Africa, that others of our race are being subsidized to turn the attention of the world toward a different desire on the part of Negroes, but men, I am so pleased to find out and to know that you have not fallen under the influence of the enemy. Keep your torchlight burning; keep it burning bright. The enemy may argue with you to show you the impossibility of a free and redeemed Africa, but I want you to take as your argument the thirteen colonies of Africa [*America*] that once owed their sovereignty to Great Britain, and that sovereignty was turned away to make us a United States of America today. Use that as your argument—that George Washington was not Jesus Christ; George Washington was not God Almighty; George Washington was a man like any Negro in this building, and if George Washington and his associates were able to make a free America, we can make a free Africa. (Applause.) Hampden,[1] Gladstone, Pitt, Disraeli were not the representatives of God in the person of Jesus Christ, they were but men. Disraeli was a man; Pitt, the Earl of Chatham, was a man; Gladstone was but a man; but in their time they worked for the expansion of the British Empire, and today they boast of a British Empire on which the sun never sets. As Pitt and Gladstone were able to work for the expansion of the British Empire, so you and I can work for the expansion of a great African empire. Voltaire was not Jesus Christ; Mirabeau was not Jesus Christ; they were but men like ourselves. They worked for the French Revolution; they worked and overturned the monarchy; they worked for the democracy that France now enjoys, and if they were able to do that we are able also to work for a democracy in Africa. Lenine is not Jesus Christ; Trotsky is not Jesus Christ; but Lenine and Trotsky were able to turn down the Czar; they were able to turn down the despotism of Russia, and today they have given to the world a social republic, the first of its kind. If Lenine and Trotsky were able to do that for Russia you and I can do that for Africa. (Applause.) Therefore let no man, let no power on earth, let no influence turn you from this sacred cause of liberty. I prefer to die at this moment rather than not to work for the freedom of Africa. If liberty, if freedom, is good for a certain sect of humanity, it is good for all. Black men, colored men, Negroes have as much right to be free as any other race that God Almighty created, and we desire a freedom that is unfettered; we desire a freedom that is unlimited; we desire a freedom that will give us a chance and opportunity to rise to the fullest of our ambitions, and that we cannot get in countries where other men rule and dominate.

I care not what the scholars of this race say; I care not what the intellectual men of this race say, there is no greater cause in the world than the cause of freedom, the cause of liberty. Liberty is man's first right; therefore men everywhere are entitled to liberty. Our philosophers and our scholars may argue from now until doomsday, they will be unable to convince the Universal Negro Improvement Association that it is not a proper thing to fight for the liberty of Africa. They are using that in opposition to us. Some of the scholarly men of the race who have no backbone, who have no race pride, who have no courage, who have nothing in common with the millions of suffering sons and daughters of Ham against whom they are using their influence to foster a counter-propaganda—the old time propaganda that of Negro subserviency; that of the Negro always being the under dog. But, thank God, we have served notice on the world already that we shall only recognize and follow leaders created by ourselves (applause) and no leader created by us can misrepresent us, because you have seen how we have tried some of our leaders in this last convention. We are in a mood not to be trifled with. We desire service on one count only; service that means the speedy redemption and the speedy freedom of Africa, and the man who cannot give it must get out of the way (applause) because we have no time to waste.

We have reached the time when every minute, every second must count for something done, something achieved in the cause of Africa. We need the freedom of Africa now. Therefore we desire the kind of leadership that will give it to us as quickly as we want it. You will realize that not only individuals but governments are using their influence against us; but what do we care about the unrighteous influence of any government? Our cause is based upon righteousness (applause) and anything that is not righteous we have no respect for, because God Almighty is our leader and Jesus Christ is our standard bearer. (Applause.) We rely on Them for the kind of leadership that will make us free, for it is that same God who inspired the Psalmist to write, "Princes shall come out of Egypt and Ethiopia shall stretch our her hands unto God." And at this hour methinks I see Ethiopia stretching out her hands unto God; and methinks I see the angel of God taking up the standard of the Red, the Black and the Green and saying, "Men of the Negro race, men of Ethiopia, follow me." And tonight we are following—we are following 400,000,000 strong. We are following with a determination that we shall be free. We must be free. Before the wreck of matter, before the doom of the world, Africa shall be free.

REDEEMING AFRICA

It falls to your lot to tear off the shackles that bind Mother Africa. Can you do it? (Cries of "Yes! Yes!") You did it in the Revolutionary War; you did it in the Civil War; you did it in the Battle of the Marne; you did it at Verdun; you did it in Mesopotamia; you did it in Togoland, in German East Africa, and you can do it marching up the battle heights of Africa. (Loud and prolonged applause.) Why should we turn back? The path is clear; it is for us to follow in the way that is made clear before us. They tell us that the Negro has no soul; they tell us that the Negro is a beast created in the image of God; they tell us that the Negro is not a man; they tell us that the Negro has no aspirations. But they speak of the Negro of the past. The Negro of the present is hoping—hoping as all men are hoping—hoping that when Gabriel blows his horn, the Negro, like all other races, shall answer "Here" in equality, socially, intellectually, physically and politically. (Cheers.)

It is a race for the life of this race of ours. Started in the race late though it be, we are on the journey, and I feel sure, with the abiding confidence I have in this race of mine that we shall answer there equally and simultaneously with others when they register here. I am calling on you to exercise your faculties to the limit, to utilize your senses to the extreme, because this is the age of the survival of the fittest. If you are not fit you will die. Must we die? (Cries of "No!") We shall live; we shall live as men or die as men. We have labored hard; we have suffered long; but we have reached the parting of the ways; we have reached the crossroads of humanity, and each race is traveling in its own direction. Let the white race travel in its own direction; let the yellow race travel in its own direction. Four hundred million Negroes are traveling toward Africa. (Applause.) The white world may despise us; the white world may scoff and spurn the idea of a free Africa because they say: "How dare you talk about Africa when Africa is in possession of England, when Africa is in possession of France, when Africa is in possession of Italy, when Africa is in the possession of Spain?" What logic have you, Mr. White Man? Have you not before you the pages of history recording the rise and fall of peoples, of races and nations[?] White Man, can you not learn by experience? Why talk about the permanency of Great Britain in Africa? Why talk about the permanency of France in Africa? Why talk about the permanency of Italy in Africa, when the Moors have driven the Spaniards without mercy out of their territory?[2] Is not that an indication of the direction in which the wind of African liberty is blowing? It took but a few unorganized Moors to drive the organized Spaniards out of the Mediterranean section of Africa. When we get there with our knowledge of the latest artillery, when we get there with our knowledge of the latest explosives, when we get there with our knowledge of the latest strategy in war, what will England do, what will France do, what will Italy do?

Let the world understand that 400,000,000 Negroes are prepared to die or live freemen. (Cheers.) Despise us as much as you care, ignore us as much as you care, we are coming, 400,000,000 strong. We are coming with our woes behind us, with the memory of sufferings behind us—woes and suffering of 300 years—they shall be our shield. My bulwark of strength in the conflict for freedom in Africa will be the 300 years of persecution and hardship left behind in this Western world. The more I remember the suffering of my forefathers, the more I remember the lynching and burning in the Southern States of America, the more will I fight on even though the battle seems doubtful. Tell me that I must turn back and I laugh you to scorn. Go on! Go on! Climb ye the heights of liberty and cease not in well doing until you have planted the standard of the Red, the Black and the Green on the hilltops of Africa. (Loud and prolonged applause.) . . .

Printed in *NW*, 20 August 1921. Original headlines omitted; speeches by William Ferris and Dr. G. E. Stewart have also been omitted.

1. John Hampden (1594–1643), English statesman and member of Parliament, was a leading opponent of Charles I. He was killed in action during the English civil war (*WBD*).

2. Postwar Spanish attempts to put down insurgent Moroccan forces led by Abd-el Krim culminated in a crushing defeat for Spain on 21 July 1921 at Anual, Morocco. Twelve thousand Spaniards died in the battle, and the suicide of the Spanish general, Fernandez Silvestre, led to a political crisis. A series of further Spanish defeats came in August 1921 (*NYT*, 5 August, 6 August, 8 August, and 31 August 1921; *EWH*, 5th ed., p. 991). Several hundred British men, most of them unemployed, reportedly applied to join the Spanish foreign legion in August 1921. The UNIA protest against British quiescence in this recruitment was reported in the London *Times*: "The International Convention of Negroes in New York has passed a resolution protesting against the enlistment of British war veterans by the Spanish Government to fight against the Moors, who are engaged in a 'fight for freedom from alien aggression'" (*Times* [London], 22 August 1921; *NYT*, 19 August and 22 August 1921).

Cyril V. Briggs to Marcus Garvey

[*New York*] August 15, 1921

My Dear Mr. Garvey:

As Executive Head of the AFRICAN BLOOD BROTHERHOOD I have been authorized by the SUPREME COUNCIL of the organization to invite you to a conference on those major questions in the work for African liberation in which both yourself and I, and our respective organizations are intensely interested.

In recognition of the fact that you are particularly busy right at present I am leaving it to you to suggest the date for such a conference. I hope, however, that you can find it convenient to have it this week in view of the fact that the agreements reached might be of a nature to importantly affect the present international Negro Congress.

I think we both of us give each other credit for being in deadly earnest in the work of African liberation. Our organizations are moving in different spheres, however. Having the same aims and ideals, we are yet approaching our object by somewhat different, though always parallel, roads. By reason of this we are bound to help each other—and that whether we consciously co-operate or not. But think of what we might be able to do for the race through conscious co-operation were we to adopt a program which would jointly represent us, without any serious compromise on either side of important tactical plans or principles.

For your information I may state that the A.B.B. is essentially a secret organization, though at present engaged in open recruiting in the Northern States (U.S.). We are organized for immediate protection purposes and eventual revolutionary liberation in Africa and other countries where Negroes constitute a majority of the population.[1] The statement sent broadcast over the United States by the Associated Press to the effect that the A.B.B. "fomented and directed the Tulsa riot"; e.g., agitated, supplied leaders, ammunition, etc., while not literally true can still give you an idea of the nature of our organization. Hoping to hear from you soon on the matter of a conference, I am, Cordially,

CYRIL V. BRIGGS
Executive Head, African
Blood Brotherhood

Printed in "Garvey Turns Informer," *Crusader* 5, no. 3 (November 1921): 1.

1. On 20 October 1921 Garvey would present this letter to Justice Renaud of the Twelfth District Magistrate Court in New York City, accusing Briggs of inviting him to help overthrow white governments.

Convention Reports

[[New York City, 15–19 August 1921]]

The second annual international convention of Negroes enters upon the fourth and most important week of its sessions with a lively sense of satisfaction over the results of its deliberations to date. There were many who, early in the month, regarded with impatience the latitude extended by the chair to delegates for ventilating divisional and other grievances and in laying bare, in many instances, the hopes and aspirations, the fears and suspicions of the various communities they represented. As the President General opined, the fruits of this are being reaped in full measure as the convention reaches its final stages. Last we[ek] delegates approached their task of corrective and constructive legislation with refreshing savoir faire. The wheat was adroitly separated from the chaff, the winnowing [p]an working with remarkable smoothness and celerity. Several excellent resolutions, aimed at the correction of past blunders, were introduced and adopted with but little debate, and legislation of a far-reaching character was enacted.

The Hon. Marcus Garvey again occupied the chair in the capacity of acting speaker. Interest in the deliberations was increased, the gallery being crowded at every session. Several delegates also joined the convention for the first time during the week under review.

As foreshadowed in his official speech, the President-General introduced a resolution having for its object the establishing of a U.N.I.A. civil service. The discussion on the measure was lengthy and enlightening and revealed the fact that the organization had suffered in the past through the ravages of irresponsible and dishonest officers who disappeared at their own sweet will with the funds, records, etc., of the branches in which they held office. The civil service was intended to remedy this condition and thereby promote confidence where distrust now reigned in the various branches, besides facilitating the work of the movement in general.

An ambitious motion by the Hon. J. D. Gibson, having for its object the establishing of medical and surgical dispensaries throughout the world, was carried by a large majority. The motion was strongly opposed by a few who thought it beyond the realms of practical politics at the present time. The sponsor of the project averred, however, that he was confident of being able to place before the Executive Council views such as would convince them that the measure was capable of fulfillment at little or no cost to the Asso[ci]ation as a whole.

A resolution echoing the sentiments of the President-General, as expressed in his official speech, re the salaries of high officials, was introduced by the Hon. Austin (Brooklyn) and carried. The resolution enacted that these salaries be placed on an incremental basis, the minimum to be one-half of the maximum.

It was decided that a printing plant be procured by the organization for doing its work, the publication of the Negro World being specially borne in mind.

Rules and regulations for the governance of the Universal African Legions, the Black Cross Nurses and the Motor Corps were carefully formulated and passed into law.

ELEVENTH DAY

U.N.I.A. CIVIL SERVICE TO BE ESTABLISHED

Nearly the whole of Monday, the 15th inst., was spent in discussing a resolution, which stood in the name of the President-General, having for its object the establishing of a civil service by the U.N.I.A. The resolution was as follows:

Be it resolved:

(a)   That a civil service be established by the U.N.I.A. from which shall be recruited all employes. A civil servant shall have precedence and preference to all persons employed by the U.N.I.A.

(b)   That an official servants' list of the U.N.I.A. shall be designated as the Civil Service and that all persons of the Civil Service shall be obliged to pass an examination and educational test as laid down by the official examiners.

(c)   All promotion in the U.N.I.A. shall be from the civil service list of the association.

(d)   All executive secretaries of divisions shall be members of the Civil Service.

(e)   All records, deeds, seals and papers belonging to local divisions shall be in the custody of the executive secretary who shall be a civil servant.

The resolution was debated at considerable length.

Re Clause (a), a motion that a clause be added to the effect that the provisions of the resolution shall apply to officials of the U.N.I.A. now in position as well as to future applicants was [l]ost by a narrow majority.

It was moved and carried by an overwhelming majority that the word "employes" be not considered to apply to officials of the association elected by that convention.

Clause (b) was adopted with the following amendments: The word "general" was inserted before "educational," and the following clause was added, "and in addition they shall be required to give evidence of their good character and honesty."

Clause (c) was adopted with little discussion, the acting speaker only explaining, in answer to a question, that is did not apply to officers elected by convention.

Clause (d) provoked considerable discussion. The President-General explained that the general secretary of a division would receive all dues and payments from the members and make a report to the executive secretary, who in turn would make a report to the officers of the division and also submit a monthly report to the parent body as coming from the executive officers of that division. The executive secretary would be subject to the Executive Board of the Division to which he was appointed, and would be withdrawn, according as the board desired, for any violation of rules, etc.

Clause (e) was adopted after a brief discussion.

It was decided that the Board of Examiners shall consist of the administrator of the U.N.I.A. and such other persons as he shall deem fit to appoint.

Other details were also left to this board to arrange.

TWELFTH DAY

RULES AND REGULATIONS FOR AFRICAN LEGION

The Order of the Day for Tuesday, the 16th inst., was the introduction of motions by delegates.

The following resolutions by the Hon. W. A. Wallace (Chicago) were carried unanimously:

1.—Be it resolved: That all officials of the Parent Body collecting money from local divisions be required to register the amounts so collected with said divisions.

2.—Be it resolved: That there shall be left with every division from which moneys are collected by Agents or Officers sent out by the Parent Body or the Executive Council a receipt stating the amount collected and what for.

Hon. A. Ford (New York) introduced a copy of rules and regulations for the Universal African Legions and the Black Cross Nurses and other auxiliaries. The book, he said, had been drafted by the Hon. Capt. E. L. Gaines, Minister of Legions, and himself, and had been referred to the Executive Council, which had referred it to a special committee for consideration and subsequently ordered that it be printed.

The President-General strongly criticized the Executive Council for permitting the book to be printed, remarking that while some parts of it were very useful, there were clauses in it which were opposed to the real aims and objects of the movement.

The members of the Executive Council present denied having given authority for the book to be printed, stating that it had, as far as they knew, never left the committee stage.

It was agreed that the book be considered by the convention, clause by clause, during the afternoon session.

This was done, all references to the Black Cross Nurses, etc. being eliminated. Various corrections, substitutions and deletions were made to the draft, which, as revised, would become the rules and regulations by which the Universal African Legions would be governed.

Thirteenth Day

Further Discussion of Regulations for
Universal African [Legion]

On the initiative of Hon. F. A. Toote, the assembly tendered congratulations to the President-General on his attaining his thirty-fourth birthday, Wednesday, the 17th inst.

The meeting then proceeded with its consideration of the rules and regulations governing the African Legions.

The task was completed by 1 o'clock, when the session was adjourned. On the resumption the following motion, introduced by the Hon. A. Ford (New York) was carried:

Be it resolved: That the President-General of the Universal Negro Improvement Association and African Communities League may, after due inquiry by the general membership, instruct the commander of a local division through the Minister of Legions, or, in his own discretion, suspend, disband, or otherwise discipline any brigade of the Universal African Legion, if such brigade, auxiliary or unit disobeys the constitution or fails to live up to the rules and regulations issued from headquarters of the Universal African Legion for their guidance.

A special committee was appointed to draft rules and regulations for the Black Cross Nurses and Motor Corps.

The remainder of the session was occupied in formulating rules for the Universal Negro Improvement Association choirs.

Fourteenth Day

Printing Plant to Be Procured

On Thursday, the 18th inst., some important resolutions brought forward by delegates were carried:

Hon. Noah Thompson (Los Angeles, Cal.):

That an Official Blue Book be published with the records of the convention.

A motion by this delegate that any transaction or transactions by the convention be subject, provided a majority percentage of the branches so desire, to be a referendum, was tabled.

Hon. Alfred Potter (Montreal, Canada):

1. That the one dollar annual tax of each member shall be charged against the local division to which the member is attached and shall be collected against the financial membership up to the 31st of December of each year.

2. That the parent body of the U.N.I.A. through its High Executive Council be authorized to procure a printing plant and outfit for the printing of and supplying in general of all literature and other printing matter in [c]onnection with the U.N.I.A. and its branches and auxiliaries; and more especially for the printing of the Negro World newspaper.

Hon. W. O. Harper (Youngstown, Ohio):

1. That a training institute be established and that all representatives of the organization be given a course in this institute before being sent out on field work.

Bureau of Justice

2. That a Bureau of Justice be established by the parent body of the U.N.I.A. and A.C.L. for the protection of all Negroes.

A committee of five appointed to draft the necessary rules and regulations to govern the Bureau of Justice submitted the following rules:

(a) The Bureau of Justice shall be composed of three members. It shall have for its head an attorney-at-law, who shall be known as Chief of the Bureau of Justice. One of the members of the bureau shall be its secretary.

(b) The bureau shall have to co-operate with it a committee of three from each local division, composed of the president and two members selected from the general membership, which committee shall be under the supervision of the bureau.

(c) The local committee shall have the power to dispose of all matters not of sufficient magnitude to require special attention of the bureau, and shall report to the bureau their action therein.

(d) The bureau with the consent and advice of the High Executive Council shall have the power to make such rules and incur such expense[s] as a[r]e absolutely necessary for the carrying out of its object.

TRAVELING AUDITORS

Hon. Rudolph Smith (New York):

1. That the Auditor General shall have under his jurisdiction at least four traveling auditors who shall audit the books of divisions and make immediate report to the Auditor General.

2. That commissioners in far off countries may be appointed by the Auditor General to perform the work of Auditors.

3. That presidents or other officers of divisions who cause the arrest of a high official, officer or representative of the parent body through certain grievances affecting him or her personally shall be forthwith removed from office.

4. That the presidents, officers and members of divisions having grievances against any representative shall pursue the proper [co]urse as stated in article III, section 61, of the constitution.

U.N.I.A. DISPENSARIES

Hon. Dr. J. D. Gibson (New York):
That the U.N.I.A. establish medical and surgical dispensaries in the various parts of the world where medical and surgical aid is in need, and said medical aid be supported by the local division.

FIFTEENTH DAY

DR. GORDON'S FIFTEEN POINTS

On Friday, the 19th inst., the committee appointed to investigate the fifteen points submitted by the Rt. Hon. the Assistant President-General Rev. Dr. J. [D.] Gordon as a basis for his resignation, reported its findings.

The committee found that certain things stated in the resignation were worthy of consideration, and others were the result of misunderstanding. It had recommended to the Assistant President-General that he withdraw his fifteen points and he had agreed to do so, providing the President-General also withdrew the remarks made publicly by him in rebuttal.

After the report had been read to the meeting, the Assistant President-General withdrew the fifteen points, adding that he referred them to the

High Executive Council for consideration. The President-General then withdrew the remarks he had made in rebuttal, with a similar rider.

It was moved and seconded that the resignation be received. After a lengthy discussion an amendment that the resignation be laid on the table was carried.

HIGH OFFICIALS' SALARIES

The following resolution brought forward by the Hon. Austin, Brooklyn, was carried:

Be it resolved, That the salaries of all elected officers to the positions of officers in the High Executive Council be regulated at a minimum and a maximum, the minimum to be fifty per cent. less than the maximum. That said officers shall commence their duties at the minimum salary, which shall be raised from time to time, according to the competence and service of the individuals, on the recommendations of the President-General and Administrator of the Universal Negro Improvement Association to the council assembled in regular session. The bill shall require a two-thirds majority vote of the members of the council to carry it.

RULES FOR AUXILIARIES

The committee appointed to draft rules and regulations for the governing of the Black Cross [N]urses and Motor Corps then made their report.

The remainder of the session was spent in perfecting and revising these rules.

The convention was assembled at 10 o'clock and continued its consideration of the rules and regulations pertaining to the Black Cross Nurses and the Motor Corps, the session adjourned at 2 o'clock when this business was completed.

Printed in *NW*, 27 August 1921. Original headlines omitted.

Article by H. Vinton Plummer

[*New York Daily Star*, 16 August 1921]

Liberty Hall will witness Saturday night [*27 August*] a scene of the most dazzling and brilliant display of Negro officialdom in full dress and uniform that has ever been seen or remembered by the oldest citizens in Harlem, yet that has ever come under the ken of man since the golden days of Solomon, when he received the Queen of Sheba from Abyssinia, the great African kingdom, or during the Ptol[e]mies of Ancient Egypt in their glory and splendor.[1]

His Highness, General Gabriel Johnson, Mayor of Monrovia, Liberia, Potentate of the Universal Negro Improvement Association and African Communities League, the official to whom all others are subordinate in rank and must pay homage on set stately oc[ca]sions, will receive his official family and their wives in courtly style at Liberty Hall, next Saturday evening. All officials of this great organization must attend in full dress if a civilian[;] uniform if of the military branch, with their wives or ladies to be introduced and received by his Highness. All deputies and delegates to the Second Annual Convention now in session with their ladies will also be out in full array to be received in court.

His Excellency the Hon. Marcus Garvey, President-General of the Negro Improvement Association and African Communit[ies] League and Provision[al] President of Africa, will receive with his Highness, surrounded by the First and Second Regiments of African Legions, commanded by Colonel Harrigan[2] and staff on the one side and the Black Cross Nurses with the Ladies' Motor Corps on the other with contingent auxiliaries. . . .

Printed in the *New York Daily Star*, 16 August 1921; reprinted in *NW*, 27 August 1921. Original headlines omitted.

1. The twentieth-century Ethiopian dynasty traced its origins to Menelik, reputedly the son of King Solomon and the queen of Sheba. The queen of Sheba, after hearing of Solomon's great fame, made her legendary visit to the Jewish king. According to Ethiopian legends, Solomon seduced Sheba, and their son, Menelik, brought Judaic customs and civil law to Ethiopia (*Encyclopedia Judaica* 6: 943; 13: 1,423).
2. Ludwig E. Harrigan was a native of the Virgin Islands.

Convention Speech by Rose Pastor Stokes[1]

[[*New York*, Aug. 19, 1921]]

The President-General thereupon resumed the chair and said:

Ladies and Gentlemen: We have with us tonight a lady visitor who has been widely made known to the public by the press the world over as belonging to that class of agitators who are endeavoring to free struggling white humanity. This lady has been proscribed against, prosecuted, and persecuted, I believe, she and her husband, for the cause they represent. She desires to say a few words to us in convention, in her own way.

It is for me to explain that Liberty Hall welcomes all friends of liberty. (Applause.) We welcome the Irish, we welcome the Jews, the Egyptians, the Hindus, and all peoples struggling for liberty, because we are in sympathy with suffering humanity everywhere. But that does not mean to say that we support every program, every method that is being used. We are in sympathy with the cause of freedom everywhere, and this lady in her own way has linked up herself with the cause of bleeding Russia. It is her feeling, it is her belief, that certain things should be done to free the struggling ones of

Russia, the oppressed people of Russia. Her cause, I believe, is dear to her, even as our cause is dear to us. She has her own way of representing herself and of representing her cause, and we want to say that, representing as she does today the friends of Soviet Russia, it will be understood that the Universal Negro Improvement Association adopts no one form of government. We are not adopting any method or the methods of any government. Having been mingled and mixed with civilization during the last two thousand years at least, we have come to the conclusion that there is good in all and in every government. Therefore we are seeking to pick out the good in each government, let that government be monarchial, let that government be democratic, republican, or Soviet, we will pick out the good that is in each, and reject the bad. So that you will not mistake us to say that we are in support of the Soviet government while we invite this friend of Soviet Russia to speak to us. We are not Soviets; we are not monarchists; we are not entirely republican; we are, rather, a part of every good government in the world. (Applause.) Coming down in history from the time of the empires of Greece, Carthage, and Rome, and extending up to the present day, we pick out the good in each of them.

I trust, therefore, that the press will not misinterpret us as being Soviets, for I repeat, we are not Soviets. The press I wish to understand us as not being ultra-radicals, because we are not radicals, nor ultra-radicals. We are an organized body of people struggling towards freedom, and we are not going to stop at anything to get freedom. (Applause.)

So we welcome this friend of Soviet Russia to tell us a little of what her people are doing to get liberty, and if we can find any good in what she says we shall certainly be quick to seize upon it and adopt it for our own benefit. I take great pleasure, therefore, in presenting to you Mrs. Rose Pastor Stokes, a member of the Soviet Friends of Russia. (Applause.)

MRS. STOKES SPEAKS

Rising, Mrs. Stokes said:

Friends and Fellow Workers: First I want to thank your president for his courtesy in permitting me to speak to you this evening. Wherever a Bolshevik like myself comes face to face with members of the working class, whether they be black, or yellow, or brown, or red, or white; whether they be Jew, or Christian, or Mohammedan, or heathen; whether they be believers or non-believers; whether they belong to one nation or another on the face of the earth—whatever their beliefs may be, whatever their color or nationality may be, the Bolsheviks are glad to face the workers, those who toil with their hands or with their brain for a living.

Friends and workers, Soviet Russia is today a government of the workers and the peasants of Russia. The working class of Russia have made their revolution; they have thrown off their backs those who oppressed them. The bourgeois[i]e, we call them; the capitalist class, those who, regardless of whether they are people of our own color or people of your color; whether they be black or white, or any other shade or any other complexion, those people who themselves may be black, or white, or red, or brown, who have the whip with which to oppress their fellow men the world over. In every government, Mr. President, I beg to say (and I am sure you wish me to express my opinion and my conviction from this platform), in every government on the face of the earth today, and wherever floats a flag, the working class, white or black, are being exploited to the limit of endurance; in the midst of industries, in the midst of factories, in the midst of technical developments, such as the world has never seen before.

We have millions of men and women unemployed in every line, hungry for work, seeking entry into those factories, seeking contact with the machinery of production, and not permitted to operate those machines. Why? Because at the present moment, fellow workers, it is unprofitable to the few who rule—those individuals, the few who are the power behind those governments—to employ every man and every woman who have the right to work, for the right to work is the right to live. Without work we cannot maintain existence. That, friends, that, fellow workers, is the condition existing in every government at the present time, and we who are Communists (and I am a Communist, I am a Bolshevik. I proclaim it from every platform where I get the opportunity to proclaim anything, for I believe in the principles of Communism), we Communists maintain that just so long as a nation, so long as a government permits the few to exploit the many for their own enrichment, just so long as capitalism, with its profit system, with its oppression of the broad masses of the people, is allowed to continue to exploit us, the working masses have but one mission, but one historic task before them, and that is to defeat, to take the power from the hands of the capitalist class and open the factories and give the land once more to the people. (Applause.)

Friends, Soviet Russia has done this thing, and Soviet Russia, to prove her faith, which is the faith of the Communists the world over, seeks not only to free herself from economic and social oppression and inequality, but it seeks to free also every people, every nation, [e]very race upon the face of the earth.

Mr. President, you must know, and fellow workers, you all must know (because you read) that the Communists of Russia, that the international Communists, are setting up a Communist convention, a congress, sitting in Moscow. They give aid, they give unstinted help to the weaker peoples, to the darker races of the East. Wherever men are oppressed we say there is neither color, nor creed, nor nation. We stand together against all oppressors.

It is quite true, men and women—I admit it; we all must admit it who know anything of conditions today—that wherever we go there is prejudice; there is prejudice against a man or a woman because he does not happen to have a white skin, or she is a little darker than I am. We know that that prejudice exists; but it exists chiefly among the ignorant masses. It exists mainly among those who do not understand that if they, themselves, would be free, that they must free all workers together. (Applause.) We can have no liberty except in the liberty of all the people of all the world. (Applause.) In Soviet Russia they have decided that Persia shall be free; that India shall be free (applause); that Africa shall be free. (Great applause.) And it is not merely words; it is not sentiment that they express; they have given of their gold; they have given of their wealth, which represents the labor power of the Russian workers and the peasants; and they have given not only of these things; they have given of their very all for the liberation of the darker races of the world. Go East and you will find the red armies of Russia are marching, shoulder to shoulder with the black men; they march with the darker races. We say we will give you not only our wealth and our labor, but we will give you of our lives when necessary. (Applause.) And whenever necessary you will find us not wanting. (Renewed applause.)

And I want to say, fellow workers, that until we can and do co-operate, and until you recognize, as we Communists recognize, that it is a matter of hard fact, a matter of clear experience, a matter of self-interest, if you please, that if we ourselves would be free, if you yourselves would be free, you must co-operate with the revolutionary working class of the world, the white working class of the world, revolutionary and determined that every oppressed people, that the oppressed classes of the world, of all colors and all races must be free; you must co-operate with them, you must come with us, just as we are willing and eager to go with you in the struggle of liberty. (Applause.)

IMPERIALISM

Friends, one other thought occurs to me—You want Africa. Africa should be yours. (Great cheering.) But Africa should be yours free, and not enslaved. Is it not true? You want a free Africa; you don't want an enslaved Africa, do you? (Cries of "No! no!") If your eyes are open to the conditions that prevail under capitalistic imperialism, you know, as well as we know, that there can be no freedom in the farthest parts of the world so long as capitalism maintains its power in the world. Do they not reach their tentacles out to the most remote places in the world? Is not imperialism placing its tentacles around Africa today? Is not Africa today the great prize, or one of the great prizes for which capitalistic imperialism is contending? It is true.

The Bolsheviki, friends and fellow workers, the Communists of Russia, and the communists of the world—and by Communists we mean the conscious revolutionary working class of the world—are seeking to destroy capitalistic imperialism, root and branch.They cannot, however, do it without the co-operation of the workers everywhere; and, fellow workers, insofar as you are workers, insofar as you live by the labor of your hands, by tilling the soil, or operating a machine, or in any other way serve your fellow-men; insofar as capitalism exploits you; insofar as you are one with us, the white workers of the world, there is a class conflict coming on in the world, and that conflict today overshadows every other element in the conflict of peoples and races and humanity. We must stand together as workers.

We must stand together as workers. We need not seek to place lines; or, I should say, on the contrary, if you prefer to draw lines, if you prefer to say: "Oh, we are black and you are white"; very well, fellow workers. But co-operation, in the interest of your own freedom, is as necessary in relation to the great revolutionary working-class struggle of the world as it is necessary for you to build your own powerful organization. (Applause.) I am glad that you concur in this. I am glad that you see that it is essential for you, as workers, to struggle with the workers of the world against the powers that oppress us all.

We fought a great war. We fought it; that is, the workers of the world fought a great war. For whom did they fight? Did they fight for their own? Did they fight in the interest of their own class—black, white, yellow, brown, anything you like? No; they did not. They fought in the interests of that imperialism which happens to be in the white world; they fought in the interest of that imperialism in (I should not say it was in the white world only; so, I will qualify that statement); they fought in the interest of that imperialism which happens to be dominant in the white world. It is also in India, in Africa, in Persia, and everywhere else in the world. You will find the rich men, you will find princes in India, and you will find Shahs in Persia, you will find the strong and the mighty who live upon the blood and the tears of the common people. You will find them hand in glove with European imperialism; they work with them and enslave their own people. In Persia, recently, they had to defeat these Shahs and these princes; they had to overthrow them,[2] and the land was brought back to the people, and all went back to the common masses for their use.

Well, then, we have capitalistic imperialism dominantly in the white world, and also in a measure wherever men can prey upon the labor of their fellows. Yes, we fought for them, but we have to strengthen the hands of those cut-throats and their crew that are trying to destroy humanity. We fought for them. What was our reward? We did not know we were fighting for them; we thought we were fighting for ourselves. And when we returned here, you comrades, you fellow workers, you who went to the war with dark skins, you who came back with dark skins, the dominant press—which is the capitalist press—continued to foment and instill in the breasts of the white people all over the country the same old, dark, antediluvian prejudice that was before the war. But you fought back; some of you fought back. I glory in the fact that you fought back. (Applause.) We Bolsheviki were proud and glad that there were black workers in this country who had the courage and the manhood to stand up against their oppressors. (Applause.) You came back from an imperialist war to fight your own battles anew; and even at this moment, men and women, even at this moment, a new, a more deadly and more widespread, a more terrible imperialist conflict is preparing. And we shall have to send—no; we shall be driven by the millions, like so many ignorant, dumb-driven cattle—through the battlefields of Europe, or upon whatever field it may be that we shall have to fight. That new war is preparing. And why? I want you to think of the causes.

PRODUCTION

There can be no peace—there can be no peace until the capitalist elements are eliminated from production and distribution. There can be no peace until capitalists are thoroughly defeated. Capital must have an outlet. We, the millions of workers in America, for instance, and in every capitalist country, produce, produce, produce; we pile up, we pile up, great huge storehouses of products by our labor; and what becomes of it? We, the masses, go hungry; we are not permitted more than a meagre wage per day; we are permitted not more than the low wage against the high cost of living will provide. The rest of it—because we produce a great deal more than we get in exchange in wages—the rest of it goes to the capitalist class; the rest of it goes to those who own and control industry, and they must have an outlet; there must be a way out. These products, these shoes, this clothing, this wheat, this food, these building materials—it must all be consumed before the workers can go on working; it must be consumed at a profit.

Do you know—have you ever seen in your newspapers the stories of food that has been destroyed; food that they have dumped into the ocean—multitudes of fruit, multitudes of eatables, multitudes of food that the people famished for? And why? Because they want to jerk up the prices! They want to keep the prices high; they want to make a large profit. They don't care about feeding us who make and produce these goods, and they must have a market; they can't destroy it all. They want to find an outlet. So here in America we go to Haiti; we go to Santo Domingo; we go to the islands of the South Seas. If you don't come to us, we go to you, and if you will not accept our enslavement, if you will not accept our capitalism, if you will not accept our profit system, if you will not accept the slave system of the present day they shoot lead into you. They destroyed over 4,000 black men in Haiti.[3] Why? Because the Haitians objected to this imperialistic game. That is why they did it, and they are determined; they are determined to enter every black man's territory, every brown man's territory; every territory that is as yet unexploited, to exploit it further, because they must keep the old system going.

Friends and fellow workers, we must destroy this system, root and branch, because every capitalist nation is trying. To conclude, every capitalist nation, every flag in the world that has any power at all, is trying to plant itself or himself in these territories. Don't you see that, like dogs for a bone, they are going to fall to fighting? They must quarrel over it, just as they quarreled in the last war as to who should exploit him. It had nothing to do with the Bolsheviks; it had nothing to do with the Hun; it had nothing to do with the Germans; it had everything to do, however, with the imperial interests of France, of England, of the United States, and other powerful nations. Just so, we shall have the old game over again. Are you going to offer yourselves as cannon fodder for the imperialistic nations of the world again? (Cries of "No!")

Soviet Russia, fellow workers, appeals to you. Soviet Russia appeals to Africa to co-operate with it in its efforts to defeat imperialism. In your own interest you must, and we in our own interests must work and co-operate with each other. I trust that you, Mr. President, and the other high officers of this organization, and the representatives who are attending this congress, I trust that before you have closed your congress you will have taken some stand in the battle.

I don't know whether I am overstepping your hospitality, or whether I am abusing your hospitality; but I believe, and I am sure, that your President must see that wherever there are workers, they must get together to fight together, to struggle onward together, to a new, a free world, until all shall have free access of the land, and wherever they want it; whether it be in Africa, in Asia or in Europe; wherever the workers want the land, there they shall have it; wherever they wish to operate industrially, there they shall have free access to it; and those who will not work shall not eat. (Loud, enthusiastic applause.)

PRESIDENT GENERAL'S REPLY

The President-General replied briefly to Mrs. Stokes' address as follows:

Mrs. Stokes: Liberty Hall being a great university, we call here to this forum of our professors from the four corners of the world. (Applause.) Tonight we have had a Soviet professor. (Laughter.) Some few nights ago we had an Irish professor. Later on we will have a Republican professor, a Democratic professor, a professor from the monarchial system of government; and then we will decide, later on what we will do. (Applause.)

I think, Mrs. Stokes, that you have made out a good cause for the Soviets. I hope that the capitalists will make out their cause; but when they come to Negroes they will find keen judges. (Applause.) We are going to give Mrs. Stokes a fair trial—after we have heard the other fellow. (Laughter.)

We give to you, Mrs. Stokes, the best wishes of the representatives of the Negro peoples of the world to the struggling workers in Russia and elsewhere. They are seeking, I understand from you, freedom from their capitalistic oppressors. We are seeking freedom in Africa. Later on, if the Soviets can help us to free Africa, we will do all we can to help free them.

In behalf of the convention, I thank you for your splendid address, which I am sure was enjoyed and appreciated by every one here. (Applause.) . . .

Printed in *NW*, 27 August 1921. Original headlines omitted.

1. Rose Pastor Stokes (1879–1933), an early Socialist and feminist, worked in a cigar sweat shop before her marriage to the Socialist millionaire and philanthropist, J. Phelps-Stokes. A

leader of the left wing of the Socialist party during World War I, she was a founding member of the American Communist party and one of those arraigned on criminal anarchy charges during the Palmer raids of 1 January 1920. In May and June 1921, as a spokesman for the faction advocating the creation of a legal Communist party, she won the support of Cyril V. Briggs, who rejected the appeals of Robert Minor to join the illegal underground faction of the party. Shortly thereafter she held a meeting at her home attended by W. A. Domingo, Hubert H. Harrison, Edgar M. Grey, Claude McKay, and Briggs, in which she apparently offered to finance the Liberty party as a vehicle for black recruitment into the Communist party. Harrison and Grey rejected this proposition (DNA, RG 65, file BS-202600-2031-7). In a report on 15 August, Bureau of Investigation special agent P-138 stated: "I am again compelled to repeat that the Communist Party of America, headed by Mrs. Rose Pastor Stokes, working through the African Blood Brotherhood, headed by Cyril Briggs, Domingo, Moore, [Arthur] Reid—all aliens and connected with the 'Crusader' magazine—are spreading dangerous propaganda among negroes in Harlem. This is especially so since the Garvey Convention has been in session" (DNA, RG 65, file BS 202600-667-78). Arthur Hilton Reid (b. 1890), Trinidadian-born radical, was a former UNIA member who left shortly after his arrest for selling BSL stock in Fredericksburg, Va., in October 1920. He subsequently joined the African Blood Brotherhood, becoming post commander of the New York branch. The ABB sent Reid to work in the South in August 1921 (DNA, RG 65, files BS 202600-2031 and 202600-667; U.S. Department of Labor, Naturalization Service, certificate no. 167132). During the address by Rose Pastor Stokes, "The Blood Brotherhood members were scattered through the audience to hear their leader Mrs. Stokes while others were busy outside giving out circulars headed by Cyril Briggs" (DNA, RG 65, files BS 198940-240 and BS-202600-667). In 1922 Stokes was appointed a delegate to the fourth congress of the Communist International (Kathleen Ann Sharp, "Rose Pastor Stokes: Radical Champion of the American Working Class, 1879–1933" [Ph.D. diss., Duke University, Durham, N.C., 1979]; Theodore Draper, *American Communism and Soviet Russia* [New York: Viking Press, 1960]; Robert K. Murray, *Red Scare: A Study of National Hysteria, 1919–1920* [New York: McGraw-Hill, 1964]; Theodore Vincent, *Black Power and the Garvey Movement* [San Francisco: Ramparts Press, 1971]).

2. In the wake of an unsuccessful British attempt to bring about the overthrow of the Bolsheviks during and after the First World War, the British and Soviets maintained occupying forces in Persia. In April 1920 Soviet troops occupied the port of Enzeli and, shortly thereafter, set up the Persian Soviet Socialist Republic of Gilan in northern Persia. They also helped to establish the Communist party in Persia, which aimed to overthrow the authority of the shahs. When growing anti-British sentiment in the area forced the British to withdraw their forces from northern Persia and to reduce their forces in the south, the Soviets also withdrew, ending the brief existence of the Persian Soviet republic. In February 1921 the Soviets signed a treaty of friendship with Persia (Amin Saikal, *The Rise and Fall of the Shah* [Princeton, N.J.: Princeton University Press, 1980], pp. 20–21).

3. The bulk of Haitian casualties, estimated by the U.S. Marine Corps at 3,250, were sustained during the 1918 and 1919 *caco* uprising led by the Haitian guerrilla leader Charlemagne Peralte. Peralte's force of several thousand men, armed mostly with machetes and knives, was finally defeated in 1919 following their attack on Port-au-Prince (Hans Schmidt, *The United States Occupation of Haiti, 1915–1934* [New Brunswick, N.J.: Rutgers University Press, 1971], pp. 102–103).

Convention Reports

[*New York, 22–26 August 1921*]

[*22 August 1921*]

... SEVENTEENTH DAY

IMPORTANT GOVERNMENT RESOLUTIONS

Before the order of the day was begun, the following communication from the secretary of the League of Nations was read:

Geneva, Aug. 5, 1921.

The Secretary, World Convention of Negroes, New York.
Sir:
I have the honor to acknowledge receipt of your telegram, dated New York, August 1, addressed to the Secretary-General of the League of Nations. I have the honor to be, sir, your obedient servant,

WM. E. RAPPARD[1]
Director of the Mandates Section for
the Secretary-General.

Hon. Marcus Garvey explained that the letter was in acknowledgement of the cablegram sent to the League of Nations on August 1, protesting against the Pan-African Congress, and informing the secretary of the League of Nations that Dr. Du Bois did not represent the present-day Negro, and that his representations would be unofficial.

It was then unanimously carried that a cablegram be sent to the League of Nations deprecating the actions of the nations against the Moors, who had declared war against the Spaniards.

The following resolutions were submitted by the administration and carried:

HIGH COMMISSIONERS TO BE APPOINTED

That a high commissioner shall be appointed to represent this organization in every country where Negroes live, and that in parts where the country is divided up into large States and different sections that a commissioner be appointed to every section and State.

That foreign high commissioners be appointed with the rank of ministers plenipotentiary or ambassadors, who shall be domiciled at the capital of all recognized governments.

Their duties shall be to keep up friendly relations with the respective governments and to protect the interest of all Negroes.

The President-General explained that an official representative of the U.N.I.A. would be assigned to such places as Cuba, Haiti, Jamaica, Barbados and Trinidad. Countries like the United States of America would be divided into States, where the State was large enough, and to each would be assigned a commissioner, who would represent officially the work of the U.N.I.A., supervise the work of the organization in that State or country, and make efforts to propagate the work of the organization.

The high commissioner would only reside in such countries as France, England and Germany. His duty would be as minister plenipotentiary to protect the interests of Negroes in those quarters and to supply information as to what is being done there to the detriment or the good of Negroes, so that the organization might have a full grasp of everything being done by those governments affecting Negroes.

PASSPORTS

That a Bureau of Passports and Identification be attached to the Secretary-General's office, and that each and every member who desires a passport of identification for the purpose of travel, or for the purpose of receiving recognition, consideration and likely help of other branches, and for proving such members' connection with a recognized organization, shall be supplied with one of these passports at any division of the organization by the executive secretary.

Each passport shall have the photograph of the bearer and his or her signature, and other details.

Each passport identification shall be issued by the Universal Negro Improvement Association from its headquarters. It shall be countersigned and stamped by the executive secretary of the division from which same has been secured.

Before a passport identification can be secured, each and every member will have to fill out a form of particulars, and only financial members whose dues and assessments have been fully paid up, and whose records are clean, shall be supplied with a passport identification.

The sum of two dollars shall be paid for the issuance of every passport identification.

That the Bureau of Justice through the office of the President-General shall see that each and every member who holds a passport identification is properly protected in case of abuse, advantage or injustice committed upon such individual.

The President-General explained that he had come into contact with hundreds of Negroes in different parts of the world, who, through being unable to establish their connection or relationship with any organization or institution, were unable to get help from the U.N.I.A. and from the governments. The passport was not intended to take the place of the passport required by governments.

AFRICAN REDEMPTION FUND

That the parent body shall raise a universal fund from all Negroes for the purpose of the redemption of Africa, and that every member of the Negro race shall be asked to contribute a sum of not less than five dollars to this fund. This shall not be a tax on active members, but a voluntary contribution from all Negroes. The fund shall be known as the "African Redemption Fund."

Each and every person who subscribes to this fund shall receive a certificate of loyalty to the cause of Africa. The certificate shall bear the signatures of the President-General and the High Chancellor.

That the purpose of the African Redemption Fund shall be to create a working capital for the building up of Africa.

VETO POWER FOR ADMINISTRATOR

That the administrator of the Universal Negro Improvement Association shall be empowered to exercise a veto power on all and any financial measures initiated by any individual or by the Executive Council that may tend to jeopardize or ruin the finance of the organization.

Such veto power shall only be used by the administration in financial matters and where, from his best judgment, he is convinced it is not to the best interest of the organization to permit the carrying out of such financial matters.

An appeal may be made to the convention against the veto of the administrator on any measure, and he shall be held responsible to the convention for his exercise of his judgment on the matter.

This resolution provoked considerable discussion. Members of the Executive Council opposed on the ground that the counsel of the many was better than that of a single individual. It would cripple the hands of the Executive Council, whose members would be mere figureheads. Delegates from the floor of the house also opposed the measure for the same reasons, and introduced amendments to the effect that the veto power may be overridden by the unanimous vote or a two-thirds' majority vote of the Executive Council. Both amendments were defeated, the original resolution being carried with only 24 dissentients.

THE ISSUANCE OF CHARTERS

The following resolutions for the granting of charters were adopted:

That on application for a charter by any seven persons, in a State where there already exists a chartered division in good standing with the parent body, that chartered division be referred to for information regarding the applicants before the charter can be issued to said applicants.

That the following paragraphs be added to Article E, Section 4, of the Constitution: That all divisions created in the same cities be under the supervision of the former chartered division and be designated as chapter charters instead of divisions, and that only a chapter charter be issued or granted by the parent body, thereby authorizing only one chartered division in the same city.

That in countries requiring the registration of charters there shall be issued one dominion, provincial or colonial charter, as the law may require, to one division, and all succeeding divisions within the charter limits shall be designated as chapters. Nothing in this provision shall be construed to give the original division any jurisdiction over the others.

[*23 August 1921*]

EIGHTEENTH DAY

MINISTRY OF INDUSTRIES AND LABOR

On Tuesday, the 23d inst., the convention dealt with the resolutions, of which notice had been given by delegates. Questions were also answered. The following resolutions were carried:—

1. That the High Executive Council of the U.N.I.A. co-operate with local divisions in starting industrial activities for the purpose of furnishing work for U.N.I.A. members.

2. That a Minister of Industries and Labor be added to the High Executive Council of the U.N.I.A.

Hon. A. Johnson (New York):
That the Bureau of Publicity and Propaganda be an attachment to the Institute of Propaganda to be established.

The above measure was brought before the House in the form of an amendment to a resolution, sponsored by Hon. H. V[inton]. Plummer[2] (New York), that such a bureau be created with a director.

Hon. J. D. Horton (West Africa):
That one or two native Africans be elected to the Field Corps of the Western Hemisphere so that they may be enabled to explain to the people the conditions in Africa.

Hon. R. H. Tobitt, West Indian Leader:

1. That the Provisional President of Africa, the American Leader and the two West Indian Leaders shall be honorary members of the High Executive Council.

2. That the Leaders of the West Indies present for the approval of the High Executive Council a budget for the proper execution of their work in their particular field, taking into consideration local economic and other conditions.

3. That Commissioners serving in the West Indies forward monthly reports to the parent body.

A resolution presented by the Hon. G. R. Weston,[3] Boston, Mass., recommending that the convention take steps towards the unification of the race under one great faith was rejected, it being the unanimous opinion that the present time was inopportune.

AMERICAN LEADER'S REPORT

During the afternoon session His Excellency, the American Leader, Dr. J. W. H. Eason, gave his departmental report. He referred at the outset to the fact that the administration had found it impossible during the year under review to establish the official residence and office of the American Leader in Washington. The year had therefore been spent in carrying out the orders of the administrator and of the Executive Council and in studying world conditions and in applying them to the conditions confronting Negroes in this country.

Dr. Eason then proceeded to give a detailed account of his work in this country and Canada, where he had settled disputes, organized successfully and promoted the welfare of the movement in general. He emphasized the need for greater respect for those in authority and recommended that a school of diplomats be established, and that an embassy be established at once in Washington. In regard to the latter recommendation, he promised that he would raise money sufficient to defray all the expenses.

[24 August 1921]

NINETEENTH DAY

THE DISAPPEARANCE OF DR. BROOKS

Wednesday, August 24, with the exception of a brief period spent in discussing some more resolutions which stood in the names of delegates, was devoted to investigating charges laid against the secretary-general, Dr. J. D. Brooks, and also a charge of dual service preferred against the chaplain-general, Dr. G. A. McGuire.

The charges against the secretary-general were: (1) incompetence, (2) violating the Constitution. They were preferred by Hon. R. Smith, New York, who initiated the discussion by moving that the office of the secretary-general be declared vacant.

The president-general said prior to his departure from the United States the secretary-general was sent out on an itinerary and did not report to the parent body for four months. He wrote Dr. Brooks, requesting that he report back at New York, but he failed to do so. He reported some time after and was told by the Executive Council not to return to the field, but he nevertheless did so. Moneys collected by him had not been properly returned to the parent body. Nothing had been heard of him since July 1. He was under a bond for $5,000.

The auditor-general said, as far as could be ascertained, a sum in the vicinity of $1,000 was due by the secretary-general to the parent body, in addition to various collections, donations, etc.

Several delegates spoke, testifying to unbecoming conduct on the part of Dr. Brooks and giving evidence which supported the statement of the auditor-general as to there being defalcations in the accounts of Dr. Brooks.

When the delegates had finished their recitals the Hon. R. Smith asked permission to substitute the following motion: That the office of the Rt. Hon. Secretary-General, Dr. J. D. Brooks, be declared vacant because of malfeasance and failure to account for moneys collected by him for this organization.

The motion was carried, there being only one dissentient.

DR. McGUIRE'S RESIGNATION ACCEPTED

The case of the chaplain-general was next dealt with.

Dr. McGuire said there was no necessity to bring any charge of dual service against him, as he had already stated in his department report his connection with the Independent Episcopal Church[4] and had made known his attitude. Further, that upon the ground that he would not in the ensuing year be able to give his entire time to the work of the association he had tendered his resignation.

It will be remembered that when Dr. McGuire tendered his resignation to the convention a few days ago it was tabled by the unanimous vote of the house.

The resignation was then taken up for discussion.

Several questions were asked by Hon. A. Taylor (New York), directed at the eliciting of information on the subject of Dr. McGuire's efforts in behalf of the Independent Episcopal Church on his recent visit to Cuba. Hon. E. V. Morales stated, in answer to Hon. Taylor's questions, that, as far as he could see, the Independent Episcopal Church services held by Dr. McGuire did not conflict with the meetings of the association nor did the interests of the latter suffer in any way. Dr. McGuire had explicitly stated to the people that the I. E. Church bore no relationship to the U.N.I.A.

A PRINCIPLE INVOLVED

Before the motion was put to a vote the president-general, in a stirring address, paid a warm tribute to the ability and excellence of the service of the chaplain-general. He declared, however, that a principle was involved, the principle requiring officers of the U.N.I.A. to give their undivided time and attention to their duty. He ended with a moving appeal to the chaplain-general to decide to give his services to the alleviation of the sufferings of the 400,000,000 Negroes of the world.

Dr. McGuire, deeply moved, replied that he, too, found that a principle was involved. He was unable to turn aside from his ministerial work in his chosen field. His desire was to serve the U.N.I.A. and the Independent Episcopal Church, which he had founded. The destiny of the two institutions was the same—the salvation of the Negro. If he were not permitted to serve both at one and the same time, he would at least pledge unsalaried support to the cause of Garveyism. Whatever service the president-general required of him he would give, as far as it lay in his power.

The resolution was then put to a vote and carried, the voting being in the proportion of 3 to 1.

Dr. McGuire was then made honorary chaplain-general of the organization by unanimous vote of the house.

[*25 August 1921*]

TWENTIETH DAY

CHARGES AGAINST EXECUTIVE OFFICERS

On Thursday, the 25th inst., the cases of several other officers of the Executive Council were dealt with.

Dr. F. W. Ellegor, high commissioner general, was charged with duality of service.

Dr. Ellegor explained that he held a small charge, a mission with about thirty-five members, and that his ministerial work there did not interfere with the faithful performance of his duties. He was only technically guilty of the charge.

The president-general stated that Dr. Ellegor was a very capable officer, one who had been a decided asset to the organization, but a principle, the same as in the case of the chaplain-general, was involved.

The house having found that the high commissioner-general had functioned in a dual capacity, the president-general called upon Dr. Ellegor to state which position he would relinquish.

Dr. Ellegor replied that he would not surrender his charge.

The president-general remarked that that amounted to a resignation.

Dr. Ellegor disagreed with this finding, and it was eventually decided that he be given twenty-four hours to place his decision before the house.

In reference to His Excellency the West Indian Leader (Eastern Province), Rev. R. H. Tobitt, against whom, it will be remembered, it was charged successfully that he had been guilty of duality of service, and had been a liability rather than an asset to the organization, it was agreed that he be employed in the office of the parent body on work commensurate with his ability at a salary not exceeding $3,000 a year.

The office of the West Indian Leader was then declared vacant.

The Assistant President-General Dr. J. [D.] Gordon, was also charged with duality of service. He intimated his desire to adhere to his ministerial duties and his unwillingness to continue in the position of assistant president-general.

The office was then declared vacant, it being, however, agreed that Dr. Gordon be given such work to perform in the interests of the organization as will not interfere with his religious duties.

It was also decided that the office of chaplain-general be left vacant for the ensuing year.

NOMINATIONS

The following nominations for offices were then received:

Assistant President-General: Hons. J. R. L. Diggs[5] (Baltimore), W. A. Wallace (Chicago), C. H. Duvall (Boston), N. D. Thompson (Los Angeles), H. A. Collins (Banes, Cuba), and W. [H.] Ferris (New York).

Secretary-General: Hons. F. A. Toote (New York), J. E. Bruce (Brooklyn), V. J. Williams (New York), W. A. Wallace (Chicago), and P. E. Paul (New York).

Second Assistant Secretary-General: Hons. A. J. Ford (New York), J. J. Cranston (Pittsburgh), R. L. Poston[6] (Detroit), W. Phillips (Boston), C. A. Bryce (Buffalo), H. V. Plum[m]er (New York), and F. O. Raines (Chicago).

Minister of Industries and Labor: Hons. Lionel Francis (Philadelphia), U.S. Poston[7] (Detroit), T. J. Carr (St. Paul, Minn.), J. DeLeon (Philadelphia), J. R. L. Diggs (Baltimore), W. O. Smyers (Detroit), Marie P. Williams (Kansas City, Mo.), W. H. Ferris (New York), C. H. Duval (Boston), and P. E. Paul (New York).

West Indian Leader of the Eastern Province: Hons. E. V. Morales (Cuba), Adrian Johnson (New York), Arden Bryan (Barbados), H. A. Collins (Banes, Cuba), R. Smith (New York), Dr. Lionel Francis (Philadelphia), E. C. West (Columbia), and C. S. Bourne (Guatemala).

Surgeon-General: Hons. Dr. J. D. Gibson and W. S. Hannah.

Speaker-in-Convention: Hons. F. A. Toote (New York), Adrian Johnson (New York), P. E. Paul (New York), W. O. Smyer (Detroit), W. A. Wallace (Chicago), C. A. Stewart (Boston), G. E. Carter (Miami), and George Taite (Preston, Cuba).

[26 *August 1921*]

TWENTY-FIRST DAY

THE BLACK STAR LINE, INC.

When business was resumed on Friday, the 26th inst., Hon. Dr. F. W. Ellegor signified that he had decided to relinquish the position he held in his church and asked for a reasonable time to do so.

It was unanimously agreed that this be determined by the President-General.

On the recommendation of the President-General, the office of an Honorary Provisional Vice-President of Africa was created. The following were then nominated to fill the office: Hon. W. H. Ferris, Hon. T. J. Carr, Hon. E. V. Morales, Hon. [L.] J. Francis and Hon. J. C. Gill.

The affairs of the Black Star Line Steamship Corporation were then discussed.

The Hon. Marcus Garvey gave a comprehensive survey of the operations of the corporation, referring to the difficulties encountered—the legal battles fought to preserve the life of the concern, the acts of disloyalty of the various crews employed and the facts leading up to the purchase of the "Frederick Douglass."

Mr. O. M. Thompson, vice-president of the Black Star Line, corroborated the statements of the president, dating back to the time he was elected to office, and outlined the difficulties and disappointments in the contracts made in connection with the "Phyllis Wheatley." He, however, expected delivery of the ship by Thursday, September 1.

When business was resumed after the luncheon recess, the discussion of the Black Star Line, Inc., was continued, several recommendations being forthcoming from delegates. The Hon. Marcus Garvey made a strong plea to the representatives of divisions to place the situation clearly before their members on their return, and emphasized that the real need of the corporation was capital. If the capital were subscribed, all the difficulties would disappear and not one, but several ships would be immediately procured.

He also announced the intention of the directors to operate the ships under the Liberian flag.

BOLSHEVISM IN FLIGHT

There was some excitement during the afternoon session when a delegate from the African Blood Brotherhood left the House in haste. The Negro Congress Bulletin, published by the African Blood Brotherhood, devoted almost the entire space of its issue of the 24th inst. to a fantastic misrepresentation of the work accomplished by the second international convention of Negroes. A member drew the attention of the House to the scurrilous pamphlet and moved that the representatives of the A.B.B., four in number,[8] who had been in attendance at the previous sessions, be required to give an explanation. Their names were called and no one responded. An examination of delegates' cards was about to be made, when a man was seen to rise hastily and scurry across the hall, plunge through the doorway, beating his way in precipitate flight towards Seventh avenue. The erstwhile indignant House rocked with laughter.

The Hon. Marcus Garvey then warned the House not to be misled as to the nature of the policy of the African Blood Brotherhood. Through its organ, the Crusader Magazine, he said, it pretended to have at heart the interests of Negroes. It was in reality the advocate of Sovietism, Bolshevism and Radicalism, the paid servant of certain destructive white elements which aimed at exploiting Negroes for their own subservient ends. Finding that the Universal Negro Improvement Association held nothing in common, it had set itself to discredit the work of this organization.

It was unanimously agreed that the delegates' cards of the four representatives be withdrawn.

FRIDAY NIGHT SESSION

ELECTION OF OFFICERS

On Friday night the election of officers took place.

The newly created office of second assistant secretary-general was first taken and was very keenly contested. By a process of elimination the field was reduced to two, Hon. R. L. P[o]ston (Detroit), the nominee of the President-General, and Hon. J. J. Cranston (Pittsburgh). The former won on the second ballot by a majority of [*torn*].

Hon. P. E. Paul declined to contest the election for Secretary-General, leaving four contestants. Hon. Fred A. Toote headed the poll, defeating Hon. J. E. Bruce, the President-General's nominee, by 29 votes.

The election of a Minister of Industries and Labor provided the closest contest of the evening. Hon. J. R. L. Diggs (Baltimore), withdrew, leaving nine contestants. On the second ballot, Hon. U. S. Poston (Detroit), the nominee of the President-General, defeated Prof. W. [H.] Ferris by three votes.

Hon. Dr. J. D. Gibson secured the position of Surgeon-General, easily defeating Dr. W. S. Hannah, of Philadelphia.

The meeting was then adjourned until Monday, the 29th inst., when the remaining offices would be filled.

Printed in *NW*, 3 September 1921. Original headlines omitted.

1. William Emmanuel Rappard (1883–1958) was a professor at the University of Geneva and a member of the Permanent Mandates Commission of the League of Nations. He was also a Swiss delegate to the assembly of the league (*NYT*, 2 May 1958).

2. UNIA director of publicity.

3. Rev. George Auesby Weston (1885–1972) was a native of Antigua in the West Indies. He came to the United States in 1905 by working his way as a coaler aboard a Norwegian steamer and was discharged at Newport News, Virginia; from there he shipped as a deckhand to Rotterdam and Cardiff. In 1906 he stowed back to America aboard a cattle boat, arriving at Baltimore. He spent the next several years working in sundry positions aboard vessels that took him from Savannah, Georgia, to Philadelphia, Boston, Maine, and Havana. In 1919 he joined the UNIA in Boston after a friend persuaded him to attend a local meeting in an AME church at which Garvey spoke. Weston was himself a preacher in the local Methodist Episcopal Church in Boston, and after joining the UNIA he was appointed chaplain of the Boston division. At the time of the UNIA's August 1920 convention, Weston was instrumental in raising the funds that allowed the attendance of delegations from his native Antigua and from St. Thomas in the Virgin Islands. Weston's presence as a delegate to the August 1921 convention came in response to a cable that was sent two days after the convention actually began, summoning him to New York. At the time, his wife was the musical director of the choir at Liberty Hall. Weston very quickly became active in the affairs of the convention, and he stood

out among the group of delegates who opposed Garvey's request for legislation that would grant him veto power over all UNIA and BSL finances. This group included, among others, Dr. Lionel Francis of Philadelphia, William A. Wallace of Chicago, and Joseph A. Craigen of Detroit. It is said that Garvey even went so far at one point as to threaten to have Weston thrown out of the convention on account of the stubbornness of his opposition. Weston subsequently took up residence in Pittsburgh, where he became the president of the local UNIA as well as district UNIA arbitrator for western Pennsylvania. From Pittsburgh, Weston moved on briefly to the Cleveland UNIA division; he then settled in New York and became vice-president of the New York division. Following Garvey's incarceration in the Atlanta penitentiary in early 1925, Weston asserted the right of the New York division, as the original chartered UNIA body, to ownership of the Liberty Hall property. In an attempt to save it financially, the New York division voted to sell the property to a holding corporation as the initial step in a commercial development plan to construct a nine-story UNIA executive office building and convention hall on the site. Meanwhile, Weston found himself in sharp conflict with Amy Jacques Garvey, who was acting as Garvey's personal representative. At an emergency convention of the UNIA called in Detroit in March 1926, Weston was ousted from the organization on charges of rebellion and encumbering Liberty Hall; yet Weston and his followers were still in physical control of the property. Garvey at this juncture described Weston as "one of the most dangerous men we have yet encountered" (*NW*, 20 March 1926). The following month the New York State Supreme Court granted to Garvey's followers a restraining order against Weston (*NW*, 8 May 1926). In the midst of this confused situation, with two rival UNIA bodies existing side by side and each claiming to represent the only "official" UNIA, Weston's group held the "Fifth International Convention of the Negro Peoples of the World" in August 1926 and voted to "expel" Garvey. Among the more important UNIA officials who were associated with Weston were G. O. Marke, William L. Sherrill, William Isles, Wesley MacDonald Holder, William H. Ferris, and W. O. Smyer. The effort proved short-lived, however, and soon thereafter Garvey's supporters were able to retake possession of Liberty Hall. In later years Weston organized a group calling itself the Pioneer Negroes of the World. He eventually returned to Antigua, and in 1953 he organized the African Orthodox Evangelical Mission, with himself as "evangelical crusader." (He was earlier ordained by F. A. Toote as a deacon in the African Orthodox church of his fellow countryman, Rev. George Alexander McGuire.) Weston died in New York City on 16 May 1972; he remained throughout his life a committed advocate of what he consistently referred to as "the Garveyan philosophy" (Interviews with Rev. George A. Weston by St. Clair Drake, October 1970; by Robert A. Hill, New York, August 1971; and by Canute Parris, New York, March 1971; MU, WEBDB; NNHR, *Universal Negro Improvement Association* v. *Marcus Garvey, Amy Jacques Garvey, Fred A. Toote, F. Levi Lord, William A. Wallace, and Uriah Gittens*, no. 34151, New York State Supreme Court, September 1926; *NW*, 6 March, 21 August, and 11 September 1926; *Chicago Defender*, 4 September and 11 September 1926; Elton C. Fax, *Garvey: The Story of A Pioneer Black Nationalist* [New York: Dodd, Mead & Co., 1972]).

4. The first Independent Episcopal Church was incorporated by McGuire in April 1920 under the statutes of New York, after he resigned from the Reformed Episcopal church and organized the Church of the Good Shepherd in November 1919. It was stated that "among other reasons, the connection of Dr. McGuire with the Universal Negro Improvement Association, of which he is now the honored Chaplain General, was the impelling factor in the decision reached by him and his members not to affiliate with any existing body of white Episcopalians, but to organize an Independent or African Episcopal Church to include Negroes everywhere, and of which the 'Good Shepherd' would be the mother church or congregation." The statement went on to disclose: "Dr. McGuire's congregation numbers 50 communicants besides other adherents. Seven other clergymen have joined him in the movement, and in addition to the congregations in the United States, work is being done in Bermuda, Cuba, and Central America. Plans are on foot to link up with a similar movement in West Africa and to plant missions in various West Indian islands. The day of the Independent Episcopal Church is at hand" ("Caustic Reply to Bishop Burch:—Rev. Dr. McGuire Refutes False and Misleading Statements," *NW*, 6 November 1920). McGuire was elected bishop of a group of Independent Episcopal churches on 16 July 1921, at a meeting held at St. Saviour's Church in Brooklyn (Richard Newman, "The Origins of the African Orthodox Church," introduction to *The Negro Churchman* [Official organ of the African Orthodox Church] [Millwood, N.Y.: Kraus Thomson Reprint Co., 1977] p. xi). While Garvey was on tour in the Caribbean, a report published in the *Negro World* stated: "The Negroes of the world in

convention [August 1920] made the Most Rev. Dr. G. A. McGuire the first prince of the Church Ethiopia. We understand that plans are under way for his enthronement at the coming Convention in August next" (*NW*, 2 April 1921).

5. James Robert Lincoln Diggs (1866–1923) was born in Upper Marlboro, Md., and educated at Wayland Seminary, Washington, D.C., Bucknell University, Lewisburg, Pa., and Illinois Wesleyan University, Bloomington, Ill., where he became the ninth black in the United States to earn a Ph.D. degree. He served as president or dean of several black colleges in the South between 1906 and 1914, when he became president of Clayton-Williams University in Baltimore. Diggs was a member of the Niagara movement, an early member of the NAACP, and national vice-president of the National Equal Rights League, which held its 1920 convention at the church Diggs pastored, Baltimore's Trinity Baptist Church. In August 1921 Diggs delivered a sermon on the closing day of the UNIA convention. By October he was president of the Baltimore UNIA division. Six months later Diggs presided over the wedding ceremony of Garvey and Amy Jacques, assuming the title of acting chaplain general of the UNIA. He also preached the annual convention sermon at the 1922 UNIA convention, where he was unanimously elected chaplain general. He died of cancer six months later (Randall K. Burkett, *Black Redemption*, pp. 99–102).

6. Robert Lincoln Poston (1891–1924) won the post of second assistant secretary-general and later became secretary-general (September 1921) and second assistant president general (August 1923). Born in Hopkinsville, Ky., Poston was the son of Ephraim and Mollie Poston, both teachers in Kentucky public schools and colleges. He briefly attended Princeton University during Woodrow Wilson's term as university president, but he was forced to leave after protesting Wilson's policy of racial segregation on campus. After serving in the U.S. Army in 1918 and 1919, he joined his brother Ulysses in publishing the *Detroit Contender* in 1920 to 1921, a newspaper that the *Negro World* claimed had "rendered signal service to the UNIA in winning Detroit against the strongest opposition that the oganization has encountered in any northern city" (*NW*, 8 July 1922). A Garvey favorite who became "Sir" Robert Poston, he rose quickly within the UNIA. He became a member of the *Negro World* editorial staff and contributed articles, commentary, and poetry regularly. In February 1924 he headed a UNIA mission to Liberia to discuss the terms for Afro-American immigration. He died of pneumonia aboard ship on the voyage back to New York. The *Negro World* obituary read: "He was a radical of the radicals in his attitude towards the white man's government and religion. . . . As long as the Negro race can father such men as Robert Lincoln Poston we need not despair of the highest service and greatest achievements for race unity and redemption possible in human aspiration and hope" (*NW*, 29 March 1924; Theodore G. Vincent, *Black Power and the Garvey Movement* [San Francisco: Ramparts Press, 1971], pp. 156–157; National Personnel Records Center, St. Louis, military service certificate no. 3 104 018).

7. Ulysses S. Poston, the younger brother of Robert Lincoln Poston, later became UNIA minister of industries and labor.

8. The four ABB delegates were W. A. Fleming, Ben Burrell, L. C. Caine, and Orry N. Deibol.

Charles L. Latham to Charles Evans Hughes

Kingston, Jamaica, August 24, 1921

No. 1157

SIR:

I have the honor to refer to my despatches No. 878 of September 12, 1920 and No. 991 of March 1, 1921, in which the Department's instructions were requested as to whether this office should grant a visa to Marcus Garvey, and to the Department's instruction of March 25, 1921, directing me to refuse him a visa in view of his activities in political and race agitation.

I have to report that Marcus Garvey arrived in Kingston on March 21, 1921 and conducted here a propaganda campaign in favor of the Universal Negro Improvement Association, and the several negro corporations organised by him in the United States.

He arrived on board the steamer KANAWHA of the Black Star Line and with him as passengers on that vessel were a number of other negroes identified with political and racial agitation[,] notably John Sidney deBourg, Henrietta Vinton Davis, Amy Euphemia Ja[c]ques and Augustus Fredericks.

When the vessel docked, Garvey who styles himself the first Provisional President of Africa landed in his so-called robes of office and Augustus Fredericks who uses the title of Lieutenant was also uniformed and carried a sword, indicating that their voyage on the KANAWHA, which had been apparently at Garvey's personal orders, was for propaganda purposes rather than commercial ones.

Garvey made a number of speeches and publications while in this Island which were of very mischievous tendencies and calculated to arouse race antagonism. He criti[ci]sed the local officials, upbraided the Jamaican negroes for their inertness and servility and sought especially to alienate support from the local preachers in this Island, most of whom are colored, on the ground that they were preaching subservience to the white man.

Garvey's movements were closely watched by the local police. It may be stated that his mission to Jamaica, where he was born and where his early record is known, was a failure, due principally to the impression that very quickly gained ground among the negroes here that his principal purpose was that of obtaining money. He made capital mistakes in overcharging for admission to hear him speak and in over emphasizing his appeals for subscriptions to his industrial corporations. In a recent speech in New York, however, he is quoted as stating that while he found Jamaica cold to his propaganda he left them enthusiastic and that the policemen here were now members of the Universal Negro Improvement Association.

A complete failure of discipline and a state of near-anarchy existed on board the KANAWHA during its stay in this port. In the opinion of this office, this condition was due to the interference with the discipline on board by the negro agitators, who remained on board while the vessel was in port.

Garvey applied for a visa to his passport on April 11, 1921 and, as directed by the Department, his application was refused. On June 25, 1921, instructions were received from the Department to grant Garvey a visa and to cable the date of his departure and this was accordingly done.

The New York newspapers indicate that he is now engaged in political agitation in New York and in a public speech he has stated that I refused to visa his passport to return to the United States but that he obtained that the Department of State directed that the visa be granted.

I am in receipt of a letter from Adrian Richardson who was formerly the Master of the KANAWHA and who left the vessel in his port as a result of disagreement with Garvey in which he states that he thinks it is "his duty to inform me of what remarks Marcus Garvey is saying and preaching in Liberty Hall here[.] [H]e says you tried to keep him out of the United States by not visaing his passport also that he applied to you for protection for the property of the Black Star Line against Charles Harris the Chief Engineer and myself and you did not give him any protection because you were a Southern cracker and you do not care to recognise negroes. He has also warned all Jamaicans to beware of you should they apply to you for anything."

The absurd charges of Marcus Garvey against the Master and the Chief Engineer of the KANAWHA were given the fullest consideration by this office and were found to have no basis except spite and chagrin, I believe they were brought for the purpose also of saving his face with the Black Star Line stockholders; the line has not been a paying enterprise commercially, it could not well be, while devoted /to/ carrying Garvey and his agitators around on propaganda tours. He was given every opportunity to present all of the evidence he desired despite the fact that most of it was obviously irre[lev]ant and false. He was given the same courteous treatment that is accorded everyone applying at the Consulate and he took advantage of it to such extent that either he or some of his fellow agitators were almost constantly in the office.

As to his remarks about myself, my convictions in regard to him and his purposes are such that I prefer that he show that I have not given any personal countenance to him or his designs. While I have no time for personal animosity towards Garvey on account of his race or color, I believe it my duty to state for the consideration of the Department that from my observation of him and his propaganda I believe him to be a clever scoundrel and that the principal purpose in all of his corporations and organizations is that of extracting money from the ignorant negroes for his own pocket. But I am convinced that there is a serious side to the matter in that for purpose of his own profit he is appealing to and inflaming every race prejudice and animosity that he can. While he is clever enough to temper his propaganda with statements that he is for the negro rather than against the white man or any Government, his speeches are not lacking in many references to fighting for negro rights and I believe that a tendency of his propaganda is to alienate the loyalty of American and British negroes to his Association or as he terms it, to Africa. Though he is certainly not an intellectual his particular propaganda and agitation is considered dangerous in that it will find a more fertile field of class divergence than Bolshevism would be likely to find in the United States.

I also believe it probable that an investigation by detectives would show that the Jamaica negro girl, Amy Euphemia Ja[c]ques, who was traveling on the KANAWHA with him as his Secretary is living with him in improper relations and that he might be found to have made himself liable to criminal prosecution on account of connection with her entry into the United States for such purpose. Evidence to this end might be obtainable from Adrian

Richardson of 14 West 107th. Street, New York, who was formerly the Master of the KANAWHA, and is now suing the Black Star Line for his wages. The vessel is understood to be in Cuba en route to the United States and the members of the crew would be available upon its arrival and might also be inclined to give evidence after their connection with the vessel had been severed. I have the honor to be, Sir, Your obedient servant,

CHARLES L. LATHAM
American Consul

DNA, RG 65, file BS 198940-268. TLS. Also in DNA, RG 59, file 000-612.

Black Star Line to Henry C. Von Struve, American Consul, Antilla, Cuba

New York [*26 August 1921*]

CAPTAIN AND CREW OF KANAWHA HAVE CARRIED SHIP OUT OF COURSE TO ANTILLA[.] COMPANY DOES NOT HOLD ITSELF RESPONSIBLE FOR THEM AND THEIR ACTION[.]

BLACK S[T]AR LINE NEW YORK

DNA, RG 84, file 885. TG, recipient's copy.

Article in the *Negro World*

[27 August 1921]

WOMEN'S INDUSTRIAL EXHIBIT

The Women's Industrial Art Exhibit, which was a feature of the Second International Convention of Negroes, closed on Tuesday, August 23. The High Commissioner General and Mrs. Mary G. Johnson, the Executive Secretary, worked indefatigably. And the needle, art and literature exhibits from America, the West Indies and Africa were a credit to Negro Womenhood, and demonstrate its possibilities. The elaborate work of Mrs. Geo. D. Tobias attracted considerable attention. It is to be hoped that sooner or later the Women's Industrial Art Exhibit will be made a permanent feature of the comprehensive work of the U.N.I.A.

Mrs. Mary G. Johnson, Mrs. Elie Garcia, Mrs. G. A. McGuire, Mrs. Smith of the N.Y. Local in charge of the cafeteria, and Mrs. Beresford B. Jemott deserve credit for co-operating with the High Commissioner in making the Women's Industrial Art Exhibit a success.

Credit must also be given to Mrs. Weeks and Mrs. Sharpison Young for the elaborate dresses they made, which made the fashion show a success.

It is significant that two ladies, Mrs. Eloise Bibbs Thompson[1] of Los Angeles, Cal., who distinguished herself as a writer and playwright, and Mrs. Maria P. Williams of Kansas City, Mo., an author and song writer, are enrolled among the delegates of this great convention.

Printed in *NW*, 27 August 1921.

  1. The wife of Noah Thompson.

First UNIA Court Reception

[Liberty Hall, August 27, 1921]

ANCIENT ETHIOPIAN CEREMONIAL COURT RECEPTION REVIVED AMID SCENES OF UNUSUAL POMP, MAGNIFICENCE AND SPLENDOR BY U.N.I.A.

Under the auspices of the Universal Negro Improvement Association and the second international convention of Negroes of the world was held tonight at Liberty Hall what must be conceded to be, without exception, the greatest state social event that has taken place among black people in the last three hundred years. It was a ceremonial that may correctly be regarded as a revival of the ancient glory, pomp and splendor of Ethiopia in the days of the Queen of Sheba, centuries long ago, of her greatness and world supremacy, comparable to similar state functions held in the ceremonial courts of England, Germany, Italy, France and the United States. It was representative, too, not only of the very best elements in the race, but representative as well of the highest Negro culture, there having been present men and women in every walk of life, as ministers, doctors, lawyers, architects, engineers, teachers, financiers, merchants, business men, dressmakers, designers, milliners, hairdressers, restauranteurs, etc. Persons of prominence and note were knighted, as in the days of old, for distinguished service rendered to the race; men and women of outstanding character and ability were presented to His Highness the Potentate, and several young misses also presented upon making their social debut.

All this took place and was done amid a gorgeous, dazzling scene that could not but evoke the highest admiration and delight of those fortunate enough to witness it, and stir to the very depths of one's soul a true feeling of race consciousness and race pride. For here one stood in a blaze of brilliant scenery—men in uniforms; ladies, young and old, in beautiful, elaborate gowns in the latest modes; gentlemen in full dress; decorations all around in the colors of the Red, the Black and the Green; bunting, flags, Japanese lanterns, flowers, palm plants and ferns tastefully arranged here and there, and here one found himself in the midst of a select assemblage of more than 1,500 persons. In short, it is no exaggeration to say that it was a scene that had never before been beheld anywhere among Negro people in this or any other part of the world in modern times.

The affair concluded with a banquet [for] the high officials of the association and delegates to the convention and 500 invited guests; a grand ball, the latter being begun by a waltz number, played for the special benefit of the newly-titled distinguished persons and the members of the High Executive Council. It was an historic event and, unlike social functions held in the past by Negro associations, fraternal and otherwise, was not an empty display of grandeur, but an occasion of far-reaching import to the Negro race in that it was a manifestation of the tremendous possibilities within the black people of the world for their future development along industrial, economic, political and social lines, and significant of their determination, through the instrumentality of the Universal Negro Improvement Association and its subsidiary branches, to put over completely the program of the redemption of Africa and absolute emancipation of the race from every form of oppression and injustice by which they are now beset. Truly, it was a wonderful occasion, one that will ever linger in the memory because of its brilliance and its meaning as the dawning of an auspicious new era for Negroes the world over; an occasion, too, that has established for them as a criterion for all time a high standard of society of their own, devoid of any slavish imitation of the social standards of other races.

PARTICULARS OF THE RECEPTION

Beginning at 7:30 people began assembling in the spacious hall, admittance to which was by ticket only, while big limousines and automobiles rolled up to the special entrance (from which extended a canopy specially erected for the occasion, leading to the curb of the street), bringing distinguished invited guests and visitors and high officials of the U.N.I.A. Within[,] everything was astir and in readiness. Ushers, either in full dress or in uniform, were stationed here and there at every important point, with guards at both entrances to take care of the people as they entered and to seat them. Liberty Hall on ordinary occasions is filled with chairs, but tonight the majority of these, particularly those that were directly in front of the rostrum, were removed, the space being covered in part with matting rugs.

Extending from the western end of the hall and stopping just at the speaker's stand, were two long rows of tables that were used for the banquet given to the high officials. These tables were beautifully decorated with fruit, viands and delicacies at the disposal at this time of the year of the caterer, the Pomona Bakery Enterprises, under the direction of Mr. H. C. Francis. Streamers in black, red and green were strung in various directions over the hall. A large red lantern hung near the ceiling and about in the center, while small Japanese lanterns, brightly illuminated, were suspended from one end of the hall to the other. On the platform was a beautiful mahogany parlor suit[e], loaned, for the occasion, by the President-General from his home. This consisted of chairs, lounging chairs and rockers, the chair placed in the center being used by his Highness, the Potentate, as the throne of the reception. Each of these had soft, artistically embroidered cushions in red, black and green colors. Back of these stood a victrola and behind that a swinging settee with canopy, and on either side, toward the end of the platform, were two settees, one of willow and one of mahogany. Directly below the rostrum, to the right, was an adjustable mirror. The platform was covered with soft green carpet. A tall lamp was placed behind the throne reception chair, its light shedding golden rays like a halo around the head of His Highness, the Potentate. The background was draped in gold effect. A tall Ethiopian vase on a hand-carved stand stood in the centre. On the wall hung pictures and banners representing Africa, Central America, North America and the West Indies.

The edges of the platform were decorated with fern leaves, interspersed with yellow and white daisies. Large fern plants were also on the rostrum, at each end, also vases with bouquets of roses that gave out fragrant odors.

The Black Star Line Band, under Prof. William Isles, was then placed below this, to the left, while off a little farther sat the choir in their white surplices and black caps, under the direction of Prof. Arnold J. Ford. The press table was stationed on the floor level, to the left of the speaker's stand, and was occupied by the official reporters of the association, Mr. I. Newton Braithwaite and his associate, Mr. James H. G. Green, and representatives of the Daily Star[1] and white press.

On the posts or pillars throughout the hall were suspended high the brilliant colored flags of several of the divisions of the U.N.I.A. There were also small American flags that appeared here and there. At one end of the rostrum was a large silk flag of the U.N.I.A., while at the other end stood a large American silk flag.

The scenic effect of the decorations was very striking. These were made under the supervision of the High Commissioner, Rev. Dr. Wilcom H. Ellegor, with the aid of Madame M. Sharperson Young, Miss Amy Jacques (Mr. Garvey's secretary), and Mr. J. M. Rodriguez, one of the ushers of Liberty Hall and its official decorator.

As the high officials entered they were escorted by uniformed members of the African Legion to the anterooms at the east end of the hall, where they awaited the time for the reception to begin. At about 8:20 o'clock a bugle call was given, announcing that all was ready. The African Legion of 60 men, under Major Ludwig Harrigan; the Black Cross Nurses, 45 in number, under Mrs. J. Williams, leader; the Women's Motor Corps of 13, under the leadership of Capt. Mary Charles; the Juvenile Corps of 22 girls, under Lieut. Rosalie Stevens, and 14 boys, under Capt. Alfred King, had been lined up in the western end of the hall. Immediately Capt. Harrigan and four of his men marched to the east end and acted as an escort to His Grace the Chaplain General, His Highness the Potentate, the Provisional President of Africa, and the American Leader, as they marched forward to review the uniformed divisions, all of whom stood at attention while the distinguished officials slowly walked past and closely inspected them.

His Highness the Potentate wore the same uniform he wore on the morning of the opening of the convention, consisting of a military hat with ostrich feather plume, black broadcloth trousers with gold stripe down the side, gold sword, gold sash over the shoulder and around the waist, white gloves and gold military cape. The Provisional President of Africa wore a military hat, very pointed, tipped with white feathers, broadcloth trousers with gold stripe down the side, a Sam Browne belt crossing the shoulder and around the waist, gold epaulets, gold and red trimmings on the sleeves, gold sword and white gloves. He looked the image of Marshal Joffre, though he seemed a trifle uncomfortable in his new, unaccustomed attire.

The American Leader also wore a uniform somewhat similar to that of the Provisional President; with sufficient difference to make a distinction between the two, his hat having an ostrich feather trimming, much like the hats worn on dress occasions by the uniformed department of the Masons. Dr. Eason, tall and of splendid physique, made a brilliant, noble looking general.

The Chaplain General wore a uniform such as Army Chaplains wear on dress occasions in the countries of Europe and England, added to which he had a vest or coat in white and black, trimmed with lace. He carried in one hand the ritual of the U.N.I.A., and in the other a brass rod shaped like a shepherd's crook. He wore white gloves and a mitre cap. Over all, he wore a red, black and green colored robe befitting his station. His appearance was that of an ecclesiastical prelate.

The inspection of the uniformed divisions being over, the high officials were escorted back to the far eastern end of the hall, whence, while the band played the national anthem of the association, the procession began, headed by the entire African Legions, and followed by all the members of the High Executive Council, accompanied by their wives, including Right Hon. Miss Henrietta Vinton Davis, International Organizer; Right Hon. Rev. Dr. G. E. Stewart, High Chancellor; Right Hon. Eli[e] Garcia, Auditor-General; Right Hon. Wilford J. Smith, Counsellor General; Right Hon. W. C. Matthews, Assistant Counsellor General; Right. Hon. Rev. Dr. [R.] H. Tobitt, leader of the Western Provinces of the West Indies; Right Hon. Rev. Dr. J. D. Gordon, Assistant President General; Hon. J. B. Yearwood, Assistant Secretary General; Right Hon. Fred A. Toote, Speaker in Convention; Right Hon. Capt. [E. L.] Gaines, Minister of Legions; Right Hon. Dr. F. Wilcom Ellegor, High Commissioner General. Dr. Tobitt also wore a military uniform, something on the order of the American Leader, but with a helmet in white like the Germans wear. The other officials wore the academic robes of their office. The procession marched down to the centre of the hall, then passed the uniformed divisions now standing in double line formation and still at attention, and continuing to the eastern end, marched back to their seats on the platform. Here His Highness the Potentate occupied the throne seat, the Provisional President of Africa sitting on his right, while the American Leader sat on his left, His Grace the Chaplain-General sitting to the right of Mr. Garvey. The uniformed divisions then marched and counter-marched in various evolutions, displaying their thorough training in military marching. Each division did well and elicited enthusiastic applause by their performance.

This was followed by the announcement by Capt. [E. L.] Gaines, Minister of Legions, that the Court Reception was about to be opened. The Chaplain-General thereupon stood and offered prayer, invoking God's divine blessing upon the occasion and upon all assembled. He then delivered the following address:

Your Supreme Highness the Potentate of the Universal Negro Improvement Association, your Excellency the Provisional President of Africa, your Excellency the American Leader, your Excellency the Leader of the Eastern Province of the West Indies, Right Hon. Members of the High Executive Council, Ladies and Gentlemen—I am instructed for the next three or four minutes to say a few words explanatory of this auspicious and momentous occasion in the history of the Negro race. In all the centuries past since the days of the ancient glories of Ethiopia the eyes of man have not seen such a glorious and gorgeous era of the sons and daughters of Africa as we witness here tonight. I believe that prophecy is about to be fulfilled, even now is being fulfilled. The ancient glories of Eth[i]opia, especially as it excelled on that splendid island of Nero, where the tributaries of the Nile surrounded that wonderful capital of ancient Ethiopia and where the men of our race revelled with pomp and with glory such as we are enjoying tonight. But those days for many centuries have gone. In this year of grace Anno Domini one thousand nine hundred and twenty-one, we see being renewed something of the ancient courts of the nations of Hamitic descent.

We are now about to set our own standards of society. For over 300 years and especially for the last 60 years we have been imitating the social standards of alien races; we have been copying their etiquette; we have been bowing down to their grooves of society. But there comes a time and this is the birthday of the new and glorious era when Negroes led on by the great genius who wrote the constitution of the Universal Negro Improvement Association and included in that constitution a provision for the annual holding of such a court. The time has come when due to this genius we see that for which we have long waited—the first Court held by Negroes under their own world leaders and Potentate. Our eyes have seen this day. Generations have long waited just as when the Messiah came it was said that Abraham rejoiced in spirit to see his day; but there came one Simeon who took the babe in his arms and said: "Lord, now lettest [thou] Thy servant depart in peace for mine eyes have seen Thy salvation."[2] There are some of the older men and women of our race who still remember the days of compulsory servitude, but before their eyes close upon this world they see with their eyes that for which they have been praying—the daybreak of new social conditions among Negroes.

On behalf, therefore, of His Supreme Highness the Potentate, on behalf of His Excellency the Provisional President of Africa, we bid welcome to the numerous delegates that have come up to this great convention from all parts of the world. In due time these delegates will be presented by name as they pass before His Supreme Highness and the Court, after which there will be special introduction to the social life of the Court, especially of certain young misses who are to make their social debut tonight in the presence of the highest elected body of men of the Negro race. These girls and young ladies will be honored by being the first young ladies to be presented in this High Court among Negroes; and also (though I mention it last, it is not least) other members of the Negro race who for the past years (ranging from 4 to 20 years) have been rendering service to their race, not merely in a locality, but work to the entire race–service to humanity of our hue—international service—four persons have been selected by the Right Honorable Commissioner to be admitted to one of the greatest Orders among Negroes today. We have heard of the Order of St. Michael and St. George and the Order of the Bath, and many other English, German, French, and other Orders. We have in the Universal Negro Improvement Association already the Distinguished Service of Eth[i]opia and also the Cross of African Redemption. Tonight, this 27th day of August, according to the action of the Potentate, the Provisional President of Africa and their cabinet will put into the history the inauguration of the Sublime Order of the Nile; and therefore your eyes shall behold a little later in the program two gentlemen of international fame, one lady of singular fame who will be admitted as Knight Commanders of the Sublime Order of the Nile; and then one young man as an example to other young men for distinguished service especially to this organization, will be admitted to the Knighthood of Distinguished Service of the Order of Ethiopia.

I thank you for your patience; I thank you for the good order that has prevailed in this Court at this time.

Following the address by the Chaplain General, the presentation of delegates, deputies and distinguished visitors took place—more than two hundred in number. Then were presented Misses Violet Robinson, Ethel Collins, Carmena Tobitt and Irene Callender, as the occasion of making their social debut.

Miss Carmena Tobitt is the eldest daughter of West Indian Leader Tobitt. She is 20 years of age, and received her schooling in Bermuda, where she was born, graduating from St. George's High School, where she afterwards became an assistant teacher. She is now pursuing a course in millinery and art work in New York. She is chaperoned by her aunt, Mrs. William Watkins of Newport, R.I.

Miss Irene Callender is the daughter of Mrs. Helen Weekes; is 14 years of age and is said to be of an exemplary character and disposition. She is attending Grammar School and is a faithful member of the U.N.I.A. choir. She is an accomplished pianist and voluntarily gave her services to Liberty Hall in its early days when there was no one else to play the piano during the services and musical programs.

Mr. Vernal J. Williams, of the Field Corps, announced the name of each individual as he or she was presented; the person being presented then made a low bow to His Highness the Potentate, who, while sitting, bowed in return.

The last presentation was that of Miss Henrietta Vinton Davis, International Organizer; Rev. Dr. William H. Ferris, M.A., Literary Editor of the Negro World; Mr. George Tobias, Treasurer of the U.N.I.A. and Black Star Line, and Mr. John E. Bruce, noted journalist and writer. These persons were presented, with the exception of Mr. Tobias, to receive the honor of Knighthood of the Sublime Order of the Nile for distinguished services rendered to the Negro race. Mr. Tobias was welcomed to the honor of Knighthood of the Order of Ethiopia. The Chaplain General delivered the address in conferring the title, the language of which in each instance was as follows, with modification according to the name of the person receiving the title and the kind of service rendered by him or her:

"Henrietta Vinton Davis, through the pleasure of his Supreme Highness the Potentate, you are called forth in the name of the Negro peoples of the world to have bestowed upon you the honor of Lady Commander of the Sublime Order of the Nile. You are thus honored by His Highness for the splendid service you have rendered your race in being a successful leader and organizer.

"Rise, Lady Henrietta, and accept this commission to go forth as a bold lady and do further service to your race and to humanity. May you, Lady Henrietta, ever hold yourself in honesty, dignity and self-respect, and thus command all men to honor and respect you for the honor conferred upon you through the graciousness of His Highness."

Dr. Ferris was honored because of his services to the race "as a successful author, journalist and lecturer." Mr. Bruce was honored because of distinguished services rendered by him to the race "as a successful statesman and journalist." Mr. Tobias was honored because of "faithful and distinguished service rendered to the Universal Negro Improvement Association." After welcoming each candidate to the honor conferred, the Chaplain General handed him or her a sealed envelope containing the certificate of Knighthood, whereupon the person thus knighted arose, bowed and thanked His

Highness the Potentate, who in turn bowed and shook the hand of the individual presented.

Miss Susie Belle Anderson then sang a solo. At this point announcement was made that a supper would be served to the high officials of the Association. As a trio, Mesdames Marie Barrier Houston, Alice Fraser-Robinson, Hattie Edwards-McVey, sang "Africa for the Africans," an original composition (words and music) by Madame McVey. Both numbers were rendered with great art and finish and the singers warmly and enthusiastically applauded. The trio represented, doubtless, the three greatest female singers of the race, such is the richness, sweetness and thorough cultivation of their voices. Miss Anderson is also a noted singer, one of great promise for the future.

The supper was then served, and lasted about an hour. When over, the Provisional President of Africa announced that the Grand Court Ball would begin; that the first number, a waltz, would be played for the special benefit of the high officials of the Association and the distinguished persons who had been knighted. Lady Henrietta Vinton Davis and His Highness the Potentate, the Auditor-General and Mrs. Garcia, Capt. [E. L.] Gaines and Mrs. Gaines, Counsellor General Wilford H. Smith and Mrs. Smith and Assistant Counsellor General W. C. Matthews and Mrs. Matthews participated in the opening dance, while the entire assemblage of people, forming a dense, closely packed ring around the dancers, looked on in admiration. Lady Davis and His Highness the Potentate danced with skill and grace, and evoked considerable applause, Lady Davis making a charming-looking belle, while her partner made a gallant knight in his brilliant and multi-colored uniform. The first number finished[,] the ball was thrown open to everyone, who, under the enchanting strains of two-steps, one-steps and waltzes played by the popular Black Star Line Band, tripped the light fantastic too. Big as the hall is, with all the chairs removed, the dancing was so crowded as to be almost uncomfortable, yet all enjoyed the occasion to the full.

Promptly at 12 o'clock, "Home, Sweet Home" was played (which the dancers thought came all too soon, so much were they enjoying themselves), thus ending the first and greatest reception of its kind ever held by Negroes for centuries past. It was an occasion that reflected great credit upon the race, and for which too high praise cannot be given to those who, in however slight a measure, contributed to its success. . . .

MENU OF THE BANQUET

The menu of the banquet was printed on a beautifully embossed card folder showing on the outside fringed lamp shades in colors of red and green, with the words below, "Menu (in gold letters), First Court Reception, U.N.I.A., at Liberty Hall, New York City, Saturday Evening, August 27,

1921["] (all this in Old English black letters); a flag in the colors of red, black and green (the emblem of the association) in the centre. On the inside was printed the dishes constituting the meal, which were:

Punch Africanos
Liberian chicken, shredded
Boiled Virginia ham
Filet of ox tongue
Sliced cold shoulder a la Monrovia
Salads
Chilled lettuce and tomato
Tropical dressing
Dessert
Liberty special ice cream
Cakes

Pomona dainty   Lady Vinton's

Black Cross Macaroons
Assorted fruits

Covers were laid for three hundred, the repast being one of unusual excellence.

News of the holding of the court reception was spread throughout the city. Owing to the hall not being large enough to accommodate unlimited numbers only 500 persons were to be admitted, though it is estimated that fully 1,500 attended. Great crowds, however, hung around the hall—the largest, it is said, that ever was attracted to any gathered there in its history. People jammed the sidewalk and street from in front of the building down to Lenox avenue on one side up to Seventh avenue on the other, and if admission had been unrestricted doubtless there wouldn't have been breathing space, much less standing room, in Liberty Hall, even though it is the largest public meeting hall in Harlem that belongs to and is used by colored people.

Printed in *NW*, 3 September 1921. Original headlines abbreviated.

1. A black daily newspaper in New York, edited by A. V. Craig and Floyd J. Calvin (*NW*, 17 September 1921). Copies of this newspaper have not been located.
2. Luke 2:29–30.

FIRST ANNUAL

COURT RECEPTION

of

His Supreme Highness

THE POTENTATE

of the

Universal Negro Improvement Asssociation

LIBERTY HALL

120 W. 138th Street
New York

Saturday, August 27th, 1921

8 P. M.

500 Guests Invited
Including House of Deputies
and Delegates

(*Source*: NN-Sc, Garvey file.)

Joseph P. Nolan to J. Harry Philbin

NEW YORK CITY, August 28, 1921

Dear Sir:

This is to advise you that the power of attorney given by the Black Star Line to Mr. Rudolph Silverston has been canceled and a new power of attorney has been issued to Charles M. Barnett, duplicate original of which power of attorney I inclose herewith.

Will you kindly in the future communicate with Mr. Barnett, and do not communicate any further with Mr. Silverston. Very truly yours,

JOSEPH P. NOLAN

Judgment Creditors of Black Star Line, Inc., exhibit no. 4.

Black Star Line to Henry C. Von Struve

New York August 29, 1921

AMERICAN CONSUL. ANTILLA.—

OWING TO DISLOYAL[T]Y OF CREW ON KANAWHA WE ARE ASKING YOU TO TRANSHIP PASSENGERS TO NEW YORK ON FIRST SHIP LEAVING ANTILLA AT OUR EXPENSE ALL PASSENGERS WHO SAILED FROM JAMAICA FOR NEW YORK[.] THIS DOES NOT MEAN THE CREW[.] YOU MAY [S]HOW THIS CABLE TO SYDNEY DEBOURG W[H]O IS ON KANAWHA[.] CABLE US HOW MUCH MONEY IS NEEDED TO TRANSHIP PASSENGERS.—

BLACK STAR LINE
Cable Address Slib New York.

DNA, RG 84, file 885. TG, recipient's copy.

Convention Reports

[*New York, 29–31 August 1921*]

[*29 August 1921*]

. . . TWENTY-SECOND DAY

PRESIDENT GENERAL'S REVIEW

Nearly the whole of Monday, the 29th ult., was occupied with a lecture by the President-General on the history and growth of the Universal Negro

Improvement Association and African Communities' League, and the delivery of a charge to the delegates with hints and suggestions for the furtherances of the cause.

At the morning session he reviewed the life of the organization. He said he first conceived the idea of founding the organization in 1914 after traveling through England, Scotland, Ireland, France, Italy, Spain, Austria-Hungary, and Germany. Extensive travels in those countries revealed to him the disabilities under which Negroes lived, politically and otherwise. It occurred to him that, if the Negro must become a recognized factor in world government, the race must solidify itself through the medium of one great organization based on international principles. With this idea in mind he sailed from England in June, 1914, arriving in Jamaica on the 5th [*8th*] of July. His plans having been mapped out on board ship, he called the first meeting of the U.N.I.A. and A.C.L. on the 20th of July, and elected officers. Soon after he wrote to the late Booker T. Washington, of Tuskegee, telling of his desire to form a world-wide organization of Negroes, and his intention to come to America to further the work. Mr. Booker T. Washington sent a very courteous reply, but the death of this gentleman, occurring shortly after, he had to abandon his trip temporarily. Eventually he sailed to New York in March 1915 [*1916*], and hastened to the shrine of the illustrious gentlemen to pay his homage.

OBSTACLES OVERCOME

The President-General then described the great obstacles he encountered in his efforts to gain a following in the United States, and stated that he had made up his mind to return to Jamaica in the spring of 1917, when he became associated with Mr. W. A. Doming[o] and Mr. Hubert Harrison. Subsequent events soon proved conclusively to him that what was wanted was real Negro leadership. He remained and started The Negro World, and organized the branch of the U.N.I.A. in New York. They started with thirteen members, and in the space of six months the membership had grown to 600. The politicians came, prompted by a desire to further their own ends, but they had to go, after a terrible fight which left him faced with the task of beginning all over again. This he did, and the work grew to the proportions it had attained on August last, in spite of opposition from the politicians and other factions.

ANOTHER STEP ONWARD

At the afternoon session the President-General continued his lecture. He resumed as follows: "The internationalization of the Universal Negro Improvement Association was amply demonstrated for the first time on August 1, last year, when delegates representing the Negro race, coming from the four corners of the globe, assembled here in Liberty Hall to convene the First International Convention of Negroes. We had representatives from far-off Africa, from the countries of the West Indies, of Central and South America, and the forty-eight States of this American Union, and they came because the U.N.I.A. through its organ, The Negro World, had intimated to them that at that convention they were to discuss the future government of the Negroes of the world, and to elect Negroes to lead the entire race. Those of you who were here last year will recall the splendid work we did. Those who were not here must have read of it. We sat for thirty-one days and thirty-one nights and enacted laws. Some were placed in the 'Constitution,' and others were classified as a Declaration of Rights of the Negro Race, and we gave those enactments to the world. They have made the circuit of the world, thereby lifting the U.N.I.A. from an ordinary State organization into a great international power. As an international power we existed for one year after the rising of convention on August 31, last year, and the strength of this international movement is further exemplified by the presence of so many delegates here today and all during this month, who have come back to this Second International Convention from the four corners of the world."

Proceeding, he said he could say with full authority that the movement was now recognized, known and appreciated not only by individuals, but by governments, and that the U.N.I.A. and A.C.L. now occupied a place not only among organizations but among governments, because it was regarded and appreciated as a government in embryo.

MISTAKES OF THE HEAD

He then referred to the unhappy statements which many lovers of the organization had sometimes made, though with the best intention, and which were opposed to the true interests of the organization. After pointing out many of the errors made, he counselled the delegates to take the constitution as their guide and inspiration.[1] In it, he declared, would be found all the texts needed by those who would preach Garveyism.

He then explained at great length the true meaning of article I, section 3, of the constitution, taking it clause by clause, and asked the delegates to explain them to their constituents as he had done.

On the conclusion of the address several delegates asked questions, eliciting information for their guidance in the work before them.

MONDAY NIGHT SESSION

ELECTION OF OFFICERS

Liberty Hall was crowded at the evening session, when the election of officers for the ensuing year was continued. The following were elected:—

Speaker in Convention—Hon. Adrian Johnson.
Assistant President-General—Sir William H. Ferris.
West Indian Leader (Eastern Province)—Hon. Rudolph Smith.

TWENTY-THIRD DAY

REGULATIONS FOR JUVENILE DEPARTMENT

On Tuesday morning, August 30, rules and regulations for the Juvenile Department were discussed and passed into law.

They provided for the establishment of the following classified system:

(1) Infant Class. (2) Girls' Souvenir Class; Boys' Souvenir Class. (3) Cadets. (4) Preparatory Nurse Class.

Rules for teachers and children were formulated.

The following resolutions, bearing on the subject, were introduced by the Hon. H. A. Collins (Banes, Cuba) and carried unanimously:

U.N.I.A. SCHOOL BOOKS

(1) Whereas, our race has suffered materially by being instructed from books written by alien teachers; and

Whereas, such instruction has tended to a great extent to destroy our racial pride and progress;

Be It Resolved, That this organization publish school books from which all children of this organization shall be taught racial pride, and that this be a part of the duty of the Propaganda Institute.

(2) Whereas, it is difficult in some countries to find suitable schools for the proper tuition of children of our race;

Be It Resolved, That this organization establish schools in divisions where necessary and where desired by the members of such divisions.

(3) Be It Resolved, that the parents of children attending the schools of this organization be required to contribute to the maintenance of such schools, the fees to be regulated by the executive board of the division to meet local demands.

The following resolution was introduced by the Hon. Mrs. Mary Johnson:

Be It Resolved, That a Central Exchange be established at the Parent Body for the industrial work of the association, and a woman at the head be a member of the staff of the Minist[ry] of Industry and Labor for the purpose of making flags for conventions and divisions; banners, Black Cross Nurses' garments and all U.N.I.A. souvenirs, such as embroidered flags, etc., representing the emblems of the U.N.I.A.; also post cards and all other accessories that can be produced from the work of our women in the various divisions.

On motion of His Grace, the Chaplain-General, Dr. G. A. McGuire, the suggestion contained in the resolution was referred to the Minister of Industry and Labor for consideration.

The remainder of the morning session was occupied by the President-General with an appeal to the male and female presidents of divisions to work in unity, and with a statement on the nature of the leadership the organization would require from those sent out to represent the organization in the various countries of the world. He hinted that the delegates' choice of officers for vacant positions had not met with his entire satisfaction, and made it clear that the new officers would have to pass the executive challenge (which would be a test of qualifications and ability) before they would be allowed to enter upon their respective duties.

OFFICE OF PROVISIONAL VICE-PRESIDENT OF AFRICA LEFT VACANT

It had been decided that the election of a candidate to the office of Honorary Provisional Vice-President of Africa take place during the afternoon session. The matter came before the House soon after the resumption of business for the afternoon, and a long drawn out and heated debate arose.

The nominees were: Sir W. H. Ferris, Hon. T. J. Carr, Hon. E. V. Morales, Hon. [L.] J. Francis and Hon. J. C. Gill.

The first named was declared ineligible in that he had been elected to the position of Assistant President-General. Hons. Carr and Francis declined to contest the election, leaving a field of two—Hons. Morales and Gill.

Hon. C. A. Reid (Panama), after the candidates had declared their policy, initiated a lengthy discussion by moving that the election be su[s]-pended until proper persons came upon the scene. He had been instructed so to act, he said, by the division he represented.

In the end it was agreed that the post be left vacant during the ensuing year, the President-General making a statement to the effect that there was nothing personal in his attitude when he supported such action, but he, too, was of the opinion that such an important office should be filled when there was a greater number of nominees to be chosen from.

[*31 August 1921*]

THE CLOSING DAY

DIVINE SERVICE

The convention was assembled on Wednesday, the 31st ult., at 10:30 A.M.

Divine service was held, conducted by His Grace the Chaplain-General, Dr. G. A. McGuire. The Scripture lesson was read by Dr. F. W. Ellegor, High Commissioner General. The sermon was preached by the Hon. J. R. L. Diggs of Baltimore, Md.

The service concluded, the President-General, in a short address, thanked the delegates and deputies for their attendance at the convention and the splendid manner in which they had conducted their deliberations and expressed his conviction that they would return to their homes with renewed spirit and energy to carry on the work for the redemption of Africa. He also read an article from that morning's "Journal of Commerce," which related the purchase of a ship from the United States Shipping Board by the Black Star Line Steamship Corporation for the African and West Indian trade.

TAKING THE OATH OF OFFICE

The oath of office was then administered to the following newly-elected officers:

Fred A. Toote, Right Honorable Secretary General.

Ulysses S. Poston, Right Honorable Minister of Industry and Labor.

Sir William H. Ferris, Right Honorable Assistant President General

Dr. Joseph Deighton Gibson, Right Honorable Surgeon General.

Rudolph Smith, Right Honorable Leader of the Eastern Province of the West Indies.

Adrian Fitzroy Johnson, Right Honorable Speaker in the Convention.

Robert Lincoln Poston, the Honorable Second Assistant Secretary General.

The oath administered, His Grace the Chaplain pronounced the benediction upon each officer.

The High Commissioner General then presented His Highness the Potentate with a banner on behalf of the delegates and the members of the New York Local in appreciation of His Highness' presence during the sessions of the convention.

His Highness expressed his thanks and promised to take the banner with him to Liberia, where it would be among his most valued possessions.

The oath of office was then administered to all the delegates and deputies by His Grace the Chaplain-General.

On Wednesday night the convention was brought to a close with the holding of a mass meeting at which the President-General, the American leader and the Chaplain-General spoke. Liberty Hall was crowded. The scene was an unforgettable one and when the meeting broke up shortly after 11 o'clock the convention of 1921 had passed into history. . . .

Printed in *NW*, 10 September 1921. Original headlines omitted.

1. In his statement "How to Teach the U.N.I.A.," which formed a section of lesson 20 of his "School of African Philosophy" (September 1937), regarding the preamble of the UNIA Constitution, Garvey wrote:

Whenever the purpose of the organization is challenged by foes particularly, quote the preamble of the Constitution. This should be done particularly where its enemies assail it before a Court of Law or before Governmenta¹ Authorities.

> This preamble was written particularly for the purpose of winning the sympathy and support of alien races where the other objects of the association were being threatened with hostility. (p. 2)

Henry C. Von Struve to the Black Star Line

Antilla, 30 August 1921

Cable eleven hundred dollars send passengers New York[.] [Y]our attitude forces crew abandon ship[.] [S]teamer threatens total loss unless looked after[.]

VON STRUVE
Consul

DNA, RG 84, file 885. TG, carbon copy.

Henry Bailey to Charles L. Latham

Antilla de Cuba 30th A[u]gust 1921

Sir

[P]lese to excuse my liberty but I am air [*here?*] as a crew of the S.S. Kanawha sail from the [U]nited State of America and sine [*sign?*] up from there leaveing my whife there for this 6 mounth trip which is expired at present[.] I married under the American flag and the law of the State I leave no elotment for my whife when I was leaveing on the count they tell me the trip will be only 6 or 7 weeks[.]

Sir I am asking you to do me the favour by consider my greavence of my family in the State without help of money and I am in a forin port where I cant help them[.]

Sir plese I am asking for no other help only to help me to get out by the first chance back to America port where I am from for our state of life air [*here?*] is afull for one to stand[.] [P]lese Sir I am asking you to see with me and help me out of this truble as there is no other to call upon but you[.]

Sir I trust you will consider over this and do what you can for me Your Respetfuly

HENRY BAILEY

DNA, RG 84, file 885. ALS, recipient's copy.

Edward J. Brennan to William J. Burns

NEW YORK, N.Y. August 30th, 1921

GENERAL INTELLIGENCE DIVISION.

Dear Sir:

In reference to Marcus Garvey, Alleged Violation Mann Act, attached herewith please find report made by Agent F. B. Faulhaber for date August 29th, 1921, concerning Marcus Garvey, together with affidavits made by Adrian Richardson and Edgar M. Gr[e]y. Further statements will be secured and forwarded to Washington at the earliest practicable time.

For your information Mr. Cleveland Jacques, residence, 156 West 131st Street, New York City, c/o Gordon, who it is believed is in possession of considerable detailed information that would tend to prove that Garvey has been violating the White Slave Act, has refused to visit this office or to make any statement whatsoever, although it appeared several days ago that Jacques was anxious to make a statement concerning the whole matter.

Your attention is particularly called to page 5 of Agent Faulhaber's report on which page appears Gr[e]y's statement relating to the payment of $2,000 in order to facilitate Garvey's entry into the United States. Very truly yours,

EDWARD J. BRENNAN
Division Superintendent

[*Stamped endorsement*] FILE G. F. R.
[*Handwritten endorsement*] FILE GBH
Enc 8/31/21

DNA, RG 65, file BS 198940-249. TLS, recipient's copy.

Enclosure

NEW YORK, N.Y. 8/30/21

IN RE: MARCUS GARVEY—ALLEGED VIOLATION
MANN WHITE SLAVE ACT

Pursuant to instructions of Special Agent C. J. Scully, and continuing investigation from my report of 8/26–29/21, based on Chief's letter of August 8th, 1921, initialed GFR:EHM, I today [*29 August*] interviewed EDGAR M. GREY, who resides at #214 West 140th Street, New York City, apartment #9.

Mr. Grey informed me that he had today gotten in touch with CLEVELAND JACQUES and requested the latter to telephone the office and ask for the writer of this report. Mr. JACQUES complied with this request and the writer spoke to him over the phone about five P.M. yesterday. Mr. JACQUES' conversation indicated a complete reversal of his desire to give information concerning the alleged violation of the Mann White Slave Act by MARCUS GARVEY and his sister, AMY JACQUES. He said he refused to give any information "of any kind" at the request of this Bureau and refused point-blank to come to this office of his own volition. Writer did not threaten him over the phone, and simply stated that further action will be taken later concerning him.

At 6 P.M. Mr. Grey called at this office, and writ[er reques]ted Mr. Grey to inform Mr. Jacques that he could either come to this office voluntarily and give information required, or await the action of the Grand Jury, which in the course of procedure, would e[ve]ntually result in his being called as a material witness and obliged to come down and give information against his wishes. This necessitates withholding further action regarding Jacques, unless he appears here willingly, until action is taken by a Grand Jury.

Mr. Grey was anxious to assist the government in this matter and made the following statement in connection with the departure of Garvey, Miss Jacques and Cleveland Jacques, and also furnished the hearsay evidence in his possession concerning the allegation that Garvey "paid someone $2000. to be allowed to re-enter the United States."

"I am thirty one years of age and reside at #214 West 140th Street, Apartment #9. I am married; a chiropractor by profession, having been engaged in this profession since May, 1921, and two years prior to that I was employed as a clerk with the Post [O]ffice Department of the U.S. Government.

"I first met Marcus Garvey in 1917, when he arrived here from Port Limon, C.R. He is a citizen of Jamaica, B.W.I., as I saw his passport on one of his trips where the statement that he is a citizen of that British possession was made. This passport was dated some time in 1919. Since I first met Garvey in 1917, exclusive of my seventeen months service in the United States Army, I have seen him continuously two or three times a day to date, and I know him personally.

"I know his legal wife, to whom I was introduced socially first on the 16th day of May, 1919, when she was MISS AMY ASHWOOD, and to date I have seen her once every two weeks and I personally know that she married Marcus Garvey on December 31st, 1919, and know her as the legal wife of Marcus Garvey.

"I also know Miss AMY JACQUES, having met her first in Marcus Garvey's office, the Universal Negro Improvement Association offices, about January 17th, 1921, and have seen her since about twice a week until she went away some time in the latter part of February or the early part of March, and since her return I have seen her as often as three times a day on an average, always in the company of Garvey.

"In the latter part of February or the early part of March of this year, 1921, Marcus Garvey settled a libel suit I had brought against him at his office at #56 West 135th Street, City, by giving me a check for $100 which was the first payment applicable on a promise to pay me $300, $250 for settlement of the suit and $50 for attorneys fees. The date of this meeting can be learned from the date of the first check. All checks were later paid and cashed by RAYMOND D. ROSE, 461 Lenox Avenue, New York City. On this date, the date he made the first payment, he volunteered to me the information that he was going abroad by way of the south, for the purpose of selling stocks for the Black Star Line and talking to keep up the morale of the c[o]lored peoples abroad.

"He further volunteered the information that he would be accompanied by MISS HENRIETTA VINTON DAVIS, CLEVELAND JACQUES and the sister of this latter man, who is known as AMY JACQUES, and that a Dr. McGuire would meet them in Cuba.

"He stated he expected to leave on this trip the following day and that he intended going by rail to Key West, Fla. I later learned from newspaper articles appearing in the "NEGRO WORLD" that he had left as he stated he would.

"On Sunday, July 31st, 1921, Marcus Garvey, in my presence and in the presence of a Mr. H. S. Boulin, (a friend of Garvey's who lives at 135 West 135th St. and has an office as President of the Berry & Ross Corp., negro doll manufacturers, at 34 West 135th St.) told us (and this incident happened in his home 135 West 129th St.) that CLEVELAND JACQUES had come down with him thru Central and South America for the purpose of carrying on the public meetings of the organization and to sell stock; that they had gotten down there and then the boy had become recalcitrant and he (Garvey) had been forced to admonish him about the way he was acting, and then that the boy had lost two stock stubs /of/ the stock books and then when they returned to the States the boy told him that he didn't know where they were and that he (Garvey) then deducted $30 from the boy's salary and the boy abused him in the office and he had been obliged to discharge him. He said that he discharged him at the office at New York, after "they had returned."

"In this conversation he stated that CLEVELAND JACQUES had accompanied him throughout his entire trip and that he had dismissed him upon their return.

"Garvey informed me that the BLACK STAR LINE paid the expenses of the boy on the trip, but did not tell me who paid the girl's expenses."

Mr. Grey volunteered the following information concerning the report that Garvey had paid someone "$2000 to re-enter the United States":

"Regarding the report that Mr. Garvey paid the sum of $2000 to some individual to be permitted to re-enter the United States, I have the following hearsay information regarding that:

"It is common gossip in the community around 135th Street, that certain representations were made by Mr. Garvey's Vice-Attorney-General, whose name is MATTHEWS, (a Harvard Graduate and practising attorney) to a HENRY LINCOLN JOHNSON,[1] Negro National Political spokesman, at Washington, D.C., asking that he use his good offices for the purpose of convincing the State Department that should Mr. Garvey not be allowed to return to the United States that negro citizens who had invested moneys in various of his organizations would sustain losses and that upon this representation, it is further rumored, Johnson called upon Secretary of State, Hughes, and so informed him; whereupon Mr. Garvey was made to promise in a written statement that he would not make any inflammatory statements in his speeches against the American government or the white people of this country, upon penalty of being deported at the first violation of this promise. In this statement, it is also rumored, he stated that he had never engaged in any political or radical propaganda against the interests either of the American government or the American people.

"It is also further rumored that for this service rendered by HENRY LINCOLN JOHNSON, aforementioned above, that he received the sum of $2000 from Marcus Garvey.

It has also been rumored that CLEVELAND JACQUES has been voluble and persistent in disseminating this rumor.

"At a meeting held last Friday night, at Liberty Hall, Garvey hinted at a contemplated trip to Europe.["]

To be continued.

F[RANK] B. FAULHABER,
Special Agent

[*Endorsement*] Copy State 9/2/21 GFR

DNA, RG 65, file BS 198940-249. TD. Handwritten endorsement.

1. Henry Lincoln Johnson (1870–1925) was named Republican national committeeman from Georgia in 1920 with the support of Warren G. Harding. Johnson was born in Augusta, Ga., and educated at Atlanta University and the University of Michigan, Ann Arbor, where he received his LL.B. degree in 1892. In 1910 President Taft appointed him recorder of deeds, and he held that position until 1913. By 1920 Johnson was regarded as the black politician with the greatest influence in Washington; that year the Republicans selected him as the "director of colored voters in the North" (*WWCA*; *NW*, 1 January 1921).

Report by Bureau Agent W. S. Bachman

Buffalo, N.Y. 8/30/21

AFRICAN LEGION—BUFFALO, N.Y.—NEGRO ACTIVITIES

Above mentioned letter handed me by Acting Agent in Charge Buchanan for attention. (This letter requested immediate investigation.)

On interviewing WILLIAM FORD of 34 Potter Street, I find that although he admits that he is a member of the Universal Negro Improvement Association (U.N.I.A.), he disclaims any leadership in any negro organization. He says that the U.N.I.A. is the official name of the "Garvey" movement. He directed me to HOWARD B. PHILLIPS, who is one of the partners conducting the Douglas Grocery at 132 Williams Street.

I found PHILLIPS to be a very intelligent, well educated young negro, and apparently well versed in matters connected with the U.N.I.A. He says that he is the Captain of the so-called AFRICAN LEGION, which he describes as being similar to the uniformed rank of various fraternal organizations such as the Knights of Pythias. He says that the African Legion in Buffalo has about 100 members and that it is their practise to drill three times a week, at which drills they have an average attendance of twelve. (Other informants state that the number drilling runs from twenty to thirty.)

The AFRICAN LEGION in Buffalo have no uniforms up to the present time, but PHILLIPS [stated] that they hope to be able to buy them soon.

PHILLIPS [stated] that the U.N.I.A. has about 3,000,000 members in the United States, and over 1,000,000 in the West Indies, beside[s] a large organization in Liberia. The . . . [*words mutilated*] in Buffalo is about 500, /and/ in the neighborhood of 450 in other branches of Lackawanna, and Tonawanda, New York. These are all [du]es paying members. The dues are 30¢ per month, of which 10¢ is sent to the main [office?] in New York and 20¢ is kept in the local treasury for the benefit of the negro population in Buffalo, particularly the members.

The President of the organization in Buffalo is ARTHUR L. LEWIS of 414 [Michigan] Avenue. The other members are Vice President——Thomas, Secretary——Burlington, and Treasurer——Harris, the first names of the last three being [unknown] to Phillips.

PHILLIPS stated that the ultimate object of the association is to form a negro government in Africa, with the population to be largely recruited from the negroes in the United States and West Indies and that this object is to be attained peacefully, if possible, but if necessary by force. He says that there are twenty negroes in Buffalo at the present time who have paid their fare to Liberia and are [awaiting?] transportation facilities, and that if transportation were available at least [200?] negro families would be ready and willing to migrate to Liberia from Buffalo.

The negro population of the city of Buffalo is between 4000 and 5000, permanent and [floating?]. A large number of negroes were brought to Buffalo about a year and a half ago to work in the [building?] of a new factory. This work stopped and they were thrown out of employment last spring. At this time a movement was started to take care of them, called the Big Brotherhood. A hall was rented and lodging and some meals were furnished to between 300 and 400 negroes, who were out of employment. The furnishing of lodging and meals has been discontinued, and the hall is now kept only as a recreation hall. There are only about 25 or 30 negroes availing themselves of the use of this hall at the present time, most of them having either left Buffalo or obtained work, at least enough to keep them going without charity.

There has been no trouble in Buffalo between negroes and the white population which has assumed anything like the proportions of race riots. There has been nothing further then a few altercations between individuals. So far as I have been able to learn the object of the AFRICAN LEGION is peaceful. They have no arms and no means of obtaining any.

/Continued/

W. S. BACHMAN

[*Endorsements*] NOTED F. D. W.
FILE G. F. R.

DNA, RG 65, file BS 202600-667-85. TD. Copies of this report were furnished to the bureau's Buffalo, N.Y., office.

Report by Bureau Agent Edward Anderson

NEW YORK, N.Y. 8/31/21

MARCUS GARVEY—ALLEGED VIOLATION OF THE MANN ACT.

Continuing my report of August 25th and 26th, agent proceeded to 135th Street to locate JACQUES, GRAY [*Grey*] and CAPTAIN COCKBURN, of whom agent was informed would be able to give information concerning the violation of the White Slave Act. Agent looked around Harlem all day trying to locate these people but was unable to do so, no one seeming to know them.

The next day, on the 29th, agent proceeded to 135th Street again to a cigar and fruit store at 122 West 135th Str. and was there informed that Gray would be in in a few minutes. About 11 o'clock, agent met MR. EDGAR GRAY and he informed me that he was unable to give any information concerning the said violation but he would do everything in his power to locate JACQUES whom he believed would be able to give information concerning same. GRAY is a speaker among the Negroes of Harlem for the NATIONAL LIBERTIES UNION and a former clerk in the U.S. Post Office. Mr. Gray and agent scoured Harlem for Jacques until 3 o'clock and were unable to find him. We learned from another Negro that Jacques was seen and had been all morning in the Convention Hall at 138th Street where MARCUS GARVEY is holding his convention, but that he had left and his whereabouts were unknown at that time.

Agent and Gray then located CAPTAIN COCKBURN who lives at 201 West 128th Street. Cockburn was former captain of the BLACK STAR LINER YARMOUTH and is willing to help this department in every way possible against MARCUS GARVEY although is unable to give any information concerned the alleged violation.

Gray and agent then went out again looking for Jacques and heard that he was in the convention hall again, whereupon agent sent a telegram into the convention hall asking Mr. Jacques to call at Captain Cockburn's home immediately. We then proceeded back to Captain Cockburn's home awaiting the arrival of Jacques. When Jacques didn't show up by 4:30, agent called the Bureau office on the telephone and agent was instructed to take up a shadow job on another matter and before leaving Mr. Cockburn's home, agent instructed Mr. Cockburn and Mr. Gray that if Jacques came there for the three of them to come to the Bureau office and see Agent Faulhaber who would take statements from them. Agent had gone about five minutes when Jacques arrived at Cockburn's home and agent learned later that Jac[q]ues absolutely refused to talk about Marcus Garvey.

For further information on this matter as to Jacques refusing to report, see Agent Faulhaber's report.

[*30 August*:] Agent today got in touch with CAPTAIN RICHARDSON who brought with him to the Bureau office, one SYRUS M. YARTER of 12 Vine Street, Brooklyn, N.Y., who corroborated Mr. Richardson in his statement. Agent Faulhaber also took signed statement from Yarter which corroborated Captain Richardson.

Agent then called Captain Cockburn on the wire and had him and Gray come to the Bureau office where statements were taken from them.

Then got in touch with one, SMITH GREEN and he was instructed to come to the Bureau office and give statement, which he did, arriving at the Bureau office about 4 P.M.

For full information regarding Garvey's alleged violation of the Mann Act, also concerning the $2,000 that Garvey was alleged to have paid someone in order to facilitate his entry into the U.S., would respectfully refer you to Agent Faulhaber's report and statement made by EDGAR GRAY which has been forwarded to the Bureau office.

Matter to be continued.

EDWARD ANDERSON[1]
Special Agent

[*Endorsement*] NOTED F. D. W.

DNA, RG 65, file BS 198940-253. TD. Stamped endorsement.

1. Edward Anderson was employed by the Bureau of Investigation as a special agent from 2 September 1919 to 6 October 1922 (DJ-FBI).

Report by Special Agent P-138

NEW YORK, N.Y. 8/31/21

MARCUS GARVEY—ALLEGED VIOLATION MANN ACT.

Today [*29 August*] I had a few minutes talk with MARCUS GARVEY at his office, 56 West 135th Street just before he left for the convention now going on at Liberty Hall. I asked him what had become of CLEVELAND JACQUES and he said that he learned that JACQUES, COCKBURN and RICHARDSON had tried to report him to the District Attorney a few weeks ago but they could not affect him as he had exercised certain strong influence and blocked their effort in that direction. He said that EDGAR M. GR[E]Y had promised to keep him posted relative to the movement and plans of his enemies—CAPTAIN COCKBURN, RICHARDSON, SMITH GREEN and JACQUES so that he could get up a case against them for conspiracy—hence he was not afraid of anything they might do. I tried to talk to him so as to learn his future plans as to whether he would plan another trip abroad but he was in a hurry to go. At any rate he told me that Edgar M. Gray was keeping him posted with his opponents.

I also had a talk with Garvey's sweetheart, AMY JACQUES, with whom he had travelled to the West Indies and South America. I asked her what had become of her brother, CLEVELAND JACQUES and whether it was true he was against her. She told me that he (her brother) accompanied her and MARCUS GARVEY on the trip and was in charge of selling stocks of the Black Star Line and Liberia Liberty Bonds. That on account of his behavior abroad and his actions in dealing with the finances by making extravagant expenses without orders from Garvey, coupled with the fact that he conveniently lost the stubs of a stockbook from which thousands of dollars of stock were sold, causing Garvey to take the cost of the book out of his salary and because she refused to advance him monies abroad whenever he called on her for same, he took objection to these things which engendered bad feeling and a complete disagreement between him, Garvey and herself after he quit the employment of the Black Star Line.

She told me that ever since their return from abroad she has been hearing rumors that her brother and Richardson were trying to report them to the government and cause them trouble but so far as she was concerned they can go ahead as in all her travels she was always accompanied by another girl the name of MISS LEMOTT [*Enid Lamos*][1] who is also an employee of the U.N.I.A. That Captain Richardson caused Garvey and herself endless trouble while they were going from Jamaica to Colón, Richardson even threatened to throw them overboard, stopped the ship two or three times and said he would kill Garvey and would some day get even with her. These acts have now left her a nervous wreck.

P-138

[*Endorsement*] NOTED F.D.W.

DNA, RG 65, file BS 198940-250x. TD. Stamped endorsement.

1. Enid Lamos (1898–1951) was born in Kingston, Jamaica, and immigrated to the United States in July 1920, although in her court testimony she claimed to have begun working for Garvey as his stenographer in October 1919. She traveled with Garvey and Amy and Cleveland Jacques during the spring and summer of 1921. With Amy Jacques she was responsible for receiving and recording money taken in at Garvey's meetings in the West Indies and Central America. She also recorded the testimony at Garvey's mail fraud trial for publication in the *Negro World*. In November 1925 Enid Lamos became a United States citizen (U.S. Department of Labor, certificate of naturalization no. 2137621; *Marcus Garvey* v. *United States*, no. 8317, Ct. App., 2d Cir., 2 February 1925, pp. 1,650–1,656; Lionel A. Francis to Amy Ashwood Garvey, 6 August 1951).

Report by Bureau Agent F. B. Faulhaber

NEW YORK, N.Y. 8/31/21

IN RE: MARCUS GARVEY; ALLEGED VIOLATION MANN
WHITE SLAVE ACT.

Continuing on above investigation pursuant to instructions of Special Agent C. J. Scully, based on Chief's letter of August 8th, 1921, initialed GFR:MEM, I interviewed Mr. Smith Green, of 111 West 143rd St., New York City.

Mr. Green informed the writer that he is an office-man by occupation, that on July 22nd, 1919, he was retained to the employ of the BLACK STAR LINE as Secretary, by Marcus Garvey personally.

Mr. Green stated he has personally known Marcus Garvey since 1916 and from then to date has seen him every day, nearly, except when Garvey was away from the city.

Informant further stated that he has known Miss Amy Jacques since about July 19th, 1919, and was introduced to her socially by Marcus Garvey personally, and from July 19th, 1919, to date informant has seen Miss Jacques on an average of at least once a day, except when she was out of town.

Informant still further states that he has met the legal Mrs. MARCUS GARVEY, who was first introduced to him as AMY ASHWOOD on the same date he met Miss Jacques, July 19th, 1919, and was present at the wedding of Miss Ashwood and Marcus Garvey at Liberty Hall, on the night of December 24th, 1919. Green was introduced to Miss Ashwood socially by Marcus Garvey personally, and from the date of introduction to the present writing he has seen her on an average of nearly every day.

He further states he met CLEVELAND JACQUES in April, the 19th, 1920, at the office of the UNIVERSAL NEGRO IMPROVEMENT ASSOCIATION and BLACK STAR LINE, who occupy offices jointly, and that he first met him in an official capacity, while Jacques was in charge of the files at the offices of the Black Star Line at 56 West 135th St. Since that time he has seen him on an average of once a week; at least, once every two weeks.

Sometime in the latter part of April, 1920, MARCUS GARVEY accompanied by Miss AMY JACQUES (Green could not give exact dates in either of the cases following) came down to Philadelphia where he was making a speech and spoke at the same meeting with him. The same night they returned to New York, leaving probably around ten or eleven P.M.

In the early part of May, 1920, Green spoke at the Academy of Music at Brooklyn and left on a train at 2.40 A.M. for Boston. The day he arrived there, he was followed by Garvey and Miss Jacques, both arriving some time the same afternoon /of the day/ he arrived, and they remained in Boston at least two days, stopping at some place [un]known to Green. While they were in Boston they called on Green several times, Garvey speaking at a meeting at which Green spoke. They met him at the office of the Black Star Line at 806 Tremont Street, Boston, Mass.

During the latter part of April or the early part of May, Garvey and Miss Jacques again came down to Philadelphia while Green was there and a meeting was scheduled for the night they arrived at which Green and Garvey spoke. They remained overnight, going to Attuck's Hotel, at 15th and Christian Streets, where Green registered under his own name; Garvey under his name, and Miss Jacques under her correct name, Miss Jacques occupying a room with a Madame Houston, now in the West.

Mr. Green stated he had been informed by Mrs. Garvey that she had received information to the effect that on some of the trips made from Philadelphia to New York in 1920 by Miss Jacques and Garvey they had both travelled in a Pullman sleeper and that she (Mrs. Garvey) "had been informed" that they had "slept together." Green, however, could furnish no definite information of the source of Mrs. Garvey's information.

On this same date, CAPTAIN JOSHUA COCKBURN called at this office with Mr. Edgar M. Grey (the latter appearing to sign affidavit) and volunteered such information as he had in his possession in this matter, stating that he could not of his own personal knowledge furnish any information concerning the alleged violation of the Mann White Slave Act by Garvey. He did, however, furnish voluntarily the information that he has personally heard considerable rumor in the community around 135th Street, to the effect that Garvey, thru a Mr. Matthews, had made representations that refusal to permit his re-entry into the U.S. would seriously injure the interests of negroes in this country. Mr. Cockburn further stated that he had "heard" that these representations had eventually been made to Mr. Hughes, Secretary of State, but could not inform the writer who had personally made such representations. He knew nothing further in this connection.

Mr. Cyrus M. Yarter, residing at #12 Vine Street, Brooklyn, New York, formerly 1st Assistant Engineer of the KANAWHA, made a statement, which is to be written in the form of an affidavit, in which he detailed his personal knowledge of improper relations conducted by Marcus Garvey and Amy Jacques on the S/S "KANAWHA" of the Black Star Line, after the vessel had left Santiago, Cuba, and was en route to Kingston, B.W.I.

None of the witnesses so far called could give any definite information concerning the trip by Garvey and Miss Jacques from New York to Key West, Fla., all information along this line having been furnished to the man interviewed in this connection by CLEVELAND JACQUES (brother of Amy) who accompanied Garvey and Miss Jacques from New York to Key West, Fla., and from New Orleans to New York upon their return. The date of the departure from New York cannot be more definitely fixed by any of the informants than "the latter part of February or the early part of March." To be continued.

F. B. FAULHABER
Special Agent

DNA, RG 65, file BS 198940-250-X. TD.

Henry C. Von Struve to H. H. McGinty

Antilla, Cuba August 31, 1921

Dear sir:

The Acting Collector of Customs of this port advises me that there is no reason why your company could not send water to the ship "Kanawha"; that the ship has been entered, the only condition of entry being that neither the crew nor the passengers should land. I shall appreciate it, therefore, if you can arrange to furnish the vessel such a supply of water as it may pay for. Very truly yours,

H. C. VON STRUVE,
American Consul

[*Address*] Mr. H. H. McGinty, Superintendent of the Terminal, City.

DNA, RG 84, file 885. TLS, carbon copy.

Black Star Line to Henry C. Von Struve

New York August 31 1921

ELEVEN HUNDRED SENT TODAY ROYALBANK CANADA FOR PASSENGER TO NEW YORK[.] PROTEST IS BEING LODGED HERE AND IN WASHINGTON AGAINST CONSPIRACY AND DESTRUCTION BY CREW.—

BLACK STAR LINE

DNA, RG 84, file 885. TG, recipient's copy.

Norman Thomas to James Weldon Johnson

20 Vesey Street, New York
August 31, 1921

Dear Mr. Johnson:

I am enclosing a copy of a list of questions I have sent Marcus Garvey. I would honestly like your opinion on his whole movement. Of course I read the articles Dr. Du Bois wrote, but that was sometime ago. I won't quote you in The Nation, or otherwise, if you don't want. I may never even write an article myself on the subject, but I probably shall write a short editorial and I want to go straight on it, and to have some standards by which to judge articles that come in. I should deeply appreciate any information you can give me, either in the form of an interview or by writing. Sincerely yours,

NORMAN THOMAS[1]
Associate Editor

DLC, NAACP. TLS on *Nation* letterhead, recipient's copy.

1. Norman Thomas (1884–1968), Socialist party leader and spokesman, became associate editor of the *Nation* in 1921, resigning in 1922 to become codirector of the League for Industrial Democracy (Murray B. Seidler, *Norman Thomas: Respectable Rebel* 2d ed., [Syracuse, N.Y.: Syracuse University Press, 1967]).

Enclosure

[*New York*] August 31, 1921

My dear Sir:

I regret the fact that you could not see me yesterday at 5 o'clock, but shall try to call Wednesday of next week. Could you not give me an earlier appointment in the afternoon than 5? It may save time in the interview if I should outline now the kind of questions I respectfully desire to ask. Perhaps I should preface these questions by assuring you how sympathetic The Nation has always been to all questions of justice to the Negro. We honestly want information.

1. What is the Membership of the U.N.I.A.?

2. Has it any organic relation to the Black Star Line, and Your other commercial ventures?

3. Do you publish statements as to the financial condition of the Black Star Line?

4. In these times, when shipping is in so bad a state, do you hope the Black Star Line will become a commercially successful venture? Do you

regard it primarily as a means of developing the racial consciousness and cohesion of the Negro?

5. Is it true, as has been alleged, that the U.N.I.A. derives its principal strength from West Indian Negroes, rather than from those who have been longer in the United States?

6. What program have you for the winning of Africa by the Negroes?

7. How will the winning of Africa improve the Negro status in the United States? Do you expect a large emigration of Negroes from the United States to Africa?

8. Have you any program for dealing with the injustices to which Negroes are subject in this country[?] For instance, did you have members of your organization in Tulsa? What were you able to do for them in connection with the terrible riots which wiped out the Negro colony?

9. What are your criticisms of Mr. Du Bois and /in/ particular, of the Pan African Congress? What are your relations with the National Association for the Advancement of Colored People?

10. What is your attitude towards such institutions as Tuskegee and Hampton?

11. Do you regard the problem of the Negro as exclusively racial, or, in part, at least, economic? Do you think that any satisfactory solution of the Negro race, or any other races, is possible under the present economic framework? How will the mass of Negroes be helped by the creation of the Negro upper class?

12. Have you a constitution of the U.N.I.A., which is public? Is your potentate an honorary figure or a governing official? What is his relation to you as provisional president of Africa?

13. I notice in your open speech that you consider war a necessary means for the winning of freedom. I am, of course, aware that you are not starting anything now, and I very much admire the spirit of some of your remarks toward the white race. Nevertheless, I should like to ask whether in view of the demonstrated terrors of modern warfare you consider it wise to preach military organization as the way out? Is not new war, racial or otherwise, simply equivalent to the suicide of mankind, irrespective of color?

I beg you to believe that these questions are not critically intended— that they are honestly designed to elicit information. I have been very deeply impressed by what I have read in the Negro World, and what I have seen and heard of your convention. Believe me, Very sincerely yours,

NORMAN THOMAS
Associate Editor

DLC, NAACP. TL, carbon copy.

Edward J. Brennan to William J. Burns[1]

NEW YORK, N.Y. August 31st, 1921

ATTENTION: GENERAL INTELLIGENCE DIVISION.
RE: MARCUS GARVEY—ALLEGED VIOLATION MANN ACT.

Dear Sir:

Supplementing my telegram of even date[2] I am transmitting herewith report of Agent Faulhaber for the 30th instant together with sworn statement of Cyrus M. Yarter, in triplicate, as well as copy of a statement made by Smith Green, who had not as yet however, called at this office to sign and swear to same.

While a perusal of these affidavits[3] could appear to prove conclusively that Marcus Garvey had illicit relation[s] with Amy Jacques while aboard the S/S Kanawha which was at the time enroute from Santiago, Cuba to Kingston, Jamaica and at other times aboard the same ship, these acts seem to have been committed while the ship was in foreign waters and not destined for the U.S.

From confidential sources it has been learned that Amy Jacques is an employee of the Universal Negro Improvement Association, of which Marcus Garvey is the President, Miss Jacques acting as Garvey's private secretary. From the same sources it has been learned that the above association was responsible for the travelling expenses of both Garvey and Amy Jacques, so that he could hardly be charged with having transported her to or from the points visited by them.

According to best information, Garvey, Amy Jacques and Cleveland Jacques, her brother, were said to have left New York for Key West, Fla. the latter part of February or the early part of March of this year and the person who would have full knowledge of what transpired during this journey is Cleveland Jacques, brother of Amy, whom according to your letter of the 8th instant, initialed GFR/EHM, had made the statement that Garvey had violated the Mann Act with his sister. Efforts have been made by this office to obtain an interview with Jacques but he has refused positively to make any statement whatever. If Cleveland Jacques ever had any intention of making a statement involving Garvey and Amy Jacques, it is quite evident that he has undergone a change of heart as he is in daily company with Garvey and spends most of his time with the latter at Liberty Hall, where the Second Congress of the U.N.I.A. is now in session.

I have today been informed by a confidential employee that a Mr. Wheaton of the law firm of Marshall, Garrett & Wheaton, Negro lawyers with offices at 2295—7th Avenue, this city, who are representing Mrs. Amy Ashwood Garvey in her suit for divorce from Marcus Garvey, is in possession of the names of two Negro porters who have stated to Wheaton that they would testify that on trips between New York and Philadelphia and return they have seen Garvey and Amy Jacques occupy the same berth. This matter will be investigated immediately and will be promptly reported upon.

It has been customary in all previous White Slave cases to obtain a statement from the alleged victim. In this case, however, this has not been done and I await your advice as to whether you wish to proceed further without interviewing Amy Jacques.

With regard to the alleged payment of $2,000 by Garvey or someone representing him, in order to secure his entrance into this country, your attention is invited to the best information obtainable at this time which is contained in attached report of Special Employee P-138. Very truly yours,

EDWARD J. BRENNAN
Division Superintendent

JGT:WED
Enclos.

[*Stamped endorsement*] NOTED F. D. W.
[*Handwritten endorsement*]
Ack 9/3/21 GFR

DNA, RG 65, file BS 198940-250. TLS, recipient's copy.

1. William J. Burns replaced Lewis J. Baley as head of the Bureau of Investigation in August 1921. He had been head of the Burns Detective Agency, where he achieved a reputation as an anti-Communist. He frequently testified before congressional committees warning of the threat of bolshevism in the United States, and he soon broadened the role of the Bureau of Investigation, launching investigations into the activities of virtually every organization thought to be radical (Robert Justin Goldstein, *Political Repression in Modern America* [Boston: G. K. Hall & Co., 1978], pp. 174–175).

2. Brennan's telegram of 31 August 1921 stated that proof of violation of the Mann Act was lacking (DNA, RG 65, file BS 198940-251).

3. With his report of 29 August 1921, agent Frank B. Faulhaber submitted affidavits by Edward D. Smith-Green, Edgar M. Grey, Cyrus M. Yarter, and Adrian Richardson. Smith-Green stated that Amy Jacques and Marcus Garvey had traveled together to Garvey's speaking engagements in Philadelphia, Brooklyn, and Boston during April and May of 1920. Grey stated that Garvey told him in July 1919 that he and Miss Jacques would be traveling together on a future promotional tour of the Caribbean, although Garvey also indicated that his entourage would include Cleveland Jacques and Henrietta Vinton Davis. Capt. Adrian Richardson, formerly of the *Kanawha*, submitted a lengthy statement claiming that on one occasion he had seen Garvey and Amy Jacques in Garvey's stateroom during their 1921 Caribbean trip. Cyrus Yarter, first assistant engineer aboard the *Kanawha*, also indicated that on one occasion he had seen Amy Jacques standing in Garvey's stateroom (DNA, RG 65, file 198940).

Report by Special Agent P-138

New York, N.Y. 8/31/21

MARCUS GARVEY: ALLEGED VIOLATION MANN ACT.

Today [*30 August*] I visited the Black Star Line offices, calling on LAWYER WILFRED SMITH, Garvey's Counsellor-General. I sat in his office and talked on general matters touching the U.N.I.A., Black Star Line, Garvey,

Convention, etc. Smith told me that he was laughing at Richardson and Garvey's other enemies who tried to keep him out of the country as he had strong influence working through the State Department which caused them to let Garvey in. That Garvey was a wonderful man and nothing can stop his progress. That he had given Garvey's ex-wife $100. to keep her away from the Richardson group as she is the most dangerous and can hurt the situation. That Counsellor Matthews, his assistant was handling all such counter-propaganda work. I tried to draw out as to whether Garvey was planning a trip abroad but could not get any definite information.

It is common knowledge among the Negroes that Garvey had to pay $2,000 to Lincoln Johnson, Negro National Committeeman to pay someone in the State Department so as to use their influence in letting Garvey return. That Counsellor Matthews, Assistant Counsellor-General of the Black Star Line, an ex-Assistant M.3. attorney in Boston and Negro politic[i]an spent over one month in Washington in his effort to reach the State Department as described above. Of course, this makes Garvey feel almost immune from governmental or other interference as he is under the impression that he can buy his way out of anything.

P-138[1]

[*Endorsement*] NOTED F. D. W.

DNA, RG 65, file BS 198940-250x. TD. Stamped endorsement.

1. This was one of P-138's last reports; his services were terminated by the U.S. attorney general's office on 31 August 1921. Born in Kingston, Jamaica, in 1873, Herbert Simeon Boulin served in the British army from 1902 until 1907. After spending most of his term of service in Africa, he returned to Jamaica in 1907. In 1908 he visited Philadelphia, where he decided to make his home. He opened up a school for teaching shorthand, but it soon failed. Afterward, he worked as a laborer at a local shipyard and then as an employee of the Pinkerton Detective Agency between 1915 and 1920. In January 1920 Boulin became a U.S. citizen. In July 1920 he was hired by the Bureau of Investigation to investigate the Garvey movement. After J. Edgar Hoover sent him a letter terminating his services in August 1921, Boulin opened his own detective agency, promoting his services by advertising his status as a former employee of the Department of Justice (DJ-FBI, NY file 65-8295; J. Edgar Hoover to T. J. Donegan, 12 August 1941, DJ-FBI).

William J. Burns to Frank Burke

[*Washington, D.C.*] August 31, 1921

My dear Mr. Burke:[1]

The Bureau has been advised by a strictly confidential source, that MARCUS GARVEY, president of the Universal Negro Improvement Association, and head of the Black Star Line, is negotiating at the present time for the purchase of a boat from the U.S. Shipping Board.

I am sure that you will recall the activities of Marcus Garvey and I am therefore, referring this information to you for such attention as you may deem advisable. Very truly yours,

W. J. BURNS
Director

DNA, RG 65, file BS 198940-251. TLS, recipient's copy.

1. Frank Burke was the head of the USSB's bureau of investigation, which was established in 1921 to handle the liquidation problems that grew out of the board's ship operation program and to manage the details of court litigation. In 1926 the USSB bureau of investigation was closed, and the Department of Justice took over its files (T. V. O'Connor [chairman of USSB] to John G. Sargent, [U.S. attorney general], 27 July 1926, DNA, RG 32, file 605-1-653).

Report by Bureau Agent F. M. Ames

Pittsburgh, Pa. Aug. 31, 1921

UNIVERSAL NEGRO IMPROVEMENT ASSOCIATION,
WOODLAWN, PA.

This report has reference to my report for August 13th, 1921, under the following caption: "WALTER GRAVES (GREAVES), 241 Todd Street, Woodlawn, Pa., President, Woodlawn Div., Universal Negro Improvement Association, (Black Star Line)".

Information was received at this office to the effect that a meeting of the UNIVERSAL NEGRO IMPROVEMENT ASSOCIATION was to be held at Woodlawn, Pa., on Sunday, August 28th, 1921, at 3:00 P.M.

Pursuant to instructions from Agent in Charge McKean, I proceeded to Woodlawn, Pa., for the purpose of attending the meeting in question.

Upon my arrival at Woodlawn, I interviewed CAPT. HARRY MAUK, who is Superintendent of the Jones & Laughlin Steel Company Police Force at that place.

Accompanied by CAPT. MAUK, I proceeded to Wykes and Davis Streets, Woodlawn, Pa., as it is at this place the meeting referred to was to take place.

Under a suitable pretext and without disclosing my identity I interviewed S. A. FRANKLIN, the District Organizer of this organization, and ascertained the following information:—

1st—MR. FRANKLIN resides at 1604 Wylie Avenue, Pittsburgh[.]

2nd—Has been a member of the above referred to organization since 1918 and has been personally acquainted with MARCUS GARVEY for the past fourteen years.

3rd—He also stated that he was personally acquainted with CHANDLER OWENS, a radical negro who resides in New York City. The said CHANDLER OW[EN]S is the editor of a radical magazine known as "THE MESSENGER".

4th—FRANKLIN stated that he is in full sympathy with the principles advocated by CHANDLER OWENS and considers MR. OWENS a very intelligent man.

5th—FRANKLIN is familiar with WILLIAM SCARVILLE, who is a member of the I.W.W. and resides at 1839 Howard Street, Pittsburgh.

For the information of the Bureau WILLIAM SCARVILLE was arrested by me during the railroad strike for distribution of I.W.W. literature.[1]

S. A. FRANKLIN is a subject of Great Britain and is a West Indies negro. He has his first papers, is very intelligent and can speak the following languages: English, Japanese, Chinese, Bulgarian, Spanish, German, Hindoo, French and Italian. He also stated that he received no salary from the UNIVERSAL NEGRO IMPROVEMENT ASSOCIATION for his services, but receives actual expenses while on the road.

A description of S. A. FRANKLIN is as follows:—

Name	—S. A. FRANKLIN
Nationality	—West Indies Negro.
Speaks English fluently.	
Height	—5 ft. 3 in.
Weight	—140 lbs.
Teeth	—Fairly good.
Appearance	—Erect.
Personality	—Fair.
Very clever talker.	

The meeting convened at 3:35 P.M., there were approximately 135 negroes present. IRVIN FRANKLIN acted as chairman during the absence of WALTER GRAVES, the President. IRVIN FRANKLIN introduced S. A. FRANKLIN, the District Organizer, who made the following speech:—

"Ladies and Gentlemen, members of the UNIVERSAL NEGRO IMPROVEMENT ASSOCIATION and friends, it gives me great pleasure to address this meeting this evening. I have a few important matters which I have received from the Parent Body in New York City that I wish to explain to you at this time. During MR. GARVEY's recent trip to West Africa [*Indies?*], I regret very much to say, some of the officials of this organization which you and I are a member of have tried the[ir] very best to prevent MR. GARVEY's return to this country, but were unsuccessful in the attempt. The President of the United States and the State Department granted him a passport to return to this country. I have been further advised that Mr. Brooks[,] one of the officials of our organization who was one of the participants in this movement[,] has embezzled $15,000.00 belonging to the organization and since MR. GARVEY's return to the United States the said Mr. Brooks has not been seen or heard of. Mr. Gordon, one of the officials who also participated in the movement objecting [to] MR. GARVEY'S return to the United States, has tendered his resignation; his reasons are covered by fifteen points[;] the principal one is that he cannot agree with the principles of MR. GARVEY.

["]The National Convention of this organization is in progress at the present time and a new set of National officers will be elected but at this time I am unable to state who they are. I am further advised that there will be a change in the Constitution and By-Laws of our organization. Our organization is very much opposed to Labor Unions[;] the Union does not benefit the Negro working man, this is one principle of our organization to abolish recognition of the Labor Union.

["]If you are not a member of the UNIVERSAL NEGRO IMPROVEMENT ASSOCIATION, join it now[,] we advocate the open shop. If you want to work and the members of the white man's Union attempt to stop you take a gun and fight your way through. (Applause by the audience). Don't go out on a strike with the white man's Union for if you do as soon as the strike is settled you will be left out in the cold without a job. (Applause by the audience).

["]Our organization is backed by the United States Government. Here just recently President Harding authorized a loan of $5,000,000.00 for the use of organization in carrying on our work and the money has been advanced by the United States Government. There are 400,000,000 negroes in the world and they are all considered as members whether they have signed up or not; they belong to the Black Race and they have quit asking England to grant the freedom of Africa; they are going to fight and shed blood for it and their freedom. (Applause by the audience). England is afraid to free Ireland, if she does she will have to free Africa."

The second speaker to take the platform was REV. R. L. SWANN, who resides at 817 Pennsylvania Avenue, Coraopolis, Pa. His chief topic was on the social equality rights of the negro. He talked for about fifteen minutes on this subject.

At different intervals during the meeting there were solos rendered by two colored ladies in the audience and later the audience sang three hymns.

A collection was taken up, but the amount collected was not announced. Investigation continued.

F. M. AMES

[*Handwritten endorsement*] 9/9/21 GFR 800
[*Stamped endorsement*] NOTED F. D. W.

DNA, RG 65, file BS 202600-824-8. TD.

1. Following the breakdown of talks between employers and the railroad brotherhoods in March 1920, an unauthorized strike of several thousand railroad switchmen broke out in Chicago and spread rapidly throughout the country. The strike was opposed by the brotherhoods themselves, who supplied strikebreakers to the railroad corporations, and on 20 September 1920 the strike was called off (Selig Perlman and Philip Taft, *History of Labor in the United States, 1896–1932* [New York: Macmillan Co., 1935] 4: 453–56).

Speech by Marcus Garvey

[[LIBERTY HALL, New York,
Aug. 31, 1921]]

MARCUS GARVEY SPEAKS

Immediately the President-General arose, smiling and bowing to the right and then to the left like a black Napoleon, whereupon the audience again broke into great cheering and hurrahing, followed by the association yell of the Junior Motor Corps girls. When the audience, after a period of about five minutes, had spent itself, and quiet was restored, the President-General spoke as follows:—

May it please your Highness the Potentate, Right Honorable Members of the Executive Council, Deputies and Delegates to the Second International Convention of Negroes of the World, Ladies and Gentlemen:—We are assembled here tonight to bring to a close our great convention of thirty-one days and thirty-one nights. Before we separate ourselves and take our departure to the different parts of the world from which we came, I desire to give you a message; one that you will, I hope, take home and propagate among the scattered millions of Africa's sons and daughters.

We have been here, sent here by the good will of the 400,000,000 Negroes of the world to legislate in their interests, and in the time allotted to us we did our best to enact laws and to frame laws that in our judgment, we hope, will help solve the great problem that confronts us universally. The Universal Negro Improvement Association seeks to emancipate the Negro everywhere, industrially, educationally, politically and religiously. It also seeks a free and redeemed Africa. It has a great struggle ahead; it has a gigantic task to face. Nevertheless, as representatives of the Negro people of the world we have undertaken the task of freeing the 400,000,000 of our race, and of freeing our bleeding Motherland, Africa. We counselled with each other during the thirty-one days; we debated with each other during the thirty-one days, and out of all we did, and out of all we said, we have come to the one conclusion—that speedily Africa must be redeemed! (Applause.) We have come to the conclusion that speedily there must be an emancipated Negro race everywhere (applause); and on going back to our respective homes we go with our determination to lay down, if needs be, the last drop of our blood for the defense of Africa and for the emancipation of our race.

The handwriting is on the wall. You see it as plain as daylight; you see it coming out of India, the tribes of India rising in rebellion against their overlords. You see it coming out of Africa, our dear motherland, Africa; the Moors rising in rebellion against their overlords, and defeating them at every turn. (Applause.) According to the last report flashed to this country from Morocco by the Associated Press, the Moors have again conquered and subdued the Spanish hordes. The same Associated Press flashes to us the news that there is a serious uprising in India,[1] and the English people are marshaling their troops to subdue the spirit of liberty, of freedom, which is now permeating India. The news has come to us, and I have a cable in my pocket that comes from Ireland that the Irish are determined to have liberty and nothing less than liberty. (Applause.)

THE LEAGUE OF NATIONS

The handwriting is on the wall, and as we go back to our respective homes we shall serve notice upon the world that we also are coming; coming with a united effort; coming with a united determination, a determination that Africa shall be free from coast to coast. (Applause.) I have before me the decision of the League of Nations. Immediately after the war a Council of the League of Nations was called, and at that Council they decided that the territories wrested from Germany in West Africa, taken from her during the conflict, should be divided between France and England—608,000 square miles—without even asking the civilized Negroes of the world what disposition shall be made of their own homeland, of their own country. An insult was hurled at the civilized Negroes of the world when they thus took upon themselves the right to parcel out and apportion as they pleased 608,000 square miles of our own land; for we never gave it up; we never sold it. It is still our[s]. (Cries of "Yes!") They parceled it out between these two nations—England and France—gave away our property without consulting us, and we are aggrieved, and we desire to serve notice on civilization and on the world that 400,000,000 Negroes are aggrieved. (Cries of "Yes!" and applause.)

And we are the more aggrieved because of the lynch rope, because of segregation, because of the Jim Crowism that is used, practised and exercised here in this country and in other parts of the world by the white nations of the earth, wherever Negroes happen accidentally or otherwise to find themselves. If there is no safety for Negroes in the white world, I cannot see what right they have to parcel out the homeland, the country of Negroes, without consulting Negroes and asking their permission so to do. Therefore, we are aggrieved. This question of prejudice will be the downfall of civilization (applause), and I warn the white race of this, and of their doom. I hope they will take heed, because the handwriting is on the wall. (Applause.) No portion of humanity, no group of humanity, has an abiding right, an everlasting right, an eternal right to oppress other sections or portions of humanity. God never gave them the right, and if there is such a right, man arrogated it to himself, and God in all ages has been displeased with the arrogance of man. I warn those nations which believe themselves above the law of God, above the commandments of God. I warn those nations that believe themselves above human justice. You cannot long ignore the laws of God; you cannot long ignore the commandments of God; you cannot long ignore human justice, and exist. Your arrogance will destroy you, and I warn the races and the nations that have arrogated to themselves the right to oppress, the right to circumscribe, the right to keep down other races. I warn them that the hour is coming when the oppressed will rise in their might, in their majesty, and throw off the yoke of ages.

The world ought to understand that the Negro has come to life, possessed with a new conscience and a new soul. The old Negro is buried, and it is well the world knew it. It is not my purpose to deceive the world. I believe in righteousness; I believe in truth; I belie[ve] in honesty. That is why I warn a selfish world of the outcome of their actions towards the oppressed. There will come a day, Josephus Daniels wrote about it, a white statesman, and the world has talked about it, and I warn the world of it, that the day will come when the races of the world will marshal themselves in great conflict for the survival of the fittest. Men of the Universal Negro Improvement Association, I am asking you to prepare yourselves, and prepare your race the world over, because the conflict is coming, not because you will it, not because you desire it, but because you will be forced into it. The conflict between the races is drawing nearer and nearer. You see it; I see it; I see it in the handwriting on the wall, as expressed in the uprising in India. You see the handwriting on the wall of Africa; you see it, the handwriting on the wall of Europe. It is coming; it is drawing nearer and nearer. Four hundred million Negroes of the world, I am asking you to prepare yourselves, so that you will not be found wanting when that day comes. Ah! what a sorry day it will be. I hope it will never come. But my hope, my wish, will not prevent its coming. All that I can do is to warn humanity everywhere, so that humanity may change its tactics, and warn them of the danger. I repeat: I warn the white world against the prejudice they are practising against Negroes; I warn them against the segregation and injustice they mete out to us, for the perpetuation of these things will mean the ultimate destruction of the present civilization, and the building up of a new civilization founded upon mercy, justice and equality.

I know that we have good men in all races living at the present time. We have good men of the black race, we have good men of the white race, good men of the yellow race, who are endeavoring to do the best they can to ward off this coming conflict. White men who have the vision, go ye back and warn your people of this coming conflict! Black men of vision, go ye to the four corners of the earth, and warn your people of this coming conflict. Yellow men, go ye out and warn your people of this coming conflict, because it is drawing nearer and nearer; nearer and nearer. Oh! if the world will only listen to the heart-throbs, to the soul-beats of those who have the vision, those who have God's love in their hearts.

I see before me white men, black men and yellow men working assiduously for the peace of the world; for the bringing together of this thing called human brotherhood; I see them working through their organizations. They have been working during the last fifty years. Some worked to bring about the emancipation, because they saw the danger of perpetual slavery. They brought about the liberation of 4,000,000 black people. They passed away, and others started to work, but the opposition against them is too strong; the opposition against them is weighing them down. The world has gone mad; the world has become too material; the world has lost its spirit of kinship with God, and man can see nothing else but prejudice, avarice and greed. Avarice and greed will destroy the world, and I am appealing to white, black and yellow whose hearts, whose souls are touched with the true spirit of humanity, with the true feeling of human brotherhood, to preach the doctrine of human love, more, to preach it louder, to preach it longer, because there is great need for it in the world at this time. Ah! if they could but see the danger—the conflict between the races—races fighting against each other. What a destruction, what a holocaust it will be! Can you imagine it?

Just take your idea from the last bloody war, wherein a race was pitted against itself (for the whole white races united as one from a common origin), the members of which, on both sides, fought so tenaciously that they killed off each other in frightful, staggering numbers. If a race pitted against itself could fight so tenaciously to kill itself without mercy, can you imagine the fury, can you imagine the mercilessness, the terribleness of the war that will come when all the races of the world will be on the battlefield, engaged in deadly combat for the destruction or overthrow of the one or the other, when beneath it and as a cause of it lies prejudice and hatred? Truly, it will be an ocean of blood; that is all it will be. So that if I can sound a note of warning now that will echo and reverberate around the world and thus prevent such a conflict, God help me to do it; for Africa, like Europe, like Asia, is preparing for that day. (Great applause.)

AFRICA'S POSSIBILITIES

You may ask yourselves if you believe Africa is still asleep. Africa has been slumbering; but she was slumbering for a purpose. Africa still possesses her hidden mysteries; Africa has unused talents, and we are unearthening them now for the coming conflict. (Applause.) Oh, I hope it will never come; therefore, I hope the white world will change its attitude towards the weaker races of the world, for we shall not be weak everlastingly. Ah, history teaches us of the rise and fall of nations, races and empires. Rome fell in her majesty; Greece fell in her triumph; Babylon, Assyria, Carthage, Prussia, the German Empire—all fell in their pomp and power; the French Empire fell from the sway of the great Napoleon, from the dominion of the indomitable Corsican soldier. As they fell in the past, so will nations fall in the present age, and so will they fall in the future ages to come, the result of their unrighteousness.

I repeat, I warn the world, and I trust you will receive this warning as you go into the four corners of the earth. The white race should teach humanity. Out there is selfishness in the world. Let the white race teach humanity first, because we have been following the cause of humanity for three hundred years, and we have suffered much. If a change must come, it must not come from Negroes; it must come from the white race, for they are the ones who have brought about this estrangement between the races. The Negro never hated; at no time within the last five hundred years can they point to one single instance of Negro hatred. The Negro has loved eve[n] under the severest punishment. In slavery the Negro loved his master; he protected his master; he saf[e]guarded his master's home. "Greater love hath no man than that he should lay down his life for another." We gave not only our services, our unrequited labor; we gave also our souls, we gave our hearts, we gave our all, to our oppressors.

But, after all, we are living in a material world, even though it is partly spiritual, and since we have been very spiritual in the past, we are going to take a part of the material now, and will give others the opportunity to practice the spiritual side of life. Therefore, I am not telling you to lead in humanity; I am not telling you to lead in the bringing about of the turning of humanity, because you have been doing that for three hundred years, and you have lost. But the compromise must come from the domina[n]t races. We are warning them. We are not preaching a doctrine of hatred, and I trust you will not go back to your respective homes and preach such a doctrine. We are preaching, rather, a doctrine of humanity, a doctrine of human love. But we say love begins at home; "charity begins at home."

We are aggrieved because of this partitioning of Africa, because it seeks to deprive Negroes of the chance of higher national development; no chance, no opportunity, is given us to prove our fitness to govern, to dominate in our own behalf. They impute so many bad things against Haiti and against Liberia, that they themselves circumvented Liberia so as to make it impossible for us to demonstrate our ability for self-government. Why not be honest? Why not be straightforward[?] Having desired the highest development, as they avowed and professed, of the Negro, why not give him a fair chance, an opportunity to prove his capacity for governing? What better opportunity ever presented itself than the present, when the territories of Germany in Africa were wrested from her control by the Allies in the last war—what better chance ever offered itself for trying out the higher ability of Negroes to govern themselves than to have given those territories to the civilized Negroes, and thus give them a trial to exercise themselves in a proper system of government? Because of their desire to keep us down, because of their desire to keep us apart, they refuse us a chance. The chance that they did give us is the chance that we are going to take. (Great applause.) Hence tonight, before I take my seat, I will move a resolution, and I think it is befitting at this time to pass such a resolution as I will move, so that the League of Nations and the Supreme Council of the Nations will understand that Negroes are not asleep; that Negroes are not false to themselves; that Negroes are wide awake, and that Negroes intend to take a serious part in the future government of this world; that God Almighty created him and placed him in it. This world owes us a place, and we are going to occupy that place.

We have a right to a large part in the political horizon, and I say to you that we are preparing to occupy that spot.

Go back to your respective corners of the earth and preach the real doctrine of the Universal Negro Improvement Association—the doctrine of universal emancipation for Negroes, the doctrine of a free and a redeemed Africa!

RESOLUTION

Be It Resolved, That we, the duly elected representatives of the Negro peoples of the world, assembled in this Second Annual Convention, do protest against the distribution of the land of Africa by the Supreme Council and the League of Nations among the white nations of the world. Africa, by right of heritage, is the property of the African races, and those at home and those abroad are now sufficiently civilized to conduct the affairs of their own homeland. This convention believes in the right of Europe for the Europeans; Asia for the Asiatics, and Africa for the Africans, those at home and those abroad. We believe, further, that only a close and unselfish application of this principle will prevent threatening race wars that may cast another gloom over civilization and humanity. At this time humanity everywhere is determined to reach a common standard of nationhood. Hence 400,000,000 Negroes demand a place in the political sun of the world.

> SECOND INTERNATIONAL CONVENTION
> OF NEGROES.
> Through the Universal Negro Improve-
> ment Association,
> Marcus Garvey, President-General.
> Wednesday, August 31, 1921. New York, N.Y.

His Grace the Chaplain General took the chair, whereupon His Excellency the American Leader, the Hon. Dr. J. W. Eason, arose to second the resolution saying that because of the fact, as expressed in the resolution, that the Negro peoples of the world, the civilized groups of Negroes in the world, are now sufficiently trained to manage their own affairs, including the territory of Africa, as well as Haiti, San Domingo, Liberia and other independent Negro republics, he heartily endorsed the resolution and recommended the adoption by the convention. Continuing, the American Leader said:

"In the next place, I second this resolution because if for no other reason than this: that the 300,000 black soldiers, representing the highest intelligence of the Negroes of North America, who went from here to France to fight to help make the world safe for democracy, and the thousands and thousands of black soldiers from Africa under the French flag and under the British flag, and even under the Belgium flag, who fought to keep the German hordes from crossing the Rhine—that they ought to be recognized in the dividing up of the spoils. (Applause.) And since we, the representatives of the Negroes of the world, assembled in this convention have understanding sufficient to realize that Europe is for the Europeans, that Asia is for the Asiatics—we are even willing to say let America be for the white man, for they have charge of it, anyhow (laughter); we therefore should adopt this resolution, which I strongly and unqualifiedly endorse. Because we firmly believe that the League of Nations ought to turn over the entire portion of Africa to the representatives of the Negroes of the world that they have taken from Germany's possession." (Applause.)

The motion was then put by the chair, and carried unanimously, expressed by a rising vote. . . .

Printed in *NW*, 10 September 1921. Original headlines and portions of the report are omitted.

   1. The uprising of Muslim Moplah peasants in Malabar, southwest India, was directed principally against Hindu landlords. Western reports, however, attributed the uprising to violent religious fanaticism, hatred of the Hindus, and agitation by Indian nationalists. Following the deaths of a number of Europeans, Indian troops were brought in to quell the uprising (*NYT*, 30 August and 31 August 1921).

Draft Memorandum by John Cooper Wiley

[Division of Western European Affairs,
Washington, D.C., August 1921]

The [Garvey] movement was launched and is fostered by a group of professional negro agitators under the leadership of Marcus Garvey. Freedom of speech and press make the United States an advantageous place for the operation of these men. It is understood that Garvey is British subject, born and mainly educated in the West Indies, and it is reported that many of his associates are also British subjects.

The war and the wide and general public discussion of the so-called principle of "self determination" undoubtedly had the effect of quickening racial consciousness in the negroes of the United States and causing among the masses the growth of a more or less vague sentiment favoring any movement which had as its objective negro nationality.

It therefore happened that the agitation and propaganda of Garvey was started at a moment when conditions were such that he was able to interest in his movement thousands of people, most of whom have no real understanding of what he is aiming to do or how he intends doing it. The adherents of this movement, may, for the most part, be regarded as dupes of men who have a considerable degree of intelligence, unfortunately directed, some organizing ability, and a great deal that suggests they are impostors. The most charitable view would be that they are visionary and impractical. But their methods and [activities?] are none the less encouraging false hopes in and misleading thousands of American Negroes.

The movement has assumed a definitely organized form. A so-called "Constitution and Book of Laws" became effective July 1918, and were revised and amended Aug. 1920. The pretentious and all-inclusive name of the "Universal Negro Improvement Association, Inc. and African Communities' League, Inc. of the World" has been adopted by the movement.

An examination of the Constitution would seem to disclose that it is a composite instrument designed manifestly to make the widest possible appeal to Negroes in the United States and elsewhere. The church, fraternal orders, organic state laws, organized management of commercial enterprises, and even African tribal customary laws, all suggest themselves as sources from which parts of the constitution and by-laws might have been taken.

The objectives toward which the organization is supposed to be working are sufficiently general and loosely defined to permit it to undertake almost any kind of activities. Specifically the major aim seems to be the founding in Africa of a great negro state through the unification of African communities by creating a strong sentiment therefor, among the negroes of the world. Commercial ventures have also received attention. The biggest thing so far attempted has been the effort to establish a steamship line. One or two vessels have been actually bought, or chartered, or have at least come under the control of the organization. Some trips have been made to the West Indies to begin trade relations. The proposed sailings to West Africa have so far not been undertaken. It may well be doubted that the business methods which are said to prevail in the organization's business management can ever procure successful results.

The parent organization has its headquarters in New York City. Numerous local societies have been organized in various cities and towns throughout the United States. These local societies are directly under the jurisdiction of the parent organization from which they receive their charter, laws of government, etc.

Executive authority is vested in the Potentate and Supreme Commissioner assisted by a highly titled corps of subordinate officials. These are maintained in office by money collected in the form of weekly dues from the membership of 25 cents per member each, also donations, collections, gifts, profits derived from business, entertainments, etc. and a tax of $1.00 per year payable on Jan. 1st by each member. It is evident that, if as [commonly?] reported the membership numbers several hundred thousand, and any considerable number of them keep up their assessments, the organization as a whole must handle considerable amounts of money.

Active propaganda is carried on chiefly through the medium of a weekly newspaper styled "The Negro World" published in New York City. Copies of this paper are sent all over the United States, West Indies, and parts of Central and South America, as well as Africa, or in short, wherever negro people may be reached. It has been reported that the British and French colonial governments of West Africa regard this publication as particularly pernicious and some have taken steps to discourage its circulation. While much of the space is devoted to extolling the virtues of Marcus Garvey and his movement, there is still a great deal published about the grievances of negroes in such a way as to unsettle their minds and produce unrest and dissatisfaction without offering any practicable solution to improve their conditions.

It may be observed, however, in this connection, that the better class of negroes in the United States appear to have very little interest in the movement and have not as yet accorded it any material support.

The organization has opened a branch office in Monrovia for the purpose of administering its West African business. The mayor of Monrovia, Gabriel M. Johnson, holds the position of High Potentate and is actively endeavoring to put the U.N.I.A. on a permanent footing in Liberia. In addition to the High Potentate, there have been present at Monrovia G. O. Marke, Supreme Deputy, and C. A. Crichlow, Resident Secretary, a builder, agriculturist, pharmacist, and surveyor. Of this group it is reported that C. A. Crichlow is the only American citizen.

The avowed program in Liberia is:

> to assist in rehabilitating the country
> to establish settlements and assist immigrants in settling therein,
> etc.

In an interview which the High Potentate, Supreme Deputy and Resident Secretary had with the acting President of Liberia, on March 22, 1921, the latter is reported to have made the following most extraordinary statement.

> I will say this among ourselves. There isn't a negro in the world who, if given the opportunity and power to do certain things, will not do them. But it is not always advisable nor politic to openly expose our secret intentions—our secret thoughts. This is the way we do—or rather don't do—in Liberia. We don't tell them what we think; we only tell them what we like them to hear—what, in fact they like to hear. (While the British and French were probably in the mind of the acting President when making the above statement, it may be noted that he would no doubt not hesitate to apply these same methods in his dealings with Americans).

A branch or local society of the U.N.I.A. has been organized in Monrovia. Some of the leading Liberians are officers and members of this society. At the last legislature it was incorporated and given the right to establish branches in any town or city within the Republic. The further rights were granted to hold real, personal or mixed property to the value of ($1,000,000.00) one million dollars to carry on commercial and industrial enterprises, to build and operate factories[,] establish steamship communications, to carry on educational pursuits, etc.

From the information at hand it may, without difficulty, be implied that the U.N.I.A. have political aims in Liberia. This is the point which should be carefully watched. A few hundred radical American Negroes shipped to Liberia might overthrow the government as now constituted and attempt to replace it by a regime dominated by the . . . [*word illegible*] of the Garvey movement, if not under the actual control of the organization itself.

Very strained relations grew up between certain of the organization's agents who have been in Liberia which led to the resignation of C. A. Crichlow[,] the Resident Secretary at Monrovia. It appears that the original cause of the difficulty was conflicting opinions [as] to policy and authority. To this were finally added misunderstandings as to money matters. Crichlow seems to have failed to carry his points and so resigned. He then turned "states evidence," so to speak[,] and appealed to the American Minister for assistance. To support his case Crichlow put in the hands of the Minister copies of the record of the organization's Liberian activities which give a fairly good outline of what has been going on.

Gabriel M. Johnson, Mayor of Monrovia, and High Potentate, is now in the United States. He came to attend the Annual Convention of the organization held at New York during the month of August.

Officially the Liberian Government is not disposed to favor the political aspirations of the movement. This attitude appears to be largely based on fear that the U.N.I.A. might become powerful enough to take control of the Republic's government from the little group of Americo-Liberians who have run things for seventy-five years. This fear as before indicated seems pretty well founded. However, it is believed that President King is treating the leaders of the movement in such a way as would render it possible for him to make use of them if it should happen to be to his advantage to do so.

[JOHN COOPER WILEY]

DNA, RG 59, file 800. AM, recipient's copy.

African Redemption Fund Appeal
by Marcus Garvey

[*New York, August 1921*]

An Appeal to the Negro Race

Negroes to be Thrown Off to Suffer and Die

My dear Comrades:

The hour has struck for universal action on the part of our Race to save itself. For three hundred years we have been held as chattel and industrial slaves in this Western World, and for five hundred years we have been robbed, exploited and killed in Africa. The world in which we live today is closing in upon us, and in a short while we will be thrown off to die as an unfit and unprepared people. We have in the past, and up to the present, been lynched, raped, jim-crowed, segregated and exploited in our labor, and after all this, it is apparent that in the great industrial struggle that is to come, we will be thrown off to suffer and to die.

Negro Race Must Be Saved

The Universal Negro Improvement Association—the strongest Negro Movement in the world—is making every effort to save the Negro Race from destruction. We are endeavoring to unite the four hundred million Negroes of the world into one solid body, for the purpose of protecting ourselves industrially, socially, educationally and politically, as also to found a great government of our own on the Continent of Africa.

Negro About To Protect Himself

Already four million members have joined the organization, and we have already moved the world to realize that the Negro is about to protect himself. But we need money to carry on the work, to start industries, to scatter our propaganda all over the world, and to provide for our people generally. We as an Organization haven't the money, but the race has it; hence we are appealing to every member of the race to do his or her part in raising a large fund of four billion dollars to capitalize the work of the Universal Negro Improvement Association, so that we can do things.

Must Have Money

It is no use talking about race improvement and adjustment without money. If Africa must be free, we must have money. If we must find employment for our own people, we must have money. If we are to become a great race and a great nation we must have money. Therefore every Negro in the world is hereby asked to contribute five dollars to this great cause.

SUBSCRIBE FIVE DOLLARS OR MORE

We are raising this money as the "African Redemption Fund" and every person with one drop of African blood in his or her veins is requested to subscribe five dollars or more. If every Negro in the world will subscribe five dollars or more to "The African Redemption Fund", in twelve months enough money will be raised to make the Negro Race permanently a power among the other races and nations of the world.

LIBERTY FOR ALL NEGROES

Now brother or sister, in the name of God, and to the glory of the race, we ask you to subscribe to this Fund. Remember the raising of the Fund means your liberty, and the liberty of all Negroes now and forever. Support one good big Negro Movement for liberty's sake.

CERTIFICATE OF RACE LOYALTY

Every person who subscribes five dollars or more to the "African Redemption Fund" will receive a certificate of race loyalty from the Universal Negro Improvement Association with the autograph signatures of the Provisional President of Africa, the Right Honorable Secretary-General and the Right Honorable High Chancellor of the Movement.

FOREFATHERS SUFFERED SLAVERY

Remember, for two hundred and fifty years in America, and for two hundred and thirty years in the West Indies, our forefathers suffered slavery. They were whipped, maimed, branded with hot irons, worked to death to make us what we are today. Now, that we are civilized, will we not subscribe five dollars or more to the Cause that means liberty to the country from whence we came, and to advance our cause of true freedom and democracy? Who can refuse the plea of the dead grandmother or father from the grave of slavery for help for posterity of the race? From the heights of Heaven our foreparents call out to us to do now for ourselves, or make up our minds to suffer worse than they did in a selfish world that is now closing in around us.

SUBSCRIBE AT ONCE TO AFRICAN REDEMPTION FUND

Turn not a deaf ear to the plea for help, but send in your subscription at once to "The African Redemption Fund". All persons who subscribe five dollars or more will receive a certificate of race loyalty and the amount will be acknowledged in the columns of "The Negro World" newspaper, and the person's name will also be published in "The Universal African Volume", to be circulated all over the world for everybody of the race and succeeding generations to know of the loyal persons who subscribed for the Freedom of Africa and the emancipation of Negroes everywhere.

All those persons who subscribe $25.00 or more besides having their names published in "The Negro World" and "The Universal African Volume," will also have their photographs published.

Send in your contribution now to

THE UNIVERSAL NEGRO IMPROVEMENT ASSOCIATION
56 WEST 135TH STREET, NEW YORK CITY, U.S.A.

I have the honor to be your obedient servant,

MARCUS GARVEY, President-General

Printed pamphlet.

APPENDIX I

Revisions to the Constitution and Book of Laws[1]

[New York, August 1921]

ARTICLE I

. . . CHAPTERS

Sec. 5.   All additional Divisions created in the same cities shall be under the supervision of the former Chartered Division. The Charters granted to such Divisions shall be called Chapter Charters, and all new Divisions so created shall be called Chapters instead of Divisions, and the Executive Secretary, who shall be a civil servant attached to the Division shall be the Supervisor of such Chapters.

DOMINION, PROVINCIAL OR COLONIAL CHARTERS

Sec. 6.   In countries requiring the Provincial or Colonial registration of Charters, there shall be issued one Dominion, Provincial or Colonial Charter, as the law may require, and all Divisions within the Charter limits shall be designated as Branches. Nothing in this provision shall be construed as giving the original Division any jurisdiction over the others other than through the parent body. . . .

ARTICLE IV

OFFICIALS, OFFICERS, APPOINTMENTS AND ELECTIONS

Section 1.   . . . a First Assistant Secretary-General, a Second Assistant Secretary-General, . . . a Minister of Labor and Industries. . . .

FAILURE OF OFFICIAL TO QUALIFY

Section 1.   No person elected to a high office of the Universal Negro Improvement Association shall hold office until his credentials as to his character and qualifications have satisfied the High Executive Council. In case a person elected to a high office is rejected by the High Executive Council, the President General and Administrator shall have the power to appoint a person to fill the position of the person rejected until the next session of the Convention.

HIGH COMMISSIONERS AND COMMISSIONERS

Sec. 2. A High Commissioner or Commissioner shall be appointed to represent the Universal Negro Improvement Association in every country where Negroes live. In parts where the country is divided up into large states and different sections a Commissioner shall be appointed to every state and section.

RANK OF MINISTER OR AMBASSADOR

Sec. 3. There shall also be appointed High Commissioners who shall be given the rank of Ministers Plenipotentiary or Ambassadors, who shall be domiciled at the Capital of all regular governments. Their duties shall be to keep up friendly relations with the respective governments and to protect the interests of all Negroes. . . .

ARTICLE V

. . . OFFICIALS AND B.S.L. STOCK

Sec. 11. It shall be obligatory that all high officials, officers and members of the Parent Body and the Local Divisions subscribe to the stocks of the Black Star Line Steamship Corporation, and shall support all enterprises by the Association in its interest. . . .

PRESIDENT GENERAL AND ADMINISTRATOR

Sec. 13. . . . He shall be empowered to exercise a Veto Power on any financial matter initiated by any individual or by the Executive Council that may tend to jeopardize or ruin the finances of the organization. Such Veto Power shall only be used by the Administrator in financial matters, and where from his best judgment he is convinced that it is not to the best interest of the organization to permit the carrying out of such financial measures. An appeal may be made to the Convention against the veto of the Administrator, on any measure, and he shall be held responsible to the Convention for the exercise of his judgment on the matter.

. . . SECOND ASSISTANT SECRETARY GENERAL

Sec. 17. It shall be the duty of the Second Assistant Secretary General to work in concert with the First Assistant and the Secretary General in the performance of the duties of that office.

... MINISTER OF LABOR AND INDUSTRIES

Sec. 28. The Minister of Labor and Industries shall be an Executive Officer of the Universal Negro Improvement Association, whose duty it shall be to regulate labor and industry among the various members of the organization throughout the world. When feasible he should have representatives in each Division, and shall thereby inform himself of the labor conditions throughout the world and formulate plans to relieve the economic condition of Negroes everywhere. He shall also lend his assistance to all matters of immigration and to the establishment of avenues of industry for the members of the organization. . . .

ARTICLE VII

... SALARIES OF DIVISIONAL OFFICERS

Sec. 4. . . . and all such salaries shall be conditional on the local Division having at its disposal sufficient funds in its treasury to make payment of such possible.

... DEPARTMENTAL ASSISTANT

Sec. 6. No department of the Parent Body shall employ an Assistant for that Department without first obtaining the approval of the President General as to the fitness and desirability of the individual to be employed.

ARTICLE VIII

... ANNUAL EXPENSE TAX

The One Dollar annual tax of each member shall be charged against the local Division to which the member is attached, and shall be collected from the financial membership of the Division as by its report on the 31st of December of each year.

... NET PROCEEDS TO DIVISIONS

Sec. 11. Fifty per cent of the proceeds of all entertainments given by auxiliaries of Divisions, Branches or Chapters shall be turned over to the Division, Branch or Chapter after all legitimate expenses incurred for such entertainments have been paid, and no auxiliary shall give any entertainment without the permission of the President of the Division, Branch or Chapter.

Sec. 12. All auxiliaries of Divisions must turn into the treasury of the Divisions to which they are attached all moneys derived from entertainments at the first meeting following such entertainments. . . .

ARTICLE XII

THE CIVIL SERVICE

Section 1.   A Civil Service shall be established by the Universal Negro Improvement Association. From this Civil Service shall be recruited all employes of the Association.

PREFERENCE OF CIVIL SERVANTS

Sec. 2.   A civil servant shall have precedence over and preference to all persons employed, or to be employed, by the Universal Negro Improvement Association.

LISTS

Sec. 3.   An official civil servants' list of the Universal Negro Improvement Association shall be compiled and designated as the Civil Service.

EXAMINATION

Sec. 4.   All persons to be placed on the Civil Service shall first be obliged to pass an examination on general educational tests as laid down by the official examiners, and in addition thereto such persons shall be required to give evidence of good moral character and honesty.

EXAMINERS

Sec. 5.   The official examiners shall be the Administrator of the Universal Negro Improvement Association and such other persons as he may appoint to serve with him.

CIVIL SERVICE COMMISSION

Sec. 6.   The persons appointed by the Administrator to serve with him as official examiners shall be known as the Civil Service Commission; and the Civil Service Commission, together with the Administrator, shall compose the Board of Civil Service Examiners. They shall designate the subjects in which applicants shall be examined, and shall also prescribe the rules and regulations governing the examinations of applicants.

CERTIFICATE

Sec. 7.   All applicants who have passed the Civil Service examination shall be given a certificate as proof thereof.

PROMOTIONS

Sec. 8.   All promotions in the Universal Negro Improvement Association shall be made from the Civil Service list of the Association.

Sec. 9.   All Executive Secretaries of local divisions shall be members of the Civil Service.

ARTICLE XIII

PASSPORT IDENTIFICATIONS

Section 1.   A Bureau of Passports shall be attached to the Secretary-General's Office.

Sec. 2.   Each and every member who desires a Passport Identification for the purpose of travel or for the purpose of receiving recognition, consideration and likely help from other branches, or for the purpose of proving connection with a regular organization or with a branch of the Universal Negro Improvement Association, shall be supplied with one of these Passports at any Division of the organization by the Executive Secretary of that Division at which application is duly made.

Sec. 3.   Each passport shall have on its face a photograph of the bearer, the signature of the bearer and such other details as may be provided in the rules and regulations of the Bureau of Passports and Identifications.

Sec. 4.   Each passport identification shall be issued by the Universal Negro Improvement Association and African Communities' League from its Headquarters. It shall be signed and stamped by the Executive Secretary stationed at the Division where the passport has been secured.

Sec. 5.   Before a passport identification can be secured each and every member shall be required to fill out a bill of particulars, and only financial members whose dues and assessments have been fully paid up and whose records are clean shall be supplied with a passport identification. No one shall be granted a passport identification until he or she shall have been in the organization for six months and shall have paid up all dues and assessments.

Sec. 6.   The sum of two dollars shall be paid for the issuance of every Passport Identification. Renewals may be made annually against the payment of a fee of twenty-five cents.

Sec. 7.   The Bureau of Justice, through the office of the President-General, shall see that each and every member who holds a passport identification is properly protected, in case of abuse, advantage or injustice committed upon such individual.

AFRICAN REDEMPTION FUND

1.   The parent body shall be empowered to raise a universal fund from all Negroes for the purpose of the redemption of Africa. Every member of the Negro race shall be asked to contribute to this fund a sum not less than $5.00 (Five Dollars). This contribution to the African Redemption Fund shall not be a tax on active members, but shall be a voluntary contribution by all Negroes.

2.   This fund shall be known as the "African Redemption Fund."

3. Each and every person who subscribes to this fund shall receive a certificate of loyalty to the cause "Afric." The certificate shall bear the signatures of the President-General, the High Chancellor and the Secretary-General of the Universal Negro Improvement Association.

4. The purpose of the African Redemption Fund shall be to create a working capital for the organization and to advance the cause for the building up of Africa.

ARTICLE XIV

BUREAU OF JUSTICE

1. That a Bureau of Justice shall be established by the parent body of the U.N.I.A. and A.C.L. for the protection of all Negroes.

2. The Bureau of Justice shall be composed of three members. It shall have for its head an attorney-at-law who shall be known as the chief of the Bureau of Justice. One of the members of the Bureau shall be its secretary.

3. The Bureau shall have to co-operate with it a committee of three from each Local Division, composed of the President and two members selected from the general membership. This committee shall be under the supervision of the Bureau.

4. The local committee shall have the power to dispose of all matters not of sufficient magnitude to require special attention of the Bureau, and shall report to the Bureau their action therein.

5. The Bureau, with the consent and advice of the President General and High Executive Council, shall have the power to make such rules and incur such expenses as are absolutely necessary for the proper carrying out of its objects.

General Laws

ARTICLE I

. . . BLUE BOOKS

Sec. 2. An official Blue Book containing the records of Convention shall be published yearly for the benefit of officers and members of divisions of the Universal Negro Improvement Association and African Communities' League. . . .

ARTICLE III

. . . OFFICERS OF LOCAL DIVISIONS

Sec. 2. . . . an Executive Secretary (who shall be a Civil Servant appointed by the President-General from the Parent Body). . . .

Executive Secretary

(a)   The Executive Secretary of each Division shall be a Civil Servant of the Parent Body. He shall be an educated and competent person. He shall keep under his control all books, papers and documents belonging to the Division, and shall be responsible to the local Division and the parent body for his conduct.

(b)   The Executive Secretary shall make up the monthly report of the Division and forward same to the parent body by the 1st of every month. He shall see that all members are financial and have paid all dues and assessments, including the death tax.

(c)   He shall be the financial representative of the parent body, and all loans, bonds or stock sold for the parent body shall be under his charge, and he shall lodge such amounts of money in the bank, separate and distinct from the funds of the local Division. Such funds shall be lodged in a special account as directed by the parent body through the office of the President General, and he shall see that every member of his Division subscribe to the official organ of the organization, "The Negro World."

(d)   The Executive Secretary shall supervise the work of all other secretaries of his Division and all Chapters in his jurisdiction. He shall be the secretary to the local executive officers of the Division. He shall instruct the General Secretary to receive the dues, collections, assessments, etc., of the members of the Division and report same to him so that he can report to the local officers and make his monthly report to the parent body.

(e)   Where the funds of the local are low and cannot pay two officers to attend to its work, the Executive Secretary shall be the only one paid, and he shall do all the work with the assistance of the honorary officers, who shall not be paid. The Executive Secretary shall give all his time to the organization and cannot be employed otherwise.

. . . Insubordination

Sec. 24.   No officer or member shall be insubordinate to those in higher authority.

Sec. 24a.   Any President or officer of local Divisions who causes the arrest or prosecution of any high official, officer or representative of the Parent Body through grievances affecting such President or officer shall be forthwith removed from office.

It shall be the duty of Presidents, officers and members of local Divisions having grievances against any representative or representatives of the Parent Body to pursue the proper course, provided by the Constitution and laid down in Article III, Section 61, of the General Laws.

No officer, members of the Field Corps, Detective Staff, or person sent to a local Division shall treat with any unofficial member of that Division. Nor shall such person or persons make any statement or statements which may prove detrimental to the harmonious working of that Division, or which may tend to foster suspicion on any officer or officers of that Division, or on any Field Representative, or on any member of the High Executive Council.

. . . PAYMENT OF DEATH GRANTS

Sec. 31a. Divisions claiming death grants from the [P]arent [B]ody for a member must send to the Secretary General a certificate of death of the member and the member's dues card.

. . . AUDITING ACCOUNTS OF LOCAL DIVISIONS

Sec. 45a. The President General shall cause a Traveling Auditor to visit all Divisions, Branches, Chapters, Societies, etc., and audit their accounts at any time.

. . . MEMBERS IN DISTRESS

Sec. 47b. A Division may help from its charitable funds any needy member in distress, where injustice had been done; and in cases where further aid is needed on the part of said member application shall be made to the Parent Body through the Bureau of Justice.

. . . COMMISSIONERS AND ORGANIZERS

Sec. 57. The Commissioner appointed to each County, State or Province shall be the national oganizer of that locality, and he shall supervise the work of all Divisions in the County, State or Province.

Sec. 57a. All Commissioners shall make a monthly report to the President General as touching the work performed by him for the organization.

. . . CHAPLAINS

Sec. 63. All chaplains of the U.N.I.A. & A.C.L. shall be intelligent persons versed in the reading and interpretation of the Universal Ritual and the Scriptures.

DISPENSARIES

Sec. 64. The Universal Negro Improvement Association and African Communities' League shall establish Medical and Surgical Dispensaries in the various parts of the world where medical and surgical aid is needed. Such Dispensaries shall be supported by the local division in the locality where such dispensaries are established.

Rules and Regulations for Universal African Legions of the U.N.I.A. and A.C.L.

ARTICLE I

(NAME AND OBJECT)

Section 1. This Auxiliary body shall be known as the Universal African Legions and shall consist of men who are active members of the Universal Negro Improvement Association and African Communities' League, and between the ages of 18 and 55 years and in good health.

Sec. 2. This Auxiliary body shall have the special designation of the Universal African Legions and shall prepare men for service by teaching them military skill and discipline and by registering them according to the various trades in which they have been trained.

There shall be among them non-commissioned officers and men of three classes, viz.: First Class Master Workmen, Second Class Skilled Workmen and Third Class Unskilled Workmen. The Master and Skilled must have trade identifications. Unskilled workmen must be grouped without trade identifications.

ARTICLE II

LOCATION

Section 1. The Quarters of the Universal African Legions shall be the Liberty Hall or the meeting place of the Division of the U.N.I.A. and A.C.L., in which they are formed and unto which they shall be attached.

Sec. 2. T[h]e Headquarters of the Universal African Legions shall be with the parent body of the U.N.I.A. and A.C.L., and shall be under the direct supervision of the Minister of the Legions.

ARTICLE III

COMMISSIONED OFFICERS

Section 1. The Minister of Legions Staff shall consist of Generals, Lieutenant Generals, Major Generals and Commanders, and such other Departmental General Officers that may be expedient for the successful conduct of the U.A.L.

Sec. 2. The Generals, Lieutenant Generals, Major Generals, etc., shall be appointed by the Minister of Legions with the approval of the President General. The President of each Local Division of the U.N.I.A. and A.C.L., by virtue of his Office, shall be the ranking Commander of his Division.

Sec. 3. Commissioned Officers of the various Divisions or Brigades when fully organized shall be as follows:—

1. Commander-President of the Local Division.
2. Colonel.
3. Honorary Colonel (inactive, except for consultation or advice).
4. Lieutenant Colonel.
5. Majors.
6. Captains.
7. First Lieutenants.
8. Second Lieutenants.
9. Cadet or Boy Scouts Commander (Second Lieutenant).

STAFF OFFICERS' INSIGNIA

General—Sphinx and six Buttons.
Major General—Sphinx and five buttons.
Lieutenant General—Sphinx and four buttons.
Commander—Sphinx and three Buttons.
Inspector General—Sphinx and two Buttons.

DIVISIONAL OFFICERS' INSIGNIA

Colonel—Six Buttons.
Lieutenant Colonel—Five Buttons.
Major—Four Buttons.
Captain—Three Buttons.
First Lieutenant—Two Buttons.
Second Lieutenant—One Button.

ARTICLE IV

NON-COMMISSIONED OFFICERS AND MEN AND MANUAL OF INSTRUCTION

Section 1. The Headquarters of the Universal African Legions shall adopt and authorize a uniform system of training and discipline which shall be used by all branches of the Legions wherever domiciled.

ARTICLE V

QUARTERMASTER AND STAFF

Section 1. There shall be established in the Unit of each Division or Brigade a Quartermaster and Staff, who shall receive moneys, collections and deposits for uniform. They shall make weekly and monthly reports to the

Commander through the General Secretary. All moneys received by the Quartermaster shall be lodged with the Treasurer of the Division for deposit in the Bank so designated, as part of the funds of the Division, for which the Legions shall be credited.

Sec. 2. The Quartermaster shall receive all moneys designated to the Universal African Legions and shall pay all debts with the approval of the Commander and issue vouchers for same.

ARTICLE VI

COMMISSARIAT AND ITS DUTIES

Section 1. Each Brigade or Division shall have a Commissary of Subsistence Department which shall be composed in ratio to the size of the Division. The head shall be known as the Commissary Captain and shall function directly under the Commander of the Division.

Sec. 2. The Commissary Officer of a Division shall be a caterer and have knowledge of feeding and refreshing his Brigade while on the march, camping or other outings. He shall under instructions of the Commander see that refreshments are prepared and served to each unit while outing, camping or hiking and with the assistance of his department insure equal distribution. In case where special catering by him is unnecessary he shall use his department to supervise those who have volunteered or are paid to do so.

Sec. 3. When the Brigade is normally at rest at its quarters and the duties of the Commissariat are not necessary, each member of the Commissariat shall muster back to his Division. When needed the Commissary Officer shall apply to the Colonel or Commanding Officer of each unit for the number wanted under orders from the Commander.

Sec. 4. When more than one Division or Brigade is on the hike or move, the Minister of the Legions shall appoint a Commissary General, who shall supervise all duties of the Commissariat hereinbefore mentioned, with the addition of sleeping and living quarters. Any inconvenience of living, sleeping or feeding by any member or unit in a Brigade shall be communicated through the Commissary Officer in Command to the Commissary General.

ARTICLE VII

YEARLY TAX AND OTHER EXPENSES

Section 1. Each member of this Auxiliary shall pay on the first day of January, each year, the sum of 25 cents into the fund of the Universal African Legion[s]. The Quartermaster of each Division shall receive the tax, issue proper vouchers and turn over the money to the Secretary of the Division, who shall forward it to Headquarters in conjunction with the general report of the parent body.

Sec. 2.   Every Division or Brigade shall bear the expenses of the Staff Officer who shall be sent from Headquarters at the invitation of said Division or Brigade to visit the whole or any unit thereof.

Sec. 3.   Any Division or Brigade may make a weekly collection from its members to finance the working thereof; such collection not to exceed 10 cents weekly for non-commissioned officers and men. Such collections have nothing whatever to do wi[th] the yearly Tax for Headquarters, neither shall it be regarded as Dues of the Local Division.

ARTICLE IX[2]

EXAMINATIONS FOR OFFICE

Section 1.   Any Officer before receiving his commission shall be required to pass an examination by an Examining Board named by the Minister of Legions.

The subjects shall be chosen from the following:—

Georgraphy of Africa.
Topography.
Mathematics.
Languages.
Writing.
Reading.
Signalling, including Morse, Semaphore Telegraphy.

And any other subjects that are necessary for the fulfilment of the duties assigned to the position for which he applies.

Each Officer shall be required to obtain 75 per cent. marks for graduation in his ability test. Each Officer shall also bring with his application 75 per cent. marks for good conduct, i.e., 75 out of a 100 ability and 75 out of a 100 good conduct.

ARTICLE X

DISCIPLINARY POWERS OF OFFICERS IN COMMAND

Section 1.   Under these regulations as ratified by the Second International Convention of the U.N.I.A. & A.C.L., and which shall be from time to time amended by succeeding Conventions, the Commanding Officer of any attachment, company or high command may, for minor offenses not denied by the accused, impose disciplinary punishments upon persons of his command without the intervention of a court-martial, unless the accused demands trial by court-martial.

Sec. 2.   The disciplinary punishments authorized by this Article shall include admonition, reprimand, withholding of privileges, extra fatigue, and

Sec. 3. The Headquarters of the Universal Negro Improvement Association and African Communities' League shall have an official representative Band, which shall be the senior Band of the Organization. The same shall be under the supervision of the Commander-in-Chief at Headquarters.

ARTICLE XV

ELECTION AND APPOINTMENT OF OFFICERS

Section 1. All Officers, except Staff Officers[,] shall be selected by the men of the Legions, examined by the examination Staff of the Minister of Legions and if qualified, commissioned by said Minister.

Sec. 2. All Staff Officers shall be appointed by the Minister of Legions with the approval of the President General.

Sec. 3. An Officer's term of service, if proven capable[,] shall be indefinite unless retired through ill health or old age, or other uncontrollable disability. In such cases an honorary retirement shall be accorded him. If, however, his conduct is faulty or he shall be proven incapable he may be dismissed and another appointed to his place in due process by the Minister of Legions.

ARTICLE XVI

CONDUCT

Section 1. There shall be two classes for conduct in the Universal African Legion[s], i.e., (Good and Bad).

The good shall be designated by "G" which shall mean "Good" and "V.G." which shall mean "Very Good"; these designations shall be placed on their cards under the photographs and shall be entered on the various lists which are compiled of the men and women. The others shall be designated by an "F" which shall mean "Fair" and "B" which shall mean "Bad."

Sec. 2. Good Conduct distinction badges shall be designed for non-commissioned Officers and men by the Minister of Legions' Staff to be worn for each year's service consistent with military regulations. Badges will be awarded only for "G." and "V.G."

Sec. 3. Any members having a clear record without a conviction during the year will receive the "V.G." A charge for which admonition or reprimand is invoked (see Art. X) shall not be registered against him to mar an otherwise good record, but if his convictions entail a withholding of privileges or other punishments it shall be registered and he may at the discretion of the Commanding Officer receive the "G."

Sec. 4. Any member receiving three convictions in a year cannot receive the "G." and forfeits all badges prior obtained. If however, on appeal a conviction or sentence is revoked by a court-martial or a superior Officer to his officer in command, his record shall be clear as regards that sentence or conviction. Five badges shall be the limit worn and shall denote five years continuous good behavior. One badge shall be allowed for every "V.G." up to five.

ARTICLE XVII

LIST OF OFFICERS AND MEN

Section 1. Besides the usual military lists there shall be a trade list designating the number of men listed under the various trades in which they are skilled. A copy of said list shall be kept in the Office of the President General. Each Division shall be required to forward one of these lists to the Minister of Legions at the beginning of each financial year.

ARTICLE XVIII

MILITARY CLASSES AND RETIREMENT

Section 1. Non-commissioned Officers and men for military service shall be divided into three military classes (i.e.), from 18 years to 36, (class 1); from 37 to 49, (class 2); and from 50 and upwards, (class 3).

Sec. 2. Any member after serving five years and at the expiration of that time be passed his 55th birthday may retire from active service with honor.

Sec. 3. Any member past 55 years of age and still feeling fit may be allowed to continue in his military service class. If, however, on medical examination he be pronounced by his Medical Examiner physically unfit, he may be honorably retired by the Commander of his Division or Brigade.

Sec. 4. No member shall be admitted to the ranks who has passed his 55th birthday.

Sec. 5. Each member before receiving his card or commission shall be examined by the Brigade's Medical Officer and proven fit, or if there is no resident Officer he shall produce a bona fide doctor's certificate of health.

ARTICLE XIX

WHEN MEN MAY BE PAID

Section 1. The U.N.I.A. and A.C.L. shall pay salaries to the men of the U.A.L., only when employed by them at the various trades or professions in which they are skilled and registered. The Association shall do its utmost to see that every man of the U.A.L. be put to useful work at his trade or profession for the rehabilitation of the ancient glories of our Motherland, Africa.

ARTICLE XX

UNIFORMS

Section 1. The uniforms of the U.A.L. shall be of one design throughout the world (except where in conflict with local authorities) and shall be that approved at headquarters by the Minister of Legions.

In various climates the materials may be suited to the temperature or climatic conditions, but the designs shall be "universal." The chevrons and other devices for non-commissioned officers and men shall be issued from headquarters only, and no other shall be used.

Sec. 2. Staff officers' uniforms shall be ordered from headquarters only, and all designs and improvements therefor submitted to the Minister of Legions. Every year ratification of the designs of all uniforms or any change therein shall be made by the Minister of Legions immediately after the yearly convention.

ARTICLE XXI

THE NATIONAL ANTHEM AND THE COLORS

Section 1. The National Anthem and the colors of the country in which any division, unit or individual of the U.A.L. is domiciled shall receive due respect and acknowledgement by each individual of the U.A.L., whenever played or presented on official occasions. The flag shall be respected at all times. Disobedience of this rule is a misdemeanor and is punishable by reprimand, withholding of privileges, restrictions or such other punishment as the gravity of the offence may warrant.

Sec. 2. Whenever the National Anthem of the U.N.I.A. and A.C.L., is played, all Officers and men of the U.A.L., in uniform and under the command of a Senior Officer, the Senior Officer alone shall salute while all other men stand at attention. Whenever not under the command of a Senior Officer all men shall salute, the right hand man giving the time. Whenever not in uniform they shall stand at attention and not salute.

ARTICLE XXII

BANKING FUNDS

Section 1. Each Unit of a Division or Brigade shall bank all funds or monies through the local Treasurer of the Division with the Banking Account of the Division. The Quartermaster shall receive from the said Treasurer a duplicate of all monies paid in: one to be kept on his file and a copy to be delivered to the Colonel. Two receipt books shall be kept for this purpose.

That fifty per cent. of the proceeds of all entertainments given by Auxiliaries be turned over to the Division, after all legitimate expenses incurred for such entertainments have been paid. No Auxiliary shall give any entertainment without the permission of the President of the Division.

Sec. 2. All Auxiliaries shall be required to deliver to the Treasurer of the Division all monies derived from entertainments at the first meeting following each entertainment.

Sec. 3. All monies or checks to be drawn through, or from the said Treasurer of the local Division shall have three signatures; the Commander's, the Colonel's and the Quartermaster's. All drafts for monies or checks shall be attested in regular meeting of the Unit before being signed. The Treasurer of the Local shall acknowledge all such legal documents and pay by cash or check to the bearer.

Article XXIII

Obedience and Courtesy

Section 1. Obedience shall be the first duty of a member of the U.A.L. No body of men without discipline and strict obedience of lawful orders can accomplish much.

A lawful order is a command given by a superior Officer relative to the service and not to self.

A superior Officer shall not only be considered by his relationship to the members, regular squadron, platoon or regiment, but of any squadron, platoon, regiment or Staff, or otherwise of the Universal African Legion[s] when in uniform.

Sec. 2. Be courteous. Let love and appreciation of one another be the rule.

For men in the ranks to be discourteous to an Officer is a misdemeanor.

Guard yourself against the enemy. Your greatest enemy and the Organization's greatest enemy is a knocker or a shirker. He can hurt and will hurt you quicker than a hostile enemy. Guard yourself against a knocker or a shirker. Do your duty with a smile on your face. Be courteous.

Sec. 3. Any member subjected to the discipline and control of the U.A.L., found guilty of "disobedience of orders[,]" shall, for first offence, suffer a penalty of twenty-five cents fine in the case of a Private; fifty cents in the case of a non-commissioned Officer; and One Dollar in the case of a commissioned Officer. These fines may be more or less based upon the gravity of the case and the discretion of the presiding Officers of the court-martial. All such fines shall be the property of the Parent Body of the U.N.I.A.

Sec. 4. Any member subjected to discipline and control of the U.A.L. found guilty of "insolence and gross insubordination," shall be liable to a fine of Two Dollars in the case of a Private; Three Dollars in the case of a non-commissioned Officer, and Four Dollars in the case of a Commissioned Officer. The person so fined shall not be permitted to appear in uniform for a fortnight. All such fines shall be the property of the Parent Body of the U.N.I.A.

If a Legionary feels himself wronged by a Corporal, he shall apply to his Sergeant for redress; if wronged by a Sergeant, he shall apply to his Platoon Commander; if wronged by a Platoon Commander, he shall apply to his Company Officer; if wronged by his Company Officer, he shall apply to his Regimental Commander; and if wronged by his Regimental Commander, he shall apply to the Minister of Legions.

Article XXIV

Disciplinary Powers of President-General

Section 1.   The President-General of the Universal Negro Improvement Association and African Communities' League shall have the power after due inquiry by the general membership to instruct the Commander of a local division through the Minister of Legions, or, in his own discretion, to suspend, disband, or in any other manner discipline any Brigade of the Universal African Legion[s], or any auxiliary or unit created by the Universal Negro Improvement Association; if such auxiliary disobeys the Constitution or fails to live up to the rules and regulations issued from the Headquarters of the Universal Negro Improvement Association and African Communities' League for their guidance.

Sec. 2.   No auxiliary, unit, brigade, member or members thereof on trial before a local division shall have a voice in the voting as to the conclusion or outcome of such trial.

Article XXV

Emblem

The Official Coat of Arms of the Universal African Legions shall be a shield or crest bearing the colors of the U.N.I.A. and A.C.L., namely the Red, Black and Green. These shall be arranged perpendicularly on the shield and surrounded by a brilliant sunburst. Above the shield shall be a globe showing the Continent of Africa and below the shield shall be scroll, with the words PRO DEO, PRO AFRICA, PRO JUSTITIA. These words shall be the slogan of the Universal African Legion[s].

Article XXVI

Oath

All members shall be required before receiving their cards or commissions to take the following vow. This vow shall be printed in small type at the back of their cards or at the bottom of their commissions.

The vow to be taken by all members of the Universal Negro Improvement Association and African Communities' League shall be as follows:—

I . . . . , in the presence of the Supreme God of the Universe and all persons here assembled, do solemnly vow, that I do here and now dedicate my whole life to the Universal Negro Improvement Association and African Communities' League and the cause of the redemption of my Mother-land Africa.

That I pledge strict obedience and support to His Highness the Potentate and all other persons designated by him or representing him.

That I shall never disgrace myself or my uniform by insubordination or contemptuous behavior of any kind.

That I shall discreetly and to the best of my ability spiritually, mentally and physically defend the cause of the U.N.I.A. and A.C.L. from all enemies within and without, and also do my utmost to build up and protect the morale of its members to the end that God's Divine purpose be speedily accomplished in the ultimate freedom of all mankind from slavery and despoliation and particularly the cause of the Redemption of Africa.

Rules and Regulations Governing the Universal African Black Cross Nurses

ARTICLE I

NAME

This Auxiliary of the Universal Negro Improvement Association shall be named the Universal African Black Cross Nurses.

ARTICLE II

OBJECT

Section 1.   The Objects of this Auxiliary shall be to carry on a system of relief and to apply the same in mitigating the suffering caused by pestilence, famine, fire, floods, and other great calamities, and to devise and carry on measures for preventing same.

Sec. 2.   To attend to the sick of the Division to which the public Auxiliary is attached and be ready for service at any time when called upon by His Highness the Potentate.

Sec. 3.   To issue pamphlets which will tend to educate the public to the use of safety devices and prevention of accident; to instruct in sanitation for prevention of epidemics; and to instruct in First Aid.

ARTICLE III

MEMBERSHIP

Section 1.   All women of Negro Blood and African Descent between the ages of sixteen and forty-five may become members of this Auxiliary.

Sec. 2.   Only active members of the Universal Negro Improvement Association shall be admitted to membership in this Auxiliary.

Sec. 3.   All women of the Race not desiring active membership may become honorary members upon payment of One Dollar or more Annually.

Sec. 4.   All men of the Race shall be permitted to become Honorary members of this Auxiliary upon payment of One Dollar or more Annually.

Sec. 5.   All Honorary members shall be known as Annual or Sustaining members.

ARTICLE IV

MANAGEMENT—CENTRAL AND LOCAL

Section 1.   The management and direction of this Auxiliary shall be entrusted to a Central Committee which shall consist of the President-General of the U.N.I.A.; a Universal Directress, who shall be a graduate Nurse of at least three years' experience; a Surgeon-General, who shall be a Bacteriologist; the Secretary-General of the U.N.I.A.[;] and the Presidents of local Divisions.

Sec. 2.   The Presidents of local Divisions shall exercise over their Units the same power of control as the Central Committee exercises over the whole Auxiliary.

Sec. 3.   All members of the High Executive Council shall be ex-officio members of the Central Committee.

Sec. 4.   The Surgeon-General shall be the Medical Director of this Auxiliary.

Sec. 5.   Each Unit of this Auxiliary shall have the following Officers: A Matron, who shall be the Lady President of the Division and Superintendent of the Auxiliary; a Head Nurse, who shall be the President of the Unit; a Secretary[;] and a Treasurer.

ARTICLE V

REVENUES AND INCOMES

Section 1.   The funds for the maintenance of this Auxiliary shall be known as "General and Special."

Sec. 2.   The General Fund shall be derived from such sources as Annual membership dues and Sustaining membership dues. The entire amount of dues of members at large shall be forwarded to Headquarters. Besides the membership dues, it shall be further derived from the interest on bank balances of the various units, the generous annual contributions given for several purposes from members or other individuals and the profits of sales of supplies and materials of all kinds.

Sec. 3.   The General Fund shall be used for the Administration expenses at the Office of Headquarters; Maintenance of First Aid Instructions; Supplies for the Nursing Service and Women's Classes in home care of the sick[;] and for all expenses in connection with the pamphlets or magazines issued by this Auxiliary and which every member shall receive.

Sec. 4.   The Special Fund shall be derived from special appeals made by or through the Central Committee.

Sec. 5.   Each local Unit shall be privileged to raise funds among its own Community for local purposes and the appeal for such funds shall only be made in the name of the local Unit. These funds may be derived from lectures, entertainments and other social functions of an innocent nature. The raising of such funds by a local Unit shall only be with the permission of the President of the local Division.

Sec. 6. All monies raised by a local Unit shall pass through the hands of the Secretary of the Unit to the Treasurer of the Unit. The Treasurer of the Unit shall then turn over such monies to the Treasurer of the Division through the General Secretary of said Division, to be lodged to the credit of the Unit in the name of the Division at the Bank designated.

Sec. 7. All monies raised by this Auxiliary shall remain in the hands of its Treasurer for a period not exceeding twenty-four hours.

ARTICLE VI

SOLICITING AND COLLECTING

No person or persons shall solicit or collect funds or materials in the name of the Universal African Black Cross Nurses unless authorized to do so and bear credentials properly signed by the President of the local Division; the Matron of the Unit, or the signatures of the Officers of the Central Body. All such credentials must bear the Seal of the Division from which the appeal is issued or the Seal of the Parent Body of the Universal Negro Improvement Association.

ARTICLE VII

UNIFORM

Each active member of this Auxiliary shall supply herself with her own uniform.

ARTICLE VIII

EMBLEMS

Section 1. Each member of this Auxiliary shall wear its emblem on a button as an indication of membership.

Sec. 2. The official button of this Auxiliary shall be a Black Latin Cross on a Red background enclosed by a Green Circle around the border.

Sec. 3. The official emblem of this Auxiliary shall be a Black Latin Cross encircled by a Red background in the center of a Green field.

Rules and Regulations Governing the Universal African Motor Corps

Article I

Name

This Auxiliary of the Universal Negro Improvement Association shall be named the Universal African Motor Corps.

Article II

Object

The object of this Auxiliary shall be to assist the Universal African Legions in the performance of their duties.

Article III

Membership and Instructions

Section 1. All active members of the Universal Negro Improvement Association between the ages of sixteen and forty-five may become members of this Auxiliary. The male membership shall, however, be confined to only those who are in active command of the units of the various Divisions. All commissioned Officers above the rank of Major shall automatically be Officers of this Auxiliary.

Sec. 2. This Auxiliary shall be trained in "Military Discipline" by the Officers of the Universal African Legions. They shall also be given such Automobile instructions as: driving, repairs, etc.

Article IV

Management

Section 1. The Universal Head of the Motor Corps shall be a Brigadier-General, who shall be a Lady. She shall be fairly educated and shall be a trained and licensed Chauffeur. She shall be attached to the office of the Minister of Legions.

Sec. 2. The local Officers of this Auxiliary shall be a Captain, a First and Second Lieutenant and such non-commissioned Officers as may be found necessary. The Captain shall be the President of the Unit and the First and Second Lieutenants shall be its Secretary and Treasurer respectively.

Sec. 3. All Divisional staff Officers, meaning Commander and the active head of each Unit of the Universal African Legion[s] shall be ranking Officers of this Auxiliary.

Rules and Regulations for Juveniles

ARTICLE I

INFANT CLASS
(1 YEAR TO 7 YEARS)
SUBJECTS:

Bible Class and Prayer. Doctrine of the U.N.I.A. and A.C.L. Facts about the Black Star Line Steamship Corporation, The Negro Factories Corporation, and History of Africa (in story book fashion).

CLASS 2 OR GIRLS' SOUVENIR CLASS
(AGE 7 YEARS TO 13 YEARS)
SUBJECTS:

Taught to make Souvenirs with cloth, needle and thread, for sale for Juvenile Department. Ritual of Universal Negro Improvement Association. Write Negro stories, taught Race pride and love. Taught Negro history and Etiquette and be given disciplinary training by the Legions.

CLASS 2 OR BOYS' SOUVENIR CLASS
(AGE 7 YEARS TO 13 YEARS)
SUBJECTS:

Will be given same training as girls of No. 2 Class, the only difference being that the boys of this class shall make souvenirs with wood and carved with tools instead of with needle.

U.N.I.A. & A.C.L. CADETS
(AGE 13 YEARS TO 16 YEARS)
TRAINING:

Ritual of U.N.I.A.; Military Training; Flag signaling; Negro History. (Books advised) "From Superman to Man," "White Capital and Colored Labor," "When Africa Awakes," "African Lore and Lyrics." This class must be taught by a member of the Legions who is acquainted with military tactics.

THE PREPARATORY NURSING CLASS
(AGE 14 YEARS TO 18 YEARS)
TRAINING:

Making uniforms for Juveniles; Negro History; Etiquette; Talk on latest topics of the day; Elementary principles of Economy; Negro Story Writing; Hygiene and Domestic Science.

This Class shall be taught in three Divisions or Classes; namely 14 years to 15 years; 16 years to 17 years; 18 years to finishing class. It shall be trained by the Black Cross Nurses.

ARTICLE II

LAWS FOR CHILDREN

Section 1.   All Juveniles of Divisions and Societies of the U.N.I.A. shall show high respect to all Officers of the Association and respect for teachers in charge of Class.

Sec. 2.   No Juvenile shall be allowed to talk, laugh or carry on any mischief while classes are in session, but must sit to attention to instruction so as to get the benefit thereof.

Sec. 3.   Any Juvenile found using profane or bad language or becoming unruly and disrespectful to his or her officer in charge shall be reported to Superintendent of Juveniles by teacher in charge and Superintendent, through Secretary, notify parents of child's conduct. If parents fail to correct child and he or she continues, same shall be expelled by Superintendent of Juveniles.

ARTICLE III

LAWS FOR TEACHERS

Section 1.   Teachers must meet once a week previous to meeting of general body of Juveniles to receive instructions, to familiarize themselves with the working of their class and department.

Sec. 2.   All teachers shall be appointed by the President of the local Division.

Sec. 3.   The Juvenile Department shall operate under the jurisdiction of the Division.

Sec. 4.   The Superintendent of Juveniles shall see that all reports are kept properly so as to avoid disputes. The Superintendent shall also have an assistant to aid in the working of its department.

Sec. 5.   The First Assistant shall be held responsible to the Superintendent for working of the department and meetings over which she presides. The Superintendent shall be held responsible to the President of the local Division.

ARTICLE IV

LOCAL STAFF

Section 1.   The Superintendent shall be a Lady Vice-President. The First Assistant shall be a loyal member. The Secretary shall be one of the best learned Juveniles (male or female). The Teachers shall be loyal members of local Divisions. Cadet Class Teacher shall be a member of the Legions and shall know all military tactics. The Preparatory Nurse Class shall have two teachers and one shall be a trained Black Cross Nurse and a responsible lady.

The Lady President of the local Division shall be the "Honorary Superintendent of the Juveniles."

Sec. 2.   There shall be a Treasurer of each local Division. All monies raised by the Juveniles shall be handed over to him (or her) through its Secretary to be turned over to the Treasurer of the Division through the Secretary of the Division to be deposited in the bank of said Division.

The Juvenile Treasurer shall not keep in his possession monies belonging to the Juveniles for a period exceeding twenty-four hours.

Rules for the Universal Negro Improvement Association Choirs

ARTICLE I

NAMES AND OBJECTS

Section 1.   This Auxiliary shall be known as the Universal Negro Improvement Association Choir. It shall consist of men and women who are active members of the Universal Negro Improvement Association and African Communities' League.

Sec. 2.   Its object shall be to furnish vocal talent in the form of solos, duets, trios, quartettes, quintettes, choruses, etc., for the various meetings and services held by the organization as may be expedient.

ARTICLE II

OFFICERS AND THEIR DUTIES

Section 1.   The officers shall be a President, a Secretary-Librarian, a Treasurer and a Musical Instructor, who shall not be the President.

Sec. 2.   Besides the foregoing officers mentioned in Section 1 of this Article, there shall be a leading soprano, a mezzo soprano, a leading alto, a first tenor and basso profundo, and a pianist and assistant instructor.

Sec. 3.   The duties of the musical instructor shall be to instruct the choir in music.

Sec. 4.   The duties of the President shall be to supervise at all meetings, rehearsals, services and other functions, and manage all affairs pertaining to the choir and its obligations to the organization.

Sec. 5.   The duties of the Secretary-Librarian are to keep a record of the members of the choir, their attendance to rehearsals, services, etc., for the information of the President of the Division. He shall write all notices, attend to the general correspondence and keep a record of the properties of the Choir. He shall receive all contributions and moneys of the Choir and turn same over to the Treasurer. He shall be solely responsible for the distribution and collection of all music designated for use on any occasion.

ARTICLE III

TERM OF OFFICE

Section 1.   The term of office for all officers shall be as long as they give satisfactory services to the membership.

ARTICLE IV

DECORUM

Section 1.   The strictest decorum must be observed by each member of the choir during all services and other functions. Any member misconducting himself shall be reprimanded by the Musical Instructor for the first offense, suspended for one month for the second offense and dismissed altogether from the choir for the third offense.

Sec. 2.   Any member absenting himself or herself for three consecutive weeks or failing to attend six rehearsals consecutively, except through sickness, forfeits automatically his or her membership in the choir.

Sec. 3.   Members failing to attend rehearsals may sing at the service, or concert rehearsals only by special permission from the Musical Instructor. If not granted they must not sit with the choir at that particular service or concert.

Sec. 4.   Any insubordinate to an officer shall be charged with disorderly conduct, especially if that officer be at the time discharging his or her duty.

Sec. 5.   Officers are expected to conduct themselves with propriety in the execution of their duties and shall not molest members of the choir unnecessarily.

Sec. 6.   Any officer absenting himself or herself from three consecutive rehearsals except by permission of the President of the Division or on account of sickness, shall forfeit automatically his or her office.

ARTICLE V

SICKNESS

Section 1.   Any member taken sick shall immediately see, if possible, that the Secretary-Librarian is notified either by letter, by announcement or otherwise.

Sec. 2.   The Secretary-Librarian shall announce all sick members at meetings, rehearsals of services, and a committee shall be appointed to visit them.

Sec. 3.   Members shall make it their duty to visit individually all sick comrades and to spare no pains to do anything to alleviate their sufferings, regardless of whatever aid they may receive from the Association.

ARTICLE VI

UNIFORM

Section 1. All members having surplices must wear them. The uniform appearance of the Choir must be preserved. Non-observance of this rule will be regarded as a misconduct.

ARTICLE VII

MUSIC

Section 1. The Local Division shall furnish the music to be used by its Choir on all occasions (except solo work for salaried soloists), such music to remain the property of the organization.

ARTICLE VIII

Section 1. The members of the Choir shall do their utmost to promote and preserve the harmony with all the other auxiliaries comprising the Universal Negro Improvement Association and African Communities' League, bearing in mind at all times that there is but One God, One Aim, One Destiny.

Constitution and Book of Laws, revised and amended in August 1921. Printed document.

1. Only the revisions to the UNIA Constitution have been printed. For the 1918 Constitution, see *Garvey Papers* 1:256–281; for the 1920 amendments, see *Garvey Papers* 2:677–681.

2. The 1921 Constitution inadvertently omitted article 8. This error was corrected in the 1922 revisions to the Constitution.

APPENDIX II

Finances of the Black Star Line, Incorporated

The following tables setting out the financial state of the Black Star Line, Incorporated, up to the end of the period covered in the present volume are excerpted from four government exhibits (nos. 134, 137, 138 and 142) printed in *Marcus Garvey* v. *United States* (no. 8317, Ct. App., 2d Cir., 2 February 1925). The tables were constructed by four government accountants, who worked full-time for two months, from stock ledgers, cashbooks, journals, vouchers, and minute books obtained under court subpoena. In the end, an entirely new ledger of the corporation's finances was produced.

Monthly Summary of Shares of Stock Issued, Cancelled, Transferred and Outstanding.

	Shares Issued	*Shares Cancelled*	*Shares Transferred*	*Shares Outstanding*
1919				
July	587	4	—	583
August	1,401	60	—	1,341
September	5,530	147	—	5,383
October	11,182	172	—	11,010
November	8,090	77	—	8,013
December	10,352	121	—	10,231
	37,142	581	—	36,561
1920				
January	9,694	150	36	9,508
February	8,192	127	115	7,950
March	10,494	55	254	10,185
April	8,357	18	36	8,303

Monthly Summary of Shares of Stock Issued, Cancelled, Transferred and Outstanding (Continued)

	Shares Issued	Shares Cancelled	Shares Transferred	Shares Outstanding
May	6,856	135	82	6,639
June	5,146	58	6	5,082
	85,881	1,124	529	84,228
July	5,690	41	46	5,603
August	4,714	35	14	4,665
September	5,233	44	25	5,164
October	4,305	86	37	4,180
November	2,615	34	16	2,565
December	2,971	13	—	2,958
	111,407	1,377	667	109,363
1921				
January	3,526	107	18	3,401
February	4,369	52	51	4,266
March	5,087	42	13	5,032
April	5,188	65	9	5,114
May	2,560	7	2	2,551
June	2,830	16	1	2,813
	134,967	1,666	761	132,540
July	15,389	13	5	15,371
August	1,074	11	1	1,062
	151,430	1,690	767	148,973

Statement of Total Income and Expense
1 July 1919 to 30 June 1921

	Period to June 30, 1920		*Year ending June 30, 1921*	
Operating Income:				
S/S Yarmouth	[$]44,779.71		[$]13,340.25	
Shadyside	2,882.63		3,306.67	
Kanawha	98.25		1,109.38	
Gross operating income		47,760.59		17,756.80
Operating Expense:				
S/S Yarmouth	138,469.55		54,644.12	
Shadyside	8,120.28		8,946.45	
Kanawha	4,060.83		117,678.36	
		150,650.66		181,268.93
Operating Loss		102,890.07		163,512.13
Office Expense (see attached)		68,329.02		55,865.89
Stock selling expense (see attached)		63,576.82		25,193.93
		234,795.91		244,571.95
Less forfeited partial payments on stock		—		35,115.61
Deficit:		234,795.91		209,456.34

Statement of Total Income and Expense
1 July 1919 to 30 June 1921

	Period to June 30, 1920	*Year ending June 30, 1921*
Office Expense:		
Rent	[$]550.00	[$]35,449.95
Salaries	34,783.61	6,316.16
Books, stationery, postage, printing	9,283.54	6,316.16
Light and heat	355.96	70.80
Telephone & telegraph	1,119.76	433.69
Legal & prof[*essional*]	8,539.56	6,636.00
Interest & discount	288.17	1,423.58
Real Estate expense	3,764.71	338.75
General	9,643.71	5,196.96
	68,329.02	55,865.89
Stock Selling Expense:		
Rent halls, etc.	6,437.47	100.00
Music	10,518.20	11,419.35
Travelling	10,649.26	8,177.97
Com. & Salaries	2,397.45	1,925.01
Stamp revenue	505.00	1,182.19
Advertising	23,369.63	3,855.45
Miscellaneous	16,724.13	1,308.50
Less miscellaneous income	[7]0,601.14	27,968.47
(a) Miscellaneous income deducted	70,601.14	27,968.47

Marcus Garvey v. *United States*, no. 8317, Ct. App., 2d Cir., 2 February 1925, government exhibit no. 137, p. 2,650.

Statement of Assets and Liabilities, at Periods Stated Below, from Analysis of Cash Book, Etc.

	December 20, 1919		June 30, 1920		June 30, 1921	
	Assets	Liabilities	Assets	Liabilities	Assets	Liabilities
Assets:						
S/S Yarmouth	[$]108,201.95		[$]189,361.65		[$]189,842.90	
Kanawha	—		66,761.47		75,339.45	
Shadyside	—		35,000.00		35,000.00	
Phyllis Wheatley					25,000.00	
Real Estate	2,500.00		26,665.00		26,665.00	
Furniture & Fixtures	1,093.75		4,681.44		6,120.23	
Delivery Equipment	1,262.81		4,440.16		4,440.16	
Total Fixed Assets	113,058.51		326,909.72		362,407.74	
Cash	8,213.04		2,025.23		1,550.31	
Loans Receivable	1,902.64		13,742.44		14,814.99	
Building Fund Notes	—		—		1,378.57	
Liberian Construction Loan	—		—		—	
Liabilities:						
Capital Stock issued		188,470.87		406,310.50		$84,812.70
Capital Stock part paid		—		32,585.98		14,611.15
Capital Stock Agents returns		—		—		38,782.43
		188,470.87		438,896.48		638,206.28

Statement of Assets and Liabilities, at Periods Stated Below, from Analysis of Cash Book, Etc. (Continued)

	December 20, 1919		June 30, 1920		June 30, 1921	
	Assets	Liabilities	Assets	Liabilities	Assets	Liabilities
Less Deficit		65,296.68		234,795.91		234,795.91
Less Deficit						209,456.34
		123,174.19		204,100.57		193,954.03
Mortgages payable		—		21,500.00		19,400.00
Notes payable		—		117,076.82		70,930.22
Loans payable		—		—		84,078.11
Account payable		—		—		4,500.00
Unearned passage Liberia		—		—		7,289.25
TOTAL ASSETS	123,174.19		342,677.39		380,151.61	
TOTAL LIABILITIES		123,174.19		342,677.39		380,151.61

Marcus Garvey v. United States, no. 8317, Ct. App., 2d Cir., 2 February 1925, government exhibit no. 138, p. 2,652.

Payments on Contract Prices of S/S Yarmouth, Shadyside and Kanawha, Showing Balances Due on Given Dates

Date	YARMOUTH		SHADYSIDE		KANAWHA		TOTAL	
	Paid	Due	Paid	Due	Paid	Due	Paid	Due
1919								
Sept. 15	[$]16,500	[$]148,500	⋯	⋯	⋯	⋯	[$]16,500	[$]148,500
Oct. 20	3,500	148,500	⋯	⋯	⋯	⋯	20,000	148,500
Oct. 31	50,000	98,500	⋯	⋯	⋯	⋯	70,000	98,500
Nov. 24	23,000	75,500	⋯	⋯	⋯	⋯	93,000	75,500
1920								
Jan. 10	20,000	55,500	⋯	⋯	⋯	⋯	113,000	55,500
Mar. 24	⋯	⋯	2,000	33,000	⋯	⋯	115,000	88,500
Apr. 10	⋯	⋯	8,000	25,000	⋯	⋯	123,000	80,500
Apr. 24	⋯	⋯	⋯	⋯	5,000	55,000	128,000	135,500
May 4	⋯	⋯	2,000	23,000	⋯	⋯	130,000	133,500
May 17	9,000	46,500	⋯	⋯	⋯	⋯	139,000	124,500
May 25	⋯	⋯	⋯	⋯	10,000	45,000	149,000	114,500
June 7	⋯	⋯	2,000	21,000	⋯	⋯	151,000	112,500
July 10	⋯	⋯	⋯	⋯	7,500	37,500	158,500	105,000
July 14	⋯	⋯	2,000	19,000	⋯	⋯	160,500	103,000
July 17	4,950	41,350	⋯	⋯	⋯	⋯	165,450	98,050
July 26	4,950	36,600	⋯	⋯	⋯	⋯	170,400	93,100

Payments on Contract Prices of S/S Yarmouth, Shadyside and Kanawha, Showing Balances
Due on Given Dates (Continued)

Date	YARMOUTH Paid	Due	SHADYSIDE Paid	Due	KANAWHA Paid	Due	TOTAL Paid	Due
Aug. 6	....	....	....	....	5,000	32,500	175,400	88,100
Aug. 12	....	....	....	....	2,500	30,000	177,900	85,600
Aug. 25	....	....	2,000	17,000	....	....	179,900	83,600
Nov. 3	2,000	34,600	....	....	....	....	181,900	81,600
Nov. 9	950	33,650	....	....	....	....	182,850	80,650
Nov. 17	....	....	1,000	16,000	....	....	183,850	79,650
Nov. 30	....	....	1,000	15,000	....	....	184,850	78,650
Dec. 3	1,000	32,650	....	....	1,500	28,500	187,350	76,150
Dec. 11	1,000	31,650	....	....	....	....	188,350	75,150
Dec. 21	500	31,150	....	....	....	....	188,850	74,650
Dec. 28	....	....	....	....	7,500	21,000	196,350	67,150
1921								
Jan. 15	1,000	30,150	....	....	....	....	197,350	66,150
Jan. 20	....	....	....	....	5,000	16,000	202,350	61,150
Jan. 24	500	29,650	....	....	....	....	202,850	60,650
Jan. 31	500	29,150	....	....	2,500	13,500	205,850	57,650
Feb. 8	500	28,650	....	....	....	....	206,350	57,150
Feb. 18	500	28,150	....	....	....	....	206,850	56,650
Feb. 21	....	....	....	....	4,000	9,500	210,850	52,650

Date							
Mar. 3	1,000	27,150	....	....	....	211,850	51,650
Mar. 10	500	26,650	....	....	....	212,350	51,150
Mar. 18	500	26,150	....	....	....	212,850	50,650
Mar. 25	500	25,650	....	....	....	213,350	50,150
Apr. 1	500	25,150	....	....	....	213,850	49,650
Apr. 26	....	....	2,000	2,000	7,500	215,850	47,650
May 2	....	....	2,000	2,000	5,500	217,850	45,650
May 17	....	....	1,000	1,000	4,500	218,850	44,650
May 21	....	....	1,000	1,000	3,500	219,850	43,650
May 25	....	....	1,000	1,000	2,500	220,850	42,650
May 28	....	....	1,000	1,000	1,500	221,850	41,650
June 18	....	....	1,000	1,000	500	222,850	40,650
June 29	....	....	1,000	1,000	500	OP 223,850	39,650
July 9	....	....	1,000	1,000	1,500	OP 224,850	38,650
Paid	143,350		20,000	15,000	61,500		
Leaving unpaid		25,150					
Less overpaid					1,500	OP	38,650

Marcus Garvey v. United States, no. 8317, Ct. App., 2d Cir., 2 February 1925, government exhibit no. 142, p. 2,657.

APPENDIX III

Bureau of Investigation Summary of the Minutes of Black Star Line Board of Directors' Meetings, 20 October 1920–26 July 1921

STOCK SELLING PLANS (FROM MINUTE BOOK):

At a meeting of the Board of Directors October 20, 1920, the President (MARCUS GARVEY) informed the Board of the conduct of H. R. Watkis, salesman for the BLACK STAR LINE who in his report of receipts and disbursements had submitted an item of $300. as "Paid to Court." The President denied knowledge of any case that required payment of such an amount or that he had authorized it. Mr. Watkis stated that he was arrested in Youngstown, Ohio, on suspicion together with Dr. J. D. Brooks and on the following morning paid $300. to two men and were released. Ordered that Watkis give a note for $300. to be paid in instalments of $5. a week.

At a meeting of the Board of Directors May 28, 1921, Mr. Garcia (Secretary) requested the Board to outline the statement to be made to the public since the various announcements made (of the sailing of the S.S. Phyllis Wheatley) were not going to be kept. Mr. Garcia also stated that owing to the conditions created by the delay in having the boat and the failure of the company to produce said boat on the various dates given to the public, the returns from the field were decreasing rapidly with but very little hope of improvement unless a sound and reasonable explanation was given.

Matthews, Toote and Garcia appointed a committee to prepare such statement, Smith and Thompson added and to consult with Mr. Nolan about the whole matter.

At a meeting of the Board of Directors June 9, 1921, the Committee reported they had related the whole matter to Mr. Nolan and pointed out that owing to the fact that the N.Y. Shipping Exchange had defaulted their contract the company was considering to call off the negotiations for the purchase of the S.S. Phyllis Wheatley and withdraw its deposit in escrow. Mr. Nolan advised the company not to do so, etc.

Mr. O. M. Thompson informed the Board that a communication had reached him the night before from the N.Y. Shipping Exchange through Mr. Silverston that the papers were signed in Washington and the vessel secured. He made known that since the contract with the N.Y. Shipping Exchange calls for delivery in New York all expenses in connection with bringing the ship to New York were to be met by the N.Y. Shipping Exchange but that to help our propaganda he had obtained the authorization to place on the ship our own crew.

After weighing carefully the prospects of financial results in Philadelphia, the Board decided that the S.S. Phyllis Wheatley stop at Philadelphia, also that the boat stop at Norfolk half a day. Committees appointed to stage meetings at both places and take care of campaign to be waged in connection with the visit of the boat:

For Norfolk—Mr. Toote and Dr. Gordon.
Philadelphia—Dr. Eason, Captn. Gaines and Mr. Garcia.

Mr. Thompson suggested and the Board approved that invitations be sent to a number of prominent men of the Race to a luncheon on the S.S. Phyllis Wheatley on July 4th, pointing out that the high standard of the ship cannot fail to impress their minds to our benefit and therefore secure their future financial and moral support. Committee on invitations—Mr. Smith, Mat[t]hews, Dr. Ellegor and Thompson.

Understanding that the S.S. Phyllis Wheatley would reach New York about June 26th, it was decided that a campaign be launched in New York from June 26 to July 4th. During this period effort to be made for the sales of stock and the sale of 30,000 tickets of admission on the ship at the cost of one dollar. Campaign committee—Dr. Stewart, Mr. Yearwood, Dr. Brooks, Mr. Walters, Mr. H. V. Plummer, Dr. Ellegor, Mr. Tobias, Miss Jenkins and Mr. Garcia.

At the regular stockholders meeting held July 26, 1921, the President (MARCUS GARVEY) gave stockholders a lengthy report of his trip to the West Indies and Central America for the purpose of developing new business and bringing new investment and related some of his unfortunate experience on board the S.S. Kanawha due to the incompetency and disloyalty of the crew.

From Thomas P. Merrilees, "Summary Report of Investigation of the Books and Records of the Black Star Line, Inc., and the Universal Negro Improvement Association, involving Marcus Garvey, Elie Garcia, George Tobias, and Orlando M. Thompson, in Violations of Sections 215 and 37 U.S.C.C., Under the Title 'U.S. vs. Marcus Garvey, et al.' " 26 October 1922, DJ-FBI.

APPENDIX IV

Delegates to the 1921 UNIA Convention

The following are some of the delegates whose names appeared in accounts of the convention printed in the *Negro World* and in the records of the Bureau of Investigation. In some cases, spellings have been standardized.

John C. Armstrong
Carrie Ashford
Reynold F. Austin
J. D. Barber
John G. Bayne
Clifford S. Bourne
I. Newton Brathwaite
A. D. Brown
John E. Bruce
Arden Bryan
Collins A. Bryce
Percival Burrows
Mr. Cargill
T. J. Carr
G. Emonei Carter
Florence Cochran
Harold A. Collins
John Collins
Rev. J. J. Cranston
George D. Creese
Arnold S. Cunning
W. D. Daniels
Henrietta Vinton Davis
John Sydney de Bourg
J. Deleon
Rev. J. R. L. Diggs

Mrs. H. A. Dowden
Dr. Charles Harris Duvall
Clara Earle
Rev. J. W. H. Eason
Rev. Francis W. Ellegor
William H. Ferris
Bruce Forbes
Arnold J. Ford
Lionel Francis
Napoleon J. Francis
Emmett L. Gaines
Elie Garcia
Marcus Garvey
Dr. J. D. Gibson
Fanny Giles
J. C. Gill
T. C. Glashen
T. H. Golden
Newton Goodridge
John Dawson Gordon
Dr. Walter S. Hannah
W. O. Harper
Ludwig Harrigan
Samuel A. Haynes
Allen Hobbs
Wesley McDonald Holder

J. D. Horton
William Isles
A. A. Johnson
Adrian F. Johnson
Gabriel M. Johnson
Joseph Johnson
Mary E. Johnson
P. E. Johnson
Wiley Kimbrough
George O. Marke
Prince Alfred McConnery
George Alexander McGuire
Rev. Samuel McIntyre
William Matthews
Edward V. Morales
Robert B. Mosely
Georgiana O'Brien
John O'Loughlin
James A. O'Meally
A. Parker
Rev. P. E. Paul
William Phillips
Robert L. Poston
U. S. Poston
Alfred Potter
Rena Powell
Frank O. Raines
C. A. Reid

Richard E. Riley
Rev. E. D. Roberts
Maggie M. Scott
Jacob Slappey
Rudolph E. B. Smith
Wilford H. Smith
G. E. Stewart
Elizabeth Sutton
George Taite
A. Taylor
Noah D. Thompson
Orlando M. Thompson
D. E. Thorpe
George Tobias
Richard H. Tobitt
Frederick A. Toote
H. W. Tucker
Philip Van Putten
William A. Wallace
Beatrice Washington
Dr. J. A. Waters
Rev. J. M. Webb
Edgar C. West
George A. Weston
Marie P. Williams
Shedrick Williams
Vernal J. Williams
James B. Yearwood

Convention Delegates by Division

CALIFORNIA

Los Angeles

John Dawson Gordon
Wiley Kimbrough
Noah D. Thompson

CONNECTICUT

Hartford

Mary E. Johnson

FLORIDA

Miami

George Emonei Carter

INDIANA

J. D. Barber

MASSACHUSETTS

Boston

Dr. Charles H. Duvall
Dr. J. D. Gibson
William Phillips
George A. Weston

MARYLAND

Baltimore

Rev. J. R. L. Diggs

MISSOURI

Frank O. Raines
Marie P. Williams

MINNESOTA

St. Paul

T. J. Carr

NEW JERSEY

Atlantic City

Carrie Ashford

Newark

John O'Loughlin
Elizabeth Sutton

NEW YORK

Brooklyn

Reynold F. Austin

Buffalo

Collins A. Bryce

New York City

John G. Bayne
I. Newton Brathwaite
John E. Bruce
Mr. Cargill
Henrietta Vinton Davis
Rev. Francis W. Ellegor
William H. Ferris
Arnold J. Ford
E. L. Gaines
Elie Garcia
Marcus Garvey
J. C. Gill
Ludwig Harrigan
William Isles
Adrian F. Johnson
George Alexander McGuire
William Matthews
Rev. P. E. Paul
Wilford H. Smith
G. E. Stewart
A. Taylor
O. M. Thompson
George Tobias
Vernal J. Williams

OHIO

Cleveland

Florence Cochran
Wesley McD. Holder
William Sherrill
Shedrick Williams
Mr. Edgar C. West

Youngstown

W. O. Harper

PENNSYLVANIA

Philadelphia

J. Deleon
Rev. J. W. H. Eason
Bruce Forbes
Lionel Francis
Dr. Walter S. Hannah
Frederick A. Toote

Pittsburgh

Rev. J. J. Cranston
Jacob Slappey

TENNESSEE

T. C. Glashen

VIRGINIA

Newport News

Samuel A. Haynes

Norfolk

Allen Hobbs

FOREIGN DIVISIONS

Barbados

Arden Bryan

British Guiana

Richard H. Tobitt

Canada

George D. Creese
Georgiana O'Brien
Alfred Potter
Richard E. Riley

Cuba

Harold A. Collins, Banes
Arnold S. Cunning
Edward V. Morales
George Taite, Preston

Guatemala

Clifford S. Bourne

Haiti

Napoleon J. Francis

Jamaica

James A. O'Meally

Liberia

Gabriel M. Johnson

Panama

C. A. Reid

Santo Domingo

Philip Van Putten

Sierra Leone

George O. Marke

West Africa

J. D. Horton

West Indies

Rudolph E. B. Smith
James B. Yearwood

DELEGATES,
AFFILIATION UNKNOWN

John C. Armstrong
A. D. Brown
Percival Burrows
John Collins
W. D. Daniels
Mrs. H. A. Dowden
Clara Earle
Fanny Giles
T. H. Golden
Newton Goodridge

A. A. Johnson
Joseph Johnson
P. E. Johnson
Prince Alfred McConnery
Rev. Samuel McIntyre
Robert B. Mosely
A. Parker
Rena Powell
Rev. E. D. Roberts
H. W. Tucker
Beatrice Washington
Dr. J. A. Waters
Rev. J. M. Webb

INDEX

A Note on the Index

An asterisk (*) precedes annotated biographical entries found in the text. A page number followed by an *n* with a digit indicates that the entry appears in the footnote cited. An entry that appears both in the text and in a footnote on the same page is indicated by the page number only, except in the case of an annotated entry. Bibliographical information can be found in the annotations that accompany the text.

When there are variant spellings of a name, the accepted spelling is used; in other instances, where there is no generally accepted usage, the spelling which seems most correct is given. Variants have not been indexed. Women are indexed under the name that first appears in the text; married names are indicated by parentheses, as, Ashwood, Amy (Garvey). Cross-references to both married and maiden names are supplied. Titled persons are indexed by title, with the family name following in parentheses if necessary.

Government agencies are listed by name. However, cross-references to the appropriate cabinet-level department are provided, as, United States Department of Justice, *See also* Bureau of Investigation.

Abd-el-Krim, 667 n. 2
Abyssinia, 309
Abyssinian riot, 174
Acosta, Julio, *379 n. 1
Adee, Alvey A., 277, 367, 422
Africa, 10, 23–24, 95, 384, 550, 630; for Africans, 16, 20, 21, 26, 42, 43, 53, 151, 175, 229, 317, 368, 411, 480, 560, 561–562, 582, 588, 611, 662, 666, 735, 738, 739–740; anthem of, 129, 213, 648, 652 n. 1; Canada and, 195, 196–197, 199, 208, 209, 210, 213; Christ in, 304; civilization in, 308–309; colonized, 77–79, 152, 198, 204 n. 6, 207–209 (*see also* Back to Africa movement; Liberia, UNIA emigration program in); as continent of light, 211; duty to, 73, 76–81; Europe in, 8, 195–199, 200, 201, 202, 203 n. 2, 206, 207, 208, 209, 210, 213, 309–310, 324, 328 n. 3, 666, 738; exploited, 198–200, 201; flag of, 42, 163, 165, 173, 541–542, 588–589, 603; Garvey plans to go to, 146, 231, 232, 234, 387; Garvey's influence in, xxxvi, 608; government for, 150, 380, 385–386,

389; imperialism in, 228–230; mandates in, 735, 739; missionaries in, 323; president of (*see* Garvey, Marcus, as provisional president of Africa); race war in, 356–357 n. 1; redemption of, 9, 73, 96, 144–145, 151, 160, 161, 162, 167, 207, 208, 209, 213–214, 215, 240, 273, 274, 374, 381, 404, 407, 408, 509, 528, 529, 576, 577, 579, 596, 599–600, 659, 660, 662, 663–664, 665, 734, 744–745; religion in, 309; republic of, 174, 259, 589–590; slavery in, 309–310; sleeping, 737; UNIA in, 231. *See also* Egypt; Ethiopia; Liberia
African Blood Brotherhood: challenges Garvey, xxxvi, 667–668; Garvey on, 691–692; manifesto, 637, 639 n. 3; *Negro Congress Bulletin and News Service* of, xxxvi–xxxvii, 637, 638 n. 1, 691; Negro World Federation of, 637, 638–639 n. 2; program of, 637, 638–639 n. 2, 667; at UNIA convention, xxxvi, xxxvii, lviii, 637–639, 681–682 n. 1, 691
African Communities League. *See* Uni-

DATE DUE